JIM MURRAY'S
WHISKY BIBLE
2012

This edition first published 2011 by Dram Good Books Ltd

10 9 8 7 6 5 4 3 2 1

For information regarding using tasting notes from Jim Murray's Whisky Bible contact:
Dram Good Books Ltd, 9 Edison Court, Wellingborough, Northamptonshire, UK, NN8 6AH
Tel: 44 (0)117 317 9777. Or contact us via www.whiskybible.com

A CIP catalogue record for this book is available from the British Library

ISBN: 978-0-9554729-6-1

Printed in England by Stanley L Hunt (Printers) Ltd. Rushden, Northamptonshire
www.stanleylhunt.co.uk

Written by: Jim Murray
Edited by: David Rankin
Design: James Murray, Jim Murray
Maps and Cover Design: James Murray
Production: James Murray, Billy Jeffrey, Ally Telfer, Dani Dal Molin
Sample Research: Ally Telfer, Julia Nourney
Cover Photograph: John Paul

Author's Note
I have used the spelling "whiskey" or "whisky" depending on how the individual distillers
prefer. All Scotch is "whisky". So is Canadian. All Irish, these days, is "whiskey", though
that was not always the case. In Kentucky, bourbon and rye are spelt "whiskey", with the
exception of the produce of the early Times/Old Forester Distillery and Maker's Mark which
they bottle as "whisky". In Tennessee, it is a 50-50 split: Dickel is "whisky", while Daniel's is
"whiskey".

JIM MURRAY'S
WHISKY
BIBLE
2012

DRAM GOOD BOOKS

Contents

Introduction

My word! What a battle...!!!

Never has a Whisky Bible taken so long to write; never has one set of taste buds been working on so many enormous whiskies from every corner of the planet.

This is the Whisky Bible which began in the Arab Spring. And 1,210 new whiskies and some 200 re-tastes later ended in the Hoodie Autumn.

And was it worth dodging tornadoes in Kentucky and riots in the UK? You bet. It is as though I have spent four solid months evaluating the Family Silver. Day after day of nosing, tasting (though, sadly, not polishing off), one after the other, the oldest crop of whiskies I have ever seen, let alone rated. The result is an increase of Whisky Bible Liquid Gold winners – that's 94 points and above – to percentage numbers I thought highly improbable when I devised the scoring method two decades ago. I know what you might be thinking. But I can assure you: no, I haven't gone soft. Am I being kind to the distillers? Not a bit of it. Am I the same demanding, unforgiving self? On that you can rely.

Once upon a time whiskies which are common or garden, age-wise, in this Bible would have been kept to the end of the week, or even book, before tasting as a treat. Now I am more likely to encounter a 30-year-old malt than I am to find a 10- or 12-year-old. Astonishing. But true. Hard to believe, but it sometimes became a relief to get my nose into a glass of something youthful and familiar to a majority of the world's whisky shelves.

Indeed, there are so many ancient whiskies for you to choose from these days (and, when the dust settles, I will set my team the task of working out how many of the 4,500 plus whiskies in Jim Murray's Whisky Bible 2012 are 21 or over) – Scotch in particular – that it took a month longer than anticipated to complete my work. For it takes much more time to properly nose and taste an oldie than a relative youngster as the whisky requires time to react to the air and temperature in very much the same way as a fine old wine.

Not that every old whisky was a success, of course. But perhaps what was so remarkable about this year is that distillers and independent bottlers were able to strike gold so consistently. Despite the magnificence of so many whiskeys from Kentucky, it was Scotland which sneaked the World Whisky of the Year Award thanks to a malt many may not be familiar with: Old Pulteney from the Pulteney Distillery, the most northern on mainland Scotland. It was the 21-year-old that pressed all the right buttons this time, though in previous years it was the 17-year-old which had underlined the distillery's potential.

Fittingly, though, Kentucky grabbed second and third spot with two muscle-bound bourbons to die for: a George T Stagg back to near perfection and a Parker's Heritage Collection which put the wheat recipe style onto a new plane. Had there been a medal struck for fourth spot, that would have gone to Thomas Handy Sazarac Rye...meaning three different types of Kentucky whiskey had created the greatest impression this year. With Buffalo Trace's Single Oak Project series now out, Kentucky is a useful place to be when in search of the extraordinary.

For the thousands of people I meet every year, don't be worried if you see less of me in future. At Christmas I weighed in at 196 pounds. Just prior to taking on the sulphured whiskies requiring cheese, tomatoes and raspberries to re-balance my palate, I was down to 161 pounds. Running after all these whiskies is keeping me fit.

Also, whilst writing this year's edition of the Whisky Bible, my daughter Tabitha gave birth to a little girl whose name was kept secret until after she was born. It was Islay-Mae. The highlight of my year, by far.

But, as part of the circle of life, it was not just hello but also goodbye. And around the Christmas period I learned of the loss of that most genuine and appreciative of whisky connoisseurs, Mike Smith of Vancouver. He had supported Jim Murray's Whisky Bible for five years, especially during a most difficult period of legal warfare. And had it not been for Mike and his wife Barbara, there would be no Whisky Bible. Fact. Thank you, my dear friend. I Crown Royal Salute you, sir...

Jim Murray
The Tasting Room
Wellingborough September 2011

How to Read
The Bible

The whole point of this book is for the whisky lover – be he or she an experienced connoisseur or, better fun still, simply starting out on the long and joyous path of discovery – to have ready access to easy-to-understand information about as many whiskies as possible. And I mean a lot. Thousands.

This book does not quite include every whisky on the market... just by far and away the vast majority. And those that have been missed this time round – either through accident, logistics or design – will appear in later editions once we can source a sample.

Whisky Scoring

The marking for this book is tailored to the consumer and scores run out just a little higher than I use for my own personal references. But such is the way it has been devised that it has not affected my order of preference.

Each whisky is given a rating out of 100. Twenty-five marks are given to each of four factors: nose (n), taste (t), finish (f), balance and overall complexity (b). That means that 50% of the marks are given for flavour alone and 25% for the nose, often an overlooked part of the whisky equation. The area of balance and complexity covers all three previous factors and a usually hidden one besides:

Nose: this is simply the aroma. Often requires more than one inspection as hidden aromas can sometimes reveal themselves after time in the glass, increased contact with air and changes in temperature. The nose very often tells much about a whisky, but – as we shall see – equally can be quite misleading.

Taste: this is the immediate arrival on the palate and involves the flavour profile up to, and including, the time it reaches maximum intensity and complexity.

Finish: often the least understood part of a tasting. This is the tail and flourish of the whisky's signature, often revealing the effects of ageing. The better whiskies tend to finish well and longer without too much oak excess. It is on the finish, also, that certain notes which are detrimental to the whisky may be observed. For instance, a sulphur-tarnished cask may be fully revealed for what it is by a dry, bitter residue on the palate which is hard to shake off. It is often worth waiting a few minutes to get the full picture of the finish before having a second taste of a whisky.

Balance: This is the part it takes a little experience to appreciate but it can be mastered by anyone. For a whisky to work well on the nose and palate, it should not be too one-sided in its character. If you are looking for an older whisky, it should have evidence of oak, but not so much that all other flavours and aromas are drowned out. Likewise, a whisky matured or finished in a sherry butt must offer a lot more than just wine alone and the greatest Islay malts, for instance, revel in depth and complexity beyond the smoky effects of peat.

Each whisky has been analysed by me without adding water or ice. I have taken each whisky as it was poured from the bottle and used no more than warming in an identical glass to extract and discover the character of the whisky. To have added water would have been pointless: it would have been an inconsistent factor as people, when pouring water, add different amounts at varying temperatures. The only constant with the whisky you and I taste will be when it has been poured directly from the bottle.

Even if you and I taste the same whiskies at the same temperature and from identical glasses – and even share the same values in whisky – our scores may still be different. Because a factor that is built into my evaluation is drawn from expectation and experience. When I sample a whisky from a certain distillery at such-and-such an age or from this type of barrel or that, I would expect it to offer me certain qualities. It has taken me 30 years to acquire this knowledge (which I try to add to day by day!) and an enthusiast cannot be expected to learn it overnight. But, hopefully, Jim Murray's Whisky Bible will help...!

Finding Your Whisky

Worldwide Malts: Whiskies are listed alphabetically throughout the book. In the case of single malts, the distilleries run A–Z style with distillery bottlings appearing at the top of the list in order of age, starting with youngest first. After age comes vintage. After all the "official" distillery bottlings are listed, next come other bottlings, again in alphabetical order. Single malts without a distillery named (or perhaps named after a dead one) are given their own section, as are vatted malts.

Worldwide Blends: These are simply listed alphabetically, irrespective of which company produce them. So "Black Bottle" appears ahead of "White Horse" and Japanese blends begin with "Ajiwai Kakubin" and end with "Za". In the case of brands being named after companies or individuals the first letter of the brand will dictate where it is listed. So William Grant, for instance, will be found under "W" for William rather "G" for Grant.

Bourbon/Rye: One of the most confusing types of whiskey to list because often the name of the brand bears no relation to the name of the distillery that made it. Also, brands may be sold from one company to another, or shortfalls in stock may see companies buying bourbons from another. For that reason all the brands have been listed alphabetically with the name of the bottling distiller being added at the end.

Irish Whiskey: There are four types of Irish whiskey: (i) pure pot still; (ii) single malt; (iii) single grain and (iv) blended. Some whiskies may have "pure pot still" on the label, but are actually single malts. So check both sections.

Bottle Information

As no labels are included in this book I have tried to include all the relevant information you will find on the label to make identification of the brand straightforward. Where known I have included date of distillation and bottling. Also the cask number for further recognition. At the end of the tasting notes I have included the strength and, if known, number of bottles (sometimes abbreviated to btls) released and in which markets.

Price of Whisky

You will notice that Jim Murray's Whisky Bible very rarely refers to the cost of a whisky. This is because the book is a guide to quality and character rather than the price tag attached. Also, the same whiskies are sold in different countries at varying prices due to market forces and variations of tax, so there is a relevance factor to be considered. Equally, much depends on the size of an individual's pocket. What may appear a cheap whisky to one could be an expensive outlay to another. With this in mind prices are rarely given in the Whisky Bible.

Bible Thumping
And the Truth Shall Make You Free

Someone comes up to you and says: "Look, here's the next 20 years of your life. Treat them preciously. By the way: what are you going to do with them?"

It is an intriguing dilemma, as few of us look at it quite that way. Most, from paying the mortgage and ensuring the kids have clothes and food on the table, just take it one step at a time, as often as not playing it safe. Trying whenever possible to keep some form of control, but knowing that we are all, to one degree or another, in the lap of the Fates.

In 20 years as a Sportsman, as a cricketer (which the 13-year-old me had wanted to be) or footballer we would watch our playing careers bloom and then wither if injury does not intervene; in civil or public service we would hope for deserved promotions when the time was ripe. In our personal lives we hope in that time to find happiness and use those years to secure and savour it.

Twenty years ago I did something bonkers. I left a very well paid job as a journalist in Fleet Street and decided to earn nothing for a very long time. I created a job which, until then, did not exist. I became a Whisky Writer. That was in late May 1992. So the life of this Jim Murray's Whisky Bible will cover the anniversary. Fittingly, I will be celebrating it while writing the 10th Edition of the Bible. How pleasingly circular is that...?

But in those 20 years I have been asked one question above all others: Why? And the answer is quite simple, really.

Let's travel back to 1992. The whisky landscape is entirely unrecognisable from the one we see today. It is barren, peopled with nervous individuals with no great belief in the future and still feeling the rawness of having seen so many distilleries close in the last decade and throughout their careers. I am not just talking about Scotland, but the USA and Canada here, too.

Anything to read about whisky is pretty thin on the ground. Wallace Milroy, an industry insider, had produced a simple and charming Single Malt guide and Michael Jackson was doing great things, too, on the book front. But Michael had long been my hero for his writings on beer – his first and great love – rather than whisky which fitted usefully into his later career, though with nothing like the same tender devotion or with any chance of it usurping his true passion. A writer called Gordon Brown, now sadly lost to us, was writing the odd piece in the nationals, but he was also as likely to give us something about Cognac, gin or vodka: he saw himself as a spirits, rather than a whisky man.

Virtually all the other meagre contributions were by wine writers who used their bylines to generate an air of knowledge on the subject that the contents of their writing revealed they did not possess.

I had spent 17 years wondering around every distillery I could get to, tasting every different whisky I could find or afford, meeting as many people from every walk of the industry I could find. Even in the mid '80s when seconded to Scotland I would spend a spare afternoon working in the Maltings at Balvenie or the still room at Benriach if a story had fallen flat on its face and I had time to kill. For 17 years I built up my reserves of knowledge until they were like a dam about to burst. By 1986 I knew that one day I would take the plunge and devote my life to whisky. But during that time letters and phone calls to publishers and Features Editors received not a single word of encouragement on the whisky front, though I was offered several jobs to write articles on wine...

What particularly stirred me was the ignorance I found in Wine Shops, when trying to track down whiskies. Some in the industry were knowledgable to a degree. Others were simply clueless and beyond Glenfiddich hadn't much of an idea, or even very much cared, what a Single Malt was, let alone the innumerable variations amongst them all. It was probably that, and the garbage that was being written in the wine columns about whisky, which made me want to do something major about it. Because if these guys in the shops – the front line of the war to win over whisky converts - knew little, then they were unlikely to be passing on much information of any use to their customers. The great void in knowledge was staring back at me every time I spoke to someone at the Spirits counter.

Therefore after nearly 20 years of slogging myself around the world, selling over half a million books, lecturing in nearly 30 different countries, dragging myself from one television or radio studio to another to preach the word, watching my hair turn from black to grey, just imagine how my heart sank when, greeted by a charming lady in a duty free outlet at a British Airport, I was informed: "All the whiskies we have here are good. There's no such thing as bad whisky."

She soon realised, by my icy response, that perhaps she had not picked quite the right phrases to greet me with.

"Well that's what I've been trained."

"Oh, by whom?"

"When we have the training sessions with the distillers."

"And what do they tell you about caramel, for instance? You know: the colouring sometimes put in a whisky."

"Oh, that. Well, it has no effect on the whisky."

"What, neither in the aroma or taste?"

"Exactly. It's neutral. They put it in just to standardise the bottling, I think. I was certainly told it has no effect in any way on the aroma or taste."

And there I stood, wondering if my 20 years had been wasted. Certainly, it told me that my next 20 years – should I have them all – will mean that my work is well and truly cut out.

I understood, exactly, where her training was coming from. Once, in Canada, I allowed a Brand Ambassador for a well known blend into a training session I was giving to the high-ups of a Liquor Board. I stopped it dead when she began telling them that the caramel makes no difference. In another country, a friend of mine, unable to make a living from his whisky writing, joined a Scotch company as a Brand Ambassador and had to give the same nonsensical spiel even though he knew it not to be true. Within a year or so he quit as his conscience had, rightly, won in the end.

Likewise, I was once giving a whisky tasting in central England. A club barman tried to interject on virtually every point I made regarding bourbon, where he made it clear I didn't have a single idea of what I was talking about. Despite the fact that I have devoted almost as much of my whisky life to Kentucky as I had the Highlands and Islands of Scotland. Puzzled by his almost aggressive stance, and some of the absolute drivel he was spouting with total conviction, I discovered that a few days earlier he had attended a course given by an American distiller's brand ambassador. That is always the danger: when training becomes a form of brainwashing.

Of course the problem stems from the fact that sometimes it is hard to know where proper independent writing and thought ends and PR begins. There is one guy whose tasting notes I have been shown online are such an amalgam of his own thoughts blended in with the official line, they are rendered useless.

So maybe that should be the next project to start my next 20 years. To carry out even more real training than I already do. Surely, if you go into a shop and ask a specialist for his opinion, you want an independent view. Not the regurgitation of a company's PR speak. Not the hard sell soft-soaped.

To make my independent voice heard even louder...

Do you know something...? I am already looking forward to it...

Review of the Whisky Year

It is as though the whisky industry is trying to make snobs of us all.

Collectively, from Scotland to Kentucky and across to Asia, distillers and independent bottlers appear to have gone out of their way to ensure that we must look again at how we should evaluate great whisky. To touch upon a point I made in the introduction to this, the 2012 Whisky Bible, we have now entered a Golden Age of Whisky. And that applies as much to its colour as anything else. For while the average age of whisky lovers appears to be getting younger, what they are being offered to buy just gets older and older.

If the whiskies placed before me for last year's Bible were among some of the most disappointing ever, this year is a complete 180 degree about turn with more breathtaking drams to choose from than I can wave a nose at. For that reason, I have decided to change the format of this chapter to summarise not what has happened outside the bottle within the industry but to take a far closer look at the 1,200 new whiskies I have found in the last twelve months. Because, as it might be said, the proof of the whisky is in the bottle...

For twenty years I have been telling the whisky-discovering world to avoid the elitist snobbery rife among a certain type of "connoisseur". My message has been clear and consistent: an older age statement does not necessarily equate to a better whisky. That was certainly the case and, to a degree, still holds good. However, what is now becoming very apparent is that a gap is starting to appear in wood quality, greatly favouring the oldies. With some of the younger whiskies struggling to escape the pincer movement of sulphur in some sherry butts and a shrinking of availability of fully seasoned bourbon barrels, the older whiskies now appear to offer a much truer and more attractive picture of the distilleries. And, consequently, a much greater appreciation of the beauty of a good oak, good spirit mix.

That does not mean that all whiskies under 18 years should simply be written off. Just one quick look through the whiskies listed in the Whisky Bible reveals that this is certainly not the case. However, single casks are more at risk, as any weakness is fully exposed with nowhere to hide. A single cask does, as the name implies, stand or fall as much by the quality of the oak as the spirit which was filled into it. So, theoretically, multi cask brands should, in the long run, be of better quality. Put in the time and effort and you should be able to select casks which can balance out the tell-tale bitter signature of an inferior bourbon barrel (reaching the end of its useful life earlier than it once did) with the sugar-sweet richness afforded by still vibrant oak. But time is money.

No less worrying are the younger blends. When the sulphur problem first started to emerge I remember one or two blenders telling me this would easily be overcome, as the contents of any faulty butt would be tipped into the bottomless vat of a blend where, like Harry Lime in the underworld of Vienna, they would simply vanish. The evidence of some of the younger to middle aged blends I tasted this year confirms that a Plan B is now urgently required...

Onslaught of the Senses

But these are the negatives. Jim Murray's Whisky Bible 2012 is exploding at every page with positives. So much so, I have never felt so exhausted and drained after completing the writing of a new edition. The sheer mental effort required to understand the working and personality of so many hundreds of enormous and compellingly beautiful whiskies is dizzying.

Some distillers have excelled in particular. Perhaps in Scotland the one distillery deserving an extra special mention in dispatches is **GlenDronach**. I have to admit that until quite recently this was the one distillery in the Highlands I knew least about because on the half a dozen times or so I randomly visited over a 30 year period, it was the one that was always closed. I had not come across many lab samples, either, while distillery bottlings had been patchy and restricted to 12-years-old. It was one of a number of distilleries that the marketing guys at **Allied** had no idea whether to twist or stick with. The fact that, like **Scapa**, it was enduring a stop-go working pattern didn't help one little bit.

Now, thanks to its new owners, I now not only know and comprehend the distillery but simply adore it. The last time I was up there with owner and blender Billy Walker he showed samples which displayed **GlenDronach** to its best and worst advantages: it is a distillery where sherry butts were often historically preferred. The odd one or two Billy showed me were sulphur-stained. Others were pristine and, frankly, hardly of this world.

This year I have been absolutely blown away by its 18- and 21-year-old vintages. While the '72, '78, '89, '91 and '92 are gems of the rarest quality. Together they make the best single year's bottled output by any distillery in the whole of Scotland, even above the continuing excellence of **Ardbeg**, **Laphroaig** and **Highland Park**, and firmly places **GlenDronach** in the Grand Crus of Scottish malt distilleries. There is, as might be expected of a distillery with its feet so firmly planted in the sherry butt camp, the odd sulphured dud, too. But the **GlenDronach** 1992 picking up the single cask of the year for its age seems a miserly return for such widespread magnificence: if there was a Whisky Bible Scotch Malt Whisky Distillery of the year, **Glendronach** would be it.

Not too far behind we would find **Bruichladdich** and **Glenfarclas**. **Bruichladdich** carries on being... well, **Bruichladdich**. One of those distilleries where you can't wait to open the sample bottle to see what is going to happen next; like **GlenDronach** the difference between their great and not-so-great bottlings can be quite wide. However, they have really hit top gear with their Octomore and Port Charlotte ranges where all the sums add up and probably lead the way when it comes to younger malts offering great complexity and personality.

Displaying, usually, a little more gentility, **Glenfarclas** is another distillery that, traditionally, leans more heavily than most on sherry butts. The fact they can wow us with the youthful and far from gentile **Glenfarclas** 105, still one of the most fabulous and distinctive whiskies of its type, and then bow us with the magisterial 40-year-old gives an indication of just how rich those Speyside warehouses of theirs must be. Plucked from them this year were further additions to their fabulous Family Casks range, the 1960, '62, and '73 being the pick of an outstandingly fine grapey bunch.

But other Scottish distilleries refused to be outdone in the Goldie Oldie stakes: The **Dalmore** EOS showed the best way of passing 59 years; **The Macallan** Lalique III 57-year-old was determined not to be outdone; **Gordon and MacPhail** followed up their improbable success with the **Mortlach** 70-year-old with a **Glenlivet** of the same improbable age, though with marginally less glory and did better with their whippersnapper 1954 bottling; **Highland Park's** 50-year-old was stupendous; **Tullibardine** chipped in with an exquisite 1962 vintage. The number of sensual, sensational single malt bottlings of between 35- and 45-years-old is simply too great to include in this summary. This was an onslaught of the senses I have never before encountered. And, if it continues, we must seriously look at building in an extra month to write this thing; certainly add an over 50-year-old award...!

Reaching New Heights

But it wasn't just the Single Malt guys. The independent bottlers **Douglas Laing** did the whisky world a favour which leaves us greatly in their debt when they launched a series of Clan Denny very old single grain bottlings. Once more, the quality exceeded anything the market has seen before with their **Cambus** – a grain plant I argued two decades ago was as good as most malt distilleries – reaching new heights. This was a mere 47-year-old and the fact it comfortably eclipsed even the stunning Clan Denny **Caledonian** 45-year-old gave some idea of its greatness.

But some of the biggest surprises have been reserved for Scotch blends. Not least with some of the older bottlings. When I heard that the proprietors of **The Last Drop** had decided to put some of their remaining stock back into butt to round up to 50 years, I thought they were taking a very risky gamble. However, it is one that has paid off handsomely with a whisky which just about matches the original for style, and by wearing an entirely new wardrobe.

During an unforgettable year worldwide another new English whisky hit the market, this time the beautiful apple-tinged **Hicks and Healey** from Cornwall. This whisky, distilled in 2004, actually predates **St George's**, though they were beaten to bottle by their Norfolk counterparts who decided, wisely, to launch with a three-year-old in 2009 to become England's first commercially available single malt in a century. For their part **St George** did their reputation no harm at all with some further fine releases. If you take the average quality of English whisky released, it has suddenly become a Premier League whisky nation. Other major European whiskies from **Penderyn** in Wales, **Mackmyra** in Sweden and **The Belgian Owl** in – err – Belgium, also kept their reputations intact.

Elsewhere around the world there has been no shortage of high quality whiskies to tuck into. Australia just gets better and better. The day I sat down with their samples was one I will remember for a long time. In fact, they were so good I had to repeat it a few days later, not only for an encore of the fun but to make sure my taste buds weren't playing tricks on me. They weren't. **The Nant** 3-year-old pretty much amazed and **Limeburners** fascinated. However, I still wasn't prepared for the glory that fell from the bottle of **Southern Coast** batch two which boasted some of the characteristics of the finest Demerara rum you could wish to find.

I fully expected that to pick up an award until the Kavalan Solist Fino Sherry from the **King Car** distillery in Taiwan arrived in my tasting room. No surprise that Dr Jim Swan had been at work with the cask choice here: probably only the **Penderyn** distillery in Wales showed better wood selection. And he is their advisor, also...

The fact that these were a match for **Amrut** in India, who again beguiled with their astonishing choice of flavour profiles which mark the enormous efforts they go to get it right, is an indication of how the whisky world outside the old established players is moving on from toddling to confident strides.

Whiskey's Big Bang

But for the most astonishing whiskeys of them all, we must return, as we so often do, to Kentucky.

Buffalo Trace, with their range of magnificent ryes and bourbons of varying mash bills is now becoming the most complete whiskey distillery in the world and the most trustworthy as regards to quality. And they have to be: it is noticeable that **Jim Beam** have upped their game considerably over the last few years while the bourbons of **Four Roses** are now showing a depth and quality that had previously been missing. **Heaven Hill**, meanwhile, though less predictable, are still guaranteed to bottle something which will have you purring into your glass with a degree of wonder. However, since their enforced move away from Bardstown, it is becoming increasingly more difficult to know just which brand will hit the highest peaks. This year it was their quite brilliant Virgin 7-year-old and their altogether different wheated mash bill version of the Parker's Heritage Collection.

Yet for pure breathtaking individuality it is back to Frankfort by the banks of the Kentucky River. For there has been taking place an experiment which, as experiments go, is the Large Hadron Collider of the whisk(e)y world: it leaves all the cask finish stuff of the last two decades looking like so many children's chemistry sets. At **Buffalo Trace** were released, in two lots so far, 24 versions of bourbon which mark the most important and fascinating brand to have been launched in my lifetime; almost certainly ever. But that is only the tip of the iceberg: over the next few years another 168 are to come.

I had heard over the years bits and pieces of some kind of The Experiment at **Buffalo Trace**, but nothing prepared me for what I was to learn at a briefing at the distillery in April. The Single Oak Project was, in effect, going to take us to the Big Bang of whiskey: we were about to discover, in a way we had never before, exactly what made a whiskey tick. During the briefing my hairs stood on end; that night I could hardly sleep... and not, for once, because of the tornado warnings.

To find out how whiskey behaved as it did during maturation, **Buffalo Trace** had selected 96 American oak trees depending on their growth history, with them having so many rings per inch. After they were felled, they were then divided into two parts, upper and lower. And from each part an individual cask was made. These casks would also differ with a variance of seasoning and charring. Next, the casks would be filled with bourbon, but as a further variance some of the whiskey included rye in the mash bill, others wheat. And there were further differences in filling proofs and warehouse locations. Finally, all the casks, which had been filled simultaneously, were dumped on the same day, too. So each whiskey was exactly the same age at the time of going into bottle.

In total there will be 192 different bottles available, each given a code number from 1-192, and no less than 1,396 variances between them with no two bottles being the same and sometimes as little as only a single difference from one type to another. But, as you will see on *page 284*, that lone difference can be quite marked.

Part of the fun is that the distillery wishes to see what the public think. So they are invited to enter their own tasting notes on the online site covering the project. To that effect I have kept my tasting notes for the whiskeys in the Whisky Bible brief. Indeed, I was not going to enter much about about them at all, but that was pointless as people couldn't help themselves and the details are already all over the internet. So I have devised a code which will mean nothing to those not wishing to know and easily decipherable for those who do.

This is the whiskey range I have waited my entire life to see. It is not about finding a whisky of rare magnificence, though that would be a bonus. It is about locating the subtle differences on both nose and palate; the slow awakening and learning. For me, at least, whisky has been a journey of discovery and here we have the chance of a voyage like no other.

As I have mentioned, tasting all these ancient whiskies over the last year has been like polishing the family silver. With the Single Oak Project it is more like discovering whiskey's very DNA...

Jim Murray's Whisky Bible Award Winners 2012

You have to go a long way to beat Jim Murray's Whisky Bible World Whisky of the Year 2012. Indeed, you have to go an even longer way to even get to where it is made...

The Pulteney Distillery is Scotland's northernmost mainland distillery, found in the town of Wick, just a short drive from John o'Groats. It is the perfect place to spend midsummer's day, as I did some years back, watching the sun set at the distillery and then whizzing up the coast to the famous landmark to see it disappear again, this time into the sea.

But although I have been a major admirer of its malts for over 30 years and always delighted to include it in my tastings, not least because I have long regarded it as one of the great undiscovered distilleries, it still came as something of a surprise to me that it blew away all the other contenders in a quite exceptional year for great whisky. Not the distillery, mind, but the particular victorious version.

I thought the George T. Stagg had it in the bag and was about to be crowned by the Whisky Bible for the first time since the 2006 edition. But then, as I worked through a hundred or so re-tastes, I encountered a malt which stopped me in my tracks. Between pouring and tasting I had been in a back room checking samples. When I returned to my table I had forgotten what I had poured and the sample bottle was sitting sideways on to me. It was only on the second mouthful it dawned on me it could well be an Old Pulteney. And I plumped for the 17-year-old version. I was out by four years: on turning the bottle in mid chew I discovered it was the 21-year-old.

The Old Pulteney 17 is unquestionably one of the greatest experiences you can have among Highland malts. However, the 21 for all its excellence always had a tendency to be a duller fellow by comparison, losing its way towards the end as toffee took hold. This sample had no such restraints and simply dazzled from the nose to the last dying embers, like the rays of the midsummer sun. Indeed, I even checked with distillery owners, Inver House, that they had sent a post- rather than pre-bottling sample. Unaware they were in line for the big one, they confirmed it came from a recent bottling: a scotch Single Malt was going to be Whisky Bible World Whisky of the Year for the first time since 2009.

On the odd occasion I include Old Pulteney in my tasting around the world as often as not only a handful, if any of those assembled, will ever have tasted it. I get the feeling that may not be the case in future years...

2012 World Whisky of the Year
Old Pulteney Aged 21 Years

Second Finest Whisky in the World
George T. Stagg

Third Finest World Whisky in the World
Parker's Heritage Collection
Wheated Mash Bill Bourbon Aged 10 Years

SCOTCH

Scotch Whisky of the Year
Old Pulteney Aged 21 Years
Single Malt of the Year (Multiple Casks)
Old Pulteney Aged 21 Years
Single Malt of the Year (Single Cask)
Scott's Selection Highland Park 1981
Best Scotch New Brand
Clan Gold Blended
Scotch Blend of the Year
Ballantine's 17 Years Old
Scotch Grain of the Year
Clan Denny Cambus 47 Years Old
Scotch Vatted Malt of the Year
Johnnie Walker Green Label 15 Years Old

Single Malt Scotch

No Age Statement (Multiple Casks)
Glenmorangie Sonnalta PX
No Age Statement (Runner Up)
Laphroaig Quarter Cask
10 Years & Under (Multiple Casks)
Ardbeg 10 Years Old
10 Years & Under (Single Cask)
SMWS 126.2 Aged 10 Years (Hazelburn)
11-15 Years (Multiple Casks)
The Macallan Fine Oak 12 Years Old
11-15 Years (Single Cask)
Berry's Own Selection Clynelish 1997
16-21 Years (Multiple Casks)
Old Pulteney Aged 21
16-21 Years (Single Cask)
The GlenDronach Single Cask 1992
22-27 Years (Multiple Casks)
Highland Park Aged 25 Years
22-27 Years (Single Cask)
Malts of Scotland Port Ellen 1983
28-34 Years (Multiple Casks)
Benromach 30 Years Old
28-34 Years (Single Cask)
Scott's Selection Highland Park 1981
35-40 Years (Multiple Casks)
Balvenie Aged 40 Years Batch 2
35-40 Years (Single Cask)
Peerless Glen Grant 40 Years Old
41 Years & Over (Multiple Casks)
Highland Park 50 Years Old
41 Years & Over (Single Cask)
Gordon and MacPhail Glenlivet 1954

Blended Scotch

No Age Statement (Standard)
Ballantine's Finest
No Age Statement (Premium)
Royal Salute 62 Gun Salute
5-12 Years
Johnnie Walker Black Label 12 Years Old
13-18 Years
Ballantine's 17 Years Old

19 - 25 Years
William Grant's 25 Years Old
26 - 50 Years
The Last Drop 50 Years Old

IRISH WHISKEY

Irish Whiskey of the Year
Powers John's Lane Release Aged 12 Years
Irish Single Malt of the Year
Sainsbury's Dún Léire Aged 8 Years
Irish Blend of the Year
Jameson Rarest 2007 Vintage Reserve

AMERICAN WHISKEY

Bourbon of the Year
George T. Stagg (143 proof)
Rye of the Year
Thomas H. Handy Sazarac (126.9 proof)

Bourbon

No Age Statement (Multiple Barrels)
George T. Stagg (143 proof)
No Age Statement (Single Barrel)
Four Roses Single Barrel
9 Years & Under
Virgin Bourbon 7 Years Old (101 Proof)
10-17 Years
**Parker's Heritage Collection Wheated
Mash Bill Aged 10 Years (124.2 proof)**
18 Years & Over (Single Barrel)
Elijah Craig 18 Years Old Single Barrel
18 Years & Over (Multiple Barrel)
Evan Williams 23 Year Old

Rye

No Age Statement
Thomas Handy Sazarac (126.9 proof)
11 Years & Over
High West Rocky Mountain 21 Year Old

CANADIAN WHISKY

Canadian Whisky of the Year
Crown Royal Special Reserve

JAPANESE WHISKY

Japanese Whisky of the Year
Hibiki Aged 21 Years

EUROPEAN WHISKY

European Whisky of the Year (Multiple)
Mackmyra Moment "Urberg"
European Whisky of the Year (Single)
Penderyn Bourbon Matured Single Cask

WORLD WHISKIES

Indian Whisky of the Year
Amrut Two Continents 2nd Edition
New World Whisky of the Year
Kavalan Solist Fino Single Cask

*Overall age category winners are presented in **bold**.*

The Whisky Bible Liquid Gold Awards (97.5-94)

Jim Murray's Whisky Bible is delighted to again make a point of celebrating the very finest whiskies you can find in the world. So we salute the distillers who have maintained or even furthered the finest traditions of whisky making and taken their craft to the very highest levels. And the bottlers who have brought some of them to us.

After all, there are over 4,500 different brands and expressions listed in this guide and from every corner of the planet. Those which score 94 and upwards represents only a very small fraction of them. These whiskies are, in my view, the elite: the finest you can currently find on the whisky shelves of the world. Rare and precious, they are Liquid Gold.

So it is our pleasure to announce that all those scoring 94 and upwards automatically qualify for the Jim Murray's Whisky Bible Liquid Gold Award. Congratulations!

97.5

Scottish Single Malt
Ardbeg Uigeadail
Old Pulteney Aged 21 Years
Scottish Blends
Ballantine's 17 Years Old
Bourbon
George T Stagg

97

Scottish Single Malt
Ardbeg 10 Years Old
Ardbeg Supernova
Brora 30 Years Old
Glenfiddich 50 Years Old
Scott's Selection Highland Park 1981
Scottish Grain
Clan Denny Cambus 47 Years Old
Scottish Blends
Old Parr Superior 18 Years Old
Bourbon
Parker's Wheated Mashbill Aged 10 Years
William Larue Weller
American Straight Rye
Thomas H. Handy Sazerac Straight Rye
Japanese Single Malt
The Cask of Yamazaki 1990 Sherry Butt
Nikka Whisky Single Coffey Malt 12 Years
Indian Single Malt
Amrut Fusion
Taiwanese Single Malt
Kavalan Solist Fino Sherry Cask

96.5

Scottish Single Malt
Ardbeg 2000 Single Cask Lord Robertson of Port Ellen KT
Ardbeg Corryvreckan
The Balvenie Aged 40 Years Batch 2
The BenRiach Single Cask 1971
Bruichladdich 1991 Valinch Anaerobic Digestion 19 Years Old
Octomore Orpheus Aged 5 Years Edition 02.2 PPM 140
Port Charlotte PC6
Berry's Own Selection Clynelish 1997
Old & Rare Glencadam Aged 32 Years
GlenDronach 18 Years Old
Glenfarclas 1979 Family Casks (3rd Release)
Gordon & MacPhail Glen Grant 1958
Private Collection Glenlivet 1959
Glenmorangie Sonnalta PX
Highland Park 50 Years Old
Laphroaig Aged 25 Years Cask Strength 2011
Gordon & MacPhail Mortlach 70
Cadenhead's Royal Brackla Aged 16 Years
Old Malt Cask Speyside's Finest Agd 43 Yrs
Scottish Blends
The Last Drop
The Last Drop 50 Years Old
Irish Pure Pot Still
Powers John's Lane Release Aged 12 Years
Bourbon
Blanton's Gold Original Single Barrel
Blanton's Uncut/Unfiltered
Four Roses Single Barrel
Parker's Heritage Collection Third Edition 2009 "Golden Anniversary"
Virgin Bourbon 7 Years Old
Japanese Single Malt
Scotch Malt Whisky Society Cask 116.14 Aged 25 Years (Yoichi)
Swiss Single Malt
Säntis Swiss Highlander Dreifaltigkeit
Welsh Single Malt
Penderyn Cask Strength Rich Madeira
Penderyn Port Wood Edition
Indian Single Malt
Amrut Intermediate

96

Scottish Single Malt
Aberlour a'bunadh Batch No. 23
Ardbeg 1977
Ardbeg Kildalton 1980
Ardbeg Provenance 1974
Auchentoshan 1978 Bourbon Cask Matured Limited Edition

Old Malt Cask Auchroisk Aged 34 Years
A.D. Rattray Benrinnes 1996
Brora 25 Year Old 7th Release
Duncan Taylor Collection Brora 1981
Octomore 5 Years Old
The Whisky Agency Bunnahabhain 34 YO
Rare Old Convalmore 1975
The Dalmore Candela Aged 50 Years
Scotch Malt Whisky Society Cask 104.13
Aged 36 Years (Glencraig)
GlenDronach Single Cask 1992
GlenDronach Single Cask 1992 Batch 4
Glenfarclas Family Casks 1967 Release V
Glenfiddich 40 Years Old
Hart Brothers Glenfiddich Aged 45 Years
Glenglassaugh 40 Year Old
Peerless Glen Grant 40 Years Old
The Whisky Fair Glen Grant 36 Year Old
Gordon & MacPhail Glenlivet 1954
Rarest of the Rare Glenlochy 1980
Glenmorangie Truffle Oak
Old Malt Cask Glenury Aged 32 Years
Highland Park Aged 25 Years
Highland Park 1973
Duncan Taylor Highland Park 1986
Rarest of the Rare Inverleven 1979
The Arran Malt 1996 'The Peacock'
Lagavulin 21 Years Old
Laphroaig Quarter Cask
Old & Rare Laphroaig 21 Years Old
Old Malt Cask Lochside Aged 18 Years
A.D. Rattray Pulteney 1982
Rosebank 25 Years Old
Cadenhead's Rosebank Aged 20 Years
Old Malt Cask Tactical Aged 18 Years
The Whisky Fair Tullibardine 1976
The Whisky Agency Speyside 39 Year Old
Scottish Vatted Malt
Big Peat
Scottish Grain
Clan Denny Caledonian 45 Years Old
Scottish Blends
Ballantine's Finest
Irish Pure Pot Still
Redbreast 12 Years Old
Irish Blends
Jameson Rarest 2007 Vintage Reserve
Bourbon
Ancient Ancient Age 10 Years Old
Buffalo Trace Master Distiller Emeritus
Elmer T Lee Collector's Edition
George T. Stagg (141.4 proof)
Old Weller Antique 107
Pappy Van Winkle's Family Reserve 15 YO
American Single Malt Rye
Old Potrero Single Malt Hotaling's Whiskey
Aged 12 Years Essay MCMVI-MMVII
American Straight Rye
Bulleit 95 Rye

Rittenhouse Very Rare 21 YO Barrel 28
Rittenhouse Rye Aged 25 Years Barrel 19
Canadian Blended
Crown Royal Special Reserve
Japanese Single Malt
Karuizawa 1967 Vintage
Japanese Blended
Hibiki Aged 21 Years
Finnish Single Malt
Old Buck Second Release
Swedish Single Malt
Mackmyra Privus 03 Rökning Tillåten
Welsh Single Malt
Penderyn Bourbon Matured Single Cask
Penderyn Rich Madeira Limited Edition
Australian Single Malt
Southern Coast Single Malt Batch 002
Indian Single Malt
Amrut Double Cask

95.5
Scottish Single Malt
Scotch Malt Whisky Society Cask 33.108
Aged 13 Years (Ardbeg)
The BenRiach Aged 12 Years Sherry Wood
Cadenhead's Benriach Aged 23 Years
Benromach 30 Years Old
Bruichladdich Redder Still 1984
Caol Ila 'Distillery Only'
Caol Ila Special Release 2010 12 Years Old
Cragganmore Special Release 2010 21 YO
The Dalmore Visitor Centre Exclusive
Adelphi Glenallachie 1973 Aged 36 Years
GlenDronach Single Cask 1972
GlenDronach Single Cask 1978
Glenfarclas 105
Glengoyne 1999 Aged 11 Years Single Cask
Norse Cask Glen Grant 1993 Aged 16 Years
The Whisky Agency Glen Grant 1973
The Glenlivet Founder's Reserve 21 Yrs Old
Gordon & MacPhail Generations Glenlivet
70 Years Old
Gordon & MacPhail Glenlivet 1974
Glenmorangie 25 Years Old
Glen Moray 1995 Port Wood Finish
Scotch Malt Whisky Society Cask 35.54
Aged 11 Years (Glen Moray)
The Whisky Castle Glenrothes 21 Years Old
Gordon & MacPhail Glenury Royal 1984
Highland Park Aged 18 Years
Highland Park Vintage 1978
Malts Of Scotland Laphroaig 1998
Gordon & MacPhail Longmorn 1968
The Macallan Fine Oak 12 Years Old
The Macallan Oscuro
Malts Of Scotland Port Ellen 1983
Provenance Port Ellen Over 26 Years
Berry's Own Selection St. Magdalene 1982
Longrow C.V

A.D. Rattray Tamdhu 1967
Old Malt Cask Tamnavulin Aged 20 Years
Malts Of Scotland Ledaig 1998
Tullibardine 1962
Elements of Islay Pe1

Scottish Vatted Malt
Compass Box Flaming Hart
Compass Box The Spice Tree

Scottish Grain
Clan Denny Invergordon 44 Years Old

Scottish Blends
Compass Box Double Single 10th Anniv.
Johnnie Walker Black Label 12 Years Old
Royal Salute "62 Gun Salute"
William Grant's 25 Years Old

Irish Single Malt
Sainsbury's Dún Léire Aged 8 Years

Bourbon
Booker's 7 Years 4 Months
Buffalo Trace Single Oak Project Barrel 63
Charter 101
Parker's Fourth Edition Aged 10 Years
Willett Pot Still Reserve

American Straight Rye
Sazerac Straight Rye Fall 09
Thomas H. Handy Sazerac Rye

American Small Batch
Stranahan's Snowflake Cab Franc
The Notch Aged 8 Years

Canadian Blended
Alberta Premium
Gibson's Finest Rare Aged 18 Years

Japanese Single Malt
Golden Horse Chichibu Aged 12 Years
Hakushu Single Malt Whisky Agd 12 Yrs
Ichiro's Card "King of Hearts"
Ichiro's Malt Aged 20 Years

Japanese Single Grain
Kawasaki Single Grain

Belgium Single Malt
The Belgian Owl Single Malt Spirit Aged 44 Months

German Single Malt
Blaue Maus Single Malt 25 Jahre

Swedish Single Malt
Mackmyra Brukswhisky

Australian Single Malt
The Nant 3 Years Old Cask Strength

95

Scottish Single Malt
Aberlour a'bunadh Batch No. 26
Ardbeg 10
Ardbeg Mor
Cadenhead's Ardbeg Aged 15 Years
Scotch Malt Whisky Society Cask 33.77
Aged 11 Years (Ardbeg)
Old Malt Cask Aultmore Aged 20 Years
The BenRiach Single Cask 1976

Connoisseurs Choice Braes of Glenlivet '75
Bruichladdich 16 Years Old
Bruichladdich 1989 Black Art 2nd Edition
Octomore 3rd Edition Aged 5 Years
Malts Of Scotland Port Charlotte 2001
Old Masters Bruichladdich Aged 20 Years
Bunnahabhain Darach Ùr Batch no. 4
Adelphi Bunnahabhain 31 Years Old
Berry's Own Selection Caol Ila 1984
Berry's Own Selection Caol Ila 2000
Scotch Malt Whisky Society Cask 53.139
Aged 27 Years (Caol Ila)
Matisse Caperdonich 1972 Highland Malt
Adelphi Clynelish 14 Years Old
The Dalmore Eos Aged 59 Years
The Dalmore 62 Years Old
Dalwhinnie 15 Years Old
Glencadam Aged 10 Years
Glencadam Agd 14 Years Oloroso Finish
GlenDronach Aged 33 Years
GlenDronach Single Cask 1989
GlenDronach Single Cask 1991
Duthies Glen Elgin 18 Years Old
Glenfarclas 1962 The Family Casks VI
Glenfarclas 1966 The Family Casks
Glenfarclas 1973 The Family Casks VI
Glenfiddich 18 Years Old
Glenfiddich 1961 47 Years Old
Glenfiddich Snow Phoenix
Glenglassaugh 1973 Family Silver
Glengoyne 1997 Aged 11 Years Single Cask
The Whisky Agency Glengoyne 37 YO
The Glenlivet French Oak Reserve 15 YO
Old Malt Cask Glen Mhor Aged 27 Years
Glen Ord 25 Years Old
Fine Malt Selection Glen Ord 12 Years Old
Berry's Own Selection Glen Scotia 1992
Scotch Malt Whisky Society Cask 16.30
Aged 22 Years (Glenturret)
Dun Bheagan Glenugie 30 Years Old
Malts Of Scotland Highland Park 1986
Murray McDavid Highland Park 1989
Scotch Malt Whisky Society Cask 4.143
Aged 20 Years (Highland Park)
The Whisky Agency Highland Park 25 YO
The Arran Malt 1997 Single Cask
Lagavulin Aged 16 Years
Malts of Scotland Laphroaig 1996
Old Malt Cask Linkwood Aged 28 Years
The Macallan Lalique III 57 Years Old
The Macallan 1949 (53 Years Old)
The Macallan 1970 (32 Years Old)
Gordon & MacPhail Macallan 1971
Rarest of the Rare North Port 1981
Old Pulteney Aged 17 Years
Rosebank Aged 12 Years
Premium Scotch Importers Springbank '98
Scotch Malt Whisky Society Cask 126.2
Aged 10 Years (Springbank)

Malts Of Scotland Strathisla 1970
Talisker Aged 20 Years
Talisker 57 Degrees North
Old Malt Cask Tamdhu Aged 18 Years
Old Malt Cask Tamdhu Aged 21 Years
Tomatin 1982
Tomintoul Aged 14 Years
Wemyss 1990 Highland "Tropical Spice"
Auld Reekie Islay Malt
Celtique Connexion Saussignac Double Matured 1997
Celtique Connexion Sauternes Agd 13 Yrs

Scottish Vatted Malt
Douglas Laing's Double Barrel Highland Park & Bowmore
Johnnie Walker Green Label 15 Years Old
Norse Cask Selection Vatted Islay 1992 Aged 16 Years
Wild Scotsman Aged 15 Years Vatted Malt

Scottish Grain
The Clan Denny Garnheath Vintage 1969 Aged 40 Years
Duncan Taylor North British 1978

Scottish Blends
The Bailie Nicol Jarvie (B.N.J)
Chivas Regal 25 Years Old
Clan Gold 3 Year Old

Irish Pure Pot Still
Midleton 1973 Pure Pot Still

Irish Single Malt
Tyrconnell Aged 11 Years
Bushmills Select Casks Aged 12 Years
Bushmills Rare Aged 21 Years

Irish Blends
Jameson

Bourbon
Buffalo Trace Single Oak Project Barrel #132
Cougar Bourbon Aged 5 Years
Maker's 46
Willett Aged 17 Years Barrel Proof
Woodford Reserve Master's Four Grain

American Corn Whiskey
Dixie Dew

American Straight Rye
Cougar Rye
High West Rocky Mountain 21 Year Old Rye
Rathskeller Rye
Rittenhouse Very Rare 21 YO Barrel 8
Sazerac Kentucky Straight Rye 18 Years Old

Canadian Blended
Alberta Premium 25 Years Old
Danfield's Limited Edition Aged 21 Years
Wiser's Legacy
Wiser's Red Letter

Japanese Single Malt
The Hakushu Aged 15 Years Cask Strength
Hakushu 1984
Ichiro's Card "Four of Spades"
The Cask of Yamazaki 1993 Heavily Peated

Yoichi Key Malt Agd 12 Yrs "Peaty & Salty"
Yoichi 20 Years Old
Pure Malt Black

Japanese Single Grain
Nikka Single Cask Coffey Grain 1992

Japanese Blended
Royal Aged 15 Years

Finnish Single Malt
Old Buck

Swedish Single Malt
Mackmyra Moment "Urberg"
Mackmyra Privus 04 Ratta Virket

Swiss Single Malt
Interlaken Swiss Highland "Classic"

Welsh Single Malt
Penderyn Sherrywood Limited Edition

Indian Single Malt
Amrut Two Continents Limited Edition
Amrut Two Continents 2nd Edition

Taiwanese Single Malt
Kavalan Solist Fino Sherry Cask

94.5

Scottish Single Malt
Aberlour Agd 16 Yrs Double Cask Matured
Aberlour a'bunadh Batch No. 29
Scott's Selection Aberlour 1989
Cadenhead's Ardbeg 1994
Adelphi Aultmore 28 Years Old
Balblair 1975
The Balvenie Aged 21 Years Port Wood
The BenRiach Aged 15 Years PX Finish
The BenRiach 30 Years Old
Benromach Vintage 1968
Bruichladdich 32 Years Old DNA 1977
Bruichladdich Infinity Third Edition
Single & Single Bunnahabhain 1976 Aged 31 Years Special Edition
Wilson & Morgan Bunnahabhain 42 YO
Matisse Caperdonich 1972 Highland Malt
The GlenDronach Grandeur Aged 31 Years
The Whisky Agency Glendullan 1981
Glenfarclas Family Casks 1990 Release V
Glenfarclas 1995 45° Heritage Collection
Glenfiddich 15 Years Old
Glen Grant Cellar Reserve 1992
Gordon & MacPhail Glen Grant 1962
Old Malt Cask Glen Grant Aged 35 Year
The Glenlivet 1973 Cellar Collection
Kingsbury's Finest & Rarest Glenlivet 1978
Malts Of Scotland Glen Ord 1999
Duncan Taylor Octave Glenrothes 40 YO
Glen Spey Special Release 2010 21 YO
The Whisky Agency Glentauchers 1975
Highland Park 1970 Orcadian Vintage
The Arran Malt Bourbon Single Cask 1998
The Arran Malt Single Sherry Cask 1998
The Arran Malt Amarone Cask Finish
Isle of Jura 1976

AnCnoc 12 Year Old
Lagavulin 12 Years Old (8th Release)
Lagavulin 12 Years Old (10th Release)
Laphroaig 27 Years Old
Old Malt Cask Laphroaig Aged 18 Years
Linkwood 12 Years Old
Hart Brothers Linkwood Aged 13 Years
Old Masters Linkwood Aged 12 Years
Gordon & MacPhail Longmorn 1969
The Macallan Fine Oak 18 Years Old
The Macallan Masters Of Photography
Albert Watson 20 Years Old
Old Malt Cask Macallan Aged 21 Years
Old Pulteney Aged 17 Years
Old Malt Cask Rosebank Aged 20 Years
The Whisky Fair Lochnagar 1972
Scotch Malt Whisky Society Cask 17.28
Aged 8 Years (Scapa)
Duncan Taylor Collection Tomatin 1976
Tomintoul Aged 16 Years
Mackillop's Choice Tominoul 1989
Tullibardine 1976
Adelphi Breath Of The Isles 15 Years Old

Scottish Vatted Malt
John McDougall's Selection Islay Malt 1993
Old St Andrews Twilight

Scottish Grain
Late Lamented North of Scotland 37 YO
Clan Denny Strathclyde 33 Years Old

Scottish Blends
Ballantine's Limited
Clan Gold Blended 18 Years Old
Highland Dream 12 Years Old
Lochside 1964 Rare Old Single Blend

Irish Single Malt
Green Spot

Irish Blends
The Irishman Rare Cask Strength

Bourbon
Ancient Ancient Age 10 Star
Benjamin Prichard's Double Barrelled
Bourbon 9 Years Old
Buffalo Trace Single Oak Project Barrel 61
Buffalo Trace Single Oak Project Barrel 164
Buffalo Trace Single Oak Project Barrel 191
Elijah Craig 18 Years Old Single Barrel
Kentucky Vintage
Knob Creek Aged 9 Years
Old Grand-Dad Bonded 100 Proof
Parker's Heritage Collection
Ridgemont Reserve 1792 Aged 8 Years

American Straight Rye
Rittenhouse Aged 25 Years Barrel 30
Van Winkle Reserve Rye Aged 13 Years Old

American Small Batch
McCarthy's
Stranahan's Colorado Whiskey Small Batch
Stranahan's Colorado Whiskey Batch 27
Stranahan's Colorado Whiskey Batch 49

Stranahan's Colorado Whiskey Batch 60

Other American Whiskey
Buffalo Trace Experimental Collection 1995
French Oak Barrel Aged

Canadian Blended
Royal Reserve Gold

Japanese Single Malt
Ichiro's "Ace of Diamonds" Hanyu 1986

Belgium Single Malt
The Belgian Owl Single Malt Age 4 Years

English Single Malt
Hicks & Healey Cornish Malt 2004 Cask 29

French Single Malt
Kornog Taouarc'h Kentan

German Single Malt
Old Fahr Single Cask Malt

Welsh Single Malt
Penderyn Madeira Apr 10
Penderyn Madeira Feb 11
Penderyn Sherrywood Edition

Indian Single Malt
Amrut Fusion
The Ultimate Amrut 2005 Cask Strength

94

Scottish Single Malt
Old Malt Cask Aberfeldy Aged 16 Years
Ardbeg Alligator 1st Release
Ardmore 100th Anniversary 12 Years Old
Ardmore 30 Years Old Cask Strength
Balblair 1978
Old Malt Cask Ben Nevis Aged 40 Years
The BenRiach "Solstice"
Exclusive Casks Bowmore 1998 Agd 10 Yrs
Scotch Malt Whisky Society Cask 3.164
Aged 17 Years (Bowmore)
Bruichladdich 1992 Sherry Edition "Fino"
Octomore 2.1 Aged 5 Years
Bunnahabhain Agd 18 Yrs (Older Bottling)
Bunnahabhain XXV Aged 25 Years
The Whisky Agency Bunnahabhain 1967
Berrys' Own Selection Caol Ila 2000
Old Malt Cask Caol Ila Aged 25 Years
Scotch Malt Whisky Society Cask 53.141
Aged 20 Years (Caol Ila)
The Scotch Single Malt Circle Caol Ila 1982
Single Cask Collection Caol Ila Agd 10 Yrs
Duncan Taylor Caperdonich 1972 cask 7422
Octave Caperdonich 38 Years Old
James MacArthur's Clynelish Agd 12 Yrs
Chieftain's Dalmore 13 YO Pinot Noir Finish
Old Malt Cask Dalmore Aged 32 Years
The GlenDronach Single Cask 1993
Glenfarclas 12 Years Old
Glenfarclas 40 Years Old
Glenfarclas 1960 The Family Casks VI
Glenfarclas 1987 Ltd Rare Bottling - No. 13
Glenfarclas 175th Anniversary 2011
Duncan Taylor Glen Garioch 1988

Mackillop's Choice Glen Garioch 1990
Glenglassaugh 21 Year Old
Glengoyne 13 Years Old Single Cask 1995
Glengoyne 1990 Aged 19 Years Single Cask
Glen Grant Cask Strength Aged 17 Years
Old Malt Cask Glen Grant Aged 32 Years
Glenkinchie Agd 15 Yrs The Distillers Edition
The Glenlivet Nadurra Aged 16 Years
The Glenlivet Nadurra Agd 16 Cask Strength
Berrys' Own Selection Glenlivet 1982
Old Malt Cask Glenlivet Aged 30 Years
Berrys' Own Selection Glenlossie 1975
Glenmorangie 10 Years Old
Glenmorangie Nectar D'or Sauternes Finish
Berry's Own Selection Glen Mhor 1982
Provenance Glen Ord Over 11 Years
Cadenhead's Glenrothes-Glenlivet 1994
The Arran Malt Open Day Single Bourbon
Cask Bottling 2011
The Arran Malt Pineau des Charentes Finish
Victoria Single Malt Club Arran 10 Years Old
Knockando The Manager's Choice
Lagavulin Special Release 2010 12 Yrs Old
Laphroaig 18 Years Old
Berry's Own Selection Laphroaig 1998
Old & Rare Laphroaig Aged 20 Years
Scotch Malt Whisky Society Cask 29.94
Aged 11 Years (Laphroaig)
The Whisky Agency Laphroaig 1990
Adelphi Linkwood 26 Years Old
Hart Brothers Linkwood Aged 19 Years
Montgomeries Longmorn 1975
Scotch Malt Whisky Society Cask 7.55 Aged
40 Years (Longmorn)
The Whisky Agency Longmorn 1975
Macallan Cask Strength
The Whisky Agency Miltonduff 1980
Old Malt Cask St Magdalene Aged 28 Years
The Secret Treasures Springbank 1970
Old & Rare Tamdhu Aged 19 Years
The Whisky Agency Tomatin 1966
The Whisky Fair Tullibardine 1976
Adelphi's Liddesdale Agd 18 Yrs Batch 1
Smokehead Extra Black Aged 18 Years
Wemyss 1981 Islay "Whispering Smoke"
Chieftain's The Cigar Malt Aged 15 Years
Scottish Vatted Malt
Sheep Dip 'Old Hebridean' 1990
Scottish Grain
Clan Denny Caledonian Aged 44 Years
Scott's Selection Dumbarton 1986
Clan Denny Garnheath 43 Years Old
Duncan Taylor Invergordon 1965 cask 15519
Duncan Taylor Invergordon 1965 cask 15528
Scottish Blends
Ballantine's Aged 30 Years
Duncan Taylor Collection Black Bull 40 YO
Grand Sail Rare Reserve Aged 18 Years
Isle of Skye 8 Years Old

William Grant's Family Reserve
Irish Pure Pot Still
Barry Crockett Legacy
Irish Single Malt
Connemara Turf Mór Small Batch Collection
Bourbon
Buffalo Trace Single Oak Project Barrel 95
Buffalo Trace Single Oak Project Barrel 100
Colonel EH Taylor Old Fashioned Sour Mash
Evan Williams 23 Years Old
John J Bowman Virginia Straight Bourbon
Single Barrel
Very Old Barton 90 Proof
Wild Turkey Rare Breed
American Straight Rye
(rī)[1]
Rittenhouse Aged 25 Years Barrel 23
Rittenhouse Aged 25 Years Barrel 29
American Small Batch
Balcones Brimstone Texas Scrub Oak
Smoked Corn Whisky
Moylan's 2004 Cherry Wood Smoked
Single Malt Cask Strength
Stranahan's Snowflake Grand Mesa
Stranahan's Colorado Whiskey Batch 41
Canadian Single Malt
Glen Breton Battle Of The Glen Aged 15
Years Special Edition
Japanese Single Malt
Scotch Malt Whisky Society Cask 120.05
Aged 17 Years (Hakushu)
Shirakawa 32 Years Old Single Malt
Yamazaki 1984
The Yamazaki Aged 15 Years Cask Strength
Nikka Whisky Yoichi 1986 20 Years Old
English Single Malt
The English Whisky Co. 7 Rum Finish
The English Whisky Co. 11 "Heavily Peated"
Cask Strength
French Single Malt
Kornog Single Malt Breton Sant Ivy 2011
German Single Malt
Schwarzwälder Whisky Weizenmalz
Sloupisti 4 Years (Cask Strength)
Liechtenstein Single Malt
Telsington
Telsington IV 3 Years Old
Swiss Single Malt
Edition Käser Castle One Single Malt
Welsh Single Malt
Penderyn bott code Jul 09
Penderyn Sherrywood Edition Jan 11
Indian Single Malt
Amrut Peated

Scottish Malts

For those of you deciding to take the plunge and head off into the labyrinthine world of Scotch malt whisky, a piece of advice. And that is, be careful who you take your advice from. Because, too often, I hear that you should leave the Islays until you have tackled the featherlight Speysiders and the bolder, weightier Highlanders. This is just complete, patronising nonsense. The only time that rings true is if you are tasting a number of whiskies in one day. Then leave the smoky ones to last, so the lighter chaps get a fair hearing.

I know many people who didn't like whisky until they got a Talisker from Skye inside them, or a Lagavulin to swamp their tastebuds with oily iodine. The fact is, you can take your map of malt whisky, start at any point and head in whichever direction you feel. There are no hard and fast rules. Certainly with nearly 3,000 tasting notes for Scottish malts here you should have some help in picking where this journey of a lifetime begins.

It is also worth remembering not always to be seduced by age. It is true that many of the highest scores are given to big-aged whiskies for reasons given in Review of the Whisky Year *(page 11)*. The truth is that the majority of malts, once they have lived beyond 25 years or so, suffer from oak influence rather than benefit. Part of the fun of discovering whiskies is to see how malts from different distilleries perform to age and type of cask. Happy discovering.

SKYE

Talisker

Tobermory

MULL

Islay

Bunnahabhain

Caol Ila

Kilchoman

Bruichladdich

Bowmore

ISLAY

Isle of

Isle of

Springbank
Glen Scotia
Glengyle

Ardbeg

Port Ellen

Laphroaig   Lagavulin

ORKNEY
ISLANDS

Highland Park
Scapa

Pultney

Clynelish
Brora

Balblair
Dalmore
Teaninich

Invergordon

Glen Ord

Glenmorangie

Glenglassaugh

Banff†
Macduff

Speyside see page 24

Knockdhu

Glenugie

Inverness
Glen Albyn†
Glen Mhor
Millburn†

Royal Brackla

Tomatin

Glendronach

Ardmore

Speyside Distillery

Glen
Garioch

Royal Lochnagar

Aberdeen

Dalwhinnie

Glenury Royal

Fettercairn

Ben Nevis
Fort William
Glenlochy

Blair Athol
Edradour

Aberfeldy

Glencadam
North Port
Lochside

Glenesk†

Dundee

Glenturret

Perth

Daftmill

Tullibardine

Deanston

Cameronbridge

Lomond
umbarton
nterieven
†Littlemill
entoshan

Glengoyne

Rosebank†
St. Magdelene†

Glenkinchie

Edinburgh
North British

Glasgow
Strathclyde
Port Dundas

Girvan
Ailsa Bay
Ladyburn†

Bladnoch

Key	
●	**Major Town or City**
▲	Single Malt Distillery
▲	(*Italics*) Grain Distillery
†	Dead Distillery

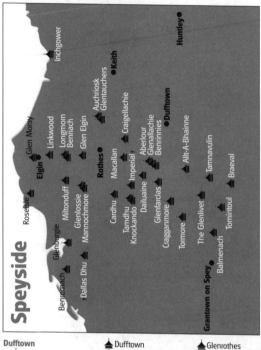

Speyside

Dufftown
- 🍺 Glenfiddich
- 🍺 Convalmore†
- 🍺 Balvenie
- 🍺 Kininvie
- 🍺 Glendullan
- 🍺 Mortlach

- 🍺 Dufftown
- 🍺 Pittyvaich†

Rothes
- 🍺 Speyburn
- 🍺 Glen Grant
- 🍺 Caperdonich†

- 🍺 Glenrothes
- 🍺 Glen Spey

Keith
- 🍺 Aultmore
- 🍺 Strathmill
- 🍺 Glen Keith
- 🍺 Strathisla

Single Malts
ABERFELDY

Highlands (Perthshire), 1898. John Dewar & Sons. Working.

Aberfeldy Aged 12 Years bott no. A44103 db **(88.5) n22.5** the signature honey aroma is still there and intact but a subtle smokiness appears to have developed adding extra depth; **t23** busy delivery with the mildly waxy barley having much to say: spice prickle early on followed by some early chocolate toffee; **f21** luxuriant mouthfeel, the honey now tends towards the honeycomb variety and then Canadian, but still plenty of toffee which hushes proceedings; **b22** a lovely whisky which could be improved overnight to true brilliance by simply increasing the strength to the 46% that malt lovers these days expect and a reduction in the colour. A non-chill filtered, non-coloured policy would see this become a Premiership dram in the time it takes to brew the coffee for the marketing meeting which decides it... 40%

Aberfeldy Aged 18 Years "Chris Anderson's Cask" db **(90) n24** brimming with enormous energy and freshness: plays the range from bourbon-rich red liquorice right down to diced kumquat; sharp, angular, bold, salty and very enticing; not a single blemish in distillate or wood...fabulous; **t23.5** sharp delivery with a mouth watering malty juiciness, but also weighty, too, with heavy oaks immediately apparent. Any threatening bitterness is seen off by a light dusting of muscovado and dried dates; **f21.5** bites deep and caramels out; **b22** had the natural caramels just not ticked over a little too exuberantly, this would have headed for a very high score. Aberfeldy in a very unusual light... 54.9%. 248 bottles.

Aberfeldy Aged 21 Years db **(91) n22** exotic fruit, under-ripe crushed ground cherry and some honey – what else..? **t23.5** sensual delivery that would be recognized and wholly appreciated by fans of Highland Park thanks to the busy honey and semi-hidden waves of smoke; a few oaky touches appear early but enhance in a toasty rather than life-threatening way; the spices rave early on then settle; f22.5 a gentlemanly exit with its honeyed head held high to the last; no oaky screaming and shouting, just a few bitter-sweet farewells; b23 a much improved dram which is far truer to the Aberfeldy style than earlier bottlings. Very high class malt which confidently underlines this distillery's excellence. 40%

Aberfeldy Aged 25 Years db (85) n24 t21 f19 b21. Just doesn't live up to the nose. When Tommy Dewar wrote, "We have a great regard for old age when it is bottled," as quoted on the label, I'm not sure he had as many as 25 years in mind. 40%. 150 bottles to mark opening of Dewar's World of Whisky.

A.D. Rattray Aberfeldy 1994 cask no. 4007, dist Jun 94, bott Dec 09 (82) n20 t23 f19 b20. All about the big upfront maltiness on delivery which is simply superb. Don't expect the same excellence from the nose and finish, though. 57.3%. A.D. Rattray Ltd.

Connoisseurs Choice Aberfeldy 1990 (85.5) n21.5 t22 f21 b21. Silky malt but perhaps a bit too much sheen on the vanilla-led finish. 43%. Gordon & MacPhail.

Duthies Aberfeldy 14 Years Old (86) n21 t21.5 f22 b21.5. Clean, almost crunchy barley. A very attractive degree of juiciness, too. 46%. Wm. Cadenhead Ltd.

Old Malt Cask Aberfeldy Aged 14 Years refill hogshead, dist Jun 94, bott Mar 09 (86) n21 t21.5 f22 b21.5. Unusual to see 'Feldy in such an aggressive mood. And, as it happens, this is pretty enjoyable fare if occasionally on the thin side. The semi-thick malt really zaps into the tastebuds but the harsh vanilla has the most profound words. 50%. Douglas Laing. 338 bottles.

⌐∺∺ **Old Malt Cask Aberfeldy Aged 16 Years** refill hogshead, dist Jun 94, bott Dec 10 (94) n23 heather, lavender and polished leather...; t24 juicy barley with a beautiful lustre to the thin treacle outlining the vanilla-rich oak; all kinds of spices buzz and fret; f23 a succession of firm barley-bourbon notes drying towards the very death; b24 a trademark top range Aberfeldy I actually recognised as being from this distillery even before I looked at what sample I was tasting! Adorable. And quite beautifully constructed. 50%. nc ncf sc. 350 bottles.

Old Malt Cask Aberfeldy Aged 26 Years refill hogshead no. DL 6214, dist Nov 83, bott May 10 (88) n23 A lovely salty tang to this one, ensuring the barley comes through loud and clear. The good age means the oak has been to work, too, offering a pleasant degree of apricot and under-ripe raspberry, as well as a hint of something slightly more south sea island-ish, as well as something a little less exotic in the form of creamy butterscotch candy; t23 immediate lift off with that barley rocketing into taste buds; a pleasant marriage of varying sugar tones; f20 disappointing bitterness from the exhausted oak; b22 goes swimmingly well until the finale. But loads of quality en route. 50% Douglas Laing. 270 bottles.

⌐∺∺ **The Whisky Agency Aberfeldy 1983** bott 2010 (86) n22.5 t23 f19 b21.5. If Perthshire does boast a honeyed style, this does little to detract from that notion. 49.9%

ABERLOUR

Speyside, 1826. Chivas Brothers. Working.

Aberlour 10 Years Old db (87.5) n22.5 plenty of grape, but there is a dry, rough edge to this, too; t22 the delivery briefly bursts with a grapey welcome which soon gives way to a grating vanilla and toffee; b21 overly dry with flecks of cocoa; b22 remains a lusty fellow though here nothing like as sherry-cask faultless as before, nor displaying its usual honeyed twinkle. I will re-taste for next year, as this is the least impressive bottling I have found for a while. Which just shows the heights and expectancy of this distillery these days. 43% ⊙⊙

Aberlour 10 Years Old Sherry Cask Finish db (85) n21 t21 f21 b22. Bipolar and bitter-sweet with the firmness of the grain in vivid contrast to the gentle grape. 43%

Aberlour 12 Years Old Double Cask Matured db (88.5) n22 pretty unsubtle grape but sweet and attractive; t22.5 serious juice at first drowns the barley but the oaky-spice heralds its return; f22 delicate barley remnants; b22 voluptuous and mouth-watering in some areas, firmer and less expansive in others. Pretty tasty in all of them. 43%

Aberlour 12 Years Old Sherry Cask Matured db (88) n23 dry sherry and make no mistake; t22 silky, juicy delivery; cramped slightly by a background bitterness; spices take their time but arrive eventually; f21 double dry finale thanks to both big oak and the sherry influence; b22 could do with some very delicate extra balancing sweetness to take it to the next level. Sophisticated nonetheless. 40%

Aberlour 13 Years Old sherry cask, hand fill db (84) n21 t22 f20 b21. Skimps on the complexity. 58.8%

Aberlour 15 Year Old Double Cask Matured db (84) n23 t22 f19 b20. Brilliant nose full of vibrant apples and spiced sultana, but then, after a complex, chewy, malt-enriched kick-off, falls surprisingly flat on its face. 40%

Aberlour 15 Years Cuvee Marie d'Ecosse db (**91**) **n22 t24 f22 b23**. This always was a deceptive lightweight, and it's got lighter still. It is sold primarily in France, and one can assume only that this is God's way of making amends for that pretentious, over-rated, caramel-ridden rubbish called Cognac they've had to endure. *43%*

Aberlour 15 Year Old Sherry Finish db (**91**) **n24** exceptionally clever use of oak to add a drier element to the sharper boiled cooking apple. And a whiff of the fermenting vessel, too. Love it! **t22** the sharp fruit of the nose is magnified here ten times for one of the strangest mouth arrivals I've ever come across: the roof of the mouth won't know what's hit it; **f23** wave upon wave of malt concentrate; **b22** quite unique: freaky, even. Really a whisky to be discovered and ridden. Once you acclimatize, you'll adore it. *43%*

Aberlour Aged 16 Years Double Cask Matured bott 23 Feb 10 db (**94.5**) **n24** a magnificent marriage between sweet, juicy fruit and lively spice; sturdy-framed but giving grape, too; **t24** the softest delivery of lightly sugared grape, salivating and sensuous; light spices struggle to free themselves from the gentle oils; **f23** pithy with the vanilla determined to ensure a drier finale; **b23.5** compensation for the disappointing 10-y-o is the elevation of the 16 to superstar status. A joyous malt reminding us of just what clean, fresh sherry butts are capable of. A malt of unbridled magnificence. *43%* ⊙⊙

Aberlour 18 Years Old db (**91**) **n22** thick milkshake with various fruits and vanilla; **t22** immediate fresh juice which curdles beautifully as the vanilla is added; **f24** wonderful fruit-chocolate fudge development: long, and guided by a gentle oiliness; **b23** another high performance distillery age-stated bottling. *43%*

Aberlour 100 Proof db (**91**) **n23 t23 f22 b23**. Stunning, sensational whisky, the most extraordinary Speysider of them all ...which it was when I wrote those official notes for the bottling back in '97, I think. Other malts have superseded it now, but on re-tasting I stand by those original notes, though I disassociate myself entirely with the rubbish: "In order to savour Aberlour 100 at its best add 1/3 to 1/2 pure water. *57.1%*

⸭ **Aberlour a'bunadh Batch No. 18** db (**93.5**) **n24.5** textbook oloroso: it is like being in the bodega as the butt is emptied. But what makes this so special is the malt which blasts through: absolutely no chance of the grape dominating for all its massive character. Full frontal finesse...; **t23.5** the dryness which catches the mid palate does not lie. But so complete is the delivery you wonder for a brief moment if you are on course for the near perfect malt. Plenty of chocolate orange helps compensate, and some Rollo toffee, too; **f22.5** some inevitable bitterness, but all kinds of toasted fudge notes; **b23** just one butt away from total brilliance. Even so, a dram to cherish. *59.7%. ncf.*

Aberlour a'bunadh Batch No. 22 db (**83.5**) **n24.5 n20 t21 f21.5 b21**. Thick grape but a docile mustiness acts as a straightjacket; overall, plenty to get on with, but never sparkles. And such is the high stall Aberlour has set itself in recent years, nothing but the best will do.... *59.3%. ncf. Chivas Bros, Italian market.*

Aberlour a'bunadh Batch No. 23 db (**96**) **n24.5 t24.5 f23 b24**. My word: just so close to being the perfect whisky. There are one or two sherry butts used in this bottling which, individually, must be verging on perfect. Even taking into account my total inability to accept anything sulphurous, I have to say this is a masterpiece of a malt and possibly one less than perfect cask away from being among the top three bottles of Speyside whisky I've ever come across. There is no doubting in my mind that this brand has now become the most eagerly anticipated of not just all Speyside's regular bottlings but the world's. Perhaps part of the fun is that there is a degree of uncertainty to just how good it will be. But when on song this is a whisky searching every liquor store you can to find. This one was just so close to being a world champion... *60.2%*

Aberlour a'bunadh Batch No. 25 db (**82.5**) **n21.5 t20.5 f20 b20.5**. Oh dear. One or two less than brilliant casks have sneaked in and spoiled the usual party. *60.4%*

Aberlour a'bunadh Batch No. 26 db (**95**) **n24.5 t23 f24 b23.5**. Another fabulous and enthralling adventure from now one of the truly wonderful brands that is always one of the highlights of the whisky-tasting year to discover. *60.6%*

Aberlour a'bunadh Batch No. 27 db (**82**) **n21 t21.5 f18.5 b21**. More than the odd dud sherry butt. Shame, because some of the intensity of the ginger and Demerara could have made for something ultra special. *60%*

Aberlour a'bunadh Batch No. 28 db (**93.5**) **n22.5** firm but fruity. A dusty dryness; **t24** thrilling delivery: puckering oak and fruit, then a slowly unravelling of liquorice, hickory and mocha; some cherry cake offers the sweeter moments; **f23.5** long, remaining massive and intact with jaffa and ginger cakes vying with the chocolate cup cake for supremacy. An irritatingly dry fade but spices and a late dememara rum surge compensate; **b23.5** those of you who like your malts to be quiet in the glass and offer little more than a barley whine, don't even bother. Though there is evidence of a mildly off key sherry butt, such is the uncompromising enormity of all else you cannot be other than blown away. X-rated malt for grownups, with the odd tart amongst class acts. *59.8%*

Aberlour a'bunadh Batch No. 29 db **(94.5) n23.5** rich coffee: very similar to pre-coloured Demerara pot still at seven or eight years; toffee apple and a touch of burnt toast; **t24** a degree of puckering dryness suggests good age, then layers of honey of varying thickness and intensity; hickory and crème brulee in the middle ground with a wonderfully moist Lubec marzipan offering the flourish; **f23.5** back to the caramel but spices arrive so late they are almost an afterthought. But they work well; **b23.5** and indulgent malt lashing on the toffee creams. Assured, with not a single false step from beginning to end. World class. *59.9%*

Aberlour a'bunadh Batch No. 30 bott Mar 10 db **(87.5) n23** a big, fruity signature with succulent dates and dried blackberries; a nipping dryness points towards a particular type of cask; **t23.5** now in its element as a huge wave of fruit and honey cascade down upon the taste buds; wonderful weight and structure and a light coppery sheen; **f19** a bitter note slowly creeps in; **b22** though a renegade cask has slipped through the net, some moments are breathtaking. Oh, what might have been...! *59.8%*

⟐ **Berry's Own Selection Aberlour 1988** cask no. 5551, bott 2011 **(85.5) n21 t22 f21 b21.5.** Starts almost too beautifully with the citrus tint to the honey on delivery the stuff of dreams. A rather tired cask does not allow much building upon this early promise. *53.2%. nc ncf sc. Berry Bros & Rudd.*

Berry's Own Selection Aberlour 1995 bott 2009 **(85) n21 t22 f21 b21.** Plenty of fresh barley and the odd wave of tannin. *46%. Berry Bros & Rudd.*

The Coopers Choice Aberlour 1992 Aged 17 Years (84) n21.5 t21.5 f21 b20. Clean, grassy, as simplistic as they come. And nothing like its 17 years. *46%*

Milroy's of Soho Aberlour 1991 hogshead, cask no. 101278, dist Sep 91, bott Feb 10 **(85) n20.5 t23 f20.5 b21.** Just one quick sniff is enough to tell you the cask isn't going to be of much use. So all the workload is borne by the quality of the malt. Thankfully, that is extremely high, so you are treated to a fabulous exhibition of mouth watering barley at its most impressively weighted. A lesser distillery than Aberlour would have buckled. *46%. Milroy's of Soho. 314 bottles.*

⟐ **Old Malt Cask Aberlour Aged 20 Years** refill hogshead, cask no. 6881, dist Oct 90, bott Jan 11 **(85.5) n21 t22 f21 b21.5.** Makes a particular point of saying as little as possible. Just very pleasant with the odd billowing barley moment. But otherwise very shy. *50%. nc ncf sc.*

Old Malt Cask Aberlour Aged 22 Years refill hogshead, dist Oct 86, bott Dec 08 **(87) n21 t22.5 f22 b21.5.** Tasted blind, I'd never have recognised this as Aberlour, except for the sprig o' mint on the nose, perhaps. Composed and steady stuff. *50%. Douglas Laing. 295 bottles.*

⟐ **Provenance Aberlour Over 12 Years** refill hogs head, cask no. 6863, dist Autumn 98, bott Winter 2010 **(87) n22** clear honey on toast; **t21.5** a bit of wobble as some aggressive oak bites. But that honeydew melon barley saves the day; **f22** spices enliven the continuing honey; **b21.5** so delicate, looks as though it could snap at any moment. But some busy bees save the day... *46%. Douglas Laing & Co.*

⟐ **Scott's Selection Aberlour 1989** bott 2011 **(94.5) n24.5** sugared Frosties soften in milk; the vaguest hint of cinnamon on the over-cooked toast; a dab of acacia honey and lime offers the required balance; **t24.5** if you can find a delivery in which the sugars are so perfectly in tune with the drier oaks, please show it to me. The natural caramels build slowly, as do the spices; enough barley to ensure maximum salivation; **f22.5** just a hint of unrequited bitterness but the caramels hold sway; **b23** around this period at Aberlour, the consistency in the quality of production went up a gear or two. Here is fabulous example: quite wonderful. *49.8%. Speyside Distillers.*

ABHAINN DEARG

Highlands (Outer Hebrides), 2008. Marko Tayburn. Working.

⟐ **Abhainn Dearg New Make** db **(92.5) n23 t23 f23.5 b23.** A technically efficient spirit. Exceptionally well made with no feints and no waste, either. Oddly salty – possibly the saltiest new make I have encountered, and can think of no reason why it should be – with excellent weight as some extra copper from the new still takes hold. Given a good cask, no reason this impressive new born son of the Outer Hebrides won't go on to become something significant. *67%*

Abhainn Dearg New Make db **(88) n21.5 t23 f21.5 b22.** OK. I admit that the 1,001st new whisky for the 2011 Bible wasn't whisky at all, but new make. But, as the Isle of Lewis has made it impossible for me not to visit there by now being an official whisky-making island, I thought it was worth celebrating. The new make in this form is rich, clean and malty but with a much heightened metallic feel to it, both on nose and taste, by comparison to other recently-opened distilleries. This is likely to change markedly over time as the stills settle in. So I had better start looking at the Cal-Mac Ferry timetables to go and find out for myself if it does... *Sample from cask at Whiskyfair Limburg 2010*

⊱ **Abhainn Dearg Spirit Of Lewis** PX cask, cask no. 122010 db **(89)** n22 t23 f22 b22. A very brave cask choice, I must say: I can think of no other more likely to throttle the personality out of the embryonic malt. But it does pass on a welcome spiciness which mixes well with the latent saltiness. A vague, distant touch of phenol but can't really tell amid the prune juice. Have to say that the spirit is standing up to the bullying of the butt rather well... *56.5%. Matured for 2 to 3 months.*

ALLT-Á-BHAINNE
Speyside, 1975. Chivas Brothers. Working.

Chester Whisky & Liquer Co. Allt-á-Bhainne Aged 12 Years dist 1996 **(78.5)** n19 t21 f19 b19.5. One of the weirder whiskies tasted for the 2010 Bible, almost worth collecting in its own right for its oddity alone. Nosed and tasted blind I would have sworn this was from a Holstein still in Germany. Even so, sweet and drinkable but nothing like I would have expected from this distillery. *54.3%*

Connoisseurs Choice Allt-á-Bhainne 1995 dist 1995 **(88)** n21.5 Lincoln biscuit: light, a hint of oil and a sugary coating; t22 fresh barley, lightly salivating as sugar leads the way; f22.5 longer and more complex thanks to the ever-increasing oak participation; b22 almost beautiful in its stark simplicity. *43%. Gordon & MacPhail.*

⊱ **Malts Of Scotland Allt-á-Bhainne 1992** bourbon hogshead, cask no. 6, dist May 92, bott Feb 11 **(89)** n19.5 the oak bludgeons the deft barley with just too heavy a hand; t24 toffee apples with copious cinnamon for good measure. The barley reaches astonishing intensity, the sweetness forming a chewy, molassed density; f22.5 quite a long fade with the sugars lingering some way beyond expectation. The apples remain, though of the windfall variety. Some fine butterscotch tart, too; b23 such is the purity and depth of the barley it frees itself from its oaky entrapment with glorious results. A real beauty. *56.1%. sc.*

⊱ **Old Malt Cask Allt-á-Bhainne Aged 13 Years** sherry butt, cask no. 6500, dist Dec 96, bott Jul 10 **(79.5)** n18 t21.5 f19.5 b20. Some sulphur but the enormity of the barley keeps the damage to an absolute minimum. *50%. nc ncf sc. Douglas Laing & Co. 266 bottles.*

Old Malt Cask Allt-á-Bhaine Aged 17 Years refill hogshead, dist Jun 91, bott Dec 08 **(84.5)** n19.5 t23 f21 b21. For all the evidence of fading glory and slightly over enthusiastic oak, there is much on the punchy, spicy, bourbon-sweetened delivery to celebrate. Almost diametrically opposed to the last Original Malt Cask 17 I tasted from this distillery!! *50%*

⊱ **Old Masters Allt-á-Bhainne 17 Years Old** cask no. 40658, dist 1993, bott Nov 10 **(88)** n22 a beautiful interplay between barley and banana; t23 fresh, mouth-puckering barley arrival almost brings a tear to the eye; the fudge-rich middle is comforting and soft but a surprise; f21.5 a massive caramel kick dampens the malty fire; b21.5 I am assuming there is no colouring, so the barrel must have given this an enormous jolt of natural caramels. Great fun, all the same. *57.9%. sc. James MacArthur & Co.*

Provenance Allt-á-Bhainnne Over 11 Years sherry cask no. 5439, dist Winter 97, bott Summer 09 **(87)** n22 older than its given years with a massive oak-barley head-on smash; t22 pretty chunky for an Allt-a. A deep glossiness to the oak cannot out-perform the barley; f21.5 good, oils keep the toasty barley lingering; b21.5 presumably from a first-fill ex-bourbon cask. *46%. nc ncf. Douglas Laing & Co Ltd.*

⊱ **Provenance Allt-á-Bhainne Over 12 Years** dist Winter 97, bott Spring 2010 **(82)** n19 t20.5 f21.5 b20. Curious. The grape appears to neuter any complexity to the big barley, giving the effect of a malt all dressed up but going nowhere. *46%. Douglas Laing & Co Ltd.*

⊱ **Provenance Allt-á-Bhainne Over 12 Years** sherry butt, cask no. 6533, dist Winter 97, bott Autumn 2010 **(83.5)** n20 t21 f21.5 b21. Heavy, heady stuff with a big liquorice middle and late spice. The hallmarks of a first fill bourbon cask with a little too much to say. *46%. nc ncf sc.*

ARDBEG
Islay, 1815. Glenmorangie Plc. Working.

Ardbeg 10 Years Old db **(97)** n24 more complex, citrus-led and sophisticated than recent bottlings, though the peat is no less but now simply displayed in an even greater elegance; a beautiful sea salt strain to this; t24 gentle oils carry on them a lemon-lime edge, sweetened by barley and a weak solution of golden syrup; the peat is omnipotent, turning up in every crevice and wave, yet never one once overstepping its boundary; f24 stunningly clean, the oak offers not a bitter trace but rather a vanilla and butterscotch edge to the barley. Again the smoke wafts around in a manner unique in the world of whisky when it comes to sheer élan and adroitness; b25 like when you usually come across something that goes down so beautifully and with such a nimble touch and disarming allure, just close your eyes and enjoy... 46% ⊙

⠿ **Ardbeg 10** bottling mark L10 152 db **(95)** n24.5 mesmerising: bigger oak kick than normal suggesting some extra age somewhere. But fits comfortably with the undulating peat and dusting of salt; captivating complexity: hard to find a ten year old offering more than this...; t23.5 a shade oilier than the norm with orange and honey mingling effortlessly with the smoke: more than a hint of icing sugar; melts in the mouth like a prawn cracker...but without the prawns...; f23.5 drying oak with cocoa powder. The oils help the sugars linger; b23.5 a bigger than normal version, but still wonderfully delicate. Fabulous and faultless. 46%. *Canadian market bottling in English and French dual language label.*

Ardbeg 17 Years Old earlier bottlings db **(92)** n23 t22 f23 b24. OK, I admit I had a big hand in this, creating it with the help of Glenmorangie Plc's John Smith. It was designed to take the weight off the better vintages of Ardbeg whilst ensuring a constant supply around the world. Certainly one of the more subtle expressions you are likely to find, though criticised by some for not being peaty enough. As the whisky's creator, all I can say is they are missing the point. 40%

Ardbeg 17 Years Old later bottlings db **(90)** n22 t23 f22 b23. The peat has all but vanished and cannot really be compared to the original 17-year-old: it's a bit like tasting a Macallan without the sherry: fascinating to see the naked body underneath, and certainly more of a turn on. Peat or no peat, great whisky by any standards. 40%

Ardbeg Guaranteed 30 Years Old db **(91)** n24 t23 f21 b23. An unsual beast, one of the last ever bottled by Allied. The charm and complexity early on is enormous, but the fade rate is surprising. That said, still a dram of considerable magnificence. 40%

Ardbeg 1977 db **(96)** n25 t24 f23 b24. When working through the Ardbeg stocks, I earmarked '77 a special vintage, the sweetest of them all. So it has proved. Only the '74 absorbed that extra oak that gave greater all-round complexity. Either way, the quality of the distillate is beyond measure: simply one of the greatest experiences – whisky or otherwise – of your life. 46%

Ardbeg 1978 db **(91)** n23 t24 f22 b22. An Ardbeg on the edge of losing it because of encroaching oak, hence the decision made by John Smith and I to bottle this vintage early alongside the 17-year-old. Nearly ten years on, still looks a pretty decent bottling, though slightly under strength! 43%

Ardbeg 1992 Single Cask No. 772 1st fill ex bourbon, dist Apr 92, bott Dec 08 db **(86.5)** n22 t22.5 f21 b21. Curious choice of cask. Rare for a distillery bottling not to take off, but this one comes at you with its hands and legs tied. The nose suggests there might be some bitterness further down the line. And there is. The citrus is engaging, though. 55.7%. 184 bottles.

Ardbeg 1995 Single Cask No. 2761 2nd fill bourbon, dist Dec 95, bott Mar 10 db **(92.5)** n22.5 light coffee; unusually floral, delicate, salty smoke; t24 mouth watering with an immediate citrus kick. Barely discernable oils, but enough to maximise the lighter than normal phenols. A lovely lemon-orange freshness clings to the palate; f23 sharp marmalade with vanilla delving into the increasingly prickly smoke; b23 textbook Ardbeg from the point of view that its complexity can be gauged only after five or six mouthfuls. A shifting sands of a dram... 53.3%. 228 bottles. For Feis Ile.

Ardbeg 1998 Single Cask No. 1189 db **(87)** n22.5 t22 f21 b21.5. This has been a vintage year for very odd new bottlings of Ardbeg. Yes, I've warmed it and reduced with water (anything!); and yes it is enjoyable. But just not up to snuff on the Ardbeg front for me... 54%

Ardbeg 1998 Single Cask No. 1190 toasted oak hogshead, dist May 98, bott Dec 08 db **(88.5)** n21.5 no surprise about the giant tannin-laced oak input: the smoke is not so much dwarfed as submerged. No shortage of chocolate, though; t23 massive: again the oak dominates beyond belief with a whole bunch of natural caramels and Jaffa cakes hanging onto its tail. The smoke appears lost and bewildered as the oils and spices invade; f22 long, tangy orange; b22 it's the oak behaving like some look-at-me merchant on an annoying reality TV show. Pretty and entertaining, but only to a point. The unique personality of Ardbeg is jettisoned and while this is a lovely if rather OTT dram, not for a second is the distillery recognisable. A fascinating experiment, nonetheless. 54.7%. 282 bottles. For Feis Ile.

Ardbeg 1998 Single Cask No. 1275 1st fill bourbon barrel, dist May 98, bott Oct 09 db **(87)** n21 dim; t22 half-hearted vanilla keeps the smoke under control, with a muscovado edge; f22 delicate vanilla with a soft smoke fade; b22 enjoyable but lacking a bit of the usual Ardbeg charisma and vitality. 55.4%. 252 bottles.

Ardbeg 1998 Single Cask No. 2763 refill sherry hogshead, dist Sep 98, bott Nov 09 db **(86.5)** n22 t22 f21 b21.5. Ardbeg in a straightjacket. The sherry influence tightens every aspect, restricting the usual effortless grace and complexity. As hard an Ardbeg as you'll ever find. 55.6%. 270 bottles.

Ardbeg 2000 Single Cask Lord Robertson of Port Ellen KT cask no. 1217, dist Apr 00, bott May 10 db (**96.5**) **n24** classic busy but relaxed nose: that delicate squeeze of young lemon dancing with such elegant peat confirms that it can be from no other distillery; **t24.5** and there we are: the delivery is at once soft and full of spices which blast you from your chair; again the lemon is quickly in and the phenols melt into cocoa and Demerara...beyond orgasmic; **f23.5** exceptionally long even by Ardbeg standards with the lightest oils to assist. Spices, mocha, citrus and smoke stretch into infinity... **b24.5** though fun, a number of the distillery bottling casks had left me a little flat. Here though is a cask not just basking in all the finest Ardbegian traditions but taking those unique characteristics and pushing them beyond the distance you thought they might go. And proof, were it needed, that Ardbeg at10 can, as it did one, two and three decades ago, offer something which is the equivalent of a whisky lover's wet dream. Whatever they ask you for this bottling, pay it. Not only is the money going to a great cause. But your experience in whisky will be equally enriched. *53%. For Lord Robertson (proceeds donated to Erskine). 202 bottles.*

⋰ **Ardbeg Alligator 1st Release** db (**94**) **n24** delicate: like a bomb aimer...steady, steady, steady...there she goes...and suddenly spices light up the nose; some coriander and cocoa, too; **t22.5** surprisingly silky, soft and light; milky chocolate hides some lurking clove in the soothing smoke; **f24** hits its stride for a magnificent finale: as long as you could possibly hope for and an-ever gathering intensity of busy, prickly spice. Mocha and a dab of praline see off any potential bitterness to the oaky fight back; **b23.5** an alligator happy to play with you for a bit before sinking its teeth in. The spices, though big, are of the usual Ardbegian understatement. *51.2%. ncf. Exclusive for Ardbeg Committee members.*

⋰ **Ardbeg Alligator 2nd Release** db (**93**) **n24** clove and black pepper; a degree of bourbony polished leather and liquorice, too; **t23** early Demerara sugars and smoke make way for that slow build up of spices again; though perhaps missing the subtlety of the first edition's quietness, it more than has its macho compensations; **f23** curiously, a short finale, as though more energy was expended in the delivery. Much drier with the oak having a good deal to say, though the spices nip satisfyingly; **b23** something of a different species to the Committee bottling having been matured a little longer, apparently. Well long enough for this to evolve into something just a little less subtle. The nose, though, remains something of striking beauty – even if barely recognisable from the first bottling. *51.2%. ncf.*

Ardbeg Almost There 3rd release dist 1998, bott 2007 db (**93**) **n23 t24 f23 b23**. Further proof that a whisky doesn't have to reach double figures in age to enter the realms of brilliance... *54.1%*

Ardbeg Blasda db (**90.5**) **n23.5** distant kumquat and lime intertwine with gentle butterscotch tart; it's all about the multi-layered barley and the most vague smokiness imaginable which adds a kind of almost invisible weight; the overall clarity is like that found swimming off a Pacific atoll; **t22.5** sharp barley hits home to almost mouth-watering effect; again there is the most pathetic hint of something smoky (like the SMWS cask, perhaps from the local water and warehouse air), but it does the trick and adds just the right ballast; **f22** soft spices arrive apologetically, but here it could do with being at 46% just to give it some late lift; **b22.5** a beautiful, if slightly underpowered malt, which shows Ardbeg's naked self to glowing effect. Overshadowed by some degree in its class by the SMWS bottling, but still something to genuinely make the heart flutter. *40%*

Ardbeg Corryvreckan db (**96.5**) **n23** excellent, thick, not entirely un-penetrable – but close – nascent smoke and a vignette of salty, coastal references save the day; **t24.5** amazing: here we have Ardbeg nutshelled. Just so many layers of almost uncountable personalities with perhaps the citrus leading the way in both tart and sweet form and then meaningful speeches from those saline-based, malty sea-spray refreshed barley notes with the oak, in vanilla form, in close proximity. The peat, almost too dense to be seen on the nose, opens out with a fanfare of phenols. It is slumping-in-the-chair stuff, the enormity of the peat taking on the majesty of Cathedral-esque proportions, the notes reverberating around the hollows and recesses and reaching dizzying heights; such is its confidence, this is a malt which says: "I know where I'm going...!"; **f24** long, outwardly laconic but on further investigation just brimming with complexity. Some brown sugary notes help the barley to come up trumps late on but it's the uniquely salty shield to the mocha which sets this apart. Simply brilliant and unique in its effortless enormity...even by Ardbeg standards; **b25** as famous writers – including the occasional genius film director (stand up wherever you are my heroes Powell and Pressburger) – appear to be attracted to Corryvreckan, the third most violent whirlpool found in the world and just off Islay, to boot, - I selected this as my 1,500th whisky tasted for the historic Jim Murray Whisky Bible 2009. I'm so glad I did because many have told me they thought Blasda ahead of this. To me, it's not even a contest. Currently I have only a sample. Soon I shall have a bottle. I doubt if even the feared whirlpool is this deep and perplexing. *57.1%. 5000 bottles.* ☺

❉ **Ardbeg Feis Ile 2011** db **(67) n16 t19 f15 b17.** If anyone asked me what not to do with an Ardbeg, my answer would be: don't put it into a PX cask. And if asked if anything could be worse, I'd day: yeah, a PX Cask reeking of sulphur. To be honest, I am only assuming this is PX, as there is no mention on my sample bottle and I have spoken to them about it. But for something to fail as completely as this my money is on PX. And sulphur. *55.4%*

Ardbeg Kildalton 1980 bott 2004 db **(96) n23 t24 f24 b25.** Proof positive that Ardbeg doesn't need peat to bring complexity, balance and Scotch whisky to their highest peaks... *57.6%*

Ardbeg Lord of the Isles bott Autumn 2006 db **(85) n20 t22 f22 b21.** A version of Ardbeg I have never really come to terms with. This bottling is of very low peating levels and shows a degree of Kildalton-style fruitiness. No probs there. But some of the casks are leaching a soft soapy character noticeable on the nose. Enjoyable enough, but a bit frustrating. *46%*

Ardbeg Mor db **(95) n24** coastal to the point of sea spray showering you, with the smell of salt all the way home until you reach the peat fire. Evocative, sharp with elements of vinegar to the iodine; **t24** one of the biggest deliveries from Ardbeg for yonks; the peat appears way above the normal 50%, thickest and gloriously bitter-sweet, the steadying vanillas carried on the soft oils; **f23** mocha enters the fray with a raspberry jam fruitiness trying to dampen the continuing smoke onslaught; **b24** quite simply Mor the merrier... *57.5%*

Ardbeg Provenance 1974 bott 1999 db **(96) n24 t25 f23 b24.** This is an exercise in subtlety and charisma, the beauty and the beast drawn into one. Until I came across the 25-year-old OMC verson during a thunderstorm in Denmark, this was arguably the finest whisky I had ever tasted: I opened this and drank from it to see in the year 2000. When I went through the Ardbeg warehouse stocks in 1997 I earmarked the '74 and '77 vintages as something special. This bottling has done me proud. *55.6%*

Ardbeg Renaissance db **(92) n22.5 t22.5 f23.5 b23.5.** How fitting that the 1,200th (and almost last) new-to-market whisky I had tasted for the 2009 Bible was Renaissance... because that's what I need after tasting that lot...!! This is an Ardbeg that comes on strong, is not afraid to wield a few hefty blows and yet, paradoxically, the heavier it gets the more delicate, sophisticated and better-balanced it becomes. Enigmatically Ardbegian. *55.9%*

Ardbeg Rollercoaster db **(90.5) n23** youthful malts dominate; a patchwork of smoke on many different levels from ashy to ethereal: almost dizzying; **t23** again, it's the young Ardbeg which dominates; the delivery is almost painful as you shake your head at the shock of the spices and unfettered peat. A genuine greenness to the malts though some natural caramels do make a smoky surge; **f23** long, buttery in part, limited sweetness; almost a touch of smoked bacon about it; **b21.5** to be honest, it was the end of another long day – and book – when I tasted this and I momentarily forgot the story behind the malt. My reaction to one of my researchers who happened to be in the tasting room was: "Bloody hell! They are sending me kids. If this was any younger I'd just be getting a bag of grist!" This malt may be a fabulous concept. And Rollercoaster is a pretty apt description, as this a dram which appears to have the whisky equivalent of Asperger's. So don't expect the kind of balance that sweeps you into a world that only Ardbeg knows. This, frankly, is not for the Ardbeg purist or snob. But for those determined to bisect the malt in all its forms and guises, it is the stuff of the most rampant hard-ons. *57.3%*

Ardbeg Still Young 2nd release dist 1998, bott 2006 db **(93) n24 t24 f22 b23.** A couple of generations back – maybe even less – this would not have been so much "Still Young" as "Getting on a Bit." This is a very good natural age for an Ardbeg as the oak is making a speech, but refuses to let it go on too long. Stylish – as one might expect. And, in my books, should be a regular feature. Go on. Be bold. Be proud say it: Ardbeg Aged 8 Years. Get away from the marketing straightjacket of old age... *56.2%. ncf.*

Ardbeg Supernova db **(97) n24.5** moody, atmospheric; hints and threats; Lynchian in its stark black and white forms, its meandering plot, its dark and at times indecipherable message and meaning...; **t24** at first a wall of friendly phenols but only when you stand back and see the overall picture you can get an idea just how mammoth that wall is; there are intense sugary gristy notes, then this cuts away slightly towards something more mouth-fillingly smoky but now with a hickory sweetness; a light oil captures the long, rhythmic waves, a pulse almost; **f24** gentle, sweetening cocoa notes evolve while the peat pulses... again...and again... **b24.5** apparently this was called "Supernova" in tribute of how I once described a very highly peated Ardbeg. This major beast, carrying a phenol level in excess of 100ppm, isn't quite a Supernova...much more of a Black Hole. Because once you get dragged into this one, there really is no escaping... *58.9%*

Ardbeg Supernova SN2010 bott 2010 (93.5) n24 youthful, punchy and spicy; vanillas and bananas add a sweetness to the molten peat; t23.5 an explosion of sharp citrus and grassy malt. Not quite what was expected but the smoke and spices cause mayhem as they crash around the palate: eye-watering, safety harness-wearing stuff; f23 the oak has a bitter-ish surprise but soft sugars compensate. Elsewhere the smoke and spice continues its rampage; b23 there are Supernovas and there are Supernovas. Some have been going on a bit and have formed a shape and indescribable beauty with the aid of time; others are just starting off and though full of unquantifiable energy and wonder have a distance to travel. By comparison to last year's blockbusting Whisky Bible award winner, this is very much in the latter category. 60.1%

Ardbeg Uigeadail db (97.5) n25 t24.5 f23.5 b24.5. Massive yet tiny. Loud yet whispering. Seemingly ordinary from the bottle, yet unforgettable. It is snowing outside my hotel room in Calgary, yet the sun, in my soul at least, is shining. I came across this bottling while lecturing the Liquor Board of British Columbia in Vancouver on May 6th 2008, so one assumes it is a Canadian market bottling. It was one of those great moments in my whisky life on a par with tasting for the first time the Old Malt Cask 1975 at a tasting in Denmark. There is no masking genius.The only Scotch to come close to this one is another from Ardbeg, Corryvreckan. That has more oomph and lays the beauty and complexity on thick...it could easily have been top dog. But this particular Uigeadail (for I have tasted another bottling this year, without pen or computer to hand and therefore unofficially, which was a couple of points down) offers something far more restrained and cerebral. Believe me: this bottling will be going for thousands at auction in the very near future, I wager. 54.2%

Ardbeg Uigeadail db (89) n25 awesome package of intense peat reek amid complex fruitcake and leather notes. Everything about this nose is broadside-big yet the massive oak never once oversteps its mark. A whiff of engine oil compliments the kippers. Perfection; t22 begins with a mind-blowing array of bitter-sweet oaky notes and then a strangely fruity peat entry; real scattergun whisky; f20 very odd finish with an off-key fruit element that flattens the usual Ardbeg grand finale; b22 a curious Ardbeg with a nose to die for. Some tinkering - please guys, as the re-taste is not better - regarding the finish may lift this to being a true classic 54.1%

Cadenhead's Ardbeg Aged 15 Years cask no. 1056, dist 1994, bott 2009 (92.5) n23 t23.5 f23 b23. Typically understated Ardbeg, where everything first appears big, but when analysed is just so delicate and almost coy. Wonderful. 58.1%

Cadenhead's Ardbeg Aged 15 Years cask no. 1057, dist 1994, bott 2009 (95) n23 t24 f23.5 b24.5. Virtually peas in a pod, are casks 1056/7. Except this is a spicier cove. And doesn't suffer for it, for those tiny differences add up to a lot. 57.3%

Cadenhead's Authentic Collection Ardbeg 1994 bott Feb 10 (94.5) n23.5 super spiced: a zillion mini explosions on the nose, each of them hitting a nerve. The smoke is dense; t24 sweetness is at a premium at any point here and after the expected eruption on delivery and scattering of spice, the odd grain of muscovado can be picked up here and there; f23.5 long, with hickory firming up the peat to a daft degree. And those peppery spices just refuse to fade. Wonderful...; b23.5 a classy, growling Ardbeg. Just a little attitude here and there, like a superstar having a grouse. 56%. Wm. Cadenhead Ltd. 268 bottles.

Connoisseurs Choice Ardbeg 1991 (93.5) n24.5 t23.5 f22.5 b23. A superb whisky unable to live up to the supernatural nose by being merely excellent on the palate. 43%

⟨⋅⟩ **Dun Bheagan Ardbeg 15 Years Old** dist Nov 94 (93) n23 above average phenols even for this distillery marked by a dry, sooty style; t23 nothing dry about the delivery: almost grist like in its juiciness; f23 long, with a far better oak accompaniment than you would ever expect from an old Allied distillery; the sugars stay to the far from bitter end; b24 effortlessly beautiful. Never quite gets out of second gear...never really has to... 53%. nc ncf. Ian Macleod Distillers.

Duncan Taylor Collection Ardbeg 1993 cask no. 1724 (92) n23 classic buzzing peat, nipping and radiating lavender and smoke; t23.5 bristling delivery: eyes on stalks stuff! The explosive spices clear a path for the smoke and liquorice as its takes a peculiarly bourbon turn for the sweeter; f23 long, with those white peppers red hot; b22.5 a tin hat malt; like an abridged version of this year's Cadenhead '94 bottling. 58.9%. Duncan Taylor & Co Ltd.

Hart Brothers Ardbeg Aged 17 Years dist Feb 91, bott Mar 08 (92) n23.5 t23 f22.5 b23. A busy and engaging Ardbeg. 46%. Hart Brothers Limited.

Old & Rare Ardbeg Aged 36 Years dist Mar 73, bott Apr 09 (76) n19 t20 f18 b19. Some serious cowshed moments on the nose: fruity, too. But, frankly, to nose and taste as uniquely weird as any Ardbeg I've come across in over 25 years of worshipping the stuff. Can't help thinking that this might become the stuff of legend in some parts of northern Germany... 44.7%. Douglas Laing. 78 bottles.

Old Malt Cask Ardbeg Aged 17 Years refill hogshead, finished in rum cask, dist Mar 91, bott Oct 08 (86.5) n21.5 t22 f22 b21. Enjoyable, juicy, candy-crisp sweet and spicy but relatively flat for an Ardbeg with the higher notes cropped by the rum. 50%. 316 bottles.

Old Malt Cask Ardbeg Aged 17 Years refill hogshead, dist Mar 91, bott Aug 08 (90.5) n23.5 t22.5 f22 b22.5. A whispering Ardbeg... 50%. 226 bottles.

Old Malt Cask Ardbeg Aged 18 Years refill hogshead, dist Mar 91, bott Apr 09 (86.5) n21.5 t23 f21 b21. A very different kind of Ardbeg with the oils really showing to maximum effect. Helps the intensity of the delivery, but perhaps not the unveiling of the more complex notes further down the line. Very pleasant, but ordinary by Ardbegian standards. 50%. 357 bottles.

Old Malt Cask Ardbeg Aged 18 Years refill hogshead no. DL 5440, dist Mar 91, bott Aug 09 (89) n21 salty and sharp; t23 juicy: tidal waves of smoky barley with a rich mocha and spice background; f22 spiced smoky chocolate; b23 a gentle version which takes time to crank itself up. But worth the wait. 50%. Douglas Laing. 208 bottles.

Scotch Malt Whisky Society Cask 33.77 Aged 11 Years 1st fill barrel, dist May 98 (95) n23.5 intriguing dusty cocoa on the briny smoke; t24 jam tart and cream: a lightly oily, fruity edge to this one. Gentle for all the peat and cask strength zap; the middle ground luxuriates in an orangey glow to the smoke; f23.5 long, more hints and whispers of fruit and bourbon tones while the peat continues its gentle cascade onto the palate; b24 it's as though this distillery does genius without even trying... 57.3%. 239 bottles.

Scotch Malt Whisky Society Cask 33.80 Aged 11 Years 1st fill barrel, dist May 98 (86) n21.5 t22 f22 b20.5. For many distilleries, this wouldn't be a bad dram; it is perfectly flavoursome, enjoyable and chewy. For an Ardbeg, though, this is rather clumsy and ill-defined. 56.5%. Scotch Malt Whisky Society. 242 bottles.

Scotch Malt Whisky Society Cask 33.84 Aged 10 Years 1st fill barrel, dist Sep 99 (92) n23 an unusual Ardbeg nose with the peat almost ash dry: spices – all of them smoky – nip at the nose; t24 powering peat in both ash and oil form. The sugars have that slightly burned feel to them. There is a sublime rhythm and pulse to this one while the bittering oak and confident, gristy sugars offer a superb balance; f22 remains on the toasty, smoky side; b23 you get the feeling this is some way above the usual 50ppm phenols! A must have for Smokeheads. 57%. Scotch Malt Whisky Society. 243 bottles.

Scotch Malt Whisky Society Cask 33.85 Aged 7 Years 2nd fill barrel, dist Nov 02 (84) n22 t21 f20 b21. I raised an eyebrow on nosing this – until I checked the age. Even so, the bitter notes suggest this may not have been filled into quite the best barrel at the distillery. 60.5%. Scotch Malt Whisky Society. 215 bottles.

Scotch Malt Whisky Society Cask 33.86 Aged 10 Years 1st fill barrel, dist Sep 99 (89.5) n23 a beguiling coastal peatiness which, like an Islay storm, builds quickly in intensity; t23 big sugary drive on delivery followed by some major smoke; plenty of fruits, not least pears – with a damn good dollop of smoky custard; the peats fizz from the first moment; f21.5 heads into a bitter-sweet siding; b22 excellent stuff. But runs off the tracks slightly towards the finish. 56.4%. Scotch Malt Whisky Society. 243 bottles.

Scotch Malt Whisky Society Cask 33.87 Aged 10 Years 1st fill barrel, dist Feb 00 (86.5) n21.5 t22 f21.5 b21.5. Surprising degree of vanilla. Deliciously smoky and sweet, but fails to engage the usual degree of subtle fruit and complexity. 576%. 255 bottles.

⚜ **Scotch Malt Whisky Society Cask 33.88 Aged 10 Years** 1st fill bourbon barrel, cask no. 1792, dist 1999 (84.5) n22.5 t21 f20 b21. Big liquorice lilt to the smoke but curiously lacking the usual deft fruitiness. But some evidence that the stills were run a little too keenly on this one. Extremely average by Ardbegian standards. 56.5%. sc. 243 bottles.

⚜ **Scotch Malt Whisky Society Cask 33.91 Aged 10 Years** refill sherry puncheon, cask no. 759093, dist 2000 (75.5) n19.5 t19.5 f18 b18.5. A thin, niggardly and hot dram. Proof that a poor cask equals a poor whisky – no matter who makes it. 64.4%. sc. 410 bottles.

⚜ **Scotch Malt Whisky Society Cask 33.96 Aged 10 Years** refill sherry butt, cask no. 1556, dist 1999 (93) n23 a pretty violent meeting between grape and smoke. And though I abhor violence...gerthcha!!! t24 knee-buckling stuff! The grapes are simply dripping juice, but the peat will not be outdone. The result is a battle which, had it been in Greek times, would have lived in the classical annals forever; f23 long, luxurious with persistent fresh grape but also big spice and ever building vanilla; b23 the grape and toffee from the oak combine to just deflect some of the higher notes of complexity. That said...wow! 56.7%. sc. 668 bottles.

⚜ **Scotch Malt Whisky Society Cask 33.100 Aged 7 Years** 1st fill bourbon barrel, cask no. 1419, dist 2003 (93.5) n23 one of the delicately peated variety where the smoke hangs by a thread and is easily challenged by citrus for supremacy; a few herbal notes offer greater tread; t24 mega sweet, but purely from a gristy perspective: virtually no oak sugars I can detect. Just barley-driven ones alone. Because of the tender years this is fabulously juicy;

f23 pretty short by Ardbeg standards. No great oils or oak contribution to lengthen it. But those delicate peats just keep drifting; the only nod to the barrel is a gentle cocoa lilt; **b23.5** in another world, the management at Ardbeg reckoned that, on the rare occasions it was bottled as a single malt, this kind of age suited it best. I don't think bourbon casks were an option then. But, even so, a memorable, must-have bottling showing the distillery at its most fragile. *60.7%. sc. 254 bottles.*

⋙ **Scotch Malt Whisky Society Cask 33.107 Aged 11 Years** refill sherry butt, cask no. 1559, dist 1999 **(91.5) n23.5** trademark big smoke but deceptively lurking in little hideaways to appear not quite as big as it is; still a little grist to be found plus mocha; also a little moist fruitcake popping up here and there; **t22** but it's that grist which shows on delivery followed swiftly by an avalanche of spices; a little cough sweet towards the middle; **f23** enters a wonderful phase of complexity. Vanillas have arrived big time, there is the most distant hint of berry fruit while the peat and spices rumble on...; **b23** Ardbeg at its most charming. *57.8%. sc. 659 bottles.*

⋙ **Scotch Malt Whisky Society Cask 33.108 Aged 13 Years** 2nd fill barrel, cask no. 1140, dist 1997 **(95.5) n24** salty, crisp barley with an oily gloss to the smoke; so complex and just about perfectly weighted; **t24** salivating and filled to the brim with juicy lemon notes. The spices kick off early but remain busy if slightly aloof, allowing the smoke full scope to mingle with the vanilla; the sugars are a constant, taking a midline in intensity and remain firmly in the muscovado style; **f23.5** a gentle praline edge to the ever more delicate smoke; **b24** my favourite cask type for Ardbeg. Juicy, elegant... frankly, sublime. *56.6%. sc. 220 bottles.*

ARDMORE
Speyside, 1899. Beam Inc. Working.

Ardmore 100th Anniversary 12 Years Old dist 1986, bott 1999 db **(94) n24 t23.5 f22.5 b24.** Brilliant. Absolutely stunning, with the peat almost playing games on the palate. Had they not put caramel in this bottling, it most likely would have been an award winner. So, by this time next year, I fully expect to see every last bottle accounted for... *40%*

Ardmore 25 Years Old db **(89.5) n21** decidedly caramel oriented with the smoke thin and crisp; **t23.5** quite brilliant delivery: not only powering, but with an unwavering Demerara and chocolate voice; lightly roasted Blue Mountain benefits from the playful spices; the smoke is little more than a background hum; **f22.5** long with a milky, orangey texture steeling in; **b22.5** a 25-y-o box of chocolates: coffee creams, fudge, orange cream...they are all in there. The nose maybe ordinary: what follows is anything but. *51.4%. ncf.*

⋙ **Ardmore 30 Years Old Cask Strength** db **(94) n23.5** the first time I have encountered a cough-sweetish aroma on an Ardmore but, like every aspect, it is played down and delicate. Melting sugar on porridge. Citrus notes of varying intensity. Fascinating for its apparent metal hand in velvet glove approach; **t23.5** sweet, gristy delivery even after all these years. And a squeeze of sharp lime, too, and no shortage of spices. Does all in its power to appear half its age. This includes blocking the oaks from over development and satisfying itself with a smoky, mocha middle; the muscovado sugars are, with the smoke, spread evenly; **f23** busy spices and a lazy build up of vanillas; **b24** I remember when the present owners of Ardmore launched their first ever distillery bottling. Over a lunch with the hierarchy there I told them, with a passion, to ease off with the caramel so the world can see just how complex this whisky can be. This brilliant, technically faultless, bottling is far more eloquent and persuasive than I was that or any other day... *53.7%. nc ncf. 1428 bottles.*

Ardmore Fully Peated Quarter Casks db **(89) n21 t23 f23 b22.** This is an astonishingly brave attempt by the new owners of Ardmore who, joy of all joys, are committed to putting this distillery in the public domain. Anyone with a 2004 copy of the Whisky Bible will see that my prayers have at last been answered. However, this bottling is for Duty Free and, due to the enormous learning curve associated with this technique, a work in progress. They have used the Quarter Cask process which has been such a spectacular success at its sister distillery Laphroaig. Here I think they have had the odd slight teething problem. Firstly, Ardmore has rarely been filled in ex-bourbon and that oak type is having an effect on the balance and smoke weight; also they have unwisely added caramel, which has flattened things further. I don't expect the caramel to be in later bottlings and, likewise, I think the bourbon edge might be purposely blunted a little. But for a first attempt this is seriously big whisky that shows enormous promise. When they get this right, it could – and should – be a superstar. Now I await the more traditional vintage bottlings... *46%. ncf.*

Ardmore Traditional Cask db **(88.5) n21.5 t22 f23 b22.** Not quite what I expected. "Jim. Any ideas on improving the flavour profile?" asked the nice man from Ardmore distillery when they were originally launching the thing. "Yes. Cut out the caramel." "Ah, right..." So what do I find when the next bottling comes along? More caramel. It's good to have influence... Actually,

I can't quite tell if this is a result of natural caramelization from the quarter casking or just an extra dollop of the stuff in the bottling hall. The result is pretty similar: some of the finer complexity is lost. My guess, due to an extra fraction of sweetness and spice, is that it is the former. All that said, the overall experience remains quite beautiful. And this remains one of my top ten distilleries in the world. 46%. ncf.

Chieftain's Ardmore Aged 17 Years dist Jun 92, bott 2010 **(88.5)** n22 deceptively rich smoke; t22 beautiful honey strands to the intense barley; the smoke adds gravitas; f22 long, light oils; buttery barley and a constant smoky, gristy, sugariness ; b22.5 a wonderfully nimble and understated dram. 46%. nc ncf. Ian Macleod.

⋰ **Chieftain's Ardmore Aged 18 Years** dist Jun 92, bott 2011 **(93)** n23 soft, slightly dry peat drifts over the relaxed oak-barley mix; t23 silky body wrapped in a deftly smoky, oak-caramel-rich shroud; f24 very long finale helped by the cleverly ingratiating smoke and those sugar-coated oils. About as soft a finish as you'll ever find – even after when the spice attack is made; b23 over the last 30-odd years it has been my good fortune to taste samples from the contents of an enormous number of Ardmore barrels: and I mean almost certainly a four figure sum. Which is why I was probably the most vociferous advocate they had ever enjoyed right up until the time the first commercial distillery bottling was launched. This gives you some idea why: it is absolutely typical of the malt for its age: not a single off note, not overly spectacular, yet effortlessly ticks every single positive box in its own delicately peaty way. 46%. nc ncf. Ian Macleod Distillers. USA release.

⋰ **L'Esprit Single Cask Collection Ardmore** refill bourbon barrel, cask no. 6487, dist Sep 03, bott Oct 10 **(80)** n22 t21 f18 b19. The nose is full of the usual Ardmore understated smoky promise which is never quite fulfilled due to the trademark bitterness of a less than brilliant ex-Allied cask. 46%. nc ncf sc. Whisky & Rhum. 121 bottles.

⋰ **L'Esprit Single Cask Collection Ardmore Cask Strength** refill bourbon barrel, cask no. 6487, dist Sep 03, bott Oct 10 **(85.5)** n22.5 t22 f20 b21. There you go: a real April the 1st moment. Or at least end of day one. Went off after tasting the last sample (above) to clean out the palate from the bitter finish. Then sat down, nosed and tasted this and actually said to myself out loud: "bugger me! This could be from the same cask as the last one!" So exasperated was I, I studied the labels...and found that they were! This, by the way, is very much better than the 46% version. The reason is quite simple: the intensity of the sugars on the malt, fatally weakened in the other version, have enough about them to see off all but the worst of flaws in the cask. Further proof, should you need it, why whisky and water don't go... 56.2%. nc ncf sc. Whisky & Rhum. 60 bottles.

⋰ **Malts Of Scotland Ardmore 1992** bourbon barrel, cask no. 5014, dist, Jun 92, bott Dec 10 **(92.5)** n22.5 smoky bacon and a distinct peppery nip to the citrus; t23.5 still some juice in the barley and the peat gathers in light layers; a gorgeous mocha middle is carefully sweetened before the dryer vanillas arrive; f23 the smoky chocolate theme continues, aided by the most choice degree of oil; b23.5 weighty but with a very deft touch. High quality malt with sublime marbelling. 49.4%. nc ncf sc. Malts Of Scotland. 185 bottles.

Old Malt Cask Ardmore Aged 12 Years refill hogshead, dist Mar 96, bott Sep 08 **(85.5)** n22.5 t20.5 f21.5 b21. Billowing smoke, with an earthy, bonfire quality; chewy, malty, pleasantly sweet in part; peppery and gristy. 50%. Douglas Laing. 348 bottles.

⋰ **Old Malt Cask Ardmore Aged 15 Years** refill hogshead, cask no. 7044, dist Feb 96, bott Mar 11 **(88)** n23 stunning: the smoke is seemingly both delicate and storming in equal measures; powdery and a tad gristy, too; t23 fabulous arrival full of peaty pleasure. A real muscovado sugar kick to this and then those gristy notes return; f20 a little bitterness bites from the tiring cask; b22 had the cask been just a little kinder, we would have had a superdram on our hands. As it is, one to hunt down and explore. 50%. nc ncf sc. 212 bottles.

Provenance Ardmore Aged 11 Years refill hogshead, dist Autumn 96, bott Summer 08 **(80)** n21 t20 f20 b19. I'd like to say this is a third-fill cask. Except it appears to have done the rounds at least once more than that. Pleasant smoke, though. 46%. Douglas Laing.

Provenance Ardmore Over 12 Years refill hogshead no. DMG 5743, dist Autumn 97, bott Winter 2010 **(84.5)** n21 t21 f21.5 b21. Light, sweet, playfully smoked; minimum oak interference. 46%. Douglas Laing.

⋰ **The Whisky Agency Ardmore 1992** bott. 2010 **(86)** n22.5 t22 f19.5 b22. Appears a lot younger than its near 20 years. Gristy, lightly smoked and fresh. 49.9%

AUCHENTOSHAN

Lowlands, 1800. Morrison Bowmore. Working.

Auchentoshan 10 Years Old db **(81)** n22 t21 f19 b19. Much better, maltier, cleaner nose than before. But after the initial barley surge on the palate it shows a much thinner character. 40%

Auchentoshan 12 Years Old db (85) n20 t23 f21 b21. Thicker and more chewy malt than is the norm for a 'Toshan. But don't get this one confused with the astonishing peaty number that was 43%!! The finish is OK, but the delivery is superb. 40%

Auchentoshan 18 Years Old bourbon cask, batch no. L092458 db (87) n21.5 retains its light frame, but bolstered by a new-found bourbon-honey sweetness; t22.5 the oak shows up early, as you might expect from a 'Toshan of this age. But a thick strata of barley and vanilla sponge in syrup sweetness give it an enjoyable polish; f21.5 dries with a wobble, but the late spices come up trumps; plenty of chewy toffee to finish with; b21.5 a much happier soul than previous years, celebrating with an extra dollop of honey. The citrus and almonds promised on the label never quite materialise. 43% ⊙ ⊙

Auchentoshan 21 Years Old db (93) n23.5 the most unblemished, desirable and surprising of all the distillery-bottled 'Toshan noses: a sprig of mint buried in barely warmed peat, all with an undercoat of the most delicate honeys; t23 velvety and waif-like, the barley-honey theme is played out is hushed tones and unspoiled elegance; f23 the smoke deftly returns as the vanillas and citrus slowly rise but the gentle honey-barley plays to the end, despite the shy introduction of cocoa; b23.5 one of the finest Lowland distillery bottlings of our time. A near faultless masterpiece of astonishing complexity to be cherished and discussed with deserved reverence. So delicate, you fear that sniffing too hard will break the poor thing...! 43%

⸭ **Auchentoshan 1977 Sherry Cask Matured** oloroso sherry cask db (89) n23 t22 f22 b22. Rich, creamy and spicy. Almost a digestive biscuit mealiness with a sharp marmalade spread. I regret the sample sent was too meagre for more detailed professional analysis. 49%. sc. Morrison Bowmore. 240 bottles.

Auchentoshan 1978 Bourbon Cask Matured Limited Edition db (96) n24.5 a nose which stops you in your tracks: Taiwanese green tea sweetened with a brave and enthralling mix of muscovado sugar and manuka honey. There is essence of Kentucky, too, with a bourbon-liquorice trait while the vanillas head at you with two or three different degrees of intensity. How subtle. How complex. So beguiling, you almost forget to drink the stuff... t24 who could ask for more from a 30-y-o malt? Certainly not I. Because I didn't expect this engrossing seduction of my palate before opening the bottle. Wonderful strands of sweetness of varying types and levels, from the lighter, fragile citrus notes to something sturdier and more honeyed; the middle ground has a few oily moments which allow all the elements to mix without bias or domination: a near perfectly balanced harmony; f23.5 long, lush with the barley now having the confidence to reveal itself while the toasted fudge ensures an attractive and fitting bitter-sweet finale; b24 if there was a Lowlander of the Year, this'd probably wipe the floor with the rest. It's as though someone was in a warehouse, stumbled across this gem and protected it with his life to ensure it was not lost in some blend or other. Whoever is responsible should be given a gold medal, or a Dumbarton season ticket. A tip, by the way. If you ignore on all other requests to do this, please ensure you taste this one at body and not room temperature for full blow-away results. 53.4%. 480 bottles.

⸭ **Auchentoshan 1998 Sherry Cask Matured** fino sherry cask db (81.5) n21 t22 f18.5 b20. A genuine shame. Before these casks were treated in Jerez, I imagine they were spectacular. Even with the obvious faults apparent, the nuttiness is profound and milks every last atom of the oils at work to maximum effect. The sugars, also, are delicate and gorgeously weighted. There is still much which is excellent to concentrate on here. 54.6%. ncf. 6000 bottles.

Auchentoshan Classic db (80) n19 t20 f21 b20. Classic what exactly...? Some really decent barley, but goes little further. 40%

Auchentoshan Select db (85) n20 t21.5 f22 b21.5. Has changed shape of late, if not quality. Much more emphasis on the enjoyable juicy barley sharpness these days. 40%

Auchentoshan Three Wood db (76) n20 t18 f20 b18. Takes you directly into the rough. Refuses to harmonise, except maybe for some late molassed sugar. 43%

A.D. Rattray Auchentoshan 1990 cask no. 17285 (86.5) n21 t23 f21 b21.5. A messy nose and confused, vanilla-clad finish is rescued in magnificent fashion by a startlingly bright delivery full of lilting, juicy barley notes. 56.5%

The Coopers Choice Auchentoshan 1991 Aged 18 Years (75.5) n18 t20 f18.5 b19. Virtually nil colour thanks to a third-fill cask and enjoys the corresponding degree of oak complexity. It's pure grist after all these years and a tad feinty, too. Don't come across many of these in the course of a year. 46%. The Vintage Malt Whisky Co Ltd.

Duthies Auchentoshan 16 Years Old (78.5) n19 t21 f19.5 b19. Tangy and somewhat hot. 46%. Wm. Cadenhead Ltd.

Duthies Auchentoshan 19 Years Old (86) n21.5 t22 f21 b21.5. Mouth-watering, juicy and boasting a lot of natural toffee. 46%. Wm. Cadenhead Ltd for Germany.

⁂ **Hart Brothers Auchentoshan Aged 11 Years** dist Jun 99, bott Nov 10 **(84.5) n22 t22 f19 b21.5.** Clean, delicate, displaying a surprising degree of oil and no shortage of sweet barley. 46%. sc.

Murray McDavid Auchentoshan 1992 (77) n19 t20 f19 b19. Creamy, fruity...but somehow not on the ball. 46%

Old Malt Cask Auchentoshan Aged 13 years refill hogshead, dis Dec 95, bott Feb 09 **(86.5) n21 t22 f21.5 b22.** Genuinely enjoyable and showing a deft touch to the barley component. The spices are located where you want them to help counter the juicy onslaught, but also not to an extent that would shut out that source of entertainment. The degree of sweetness if also spot on. Always good to come across a 'Toshan at this calibre. 50%. 365 bottles.

⁂ **Old Malt Cask Auchentoshan Aged 20 Years** refill hogshead, cask no. 6479, dist Aug 90, bott Aug 10 **(91) n22.5** obviously Auchentoshan is in Kentucky: almost pure bourbon...but with some extra walnut oil; **t23** yee-ha! Here we go again: a ridiculous amount of liquorice and tannin bolsters the busy barley; **f22.5** lush, copper-rich and still a light honeyed Kentuckian feel; **b23** a decided Blue Grass tint to this Lowland gold...; 50%. nc ncf sc. 298 bottles.

⁂ **Old Masters Auchentoshan 12 Years Old** cask no. 102338, dist 1998, bott Jun 11 **(86) n21 t22 f21.5 b21.5.** Freshly cut grass...and makes hay but giving the barley a massively juicy role. Lots of Toffo candy on the finale. 62.9%. sc. James MacArthur & Co.

⁂ **Premier Barrel Auchentoshan 12 Years Old** **(83) n20 t22 f20 b21.** Simplistic big barley. 46%. nc ncf sc. Douglas Laing & Co. 319 bottles.

⁂ **Provenance Auchentoshan Over 9 Years** refill hogshead, cask no. 6291, dist Autumn 00, bott Summer 2010 **(77) n19 t21 f18 b19.** Clean, juicy but undercooked. 46%. nc ncf sc.

Provenance Auchentoshan Over 11 Years refill hogshead 5586, dist Autumn 98, bott Autumn 09 **(86) n22 t22 f21 b21.** Fresh, clean and bursting with triple-distilled lightness. A decent early day dram. 46%. nc ncf. Douglas Laing & Co Ltd.

Provenance Auchentoshan Aged 12 Years refill hogshead, dist Winter 96, bott Spring 09 **(73) n18 t20 f17 b18.** Thin, mildly off key. 46%. Douglas Laing.

⁂ **Provenance Auchentoshan Over 12 Years** refill hogshead, cask no. 6862, dist Winter 98, bott Winter 2010 **(86) n21 t22.5 f21 b21.5.** Outwardly thin, but closer examination reveals a malt bristling with barley and at times a sensuously juicy demeanour. 46%. nc ncf sc.

Scotch Malt Whisky Society Cask 5.25 Aged 9 Years refill barrel, dist Jun 99 **(88.5) n22.5 t22.5 f21.5 b22.** A fine, hugely enjoyable example of a (probably) 2nd fill cask allowing a relatively young malt to do its own thing. 57.8%

Old Malt Cask Auchentoshan Aged 18 Years refill hogshead, dist Aug 90, bott Nov 08 **(83.5) n22 t22 f19.5 b20.** At times unashamedly throat-ripping but plenty of ginger-led fun for those who want to go for the white knuckle ride. 50%. Douglas Laing. 335 bottles.

⁂ **Vom Fass Auchentoshan 12 Years Old (79) n20 t21 f18 b20.** Gooseberries on the nose and intense malt on the delivery. But ultimately betrayed by an old, expiring cask. 40%

AUCHROISK
Speyside, 1974. Diageo. Working.

Auchroisk Aged 10 Years db **(84) n20 t22 f21 b21.** Tangy orange on the nose, the malt amplified by a curious saltiness on the palate. 43%. Flora and Fauna.

⁂ **Auchroisk Special Release 2010 20 Years Old** American and European oak db **(89) n22.5** no little mocha and praline to this; some attractive herbal notes, too; **t22** lively malt is buffeted around the palate by a spicy attack; light oils – not normally associated with this distillery – offer suspension; **f22.5** back to a big, soft death by chocolate finale; **b22** can't say I have ever seen Auchroisk quite in this mood before. Some excellent cask selection here. 58.1%. nc ncf. Diageo. Fewer than 6000 bottles.

Auchroisk The Manager's Choice bodega sherry European oak, cask no. 11323, dist 1999, bott 2009 db **(84.5) n19 t21.5 f22.5 b21.5.** The astringent nose offers little hope but an entirely different story on delivery. Even though there is the odd spirity weakness on arrival, the thumping barley back-up chased by a light mocha follow through ensures a pleasant few minutes with the glass. 60.6%. 622 bottles.

Chieftain's Auchroisk Aged 11 Years Medoc Finish (79) n20 t22 f18 b19. Salivating but thin. 43%. Ian Macleod.

Connoisseurs Choice Auchroisk 1993 (78) n19 t21 f19 b19. Simplistic malt essay of few words. 43%. Gordon & MacPhail.

Duthies Auchroisk 20 Years Old (63.5) n16 t16 f16.5 b15. Oops! Should sell well in Germany. 46%. Wm. Cadenhead Ltd.

Kingsbury's "The Selection" Auchroisk 7 Years Old 2002 (81) n20 t21.5 f19 b20.5. Clean and refreshingly malty. 43%. Japan Import System.

Old Malt Cask Auchroisk Aged 16 Years (81) n21 t20 f20 b20. Pear drops and barley. 50%

:·· **Old Malt Cask Auchroisk Aged 21 Years** refill hogshead, cask no. 7045, dist Feb 90, bott Mar 11 (85.5) n21 t21 f22 b21.5. For such a light distillate the malt is stretched to impressive lengths. Surprisingly fresh and juicy. 50%. nc ncf sc. Douglas Laing & Co. 244 bottles.

Old Malt Cask Auchroisk Aged 34 Years refill hogshead 5522, dist Apr 75, bott Sep 09 (96) n24 quite superb: a wonderful tangle of delicate floral notes, the faintest dab of citrus and a medley of vanilla-based, weightier oaky tones. All bound together by a nimble barley hand. Not even remotely what I expected...; t24.5 sensual...there is no other word. The barley is on maximum sweet-shape mode and brings to the table other delicious issues amid the juiciness, like an over-toasted butterscotch tart and caramelised coffee biscuits...dangerously delicious; f23.5 long with countless strands of vanilla, each of varying degrees of dryness; b24 this may not be Whisky of the Year, but it could qualify as "Shock Whisky of the Year"...on two counts. Firstly, is this really 34-years-old...? Hell, I am getting old!!! I remember like yesterday waiting for my local merchant to ring to tell me the first-ever bottling arrived...as a 12 year-old...(the whisky, not me)!! And secondly, the quality. The blender in charge of Auchroisk during its infant years, Jim Milne, would have given this malt about as much chance of reaching this degree of quality after 34 years as Aberdeenshire winning the County Cricket Championship: none. How one of Speyside's most light and brittle whiskies has not only survived this amount of time in the barrel but actually thrived, showing not a single trace of defamatory over-aging, has to be one of the great malt whisky mysteries of recent years. Astonishing. 50%. 228 bottles.

:·· **Old Malt Cask Auchroisk Aged 35 Years** refill bourbon barrel, cask no. 6703, dist Apr 75, bott Oct 10 (88) n21.5 the usual exotic fruit expected from an aged, ultra-light malt; t21.5 a big, mouth-watering dust up between belligerent oak and squawking barley: the spices towards the middle suggest the oak wins; f23 spiced up vanilla and the inevitable chocolate milkshake; b22 to think: I can still remember waiting for the delivery of – and receiving from a wine store in Manchester - the first ever bottling of this, a 12-year-old in the mid 80s. God...I'm getting bloody old... 47.2%. nc ncf sc. Douglas Laing & Co. 224 bottles.

Scotch Malt Whisky Society Cask 95.11 Aged 19 Years refill barrel, dist Jun 90 (86) n22 t22 f21 b21. Creamy, fruity and, despite the balmy finale, occasionally sharp and lively. 58.2%. Scotch Malt Whisky Society. 192 bottles.

Scotch Malt Whisky Society Cask 95.13 Aged 19 Years refill barrel, dist Jun 90 (87) n20 malty but rather drab; t22.5 didn't expect that...!! Superb versatility on the delivery with the malt jumping through hoops as it moves rapidly between crunchy and sharp and lightly sugar-coated; f22 long with an unusual light oiliness for this distillery; b22.5 puckeringly intense and full of mischief. 60.2%. Scotch Malt Whisky Society. 192 bottles.

AULTMORE

Speyside, 1896. John Dewar & Sons. Working.

Aultmore 12 Years Old db (86) n22 t22 f20 b22. Do any of you remember the old DCL distillery bottling of this from, what, 25 years ago? Well, this is nothing like it. 40%

:·· **Adelphi Aultmore 28 Years Old** cask no. 2233, dist 1982, bott 2011 (94.5) n24 if I had the time, I could nose this all evening: the crystalline Demerara attached to the light cinnamon on cooking apple is simply to die for...; t23.5 brilliantly bright delivery: the barley is virtually granite-like while the oak and fruit orbit it like so many moons; the sugars are pure and entirely unrefined; f23 long with still a wonderfully juicy element complementing the complex spices; b24 after tasting a lot of, frankly, rubbish whisky today, this one is standing out like a sore thumb. People from Adelphi: I salute you...this is the sheer class my put upon palate was craving for. 57.6%. sc. Adelphi Distillery. 179 bottles.

:·· **Berry's Own Selection Aultmore 1991** cask no. 7432, bott 2011 (86) n21.5 t22 f21 b21.5. Unmistakably Aultmore in its crunchy barley guise. But a massive attack of natural oak-generated caramels has kept the usual complexity under wraps. Demands a refill, though. 52.8%. nc ncf sc. Berry Bros & Rudd.

:·· **Chieftain's Aultmore Aged 13 Years** German oak finish, dist May 97, bott 2011 (84) n20.5 t21.5 f21 b21. Sweet, malty and very proudly Speyside. 54.9%. nc ncf. Ian Macleod Distillers.

Dun Bheagan Aultmore 12 Years Old Sherry Butt Finish dist May 97 (84) n22 t22 f19.5 b20.5. Fruity and mildly feisty, the most compelling fun is condensed into the generously rich delivery. A tad thin and a little warming elsewhere. 50%. nc ncf. Ian Macleod.

Dun Bheagan Aultmore Aged 15 Years (76) n19 t19 f19 b19. A bit dense, monosyllabic and bitter. 43%. Ian Macleod.

:·· **Gordon & MacPhail Connoisseurs Choice Aultmore 1997** (92) n23 lively, lithesome barley seemingly bubbling in the glass. Dangerously alluring...; t22.5 prickly, tingly malt at first closed and then opens out so the sugars bring the barley into full grassy play; f23.5 heads at first down a mocha route, but decides instead to go honeycomb; **b23** tender Speyside malt in full spate. It's what G&M do so naturally... *43%. Gordon & MacPhail.*

Norse Cask Selection Aultmore 1992 Aged 16 Years barrel no. 3839, dist 1992, bott 2008 **(91) n23 t24 f21.5 b22.5.** What a treat to find Aultmore in this kind of mood. Great fun! *56.8%*

Old Malt Cask Aultmore Aged 12 Years sherry butt, dist Jan 96, bott Sep 08 **(79) n20 t21 f18.5 b19.5.** Ferociously hot on delivery, you will hunt the grape in vain. Plenty of malt, though. *50%. Douglas Laing. 687 bottles.*

Old Malt Cask Aultmore Aged 18 Years dist Sep 90, bott Jul 09 **(89) n21 t23 f22 b23.** A fizzing beaut! *50%*

⋙ **Old Malt Cask Aultmore Aged 20 Years** refill hogshead, cask no. 6839, dist Sep 90, bott Nov 10 **(95) n22.5** sweet and crusty like an old bakery. And a bit dusty, too; **t24.5** oh my word! What a delivery...!! This must be one of the most intense barley deliveries I have come across in the last four or five years. This is concentrated barley: the sugars have almost a syrupy quality, but the clarity of the barley leaves you almost nonplussed; **f24** long, lightly oiled and softly spiced. A slow descent from the barley mountain of before; **b24** this distillery is quite capable of greatness. But I have never expected to see it in quite this form. A malt you will remember all your born days. *50%. nc ncf. Douglas Laing & Co. 274 bottles.*

⋙ **Old Malt Cask Aultmore Aged 36 Years** refill hogshead, cask no. 3741, dist Apr 75, bott Jul 10 **(83) n21 t20 f21 b21.** Stretches out the barley and spice the best it can. But the oak is just a little too advanced... *50%. nc ncf sc. Douglas Laing & Co. 168 bottles.*

⋙ **Premier Barrel Aultmore Aged 12 Years (78) n19 t20 f20 b19.** Intense and oily. But intense and oily what? This is never quite fully answered. *46%. nc ncf sc. 449 bottles.*

Provenance Aultmore Aged 9 Years sherry butt no. DMG 6211, dist Autumn 2000, bott Spring 2010 **(88) n22** new mown grass drying in the sun; **t22** fantastically juicy with a slow build up of heavier fruit; the middle ground is lush but maltily flighty, too; **f22** light vanillas enter but don't break the spell; **b22** from a sherry butt it may be, but rarely (thankfully!) does the grape interfere with the bracing malty freshness. *46%. Douglas Laing.*

Provenance Aultmore Aged 11 Years sherry butt, dist Autumn 1996, bott Summer 2008 **(86) n22.5 t21.5 f21 b21.** Perplexing in style, with loads of crystalised brown sugar ensuring a solidity you would hardly expect. The malt is deliciously flinty; crunchy almost. *46%*

⋙ **Provenance Aultmore Over 12 Years** refill hogshead, cask no. 7477, dist Autumn 2000, bott Summer 2011 **(86) n21.5 t22 f21.5 b21.** When I nosed this without seeing what I had in the glass, I thought some new make was before me. For all the input of the oak, it might as well be. You will find some citrus if you look hard enough! But no off notes and, all in all, sweet, refreshing and entirely enjoyable. Not a bad word to say against it. *46%. nc ncf sc.*

Provenance Aultmore Aged 13 Years sherry butt, dist Winter 1996, bott Winter 2009 **(77.5) n19 t21 f19 b18.5.** Tangy with the odd distinctive unhappy note. The colour is excellent but the oak somehow doesn't quite gel. *46%. Douglas Laing.*

⋙ **Scotch Malt Whisky Society Cask 73.42 Aged 28 Years** refill butt, cask no. 1673, dist 1982 **(92.5) n22.5** fruit driven, but it's all rather subtle. Diced greengage with a squeeze of kumquat all embedded in a spotted dog pudding, complete with an over-ripe physalis on top; **t23.5** salivating barley offers a crisp and delicious skeleton; lighter sultana notes do nothing to soften the impact; **f23** long, clean with an entirely pleasing denouement of mildly puckering fruit aiding the lightly sweetened vanillas and persistent barley; **b23.5** a class act without even breaking sweat. *51.1%. sc. 181 bottles.*

The Whisky Agency Aultmore 1990 (82) n21 t21 f20 b20. Once a relatively common malt now in rare supply these days. So a shame that the cask has done little to help this one hit the heights. *56.3%*

BALBLAIR
Highlands (Northern), 1872. Inver House Distillers. Working.

Balblair 10 Years Old db **(86) n21 t22 f22 b21.** Such an improved dram away from the clutches of caramel. *40%*

Balblair Aged 16 Years db **(84) n22 t22 f20 b20.** Definitely gone up a notch in the last year. The lime on the nose has been replaced by dim Seville oranges; the once boring finish reveals elements of fruit and spice. It's the barley- rich middle that shines, though, and some more work will belt this up into the high 90s where this great distillery belongs. *40%*

Balblair 1975 db **(94.5) n24.5** one of the most complex noses in the Highlands with just about everything you can think of making a starring, or at least guest, appearance at some time. That's not a taster's get-out. Nose it and then defy me...For starters, watch the clever bourbon edge alongside the crème brulee and ground cherry topping...hunt the smoke down, also... **t23.5** silk. No, wait...it could be velvet. No, definitely silk. The barley descends in the most gentle manner possible but this does not detract from the intensity: wave upon wave of barley melts upon the tastebuds, varying only in their degree of sweetness; f23 a few more bitter oak noises, but it remains barley all the way, even at this age. Amazing...; b23.5 essential Balblair. 46%

Balblair 1978 db (**94**) n24 evidence of great antiquity hangs all over this nose, not least in the exotic fruit so typical of such vast aging; there is smoke, too: a delicate peat more common at the distillery in those days is evident and most welcome; t24 the lush delivery offers up an improbably malty juiciness. But this is almost immediately countered by a spicy oakiness which offsets with great charm the salivating barley chorus and layers of delicate fruit and almost nutty vanilla: not for a second is elegance compromised; f23 those of you with a passion for older Ballantine's will not be much surprised that this was, in its Allied days, once a vital ingredient: such is the clarity of the vanilla-led silkiness. Again, great age is never in doubt. Towards the very death the wisps of smoke found on the nose make a lingering reappearance; b23 just one of those drams that exudes greatness and charm in equal measures. Some malts fall apart when hitting thirty: this one is totally intact and in command. A glorious malt underlining the greatness of this mostly under-appreciated distillery. 46%

Balblair 1989 db (**91**) n23 t23 f22.5 b22.5. Don't expect gymnastics on the palate or the pyrotechnics of the Cadenhead 18: in many ways a simple malt, but one beautifully told. Almost Cardhu-esque in the barley department. 43%

Balblair 1990 db (**92.5**) n24 big, mildly syrupy with figs and pears of exploding ripeness, and a thick layering of barley-oak mix; that there is good age to this is indisputable by the evidence of the nose, as is its extraordinary dexterity and finesse: a nose to spend a good 20 minutes alone with...; t23.5 fabulous spice explosion on arrival and then a ridiculously soothing massage of lightly sugared oak and gentle fruits; amid all this, the barley is juicy, fresh and almost like a three-year-old in its clarity; f22 long, lightly waxed and luxuriant; b23 tangy in the great Balblair tradition. Except here this is warts and all with the complexity and true greatness of the distillery left in no doubt. 46%

Balblair 2000 db (**87.5**) n21.5 gristy and grassy; t22.5 the freshness on the nose is fully accentuated by a juicy, clean barley delivery; f21.5 dries markedly towards powdery cocoa; b22 no toffee yet still a clever degree of chewy weight for all the apparent lightness. 43%

.·: **Balblair 2001** db (**90.5**) n23.5 gooseberries at varying stages of ripeness; barley so clean it must be freshly scrubbed; the kind of delicate spice prickle that is a must; t23.5 majestic delivery: hard to imagine barley making a more clean, intense and profound entrance than that. The malt forms many layers, each one sugar accompanied but taking on a little more oak; f21.5 dries, spices up but bitters a little; b22.5 a typically high quality whisky from this outrageously underestimated distillery. 46%

A.D. Rattray Balblair 1991 cask no. 09/03070 (**88**) n24 superbly salty and bracing: it is as though the Balblair warehouses have been moved ashore where the stormy seas never cease. One of the most delightful Highland noses of the year; t21.5 tangy with the malt and lazy fruit really trying to fend off some bitter oak incursions; f21.5 a touch oily with an injection of late sugars; b21 the nose perhaps demands too much for the flavours to live up to. By no means your common or garden single malt: a wonderful experience all the same. 46%

.·: **Gordon & MacPhail Rare Vintage Balblair 1979** (**88.5**) n22 chocolate ginger; t22.5 big oak but saved by the weight of barley and sharpness of the salt; f22 dry, almost martini-like, with just enough late melting honey, caramel and cocoa to see this one safely home; b22 like a glorious old manor house suffering from woodworm: not entirely sound but still an object of beauty. 43%

Old Distillery Label Balblair Aged 10 Years (**92**) n22 t23.5 f23 b23.5. I'm a sucker for these juicy, big-malted flawless numbers. And this one certainly leaves you sucking hard as you pucker up. A top-notch thirst-quencher. 43%. Gordon & MacPhail.

.·: **Old Malt Cask Balblair Aged 20 Years** refill sherry butt, cask no. 6340, dist Jun 90, bott Jul 10 (**85.5**) n23.5 t21 f20 b21. How deceptive! The nose announced a stunning cask, the oaky battering on the taste buds told of a malt prematurely aged. Still worth finding for the nose alone: the balance of the salt, pepper and butterscotch-barley is the stuff of dreams. 50%. nc ncf sc. Douglas Laing & Co. 637 bottles.

BALMENACH
Speyside, 1824. Inver House Distillers. Working.

Balmenach Aged 25 Years Golden Jubilee db (**89**) n21 t23 f22 b23. What a glorious old charmer this is! An essay in balance despite the bludgeoning nature of the beast early on. Takes a little time to get to know and appreciate: persevere with this belter because it is classic stuff for its age. 58%. Around 800 decanters.

Berry's Own Selection Balmenach 1979 (87.5) n22 polite, almost subdued. Barley for sure, but bread and butter pudding, too...; t22 intense oak to begin, but always enough sugars to handle the age; f21.5 the malt fights back amid the half cooked toast; b22 Auld Balmenach pretty much nutshelled: light and attempting to be barley dominant...but not always achieving. 56.3%. Berry Bros & Rudd.

The Cärn Mör Vintage Collection Braes of Balmenach 2001 barrel, cask no. 800412, dist 2001, bott 2009 (85.5) n20.5 t22 f21.5 b21.5. Light, crisp, sweetly malted and a pleasing spiciness. 46%. The Scottish Liqueur Centre.

Chieftain's Balmenach 15 Years Old Hogshead (77) n19 t21 f18 b19. Fruity and pleasant, but a fraction too over-oaked. 43%. Ian MacLeod.

Connoisseurs Choice Balmenach Aged 18 Years first fill sherry butt, dist 1990, bott 2008 (76) n19 t20.5 f18 b18.5. Sufficient sulphur to take the shine from the experience. 43%

Connoisseurs Choice Balmenach 1991 (88) n22 t22 f22 b22. Firm, steady-as-she-goes malt which would not have improved with further aging. A musty-have though for those who prefer their dram spiced up and chunky. 43%. Gordon & MacPhail.

Connoisseurs Choice Balmenach 1993 (85) n22 t21.5 f20.5 b21. My glass runneth over with docile vanilla and even more sleepy barley. A few spices and a tang indicate the cask has been taken to its limit. 43%. Gordon & MacPhail.

Deerstalker Balmenach Aged 12 Years bott Apr 10 (77) n19 t20 f19 b19. Even more gooseberry-ish than the super-plump gooseberries in my old mum's garden. However, each time I come to this one, I put it back in the pool as something troubled me. Now I finally analyse this, there is, indeed, a detectable odd note: sweetened butyric...? Deerstalker is usually a whisky you can put your hat on for quality. Perhaps not this bottling, alas. 46%. Aberko Ltd.

Deerstalker Balmenach Aged 18 Years (86) n22.5 t22 f21 b21. Not quite in the same sparkling mode as many previous Deerstalkers, though the fruitiness does have a spicy tang. 46%. Aberko Ltd.

🔅 **Gordon & MacPhail Connoisseurs Choice Balmenach 1999** (85) n21 t21.5 f21 b21.5. Those with a soft spot for spicy suet pudding will find this irresistible. 43%

Old Malt Cask Balmenach Aged 18 Years dist Oct 90, bott Jul 09 (87.5) n21 t24 f21 b21.5. Excellently weighted and shows some fine touches. 50%. Douglas Laing.

🔅 **Old Malt Cask Balmenach Aged 27 Years** refill hogshead, cask no. 7148, dist Sep 83, bott Apr 11 (82) n22 t22 f18 b20. A real mish-mash. On the nose, green and a little sharp. On the finish, vivid signs of a flailing cask. But elsewhere juicy, malty and fun. Never for a moment, though, does it ever act its 27 years... 50%. nc ncf sc. Douglas Laing & Co. 268 bottles.

Provenance Balmenach Aged 8 Years refill hogshead, bott Winter 99, bott Autumn 08 (86) n21 t22 f21.5 b21.5. Clean, simplistic but delightfully malty. 46%. Douglas Laing.

Provenance Balmenach Over 11 Years refill hogshead 5734, dist Spring 98, bott Winter 2010 (78) n20.5 t20 f18.5 b19. Distilled from helium. Sweet grist. 46%. nc ncf.

🔅 **Scotch Malt Whisky Society Cask 48.24 Aged 22 Years** refill hogshead, cask no. 1118, dist 1988 (84) n21.5 t21 f20.5 b21. A bit of nag: the sharp barley and vivid oak overstates the case just a little too tartly. 49.3%. sc. 265 bottles.

🔅 **Scotch Malt Whisky Society Cask 48.25 Aged 22 Years** refill butt, cask no. 1080, dist. 1989 (86.5) n22 t22.5 f21 b21. Clean and mouthwatering, there is an engaging and dogged persistence to this one. Good sugar-spice balance. 56.2%. sc. 268 bottles.

THE BALVENIE
Speyside, 1892. William Grant & Sons. Working.

The Balvenie Aged 10 Years Founders Reserve db (90) n23 astonishing complexity: the fruit is relaxed, crushed sultanas and malty suet. A sliver of smoke and no more: everything is hinted and nudged at rather than stated. Superb; t24 here we go again: threads of malt binding together barely detectable nuances. Thin liquorice here, grape there, smoke and vanilla somewhere else; f20 Light muscovado-toffee flattens out the earlier complexity. The bitter-sweet balance remains brilliant to the end; b23 just one of those all-time-great standard 10-year-olds from a great distillery – pity they've decided to kill it off. 40%

The Balvenie Double Wood Aged 12 Years db (80.5) n22 t20.5 f19 b19. OK. So here's the score: Balvenie is one of my favourite distilleries in the world, I confess. I admit it. The original Balvenie 10 is a whisky I would go to war for. It is what Scotch malt whisky is all about. It invented complexity; or at least properly introduced me to it. But I knew that it was going to die, sacrificed on the altar of ageism. So I have tried to get to love Double Wood. And I have tasted and/or drunk it every month for the last couple of years to get to know it and, hopefully fall in love. But still I find it rather boring company. We may have kissed and canoodled. But still there is no spark. No romance whatsoever. 40% ☉

The Balvenie Signature Aged 12 Years batch 001 db (93) n25 t23 f21 b24. This whisky was created by Grant's blender David Stewart and bottled to mark his 45 years in the industry. For my money, he's now the best in the business and has been for a little while. But it is a great shame that the marketing guys didn't insist on this being an apposite 45% because, for all the subtle wizardry going on here and the fact that the nose should immediately become the stuff of whisky legend, this is dreadfully underpowered. 40%

Balvenie Signature Aged 12 Years batch 003 db (89) n24 nothing like as rich as the first Batch: this aroma is about innuendo and strands. Where once there was powering, fresh-out-of-the-oven fruitcake, now there is more of the mixing bowl with the emphasis on the flour rather than the dried fruit. Even so, there is sufficient orange peel to freshen things up; t23.5 against the odds the barley shows first, only briefly, mind, before a dizzying welter of fruity blows knocks it from the scene. The mouthfeel is silky but roughens up towards the middle ground; f19 a hint of discord and fluffy dryness; b22.5 if you don't taste this at body temperature you are doing both yourself and this whisky a huge disservice. One of the great benefits of Balvenie is that it can shine at virtually any age: at 10 it is truly magnificent – though sadly you'll rarely get the chance to discover this these days – and when a couple of years old still the barley has enough charisma to talk a beautiful game. The fruits have a bitter-sweet effect – literally – by helping to map out a wonderful nose but lessening the value of the finish. Enjoyable whisky all the same and what a pity it isn't at 47%... 40%

⠿ **The Balvenie Signature Aged 12 Years** batch 004 db (92) n23.5 back to its dried dates origins, helped along by some muscovado sugars keeping a lightness to the vanilla; the spices are little more than a whisper; t23.5 soft, as you might expect, but with an early noise of some bitterish oak...the price often paid by breaking down the oils by adding too much water. But the reinstatement of the dates – juicier now than on the nose – and a doughy plum pudding restores the balance; f22 the vague bitterness returns, predictably, as but there is a double helping of Cornish vanilla ice cream...without the ice... b23 it is a relief to know that the unparalleled talent in the scotch whisky industry that is David Stewart has not been entirely lost to us, with the legendary blender still working on the Balvenie brand. Next time I see him, I will still insist on knowing why this wonderful whisky, so cleverly complex, remains so woefully underpowered. 40%

The Balvenie 14 Years Old Cuban Selection db (86) n20 t22 f22.5 b21.5. Unusual malt and tasted blind you wouldn't recognise the distillery in a million years. No great fan of the nose but the roughness of the delivery grows on you; there is a jarring, tongue-drying quality which actually works quite well and the development of the inherent sweetness is almost in slow motion. Some sophistication here, but also the odd note which, on the nose especially, is a little out of tune. 43%

The Balvenie 14 Years Old Golden Cask db (91) n23.5 mildly tart: rhubarb and custard, with a vague sprinkling of brown sugar; bourbon notes, too; t23 mouth-watering and zingy spice offer up a big delivery, but settles towards the middle towards a more metallic barley-rich sharpness; f22 soft spices peddle towards the finish and a wave or three of gathering oak links well with the sweetened barley strands; b22.5 a confident, elegant malt which doesn't stint one iota on complexity. Worth raiding the Duty Free shops for this little gem alone. 47.5%

The Balvenie Roasted Malt Aged 14 Years db (90) n21 t23 f22 b24. Balvenie very much as you've never seen it before: it takes time to settle, but when it does it becomes an absolute, mouth-filling cracker! 47.1%

The Balvenie Rum Wood Aged 14 Years db (88) n22 t23 f21 b22. Tasted blind I would never have recognized the distillery: I'm not sure if that's a good thing. 47.1%

Balvenie 17 Years Old Rum Cask db (88.5) n22 green bananas and oak: curious... t22.5 initially dry with the oak elbowing in first; several levels of barley battle back while some fudge enters the middle ground; f22 remains fudgy, with a touch of oily butterscotch tart, but the emphasis is on the dryer, flaky tart; b22 for all the best attentions of the rum cask at times this feels all its 17 years, and perhaps a few Summers more. Impossible not to love, however. 43%

The Balvenie Aged 15 Years Single Barrel db (90.5) n22 t23.5 f22.5 b23. Sadly, unable to discover which cask this was from or for which market. So one takes this as a generic Balvenie at its new strength. 47.8%

Balvenie New Wood Aged 17 Years db (85) n23 t22 f19 b21. A naturally good age for Balvenie; the nose is lucid and exciting, the early delivery is thick with rich malt. This, though, has sucked out lots of caramel from the wood to leave an annoyingly flat finish. 40%

The Balvenie Aged 17 Years Old Madeira Cask Madeira finish, bott 2009 db (93.5) n24 classically two-toned, with a pair of contrasting tales being told simultaneously yet in complete harmony. One is fruity (especially apple) and ripe and blended with the weighty oak; the other is barley-sweet and refreshing. What a treat...; t23.5 the juicy grape takes the higher ground, joining forces with the juicier barley; some distance below the oak throbs contentedly...; **f23** a little oak prickle and a hint of sweet mocha on the vanilla; **b23** an essay in deportment. Every aspect appears to have been measured and weighed. Hurry this imperious whisky at your peril. *43%*

The Balvenie 17 Year Old Sherry Oak db **(88) n23 t22.5 f21 b21.5.** Clean as a nut. High-class sherry it may be but the price to pay is a flattening out of the astonishing complexity one normally finds from this distillery. Bitter-sweet in every respect. *43%*

The Balvenie Aged 21 Years Port Wood db **(94.5) n24** chocolate marzipan with a soft sugar-plum centre; deft, clean and delicate; **t24** hard to imagine a delivery more perfectly weighted: a rich tapestry of fruit and nut plus malt melts on the palate with a welter of drier, pithy, grape skin balancing the vanillas and barley oils; **f23** delicately dry with the vanilla and buttered fruitcake ensuring balance; **b23.5** what a magnificently improved malt. Last time out I struggled to detect the fruit. Here, there's no escaping. *40%* ⊙⊙

The Balvenie Thirty Aged 30 Years db **(92) n24** has kept its character wonderfully, with a real mixture of varied fruits. Again the smoke is apparent, as is the panting oak. Astonishing thet the style should have been kept so similar to previous bottlings; **t23** big, full delivery first of enigmatic, thick barley, then a gentle eruption of controlled, warming spices; **f22** much more oaky involvement but such is the steadiness of the barley, its extraordinary confidence, no damage is done and the harmony remains; **b23** rarely have I come across a bottling of a whisky of these advanced years which is so true to previous ones. Amazing. *47.3%*

⋰⋱ **The Balvenie Aged 40 Years Batch 1** bott 2010 db **(79) n22 t20 f18 b19.** The makings of a great nose: a real nutty Dundee cake special. But a bitter let down on the palate. *48.5%*

⋰⋱ **The Balvenie Aged 40 Years Batch 2** db **(96.5) n25** unless you have a good two hours that you know will be uninterrupted and unspoiled by cooking and other extraneous aromas, don't even think about opening this bottle. Once you have, sit back and experience something just a little special... eyes closed, you might fancy the odd, playful, peek-a-boo atom of peat. You'd be right..it is there. Likewise, for a moment you will be drifting off to Kentucky and breathing in the honeyed charms of a very old bourbon. A hint of cucumber...? Tick. Coconut? Yes. Sultana? Maybe. If so, as voluptuous as a female opera singer. Ah, Greengages! Spilling out their over-ripened juices. And lychee! Does it need a shake of salt to embolden the aromas? No, thanks to the oak, it is already there. Hang on: the oak? What is that up to, exactly? Well, apart from the salt, it is adding some weight. Not so it will drag the whisky down. But rather so it holds all else in place. How do I locate it exactly...? Try looking for those delicate herbs singing apart from the spice; **t24** could never quite live up to the nose and the early, roaring oak is bolder on delivery than it ever was on aroma. But this works, too. Because, against all the odds, there is a juicy barley lustre to this guy which sits comfortably with those big tannins. The sugars are deep and meaningful and magically in sync with all else around it. The spices are deft but build in weight; **f23.5** shows just a few late cracks, as it has every right to do. The light sugars still see off the more militant of the oaky notes; **b24** gets it so right in every department where Batch 1 got it so lamentably wrong. My only sorrow was that I could give the nose only 25 points... A near faultless glass of honour to one of the great distilleries of the world. Have no idea of the price. Double whatever it is, and you'd still have a bargain. *48.5%*

The Balvenie 1993 Port Wood db **(89) n21 t23 f22 b23.** Oozes class without getting too flash about it: the secret is in the balance. *40%*

BANFF

Speyside, 1863–1983. Diageo. Demolished.

Cadenhead's Banff 29 Years Old **(73) n19 t19 f18 b17.** Too heavily oaked: should have been bottled at 25. *52%*

Cadenhead's Banff Aged 32 Years dist 1976, bott 2009 **(85) n22.5 t21 f20.5 b21.** Valiantly offers all the barley it can muster, and even a touch of defiant sweet grassiness, but the passing years and accumulated oak have the biggest say. *47.1%*

Celtic Heartlands Banff 1975 bott 2008 **(93) n23 t23.5 f23 b23.5.** Pure, unambiguous quality. *48.1%. Bruichladdich Ltd. 449 bottles.*

Old & Rare Banff Aged 38 Years dist Mar 71, bott Aug 09 **(86) n22 t21.5 f21 b21.5.** Now here's something that might take 38 years to fathom. An old peculiar Banff carrying a tired, bitter oak note which runs directly under the strata of smoke. The result is a very unusual personality which some might find hard to understand. Elsewhere the barley shimmers and there is just enough muscovado sugar to raise a light fruit profile. But it is that almost unique peat-oak combination which will dominate the experience – and entirely baffle - most who encounter this. *53.4%. Douglas Laing & Co Ltd. 324 bottles.*

Old Malt Cask Banff Aged 32 Years refill hogshead, dist Nov 75, bott Aug 08 **(89)** **n22** **t23** **f21.5** **b22.5** funny how age works on some distilleries and not others. Technically, this probably has too much oak. Yet such is the overall richness and class of this enchanting dram, you can easily forgive its weaknesses. *48.7%. Douglas Laing. 164 bottles.*

⊹⊱ **Rarest Of The Rare Banff 35 Years Old** dist 1975, cask no. 3352 **(86.5)** **n21** **t22** **f22.5** **b21.** Hangs in hard to stay the right side of good. The over enthusiastic oaks do some damage, but also ultimately save the day by carrying out the required repairs offering a fantastic degree of milky chocolate, sweetened by muscovado sugars, along the way. Somehow, it is a triumph! *42.5%. sc. Duncan Taylor & Co.*

The Whisky Agency Banff 1975 **(89.5)** **n23** can't remember the last time I got this amount of honey from a 35-y-o malt which wasn't HP...; an almost pathetic puff of smoke; **t23** here we go again...!! Honey in a multitude of guises, though the oak bites hard; vanillas fill the middle ground as does a little pine and eucalyptus; **f21.5** oily, with a little liquorice attached to the honey and vanilla; **b22** distilled by bees. Matured by squirrels. *44.9%*

BEN NEVIS
Highlands (Western), 1825. Nikka. Working.

Ben Nevis 10 Years Old db **(88)** **n21** enormously chunky and weighty: for a 10-y-o the oak is thick, but sweetened medley of ripe fruits; **t22** an almost syrupy mouth feel: a tad cloying but the malt is something you can so get your teeth into; **f23** long with traces of liquorice and hickory; **b22** a massive malt that has steadied itself in recent bottlings, but keep those knives and forks to hand! *46%*

Ben Nevis 14 Years Old Single Sherry Cask dist Sep 92, bott Jan 07 db **(88.5)** **n21** **t22.5** **f22** **b22.5.** Talk about brinkmanship! This sherry butt has been introduced to sulphur. Luckily, its acquaintance was a passing one only, otherwise the marks would have tumbled frighteningly; but they shook hands sufficiently for five or six points to be lost here. That said, the integrity of the actual distillate is so high it comes through as a serious dram to savour. Mind you, I know a few Germans who would do anything for this kind of malt...well almost... *46%. 815 bottles.*

Ben Nevis 1984 Single Cask double wood matured cask no. 98/35/1, dist Dec 84, bott Jan 10 db **(73.5)** **n18.5** **t19** **f17** **b19.** Formidable sherry and some early grape. But once the sulphur gets hold, it refuses to let go. *56%. ncf.*

Ben Nevis 1996 Single Cask bourbon cask, dist May 96, bott Jan 09 db **(90)** **n22** malt concentrate man marked by clean, proud oak; **t23** not often you get a delivery this barley entangled. Rich malt head in every direction, enriched by Demerara sugars and a light liquorice: a quasi-bourbony feel to this; **f23** a long, impressive trail of intense malt and lighter vanillas; **b22** a thick-set little gem of a whisky. *56.8%. For Swedish Whisky Society TKS.*

Ben Nevis 1997 Single Cask Port Finish for TKS port bodega butt, double wood matured, dist Feb 97, bott Jul 07 db **(79)** **n18.5** **t22** **f18.5** **b20.** The quite magnificent rose colouring is not quite matched by the thick, almost impenetrable nose. But things take a turn for the better as the enormity of the fruit makes its mark on delivery. The finish, though, still leaves a little to be desired. *46%. ncf. For Swedish whisky Society TKS.*

Ben Nevis 1998 Single Cask sherry butt no. 358, dist Jun 05, bott Oct 09 db **(67)** **n16** **t17** **f17** **b17.** Uncompromising sulphur. *46%. ncf. For Swedish Whisky Society TKS.*

A.D. Rattray Ben Nevis 1996 cask no. 2214, dist Dec 96, bott Mar 10 **(72.5)** **n17** **t19** **f18.5** **b18.** Looks like the stillman's watch had stopped when he was working out the cut times. Still, can't say it's not interesting... *58.2% A.D. Rattray Ltd*

Berry's Own Selection Ben Nevis 1996 bott 2009 **(86.5)** **n21.5** **t21** **f22.5** **b21.5.** One of those almost impenetrably dense malty affairs this distillery conjours up from time to time, this one showing some fabulous sweet touches to the barley late on. Serve with a spoon. *56.9%. Berry Bros & Rudd.*

The Càrn Mòr Vintage Collection Ben Nevis 1997 hogshead no. 252, dist 1997, bott 2009 **(83.5)** **n19.5** **t22** **f21** **b21.** Big, busty, at times bruising, but always malty and sweet. *46%. nc ncf. 1275 bottles.*

Dancing Stag Ben Nevis 1996 **(89.5)** **n23.5** so complex and delicate! The odd hint of smoke here and there counters the light, fruity sparkle of the barley; just the mocha note hanging around, too; **t22.5** silky with a puff of smoke arriving early, followed swiftly by busy barley; **f21.5** quietens as the toffee arrives; **b22** a beautifully made and matured whisky. *46%. Robert Graham Ltd.*

Duncan Taylor Collection Ben Nevis 1995 rum cask **(86)** **n21** **t23** **f21.5** **b21.5.** Almost eye-wateringly juicy. The crisp barley is helped out by a sugary firmness, presumably offered by the rum. Narrow but a joy. *46%. Duncan Taylor & Co Ltd.*

The Golden Cask Ben Nevis 1997 cask no. CM141, dist 1997, bott 2009 **(88)** n21.5 salt sprinkled on custard; t22 malty, wonderfully busy with the barley breaking down into an almost bourbon small grain buzz; f22.5 a mix of malt and chocolate milkshake; b22 oily textured and tests the palate. *56%. The House of MacDuff. 310 bottles.*

·⊰:·· **Kingsbury Finest and Rarest Ben Nevis 44 Years Old** dist 1966 **(92)** n23.5 a herb garden bordered by lavender; t23 softly oiled barley delicately lined with honey. Charming degrees of hickory and vanilla tick all the age boxes; f22.5 reverts back to a malty colossus. Very usual, and highly attractive, way of ending a 44 year sojourn; b23 at times plays the part of a bourbon with more gusto than it does a malt. However, the late malty revelation at the finale dispels any doubts. An unusual and wonderfully gifted malt. *40.7%. nc ncf sc. Japan Import Systems.*

Malts of Scotland Ben Nevis 1996 sherry hogshead no. 1466, dist Oct 96, bott Jan 10 **(89.5)** n22.5 curious: big bodied, but the malt and grape elements, though clear and precise, are pretty lightweight; t23 the fruity exoskeleton ensures a slow barley build up; f22 medium length, clean and every bit as dapper as the nose and delivery; b22 a delicious, quite flawless, experience. *571%. Malts of Scotland. 192 bottles.*

Milroy's of Soho Ben Nevis 1996 refill sherry butt, cask no. 1670, dist Oct 96, bott Jul 08 **(90.5)** n21.5 t22 f24 b23. Hard not to be seduced by the rich and silkily-textured finish. A malt of great character. *46%. 198 bottles.*

Old & Rare Ben Nevis 1966 Aged 43 Years dist 1966, bott Nov 09 **(91.5)** n23 almost a bourbon feel to this with a roastiness to the sugars of the oak; some fruit around still, as is a dying smokiness; t22.5 silky: the oak offers a degree of mocha and toasty vanilla; a tad off key, but no damage done; f24 light spices and soft vanilla; that hint of smoke returns with a light, milk chocolate fade and some lovely late kumquat; b22 one of those drams which looks as though it just ain't gonna cut it...and then does with a sly flourish. *43.8%. Douglas Laing & Co Ltd.*

Old Malt Cask Ben Nevis 13 Years Old refill hogshead no. 5599, dist Nov 96, bott Nov 09 **(91)** n22.5 you wouldn't find this nose out of place in Kentucky... t23.5 chewy, beautifully full bodied and forever building up the Demerara sugar and burnt honeycomb theme; f22.5 long and vanilla saturated. That sugary sweetness persists to the end; b22.5 a fabulous cask absolutely bulging with high grade personality. *50%. Douglas Laing & Co Ltd. 334 bottles.*

·⊰:·· **Old Malt Cask Ben Nevis Aged 40 Years** refill hogshead, cask no. 6991, dist Mar 71, bott Mar 11 **(94)** n23.5 nosed blind, this is almost identical to the oldest whiskeys stored at the old Tom Moore distillery. Almost rabid, yet wonderfully alluring, red liquorice emboldened by spice and a small grain pithiness: complex to the point of intriguing...; t23.5 a busy mixture of oak and barley pepper the palate. Virtually no oil present, which makes for a profound intensity; the sweetness of the barley is lightly sugar coated and suits the drier oaks to a tee; f23 long, despite the lack of the usual creamy oils you associate with this distillery, and doubles up on the vanillas; b24 reminds me not of just the wild west of Scotland, near where this distillery is situated. But the 18th century world west of the USA, too: Kentucky. All kinds of bourbon fingerprints on this, which means it has survived four decades with aplomb. Simply fabulous. *45.8%. nc ncf sc. Douglas Laing & Co. 188 bottles.*

Old Masters Ben Nevis Aged 10 Years cask no. 172, dist 1998, bott 2008 **(86)** n22 t22.5 f20.5 b21. Typical Nevis thick barley soupiness with the sharpness of the malt and bourbony nose. A real early delight. *579%. James MacArthur & Co. Ltd.*

·⊰:·· **Provenance Ben Nevis Over 11 Years** refill hogshead, cask no. 6922, dist Autumn 99, bott Winter 2011 **(77.5)** n18 t22 f18.5 b19. Huge, delicious, richly-flavoured malt does all it can to clamber over some unfriendly oak. *46%. nc ncf sc. Douglas Laing & Co.*

Provenance Ben Nevis Over 12 Years refill hogshead no. DMG 6190, dist Autumn 97, bott Spring 10 **(80.5)** n18.5 t21.5 f19.5 b21. If you know a whisky bottled this year more uncompromisingly malty, then show me it. *46%. nc ncf. Douglas Laing.*

·⊰:·· **Provenance Ben Nevis Over 12 Years** sherry finished hogshead, cask no. 7121, dist Autumn 98, bott Spring 2011 **(85.5)** n19.5 t23 f21.5 b21.5. This distillery does a honeycomb and Demerara sugar mix better than most. Here it is in top gear, but the engine misfires slightly due to some unturned oak. A scintillating, sparks flying ride, nonetheless! *46%. nc ncf sc.*

·⊰:·· **Vom Fass Ben Nevis 12 Years Old (80)** n19 t21.5 f19.5 b20. Juicy barley aplenty. And an almost jammy creaminess, note unlike a Swiss roll. *40%*

·⊰:·· **The Whisky Agency Ben Nevis 1968** bott 2010 **(80.5)** n21 t20 f19.5 b20. Not sure the sample I have was sent at 40% abv...certainly not enough here to carry out an analysis. But, even taking a degree of evaporation into context, the oaks have got their hooks into this one just a little too vehemently, though the honey peddles flat out to make up for the lost ground. *40%*

BENRIACH
Speyside, 1898. The BenRiach Distillery Co. Working.

The BenRiach db (86) n21 t22 f21.5 b21.5. The kind of soft malt you could wean nippers on, as opposed to Curiositas, which would be kippers. Unusually for a BenRiach there is a distinct toffee-fudge air to this one late on, but not enough to spoil that butterscotch-malt charm. No colouring added, so a case of the oak being a bit naughty. 40%

The BenRiach Curiositas Aged 10 Years Single Peated Malt db (90.5) n23 the thin smoke is losing out to the honey-fudge; t23 the peat takes a little time to gather its speech, but when it comes it is fine and softly delivered. In the meantime soft barley and that delicious but curiously dampening sweet fudge struts its stuff; f22 chalky vanillas and a squirt of chocolate like that found on ice cream cones; b22.5 "Hmmmm. Why have my research team marked this down as a 'new' whisky" I wondered to myself. Then immediately on nosing and tasting I discovered the reason without having to ask: the pulse was weaker, the smoke more apologetic...it had been watered down from the original 46% to 40%. This is excellent malt. But can we have our truly great whisky back, please? As lovely as it is, this is a bit of an imposter. As Emperor Hadrian might once have said: "ifus itus aintus brokus..." 40%

The BenRiach Aged 12 Years db (82.5) n21 t20 f21 b20.5. More enjoyable than the 43% I last tasted. But still a very safe, entirely inoffensive malt determined to offer minimal complexity. 40%

The BenRiach Aged 12 Years db (78.5) n21.5 t20 f18 b19. White peppers on the nose, then goes uncharacteristically quiet and shapeless. 43%

The BenRiach Aged 12 Years Dark Rum Wood Finish db (85.5) n21 t22 f21 b21.5. Does exactly what it says on the tin. More than a decade ago, long before it ever became fashionable, I carried out an extensive programme of whisky maturation in old dark rum casks. So, if someone asked me now what would happen if you rounded off a decently peated whisky in a rum cask, I'd say – depending on time given for the finish and type of rum – the smoke would be contained and there would be a ramrod straight, steel-hard sweetness ensuring the most clipped whisky you can possibly imagine. And this here is exactly what we have... 46%

The BenRiach Aged 12 Years Matured In Sherry Wood db (95.5) n23.5 big, juicy, compelling grape. Absolutely clean and stupendous in its multi-layering; t24 quite magnificent! How I pray whiskies to be on delivery, but find they so rarely are. Some caramels are caught up in the genteel squabble between the grape juice and the rich barley; f24 long, faultless and ushering in a chocolate raisin depth; late vanilla and any amount of spice...; b24 since i last tasted this the number of instances of sampling a sherry wood whisky and not finding my taste buds caked in sulphur has nosedived dramatically. Therefore, to start my tasting day at 7am with something as honest as this propels one with myriad reasons to continue the day. A celebration of a malt whisky – in more ways than you could believe... 46%. nc ncf. ⊙⊙

The BenRiach Aged Over 12 Years "Arumaticus Fumosus" richly peated style, ex-dark rum barrels db (91) n23 t23 f22 b23. Very often finishing in rum can sharpen the mouthfeel yet at the same time add a sugary sheen. This little gem is no exception. 46%

The BenRiach Aged Over 12 Years "Heredotus Fumosus" peated PX finish db (92.5) n23 the peat is so thick you could grow a grape vine in it; t23 the sweetness of the grape arrives in spicy waves, comfortably supported by the thick, oily peat; f23 long, more sugared smoke and cocoa; b23.5 at last a PX-peat marriage not on the rocks. What an improvement on the last bottling. Smokograpus Miraculus. 46%. nc ncf. ⊙⊙

The BenRiach Aged Over 12 Years "Importanticus Fumosus" richly peated style, ex-port hogshead db (87) n22 t22 f21 b22. Hardicus asius Nailsus. 46%

The BenRiach Aged 12 Years "Importanticus Fumosus" Tawny port wood finish db (91.5) n23 no matter here had it been finished in Short-eared, Long-eared, Little, Barn or Tawny Port, the peat would have come out tops. The smoke is enormous: owl do they do it...? t22.5 a peaty custard pie in the mush: enormous impact with more early vanilla than fruit; f23.5 now the grape begins to get its head above the smoky parapet; a beautiful balance with the smoke, vanilla and minor spices; b22.5 you'd be a twit not to buy two of 'em. 46%

The BenRiach Aged 13 Years "Maderensis Fumosus" peated madeira finish db (85.5) n20 t23.5 f21 b21. Never a shrinking violet, this still enjoys some pretty off the wall moments. But for a brief success on delivery where the richness of the sugars and smoke work in astonishing harmony, the remainder of the journey is one of vivid disagreement. 46%. nc ncf. ⊙⊙

The BenRiach Aged 15 Years Dark Rum Finish db (86) n20 t22 f22 b22. Drier, spicier than before. Old Jamaica chocolate candy. 46%. nc ncf. ⊙⊙

The BenRiach Aged 15 Years Madeira Wood Finish db (89.5) n22.5 fascinating dry farmhouse cider gives a deliciously unusual edge; t21.5 as sharp and tangy as they come: the first three or four waves are all about the grape finish, then the barley has a clear run; f23 settles rather beautifully with the barley and cocoa-dusted oak offering an excellent exit; b22.5 very much drier than most Madeira finishes you will find around. Once the scramble on delivery is over, this bottling simply exudes excellence. A collector's must have. 46%

The BenRiach Aged 15 Years Pedro Ximénez Sherry Wood Finish db (94.5) n25 a delicate PX influence? This is magnificent...can't be... I'll stop and start again...(15 mins later...) Nope, I was right first time: a PX which is subtlety whiskified. Astonishing layering, each one delicate and fragile: vanilla and lime; gooseberry; barley; grape...a buzz of spice. All clean: not a single bitter or off note...wow! This is one of the world whisky noses of the year: absolute perfection; t23.5 mouth-filling barley then a spreading of a sugary but fruity theme, especially to the roof of the mouth where it sticks on a light oil; in the meantime there is a slow burn of increasing spice; f22.5 long, absolutely thick with butterscotch barley, framed by a constant drone of spicy, sugared grape; b23.5 some of the strangest Scotch malts I have tasted in the last decade have been fashioned in PX casks. And few have been particularly enjoyable creations. This one, though, bucks the trend thanks principally to the most subtle of spice imprints. All the hallmarks of some kind of award-winner. 46%

The BenRiach Aged 15 Years Tawny Port Wood Finish db (89.5) n21.5 confused and heavy. The fruit has little give; t23 comes together on the palate with a rare degree of grace. The kicking expected from the fruit never materialises and instead there is a soft malt and firm fruit double whammy; the fruit and nut chocolate arrives earlier than expected; f22.5 long, with a sustained gracefulness as the malt continues to have an impressive say; a soupcon of furry bitterness at the death; b22.5 now that really is the perfect late night dram after a bastard of a day. 46%

The BenRiach Aged 16 Years db (83.5) n21.5 t21 f20 b21. How extraordinary: just checked the scoring for its old 43% incarnation...and it's identical right along the line. Which is a shame. Because although maltily enjoyable, if over dependent on caramel flavours, you get the feeling that a full works 46% version would offer something more gripping and true to this great distillery. 40%

The BenRiach Aged 16 Years db (83.5) n21.5 t21 f20 b21. Pleasant malt but now without the dab of peat which gave it weight; also a marked reduction of the complexity that once gave this such a commanding presence. Doubtless next time I come across this it'll be back to its brilliant old self. 43%. nc ncf. ⊙

The BenRiach Aged 16 Years Sauternes Wood Finish db (85) n19.5 t23 f21.5 b21. One of the problems with cask finishing, is that there is nothing like an exact science of knowing when the matured whisky and introduced wood gel to their fullest potential. BenRiach enjoy a reputation of getting it right more often than most other distillers and bottlers. But here it hasn't come off to quite the same effect as previous, quite sensational, versions I have tasted of the 16-y-o Sauternes finish. No denying the sheer joy of the carpet bombing of the taste buds on delivery, though, so rich is the combination of fresh grape and delicate smoke. 46%

The BenRiach Aged 18 Years Gaja Barolo Wood Finish db (89) n22 clean: bag of semi-sweet wine gums and gristy barley sub-plot; t23 brilliant delivery where the taste buds are washed in something approaching grape juice and barley water; f21.5 bitters and spices out as the oak gets a foothold; b22.5 the delivery gives one of the most salivating experiences of the year. Love it. 46%

The BenRiach Aged 18 Years Moscatel Wood Finish db (92.5) n23.5 one of those sublime noses where everything is understated: the fresh apples and grape, the most delicate of smoke, the jam on toast, the vanilla...; t23.5 textbook delivery: every note clean and clear, especially the juicy fruits melting into the lush barley. A buzz of distant background smoke all helped along by the most subtle of oils; f22 leans towards the vanilla; b23.5 one of those rare whiskies which renews and upholds my belief I have for cask finishing. Superb. 46%

◦◦◦ **The BenRiach Aged 20 Years** db (85.5) n21.5 t23 f19 b22. A much more attractive version than the American Release 46%. Here the barley offers a disarming intensity and sweetness which makes the most of the light oils available. Only a bittering finish shuts the gate on excellence. 43%. nc ncf.

The BenRiach Aged 20 Years db (78) n19 t20 f19 b20. This is big, but not necessarily for the right reasons or in the right places. A big cut of oiliness combines with some surging sugars for a most un-BenRiachy ride. 46%. US Market.

The BenRiach Aged 21 Years "Authenticus" Peated Malt (85.5) n22 t21.5 f21 b21. A heavy malt, though the smoke only adds a small degree to its weight. The barley is thick and chewy but the oak has a very big say. 46%

The BenRiach 25 Years Old db (87.5) n21.5 sharp and intense: a fruitcake with extra sultanas but the oak bites...; t23 not the most subtle of deliveries: the oak rushes in for an eye-wateringly tart and juicy start, but simmers down with hazelnuts and walnut cream cake; on a higher level there is a far more relaxed fruitcake theme pepped up by subtle spice; f21 the spice continues but there is a furry, chalky dryness; b22 the tranquillity and excellent balance of the middle is the highlight by far. 50%

The BenRiach 30 Years Old db (94.5) n24 the fruit, though very ripe and rich, remains uncluttered and clean and is helped along the way by a superb injection of sweetened cloves and Parma Violets; the oak is present and very correct offering an egg custard sub-plot; t24 how ridiculously deft is that? There is total equilibrium in the barley and fruit as it massages the palate in one of the softest deliveries of a 30-y-o around; the middle ground is creamy and leans towards the vanilla; even so, there are some amazingly juicy moments to savour; f23 long, very lightly oiled and mixing light grist and rich vanilla; b23.5 it's spent 30 years in the cask: give one glass of this at least half an hour of your time: seal the room, no sounds, no distractions. It's worth it...for as hard as I try, I can barely find a single fault with this. 50%

The BenRiach Single Cask 1970 PX finish, cask no. 1035 (93.5) n23 the odd soapy tired note is soon swamped by a lightly spiced, massively graped tsunami. Talk about old and new... t24 a quite sublime delivery: buttery barley stands shoulder to shoulder with a feisty, lightly spiced grape. The result is a pulsating encounter which stimulates every working taste bud... f23 long, creamy...a bit like a spiced, fruity iced cream; b23.5 admission time: I was wholly sceptical that a malt like Benriach at this age would have what was needed to carry the load of something so hefty and uncompromising as a PX cask. I suspect the blender probably thought the same thing. But, against the odds I would say, this has worked...and with aplomb. 49.1%. 250 bottles.

⠐⠄ **The BenRiach Single Cask 1971** batch 8, hogshead, cask no. 1947, dist 21 Apr 71, bott 2011 db (96.5) n23.5 gooseberry tart and mint; a slice or two of lime breaks up the honeyed-tannin background; t25 the delivery is nearly impossible to properly read: not only are the notes delicate but they are myriad and short-lived. There is a hint of sweetened cocoa, but that's only after the taste buds have been confused, seduced and then made near perfect love to by at least a dozen tantalising flavours. Being a mere human, perhaps it is best described as a wondrous bourbon style with a big accent on the small grains. It is hard to tell exactly which are fruit notes and which are sugars. For sure, though, delicate spices play a significant role. This is an absolutely perfect whisky experience. f23.5 like some kind of whisky orgasm, hard to know where the middle and ending is exactly. A late flourish of chocolate ice cream ensures a happy ending with not a single off note to be detected; b24.5 a cask of unreconstituted magnificence. I have tasted some astonishing whiskies this year: this, so far, tops the lot. 49.8%. nc ncf sc.

⠐⠄ **The BenRiach Single Cask 1972** batch 8, hogshead, cask no. 802, dist 18 Feb 72, bott 2011 db (90.5) n23 plenty of natural vanilla. But it is the blend of near black banana, physalis and gooseberry which takes the plaudits; t23 the unmistakable sharpness of a malt on the edge as the oak burrows into the taste buds. But that lasts no more than a moment: the layering of sugars and fudge rescue the situation and builds a platform for those exotic fruits to re-surface; f22 sweetened lemon and lime amid the vanilla; b22.5 from the exotic fruit school of malt...and picked just in the nick of time... 40.1%. nc ncf sc.

The BenRiach Single Cask 1975 Tawny port finish, cask no. 4450 db (83) n20.5 t22.5 f19 b21. A massive malt which perhaps I should enjoy more than I do. When the grape is clean it is a sweet thing of wonder. But there is a dull note in there which lets the side down 52.2%. 648 bottles.

The BenRiach 1975 Vintage Single Cask Campaign No. 4 ex port pipe, cask no. 4451, bott Jun 07 db (91) n23 t23 f22 b23. The Port has certainly breathed life into this old 'un. The complexity and enormity of the experience means it takes about 20 minutes to even begin to fathom this one out. 53.9%. 650 bottles.

⠐⠄ **The BenRiach Single Cask 1976** batch 8, butt, cask no. 6942, dist 14 Oct 76, bott 2011 db (95) n23.5 enormous but leading fruitcake brimming with cherry and molasses; t24 mouth- watering and fresh way beyond – or below? – its years. The sharpness of the fruit appears to have a salty bite as the superior oak make its presence felt; the spices have almost perfect impact; f23.5 long, entirely without a blemish and fading with molasses on toast; b24 strikingly beautiful. 578%. nc ncf sc.

The BenRiach Single Cask 1977 virgin American oak, cask no. 3798 db (76.5) n21 t19 f18 b18.5. Proof, were it needed, that there is only so much fun you can have with an old virgin... 43.2%. 292 bottles.

⮿ **The BenRiach Single Cask 1977** batch 8, PX hogshead, cask no. 1034, dist 15 Apr 77, bott 2011 db **(80.5)** n20.5 t20.5 f19 b19.5. Huge grape: struggles manfully but unsuccessfully to find a second dimension... 54.3%. nc ncf sc.

The BenRiach Single Cask 1978 Gaja Barolo finish, cask no. 4414 db **(88)** n22 huge battle between thumping grape and significant oak; t22.5 eye-watering in the usual Gaja Barolo style, but here tempered by a very confident butterscotch tart and smoked cheese duet; f22 dry with pithy grape and quietly unfolding vanillas; b21.5 a bit leaden footed at times, but where it works it does so splendidly. 51.2%. 245 bottles.

⮿ **The BenRiach Single Cask 1978** batch 8, virgin oak hogshead, cask no. 4387, dist 15 Dec 78, bott 2011 db **(86.5)** n22 t22 f21 b21.5. no shrinking violet, this: the flavours virtually scream at you. After the carpet bombing by toasty sugars comes a surprising degree of bitterness. 50.9%. nc ncf sc.

⮿ **The BenRiach Single Cask 1979** batch 8, ASB cask no. 11195, dist 14 Dec 79, dist 14 Dec 79, bott 2011 db **(86.5)** n21.5 t23 f21 b21. Pleasing: the sugars and spices are a treat on the fabulous delivery. Between the massive oils and light peat almost everything else vanishes. 50.3%. nc ncf sc. Heavily peated.

⮿ **The BenRiach Single Cask 1980** batch 8, virgin oak hogshead, cask no. 2531, dist 28 May 80, bott 2011 db **(92)** n24 fans of bourbon will appreciate this: red liquorice, old waxed leather, honey comb...all the big, aged Kentucky regulars in there big time...; t23 this is one yielding virgin, believe me... Rare that such a dynamic nose is followed up by such a docile delivery: layer upon layer of light, sometimes vaguely molassed sugars...but where is the skeleton? A touch of hickory meets the middle; f22.5 stays on its blancmange style course, though the late rays of honey are magnificent; b22.5 an odd customer. To say it melts in the mouth implies it had some substance in the first place. That is never the case: this, very unusually, is always about flavour rather than structure. Of all the fluids found in this malt, none of it is spinal... 49.8%. nc ncf sc.

The BenRiach Single Cask 1984 PX finish, cask no. 1048 db **(90.5)** n23.5 peatius fruitus magnificus; t22.5 chewus significus; grapum sucrus smokum; juicius maximus amazingus; f22 dullus rubberius primarius; extendos grappa and Cadburyus fruitus and nutus chocolateus; b22.5 at first just reminded me too much of the Lagavulin PX finish. Enjoyable, but feeling that the peat and sweet grape refuse to be on quite the same wavelength. Massive and enjoyable whisky without a doubt, but a bit like watching your football team winning a game by a decent score without really ever getting into their normal rhythm. In many ways, the 15-y-o version worked far better, I thought. Then remembered that this kind of malt was a mood thing. So held back for another time. Only on a second tasting when in a little darker frame of mind did it all come together... (score on first mood: n22 t21.5 f21.5 b21) 49.2%. 279 bottles.

⮿ **The BenRiach Single Cask 1984** batch 8, virgin oak hogshead, cask no. 7193, dist 03 Oct 84, bott 2011 db **(88.5)** n23.5 the peat is oiled on but has some major molasses to contend with; t22 the smoke and liquorice notes trip over each other in a jumbled display on the palate. Great fun...and you never quite know what is going to happen next; f21.5 back to the smoked molasses; b21.5 a perverse whisky: a kind of peated bourbon... 54.3%. nc ncf sc. Richly peated.

The BenRiach Single Cask 1988 Gaja Barolo finish, cask no. 4424 db **(93.5)** n23.5 a rich, weighty bag of tricks with the grape mingling attractively with delicate smoke; t24 the sharp, intense fruitiness of a mildly unripened grape results in the same salivating tendencies as the 18-y-o version; the most delicate soft smoke imaginable acts as the perfect foil and leads to a fabulous mocha middle; f22.5 again bitters out but still plenty of life and depth to keep the party going; b23 superficially, a very similar re-run of the 18-y-o Gaja Barolo. But in reality, much more complex and complete, with the finish intact and the smoke more telling. Another all-round stunner from the wonderful distillery. 54.3%. 322 bottles.

⮿ **The BenRiach Single Cask 1989** Sauternes hogshead, cask no. 4813, dist 25 Jan 89, bott 2011 db **(74.5)** n19 t19 f18 b18.5. Never gets the chance to open out. 49.1%. nc ncf sc.

⮿ **The BenRiach Single Cask 1989** virgin oak hogshead, cask no. 5620, dist 21 Apr 89, bott 2011 db **(91.5)** n23 telling, almost bolshie but the firm layering of sugars make it less of an ogre; t24 fabulous, eye-rolling delivery: the barley explodes like a mushroom cloud on the palate. The sugars become particularly noticeable in the fallout but are then immediately toughened by a backbone of drier, intense tannin; f22 more tannin on the fade; b22.5 at times like sucking a malt whisky candy... 50.6%. nc ncf sc.

The BenRiach Single Cask 1990 cask no. 970 db **(89.5)** n21.5 clean, heavy vanilla presence; t23 it's salivating, lip-smacking barley all the way with an improbably gristy sweetness retained throughout; f22 the malt continues to an astonishing degree; b22.5 another mind-blowing ultra clean maltfest from this distillery. With Cardhu, Glen Moray and Tomatin, no-one can do malt quite like this. 57.1%. 195 bottles.

⟨⟨~ **The BenRiach Single Cask 1992** batch 8, Tawny Port hogshead, cask no. 972, dist 19 Feb 92, bott 2011 db **(93)** n24 beautiful, clean and sparkling exuberance to the grape: rather more like I expected their Sauternes to be...; **t23.5** more of the same but now with a puckering sharpness and some real needle in the spice; **f22.5** a few controlled bitter notes headed off by a slice of fruitcake washed down with creamy mocha; **b23** yet another delight from this outstanding distillery. 55.6%. nc ncf sc.

⟨⟨~ **The BenRiach Single Cask 1993** batch 8, Barolo hogshead, cask no. 7415, dist 27 May 93, bott 2011 db **(92.5)** n23.5 a rare display of tight, almost paranoidly intense fruit with almost paranoidly intense oak. The combination is sweet, intense bliss; **t23** the silky arrival does nothing to prepare you for the barrage of white hot spices which sear the palate; like the nose, so thick you could carve the distillery's name into it; **f23** concentrates on the tannins. But no off notes, no bitterness of any kind...just an elegant, roast fudge fade; **b23** unique flavour profile: there is no other offering anything quite like this in the world, trust me... 56.1%. nc ncf sc.

The BenRiach 1994 Limited Release Madeira Finish Aged 15 Years cask no. 4810, bott Sep 09 db **(87)** n23 richly layered and textured fruit on a bedrock of cement-like barley; **t22** good grief! Mouth-watering but the barley is hard enough to crack your teeth **f20.5** disappointing compared to the bare-knuckle entertainment of before: a distinctive bitter note; **b21.5** gives the impression of having been distilled from granite... 57.1%. Exclusive to Kensington Wine Market.

The BenRiach "Heart of Speyside" db **(85.5)** n21.5 t22 f21 b21. A decent, non-fussy malt where the emphasis is on biscuity barley. At times juicy and sharp. Just a tease of very distant smoke here and there adds weight. 40%

⟨⟨~ **The BenRiach "Horizons"** db **(87)** n22 a plethora of natural caramel notes; **t22.5** a simple barley/caramel weight and counterweight; the sugars are even and toasty; **f21** heads off along one very long, straight caramel-vanilla path as far as the eye can see...; **b21.5** few mountains or even hills on this horizon. But the view is still an agreeable one. 50%. nc ncf.

⟨⟨~ **The BenRiach "Solstice"** db **(94)** n23.5 gorgeous non-coastal peat. By which I mean, intense smoke, but none of the brine and rock pools which sometimes accompanies it. This is simply clean, lumbering phenols, thickened still further by a good dollop of lascivious fruit...; **t24** a barrage of firm brown sugars are first to show, followed soon after by a cream sundae fruitiness. The smoke is all pervasive and intensifies as the flavours play out; there is also a decent showing of peppery spice pulsing in its intensity; **f23** an enormously long fade, a bit like a midsummer sunset. No surprises, bitterness or off notes whatsoever. Just a slow dimming of all that has gone on before; **b23.5** on midsummer's day 2011, the summer solstice, I took a rare day off from writing this book. With the maximum light available in my part of the world for the day I set off at daybreak to see how many miles I could walk along remote country paths stopping, naturally, only at a few remote pubs on the way. It was a fraction under 28 miles. Had this spellbinding whisky been waiting for me just a little further down the road, I am sure, despite my troubled left knee and blistered right foot, I would have made it 30... 50%. nc ncf.

Birnie Moss Intensely Peated db **(90)** n22 youthful, full of fresh barley and lively, clean smoke; **t23.5** juicy, fabulously smoked, wet-behind the ears gristy sugars; **f22** some vanillas try to enter a degree of complexity; **b22.5** before Birnie Moss started shaving... or even possibly toddling. Young and stunning. 48%. nc ncf. ☉☉

Cadenhead's Benriach Aged 23 Years bott 2009 **(95.5)** n24 t24 f23.5 b24. How blenders for so long considered this very much a second rate distillery is entirely beyond me. 53.3%

The Càrn Mòr Vintage Collection Benriach 1985 barrel no. 5494, dist 2009 **(89.5)** n22.5 a squeeze of lemon on the clean barley; **t23** clean, salivating and intensifying in barley input through to the fudgy middle; the citrus plays peek-a-boo throughout and some nut oil adds needed weight; **f22** long barley-rich fade with an increasing amount of natural caramels; **b22** very attractive in its light citrusy mode. Just don't expect a brooding malt of some 25 years, complete with thick eyebrows and a stoop...this is a dandy, but one which will charm the life out of you. 46%. 819 bottles.

Connoisseurs Choice Benriach 1987 **(82.5)** n20 t22 f20 b20.5. Pretty oak-laden, even for its age. Attractive barley sugar attack, though. 43%. Gordon & MacPhail.

Dun Bheagan Benriach Aged 10 Years **(86)** n21 t22 f21 b22. A delicate, delicious and youthful Benriach in full blending colours. 43%. Ian Macleod.

Duncan Taylor The NC2 Range Benriach Aged 12 Years dist 1996, bott 2008 **(85.5)** n22 t21 f21.5 b21. Has soaked up no shortage of oak in its dozen years, but the barley and spice fizz, topped with plain chocolate, evens things out. 46%

⟨⟨~ **Hart Brothers Benriach Aged 14 Years** dist Mar 96, bott Jan 11 **(86.5)** n21 t22 f22 b21.5. Doesn't even bother to play the complexity card. Just big, sweet chest-beating barley all the way. 46%. sc.

Old Malt Cask Benriach Aged 15 Years refill hogshead, cask no. 6990, dist Mar 96, bott Mar 11 **(93) n22** mildly shallow but oozing a brassy saltiness; **t24** much more like it: intense with the juicy malt and vanilla intact and in harmony. Those briny notes remain, but some surprising honeycomb and hickory prop up the middle ground; **f23** loads of toffee and milk chocolate and a few embers of warming spice; **b23.5** one of those malts that doesn't shout its greatness at you. You have to possess a bit of cunning and understanding to discover the hidden gems here. *50%. nc ncf sc. Douglas Laing & Co. 332 bottles.*

Old Malt Cask Benriach Aged 19 Years refill hogshead, dist Feb 90, bott Apr 09 **(83.5) n20 t22 f20 b21.5.** It's all about the malty delivery: exceptional balance to the sweetness. Light latte, too. *50%. Douglas Laing. 235 bottles.*

Old Masters Benriach 14 Years Old cask no. 43219, dist 1996, bott Feb 11 **(72) n17 t19 f17.5 b18.5.** Not quite the greatest cask in the world, Mr MacArthur! *54%. sc. James MacArthur & Co.*

Provenance Benriach Aged 11 Years refill hogshead DMG 5740, dist Spring 98, bott Winter 2010 **(89) n23** rarely comes more cleanly malty than this; **t23** spot on! The degree of gristy sugars mixing with the blooming oaky vanillas just can't be faulted; weight and mouth-feel tick all the right boxes; **f21** heads back towards the vanilla. A degree of toasty bitterness, but the barley is never far away; low level spices kick in at the very death and extend the finale considerably; **b22** top rate Benriach, not only at its very maltiest but in an uncommonly excellent cask. For nose and delivery alone, a minor gem of its type showing why some blenders prize this distillery so highly. *46%. Douglas Laing & Co Ltd.*

Provenance Benriach Over 11 Years refill hogshead, cask no. 6821, dist Spring 99, bott Autumn 2010 **(86.5) n22 t22 f21 b21.5.** An intense, compact and natural caramel spined maltfest. *46%. nc ncf sc. Douglas Laing & Co.*

The Whisky Agency Benriach 1975 bott 2010 **(93) n23** entirely intact with coconut dipped in syrup. The tannins are present but muscovado sugars pepper it with purpose; **t23.5** toasty with sweet oak notes scrambling around the palate; the lightness of touch of the honey is commendable; the spices need locating, but once found play a very clever role; **f23** a real custard pie of a finale with the vanillas in the ascendency; the spices persist to the end; **b23.5** the secret of this malt's success is the alliance between the oils and rich sugars. Fabulous. *50.6%*

The Whisky Agency Benriach 1985 bott 2010 **(86.5) n21 t22 f21 b21.5.** Plenty of malty juices flowing, but feels the oak perhaps just a little too keenly. *48.1%*

Whisky Doris Benriach 12 Year Old cask no. 45757, dist Mar 96, bott Oct 08 **(88) n22 t22 f23 b21.5.** See 52.1% below. Works very fractionally better at this strength as the honey just gets a slightly higher profile and there is less jarring. On the minus side, there is much less character and is a little too suave. *46%*

Whisky Doris Benriach 12 Year Old cask no. 45757, dist Mar 96, bott Oct 08 **(87.5) n22 t21 f23 b21.5.** Bit of a stop-start merchant, never quite finding a rhythm. That said, the goods parts really are excellent...! *52.1%*

The Whisky Fair Benriach 33 Year Old dist 1976, bott 2009 **(84.5) n21.5 t21.5 f21 b21.** Has all the exotic fruit flourishes to mark the years - and a touch of coppery sheen on the palate, but perhaps a fair few splinters, too. *46.2%. The Whisky Fair, Germany.*

The Whisky Fair Benriach 33 Year Old dist 1976, bott 2009 **(84.5) n21.5 t21.5 f21 b21.** The absolute twin of the 46.2% version, other than a quick, briefly passing explosion of juicy barley. *47.4%. The Whisky Fair, Germany.*

BENRINNES
Speyside, 1826. Diageo. Working.

Benrinnes Aged 15 Years db **(70) n16 t19 f17 b18.** What a shame that in the year the independent bottlers at last get it right for Benrinnes, the actual owners of the distillery make such a pig's ear of it. Sulphured and sicklysweet, this bottling has little to do with the very good whisky made there day in day out by its talented team. Depressing. *43%. Flora and Fauna.*

Benrinnes The Manager's Choice refill American oak, cask no. 8994, dist 1996, bott 2009 db **(89.5) n21.5** thick, pulpy gooseberry; a bit of a thin, biting note, too, but vanilla-barley layering also attractive; **t23.5** excellently active barley really hitting some glorious clean and eye-wateringly sharp notes; for a triple distilled malt, the light, malty oils are a bit of a surprise...and a treat; **f22** simplistic like the delivery and thins again. But some attractive powdery oak suggests good cask selection and age...and enough controlled dryness to balance the continuing fresh barley; **b22.5** great to see the distillery in this kind of outstanding form. *59.7%. 328 bottles.*

A.D. Rattray Benrinnes 1996 cask no. 6461, dist Jun 96, bott Sep 09 **(89) n20** somewhere, amid this soupy fruit, there has to be some whisky...hasn't there...? **t22** thundering delivery of the most intense grape and barley imaginable. I say barley...something which offers a juicy element is in there somewhere; quite metallic and spicy, too; **f23** settles down from the pell-mell of the nose and delivery and heads in a much more refined cocoa and custard direction. But the lingering burned raisin drifts on forever... **b22** the nose has more rum about it than Scotch whisky in many respects. But such is the lack of discipline and shape here, it's bloody impossible to tell what is going on. Just put on a tin hat and go for the bumpy – and undeniably fun – ride. *57%. A.D. Rattray Ltd.*

⋯ **A.D. Rattray Benrinnes 1996** cask no. 6463 **(96) n25** absolutely terrifying degree of sherry: a butt from the old school – 100% sulphur free and dripping with toasted raisin and voluptuous dates. Malt, layered with Demerara and soft spice. This is perfection...; **t24** nothing short of magnificent: a controlled, slow-motion explosion of spices and a fanning out into all directions of the palate of chestnuts, liquorice, burnt fudge and even barley...; equally as vital is the weight and texture, which both tick the right boxes; **f23** dries towards a big vanilla exit but with a pithy quality to the fruit. Here a triple-distilled malt does not quite have the body to take the finale on that extra few notches; **b24** if you ever hear some self invented, industry toadying "whisky expert" saying that today's average sherry butt is fine, and no different to how they used to be, just get them to investigate a bottle of this. This is oloroso enriched malt the way I was first weaned on it nearly 40 years ago. The butt is devoid of a single off note: it is clean and could be easily mistaken for a Macallan bottling of the 70s and 80s. This is the way the majority of fresh sherry butts used to be: the industry norm by which I still, to the chagrin of certain others, measure today's malt. I fear that there may now be an entire generation of whisky lovers who have yet to experience anything quite like this mahogany-coloured masterpiece. For there is not a single molecule giving you trouble on the nose and, as that indicates, the entire experience is free from any pressing of the self destruct button. A dram which certain people in, or on the periphery of, today's Scotch whisky industry who deceive themselves and others into thinking they know something about this game should taste...and, if they are capable (which in many cases I doubt), learn from. And it is a bottle I would love to ram up their collective rear ends to stop them talking the absolute drivel which ultimately does the industry – and you the consumer – such a massive disservice. *56.1%. sc. A.D. Rattray.*

The Càrn Mòr Vintage Collection Braes of Benrinnes 2002 hogshead, cask no. 5, dist 2002, bott 2009 **(80) n19 t21 f20 b20.** An entirely competent example of sweet, malty blending fodder untroubled by oak. *46%. The Scottish Liqueur Centre.*

Connoisseurs Choice Benrinnes 1975 (85.5) n22 t21.5 f20.5 b21.5. I remember as a nipper going annually to Epsom Downs, close to my Surrey home, on Derby Day in the very early '60s. The two most important things to get my parents to buy me were a) a blue and white quartered riding cap and b) a toffee apple from the fair they used hold there in those days. This reminds me very much of those old-fashioned toffee apples. The stick was made of wood, like that used in lollies. And after chomping through the toffee and apple, I would then give the wood a good gnaw to extract every last piece of flavour. Who would have thought that over 45 years ago this would have been made from Benrinnes casks...? *43%. Gordon & MacPhail.*

⋯ **Old Malt Cask Benrinnes Aged 19 Years** sherry butt, cask no. 7232, dist Jan 92, bott May 11 **(71) n16 t20 f18 b19.** After the horror nose, the malty, chocolate-infested story told on the palate is a comparative treat. *50%. nc ncf sc. Douglas Laing & Co. 286 bottles.*

Old Malt Cask Benrinnes Aged 21 Years refill hogshead, dist Mar 88, bott May 09 **(91.5) n23 t23 f22.5 b23.** Heart-warming to see Benrinnes in this outstanding nick and so clean on nose and delivery. A distillery classic. *50%. Douglas Laing. 276 bottles.*

Provenance Benrinnes Over 11 Years bourbon cask no. 5238, dist Spring 98, bott Summer 09 **(84.5) n21 t21 f21.5 b21.** Eye-watering barley in sharp, concentrated form...and with raspberry jam for good measure. Great fun. *46%. nc ncf. Douglas Laing & Co Ltd.*

⋯ **Provenance Benrinnes Over 12 Years** sherry butt, cask no. 6506, dist Winter 97, bott Summer 2010 **(67) n18 t18 f15 b16.** Starts badly. And gets a lot worse... *46%. nc ncf sc.*

⋯ **Robert Graham's Dancing Stag Benrinnes 1988** hogshead, dist 10 Mar 88, bott 09 Jun 11 **(77.5) n20.5 t20 f18 b19.** Big, single tracked malt early on. But almost a collectors' item to find a whisky with so little taste on the finish. *46%. nc ncf sc. 277 bottles.*

Scotch Malt Whisky Society Cask 36.44 Aged 20 Years refill butt, dist May 88 **(74.5) n18.5 t19 f18 b19.** Lively, tangy, some interesting cocoa but with its many flaws really would have been better suited to a blend. *60.5%*

Stronachie Benrinnes Aged 12 Years 2009 batch **(75.5) n18.5 t20 f19 b19.** Big malt but, technically, not quite at the races. *43%. A.D. Rattray Ltd.*

⋯ **Vom Fass Benrinnes 11 Years Old (83.5) n22 t22 f20.5 b19.** For those who like their barley in fresh, clean concentrated form...and to rip directly into their taste buds. And, some cocoa on the finale apart, not much else besides! Delicious! *578%*

BENROMACH
Speyside, 1898. Gordon & MacPhail. Working.

Benromach 10 Years Old matured in hand selected oak casks db (87.5) n22 how you might expect a chocolate peat bar to be when grated. The odd blood orange note, too; t22 a gristy sweetness imparts a delicate smoke which mingles with the vanilla; f21.5 surprising degrees of sugars see off the worst of a bitter oakiness; b22 for a relatively small still using peat, the experience is an unexpected and delicately light one. 43%

Benromach 21 Years Old db (91.5) n22 some exotic fruit and green banana is topped off with a splodge of maple syrup; t23.5 excellent interplay between the sweeter, barley-rich components and the elegant, spiced oaky backbone; virtually no bite and softened further by an unfurling of vanilla on the middle; f23 long, oak-edged with a slow, tapering dryness which does nothing to confront the sugared backnotes or even the suggesting of the most delicate smoke; b23 an entirely different, indeed lost, style of malt from the old, now gone, big stills. The result is an airier whisky which has embraced such good age with a touch of panache and grace. The sweetness has been underlined in the last few seconds by attracting a tiny fruit fly which, whilst writing these notes, has chosen this to dive into and drown in. What a way to go: you could hardly wish for a classier end... 43%

Benromach 22 Years Old Finished in Port Pipes db (86) n22 t23 f20 b21. Slightly Jekyll and Hyde. 45%. 3500 bottles.

Benromach 25 Years Old db (92) n24 seriously sexy with spices interplaying with tactile malt: the bitter-sweet balance is just so. There is even the faintest flicker of peat-smoke to underscore the pedigree; t22 an early, surprising, delivery of caramel amongst the juicy barley; f23 lots of gentle spices warm the enriched barley and ice-creamy vanilla; b23 a classic old-age Speysider, showing all the quality you'd hope for. 43% ⊙

⋗ **Benromach 30 Years Old** db (95.5) n23.5 spiced sultana, walnuts and polished bookcases; t24 no malt has the right to be anything near so silky. The sugars are a cunning mix of molasses and muscovado; the honey is thinned manuka. Still the barley gets through, though the vanilla is right behind...; f24 drier, but never fully dries and has enough spotted dog in reserve to make for a moist, lightly spiced finish. And finally a thin strata of sweet, Venezuelan cocoa; b24 you will struggle to find a 30-year-old with less wrinkles than this.. Magnificent: one of the outstanding malts of the year. 43%

Benromach Cask Strength 1981 db (91) n21.5 t23 f23.5 b23. Really unusual with that seaweedy aroma awash with salt: stunningly delicious stuff. 54.2%

⋗ **Benromach Cask Strength 2001** db (89) n21.5 a pretty closed road: the peat stands by a blockage and allows little else to pass; t23 an amalgamation of soft oil, big alcohol and venomous spice allows the taste buds to be truly duffed up in a splendidly macho manner. Like a bunch of East End gangsters, they kick their way through all closed doors until they reach their quarry. Luckily, by the time they get to the middle ground, their guns have transformed into pea-shooters popping out nothing more deadly than muscovado sugars; f22 yet more layers of smoky vanilla and sugar; b22.5 just fun whisky which has been very well made and matured with total sympathy to the style. Go get. 59.9%

Benromach 2002 Sassicaia Wood Finish db (86) n21 t22 f21 b22. Again this entirely idiosyncratic wood-type comes crashing head to head with the smoke to form a whisky style like nothing else. Dense, breathless and crushed, there is little room for much else to get a word in, other than some oak-extracted sugars. A must experience dram. 45%

Benromach Latitude 57° cask no. 580 db (73.5) n18.5 t19 f18 b18. I'm afraid with that sulphur evident it shows the wrong kind of latitude altogether... 57%. 330 bottles.

Benromach Madeira Wood db (92) n22 some rolling smoke and chunky dried fruits almost cancel each other out...almost...; t24 voluptuous body displaying soft oils which coat the mouth with a spot on peat which is at once full and chewy yet light enough to allow the layered fruits full reign; the bitter-sweet balance just couldn't be better; f23 long with some touches of almost Jack Daniel hickory amid the circling smoke and juiced up fruit; mind-boggling complexity to this for so long... b23 good grief! If you want a boring, safe, timid malt, stay well away from this one. Fabulous: you are getting the feeling that the real Benromach is now beginning to stand up. 45%

Benromach Marsala Wood db (86.5) n21.5 t22 f22 b21. Solid, well made, enjoyable malt, which in some ways is too solid: the imperviousness of both the peat and grape appears not to allow much else get through. Not a dram to say no to, however, and the spices in particular are a delight. 45%

Benromach Organic db (91) n23 massive oak input and the freshest oak imaginable. But sits comfortably with the young pulsing malts. Wow!!; t23 oak arrives first again, but has enough deftness of touch to allow the rich, mouthwatering malts to prosper; f22 plenty of vanillins and natural, sweet toffee; **b23** young and matured in possibly first fill bourbon or, more likely, European (even Scottish) oak; you cannot do other than sit up and take notice of this guns-blazing big 'un. An absolute treat! *43%. nc ncf.*

⁘ **Benromach Organic Special Edition** db **(85.5) n22 t21 f21.5 b21.** The smoky bacon crisp aroma underscores the obvious youth. Also, one of the driest malts of the year. Overall, pretty. But pretty pre-pubescent, too... *43%*

Benromach Origins db **(84.5) n20 t22 f21 b21.5.** You'd think after tasting over 1,250 whiskies in the space of a few months you'd have nosed and tasted it all. But no: here is something very different. Discordant noises from nose to finish, it is saved by the extraordinary richness of the coppery input and a vague smoky richness finishing with cold latte. Very different, indeed. *50%*

⁘ **Benromach Origins Batch 1 "Golden Promise"** dist 1999 db **(69.5) n17 t17.5 f17.5 b17.5.** The nose is less than promising. And with good reason. *50%*

⁘ **Benromach Origins Batch 2 "Port Pipe"** dist 1999 db **(86) n22 t20.5 f23 b20.5.** Dense whisky with huge spice. But it is as if in concentrate form with little room for complexity to develop into its full potential. Some charming chocolate and toffee on the finish. *50%*

⁘ **Benromach Origins Batch 3 "Optic"** dist 2000 db **(83.5) n21 t20 f21.5 b21.** Another chunky, tight malt from the new Benromach. Some serious chewing, but a few feints on which to chew... *50%*

Benromach Peat Smoke Aged 6 Years 2nd edition 1st fill bourbon barrel, dist 2002, bott 2008 db **(92) n22.5 t23.5 f23 b23.** This is Benromach getting it right at every turn, including bottling at such tender years. Proof that excellence can be achieved with first class wood selection and fine work in the still house, rather than simply Summers spent in the warehouse. *46%*

⁘ **Benromach Peat Smoke Batch 3** db **(90.5) n22** excellent nose: pretty decent levels of peak reek evident but dried, rather than cured...; **t23** now that is impressive: the dry peat builds in intensity, though not after the clean and powering barley makes the first speech; **f22.5** dry, chalky and compact; damn it – this is very good, indeed! **b23** an excellent malt that has been beautifully made. Had it been bottled at 46 we would have seen it offer an extra degree of richness. *40%*

Benromach Sassicaia Wood Finish bott 2007 db **(86) n23 t20 f22 b21.** Benromach in very different clothing here – in fact, there is no other malt with the elements so portrayed. Particularly pleasing is the beauty of the balance between the soft smoke and the varied oaky tones – very European. The arrival is a little confused (a touch of the Italian tantrums at one point) but it eventually pans out into an attractively sweet, and again softly peated, little charmer. Unique. *45%*

Benromach Traditional db **(86) n22 t21 f21.5 b21.5.** Deliciously clean and smoky. But very raw and simplistic, too. 40% ⊙ ⊙

⁘ **Benromach Wood Finish Hermitage** dist 2001 db **(84) n19 t23 f21 b21.** A sweet, tight dram with all the shape crushed out of it. It does have its moment of greatness, though: about three or four seconds after arrival when it zooms into the stratosphere on a massively fruity, sensuously spiced rocket. Then it just fades away... *45%*

⁘ **Benromach Wood Finish Pedro Ximénez** dist 2002 db **(85.5) n21 t22.5 f21 b21.** Combining PX with peated whisky is still probably the hardest ask in the maturation lexicon. Lagavulin are still to get it right. And they have not quite managed it here, either. It's a bumpy old ride, though some of the early chewing moments are fun. Not a bad attempt, at all. Just the learning curve is still on the rise... *45%*

⁘ **Benromach Vintage 1968** db **(94.5) n23** theoretically way over the top oak. But the sherry acts as a sponge...or, to be more precise, a very well aged fruit cake; some mega juicy plums and figs; **t23** can't fault the marbelling with the fruit running thickly into the spicier, almost bourbony meat. Again the oak is over the top, yet, thanks to the depth of the cocoa and juicy grape, somehow gets away with some outrageous splinters; **f24.5** now completely dazzles as all the more militant elements of the oak have been pacified and we are left with not only a sherry trifle/fruitcake mix, but chocolate cream/raspberry roll for good measure... **b24** a 40 year plus whisky of astonishing quality...? A piece of cake... *45.4%*

BLADNOCH
Lowlands, 1817. Armstrong Brothers. Working.

Bladnoch Aged 6 Years Bourbon Matured db **(91) n21.5** young, yes. But the soft feints have nothing to do with that; **t22.5** a youthful, oily delivery, not exactly a picture of harmony, gives way to a brutal coup d'etat of ultra intense prisoner-slaughtering barley; **f24** I'm in barley heaven: intense barley-concentrate oils offer a perplexing array of sweet, grassy tones;

you simply chew and chew until the jaw aches. Cocoa at last arrives, all with a spiced buzz and a smearing of vanillas. Meanwhile your tongue explores the mouth, wondering what the hell is going on... **b23** ignore the mildly feinty nose and delivery. The fun starts with the late middle, where those extra oils congregate and the taste buds are sent rocking. Great to see a Lowlander bottled at an age nearer its natural best and even the smaller cut, in a roundabout way, ensures a mind-blowing dram. *57.3%*

Bladnoch Aged 6 Years Lightly Peated db (93) **n23** a peat fire just bursting into life; **t23** firm, bitter-sweet; the layering of the peat is awesome, with the youth of the malt adding an extra dimension; some citrus notes help lighten the load; **f23.5** smoky hickory; the vanillas make a feeble entry, a gentle oiliness persists; **b23.5** the peat has nothing to do with the overall score here: this is a much better-made whisky with not a single off-note and the cut is spot on. And although it claims to be lightly peated, that is not exactly true: such is the gentle nature of the distillate, the smoke comes through imperiously and on several levels. "Spirit of the Lowlands" drones the label. Since when has outstanding peated malt been associated with that part of the whisky world...?? *58.5%*

Bladnoch Aged 6 Years Sherry Matured db (73.5) **n18 t19 f18.5 b18**. A sticky, lop-sided malt where something, or a group of somethings, conjures up a very unattractive overture. Feints on the palate but no excellent bourbon cask to the rescue here. *56.9%*

Bladnoch Aged 10 Years db (94) **n23** lemon and lime, marmalade on fresh-sliced flour-topped crusty bread; **t24** immensely fruity and chewy, lush and mouthwatering and then the most beguiling build-up of spices: the mouthfeel is full and faultless; **f23** long, remains mildly peppery and then a dryer advance of oak. The line between bitter and sweet is not once crossed; **b24** this is probably the ultimate Bladnoch, certainly the best I have tasted in over 25 years. This Flora and Fauna bottling by then owners United Distillers should be regarded as the must-get-at-all-costs Bladnoch. If the new owner can create something even to hang on to this one's coat-tails then he has excelled himself. For those few of us lucky enough to experience this, this dram is nothing short of a piece of Lowland legend and folklore. *43%. For those of you with a nervous disposition, the author would like to point out that not a single drop of this whisky was spat out during the creation of these tasting notes.*

Bladnoch Aged 15 Years db (91) **n22.5** remnants of zest and barley sit comfortably with the gentle oaks; **t22.5** excellent delivery and soon gets into classic Bladnoch citric stride; **f23** wonderfully clean barley belies the age and lowers the curtain so delicately you hardly notice; **b23** quite outstanding Lowland whisky which, I must admit, is far better than I would have thought possible at this age. *55%*

Bladnoch Aged 16 Years "Spirit of the Lowlands" db (88) **n22 t22 f22 b22**. Really lovely whisky and unusual to see a Lowlander quite this comfortable at such advanced age. *46%. ncf.*

Bladnoch 18 Years Old db (88.5) **n21** dulled with oak; **t23.5** fabulous balance between juicy fruit and juicy barley. The gooseberries are green, fat and splitting at the sides...; **f22** vanilla and a trail of light oil allows the barley an extended stay **b22** the juiciness and clarity to the barley, and especially the big gooseberry kick, early on makes this a dram well worth finding. *55%*

Berrys' Own Selection Bladnoch 1990 (86) **n21.5 t22 f21 b21.5**. Not your typical Bladnoch, with the usual ultra malty personality being moved by a sharper, apple-accented nose and delivery. Angular and entertaining with a touch of severity. *50.4%*

Berry's Own Selection Bladnoch 1990 bott 2009 (89) **n23 t22 f22 b22**. Some people will be disappointed with this as an 18-year-old, as it doesn't actually do much. And they might have a point. But on the other hand, how can you not be charmed by something so crystalline. *43%*

⋯ **Berry's Own Selection Bladnoch 1990** cask no. 2462, bott 2011 (75) **n18 t20 f18 b19**. Malty but persists with a strangely off key, mouldy hay persona. *51.2%. nc ncf sc.*

Cadenhead's Bladnoch Aged 17 Years dist 1992, bott 2009 (92.5) **n23.5 t23.5 f22.5 b23**. An exceptional cask full of charisma and quality. *55.1%*

Chieftain's Bladnoch 16 Years Old hogshead, dist Nov 92, bott 2009 (84.5) **n21 t21.5 f21 b21**. Distilled during its lighter body phase, this still juicy offering holds up well, though the slightly sawdust-like oakiness does play the most prominent role. *48%. nc ncf. Ian Macleod.*

Connoisseurs Choice Bladnoch 1993 (88.5) **n22.5 t21.5 f22.5 b22**. One of those drams which on the oaky face of it shouldn't work..but deliciously does. *43%. Gordon & MacPhail.*

John McDougall's Selection Bladnoch 1990 cask no. CM101, dist 1990 (83.5) **n22 t21 f20 b20.5**. Clean and crammed with big malt. But on the hot and thin side. *54.2%. 260 bottles.*

John McDougall's Selection Bladnoch 1990 cask no. CM124, dist 1990 (92) **n23.5 t23 f22.5 b23**. Just wonderful malt, showing Bladnoch in a clear and excellent light. The structure and layering is sublime. *53.3%. House of Macduff. 240 bottles.*

⋯ **Old Malt Cask Bladnoch Aged 18 Years** refill hogshead, cask no. 6909, dist Nov 92, bott Jan 11 (73.5) **n19.5 t19 f17 b18**. More Major Bloodnok, I'm afraid... *50%. nc ncf sc. 187 bottles.*

⠬ **Scotch Malt Whisky Society Cask 50.41 Aged 20 Years** refill hogshead, cask no. 30538, dist 1990 **(92) n23** attractive flecks of fruit appear to conflict with an almost bourbon-style oakiness. Well measured and weighted: delicate and complex; **t23** charming delivery which fulfils the promise of complexity on the nose. Again, there is a discreet honey-liquorice sweetness which points in a Kentucky-ish direction while elsewhere the barley and vaguely fruity sugars ensure a massive degree of small talk; **f22.5** spices up as the barley levels go down; **b23.5** one of those outstanding drams which keeps you guessing and entertained forever. *54.5%. sc. 162 bottles.*

⠬ **Scotch Malt Whisky Society Cask 50.44 Aged 18 Years** refill hogshead, cask no. 3835, dist 1992 **(82) n19 t21.5 f20.5 b21.** A big, malty fellow. But goes easy on the finesse. *56.5%. sc. 282 bottles.*

⠬ **Single Cask Collection Bladnoch Aged 21 Years** bourbon hogshead, cask no. 134, dist Jan 90, bott Feb 11 **(83) n18 t23 t20.5 b21.5.** Recovers after a less than promising start on the nose. The clean intensity of the barley is a stark contrast and with its citrus sub-plot gives a good showing of the malt at its most simplistic self. *51.9%. nc ncf sc. 288 bottles.*

Wilson & Morgan Barrel Selection Bladnoch Aged 18 Years rum finish, dist 1990, bott 2008 **(93) n22.5 t24 f23 b23.5.** A glittering malt whose delivery is nothing short of sublime. *51%*

BLAIR ATHOL
Highlands (Perthshire), 1798. Diageo. Working.

Blair Athol Aged 12 Years db **(77) n18 t19 f21 b19.** Thick, fruity, syrupy and a little sulphury and heavy. The finish has some attractive complexity among the chunkyness. *43%. Flora and Fauna.*

Connoisseurs Choice Blair Athol 1995 (76) 20 **t20 f18 b18.** Clean and malty. But straight as a dye. Zero complexity. *43%. Gordon & MacPhail.*

Old & Rare Blair Athol Aged 32 Years dist Jun 76, bott Aug 08 **(86.5) n22 t22.5 f21 b21.** Belies its years in any number of ways, not least in how the oak is so easily accommodated. Hugely enjoyable, especially on the lightly smoked, gingerbread nose and early Parkin Cake delivery, and even though not one to exactly raise the pulse there is a very agreeable degree of complexity. *55.4%. Douglas Laing. 119 bottles.*

Old Malt Cask Blair Athol Aged 9 Years sherry butt, dist Sep 99, bott Mar 09 **(81) n19 t20 f21 b21.** Sweet, warming and clean. *46%. Douglas Laing.*

Old Malt Cask Blair Athol Aged 10 Years sherry butt, dist Dec 98, bott Jul 09 **(73) n18 t20 f17 b18.** More Blair Witch. *50%. Douglas Laing.*

⠬ **Old Malt Cask Blair Athol Aged 15 Years** sherry butt, cask no. 6814, dist Nov 95, bott Nov 10 **(77) n19 t21 f18 b19.** Appears terrified to get going. Malty but refuses to find any complexity. *50%. nc ncf sc. Douglas Laing & Co. 545 bottles.*

Old Malt Cask Blair Athol Aged 35 Years refill hogshead no. 5572, dist Oct 74, bott Oct 09 **(86) n21 t22 f22 b21.** from the days when Bells ruled the distillery...what the bloody hell was going on here? Was this some attempt to create an Islay-style malt? If so, they failed...spectacularly. No: I think just mucky, overworked stills at play here. Enormous and bordering on the manic. Thick, incomprehensible...but magnificent fun! *50%. Douglas Laing. 217 bottles.*

Premier Barrel Blair Athol Aged 10 Years sherry cask **(78) n18 t20 f20 b20.** A very sweet and simple barley-fest. The oak is mainly conspicuous by its absence. *46%. 651 bottles.*

⠬ **Premier Barrel Blair Athol Aged 10 Years** sherry cask **(86.5) n21.5 t22 f21.5 b21.5.** Any more baby bum-soft casks like this and I might start really warming to this distillery. The grape really is a treat. *46%. nc ncf sc. Douglas Laing & Co. 330 bottles.*

⠬ **Premier Barrel Blair Athol Aged 13 Years** **(87) n21** vanilla and barley; **t23** melt-in-the-mouth malt with a delightful cocoa subplot; the barley intensifies beautifully for the middle; **f21** thins to allow in the oak; **b22** soft, malty and easy going. *46%. nc ncf sc. 468 bottles.*

Provenance Blair Athol Aged 10 Years sherry butt, dist Autumn 99, bott Autumn 08 **(85) n20 t22 f21.5 b21.5.** Beautifully spiced, chewy and juicy for all its weight. *46%. Douglas Laing.*

⠬ **Provenance Blair Athol Over 11 Years** refill hogshead, cask no. 7508, dist Winter 99, bott Summer 2011 **(85) n21 t22 f21 b21.** Similar to an Aultmore I tasted yesterday, matured for a similar time in relatively inert casks. Also decently sweet and pleasant with no off notes, but this is oilier and more barley intense. *46%. nc ncf sc. Douglas Laing & Co.*

⠬ **Single Cask Collection Blair Athol Aged 12 Years** bourbon hogshead, cask no. 2767, dist Apr 98, bott Feb 11 **(92.5) n23.5** a sublime mix of delicate lavender and crushed toasted almond; **t23** a smattering of honey on the intense barley; **f23** a few spices melt into the bourbony fade; gorgeously layered; **b23** a superb cask showing the distillery at its very best. Sophisticated and makes a mockery of its strength. *60.3%. nc ncf sc. 337 bottles.*

BOWMORE
Islay, 1779. Morrison Bowmore. Working.

Bowmore Aged 12 Years db (**91**) **n22.5** light peats, the air of a room with a man sucking cough sweets; sweet pipe smoke; **t23.5** soft, beautiful delivery of multi-layered peats; lots of effervescent spices and molassed sugars; spices abound; **f22.5** much drier with sharper berries and barley; the peat still rumbles onwards, but has no problems with the light, sawdusty oaks; **b23.5** this new bottling still proudly carries the Fisherman's Friend cough sweet character, but the coastal, saline properties here are a notch or three up: far more representative of Islay and the old distillery style. Easily by far the truest Bowmore I have tasted in a long while with myriad complexity. Even going back more than a quarter of a century, the malt at this age rarely showed such relaxed elegance. Most enjoyable. *40%*

Bowmore "Enigma" Aged 12 Years db (**82**) **n19 t22 f20 b21**. Sweet, molassed and with that tell-tale Fisherman's Friend tang representing the light smoke. This Enigma hasn't quite cracked it, though. *40%. Duty Free.*

Bowmore "Darkest" Aged 15 Years db (**83**) **n20 t23 f19 b21**. In recent years a dram you tasted with glass in one hand and a revolver in the other. No more. But for the sulphur present, this would have been a much higher score. *43%* ⊙ ⊙

Bowmore "Mariner" Aged 15 Years db (**79**) **n19 t21 f19 b20**. There are two ways of looking at this. As a Bowmore. Which is how I have marked it. Or a something to throw down your neck for pure fun. Which is probably worth another seven or eight points. Either way, there is something not entirely right here. *43%. Duty Free.*

Bowmore Aged 17 Years db (**77**) **n18 t22 f18 b19**. For all the attractiveness of the sweet fruit on delivery, the combination of butt and cough sweet makes for pretty hard going. *43%*

Bowmore Aged 18 Years db (**79**) **n20 t21 f19 b19**. Pleasant, drinkable Fisherman's Friend style – like every Bowmore it appears around this age. But why so toffee-dull? *43%*

Bowmore Aged 25 Years db (**86**) **n21 t22 f21 b22**. Not the big, chunky guy of yore: the age would surprise you if tasted blind. *43%*

Bowmore Aged 30 Years db (**94**) **n23** intense burnt raisin amid the intense burnt peat; a deft rummy sweetness strikes an improbable chord with the sweetened lime; the oak is backward coming forward but binds beautifully with both peat and fruit; **t24** near flawless delivery showing a glimpse of Bowmore in a form similar to how I remember it some 25 years ago. The peat, though intense - much bigger than you will find today - does have a hint of the Fisherman's Friend about it, but not so upfront as today. For all the peat this is clean whisky, moulded by a craftsman into how a truly great Islay should be; **f23** dries sublimely as the oak contains the peat and adds a touch of coffee to it in unsugared form. Gentle oils cling tightly to the roof of the mouth but it is at once gentle yet enormous; **b24** frankly, a Bowmore that no Islay scholar should be without. Shows the distillery at its most intense yet delicate; an essay in balance and how great oak, peat and fruit can combine for those special moments in life. Unquestionably one of the best Bowmores bottled this century. *43%*

Bowmore 1971 Vintage Aged 34 Years sherry cask db (**86**) **n23 t22 f20 b21**. Loses it on the finish. But one for those who like their whisky big and with splinters aplenty. *51%. 960 bottles.*

Bowmore Legend db (**88**) **n22** big peat fire; dry, but really attractively so; **t22.5** Ok, Fisherman's Friend cough sweet maybe, but the countering barley and brown sugar sweetness appears to dissipate the worst of the effect: the result is big peat, very evenly spread; **f22** gentle finale with a vanilla flourish; **b22.5** not sure what has happened here, but it has gone through the gears dramatically to offer a substantial dram with both big peat and excellent balancing molasses. Major stuff. *40%*

Bowmore Tempest Aged 10 Years Small Batch Release No.1 db first fill bourbon, bott 2009 (**87**) **n22.5** attractive salty kick to the gentle smoke: about as coastal as it comes. Welcome traces of citrus and lavender, too; **t22** tangy, with a pretty full-bodied layering of thick, stubby vanillas: dates and Demerara almost outweigh the shy smoke; a few saintly spices bubble away in a most contented and friendly manner; **f21** pretty full on caramel fudge with just a touch of creamy mocha to soften things slightly; just enough smoke to get through to the final moments; **b21.5** a very different Bowmore which is perhaps too dependent on the fudgy character. When given a chance, its coastal attributes are set off to excellent effect. *55.3%*

⋄ **Bowmore Tempest Aged 10 Years Small Batch Release No.2** 1st fill bourbon, bott 2010 db (**93**) **n23.5** a rousing and strangely subtle mixture of dusty, bone-dry phenols not uncommon to non-island peated malts and a sweeter, tangier smoke, much more reminiscent of lums reeking their winter warmth; all this charged and emboldened by sly degrees of golden syrup and juicy figs; **t23.5** sturdy delivery. Just a light introduction of oils help the easy passage of a more fulsome earthiness, like the nose assisted by sugars, much more gristy this time. There is also a youthful citrus tone to this, though the dissolving vanilla and icing sugars do much good work; **f23** a hint of bitterness from the oak, but the smoke and spices bombard the taste buds. Some muscovado sugars and even the most playful hint of molasses ensures the salty, coastal notes don't take too great a hold...; **b23.5** just turned the bottle round to find some tasting notes banging on about "lemon pepper" here there and everywhere. That is only part of the tale: this is one of the better distillery bottlings to be found at Bowmore in recent years and does much to restore a slightly jaded reputation. Less a tempest than a glide across the Sound of Islay on a sunny day, cheese and tomato sandwich in hand.. But a massive statement by Bowmore, nonetheless. *56%. ncf.*

Adelphi Bowmore 2001 Aged 8 Years sherry butt, cask no. 1126, bott 2010 **(89.5) n23** fantastically crisp and roasty aspect to the barley: almost like chocolate malt · but made all the better thanks to a beautiful smoky crust. Impressive... **t22.5** like the nose, firm and malt-studded. And again the smoke drifts on a slightly different plane, bringing with it some pretty significant sweetness; the middle ground lightens towards that chocolate again, only this time spiced; **f21** a touch of forgivable oak bitterness, but gristy sugars do their best to compensate; **b22.5** now why can't more bottlings of Bowmore be this wonderful? *59.9%. Adelphi Distillery Ltd. 583 bottles.*

A.D. Rattray Bowmore 1991 sherry butt, cask no. 2060, bott Nov 08 **(85.5) n21 t22.5 f20.5 b21.5.** Dry, ashy, sooty, with an excellent thick, fruity swirl and flourish; but ultimately over bitters out. *56.2%*

A.D. Rattray Bowmore 1996 cask no. 960028, dist Mar 96, bott Mar 10 **(90) n23** custard and smoke: a clean and attractive combination; **t23** sweet delivery but the bite and spice are a treat; **f22** soft oils and a touch of smoky chocolate mousse; **b22** now that's much more like it!! Memories of Bowmore from 30 years ago: assertive but with a touch of poise. Exemplary. *46%*

∴ **Berry Brothers Bowmore 2000** cask no. 800271, bott 2010 **(85.5) n21 t22 f21 b21.5.** Fascinating lightly toasted wholemeal bread on the gently smoked nose. Elsewhere the light oils and roasted almonds give a good account of themselves. *58.2%. nc ncf sc. For The Vintage House. 240 bottles.*

Berry's Own Selection Bowmore Aged 11 Years (84) n20 t23 f21 b20. To see Bowmore like this from a second- (or even third) - filled bourbon cask makes for interesting tasting: such is the mouthwatering malt intensity, and so retiring is the peat, this could almost pass for lightly smoked Speyside. *56.2%. Berry Bros & Rudd.*

Berry's Own Selection Bowmore 1989 bott 2008 **(89) n22 t23 f22 b22.** Technically, Berry's 1994 bottling is a superior whisky. But here you just have to admire the structure and complexity. *53.5%. Berry Bros & Rudd.*

∴ **Berry's Own Selection Bowmore 1989** cask no. 7619, bott 2010 **(88.5) n21.5** usual hints of Fisherman's Friend; dry and distinctly unusual; **t22.5** big, pulsing peat, a slight invasion of oils and then a propane-based acceleration of spices; **f22.5** outwardly thin and niggardly, there is a compelling enjoyment to the smoke clinging to the spice; **b22** This guy rips into you like a lion into the throat of a wildebeest. Bracing, uncompromising and actually quite a treat...in a brutal kind of way... *50.9%. nc ncf sc. Berry Bros & Rudd.*

Berry's Own Selection Bowmore 1994 bott 2008 **(86.5) n21 t22.5 f21.5 b21.5.** A must for those looking for something very sweet and moderately smoky yet exceptionally clean. *53.5%*

∴ **Berry's Own Selection Bowmore 1999** cask no. 800348, bott 2010 **(86) n20 t22.5 f21.5 b22.** Fisherman's Friend meets Liquorice Allsorts. The finish, though, is pure kipper. Not sure if I should be drinking or eating this one... *56.4%. nc ncf sc. Berry Bros & Rudd.*

∴ **Berry's Own Selection Bowmore 2002** cask no. 800420, bott 2011 **(84) n20.5 t21.5 f21 b21.** A sweet, seaweedy, earthiness as well as a vaguely bitterness. Curiously, appears to be missing a little bit of copper in the mix. *46%. nc ncf sc. Berry Bros & Rudd.*

The Coopers Choice Bowmore 1998 Aged 10 Years (85) n20 t21 f22.5 b21.5. After an inconsequential nose and delivery the smoked chocolate of the middle ground is an absolute treat! *46%. The Vintage Malt Whisky Co Ltd.*

Douglas of Drumlanrig Bowmore Aged 11 Years refill hogshead no. LD 5593, dist Sep 98, bott Oct 09 **(88) n22.5** clean grist with light, sweet smoke untroubled by oak; **t22** think of new make with just enough clear vanilla to soak up the more youthful edges; **f22** medium length with the barley and smoke having all the final words; **b21.5** beautifully made, minimum fuss and spic and span. *46%. Douglas Laing. 210 bottles.*

Duncan Taylor Collection Bowmore 1982 cask no. 85030 **(82) n20.5 t20 f21 b20.5.** Had to laugh when I lined up this latest bunch of DT Bowmores. Talk about déjà vous...!! It was like opening up a packet of Fisherman's Friends, that cough sweet style unique for a while at this distillery. And I thought: didn't DT do something like this last year? Well, on consulting my notes, yes they did. And here are half a dozen more or so from the same batch – peas from the same pod. The thing is, you can't not like them. Nor do they blow you away: they simply offer a quite different whisky style, one that no other distillery has done before or since. *50.1%*

Duncan Taylor Collection Bowmore 1982 cask no. 85031 (86.5) n21.5 t23 f21 b21. By far and away one of the best casks in the set: everything is a tad sharper and more intense. The barley is truly salivating and there is even a thread of honey woven through the smoke and liquorice. Lovely. *52.1%*

Duncan Taylor Collection Bowmore 1982 cask no. 85032 (83) n20 t21 f21 b21. A bit of a hot-head, this. The nose is a dullard, but a bit of zip on the palate compensates and really cranks out the cough sweet side of things. *53.7%*

Duncan Taylor Collection Bowmore 1982 cask no. 85057 (86) n23 t22 f20 b21. We have moved on a few casks and the whisky has moved on in style, slightly, too. To nose, some real butterscotch on the cereals and smoke ensure a touch of class and there is shades of demerara and liquorice on delivery before the finish bitters and flattens. *53.5%*

Duncan Taylor Collection Bowmore 1982 cask no. 85064 (84) n21 t22.5 f20 b20,5. Slightly in the style of 85032 but with a touch of extra citrus and finesse. *54.9%*

Duncan Taylor Collection Bowmore 1982 cask no. 85068 (84) n21 t21 f21 b21. A fleet of Fishermen's Friends: sweet, but uncompromising in the cough sweet department. *53.8%*

Duncan Taylor Collection Bowmore 1982 cask no. 85072 (83.5) n20 t21.5 f21 b21. A bit of a softie, but sticks to the cough sweet script for all the best vanilla-led intentions. *50.4%*

Duncan Taylor Collection Bowmore 1982 cask no. 85162 (78) n19.5 t20 f19 b19.5. Date drawn: 9.9.9. But no need to call the Fire Brigade as the smoke is easily doused. *50.5%*

Duncan Taylor Collection Bowmore 1982 cask no. 378770 (80.5) n19 t21 f20 b20.5. A rough hewn blighter and one of the Fishermen's Friend variety. *50.6%*

⌐☞ **Duncan Taylor NC² Bowmore 1998** (85.5) n22 t21 f21.5 b21. Lightly smoked, softly oiled, delicately oaked and as though any excess sweetness has been extracted from it. *46%. nc ncf.*

Duthies Bowmore 17 Years Old (86.5) n20 t22.5 f22 b22. Unusually crisp for a Bowmore with the smoke little more than an afterthought. Adore the clarity of the barley and the almost husky crunchiness. Worth seeking. *46%. Wm. Cadenhead Ltd.*

Exclusive Casks Bowmore 1998 Aged 10 Years American oak (94) n24 t23.5 f23 b23.5. A gold nugget of a cask that is worth a trip to the walled city for alone... *52.7%*

⌐☞ **Fine Malt Selection Bowmore 10 Years Old** (76.5) n19 t21 f18 b19.5. Lightly smoked, liberally sugared but bitterly oaked. *45%. sc. James MacArthur & Co.*

⌐☞ **Fortnum & Mason Bowmore Aged 9 Years** (88) n22.5 Palma violets with a lavender and mint surround; t22.5 a friendly muscovado sweetness helps soften the smoky blow; loads and loads of light, vaguely sawdusty vanilla; f21.5 suffers slightly from the weak strength as the backbone begins to give way early; b22 about 20 years ago I became the first person to give a series of whisky tastings at Fortnum and Mason. I advised then not to add water. On the label of this whisky they do: I shall remind them...add water to this, and it simply is no longer whisky...!! *40%. nc ncf. Fortnum & Mason.*

Hart Brothers Bowmore Aged 10 Years dist Apr 98, bott Jun 08 (85) n21.5 t21 f21.5 b21. Sweet, simplistic but with a pleasing degree of peat ash. *46%. Hart Brothers Limited.*

Hart Brothers Bowmore Aged 11 Years dist Apr 97, bott Oct 08 (77) n20 t20 f18 b19. Interesting farm yard nose. But, overall, a bitter experience. *46%. Hart Brothers Limited.*

Hart Brothers Bowmore Aged 18 Years dist May 90, bott Jun 08 (86.5) n22 t22 f21 b21.5. Very pleasing malt with a distinctively fresh, fruity edge to the smoke. *46%*

James MacArthur's Old Masters Bowmore 1996 Aged 13 Years cask no. 960003, bott Nov 09 (87.5) n22 decent mixture of thick and lighter, punchy phenols; t22 a hint of chocolate marzipan at the well smoked heart of this; f21.5 a touch of bitterness to the oak; b22 attractively sweet and viscous. *58.8%. James MacArthur & Co Ltd.*

The John Milroy Selection Bowmore 21 Years Old dist 1987, bott 2009 (84) n21 t21.5 f20.5 b21. Heads down for the absolutely unique "Hughsey" style of Victory V and Parma Violet smokiness. *45%. Berry Bros & Rudd.*

The John Milroy Selection Bowmore 22 Years Old (85.4) n21 t22 f21 b21.5. Very lightly smoked and with myriad forms of sugared toast. *48.4%. Berry Bros & Rudd.*

Kingsbury's Bowmore 1997 (87) n21.5 more Bow-less than Bow-more...the peat is little more than a whisper, very much outshouted by the barley; t22 excellent mouthfeel with the juicy barley brushing aside the lightest of smoky strokes; f21.5 a soft smoky burr to the developing cocoa; b22 those looking for a smoky experience will feel a little short-changed. But a well made and attractive malt nonetheless. *57.4%. Japan Import System.*

Malts of Scotland Bowmore 1995 Clubs sherry butt no. 113, dist May 95, bott Nov 09 (81.5) n20.5 t20 f21 b20. Peat and anthracite nose but with an attractively sweet and mildly sticky pay off. *56.7%. 192 bottles.*

⁘ **Malts Of Scotland Amazing Casks Bowmore 1995** bourbon barrel, cask no. 177, dist May 95, bott Sep 10 **(89.5) n22** from the distillery's infamous "Fisherman's Friend" school of cough sweet peatiness. A lovely lemon curd tart edge to the barley combines well; **t24.5** fabulous delivery: chocolate liquorice allsort is bombarded by waves of lightly oiled, very polite peat. The Fisherman Friend character is evident from the midpoint onwards, but the spices and Demerara sweetened mocha keep the impact to manageable levels; **f20.5** tired as the cask collapses slightly; **b22.5** in some ways this is an Amazing Cask. Every single aspect of this whisky is instantly recognisable to those few of us who have dealt with this malt in all its varied forms over the last 30 years. Where is takes the breath away is how everything fits together for a minute or two on delivery and just beyond. The finish, sadly, is a let down by comparison. The star may have shone for only a short while. But while it did, it did so very brightly, indeed. 56.4%. nc ncf sc. 222 bottles.

Master of Malt Bowmore 26 Years Old bott 2009 **(88) n21.5 t21 f23 b22**. Now that's something completely different: the nose and early delivery has you checking the paper for the date: nope, it really isn't April 1st. Where the hell is all that sweetness coming from...? Then it starts to settle towards something recognisable as very good whisky and from then onwards you are served up a minor treat. 53.4%. Master of Malt.

⁘ **Old Malt Cask Bowmore Aged 14 Years** refill hogshead, cask no. 6837, dist Dec 96, bott Jan 11 **(84.5) n21 t21 f21.5 b21**. The type of sweet, lightly smoked malt which adds ballast to a blend. 50%. nc ncf sc. Douglas Laing & Co. 277 bottles.

Old Malt Cask Bowmore Aged 21 Years refill hogshead, dist Jun 87, bott Sep 08 **(88) n21.5 t23 f21.5 b22**. A cask taken as far as it dare go but the light radiation of peat is lovely. 50%. nc ncf sc.

⁘ **Old Malt Cask Bowmore Aged 21 Years** refill butt, cask no. 7460, dist Nov 89, bott Jun 11 **(84) n20 t22 f21 b21**. It may be 21, but it would never be served in the USA, so immature is it for its age. Even so, lightly smoked and very tasty... 50%. nc ncf sc. 298 bottles.

Old Malt Cask A Fine Cigar's Pleasure Bowmore Aged 9 Years refill hogshead **(84) n21 t21 f22 b21**. Lots of natural caramel wrapped in chocolate. 50%. Douglas Laing. 354 bottles.

Old & Rare Bowmore Aged 22 Years sherry finished hogshead, dist Nov 87, bott Apr 10 **(80) n19 t20 f21 b20**. Fisherman's Friend concentrate. 56.1%. nc ncf. 244 bottles.

Premier Barrel Bowmore Aged 9 Years (80) n19 t20 f21 b20. When I tell people that I remember the days, 20 years ago, when Bowmore was sold by Oddbins as a five-year-old, I tend not to be believed. Especially when I explained it was a more than enjoyable dram. Here is something which reminds me a little of those days, though, for all its simplistic charm, this doesn't have quite the same cut and dash. 46% nc ncf Douglas Laing & Co Ltd. 362 bottles.

Premier Barrel Bowmore Aged 9 Years (83.5) n21.5 t22 f20 b20. Pleasantly sweet before running out of legs. 46%. Douglas Laing. 302 bottles.

⁘ **Premier Barrel Bowmore Aged 12 Years (62) n15 t16 f15 b16**. Not even peat stands a snowflake's chance in this kind of sherry butt... 46%. nc ncf sc. Douglas Laing & Co. 451 bottles.

⁘ **Premier Barrel Bowmore Aged 13 Years (90.5) n23** wonderfully layered smoke entwined with chocolate mint; **t23** textbook interweaving between light smoke and rich barley. The mocha is a delight; **f22** the smoke effect virtually vanished but the sweet malt rumbles on; **b22.5** a sexy, beautifully shaped little belter. 46%. nc ncf sc. 174 bottles.

⁘ **Provenance Bowmore Over 10 Years** refill hogshead, cask no. 6818, dist Autumn 00, bott Autumn 2010 **(78) n19 t21 f19 b19**. A pleasant, gristy countenance. But the ancient cask adds nothing positive. 46%. nc ncf sc. Douglas Laing & Co.

Secret Stills 4.9 Islay 1991 bott 2008 **(89.5) n23** no secret about this being a top-notch nose: the peat is controlled and quite refined, the citrus is little more than an echo, the sugars in total harmony with the vanillas and a speck or two of salt just to up the tang a little; **t22.5** a distant murmur of cough sweet gives the game away regarding identity, but to the foreground there is a relaxed gristy sweetness with the smoke melting on the tongue; **f22** weightier as the oaks and spices roll in; **b22** the perfect malt for those who like smoky but not heavily peated whisky. The style tells me this is likely to be from one distillery only. And though it is a secret, and I thought I just heard a door creak behind me, I am certain this has all the hallmark of a B...aarrrhhhh......!! 45%. Gordon & MacPhail.

Scotch Malt Whisky Society Cask 3.155 Aged 21 Years refill hogshead, dist Dec 87 **(88.5) n22** passion fruit and peat...an unlikely, but lovely combination...; **t22.5** the nature of the exotic fruit is a bit of a giveaway regarding the age while the strained cough mixture note equally spills the beans on the identity; **f22** some vanilla is added to the unusual mix; **b22** for those who like their peat – or cough sweets - a little exotic... 49.1%. 214 bottles.

Scotch Malt Whisky Society Cask 3.160 Aged 10 Years 1st fill barrel, dist May 99 **(86) n21 t22 f21.5 b21.5**. Malty with a surprising hint of mango. The smoke is lethargic, distant and little more than an echo. 60.1%. Scotch Malt Whisky Society.

Scotch Malt Whisky Society Cask 3.161 Aged 11 Years refill sherry butt, dist Feb 99 **(85)** n21 t22.5 f21 b21. Juicy, fruity, lightly smoked and no shortage of zip and nip. Surprising degree of oak, too. 58.4%. Scotch Malt Whisky Society. 204 bottles.

Scotch Malt Whisky Society Cask 3.162 Aged 17 Years 2nd fill hogshead, dist Sep 92 **(78.5)** n20 t21 f18 b19.5. Get the feeling that this is not firing on all cylinders, in spite of its early decadence. Thin, biting and a little unforgiving. 56%. Scotch Malt Whisky Society. 209 bottles.

⁖ **Scotch Malt Whisky Society Cask 3.164 Aged 17 Years** 2nd fill hogshead, cask no. 4177, dist 1992 **(94)** n23 a slight hint of Victory V. But the molasses and the Palma Violet offer superb depth to the excellent oaks; t23.5 mesmerising degree of layering. The vanillas offer both a degree of sweetness and dryness; the smoke offers depth and spice; the sugars also offer unusual ballast as well as balance; f23.5 long, playing out the same way as the delivery and middle, but just a notch drier; b24 I need not have checked the age of this one. For some reason 17 years so often appears to agree with this distillery... especially when in wood as good as this. 54%. sc. 195 bottles.

⁖ **Scotch Malt Whisky Society Cask 3.168 Aged 11 Years** 1st fill sherry butt, cask no. 390008, dist 1999 **(84)** n22 t21 f21 b20. The deluge of dripping oloroso combines lopsidedly with the smoke to make for a clean, chewy, but, ultimately, ungainly dram. 60.4%. sc. 269 bottles.

⁖ **Scotch Malt Whisky Society Cask 3.169 Aged 16 Years** refill sherry butt, cask no. 562, dist 1994 **(83.5)** n21 t21 f20.5 b21. Fails to hit a rhythm so even its usual cough sweet persona is only partially developed. As Ed Reardon might observe: less a Fisherman's Friend, more a holiday acquaintance. 56.6%. sc. 589 bottles.

⁖ **Scotch Malt Whisky Society Cask 3.176 Aged 20 Years** refill barrel, cask no. 1181, dist 1990 **(87.5)** n22 a squirt of lemon and lime into the undemonstrative smoke; some molten icing sugar, too; t20 a bizarre criss-crossing of tart fruits and unhappy peat which struggles to find a place to land; f23.5 settles into a quite beautiful, buttery, lightly smoked French-toast finale; long with the peat finding feet and the balance improving by the second; b22 an unusual, almost bizarre, malt which takes a great amount of time to come to terms with its age. But when it gets there, it makes every moment count. 49.4%. sc. 51 bottles.

⁖ **Scotch Malt Whisky Society Cask 3.177 Aged 9 Years** 1st fill barrel, cask no. 800538, dist. 2001 **(92.5)** n22.5 lazy but somehow stirring layers of smoke. Charmingly gristy; t23.5 excellent balance between the sugars and burgeoning spicy phenols; outstanding mouthfeel and a degree of oil; f23 a surprising injection of late oak ramps up the vanilla and confirms the 1st fill pedigree; some citrus clings to the gorgeously weighted smoke; b23.5 Bowmore at its most benign and beautifully made and matured. 61.3%. sc. 223 bottles.

Single & Single Bowmore 2000 Aged 8 Years Limited Release (81.5) n21.5 t22 f18 b20. Stereotypical, decent quality, young-ish peated Islay early on, but then let down on the finish. Almost Caol Ila-esque in its early, lightly oiled, approach. 46%. South Africa.

⁖ **Vom Fass Bowmore 13 Years Old (91.5)** n23 delicate, sugar-shrouded smoke; t23 one the most mouth-watering peaty malts you are likely to encounter this year. Fabulous barley has no problem being heard while the peat adds both a light anchoring role and something to get your teeth into; f22 a touch of tired cask bitterness evident but the sugars cock a sweetening snook; b23.5 it is probably near impossible to locate a Bowmore more true to the distillery than this. A gem of its type. 40%

⁖ **The Whisky Agency Bowmore 1993 (87.5)** n22 clean with oak having surprisingly little impact on the higher-than-usual peat; t22.5 all kinds of citrus amid the smoky embers; f21.5 the sugars recede exposing the vanilla; b22 makes a mockery of its age by acting only half its years. And that's no bad thing... 53.8%. The Whisky Agency.

⁖ **The Whisky Agency Bowmore 1995** bott 2010 **(76)** n18 t21 f18 b19. An unfortunate cask, whose faults will, to some, be obscured by the swirling smoke. 54.1%.

⁖ **The Whisky Agency Bowmore 1998** bott 2010 **(77.5)** n18.5 t21 f19 b19. Sugary sweet, smoky and virtually colourless for its age. No perceivable complexity. Throw a whisky into an inert cask and you'll get an inert dram. 51.8%. The Whisky Agency.

The Whisky Fair Bowmore 10 Year Old dist 1998, bott 2009 **(93)** n23 t24.5 t22.5 b23. Simply and beautifully made whisky matured in a cask which gives full view to the malt. 59.8%. The Whisky Fair, Germany.

Whisky Galore Bowmore 2002 (87.5) n22.5 gristy, guttural smoke. No attempt at refinement or even great complexity: just honest, relatively young Bowmore with a natural barley sweetness; t22 like the nose, there are no pretensions here and all is based on simplicity: the smoke does have a degree of citrus to lighten it, though; f21 the oak eases in to offer a little green tea bitterness; b22 Ah-ha!! I see the Whisky Galore brand is back. There are those who probably still have a touch of the vapours when the name is mentioned, as a decade or so ago it was well, a bottle of caramel with some whisky in it. Well, of course it wasn't, but that's how it sometimes seemed. Not anymore. Lessons have obviously been learned. And for those who produce a natural tick whenever the name is mentioned...it is safe to come out now...!!! If this bottling is anything to go by, then go buy: for you are getting malt very much as nature intended. Except for the impurity of that irritating splash of water, taking it down to 46%, of course. 46%

⸫ **Wilson & Morgan Barrel Selection Bowmore Twenty Years Old** cask no. 22555/56, dist 1989, bott 2010 (86) n22 t22 f21 b21. Distilled from smoked granite... 46%

BRAEVAL
Speyside, 1974. Chivas Brothers. Working.

The Càrn Mòr Vintage Collection Braes of Glenlivet 1989 hogshead, cask no. 997, dist 1989, bott 2009 (88) n22.5 t22 f21.5 b22. Charming, simplistic but beautifully made malt. 46%

⸫ **Chieftain's Braeval Aged 13 Years** petrus gaia finish, dist Nov 98, bott 2011 (71.5) n18 t18 f17 b17.5. In the whisky game, you wine finish at your peril. 43%. nc ncf Ian Macleod.

Connoisseurs Choice Braes of Glenlivet 1975 (95) n23.5 t24.5 f23.5 b23.5. An astonishing time capsule of a dram. We are tasting a malt made within months of the distillery being opened, nearly 35 years on. The result is one of the malts of the year: how it has survived so flawlessly should keep connoisseurs in heated debate for a very long time. Spectacularly elegant and beautiful. And an all time Braes classic, never to be forgotten. 43%

Dun Bheagan Braeval Aged 13 Years Manzanilla sherry butt, dist Jun 95 (83) n20 t23 f20 b20. The fade is just too bitter. 46%. Ian Macleod Distillers Ltd.

⸫ **Fortnum & Mason Braeval Aged 9 Years** (91) n23.5 magnificent: the ginger also appears to have a distant hint of juniper attached. But the butterscotch barley shines brightest; t23 effortlessly elegant. The barley makes a carefree entrance and appears to pick up some oils and sugared vanilla along the way; f22 the oaks begin to make a noise; b22.5 another touch of understated class in Piccadilly. 40%. nc ncf. Fortnum & Mason.

Old Malt Cask Braeval Aged 12 Years sherry butt, dist Jul 96, bott Sep 08 (88) n20 t23 f22.5 b22.5. Makes the nose something of a liar. An ultimately fine dram with a tale to tell. 50%. 665 bottles.

Old Malt Cask Braes of Glenlivet Aged 20 Years refill hogshead no. DL 5717, dist May 89, bott Dec 09 (84.5) n22 t20 f21.5 b21. The oak has much to say, some of it a little bitterly. But the oratory of the malt is much more uplifting. 50%. Douglas Laing.

⸫ **Old Malt Cask Braes of Glenlivet Aged 20 Years** refill hogshead, cask no. 6383, dist May 90, Jul 10 (80) n19.5 t19 f22 b19.5. Struggles early on. But the stupendous malt present, aided by some sterling cocoa, makes a pleasant experience of it. 50%. nc ncf sc. 329 bottles.

Premier Barrel Braeval Aged 10 Years sherry cask, dist Sep 99 (77) n18.5 t21 f18.5 b19. Grapey and...I bet this'll be as popular in Germany as Joachim Loew... 46%. 582 bottles.

Premier Barrel Braeval Aged 11 Years (79.5) n20 t20.5 f19 b20. Everything about this screams that it is a competent dram made to bulk up the malt content – and maltiness – in a blend. 46%. nc ncf 180 bottles.

⸫ **Premier Barrel Braeval Aged 11 Years** sherry cask (89.5) n22.5 a few atoms of smoke go a very long way in a malt this delicate; the degree of sweetness is beautiful, especially when balanced by a squeeze of lemon; t23 mouth-watering. A very slow, sexy strip-tease revealing the juicy barley, delicate fruits and, again, that most distant puff of smoke; moves towards mocha for the middle; f21.5 the oak bites and slightly bitters out the outside edges; b22.5 a deceptively complex and weighty Speysider. 46%. nc ncf sc. 298 bottles.

Provenance Braeval Aged 10 Years sherry butt, dist Summer 98, bott Autumn 08 (73) n18 t19 f18 b18. Some grand barley does its best to negate the lightly sulphured flaws. 46%

⸫ **Provenance Braeval Over 11 Years** refill hogshead, cask no. 6293, dist Spring 99, bott Summer 2010 (81) n20 t20 f20.5 b20.5. The mocha from the middle through to the finish emphasises the surprising lack of meat on the bone. 46%. nc ncf sc. Douglas Laing & Co.

⸫ **Provenance Braeval Over 11 Years** sherry butt, cask no. 6886, dist Autumn 99, bott Winter 2010 (75.5) n19 t19 f18.5 b19. Thin but with some biscuity barley: never quite gets off the ground. 46%. nc ncf sc. Douglas Laing & Co.

⸫ **Vom Fass Braeval 11 Years Old** (86) n22 t22 f21 b21. Excellent ginger and butterscotch mix with light spices and a buttery body. Tasty. 40%

⸫ **The Whisky Castle Distilled in the Park Braeval "Cairngorm's Dew"** (92) n23 lovely marmalade on toast intertwining with walnut oil; t23.5 dreamy delivery: ultra soft delivery with the barley in fresh but creamy form melting alongside a light coating of Golden Syrup; f22.5 long thanks to the oils with the barley, alongside the vanilla, proud to the end; b23 this distillery is more than capable of producing a cracking malt: here's proof. 46%. nc ncf sc. Douglas Laing & Co for The Whisky Castle.

BRORA

Highlands (Northern), 1819–1983. Diageo. Closed.

Brora 25 Year Old 7th Release bott 2008 db **(96) n24** even with the lowest peating levels you ever have nosed from this distillery, the aura of beauty is unmistakable: the soft phenol molecules appears to be perfectly matched with the oak ones. Meanwhile fragile citrus ensures a youthful charm; somewhere there is a hint of bourbon; **t24.5** superb barley kick off, absolute waves of juices running about the palate, and still the smoke holds back, no more than a background murmur; as the middle fills, that bourbon on the nose become more pronounced with shades of honeyed liquorice; **f23.5** long, with the sugars hanging in there allowing the vanillas to form very slowly; **b24** as the distillery closed in March 1983, if memory serves me correctly, this must be coming to the end of the road for the true 25-year-old. Those looking for the usual big peat show might be disappointed. Others, in search of majesty, sophistication and timeless grace, will be blown away. 56.3%

Brora 30 Years Old db **(97) n24 t25 f24 b24.** Here we go again! Just like last year's bottling, we have something of near unbelievable beauty with the weight perfectly pitched and the barley-oak interaction the stuff of dreams. And as for the peat: an entirely unique species, a giant that is so gentle. Last year's bottling was one of the whiskies of the year. This even better version is the perfect follow-up. 56.4%

⁖ **Brora 30 Years Old Special Release** refill American and European oak db **(89) n22** the smoke is receding like a balding pate and exotic fruit is taking its place...; **t23.5** the juiciest of juicy barley; the most exotic of exotic fruits; the most delicate of delicate spices, the most non-existent of smoke; **f21.5** practically yawning, so tired is it. But the custard sweetness mixes beautifully with the spice; **b22** seeing as I was the guy who proudly discovered this whisky over 20 years ago, I take more than a keen interest. But like a loved and cherished old relative, you can still adore its personality and unique independence but be aware that it is slowly fading away... 54.3%. nc ncf. Diageo. 2958 bottles.

Brora 30 Years Old Special Release 2006 db **(92) n23 t24 f22 b23.** Showing a degree of age decay but even so the sheer beauty of this malt leaves you gasping. 55.7%

Brora 30 Years Old Special Release 2007 db **(88.5) n21.5 t23.5 f21.5 b22.** Not in the highest echelons of old Broras with a degree of lactic being milked from the oak. But close your eyes, concentrate on the more delicate smoke tones – especially on arrival – and still be amazed. 55.7%. 2,958 bottles.

Chieftain's Brora 26 Years Old oloroso butt, dist Dec 81 **(92.5) n24 t22 f23.5 b23.** On delivery there is a fear that the great nose of the work will be undone. But hang on in there: the ending is a happy one. 48%. Ian Macleod Distillers Ltd.

Duncan Taylor Collection Brora 1981 cask no. 291 **(96) n23.5** playful and succulent, the smoke enjoys equal billing to the citrus and cherry cake; **t24.5** we are talking near perfect weight, sweetness, injection of oil, control of smoke, slow infusion of cocoa, almonds and other delicate flavours and involvement of spice...; **f23.5** hard to know where the middle ends and the finish begin...like some kind of lightly peated orgasm; a very light degree of oaky bitterness, but it is a trifle; **b24.5** you won't ever want to wash your glass again after tasting this one. 51.3%

Old & Rare Brora Aged 28 Years sherry cask, dist Jun 81, bott Nov 09 **(91) n23** buzzing, nipping peat with a real farmyard feel; **t22.5** at first a wave or two of crusty molasse sugar, giving way to an earthy peatiness; **f23** the vanillas arrive in force, but the smoke drifts around on an oily carpet; **b22.5** a beautifully dirty tasting whisky: you will have to taste it to see exactly what I mean...! 57.4%. Douglas Laing. 93 bottles.

BRUICHLADDICH

Islay, 1881. Bruichladdich Ltd, Working.

Bruichladdich 10 Years Old db **(90) n22** beautifully clean and zesty, the malt is almost juvenile; **t23** sweet, fruity then malty charge along the tastebuds that geets the mouth salivating; **f23** the usual soft vanilla and custard but a bigger barley kick in the latter stages; **b22** more oomph than previous bottlings, yet still retaining its fragile personality. Truly great stuff for a standard bottling. 46%

Bruichladdich 12 Years Old 2nd Edition db **(88) n23** big barrage of fruit; crisp barley beautifully integrates with oak; **t22** an uneven, mildly uncertain, delivery due to the grape being out of sync with the big barley; give it about eight-ten seconds and they have found a delicious degree of harmony; **f22** long with the intense, chiselled flavours still slightly at odds, but calming down with some oils; **b21** a similar type of wine involvement to "Waves", but this is oilier in the old-fashioned 'Laddie style and lacks a little of the sparkle. The fruit on the finish is outstanding, though, and I don't think you or I would turn down a third glass... 46%

Bruichladdich 15 Years Old 2nd Edition db (86) n22 t23 f20 b21. Delicious, as usual, but something, possibly fruity, appears to be holding back the show. 46%

Bruichladdich 16 Years Old bourbon cask db (89) n22.5 sweet barley hangs from sturdy oak beams; t22.5 remains firm yet sweet with a charming honeyed streak; again the oak plays a major role but its obvious dry input remains contained; f22 dries further, with vanilla replacing the honey; some superb spices; b22 plucked from the cask in the nick of time. In this state rather charming, but another Summer or two might have seen the oak take a more sinister turn. 46%

Bruichladdich 16 Years Old bourbon/Chateau d'Yquem cask db (95) n24 if you've got a good half an hour to spend, try using it intelligently by sticking your nose in this for a while: the grape is sweet and sultana juicy; the understated spices somehow hit just the right point to satisfy grape, oak and barley in one hit: some achievement... t23.5 sweet, as the nose suggests, but the arrival is not all about grape. That sweetness also contains pristine barley... f23.5 just so soft and subtle with the vanillas offering a discreet escort to the barley-grape marriage; b24 possibly the most delicate and understated of all the truly great whiskies of the year. Not one for the ice and water brigade. 46%

Bruichladdich 16 Years Old bourbon/Chateau Haut Brion cask db (81.5) n21 t21.5 f19 b20. fruity and busy for sure. But just not the kind of wine barrel effect that does much for me, I'm afraid, not least because of the background buzz on the palate. 46%

Bruichladdich 16 Years Old bourbon/Chateau Lafite cask db (89) n24 t22.5 f21.5 b21.5. Ridiculously soft. Could just do with an injection of something to propel it into greatness. 46%

Bruichladdich 16 Years Old bourbon/Chateau Lafleur cask db (92.5) n23 t23.5 f23 b23. So luminous on the palate, it's positively Lafleurescent... 46%

Bruichladdich 16 Years Old bourbon/Chateau Latour cask db (84.5) n21 t21.5 f21 b21. Enjoyable. But there is a strange aggression to the spice which doesn't altogether sit as comfortably as it might. The fruit heads off into not just grapey but citrus territory, but there is a always a but about the direction it takes... 46%

Bruichladdich 16 Years Old bourbon/Chateau Margaux cask db (78.5) n20.5 t20 f19 b19. Not 1st Cru Bruichladdich, I'm afraid. 46%

Bruichladdich XVII Aged 17 Years bourbon/renegade rum db (92) n23 typical rum "clipped" nose; this one with just a shade of soft, rich rubber typical of certain Guyana (especially Enmore) or Barbados marks; a rather lovely lemon tint to the vanilla works a treat; t23.5 super dry delivery, too, with the sugars taking time to arrive. When they do, they weld with the barley attractively; formidable balance between the barley and spices while a light sprinkling of salt seems to up the spicy oak input to counter the sugars; f22 mainly dry and attractively layered with short, sweet bands; b23.4 no shortage of sophistication here. Always good to see the casks of drier, more complexly structured rums being put to such intelligent use. My sample doesn't tell me which rums casks were used, but I was getting vivid flashbacks here of Ruby-Topaz Hummingbirds flitting from flower to flower in the gardens of the now closed Eigflucht distillery in Guyana in the long gone days when I used to scramble around the warehouses there. That distinctive dryness though is pure Enmore, though some Barbadian rum can offer a similar effect. Something very different and a top quality experience for late at night or to get the taste buds aroused as dinner is prepared. 46%. nc ncf.

Bruichladdich 18 Years Old bourbon/cognac cask db (84.5) n23.5 t21 f20 b20. Big oak-spice buzz but thin. Sublime grapey nose, for sure, but pays a certain price, ultimately, for associating with such an inferior spirit... 46%

Bruichladdich 18 Years Old bourbon/opitz cask db (80.5) n19 t22 f19.5 b20. Dry, complex; at times oak-stretched. 46%

Bruichladdich 18 Years Old 2nd Edition bourbon/jurancon db (86) n22 t21.5 f21 b21.5. Plenty of fruit, including medium ripe greengages and slightly under-ripe grape. Juicy and sweet in the right places. 46%

Bruichladdich Flirtation Aged 20 Years 2nd Edition db (86) n21 t22 f22 b21. Hi sugar! A Laddie for those with a sweet tooth. 46%

Bruichladdich 21 Years Old oloroso cask db (76.5) n18.5 t21 f18 b19. Oops! 46%

·:·· **Bruichladdich 32 Years Old DNA 1977** bourbon cask db (94.5) n23 there are so many bourbon tags on this, especially the waxiness to the honey, that just for a fleeting, off-guard moment I thought I was back nosing Kentucky whisky again. Then a giveaway salty tang coupled with a delicate hint of barley reminded me that I was in the land where the bagpipe abounds...; t24 ridiculous! I mean, bloody outrageous! No whisky has the right to a delivery that perfect with the lightly oiled texture seemingly holding both oak and grain in equal measures. Buttery and rich, it then pans out back towards Kentucky with some liquoricy and threads of honey. Then propels back to Scotland with a uniquely salty toffee middle; f23.5 relatively easy going and simplistic. But the cream toffee hangs in there and then a late breakdown of almost clichéd bourbon notes from honey to hickory...; **b24** absolutely top of the range, profound and virtually faultless whisky which makes you remember the reason why you fell so deeply in love with this stuff all those many years ago. How fitting that when this was made Laddie was the Scotch distillery closest to America. For this is as much a bourbon in style as Scotch. But who cares? It doesn't matter: great whisky is great whisky. Full stop. *47.4%*

Bruichladdich 37 Years Old DNA 80% bourbon/20% sherry cask, aged in Le Pin wine casks db **(87) n23.5** a beautiful, if potentially dodgy, counter between some gray-haired oak and pre-pubescent grape; **t22** nothing is settled with this one: the oak charges about in one direction, grapey waves soothes in another. A real flavour factory, especially with some light mocha in the middle ground, but don't look for a story here; **f20.5** a bit bitter, furry and nibbling; **b21** balance..? What balance...? Actually, somehow, this crazy thing does find some kind of equilibrium... *41%*

Bruichladdich 1984 Golder Still bourbon cask, db **(88.5) n22 t23 f22 b21.5.** A huge amount of natural caramels leached from the oak does the joint job of ensuring extraordinary softness and eroding the higher notes. Still, there is enough eye-rolling honey and spice to keep anyone happy and the rich bourbony character on delivery really is dreamy stuff. *51%*

Bruichladdich 1984 Redder Still db **(95.5) n23.5 t24 f23.5 b24.5.** Now it's finding whiskies like this that I became the world's first-full time whisky for. I dreamed of discovering drams which stretched my tastebuds and spoke to me with eloquence, charisma and unmistakable class. This is one such whisky: the style is highly unusual; the cleverness of the layering almost unique. This is the kind of near flawless whisky for which we were given tastebuds. Oh, and a nose... *50.4%*

Bruichladdich 1989 db **(75.5) n20 t19 f17.5 b19.** Ouch! *52.9%. Special bottling for Alberta.*

Bruichladdich 1989 Black Art Aged 19 Years bourbon/wine casks db **(78.5) n20 t21.5 f19 b18.** Good grief...!! What was all that about? About as much balance as England and West Ham goalkeeper Robert Green trying to catch a tame shot. You have to admire the ruthless grape delivery, but the remainder is pretty shapeless and without a coherent plan...a bit like Mr Green's team mates... *51.1%. nc ncf. 6,000 bottles.*

◈ **Bruichladdich 1989 Black Art 2nd Edition** bourbon cask db **(95) n24** a thick fruit composite of probably the juiciest dates you'll find south of the Sahara and a dense hickory and honey strain of bourbon... Not just compelling. But absolutely magnificent...and just so right!!! Sulphur? Can it be? Yes, no...? Can't quite make it out...; **t24** how many deliveries allow the spice ahead of the main thrust? Perhaps more accurately, alongside. Still pretty rare and the way in which the chocolate fruit and nut melts in with the honey and liquorice bourbon notes, you feel anything can happen...; **f23** long, with some wonderful oils helping those dates and now walnuts, too, all embedded in light cocoa, to their final spicy farewell; **b24** it is close to 1am in the morning as I continue trying to hit the deadline. My head spins; not from the alcohol: I spit. But simply, after a 15 hour tasting day, to work out how the hell this whisky works. Bourbon cask, it says. Right. But how did those lush dates get in there? Also, there even appears to be the very faintest (and I mean the odd molecule) of sulphur. But so miniscule it does no damage whatsoever. This is a whisky that asks ten times more questions than it answers. Time, though, not to wonder why, but just bloody well enjoy, for this is one of the great whiskies of the year. Now, as I deserve it, I'll swallow the very last mouthful before calling it a day. Or very early morning, maybe.. *49.7%*

Bruichladdich 1990 Aged 18 Years db **(85.5) n22.5 t21 f21 b21.** Enlivened by citrus and emboldened by soft salt. *46%*

Bruichladdich 1990 Aged 18 Years cognac cask db **(81.5) n20.5 t21 f20 b20.** Wouldn't be a far greater benefit to the spirit world if Cognac was matured in a Bruichladdich cask...? *46%*

Bruichladdich 1991 Aged 16 Years Chat Margaux finish db **(94) n23 t25 f22.5 b23.5.** A true Premier Cru malt...I have been almost certainly the most outspoken critic of whisky finishes: trust me, if they were all like this, you would never hear the merest clack of a dissenting typing key from me again... *46%*

◈ **Bruichladdich 1991 Valinch Anaerobic Digestion 19 Years Old** bourbon & madeira casks db **(96.5) n24.5** huge, yet cleverly weighted fruit with spiced boiled greengages oozing from the glass but very happy to allow golden syrup to share some of its limelight; **t24** if the nose was excellent, the delivery is of no less quality. A light, oily bed allows the grape and sugars to land gently, then a light spicy layer forms another level entirely. All the hallmarks of a juicy first fill Madeira cask at work here...and working well; **f24** perhaps drier than all else before with the spices chipping away and a burnt raisin sharpness mingling with the latent honey; virtually a never ending tale...; **b24** about 20 minutes ago I could name you 250 excellent reasons to go and visit this distillery. I can now name you 251...A potential world whisky of the year that manages to do just about everything right...!!! *52.5% ncf sc. Only available at distillery.*

Bruichladdich 1992 Sherry Edition "Fino" Aged 17 Years bourbon/fino sherry db (**94**) n23.5 dry, suety, spotted dick; in the background, dried dates lurk deliciously; wonderful balance; t24 fabulously subtle malt-generated sweetness sits comfortably with a much drier, juicier sub-plot; the mouthfeel hovers around perfection with just enough light oil to grease the roof of the mouth and keep the barley in the ascendancy; f23 lots to chew here as the vanillas offer a custardy edge, though sugars – whilst present - are at a premium. Again we are back to the dregs of dried dates; b23.5 exceptionally good: a rare showing of Fino at its most sophisticated and unblemished. 46%. nc ncf.

Bruichladdich 1992 Sherry Edition Pedro Ximénez Aged 17 Years bourbon/PX db (**83**) n22 t22 f18.5 b20.5. Semi-puckering delivery: my word, that grape really does fly relentlessly at the taste buds. Probably the hardest sherry type to get right and here it works pretty well for the most part. 46%. nc ncf.

⋯ **Bruichladdich 1993 14 Years Old** Bolgheri French oak db (**85.5**) n23 t21 f21.5 b20. The fabulous nose doesn't quite translate once on the palate. The big natural caramels and barley combo never quite gets it together with the grape. Now the nose...yummy: that's a different matter! 46%

⋯ **Bruichladdich 1993 14 Years Old** Sassicaia French oak db (**83**) n20 t21 f20.5 b21. From a too tight nose to a too limp body. Just not my sac... 46%

Bruichladdich 1994 Valinch Blandola bourbon/Chateau d'Yquem casks, dist Sep 94 db (**87**) n21.5 t22.5 f21 b22. A bit muddled here and there but, like the distillery and staff, no shortage of personality. 55.3%. Available only from Bruichladdich's distillery shop.

Bruichladdich 1994 "Kosher" Aged 12 Years db (**85.5**) n22 t21 f21 b21.5. Clean. What else, my dear? 46%

Bruichladdich 1998 db (**89**) n22 t22.5 f22.5 b22. A truly unique signature to this but absolute class in a glass. 46%

Bruichladdich 1998 bourbon/oloroso cask, dist 1998 db (**87.5**) n22.5 t22.5 f21 b21.5. Surprisingly conservative. But, joy of joys, not an atom of sulphur to be found...!! 46%

Bruichladdich 1998 bourbon/Manzanilla cask, dist 1998 db (**82.5**) n21 t21 f20 b20.5. Fruity. But bitter where it should be sweet. 46%

⋯ **Bruichladdich 1998 Ancien Regime** db (**84.5**) n22 t21.5 f20 b21 An easy, slightly plodding celebration of all things malty, caramelly, oily and vanilla... 46%

⋯ **Bruichladdich 2001 Renaissance** db (**91**) n23 lively with the smoke and oak in particular going hammer and tongs; t23 brilliant delivery! Varying fruit tones hit the palate running but there is a bit of barley reinforcement flexing some considerable muscle. But the star is the ubiquitous smoke which shows a gentle iron fist; f22.5 a big surge of natural caramels but the spices make a scene; b22.5 a Big Laddie. 46%

Bruichladdich 2001 The Resurrection Dram 23.10.01 bourbon cask, dist 2001, bott 2009 db (**90.5**) n23 so subtle! Spiced sultana on malt, laced with golden syrup; t23 grist dissolves in the mouth: molten (fruitless) barley again with a sugary sheen. Simplistic, but beautifully effective; f21.5 long, vanilla-led, spiced and a little bitter; b23 now, be honest. How can you not have a first class Resurrection in the Bible...? 46%. 24,000 bottles.

Bruichladdich 2004 Islay Barley Valinch fresh sherry butt db (**89.5**) n22.5 positively porridgey, complete with brown molten sugar; someone's tipped a sherry trifle into this one, too...; t24 waaaaowww...!! That is some delivery: the thickest, most uncompromising Laddie of the year. Forget about sticking a spoon in it: this could easily accommodate a pitch fork. The fruit plays along with the porridge character and there is fudge, sundry spices, and tannin-shaded barley; f21 quite bitter, but the mocha effect works well; b22 yet another quite fabulous bottling from Bruichladdich, this one really cranking up the flavours to maximum effect. Having said all that, call me mad if you will...but seeing as this is Islay barley, would it not have been a good idea to shove it into a bourbon barrel, so we could see exactly what it tastes like? Hopefully that is on its way... 57.5%

Bruichladdich Full Strength Special Edition - The International Malt Whisky Festival, Gent 2008 db (**94**) n23 t23.5 f23 b24.5. The only thing more beautiful than this I came across for the first time at Gent was the girl selling my books. Both are enough to drive you inSanne with desire. 56.5%. nc, ncf.

Bruichladdich Infinity Second Edition bourbon/rioja db (**94**) n24 t24 f23 b23. Wasn't it Daffy Duck who used to put on his cape and shout: "Infinity and Beyond" ? Oh, no... it was Buzz Lightyear. Anyways, he must have been thinking of this. And there's certainly nothing dethspicable about this one... 52.5%

Bruichladdich Infinity Third Edition refill sherry tempranillo db (**94.5**) n24 the smokiness appears to have a life of its own: still cured bacon, as in previous Infinities (actually can there be such a thing...?) but perhaps a touch of Bavarian smoked cheese, perhaps, as a side dish, next to a freshly diced apple? I adore the lack of oils on the nose; the teasing dryness compensated by a distant fruit freshness; **t24** and its more of the same: just so dry, the palate is parched in seconds. The smoke is ashy, the vanilla is powdery, the malt gristy...just flakes of flavour wafting into every crevice like snow falling on a silent day; **f23** long, with the inevitable build up of dry, powdery spices which match the vanilla for weight and impact; **b23.5** I dare anybody who says they don't like smoky whisky not to be blown away by this. Go on...I dare you... *50%*

⁂ **Bruichladdich Laddie Classic Edition 1** db **(89.5) n23** salt-lashed and coastal, the barley is shimmering in the glass; **t23** a big barley delivery, but also enjoying a thick, almost fruit-cakey sub-plot, with dark, molassed depth. The piquancy seems to be maximised by the lingering salt; **f21** a degree of bitterness amid the big caramels; **b22.5** you probably have to be a certain vintage yourself to fully appreciate this one. Hard to believe, but I can remember the days when the most popular malt among those actually living on Islay was the Laddie 10. That was a staunchly unpeated dram offering a breezy complexity. Not sure of the age on this Retroladdich, but the similarities almost bring a lump to the throat... *46%*

Bruichladdich Legacy Series 3 Aged 35 Years db **(91) n22 t22.5 f23.5 b23**. So they managed to find a whisky exactly the same age as Ladie distiller Jim. *40.7%*

Bruichladdich Links "Carnoustie" 14 Years Old db **(78) n19 t20 f19 b20**. Hits some unexpected rough. *46%*

Bruichladdich Links K Club Ireland "16th Hole" 14 Years Old bourbon/syrah, dist 1992, bott 2007 db **(93) n23 t23 f23 b24**. I quite like this, though as hard as I try I can't quite love it. The spices offer great entertainment value and the juiciness on delivery is astonishing, but... My tongue is investigating every crevice in my mouth with some urgency, so I know it's complex – and very unusual, but... It's gossamer light. It kind of teases you. It's playful. But it's not beautiful. Is it...? Third mouthful in and I'm getting hooked. Oh, sod it! I've just upped it from a 86 to 93. What can I do? I'm in love... *46%. nc ncf. 12,000 bottles.*

Bruichladdich Links "Torrey Pines" 15 Years Old db **(89.5) n23 t22.5 f22 b22**. As clean as the perfect tee shot from the 15th... *46%*

Bruichladdich Organic 2003 Anns An T-Seann Doigh bourbon db **(84.5) n22 t22 f20 b20.5**. Thick barley carrying a soft smoke. A slight bitterness threads in and out of the proceedings. *46%. nc ncf. 100% Scottish barley.*

⁂ **Bruichladdich Organic Multi Vintage** bourbon cask db **(87.5) n22** subtle smoke; elements of grist; delicate citrus; **t22** sweet delivery but an immediate bitter-ish back up; coffee ice cream fills the middle; **f20.5** soft oils develop, as does the bitter tang; **b22** genteel. *46%*

⁂ **Bruichladdich Peat** db **(89.5) n23** peat; **t22.5** peat; **f22** peat; **b22** peaty. *46%*

Bruichladdich Rocks db **(82) n19 t22 f20 b21**. Perhaps softer than you'd imagine something called "rocks"! Beautiful little malty charge on entry. *46%* ☉

Bruichladdich Sherry Classic Fusion: Fernando de Castilla bourbon/Jerez de la Frontera db **(91) n23** a warm oaky spiciness adds attitude to the otherwise clean grape barley mix; a real dank warehouse backdrop to this one; **t23** a barley-grape see-saw which moves effortlessly into a dry winey middle; the malt when apparent appears youthful and lithe; **f22** some late prickly spice helps to really emphasise the subtlety of the oak; **b23** what a fantastically stylish piece of work! I had an overwhelming urge to sing Noel Coward songs while tasting this: for the Dry Martini drinkers out there who have never thought of moving on to Scotch... *46%*

⁂ **Bruichladdich Waves** db **(81.5) n20.5 t21.5 f19.5 b20**. Not sure if the tide is coming in or out on this one. Got various sugar and spice aspects which appeals, but there is something lurking in the depth that makes me a little uneasy... *46%*

Bruichladdich WMD II - The Yellow Submarine 1991 db **(75) n20 t19 f18 b18**. This one just doesn't have the balance and sinks. *46%*

Bruichladdich X4 db **(82) n18 t22 f21 b21**. Frankly, like no new make I have ever come across in Scotland before. Thankfully, the taste is sweet, malty and compact: far, far better than the grim, cabbage water nose. Doesn't really have the X-Factor yet, though. *50%*

Bruichladdich X4 +3 Quadruple Distilled 3 Aged Years bourbon db **(86) n21.5 t22 f21 b21.5**. It is as if the sugars in the barley have been reduced to their most intense form: this is all about huge barley of eye-watering intensity. A novel and not unattractive experience. *63.5%. nc ncf. 15,000 bottles.*

Octomore 5 Years Old db **(96) n23.5** seeing how Octomore is actually a farm on Islay, it is rather fitting that the massive peat here yields a distinctly farm-yardy aroma. Yet this is curiously low on peat reek for a dram boasting phenomenal phenols at 131 parts per million – Ardbeg is about 50; the much smokier PC7 is just 40. That said, obviously peaty, yet an age-related lemon lightness, too...and a herd of cattle...; **t24.5** the oils are absolutely perfect, as is the slow unfurling of the myriad strata of peat; those youthful, zesty, citrus notes have been enriched with a perfect degree of golden syrup; a near-perfect sprinkling of spice enriches further...; **f24** a wonderful array of vanillas lighten not just the peat but the sweetened mocha which is now making its mark. Long, relaxed and very assured for a malt so young... **b24** forget about the age. Don't be frightened by the phenol levels. Great whisky is not about numbers. It is about excellent distillation and careful maturation. And here you have a memorable combination of both... 63.5%

Octomore Edition 2.1 Aged 5 Years (140 ppm) bourbon cask, bott Jun 09 db (**94**) **n23** a snug nose of tight, thick peat: needs a chainsaw to cut through it; **t24** surprisingly sweet delivery with more than a hint of citrus: a massive gristy surge which is about as mouthwatering as heavily peated malt ever gets; the smoke is all enveloping; **f23** long with some vanilla at last getting into the act; some excellent late mocha and marzipan thins the smoke; **b23** talk about a gentle giant: as though your taste buds are being clubbed to death by a ton of smoky feathers. 62.5%. nc ncf. 15,000 bottles.

Octomore Edition 2.2 "Orpheus" Aged 5 Years (140 ppm) bourbon/chateau Petrus, bott 2009 db (**96.5**) **n24** when you clean out the ashes of fire that had been fed 100% by peat, that morning after the night before task, this is what you get. Well, partially. You will have to have one hand in the grate, the other around a glass of Petrus...; **t24.5** let's get this right: 140ppm phenols? Check. 61% abv? Check. How then, can the landing on the palate be like jumping onto a bed of feathers? The Demerara-gristy sweetness helps. So does the smoke, which envelopes the mouth. But the peat is also dry and that means a magnificent balance with those gristy sugars, so all seems to be in harmony. Brilliant! **f23.5** long, and just a gentle wind down of all before. Maybe a bit of extra fruit visible later on, as well as some Liquorice Allsorts; **b24.5** a standing ovation for this massive performance...the quite perfect way to bring up my 900th new whisky for the 2011 Bible. Everything works; the age and freshness of the barley, the controlled enormity of the smoke...even the entirely sulphur-free wine barrel. For those with a bit of hair on their chest...and want even more. 61%. 15,000 bottles.

⠴ **Octomore 3rd Edition Aged 5 Years** bourbon cask db (**95**) **n24.5** as someone who grew up in the countryside and, to this day, spends as much of what little spare time I get traipsing around fields and farmsteads, this is an aroma I know too well... cowsheds! Except here there is that extra element of peat, but that intense sweetness is unmistakable: Octomore: once the home of the cowshed itself once upon a time, come to think of it. It may only be a young 'un, and the youth is noticeable, but it remains one of the most distinguished and most flawless of all Scotland's whisky aromas...; **t24** as soft to the palate as a view of the sea from Port Charlotte is to the eye... The peat does not compromise, yet nor does it bully, allowing any amount of Demerara sugars to form and intensify with the vanilla and natural caramels from, I suspect, from first fill oak; **f23** much quieter than you might expect from the nose, but there is a touch of the Horlicks about the finale...but smoked Horlicks, of course...; **b23.5** I usually taste this late on in the Bible writing cycle: it is so important to be rewarded at the end of a long journey. This hasn't let me down and here's the rub: how something which looms so large be made from so many traits so small...? 59%

⠴ **Octomore 4th Edition Aged 5 Years** (167 ppm) db (**92**) **n21.5** hardly believable as an Octomore: the smoke appears locked in a caramel bubble...; **t23.5** sheer power seems to allow the smoke to burst away from its shackles, but it has to work hard. But there is none of the normal peaty dryness. Instead we are directed towards a delicious praline thread with the nut oils building and a non-specific fruitiness offering little more than a hint; **f23.5** 80% cocoa smoked chocolate...outrageous! **b23.5** Choctomore, surely? 62.5%

⠴ **Port Charlotte An Turas Mor Multi Vintage** bourbon cask db (**85.5**) **n23 t22 f20 b20.5** Does much right, especially the intriguing bullying of the colossal peat over what probably passes for grape. But bitters out and struggles to find a balance or plot line to keep you wanting to discover more. 46%

Port Charlotte PC6 db (**96.5**) **n24.5** ohhhhhh... arrrrrrrhh... mmmmmmmmmm... oh, the peat, the peat... yessssss... oh my god... mmmmmmm... ohhhhhhh... **t24** first you get the smoky... ooooohhhhhh... arrrrrrrrr... then the sweeter... mmmmmmmm... arrrrooooohhhh... **f24** it finishes with a more gentle arghoooo... mmmmmmm... oooophhhhhh... arrrrrrrr... **24** not many whiskies have a truly unmistakable nose... and... but this is, this... is... this... mmmmmmm..., arrrrrhh. Ohhhhhhhh... 61.6%

Port Charlotte PC7 dist 2001 db (**93.5**) **n24** dry. The most profound peat fire ashes: not for peaty amateurs... **t24** a few drops of sweetness added; a liquorice/molassed melt to the massive smoke: the phenols seems a lot higher than the 40ppm they talk about; **f22** drops down a gear or two as some bitterness creeps in, as does a secondary fizz to the spice; **b22.5** not quite as orgasmic as last year, sadly. But should still be pretty stimulating... 60.5%

Port Charlotte PC8 bourbon, dist 2001, bott 2009 db (**88**) **n22** the bourbon and smoke appear to be rather too in cahoots; **t23** beautifully rounded with the smoke taking off. But the oak is very caramel-centric and lacks complexity; **f21** cartloads of natural caramel; some injury time spice; **b22** enjoyable, but muted by PC standards... 60.5%. 30,000 bottles.

⋄ **Berry's Own Selection Bruichladdich 1991** cask no. 2996, bott 2011 **(78) n20 t21 f18 b19.** Malty, but the nose accurately foretells the bitter oak influence which is to follow later. 50.1%. nc ncf sc. Berry Bros & Rudd.

The Golden Cask Bruichladdich 1992 cask no. CM114 **(93) n23.5 t24 f22.5 b23.** A quite truly golden cask... 54.2%. 223 bottles.

Hart Brothers Bruichladdich Aged 15 Years dist Dec 94, bott Apr 10 **(89) n22** firm, lightly salted barley but with just a hint of smoke on the breeze; **t23** intense but always clean and fresh malt, again with that lightly salted, marginally smoked feel, but now with cream and jam sponge in the middle ground; gristy barley sugar throughout; **f22** spices up very late on; **b22** a delight of a near flawless bottling. 46%. Hart Brothers, for the Whiskyfair Limburg 2010.

Malts of Scotland Port Charlotte 2001 sherry hogshead, cask no. 829, dist Dec 01, bott Mar 09 **(93.5) n23** when worlds collide: dense grape... impenetrable peat... not for the faint hearted...; **t23.5** my taste buds have just been lost under a deluge of... errr... something. Seeing that the book has to be finished this year, I'll try and take a stab at what: errr... sherry... errr... peat... errrr... **f23** no, not technically the soundest finish, but then this is all about the experience... and does it ever end...? **b23** if this was any more weighty and solid it'd probably have its own gravity... 66.2%. Malts of Scotland. 96 bottles.

Malts of Scotland Port Charlotte 2001 bourbon barrel, cask no. 967, dist Dec 01, bott Feb 10 **(91) n23.5** bonfires and smoked Hungarian sausage; **t22.5** sweet, fabulously grist-malty delivery with excellent early buttery-vanilla layering; **f22** back to the bonfires as the ash comes through; the degree of smoke drifts and wafts around the palate while the degree of sweetness likewise pulses: how very clever...; **b22** impossible not to enjoy. Unless you don't like peat... 60.2%. Malts of Scotland. 192 bottles.

Malts of Scotland Port Charlotte 2001 sherry hogshead, cask no. 833, dist Dec01, bott Feb 10 **(73.5) n18.5 t20 f17 b18.** Strange, isn't it. Cask 829 works a treat. This one...well, doesn't. That's present day sherry butts for you. Like playing Russian roulette. Only with significantly more than one bullet in the chamber... 61.6% Malts of Scotland. 192 bottles.

⋄ **Malts of Scotland Port Charlotte 2001** zinfandel barrel, cask no. 969, dist Dec 01, bott May 10 **(95) n24** good grief! A Russian doll of peat and grape...; seemingly huge, but after a while lightens to the point of near fragility; **t24.5** fabulously juicy. Certainly the wine plays a big part, but you almost fancy there is some barley tucked up in there, too. The peat comes in thick tranches, but there is a wonderful degree of treacle oiling its path; the middle is lightly sugared, medium roast Blue Mountain Jamaican...or at least about as close an approximation a whisky might achieve; **f23.5** the grape takes over the steering from here on in; **b24** it didn't take long, but my taste buds soon hoisted the white flag on this one. Insane amounts of peat, a faultless wine barrel churning out thick fruit. Not the easiest experience to make sense of. But give the whisky time – and yourself to acclimatise – and it begins to make sense. Then it becomes truly unforgettable: an outrageous whisky which pays off...and with interest. 60.6%. nc ncf sc. Malts Of Scotland. Exclusive bottling for Whisky Fair Limburg 2010. 212 bottles.

⋄ **Malts Of Scotland Port Charlotte 2002** bourbon barrel, cask no. 77, dist May 02, bott Oct 10 **(93.5) n23** tight, thick nose with the peat forming a near impenetrable layer around all else. Most smoky whiskies are sweet to nose: this is very dry; **t24** the sugars missing on the nose dissolve on the palate on impact, though the diamond-hard peat which follows directly behind crashes into the taste buds without a scratch; the middle ground is far better balanced with a touch of hickory and coffee offering respite; **f23** a long finish as the peat unfurls in countless layers like an onion of near infinity; light sugars and vanilla add the required back up; **b23.5** some might say this one is for x-rated peat whisky lovers only. My message would be: if you don't like smoky whisky, see what you think when taking it to the max... Superb! 61.1%. nc ncf sc. Malts Of Scotland. 218 bottles.

⋄ **Malts Of Scotland Port Charlotte 2002** bourbon hogshead, cask no. 1172, dist Nov 02, bott Sep 09 **(85.5) n21.5 t21 f21.5 b21.5.** Heavily smoked cream toffee. 64.2%. nc ncf sc. Malts Of Scotland. 306 bottles.

Old Malt Cask Bruichladdich Aged 15 Years refill hogshead, dist Nov 93, bott Nov 08 **(91) n22.5 t23 f22.5 b23.** Very similar to the old Invergordon bottlings at this age. 50%. 353 bottles.

⋄ **Old Malt Cask Bruichladdich 16 Years Old** refill hogshead, cask no. 6384, dist Nov 93, bott Jul 10 **(84) n22 t22 f19 b21.** Charmingly light, gristy and simple. 50%. nc ncf sc. 346 bottles.

Old Malt Cask Bruichladdich Aged 18 Years refill hogshead, dist Nov 89, bott Aug 08 **(76) n20 t21 f17 b18.** Sweet, fat and juicy early on. But never gets into a stride and the finish is rather inevitable. 50%. Douglas Laing. 350 bottles.

∷ **Old Malt Cask Bruichladdich 20 Years Old** refill hogshead, cask no. 6307, dist Nov 89, bott Jun 10 **(85.5)** n23 t22 f19.5 b21. Big malt statement with some salient saline. *50%. nc ncf sc. Douglas Laing & Co. 289 bottles.*

Old Masters Bruichladdich Aged 20 Years cask no. 1883, dist 1988, bott 2008 **(95)** n24 t23.5 f23.5 b24. A beautiful version of the old-fashioned peatless Bruichladdich 10, which was once the most popular malt on the island. Twice as old and twice as intense. An indisputable must-have malt for the Islayphile, whether you are peathead or not, for this is one of the true classic Islays of the year. *52.6%. James MacArthur & Co Ltd.*

∷ **Old Masters Bruichladdich 20 Years Old** cask no. 2493, dist 1991, bott Jun 11 **(90.5)** n22.5 sharp barley; clean but some light, salty tannins offering weight and extra piquancy; t23 perhaps the cleanest barley you'll find this year. Light sugars help along the vanillas; f22.5 medium length and refusing to stray from the malty path; b22.5 faultlessly clean, simplistic malt which has been excellently distilled and matured. A treat. *51.5%. sc. James MacArthur & Co.*

Port Sgioba Private Cask Port Charlotte Aged 8 Years refill sherry hogshead, cask no. 826/2001, dist Dec 01, bott Mar 10 **(93.5)** n24 how can some be at the same time enormous, and yet on another level feather-light in its touch? Sherry and peat have a history of occasionally becoming unhappy barrel fellows. But not here. Both the grape and smoke are pristine and confident. They are both full bodied, but not for a second shout the other aspect down. Frankly, brilliant... t24 it's not just the unlikely marriage of juicy grape and intense peat that works here, but the weight also. All three combine memorably – and to jaw-aching, lip-smacking effect. Black cherry tops off the thickest of the smoke; hickory softens the middle ground; f22.5 although only eight, tires a bit at the death with a shadow of oaky bitterness visible, but the peaty smog fills in the cracks while the lingering sugars ensure fair play; b23 this is a cask from the whisky syndicate, FOAH... Friends Over A Hogshead. This is not to be confused the blackmailing syndicate, FOAB... Friends Over A Barrel. However, kidnap a few cases of this and you'll be able to hold these guys to ransom. *66%. For FOAH Syndicate.*

∷ **Scotch Malt Whisky Society Cask 23.66 Aged 17 Years** refill bourbon hogshead, cask no. 34, dist 1993 **(80)** n20 t21 f19 b20. Lots of malt and caramel. But steadfastly refuses to go anywhere interesting. *53.5%. sc. 217 bottles.*

∷ **Scotch Malt Whisky Society Cask 23.67 Aged 8 Years** refill barrel, cask no. 520, dist 2002 **(86)** n22 t21.5 f21 b21.5. Sweet, moderately peated and has taken a surprisingly hefty amount of caramel from the oak. *62.5%. sc. 259 bottles.*

∷ **Scotch Malt Whisky Society Cask 23.69 Aged 17 Years** 2nd fill hogshead, cask no. 1552, dist 1993 **(86.5)** n20.5 t22.5 f21.5 b22. A much happier malt than 23.66, having lived for 17 years in much classier surroundings. However, the view is quite similar and although the sugars make a healthy contribution to the wellbeing of the whisky, it is still frustratingly limited in its self expectation. *53.8%. sc. 270 bottles.*

∷ **Scotch Malt Whisky Society Cask 127.1 Aged 8 Years** refill bourbon barrel, cask no. 947, dist 2001 **(88.5)** n21.5 sharp, chattering peat offers a bit of attitude; t23 big, puckering delivery. The oak is a bit scruffy but the bite and pugnaciousness of the peat is rather thrilling; the vanilla and sugars in the middle ground balance the spices rather well; f21.5 heavy going with the caramels forming a dam; the spices continue running riot; b22.5 really enjoyable dramming. But you get the feeling the malt is working overtime to overcome a pretty average cask. *66.5%. sc. 231 bottles.*

∷ **Scotch Malt Whisky Society Cask 127.6 Aged 8 Years** refill bourbon barrel, cask no. 842, dist 2001 **(82.5)** n22 t21 f19.5 b20. Compared to 127.1, just shows what a sluggish cask can do. Even the complex peat can't overcome the more bitter notes. *65.2%. sc. 231 bottles.*

∷ **Scotch Malt Whisky Society Cask 127.12 Aged 8 Years** refill barrel, cask no. 383, dist 2002 **(86.5)** n22 t22 f21 b21.5. An enjoyable malt. But an excess of caramel makes it a little sluggish. *66.2%. sc. 160 bottles.*

∷ **Vom Fass Bruichladdich 20 Years Old** **(87.5)** n22.5 some delightful honey amid the toffee; t22 a few spice notes raises the profile and complexity; f21.5 thick natural caramels, bitters slightly; b21.5 best left in the glass for a while for the honeys to develop. *46%. sc.*

∷ **Whisky Doris Port Charlotte 7 Year Old** hogshead, cask no. 1171, dist Nov 02, bott Sep 10 **(82.5)** n20 t21 f20.5 b21. A crazy mixed up kid: the peats and caramels lurch drunkenly all over the palate. *63.5%. Whisky Doris.*

BUNNAHABHAIN

Islay, 1881. Burn Stewart Distillers. Working.

Bunnahabhain 12 Years Old (Older Bottling) db **(80)** n19 t21 f20 b20. Pleasant in its own clumsily sweet, smoky way. But unrecognisable to the masterful, salty Bunna 12 of old. *43.3%. nc ncf.*

⌖ **Bunnahabhain Aged 12 Years** db (85.5) n20 t23 f21 b21.5. Lovers of Cadbury's Fruit and Nut will adore this. There is, incongruously, a big bourbony kick alongside some smoke, too. A lusty fellow who is perhaps a bit too much of a bruiser for his own good. Some outstanding moments, though. But, as before, still a long way removed from the magnificent Bunna 12 of old... 46.3%. nc ncf.

Bunnahabhain Aged 16 Years Manzanilla Sherry Wood Finish db (87) n20.5 t23 f21.5 **b22.** The kind of undisciplined but fun malt which just makes it up as it goes along... 53.2%

Bunnahabhain Aged 18 Years (Older Bottling) db (94) n24.5 chestnut colour and, fittingly, roast chestnut on the fruitcake nose: the health-conscious might say there is too much salt in the mix, but it works perfectly here...; **t24** outstanding oloroso with the clean, faultless grape dripping of the salty barley; the oak again offers a nutty background, while Demerara sugars form a crisp counter to the invading salt; burnt raisin underscores the fruitcake character; **f22.5** light mocha, as a very slight bitterness steels its way in; **b23** a triumph for the sherry cask and a reminder of just how good this distillery can be. It's been a long time since I've enjoyed a distillery bottling to this extent. 43%

⌖ **Bunnahabhain Aged 18 Years** db (93.5) n24 a sumptuous amalgam of lightly salted roasted hazelnut shimmering within its own oil. Oloroso bulging with toasted, slightly singed currants, a sliver of kumquat and topped by thick vanilla. Irresistible... **t24.5** almost impossible to fault: the oloroso grandly, almost pompously, leads the way exuding thick, Christmas pudding depth; a light muscovado sugar top dressing counters the deeper, lightly salted vanillas which begin to emerge; **f22** a very slight sulphury note sullies the tone somewhat, but there is still enough rich vanilla and spotted dick for some enjoyable afters; **b23** only an odd cask has dropped this from being a potential award winner to something that is merely magnificent... 46.3%. nc ncf.

Bunnahabhain XXV Aged 25 Years (Older Bottling) db (91.5) n23 hard to imagine a more coastal aroma than this: the grape tries to get a word in edgeways but the salt has formed a crusty doorway; what fruit does get through is top quality; **t23** excellent arrival, the grape forcing the pace but with a tell-tale tang of saltiness; busy with a sneaky arrival of malt through the middle; **f22.5** chocolate fruit and nut... and salt; **b23** an intense and fun-packed malt for those who like a fine sherry and a sea breeze. 43%

⌖ **Bunnahabhain XXV Aged 25 Years** db (94) n23 you almost need a blow torch to cut through the oloroso, so thick is it. A little tight thanks to a minor distortion to a butt, but I am being picky. Salty and seaweedy, the ocean hangs in the air...; **t24** glorious weight and sheen to the delivery. The early balance is nearly perfect as the thick fruit is thinned by the proud barley. The early, contemplative sweetness, buttressed by a wonderful mixture of sultana and Demerara, gives way to the drier oaks and the tingly, chalky signs of a mildly treated butt; **f23** despite the winding down of the sugars the residual fruit manages to overcome the small obstacles placed before it; **b24** no major blemishes here at all. Carefully selected sherry butts of the highest quality (well, except maybe one) and a malt with enough personality to still gets its character across after 25 years. Who could ask for more...? 46.3%. nc ncf.

⌖ **Bunnahabhain Cruach-Mhòna** batch no.1 db (83) n17.5 t24.5 f21 b20. It appears that there is a new house style of being strangely and at times spectacularly off balance and less than brilliantly made, but making amends by offering a blistering maltiness which leaves one almost speechless. The delivery alone, with its light smokiness mixing in with the Demerara sugars and Grenadine spices, is the stuff of Islay legend. All else is bizarrely skewed and out of sync. Unique, for sure. 50% nc ncf.

Bunnahabhain Darach Ùr Batch no. 1 db (87) n21.5 a real fruit and barley soup; **t22.5** a wall of flavours hit the palate on entry, but it is the near impenetrability of the barley mouth feel amid soft fruit which catches the eye; **f21** bitters and fault lines show; **b22** almost milkshake thick. Not exactly a technical triumph but high marks for entertainment value! 46.3%

⌖ **Bunnahabhain Darach Ùr Batch no. 4** db (95) n24 good grief; as though matured in a barrel full of plump sultanas... but from the depth of sweetness, rather than the fruit... if you get my drift. Just a hint of spice as well as coconut and honey. Fabulous in a bourbon kind of salty, Hebridean way...; **t24.5** as thick and richly-textured as any malt you'll find this year. Intense, lightly salted barley is a match for the brimming, fruit-like sweetness; with a salivation factor which disappears through the roof, wonderful bourbon over- and under-tones link wonderfully to the mega sugars attached to the vanilla; **f23** much drier with a tangy, kumquat fade but plenty of vigorous spice; **b23.5** because of my deep love for this distillery, with my association with it spanning some 30 years, I have been its harshest critic in recent times. This, though, is a stunner. 46.3%. nc ncf.

Bunnahabhain Toiteach db (78) n19 t21 f19 b19. Cloying, sweet, oily, disjointedly smoky. Had you put me in a time capsule at the distillery 30 years ago, whizzed me forward to the present day and given me this, it would have needed some serious convincing for me to believe this to be a Bunna. 46%

⁘ **Bunnahabhain Toiteach Un-Chillfiltered** db (75.5) n18 t21 f17.5 b19. A big gristy, peaty confrontation on the palate doesn't hide the technical fault lines of the actual whisky. 46%. ncf.

⁘ **Adelphi Bunnahabhain 11 Years Old** cask no. 6037, dist 1998, bott 2010 (81) n19 t22 f20 b20 Perhaps an interesting way to look at this whisky is how we might the condition of the average present day chap compared to his counterpart of a generation ago. It is agreed that, in the western world, there is a higher percentage of flabby individuals now than in the 1980s, where their condition is far from conducive to good health. Where there was once muscle and tone there is now fat and paunch. That somehow sums up this malt: Bunna, once upon a time, was an impressively taught individual, on whom the malt and salt was found in perfect proportion on its firm frame. Not of late. And though the sherried clothes it wears may well be Saville Row, what lies underneath could do with a very major workout. 53.4%. sc. 538 bottles.

⁘ **Adelphi Bunnahabhain 31 Years Old** cask no. 8893, dist 1979, bott 2011 (95) n23.5 a classic oloroso butt, dripping with the juices of fat sultana over burnt raisin...the Demerara sugars help reinforce the Melton Hunt cake style. Barley at a premium but decent salt injection; t24 wow! A volley of black cherry helps dissipate the bulging oak. Good aged bitterness – as opposed to negative, shagged out cask bitterness – goes alongside oloroso dryness and the whole chewy, mature fruitcake theme; as for the spices, the nutty layering, the glorious juiciness...where do I start...? f23.5 even more black cherry, were that possible...! Those toasted raisins don't give up without a fight, either. b24 as you know, I am not one for matching food with whisky. But this is already like a frazzled piece of Melton Hunt cake one might have originally found in Dickinson and Morris' Nottingham Street shop and left at the back of a cupboard for a few years. By which I mean...bloody scrummy! 46.5%. sc. 516 bottles.

Adelphi Bunnahabhain 1968 Aged 41 Years sherry butt, cask no. 12401/3, bott 2010 (84) n22 t21 f20 b21. A procession of sticky treacle notes stave off the staves. Every one of those 41 years is on show. 41.2%. Adelphi Distillery Ltd. 719 bottles.

Adelphi Bunnahabhain 1997 Aged 11 Years sherry butt, cask no. 5368, bott 2009 (93.5) n23.5 they've caught some kippers in the Sound of Islay...; t23.5 beautiful mouth feel with the peat offering both soft smoke and sharper, more biting earthiness; some lovely muscovado sugars throughout; f24 the degree of excellent nip and bite one would demand from its age; the smoke continues on its own, literally sweet, way; b22.5 a beautifully made Bunna where the peat has a life of its own. A gem of a bottling. 58.6%. Adelphi Distillery Ltd. 610 bottles.

A.D. Rattray Bunnahabhain 1974 cask no. 7111, dist Jul 74, bott Dec 09 (81.5) n21.5 t20 f19 b20. Silky and savoury. But the big oakiness has bitten just a little too deep. That said, there is a sharpness to the barley which bites back rather beautifully. 44.3%. A.D. Rattray Ltd.

A.D. Rattray Bunnahabhain 1974 cask no. 5448 (85) n21.5 t22.5 f20 b21. Dense, brooding and a tad cloying. Huge presence in the glass and you can chew this stuff until your jaw aches. But doesn't really open up enough to ever get to know the true personality...a veritable Heathcliffe of a malt. 53.7%. A.D. Rattray Ltd.

Celtic Heartlands Bunnahabhain 1973 bott 2008 (91) n20 t24 f23.5 b23.5. The tired, slightly through-the-wood nose warns you of the worst...then the delivery blows you away...!! 46.1%. Bruichladdich Ltd. 669 bottles.

Douglas of Drumlanrig Bunnahabhain Aged 9 Years refill hogshead no. LD 3844, dist Dec 99, bott Oct 09 (88) n22 malt 'n' salt; t22.5 lightly oiled sweet malt; f21.5 strands of vanilla... clinging to malt; b22 quite possibly the maltiest whisky I have tasted this year. 46%. Douglas Laing. 180 bottles.

Dun Bheagan Bunnahabhain Aged 10 Years Manzanilla Finish (86) n22 t22 f20 b22. Distinctive fruity bite to this. 46%. Ian Macleod.

Dun Bheagan Bunnahabhain 14 Years Old Medoc Finish dist Apr 95 (88) n22 something of the rose garden about this one; even a little earthy; t22 chewy and juicy with excellent salt/oak and fruit interplay; f22 remains intact throughout with a very attractive vanilla and liquorice fade; b22 A very steady malt. 46%. nc ncf. Ian Macleod.

Dun Bheagan Bunnahabhain 24 Years Old barrel, dist Jun 85 (92.5) n23 fruit pastels (especially the green ones) but really it is the barley dominating with citrus, salt and surprising smoke always there or thereabouts; t23.5 classic Bunna body: thick malt and a hint of a something saline. But gentle waves of chocolaty peat are anything other than the norm for this distillery at the time...; f23 long with a wonderful, light peppery residue. Mocha appears to hang around forever... b23 amazingly, I holidayed in the old workman's cottage above the distillery a month or two after this was distilled. And I do remember being told of a peated run as a complete one-off that had been made just prior to my arrival...and tasting some of the still virtually new make in one of the warehouses. Miraculously, one of the casks has, some quarter of a century later, turned up in my tasting lab. It appears to have fared better than I over the years... 48.1%. nc ncf. Ian Macleod.

Duncan Taylor Collection Bunnahabhain 1970 cask no. 4075 **(81)** n20.5 t20 f20.5 b20. Clung like a limpet to retain its whisky life. In so doing has taken on nougat and honey clothing with just enough depth and sharpness to the barley to see off the mounting resin. Yet, for all its best effort, unwieldy and inelligent. 40.2%

Kingsbury's Bunnahabhain 11 Years Old 1997 **(84.5)** n21 t22 f20 b21.5. For all the charming, ashy smokiness found on this, it is a malt which still lacks conviction. Somehow the salty, rich body, which used to be such a vibrant part of this distillery's DNA, is missing. So, attractive as this may be - and it is well worth a visit - for a Bunna you can't help thinking that there perhaps should be so much more... 54.5%. Japan Import System, Celtic Series.

⠿ **Liquid Sun Bunnahabhain 1968** refill sherry, bott 2011 **(83.5)** n21 t20.5 f21 b21. Salty and buttery... perhaps overdoes the age, but an attractive number for those who like butter on an over toasted current bun. 47.8%. The Whisky Agency.

⠿ **Malts Of Scotland Bunnahabhain 1967** bourbon hogshead, cask no. 3315, dist Mar 67, bott Jun 10 **(90)** n22.5 guava and salty kiwi fruit abound t23 the delivery is a barrage of oak. But a flotilla of sugars sail to the rescue, most of them of the muscovado variety. Spices ting randomly around the palate with increasing intensity; f22 the spices rage long and remorselessly. Creamy butterscotch creates balance; b22.5 An improbably enjoyable Bunna displaying a rare degree of old- age exotic fruit. No shortage of brine amid the oak, either, and some lovely juiciness here and there. As far as age is concerned, the areas of gray have turned white...but the joints have not seized up. 41.1%. nc ncf sc. 147 bottles.

⠿ **Malts Of Scotland Bunnahabhain 1968** bourbon hogshead, cask no. 12291, dist Dec 68, bott Jun 10 **(82.5)** n21.5 t21 f20 b20. Fascinating that the 12-y-o I first tasted at the distillery would have come from similar stock to this. Those were in the days before then owners, Highland Distillers, ran amok with sherry butts in the warehouse...the percentage ratio was far greater on the bourbon barrel side than now. Of course, those bourbon casks were filled for early blending or, just maybe, the single malt. They were certainly not laid down to last over 30 years, and this one is showing multiple signs of age distress. Teaming with character and history and the odd barley note of bravado, for sure. But a good dozen summers beyond greatness... 40%. nc ncf sc. Malts Of Scotland.

⠿ **Malts Of Scotland Bunnahabhain 1970 "Thomas Ewers" 40 Years Old** bourbon hogshead, cask no. 4066, dist Jun 70, bott Jun 10 **(92.5)** n23.5 some sawdust is scattered over a sweet coconut and exotically fruity theme. As if distilled on some exotic island...other than Islay! t22 improbably silky beginning and then a massive kick of OTT oak. Just when you think this has killed this one off, it returns from the dead with a wonderful mix of honey and red liquorice; f24 the hints of bourbon that can be heard towards the middle now come into full view. A fabulous recovery where the barley and oak defy all the odds to speak as one; b23 this one has escaped the clutches of old Father Time just enough to tell a beautifully honeyed life story... 40.5%. nc ncf sc. Malts Of Scotland. 299 bottles.

Malts Of Scotland Bunnahabhain 1976 sherry butt no. 6388, dist Nov 76, bott Mar 09 **(93.5)** n24 astonishing: the clarity of the grape cocks a snook at appalling butts which ended up in the warehouses a decade later. This is exemplary stuff: cucumber spiciness sits so well with the fragile vanillas and lightly sweetened sherry note. One of the great noses of the year... t23.5 deft fruit delivery on the palate actually gets the juices up and running; something you'd hardly expect of a 33-y-o Bunna! Everything comes into play early on: the barley, grape and oak but only towards the middle, as the drying begins, does a cedar wood and red liquorice complexity kick in...; f23 for all the obvious late-spiced oak and gathering dryness, a stubborn barley sit in ensures a high quality finale; b23 ridiculously good for its age. 52%. 96 bottles.

⠿ **Malts Of Scotland Bunnahabhain 2005** oloroso barrel, cask no. 3990, dist Dec 05, bott Oct 10 **(86)** n22 t22 f21 b21. An aggressive example of the new, lightly smoked but intense Bunna style. Thick bodied delivery: almost malt concentrate. 55.9%. nc ncf sc. 242 bottles.

Murray McDavid Mission Bunnahabhain 1966 oloroso **(86)** n21 t23 f20 b22. Creaks a fair bit, but never goes snap... 40.3%. 500 bottles.

Old & Rare Bunnahabhain Aged 34 Years dist May 74, bott Sep 08 **(93.5)** n23 t23 f24 b23.5. Ah, pride of my heart, my own love... 58.3%. 333 bottles.

Old Malt Cask Bunnahabhain Aged 13 Years refill hogshead no. DL 5811, dist Sep 96, bott Feb 10 **(81)** n20 t21 f20 b20. Gristy, malty, a molecule of smoke here and there. Pleasant but never quite reaches second gear. 50%. Douglas Laing & Co Ltd. 347 bottles.

Old Malt Cask Bunnahabhain Aged 19 Years dist Feb 90, bott Jul 09 **(73.5) n18 t19 f18 b18.5.** Typical Bunna sherry cask of the era. Alas. *50%. Douglas Laing.*

Old Malt Cask Bunnahabhain Aged 30 Years refill butt, dist Dec 78, bott Apr 09 **(87) n23.5 t20.5 f22 b21.** Ground to a halt on delivery just through old age, but there's still some fabulous life to be found. *50%. Douglas Laing. 566 bottles.*

Premier Barrel Bunnahabhain Aged 12 Years (80.5) n19.5 t21 f20 b20. Simplistically malty but with a tang and twang. *46%. nc ncf. Douglas Laing. 310 bottles.*

Provenance Bunnahabhain Aged 9 Years refill hogshead, dist Winter 99, bott Winter 08 **(79.5) n18.5 t20 f21 b20.** I have spent many a Summer at Bunna. And from the early '80s got to know its whisky uncommonly well, at all ages and in all casks. It was never like this, though; a mixture of sweet, sticky barley and an assortment of vague off notes. *46%*

⌖ **Provenance Bunnahabhain Over 9 Years** sherry butt, cask no. 6940, dist Autumn 01, bott Spring 2011 **(76.5) n18 t20.5 f19 b19.** Soupy, sweet and sour. And thick. Not sure if the cut on this spirit could have been any wider had they tried... *46%. nc ncf sc.*

⌖ **Provenance Bunnahabhain Over 10 Years** refill hogshead, cask no. 6305, dist Winter 99, bott Summer 2010 **(85) n22 t21.5 f20.5 b21.** Thumping malt. But this is as puckeringly dry as they come. *46%. nc ncf sc. Douglas Laing & Co.*

Provenance Bunnahabhain Over 11 Years refill hogshead no. DMG 5812, dist Autumn 98, bott Winter 2010 **(77) n18 t20 f19 b19.** Juicy in part. But thinner than you might expect. *46%*

Scotch Malt Whisky Society Cask 10.69 Aged 11 Years refill hogshead, dist Dec 97 **(79) n18.5 t22 f19 b19.5.** One of those highly peated Johnnies from Bunna which, for what it badly lacks in technical quality, makes up for with a quite extraordinary smoky grunt. *55.4% Scotch Malt Whisky Society. 276 bottles.*

⌖ **Scotch Malt Whisky Society Cask 10.73 Aged 12 Years** refill hogshead, cask no. 5410, dist 1997 **(85) n21 t22 f21 b21.** Violently sugary and hot. Not that that's all bad, and certainly engenders some major entertainment value while the peat is ladled on to overflowing. But something, due I think to the indolent posture of the body, naggingly second class about the whole affair. *55.8%. sc. 311 bottles.*

Single & Single Bunnahabhain 1976 Aged 31 Years Special Edition sherry cask no. 592 **(94.5) n23.5** one of those noses where the many varied fruit, spice and malt elements merge into a single, delicious, soup...which has been lightly seasoned...; **t24** the delivery is also a case of dazzling bitter-sweet notes breasting the tape together; no overall victor, though the spices work particularly well, while the malt appears to absorb a pruney fruitiness easily; **f23.5** long, date and walnut cake and a late sprinkle of salt; **b23.5** Bunna has long held a special place in my heart and when you taste this you'll discover why its malt was quite so special during the early and mid 80s. The question is: in 31 years time, is it likely you will find a Bunna of this quality emptied from a sherry butt? *479%. Single & Single, South Africa.*

The Single Malts Of Scotland Bunnahabhain Aged 29 Years dist 1979, bott Aug 09 **(87) n23** a beautiful mishmash of vanilla and coriander with some salty orange pith thrown in for good measure; **t22** the mouthfeel is outstanding though some aggressive oak does its best to interfere a little way in. The intense, fruit-edged barley keeps the malt on course but that is one struggle going on; **f20.5** fades as soon as the oak gains the inevitable upper hand and dries intensely; **b21.5** not a malt usually noted for staying the course and this one struggles gamely over the line. Some delightful moments amid the fading light, but it is the nose which really shines. *44%. Speciality Drinks Ltd.*

⌖ **Vom Fass Bunnahabhain 12 Years Old (86.5) n21.5 t22.5 f21 b21.5.** Competent if simplistic peated Bunna which is rather youthful for its years. *40%*

⌖ **The Whisky Agency Bunnahabhain 8 Years Old** sherry cask, dist 2001 **(89) n22** spiced tomato. The malt is in strong arm warfare with the grape: the grape wins... **t23** big silky notes are soon under a big grapey lake. The spices settle early and stay put...; **f22** just a frison of cocoa to make for a chocolate and raisin bar finale; **b22** swamped with grape, be assured there is not a single off note. A real rarity. *54%. The Whisky Agency.*

The Whisky Agency Bunnahabhain 32 Year Old fino cask, dist 1976, bott 2008 **(92.5) n23 t24 f22.5 b23.** This is one very sophisticated dram. *53.7%. The Whisky Agency, Germany.*

The Whisky Agency Bunnahabhain 34 Year Old dist 1974, bott 2008 **(96) n24 t24.5 f23.5 b24.** As magnificent and mighty as The Paps which looked down upon this whisky being made and matured... *59.3%. The Whisky Agency, Germany.*

The Whisky Agency Bunnahabhain 35 Year Old dist 1973, bott 2008 **(78) n17 t21 f19 b21.** Tastes better than its noses, which is hardly difficult. *50.1%. The Whisky Agency, Germany.*

⌖ **The Whisky Agency Bunnahabhain 1965** refill hogshead, bott 2010 **(78) n20 t19 f20 b19.** Recovers with a welcoming degree of lime. But the oak is uncompromising. *40%. The Whisky Agency, Germany.*

The Whisky Agency Bunnahabhain 1967 sherry cask **(94) n23.5** moist Jamaican ginger cake dappled with salt and orange peel; **t24** oak all the way, but so invigorating are the sugars and fruits that never for a moment does it pose a threat to the general excellence; **f23** the silky texture continues, even as the drier vanillas arrive. A burned raisin bitterness, too, but the molasses negate the effects; **b23.5** impossible not to be mesmerised by. 40.5%

⟳ **The Whisky Agency Bunnahabhain 1968** bott 2010 **(86) n22 t22 f21 b21.** Sets me in mind of the Liquid Sun bottling from the same company. Very similar traits, but moved around in position slightly. More citrus on the nose and much more fat – and life - to the body. 47.8%. The Whisky Agency.

⟳ **The Whisky Agency Bunnahabhain 1974 (89)** n23.5 one of the saltiest drams of this and many a year: sea spray covers the marmalade and vanilla lead so conclusively you can almost hear the waves breaking...; **t21.5** sharp with an almost vicious oak delivery. Somehow a few remaining drops of honey have kept position to ward off the worst; **f22.5** a few oils form, helping to enrich the mocha; **b21.5** a malt which should have died but somehow defies the odds by showing some fabulous signs of life. They say salt is a good preservative... 47.3%

⟳ **Wilson & Morgan Barrel Selection Bunnahabhain 42 Years Old** cask no. 12408, dist 1968, bott 2011 **(94.5) n24.5** does the exotic fruit come from the Gulf Stream which runs close to this distillery? Of course not, but it would be romantic to think so. Rather, we are talking excellent oak intermingling with the barley to truly sophisticated effect. You get this only with ancient malt. But ancient malt which has been fortunate enough to find a first class home for in excess of 35 years. The added saltiness is just too good to be true; **t24** gorgeously lithe with the barley forming a lightly sugared sheen and the softest of spices adding a mild degree of attitude to the juiciness. The oak could not be better behaved, or more elegant; **f22.5** a bitter marmalade edge creeps into the fruit and vanilla yoghurt finale; **b23.5** if you don't have a couple of hours to spare, don't even think about pouring a glass... 44.1%. sc. 436 bottles.

⟳ **Wilson & Morgan Barrel Selection Bunnahabhain 1997 Heavy Peat** cask no. 5376/77, bott 2010 **(85.5) n21 t22 f21 b21.5.** Big, unwieldy and were it not for the enormous chunkiness of the body, it would collapse under the weight of smoke and sugar. Something to seriously chew upon. 46%. Wilson & Morgan.

CAOL ILA
Islay, 1846. Diageo. Working.

Caol Ila Aged 8 Years Unpeated Style dist 1999, bott 2007 db **(93.5) n23 t24 f23 b23.5.** Oh well, here goes my reputation...honest opinion: on this evidence (backed by other samples over the years) Caol Ila makes better straight malt than it does the peated stuff. Sorry, peat lovers. This should be a, if not the, mainstay of the official Caol Ila portfolio. 64.9%

Caol Ila Aged 8 Years Unpeated Style 1st fill bourbon, dist 2000, bott 2008 db **(91.5) n23** a touch maltier than the previous bottling; salty digestive biscuit; **t23** beautifully refreshing with a real puckering, salty tartness to the barley; I seem to remember citrus here last year. But this time we have butterscotch and toffee; **f22.5** long, very delicately oiled with the vanillas and toffee in decent harmony; **b23** a bit more of a pudding than last year's offering, but delicious dramming all the way. 64.2%

Caol Ila Aged 10 Years "Unpeated Style" bott Aug 09 db **(93.5) n24** a beautiful medley of pear and lime with a thin spread of peanut butter for good measure...not exactly what one might expect...!!! **t23.5** the barley is just so juicy from the kickoff: the citrus on the nose reappears, though any hopes of pear vanishes; the barley, so rarely heard in a Caol-Ila grows in confidence and intensity as the delivery develops; **f23** not as oily as you might expect, allowing extra oak to emerge; **b23** always fascinating to see a traditional peaty Islay stripped bare and in full naked form. Shapely and very high class indeed. 65.4%. Only available at the Distillery.

Caol Ila Aged 12 Years db **(89) n23** a coastal, salty biting tang (please don't tell me this has been matured on the mainland!) with hints of rockpools and visions of rock pipits and oystercatchers among the seaweed; **t23** enormously oily, coating the palate with a mildly subdued smokiness and then a burst of gristy malt; **f21** caramel and oil; **b22** a telling improvement on the old 12-y-o with much greater expression and width. 43%

Caol Ila Aged 18 Years db **(80) n21 t20 f19 b20.** Another improvement on the last bottling, especially with the comfortable integration of citrus. But still too much oil spoils the dram, particularly at the death. 43%

Caol Ila 1979 db **(74) n20 t19 f17 b18.** So disappointing. I could go on about tropical fruit yada, yada, yada. Truth is, it just conks out under the weight of the oak. Too old. Simple as that. 58.6%

Caol Ila 1997 The Manager's Choice db **(93.5) n24** dry, ashy peat sweetened less by grist but mango chutney; **t23.5** now the grist does arrive and sharpens up quickly: a barley juiciness sets in as Lincoln biscuit/garibaldi dunked in peat hogs the middle ground; hickory and liquorice begin the form...; **f23** a tad dusty but the liquorice and smoke hold sway; **b23** when this malt is not enveloped in in taste bud-clogging oil, it really can be a little special. Here's further proof. *58%*

Caol Ila 'Distillery Only' bott 2007 db **(95.5) n24 t24 f23.5 b24**. Caol Ila is the third hardest distillery to get to in Scotland: however should you do so some time soon you can reward yourself by picking up a bottle of this. I can say honestly that the journey will be very much worthwhile... *58.4%. 5,000 bottles. Available only from the Caol Ila Distillery shop.*

⠿ **Caol Ila Moch** db **(87) n22** dry. Ground roast coffee which is decently smoked; **t22** a green barley delivery: sharp, juicy and a slow build up of oil and cocoa; **f21** vanilla but with a touch of bittering oak; **b22** easy drinking Islay. Though I think they mean "Mocha"... *43%*

⠿ **Caol Ila Special Release 2010 12 Years Old** 1st fill bourbon oak cask, dist 1997 db **(95.5) n23** the smoke is almost an afterthought to the red liquorice lead. Bracing, tangy, full of energy...; **t24** to die for. The trademark oils arrive only as an apologetic afterthought to the delivery which takes at least six mouthfuls to get the measure of. Uniquely, the lead characteristic is sweetened cocoa, something of a bourbon front which is further backed by toasted honeycomb. The smoke offers no more than ballast and refuses to assert any authority on the salivating malt; **f24** now the limited oils have arrived they are put to excellent use by lengthening the finale. The vanillas are sweetened; the barley is galvanised by a curiously fruity earthiness and the most delicate spices imaginable tiptoe across the taste buds...; finally, a discreet muscavado sugar fanfare pipes the experience to its majestic close... **b24.5** the peat more or less takes a back seat in what is a masterful display of force and diplomacy on the palate. Most probably the best Caol Ila I have tasted in recent years. And this in a year of magnificent Caol Ilas. *576%. nc ncf. Diageo. Unpeated, fewer than 6000 bottles.*

A.D. Rattray Caol Ila 1995 cask no. 10035 **(92) n24 t23.5 f21.5 b23**. The nose and delivery is pure textbook. *60.4%*

⠿ **Berry's Own Selection Caol Ila 1980** cask no. 4938, bott 2011 **(90) n22.5** clean, almost hock-like in its delicate sweetness...except for the rumbling smoke; there is also a curious juniper/rye sharpness... **t23** mouth-watering, the barley is stretched and the smoke sweet and all-encompassing; the usual oils fill the middle ground alongside a brief array of brown sugars; **f22** good length with a distinct build up of spice and cocoa; **b22.5** charming and elegant throughout. *55.6%. nc ncf sc. Berry Bros & Rudd.*

⠿ **Berry's Own Selection Caol Ila 1984** cask no. 5389, bott 2010 **(95) n23** mesmerising. A gentle citrus flourish to the nutty smoke; coal dust; **t24** fabulous. The delivery is a near perfect arrival of orange-dusted barley, all in an understated soup of liquorice and smoke; **f24** delicate. More of the same, but at half the voltage... **b24** spellbinding! Another Caol Ila which shows its brilliance in no small part thanks to the lack of the usual oils. If Doug McIvor can keep unearthing Caol Ilas of this quality, he is in danger of helping Diageo put this distillery on the Premier Whisky league map... *53.7%. nc ncf sc. Berry Bros & Rudd.*

Berry's Own Selection Caol Ila 1995 bott 2008 **(93) n23 t24 f23 b23** Now that's the way a Caol Ila of this age should behave... *58.9%. Berry Bros & Rudd.*

Berrys' Own Selection Caol Ila 2000 (94) n23.5 a beautiful mix of banana skins and dry, cindery peat: exceptionally fine in its style; **t23.5** playfully aggressive delivery with the sweetness of the barley interlocking with the much drier smoke; the middle ground is like smoked draff biscuits; **f23.5** medium length but with a citrus swirl lightening the intensity of the smoke...just so delicate and precise; **b23.5** benefits hugely from the limited oils present. This is the way I love to see Caol Ila, rather than in its oily, shapeless form. A classic. *58.9%*

⠿ **Berry's Own Selection Caol Ila 2000** cask no. 309878, bott 2011 **(95) n23.5** quite stunning, lilting, hugely smoked grist. Hard to imagine a more balanced interplay between light sugars and drier oak; Palma violets, the most distant hint of juniper, and even a touch of honey on butter; the peat is far more weighty than is the norm for this distillery, though it may not be obvious due to the beautiful balance; **t23.5** eschewing the usual oiliness, the whisky celebrates its high peat personality (appears, as does the nose, a distance above the 35ppm norm) with an uninterrupted view of the dissolving sugars and the layering of the phenols and cocoa; the pace of the spice makes one purr...; **f24** wow! How elegant is that? Really long, as should be expected from such a major degree of smoke and a slow unravelling of the light sugars, delicate spices and vanillas. Sublime...; **b24** I think it would be hard to find a better cask of Caol Ila at this age if you spent all year trying. Also, if this doesn't confirm that this has to be around the distillery's best age, I don't know what does. *576%. nc ncf sc.*

Cadenhead's Authentic Collection Caol Ila 1984 bott Feb 10 **(88) n21** smoky, but strangely under-ripe: not the cleanest...; **t23** didn't expect that...!! Wow!! An absolute explosion of sweetly confectioned smoke, with boulders of oak and spice...and all this played out in the most juicy barley imaginable; **f21.5** confirms the nose's message that all is not technically right, but the pulsing spices and smoke is pretty disarming; **b22.5** while the nose may not be particularly alluring, what follows next is sheer joy. *55.5%. Wm. Cadenhead Ltd. 250 bottles.*

The Càrn Mòr Vintage Collection Caol Ila 1983 hogshead no. 4801, dist 1983, bott 2009 **(87.5) n21.5** a nose which simply can't make up its mind: concentrated vanilla pod against sweetened peat...neither wish to win the battle; **t23** works well enough here as the initial waves ignore the nose and come through as rich barley. The smoke and vanilla play catch up, but with the phenols always ahead; **f21** a bit tired as the oak shows a more bitter side; **b22** an intriguing battle between vanilla and peat... *46%. nc ncf. 1203 bottles.*

Cask Strength Caol Ila 1998 (73) n19 t19 f17 b18. I tasted this a month or so apart from the CC Caol Ila, as it had been filed in the wrong place. But we can safely assume it is from the same batch of casks. *58.8%. Gordon & MacPhail.*

Chester Whisky & Liqueur Co. Caol Ila Aged 13 Years dist 1995 **(84) n22 t21.5 f20 b20.5.** Excellent ashy dryness to the smoky nose and soft oils on delivery. *50.6%*

Chieftain's Caol Ila Aged 12 Years hogshead **(77) n19 t20 f19 b19.** Pleasant and plodding in its own way, but has little to say. *43%. Ian Macleod.*

Chieftain's Caol Ila 12 Years Old Rum Finish (83) n22 t20 f20 b21. Slightly too oily and thick to fully take advantage of the proffered rum influence. But the peat is more polished than it might be. *46%. Ian Macleod.*

Connoisseurs Choice Caol Ila 1998 (74.5) n19 t20 f17.5 b18. The odd blast of liquorice. But the finish is far from great. *43%. Gordon & MacPhail.*

The Coopers Choice Caol Ila 1981 Aged 28 Years (83.5) n22 t21 f20 b20.5. Oily and old, the malts work exceptionally hard to keep the whisky's integrity against the marauding oak. Success is only partial. *46%. The Vintage Malt Whisky Co Ltd.*

The Coopers Choice Caol Ila 1992 Aged 17 Years (90.5) n22.5 oily and monosyllabic for the most part, a little vanilla battles through after 17 years, but enough to generate some serious sophistication; **t23** sweet, but with a half-hearted spice jab to the palate; the oils are well ordered and carry the barley away from the background smoke; the oak in the meantime goes through a number of vaguely fruity lives; **f22.5** some citrus battles through on the coat-tails of the vanillas; **b22.5** the distillery at its most disarmingly erudite. Though it makes little attempt to offer more than its smoke and oil early on, the degrees of sweetness and slow are quite charming. *46%. The Vintage Malt Whisky Co Ltd.*

Demijohn Caol Ila 1991 Single Malt (91) n23 t23 f22 b23. Tip top Caol Ila at its gristiest. *46%. Demijohn Ltd, UK.*

Douglas of Drumlanrig Caol Ila Aged 11 Years refill hogshead no. LD 5218, dist Sep 97, bott May 09 **(85.5) n21.5 t22 f21 b21.** Just about the perfect whisky for those looking for a peaty – but not too peaty – dram with soft oils to make the friendliest of glides down the gullet. *46%. Douglas Laing. 287 bottles.*

Dun Bheagan Caol Ila Aged 15 Years hogshead, dist Jun 93 **(86.5) n22.5 t22 f21 b21.** From the slightly slithery, oily school of Caol Ila. The dry nose and sharp delivery are a treat, though. *50%. Ian Macleod Distillers Ltd.*

⋰ **Duncan Taylor Octave Caol Ila 28 Years Old** cask no. 400926, dist 1983 **(93.5) n23** the peat is lazy and distinctly of the farm yard variety: cows are definitely offering a pastoral symphony...; **t23** beautiful delivery of early sugars. The standard Caol Ila oiliness here works to good effect by intensifying the scraps of flavours offered. The peat begins deftly but builds momentum; **f(23.5** even some flecks of barley added to the worty sugars. Excellent control from the oak while the peat continues to insist on adding the backing only; **b24** if you are ever to have one whisky over the eight, you could do worse than this very complex Caol Ila. A dram which after a slow starts builds to a moving crescendo. *51.7%. sc.*

Duncan Taylor Collection Caol Ila 1981 cask no. 3491 **(86.5) n20.5 t21 f23 b22.** Attractively sweet and spicy with the rampaging sugars compensating for the mild excesses of the old oak. Pleasantly complex mocha, too. *55.2%*

Duncan Taylor Collection Caol Ila 1982 cask no. 2736 **(91) n22** evening primroses amid the peat; **t23** the fabulous sweet and lush phenols counter the drier oaks with aplomb; **f22.5** spicy, soft and with some excellent custard tart to balance the ashier peats; **b23.5** very complex and excellently balanced. *55.4%*

Duncan Taylor Collection Caol Ila 1982 cask no. 2741 **(84) n20.5 t21 f21.5 b21.** Full-flavoured. But never less than sharp and hot. *55.9%*

Duncan Taylor Collection Caol Ila 1984 cask no. 6275 **(87.5) n23** the nose is pure fun: almost a self parody of a big, salty Islay...; **t20.5** begins sweetly and brightly but hits a sharp, almost bitter note in midstream; **f22** sweet, malty, gloriously smoky notes come galloping to the rescue like white blood cells to a wound. The finish is transformed back to something closer to what the nose promised...; **b22** a real character of a dram. *53.8%. Duncan Taylor & Co Ltd.*

Duthies Caol Ila 13 Years Old (90.5) n23 t23 f22 b22.5. Young and green (in every sense) for its age. But a sweet, refreshing delight. 46%. *Springbank Distillers for Germany.*

Exclusive Casks Caol Ila 1980 Aged 28 Years American oak (92) n23.5 t24 f22 b22.5. You never quite know what you are going to get from this distillery. This one's a winner. 50.5%. *Chester Whisky & Liqueur Co.*

⁘ **Fine Malt Selection Caol Ila 10 Years Old** dist 2000, bott May 11 (90) n22 eschewing the usual oils, the peat is in clean and beautifully defined form: mildly gristy but with some invigorating citrus; t23 you won't find a cleaner Islay delivery this year: the delicate oils ramp up the sugars, lightly dulling the smoke but ensuring a wonderful whole...; f22 smoked molten icing sugar with a gradual build up of vanilla and kumquat; b23 an absolutely typical, on the money bottling from James MacArthur. 45%. sc. *James MacArthur & Co. USA release.*

Hart Brothers Caol Ila Aged 11 Years dist Aug 96, bott Jun 08 (84.5) n21.5 t21 f21 b21. A quiet dram, happy to rumble along with gentle peat and dry vanilla. 46%

James MacArthur's Old Masters Caol Ila 1995 Aged 14 Years cask no. 10042, bott May 10 (85.5) n21 t22 f21 b21.5. Stereotypical Caol Ila unplugged which makes an enjoyably peaty noise without having any meaningful lyrics. 58.4%. *James MacArthur & Co Ltd.*

The John Milroy Selection Caol Ila 29 Years Old (84) n21.5 t20.5 f21 b21. Such is the antiquity here, the peat is breaking down seemingly into constituent parts and heading back towards its floral past. Some exotic fruit tries to get off the ground but is smothered by smoke. Painfully enjoyable and a fine example of a whisky that had once seen better days. 57.2%

Kingsbury's Caol Ila 1984 24 Years Old Cask Strength (92) n23.5 t23.5 f23 b22.5. Classy little cask. 53.2%. *Japan Import System.*

⁘ **Kingsbury Celtic Caol Ila 24 Years Old** dist 1984 (89.5) n22.5 dry peat but thick and generously layered; t23 soft oils first transport the smoke to all points around the palate and then a plethora of sugars; f21.5 the bitterish oak insures a balance with those pounding sugars; a bit like a Japanese tea with three or four sugars; b22.5 catches the essence of the distillery remarkably well. Delightful. 53.2%. nc ncf sc. *Japan Import Systems. 229 bottles.*

Kingsbury's Finest & Rarest Caol Ila 1982 (90.5) n23 t23 f22 b22.5. Another tip-top Caol Ila from Kingbury. 58.9%. *Japan Import System.*

Kingsbury "The Selection" Caol Ila 6 Years Old 2000 (85) n21 t22 f21.5 b21.5. Not as peaty as you might expect, allowing the grassy citrusy notes full voice. Charming. And perhaps one of the most refreshing drams of the year! 43.0%. nc ncf. *Japan Import System Co Ltd.*

Kingsbury's "The Selection" Caol Ila 8 Years Old 2000 (86.5) n21.5 t22 f21 b22. Lovely stuff, indeed. Celebrates its youthful simplicity by getting the balance of banana and vanilla amid the peat spot on. 43%. *Japan Import System.*

⁘ **Liquid Library Caol Ila 1984** bourbon hogshead, bott 2010 (86) n21 t22 f21.5 b21.5. A rare occasion when oil quenches the fire. At times tight and very hot with an over abundance of sugar. But brought under control by the oils for quite a memorable experience. 59%

⁘ **Malts Of Scotland Caol Ila 1981** bourbon hogshead, cask no. 4807, Mar 81, Sep 10 (85.5) n21 t22 f21 b21.5. Some fabulously violent, alcoholic aggression helps paper over some cracks in the oak. Absolutely nothing wrong with the peat involvement, though! 59.8%. nc ncf sc. *Malts Of Scotland. 216 bottles.*

Malts of Scotland Caol Ila 1998 bourbon hogshead no. 12374, dist Dec 98, bott Mar 09 (88) n21.5 quite tight and confined with the smoke and oak fighting the same territory; t21.5 like the nose, the delivery appears restricted with everything working within a crisp, sugary frame; f23.5 at last throws off the shackles as a light oiliness unfurls, bringing with it a much more relaxed maltiness and a lighter, ashy, peatiness; b22 takes a little time to find its feet, but leads you on a smoky dance when it finally does. 60.9%. *Malts of Scotland. 96 bottles.*

⁘ **Master Of Malt Caol Ila 30 Year Old** refill hogshead, dist 1980, bott 2010 (88.5) n22.5 earthy, dank bluebells; tip-toeing peat yet clean, moody and thick despite a hint of honey; t23 wonderful delivery of diluted Golden Syrup with a light, smoky strata; excellent spice attack amid the oily vanilla thread; f21 a little bitter tiredness to the oak, but entirely forgivable; b22 gains dramatically from the intensity of the strength. A real fun experience with a malt which wears its age with aplomb. 57.4%. nc ncf sc. *Master Of Malt. 154 bottles.*

Murray McDavid Mission Caol Ila 1984 gold series, bourbon/grenache Vincent Le Grand (91) n24 t22 f23 b22. The big question is: is it an Islay or a French rock pool? I'm sure this is near the Singing Sands... 54.1%

Old Malt Cask Caol Ila Aged 12 Years dist Sep 96, bott Jul 09 (88) n22 pepper, smoky style; t22 soft at first, then ker-pow-fizz...!! Those peppers on the nose bite... f22 smoky and sweet; b22 sweet, but with attitude. 50%. *Douglas Laing.*

⁘ **Old Malt Cask Caol Ila Aged 14 Years** refill hogshead, cask no. 6535, dist Sep 96, bott Sep 10 (90) n22.5 dry, old lum peat reek; t23 no such dryness on delivery: various degrees of sugar help balance the smoky impact; **f22** lightly smoked butterscotch and bread and butter pudding; **b22.5** unusually sweet without displaying a gristy complexion. Another Caol Ila making the most of a lack of oil. *50%. nc ncf sc. Douglas Laing & Co. 329 bottles.*

Old Malt Cask Caol Ila Aged 18 Years refill hogshead no. DL 5556, dist Mar 91, bott Oct 09 **(84) n21.5 t21 f20.5 b21.** Feathered peat and enjoyable grist. *50%. Douglas Laing.*

Old Malt Cask Caol Ila Aged 19 Years claret finish, bott 2009 **(82) n20 t21 f21.5 b20.5** For a cask finish, especially wine, to work well, the barley, oak and fruit have to somehow integrate to reach a harmony. It is always more much difficult when big peat is thrown in the mix. This one shows you just how difficult it can be. *50%. Douglas Laing.*

◌ **Old Malt Cask Caol Ila Aged 21 Years** refill hogshead, cask no. 6912, dist Mar 90, bott Mar 11 **(80) n20.5 t20.5 f19 b20.** Extremely tight with the oak in confrontational mood. *50%. nc ncf sc. Douglas Laing & Co. 148 bottles.*

Old Malt Cask Caol Ila Aged 25 Years refill hogshead, dist Jan 84, bott Apr 09 **(84) n21.5 t22 f20 b20.5.** Attractively floral in part and well weighted. But showing distinct sign of fatigue. *50%. Douglas Laing. 309 bottles.*

Old Malt Cask Caol Ila Aged 26 Years refill hogshead no. DL 6207, dist Jan 84, bott May 10 **(94) n23** the liquorice and hickory sits well with the smoke; a hint of honeycomb helps disguise the ravages of old age so well that you can't actually see any...; **t24** sublime: the honey sits in immediately and, in its holding role, allows the liquorice and smoke to raid every crevice of the palate; light vanillas help form the middle ground, underlining the high quality of the cask; **f23.5** not a single trace of bitterness marks this out not only as a rare cask, but a truly classic Caol Ila; **b23.5** usually a distillery which ages like a smoker. This, though, is a cracker of a dram: one of the best old 'uns from the Sound of Islay for a very long while. *50%. 268 bottles.*

Old Malt Cask Caol Ila Aged 29 Years refill hogshead, dist Feb 79, bott Aug 08 **(93) n24 t23.5 f22.5 b23.** Melts on the nose and mouth and shows that even big Islays like this can be purring, graceful pussycats even after the best part of three decades. A classic. *50%. Douglas Laing. 238 bottles.*

Old Malt Cask Caol Ila Aged 30 Years refill butt, cask no. 5731, dist Nov 79, bott Jan 10 **(89) n22.5** fresh, perky barley; green banana and sugared smoke; **t23** a softy, with a youthful barley streak; the oak arrives with a forceful jolt midway through but is nudged out again once the sugars reform; **f21.5** chewy, well smoked vanilla; **b22** refuses to grow up and show its age. So bravo for that!! *50%. Douglas Laing & Co Ltd. 266 bottles.*

◌ **Old Malt Cask Caol Ila Aged 30 Years** refill hogshead, cask no. 7182, dist Sep 80, bott May 11 **(86.5) n23 t21 f21.5 b21.** A fascinating bottling which held up my early start to the day as I took extra time to try and figure this one out. The peat is only in trace form and instead we are treated to a display of candy store fruits. The lack of smoke, however, means the age of the cask is felt at times profoundly. Even so, the sort of dram that deserves time and respect. *50%. nc ncf sc. Douglas Laing & Co. 270 bottles.*

◌ **Old Malt Cask Caol Ila Aged 30 Years** refill hogshead, cask no. 6858, dist Nov 80, bott Jan 11 **(79) n21 t21 f18 b19.** Some serious bitterness at play here. *50%. nc ncf sc. 318 bottles.*

Old Masters Caol Ila Aged 13 Years cask no. 10046, dist 1995, bott 2008 **(92) n23.5 t22.5 f23 b23.** A quite beautifully constructed malt. *59.8%*

Old Masters Caol Ila Aged 26 Years cask no. 733, dist 1982, bott 2008 **(86) n22.5 t21.5 f21 b21.** Some lovely lavender mingles charmingly with the smoke on the nose, but a big thrust of natural caramel limits the complexity of the salty but gentle palate. *55.2%. James MacArthur.*

◌ **Provenance Caol Ila Over 9 Years** refill hogshead, cask no. 6802, dist Winter 01, bott Autumn 2010 **(78.5) n20 t19 f20 b19.5.** Oily, sweet, pleasant yet a few cylinders have packed in. *46%. nc ncf sc. Douglas Laing & Co.*

◌ **Provenance Caol Ila Over 10 Years** refill hogshead, cask no. 7237, dist Winter 01, bott Summer 2011 **(84.5) n22.5 t21 f21 b20.** After the initial gristy big peat burst, quietens down to little more than a near oakless whisper... *46%. nc ncf sc. Douglas Laing & Co.*

Provenance Caol Ila Aged 11 Years dist Sep 97, bott Jul 09 **(89.5) n23 t22 f22.5 b22.** A spot on cask. *46%. Douglas Laing.*

Provenance Caol Ila Aged 11 Years refill hogshead, dist Summer 09, bott Winter 09 **(88) n23 t22 f21 b22.** Sweet and delicious. *46%. Douglas Laing.*

Provenance Caol Ila Over 12 Years refill hogshead no. 5720/5721, dist Autumn 97, bott Winter 09 **(80.5) n21 t20.5 f19 b20.** Regulation Caol Ila from a blending cask. *46%*

◌ **Rare Auld Caol Ila 27 Years Old** dist 1983, cask no. 3620 **(88) n22** phenolic cumquats; **t23** eye-wateringly sharp in its tart cirtrus and barley impact. The smoke descends like ash on Pompeii; **f21** bitters as the cask buckles slightly **b22** not sure the cask was designed for this kind of age. But the malt certainly was... *52.7%. sc. Duncan Taylor & Co.*

Scotch Malt Whisky Society Cask 53.134 Aged 9 Years refill hogshead, dist Nov 99 (91) n23 a delight for its sheer simplicity: a real smoke thump, but never all consuming, allowing the barley-side of the malt to be heard; t23 crisp barley offers smoke of varying levels of sweetness and youthful intensity. Just so clean and almost sparkles on the palate; f22.5 excellent burst of mocha attaches itself to the well-behaved smoke; b22.5 when a whisky is this well made and matured in such an exemplary cask, you cannot ask for too much more. 67.3%. Scotch Malt Whisky Society.

Scotch Malt Whisky Society Cask 53.136 Aged 17 Years refill hogshead, dist Jan 92 (92.5) n23 freshly squeezed lemon on peated grist; t23.5 breathtakingly refreshing, clean and vibrant with alternating smoke and juicy barley waves; f23 long, a slow building of oils and a little bourbony liquorice adding lustre; b23 don't you just love it when whisky is this damned simple... 55%. Scotch Malt Whisky Society. 256 bottles.

Scotch Malt Whisky Society Cask 53.137 Aged 17 Years refill hogshead, dist Jan 92 (79) n20 t22 f18.5 b19.5. Pleasantish - soft. But, frankly, a little dull... 56.2%. Scotch Malt Whisky Society. 284 bottles.

Scotch Malt Whisky Society Cask 53.139 Aged 27 Years refill hogshead, dist Feb 82 (95) n24 the smoke appears to have given up any attempt at the macho stuff and acceded to the graceful and dulcet tones of lightly honeyed vanilla and toffee apple; on a deeper level you can find some earthier notes with a tantalising hint of cucumber; t24 a beautiful natural fudge delves into the smoke at regular intervals ensuring a delicate layering of sugared barley amid the peat; every facet to this is rounded and elegant and even the spices - which descend about a third of the way in - are on tip-top behaviour; f23.5 every bit as graceful as all that has gone before with a gentle, artful mocha attaching to the dying rays of the peat; b23.5 the stuff of whisky genius... 55.2%. Scotch Malt Whisky Society. 256 bottles.

Scotch Malt Whisky Society Cask 53.141 Aged 20 Years refill hogshead, dist Dec 89 (94) n24 fabulous multi-dimensional nose: ultra-ripe greengages meet bananas head on; elsewhere, several layers of barley offer gristy sugars and the most delicate smoke notes: sublime... t23.5 every bit as fresh and invigorating as the nose promises with an initial soft barley introduction, then wave upon wave of Demerara, followed by hickory-tipped phenols; f23.5 so long, yet proudly continues along the same complexly smoked lines, always with a hint of something citrusy up its sleeve...; b23 a spot on barrel: the type you dream of from this distillery...but so rarely find. 52%. Scotch Malt Whisky Society. 259 bottles.

⠿ **Scotch Malt Whisky Society Cask 53.142 Aged 20 Years** refill hogshead, cask no. 5427, dist 1989 (89.5) n22 plenty of banana in the peaty mix; t22.5 lightly oiled but the barley powers through. The smoke is a delightful backdrop; f22.5 some coffee and cocoa amid the vanilla and phenols; b22.5 a relaxed bottling which wears its 20 years with ease. Attractively delicate throughout. 55.9%. sc. 209 bottles.

⠿ **Scotch Malt Whisky Society Cask 53.146 Aged 17 Years** refill sherry butt, cask no. 10904, dist 1993 (85) n21 t22 f21 b21. The barley is pugnacious and juicy. But shows minimal complexity and development for its age. 60.9%. sc. 553 bottles.

⠿ **Scotch Malt Whisky Society Cask 53.148 Aged 10 Years** refill hogshead, cask no. 310827, dist 1999 (84.5) n22 t21.5 f20 b21. Big on alcohol, limited on depth and development. 66.1%. sc. 271 bottles.

⠿ **Scotch Malt Whisky Society Cask 53.152 Aged 14 Years** refill hogshead, cask no. 2757, dist 1997 (89) n22 light and distinctly citrusy; t22.5 clean and exceptionally salivating; f22.5 a light smokiness accompanies the persistent citrus; b22 almost purifies the palate: not something said too often about a Caol Ila... 57.7%. sc. 291 bottles.

The Scotch Single Malt Circle Caol Ila 1982 cask no. 2724, dist Apr 82, bott Oct 08 (94) n23.5 t24 f23 b23.5. Hardly one for those with a heart condition. Big, rousing. Beautifully made and matured.And bloody delicious. 62.7%. German market.

⠿ **Scott's Selection Caol Ila 1981** bott 2011 (74) n19 t19 f18 b18. The huge smoke does all in its power to overcome the weakness of the oak. In the end, an unequal struggle. 61.7%. Speyside Distillers.

Scott's Selection Caol Ila 1982 bott 2008 (86) n23 t21.5 f21 b21. The nose gets top billing where the smoke churns out with a sweet, Madeira cake twist. The remainder, though, is reduced by tired, burnt, toasty oak. 60.6%. Speyside Distillers.

Scott's Selection Caol Ila 1982 bott 2008 (76.5) n20 t19.5 f18 b19. Oily and austere, despite the smoke and strength. 61.2%. Speyside Distillers.

⠿ **Single Cask Collection Caol Ila Aged 10 Years** bourbon hogshead, cask no. 309889, dist Nov 00, bott Feb 11 (94) n23.5 fizzing, thick peat. But enough grist and top spin to make for something stirring; the oak engineers a surprising early cocoa and liquorice sub plot...wow!! t24 superb delivery. Helped monumentally by the usual lack of oil, allowing the peat and rich sugars unrestricted access to the taste buds; f23 some natural caramels dull things slightly. But the smoke and spices roll on...; b23.5 a quite superb, beautifully above average bottling which works on countless levels. 58.5%. nc ncf sc. Single Cask Collection. 235 bottles.

⇛ **Single Cask Collection Caol Ila Aged 27 Years** sherry butt, cask no. 3623, dist May 83, bott Sep 10 **(88.5)** n22.5 succulent grape, lightly seasoned with allspice...and peat; t23 soft to the point of dissolving on the palate like a sugar candy: plenty of over-ripe greengage amid the spice; f20.5 bitters out slightly disappointingly; b22.5 overall, a sound butt allowing the grape to cohabit comfortably with the peat: not the most common of phenomena. 51.5%. nc ncf sc. Single Cask Collection. 64 bottles.

The Whisky Agency Caol Ila 26 Year Old dist 1982, bott 2009 **(85.5)** n21 t22 f21 b21.5. Softly oiled, lightly smoked and very pleasant without ever bothering about complexity. 63%

The Whisky Agency Caol Ila 27 Year Old dist 1982, bott 2009 **(87)** n21 t23 f21 b22. This one was probably on the way down and was plucked from the cask in the nick of time. Some great moments, but a few dodgy ones too. 62.4%. The Whisky Agency, Germany.

The Whisky Agency Caol Ila 27 Year Old Rum Finish dist 1982, bott 2009 **(80.5)** n20 t21 f19.5 b20. A disappointingly tart, closed and very average bottling from this normally first-class bottler. 50%. The Whisky Agency, Germany.

⇛ **The Whisky Agency Caol Ila 1979** bourbon hogshead, bott 2011 **(89.5)** n22.5 some serious oaky age mingles with the fading smoke; t23.5 no doubting the great vintage. But the delivery and its immediate aftermath is truly gorgeous: somehow a shimmering malty juiciness thrives and is met not just by a spiced smokiness but also a build up in barley intensity which defies belief; f21.5 just a little shine falls from the lustre as the oak offers up a telling tang; b22 shows many a sign of great age. But worth finding for the astonishing delivery alone. 52%. The Whisky Agency.

Whisky Doris Caol Ila 1992 dist 1992, bott 2009 **(85.5)** n22 t21 f21.5 b21. A very pleasant, medium- sweet and safe Caol Ila which doesn't overly depend on its natural oils and accentuates some gristy qualities. 46%

Wilson & Morgan Barrel Selection Caol Ila Aged 20 Years dist 1988, bott 2008 **(76)** n19 t20 f18 b19. You know that grating sound when the bagpipes first start up? Yep, as off key as that... 46%

Wilson & Morgan Barrel Selection Caol Ila 20 Years Old cask no. 4224/4225, dist 1988, bott 2008 **(90.5)** n23 how soft can a full-bodied peatiness be? The sub plot of lilacs helps...; t22.5 elegant and delicate, the soft coating of Demerara blends superbly with the billowing smoke; f22.5 light spices and a touch of cocoa trumpets the playfully oaky finale; b22.5 absolutely charming. 46%. Wilson & Morgan.

Wilson & Morgan Barrel Selection Caol Ila 25 Years Old cask no. 3133, dist 1984, bott 2009 **(89)** n23 some really sexy milk chocolate mixes in with a cut-grass freshness which is unusual for a Caol Ila. Actually, rather than newly cut grass, think the stuff that dried out in the sun for a few days to make hay... t22.5 sweet, surprisingly juicy, barley barely troubled by smoke; f21.5 the oak makes a drying entry; b22 a dram that's making hay in many ways... 46%. Wilson & Morgan.

Wilson & Morgan Barrel Selection Caol Ila 1995 refill butt, bott 2008 **(87)** n22 t22.5 f21 b21.5. For those who like their peat to tease them... 46%

⇛ **Wilson & Morgan Barrel Selection Caol Ila 1998 Limited Edition** cask no. 10729-38, dist 2010 **(79)** n19 t21.5 f18.5 b20. From the stridently oily school of Caol Ilas. Some profound bitterness evident. 48%. Wilson & Morgan.

Wilson & Morgan Barrel Selection Caol Ila 2000 cask no. 310262/310269, dist 2000, bott 2010 **(87.7)** n22 peat and mocha in dapper doses; t22 juicy, young with a developing sweet lemon character; f21.5 oaks out quietly; the smoke remains shy; b22 steady, clean and delicate. 48%. Wilson & Morgan, Limited Edition.

CAPERDONICH

Speyside, 1898. Chivas Brothers. Closed.

Connoisseurs Choice Caperdonich 1972 (83) n20.5 t18 f22.5 b20. A very strange creature, this: a kind of topsy-turvy dram which actually repairs itself after apparently being inflicted by fatal oaky damage. The initial intensity of the oak is such that you actually close your eyes and shudder. But so good is the sherry that the grape softens the blow to the extent that a beautiful mocha finish makes you just about purr. A real oddity...and not without moments of magic. 46%. Gordon & MacPhail.

Connoisseurs Choice Caperdonich 1994 (88) n22 pretty clean barley with a blancmange and floral subplot; t22.5 perfectly attractive, juicy malt with myriad levels of sugar and light oak **f21.5** light and sawdust-like but still enough lingering barley to make a impact; **b22** an unusual Caper, as this one appears to have the guts to go the distance. Quality. 46%

Duncan Taylor Collection Caperdonich 1970 cask no. 4376 **(84.5) n22 t21.5 f21 b20.** A drowsy ride along barley sewn on oaky ground. 42.3%

Duncan Taylor Collection Caperdonich 1970 cask no. 4377 **(86.5) n21.5 t22.5 f21.5 b21.** Punchier, weightier, tellingly more intense than 4376 and for a while a real malty treat. But still the complexity is at a premium and we are finding Caper at its most simplistic and undemanding, taking into account the whisky's great age. Some flakes of chocolate do help at the end. 45.9%

Duncan Taylor Collection Caperdonich 1970 cask no. 4381 **(82.5) n20 t21 f21.5 b20.** Some sharp barley and waxy vanilla, but you get the feeling this was once a hot whisky, which may explain the limited development on its sister casks. 46.8%

Duncan Taylor Collection Caperdonich 1972 cask no. 3246 **(94) n24 t23 f24 b23.** Any number of distilleries reach the "exotic fruit" stage of old age, but none seem to master the genre with such panache as Caper. What a treat! 46.5%

⋙ **Duncan Taylor Caperdonich 1972** bott Sep 10, cask no. 6735 **(78) n19 t19 f20 b20.** Puckering... 51.4%. Duncan Taylor & Co.

Duncan Taylor Collection Caperdonich 1972 cask no. 7421 **(87) n22.5 t22.5 f21 b21.** Oooh, so borderline!! I have given this one the benefit of the doubt. The march of the oak towards the late middle and finish is relentless. 55.6%

Duncan Taylor Collection Caperdonich 1972 cask no. 7422 **(94) n23.5 t24 f23 b23.5.** Tasted against its sister cask, 7421, here is a display of how one barrel can absorb the years and come out positively gleaming, while the other is tarnished and hanging on to its fading beauty grimly. This is truly stunning malt. 54.8%

Duncan Taylor Collection Caperdonich 1972 cask no. 7449 **(81) n21 t22 f18.5 b19.5.** Old Capers – especially from this bottler - have in recent years shown an astonishing beauty once the tell-tale exotic fruit kicks in. This one bears all the hallmarks of a whisky which has gone through the back of greatness, with those fruits now faded and much drier, more substantial – and unforgiving – oak taking its place. The first few bars of the delivery, though, remains a definite treat. 47.8%. Duncan Taylor & Co Ltd.

Lonach Caperdonich 1969 **(83.5) n22 t21 f20 b20.5.** Curious. Nothing like the famed ancient Caper fruitfest I imagined I'd get. Instead, we have a malt which has been submerged in oak, but has retained enough oxygen in the form of barley to keep alive. Just. 42.4%

⋙ **Malts Of Scotland Caperdonich 1972** sherry hogshead, cask no. 1144, dist Oct 72, bott Mar 11 **(91) n21** a bit of a train wreck; oaky splinters everywhere and some hybrid bourbon notes despite the fruity undertone; **t22.5** at first the taste buds are rushed head on by a bizarre legion of kamikaze oak. Then, in the matter of a nanosecond, the fuss ends and a clearer picture of salivating honey and barley emerges. As this comes more into focus, a very soft smokiness drifts over the scene and butterscotch fills the middle ground; **f24** no OTT oak now. A beautifully serene fade of butterscotch tart and light honey and even some traces of Melton Mowbray Hunt cake; **b23.5** at times looks as though done for by the oak. But salvaged in impressive fashion by the steady input of honey and raisin. Just gets better and better as it goes along. 57.4%. sc. Malts Of Scotland.

⋙ **Malts Of Scotland Caperdonich 1972** sherry hogshead, cask no. 1145, dist Oct 72, bott Mar 11 **(81.5) n20.5 t19 f21 b21.** Never comes close to matching the brilliance of its sister cask, 1144. Goes into the same oaky dive, but is unable to pull out in sufficient time. 52.4%. sc.

Matisse Caperdonich 1972 Highland Single Malt bott Jul 09 **(94.5) n23.5** soft exotic fruit, but over ripened gooseberries enjoy equal star billing; **t24** the whisky spiders have been busy producing the finest silk from sugar almond barley touched by acacia honey; **f23.5** an almost inevitable mocha to this with golden syrup and malt shake add the lingering sweetnes; **b23.5** sometimes these exotic fruit types are a bit of a let down; others are the very reason why whisky was invented. This, comfortably, falls into the latter. 47.5%

Matisse Caperdonich 1972 Highland Single Malt cask no. 7447, bott Jul 09 **(92.5) n24** battling sharpness: almost kiwi fruity, but sweetened by lime and liquorice; **t23.5** again, an immediate impact which brings a tear to the eye: barley in concentrate form; the oak is sugared vanilla pods; citrus abounds; **f22.5** after all that work, no wonder it begins to feel tired; **b22.5** a more aggressive version of that 47.5% cask. In your face, but pays the price in sophistication. Fabulous, though! 50.5%. Matisse Spirits Co Ltd.

Matisse Caperdonich 1972 Highland Single Malt cask no. 7448, bott Jul 09 **(95) n24** inevitable exotic fruit, rather simplistic other than the extra spices; a surprising puff of something peaty; **t24** good grief! I wasn't joking about the spices on the nose as they seer into the palate without asking for an invite; the barley is clean, rich and salivating with sugared almonds and vanilla filling the middle ground; **f23.5** elegant with a slow denouement of light smoke and golden syrup; **b23.5** I've said it before and I'll say it again: had Caper been half this quality a malt when in its vital three to five years, it wouldn't now be part of a copper works. The most sophisticated of Matisse's three exceptional casks. *49.7%. Matisse Spirits Co Ltd.*

⟡ **Octave Caperdonich 38 Years Old** dist 1972, cask no. 414293 **(94)** **n23.5** spellbinding blend of medium roast Java and kumquat. Here, though, salt appears to be added, rather than sugar...; **t24** genuinely impressed: the delivery has the unusual distinction of being both firm and oily at once. The levels of tannin, leavened by hickory and molasses, are as complex as they are impressive; some real bite despite the lightness of touch to the biscuit barley; **f23** takes a more genteel spiced vanilla route back home; **b23.5** an unusual old Caper, as this one has not gone down the famous exotic route it usually prefers to take. Instead, a high dose of extra high-quality oak has moved it along a more cocoa enriched path which suits it well. Top draw Caper with not a single shred of evidence pointing towards degenerative aging, despite the oak having a big say... *52.5%. sc. Duncan Taylor & Co.*

⟡ **Old Malt Cask Caperdonich 28 Years Old** refill hogshead, cask no. 6623, dist Jun 82, bott Sep 10 **(69)** **n18 t18 f16 b17**. Had all this late distillery's output been this bad, I would have turned up with a ball and chain myself... Curious that an anagram of the letters found between the C and the H in Caperdonich is: "I Done Crap"... *50%. nc ncf sc. 310 bottles.*

Provenance Caperdonich Aged 12 Years refill hogshead, dist Spring 96, bott Winter 08 **(81.5)** **n22 t20.5 f20 b19**. An uncommon Caper at this age, but a good example of a malt which flatters to deceive – and why the owners despaired so. The under-ripe greengage nose is attractive but the thinness of the body underwhelms. *46%. Douglas Laing.*

Provenance Caperdonich Over 12 Years refill hogshead no. DMG 5569, dist Spring 97, bott Autumn 09 **(85)** **n22.5 t21.5 f20 b21**. While it might be fair to say that this, as Caper has a tendency to do, lacks substance; what it does do, it does very well. The barley is light and precise, the malt dissolving before being able to take the complexity much further. But, for all that, a refreshing dram for an early part of the day and better for its age than much of the stuff that came from this distillery over the previous three decades. By coincidence, the day before I tasted this I happened to see part of the distillery dismantled. Sad. *46%. Douglas Laing.*

⟡ **Rarest Of The Rare Caperdonich 38 Years Old** dist 1972, cask no. 7461 **(91.5)** **n22** plenty of red liquorice and hickory sets this on a bourbon footing; **t23** the oak certainly makes an early song and dance, but the light honeycomb and golden syrup completes an excellent balancing job; **f23** again the oak is profound..and yet again there is sugars enough to ensure equilibrium... and even allow a few juicy barley notes to be heard at the very end: impressive; **b23.5** plenty of feel good factor. One for the sweet toothed amongst us. *54.6%. sc. Duncan Taylor & Co.*

⟡ **Scotch Malt Whisky Society Cask 38.20 Aged 16 Years** refill hogshead, cask no. 64211, dist 1994 **(83)** **n20 t22 f20.5 b20.5**. Huge, clean juicy barley distilled in a bit of a rush. Hot, intense and invigorating, it is fascinating as a Caper but does little to set the pulse racing in the Great Whisky Scheme of things. *57.4%. sc. 254 bottles.*

Whisky Doris Caperdonich 36 Year Old cask no. 7425, dist Nov 72, bott Feb 09 **(89.5)** **n22 t22.5 f23 b22**. A must for lovers of Crunchie bars or just those with a sweet tooth who like to chew the toothpicks. *54.4%*

The Whisky Fair Caperdonich 1972 refill sherry hogshead, dist Nov 72, bott Aug 08 **(93.5)** **n22.5 t24 f23 b24** Just fantastic... *48.3%*

CARDHU
Speyside, 1824. Diageo. Working.
Cardhu 12 Years Old db **(83)** **n22 t22 f18 b21**. What appears to be a small change in the wood profile has resulted in a big shift in personality. What was once a guaranteed malt love-in is now a drier, oakier, fruitier affair. Sadly, though, with more than a touch of something furry. *40%* ⊙⊙

CLYNELISH
Highlands (Northern), 1968. Diageo. Working.
Clynelish Aged 15 Years "The Distillers Edition" double matured in oloroso-seco casks CI-Br: 169-1f, bott code L6264CM000 03847665, dist 1991, bott 2006 db **(79)** **n20 t20 f19 b20**. Big in places, distinctly oily in others but the overall feel is of a potentially brilliant whisky matured in unsympathetic barrels. *46%*

Clynelish The Manager's Choice first fill bourbon American oak, cask no. 4341, dist 1997, bott 2009 db **(90.5)** **n22.5** friendly barley which is both intense and relaxed but the oak is a little uptight by sending out some major natural caramels; **t23** puckeringly sharp barley helped by breathtakingly clean oak. A little spice nip, but simply underlines the barley's credentials; **f22.5** custardy vanilla but still it is the barley which dominates with a profound clarity; **b22.5**

excellent cask selection. Everything is geared towards accentuation the untarnished richness of the malt. *58.5%. 232 bottles.*

A.D. Rattray Clynelish 1997 cask no. 4664, dist Apr 97, bott Dec 09 **(87)** n22 dry custard tart...with the emphasis on the tart; t22 a light honey topping to the delicate barley-vanilla; f21.5 mildly bitters; b21.5 a very pleasant sheen throughout. *594%. A.D. Rattray Ltd.*

⠶ **Adelphi Clynelish 14 Years Old** cask no. 4715, dist 1997, bott 2011 **(95)** n24.5 imagine concentrated butterscotch on a slightly overcooked pastry; you then find a lime, a kiwifruit and a physalis...you mix the juices together and pour onto the tart. And then, just to send your senses to another plane, take the richer elements of the kind of honeycomb and hickory found in the finest bourbons...and stir in gently...oh...my...god...!!! t24.5 so many whiskies with a great nose are a let down on delivery: not this one, buster! Near perfect weight and oil involvement makes for an entrance which borders on the sublime. A cross section of Demerara and muscovado sugar combine with watered-down dark treacle to take on the spices head to head. It is a near perfect match, though elsewhere the barley even manages to say a juicy 'hullo' and the honeycomb shines; f22 huge vanilla. But the spices keep warbling; b24 Adelphi are impressing me with a number of their bottlings right now. And this is another that is to be hunted down at all costs. *59.5%. sc. Adelphi Distillery. 247 bottles.*

⠶ **Berry's Own Selection Clynelish 1997** cask no. 4706, bott 2010 **(96.5)** n24 a fruit shop on a warm day in southern France. You almost expect to hear wasps in the background...; bananas and exploding greengages abound. But rather than wasps, you get spicy bees, as a little spiced honey goes a long way...; t24 does whisky arrive on the palate in any better shape than this? Perhaps only a layer of caramel, blunting some of the more complex notes, prevents a perfect score here. Instead, you have to deal with enough spices to keep a Moroccan market going for a month, and a whiole string of varying honey and barley notes which ying and yang from one side of the palate to the other; f23.5 downgrades to merely brilliant on the finale with a disappointing number of fabulous oak and fruit notes turning into a banana and custard dessert from heaven. Blast! I was hoping for so much more...; b24 absolutely everything you can ask from this distillery at this age and from this type of cask. Taste this without sighing...I challenge you..! One of the whiskies of this and many a year. *56.8%. nc ncf sc. Berry Bros & Rudd.*

Cadenhead's Authentic Collection Clynelish 1993 bott Feb 10 **(86)** n21 t22 f21.5 b21.5. Very enjoyable malt, though sharp and citrusy by Clynelish standards. Just a bit of attitude from the cask, I feel... *56.8%. Wm. Cadenhead Ltd. 315 bottles.*

The Cárn Mór Vintage Collection Clynelish 2003 hogshead, cask no. 2223, dist 2003, bott 2009 **(78.5)** n22 t20 f18 b18.5. Lovely nose but all the signs of a cask that would add little in 60 years, let alone six... *46%. The Scottish Liqueur Centre.*

Connoisseurs Choice Clynelish 1994 **(85.5)** n21.5 t22 f21 b21. Pleasingly dry with the odd honeyed note quickly counter-balanced. *43%. Gordon & MacPhail.*

Dun Bheagan Clynelish 13 Years Old hogshead **(79)** n20 t21 f19 b19. Some pleasant shards of honey and butterscotch cannot disguise the relatively hot nature of this one. *46%*

Dun Bheagan Clynelish Aged 17 Years butt, dist Dec 90 **(89)** n23.5 t23 f21 b22.5. There is no silencing a fine distillery and here it crows effortlessly. Beautiful. *46%*

Duthies Clynelish 14 Years Old (74) n17 t19 f18 b18. The nose is a good indicator of what is to follow. *46%. Wm. Cadenhead Ltd.*

Finest Whisky Clynelish 37 Years Old 80 Proof **(89.5)** n22.5 stewed rhubarb in thick custard; t23.5 early wave of fresh barley followed by a thick, but short-lived puff of peat; the middle ground is coffee-cream biscuit with a firm sugary lip; f22 an aged sheen to this with the barley remaining crunchy and firm; b21.5 no doubting its antiquity. Hangs on stoically against the gathering oaks and has plenty in reserve. *46%. Speciality Drinks Ltd. Bottled for The Whisky Exchange's 10th Anniversary.*

The Golden Cask Clynelish 1997 cask no. CM146, bott 2009 **(91)** n22 dry oak amid the honey; t23 superb delivery: some waspish oak-spice livens up the butterscotch and vanilla middle; f22.5 mocha and plenty more oak; b22.5 has aged ahead of its time. But the result is a lively treat. *58.2%. The House of MacDuff. 255 bottles.*

Gordon & MacPhail Cask Strength Clynelish 1997 (91.5) n23 t22.5 f23 b23. Plenty of class and more age than you would expect. *59.7%*

James MacArthur's Fine Malt Selection Clynelish Aged 12 Years cask no. 11828, bott May 10 **(94)** n24 spot-on nose: a light citrus note melts into the Summer garden lavender ...one of the most exquisite perfumes for any malt aroma this year. Delicate butterscotch represents the understated oak; t23 very clever: all kinds of fresh fruit and barley notes, but none of them sweet. The oak forms a drier boundary inside which there are numerous juicy elements, but none really pushing it with the sugars: a rare case of being malty, but without the usual barley water effect; **f23** elongated by a soft oil, a return of the pastry-dominant butterscotch but an intense and tapering barley; **b24** an excellent cask from a fabulous and still under-rated distillery: not a single hint of bitterness, yet no OTT sweetness, either. Of a style once common, now a bit of a rarity these days. 45%. MacArthur & Co Ltd for the USA market.

Kingsbury's "The Selection" Clynelish 7 Years Old 1999 (81.5) **n20 t21 f20 b20.5**. Fresh, malty, uncomplex. 43%. Japan Import System.

Lombard's Jewels of Scotland Clynelish 1982 Aged 21 Years (88) **n21 t23 f22 b22**. A busy and quite joyous bottling. 50%. Lombard Brands.

Malts of Scotland Clynelish 1982 bourbon hogshead no. 5895, dist Dec 82, bott Jan 10 (91) **n22.5** hardly surprising this is from a bourbon barrel: bourbon is perhaps the main theme. Toasty and full of Demerara rum and hickory notes; **t23.5** those sugary notes really pound through, meeting the unforgiving barley with a whack. Salivating early on then a subtle wave of spice as the oak thuds home; **f22.5** back to the hickory and a touch of liquorice, too. How wonderfully bourbony...in a malty kind of way...; **b22.5** uncompromisingly delicious. 51.5%. Malts of Scotland. 192 bottles.

Malts of Scotland Clynelish 1996 sherry butt no. 8245, dist Oct 96, bott Mar 09 (69) **n17.5 t17.5 f17 b17**. I remember the day this was distilled very well: it was my son James' 10th birthday. Sadly, the spirit was filled into a less than memorable cask. 58.1%. 96 bottles.

Norse Cask Selection Clynelish 1995 Aged 12 Years sherry butt no. 12773, dist Dec 95, bott Nov 08 (69) **n17.5 t18.5 f16 b17**. Sulphured. 57.3%. Qualityworld for WhiskyOwner.com.

⁙ **Old Malt Cask Clynelish 13 Years Old** refill hogshead, cask no. 6055, dist Apr 97, bott Apr 10 (86.5) **n21 t22 f22 b21.5**. Surprisingly simplistic for a Clynelish. But while little it does, it does with effortless charm. 50%. nc ncf sc. Douglas Laing & Co. 343 bottles.

Old Malt Cask Clynelish Aged 14 Years refill hogshead no. DL 5724, dist Jun 95, bott Jan 10 (81) **n21 t22 f18 b20**. Malts as underdeveloped for its age as this tend to be all upfront on delivery and struggle on the finish. This one is true to type. 50%. Douglas Laing & Co Ltd.

Old Malt Cask Clynelish Aged 20 Years bott 2009 (92.5) **n22 t23 f24 b23.5**. An excellent must-have example of typically classy from this great distillery. 50%. Douglas Laing.

⁙ **Old Malt Cask Clynelish Aged 21 Years** refill hogshead, cask no. 6939, dist Jan 90, bott Feb 11 (90.5) **n22.5** teasing citrus and vanilla with the lightest smattering of spice and an even more deft hint of smoke; **t23.5** juicy lime and tangerine blend; the middle confirms the spicy smoke on the nose; **f22** light oils plus a touch of caramel-chocolate; **b22.5** delicate and delicious. 50%. nc ncf sc. Douglas Laing & Co. 265 bottles.

Old Malt Cask Clynelish Aged 38 Years refill hogshead, dist Mar 71, bott Mar 09 (91) **n23 t23.5 f22 b22.5**. An absolute class act which grows on you with every single, ultra-complex mouthful. Unusually, the obvious age wrinkles somehow add to the charm. 47.9%. 145 bottles.

⁙ **Old Masters Clynelish 13 Years Old** cask no. 4643, dist 1997, bott Sep 10 (92) **n23** zesty and packed with honey notes. Just a slight hint of bigger oak than usual for the age; a molecule or two of smoke, too; **t23.5** gorgeously fresh honey but again the oak has an essence of pine feel; the malt is powerful enough to bounce back; that smoke thinks it's got away without being spotted...but failed...; **f22.5** milky cocoa topped with melt-in-the-mouth icing sugar; **b23** brimming with all the honeyed beauty you might expect from this sublime distillery. A real, top-class bottling. 52.1%. sc. James MacArthur & Co.

Provenance Clynelish Over 10 Years refill hogshead no. DMG 5236, dist Autumn 98, bott Summer 09 (92.5) **n23** porridge topped with melting brown sugar; some coal dust hangs around; **t23.5** always fresh and energetic on the palate without ever going on the attack: the barley is duo-toned with a wonderful interplay between crisp barley and an altogether more yielding maltiness; **f23** dries as the oak makes its polite and elegant entry; something lightly smoked simmers in the background; **b23** shows what an excellent malt can do in a less than excellent cask. 46%. Douglas Laing & Co Ltd.

Provenance Clynelish Over 12 Years refill hogshead no. DMG 5609, dist Autumn 97, bott Autumn 09 (84.5) **n22 t21 f20.5 b21**. Unusual degree of citrus for the distillery. 46%

Provenance Clynelish Over 12 Years refill hogshead, cask no. 6057, dist Spring 98, bott Spring 2010 (92.5) **n23** lemon squeezed on honey-sweetened pancakes; **t23.5** clean barley, light and sensuously juicy; **f23** more citrus as the vanilla adds weight. Clean and very classy; **b23** a dream of a bottling revealing unambiguously through the medium of a well used but intact cask the distillery's brilliance. The citrus here combines with the honey quite charmingly but there is always that richer, bigger, more complex picture. 46%

Scotch Malt Whisky Society Cask 26.62 Aged 26 Years refill hogshead, dist May 83 (92) **n23** an attractive combination of over-ripe tangerine and delicate smoke; **t23** a chunky, big-bodied delivery with shards of Demerara sugar ducking and weaving with the thin smoke cloud; **f23.5** the smoke lingers as late spice and latte arrives; **b22.5** sounds odd, I know, but there is a touch of blue fruit mould, especially to nose and delivery, to this...but it's actually attractive and sits with the gentle smoke very comfortably. 55%. 155 bottles.

Scotch Malt Whisky Society Cask 26.63 Aged 12 Years refill butt, dist Oct 96 (85.5) n22.5 t22.5 f19.5 b21. Fabulous nose: not entirely unlike the inside of a fruit-scented wooden trinket box. The delivery briefly sparkles but the finish is sub-prime. 54.9%. 580 bottles.

Scotch Malt Whisky Society Cask 26.67 Aged 25 Years refill sherry butt, dist Dec 84 (86.5) n21.5 t22 f21 b22. The oak makes some heavy demands which the barley just about resists. But at times it's touch-and-go. 48.9%. Scotch Malt Whisky Society. 60 bottles.

❖ **Scotch Malt Whisky Society Cask 26.69 Aged 10 Years** refill bourbon hogshead, cask no. 51, dist 2000 (84) n20 t22.5 f20.5 b21. Clean, juicy barley but strictly limited. Even for a great distillery such as Clynelish, you need good oak to flourish. 57%. sc. 252 bottles.

❖ **Scotch Malt Whisky Society Cask 26.73 Aged 15 Years** refill sherry butt, cask no. 6117, dist 1995 (74.5) n18 t18 f19 b18.5. Weird. At times shows outlines of the Fisherman's Friend character better known at Bowmore...but without the peat. Really would like to know why this was bottled. 55%. sc. 283 bottles.

❖ **Scotch Malt Whisky Society Cask 26.77 Aged 27 Years** 2nd fill hogshead, cask no. 2584, dist 1983 (86.5) n22 t22 f21 b21.5. Lots of ticks, but few gold stars. A sound dram with a touch of nip and aggression. But the oak is a little lopsided and the resulting caramels are laid on thick. 55.1%. sc. 204 bottles.

❖ **Scotch Malt Whisky Society Cask 26.80 Aged 19 Years** 2nd fill hogshead, cask no. 4435, dist 1992 (90.5) n22 a major injection of oak sits comfortably with the sturdy barley. Usually there is some honey around, though here it is in delicate amounts outweighed by the citrus; t22.5 fabulous tannins add instant spice while a tart, mildly eye-watering and shrill honey-sugar note rips into any drier vanillas; f23 settles impressively with those spices still radiating and the tannins heading towards Kentucky. But it is the clever interplay with those sugars which really hit the high spots; b23 I was beginning to wonder if the SMWS were losing their touch slightly with distillery 26. But, at last, a sample which is busy and challenging and absolutely brimming with all the right stuff. Hurrah! 53%. sc. 97 bottles.

The Scotch Single Malt Circle Clynelish 1995 cask no. 12780, dist Sep 95, bott Aug 08 (88) n21 t23 f22 b22. Impressive, well-made malt with a particularly well-balanced entry. 60.6%. German market.

The Whisky Agency Clynelish 14 Years Old dist 1995, bott 2010 (88) n21.5 fruity, a light dab of coal smoke and oak; t22.5 salivating marmalade and manuka honey; f22 more fruity sugars with a surprising lack of age; b22 great fun: get the feeling this one is still warming up. 48%

The Whisky Agency Clynelish 27 Year Old dist 1982, bott 2009 (90) n22 t22.5 f22 b22.5. Holds its age stupendously: like a Highland Park without the peat. 53.9%

❖ **The Whisky Agency Clynelish 1972** sherry cask (86) n21 t23.5 f20 b21.5. In over 30-odd years, I can count the number of times I have seen Clynelish in this ultra sherry state on one hand. Pretty shagged out, but worth finding to extend your whisky knowledge, alone. 45.8%

Wilson & Morgan Barrel Selection Clynelish Aged 12 Years marsala finish, dist 1996, bott 2008 (84.5) n23 t21.5 f19 b21. Wow...!! Well, that's different. This is quite massive with about as much prickle as you might find at a porcupine convention. There has been a touch of sulphur involved somewhere, but the sulphur stick must have passed through like and an express as the damage is manageable. The nose is just one salivating chorus of sultana fruitcake and the intensity on the palate is something else besides. The marauding chocolate later on is pretty telling, too. For those who never detect sulphur, or perhaps even like it, you might mark this one well in the 90s... 58.6%

❖ **Wilson & Morgan Barrel Selection Clynelish 1995 Sherry Finish** bott 2010 (73.5) n17 t21.5 f17 b18. Here's a good example why the two words "finish" and "sherry" make me shudder when rearranged and placed side-by-side. The tragedy is that this was obviously a sublime cask before its fate was sealed in the sherry butt. 46%. Wilson & Morgan.

Wilson & Morgan Barrel Selection Clynelish 1996 bott 2008 (79.5) n20.5 t20 f19 b20. Dry, occasionally to the point of austerity, and locates far too many cul-de-sacs. 46%

COLEBURN

Speyside, 1897–1985. Diageo. Closed.

Connoisseurs Choice Coleburn 1981 (81) n21 t21 f19 b20. Usual thin, hot stuff from Coleburn but benefits from a big malt kick. Way above the norm. 43%

The Whisky Agency Coleburn 26 Year Old dist 1983, bott 2009 (88.5) n22 t23 f21.5 b22. Coleburn is a rare whisky. A thoroughly enjoyable Coleburn is rarer still. So here's one you've just got to go and track down... 49.5%. The Whisky Agency, Germany.

CONVALMORE
Speyside, 1894–1985. William Grant & Sons. Closed.
Convalmore 1977 bott 2005 db **(91)** n23 t23 f22 b23. Must be blended with Botox, as there is no detrimental ageing to either nose or delivery. A quite lovely and charming whisky to remember this lost – and extremely rare - distillery by. 57.9%. 3900 bottles.

Connoisseurs Choice Convalmore 1984 (88.5) n23 t22 f21 b22.5. One of the younger Convanmores to have found its way on the market of late, having been distilled shortly before its fatal closure. This is crisper than older expressions, yet celebrates the finesse so often found from the older versions. An historic treat. 43%. Gordon & MacPhail.

Rare Old Convalmore 1975 (96) n24.5 that coal dust character which pops up in this distillery from time to time is more evident than usual here and works pretty well with the watery kiwi fruit and greengage tart; a sprig of lavender pays homage to the oak; one of the great noses of the year...; **t24** wow!! A real sprinkling of light peat, clearer than usual, adds a lovely weight to the surprisingly agile barley which sets the ball rolling; there is also the most delicate of spicy threads imaginable, too; **f23** the light peaty dusting continues and dovetails well with the drier vanillas and spices; husky barley ensures an improbable freshness; **b24.5** a caressing, ambient dram: certainly shows great age but does it in a style and manner which demands total respect. A true classic and yet another example of a distillery lost to us hitting heights of which other can only dream. 43%. Gordon & MacPhail.

CRAGGANMORE
Speyside, 1870. Diageo. Working.
Cragganmore Aged 12 Years db **(81.5)** n20 t21 f20 b20.5. I have a dozen bottles of Cragganmore in my personal cellar dating from the early 90s when the distillery was first bottled as a Classic Malt. Their astonishing dexterity and charm, their naked celebration of all things Speyside, casts a sad shadow over this drinkable but drab and instantly forgettable expression. 40%

Cragganmore Aged 14 Years The Distillers Edition finished in port casks, dist 1993, bott 2007 db **(85)** n22 t21 f21 b21. The tightly closed fruit on the palate doesn't quite match the more expansive and complex nose. 40%

⸬ **Cragganmore Special Release 2010 21 Years Old** refill American oak, dist 1989 db **(95.5)** n23.5 huge age, but the close knitted nature of the clean barley ensures all the strength required to keep the oak in check; the odd pine-laden tannin and even a touch of pineapple and honeydew melon gives the nod towards something a little exotic; **t24** you can ask little more from a Speyside-style delivery at this age and from bourbon. The barley is so wholesome and well integrated that the palate goes into immediate barley-juice overdrive; the oaks offer up some half-hearted cocoa but some full blown molasses. The result is a single malt of unstinting enormity, yet unambiguous magnificence; **f23.5** some light liquorice joins forces with the cocoa and molasses to underline the bourbon credentials. Massive age, the odd creak here and there. But never for a second is the quality breeched; **b24.5** what a fascinating, awe-inspiring dram. More or less at the very time this malt was being made, I remember talking to the manager at the then barely known Speyside distillery. He told me that the new Classic Malt 12-year-old was selected at that age because it was felt that, as a singleton (though not for blending), Cragganmore did not give its best over that age. I still tend to agree, in general. But here is a bottling which is making me look at this distillery is a new light...and that light is a beacon. I think the manager and I would have stood in amazement if we knew just how fine that young spirit would be when entering its 21st year. 112 per cent proof that you should never say never... 56%. nc ncf. Diageo. Fewer than 6000 bottles.

A.D. Rattray Cragganmore 1997 cask no. 1491, dist Mar 97, bott Mar 10 **(88)** n22.5 cut grass, clean barley and celery; **t22** juicy, spicy and brimming with barley; **f21.5** light oils circle and lengthen the vanilla **b22** an excellent Speysider showing why blenders love this stuff. 46%. A.D. Rattray Ltd.

⸬ **Berry's Own Selection Cragganmore 1989** cask no. 2880, bott 2010 **(86.5)** n22 t21.5 f21.5 b21.5. A grassy, hay loft kind of malt which is happy to explore its own cereal roots. As a single malt, enjoyable but perhaps a little limited. For a blend, this would have done one hell of a job upping the malt signature. 53.5%. nc ncf sc. Berry Bros & Rudd.

Berry's Own Selection Cragganmore 1997 (93.5) n24 ultra complex with a beguiling collection of barley and oak notes interlinking to outstanding sweet-dry effect; no shortage of floral notes, too, but it's that delicate, lemon-tinged manuka honey which really wins it; **t24.5** a beautiful, textbook, delivery with not a single note out of sync; the barley is delightfully salivating and clean and the sugars simply melt-in-the-mouth; just the lightest of spice buzzes ensures the oak offers more than just butterscotch; **f22** perhaps a little on the dry side; **b23** to be honest, I have just tasted a whole raft of pretty substandard malts. To come across something as technically excellent as this is as much a relief as it a joy...a go get bottling. *58.6%. Berry Bros & Rudd.*

᠅ **Berry's Own Selection Cragganmore 1997** cask no. 1513, bott 2010 **(87) n21.5** a little kiwi fruit adds further nip to the snarling barley; **t21.5** the palate vanishes under an explosion of intense barley; **f22** settles down but it's still one for the barleyphiles...; **b22** one very aggressive Speysider with limited conversation. *58.3%. nc ncf sc. Berry Bros & Rudd.*

Duthies Cragganmore 15 Years Old (84) n20.5 t22 f20.5 b21. Does its best in a tight cask. *46%. Cadenhead's for Germany.*

Kingsbury's Cragganmore 1989 18 Years Old Cask Strength **(84.5) n21.5 t23 f20 b20.** Big, intense barley with massive early maple syrup kick. Fades as the bitter-ish oak takes charge. *54.8%. Japan Import System.*

Murray McDavid Mission Cragganmore 1985 Aged 21 Years bourboun/syrah enhanced in Guigal Côte Rôtie **(82) n23 t21 f19 b19**. When they say bourbon, they aren't kidding: parts of this is pure Kentucky, especially on the glorious nose. But the truth is that it's gone through the wood and after the brain-blowing entry, things slip downhill. *56.5%. nc ncf. 665 bottles.*

᠅ **Old Malt Cask Cragganmore Aged 13 Years** refill hogshead, cask no. 6497, dist 1997, bott Aug 10 **(70.5) n18 t18 f17 b18.5.** Faltering and never hits its stride. More a case of Craggan-less... *50%. nc ncf sc. Douglas Laing & Co. 349 bottles.*

᠅ **Old Malt Cask Cragganmore Aged 19 Years** refill hogshead, cask no. 6547, dist Mar 91, bott Sep 10 **(86) n21 t21.5 f22 b21.5.** Not the most sympathetic cask. But here is another journey down memory lane. Soon after turning the world's first full time whisky writer back in 1992, I managed to get a whole bunch of new make samples from the previous 12 months. And I remember a very lightly smoked Cragganmore which both surprised me and caught my eye. Now here it is as a strapping 19 year-old...or would be had it been in a cask that did it full justice. Even so, a real sweet, earthy charmer. *50% nc ncf sc. Douglas Laing & Co. 308 bottles.*

Old Malt Cask Cragganmore Aged 20 Years refill hogshead no. DL 5577, dist Oct 89, bott Oct 09 **(87) n22.5** delicate and complex with a light dusting of cocoa on the cucumber and vanilla; **t22** juicy malt delivery; leaking some oak, but the barley is easily big enough to cope; **f21** the barley gives way to the drying vanillas; **b21.5** another first-class malt from this outstanding distillery. Here the oak is taken as far as is comfortable. *50%. 317 bottles.*

᠅ **Provenance Cragganmore Over 11 Years** refill hogshead, cask no. 7189, dist Summer 00, bott Summer 2011 **(87.5) n21.5** slightly mashy and fresh; **t22** uncomplicated and fabulously juicy barley; **f22** carries on it's malty way; **b22** even from what is probably a third fill cask, the quality sparkles. *46%. nc ncf sc. Douglas Laing & Co.*

Scotch Malt Whisky Society Cask 37.44 Aged 16 Years 1st fill sherry butt, dist Mar 93 **(79) n22 t20 f18 b19.** A real pea-souper of a dram which for all the rich, fruity promise on the nose, doesn't begin to live up to on the palate. *56%. Scotch Malt Whisky Society.*

᠅ **Scotch Malt Whisky Society Cask 37.47 Aged 23 Years** refill butt, cask no. 179, dist 1988 **(83.5) n21.5 t21 f20.5 b20.5.** Plenty of citrus and juicy barley but rather overbearing oak. Decent enough, but would have done a better job in a blend. *54.9%. sc. 148 bottles.*

CRAIGELLACHIE

Speyside, 1891. John Dewar & Sons. Working.

Cadenhead's Craigellachie Aged 14 Years dist 1994, bott 2009 **(91) n23 t24 f21.5 b22.5.** Can't have it all: the indifferent, though not unpleasant, finish is the devil's trade off for some earlier heaven. *56.5%*

The Càrn Mòr Vintage Collection Craigellachie 1999 barrel no. 137, bott 2009 **(74.5) n19 t20 f17.5 b18.** Another half-cocked Craigellachie. Just no oak inspiration at all. *46%. nc ncf. 1041 bottles.*

᠅ **Duncan Taylor Octave Craigellachie 11 Years Old** cask no. 752330, dist 1999 **(73.5) n17 t19 f19 b18.5.** A score of wrong notes. *54.8%. sc.*

Hart Brothers Craigellachie Aged 11 Years dist Dec 97, bott Nov 09 **(74) n18 t19 f19 b18.** An inert cask means the malt is acting half its age. Juicy, though. *46%. Hart Brothers.*

᠅ **Hart Brothers Craigellachie Aged 14 Years** dist Nov 96, bott Jan 11 **(86) n21.5 t22 f21 b21.5.** Just a little oak interference at the finish. Nothing too serious, gladly. For this is a busy little creature with a curious salty sharpness to its big malt chorus. *46%. sc.*

᠅ **Old Malt Cask Craigellachie 14 Years Old** hogshead & claret barrels, cask no. 6278, dist Feb 96, bott Jun 10 **(79) n19 t20.5 f19 b20.** Does its best to raise its game despite an obvious light flaw. The rich malty oils are impressive. *50%. nc ncf sc. Douglas Laing & Co. 275 bottles.*

᠅ **Premier Barrel Craigellachie Aged 11 Years** sherry cask **(91.5) n23.5** a beautiful summer garden perfume to add to the clean ripe fruit; **t23** lush and juicy with a swooning degree of spice; **f22** a very light bitter fuzz, but the grape is so beautifully drawn there is no damage done; **b23** dangerous malt; the kind of stuff that can be drank all day, every day... 46%. nc ncf sc. Douglas Laing & Co. 156 bottles.

Premier Barrel Craigellachie Aged 10 Years sherry cask **(86) n21 t22 f21.5 b21.5.** An understated little charmer, this. The delicate, salivating barley and playful spice appear to wander around the palate hand-in-hand. Even a hint of smoke here and there. 46%

Provenance Craigellachie Over 10 Years sherry finished butt no. DMG 5813, dist Summer 99, bott Winter 2010 **(76.5) n19 t20 f18 b18.5.** Sharp, a little abrasive and never quite finds its rhythm. 46%. Douglas Laing.

⁘ **Provenance Craigellachie Over 12 Years** sherry butt, cask no. 7507, dist Summer 99, bott Summer 2011 **(82.5) n19 t21 f21.5 b21.** Better than the nose suggests and even tries to raise the game with a late injection of salty cocoa. 46%. nc ncf sc.

Scotch Malt Whisky Society Cask 44.39 Aged 15 Years refill barrel, dist Aug 93 **(91) n22.5 t23 f22.5 b23.** Some serious bourbon notes to this, from first nosing right through to the dying embers of oak on the finish. 58.1%

Scotch Malt Whisky Society Cask 44.40 Aged 9 Years refill butt, dist Aug 99 **(89.5) n22 t23.5 f22 b22.** As mouth-watering as you might expect from a malt of this age, and the odd zingy injection. But grapey remnants and a big vanilla surge minimally limit the range of the higher notes and complexity. 58.5%

DAILUAINE

Speyside, 1854. Diageo. Working.

Dailuaine 1997 The Manager's Choice db **(87.5) n21.5** intriguing... **t23** wow!!! Well, what do you know: a Dailuaine going on a charm offensive. On one hand the big malty body thumps into the taste buds, then several layers of honey wash over the wounds. Superb...; **f21** tails off rather too quickly towards the bittering oak; **b22** one of the most enjoyable (unpeated!!) Dailuaines I've come across in an age. There is the usual distillery biff to this, but not without a honeyed safety net. Great fun. 58.6%

Dailuaine Aged 16 Years bott lot no. L4334 db **(79) n19 t21 f20 b19.** Syrupy, almost grotesquely heavy at times; the lighter, more considered notes of previous bottlings have been lost under an avalanche of sugary, over-ripe tomatoes. Definitely one for those who want a massive dram. 43%

⁘ **Adelphi Dailuaine 27 Years Old** cask no. 4319, dist 1983, bott 2011 **(81.5) n20 t20 f21 b20.5.** Good grief...! I found fingernail scratches in my chair after tasting this. They came from me, I assume, as I gripped for grim life as spasms passed. Walnut and dates. With a spectacularly vicious kick in the walnuts... 58.1%. sc. Adelphi Distillery. 219 bottles.

⁘ **Berry's Own Selection Dailuaine 1973** cask no. 10418, bott 2010 **(83) n22 t21 f20 b20.** Very rarely do you find a whisky with so much age and so little give. Outwardly juicy, but absolutely hard as granite. 50.6%. nc ncf sc. Berry Bros & Rudd.

Cadenhead's Authentic Collection Dailuaine-Glenlivet 1989 bott Feb 10 **(85.5) n21 t21.5 f22 b21.** Dense, malty and hot it may be; showing all the elegance of a one-legged giraffe, certainly; as technically brilliant as a Sunday League pub player on the Inter Milan training ground, for sure. But just one of those fabulously eccentric drams you cannot help but love. 56.5%. Wm. Cadenhead Ltd. 256 bottles.

⁘ **Chieftain's Dailuaine Aged 12 Years French** oak finish, dist Mar 99, bott 2011 **(69.5) n17 t18.5 f17 b17.** Just occasionally, and I mean very occasionally, you find a cracking French oak finished malt. This isn't it. 46%. nc ncf. Ian Macleod Distillers.

Harris Whisky Co. Dailuaine Aged 10 Years "Bright Young Things" cask no. cask 000090, dist May 00, bott Jul 10 **(86) n21.5 t22 f21 b21.5.** The barley shines and the sugar sparkles. So, yes, it is certainly bright. 46%. Harris Whisky Co. 304 bottles.

Hart Brothers Dailuaine Aged 11 Years dist Mar 97, bott Jun 08 **(74) n16 t20 f19 b19.** Typically feinty, though some of the oils do have a scarred attractiveness. 46%

⁘ **Old Malt Cask Dailuaine Aged 14 Years** bourbon barrel, cask no. 6995, dist Apr 97, bott Apr 11 **(80) n19 t20.5 f20 b20.5.** Pleasant, malty but somewhat featureless blending fodder. 50%. nc ncf sc. Douglas Laing & Co. 265 bottles.

Old Malt Cask Dailuaine Aged 27 Years Old refill hogshead no. DL 5809, dist Feb 83, bott Feb 10 **(93.5) n23** bloody hell...smoke!!! And we're not talking a couple of ppms, either. Sweet, almost a touch of cloves, to dance with the phenols; **t24** probably the best delivery from this distillery I've come across in 20 years. Not only is the peat chewy, but there are sumptuous waves of Demerara blending in perfectly; the middle is entirely consumed with vanilla and barley, with the smoke drifting around the back of the palate: what a treat... **f23** the usual distillery leaden-footed lushness works to good effect here as the smoked honey goes the full length... **b23.5** don't get me wrong. I am not just marking this up because it is a peaty malt. There are any number in this book which have underwhelmed me, as you can see. No, this is all about the sublime marriage between the smoke and varying sugary notes. A real journey of a dram...what a discovery!! *50%. nc ncf. Douglas Laing & Co Ltd.*

∴ **The Perfect Dram Dailuaine 1971** bourbon hogshead, bott 2010 **(78.5) n19.5 t19 f20 b20.** Pleasant and engaging in its own limited way, though shows a piney, creosotey tendency as it embraces old age. Memo to the powers that be at The Whisky Agency: if you are in search of The Perfect Dram, Dailuaine isn't the place to start... *46.6%. The Whisky Agency.*

Provenance Dailuaine Aged 9 Years sherry butt, dist Autumn 99, bott Autumn 08 **(67) n15 t19 f16 b17.** Badly made and matured. *46%. Douglas Laing.*

Provenance Dailuaine Over 9 Years refill hogshead no. DMG 6213, dist Summer 00, bott Spring 2010 **(87.5) n22.5** the usual ballsy, thick malt with a light citrus edge to the vanilla; **t22** coats the mouth with a mildly thuggish maltiness, seemingly all knuckles against the floor and little finesse. But the odd sharp note offers something that resembles layering; **f21.5** slapped on barley vies with the simple vanilla; **b21.5** I know one or two blenders who are not great fans of this stuff. And I remember one distillery manager at Dailuaine telling me many years back that he'd made "better spirit elsewhere." But this isn't half bad, and appears to enjoy its mildly quirky maltiness. *46%. nc ncf. Douglas Laing.*

Provenance Dailuaine Over 10 Years sherry butt no. DMG 5747, dist Autumn 99, bott Winter 2010 **(84.5) n20.5 t22 f21 b21.** Pleasant and at its best when the honeyed barley is showing, as opposed to the grape. *46%. Douglas Laing.*

Scotch Malt Whisky Society Cask 41.42 Aged 23 Years refill hogshead, dist May 86 **(85) n22 t22 f20 b21.** Big, uncomplicated, thumping malt. Perfect for bulking up in blends, and not bad here as a tart, malty mouthful. *57.2%. Scotch Malt Whisky Society. 220 bottles.*

∴ **Scotch Malt Whisky Society Cask 41.47 Aged 7 Years** 1st fill bourbon barrel, cask no. 800243, dist 2003 **(86) n22 t21 f21.5 b21.5.** There you go. All those old Dailuaines letting you down time and time again. When its forte was being bottled at what I think is always a fascinating age in Scotland when the malt gets a chance to say its piece, especially when in first fill cask. Can't escape the fire, but you must have a heart of steel not to enjoy the oak-barley tapestry. *61.2%. sc.*

∴ **Scotch Malt Whisky Society Cask 41.49 Aged 30 Years** 2nd fill sherry butt, cask no. 9137, dist 1980 **(83) n21.5 t21 f20 b20.5.** A tart monster of a dram which has you thumping the back of your own head to restore you to life. The sherry offers a lot more refinement on the nose than the palate where it fails to cope with the distillery's, rolled-sleeve, aggressive style. *50.9%. sc. 51 bottles.*

DALLAS DHU
Speyside, 1899–1983. Closed. Now a museum.

Duncan Taylor Collection Dallas Dhu 1981 cask no. 389 **(90) n21.5** a curious mixture of acacia honey and dry, mildly soaped pummace stone; **t21.5** honeyed silk - and then a screeching delivery of nippy spices; settles in the middle to something more comfortably vanilla and cocoa; **f24** now really comes into its own as the barley finds a foothold to ensure a charming complexity to the vanilla and mocha. Sheer class; **b23** until the finale, it's difficult to know where this one is going. Or even that it is Dallas Dhu, as this is a much wilder, kick ass version than most... *55.1%*

DALMORE
Highands (Northern), 1839. Whyte and Mackay. Working.

The Dalmore 12 Years Old db **(90) n22** mixed dates: both dry and juicy; **t23** fat, rich delivery with a wonderful dovetailing of juicy barley and thick, rumbling fruit; **f22.5** lots of toffee on the finish, but gets away with it thanks to the sheer depth to the barley and the busy sherry sub-plot; **b22.5** has changed character of late yet remains underpowered and with a shade too much toffee. But such is the quality of the malt in its own right it can overcome any hurdles placed before it to ensure a real mouth-filling, rumbustious dram. *40%*

The Dalmore Dee Dram 12 Years Old db **(63.5) n15.5 t17 f14 b16.** Words fail me...*40%*

The Dalmore 15 Years Old db **(83.5) n21 t21 f20.5 b21.** Another pleasant Dalmore that coasts along the runway but simply fails to get off the ground. The odd off note here and there, but it's the blood orange which shines brightest. *40%*

The Dalmore 18 Years Old db **(76.5) n19 t21 f18 b18.5.** Heaps of caramel and the cask choice might have been better. *43%*

The Dalmore 21 Years Old db **(87) n22** just how many citrus notes can we find here? Answers on a postcard... on second thoughts, don't. Just beautifully light and effervescent for its age: a genuine delight; **t23** again, wonderfully fruity though this time the malt pushes through confidently to create its own chewy island: fabulous texture; **f20** simplifies towards toffee slightly too much in the interests of great balance. A lovely coffee flourish late on; **b22** bottled elegance. 43%

The Dalmore Forty Years Old db (82) n23 t20 f19 b20. Doubtless my dear friend Richard Paterson will question whether I have the ability to spot a good whisky if it ran me over in a ten ton truck. But I have to say here that we have a disappointing malt: I had left this too late on in writing this year's (2008) Bible as a treat. But it wasn't to be. A soft delivery: but of what? Hard to exactly pin down what's going on here as there is so much toffee and fruit that the oak and barley have been overwhelmed. Pleasant, perhaps, but it's all rather dull and passionless. Like going through the motions with an old lover. Adore the sherry-trifle/toffee mousse nose, though... 40%

⋰⋱ **The Dalmore Astrum Aged 40 Years** db (89) n23.5 I think this is as far as you can take oak and still be on the credit side: a rich saltiness seems to inject life and extra sharpness to the blackcurrants, dates, plums and stewed cooking apples which abound. The very lightest dusting of allspice furthers the piquancy; **t21** for a moment the fruit – and even stratum of barley - looks intact, but soon the oak arrives with a brutal vengeance. The middle ground becomes puckeringly tight; **f22** relaxes as sugars are released and some vanillas arrive but at the very death the bitter oaks dominate; meanwhile a fruity sub-note rumbles...; **b22.5** this guy is all about the nose. The oak is too big for the overall framework and the balance hangs by a thread. Yet somehow the overall effect is impressive. Another summer and you suspect the whole thing would have snapped... 42%

⋰⋱ **The Dalmore Aurora Aged 45 Years** db (90.5) n25 unquestionably an intriguing and engaging nose, full of subtleties and quirky side streets. Initially, all these sub plots and intrigues are to do with oak and very little else. However, the spices once located are a treat and open the door to the delicate boiled fruit which, after making a tentative entrance, begins to inject the required sweetness; give ten minutes in the glass to discover something quite sublime and faultless... **t22** rounded on delivery but again it's all about the oak which piles up untidily on the palate, though the odd exotic fruit note can be detected. Salt dovetails with that fruit but it is heading downhill... **f21.5** some vaguely malty vanilla but the oak is now dominating though some mocha does come to the rescue; **b22** sophisticated for sure. But so huge is the oak on the palate, it cannot hope to match the freakish brilliance of the nose. 45%

The Dalmore 50 Years Old db (88) n21 buxom and bourbony, the oak makes no secret of the antiquity; **t19** oak again arrives first and without apology, some salty malt creaking in later. Ripe cherries offer a mouthwatering backdrop; **f25** comes into its own as harmony is achieved as the oak quietens to allow a beautiful malt-cherry interplay. Spices arrive for good measure in an absolutely has-it-all, faultless finish: really as much a privilege to taste as a delight; **b23** takes a while to warm up, but when it does becomes a genuinely classy and memorable dram befitting one of the world's great and undervalued distilleries. 52%

The Dalmore Candela Aged 50 Years db (96) n25 there you go: that's the next half hour to 45 minutes taken up...trying to unravel this one. Fresh fruity frame, but the picture in the middle is far more difficult to understand. Dates – both dried and juicy – mingle with finest quality Lubec marzipan paste (sans chocolate) while a few spices nip in to say 'hullo'; clean, relaxed...and very sprightly for its age; **t24** immediate onrush of oaks, offset by a cherry sauce and later plain chocolate fondant to ensure any bitterness is kept in check; elsewhere an improbable layering of barley juice and fruit again makes a mockery of the age; **f23.5** for a whisky reaching half a century, curiously reserved with the oaks now really starting to get a degree of bitterness generated; a thin line of chocolate and raisin helps keep that bitterness at acceptable levels; **b23.5** just one of those whiskies which you come across only a handful of times in your life. All because a malt makes it to 50 does not mean it will automatically be great. This, however, is a masterpiece, the end of which seemingly has never been written... 50% (bottled at 45%). Whyte & Mackay. 77 bottles.

The Dalmore Selene 58 Years Old cask no. 1781/1782 dist Jun 51 db (87.5) n23 the oak let's you know it has been around a while; eggnog and spiced spotted dick make an unlikely backdrop combination; **t22** the oak bites with a viciousness that is enough to cause the eyes to close; the middle ground fills with chocolate caramel and spices begin to really kick in; **f21** tired and monumentally oaky but enough natural caramels to ensure a light finish; the spices keeps the whisky ticking pleasantly **b21.5** a fascinating experience, but in terms of quality, though very good indeed for its range alone, not in the same league as the Dalmore 50 or 60-y-o. A great present for anyone born in 1951, or supporters of Queen of the South marking the 60th anniversary of their winning the Scottish Div 2 title. But as a whisky spectacle: great nose, decent delivery and then after that...you are on your own. 44%. Whyte & Mackay. 30 bottles.

⸫ **The Dalmore Eos Aged 59 Years** db (95) n24.5 extraordinary pulsing of rich, dry sherry notes: nutty and polished oak in one of the finer Mayfair antique shops or clubs. The moistest, choicest Lubeck marzipan with a thread of Jaffa jam and, as the whisky settles into its stride, this moves to Jaffa cakes with heavy dark chocolate; very limited spice, but the salt levels grow..; t24 ultra dry delivery despite the juices flowing from the very first moment: the grape is beautifully firm and holds together light oils and burgeoning oak which threaten to inject a weighty toastiness; the mid ground though is a triumph of glorious lightly molassed vanilla notes with strands of barley; spices buzz and fizz and add even further life; f22.5 a light off-key bitterness knocks off a mark or two, but the cocoa and burnt raisin charge to the rescue; b24 for those of you who thought this was a camera, let me put you in the picture. This is one well developed whisky, but by no means over exposed, as it would have every right to be after nearly 60 years. Indeed: it is one of those drams which utterly confounds and amazes. I specially chose this as the 1001st new whisky for the 2012 Bible, and those of us old enough to be young when most of its sister casks were hauled off for blending, there was an advert in the '60s which said: "1,001 cleans a big, big carpet...for less than half a crown." Well this 1001 cleans a big, big palate. But I can't see a bottle of this majestic malt going for as little as that... 44%

The Dalmore 62 Years Old db (95) n23 PM or REV marked demerara potstill rum, surely? Massive coffee presence, clean and enormous, stunning, topdrawer peat just to round things off; t25 this is brilliant: pure silk wrapping fabulous moist fruitcake soaked in finest oloroso sherry and then weighed with peat which somehow has defied nature and survived in cask all these years. I really cannot fault this: I sit here stunned and in awe; f24 perfect spices with flecks of ginger and lemon rind; b24 if I am just half as beautiful, elegant and fascinating as this by the time I reach 62, I'll be a happy man. Somehow I doubt it. A once-in-a-lifetime whisky – something that comes around every 62 years, in fact. Forget Dalmore Cigar Malt – even I might be tempted to start smoking just to get a full bottle of this. 40.5%

The Dalmore 1263 King Alexander III db (86) n22 t22.5 f20 b21.5. Starts brightly with all kinds of barley sugar, fruit and decent age and oak combinations, plus some excellent spice prickle. So far, so good...and obviously thoughtfully and complexly structured. But then vanishes without trace on finish. 40%

⸫ **The Dalmore 1978** db (89.5) n23.5 moist sponge cake with a generous layer of golden syrup; a few delicate citrus notes lighten further but a plumy counterweight excels; t22 juicy delivery with a fine array of early barley and fruit. But there is a big oaky surge, though never to an overall detriment; f21.5 finishes as a coffee cake with the odd bitter bean; b22.5 a seriously lovely old dram which is much weightier on the palate than nose. 47.1%. 477 bottles.

⸫ **The Dalmore 1979** db (84) n21 t21.5 f20 b21.5. Hard to find a more rounded malt. Strangely earthy, though. 42%. 487 bottles.

The Dalmore 1980 db (81.5) n19 t21 f20.5 b21. Wonderful barley intensity on delivery does its best to overcome the so-so nose and finale. 40%

⸫ **The Dalmore Matusalem 1981** db (91.5) n23 muscular and beautifully primed with soft herbs amid the fruit; marmalade at the bottom of an old jar; t23.5 now, do I love that delivery! Waxy and thick in a uniquely Whyte and Mackay style, there is a clever muscovado-molasses mix which not just ramps up the sugars but the weight and depth, also; f22.5 some tangy notes while the sugars fight a rearguard action with the bittering oak; b22.5 had someone tied me to a rack and kept pulling until I said this could be something other than a W&M production, I would have defied them to the bitter end... 44%. 497 bottles.

The Dalmore 1981 Amoroso Sherry Finesse amoroso sherry wood cask db (85.5) n21 t22 f21.5 b21. A very tight, fruity, dram which gives away its secrets with all the enthusiasm of an agent under torture. Enjoyable to a degree... but bloody hard work. 42%

The Dalmore Mackenzie 1992 American oak/port pipes, bott 2009 db (88.5) n23 a dripping nose: dripping of fresh grape juice, that is. Mostly clean, with a slow unveiling of delicate spices and further fruit notes, especially a well disguised kiwi; really very seductive, indeed... t22 on one level a sharp, almost metallic delivery, crushed fruit stone, at first finding it hard to hit a rhythm; on the other, immediately soft, creamy and luxuriant. Finally some vanillas get a grip and the fruit now has somewhere to go; f21 after a short bitter burst, settles towards a gentle sherry trifle finale; a late furry bitterness develops... b22.5 I suppose you could say that such is the influence of the grape that this is a tad one dimensional. But such is the grim state of the wine casks in the industry today, one is forgiven for falling on bended knee and kissing the bottle. Though even this isn't without its sulphury failings... 46%

⸫ **The Dalmore Vintage 2001 Limited Edition** db (84.5) n21 t22 f20.5 b21. Ah... a Dalmore of straw colour displaying such delicate intricacies with the barley...complex, especially with the varying degrees of malt to the oils... What???? I was asleep? I was dreaming...? What do we have here? Oh. Yet another mahogany-coloured Dalmore. Another Dalmore so thick, nutty-toffeed and chewy you can hardly tell where the story starts and ends. Or exactly what the story is that differs from the others... Yes, overall a generally pleasant experience but the feeling of déjà vu and underachievement is depressingly overwhelming. 48%

⁖ **The Dalmore Rivers Collection Dee Dram Season 2011** db (81.5) n20 t22.5 f19 b20. Where the previous bottling was a complete disaster, this one is friendly and approachable. Still don't expect anything two dimensional on the finish as the caramel attack and a strand of bitterness dries your taste buds to squeaking point. But the delivery is a very pleasant, chewy affair for sure. 40%

⁖ **The Dalmore Rivers Collection Tweed Dram Season 2011** db (86) n21 t22 f21.5 b21.5. Silky and slinky, a real soup of a malt in which the barley occasionally rises high to deliciously juicy effect. 40%

⁖ **The Dalmore Rivers Collection Tay Dram Season 2011** db (86.5) n22.5 t23 f20 b21. Despite the house toffee-neutered finale and the odd but obvious cask-related off note, there is still plenty to enjoy here. 40%

The Dalmore Cabernet Sauvignon db (79) n22 t19 f19 b19. Too intense and soupy for its own good. 45%

⁖ **The Dalmore Castle Leod** db (77) n18.5 t21 f18.5 b19. Thumpingly big and soupy. More fruit than you can wave a wasp at. But, sadly, the sting comes with the slightly obvious off note. 46%

⁖ **The Dalmore Cigar Malt Reserve Limited Edition** db (73.5) n19 t19.5 f17 b18. One assumes this off key sugarfest is for the cigar that explodes in your face... 44%

The Dalmore Gran Reserva sherry wood and American white oak casks db (82.5) n22 t21.5 f19 b20. An improvement on the near nonentity this once was. But still the middle and finish are basic and lacking sophistication or substance outside a broad sweet of oaky chocolate toffee. Delightful mixture of blood orange and nuts on the approach, though. 40% ⊙⊙

⁖ **The Dalmore Visitor Centre Exclusive** db (95.5) n25 this isn't just about fruit: this is a lesson in a nosing glass in how the marriage and equilibrium between salt, sugars, barley and delicate fruit juices should be arranged. There is not an off note; no party dominates; the complexity is beguiling as the picture shifts and changes in the glass every few seconds. Also, how the weight of the whisky is essential to balance. It is, frankly, the perfect malt whisky nose... t24 so off we go on a journey around about fifteen fruit levels, half that number of sugar intensities and a fabulous salty counter. Close your eyes and be seduced...; f22.5 a minor blemish as a vaguely bitter note from the oak interjects. Luckily, the thick barley sugar is in there to repair the damage; remains salty to the very end; b24 not exactly the easiest distillery to find but a bottle of this is worth the journey alone. I have tasted some sumptuous Dalmores over the last 30-odd years. But this one stands among the very finest. 46%

A.D. Rattray Dalmore 1999 cask no. 3080 (86.5) n21.5 t23 f20.5 b21.5. With all that intense malt and gooseberry running about, there will be a few blenders wanting to lay their hands on this stuff. 59.1%. A.D. Rattray Ltd.

Chester Whisky & Liquer Co. Dalmore Aged 10 Years dist 1999 (84) n21.5 t21.5 f21 b20. Evidence of feints backed up by the oiliness and near black bone-like mass of this blighter. Prisoners barely taken as the molten Rollo toffee/chocolate sticks to all corners of the palate. Enjoyable and fun, but not without its flaws and hardly one for the purest. 54.8%

Chieftain's Dalmore 13 Years Old Pinot Noir Finish dist Jun 96, bott 2010 (94) n23 a curious phenol note to this is neither peaty nor coal-dusty. But it appears to give the grape an extra degree of weight and thrust. Some lovely bourbony sweetness to this, too; t24 a deliciously schizophrenic and stunning delivery: on one hand it appears light and incapable of complexity, yet elsewhere moody barley grows in intensity and the fruits begin to thicken wonderfully; f23.5 long and lingers with a tingling but profound spiciness that tags on to the ever intensifying barley; there is an unusual coffee and cola union towards the finish. But this is ground-breaking stuff all the way... b23.5 bravo!! A wine finish which appears be in total sympathy with the malt. Not sure whether to drink it or mount it on the wall... Definitely worth hunting down as this is a minor classic in its own right. 56.7%. nc ncf. Ian Macleod.

Chieftain's Dalmore Aged 14 Years Rum Finish dist Dec 95, bott 2010 (85.5) n22 t21 f21.5 b21. A very tight example of rum at work. Usually you get a clipped sugary style. Here a dry Demerara-style cask appears to have been used which happily squeezes every spare bit of sweetness out of it, even though there a few oils to spare. Conservative, enjoyable and just a little bit different. 46%. Ian Macleod.

Connoisseurs Choice Dalmore 1992 (81) n20 t21 f20 b20. Sweet, sticky and spiced, without offering much in the way of form or format. Not the distillery at its finest. 40%

Duncan Taylor Collection Dalmore 1990 cask no. 7329 **(87) n22 t23 f20.5 b21.5.** Brimming with esters and quite a few acceptable feints and spice this is absolutely enormous whisky which might equally appeal to rum freaks. *56.7%*

⟚ **Old Malt Cask Dalmore Aged 12 Years** refill butt, cask no. 7096, dist Apr 99, bott Apr 11 **(86) n22** the odd blood orange amid the walnuts; **t22** an enormous outpouring of gorgeously textured barley; a glowing sugary sheen amplifies the malt; **f22.5** really comes into its own as the oak and barley dance effortlessly together amid the gathering oils; **b22.5** an endearing malt which grips your attention the further along the track it travels. The barley and light citrus are superb. *50%. nc ncf sc. Douglas Laing & Co. 429 bottles.*

Old Malt Cask Dalmore Aged 19 Years dist Apr 90, bott Jul 09 **(83) n20 t22 f21 b20.** Pleasant but perhaps over sweet. *50%. Douglas Laing.*

⟚ **Old Malt Cask Dalmore Aged 20 Years** refill butt finished in amontillado sherry butt, cask no. 6838, dist Apr 90, bott Nov 10 **(90) n23** dense, almost impenetrable fruit; mainly blood orange, but some freshly grilled liver, too...talk about meaty...; **t23.5** thicker than a medieval castle wall, but with a lot more yield. Salivating as the onrush of barley carries with it traces of lemon and brown sugars; **f21.5** bitters as we are back to that meaty strata; lots of vague feinty notes; **b22** knife and fork required... *50%. nc ncf sc. Douglas Laing & Co. 224 bottles.*

Old Malt Cask Dalmore Aged 32 Years refill hogshead dist Dec 76, Apr 09 **(94) n23 t24 f23 b24.** Quite a triumph of age over probability. Oh, if only the distillery bottlings were regularly this fresh and breathtaking. *50%. Douglas Laing. 306 bottles.*

⟚ **Old Malt Cask Dalmore Aged 33 Years** rum finished hogshead, cask no. 6632, dist Dec 76, bott Oct 10 **(70) n18 t18 f17 b17.** That's odd. I always associated butyric with something a lot younger than this! *50%. nc ncf sc. Douglas Laing & Co. 98 bottles.*

Old Masters Dalmore Aged 12 Years cask no. 5603, dist 1997, bott 2009 **(90) n22 t23 f22.5 b22.5.** If they were to make a Scottish Mint Julip... *59.8%. James MacArthur & Co Ltd.*

⟚ **Premier Barrel Dalmore 12 Years Old (85.5) n19.5 t22 f22 b22.** Great fun with this characterful malt taking your taste buds on a rollercoaster ride. The nose isn't exactly great, but there is a gorgeously spiced fruit cake quality to this...without the grapes being present. Forget about an evening of romance and sophistication: this is a lovely bit of rough. *46%. nc ncf sc. Douglas Laing & Co. 146 bottles.*

⟚ **Provenance Dalmore Over 11 Years** refill butt, cask no. 6566, Spring 99, Autumn 2010 **(87.5) n23** a charming, if distantly feinty, cross of freshly ground hazelnut and sweeter marzipan paste; some kumquat provides a citrusy sharpness; **t22** fat and slightly earthy as if the vague feints on the nose come to oily fruition; again there is a wonderful citrus fruit cocktail but the middle is perhaps a tad too oily; **f21** those oils cling gamely to the roof of the mouth, allowing the chewy nuttiness to return; **b21.5** Dalmore as it should be, but is so rarely seen: in all its meaty nakedness. The cut here is much wider than you might expect a mainstream pot still single malt, but it ensures character abounds. *46%. nc ncf sc. Douglas Laing & Co.*

DALWHINNIE
Highlands (Central), 1898. Diageo. Working.
Dalwhinnie 15 Years Old db **(95) n24** sublime stuff: a curious mixture of coke smoke and peat-reek wafts teasingly over the gently honied malt. A hint of melon offers some fruit but the caressing malt stars; **t24** that rarest of combinations: at once silky and malt intense, yet at the same time peppery and tin-hat time for the tastebuds, but the silk wins out and a sheen of barley sugar coats everything, soft peat included; **f23** some cocoa and coffee notes, yet the pervading slightly honied sweetness means that there is no bitterness that cannot be controlled; **b24** a malt it is hard to decide whether to drink or bath in: I suggest you do both. One of the most complete mainland malts of them all. Know anyone who reckons they don't like whisky? Give them a glass of this – that's them cured. Oh, if only the average masterpiece could be this good. *43%*

DEANSTON
Highlands (Perthshire), 1966. Burn Stewart Distillers. Working.
Deanston 6 Years Old db **(83) n20 t21 f22 b20.** Great news for those who remember how good Deanston was a decade or two ago: it's on its way back. A delightfully clean dram with its trademark honey character restored. A little beauty slightly undermined by caramel. *40%*

Deanston 12 Years Old db **(74) n18 t19 f18.5 b18.5.** It is quite bizarre how you can interchange this with Tobermory in style; or, rather, at least the faults are the same. *46%. ncf.*

⟚ **Deanston Aged 12 Years** db **(75) n18 t21.5 f17.5 b18.** The delivery is, for a brief moment, a malty/orangey delight. But the nose is painfully out of sync and finish is full of bitter, undesirable elements. A lot of work still required to get this up to a second grade malt, let alone a top flight one. 46.3%. ncf. Burn Stewart.

Deanston Aged 12 Years Un-Chill Filtered db (71) n18 t18 f17 b18. Someone told me I would enjoy this new version of Deanston 12 far more than the old un-chill filtered one, which I didn't care for at all. They were wrong. 46.3%

Deanston Aged 12 Years Un-Chill Filtered db (84.5) n21 t21.5 f21 b21. A decent, attractive Deanston which is a definite step in the right direction. Nutty for sure, but some attractive barley sweetness flits about the palate. A wide cut at work here, one feels, but plenty to chew on. 46.3%

Deanston 1967 casks 1051-2, filled Friday 31st Mar 67 db (90) n23 t23 f21 b23. The oak is full on but there is so much class around that cannot gain control. A Perthshire beauty. 50.7%

Deanston Virgin Oak db (90) n22.5 does exactly what it says on the tin: absolutely brimming with virgin oak. To the cost of all other characteristics. And don't expect a bourbon style for a second: this is sharp-end tannins where the sugars have their own syrupy point of entry; t23 now those sugars dissolve with some major oak attached: many years back, I tasted a paste made from roasted acorns and brown sugar...not entirely dissimilar; f22.5 continues to rumble contentedly in the oakiest possible manner...but now with some fizzy spice; b22 quirky. Don't expect this to taste anything like Scotch... 46.3%

⋰ **Marks & Spencer Deanston Aged 12 Years** db (84.5) n20.5 t22 f21 b21. It's been a while since I found so much honeyed malt in a Deanston. Echoes of 20 years ago. 40%. UK.

⋰ **Marks & Spencer Deanston Aged 17 Years Limited Edition** db (88.5) n20 something not quite right being put into place by something that very much is...haughty yet unbalanced; t23.5 gooseberry pie...with a few under-ripe gooseberries thrown in for good measure; plenty of ripping spice, too: luckily the salivating barley helps keep the fire to controllable levels; f22.5 the spices continue to throb; lots of vanilla on the finale; b22.5 overcomes a taught, off-key nose to open into something full of juice, fruity intrigue. Really enjoyed this one. 46.3%. ncf. 979 bottles.

Old Malt Cask Deanston Aged 15 Years refill butt DL 6043, dist Jun 94, bott Apr 10 (76) n18 t21 f18 b19. Huge, almost immeasurable, barley. But found technically wanting. 50%. nc ncf. Douglas Laing & Co Ltd. 391 bottles.

Old Malt Cask Deanston Aged 16 Years refill hogshead, dist Dec 92, bott Mar 09 (90) n21.5 t23.5 f22.5 b23. Distinctly a cut above for this distillery of late: indeed, much more what this place was about 20-odd years ago. 50%. 330 bottles.

⋰ **Robert Graham's Dancing Stag Deanston 1995** hogshead, dist 14 Jul 95, bott Oct 10 (86) n21.5 t22 f21.5 b21. An enjoyable maltfest if you can cope with the sugars. And the fact that a 15-year-old malt has the sophistication of a whisky half that age... 46%. nc ncf sc. 186 bottles.

DUFFTOWN

Speyside, 1898. Diageo. Working.

Singleton of Dufftown 12 Years Old db (71) n18 t18 f17 b18. A roughhouse malt that's finesse-free. For those who like their tastebuds Dufft up a bit... 40% ⊙

Cadenhead's Dufftown Aged 31 Years dist 1978, bott 2009 (84) n21.5 t21.5 f21 b20. No surprise about the syrupy fruit. Behaves itself to offer a pleasant chewy dram. 48.6%

Connoisseurs Choice Dufftown 1997 (81) n20 t22 f21 b21. Sticky, syrupy and one-dimensional for sure. But the malt is rich and intact. Not at all bad. Indeed, honestly enjoyable. 43%. Gordon & MacPhail.

The Golden Cask Dufftown 1979 cask no. CM144, bott 2009 (77) n19 t22 f17 b19. No matter how golden the cask is, if it's from Dufftown chances are it's going to be a little tarnished. 54.8%. The House of MacDuff. 282 bottles.

Kingsbury's "The Selection" Dufftown 7 Years Old 1999 (81) n19 t21 f20 b21. Big oils, intense malt, hints of Demerara and, in this form, quite decent fun. 43%. Japan Import System.

⋰ **Kingsbury Finest and Rarest Dufftown 34 Years Old** dist 1975 (74) n19 t19 f18 b18. Stodgy, podgy and totally bereft of finesse. But probably the only place where the words "Finest" and "Dufftown" will be found on the same line... 45.9%. nc ncf sc. Japan Import Systems.

Old Malt Cask Collection Dufftown Aged 14 Years refill butt, dist Aug 94, bott Oct 08 (84.5) n19 t22 f21.5 b21. Syrupy and spicy. Faintly trashy and certainly not one to take home to your parents, but some nice curves in some of the right places and a sweet heart. 50%

Old Malt Cask Collection Dufftown Aged 28 Years sherry cask, dist May 80, bott Oct 08 (80) n18 t22 f21 b19. An outrageous dram. Rumbustious, rollicking, uncouth, more oak than a Henry VIII battleship and a few more explosions, too. And dirtier than the filthiest Jolly Jack Tar. But for its myriad faults, it's fun, by gum! 50%. Douglas Laing. 302 bottles.

⋰ **Old Malt Cask Dufftown Aged 28 Years** refill hogshead, cask no. 7147, dist Nov 82, bott Apr 11 (78.5) n18.5 t19.5 f21 b19. Overly sweet and overly fiery, though the milky mocha on the finale works hard to compensate. Overall, though, ordinary whisky from a distinctly ordinary distillery. 50%. nc ncf sc. Douglas Laing & Co. 247 bottles.

Provenance Dufftown Over 11 Years rum finished cask no. DMG 5169, dist Autumn 97, bott Spring 09 (74) n18 t19 f18 b19. Malty, a tad spicy but always muddled. A little too nutty for its own good. 46%. nc ncf. Douglas Laing & Co Ltd.

EDRADOUR

Highlands (Perthshire), 1837. Signatory Vintage. Working.

Edradour Aged 10 Years db (79) n18 t20 f22 b19. A dense, fat malt that tries offer something along the sherry front but succeeds mainly in producing a whisky cloyingly sweet and unfathomable. Some complexity to the finish compensates. 43%

Edradour Ballachin #1 The Burgundy Casks db (63) n17 t16 f15 b15. A bitter disappointment in every sense. Were the Burgundy casks sulphur treated? I'd say so. Something completely off-key here. A shocker. 46%

Edradour Ballachin #2 Madeira Matured db (89) n22 t22 f23 b22. On the nose and entry I didn't quite get the point here: putting a massively peated malt like this in a Madeira cask is a bit like putting Stan Laural into bed with Marylyn Munro. Thankfully doesn't come out a fine mess and the Madeira certainly has a vital say towards the beautifully structured finale. It works! I feel the hand of a former Laphroaig man at work here. 46%

FETTERCAIRN

Highland (Eastern), 1824. Whyte and Mackay. Working.

Fettercairn 12 Year Old db (66) n14 t19 f16 b17. If the nose doesn't get you, what follows probably will...Grim doesn't quite cover it. 40%

∵ **Fettercairn 30 Years Old** db (73) n19 t18 f18 b18. A bitter disappointment. Literally. 46.3%

∵ **Fettercairn 40 Years Old** db (92) n23 technically, not exactly how you want a 40-y-o to be: a bit like your old silver-haired granny knitting in her rocking chair...and sporting tattoos. But I also have to say there is no shortage of charm, too...and like some old tattooed granny, you know it is full of personality and has a tale to tell... t24 I was expecting dates and walnuts...and I have not been let down. A veritable date and walnut pie you can chew on until your jaw is numb; the sharp raisiny notes, too, plus a metallic sheen which reminds you of its provenance...; f22 those burned raisins get just a little more burned...; b23 yes, everyone knows my views on this distillery. But I'll have to call this spade a wonderfully big, old shovel you can't help loving...just like the memory of me tattooed ol' granny... 40%. 463 bottles.

Fettercairn 1824 db (69) n17 t19 f16 b17. By Fettercairn standards, not a bad offering. Relatively free from its inherent sulphury and rubbery qualities, this displays a sweet nutty character not altogther unattractive – though caramel plays a calming role here. Need my arm twisting for a second glass, though. 40%

∵ **Fettercairn Fior Limited Release** (80) n18.5 t22 f19.5 b20. Fat, sweet and relatively shapeless on the palate, bitter on the finish and very dark in the glass. No more than you might expect. But by about the sixth mouthful it does grow on you a bit, and you begin to relish the short-lived but excellent malt juiciness backed by spice and myriad rough edges. It is to be enjoyed like you might a game of football down the park on a Sunday morning. Absolutely no finesse, obvious limited quality, but great grunt and groan effort in the mud. This whisky is technically to, say, a Glenmorangie or a Highland Park what the Dog and Duck Reserves are to Barcelona. But don't whisper it too loudly: for this outrageous bottling, I'm a fan... 42%

∵ **Old Malt Cask Fettercairn Aged 19 Years** refill hogshead, cask no. 6382, dist Dec 90, bott Jul 10 (82) n20.5 t23 f18.5 b20. Refreshing delivery with a very attractive crispness to the barley. 50%. nc ncf sc. Douglas Laing & Co. 318 bottles.

∵ **Provenance Fettercairn Over 9 Years** refill hogshead, cask no. 5434, dist Autumn 00, bott Summer 2010 (68) n16 t18 f17 b17. Grimly ordinary for all the big malt. 46%. nc ncf sc.

∵ **Provenance Fettercairn Over 10 Years** refill hogshead, cask no. 6919, dist Autumn 00, bott Winter 2011 (67.5) n15.5 t18 f17 b17. The next time Fettercairn blender Richard Paterson tells me how great this distillery is, he'll get a pie full of shaving foam in his face. It will be a lot kinder than making him drink this nonsense. 46%. nc ncf sc. Douglas Laing & Co.

The Whisky Agency Fettercairn 34 Year Old dist 1975, bott 2009 (75.5) n18 t17.5 f21 b19. A sweet, nutty finish compensates for some of the earlier crimes against the tastebuds. 57%

GLEN ALBYN

Highlands (Northern) 1846–1983. Diageo. Demolished.

Old Malt Cask Glen Albyn 35 Years Old dist 26 Sep 69, bott Jul 05 (90) n24 a star-studded aroma for something this ancient: the oak weaves delicate vanilla patterns around the apple-honey-barley lead. As aromas go, a veritable gold nugget for its age; **t23** early barley absolutely rips through the tastebuds helped along the way by a glossy sweetness and a puff of smoke and cocoa; **f21** the drying oak lays claim with tolerable force; **b22** understandable signs of longevity, but overall this is simply wonderful. 50%. Douglas Laing. 229 bottles.

Rarest of the Rare Glen Albyn 1979 cask no. 3960, dist Dec 79, bott Mar 06 **(91)** **n23** melon and barley play host to a clever, nose-nipping spiciness. So relaxed: supreme confidence here; **t23** the incredibly fresh, salivating barley intertwines with glorious vanilla to give a drier tier to the delicately sweet malt; **f22** some chalky vanilla and mocha but the barley holds true; **b23** of Scotland's disappearing malts, this is going with flourish. 57.3%. Duncan Taylor. 244 bottles.

GLENALLACHIE
Speyside, 1968. Chivas Brothers. Working.

Glenallachie 15 Years Old Distillery Edition db **(81)** **n20 t21 f19 b19.** Real battle between nature and nurture: an exceptional sherry butt has silk gloves and honied marzipan, while a hot-tempered bruiser lurks beneath. 58%

⋅⋅ **Glenallachie Aged 35 Years Anniversary Selection** first fill sherry, bott 2010 **(84.5)** **n21 t21 f22.5 b20.** OTT... No doubting the high quality of the sherry butt. But for the alchemy to work, it must combine with the malt to magical effect. Sadly, it doesn't, mainly because the malt just doesn't have the wherewithal to engage. 46.9%. nc. Speciality Drinks Ltd.

Adelphi Glenallachie 1973 Aged 36 Years bourbon hogshead,cask no. 1873, bott 2010 **(95.5)** **n24** wears exotic fruit of antiquity like a Lord wears his robes. An injection of green apple takes it away from the norm for these kind of old whiskies, suggesting a devilment and youth which, frankly, it never sported in the years it originally had the chance; here's a surprise though; a playful few molecules of peat...; **t23.5** silky and soft, as opposed to steely and hard when a quarter of a century younger. There is a buzz nipping at the back of the throat suggesting great composure and spice; in fact it is the distillery bite which no number of years can even out. But in these lush surroundings it now works rather well; **f24** graceful and long, retaining that rock-hard exoskeleton, but inside it softens as that light peat returns with charming degrees of cocoa, vanilla and barley. Not a bitter note; not a single hint of disharmony...astonishing... **b24** a whisky which really makes you laugh inwardly and outwardly. Like nearby Caperdonich, this malt was way too harsh and thin for enjoyment in its prime years. Now in great age, it takes on the Elder Statesman mantle like to the warehouse born. Some whiskies are born great. Some achieve greatness. Others have greatness thrust upon them (usually by marketing departments). Trust me when I tell you that this one fluked it. But hats off to a 24 carat stunner all the same...and what a way to bring up my 500th new whisky of the 2011 Bible...!!! 48.1%. 201 bottles.

The Càrn Mòr Vintage Collection Braes of Glenallachie 1992 barrel, cask no. 587, dist 1992, bott 2009 **(82)** **n20 t21 f21 b20.** Thin and malty in the typical house style. No off notes, but no real development, either. 46%. The Scottish Liqueur Centre.

The John Milroy Selection Glenallachie 11 Years Old hogshead, dist 1999, bott 2010 **(84.5)** **n20.5 t22 f21 b21.** Clean, malty blending fodder this may be but you cannot but marvel at the degree of vanilla. 56.4%. Berry Bros & Rudd.

⋅⋅ **Malts Of Scotland Glenallachie 1995** bourbon hogshead, cask no. 1257, dist Mar 95, bott Apr 11 **(81.5)** **n20 t21 f20.5 b20.** Hot and painfully thin in the distillery style. But some delightful mouth-watering malt and late chocolate, too. Surprisingly attractive. 53%. sc.

Old Malt Cask Glenallachie Aged 38 Years dist Feb 71, bott May 09 **(72)** **n20 t17 f17.5 b17.5.** I don't think they had quite got to grips with the stills 38 years ago, or the casks: typical of the period in being spectacularly off key almost to the point of vulgarity. 50%

⋅⋅ **Old Malt Cask Glenallachie Aged 38 Years** refill butt, cask no. 6498, dist Mar 72, bott Aug 10 **(83.5)** **n23.5 t20.5 f19.5 b20.** Fabulous aroma, full of bright barley. But the severe limitations of the distillery become more apparent once you get to taste it. 50%. nc ncf sc. 384 bottles.

⋅⋅ **Old Malt Cask Glenallachie Aged 38 Years** sherry butt, cask no. 6880, dist Mar 72, bott Jan 11 **(92.5)** **n24** potentially the sherry butt of the year: in perfect condition, not even the vaguest hint of a hint of a hint of a hint of an off-sulphury note. Just juicy grape and pith, fortified by the trademark big Glenallachie malt swirl; **t23** a juicy tour de force of spiced grape and vivid barley; **f22.5** grape and vanilla; **b23** I will have to take their word for this being a Glenallachie. All reference points to the distillery have been obliterated by a stonkingly beautiful, and quite faultless sherry butt. You just can't go wrong with a bottle like this. 50%. nc ncf sc. 302 bottles.

Provenance Glenallachie Aged 9 Years refill hogshead, dist Spring 99, bott Autumn 08 **(79)** **n20.5 t20.5 f19 b19.** Clean, malty, gristy, slightly yeasty, well made, under-matured (from the point of view of being in an over-aged cask) blending fodder. 46%. Douglas Laing.

⸭ **Robert Graham's Dancing Stag Glenallachie 1995** hogshead, dist 10 Nov 95, bott Sep 10 **(82) n21 t21 f20 b20.** A very good example of this distillery at its usual malt in a straight jacket self. 46%. nc ncf sc. Robert Graham. 168 bottles.

⸭ **The Whisky Agency Glenallachie 1971** bott 2010 **(86.5) n21 t22 f22 b21.5.** Back in the early 80s, this would not have been much of a success as a 10 to 12 years-old, so emaciated would it have been. However, it has progressed with time, even somehow adopting a slight citrusy poise. Quite charming, if still a little undercooked. 51.2%. The Whisky Agency.

⸭ **The Whisky Agency Glenallachie 1972** bott 2010 **(73) n19 t19 f17 b18.** Soapy rocket fuel. 49.9%. The Whisky Agency.

GLENBURGIE
Speyside, 1810. Chivas Brothers. Working.

Glenburgie Aged 15 Years bott code L00/129 db **(84) n22 t23 f19 b20.** Doing so well until the spectacularly flat, bitter finish. Orangey citrus and liquorice had abounded. 46%

⸭ **Berry's Own Selection Glenburgie 1983** cask no. 9806, bott 2011 **(92.5) n23** blazes a spectacularly malty trail. The barley is almost in concentrated form; the sugars seem to be both on the periphery, yet somehow attached...thrillingly rich and complex; **t23.5** not just a case of the taste following the nose but even embellishing upon it. The malt seems to arrive in one huge mass and then radiates beautiful, lightly sweetened barley around the palate; **f23** the usual Burgie natural caramel...and barley...; **b23** confident, competent, beautifully distilled and matured. And if there were a Richter Scale of maltiness, this would come flying off the gauge... 56.3%. nc ncf sc. Berry Bros & Rudd.

⸭ **Dun Bheagan Glenburgie 11 Years Old** bourbon hogshead, dist Nov 98 **(86.5) n22 t22 f21 b21.5** A pretty accurate and attractive account of a Burgie at this age in ex-bourbon: on one hand massive barley drive, on the other natural caramels and delicate bourbony notes come in to play. 43%. nc ncf. Ian Macleod Distillers.

Duncan Taylor The NC2 Range Glenburgie 1996 Aged 11 Years **(86.5) n22 t22 f21.5 b21.** Youthful, slightly raw, ultra-clean...the barley appears to be gleaming on both nose and palate. Superficial development, perhaps, but as a good old fashioned slap around the tastebuds...well, it doesn't come much better! 46%

The Golden Cask Glenburgie 1983 cask no. CM145 **(92.5) n23** burned honeycomb infused with crushed leaves; earthy and floral; **t23.5** punchy delivery, again with a touch of honey but also red liquorice and muscovado sugar; teasing Danish marzipan plays with the spices; **f23** fruitier finale, sharp and full of vigour to the very chocolatey end; **b23** I have been well known over the years for telling people at tastings that Burgie is a malt which Allied should have done much more with when they owned it. And I hoped Chivas would now open doors for it. Grab a bottle of this, and you'll see why... 57.7%. The House of MacDuff. 224 bottles.

Gordon & MacPhail Distillery Label Glenburgie 10 Years Old **(77) n20 t20 f18 b19.** Sweet, toffeed and dull. 40%

Gordon & MacPhail Rare Vintage Glenburgie 1963 **(86) n20.5 t22 f22.5 b21.5.** For all its chewiness and enormity, as lovely as the spiced fruit and liquorice is: you can't get over the fact that just a too much oak has entered the system. Still, those lingering coffee and walnut cake notes are a delight. 43%

Kingsbury's Hand Writing Label Glenburgie 23 Years Old dist 1980 **(89) n23** earthy, even with a touch of grated carrot. But all aroma roads lead to something a touch bourbony; **t23** profoundly juicy despite the big bourbony oak statement with honey-softened hickory filling the middle ground; **f21** dries in the manner expected; **b22** I can see this doing some great work in an older blend as this is multi-faceted. Even as a singleton, and despite the age impact, it is a busy little gem. 54.4%. Japan Import System.

Old Malt Cask Glenburgie Aged 20 Years dist Sep 89 **(90) n22** mid range barley with excellent oak-sugar balance; **t23** just stunning delivery with the most mouth-watering of Speyside deliveries; the fifth and sixth flavour waves are uncluttered citrus; **f22.5** custardy vanillas and powdery oak; **b22.5** one of the great Speyside distilleries deserving a much wider field of appreciation. Well done, Laing brothers, for giving people a chance to discover this little gem. 50%. Douglas Laing & Co Ltd.

Old Malt Cask Glenburgie Aged 20 Years dist May 89, bott Jul 09 **(91) n22 t23 f22.5 b22.5.** Hardly a gray hair...! 50%. Douglas Laing & Co Ltd.

Provenance Glenburgie Over 11 Years refill hogshead no. DMG 6001, dist Autumn 98, bott Spring 2010 **(86) n21.5 t22 f212 b21.5.** Coats the taste buds in barley with a trowel. Juicy and lively all the way. 46%. nc ncf. Douglas Laing & Co Ltd.

Provenance Glenburgie Aged 12 Years refill hogshead, dist Spring 96, bott Autumn 08 **(81) n20.5 t21.5 f19 b19.** Pear-drops, anyone? 46%. Douglas Laing & Co Ltd.

GLENCADAM
Highlands (Eastern), 1825. Angus Dundee. Working.

Glencadam Aged 10 Years db (95) n24 crystal clarity to the sharp, ultra fresh barley. Clean, uncluttered by excessive oak, the apparent lightness is deceptive; the intensity of the malt carries its own impressive weight and the citrus note compliments rather than thins. Enticing; t24 immediately zingy and eye-wateringly salivating with a fabulous layering of sweet barley. Equally delicate oak chimes in to ensure a lightly spiced balance and a degree of attitude; f23 longer than the early barley freshness would have you expecting, with soft oils ensuring an extended, tapering, malty edge to the gentle, clean oak; b24 sophisticated, sensual, salivating and seemingly serene, this malt is all about juicy barley and balance. Just bristles with character and about as puckeringly elegant as single malt gets...and even thirst-quenching. My God: the guy who put this one together must be a genius, or something... 46%

Glencadam Aged 12 Years Portwood Finish db (89.5) n22.5 oaky vanillas manage to shape this attractively while delicate, clean grape bends this towards a subtle fruit and custard effect: soft, playful and teasing; t22.5 attractive marriage of those drier vanillas promised on the nose with that fragile fruit; for all the softness there is a playful nip to be had, too; a youngish barley flashes keenly about the taste buds; f22 a rumble of prickly spice and cocoa but that clean fruit, as light as it is, lasts the distance; b22.5 after coming across a few disappointing Port finishes in recent weeks, just wonderful to experience one as you would hope and expect it to be. 46%

Glencadam Aged 14 Years Oloroso Sherry Cask Finish bott May 10 db (95) n24 pinch me: I'm dreaming. Oloroso exactly how it should be: classically clean with a dovetailing of dry and sweeter grape notes which are weighty, but not heavy enough to crush the lighter barley and vanillas from adding to the sumptuous and elegant mix; t23.5 mouth-filling with firstly fat grape then a second flavour round of spices and custardy vanillas; f24 much drier now with the accent on the barley but still that light spice persists, actually increasing in weight and effect as it goes along; b23.5 what a total treat. Restores one's faith in Oloroso whilst offering more than a glimpse of the most charming infusion of fruit imaginable. 46%

Glencadam Aged 15 Years db (90.5) n22.5 soft kumquats mingle with the even softer barley. A trace of drier mint and chalk dust points towards the shy oak. Harmonious and dovetails beautifully; t23 sharp, juicy barley - almost fruity - fuses with sharper oak. The mouth-watering house style appears to fatten out as gentle oils emerge and then give way for a spicy middle; f22 long, with those teasing, playful spices pepping up the continued barley theme. Dries as a 15 year old ought but the usual bitterness is kept in check by the prevailing malt; b23 the spices keep the taste buds on full alert but the richness and depth of the barley defies the years. Another exhibition of Glencadam's understated elegance. Some more genius malt creation... 46%

Glencadam Aged 21 Years "The Exceptional" bott May 10 db (81) n21.5 t22 f17.5 b20. For a little distillery with a reputation for producing a more delicate malt this is one big whisky. Sadly, the finish is out of kilter, for the delivery is a knife and fork job, offering some extraordinary variations on a fudgy-maple syrup theme which promises much. 46%

Glencadam 25 Years Old Single Cask cask no. 1002, dist Apr 08 db (76.5) n20.5 t21 f16 b19. One of those "oh what might have been" casks. Or, if you are German or Swiss, one of the best experiences you will have for a very long time. Those who can't pick up sulphur will have a new love in their lives. The rest of us will continue to sob quietly... 46%

⋄ **Glencadam Single Cask 1978** sherry cask, cask no. 2332, dist Apr 78, bott Sep 10 db (88) n21.5 about as dry a fruitiness as you are ever likely to find: borders on tight, perhaps through, amongst other things, a little pine seeping in. Fruit cake baked with minimum sugars; t22.5 the delivery is also a shy, conservative affair but at least with a build up of increasingly strident molasses; f22 again, heads back towards a dry, toasty fruitiness with a little bitterness battling the fading sugars; b22 what to make of a malt like this. Absolutely refuses to open up, yet so much is quietly said...or not. Intriguing. 46%. nc ncf sc. 405 bottles.

Glencadam Single Cask 1978 cask no. 2335, bott no. 554, dist Apr 78, bott Mar 09 db (93.5) n24 this is very much how a sherry cask should be. Regard: intense nutty fruitcake. You will observe the dappling effect of the spices. Note how this gives great vitality to the whisky after 30 years and the manner in which none of the constituent parts dominate. For those who have joined the whisky industry in the last 15 years, please also take note that contrary to what you may think is the norm and perfectly acceptable, sulphur is playing no part in the proceedings; t24 melt-in-the-mouth grape. The controlled muscovado and juicy date sweetness fuse and allow a build up of playful spice and vanillas; natural caramels seep into the mix, as does a biscuity malt character; f22.5 despite the grape's enormity, there is still room for the oak to flourish and, mingling with the grape, creating a blood orange bitterness to balance with the continuing sugars; **b23.5** a fabulous distillery which is coming out of the shadows since its confidence-sapping Allied days and is now putting Brechin on the map. Its secret is that the malt is of a consistently high standard; one willing and able to get the best out of any cask type used. Some malts can't handle sherry, failing to get their personality across. This one appears able to do just that without batting an eyelid. *46%. nc ncf. 615 bottles.*

⠠⠠⠠ **Berry's Own Selection Glencadam 1990** cask no. 5982, bott 2011 **(85.5) n22 t21 f21 b21.5** Bright and pulsing in the Glencadam style. But just a little more hot and aggressive than should be expected. Can't not delight in the barley, though. And the chocolate dessert on the finale. *56.6%. nc ncf sc. Berry Bros & Rudd.*

Connoisseurs Choice Glencadam 1987 (87.5) n23 t22 f21 b21.5. Charming and fruity. *43%*

Dun Bheagan Glencadam 20 Years Old Hogshead (80) n20 t19 f21 b20. For all its age it remains hot stuff. The honey influence will win friends, though. *48%*

⠠⠠⠠ **Malts Of Scotland Glencadam 1985** bourbon hogshead, cask no. 3990, dist Jun 85, bott Nov 10 **(89) n21.5** a little hickory and tannin does no harm at all; **t22.5** feisty and spicy, the oak strikes home early but with barley not far behind; **f22.5** the spices persist while the sugars temper the raucous oak; **b22.5** not for the lily-livered. Bursting from the glass with controlled aggression and attitude. *55.4%. nc ncf sc. Exclusive bottling for Interwhisky 2010.*

Montgomerie's Glencadam 1990 cask no. 5990, dist Aug 89, bott Mar 08 **(87) n24.5 t21.5 f20 b21.** Taste-wise, the oak has gone through the barley. But the nose is simply exceptional, one of the best malts of the year, and the delivery is no mug, either. *43%*

Old & Rare Glencadam Aged 32 Years sherry cask, dist Apr 77, bott Oct 09 **(80) n19 t22 f19 b20.** Thick grape. A bit on the minty side here and there. But a furry dryness, too. *54.9%. Douglas Laing & Co Ltd. 296 bottles.*

Old & Rare Glencadam Aged 32 Years dist Apr 77, bott Jul 09 **(96.5) n25 t24 f23.5 b25.** From Brechin to Bardstown in 32 years: brilliant! Worth getting just to nose alone... *58.6%*

Single & Single Glencadam 1991 Aged 16 Years (81.5) n21 t21.5 f19 b20. Decent barley sharpness but elsewhere there is a constant drone of caramel like bagpipes at a haggis convention. *46%. Single & Single. South Africa.*

GLENCRAIG

Speyside, 1958. Chivas Brothers. Silent.

Rare Old Glencraig 1975 (87.5) n22.5 a soothing mixture of exotic fruit and more prosaic rhubarb tart; **t22** what was once background caramel leaking from the oak has now become the main theme; soft spices offer a puckering depth; **f21.5** just enough barley to manage the major oak on show; **b21.5** signs are showing that the Glencraigs are reaching the end of their natural range. *43%. Gordon & MacPhail.*

Rarest of the Rare Glencraig 1974 cask no. 2923 **(89) n22.5 t22 f22.5 b22.** Such an elegant dram which feels very at home with its age. After all these years, a bottling worth waiting for. *40.9%. Duncan Taylor.*

Rarest of the Rare Glencraig 1974 cask no. 2929 **(89.5) n22.5 t23 f22 b22.** Rarest of the Rare, alright; the smallest sample I have ever been sent for the Whisky Bible. Must have gone out on April 1st. Come on guys: give me – and the whisky – a chance!! *40.8%. Duncan Taylor.*

⠠⠠⠠ **Scotch Malt Whisky Society Cask 104.13 Aged 36 Years** refill barrel, cask no. 7825, dist 1974 **(96) n(24)** wonderful aroma: heavyweight stuff with all the characters playing at full throttle but within a seemingly confined space. So the bananas and ripe oranges would explode from the glass, except the thick bourbon is holding them by the lapels. Massive, magnificent...and very different...; **t(24)** the first oak notes to burn off are over the top and spent. But after about the third wave it settles down with the introduction of telling muscovado sugars and a seemingly roasty maltiness; spices dovetail with an almost cooing gentleness while slowly, but unmistakably, the barley builds up enough intensity to make a salivating contribution; **f(23.5)** the spices persist while the bourbon characteristics hold sway. The dryness of the sawdusty oak never hints at bitterness while the kumquats and figs ensure a distant softness; **b(24.5)** don't get many of these guys to the dozen. What a relief this one's a cracker! If you are to buy only one major whisky this year, make it this. *50.6%. sc. 179 bottles.*

GLENDRONACH

Highlands, 1826. The BenRiach Distillery Co. Working.

⠠⠠⠠ **The GlenDronach Aged 8 Years "Octarine"** db **(86.5) n23.5 t23 f19 b21.** Juicy yet bitter: a bipolar malt offering two contrasting characters in one glass. *46%. nc ncf.*

The GlenDronach 12 Years Old db **(92) n22** some pretty juicy grape in there; **t24** silky delivery with the grape teaming with the barley to produce the sharpest delivery and follow through you can imagine: exceptionally good weight with just enough oils to make full use of the delicate sweetness and the build towards spices and cocoa in the middle ground is a wonderful tease; **f22.5** dries and heads into bitter marmalade country; **b23.5** an astonishingly beautiful malt despite the fact that a rogue sherry butt has come in under the radar. But for that, this would have been a mega scorer: potentially an award-winner. Fault or no fault, seriously worth discovering this bottling of this too long undiscovered great distillery *43%*

The GlenDronach Aged 12 Years "Original" db (86.5) **n21 t22 f22 b21.5**. One of the more bizarre moments of the year: thought I'd got this one mixed up with a German malt whisky I had tasted earlier in the day. There is a light drying tobacco feel to this and the exact same corresponding delivery on the palate. That German version is distilled in a different type of still; this is made in probably the most classic stillhouse on mainland Scotland. Good, enjoyable whisky. But I see a long debate with distillery owner Billy Walker on the near horizon, though it was in Allied's hands when this was produced. *43%*

The Glendronach Original Aged 12 Years Double Matured db (88) **n23 t21 f22 b22**. Vastly improved from the sulphur-tainted bottling of last year. In fact, their most enjoyable standard distillery bottling I've had for many years. But forget about the whisky: the blurb on the back is among the most interesting you likely to find anywhere. And I quote: "Founder James Allardice called the original Glendronach, 'The Guid Glendronach'. But there's no need to imitate his marketing methods. The first converts to his malt were the 'ladies of the night' in Edinburgh's Canongate!" Fascinating. And as a professional whisky taster I am left wondering: did they swallow or spit... *40%*

⸭ **The GlenDronach 14 Years Old Sauternes Finish** db (78.5) **n18 t22 f19 b19.5**. That unique Sauternes three dimensional spiced fruit is there sure enough...and some awesome oils. But, with so much out of key bitterness around, not quite I had hoped for. *46%. nc ncf.*

⸭ **The GlenDronach 14 Years Old Virgin Oak** db (87) **n22.5** what a naughty virgin! All kinds of tempting vanilla and butterscotch notes...and spice, of course...; **t22** a little flat-chested with the barley vanishing under a sea of oily, natural caramel; **f21** caramel and vanilla; **b21.5** charming, pretty, but perhaps lacking in passion... *46%. nc ncf.*

The GlenDronach 15 Years Old db (77.5) **n19 t18.5 f20 b20**. The really frustrating thing is, you can hear those amazingly brilliant sherry butts screaming to be heard in their purest voice. Those alone, and you could, like the 12-y-o, have a score cruising over 95 mark. I can't wait for the next bottling. *46%*

The GlenDronach 15 Years Old db (83) **n20 t22 f20 b21**. Chocolate fudge and grape juice to start then tails off towards a slightly bitter, dry finish. *40%*

⸭ **The GlenDronach 15 Years Old Moscatel Finish** db (84) **n19 t22.5 f21.5 b21**. Such is the intensity of the grape, its force of life, it makes a truly remarkable recovery from such a limited start. But it is hard to be yourself when shackled... *46%. nc ncf.*

⸭ **The GlenDronach 15 Years Old Tawny Port Finish** db (84.5) **n21 t22 f20.5 b21.5**. Quite a tight fit for the most part. But when it does relax, especially a few beats after delivery, the clean fruit fairly drips onto the palate. *46%. nc ncf.*

The GlenDronach Aged 15 Years "Revival" db (88.5) **n22** almost impenetrably thick malt, further strengthened by an oak-muscovado exoskeleton; **t23** again the malt takes on massive form; the fruit marches along as a sub-plot; **f21.5** vanilla and malt, a slightly bitter finale; **b22** unambiguously Scottish... A fantastically malty dram. *46%*

The GlenDronach 18 Years Old db (96.5) **n24** groaning under the weight of sublime, faultless sherry and peppers; **t24** puckering enormity as the saltiness thumps home. Black forest Gateaux complete with cherries and blended with sherry trifle. The spices have to be tasted to be believed. The sugars ranges from Demerara to light molasses; **f24** so, so long. Again the sugars are in perfect position to ramp up the sweetness, but the grape, vanilla and spices are the perfect foil... **b24.5** the ultimate sherry cask whisky. Faultless and truly astounding! *46%. nc ncf.* ☉☉

The GlenDronach Aged 18 Years "Allardice" db (83.5) **n19 t22 f21 b21.5**. Huge fruit. But a long-running bitter edge to the toffee and raisin sits awkwardly on the palate. *46%*

⸭ **The GlenDronach 21 Years Old** db (91.5) **n23.5** thumping sherry of the old fruitcake school; a serious number of toasty notes including, somewhat perversely, hickory of a bourbon style; **t23.5** no less lush delivery than the nose portends; the follow up layerings of burnt raisin and cremated fudge are pretty entertaining; **f22** like burnt toast, a touch of bitterness at the death; **b22.5** a quite unique slant on a 21-year-old malt: some aspects appear very much older, but some elements of the grape occasionally reveal a welcome youth. Memorable stuff. *48%. nc ncf.*

The GlenDronach Grandeur Aged 31 Years db (94.5) **n23.5** dry, mildly peppery vanilla; crushed golden raisin counter-plot; **t24** spice-dusted grapes explode on the palate on entry; the mouth-feel plays a key role as the early lushness carries the fruit only so far before it begins to break up, allowing a fabulous spicy complexity to develop; **f23.5** beautiful intertwining between those golden raisins and coffee. The spices are never far away...; **b23.5** just one hell of an alpha sherry butt. 45.8%

The GlenDronach Aged 33 Years oloroso db **(95)** n24 t24 f23 b24. Want to know what sherry should really nose like: invest in a bottle of this. This is a vivid malt boasting spellbinding clarity and charm. A golden nugget of a dram, which would have been better still at 46%. 40%

The GlenDronach Single Cask 1971 oloroso cask no. 483 **(80)** n20 t22 f19 b19. Plenty of marmalade to be getting on with here. The finish is tight and bitter. 49.4%. 544 bottles.

⊰ **The GlenDronach Single Cask 1971** batch 4, PX puncheon, cask no. 1436, dist 25 Feb 71, bott 2011 db **(89)** n22.5 big peppery grape; **t22** mint humbug complete with toffee; **f22.5** a thread of barley and vanilla adds an extra dimension; **b22** silky, fresh, never less than delicious but maybe not the most complex 40-year-old on the market. 48.5%. nc ncf sc.

⊰ **The GlenDronach Single Cask 1972** batch 4, oloroso cask no. 712, dist 02 Mar 72, bott 2011 db **(95.5)** n24.5 the rare beauty of an entirely faultless sherry butt. The grape is heavily cratered by oak and some beautiful spices, dried orange pith and floral notes (especially lilacs) ensure the complexity is never less than astonishing...; **t24** for a brief second the grape puffs out its chest like a proud wood pigeon, but the oak is not very far behind; a fabulous, very delicately oiled ensemble of impressive molassed notes and some other earthy, roasty controlled honey moments; **f23** the oak, inevitably, takes command and bitters out the buttery notes; **b24** if you can head back in time to the late 80s, the Glendronach 12 had a nose not dissimilar to this: absolutely faultless sherry. Then it was too faultless and quite drowned out anything the barley had to say. The barley is still silent. But the oak has the megaphone towards the end... However, the overall play is one of the finest veteran actors squeezing every nuance out of their lines and, taking the pathos to just bearable proportions, reminding us of what we will be missing in the years to come due to the near wiping out of sherry butts like these... 49.9%. nc ncf sc.

⊰ **The GlenDronach Single Cask 1972** batch 5, oloroso cask no. 716, dist 02 Mar 72, bott 2011 db **(88)** n23 a tight, dense nose, lacking many of the intricacies of its sister cask but winning over the heart with its studied portrayal of both elegant grape and oak. Intriguingly, the lack of grape reveals a trace of smoke that is not at all apparent on Batch 4; **t22.5** much juicier on delivery with an impressive early volley of cracked grape and gooseberries. When the oak arrives, it does so with maximum impact; **f20.5** oaky...; **b22** unmistakably related to cask 712, though this does not enjoy quite so much swirling grape. This was bottled at a time when it was unlikely ever to improve in the barrel and just one more summer might have allowed the oak to have spoiled the party. As it is: a delight! 54.4%. nc ncf sc.

⊰ **The GlenDronach Single Cask 1978** batch 5, oloroso puncheon, cask no. 1067, dist 29 Dec 78, bott 2011 db **(95.5)** n24 good god...! Not just sulphur free (well, 99.25%!). But not even the vaguest hint of tired oak or gratuitous sweetness. What we have is a spotless assembly of grape, of at least six different sweetness and intensity values I could count. Some spice spills, inevitably, into the picture. But the big surprise is the shadow of barley spotted moving slowly beneath it all...; **t24** a fabulous arrival on the palate: all shimmering yet somehow puckering grape, both fresh and burnt to a crisp. The oak notes are firm and bulging with vanilla; various blackberries and weeping, over-ripe cherries fill in the middle; **f23.5** that .75% comes back to haunt, but such is the integrity of the grape, it is barely noticeable; **b24** when I first visited this distillery under its new management, its owner, Billy Walker, told me that he had found some one of the best sherry casks he had ever encountered in his long career. I would not be remotely surprised if this is one of them... This is, as nigh as damn it, faultless... 50.1%. nc ncf sc.

⊰ **The GlenDronach Single Cask 1989** batch 4, PX puncheon, cask no. 2917, dist 07 Dec 89, bott 2011 db **(86)** n22 t21.5 f21 b21.5. Lashings of sugar candy grape: it is like a high alcohol boiled sweet. But a little bit of interference in Jerez has stunted the development somewhat. 54.1%. nc ncf sc.

⊰ **The GlenDronach Single Cask 1989** batch 5, PX puncheon, cask no. 3314, dist 09 Nov 89, bott 2011 db **(95)** n24.5 if my life were not dictated by deadlines, it would be tempting to take a morning off and just spend a blissful few hours nosing this: you are unlikely ever to find a more relaxed and magnificent balance between sultry grape and scandalous spice...; **t24** almost disappointingly well behaved on the palate: the sherry has too much to say and at first overwhelms all else. Even the spices retreat for cover after the briefest of early flourishes, But I say "almost": further exploration reveals a plumy depth and a slow build up of quite unexpected barley notes on oil; **f23** clean, if mildly uninspired grape; the spices regroup for a late, delicious, rally; **b23.5** what do make of a cove like this? The nose suggests a potential whisky of the year. Though the experience on the palate is a lot more urbane, given time it reveals itself as a pretty complex piece of work. Always a treat (and bloody rare), though, to find a sherry cask entirely free of sulphur. 53.5%. nc ncf sc.

The GlenDronach Single Cask 1990 batch 4, PX puncheon, cask no. 1032, dist 29 Aug 90, bott 2011 db (81) n21.5 t20 f19.5 b20. Plenty of fruit juice. But the furry bitterness tells its own tale. I predict this to be a knockout in mainland Europe, however. 53.3% nc ncf sc.

The GlenDronach Single Cask 1991 batch 5, oloroso cask no. 2406, dist 01 Nov 91, bott 2011 db (95) n24 an absolutely honest aroma showing the style of sherry at its healthiest and most confident: dry with the grape sharing equal billing with the oak; t24 the delivery of your dreams: the grape is firm yet juicy, the sugars are nearby but controlled. Charismatic and elegant from the off, the dry sherry style is endearing; f23.5 dries towards burnt raisin as the oaks impact; b23.5 of its type, dry oloroso, you cannot find finer. 55.4%. nc ncf sc.

The GlenDronach Single Cask 1992 cask no. 401 db (96) n24 t23.5 f24.5 b24. Ultra distinctive with that firm sheen offering a very unusual dimension. However, the unmistakable rum character on a sherry theme really makes for a memorable and massive malt which never quite tastes the same twice and alters in weight and complexity considerably depending on heat and time applied. Outrageously excellent. The distillery at its most complex. 60.2%. BenRiach Distillers exclusively for Parkers Whisky.

The GlenDronach Single Cask 1992 oloroso butt no. 1140 db (93.5) n23.5 sharp, incisive grape with tannins running amok. Under all this, some barley stirs... t24.5 quite beautiful grape, almost three dimensional in its shape, form and structure. Clean, intact, marginally juicy but relaxed enough to allow both the barley and vanilla a free run; f22.5 plenty of coffee notes to give that usual rummy character which so often attaches itself to Glendronach. Some very late fuzzy bitterness...; b23 yes, it is feeling a little tired. Yes, it occasionally lurches about the palate as if under the influence of its own fumes. But we are talking a sherry butt under 20 years old with only the odd sulphur molecule in sight, before the Bodegas went insane with the stuff. Or so it appears to my poor, jaded taste buds as I near the end of this Bible. A relative wonder to behold... 57.2%. 598 bottles.

The GlenDronach Single Cask 1992 batch 4, oloroso cask no. 161, dist 22 May 92, bott 2011 db (96) n24.5 anyone into Basset's Liquorice Allsorts will recognise this one: chocolate and liquorice (the brown and black ones) squashed in the fingers, while elsewhere a glass of oloroso fills the room with rich grapey notes. Of course, spices abound, as they must... or do I mean Musto...? t25 Is it sweet? Is it sour? Does it have the fruity pungency of Granny's Voice Cough drops? Does is radiate toffee apple recently bitten into? Does it somehow posses a bourbony rich, old honeyed depth? Yes, it does...and so much more...; f22.5 a degree of taught bitterness creeps in, though it would be churlish to begrudge its presence. The oils up their game, too. But it makes for a very long, toasty, burnt hot-cross bun finale...; b24 this was distilled almost to the week that I became the world's first full-time whisky writer. Perhaps I should buy a cask as good as this to bottle in celebration...now there's an idea... Because it would be hard to find a whisky of even more of the magnitude than this to represent all that I stand for..This just has to be the Single Cask of the Year... 59.2%. nc ncf sc.

The GlenDronach Single Cask 1993 oloroso butt no. 523 db (94) n23.5 salted sherry; malted Mysore; t24.5 succulent sugars; spine-tingling spices; gregarious grape, magnificent mocha; f22.5 more Mysore; savoury staves; vanishing vanilla; b23.5 sulphur-less. Sophististicated. Sensational. 60.4%. 634 bottles.

The GlenDronach Single Cask 1993 batch 5, oloroso cask no. 1, dist 15 Jan 93, bott 2011 db (78) n21 t20 f18 b19. It would be hard to find a juicier butt than this. But a sulphur candles has the ability to strangle so many things at birth. 54.9%. nc ncf sc.

The GlenDronach Single Cask 1994 cask no. 2311 db (91.5) n21.5 t23 f23.5 b23.5. About the closest I have ever tasted to the long defunct 12-year-old bourbon cask Glendronach, a legendary single malt in the old Allied armoury. A malt which really needs to be warmed to body temperature to see it in its full glory and form, one quite unique to this little-known distillery. Fascinating and fabulous. 59.4%. BenRiach Distillers exclusively for Parkers Whisky.

The GlenDronach Single Cask 1994 batch 4, oloroso cask no. 97. dist 28 Jan 94, bott 2011 db (90) n22.5 wonderfully nutty, with walnut oil mixing with crushed toasted hazelnuts; apples and oranges dilute the thick, sweet grape; just a mild discordant note at the back; t24 top quality mouth feel and body: minimum oils, maximum lushness. The middle could almost be a bourbon with its honeycomb and liquorice theme; f21 a little tight, burnt out bitterness; b22.5 like a flower in the sun, leave in the glass for a good 20 minutes for it to open properly. 60.1%. nc ncf sc.

The GlenDronach Single Cask 1996 oloroso butt, cask no. 193 db (88.5) n22 you'd be hard pressed to find an old Demerara rum with this degree of salty, fruity intensity; t23.5 taste buds coated with several layers of sherry tar, each about three inches thick: eye-watering in intensity, a middle ground of coffee and chocolate crèmes lightening the load; f21 more coffee, but a little on the burnt side; b22 an almost frightening whisky. The ferocity of the sherry might have some hiding behind their sofas. 59.4%. 399 bottles.

Dun Bheagan GlenDronach Aged 34 Years hogshead, dist Jun 75 (**88.5**) **n22** you'd be hard pressed to find an old Demerara rum with this degree of salty, fruity intensity; **t23.5** taste buds coated with several layers of sherry tar, each about three inches thick: eye-watering in intensity, a middle ground of coffee and chocolate crèmes lightening the load; **f21** more coffee, but a little on the burnt side; **b22** an almost frightening whisky. The ferocity of the sherry might have some hiding behind their sofas. 47.8%. Ian Macleod.

Duncan Taylor Collection GlenDronach 1975 cask no. 706 (**87.5**) **n22.5 t22 f22 b21.5**. Maybe at 25 years you might be looking for a touch more variance. But on the other hand, what it does it does very well... 51.4%

Old Malt Cask GlenDronach Aged 14 Years Old refill butt, cask no. DL 5671, dist May 95, bott Jan 10 (**85**) **n21.5 t21.5 f21 b21**. Salty, tangy, lively, oddly coastal-style. Barley dominates but sugars not far behind. 50%. Douglas Laing & Co Ltd. 240 bottles.

⋯ **Old Malt Cask GlenDronach Aged 18 Years** refill hogshead, cask no. 6910, dist May 95, bott Jan 11 (**84.5**) **n21 t21 f21.5 b21**. Enjoyably simplistic: dense, malty and quietly satisfying. 50%. nc ncf sc. Douglas Laing & Co. 346 bottles.

GLENDULLAN (see also below)
Speyside, 1972. Diageo. Working.

Glendullan Aged 8 Years db (**89**) **n20** fresh, gingery, zesty; **t22** distinctly mealy and malty. **f24** brilliant – really stunning grassy malt powers through. Speyside in a glass – and a nutshell; **b23** this is just how I like my Speysiders: young fresh and uplifting. A charming malt. 40%

Glendullan The Manager's Choice European oak, cask no. 12718, dist 1995, bott 2009 db (**93.5**) **n24.5** just a near flawless nose: an absolute perfection of balance between purring barley and fresh fruit, especially apples. Just love the new-mown hay... in fact, everything about this, especially that mix of old and new characteristics ...; **t23.5** intriguing combination of ripening fruit and young-ish make: has a suet pudding feel but with the extra addition of thick sultana and reduced plum sauce; **f23** a long, leviathan of rich fruit, dappled with barley and vanilla; **b22.5** a bit like finding a perfectly preserved old Merc with low mileage: performs as beautifully as it does effortlessly and offers a priceless symmetry between simplicity and style. Whoever chose these casks deserves a medal struck. And take this one at body temp only. 58.7%. 635 bottles.

Singleton of Glendullan 12 Years Old db (**87**) **n22** significant oak hides some of the Jamaican ginger; **t22** a gutsier barley character with stifled honey and the oak dives in again; **f21** dry with a slight return of ginger; **b22** much more age than is comfortable for a 12-y-o. 40%

⋯ **Fine Malt Selection Glendullan 14 Years Old** dist 1997, bott May 11 (**86**) **n23.5 t23.5 f18 b21**. A disappointingly bitter ending to a lively story full of delightful surprises 45%. sc. James MacArthur & Co. USA release.

Hart Brothers Glendullan Aged 11 Years dist Jun 98, bott Sep 09 (**61**) **n17 t18 f12 b15**. A very poor cask. Simple as... 46%. Hart Brothers.

Old Masters Glendullan Aged 12 Years cask no. 5059, dist 1997, bott 2009 (**85**) **n21.5 t22 f20.5 b21**. Decent, thoroughly enjoyable, simplistic malt with a good, refreshing zing to the barley delivery. 56.1%. James MacArthur & Co Ltd.

⋯ **Provenance Glendullan Over 11 Years** refill hogshead, cask no. 7191, dist Autumn 99, bott Spring 2011 (**86**) **n22 t22 f21 b21**. Soft, sweet, ultra malty blending fodder which is low on complexity but high on charm. 46%. nc ncf sc. Douglas Laing & Co.

Provenance Glendullan Aged 12 Years refill hogshead, dist Summer 96, bott Autumn 08 (**80.5**) **n21.5 t20 f19 b20**. Very happy to steer a malty course, causing minimum wake. 46%

Scotch Malt Whisky Society Cask 84.12 Aged 12 Years refill hogshead, dist Sep 97 (**92.5**) **n23** the gentle feed of delicate watermelon and under-ripe papaya suggests a malt older than its years; **t22.5** amazingly light delivery, almost apologetic and takes a while for oils to build and the malts to begin to offer a distinct weight and chewiness; **f24** now goes in to overdrive as those fledgling fruity notes return, but with enough substance to take on the gathering vanilla and spice; **b23** a rare malt where the finish trumps all else. 59.1%. 296 bottles.

The Whisky Agency Glendullan 1981 (**94.5**) **n23.5** freshly diced celery complete with peppery kick; green under-ripe gooseberry; a hint of smoke; **t24** so salivating! Spices tumble around the palate as the barley goes into overdrive; still the fresh fruit and veg echo, though now some pink raspberry joins in, too; rarely to whiskies produce so much juice and spice for quite so long: exceptional; **f23.5** long, sharp and barley at its most jagged and angular; **b23.5** it is nigh impossible to find a cask of such age that could be any fresher and revitalising. Track down a bottle of this at all costs. Fabulous!! 49.6%

GLENDULLAN (see also above)

Speyside, 1898–1985. Closed.

Glendullan 1978 Rare Malt db **(88) n23** exceptional piquancy to this with the quietness of the oak shattered by a lemon-citrus shrill. Genuinely wonderful; **t22** a lovely, tart start with that citrus making a crashing entry but the oak barges in soon after and coffee is soon on the menu; **f21** more coffee and lemon cake, though it by now a very small slice; **b22** Sherlock Holmes would have loved this one: he would have found it lemon-entry. 56.8%

GLEN ELGIN

Speyside, 1900. Diageo. Working.

Glen Elgin Aged 12 Years db **(89) n23** blistering, mouthwatering fruit of unspecified origin. The intensity of the malt is breathtaking; **t24** stunning fresh malt arrival, salivating barley that is both crisp and lush: then a big round of spice amid some squashed, over-ripe plums. Faultless mouthfeel; **f20** the spice continues as does the intense malt but is devalued dramatically by a bitter-toffee effect; **b22** absolutely murders Cragganmore as Diageo's top dog bottled Speysider. The marks would be several points further north if one – rightly or wrongly – didn't get the feeling that some caramel was weaving a derogatory spell. Brilliant stuff nonetheless. States Pot Still on label – not to be confused with Irish Pot Still. This is 100% malt... and it shows! 43% ☺

Cadenhead's Glen Elgin Aged 30 Years dist 1978, bott 2009 **(92) n23 t24 f22 b23.** Worthy of this excellent distillery. 49.1%

Duthies Glen Elgin 18 Years Old (95) n24.5 oh my word...this promises to be a little special...; one of the most delicate noses I have come across this year landing with all the impact of a budgie's down feather during a good moult. With a wonderfully floral edge, the sweeter elements are provided by a freshly opened biscuit tin. Truly fabulous...; **t24** melts in the mouth, in much the same manner that the aroma lands on the nose; just layer upon layer of grist and lightly toffeed honey...and then a light coat of liquorice; **f23** even though the oak pokes through to bitter out, the burnt Demerara maintains the balance sublimely; **b23.5** spellbindingly beautiful... 46%. Wm. Cadenhead Ltd.

Old Malt Cask Glen Elgin Aged 24 Years bott Jul 09 **(83) n21.5 t21 f20 b20.5.** One of my favourite Speyside distilleries here feels the oaky pace. Pleasant natural caramels. 44.9%

⋅∴⋅ The Whisky Agency Glen Elgin 1975 bourbon hogshead, bott 2011 **(83.5) n22 t21 f20 b20.5.** Competent whisky showing just a little too much oak than it requires for greatness. Puckeringly tart in part, but there is still a depth to the barley which endears. 51.5%

GLENESK

Highlands (Eastern), 1897–1985. Diageo. Demolished.

Duncan Taylor Collection Glenesk 1981 cask no. 932 **(57) n14 t15 f14 b14.** I say! Sulphur, anyone? 54.3%

Duncan Taylor Collection Glenesk 1981 cask no. 933 **(84) n22 t20 f21 b21.** I say! Sherry anyone? 56.9%

Duncan Taylor Collection Glenesk 1983 cask no. 4930 **(89.5) n22 t23 f22 b22.5.** By far the best Glen Esk I've tasted in years. Perhaps not the most complex, but the liveliness and clarity are a treat. 52.1%

GLENFARCLAS

Speyside, 1836. J&G Grant. Working.

Glenfarclas 8 Years Old db **(86) n21 t22 f22 b21.** Less intense sherry allows the youth of this malt to stand out. Mildly quirky as a Glenfarclas and enormous entertainment. 40%

Glenfarclas 10 Years Old db **(80) n19 t20 f22 b19.** Always an enjoyable malt, but for some reason this version never seems to fire on all cylinders. There is a vague honey sheen which works well with the barley, but struggles for balance and the nose is a bit sweaty. Still has distinctly impressive elements but an odd fish. 40% ☺

Glenfarclas 12 Years Old db **(94) n23.5** a wonderfully fresh mix of grape and mint; **t24** light, youthful, playful, mouthwatering. Less plodding honey, more vibrant Demerara and juiced-up butterscotch; **f23** long, with soft almost ice-cream style vanillas with a grapey topping; **b23.5** a superb re-working of an always trustworthy malt. This dramatic change in shape works a treat and suits the malt perfectly. What a sensational success!! 43% ☺ ☺

Glenfarclas 15 Years Old db **(85.5) n21.5 t23 f20 b21.** One thing is for certain: working with sherry butts these days is a bit like working with ACME dynamite....you are never sure when it is about to blow up in your face. There is only minimal sulphur here, but enough to take the edge off a normally magnificent whisky, at the death. Instead it is now merely, in part, quite lovely. The talent at Glenfarclas is unquestionably among the highest in the industry: I'll be surprised to see the same weaknesses with the next bottling. 46% ⊙⊙

Glenfarclas 17 Years Old db (93) n23 just so light and playful: custard powder lightens and sweetens, sultana softens, barley moistens, spice threatens...; t23 the relaxed sherry influence really lets the honey deliver; delightfully roasty and well spiced towards the middle; f23 when I was a kid there was a candy – pretend tobacco, no less! – made from strands of coconut and sweetened with a Demerara syrup. My, this takes me back...; b24 an excellent age for this distillery, allowing just enough oak in to stir up the complexity. A stupendous addition to the range. 40%

Glenfarclas 21 Years Old db (83) n20 t23 f19 b21. A chorus of sweet, honied malt and mildly spiced, teasing fruit on the fabulous mouth arrival and middle compensates for the blips. 43% ⊙

Glenfarclas 25 Years Old db (84) n20 t22 f20 b22. A curious old bat: by no means free from imperfect sherry but compensating with some staggering age – seemingly way beyond the 25-year statement. Enjoys the deportment of a doddering old classics master from a family of good means and breeding. 43% ⊙⊙

Glenfarclas 30 Years Old db (85) n20 t22 f21 b22. Flawed yet juicy. 43% ⊙

Glenfarclas 40 Years Old db (94) n23 old Demerara rum laced with well aged oloroso. Spicy, deep though checked by vanilla; t23 toasty fruitcake with just the right degree of burnt raisin; again the spices are central to the plot though now a Jamaican Blue Mountain/Mysore medium roast mix makes an impressive entrance; f24 long, with the oak not just ticking every box, but doing so with a flourish. The Melton Hunt cake finale is divine... b24 couldn't help but laugh: this sample was sent by the guys at Glenfarclas after they spotted that I had last year called their disappointing 40-year-old a "freak". I think we have both proved a point... 46% ⊙⊙

Glenfarclas 40 Years Old Millennium Edition db (92) n23 t23 f23 b23. An almost immaculate portrayal of an old-fashioned, high-quality malt with unblemished sherry freshness and depth. The hallmark of quality is the sherry's refusal to dominate the spicy, softly peated malt. The oak offers a bourbony sweetness but ensures a rich depth throughout. Quite outstanding for its age. 54.7%. nc ncf.

Glenfarclas 50 Years Old db (92) n24 Unique. Almost a marriage between 20-y-o bourbon and intense, old-fashioned sherry. Earthy, weighty stuff that repays time in the glass and oxidization because only then does the subtlety become apparent and a soft peat-reek reveal itself; t23 an unexpected sweet – even mouthwatering - arrival, again with a touch of peat to add counter ballast to the intense richness of the sherry. The oak is intense from the middle onwards, but of such high quality that it merely accompanies rather then dominates; f22 warming black peppers ping around the palate; some lovely cocoa oils coat the mouth for a bitter-sweet, warming and very long finish; b23 Most whiskies cannot survive such great age. This one really does bloom in the glass and the earthy, peaty aspect makes it all the more memorable. It has taken 50 years to reach this state. Give a glass of this at least an hour's inquisition, as I have. Your patience will be rewarded many times over. 44.4%

⋯ **Glenfarclas 105** db (95.5) n23.5 the youthful grape comes in clean, juicy bunches; the herbs and spices on a rack on the kitchen wall; t24 any lovers of the old Jennings books will here do a Mr Wilkins explosive snort as the magnificent barley-grape mix is propelled with the force of dynamite into the taste buds; survivors of this experience still able to speak may mention something about cocoa notes forming; f24 long, luxurious, with a pulsing vanilla-grape mix and a build up of spices; light oils intensify and elongate; b24 I doubt if any restorative on the planet works quite as well as this one does. Or if any sherry cask whisky is so clean and full of the joys of Jerez. A classic malt which has upped a gear or two and has become exactly what it is: a whisky of pure brilliance... 60%

Glenfarclas 1952 The Family Casks (3rd Release) plain hogshead, cask no. 1713 db (81) n20.5 t20 f20.5 b20. For a curious moment there is an almost hoppy bitterness to this one: a dram for the Campaign For Real Whisky. Just too much oak for greatness, I'm afraid. 47.3%

Glenfarclas 1953 The Family Casks sherry cask no. 1678 db (87) n23 t21 f22 b21. Myriad battles are fought to keep the oak in check. Most are won. 53.7%. 480 bottles.

Glenfarclas 1954 The Family Casks sherry cask no. 444 db (94) n22 t24 f24 b24. Simply defies time and belief. Carries the scars of 52 Summers, for sure. But with the same pride a legionnaire would wear his trophies of combat. 52.6%. 406 bottles.

Glenfarclas 1955 The Family Casks sherry cask no. 2211 db (88) n23 t21 f22 b22. A proud dram gallantly hanging on to its last sweet traces. 46.1%. 545 bottles.

Glenfarclas 1956 The Family Casks sherry cask no. 1758 db (83) n24 t21 f19 b19. Great nose but relentless oak. 47.3%. 435 bottles.

Glenfarclas 1957 The Family Casks (3rd Release) sherry hogshead, cask no. 2 db (**91.5**) n25 t22.5 f22 b22. To mark my 50th birthday in 2007, I had planned on buying a cask of Glenfarclas 1957 and bottling it. Sadly, I was simply too busy to make it happen; had I done so this might possibly have been the cask I chose. It is a couple of Summers past its best – well, probably more. But back in '07, I might just have been able to prevent some of the oaky excess. Then again, maybe not. What cannot be denied is that the nose would probably be Nose of the Year for this Bible, were there such an award. And that even though, like the rest of us from that vintage, it has seen better days, there is no denying that this is less a whisky but more of a life experience. And it is certainly as good and privileged a way I can think of wrapping up all my new whiskies for 2010, this being something like number 920 (actually I have lost count – we'll have to do a final tally by computer), because astonishing whiskies like this don't grow on trees: they simply mature in bits of them...if they are very, very lucky... 46.2%

Glenfarclas 1958 The Family Casks sherry cask no. 2245 db (**88**) n24 t22 f20 b22. Keeps its head above the oaky water - just. 51.6%. 455 bottles.

Glenfarclas 1959 The Family Casks (3rd Release) sherry hogshead, cask no. 3227 db (**79.5**) n23 t20 f17.5 b19. Huge gooseberry and grape. But appears to have suffered from a little renovation work. 50.9%

⚜ **Glenfarclas 1960 The Family Casks Release VI** sherry hogshead, cask no. 1772 db (**94**) n25 I remember having some Melton Hunt cake once which lay forgotten in a kitchen cupboard for about four years. This really does remind me of it: fruity, thick, raisins not so much toasted as charred, dripping with molasses and yet showing a spicy defiance. A nose of such complexity it commands an absolute minimum of 30 minutes attention...At about 20 minutes in it announces its perfection... t24 you actually laugh to yourself at the delivery: it is so outrageously good! Where does such juiciness come from after half a century of being cooped up in a cask? Lots of toasted fruit but the honeycomb and Danish marzipan do a magnificent job of keeping the balance; f21.5 inevitably a price has to be paid and it comes on the exhausted, bitter finale. But it is entirely forgiven... b23.5 this is the 999th whisky tasted for Whisky Bible 2012. And what a choice – what a whisky! Let's just say that the 1960 is drinking well... 47%. sc.

⚜ **Glenfarclas 1961 The Family Casks Release VI** sherry hogshead, cask no. 1326 db (**91**) n25 it is ridiculous! How is any human supposed to describe this? Like the 1960 Release VI, it is faultless: different, but faultless. Here we have blackberries in both juicy and jam form, the latter spread over slightly burnt toast, of course. There is a swirl of salted butter in there, too. Nearby a slightly more roasted than the norm cup of Jamaican Blue Mountain coffee gently steams...; t23 hickory and molasses link with the most toasty raisins imaginable; toasted honeycomb...which becomes toastier by the moment...; f20 bitters out like a coffee struck by water too far on the boil; b23 up until the bitterness forming towards the middle, this was on course for World Whisky of the Year... I need say no more. 54.4%. sc.

⚜ **Glenfarclas 1962 The Family Casks Release VI** sherry hogshead, cask no. 2649 db (**95**) n22.5 hardly usual to find a whisky this age...and even more unusual to find one with a nose like this: unique, I'd say. Not often an aroma comes up that I don't recognise or can't pigeonhole. But there is one here! I would say it was from the wine influence, rather than the actual oak, but I could be wrong. It is dry, halfway to being vaguely vegetable but seems to keep the grape grounded and allow the spices to fly; t24.5 oh, my word! And do those spices fly!!!! A magnificent delivery with the grape now out of its shackles and accompanied by some muscular sugars, too. Lots of juicy plum jam and toasted raisin, but no bitterness at all; f24 a brilliant finale which somehow flips from a fruit influence to a more bourbon style with honeycomb, liquorice and a hint of molasses doing an outstanding job; b24 a quite unique whisky with countless twists and turns and displaying a personality the like of which I have never seen before. Might be a bit scary early on, but stick with it. You will be rewarded more than handsomely. 55.7%. sc.

Glenfarclas 1963 The Family Casks sherry cask no. 4098 db (**87**) n24 t22 f19 b22. Borderline. The oak really is big, but the grape holds out – just. The nose is different matter. 56.7%. 420 bottles.

Glenfarclas 1964 The Family Casks sherry cask no. 4717 db (**92**) n23 t24 f22 b23. A gentleman dram which speaks quietly despite the obvious power at hand. 53.1%. 415 bottles.

Glenfarclas 1965 The Family Casks Release V cask no. 4362, bott May 10 db (**91.5**) n24 classic fruitcake...this one with high percentage of overcooked cherry. There is a toasty, spicy oak imprint, but such is the clarity and intensity of fruit that this is one for those who dream of sherried Speysiders of the old school; t23.5 after the brief silky grape opening score, all kinds of spices ping around the palate as the grape goes to work injecting a muscovado sugar balance; the oak drills deeply into the palate and nearly goes OTT. But those big fruits and sugars keep the delivery and middle ground intact; f21.5 finally dries and bitters out with a stain of coffee; **b22.5** as silky a whisky as you might ever find. Needs a minimum half hour in the glass to open properly. *51.9%*

Glenfarclas 1966 The Family Casks sherry cask no. 4177 db **(95)** n25 t23 f23 **b24**. How fitting this whisky is the same colour as Alan Ball's hair. Because there is no greater way of toasting the memory of the man who was 1966. *51.5%. 104 bottles.*

Glenfarclas 1967 The Family Casks Release V cask no. 5110, bott May 10 db **(96)** n24 cuts a nutty dash to seriously underscore the big fruitcake quality here; no shortage of bourbon, orange peel and liquorice characteristics, either; **t24.5** like sneezing, tasting this is something it's impossible to do with your eyes open...helped by an extraordinary alcohol kick of its age, the soupy intense kumquat, over-ripened banana and sherry (as it is sherry you get here, not grape...!!) form an indestructible alliance, refusing to allow even 43 years of oak to make any kind of telling impact, other than to offer a tame and friendly vanilla frame in which the fruit can take centre stage; elsewhere brown sugars and spices adorn the picture and the odd little liquorice bourbon feature makes a cameo appearance; **f23.5** the milky cocoa makes a much later start than you'd expect, thanks to the bullying fruit; tangy orange peel and banana milkshake sticks to the very end; **b24** one of those whiskies once tasted, never forgotten. A malt which hasn't grown old gracefully: it has simply become a fruity Lothario, seducing every taste bud in sight. And taking it by force if it has to... *60.8%*

⠿ **Glenfarclas 1968 The Family Casks Release VI** sherry hogshead, cask no. 534 db **(86.5)** n22.5 t21 f21.5 **b21.5**. Some milky mocha softens the impact but the oak is very keenly felt. *49.5%. sc.*

⠿ **Glenfarclas 1969 The Family Casks Release VI** sherry hogshead, cask no. 3187 db **(89.5)** n23.5 the oak takes first, second and third positions in dominance here with burned raisin and cherry fruitcake hanging on for dear life; some exemplary spice; **t22.5** fruit takes first and third place; oak second. Massively chewy with a mocha subplot and the burned raisin becoming more intense by the moment; **f21.5** tires and bitters as caramel begins to increase; **b22** nothing shy about the oak here. *56.2%. sc.*

Glenfarclas 1970 The Family Casks sherry cask no. 566 db **(94)** n24 t23 f23 **b24**. Seriously elegant and complex malt that shows not a single blemish despite the extraordinary great age. A Glenfarclas Great. *53.6%. 497 bottles.*

Glenfarclas 1971 The Family Casks sherry cask no. 140 db **(93)** n24 t24 f22 **b23**. A noble dram. *57.1%. 459 bottles.*

Glenfarclas 1972 The Family Casks sherry cask no. 3546 db **(83)** n21 t21 f21 **b20**. Dry, a tad dull and much more natural toffee here. *51.1%. 645 bottles.*

⠿ **Glenfarclas 1973 The Family Casks Release VI** sherry hogshead, cask no. 2567 db **(95)** n(24.5) there are fruitcakes of varying intensity of flavour. This portrays the finest type, those that cost an arm and a leg at Christmas. This is rocking under its own weight in heavily toasted raisin. Big molasses and chunky almonds still sizzling in their own oils; distant hint of freshly ground high roast Java; teasing clove and other vague, lesser spices...; a little orange peel and maple syrup joins the fray as the whisky oxidises; **t24** the weight is exceptional, it's vitality and intensity thrilling; perfect balance of sweeter honeys and drier, more bitter raisin and then a slow lift off of spices which reach great heights; a wave of natural caramels slightly oil the wheels further; **f22.5** the caramel tends to take over, though a bitterness from the oak persists; a little treacle helps counter this; **b24** a whisky which speaks for itself and with spellbinding eloquence. A portrait of just how a sherried whisky should be. If you are lucky enough ever to see this, take a hammer to the piggy bank. *51.4%. sc.*

Glenfarclas 1974 The Family Casks sherry cask no. 5786 db **(93)** n23 t23 f23 **b24**. What a real brawling dram! A kind of Oliver Reed of malts; shows that touch of class despite those rough diamond edges. *60.8%. 555 bottles.*

Glenfarclas 1975 The Family Casks refill hogshead, cask no. 5038 db **(92)** n23 t22 f24 **b23**. Dry yet balances wonderfully. Another spicy number. *51.4%. 187 bottles.*

Glenfarclas 1976 The Family Casks refill butt, cask no. 3111 db **(92)** n23 t23 f23 **b23**. No whisky that's 30 years old has any right to be this juicy and fresh. A malt to take your time over. *49.4%*

Glenfarclas 1977 The Family Casks refill butt, cask no. 61 db **(90)** n22 t23 f22 **b23**. A class, understated act from nose to finale. *59%. 582 bottles.*

Glenfarclas 1978 The Family Casks (3rd Release) plain hogshead, cask no. 626 db **(88)** n22 21.5 f23.5 **b22**. The oak grabs hard early on but lets go gently to allow the barley to escape unscathed. *57.6%*

Glenfarclas 1979 The Family Casks (3rd Release) plain hogshead, cask no. 2216 db **(96.5)** n24.5 t24 f24 **b24**. Proof, not that it was ever needed, that this quite brilliant distillery does not need sherry to bolster its quality. On this evidence, there could be an argument put forward that sherry actually detracts from the greatness of the distillate. At 30 years there appears to be a marriage forged in heaven between the honey-rich barley and the oak. But to achieve this kind of style and depth, it is the raw spirit which must stand up and be counted. Game set and match against those who reckon Glenfarclas a one trick pony: if this isn't proof that the foundations of complexity aren't laid by the make, then I have no idea what is. 50.6%

Glenfarclas 1980 The Family Casks refill sherry cask no. 1942 db **(80) n19 t21 f20 b20.** Soft toffee apple, but not entirely flawless. 50.1%. 681 bottles.

Glenfarclas 1981 The Family Casks Release V cask no. 58, bott May 10 db **(88.5) n22.5** dense. Sherry trifle, with extra custard; **t23** sharp delivery with the barley and fruits crammed into the first few crashing waves; a tad salty and tangy with the middle ground giving way to an orgy of Fruit Pastilles; **f21** flaky vanilla, the most bitter orange...continues on its eclectic way...; **b22** as cluttered and intricate as a Victorian sitting room. And in its own way, just as classically beautiful, too. 50.9%

Glenfarclas 1982 The Family Casks Release V cask no. 633, bott May 10 db **(87) n23** classy, classy, classy...!!! Firm, clipped, sugary: similar to rum cask influence but with an extra semi-ripe greengage fruitiness; **t22.5** more of the same; a re-run of the nose with those vaguely fruited sugars dissolving around the palate; **f20** a tad thin and bitter; **b21.5** a long way from the Glenfarclas norm, but an enjoyable diversion! 54.2%. 216 bottles.

Glenfarclas 1983 The Family Casks refill hogshead, cask no. 50 db **(88) n20 t22 f24 b22.** A sunshine after a rainy afternoon malt 56%. 302 bottles.

Glenfarclas 1984 The Family Casks plain hogshead, cask no. 6028 db **(93) n23 t23 f23 b24.** At first I thought I had been poured malt from the wrong distillery until I saw the cask type. By no means the first non-sherry Glenfarclas, but perhaps the most lemony-fresh and palate-cleansing at this age. So, so lovely! 51.3%. 267 bottles.

Glenfarclas 1985 The Family Casks refill sherry hogshead, cask no. 2826 db **(91) n23 t23 f22 b23.** What a tart! And a fruity one at that... 46.3%. 329 bottles.

Glenfarclas 1986 The Family Casks refill sherry puncheon, cask no. 3434 db **(87) n22 t22 f21 b22.** The fight on the nose and delivery isn't matched by the sleepy follow through. 56.5%

Glenfarclas 1987 Limited Rare Bottling - Edition No. 13 cask no. 6806-6809, dist Dec 87, bott Sep 08 db **(94) n24 t23.5 f23.5 b23.** The grape grazes serenely around the tastebuds without a single note of discord. Simply delicious malt whisky which brings the major elements into play without any major conflict. 46%

Glenfarclas 1988 Quarter Casks cask no. 251-261, dist Jan 88, bott Feb 08 db **(91) n23 t23.5 f22 b22.5.** Chocolate fruit and nut bar lovers will be happy with this one, as will devotees of unspoiled sherry casks. 46.1%. German market. 1,478 bottles.

Glenfarclas 1989 The Family Casks sherry cask no. 11721 db **(94) n23 t24 f23 b24.** The 1989 and 1990 could be twins born a year apart – astonishing! 60%. 600 bottles.

Glenfarclas 1990 The Family Casks Release V cask no. 5095, bott May 10 db **(94.5) n23.5** big clean grape, but the coffee aspect hints of dark rum, too; **t24.5** juicy, beautifully sweetened and structured grape; strata of Lubec marzipan and elsewhere a butterscotch-barley intrigue; **f23** long with the fruit mingling confidently with a busy, peppery spice; always Demerara sugars keep the spices and vanillas in very good shape; **b23.5** you will dream of dusty bodegas if you drink this late at night. Massive sherry, but excellent balance and complexity, too. The delivery and early complexity ranks among the best whisky moments of the year. Strikingly gorgeous. 56.5%. 459 bottles.

Glenfarclas 1991 The Family Casks sherry cask no. 5623 db **(92) n24 t23 f22 b23.** An entrancing malt which has your tastebuds on full alert. 57.9%. 613 bottles.

Glenfarclas 1992 The Family Casks sherry cask no. 264 db **(89) n23 t22 f22 b22.** Big, gutsy, oily stuff. 55.5%. 669 bottles.

Glenfarclas 1993 The Family Casks Release V cask no. 3942, bott Apr 10 db **(72) n17.5 t19.5 f18 b18.** All over the place. The black sheep of the family... 59.7%. 566 bottles.

Glenfarclas 1993 Premium Edition Limited Rare Bottling oloroso cask no. 29 & 30, dist Feb 93, bott Dec 08 db **(75.5) n18 t20 f18.5 b19.** Lots of grape and chocolate. But one of these casks just wasn't right to begin with. 46%. German market. 3,600 bottles.

Glenfarclas 1994 The Family Casks Release V cask no. 3629, bott Apr 10 db **(86) n22 t21 f22 b21.** So dripping in clean, rich sherry that all barley traces have been expunged. Eye-watering, lightly spiced, entirely sulphur-free, and, even if a little heavy -handed here and there, in its more lucid moments of a style now almost unique to this distillery. 59.3%. 609 bottles.

⟾ **Glenfarclas 1995 The Family Casks Release VI** sherry hogshead, cask no. 6778 db **(71) n17.5 t18.5 f17 b18.** Tarnished family silver. 60.1%. sc.

Glenfarclas 1995 45° The Heritage Malt Collection sherry cask, dist Nov 95, bott Sep 06 db **(94.5) n24 t23.5 f23.5 b23.5.** Exceptional. Absolutely everything you could demand from a sherried malt of this age. Not a single off note and the freshness of comparative youth and complexity of years in the cask are in perfect harmony. 45%. Spain.

Glenfarclas 1996 Premium Edition matured in sherry casks, cask no. 678 & 679, dist Feb 96, bott Sep 08 db (75) n17.5 t20 f18.5 b19. Plenty of excellent grape. But spoiled by the obvious fault. I am told that quite a number of Germans actually enjoy sulphured casks. Then this should be right up their strasse. 46%. German market.

Glenfarclas 1997 Cask Strength Premium Edition matured in sherry casks, cask no. 642-648, dist Feb 97, bott Mar 09 db (77.5) n18.5 t20 f19.5 b19.5. In their defence, the quality of some of the casks that have gone into this are so good, it may have been possible to have missed the obvious problem. But it is there, and unmistakably so 55.5%. German market.

⁖ **Glenfarclas 175th Anniversary 2011** db (94) n23.5 crisp and precise fruit: clean and hedging towards bon bons. The very vaguest hint of smoke adds extra depth; vanilla and spice fly the other way; t24 fabulous delivery: every aspect dissolves on impact. The fruits are again subtle yet lush, the sweetness initially from gristy icing sugar, though towards the middle more muscovado. Again, the lightest imaginable wisps of smoke and more profound spices; f23 cream toffee; burnt raisin; b23.5 hard to imagine an experience more gentle than this where alcohol is concerned. No slam bam stuff here. Every moment is about whispers and brushes of the nerve endings. Sensual magic. 43%. nc. J&G Grant. 6000 bottles.

Kaleu's Own #2 Private Edition Glenfarclas Aged 20 Years hogshead, cask no. 2116, dist Feb 89, bott Jul 09 (77) n19.5 t22 f17.5 b19. Big, malty, eye-wateringly tart but the suspicion, confirmed on nose and finish, is that the cask itself could be a little more sympathetic. 58.5%

Kaleu's Own #3 Private Edition Glenfarclas Aged 12 Years hogshead, cask no. 1372, dist Mar 97, bott Jul 09 (85.5) n21.5 t21.5 f21.5 b21. A rare chance to dissect a Glenfarclas. Matured in what looks like a decent quality third fill bourbon barrel we can see just how excellently constructed this malt is, and even locate the deftest smoke. 54.8%

Kingsbury's Finest and Rarest Ballindalloch 34 Years Old 1971 (84.5) n22.5 t21.5 f20 b20.5. More oak than a Tudor battleship. But there are some enjoyable marmalade notes to form the ballast. 51.2%. Import System.

⁖ **Luvians Open Bottle 2010 Glenfarclas 17 Years Old** sherry butt (90) n22 light fruitcake with a honey middle; t23 soft delivery with an unusual vanilla arrival ahead of the fruit. The middle reverts to vanilla and butterscotch with an attractive chalky feel; f22.5 a hint of burnt raisin but there is the late honeycomb, too; b22.5 underplays the fruit and homes in on the honey. Deliciously different. 43%. Luvians Bottle Shop.

Old Malt Cask Glenfarclas Aged 42 Years dist Jun 66, bott 2008 (92) n23 t22.5 f23 b23.5. Another beautiful Glenfarclas which absolutely defies the years. 48.8%. Douglas Laing.

Scotch Malt Whisky Society Cask 1.146 Aged 42 Years refill hogshead, dist Dec 66 (78.5) n23 t20 f17.5 b18. If you invest in this one, do so for the fabulous nose. Elsewhere the oak is shot, a thin sweet fudgy thread keeping this one alive. So just breathe in the glorious gooseberry and butterscotch tart and enjoy. 44.4%. 76 bottles.

Scotch Malt Whisky Society Cask 1.147 Aged 39 Years refill hogshead, dist Feb 70 (93) n23.5 a big oaky signature but the fruit has managed to maintain a degree of freshness; delicate smoke and butterscotch fills in the background; t23.5 quite enormous: the taste buds are placed on full alert as a succession of big, noisy flavours bombard every inch of the palate. The fruits manage to keep the bigger oaks at bay, allowing the middle ground to be occupied by a milkshakey mocha; f23 the odd sharp splinter here and there, but the excellence of the mocha and spice ensures a classic finale; b23 proving that you aren't always going to seed at 39... 53.5%. 124 bottles.

Scotch Malt Whisky Society Cask 1.154 Aged 40 Years refill hogshead, dist Feb 70 (77) n21 t18.5 f19 b18.5. A great number of people enjoy this nougat-rich style of over-matured malt, especially when the creosote kicks in. And though it has the odd, fleeting, enjoyable moment, I can't say I'm a great fan. If 1.147 was the SMWS's Brazil of their 1970 bottlings, then this is their Italy... 43.4%. 61 bottles.

⁖ **Scotch Malt Whisky Society Cask 1.158 Aged 11 Years** 1st fill barrel, cask no. 800062, dist 1999 (91.5) n23 charmingly gristy, despite life in a first fill cask! Surprisingly delicate, though there are some curious vanilla explosions with the spice; t23.5 fabulously sharp malt is thrown forwards by a secondary surge of oak; in the wake is a highly complex ebbing and flowing of varying bourbon notes, with slivers of honeycomb and peppered hickory noticeable; f22 a burned toast bitterness on the fudge; those complex bourbon notes just keep on going; b23 complexity is the key but most impressive is the intensity: a dram I could enjoy all night. Not that it was ever needed, but what a way to prove that the excellence of this distillery has nothing to do with sherry... 61.8%. sc. 231 bottles.

GLENFIDDICH
Speyside, 1887. William Grant & Sons. Working.

Glenfiddich 12 Years Old db (85.5) n21 t22 f21 b21.5. A malt now showing a bit of zap and spark. Even displays a flicker of attractive muscovado sugars. Simple, untaxing and safe. 40% ⊙ ⊙

Glenfiddich 12 Years Old Toasted Oak Reserve (92.5) n22.5 t23.5 f22.5 b24. Another bottling to confound the critics of Glenfiddich. This is as fine an essay in balance, charm and sophistication as you are likely to find in the whole of Speyside this year. Crack open a bottle... but only when you have a good hour to spend. 40%

Glenfiddich Caoran Reserve Aged 12 Years db (89) n22.5 t22 f21.5 b23. Has fizzed up a little in the last year or so with some salivating charm from the barley and a touch of cocoa from the oak. A complex little number. 40%

Glenfiddich Rich Oak Over 14 Years Old new American & new Spanish oak finish db (90.5) n23 fascinating: there is a nod towards Japanese oak in the naked wood profile here. Toned down, though, by a huge pithy kumquat presence. That this is virgin oak there can be no doubt, so don't expect an easy ride; t22 soft oils help for a quiet landing: like lonely oaks falling in a forest...there is a brief sensation of passing barley. Then it returns again to a number of oak-laden notes, especially the spices which move towards a creamy mocha territory; f23.5 possibly the best phase of the experience. The vivid, surging oak has cooled and some barley oils mingle in a relaxed fashion with the sweetening, very mildly sugared mocha; b22 from the moment you nose this, there is absolutely no doubting its virgin oak background. It pulls towards bourbon, but never gets there. Apparently European oak is used, too. The result is something curiously hinting at Japanese, but without the crushing intensity. Delicious, thoughtful whisky and one to tick off on your journey of malt whisky discovery. Though a pity we don't see it at 46% and in full voluptuous nudity: you get the feeling that this would have been something really exceptional to conjure with. 40%. William Grant.

Glenfiddich Aged 15 Years Old db (94.5) n23 such a deft intermingling of the softer fruits and bourbon notes...with barley in there to remind you of the distillery; t23 intense and big yet all the time appearing delicate and light; the most apologetic of spices help spotlight the barley sweetness and delicate fruits; f24.5 just so long and complex; something of the old fashioned fruit salad candy about this but with a small degree of toffee just rounding off the edges; b24 if an award were to be given for the most consistently beautiful dram in Scotland, this would win more often than not. This under-rated distillery has won more friends with this masterpiece than probably any other brand. 40% ⊙

Glenfiddich Aged 15 Years Cask Strength db (85.5) n20 t23 f21 b21.5. Improved upon the surprisingly bland bottlings of old, especially on the fabulously juicy delivery. Still off the pace due to an annoying toffee-ness towards the middle and at the death. 51%

Glenfiddich Distillery Edition 15 Years Old db (93.5) n24.5 banana skins, but there is no slip up here as the aroma spectrum moves from ultra fat sultanas on one side to dried coconut on the other. You'll find countless other reference points, including lightly salted celery and even molten candle wax. Quite astonishing and, even with its spice nip, one of the great whisky noses of 2010; t24 my word!! Just so lively...enormous complexity from the very first mouthful. The mouthfeel is two-toned with heavier fruit not quite outstripping the flightier barley. All kinds of vanilla – both dry and sweet – and a dusty spiciness, too; f22 tones down rather too dramatically, hedging much more towards the more docile banana-vanilla elements; b23 had this exceptional whisky been able to maintain the pace through to the finish, this would have been a single malt of the year contender - at least. 51%. ncf.

Glenfiddich Aged 15 Years Solera Reserve (see Glenfiddich 15 Years Old)

Glenfiddich 18 Years Old db (95) n23.5 the smoke, which for long marked this aroma, appears to have vanished. But the usual suspects of blood orange and various other fruit appear to thrive in the lightly salted complexity; t24.5 how long are you allowed to actually keep the whisky held on the palate before you damage your teeth? One to really close your eyes and study because here we have one of the most complex deliveries Speyside can conjour: the peat may have gone, but there is coal smoke around as the juicy barley embeds with big fat sultanas, plums, dates and grapes. Despite the distinct lack of oil, the mouthfeel is entirely yielding to present one of the softest and most complete essays on the palate you can imagine, especially when you take the bitter-sweet ratio and spice into balance; f23 long, despite the miserly 40% offered, with plenty of banana-custard and a touch of pear; b24 at the moment, the ace in the Glenfiddich pack. If this was bottled at 46%, unchilfiltered etc, I dread to think what the score might be... 40% ⊙

🔅 **Glenfiddich Age Of Discovery Aged 19 Years Madeira Cask Finish** db (88.5) n22.5 mixed fruit but emboldened by gentle, oak-enriched spices. Delicate yet confident and, as the drier elements take hold, one is reminded of gooseberry jam on mildly burnt toast...; **t22.5** a soft, almost lightweight delivery...maybe too gentle due to the strength. Or lack thereof. The fruits are again evident with a touch of physalis adding a little piquancy to the more obvious grape; juicy and well-balanced; **f21** flattened by an onslaught of caramels and vanilla; **b22.5** oddly enough, almost a breakfast malt: it is uncommonly soft and light yet carries a real jam and marmalade character. 40%

Glenfiddich 21 Years Old db (86) **n21 t23 f21 b21.** A much more uninhibited bottling with loads of fun as the mouth-watering barley comes rolling in. But still falls short on taking the hair-raisingly rich delivery forward and simply peters out. 40%

Glenfiddich 30 Years Old db (93.5) **n23** always expect sherry trifle with this: here is some sherry not to be trifled with... salty, too; **t23.5** the juiciest 30-y-o I can remember from this distillery for a while: both the grape and barley are contributing to the salivation factor...; the mid ground if filled with light cocoa, soft oils and a delicate hickory-demerara bourbon-style sweetness; **f23.5** here usually the malt ends all too briefly. Not this time: chunky grape carries on its chattering with the ever-increasing bourbon-honeycomb notes; a vague furry finale...; **b23.5** a 'Fiddich which has changed its spots. Much more voluptuous than of old and happy to mine a grapey seam while digging at the sweeter bourbon elements for all it is worth. Just one less than magnificent butt away from near perfection and a certain Bible Award... 40% ⊙ ⊙

⋰⋰ **Glenfiddich 40 Years Old** batch 7 db (96) **n24** it's the spices which win hands down here. Yes, there is all kinds of juicy, voluptuous fruit...this nose is dripping with it. But the spices are the rudder steering a path through spectacular scenery...; **t24** ...so no surprises it is the eloquent spices which speak first on delivery. Nothing brash. No violence. Just considered and balanced, bringing the most from the oak and allowing a juicy degree of salt to enliven things further; to work properly sugars are required and sublime traces of muscovado sugars appear to bring the fat sultanas to bursting; **f23.5** now we get to the burnt raisin bit of the fruit cake effect. That's just how it should be...; oh, and did I mention the spices...? **b24.5** for the 750th New Whisky for the 2012 Bible, I decided to select a distillery close to my heart... and the age I'll be next birthday... Believe me: this guy didn't let me down. Full frontal fruit and spice. Perfectly toned and all the curves in all the right places. Rrrrr!!! 45.8%. 600 bottles.

Glenfiddich Rare Collection 40 Years Old db (86.5) **n22.5 t23 f20 b21.** A quite different version to the last with the smoke having all but vanished, allowing the finish to show the full weight of its considerable age. The nose and delivery are superb, though. The barley sheen on arrival really deserves better support. 43.5%

Glenfiddich 50 Years Old db (97) **n25** we are talking 50 years, and yet we are still talking fresh barley, freshly peeled grape and honey. Not ordinary honey. Not the stuff you find in jars. But the pollen that attracts the bees to the petunia; and not any old petunia: not the white or the red or pink or yellow. But the two-toned purple ones. For on the nose at least this is perfection; this is nectar... **t24** a silky delivery: silky barley with silky, watered down maple syrup. The middle ground, in some previous Glenfiddich 50-year-olds a forest of pine and oak, is this time filled with soft, grassy barley and the vaguest hint of a distant smoke spice; **f24** long, long, long, with the very faintest snatch of something most delicately smoked: a distant puff of peat reek carried off on the persistent Speyside winds, then a winding-down of vanillas, dropping through the gears of sweetness until the very last traces are chalky dry; **b24** for the record, my actual words, after tasting my first significant mouthful, were: "fuck! This is brilliant." It was an ejaculation of genuine surprise, as any fly on the wall of my Tasting Room at 1:17am on Tuesday 4th August would testify. Because I have tasted many 50-year-old whiskies over the years, quite possibly as many as anyone currently drawing breath. For not only have I tasted those which have made it onto the whisky shelves, but, privately, or as a consultant, an untold number which didn't: the heroic but doomed oak-laden failures. This, however, is a quite different animal. We were on the cusp of going to press when this was released, so we hung back. William Grant blender David Stewart, whom I rank above all other blenders on this planet, has known me long and well enough to realise that the surrounding hype, with this being the most expensive whisky ever bottled at £10,000 a go or a sobering £360 a pour, would bounce off me like a pebble from a boulder. "Honestly, David," he told my chief researcher with a timorous insistence, "please tell Jim I really think this isn't too oaky." He offered almost an apology for bringing into the world this 50-year-old babe. Well, as usual David Stewart, doyen of the blending lab and Ayr United season ticket holders, was absolutely spot on. And, as is his want, he was rather understating his case. For the record, David, next time someone asks you how good this whisky is, just for once do away with the Ayreshire niceness installed by generations of very nice members of the Stewart family and tell them: "Actually, it's bloody brilliant if I say so myself! And I don't give a rat's bollocks what Murray thinks." 46.1%

Glenfiddich 1955 Vintage cask no. 4221 db (**93**) n23 t23 f23 b24. A real surprise package, because even without sherry or peat to hide behind there is enough complexity and, at times, utter brilliance to dazzle the most demanding of commentators. And, believe me; this is one sample I didn't spit... Over 50 years old and quite majestic. Truly classic stuff. 52.6%

Glenfiddich 1958 Vintage cask no. 8642 db (**78**) n23 t18 f18 b19. Oak can be such an unforgiving master. Fabulous old oloroso nose, though. 46.3%

Glenfiddich 1959 Vintage cask no. 3934 db (**89**) n23 t22 f22 b22. From the year Jacky Cox led Ayr United to the old Scottish Second Division Championship, something equally as rare! Glenfiddich showing something of a rummy side to its character with lots of copper and ester in the mix. The oak is profound, but sits comfortably in the scheme of things. One for late at night, closed eyes and memories of long-lost days at Somerset Park. 48.1%

⚖️ **Glenfiddich 1961 47 Years Old** cask no. 9016 db (**95**) n24.5 massive bourbon flourish: all kinds of liquorice, hickory and dates, over toasted honeycomb. All this topped by molten chocolate caramel. The massive oak is outwardly OTT, but those sweeter bourbon notes and a number of herbal and ginger strands compensate: lots of what might be construed as negatives make one very big positive; t24.5 some dark sugars and salivating prune juice sweeten the way and allow a lush cushion for the oaky explosion you just know is about to happen; it arrives in the middle ground. But by now the chocolate and caramel evident on the nose has already formed a welcoming committee, backed by those dates and burgeoning fudge; f22 annoyingly tired with the oak claiming early victory, but still the depth of so many enormous facets strike back with not just style but with an imperious inevitability; b24 taste this whisky within a few minutes of opening the bottle and judge at your peril. Leave for a good half hour and then the full portrait is unveiled. For all its excellence, the oak is far too rampant for true greatness to be achieved. Or so you might reasonably think. The truth, however, must be revealed: this makes for a stunningly fine whisky experience. 43.8%. sc.

Glenfiddich 1964 Vintage cask no. 13430 db (**80**) n22 t22 f17 b19. The nose is pure bourbon – and very old bourbon at that. Wobbles a bit in both aroma and delivery but for all its oaky over- zestfulness – and even a touch of the soaps (especially on the finish) – you still cannot help but enjoy this one. To say it is a character is something of an understatement...!! 45.6%

Glenfiddich 1973 Vintage cask no. 9874 db (**94**) n23 t23 f24 b24. I've been tasting these special casks from this distillery since before my hair went grey. I've sampled some good 'uns. This is possibly the best of the lot. 48.1%

Glenfiddich Vintage Reserve 1973 cask no. 9874 db (**92**) n23 t23 f22 b24. Whisky picked at its very ripest! The juices are still flowing despite a massive oak threat. But such is the sheer élan and fruit and sweet edges that an astounding and beautiful experience is assured. 46.5%

Glenfiddich 1976 cask no. 16389, bott 2007 db (**87**) n23.5 t22 f20 b21.5. Bottled in the nick of time. The vast majority of Glenfiddichs crash and burn by this age: it is not a malt, peaking in age as it does in the 15 to 18 region, that can usually stand up to great years in the cask. Here it manages it, just, and for good measure offers a truly memorable nose. 47.4%. Exclusively for Willow Park, Calgary.

Glenfiddich Vintage Reserve 1976 cask no. 516, bott 2007 db (**93.5**) n23 t24 f23 b23.5. I still say that Glenfiddich is not naturally disposed to old age. However, the odd ancient gem crops up...and this is one. 51.9%. 549 bottles.

⚖️ **Glenfiddich Snow Phoenix** bott 2010 db (**95**) n23.5 graceful and delicate, there is obviously some age lurking, lord-like, in the background. But it is the younger malts, reminiscent of the long-lost, original, no-age statement version that steals the show, imprinting the unique grassy, tingly signature into the glass; t24 a time machine has taken me back 25 years: it is like the original Glenfiddich at its juicy, ultra-salivating youthful finest but now with a honey enriched backbone and some real belief in the oaky spices, where they were once half-hearted a generation ago; f23 long, with that honeyed sheen remaining impressively attached to the dynamic barley; b24.5 it is no easy task for blender Brian Kinsman to emerge from the considerable shadow of the now retired David Stewart, the world's finest blender of the last 20 years. But here he has stepped up to the plate to create something which captures the very essence of the distillery. It is almost a deluxe version of the original Glenfiddich: something that is so far advanced of the dull 12-year-old, it is scary. This is sophisticated whisky, have no doubt. And the first clear, impressive statement declaring that Glenfiddich appears to remain in very safe hands. Whatever Brian did from those casks, exposed to the bleak Speyside winter, he should do again. But to a far wider audience. 47.6%. ncf.

Hart Brothers Glenfiddich Aged 45 Years 1st sherry hogshead filled, dist Sep 64, bott Oct 09 (**96**) n25 what a wonderful marriage of over-ripe dates, mid roast Mysore coffee, blackened banana and the fruitiest of old Demerara pot still rum-seasoned fruitcake... Perfection, it has to be said... t24 the oak shows up early but immediately states that it shall go so far and not encroach on the overall balance. Just as well because the balance between the sharpness and richness of toasted raisin is spot on; there is burnt toast sweetened with plum jam and Demerara-lightened coffee; **f23** an understandable degree of bitterness – a mixture of that toast again and cocoa – but offset by a fabulous burnt fudge sweetness; **b24** to think this was distilled in 2 BR: 2 Before Ramsey, that is 1964...two years before England first won the World Cup. Now, having spent the last half hour being blown away by this, I leave my tasting lab to watch England take on the Germans in the hope (never expectation) that we might continue on course to do it again. This time, though, with some of the finest malt Scotland is currently able to offer. How ironic is that...? 55.6%. Hart Brothers Ltd.

GLEN GARIOCH
Highlands (Eastern), 1798. Morrison Bowmore. Working.

Glen Garioch 8 Years Old db **(85.5) n21 t22 f21 b21.5**. A soft, gummy, malt – not something one would often write about a dram of this or any age from Geary! However, this may have something to do with the copious toffee which swamps the light fruits which try to emerge. 40%

Glen Garioch 10 Years Old db **(80) n19 t22 f19 b20**. Chunky and charming, this is a malt that once would have ripped your tonsils out. Much more sedate and even a touch of honey to the rich body. Toffeed at the finish. 40%

Glen Garioch 12 Years Old db **(88.5) n22** gooseberries and fudge...and a touch of smoke...!!!!; **t23** mouth filling with a delicious degree of sharp maltiness; **f21.5** toffees out, though a little smoke drifts back in; **b22** a significant improvement on the complexity front. The return of the smoke after a while away was a surprise and treat. 43%

Glen Garioch 15 Years Old db **(86.5) n20.5 t22 f22 b22**. In the bottling I sampled last year the peat definitely vanished. Now it's back again, though in tiny, if entertaining, amounts. 43%

Glen Garioch 21 Years Old db **(91) n21** a few wood shavings interrupt the toasty barley; **t23** really good bitter-sweet balance with honeycomb and butterscotch leading the line; pretty juicy, busy stuff; **f24** dries as it should with some vague spices adding to the vanilla and hickory; **b23** an entirely re-worked, now smokeless, malt that has little in common with its predecessors. Quite lovely, though. 43%

Glen Garioch 1797 Founders Reserve db **(87.5) n21** fruit toffee fudge; **t22** some fizz on delivery followed by a rampaging barley juiciness; much lighter and softer than the strength indicates; **f22.5** excellent mocha accompanies the fruit with aplomb; **b22** impressively fruity and chewy: some serious flavour profiles in there. 48%

Glen Garioch 1958 db **(90) n24 t21 f23 b22**. The distillery in its old smoky clothes: and quite splendid it looks! 43%. 328 bottles.

⁘ **Adelphi Glen Garioch 20 Years Old** cask no. 2691, dist 1990, bott 2010 **(85.5) n21 t22.5 f21 b21**. A pleasant alpha barley experience. But the massive sugars make matters a little one dimensional. 54.9%. sc. Adelphi Distillery. 234 bottles.

Duncan Taylor Collection Glen Garioch 1988 cask no. 1988 **(94) n23 t24 f23 b24**. Glorious whisky with attitude. A must get malt: simple as that! 54.4%

⁘ **Liquid Sun Glen Garioch 1990** bourbon hogshead, bott 2011 **(85) n21 t22.5 f20.5 b21**. Lovely, juicy barley but very few trimmings. 54%. The Whisky Agency.

Mackillop's Choice Glen Garioch 1990 dist Apr 90, bott Feb 10 **(94) n23** well, what do you know? A touch of dark, earthy peat... a throwback to the days when their kiln was still working (and I'd throw on some of the turf) I assume; **t24** big, uncompromisingly full bodied with wonderful thick malt; touches of light smoke and cocoa work wonderfully together; best of all, though, is the house style of nip and pinch on the palate...just love it! **f23.5** long with a light citrus flourish to the half-hearted spice and smoke; **b23.5** almost brings a tear to the eye when I find a ye-olde style Geary with a touch of smoke. A bit rough and ready, but absolutely gorgeous! And a type of Geary I haven't tasted in years. 56.6%. Iain Mackillop & Co Ltd.

⁘ **Malts Of Scotland Glen Garioch 1991** bourbon hogshead, cask no. 3175, dist May 91, bott Jul 10 **(86) n21.5 t23 f20 b21.5**. Some marvellous sugars adds lustre to the juicy malt before it tapers out. 50.1%. nc ncf sc. Malts Of Scotland. 142 bottles.

Provenance Glen Garioch Over 9 Years refill hogshead, cask no. 6299, dist Autumn 00, bott Summer 2010 **(87.5) n21.5** teasing smoke; **t22** clean with minimum oak infusion but a lovely smokiness slowly adds gravitas to the barley; **f22** the delicate smoke lingers; **b22** a Geary with fascinating echoes of its past. 46%. nc ncf sc. Douglas Laing & Co.

⁘ **Rare Auld Glen Garioch 19 Years Old** dist 1991, cask no. 3855 **(90) n22** a fine balance between the peppery oak and crisp malt; **t23.5** superb arrival with excellent intensity to the clean, beautifully-layered barley; **f22** a flicker of gooseberry to the malt; **b22.5** a sophisticated, wonderfully complex dram worth hunting down. 51.1%. sc. Duncan Taylor & Co.

Scotch Malt Whisky Society Cask 19.44 Aged 20 Years refill hogshead, dist Oct 88 **(79)** n21 t20 f19 b19. Thin with a touch of the malty paint stripper about it. *53.3%. 251 bottles.*

GLENGLASSAUGH

Speyside, 1875. Scaent Group. Working.

Glenglassaugh 21 Year Old db **(94)** n23.5 elegant and adroit, the lightness of touch between the citrus and barley is nigh on mesmeric: conflicting messages of age in that it appears younger and yet you feel something has to be this kind of vintage to hit this degree of aloofness. Delicate and charming...; **t24.5** again we have all kinds of messages on delivery: the spices fizz around announcing oaky intentions and then the barley sooths and sweetens even with a degree of youthful juiciness. The tastebuds are never more than caressed, the sugar-sweetened citrus ensuring neither the barley or oak form any kind of advantage; impeccably weighted, a near perfect treat for the palate; **f22.5** white chocolate and vanilla lead the way as the oak begins to offer a degree of comparative austerity; **b23.5** a malt which simply sings on the palate and a fabulous benchmark for the new owners to try to achieve in 2030...!! *46%*

Glenglassaugh 26 Years Old db **(78.5)** n19 t21.5 f18.5 b19.5. Industrial amounts of cream toffee here. Also some odd and off key fruit notes winging in from somewhere. Not quite the gem I had hoped for. *46%*

Glenglassaugh 30 Year Old db **(89)** n23 the grape of noble rot stands haughtily beside the oak without blot; **t23** fruity, silky, if in some places a little flat. Lots of dried dates, demerara, chocolate raisins, a little of this, a little of that... **f21** against every wish, drifts away incoherently, mumbling something coffee-ish; **b22** sheer poetry. Or not... *43.1%*

⋰ **Glenglassaugh Aged 37 Years** db **(92)** n23.5 honeycomb and hickory; burnt (or with the vaguest hint of smoke, is that burning?) date and walnut cake with liberal helpings of Demerara sugar; a hint of spice on the ever thickening vanilla. Not a single off note, or hint of over exertion...; **t23** excellent honey and spice delivery. First-class oils and beeswax ensure the sugars glide around the palate as if on skates; a curious subplot of glazed cherry ups the salivation factor even further; **f22** more vanillas and a little (smoky?) praline for a finale flourish; **b23.5** after all those years, dementia has set in: it thinks it's a bourbon... And not any old bourbon, believe me... *54.8%. nc ncf.*

Glenglassaugh 40 Year Old db **(96)** n24.5 the kind of oak you'd expect at this age – if you are uncommonly lucky or have access to some of the most glorious-nosing ancient casks in all Scotland - but there is so much else on the fruity front besides: grape, over-ripe yam, fat cherries...And then there is a bourbony element from molassed hickory and sweetened vanilla: wake me, I must be dreaming...on second thoughts, don't; **t24.5** pure silk on delivery. All the flavours arrive in one rich wave of consummate sweetness, a tapestry celebrating the enormity of both the fruit and oak, yet condensed into a few inches rather than feet; plenty of soft medium roast Jamaican Blue Mountain and then at times mocha; on the fruity front there is juicy dates mulched with burned raisin; **f23** the relative Achilles heel as the more bitter, nutty parts of the oak gather; **b24** it is as if this malt has gone through a 40-year marrying process: the interlinking of flavours and styles is truly beyond belief. *44.6%*

⋰ **Glenglassaugh Aged 43 Years** db **(91)** n23.5 a nose of rare clarity for its age. Or it is once it has been in the glass for a good 15 minutes. Then the wrinkles vanish and we are left with a vibrant, juicy nose offering a sweetness that runs the full gamut from fruit to biscuit... Not surprisingly there is a death by chocolate feel to this one, too. And even a little smoke; not entire free of the odd gremlin, but not too much damage done; **t24** you really don't spit this kind of whisky, however professional you are. Not sure if the silkworm has been bred yet that can produce something as silky as this guy. A few random spices here, a splash of walnut oil there; **f21** a slight Achilles heel: some weaknesses show as a mild bitterness leaks in. But I am not quibbling; **b22.5** another ridiculously magnificent malt from a distillery which should never have been closed in the first place... *48.7%. nc ncf.*

⋰ **Glenglassaugh Andrea Cammineci 1972** refill butt db **(92.5)** n23.5 spiced bonbons, with some black cherry for good measure; the sweetness is dull, of the liquorice variety as well as toasty raisin; **t24** those looking for a big sherry statement are in for a shock: the delivery is nearer Kentucky with tidal waves of waxy honeycomb and natural caramels; the odd piece of fruitcake can be spotted bobbing around; **f22** enters a no-man's-land for a while where there is a lack of anything much. Then, slowly, a fruitcake toasty dryness emerges, along with walnut oil; **b23** one of those rare hybrids that manages to get the best of both worlds; will appeal to high quality bourbon lovers every bit as those looking for sumptuous sherried drams... *59.1%. nc ncf sc. For German distribution.*

Glenglassaugh 1973 Family Silver db **(95)** n23 t24 f24 b24. From first to last this whisky caresses and teases. It is old but shows no over-ageing. It offers what appears a malt veneer but is complexity itself. Brilliant. And now, sadly, almost impossible to find. Except, possibly, at the Mansefield Hotel, Elgin. 40%

⚜ **Glenglassaugh The Manager's Legacy No.1 Jim Cryle 1974** refill sherry hogshead db (90.5) n21.5 citrus and various salty, herbal notes try to prop up a crumbling castle as an incoming tide of oak begins to wash it away...; t23.5 where did that come from? Early oak, but then a magnificent recovery in the form of sharp old orange peel and a salty, mega malty thrust. Some dried fruit, mainly old dates and plums, build further bridges and as the saline quality intensifies, the juicier it all becomes; f22.5 long with spices and plenty of cream toffee; b23 talk about blowing away the cobwebs! The nose trumpets all the hallmarks of a tired old malt in decline. What follows on the palate could not be more opposite. Don't you just love a surprise! 52.9%. nc ncf sc. 200 bottles.

⚜ **Glenglassaugh The Manager's Legacy No.2 Dod Cameron 1986** refill sherry butt, dist Dec 86 db (92) n23.5 the sherry residue must have been as thick as tar when they billed this butt: an enormous welter of pithy and juicy grape married with the aroma one might expect at a Fruitcake Fest. The odd roasty bitter note counters the sweeter Demerara tones. Wow! t24 a near perfect delivery with that thick grape arriving hand-in-hand with sublime spices; again a burnt toast bitterness battles it out with some macho sugars; f22 back to a more Dundee cake style, with a few natural caramels thrown in; b22.5 did anyone mention this was from a sherry butt...? A vague, mildly out of kilter, bitterness knocks the odd mark off here and there, but a dram to kick the shoes off to and savour. 45.3%. nc ncf sc. 500 bottles.

⚜ **Glenglassaugh The Manager's Legacy No.3 Bert Forsyth 1968** refill sherry butt, dist Dec 68 db (89) n22 almost Amazonian amounts of oak but there is enough black cherry and dried dates to offer charm and complexity. A twist of salt doesn't hurt, either; t23 the oak has most of its own way on delivery. But there is a slow clawing back of vital ground as juices begin the flow and sugars come out of hiding; the odd exotic fruit moment, too; f22 any residual bitterness is absorbed by the mocha; b22 a kind of upside down whisky: usually the big oaks arrive at the death. Here they are all upfront... An excellent whisky that, by rights, should never be... 44.9%. nc ncf sc. 300 bottles.

⚜ **Glenglassaugh The Manager's Legacy No.4 Walter Grant 1967** refill sherry hogshead, dist May 67 db (86.5) n19.5 t22 f23 b22. Despite the oaky wounds to the nose, the palate is far more open and somehow reaches a degree of depth and complexity which makes for an excellent and unexpected experience. 40.4%. nc ncf sc. 200 bottles.

Glenglassaugh The Spirit Drink db (85) n20 t22 f21.5 b21.5. A pretty wide margin taken on the cut here, it seems, so there is plenty to chew over. Richly flavoured and a tad oily, as is to be expected, which helps the barley to assert itself in midstream. The usual new make chocolaty element at work here, too, late on. Just great to see this distillery back in harness after all these years. And a great idea to get the new spirit out to the public, something I have been encouraging distilleries to do since my beard was still blue. Look forward to seeing another version where a narrower cut has been made. 50%. 8,160 bottles.

⚜ **Glenglassaugh The Spirit Drink Fledgling XB** db (91) n22 t23.5 f22.5 b23. Outstandingly well made malt. The barley arrives unblemished and makes a proud, juicy stand. A surprising degree of early natural caramel. Prefer this over the peat, to be honest, and augers well for the distillery's future. 50%

⚜ **Glenglassaugh The Spirit Drink Peated** db (89.5) n22 t23 f22 b22.5. Enjoyable and doesn't appear close to its 50%abv. But it's not about the bite, for there is a welcome citrus freshness to this, helped along the way by a peatiness which is big but by no means out to be the only important voice. 50%

Glenglassaugh The Spirit Drink That Blushes to Speak Its Name db (85) n22 t21.5 f21 b21. Not whisky, of course. New make matured for a few months in wine barrels. The result is a Rose-looking spirit. Actually takes me back to my early childhood – no, not the tasting of new make spirit. But the redcurrant aroma which does its best to calm the new make ruggedness. Tasty and fascinating, though the wine tries to minimalise the usual sweetness you find in malt spirit. 50%

Adelphi Glen Garioch 1990 Aged 19 Years bourbon hogshead, cask no. 2697, bott 2009 (83) n21.5 t21 f20 b20.5. Pretty one dimensional malt, but helped along the way with a nod towards a pleasing bourbony sweetness. 53.8%. 234 bottles.

Highland Malt Glenglassaugh 31 Years Old 1978 bott 2009 (87) n23 from the polished leather and boiled candy school of aged sweetness: t22 immediate oaky impact but weathered by the sharpness of barley which rages ages the age; f20.5 pretty tired and rickety; b21.5 a cask on the brink. But enough life left in there, just, for some excellent moments. 44.6%. Speciality Drinks Ltd, bottled for TWE's 10th Anniversary.

Old Malt Cask Glenglassaugh Aged 25 Years sherry butt, cask no. DL 5362,dist Jul 84, bott Jul 09 **(71) n17.5 t20 f16.5 b17.** Bottled in Rotarua, one suspects... *50%. 624 bottles.*

GLENGOYNE

Highlands (Southwest), 1833. Ian Macleod Distillers. Working.

Glengoyne 10 Years Old db **(90) n22** beautifully clean despite coal-gas bite. The barley is almost in concentrate form with a marmalade sweetness adding richness; **t23** crisp, firm arrival with massive barley surge, seriously chewy and textbook bitter-sweet balance; but now some oils have tucked in to intensify and lengthen; **f22** incredibly long and refined for such a light malt. The oak, which made soft noises in the middle now intensifies, but harmonises with the intense barley; an added touch of coffee signals some extra oak in recent bottlings; **b23** proof that to create balance you do not have to have peat at work. The secret is the intensity of barley intermingling with oak. Not a single negative note from first to last and now a touch of oil and coffee has upped the intensity further. *40%*

Glengoyne 12 Years Old db **(91.5) n22.5** salty, sweet, lightly fruity; **t23** one of the softest deliveries on the market: the fruit, gristy sugars and malt combine to melt in the mouth: there is not a single hint of firmness; **f23** a graduation of spices and vanilla. Delicate and delightful...; **b23** the nose has a curiously intimate feel but the tasting experience is a wonderful surprise. *43%*

Glengoyne 12 Years Old Cask Strength db **(79) n18 t22 f19 b20.** Not quite the happiest Glengoyne I've ever come across with the better notes compromised. *57.2%. nc ncf.*

Glengoyne 12 Years Old Scottish Merchant's Choice 1996 sherry hogshead no. 3447 db **(88.5) n22** pots of marmalade; **t23** lush, quite wonderful dovetailing between juicy barley and no less juicy grape; **f21.5** dries and bitters slightly but enough vanilla to cope; **b22** high quality sherry influence. *57.8%*

Glengoyne 13 Years Old Single Cask 1995 European oak sherry hogshead no. 2082, dist Oct 95 db **(94) n24** just one of those fabulous, weakening of the knees, moments you used to get in the warehouse many years ago: a 12 to 15 whisky maturing in a top form oloroso butt...the bung is pulled out and you stick your nose in the barrel. You used to get...this. But very rarely now, alas. That unique slightly burnt raisin, slightly concentrated orange pith, dank heavy mixture with a custardy oakiness and a sweeter, fresher edge. Priceless... **t24** just awe inspiring. Almost a perfect weight on the palate as those burnt raisins and sultanas battle it out, with that orangey fruitcake background which this kind of malt demands; **f23** a touch bitter. Just burnt raisin in excess, or was a sulphur stick waved around here for a second or two thirteen years ago...? I'll go with the raisins...; **b23** for those of you wandering what a 1990s non sulphured sherry butt tastes like – and I am sure some of your still don't know for certain – grab some of this. And just jump into that glass: it's safe and wonderful! *56.1%. Ian Macleod.*

⌐ **Glengoyne Aged 14 Years Limited Edition** oloroso cask **(77) n19 t20 f19 b19.** A vague sulphur taint. But rather underpowered anyway. *40%. nc. Marks & Spencer UK.*

Glengoyne 16 Years Old Single Cask 1993 American oak sherry hogshead no. 899 db **(86) n22 t22 f21 b21.** Hold the front page, for here's the amazingly good news: sherry hogshead used...no sulphur. The not quite such good news is that the grape is so dominant, not much else gets a look in. Some lovely coffee notes to cling on to, and all-in-all a dram worthy of a second glass. *53.9%. For Dr Jekyll's Pub, Oslo.*

Glengoyne 17 Years Old db **(86) n21 t23 f21 b21.** Some of the guys at Glengoyne think I'm nuts. They couldn't get their head around the 79 I gave it last time. And they will be shaking my neck not my hand when they see the score here...Vastly improved but there is an off sherry tang which points to a naughty butt or two somewhere. Elsewhere mouth-watering and at times fabulously intense. *43%*

Glengoyne 18 Years Old Ambassador's Choice 1990 bourbon cask no. 2850, dist Nov 90 db **(92) n23** thick natural caramels offer clean barley, oranges and a number of delicate sugars; **t23.5** excellent barley layering on delivery: sweet despite some prickle and nip. Mouthwatering yet creamy...this is a complex hombre; **f23** remains big and returns to those caramels on the nose; **b22.5** I am assuming that the Ambassador who chose this isn't Scotland's Ambassador to England. No, I think they mean the guy who turns up wearing a kilt at some whisky festival or other and tells you Glengoyne/Talisker/ Glenmorangie, or whoever he (or she) is representing, is the dog's. Well, take a bow Mr Glengoyne Ambassador: you obviously know your casks. This is a charmer with hobnail boots. *59.9%*

Glengoyne 21 Years Old db **(90) n21** closed and tight for the most part as Glengoyne sometimes has a tendency to be nose-wise, with the emphasis very much on coal gas; **t22** slow to start with a few barley heads popping up to be seen; then spices arrive with the oak for a slightly bourbony feel. Gentle butterscotch and honey add a mouth-watering edge to the drier oaks; **f24** a stupendous honey thread is cross-stitched through the developing oak to deliver near perfect poise and balance at finish; **b23** a vastly improved dram where the caramel has vanished and the tastebuds are constantly assailed and questioned. A malt which builds in pace and passion to delivery a final, wonderful coup-de-grace. Moments of being quite cerebral stuff. 43%

Glengoyne 21 Years Old Sherry Edition db (93) n22 t24 f23 b24. The nose at first is not overly promising, but it settles at it warms and what follows on the palate is at times glorious. Few whiskies will match this for its bitter-sweet depth which is pure textbook. Glengoyne as few will have seen it before. 43%

Glengoyne 23 Years Old Single Cask 1986 European oak sherry butt no. 399 db (85) n22 t22 f21 b21. Though from a sherry cask, fascinating just how many bourbon attributes sneak onto the nose. An enjoyable malt, but not without the odd flaw. 53.6%

Glengoyne 40 Years Old db (83) n23 t21 f19 b20. Thick fruit intermittently pads around the nose and palate but the oak is pretty colossal. Apparent attempts to reinvigorate it appear to have backfired. 45.9%

Glengoyne 1989 Single Cask Billy's Choice Amontillado hogshead, cask no. 1202 db (65.5) n15 t17 f16.5 b17. You genuinely shudder with this one. Seriously, sulphurously grim. 54.1%

Glengoyne 1989 Single Cask Robbie's Choice ruby port hogshead, cask no. 328 db (89) n21.5 t22 f23 b22.5. Robbie 1, Billy 0. 55.1%

Glengoyne 1990 Aged 17 Years Single Cask Amontillado butt, cask no. 1523 db (63) n14 t17.5 f15.5 b16. The grape fights bravely against the sulphur, but it's a bloodbath. 56.3%

⁙ **Glengoyne 1990 Aged 19 Years Single Cask** bourbon hogshead, cask no. 2848, dist 28 Nov 90 db (94) n22 slightly meaty: pan fried calf's liver. With a celery side dish. Don't believe me...? Try it and then let me know... **t24** the kitchen has been done away with and we are now in a world of honey comb barley. The spices at first tip toe slowly, then run...; the juices flow while the sugars punctuate at the right time in the right place; **f24** quite magnificent. The spices are virile and peppery. The vanillas have a go at trying to dominate... but fail miserably. Still those barley notes keep on coming...; **b24** could there be a more eloquent example of just why every Glengoyne should be matured in ex-bourbon cask? 59.6%. nc ncf sc. Exclusively available on the Whisky Exchange.

⁙ **Glengoyne 1990 Single Cask Ambassador's Choice** bourbon hogshead, cask no. 2850, dist 28 Nov 90 db (91.5) n22 a vigorous examination by vanilla and butterscotch; **t23.5** absolutely no faulting the magnificent parity between the honey and the toffee. Spices abound and the barley is fresh and salivating; **f22.5** more toffee vanilla, but the sugars are pretty consistent; **b23.5** don't expect this Ambassador to be expelled in a hurry... 59.9%. nc ncf sc. German release.

Glengoyne 1992 Aged 16 Years Single Cask refill hogshead, cask no. 2078, dist Sep 92 db (87) n21 t22 f21.5 b22.5. Have to admit: than the nose suggests: at times a sugar sprinkled (mildly flawed) charmer... 52.3%

Glengoyne 1993 Aged 14 Years Single Cask American oak, sherry hogshead, cask no. 832 db (90) n23 t22 f22.5 b22.5. I suppose a curmudgeon would grumble about there being too much sherry. Perhaps. But then I would counter argue that in this day and age to find a cask so not screwed by sulphur is in itself something to really celebrate. 59.6%

Glengoyne 1993 Aged 14 Years Single Cask PX hogshead, cask no. 876 db (91.5) n23.5 t23 f22.5 b22.5. For those of us who are rapidly losing confidence in whisky held in sherry (and from what I understand I am by no means alone), here is something to restore your faith. Well, a little bit, anyway... 57.9%. German Market.

Glengoyne 1993 Aged 15 Years Single Cask oloroso hogshead, cask no. 845, dist Apr 93 db (92.5) n24 t22.5 f23 b23. Sherry as it used to be and a strange choice for the Germans, as they appear to be the one nation that can cope with the sulphur with minimum fuss. 55.5%. German market.

⁙ **Glengoyne 1995 Aged 15 Years Single Cask** European oak sherry hogshead, cask no. 2093, dist 26 Oct 95 db (91.5) n22.5 crushed walnuts and dates; **t23.5** the big spice explosion on delivery is unexpected given the relatively dormant nature of the nose; the fruit is thick and abiding, showing big fat sultana amid confident oak; **f22.5** heads towards a big mocha finale and a style much older than its years; **b23** positively yodels in gorgeous integrity. 56.1%. nc ncf sc. Swiss release.

Glengoyne 1996 Aged 11 Years Single Finish Cask La Nerthe cask finish db (88) n21.5 t21.5 f22.5 b22.5. Beautifully textured and weighted: a real delight. 52.5%. German Market.

Glengoyne Port Cask Finish 1996 db (74) n17 t20 f18.5 b18.5. Decent fruit on delivery, but elsewhere proof that in whisky there is no such thing as any port cask in a storm... 46%. Ian Macleod.

⋰ **Glengoyne Vintage 1996** db **(70)** n16 t18 f18 b18. Creamy, but off key. *43%. nc ncf. USA.*

Glengoyne 1997 Aged 11 Years Single Cask European oak sherry hogshead, cask no. 2692, dist Jun 97 db **(93)** n24 t23 f24 b23. I bet you 20 years ago I might have given this a 89 or so. However, such has been the damage done by the influx of sulphur-ruined or -damaged sherry butts into the industry, and so wide their rotting net, that you just have to give the rare, wonderful specimens such as this a standing ovation. The first two or three mouthfuls are overwhelming: when your tastebuds adjust you will be in for a rare treat. *56.3%*

Glengoyne 1997 Aged 11 Years Single Cask cask no. 2725, dist Jun 97 db **(95)** n24 t24.5 f23 b23.5. Taking into account that Norway has to be the most expensive place on this planet, this still will have been worth twice whatever price was asked for it. *56.5%. Bottled for the Oslo Whisky Festival.*

⋰ **Glengoyne 1997 Single Cask English Merchant's Choice** sherry hogshead, cask no. 2716, dist 17 Jun 97 db **(89)** n22 burned fruit cake...in which someone has forgotten to add the dough...; t23 sherry trifle...in which someone forgot to add the sponge...; f22 grapey, spiced barley...in which someone forgot to add the barley...; b22 a young fogey of a malt. Elsewhere in the Bible I have lamented this virtually lost style of sherried whisky: something akin to a size 46 overcoat placed on a five year old lad, who vanishes under the cloth. The malt may have been similarly swamped by the grape, but it does offer a degree of entertainment...and not an atom of sulphur to be had! *54.6%. nc ncf sc.*

⋰ **Glengoyne Vintage 1997** db **(68)** n16 t18 f17 b17. The "S" word strikes. And with a vengeance. *43%. nc ncf. German release.*

⋰ **Glengoyne 1999 Aged 11 Years Old Single Cask** sherry hogshead, cask no. 2163, dist 22 Sep 99 db **(95.5)** n23.5 thumping, clean grape. Some lovely candy shop notes, especially of the old granny cough sweet variety; t24 not just voluptuous, but absolutely mouth-watering to the point of having to salivate like a rabies victim. The spices swill about the palate as though they own the place. The layering of green apples and greener peach is astonishing; f24 softens, though the spices continue to maraud. The analogy to a cough sweet becomes even more pertinent; b24 entirely impressed. One of the best sherry butts for its tender years for a good while. Time to start looking for Easyjet tickets... *57.4%. nc ncf sc. German release.*

Glengoyne 1999 Single Cask Deek's Choice refill hogshead, cask no. 16 db **(83.5)** n20.5 t21.5 f21 b21. Crisp, juicy barley and emerging vanilla. Some bitter orange, too. *60.9%*

Glengoyne 'Glen Guin' 16 Year Old Shiraz Finish db **(79)** n18.5 t20 f19.5 b20. Some oily depth here. *48%*

Glengoyne Burnfoot db **(84)** n21 t21 f21.5 b21. A clodhopping bruiser of a malt. Good honey, though. *40%. Duty Free Market.*

Berrys' Own Selection Glengoyne 1999 cask no. 500781 **(83.5)** n21.5 t21.5 f20.5 b20. A plodding though pleasant malt. *46%. Berry Bros & Rudd.*

The Càrn Mòr Vintage Collection Glengoyne 2000 hogshead, cask no. 438, dist 2000, bott 2009 **(76.5)** n18.5 t18.5 f19.5 b19. Even taking into account its age, there should be a lot more offered than this. Settles only when the natural caramels kick in late on. *46%*

Hart Brothers Glengoyne Aged 12 Years dist Jun 95, bott May 08 **(85.5)** n22 t22 f20.5 b21. Magnificently clean and malty. But too much a straight bat and the finish is smothered by natural caramel. *46%. Hart Brothers Limited.*

⋰ **Kingsbury "The Selection" Glengoyne 9 Years Old** butt, cask no. 389, dist Mar 01, bott Aug 10 **(72)** n18 t18 f18 b18. Mr. Tanaka, my dear old friend. Let us dine at your favourite restaurant, Claridges. Or at my Club next door. Either way, I'll pay. Providing, that is, you give sherry butts the widest possible berth when bottling for Kingsbury... *43%. nc ncf sc. Japan Import Systems. 822 bottles.*

Malts of Scotland Glengoyne 1972 sherry butt no. 3195, dist Sep 72, bott Jun 09 **(85)** n22.5 t22 f20 b20.5. The marmalade is perhaps a tad too bitter. Elsewhere the honey and spice delights. *52.8%. Malts of Scotland. 192 bottles.*

Malts of Scotland Glengoyne 1973 bourbon barrel no. 677, dist Feb 73, bott Jun 09 **(92)** n24 magnificent! Has started on the road to old aged exotic fruit, but been diverted somewhere along the line and ended up on a much more floral route. Even some crushed, lightly salted macadamia nut. With a tiny dollop of acacia honey for good measure, it just needs a good half hour even before tasting...; t23 how can something approaching 40 years of age be this juicy? Well, except probably my neighbour. But that apart, the barley has no problem fending off the close attentions of the oak and makes a complex fist of it; f22.5 does dry now but still enough soft honey to do the job; b22.5 Glengoyne + very good bourbon barrel = excellence. Usually. *55.1%. Malts of Scotland. 192 bottles.*

⋰ **Malts Of Scotland Glengoyne 1973** bourbon barrel, cask no. 678, dist Feb 73, bott Mar 10 **(87.5)** n21.5 floral yet firm; t22 melted Mars bars; the oak adds a proud pungency; f22 lashings of natural toffee; **b22** knife-edge malt, saved by natural sugars. *50.4%. nc ncf sc. Malts Of Scotland. 97 bottles.*

Malts of Scotland Glengoyne 1997 sherry butt no. 582, dist Feb 97, bott Jun 09 **(62) n16 t15.5 f15 b15.5.** Sulphur, anyone? *57.2%. Malts of Scotland. 192 bottles.*

Malts of Scotland Glengoyne 1998 sherry butt, cask no. 1131, dist Apr 98, bott Feb 10 **(77.5) n19 t20.5 f19 b19.** Sumptuous grape. But very tight with a furry buzz. Much better than cask 1132. The thing is: would Brian Eno's Subtlety Spectrograph have spotted the difference? *54.8%. Malts of Scotland. 192 bottles.*

Malts of Scotland Glengoyne 1998 sherry butt, cask no. 1132, dist Apr 98, bott   Feb 10 **(70.5) n18 t19 f16.5 b17.** Beautiful colour. *55.2%. 192 bottles.*

꽃 **Malts Of Scotland Clubs Glengoyne 1998** sherry hogshead, cask no. 1135, dist Apr 98, bott Oct 10 **(85.5) n21 t22 f21 b21.5.** A sulphur-free, clean sherry hoggy, for sure. But the enormity of the grape drowns out much chance to see the malt develop beyond a spicy mocha theme. *52.9%. nc ncf sc. Malts Of Scotland. 280 bottles.*

Old Malt Cask Glengoyne 13 Years Old refill hogshead no. DL 5727, dist Dec 96, bott Jan 10 **(89) n22** grassy...drying hay; **t22** flinty barley just hardens further; **f23** unusually long for a Glengoyne with a delicate oiliness helping to maximise the muscovado sugars and tangy spice; **b22** solid as a rock. Not exactly complex, but when you get top quality barley all the way it doesn't need to be. Fabulous spices towards the end, though. *50%. 311 bottles.*

꽃 **The Perfect Dram Glengoyne 1972** bott 2011 **(86) n20 t22 f22 b22.** Makes up for the so-so nose with a well mannered display of sharp but lively barley. Tasted blind, hard to believe this is almost reaching the big 4-0. But the minimalist impact from the lazy oak has certainly allowed the barley to sparkle. *46.3%. The Whisky Agency.*

Provenance Glengoyne 10 Years Old refill hogshead no. DMG 5737, dist Autumn 99, bott Winter 2010 **(86.5) n20.5 t23 f21.5 b21.5.** Malty – almost with a Horlicks creaminess – but not that many other tricks. Not one to say no to. *46%. Douglas Laing & Co Ltd.*

Provenance Glengoyne Aged 10 Years refill hogshead, dist Autumn 97, bott Summer 08 **(82.5) n19 t22.5 f21 b20.** Soaring, intense barley. Given a better cask, and this would have been some dram. *46%. Douglas Laing.*

꽃 **Provenance Glengoyne Over 12 Years** refill hogshead, cask no. 6859, dist Autumn 98, bott Winter 2010 **(81) n21 t21 f19 b20.** A spotty-faced youth by Glengoyne standards. Malty, sweet but limited in scope. *46%. nc ncf sc. Douglas Laing & Co.*

꽃 **The Whisky Agency Glengoyne 37 Years Old** sherry cask, dist 1972, bott 2010 **(95) n24** a sherry trifle – though mainly of custard – is splattered into your face...; all kinds of crushed nut, too plus the unmistakable sweetness of biscoito de polvilho doce; **t24** now that is pretty classy: a crisp, malty delivery sweetened by grape-flecked sugars. The spices are a side dish wanting main course exposure. But a beautiful butterscotch middle bugles in the oak; **f23** how many different types of vanilla are there...? **b24** this is the year of the great old malt. Few, though, offer the evenly-loaded complexity found here. A 37 year old whisky, which might take just as many years to get to the bottom of... *57%. The Whisky Agency.*

The Whisky Agency Glengoyne 1972 sherry cask **(90) n21.5** uncompromising oak. A little Demerara lightens things a little; **t22.5** a bit of a mess as the oak tries to play big shot; some decent oils and sharp fruit: for those who like a bit of the rough stuff; **t24.5** one of the great finishes of any OAP malt this year: the chocolate fruit and nut needs experiencing for believing...; **b22** the oak gets tossed around the palate like logs on a raging river. Amazingly finds something to cling to at the end. An amazing malt you are unlikely to forget in a hurry. *63.5%*

GLEN GRANT

Speyside, 1840. Campari. Working.

Glen Grant db **(87) n21.5** young barley, new-mown grass and a smudge of toffee; **t23** huge flavour explosion led by juicy, young malt. Soft spices reveal an oaky interest, too; **f21** over-laced with caramel; **b21.5** this is a collector's malt for the back label alone: truly one of the most bizarre I have ever seen. "James Grant, 'The Major'" it cheerfully chirrups, "was only 25 when he set about achieving his vision of a single malt with a clear colour. The unique flavour and appearance was due to the purifiers and the tall slender stills he designed and the decision to retain its natural colour..." Then underneath is written: "Farven Justeter Med Karamel/Mit Farbstoff"" Doh! Or, as they say in German: "Doh!" Need any more be said about the nonsense, the pure insanity, of adding colouring to whisky. *40%*

Glen Grant 5 Years Old db **(89) n22 t22.5** dry and herbal with crushed celery, grist, agave, a sprinkle of pepper; **t22** crisp, firm barley with the sweetness handcuffed by a quick spurt of vanilla; semi-serious spice; **f21.5** clean, late oils and warming peppers; **b23** elegant malt which has noticeably grown in stature and complexity of late. *40%*

Glen Grant 10 Years Old db (88) n22 fine, flinty grain, quite hard and with limited oak interference; t22 really mouthwatering, clean and fresh: not an offnote in sight; f22 gentle, almost half sleeping, just malt and a faint buzz of oak; b22. a relaxed, confident malt from a distillery that makes great whisky with effortless charm and each mouthful seems to show that it knows it. And on re-taste it appears a honey and spice element has been upped slightly. 40%

Glen Grant 15 Years Old Cask Strength Limited Edition Cask no.17163 dist Feb 92, bott Sep 07 db (86) n20 t23.5 f21 b21.5. Such a frustrating bottling: thumping caramel makes its mark on both the nose and finish. 599%

Glen Grant Aged 16 Years bott Mar 10 db (91.5) n23 a lovely under-ripe banana sharpness to this while the malt snuggles up to the crunchy green apple; a playful molecule of smoke wafts around; t23.5 salivating, fresh, slightly green ...and that's just the first few nano-seconds of the delivery! Next comes a lengthy, relaxed wave of oilier barley with a coppery, honeyed depth; tangy vanilla fills the middle ground; f21.5 medium length, more oils and barley but with a degree of bitterness; b22 about the finish doesn't do justice to the earlier jousting on the nose and palate. The label talks about orchard fruits, and they are absolutely spot on. Apples are order of the day, but not sure about the ripe bit: they appear slightly green to me... and that suits the nature of the crisp malt. A gorgeous whisky I fully expect to see improve over coming batches: it's one that has potential to hit superstar status. 43%

Glen Grant Cask Strength Limited Edition Aged 17 Years cask no. 17152, dist Feb 92, bott May 09 db (94) n23.5 handsomely elegant and bolstered with an embracing degree of old-fashioned Speyside smoke, this nose demands some study. Curiously salty and studded with dried orange peel, the grain is not exactly its usual crisp self: maybe a degree of toffee has something to do with this; t24 the initial note on delivery is crisp barley. But this is soon smothered by a sweet, warming, lightly oiled smokiness which brings with it a degree of cocoa. On another level there is toffee fudge and honeycomb: together one is left salivating, with the tongue dementedly pounding the roof of the mouth; f23.5 continues along the very long road, the sweetness fluctuating with a hint of molasses here and liquorice there; b23 the nose suggests there maybe some added caramel; the whopping bourbon notes suggests it could be natural. Either way, strip a little toffee away and you might be left with what would have been a contender for Scotch single malt of the year. The balance and artistry beggars belief. Glen Grant distillery really is capable of producing some of the most monumental malt moments you can find on the whisky shelves today. 58.8%. 360 bottles.

Glen Grant Cellar Reserve 1992 bottled 08 db (94.5) n23 a beguiling array of crisp barley and crystalised sugary notes; if a nose can be crunchy and brittle, then this really is it; t24 the tastebuds virtually swoon under this glorious bathing of barley and sugar; unbelievably juicy and mouth-watering for its age, the oak is there to ensure backbone and fair play and does nothing to subtract from the most graceful notes, except perhaps to pep up slightly with a teasing spiciness; f24 long, with more playful spices and a chocolate fudge lending weight to the glassy barley edge; one to close the eyes to and be consumed by; b23.5 one of the great world distilleries being revealed to the us in its very finest colours. They tend to be natural, with no colourings added, therefore allowing the extraordinary kaleidoscope of subtle sweetnesses to be deployed and enjoyed to their fullest. I defy you not to be blown away by this one, especially when you realise there is not a single big base note to be heard... 46%. nc ncf.

Glen Grant 170th Anniversary db (89) n23.5 light and spiky for all the obvious fruitiness. Loads of warm sultana underpinning a butterscotch/vanilla spine. A little sharp and prickly in places, like fruit pastille candy, and just a hint of something that might appeal to the Germans...; t23.5 immediately busy with a dual personality of (house style) juicy, crunchy barley and a spicier, much fruitier alter-ego; f20 a tell-tale fuzzy bitterness to the finale reveals an Achilles heel; b22 the odd mildly sulphured cask has slipped through the net here to reduce what was shaping to be something magnificent. Still enjoyable, though. 46%

Glen Grant The Major's Reserve bott Mar 10 db (85.5) n21.5 t23 f20 b21. Forget about the so-so nose and finish. This is one of those drams that demands you melt into your chair on delivery, such is the fresh beauty of the malt and stunning honeycomb threads which tie themselves around every taste bud. Pity about the ultra dry, puffy, caramel-rich finish, but apparently nearly all the sherry butts have now been used up at the distillery. Thank gawd for that. 40%

A.D. Rattray Glen Grant 1985 cask no. 12364, dist Sep 85, bott Mar 09 (90.5) n22.5 some major toffee apple moments, there... t23 wow!! What a spicy little animal we have here: some serious viscosity adds to that toffeed effect on the nose and the ability to give those warming spices a damned good chew.. f22.5 simmers down and thins to reveal a malty tail;

b23 can't help feeling that there is something at play here regarding those old rummagers that used to clatter about the stills. A different kind of Glen Grant, but eternally wonderful. 55.8%. A.D. Rattray Ltd.

Berrys' Own Selection Glen Grant 1972 (90) n24 old, for sure. But the barley-honey notes are so faint and beautifully interwoven amid the more vigorous vanillas that it's a hard one to put down...; t23 relatively full bodied by GG's standards with soft oils helping the toasty-spiced butterscotch barley to have a big say; f21 some cocoa does its best to cover the thickening oak; b22 a bit gruff and throaty at the finale, but at this age it has every right to be. A beautiful dram: why can't they all be this charming? 51.8%. Berry Bros & Rudd.

Càrn Mòr Glen Grant 1993 hogshead, cask no. 121910, dist 1993, bott 2009 (87.5) n22 t23.5 f20.5 b21.5. To be honest, I would have been willing, just from the nose alone, to have bet that this would be a tired, bitter finish. From this kind of third-time around cask you are unlikely to get much else. But the virgin freshness to the barley on both nose and delivery is worth the compromise. 46%. The Scottish Liqueur Centre.

The Coopers Choice Glen Grant 1977 Sherry Wood Aged 30 Years (91) n22 t23 f23 b23. Quite beautiful whisky. 46%. ncf sc. The Vintage Malt Whisky Co.

Distillery Malt Glen Grant 1990 (88) n22 t23 f21 b22. Only a slight bitterness to the finale detracts from an otherwise excellent malt. 40%. Gordon & MacPhail.

Duncan Taylor Collection Glen Grant 1970 cask no. 3492 (85.5) n21 t22.5 f21 b21. Retains a touch of the debonair despite the obvious oak intrusion. But now the grey temples have been lost in a sea of white... 49.1%. Duncan Taylor & Co Ltd.

Duncan Taylor Collection Glen Grant 1970 cask no. 3494 (88) n21 t22.5 f22 b22.5. Only exceptionally well made spirit can absorb oak with such seemingly effortless aplomb. Classy stuff. 49.9%

Duncan Taylor Collection Glen Grant 1972 cask no. 8948 (85.5) n21.5 t22.5 f20.5 b21. Barley and gooseberries fight off the spicy oaks. Almost. 46.2%

Duncan Taylor Collection Glen Grant 1972 cask no. 8950 (88) n22 t23 f21.5 b21.5. The barley and oak have reached a pleasant understanding. 45%

⠿ **Duncan Taylor Glen Grant 1972** cask no. 446483, bott Sep 10 (86) n19 t22 f23 b22. A much better whisky than the out of sorts nose suggests. Builds not just in confidence but fruity aggression for a decent late night dram. 54.8%. Duncan Taylor & Co.

Duncan Taylor Collection Glen Grant 1974 cask no. 16574 (86.5) n21 t22 f22.5 b21. At times a seeringly hot, though by no means unpleasant. Massively malty, sharp and no shrinking violet. 55.6%

Duncan Taylor Collection Glen Grant 1974 cask no. 16575 (92) n23.5 almost a touch of slivovitz to this with plum tart and honeydew melon for good measure; the odd peat molecule drifts about; t24 melt-in-the-mouth acacia honey followed by a virile volley of barley. Mocha descends into the middle ground; f22 an oaky burst which is quickly spent and the vanilla-barley keeps position..; b22.5 another Glen Grant which somehow fights off the obvious age to show some serious quality. 51.5%. Duncan Taylor & Co Ltd.

Duncan Taylor Collection Glen Grant 1974 cask no. 16576 (85) n22 t21 f21 b21. Malty, clean, juicy, vanilla-flecked but ultimately runs out of ideas. 48.4%

Duncan Taylor Collection Glen Grant 1974 cask no. 16577 (81) n21 t19 f21 b20. Vaguely similar in style to cask 16574, but thinner, hotter and generally lacking its charisma. 54.5%

Duncan Taylor Collection Glen Grant 1974 cask no. 16578 (82.5) n21 t20 f21.5 b20. A cheery, unsophisticated dram which slaps the barley on as paste might be brushed onto wallpaper. Thin, but some buttery notes help out at the death. 52.2%

Duthies Glen Grant 13 Years Old (74.5) n18 t21.5 f17 b18. Sparkles on the palate for a few moments, but the remainder is hard work. A style which might be appreciated by certain sections of the German whisky market. But in pure technical terms, a real disappointment. 46%. Cadenhead's for Germany.

The Golden Cask Glen Grant 1997 cask no. CM142, bott 2009 (86.5) n22 t22 f21 b21.5. Beautifully distilled and so juicy. Just lacking some oaky back up. 56.5%. The House of MacDuff. 224 bottles.

Gordon & MacPhail Distillery Label Glen Grant 25 Years Old (93) n24.5 t23 f22.5 b23. The type of malt us long-in-the-tooth whisky specialists dream off, but too rarely find. The nose, though, defies belief. 43%

Gordon & MacPhail Distillery Label Glen Grant 1993 (92.5) n23 outwardly simple: sniff longer and more delicately and be astonished by its butterfly-like weight of malt; t23.5 crisp and malty, yet at the same time soft and vanilla-clad; does sweetness ever come so gossamer-like...? f23 long, with a gathering of light oils to add a malty lustre to the delicate oak; b23 eye watering: both in its juicy effect and also for its sheer beauty... 40%

Gordon & MacPhail Rare Vintage Glen Grant 1958 (96.5) n24 t24 f24 b24.5. Virtually no grey hairs on this 50-year-old which has embraced half a century with an unbelievable degree of finesse and grace. One of the truly great Glen Grants – indeed, Speyside malts – of recent years, this is textbook stuff as to regard how to showcase enormous age with virtually no blemishes to speak of. One of the all time great Old Timers. And if you can't afford Glenfiddich 50-year-old at £10,000 a throw, then settle for this one that is just half a point and £9,850 behind... 40%

Gordon & MacPhail Rare Vintage Glen Grant 1962 (94.5) n22.5 t24 f24 b24. Almost faultlessly weighted and a wonderful example of where great oak is used to add nothing but a positive slant. A stunner. And cements my belief, along with the amazing 1958 vintage, that G&M understand this distillery in a way the more recent blender(s) of the previous owners never came close to. 40%

Harris Whisky Co. Glen Grant Aged 35 Years cask no. 6650, dist Jul 73, bott Sep 08 (87) n20.5 t22 f22 b21.5. An injection of sugar concentrate helps negate the overenthusiastic oak. Not one for those looking for a sedate dram... 57.5%. 100 bottles.

Hart Brothers Glen Grant Aged 11 Years dist Oct 97, bott Sep 09 (79) n20 t22 f18 b19. From the slightly tobacco-flecked nose through the big, pleasant sugars on the palate to the unevenly bitter finish, there is something altogether odd about this one. 46%. Hart Brothers Ltd.

Kingsbury's Single Cask Glen Grant Aged 12 Years dist Jul 96, bott Jul 08 (84) n21.5 t22 f20 b20.5. Hard nosed and hard arsed. Little give but the crunchy barley offers some juicy sweetness. 46%. Japan Import System.

Lonach Glen Grant 31 Years Old (84) n21 t22 f21 b20. Exceptionally firm barley for its age; enjoys a sugar-coated lustre and good depth. 42.3%

Lonach Glen Grant 35 Years Old (83) n20 t21 f21 b21. Creaks a bit, but some lovely barley sugar and liquorice. 41.8%. Duncan Taylor.

Lonach Glen Grant 1969 (87) n21 t21 f23 b22. Talk about an over-aged malt. Far too old. Yet such is the enormity of the fruit and barley character, it somehow sees off the excesses of the oak which spoils the start and offers instead a very late alternative. A rare style, indeed. 51.7%

Norse Cask Selection Glen Grant 1993 Aged 16 Years hogshead cask no. 121914, dist 1993, bott May 09 (95.5) n23.5 t25 f23 b24. A truly great cask from a great distillery: this, surely, is what drinking single malt Scotch should be about... 578%

Old Malt Cask Glen Grant Aged 14 Years refill hogshead no. DL 5980, dist Oct 95, bott Mar 10 (84) n21 t22 f20 b21. Sharp, sough dough and massive malt. 50%. 339 bottles.

Old Malt Cask Glen Grant Aged 20 Years sherry butt no. DL 5971, dist Mar 90, bott Mar 10 (73) n18 t19 f17 b19. Sweet, honeyed. But a sherry butt let down by a dose of you-know-what... 50%. Douglas Laing & Co Ltd. 362 bottles.

Old Malt Cask Glen Grant Aged 32 Years sherry butt, dist Dec 76, bott Mar 09 (94) n23.5 t24 f23 b23.5. An old school sherry butt. And just like old schools, tends to be far more correct and exacting in standards. The flavour of a nearly lost world. 50%. 266 bottles.

Old Malt Cask Glen Grant Aged 34 Years refill hogshead no. DL 5597, dist Apr 75, bott Nov 09 (90) n23.5 exotic fruit and ginger is a giveaway regarding age; t23 the barley remains improbably crisp and clean despite some softly fruited oaky attention; f21.5 a tad tangy; b22 at this age almost a relative to neighbouring Caper. But just that little more crunchy. 50%. Douglas Laing & Co Ltd. 278 bottles.

⬩ **Old Malt Cask Glen Grant Aged 35 Years** brandy butt, cask no. 6279, dist Apr 75, bott Jun 10 (94.5) n23.5 one of the most Summery noses I have encountered this year: ripe greengages falling off the tree – I could be in France (eating their fruit, not drinking their brandy). I don't think the spices could be better paced or the combined oak/fruit depth more in tune to receive; t23 silk body with the fruit and barley ridiculously well matched; f21 improbably long, the vaguest hint of oil and a slow rolling out of the icing sugars and delicate sultanas; b24 I absolutely guarantee that whatever brandy was originally in this butt, it wasn't a patch on the whisky in this bottle... 50%. nc ncf sc. Douglas Laing & Co. 371 bottles.

⬩ **Old Masters Glen Grant 19 Years Old** cask no. 35955, dist 1992, bott Mar 11 (87.5) n22 mixed messages of good cop/bad cop cask, but enough power in the malt to seduce; t22 unusual oils holding good cop vanilla. But it's the breadth of the malt range which astounds; f21.5 bad cop oak bitterness tries to invade, but the barley sugars form a limited shield; b22 never for a moment thinks about letting up in its intensity. 594%. sc. James MacArthur & Co.

⬩ **Peerless Glen Grant 40 Years Old** dist 1970, cask no. 3497 (96) n24 almost defies belief as the barley absolutely sparkles; gooseberries punctuated with oak; nothing is out of place...it is almost too perfect... t24 nigh on perfect weight on delivery. There is a stunningly crisp sheen to the barley, which appears coated by Demerara sugar crystals. The oak offers a deep, semi-earthy Java coffee background...and is probably behind the slow swelling of spice that sits so comfortably in the nougat-vanilla middle; **f24** confirms itself as a malt of the rarest quality: the barley continues its sugar-led path, the spices beet out their delicate tattoo, the oaks weave a vanilla-butterscotch tapestry and various random fruit notes pop up here and there...; **b24** more Cary Grant...just how sophisticated is this...? A whisky which I found almost impossible to spit and shows just why the very greatest whiskies you ever taste are things of not just unique beauty, but experiences never to be forgotton. 48.5%. sc. Duncan Taylor & Co.

⁘ **Premier Barrel Glen Grant Aged 12 Years** (88) **n22** ultra clean, grassy barley; **t23** salivating with the barley, backed by golden syrup, going for gold; **f21.5** bitters very slightly; a touch of spice; **b21.5** if this were a steak, it'd be red raw. But try and find one juicier than this... 46%. nc ncf sc. Douglas Laing & Co. 324 bottles.

Provenance Glen Grant Over 12 Years refill hogshead no. DMG 5736, dist Autumn 97, bott Winter 2010 (83.5) **n21 t21.5 f20 b21.** Gristy and dry, but a little reined in by the cask. 46%. nc ncf. Douglas Laing & Co Ltd.

Provenance Glen Grant Aged 12 Years refill hogshead, dist Autumn 96, bott Winter 08 (86) **n20 t22 f22 b22.** Recovers spectacularly from a dodgy nose to a real clean barley salvo. Lots of spice and barley sugar. 46%

Scotch Malt Whisky Society Cask 9.44 Aged 11 Years refill hogshead, dist Apr 97 (85.5) **n22.5 t21 f21 b21.** Attractively malty but makes a point of not making a point. 59.4%

⁘ **The Whisky Agency Glen Grant 1972** refill sherry, bott 2011 (89) **n23** not just classic fruit cake, but the odd glazed cherry, too...; **t22** busy with the oaks pinging around charmingly and the burnt raisin trying not to look too aggressive; **f22** lots of natural caramel and vanilla; **b22** an old speysider just about on the edge, but the quality is glorious! 52.8%

⁘ **The Whisky Agency Glen Grant 1973** (95.5) **n24.5** wow! By which I mean: fruitcake concentrate, but in the cleanest, almost Sauternes-sweet/spicy way. Actually, more of a cor-blimey...wow-wow-wow..., bordering on the f**me sideways..!!! **t24** the oak is every bit as big as it should be. Yet so sublimely well structured and weighted in the fruit and barley interplay, it makes absolutely no negative impact. The secret, though, is the fabulous weight to the oil, which does a great job of carrying the spices and spreading the sugars, but heroically refuses to deaden the whole. Wondrous...; **f23.5** just the vaguest hint of oak weariness, but no more than an aged film star panting at the end of a long chase. But it is a distant cry of bitterness which can barely be heard amid the contended and very long afterglow of the fruit-spice-barley orgy of before...; **b24** knocking on the door of being the finest single cask I have tasted this year...Pity it was up against the Peerless Glen Grant 38... 52.4%

⁘ **Whisky Doris Glen Grant 38 Years Old** refill sherry, cask no. 1650, dist Feb 72, bott Mar 10 (86.5) **n21 t22 f22 b21.5.** Exceptionally oily for a Glen Grant. Even so, pleasingly rough enough to give you a good punch in the kisser where you might have hoped for something a little more delicate and fruity. 53.6%

The Whisky Fair Glen Grant 36 Year Old sherry hogshead, dist 1972, bott 2009 (96) **n24 t24 f24 b24.** This, in a bottle, is the very point of sherried malt whisky. 56.3%

GLENGYLE
Campbeltown, 2004. J&A Mitchell & Co. Working.

Kilkerran Single Malt db (80) **n19** very young, slightly Shredded Wheaty, a touch of tobacco leaf, mint and some heavy oils; **t20** ungainly arrival with big barley, big oils, big natural caramel; **f21** settles towards a light, slightly sweeter and gristier fade; **b20** Glyngyle's first offering doesn't rip up any trees. And maybe the odd flaw to its character that you won't see when the distillery is fine-tuned. But this is the first-ever bottling from this brand new Campbeltown distillery and therefore its chances of being a worldbeater as an untried and untested 3-y-o were pretty slim. I will be watching its development with relish. And with heart pounding... 46%. Available exclusively from distillery direct from cask.

Kilkerran Single Malt bott 22 May 07 db (84) **n20 t21 f22 b21.** Sadly, I was out of the country and couldn't attend the Coming of Age of Kilkerran, when its first casks turned three and became whisky. Very kindly, they sent me a bottle as if I was there and, therefore, these are the notes of the very first bottling handed out to visitors. Interestingly, there is a marked similarity in distillery style to the 46% bottling in that the malt offers a crescendo of quality. This is only three year old whisky, of course, and its fingerprints will alter as it spends longer in the cask. 62%. nc ncf.

Kilkerran 'Work in Progress' db (88) **n22.5** youthful, malty and a pinch of salt creeping into this one.. **t22** a simple malty delivery is the prologue to a simple, barley-rich tale. Dries to a surprising degree after the initial quick burst of barley sugar with the vanillas kicking hard, followed even by some spice; **f21.5** lots of natural caramel with the malt; **b22** doing very well. 46%

GLEN KEITH
Speyside, 1957. Chivas Brothers. Silent.

Glen Keith 10 Years Old db (80) n22 t21 f18 b19. A malty if thin dram that finishes with a whimper after an impressively refreshing, grassy start. 43%

Cadenhead's Authentic Collection Glen Keith-Glenlivet 1996 bott Feb 10 (85) n21 t22.5 f20.5 b21. What I suspect is a third fill cask has kept the oak at arm's length, allowing the very lightly peated malt to show its eye-watering sharpness to enjoyable effect. 54.2%. 303 bottles.

Connoisseurs Choice Glen Keith 1968 (86) n21 t21.5 f22 b21.5. Becomes much more relaxed and enjoyable when it throws off any pretence of being a good old-fashioned Speysider and revels in its newly-found bourbony-ness. The spirit from this distillery was much thinner back in the 60s than the malt made in its latter years. So it has embraced the oak with both hands, making this a must find for those who enjoy a good Heaven Hill... 46%

Malts Of Scotland Glen Keith 1970 bourbon hogshead, cask no. 6042, dist Sep 70, bott Feb 11 (92) n24 classic oak-induced exotic fruit with pineapple and crushed physalis to the fore plus some pleasing spices on the vanilla. Creaking with great age, but complex and classy; t22 perhaps slightly too active on the oak front early on, but soon settles and the fruits return with the delicate, lemon sheen; f23 back to full complexity with a touch of spice to the mocha; b23 it's extraordinary how often a malt renowned for being average at best in its early and mid life somehow achieves a degree of exotic fruity greatness in its dotage. 49.1%. sc.

Malts of Scotland Glen Keith 1990 bourbon barrel no. 13678, dist Mar 90, bott Jan 10 (83.5) n20.5 t22 f21 b20. Chunky and packed thick with barley. A curious creamless Oreo biscuit finish. 52.1%. Malts of Scotland. 192 bottles.

Old Malt Cask Glen Keith Aged 18 Years refill barrel, dist Mar 90, bott Dec 08 (93.5) n23 t24 f23 b23.5. This has never been one of the sexy Speysiders, but now and again a superb bottling rears its head – and here's the best of the lot. Occasionally a peated version was produced here by Chivas. Though this isn't peaty, as such, there is a subtle, smoky echo to this one which does it no harm whatsoever. A distillery classic and must have. 50%. 259 bottles.

Old Malt Cask Glen Keith Aged 20 Years refill hogshead no. DL 5992, dist Mar 90, bott Mar 10 (79.5) n19 t21.5 f19 b20. Stodgy though pleasantly sweet. Don't expect too much complexity, though. 50% Douglas Laing & Co Ltd. 257 bottles.

The Whisky Agency Glen Keith 1970 bott 2010 (81) n21 t19 f20.5 b20.5. Yet another bottling from the Whisky Agency displaying more oak than Henry VIII's Compass Rose...and is close to befalling a similar fate. 45.1%. The Whisky Agency.

The Whisky Agency Glen Keith 1970 (92) n21.5 déjà oak...; t23.5 didn't expect that! Fabulous!! Not only is the barley intact, but it pulses out giggawatts of sharp sugars and bourbon honeycomb and liquorice; f23.5 a massive orangey tang at the back of my palate. All topped up with spiced dark Columbian cocoa; light oils work a form of magic; b24 a real livewire of a dram that offers little on the nose but takes you into new worlds once it hits the palate. Sensational. 54.2%. The Whisky Agency.

GLENKINCHIE
Lowlands, 1837. Diageo. Working.

Glenkinchie 12 Years Old db (85) n19 t22.5 f21.5 b22. The last 'Kinchie 12 I encountered was beyond woeful. This is anything but. Still not firing on all cylinders and can definitely do better. But there is a fabulous vibrancy to this which nearly all the bottlings I have tasted in the last few years have sadly lacked. Impressive. 43% ☺ ☺

Glenkinchie Aged 15 Years The Distillers Edition Amontillado finished, dist 1992, bott 2007 db (94) n23.5 t24 f23 b23.5. Now this is absolutely top class wine cask finishing. One of my last whiskies of the night, and one to take home with me. Sophisticated, intelligent and classy. 46%

Glenkinchie 20 Years Old db (85.5) n21 t22 f21.5 b21. When I sampled this, I thought: "hang on, haven't I tasted this one before?" When I checked with my tasting notes for one or two independents who bottled around this age a year or two ago, I found they were nigh identical to what I was going to say here. Well, you can't say its not a consistent dram. The battle of the citrus-barley against the welling oak is a rich and entertaining one. 58.4%

Glenkinchie Special Release 2010 20 Years Old refill American oak, dist 1990 (86.5) n23 t22 f21 b21.5. Workhorse malts like Kinchie were hardly designed for 20 years in the cask. So although this one is hemmed in by oak from all sides, what a treat to see the nose, at least, offer a malty sparkle and fruity, mildly herbal depth of complexity. Some juiciness and residual sugars on the delivery, too. 55.1%. nc ncf. Diageo. Fewer than 6000 bottles.

Glenkinchie 1992 The Manager's Choice db (78) n19 t22 f18 b19. Has a lot going for it on delivery with a barley explosion which rocks you back in your chair and has you salivating like a rabies victim. But the rest of it is just too off key. 58.1%. Diageo.

Cadenhead's Glenkinchie Aged 21 Years dist 1987, bott 2009 **(89) n22 t23 f22 b22.** Has no right to be excellent whisky, yet somehow is... *51.6%*

Malts of Scotland Glenkinchie 1975 sherry hogshead no. 2968, dist Aug 75, bott Mar 09 **(91) n23.5** the kind of sherry butt which brings a tear to an aging man's eye. This is the way they were...and always should have been; **t23** the immediate honey/liquorice impact is heart- and palate-warming; layer upon layer of indulgent, lightly spiced bourbon character on a bed of pithy grape; the barley remains alive and salivating, though.; **f22.5** drier but with a decent line in chocolate-covered grape; **b22.5** oloroso meets Kentucky to stunning effect... *57.2%*

THE GLENLIVET
Speyside, 1824. Chivas Brothers. Working.

The Glenlivet Aged 12 Years db **(79.5) n22 t21 f18 b18.5.** Wonderful nose and very early development but then flattens out towards the kind of caramel finish you just wouldn't traditionally associate with this malt, and further weakened by a bitter, furry finale. *40%*

The Glenlivet Aged 12 Years Old First Fill Matured db **(91) n22.5 t22.5 f23 b23.** A quite wonderful whisky, far truer to The Glenlivet than the standard 12 and one which every malt whisky lover should try once in their journey through the amber stuff. Forget the tasting notes on the bottle, which bear little relation to what is inside. A gem of a dram. *40%*

The Glenlivet 15 Years of Age db **(80) n19 t21 f20 b20.** There is an undeniable charm to the countless waves of malt and oak. But don't expect much in the way of complexity or charisma. *40%*

⫶ **The Glenlivet French Oak Reserve 15 Years of Age** Limousin oak casks db **(95) n22.5** oo la la citrus; avec spice; **t23** comme ci comme ca caramels rescued by an uplifting injection of sweet barley; the juicy, salivating qualities are quite startling if not profound; **f22.5** long, with a fabulous butterscotch fade and a slow dissolving of dark sugars; **b23** really impressed (tres impressed!). Though have to say that after tasting nearly 800 cask strength whiskies, to come across something at the ancient 40% is a shock to the system. My taste buds say merci... And, what is more, a bottle of this shall remain in my dining room for guests. Having, a lifetime ago, lived with a wonderful French girl for three years I suspect I know how her country folk will regard that... Oh, and forgive a personal message to a literary friend: Bobby-Ann...keep a bottle of this beside the Ancient Age... *40%*

The Glenlivet Nadurra Aged 16 Years American oak bourbon, bott code LR10039 db **(94) n23.5 t24 f23 b23.5.** How curious: when I first nosed this one I thought: "hmmmm, stem ginger". Then looking up my previous entry saw ginger was included there, too. This time, though, the chocolate is conspicuous by its absence and a more bourbon character prevails. Remains the "must have" official Glenlivet for me to pour guests. *40%*

⫶ **The Glenlivet Nadurra Aged 16 Natural Cask Strength** batch no. 0808F, bott Aug 08 **(94) n23.5** Glenlivet in concentrate: literally. Delicate, juicy barley with the oak offering little more than a dais for the malt to make its lilting speech; **t24** every bit as salivating as the nose suggests. A fabulous brittleness and just a light puff of smoke helps soften things. Strands of citrus everywhere but it's the mouth-feel that has you whimpering with pleasure; **f23** dries at full pelt but that massive malt sees it through the turbulence; **b23.5** Glenlivet in its purest and most delicious form. Truly classic Speyside. *57.6% Canada market.*

The Glenlivet Aged 18 Years bott Feb 10 db **(91) n22** attractive mixture of honeycombed bourbon and fruitcake; **t23.5** oh...just didn't expect that...!! Fabulous, honey-sweet and slightly sharp edge to the barley: excellent weight and mouthfeel with the honeycomb on the nose making slow but decisive incursions; **f23** a very slight technical flaw drops it half a point, but there is no taking away from the improbable length of the dissolving honey and barley...some gentle chewing is required, especially with the late juices and vanilla arriving; **b23** a hugely improved bottling seriously worth discovering in this form. Appears to have thrown off its old shackles and offers up an intensity that leaves you giving a little groan of pleasure. *43%*

The Glenlivet Archive 21 Years Old batch no. 0508B bott Nov 08 db **(87.5) n22 t23.5 f20 b22.** Forget the nondescript finish: just settle down and be royally entertained by the enormity and panache of the big honey arrival. *43%*

The Glenlivet Archive 21 Years Old batch no. 1109D, bott Dec 09 db **(86.5) n22.5 t23 f20 b21.** Against the undisputed glory of a 60-second purple patch on delivery when the thick fruit, honey, spice and weight are in total harmony, the rest is comparatively humdrum with a very slight flaw helping to restrict the development to take this to where it belongs. *43%*

⫶ **The Glenlivet Founder's Reserve 21 Years Old** db **(95.5) n23.5** initially tight and, even after 20 minutes in the glass, allows the grape to unfurl in the most niggardly fashion. Thing is: the few notes, in tandem with some gorgeous Columbian cocoa, spices, orange peel and rich dates, reveals that much is to come on the palate... **t24.5** those spices are the first to flee the confines of the thick grape, but so many layers of grape skin and mocha follow that you can sit there for a good five minutes and still not entirely work out what is going on; the spices are not just persistent but simply magnificent; f23.5 long, with (milky) cocoa and dates (of the juicy rather than dried variety) leading the way; a light sulphur note detracts half a mark, but it is testament to the malt that it barely detracts from the moment; b24 on this evidence, one of the whiskies of the year for sure. I really don't think my 800th new single malt of the year could have been a more inspired – or lucky - choice. 55.6%. ncf 1824 bottles.

The Glenlivet XXV 25 Years Old batch no. 50416, bott Oct 08 db (91) n23 t24 f21.5 b22.5. Possibly the ultimate non-peated late night dram. One cask away from a massive score and a certain award... 43%

The Glenlivet 1973 Cellar Collection bott Oct 09 db (94.5) n24 luxurious stewed sultanas in a custard tart; yet for a malt heading towards 40, improbable grist, too: clean, complex, thick and simply spellbinding... t24 just melts into the taste buds with the freshest, cleanest, juiciest charm you could possibly imagine, yet always with a nibbling spice darting around the side of the tongue; f23 a touch of oaky bitterness, but a mere detail: the late oils are sympathetic and contain a surprising degree of vanilla; b23.5 for Glenlivet lovers, I point you towards something a little special... 49%. Chivas.

The Glenlivet Nadurra 1991 batch no. 0809A, bott Aug 09 db (89) n22.5 an oaky buzz and nip; some Fox's chocolate ginger usually seen in younger versions; implausibly fresh for its age yet showing just the right texture for an old un: how paradoxical; t23 quite exemplary and juicy delivery: light oils fill the palate and allow the slow release of tangy blood orange, softly honeyed malt and some unmistakable Kentucky characteristics though toffee does start thickening things; f21 long with more barley, toasted mallow and spot of liquorice; not a single sign of bitterness or tiredness from the casks; the caramel builds in intensity; b22.5 ah, had they only been a little more circumspect with the caramel... 48%

The Glenlivet Nadurra 1991 batch no. 0310B, bott Mar 10 db (78) n19 t22 f18 b19. A sulphurous sherry butt or two leaves you wondering what might have been. 48%. Chivas.

∴ **The Glenlivet Master Distiller's Reserve** db (86.5) n22.5 t22 f20.5 b21.5. I chose this as my 800th whisky for this Bible against the Founder's Reserve on the strength of the nose over the first 30 seconds. Oh, well. Shows you the pricelessness of time when evaluating a whisky... 40%

Berry's' Own Selection Glenlivet 1972 Aged 32 Years (86) n19 t23 f22 b22. A fascinating cask which cherishes its vitality. 46%. Berry Bros & Rudd.

Berry's Own Selection Glenlivet 1974 Aged 32 Years (84) n19 t22 f21 b22. A well-mannered dram offering barley-sugar in all the right places. But has a few bags under the eyes. 46%

Berry's Own Selection Glenlivet 1975 bott 2008 (87.5) n22 t23 f21 b21.5. Typically non-committal, as this distillery has a tendency to be, but has that little touch of class. 46%

∴ **Berry's Own Selection Glenlivet 1976** cask no. 18081, bott 2010 (80.5) n20 t21.5 f19 b20. No particular faults and shows a disarming sweetness early on. Just an exhausted malt at the end of a very long life, I'm afraid. 46%. nc ncf sc. Berry Bros & Rudd.

Berry's Own Selection Glenlivet 1977 bott 2008 (85) n21 t21 f22 b21. Very even: silky-soft with mature vanilla. 46%. Berry Bros & Rudd.

Berrys' Own Selection Glenlivet 1982 (94) n24 leathery, fruitcake and marzipan, and attractively oaked; something of the pre-coloured Demerara rum to this one, too; t23.5 one of those big raisin and fudge numbers which bite deep and smuggle some mocha into the act for extra intensity; still that pot still rum richness; f23 dries as the oak makes a thundering but, thankfully, Christmas cake intense speech; b23.5 for all the flying sawdust, still one hell of a bottling. And if you happen to have a love for high quality old Demerara rum, then this will be a double whammy for you. 52.2%. Berry Bros & Rudd.

∴ **Berry's Own Selection Glenlivet 1994** cask no. 58453, bott 2011 (71) n18 t18.5 f17 b17.5 Thank you. Next...! 58.9%. nc ncf sc. Berry Bros & Rudd.

Celtic Heartlands Glenlivet 1975 bott 2008 (85) n21.5 t21.5 f21 b21. oak in as many guises as you can imagine here. Bit OTT on that front, to be honest, but you cannot be blown away by some aspects of the bourbony intensity. 51.2%. Bruichladdich Ltd. 450 bottles.

The Coopers Choice Glenlivet 1997 Aged 12 Years (82.5) n21.5 t21 f19.5 b20.5. A typically juicy but weightless example of its blending style. 46%. The Vintage Malt Whisky Co.

The Coopers Choice Glenlivet 1998 Sherry Wood Aged 11 Years (78.5) n18.5 t21 f19 b20. At times, there are wonderful signs of true grapeness, backed by a spicy chorus. But undone somewhat by you-know-what.. 46%. The Vintage Malt Whisky Co.

Duncan Taylor Collection Glenlivet 1970 cask no. 2002 (87) n22.5 you almost need a spoon to get the intensely thick fruitiness out of the glass; t23 like cask 2017 but probably twice as concentrated with a mercurial maple syrup quality fighting off the oak; f19.5 just too well aged; **b21.5** were it not for the resistance of the fruit and syrup, this would be a goner. But the battle to keep a grip on life is fascinating. *54.3%. Duncan Taylor & Co Ltd.*

Duncan Taylor Collection Glenlivet 1970 cask no. 2009 (83.5) **n21 t21 f21.5 b20**. Eye-watering oak offers ample evidence of a few Summers too far. The middle, though, broadens out as some bitter-sweet barley counters beautifully, before crushed without pity by the wooden weight at the death. *52.6%*

Duncan Taylor Collection Glenlivet 1970 cask no. 2017 (85.5) **n22.5 t22 f20 b21**. Radiates the classic exotic fruit old age charm on nose and delivery, but the middle and finish creak a bit. *50.9%. Duncan Taylor & Co Ltd.*

Gordon & MacPhail Distillery Label Glenlivet 15 Years Old (88.5) **n22.5** weighty, malty with a soft, oily sheen upping the intensity; **t22** beautiful poise with just a touch of nuttiness to the barley; **f22** coconut strands dipped in golden syrup; **b22** sturdy with lots of malty weight and an unusual degree of oil. *43%. Gordon & MacPhail.*

Gordon & MacPhail Distillery Label Glenlivet 21 Years Old (88.5) **n22 t23 f21.5 b22**. Always merits a refill. *43%*

⁙ **Gordon & MacPhail Generations Glenlivet 70 Years Old** dist 1940 (95.5) **n24.5** the very first notes have a diced ginger quality to it: understated, but there. As that fades, a recognisable trait of great age begins to creep in: something akin to exotic fruit. This variety is a little dryer than some, perhaps with banana skins trying to inject a vanilla element. Slowly, spices begin to emerge – never rabid but a buzzing heard above the general murmur. Is it the ancient remnants of smoke? Or just some oaky attitude? Difficult to say at first, but then a clue: as the whisky oxidizes the oak has a more vociferous note and the drying process begins in earnest. 20 minutes in and the gingers and exotic fruits have been replaced by earthier oak notes and a touch of clove, too...and very late on...could it be? Is that the odd (non-spiced) molecule of peat...? Actually, leave the empty glass to dry of its own accord (when it hits 25/25), and you will be left in little doubt; **t23.5** if tasted early, the oaks are slightly OTT. So don't! Leave for about 15 minutes, then start tasting: a thick amalgamation of natural caramels and barley; shows almost a nougat quality at times with the toffee carrying with it a squeeze of sultana; actually becomes juicier in the middle for a while; the spices nibble and buzz, but no more viciously than your partner around your neck...; **f24** long. Not a threat of bitterness: just magnificent oak. Moves into a mocha mode. And as it oxidises, the creamier it becomes, helped along the way by an extra quarter spoonful of Demerara every now and again...; **b24** you may not be too surprised that I selected this as the 1,000th whisky to be officially tasted for the Whisky Bible 2012. Like an ancient glacier, it's a malt on the move: so slowly, it is imperceptible. I have tried to capture the path it takes over time and the scores are the average ones over a good hour. This is nothing like G&M's previous 70-year-old. It does have something in common, though: the kind of oak influence that, were it possible to return in 70 years time, I would be surprised if today's casks could come even close to matching. This whisky seemingly defies nature. It absolutely refuses to seek shelter under a honeyed umbrella and somehow plots a course from its hushed hello as it is poured to its exquisitely elegant denouement by taking us through a journey of hints, might-bes, and whispers. For the lucky ones amongst us, it is a unique journey of a lifetime. *45.9%*

⁙ **Gordon & MacPhail Private Collection Glenlivet 1954** (96) **n24** Bassett's chocolate liquorice. An outline of earthy smoke plus toffee apple with a surprising degree of Golden Delicious. I really have no idea how a whisky this old can be so devoid of any off notes – well, apart from the fact the oak was so much better in those days; **t23.5** first up come some oak-led spices, but all very civil. A charming soft oil lubricates the taste buds without them really noticing; there is a very brief puckering sharpness from the oak, but a wave of barley-tinged fruitcake fills the middle; **f24.5** such a wonderfully weighted finale it borders on the ridiculous. Understated but evident layers of chocolate sponge, walnut cake (with cream) and a liberal smattering of dates makes for a finish bordering on perfection. Especially if you can pick up on that delicate smoke which re-enters the picture and seems like the glow from a swallowed and well matured Melton Hunt cake... **b24** if there is a heaven, I think I have just entered it. For no company in the world does this kind of veteran whisky better than Gordan and MacPhail and here they have exceeded even themselves. Guessed this would be an outstanding whisky to mark my 700th specifically tasted for the Bible 2012, and 600th new entry. My word: was I right...! *50.6%*

⁙ **Gordon & MacPhail Private Collection Glenlivet 1963** (88) **n23** thin ginger and myriad vanilla tones, some displaying citrus; **t21.5** oils and cocoa make for a delightful start; the oaks threaten like storm clouds passing by slightly to the north...; **f21.5** a big oaky buzz. A little muscovado sugar and mocha keeps the balance; **b22** defies the odds to stay together. A malt that feels its age, but can still get around. *40.6%*

Gordon & MacPhail Private Collection Glenlivet 1974 (95.5) n24.5 this is ridiculous. How, with a mere human nose (albeit a pretty fine-tuned one, apparently), am I supposed to work out all that is going on here? Well, let's start with the grape: hard to begin anywhere else. A distinct musto quality to this, alongside the usual Melton Hunt cake mature fruitiness. Nuts, too: brazils and pecans in abundance; and just don't get me started on the molasses...; t23.5 this time the sugars kick off the proceedings: naturally they tend to be dark in character with molasses leading the way. The grape is thick and wonderfully overcooked; f24 normally, bitterness on a finish is the kiss of death for a whisky: not here. This is not from exhausted oak. It is, as it should be, an amalgam of big tannin and even bigger grape. And all coated with virtually flawless molasses and toasty natural caramel. There is some sharp marmalade, too, just to finish it – and you - off...; b24 I have been seriously thinking about investing in an MG Roadster 1974 vintage. One reason is because I remember at school being friends with next desk buddy, Legin Reltub (aka Nigel Butler) and my long ago tragically lost amigo Ian Lovell the merits of this then newly released car which featured prominently in Playboy. I told them, one day, when I had made my pile, I would be the proud owner of the babe magnet which radiated from the glossy pages before us. I owe it to my loyal sidekick Ian at least to keep to my word. Why am I thinking of that now? Well, because this whisky just reminded me of it. All sleek lines, elegant oomph and come-to-bed classicism. This one, dear, much missed Ian, is to you, mate... 50.1%

Gordon & MacPhail Private Collection Glenlivet 1980 (85.5) n21 t23.5 f20 b21. A subdued, slightly soapy number which enjoys its best, toasty moments on delivery and with some honey comb soon after. 48.5%

Gordon & MacPhail Private Collection Glenlivet 1991 (93) n23 apple and pear stew, sweetened only by a thin sprinkling of Demerara sugar; vanilla ice cream with raspberry sauce...; a light but telling oaky spiciness; t23 mouth-watering malt on delivery enjoying just about perfect weight. The oaks are raring to go, but a light butterscotch and burnt honeycomb middle set up the mocha middle; f23.5 a ridiculously elegant fade involving gentle nuances of mocha and Demerara...and still some barley...! b23.5 a faultless bottling, allowing the malt an uninterrupted speech. Probably an independent bottling by which others from this distillery should be measured for the age. 54.5%

Gordon & MacPhail Rare Vintage Glenlivet 1965 (87) n22.5 t21.5 f22 b21. Takes the oak to the limit but somehow works. 40%

Kingsbury's Finest & Rarest Glenlivet 1978 (94.5) n23.5 t24 f23 b24. Does and says all the right things for its age. Premier class malt. 52.6%. Japan Import System.

Kingsbury's Single Cask Glenlivet Aged 15 Years dist May 93, bott Jun 08 (79) n21 t20 f18 b18. Bitter-sweet. But mainly bitter: certainly not as the distiller intended... 46%

Old Malt Cask Glenlivet Aged 13 Years sherry butt no. DL 5537, dist Apr 96, bott Oct 09 (68) n16 t18 f16.5 b17.5. The grape fights valiantly against the sulphur. 50%. 432 bottles.

Old Malt Cask Glenlivet Aged 17 Years bourbon cask, dist Apr 92, bott Jul 09 (90.5) n23 t23 f22 b22.5. Amazing how lovely this distillery can be in the right cask and with no colouring. Grab this dazzler if you see it. 50%. Douglas Laing.

Old Malt Cask Glenlivet Aged 18 Years rum cask, dist Sep 90, bott Sep 08 (85) n20 t22 f21.5 b21.5. Well made and delivers on the maltiness. 50%. Douglas Laing. 272 bottles.

Old Malt Cask Glenlivet Aged 30 Years refill hogshead, dist Jun 78, bott Apr 09 (94) n23 t24 f23 b24. From the days when The Glenlivet had body enough to cope with 30 years with nothing more than a shrug. Glorious. 50%. Douglas Laing. 205 bottles.

Old Malt Cask Glenlivet Aged 30 Years refill hogshead no. DL 5438, dist Aug 79, bott Aug 09 (93.5) n24 seemingly strangulated by oak, a more careful look under the natural caramels reveals a few molecules of smoke trying to escape as well as a deliciously elegant lychee/papaya hybrid; t23.5 some soaring oak but there is always the backdrop of prickly barley... and that wonderful echo of smoke; f23 holds out without further oak damage with a touch of smoky chocolate mousse – lightened by a sprinkling of muscovado sugar - as a final flourish; b23 textbook complexity and benefits with being lightly warmed in the glass for a good 15-20 minutes before nosing and tasting. 50%. Douglas Laing & Co Ltd. 217 bottles.

Old Malt Cask Glenlivet Aged 32 Years refill hogshead no. DL 5969, dist Jun 77, bott Mar 10 (89.5) n21 sherbet lemon; t23 fizzy barley with charming sweet-sharp interplay; f22.5 drier vanilla with the odd, leathery strand of hickory and honeycomb; b22.5 limited complexity for its age but maximum early juiciness. 50%. Douglas Laing & Co Ltd. 280 bottles.

Old Malt Cask Glenlivet Aged 34 Years refill hogshead, cask no. 7192, dist Jun 77, bott Jun 11 (90.1) n23 honey and citrus ladled into the vanilla. Excellent weight; t23 the delivery hangs on the richness of the oils. Again honey at the foreground though an undertow of mildly bitter oaks ensures parity. Spices bounce with abandon; f22 now those peppery spices take command, warming the palate. Still the honey lingers, though: impressive! **b22.5** rarely does a Glenlivet show this degree of honey and spice. Superb. *50%. nc ncf sc. 210 bottles.*

Old Masters Glenlivet Aged 12 Years cask no. 906680, dist 1996, bott 2008 **(82) n22 t21 f19 b20.** Sharp, tasty barley but the feeling is that not all is well with the cask *57.8%*

Old Masters Glenlivet Aged 30 Years cask no. 1975, dist 1978, bott 2008 **(85) n22 t22 f20.5 b20.5**. A malt of two halves: the nose shows signs of enormous age with its hints of exotic fruit, but works pleasantly, as does the juicy malt arrival with its delightful, eye-watering zinginess. After that the splinters are harder to remove though some praline does ensure the overall experience is an enjoyable one. *57.6%. James MacArthur & Co. Ltd.*

Private Collection Glenlivet 1959 (96.5) n24.5 sure; there is oak, and plenty of it. But that is not a problem when there is a veritable basket of juice-oozing fruit to soften the blow. The mix between delicate kiwi and greengage is a treat, and this in turn blends in with the ripe dates and figs. Beyond wonderful **t24** fabulous: 50-years-old and still the juice spills all over the taste buds on arrival before a delicately sweetened natural caramel and juicy oak fizz toss some weight in there; **f24** long and now those spices take shape; they thin and fizz while the vanillas carry a light coating of barley; **b24** how reassuring it is to know I can still find a world-class whisky older than any of the women in my life... lithe, velvety textured, juicy, caresses the tongue...yes, and this 50-year-old whisky does all those things, too... *47.5%. Gordon & MacPhail.*

Scotch Malt Whisky Society Cask 2.74 Aged 15 Years refill hogshead, dist May 93 **(89.5) n22.5 t22.5 f22 b22.5.** Attractively shaped and curves in all the right places. *57.2%*

⋰⋱ **Scott's Selection Glenlivet 1980** bott 2011 **(91) n22.5** crystal ginger; some evidence of tired oak, but the barley has a juicy edge, backed up by some serious sugar; **t23** throw back your head and chew for a good five minutes. The spices are spot on, though the oak still has a distinctly aggressive stance. But hints of mocha and butterscotch help settle matters while proud barley thrusts a jutting jaw of muscovado; **f22** pretty long considering the distinct lack of oils; the spices persist; the barley remains governing and almost aloof; **b23.5** I must admit; the nose had me worried. But there was enough sweetness lurking in there somewhere for hope. And my wishes were granted. A charmer which takes you seemingly day by day through every one of its 30 years... *45.5%. Speyside Distillers.*

Wilson & Morgan Barrel Selection Glenlivet Aged 30 Years cask no. 13501, dist 1978, bott 2008 **(84.5) n21 t22 f20.5 b21**. Very much in the Glenlivet mould for older bottlings: starts off at a cracking pace on the barley and soft fruits and then flags as the vanillas drive home. *46%*

GLENLOCHY
Highlands (Western), 1898–1983. Diageo. Closed.

Rarest of the Rare Glenlochy 1980 cask no. 2454 **(96) n24 t24.5 f23.5 b24**. This does what it says on the tin: this really is the rarest of the rare. I do not often see this stuff either in bottled form or privately through a whisky year. It makes hen's teeth look pretty two-a-penny. But then one must ask the question: why? Any distillery capable of making malt this good should still be working, rather than being turned into a small hotel. (Jim Murray and all at Dram Good Books Ltd would like to assure readers of a nervous disposition that no whisky was spat out during the tasting of this sample.) *54.8%. Duncan Taylor.*

GLENLOSSIE
Speyside, 1876. Diageo. Working.

Glenlossie The Manager's Choice first fill bourbon American oak, cask no. 14098, dist 1999, bott 2009 db **(92.5) n23.5** a delicate trace of lime to the barley: what an understated, fragile, uber sexy nose...; **t23.5** unusual in that the first wave on delivery appears to be a thin, oily note. This is promptly followed by the young barley water, threatening a sharpness but dampened by the lightest scattering of icing sugar; mouth watering and youthful; **f23** even with the custard powder arrival, never a hint of anything that is remotely not kindergarten; **b22.5** one of the most impressive examples of Speyside malt, apparently not even out of nappies but treating you to a spectacular display of barley in all its beauty. Confirmation, barely needed, that with Clynelish, this has to be Diageo's most under-rated distillery. *59.1%. 207 bottles.*

Berrys' Own Selection Glenlossie 1975 (94) n23.5 exquisite Lossieness: soft contours of exotic fruit sharpened by a livelier zestiness but with a brittle maltiness just below the surface. Custard topping completes the experience for those who remember Zoom ice lollies...; **t24** pure Lossie-mouth: as delicate as the nose despite the obvious early oak prickle. This soon loses ground to the stupendous lush barley which evolves on a lightly oiled bed of muscovado sugars; **f23** those oils ensure a real length to this one with the oaks reforming, as they have every right, but never at a cost to the overall elegance; vanilla and barley dominate the fade; **b**23.5 a quite magic cask, despite the obvious signs of age. Miss at your peril. 49.8%. Berry Bros & Rudd.

⁘ **Berry's Own Selection Glenlossie 1975** cask no. 5951, bott 2010 **(87.5) n**22 soft ginger and lavender; signs of big age; **t**22 the oaks gather first, but sufficient acacia honey soften the impact; peppers give some indication of continuing life; **f**22 light vanillas and some milky chocolate but gathering drier oaks loom; **b**21.5 worth some serious time to enjoy. But please accept the wrinkles of great age. 49.7%. nc ncf sc. Berry Bros & Rudd.

Cadenhead's Authentic Collection Glenlossie-Glenlivet 1993 bott Feb 10 **(78) n**21 **t**21 **f**18 **b**18. A bit of a head scratcher, this. Where did those lightly smoked cabbage notes come from? When pitched in with a wine cask fruitiness, the result is a real hit and miss affair with more misses than hits. 55.8%. Wm. Cadenhead Ltd. 265 bottles.

The Càrn Mòr Vintage Collection Glenlossie 1984 sherry butt, cask no. 2537, dist 1984, bott 2009 **(73) n**18 **t**19 **f**18 **b**18. Sulphur-affected cask. 46%. The Scottish Liqueur Centre.

⁘ **Hart Brothers Glenlossie Aged 11 Years** dist Nov 98, bott Oct 10 **(88.5) n**22.5 grassy, clean barley; the very vaguest hint of smoke; **t**22 every bit as juicy as the nose promises, with the barley in the driving seat; **f**22 soft oils lengthen the gristy sugars; **b**22 a beautiful vehicle for the distillery to show its elegance. 46%. sc.

Old Malt Cask Glenlossie Aged 16 Years sherry butt no. DL 5530, dist Sep 93, bott Sep 09 **(77.5) n**20 **t**20.5 **f**18 **b**19. A lightweight gristiness. 50%. Douglas Laing & Co Ltd. 541 bottles.

GLEN MHOR
Highlands (Northern), 1892–1983. Diageo. Demolished.

Glen Mhor 1976 Rare Malt db **(92.5) n**23 **t**24 **f**22 **b**23.5. You just dream of truly great whisky sitting in your glass from time to time. But you don't expect it, especially from such an old cask. This was the best example from this distillery I've tasted in 30 years...until the Glenkeir version was unleashed! If you ever want to see a scotch that has stretched the use of oak as far it will go without detriment, here it is. What a pity the distillery has gone because the Mhor the merrier... 52.2%

Berry's Own Selection Glen Mhor 1982 (94) n24 wow! Now there's a nose for me to start the day with: need all the old nose buds in full working order for this one. It's like being in a honey- and peat-selling florists...who have orange blossom on special offer...; **t**23.5 again, it's all about the honey: just one soft layer after another but of ever altering intensity. Luckily weighed down by a hint of smoke, otherwise it would all float off...; **f**23 long, a touch of lingering smoke to the honey-sweetened mocha; **b**23.5 the best start I've had to a Bible tasting day...and it's late August. Although it is obvious that the oaks are just beginning to crack, everything about this malt is right. 46%. Berry Bros & Rudd.

Cadenhead's Glen Mhor 1982 sherry cask, bott Feb 10 **(88) n**22 the oak is in the process of getting its pension but enough crisp barley for an interesting development; **t**22 immediate spice fizz softened by a juicy, vaguely fruity second string; **f**22 still the unmistakable sign of OTT oak, but some lovely zest, too; **b**22 firm and spicy. Enough oak to fell a charging rhino, yet somehow the fruity richness of the barley lightens and brightens to make for a lovely dram. 56.8%. Wm. Cadenhead Ltd. 236 bottles.

⁘ **Glen Mhor Private Collection 1966 (91) n**23.5 thick, toasty oak seasoned further by a touch of salt; not quite piny, but thinking about it. There is a pretty impressive marmalade on burnt toast in the next room quality about it and, as it oxidises, the natural caramels begin to have a presence; very late on into oxidisation we enter sumptuous date and walnut territory; **t**23 sharp, juicy delivery then massive amounts of silky caramels keep an oaky undertow at bay; relatively simplistic but a few dates and walnuts to be had relatively early on; **f**22 some residual bitterness, but still the caramels dominate; **b**22.5 the trick with any very old whisky is that you must give them time to be themselves. After being cooped up for years in oak and then glass, it takes time for them to come fully alive: a classic case in point here. Virtually undrinkable upon opening the bottle to being a treat, if of limited complexity, after 20 minutes in the glass. These guys are so rare I don't honestly expect to come across another one distilled in the 60s that will give me much more than this. Sad, as one of my first experiences in the Scottish whisky shop, in the mid 70s, involved a guy trying to sell me a bottle of G&M Glen Mhor. The Glen Mhor are getting less. And lesser... 45%. Gordon & MacPhail.

Gordon & MacPhail Distillery Label Glen Mhor 1980 (77) n19 **t**21 **f**18 **b**19. A lesser Mhor. 43%

Old Malt Cask Glen Mhor Aged 27 Years refill hogshead no. DL 5420, dist Aug 82, bott Aug 09 **(95) n**24 peat-smoked oak; vanilla cream Swiss roll...simply gorgeous; **t**24 smoked-spiced delivery with several layers of lime and caramelised ginger; juicy and improbably sensuous with the peat returning to fill the middle rather nimbly; f23.5 tires but there is enough Demerara to see off the worst of the oak; the smoke-laden spice is a constant – rather delicious – noise to the very end and helped by a very light oil; b23.5 more time on its dial than Big Ben. But plenty of the smoky spice of life... this is astonishingly good. 50%

Rarest of the Rare Glen Mhor 1975 cask no. 4035 **(85) n21 t22 f21 b21.** Exceptionally gentle to the point of being docile. At one stage, threatens to go down the dramatic olde worlde exotic fruit road, decides against it and, a few spice prickles apart, glides to the finish line. 40.2%

Rarest of the Rare Glen Mhor 1975 cask no. 4041 **(85.5) n21 t21.5 f22 b21.** Never quite know what you are going to get from this batch of casks. They can be ordinary or stupendous. Here we have something of a halfway house, though tending towards the Mhor ordinaire. Wallpaper pasty in part but the crystal brown sugar edge to the barley is quite a treat. Very drinkable and for its age in pretty good nick. Just don't expect to be blown away by the complexity. 40.6%

GLENMORANGIE
Highlands (Northern), 1843. Glenmorangie Plc. Working.

Glenmorangie 10 Years Old db **(94) n24** perhaps the most enigmatic aroma of them all: delicate yet assertive, sweet yet dry, young yet oaky: a malty tone poem; **t22** flaky oakiness throughout but there is an impossibly complex toastiness to the barley which seems to suggest the lightest hint of smoke; **f24** amazingly long for such a light dram, drying from the initial sweetness but with flaked almonds amid the oakier, rich cocoa notes; **b24** you might find the occasional "orange variant", where the extra degree of oak, usually from a few too many first-fill casks, has flattened out the more extreme peaks and toughs of complexity (scores about 89). But these are pretty rare – almost a collector's item – and overall this remains one of the great single malts: a whisky of uncompromising aesthetic beauty from the first enigmatic whiff to the last teasing and tantalising gulp. Complexity at its most complex. 40% ⊙

Glenmorangie 15 Years Old db **(90.5) n23** chunky and fruity: something distinctly sugar candy about this one; the barley's no slouch, either; and, just to raise the eyebrows, just the faintest waft of something smoky...; **t23** silky, a tad sultry, and serious interplay between oak and barley; a real, satisfying juiciness to this one; **f22** dries towards the oaky side of things, but just a faint squeeze of liquorice adds extra weight; **b22.5** exudes quality. 43%

Glenmorangie 15 Years Old Sauternes Wood Finish db **(68) n16 t18 f17 b17.** I had hoped – and expected – an improvement on the sulphured version I came across last time. Oh, whisky! Why are you such a cruel mistress...? 46%

Glenmorangie 18 Years Old db **(91) n22** pleasant if unconvincing spotted dick; **t23** sharp, eye-watering mix of fruit and mainly honeyed barley; nutty and, with the confident vanillas, forming a breakfast cereal completeness; **f23** Cocoa Krispies; **b23** having thrown off some previous gremlins, now a perfect start to the day whisky... 43% ⊙ ⊙

Glenmorangie 25 Years Old db **(95.5) n24** it's strap yourself in time: this is a massive nose with more layers, twists and turns than you can shake a thief at. Soft, mildly lush Lubec marzipan is sandwiched between fruit bonbons and myriad barley tones. Worth taking half an hour over this one, and no kidding... **t24** the clarity on the nose is matched here. Every single wave of flavour is there in crystal form, starting, naturally, with the barley but this is soon paired with various unidentified fruits. The result is salivation. Towards the middle the oak shows form and does so in various cocoa-tinged ways; every nuance is delicately carved, almost fragile, but the overall picture is one of strength; **f23.5** medium length with the cocoa heading towards medium roast Java **b24** every bit as statesmanlike and elegant as a whisky of this age from such a blinding distillery should be. Ticks every single box for a 25-year-old and is Morangie's most improved malt by the distance of Tain to Wellingborough. There is a hint of genius with each unfolding wave of flavours with this one: a whisky that will go in 99/100 whisky lover's top 50 malts of all time. And that includes the Peatheads. 43% ⊙

Glenmorangie 30 Years Old db **(72) n17 t18 f19 b18.** From the evidence in the glass the jury is out on whether it has been spruced up a little in a poor sherry cask – and spruce is the operative word: lots of pine on this wrinkly. 44.1%

Glenmorangie Vintage 1975 db **(89) n23** clementines! It must be Christmas...; **t23** improbably clean malt for something so aged, then a layer or three of fruit and spiced vanilla; **f21** bitters out as an oaky trench is found; **b22** a charming, fruity and beautifully spiced oldie. 43%

Glenmorangie 1977 db **(92) n24 t23 f22 b23.** Excellent, but a trifle underpowered...what would this have been like at 46%...??? Shows little of its great age as the oak is always subservient to the sweet barley and citrus. 43%. Exclusively at Harrods.

⸬ **Glenmorangie Pride 1981** dist Oct 81, bott 2010, Sauternes barrique db **(77.5) n18 t22 f18 b19.5.** The Pride before a fall...? I know that gifted blender Bill Lumsden feels that a touch of sulphur can sometimes bring good to a dram. He and I share many similar views on whisky. But here we very much part company. For me, sulphur is a fault. Nothing more. Nothing less. The entire reason for stills to be made from copper is so sulphur compounds are removed. So by adding them back in, as they obviously have here via the barriques, can be nothing other than a negative step. Perhaps I am at fault for having a zero tolerance on sulphur. But when, for me, it spoils the nose, muddies the middle and bitters the finish, how can I do anything other than judge accordingly? The tragedy here is that it is obvious that some astonishing elements are at play. Even through the bitter haze I could detect some gorgeous honey and glazed fruits and stems; so excellent, in fact, that for a few brief moments the faults are silenced. But that is only a respite. Those unable to spot sulphur, through smoking or their DNA, will doubtless find much to enjoy and wonder why I have marked this down. But I cannot join the general back-slapping on this whisky. I have been told that someone has suggested the sulphur on this soon goes away. It doesn't: it never does – that is absolutely ridiculous. And why some whisky critics can't nose sulphur is beyond me. About as useful as a wine writer unable to spot a corked wine; or a music critic unable to hear the cello playing in entirely the wrong key. Sorry. But I have to be the sole dissenting voice on this one. 56.7%

Glenmorangie Artisan Casks db (93) n23 t23.5 f23 b23.5. If whisky could be sexed, this would be a woman. Every time I encounter Morangie Artisan, it pops up with a new look, a different perfume. And mood. It appears not to be able to make up its mind. But does it know how to pout, seduce and win your heart...? Oh yes. 46%

Glenmorangie Astar db (88) n21 t23 f22.5 b22. Decidedly strange malt: for quite a while it is as if someone has extracted the barley and left everything else behind. A star is born? Not yet, perhaps. But perhaps a new breed of single malt. 57.1% ⊙

Glenmorangie Burgundy Wood Finish db (72) n17.5 t19.5 f18 b18. Sulphured whisky de table. 43%

Glenmorangie Burr Oak Reserve db (92) n24 t24 f22 b22. Fades on the finish as a slightly spent force, but nose and arrival are simply breathtaking. Wouldn't be out of place in Kentucky. 56.3%

Glenmorangie Cellar 13 Ten Years Old db (88.5) n22 t22.5 f22 b22 oh, if only I could lose weight as efficiently as this appears to have done... oh, I have! My love and thanks to Nancy, Nigel and Ann Marie. 43%

Glenmorangie Elegance db (92) n22 quite herbal and soothing; t24 the thinnest layer of icing sugar coats the silk-soft malt; every bit as gentle as the nose suggests; f22 medium to short with some attractive rolling vanilla; b24 a surprise package that is not entirely dissimilar to the Golden Rum, only a tad sweeter. 43%

Glenmorangie Finealta db (84.5) n21 t22 f20.5 b21. Plump and thick, one of the creamiest malts around. For what it lacks in fine detail it makes up for in effect, especially the perky oaky spices. 46%

Glenmorangie Lasanta sherry casks db (68.5) n16 t19 f16 b17.5. The sherry problem has increased dramatically rather than being solved. 46% ⊙ ⊙

Glenmorangie Madeira Wood Finish db (78) n19.5 t20.5 f19 b19. One of the real problems with wine finishes is getting the point of balance right when the fruit, barley and oak are in harmony. Here it is on a par with me singing in the shower, though frankly my aroma would be a notch or two up. 43%

Glenmorangie Margaux Cask Finish db (88) n22 t22 f22 b22. Even taking every whisky with an open mind, I admit this was better than my subconscious might have considered. Certainly better than the near undrinkable Ch. Margaux '57 I used to bring out for my birthday each year some 20-odd years ago... 46%

Glenmorangie Nectar D'or Sauternes Finish db (94) n23 delicate cinnamon on toast and a drizzle of greengage and sultana; t24 equally refreshing and dense on the palate as the bitter-sweet battle goes into overdrive; excellent weight and body; f23 remains clean and precise, allowing some custard onto the apple strudel finale; b24 great to see French casks that actually complement a whisky – so rare! This has replaced the Madeira finish. But there are some similar sweet-fruit characteristics. An exercise in outrageously good sweet-dry balancing. 46% ⊙

Glenmorangie Quinta Ruban Port Finish db (92) n24 typical Morangie complexity, but the grape notes added act almost like a prism to show their varied hues; t23 fruit and spice about as the oak goes in search of glory: barley stands in its way; f22 light, deftly sweetened and juicy to the end; b23 this replacement of the original Port finish shows a genuine understanding of the importance of grape-oak balance. Both are portrayed with clarity and confidence. This is a form of cask finishing that has progressed from experimentation to certainty. 46% ⊙

Glenmorangie Sherry Wood Finish db (84) n23 t21 f20 b20. Stupendous clean sherry nose, then disappoints with a somewhat bland display on the palate. 43%

Glenmorangie Signet db (80.5) n20 t21.5 f19 b20. A great whisky holed below the waterline by oak of unsatisfactory quality. Tragic. 46% ⊙ ⊙

Glenmorangie Sonnalta PX db (96.5) n24 now this works: has that heavy-handed feel of a sweet sherry butt (or five) at work here, usually the kiss of death for so many whiskies. But an adroit praline sub-plot really does the trick. So with the malt evident, too, we have a three-pronged attack which somehow meshes in to one. And not even the merest hint of an off-note...goodness gracious: a new experience...!!! t24 Neanderthal grape drags its knuckles along the big vanilla floor before a really subtle light Columbian coffee kick puts us back on course; sharper vanillas from some awkward oak threatens to send us off course again but somehow it finds a settled, common ground; f24.5 now goes into orgasmic overdrive as Demerara sugar is tipped into some gorgeous, cream-lightened mocha. This is obviously to wash down the Melton Hunt cake which is resplendent in its grape and roast nut finery... phew!!! It is, unquestionably, the perfect whisky finish... b24 remains a giant among the tall stills. A mesmeric whisky... 46% ⊙ ⊙

Glenmorangie Traditional db (90.5) n22 orange blossom, barley sugar and chalk dust; t23 delicate delivery revelling in gentle complexity: really playful young-ish malt makes for a clean start and middle; f22.5 soft mocha notes play out a quiet finish; b23 an improved dram with much more to say, but does so quietly. 57.1%

Glenmorangie Truffle Oak db (96) n24 t24 f25 b23. The Glenmorangie of all Glenmorangies. I really have to work hard and deep into the night to find fault with it. If I am going to be hyper-critical, I'll dock it a mark for being so constantly sweet, though in its defence I have to say that the degree of sweetness alters with astonishing dexterity. Go on, it's Truffle oak: make a pig of yourself...!! 60.5%

Scotch Malt Whisky Society Cask 125.26 Aged 16 Years dist May 93 (83) n23.5 t21.5 f19 b19. Fabulous, rich chocolate-caramel bourbon nose...then on the palate a severe case of over-aging. 52.2%. 243 bottles.

Scotch Malt Whisky Society Cask 125.35 Aged 16 Years sherry butt, dist Feb 94 (68) n14 t19 f17 b18. Very thoughtful of the SMWS to throw in a cask to show its members why sulphur-treated casks are close on undrinkable. Sadly, as my 600th new whisky for the 2011 edition...a serious party pooper. 52.1%. 367 bottles.

Scotch Malt Whisky Society Cask 125.39 Aged 18 Years dist Feb 92 (85) n20 t22.5 f21 b21.5. A kind of 125.26 in reverse: here the nose is dull and unrewarding but the delivery sparks into life with the most intense orangey-bourbon arrival imaginable. Pretty close to the edge, though, and another Summer might have been one too many. 55.7%. 234 bottles.

⌁ **Scotch Malt Whisky Society Cask 125.43 Aged 18 Years** 1st fill bourbon hogshead, cask no. 10895, dist 1991 (88) n24 crushed Crunchie candy, with honeycomb biscuit to the milk chocolate; some bit into toffee-apple, too; the vanilla appears in sawdust-dry form; t23 the type of delivery which makes you groan out loud; perfect weight to the barley and oil, then a slow dissolving of Malteasers, honey and red liquorice; light spicing but the oils are divine...; f19 bitters out slightly too enthusiastically; b22 the barrel type is never in dispute: more bourbon notes than Scotch ones... 54.6%. sc. 140 bottles.

⌁ **Scotch Malt Whisky Society Cask 125.47 Aged 15 Years** 1st fill hogshead, cask no. 13230, dist 1995 (91) n23.5 a sharp barley edge pierces the natural caramels; a number of pre-bourbon notes become pure bourbon as it oxidises...; t22.5 mouth-watering, as that sharpness on the nose foretells; a lovely build up of spices dazzle; f22.5 remains spicy despite the chewy vanilla and light hickory; b22.5 a delightful malt that may also impress diehard Kentuckians. 56.1%. sc. 310 bottles.

⌁ **Scotch Malt Whisky Society Cask 125.49 Aged 9 Years** refill Burgundy barrique, cask no. 12210, dist 2001 (84) n21.5 t21 f20.5 b21. A bitter-sweet affair. 60.8%. sc. 282 bottles.

GLEN MORAY
Speyside, 1897. La Martiniquaise. Working.

Glen Moray Classic 8 Years Old db (86) n20 t22 f21 b23. A vast improvement on previous bottlings with the sluggish fatness replaced by a thinner, barley-rich, slightly sweeter and more precise mouthfeel. 40%

⌁ **Glen Moray 10 Years Old Chardonnay Matured** db (73.5) n18.5 t19 f18 b18. Tighter than a wine cork. 40%

Glen Moray 12 Years Old db (90) n22.5 gentle malt of varying pitch and intensity; t22 a duller start than it should be with the vanilla diving in almost before the barley but the juicy, grassy notes arrive in good time; f23 long, back on track with intense malt and the custardy oak is almost apologetic but enlivened with a dash of lime: mmmmm... pure Glen Moray! **b22.5** I have always regarded this as the measuring stick by which all other malty and clean Speysiders should be tried and tested. It is still a fabulous whisky, full of malty intricacies. Something has fallen off the edge, perhaps, but minutely so. Still think a trick or two is being missed by bottling this at 40%: the natural timbre of this malt demands 46% and no less.... *40%*

Glen Moray 16 Years Old db (74) n19 t19 f18 b19. A serious dip in form. Drab. *40%*

Glen Moray 16 Years Old Chenin Blanc Mellowed in Wine Barrels db (85) n20 t22 f22 b21. A fruity, oak-shaded dram just brimming with complexity. *40%*

Glen Moray 20 Years Old db (80) n22 t22 f18 b18. With so much natural cream toffee, it is hard to believe that this has so many years on it. After a quick, refreshing start it pans out, if anything, a little dull. *40%*

Glen Moray 30 Years Old db (92.5) n23.5 it's probably the deftness of the old-fashioned Speyside smoke in tandem with the structured fruits that makes this so special; t23.5 for a light Speysider, the degree of barley to oak is remarkable: soft, oil-gilde d barley is met by a wonderful, if brief, spice prickle; f22.5 deft layering of vanilla and cocoa; a sprinkle of muscovado sugar repels any darker oak notes; b23 for all its years, this is comfortable malt, untroubled by time. There is no mistaking quality. *43%*

Glen Moray 1959 Rare Vintage db (91) n25 t23 f21 b22. They must have been keeping their eyes on this one for a long time: a stunning malt that just about defies nature. The nose reaches absolute perfection. *50.9%*

Glen Moray 1962 Very Rare Vintage Aged 42 Years db (94) n23 t24 f23 b24. The first temptation is to think that this has succumbed to age, but a second and a third tasting reveal that there is much more complexity, integrity and balance to this than first meets the tastebuds. The last cask chosen by the legendary Ed Dodson before his retirement from the distillery: a pretty perceptive choice. A corker! *50.9%. sc.*

Glen Moray 1984 db (83) n20 t22 f20 b21. Mouthwatering and incredibly refreshing malt for its age. *40%*

Glen Moray 1989 db (86) n23 t22 f20 b21. Doesn't quite live up to the fruit smoothie nose but I'm being a little picky here. *40%*

Glen Moray 1992 Single Cask No 1441 sherry butt db (74) n17 t21 f18 b18. Oops! Didn't anyone spot the sulphur...? *596%*

Glen Moray 1995 Port Wood Finish bott Dec 09 db (95.5) n23 a surprising liquorice base to the healthy spiced fruit; t24 vivid grape: clean, intense and, for a while, dominant. The oak surges back with a few tricks of its own, the most impressive being a liquorice-hickory thrust and a soothing custardy topping. Meanwhile, the grape offers spice and a sheen; f24.5 a wonderful array of spicy chocolate and raisin notes that appear to continue indefinitely. Needs to be tasted to be believed. b24 possibly the most satisfying wine finish of the year. *56.7%*

Glen Moray 1995 Single Sherry Cask sherry butt db (56) n15 t14 f13 b14. So stunned was I about the abject quality of this bottling, I even looked on the Glen Moray website to see if they had said anything about it. Apparently, if you add water you find on the nose "the lingering soft sulphury smoke of a struck match". Well, here's the news: you don't need water. Just open the bottle and there's Rotorua in all it's stink bomb finery. And errr...hullo, guys... some further news: that means it's a bloody faulty, useless cask. And has no right to be put anywhere near a bottling hall let alone set loose in a single bottling. This, quite frankly, is absolutely rank whisky, the type of which makes my blood boil. I mean, is this really the best cask that could be found in the entire and considerable estate of Glen Moray..???? Am I, or is it the whisky world going mad...? *596%*

⦂⦂ **Glen Moray 2001 Single Chenin Blanc Cask** cask no. 1839 db (74.5) n19 t19 f18 b18.5. I have to be honest: if I was going to mature a malt in a French wine cask, I would be a little - no, make that very - nervous. And here you can see why. A real battle between stupendous grape which boasts almost a perfection of sugars and a barrel which is typically flawed. People in different parts of the world may view this whisky with enormous fluctuation in the results. *60.7%. sc.*

Glen Moray Classic db (86.5) n22 t21.5 f21.5 b21.5. The nose is the star with a wonderful, clean barley-fruit tandem, but what follows cannot quite match its sure-footed wit. *40%*

Glen Moray Wine Cask Edition bott Sep 09 db (83.5) n20 t23 f20 b20.5. When in full flow this is just bursting with some of the juiciest fruit you are likely to encounter. But a familiar bitter buzz – not as bad as some, thankfully, but still enough – brings down the value. How sad. *59.7%*

Duncan Taylor Collection Glen Moray 1975 cask no. 64 (89) n22.5 thinks about the exotic fruit possibility but takes the malty-oaky finesse option...; t23 silky barley with now a rich, creamy fruitiness followed by a burst of vanilla and thin honey; f21.5 an elegant succession of bourbon tones; **b22** for a malt not renowned for its backbone, withstood 35 years with remarkable ease. *52.7%*

Murray McDavid Glen Moray 1992 bourbon/madeira (88) **n23 t20 f22 b23**. The rich malt canvas of the Glen Moray gives the Madeira an unrestricted medium to do its stuff. *46%*

⟐ **Old Malt Cask Glen Moray Aged 19 Years** refill hogshead, cask no. 6637, dist Oct 91, bott Oct 10 (87) **n21.5** mossy, with a green tinge to the malt; **t22.5** clean barley offering excellent balance between sweetness and tartness; **f21** over simplifies as it heads towards a fudgy finale; **b22** this malt and I have a lot in common. Firstly, it is where us Murrays get our name. And it also appears a lot younger than it actually is... *50%. nc ncf sc. 286 bottles.*

⟐ **Provenance Glen Moray Over 11 Years** refill hogshead, cask no. 6816, dist Autumn 99, bott Autumn 2010 (89) **n22 t23 f22 b22**. Don't bother looking for meaningful mouthfuls and hidden depth. This is simply rollicking malt, of the very simplest kind. Fabulous quality eschewing complexity for effect. Lively and luscious...love it!! *46%. nc ncf sc.*

⟐ **Rare Auld Glen Moray 24 Years Old** cask no. 2858, dist 1986 (91.5) **n22** excellent marriage between lively salts and wonderfully grassy, invigorating barley; **t23** puckering sharpness on delivery, then a slow striptease of the barley, slowly revealing its naked self; **f23.5** long, with the saline nose returning for a big but beautifully proportioned finale. The barley remains clean and profound; **b23** brimming with juicy life: a sheer joy! *55.6%. sc. Duncan Taylor & Co.*

⟐ **Rare Auld Glen Moray 37 Years Old** dist 1973, cask no. 7050 (92) **n23.5**. any grapier and you would have to buy the whisky by the bunch... just love the cinnamon swirl on the apple crumble; **t24** the grape plasters itself around the palate and clings to it like a tart to a millionaire; a beautiful, if slightly furtive, blood orange injection causes a welcome degree of salivation; **f21.5** spent oak and burnt fruitcake going back into the oven... **b23** technically, so many things not quite right. But bollocks to that: sometimes you have to let your hair get blown in the wind and savour the rough with the smooth. A minor Speyside gem...for those who can see it. Oh, and a classic for nosing the empty glass first thing in the morning... The 500th whisky tasted for the 2012 Bible and it was a fitting choice. *49.3%. sc. Duncan Taylor & Co.*

Scotch Malt Whisky Society Cask 35.30 Aged 9 Years 1st fill barrel, dist Feb 00 (87) **n23.5** diced apple and rhubarb pie; closer to bourbon than scotch; **t22** powering malt and bourbony Demerara suddenly hit a thick vanilla wall; **f20** a little bitter and bready; **b21.5** strange one: starts off like a train, deliciously confident then gets slightly derailed. *60.4%. Scotch Malt Whisky Society. 215 bottles.*

Scotch Malt Whisky Society Cask 35.38 Aged 9 Years 2nd fill ex chardonnay, dist May 00 (68.5) **n18 t18 f16 b16.5**. Starts badly...and gets worse. *60%. 265 bottles.*

Scotch Malt Whisky Society Cask 35.39 Aged 9 Years fill chardonnay barrique, dist May 00 (58.5) **n15 t15 f14 b14.5**. Someone's going to have to give the panel a crash course in identifying sulphur. Jesus...what on Earth were you thinking of...??? Actually, why bother? I have recently taken up archery. Please allow those responsible for this debacle of a bastard bottling to be my targets...and I promise to make it a long, slow, painful death... *59.4%. Scotch Malt Whisky Society. 258 bottles.*

Scotch Malt Whisky Society Cask 35.34 Aged 13 Years new charred oak, dist Mar 96 (87) **n22** kumquats and figs, but just a little crushed and stifled; **t23** thick and searingly hot barley/ red liquorice; chewy in a vaguely but not quite bourbony kind of way; **f20** unravels towards a burnt toast bitterness; **b22.5** almost stunning...but not quite. For that you'll have to mosey on down to bottling 35.35. *57%. Scotch Malt Whisky Society. 281 bottles.*

Scotch Malt Whisky Society Cask 35.35 Aged 13 Years new charred oak, dist Mar 96 (93.5) **n24** Buffalo Trace at nine years? A Wild Turkey, maybe? Either way, this is all about the cask...just liquorice and honey engulfed vanillin...and a whole bowl of kumquats. A rye mash bill? Might as well be for the intrinsic fruitiness...; **t23.5** yeee-haaar...y'all find some of that darned barley in that honeyed liquorice ye ken... **f23** well...if this ain't a virgin cask with all that orangey stuff an' all, or as near as damned close to it as possible, then I'll be a five-legged racoon... **b23** when then distillery manager Ed Dodson took some time out to work in Kentucky, I wonder if he came back determined to create a Glen Moray bourbon... if so, he succeeded. And some...!! *56.6%. Scotch Malt Whisky Society. 252 bottles.*

Scotch Malt Whisky Society Cask 35.31 Aged 19 Years 1st fill barrel, dist Jan 90 (76.5) **n20 t18 f19 b19.5**. The odd lemon note here and there. But distinctly hot and rough around the edges. *58.4%. Scotch Malt Whisky Society. 231 bottles.*

⟐ **Scotch Malt Whisky Society Cask 35.41 Aged 35 Years** refill hogshead, dist Jan 75 (84) **n22 t21.5 f20 b20.5**. The citrus is out in force, but it's a case of damage limitation against the marauding oak. Some pretty major moments, though. *56.1%. 179 bottles.*

⟐ **Scotch Malt Whisky Society Cask 35.44 Aged 35 Years** refill hogshead, cask no. 84, dist 1975 (82) **n19 t21 f20 b21**. Ancient, impenetrable forests of oak on the nose; some pleasing sugars fight a rearguard action. I doubt if the people who made this whisky saw it being bottled as a 34-year-old single malt, simply as I know they never felt it had the legs. For all its big neo-bourbon mannerisms and crude attempts towards a sugary-citrussy greatness, you can perhaps see why. 55%. sc. 167 bottles.

⁓ **Scotch Malt Whisky Society Cask 35.50 Aged 47 Years** refill hogshead, cask no. 174, dist 1962 (92.5) **n23** some shy barley notes pop their head above the oaky parapet. If anyone remembers their wooden school floors being sandpapered and then polished (probably at exactly the same time this whisky was being made) will recognise the effect...; **t24** a pretty polished performance on delivery, too: heads towards a beautiful light honeycomb status but the toastiness is delayed by the slow dissolving of a mixing of icing and muscovado sugars; the vanilla filling the midground is acceptably sawdusty; **f22.5** surprisingly long, given the distinct lack of oils. Hints of bitterness remain just that while the vanilla intensity is turned up a notch; **b23** not often the SMWS come up with something quite as old as this and pretty unusual for a Glen Moray to remain intact after so many Elgin winters. Not exactly unscathed, but it wears its oaky scars with pride: an Elgin Marvel... 40%. sc. 201 bottles.

⁓ **Scotch Malt Whisky Society Cask 35.52 Aged 34 Years** refill hogshead, cask no. 1259/3, dist 1976 (93.5) **n22.5** some heavyweight citrus sometimes appears crushed under the weight of the oak. Some oxidization though manages to help forge a fragile balance; **t24** rare for a Glen Moray to show this degree of juiciness at such age; the barley flexes its muscles but the butterscotch and vanillas reveal equal stamina; the spices and light, granular honey tones embark on a journey of setting right some oaky wrongs; **f23.5** long, some excellent late oils, and the return of some eye-watering citrus notes to thin the vanillas; **b23.5** there is a lightness of touch here which manages to keep the greatest excesses of the oak at bay and actually formulates a surprisingly well structured dram. Requires at least 20 minutes in the glass to open and relax, though, before drinking. Not a distillery which, as a rule, openly embraces great age. But when it gets it right, has the ability to totally astonish. 52.3%. sc. 110 bottles.

⁓ **Scotch Malt Whisky Society Cask 35.54 Aged 11 Years** 1st fill bourbon barrel, cask no. 4474, dist 1999 (95.5) **n23.5** lovely sandalwood plus light spices; someone appears to come up with just the right degree of salt to add to malt; **t24** several layers of barley with varying degree of maple syrup; the star quality is ensured by the near perfection to the weight and oils; the spicing could not be bettered while the light saline quality draws out and amplifies the considerable complexity to the midground; **f24** long and makes every atom of oak count; honey spread over digestive biscuit **b24** such a bottling shows exactly why for the last quarter of a century I have greatly prized this malt... Flawless. 57%. sc. 245 bottles.

⁓ **Scotch Malt Whisky Society Cask 35.55 Aged 39 Years** refill hogshead, cask no. 1163/1, dist 1971 (82) **n20 t21 f20.5 b20.5**. Hangs on with grim death to the last vestiges of life. The over-oaked nose is clear statement of intent and just enough natural sugars from the hoggy survive, though its overall balance and integrity suffers. 50.3%. sc. 278 bottles.

GLEN ORD
Highlands (Northern), 1838. Diageo. Working.

Glen Ord Aged 12 Years db (81) **n20 t23 f18 b20**. Just when you thought it safe to go back...for a while Diageo ditched the sherry-style Ord. It has returned. Better than some years ago, when it was an unhappy shadow of its once-great self, but without the sparkle of the vaguely-smoked bottling of a year or two back. Nothing wrong with the rich arrival, but the finish is a mess. I'll open the next bottling with trepidation... 43%

Glen Ord 25 Years Old dist 1978 db (95) **n24 t24 f23 b24**. Some stupendous vatting here: cask selection at its very highest to display Ord in all its far too rarely seen magnificence. 58.3%

Glen Ord 28 Years Old db (90) **n22 t23 f22 b23**. This is mega whisky showing slight traces of sap, especially on the nose, but otherwise a concentrate of many of the qualities I remember from this distillery before it was bottled in a much ruined form. Blisteringly beautiful. 58.3%

Glen Ord 30 Years Old db (87) **n22 t21 f23 b21**. Creaking with oak, but such is the polish to the barley some serious class is on show. 58.8%

Glen Ord 1997 The Manager's Choice db (93.5) **n24** oh my word...what have we here...? Just the most enticing little fruit pastel number you could ask for, and all played out on the softest malty field imaginable. Genuinely complex and enticing with the nose being teasingly caressed; **t23.5** then, just to shock, a real injection of bite and nip on delivery with a tangy blood orange thread which follows from the nose; **f23** custard powder oakiness with some late hickory and toffee; **b23** when given the chance, Glen Ord offers one of the fruitiest drams on the market. Here it is in its full blood orange element. A beauty! 59.2%

Singleton of Glen Ord 12 Years Old db (89) n22.5 no-one does blood orange quite like Glen Ord...; t22.5 salivating arrival with the malt elbowing its way past the persistent fruit; f22 vanilla and some clever spices; b22 a fabulous improvement on the last bottling I encountered. Still possesses blood oranges to die for, but greatly enhanced by some sublime spices and a magnificent juiciness. 40% ⊙ ⊙

Singleton of Glen Ord 32 Year Old db (91) n23.5 t23 f22 b22.5. Delicious. But if ever a malt has screamed out to be at 46%, this is it. 40%

The Cärn Mör Vintage Collection Glen Ord 2004 hogshead, cask no. 55, bott 2009 (84) n22 t21.5 f20 b20.5. Beautiful citrus and barley though always new makey. 46%

✷ **Fine Malt Selection Glen Ord 12 Years Old** dist 1998, bott May 11 (95) n23.5 the delicate smoke threads its way between light honey and juicy green grass. The barely noticeable oak offers only so much weight. Not a single off note, or character out of line...; t23.5 melt-in-the-mouth barley is followed home by that playful smoke promised on the nose. The sweetness is identical to that found in cake mix you lick from your mum's bowl...; f24 citrus darts around the more stubborn vanillas. The smoke dovetails with the muscovado and glazed cherries; b24 if you are looking for a Glen Ord which shows all its characters in a very bright light, look no further. A classic in every sense. An irresistible tour de force for this magnificent distillery. 45%. sc. James MacArthur & Co. USA release.

✷ **Liquid Sun Glen Ord 1996** bourbon hogshead, bott 2011 (87) n22 a dab of smoke on this fellow provides the weight on a lively barley aroma; t22.5 juicy with a healthy gamut of crisp sugars; f21 boringly caramel persistent; b21.5 naggingly pleasant. 53%. The Whisky Agency.

✷ **Malts Of Scotland Glen Ord 1996** bourbon hogshead, cask no. 2171, dist Mar 96, bott Apr 11 (86.5) n21 t22 f22 b21.5. The intense sweetness – and puckering sharpness - of the barley is not even slightly bothered by the oak. This is from a pretty spent cask, but at least one gets the opportunity to see the malt, warts and all... Also, a surprising degree of smoke to be found. Lovely stuff. 53.3%. sc. Malts Of Scotland.

✷ **Malts Of Scotland Glen Ord 1999** bourbon hogshead, cask no. 31212, dist Mar 99, bott Mar 10 (94.5) n23.5 for a bourbon hoggy, there is a strange semi-grapey depth to this; t24 fantastic spice attack on delivery. Followed by strata of honey of varying intensity; f23.5 a curious burnt raisin fruit cake intensity which flies in the face of the bourbon liquorice and honey doing the rounds elsewhere. The spices congregate and accelerate in their effect; b23.5 further proof that the owners of this distillery appear to not quite realise the goldmine they are sitting on. Beautiful! 54.5%. nc ncf sc. Malts Of Scotland. 289 bottles.

✷ **Old Malt Cask Glen Ord Aged 14 Years** refill hogshead, cask no. 7478, dist Apr 97, bott Jul 11 (85) n21.5 t22 f21 b21.5. Juicy, spicy, still wet behind the ears. A Peter Pan of a malt. 50%. nc ncf sc. Douglas Laing & Co. 149 bottles.

✷ **Old Malt Cask Glen Ord Aged 21 Years** refill butt, cask no.6538, dist Jan 89, bott Sep 10 (86) n20.5 t22 f22 b22. Juicy, teaming with barley, spicy; coconut and cocoa anchored yet somehow younger than its years. Would never have quite recognised this as a Glen Ord, had I not known. But some golden nugget moments here, make no mistake. 50%. nc ncf sc. Douglas Laing & Co. 361 bottles.

Provenance Glen Ord Aged 11 Years dist mar 98, bott Jul 09 (83) n21 t21.5 f20.5 b20. Attractive, simple malty but standard Ordie for an oft recycled cask. 46%. Douglas Laing.

Provenance Glen Ord Over 11 Years refill hogshead no. DMG 5570, dist Spring 98, bott Autumn 09 (86) n21 t22 f21.5 b21.5. A distinct, lightly fruity edge to the delicious gristy barley. The oak plays only a minor role. 46%. Douglas Laing & Co Ltd.

✷ **Provenance Glen Ord Over 11 Years** refill hogshead, cask no. 6725, dist Spring 99, bott Autumn 2010 (94) n23 a potpourri of dried flowers and herbs; t24 heather-honey almost of a Highland Park style, complete with a squirt of something smoky; f23.5 golden syrup with a heathery dryness; b23.5 if Diageo want to compete head to head with Highland Park, they had better grab a bottle of this and send it to the lab... One of the must have whiskies of the year. 46%. nc ncf sc. Douglas Laing & Co.

✷ **Scotch Malt Whisky Society 77.21 Aged 23 Years** refill hogshead, cask no. 3367, dist 1987 (86) n20.5 t20.5 f23 b22. As charming as this very well might be, one wonders why this isn't making magic in a 21-year-old blend where its orangey notes would make whoopee. As a singleton, languid to start then finally finds its voice and balance to magnificent effect. Certainly, the spices and fruit towards the finish make for a malt to enjoy late in the evening when patience is a virtue and contemplation comes naturally. 57.2%. sc. 237 bottles.

✷ **Scotch Malt Whisky Society 77.23 Aged 23 Years** 2nd fill hogshead, cask no. 3370, dist 1987 (86) n22 t22.5 f20.5 b21. An initially mouth-watering suet and sawdust merchant that lives as long on the palate as it does the memory. 56.8%. sc. 226 bottles.

GLENROTHES
Speyside, 1878. Edrington. Working.

The Glenrothes 1978 dist Nov 78, bott 2008 db **(90.5) n23** over-ripe gooseberries mixed with dry tobacco; suet pudding and vanilla pods: attractively intriguing; **t23** relaxed, lush barley coats the mouth with a muscovado sugar edge; **f22** mushy sultana and toasty oak; **b22.5** sheer – and delicious – entertainment. 43%

The Glenrothes 1979 Single Cask No. 13458 db **(68) n18 t19 f15 b16.** Wrecked by sulphur. In whisky terms, tragic. 57%

The Glenrothes 1979 Single Cask No. 13459 db **(75) n20 t20 f17 b18.** This twin cask to 13458 has also seen a sulphur stick at work, but it wasn't kept inside anything to lie so long. Even so, enough damage to the finish undoes the promising big fruit start. 56.6%

·:·· **The Glenrothes 1988 Vintage** dist 16 Dec 88, bott 04 Nov 08 db **(93) n22** stunning toasted honeycomb **t24.5** exceptional delivery. Not only is the mouth feel quite perfect, the deft marriage of honey, honeycomb, treacle and maple syrup has to be tasted to be believed...; **f23** dries and spices up as the oaks grab hold; **b23.5** a gorgeous bottling still doing the rounds...and should be hunted down and polished off. 43%

The Glenrothes 1988 Vintage bott 2010 db **(74) n18.5 t19 f18 b18.5.** For all the obvious high quality sugars present, it still can't overcome the Spanish imposition. 43%

The Glenrothes 1994 dist Oct 94, bott 2007 db **(77) n19 t20 f19 b19.** The citrus appears as promised on the label, but sadly a few unadvertised sulphured butt-related gremlins are present also. 43%

·:·· **The Glenrothes 1995 Vintage** dist 26 Oct 95, bott 06 Sep 10 db **(87.5) n20** distilled vanilla...? **t22** one of the laziest deliveries you'll find: a pretty nondescript malt-oak job with a mouth feel which lies there like a doormat. Slowly, though, there is a twitching of spices, a little liquorice and the odd fruity yoghurt note; **f23** carries on in the same delicate and now complex and vaguely toasty manner: rather wonderful; **b22.5** like an old grump that takes its time to wake and finally has to be kicked out of bed. Once up, certainly does the biz. 43%

·:·· **The Glenrothes 1998 Vintage** dist Dec 98, bott Feb 09 db **(66) n16 t20 f14 b16.** Really would have thought they would have got the hang of this sulphur lark by now... 43%

The Glenrothes 1998 Vintage bott 2010 db **(73.5) n20 t19 f16 b18.5.** Talk about bitter-sweet...!!! 43%

The Glenrothes Alba Reserve db **(87.5) n22** muted honey and spices rising from the flattish nosescape; **t22** silky, malty delivery with some toffee turning up in the middle ground; **f21.5** decent length with more of the same and just a hint of a liquorice flourish; **b22** you know that very smartly groomed, unfailingly polite but rather dull chap you invariable get at dinner parties...? 40%

The Glenrothes John Ramsay bott 2009 db **(89.5) n22.5** almost a touch of the Highland Parks about this, only without the smoke. The honey has a pronounced softness, as does the toffee and very mildly floral vanilla notes; **t23.5** spices begin sparring from the first nanosecond: absolutely contrary to everything the nose has been telling you. And these are micro spices: tiny, busy little things like you sometimes get from the small grains kicking off in bourbon; in the middle ground you get your first clear sighting of unruffled barley; **f21.5** back to a lightweight, sweetening toffee; **b22** elegant and charming. What else did you expect...? 46.7%. 1400 bottles.

The Glenrothes Robur Reserve db **(81.5) n20.5 t22 f19 b20.** With the youthful barley prominent early on, one of the sweetest distillery bottling from Glenrothes I've come across. Bitter cask fade, though. 40%

The Glenrothes Select Reserve db **(80) n17.5 t22 f20.5 b21.** Flawed in the usual Glenrothes sherry places, but the brilliance of the sharp barley wins your heart. 40%

The Glenrothes Three Decades bott 2009 db **(90.5) n23.5** to say this is somewhat fruity is like saying that Everest is a pretty large mountain...works rather beautifully because there is a pugnacious element to this, and, under the softer grape, a message comes through on the oaky spice suggesting that this might be happy to rip your head off... **t24** fabulous delivery with the double whammy of intense but controlled oak and grape concentrate; **f21.5** a touch of bitter marmalade and something a little salty, too; **b22.5** not without a minor blemish here and there, but the overall magnitude of this allows you to forgive quite easily. The distant sulphur apart, a stunner. 43%. Duty Free exclusive.

A.D. Rattray Glenrothes 1990 cask no. 35468, dist Nov 90, bott Mar 09 **(90) n23.5** a molecule of smoke adds a touch of weight to the gooseberries and custard; **t22.5** maple syrup on yoghurt; **f22** long, delightfully textured with still that light syrup tinge to the custard; **b22** am I alone in preferring ex-bourbon Glenrothes to the sherried variety? This one exudes effortless charm. 49.9%. A.D. Rattray Ltd.

⟐ **Adelphi Glenrothes 20 Years Old** cask no. 12898, dist 1990, bott 2011 **(86) n**21.5 **t**20 **f**23 **b**21.5. An enjoyably clean sherry butt, but it's a hard slog through the gears. 58.6%. sc. Adelphi Distillery. 527 bottles.

Cadenhead's Authentic Collection Glenrothes-Glenlivet 1994 bott Feb 10 **(94) n**23.5 subtle and delicate; gently spiced bourbon edge; **t**24 superb...absolutely perfect mouthfeel and weight with the barley zipping around with purpose and intensity; the development is slow but aided by the most gentle of sugary inputs and embraces the almost inevitable cocoa middle warmly; **f**23.5 the spices are a long time coming but fizz and nip playfully when they arrive. The cocoa continues, at times sweetened by late grist; **b**23 you really can't ask for much more than that from this distillery. Not a single fault. 53.8%. Wm. Cadenhead Ltd. 244 bottles.

The Coopers Choice Glenrothes 1999 Port Wood Finish Aged 10 Years (76) n18.5 **t**21 **f**18.5 **b**18. The pinkness of the Port is almost a parody of the type, as there really cannot have been any other colour in the whisky to mingle with it. Though a ten year old, the input of the previous barrel had been next to non-existent in that the barley has all the traits of a three-year-old. You certainly don't find samples like this every day... 46%

Dun Bheagan Glenrothes 12 Years Old sherry finish **(79) n**20 **t**21 **f**19 **b**19. A cleanish, sound sherry cask but short changes in the complexity department. 43%. Ian Macleod.

⟐ **Duncan Taylor Octave Glenrothes 40 Years Old** cask no. 495777, dist 1970 **(94.5) n**23 elegant and deft, a soft peach note sits prettily with the vanilla and, one almost fancies, the most delicate hint of smoke imaginable; **t**23.5 the oaks arrive hurriedly, but mainly carrying with it caramels. The barley still has enough freshness to offer a juicy diversion; **f**24 spices arrive late but entirely in keeping with the understated nuances of all the other characteristics; the softness is concluded by melt-in-the-mouth chocolate ice cream... **b**24 quite fantastic malt which is unerringly subtle. 40.6%. sc.

⟐ **Duncan Taylor Octave Glenrothes 40 Years Old** cask no. 495780, dist 1970 **(86) n**21.5 **t**22.5 **f**20.5 **b**21.5. A Braveheart of a dram. Creaking here and there and obviously feeling its age, somehow it has the sheer willpower and class to cobble together a bunch of vivid barley-mocha notes to go down guns blazing. 40.9%. sc.

Duncan Taylor Collection Glenrothes 1969 cask no. 12889 **(88.5) n**22.5 **t**21.5 **f**22.5 **b**22. Very similar to 12890, except here, on the nose and sometimes elsewhere, this has managed to find a bourbony edge to the oak encroachment. Because of this the body feels fuller and healthier. 46.5%

Duncan Taylor Collection Glenrothes 1969 cask no. 12890 **(85.5) n**21 **t**21 **f**22.5 **b**21. Fascinating to compare this to the DTC 1970 I have just tasted. So many similarities that they appear closely related. But here the oak has delved deeper and upset the vital balance. Pleasant and thoroughly enjoyable and the muscovado-sweetened mocha finish is quite lovely. But you know this cask has crossed the Rubicon. Just. 45.5%

Duncan Taylor Collection Glenrothes 1970 cask no. 10557 **(93) n**23.5 **t**23 **f**23.5 **b**23. Always endearing to find a malt some 40-year-old with this kind of playful persona and so little bothered about oak. Charismatic and full of mouth-watering fun. A minor classic of its type. 42.3%

Duthies Glenrothes 15 Years Old (85.5) n22 a hint of eggnog to the barley; **t**21.5 dry delivery with tight but not OTT oak having an early impact; **f**22.5 spreads out and relaxes with sugary malt development; **b**22.5 high quality Speysider. 46%. Wm. Cadenhead Ltd.

⟐ **Malts Of Scotland Glenrothes 1968** bourbon hogshead, cask no. 13509, dist Nov 68, bott Feb 11 **(86) n**21 **t**22 **f**21.5 **b**21.5. Enough honey and spice to fend off some hairy oak. At times looks as though the years have taken too great a toll...but there is no denying the life force is strong. 45.2%. sc. Malts Of Scotland.

Old Malt Cask Glenrothes Aged 12 Years refill butt, dist May 96, bott Feb 08 **(77) n**19 **t**20 **f**19 **b**19. Give me a prod when something happens...zzzz. 50%. Douglas Laing. 657 bottles.

Old Malt Cask Glenrothes Aged 14 Years red wine cask, bott 2009 **(88) n**21 **t**22.5 **f**22.5 **b**22. Begins jerkily a bit like a train in a shunting yard before heading off on a frictionless journey. 50%. Douglas Laing.

Old Malt Cask Glenrothes Aged 18 Years refill hogshead, dist Nov 90, bott Apr 09 **(84) n**18 **t**21.5 **f**22.5 **b**22. The broken nose is compensated by the fine, if slightly fizzy, malty recovery. Delicious Maltesers at the death. 50%. Douglas Laing. 295 bottles.

Old Malt Cask Glenrothes Aged 32 Years refill hogshead, dist Dec 75, bott Aug 08 **(92) n**24 **t**22.5 **f**22.5 **b**23. First class bottling just dripping with quiet dignity. 50%. 253 bottles.

⟐ **Peerless Glenrothes 41 Years Old** cask no. 12881, dist 1969 **(85) n**20 **t**21.5 **f**22 **b**21.5. Peerless. But not ageless... 44.2%. sc. Duncan Taylor & Co.

⟐ **Provenance Glenrothes Aged 11 Years (86) n**21 **t**22 **f**21.5 **b**21.5. A pithy little number seemingly distilled and matured in an orangery. 46%

Provenance Glenrothes Aged 12 Years refill hogshead, dist Autumn 96, bott Autumn 08 **(85.5) n20 t21 f23 b21.5.** Elegant if simple malt where somehow less is more: the clean barley delivery mutates into a light custard tart and bourbon biscuit as if in slow motion. *46%*

⫷ **Scotch Malt Whisky Society Cask 30.64 Aged 18 Years** 2nd fill hogshead, cask no. 8601, dist 1992 **(88.5) n23** excellent barley/oak balance with the emphasis sweet lemon-mint tea; **t22** natural caramels act as a pedestal to the barley; sharp and tangy; **f21.5** those toffees dominate the finale; **b22** always great to see this get the chance to strut its malty stuff away from a sherry butt. *55.7%. sc. 244 bottles.*

Scott's Selection Glenrothes 1986 bott 2008 **(84) n21.5 t19.5 f22 b21.** Decidedly on the hot side, but otherwise solid and occasionally sweet with a generous late middle barley development. *52.2%. Speyside Distillers.*

⫷ **Scott's Selection Glenrothes 1986** bott 2011 **(88.5) n21.5** one of those inbetweeners: too much oak for comfort so going for exotic fruit for greatness...but hasn't yet arrived...; **t21.5** very comfortable delivery, not least thanks to a wonderfully silky texture. But again the oak is too vivid too early...; **f23.5** saved at the bell. Somewhere at the end of the middle, or at the beginning of the end, a surge of juicy barley breathes life back into a dying whisky; **b22** a rollercoaster of a dram, at times heading for oaky oblivion but pulls out of the dip with a dramatic late winner. Phew! Probably the most complicated and hardest malt to judge this year: like a fabulous lover with a crap personality. One minute you love her...then you hate her...then you love her... *51.7%. Speyside Distillers.*

⫷ **The Whisky Agency Glenrothes 39 Years Old** dist 1970, bott 2009 **(90.5) n22.5** surely a bourbon in disguise... **t23** a teasing, semi-spiced array of red liquorice, hickory and other delicious bourbon notes, especially honey; **f22.5** long, lightly oiled and magnificently spiced; **b22.5** a malt to be celebrated and one more happy to wear the flag of Kentucky than The Saltire *48.1%. The Whisky Agency.*

⫷ **The Whisky Agency Glenrothes 1980 (92.5) n23.5** gentle measures of barley, ginger, lime and kumquat bound together by the very softest smoke; **t24** quite brilliant delivery: the sugars are crisp and beautifully defined, strengthened by a rod of oak. The spices are in tandem and build into something meaningful; **f22** flattens as the vanillas and higher tannins arrive; **b23** a genuine Speyside gem. *50.9%. The Whisky Agency.*

⫷ **The Whisky Castle Raw Cask Glenrothes 21 Years Old** sherry butt, cask no. 7471, dist 02 May 89, bott Oct 10 **(95.5) n23** dripping with fat sultanas and sublimely spiced; **t24.5** near enough the perfect delivery: the fruit is sweet, but immediately balanced by some pulsing spices and cocoa and a fabulous and unexpected puff of smoke; the subsequent layers talk up the spices and allow a gorgeous butterscotch and light honey thread... wow! **f24** long with spotted dick (which is something I urge you to get your kisser around at least once in your life... and I'm talking the pudding here...) and the most extraordinary trail of diminishing but gorgeous honey; **b24** oh, if only all Glenrothes sherry bottling were like this... If this doesn't get people beating a path to the shop, nothing will... sublime whisky: one of the finest casks of the year. *54%. nc ncf sc. Blackadder for The Whisky Castle.*

GLEN SCOTIA
Campbeltown, 1832. Loch Lomond Distillers. Working.

Glen Scotia 12 Years Old db **(73.5) n18 t19 f18 b18.5.** Ooops! I once said you could write a book about this called "Murder by Caramel." Now it would be a short story called "Murder by Flavours Unknown." What is happening here? Well, a dozen years ago Glen Scotia was not quite the place to be for consistent whisky, unlike now. Here, the caramel is the only constant as the constituent parts disintegrate. *40%*

Glen Scotia 1999 heavily peated, cask no. 518, dist 23 Jul 99 db **(92) n22 t23 f23 b24.** This is pretty big and quite beautifully made malt. Forget the age. Enjoy a touch of class. *45%*

Glen Scotia 1999 heavily peated, cask no. 525, dist 23 Jul 99 db **(85) n21 t22 f22 b20.** Tasty, but relatively blunt, nothing like so together or complex as cask 518. *45%*

⫷ **Glen Scotia 2000** bourbon barrel, cask no. 087, dist 06 Jun 00, bott 28 Jul 11 db **(87) n22** a touch tight but very malty; **t22** juicy barley punches through a wall of caramel; **f21** slightly bitter as the oak ups the ante; **b22** very similar to cask 627 from year 2001. Only here the barley and oak have combined to add a degree of attitude and the barrel is less helpful. *45%. nc ncf sc. 320 bottles.*

⫷ **Glen Scotia 2001** bourbon barrel, cask no. 627, dist 05 Nov 01, bott 28 Jul 11 db **(91.5) n22.5** gristy clean malt allowing the sugars unrestricted access; **t23** huge amount of natural caramels, but for those who like Malteser candy...beware! **f23** long, with the malt stretching out forever and a day; **b23** dangerous: the kind of seemingly simple and undemonstrative whisky that you could end up spending all day, every day drinking. *45%. nc ncf sc. 330 bottles.*

⋮ **Glen Scotia 2002** American oak hogshead, cask no. 164, dist 22 Apr 02, bott 28 Jul 02 db **(77.5) n19 t21.5 f18 b19.** I know the maturing casks from this distillery quite well and this is not representative of what is sitting in their warehouse. This is a rather feeble effort, for all its big barley. And in a sub-standard cask, too. *45%. nc ncf sc. 410 bottles.*

⋮ **Glen Scotia 2007** bourbon barrel, cask no. 225, dist 23 Apr 07, bott 28 Jul 11 db **(86.5) n22 t22 f21 b21.5.** Huge clouds of natural caramels drift around the palate. But the sugars are secure and the odd molecule of smoke adds a curious balance. Very different. *45%. nc ncf sc. 370 bottles.*

A.D. Rattray Glen Scotia 1977 cask no. 985 **(92) n23.5** no doubting the cask type with the grape in dominant and, essentially, clean form: clean enough for the barley and the vaguest hint of salt and smoke to peep through; **t23** astonishing firepower for an oldie: not all of it is technically brilliant and the spices derive more from distillation than maturation. But such is the huge quality of the sherry butt this malt has been housed in for the last 30-odd years that the rougher edges are softened and the grape pushes the boundaries. Molasses and dates offer up a burned fruitcake feel, but there is also seared ginger and a light hint of smoke in there somewhere, too; **f23** long, almost powder dry vanilla pepped up by the remaining layers of grape; **b22.5** proof that a first class barrel can take a third class distillate and turn it into something top quality... *57%. A.D. Rattray Ltd.*

A.D. Rattray Glen Scotia 1992 cask no. 1, dist Mar 92, bott Dec 09 **(64) n15 t17 f16 b16.** If anyone wants to see why I am so unforgiving of sulphured casks or experience the change in sherry cask quality I have seen in the last 30 years, then I strongly suggest you buy a bottle of this and Rattray's superb '77 bottling and simply compare... *59.4%. A.D. Rattray Ltd.*

Berry's Own Selection Glen Scotia 1992 bott 2008 **(95) n24 t24 f23.5 b23.5.** From among the earliest days of smoked Scotia (well since World War II, certainly), here's a peaty nugget. I bet Berry's very own Dougie McIvor made a pact with the devil for his beloved Charlton to be relegated to their natural place in the third tier of English football in exchange for getting hold of a cask like this. A good bit of business, Dougie, my son...see you soon at The Valley!! *55.7%.*

Cadenhead's Authentic Collection Glen Scotia 1992 bott Feb 10 **(78) n18.5 t21 f18.5 b20.** Juicy and sizzling: pretty much on the mark for the distillery at this period of its history. *52.1%. Wm. Cadenhead Ltd. 260 bottles.*

Duncan Taylor Collection Glen Scotia 1991 cask no. 71375 **(73.5) n19 t19 f17.5 b18.** Malty firewater. *57.6%. Duncan Taylor & Co Ltd.*

Duthies Glen Scotia 17 Years Old (80.5) n20 t21 f19 b20.5. Busy, mouth-watering...and yet. Definitely not quite the best wood a spirit has ever been filled into. *46%*

Exclusive Malts Glen Scotia 1992 Aged 16 Years dist 1992 **(89.5) n20 t24 f23 b22.5.** An imposing malt impossible not to love: a real rough diamond... *52.1%*

Hart Brothers Glen Scotia Aged 16 Years 1st fill sherry hogshead, dist Dec 92, bott Dec 08 **(68) n17 t18.5 f15.5 b17.** Having run through an entire thesaurus of whisky lab terms in my head, the word which most succinctly sums this one up is... "weird". *46%. Hart Brothers Ltd.*

⋮ **Hart Brothers Glen Scotia Aged 18 Years** dist Feb 92, bott Jan 11 **(66) n15.5 t18 f15.5 b17.** Dear, oh dear, oh dear... *46%. sc.*

Kingsbury's Glen Scotia 1992 (86.5) n21 t22.5 f21.5 b21.5. Something of the Sugar Frosties about this: a sweet, malty cereal feel – and a bit crunchy, too. But the most impressive quality is its intense Kentucky kick, perhaps due to the heady mix of muscovado and soft cocoa. *66.2%. Japan Import System.*

⋮ **Malts Of Scotland Glen Scotia 1972** bourbon hogshead, cask no. 1926, dist Sep 72, bott May 10 **(88) n21.5** huge Palma violet explosion; **t22.5** soft interplay between aged marmalade and a liquorice enriched spice; **f22** butterscotch and vanilla ice cream; **b22** creaks more than a haunted house. But hangs on in there determined to entertain. And succeeds. *45.1%. nc ncf sc. Malts Of Scotland.*

⋮ **Malts Of Scotland Glen Scotia 1972** bourbon hogshead, cask no. 1931, dist Sep 72, bott May 10 **(89) n22** so many over the top bourbon notes, it borders on brilliant; **t22** more exhausted oak. Yet again, though, the depth of the sugars and tannin borders on the awesome; **f23** at last hits a patch of ground in which the cocoa and barley notes meet in stunning harmony; the blood orange is almost too good to be true; **b22** the malt disappears under an avalanche of oak-extracted sugar. But the bourbon effect, combined with the never-say-die oak, rescues this dramatically. *45.7%. nc ncf sc. Malts Of Scotland.*

Old Malt Cask Glen Scotia Aged 17 Years bott 2009 **(92.5) n23 t23.5 f23 b23.** Fabulous fun: if this doesn't shake some life into your tastebuds, nothing will. *50%. Douglas Laing.*

⋮ **Old Malt Cask Glen Scotia Aged 18 Years** bourbon barrel, cask no. 6481, dist Mar 92, bott Aug 10 **(85.5) n20.5 t22 f21.5 b21.5.** Sugary enough to rot your teeth. Enjoyable, though, I must admit! *50%. nc ncf sc. Douglas Laing & Co. 312 bottles.*

⁘ **Scotch Malt Whisky Society Cask 93.44 Aged 11 Years** refill barrel, cask no. 505, dist 1999 **(93)** n22.5 clean, even peating with more of a crofter's fireside than a sea shore...; **t(23)** molassed liquorice keeps apace with the full blown peat; surprisingly juicy with the barley occasionally visible; **f(24)** a stunning finish: a slow injection of butterscotch and vanilla helps the peat to unravel. The manner in which it slowly dries and breaks down into its complex, constituent parts is a revelation...; **b(23.5)** Campbeltown has obviously drifted on a tectonic plate out to sea to Islay... 61.8%. sc. 220 bottles.

⁘ **The Whisky Agency Glen Scotia 1972** bott 2010 **(79)** n20 t19 f20 b20. Even exotic fruit has a sell by date... 40.1%. The Whisky Agency.

GLEN SPEY
Speyside, 1885. Diageo. Working.

Glen Spey Aged 12 Years db **(90)** n23 the kind of firm, busy malt you expect from this distillery plus some lovely spice; t22 mouthwatering and fresh, a layer of honey makes for an easy three or four minutes; f22 drier vanilla, but the pulsing oak is controlled and stylish; b23 very similar to the first Glen Spey I can remember in this range, the one before the over-toffeed effort of two years ago. Great to see it back to its more natural, stunningly beautiful self. 43%

⁘ **Glen Spey Special Release 2010 21 Years Old** sherry American oak cask, dist 1988 db **(94.5)** n23 a huge nose by this distillery's standards. There are elements of fruit, but more delicious are the controlled oaky bourbony offerings. Honeydew melon, vanilla and red liquorice abounds...telling you something about the variation of weight; t24 the delivery is silky and positively melts into the taste buds, making a mockery of the strength. The honey is stupendously well proportioned and carries spices which prickle as much as the sugars sparkle; f23.5 long, with a wonderful butterscotch/lemon curd tart ensemble. There is a distant fruitiness, burned raisin more associated with aging oak than grape; b24 have to say I am blown away by this. Glen Speys of this age tended to find their way into blends where they would beef up the sweeter malt content. Sometimes they were used to impart clean sherry or at least fruit, but otherwise give nothing of themselves. This bottling tends to take both strands and then ties them up in a complex and compelling fashion. Wonderful. 50.4%. nc ncf. Diageo. Fewer than 6000 bottles.

⁘ **Old Malt Cask Glen Spey Aged 14 Years** refill hogshead, cask no. 6955, dist Feb 97, bott Feb 11 **(89)** n22 new mown hay and grist; t22 clean, barley sugar...almost worty; f23 a loud and delicious build up of spice and mocha; b22 probably as true to the house style as you are likely to find. 50%. nc ncf sc. Douglas Laing & Co. 338 bottles.

Old Malt Cask Glen Spey Aged 32 Years refill hogshead no. DL 5523, dist Dec 76, bott Sep 09 **(90.5)** n22.5 here we go: first rate exotic fruit, though given a dab of allspice just to ginger it up; t23 way beyond being recognisable as a Glen Spey: the light oils proudly carry the liquorice and burnt honey of major age, but all with a light sugary sheen; f22.5 much drier, but the buttery toast still doesn't show negative traits to the aging; b22.5 fruity exoticism all the way...wonderful! 50%. Douglas Laing & Co Ltd.

Old Malt Cask Glen Spey Aged 32 Years (87) n23 rose petals and vanilla: delicate to the point of disintegration; t21.5 a brief arrival of light, juicy barley and lime, quickly met by dried banana; f21 almost a papery vanilla moistened by a spot of oil; b21.5 for one of the lightest malts on Speyside this has withstood the test of time with apparent ease. This must have been one hell of a good cask for it not to have inflicted any telling damage. Naturally it is the vanillins which have the greatest say, but they dovetail gracefully with the softest of oils offered and half-hearted limey sugars. The rose petal nose is also a surprising bonus. 54.5%. Speciality Drinks Ltd. Anniversary Selection.

⁘ **Provenance Glen Spey Over 12 Years** refill hogshead, cask no. 7190, dist Spring 99, bott Spring 2011 **(78.5)** n19 t20 f19 b19.5. A pleasant enough malt. But always a little tight, sweet and nutty... 46%. nc ncf sc. Douglas Laing & Co.

GLENTAUCHERS
Speyside, 1898. Chivas Brothers. Working.

The Cärn Mör Vintage Collection Glentauchers 2006 barrel, cask no. 9, dist 2006, bott 2009 **(85)** n22 t21 f21 b21. A three year-old still in its new make nappies thanks to absolute minimum oak input. Shows the high quality malty distillate at its most naked. And refreshing. 46%. The Scottish Liqueur Centre.

Chieftain's Glentauchers 17 Years Old Pinot Noir Finish dist Sep 92, bott 2010 **(82.5)** n21.5 t21 f19.5 b20.5. Had to laugh: as I poured this, the label was facing the other way. Saw the colour and thought: "Must be a Chieftain's"...!! Just a little too cramped and frantic for the grape to take full effect while the spicy oak bites deep at the death. 50%. nc ncf. Ian Macleod.

Dun Bheagan Glentauchers Aged 15 Years hogshead, dist Sep 92 **(85) n22 t22 f20 b21.** Some really wonderful barley and citrus touches to this but a bitter finish undermines some of the good work. No doubt a better cask would have produced a sparkling gem. 43%

Gordon & MacPhail Distillery Label Glentauchers 1991 (83) n21 t22.5 f19.5 b20. Hardly does this under-rated distillery justice: the nose is lagged down by a vague lactic note from some exhausted oak while the finish is thin and unhappy. Yet the show is saved by a genuinely vivid barley dash on delivery. 43%

Old Malt Cask Glentauchers Aged 13 Years refill hogshead, dist Nov 95, bott Feb 09 **(87) n22 t22 f21.5 b21.5.** Simple, clean, elegant and very drinkable. 50%. 334 bottles.

Provenance Glentauchers Aged 8 Years sherry butt, dist Summer 00, dist Autumn 08 **(85.5) n21.5 t22 f21 b21.** Another 'Tauchers bottling struggling against indifferent oak. Thankfully there is enough low-key complexity and biscuity barley to ensure a pleasant time. 46%

Provenance Glentauchers Over 9 Years refill cask no. DMG 5706, dist Autumn 00, bott Winter 09 **(80) n20.5 t20 f19 b19.5.** An essay in bantamweight gristiness. 46%

⫶ **Provenance Glentauchers Over 10 Years** refill butt, cask no. 6522, Mar 83, Jul 10 **(91) n23** a light caress of peat is almost lost amid the sharpness of the barley; **t24** beautifully structured; the degree of oils is close to perfection while that strand of delicate smoke gives extra earthiness and depth to the clear, grassy malt; **f21.5** still light enough for the vanillas to show; **b22.5** a slightly beefier 'Tauchers than the norm, even sporting the faintest degree of smoke. The malt intensity to the delivery is a rare treat. A chance to see why this malt is a consistent blender's delight. 46%. nc ncf sc. Douglas Laing & Co.

Scotch Malt Whisky Society Cask 63.25 Aged 20 Years refill barrel, dist Dec 89 **(84.5) n22 t22.5 f20 b20.** The citrus notes are hugely desirable and ensure a zestiness to the barley. But just a little too over aged. 55%. Scotch Malt Whisky Society. 211 bottles.

⫶ **Scotch Malt Whisky Society Cask 63.26 Aged 21 Years** 2nd fill hogshead, cask no. 5626, dist 1989 **(92.5) n23** a very equal balance between the oak and barley; clean and showing a delightful Malteser candy quality; **t23** firm, sound barley which makes the most of the sharp maltiness. The oak offers light salt to balance the delicate sugars; **f22.5** back to the Maltesers...; **b24** high quality Speyside of limited complexity but showing just why this is prized for its sincere malty qualities in older blends. Quietly superb. 52.6%. sc. 161 bottles.

⫶ **The Whisky Agency Glentauchers 1975** bott 2010 **(94.5) n23** the oak is trying to crush all the life out of this one, but some old banana takes on the challenge; **t23.5** beautifully soft and you fancy some barley melts in the mouth along with the vanilla concentrate. Gorgeously refined; **f24** a stupendous essay of vanilla and chocolate ice cream...I don't think I have ever tasted a malt softer on the palate than this... **b24** at first it seems the clock has ticked once too many times for this Tauchers. However, a little oxidisation in the glass brings some barely believable life into the Old Timer. Indeed, these notes are taken at its imperious height at about 12 minutes. Then, it hits extraordinary greatness and a lightness of touch which I have rarely encountered before: it is as though it has been distilled from feathers. But don't leave it too long in there: it soon fades away... 47.3%. The Whisky Agency.

GLENTURRET

Highlands (Perthshire), 1775. Edrington. Working.

Glenturret Aged 8 Years db **(88) n21** some sma' still randomness; **t22** silky honey, a few feinty oils perhaps, but attractive; **f23** honey overdrive with spice; **b22** technically no prizewinner. But the dexterity of the honey is charming, as this distillery has a tendency sometimes to be. 40%

The Glenturret Aged 10 Years db **(76) n19 t18 f20 b19.** Lots of trademark honey but some less than impressive contributions from both cask and the stillman. 40%

The Glenturret Aged 15 Years db **(87) n21 t22 f22 b22.** A beautifully clean, small-still style dram that would have benefitted from being bottled at a fuller strength. A discontinued bottling now: if you see it, it is worth the small investment. 40%

Glenturret 1991 Aged 15 Years cask no. 638 db **(82) n20 t21 f21 b20.** Honeycomb and chocolate: liquid fruit jelly. Heavyweight stuff and at times a little stodgy. 55.3%

Glenturret 1992 Aged 14 Years cask no. 855 db **(72) n18 t19 f17 b18.** A tad feinty and never quite finds the right key despite the best efforts of the honey and spice. 59.7%

Glenturret 1993 cask no. 840 db **(83.5) n21 t20 f21.5 b21.** I'm afraid the heat on this one isn't simply down to the giant strength. This is hot whisky but with some attractively sharp notes. 59.5%

⫶ **The MacPhail's Collection Glenturret 1998 (85) n19 t21.5 f22.5 b22.** Always a delight to come across a rare bottling like this. Technically, not quite Premier League. But the honeycomb and forceful barley are a source of joy. 40%

Old Malt Cask Glenturret Aged 19 Years refill hogshead, bott Mar 09 **(91)** n23 t23.5 f22 b22.5. One of the few bottlings of late which shows off the Glenturret character to its fullest degree. And at the higher quality found in the early 1990s. A must get malt. *50%. 298 bottles.*

⬩ **Scotch Malt Whisky Society Cask 16.30 Aged 22 Years** 2nd fill hogshead, cask no. 829, dist 1988 **(95)** n23.5 polished leather and beeswax; a vague hint of molasses but rather distant and the pollen has a bigger say; t24 a wonderful sheen gives a polished effect to the barley. Honey is a Glenturret trait and here it builds up to wonderful levels, offset splendidly by busy spices; f23.5 the oak behaves (or is that beehives?) with great aplomb, offering little more than a wooden crutch for the vanilla, honey and spice to perform its magic; the late balance between the dry vanilla oak and the light honeyed barley is worth buying the bottle for alone; b24 a notoriously temperamental whisky, not least because of the small stills. However, this shows the distillery to advantage from just about every angle...a Perthshire classic and, remarkable to relate, better than anything I have ever seen bottled by the proprietors themselves. *51.6%. sc. 206 bottles.*

⬩ **The Whisky Agency Glenturret 1980** bott 2010 **(90)** n22 tries to be honeyed. But the vanilla has the bigger say; there is even an unusual fresh cabbage note; t23.5 excellent delivery and early follow through. Distinct signs of tiredness. But the waxiness of the honey seems to fill in the cracks; some liquorice arrives in the middle ground; f22 the beeswax is waning...; b22.5 a really superb whisky which makes light of a few age problems not least thanks to the most attractive mouthfeel. Lovely stuff. *50.9%. The Whisky Agency.*

GLENUGIE
Highlands (Eastern). 1834–1983. Whitbread. Closed.

⬩ **Deoch an Doras Glenugie 30 Years Old** dist 1980, bott 2011 **(87)** n22 marzipan and oranges offer some controlled sweetness. A thread of recognisable bitterness is apparent but remains attractive and even slightly aloof; t23.5 the delivery is a technical dream as far as sherry butts are concerned. A combination of rich, juicy fruit sharpened by the feel of a coppery zestiness (not something I often past associated with this distillery) and then a middle ground of intense caramels; f19.5 grinds out bitter finale; b22 now there's something I didn't expect to see again: a distillery bottling of Glenugie. Well, technically, anyway, as Glenugie was part of the Chivas group when it died in the 1980s. As far as I can remember they only brought it out once, either as a seven- or five-year-old (it was a long time ago and I can't now remember). I think that went to Italy, so when I walked around the old site just after it closed, it was a Gordon and MacPhail bottling I drank from...and it tasted nothing like this! Just a shame there is a very slight flaw in the sherry butt, but just great to see it in bottle again. *52.13%. nc ncf. Chivas.*

⬩ **Dun Bheagan Glenugie 30 Years Old** butt, cask no. 5375, dist Sep 80 **(95)** n23.5 a rare clarity of clean grape, with minimal barley or oak interference. And of sulphur...not a single atom at all...; sometimes you fancy there is a little swell of smoke in there...no, surely not...; t23.5 the delivery concentrates on the unusually clean grape and a backbone of crisp sugars; there is a mild and strangely welcome bite to the spirit but this heralds a soft vanilla entry; f24 what an outstanding finish: a stunning display of sugars at varying levels of intensity backed by a marzipan depth and a gooseberry flourish; b24 I am old and ugly enough to have bought Glenugie from a shop in Peterhead for a matter of less than ten quid. These days it is near enough impossible to find. But I can probably count on my two hands the number of times I have encountered a sherried version. If this is the cask I am thinking of, I have encountered it many times in the warehouses of Ian MacLeod over the years and occasionally tested its progress. I think they have bottled at probably the optimum time. What sets this guy apart from even the very high quality bottlings of the last five years is the extraordinary integration of the parts. Hot as Hades when a youngster, it now has the ability to bring every single nuance into play. Astonishing: for my money the best from this distillery I have encountered in some 30 years. Oh, and for the avoidance of doubt; I didn't spit a drop... *50%. sc. Ian Macleod Distillers.*

Old Malt Cask Glenugie Aged 26 Years bourbon cask, dist Mar 82, bott Oct 08 **(92.5)** n23.5 t23.5 f22.5 b23. It is possible I have tasted more bottled versions of Glenugie over the years as anyone else out there. And although it has made many of its usual statements, the manner in which they have been delivered opens new ground; the softest Glenugie and possibly most elegant of them all. *50%. Douglas Laing. 265 bottles.*

Old Malt Cask Glenugie Aged 27 Years bourbon cask, dist Mar 82, bott Mar 09 **(86)** n21.5 t21 f22.5 b21. Pleasantly and intensely malty. A tad thin for the real Glenugie purists and showing a hot streak, too. But seriously enjoyable from first to last, especially last. *50%*

Rare Old Glenugie 1970 (90.5) n24 classic old age exotic fruit but so much more: the barley is intact and whether you describe gooseberries as exotic...certainly one of the most delightful old timer noses of the year **t22.5** what was once a thin delivery has, over the years, turned into a crisp one: the barley is ridiculously juicy for a 40-y-o and the oak continues to chip in with the fruit; **f22** returns to its more metallic roots...; **b22** running across a Rare Old classic like this is certainly a true perk of the job... *43.5%. Gordon & MacPhail.*

GLENURY ROYAL
Highlands (Eastern), 1868–1985. Diageo. Demolished.

Glenury Royal 36 Years Old db (89) n22 t23.5 f21.5 b22 With so much dark, threatening oak around, the delivery defies belief or logic. Cracking stuff!! *57.9%*

Glenury Royal 36 Years Old db (89) n21 t23 f22 b23. An undulating dram, hitting highs and lows. The finish, in particular, is impressive: just when it looks on its last legs, it revives delightfully. The whole package, though far from perfect, is pretty astounding. *50.2%*

Glenury Royal 50 Years Old dist 1953 db (91) n23 marvellous freshness to the sherry butt; this had obviously been a high quality cask in its day and the intensity of the fruit sweetened slightly by the most delicate marzipan and old leather oozes class; a little mint reveals some worry lines; **t24** the early arrival is sweet and nimble with the barley, against the odds, still having the major say after all these years. The oak is waiting in the wings and with a burst of soft liquorice and velvety, understated spice beginning to make an impression; the sweetness is very similar to a traditional British child's candy of "tobacco" made from strands of coconut and sugar; **f22** masses of oak yet, somehow, refuses to go over the top and that slightly molassed sweetness sits very comfortably with the mildly oily body; **b22** I am always touched when sampling a whisky like this from a now departed distillery. *42.8%*

Gordon & MacPhail Rare Old Glenury Royal 1972 (90) n22 t23 f22 b23. A thumping malt showing good age but wears it effortlessly. Just beautiful. *40%*

Gordon & MacPhail Rare Old Glenury Royal 1984 (95.5) n25 t24 f23 b23.5. Royal and Ancient...another lost distillery comes back to haunt those with the wrecking ball. *43%*

Old Malt Cask Glenury Royal Aged 32 Years refill hogshead, dist Mar 76, bott Oct 08 (96) n23.5 t23.5 f24.5 b24.5. Imagine a night of passion consisting solely of long fingernails running over your body and little else, except maybe your head being massaged at the same time. Teasing, beautiful, delectable; impossible not to release a sigh of pleasure when nosing and tasting - and a serious contender for World Whisky of the Year. *50%. Douglas Laing. 37 bottles.*

The Whisky Agency Glenury Royal 1973 bourbon hogshead, bott 2011 (84.5) n19 t22.5 f21.5 b21.5. An absolutely creaking old Royal very much at the end of its reign. Yet it has enough regal know-how to somehow play down the worst excesses of the oak and maximise every last nuance of its majesty. Here we can still locate some sumptuous honey threads and the odd vanilla pod to die for. *43%. The Whisky Agency.*

HAZELBURN *(see Springbank)*

HIGHLAND PARK
Highlands (Island–Orkney), 1795. Edrington. Working.

Highland Park 8 Years Old db (87) n22 t22 f22 b21. A journey back in time for some of us: this is the orginal distillery bottling of the 70s and 80s, bottles of which are still doing the rounds in obscure Japanese bars and specialist outlets such as the Whisky Exchange. *40%*

Highland Park Aged 12 Years db (78) n19 t21 f19 b19. Let's just hope that the choice of casks for this bottling was a freak. To be honest, this was one of my favourite whiskies of all time, one of my desert island drams, and I could weep. I will make sure I re-taste next year and pray that the faults from the sherry butts used in this sample have been spotted and eradicated... *40%* ☺☺

Highland Park Saint Magnus Aged 12 Years 2nd edition db (76.5) n18.5 t21 f19 b19. Tight and bitter 2nd edition. *55%*

Highland Park Aged 15 Years db (85) n21 t22 f21 b21. Had to re-taste this several times, surprised by just how relatively flat this was. A hill of honey forms the early delivery, but then... *40%* ☺☺

Highland Park Earl Magnus Aged 15 Years 1st edition db (76.5) n20 t21 f17.5 b18. Tight and bitter. *52.6%. 5976 bottles.*

Highland Park 16 Years Old db (88) n23 softly softly strains of oranges, honey and vanilla; **t23** mouthwatering and delightfully weighted barley with soft nuances of liquorice and smoke; **f20** toffee-vanilla: just a little too quiet; **b22** I tasted this the day it first came out at one of the Heathrow whisky shops. I thought it a bit flat and uninspiring. This sample, maybe from another bottling, is more impressive and showing true Highland Park colours, the finish apart. *40%. Exclusively available in Duty Free/Travel Retail.*

Highland Park Aged 18 Years db **(95.5) n23.5** a thick dollop of honey spread across a layer of salted butter; in the background the ashes of a peat fire are emptied; **t24** eye closing beauty: immediate glossy impact of rich, vaguely metallic honey but upped in the complexity stakes by the subtle intense marbling of peat; the muscular richness, aided by the softness of the oil ensures that maximum intensity is not only reached but maintained; **f24** long continuation of those elements found in the delivery but now radiating soft spices and hints of marzipan; **b24** if familiarity breeds contempt, then it has yet to happen between myself and HP 18. This is a must-have dram. I show it to ladies the world over to win their hearts, minds and tastebuds when it comes to whisky. And the more time I spend with it, the more I become aware and appreciative of its extraordinary consistency. The very latest bottlings have been astonishing, possibly because colouring has now been dropped, and wisely so. Why in any way reduce what is one of the world's great whisky experiences? Such has been the staggering consistency of this dram I have thought of late of promoting the distillery into the world's top three: only Ardbeg and Buffalo Trace have been bottling whisk(e)y of such quality over a wide range of ages in such metronomic fashion. Anyway, enough: a glass of something honeyed and dazzling calls... *43%*

Highland Park Aged 21 Years db **(82.5) n20.5 t22 f19 b21**. Good news and bad news. The good news is that they appear to have done away with the insane notion of reducing this to 40% abv. The bad news: a sulphured sherry butt has found its way into this bottling. 47.5% ⊙ ⊙

Highland Park Aged 25 Years db **(96) n24** big aged oak amid the smoke and honey: it appears something a lot older has got in here...; uniquely complex and back to its very best; **t24** silky and confident, every usual box is ticked – or even double ticked. Much more honey and smoke than I have seen here for a while and it's not all about quantity. What quality! **f24** long with amazing degrees of oil, almost of the bourbony-corn variety! Helps keep those mind-bending honeys coming! **b24** I am a relieved man: the finest HP 25 for a number of years which displays the distillery's unmistakable fingerprints with a pride bordering on arrogance. One of the most improved bottlings of the year: an emperor of a dram. 48.1% ⊙ ⊙

Highland Park Aged 30 Years db **(90) n22** a fascinating balancing act between juicy fruit and very tired, splintered oak; **t22.5** the age waters the eye, so powerful is the oak. But it settles into an oily sweetness displaying both a lazy smokiness and burnt raisin; **f23** some real complexity here with oils filling in the drier vanilla moments; **b22.5** a very dramatic shift from the last bottling I tasted; this has very much taken a fruity route. Sheer quality, though. 48.1% ⊙ ⊙

Highland Park 40 Years Old db **(90.5) n20.5** tired and over-oaked but the usual HP traits are there in just enough force to save it from failing with an extra puff of something smoky diving in to be on the safe side; **t22.5** even after 40 years, pure silk. Like a 40-year-old woman who has kept her figure and looks, and now only satin stands in the way between you and so much beauty and experience...and believe me: she's spicy...; **f24** amazing layering of peat caresses you at every level; the oak has receded and now barley and traces of golden syrup balance things; **b23.5** I have to admit to picking splinters from my nose with this one. Some of the casks used here have obviously choked on oak, and I feared the worst. But such is the brilliance of the resilience by being on the money with the honey, you can say only that it has pulled off an amazing feat with the peat. Sheer poetry... 48.3% ⊙

⋅⋅⋅ **Highland Park 50 Years Old** dist Jan 60 db **(96.5) n24.5** mint, cloves and a thin coat of creosote usurp the usual deft heather and smoke to loudly announce this whisky's enormous age. Don't bother looking for honey, either. Well, not at first... However, there is a growling sweetness from the start: deep and giving up its part molten Demerara-part treacle character with miserly contempt, as though outraged by being awoken from a 50-year slumber. Of course, as the whisky oxidises there is a shift in pattern. And after about ten minutes a wine effect – and we are talking something much more akin to a First Growth Bordeaux than sherry - begins to make a statement. Then the sugars transmogrify from treacle...to molasses...to manuka honey...; **t24** certain sugars present on the delivery, though at first hard to quite make out which. Some surprising oil ensures suppleness to the oak; there is also a wonderful marriage, or perhaps it is a threesome, between old nutty fruitcake, tangy orange-enriched high quality north European marzipan, and ancient bourbon...; **f24** silky with some wonderful caramels and toasted fudge forming a really chewy finale. As well as ensuring any possible old-age holes are plugged; **b24** old whiskies tend to react to unchartered territory as far as time in the oak is concerned in quite different ways. This grey beard has certainly given us a new slant. Nothing unique about the nose. But when one is usually confronted with those characteristics on the nose, what follows on the palate moves towards a reasonably predictable path. Not here. Truly unique – as it should be after all this time. 44.8%. sc. 275 bottles.

Highland Park 1964 Orcadian Vintage refill hogshead, bott 2009 db **(90.5) n23** a spiced up marriage of light smoke, vanilla and soft fruits. For once the trademark honey is nowhere to be seen...; **t22** soft and immediately smoky – almost chunkily so – and though there is a raisin and burnt toast shape to this, the silk is never for a moment compromised; **f23** the oak makes for a slightly eye-watering finish but there are residual sugars to not only lighten the burden but make for a refreshing finale which vanishes, fittingly, in a puff of smoke...; **b22.5** at times you think the old oak is going to sink without trace, taking the whisky with it. But such is the pedigree of the HP make, that it not only fights back but regains control. An honour to experience. 42.2%. 290 bottles.

Highland Park 1968 Orcadian Vintage refill casks, bott 2009 db **(88.5) n20** thumping staves of oak; **t23.5** tangy with all kinds of curled up orange peel; a huge, unexpected wave of oily, caramelised barley; **f23** some fabulous sugar and chocolate toffee moments, **b22** the spicy oak has taken too firm a grip for true greatness. But some of the passages offer wonderful moments of contemplation. 45.6%. 1550 bottles.

Highland Park 1970 Orcadian Vintage db **(94.5) n23.5** much smokier than present day HP..would love to have nosed the new make 40 years ago: it would have been massive; helped along here with a squeeze of blood orange; **t24** splinters on delivery – in both senses - but the silky malt-honey body is able to absorb everything thrown at it; the degrees of sweetness run from honey, through light sugars to subtle Lubec marzipan: sublime; **f23.5** long, again with a distinctive orangey note clinging to the sweet, lightly smoked barley: elegant...; **b23.5** most other malts would have disintegrated under the weight of the oak. This takes it in its stride, and actually uses the extra vanilla to excellent effect. Memorable. 48%

Highland Park 1973 bott 2010 db **(96) n24** what could be better than a standard HP nose, complete with all that delicate smoke and honey? An HP nose with a decent smidgeon of high quality bourbon! Well that's what those extra years in the cask has gone and given you...; **t25** mouth-watering barley enters the arena hand-in-hand with the most pristine acacia honey. Directly behind is two-tone smoke: one firm, lightly peated and spiced, the other a softer, billowing safety net; the middle ground concerns molten manuka honey and muscovado sugar thickened with vanilla...and then the lightest hint of mocha...frankly, perfect...; **f23** lighter, lengthy with toffee and liquorice; **b24** now that, folks, is Highland Park and make no mistake! 50.6%

⸭ **Highland Park Vintage 1978** db **(95.5) n24** some thumping oak is of such high quality it only adds to the mix, rather than detracts. The smoke level is pretty high considering it's had so long in the cask and this helps fend off any oaky excess. Elsewhere tangy kumquats mix with physalis and greengages. The usual honey has given way to soft molasses; **t24** I hope the flight is a long one if you have bought this Duty Free: you really need a good hour alone with this guy to begin to understand his foibles and complexities. The delivery offers a surprising degree of sharpness and life, in which those citrus notes formulate. Then a gentle mixing of delicate, vaguely weary smoke and an almost bourbony red liquorice and light honeycomb mix...; **f23.5** a very light oiliness has formed and provides all that is required to give an extra polish to those soft oaky tones. An equally understated mocha and molasses creamy sweetness ties up the loose ends; **b24** if you are buying this in Duty Free, a tip: get it for yourself...it's too good for a gift!! This purrs quality from first to last. And is quite unmistakably Highland Park. A noble malt. 47.8%. Available in Global Travel Retail.

Highland Park 1990 bott 2010 db **(90) n23** a sprig of lavender (probably in lieu of standard heather) dovetails jauntily with ubiquitous honey and a puff of smoke; **t23** sublime delivery: an almost perfect degree of oil to help the honey slither into its rightful place at the head of the flavour queue with some toffee vanilla not far behind. Just a hint of soapiness; **f22** long, with a buzzing smokiness...and late toffee pudding; **b22** much more like it...!! 40%

Highland Park 1994 bott 2010 db **(87) n23** ah-ha!! Recognisable light smoke and honey sparked by that uniquely enigmatic sweetness...; **t22** a toffee-raisin thread to the honey; **f20.5** inexplicably vanishes off radar; **b21.5** I am not sure what is happening here. HPs of this vintage should be soaring into the comfortable 90s. But again the finish is dull and the usual complexity of the malt is vanishing behind a murky veil. 40%

⸭ **Highland Park 1997 "The Sword"** db **(79.5) n19 t23 f18 b19.5.** Shows its cutting edge for only a brief while on delivery – when it is quite spectacular. Otherwise, painfully blunted. 43%. Available in Taiwan.

Highland Park 1998 bott 2010 db **(85) n22 t22 f20 b21.** They must have special Orcadian spiders to spin a silk this fine. But, though pleasant, disappointing by HP standards as it never gets to spread its wings. The whisky, that is: not the spider. 40%

⸭ **Highland Park Earl Haakon** db **(92) n22.5** the smoke is unusually fishy – something of the Arbroath Smokie. But there are massive tracts of oak waiting in the wings – fresh, red-blooded and happy to keep the honey company; **t24** even by HP's extraordinary standards, the mouth feel on this guy makes the knees tremble. Aided by spices which shimmy and contort all over the palate, the first five or six waves are as good as any malt I have tasted this year; heads towards a surprisingly lightweight butterscotch middle; **f22.5** caramels are happy to lead the fade; **b23** a fabulous malt offering some of the best individual moments of the year. But appears to run out of steam about two thirds in. 54.9%. 3,300 bottles.

Highland Park Hjärta db **(79.5) n18.5 t22 f19 b20.** In part, really does celebrate the honeycomb character of Highland Park to the full. But obviously a major blemish or two in there as well. 58.1%. 3924 bottles.

⋆ **Highland Park Leif Eriksson** bourbon and American oak db **(86) n22 t22 f21 b21.** Has taken Leif of the normal HP senses. The usual distillery traits have gone AWOL while all kinds of caramel notes have usurped them. That said, this has to be one of the softest drams you'll find. 40%. Edrington.

Highland Park New Make Spirit Drink dist Feb 10, bott Mar 10 db **(85.5) n21 t22 f21 b21.5.** Really had to smile when I saw this. Some 15 or 16 years I ago, I remember sitting in the distillery manager's office at HP discussing whisky trends with the then incumbent. I told him that I couldn't understand why every distillery did not sell new make. People drank white spirit... in fact, I explained that, annoyingly, vodka and white rums were going up in popularity big time. Why not new make whisky in Scotland...and White Dog in Kentucky...to show white spirit could have a personality, too? His answer, as far as I remember, centred around people expecting a whole lot more if the bottle had the Highland Park, or some other famous distillery, brand visible. My counter argument was that you could find chocolate and sauces with household whisk(e)y brand names: new make would not damage a distillery's reputation. And I particularly argued that HP was a prime example of new make which should do well because of the very soft peat that you pick up on the nose. Well, now it has happened: here is new make HP Ironically, this sample doesn't have the degree of smoke normally associated with the distillery; and it has been reduced to 50%. Why not just have it at natural strength? This one doesn't boast the usual degree of ultra rich texture of new make HP – even when reduced – and though sweet, malty and enjoyable, with its few extra metallic molecules not exactly how I recently tasted new make HP in a blending lab. A curious choice. 50%. Venture Whisky Ltd.

A.D. Rattray Highland Park 1995 cask no. 1479, dist Jul 95, bott Sep 09 **(89.5) n23** some perky peat hits some hands on honey...; **t23** again the honey smothers the taste buds but there is a sublime smoked spiced sub plot which really ramps up the complexity; **f21.5** caramel flattens the fade somewhat; **b22** pity about the natural toffees. But don't drink this one where there may be bears about... 57.5%. A.D. Rattray Ltd.

A.D. Rattray Highland Park 1998 cask no. 5789 **(84.5) n21.5 t22 f19.5 b21.** Something of the lightly smoked sugar almonds about this one. 46%. A.D. Rattray Ltd.

⋆ **Adelphi Highland Park 12 Years Old** cask no. 714, dist 1998, bott 2011 **(87.5) n20.5 t23 f21.5 b21.5.** Fascinating: an unusual, forthright, more Kentucky than Kirkwell signature to this one. 58.2%. sc. 95 bottles.

Cadenhead's Highland Park Aged 17 Years dist 1992, bott 2009 **(87) n23 t22.5 f20 b21.5.** Nose and delivery are the essence of HP. 64%

Cask Strength Highland Park 1995 (89) n22 t22 f22 b23. Not immediately recognisable as from Orkney. What is genuinely amazing is that here we have a not entirely spotless cask, yet despite the odd trace of it, we still have a true corker. 57.2%. Gordon & MacPhail.

Duncan Taylor Collection Highland Park 1986 cask no. 2254 **(89.5) n21 t23 f23 b22.5.** Bit of a Lazarus malt, this... 55.7%

Duncan Taylor Collection Highland Park 1986 cask no. 2318 **(96) n24** exemplary: intense, cut-it-with-a-knife barley and smoke combination with the usual honeyed sweetness tempered by a warming floral note and bitter marmalade; **t24** my word!! What a body...just feel those curves!!! Look at the way the tongue finds all that honey! A touch of salt makes it a little sultry and sweaty, too... **f24** a long, lingering, sweet, pulsing finish. As you might expect... **b24** just about all you could ask for from an HP, and even a little more besides. 54.2%

Duncan Taylor Collection Highland Park 1987 cask no. 1529 **(86.5) n21.5 t22.5 f21 b21.5.** Enjoyable, for sure. But you can't get past the fact the oak has too big a toe hold here. Even so, the shinier edges on the first delivery certainly do reveal some talented honey and there is a good smoke-cocoa element, too. 50.4%

Duncan Taylor Collection Highland Park 1991 cask no. 8088 **(91) n21.5 t23 f23.5 b23.** A stand up and be counted malt with much to say about itself. 55.2%

Duncan Taylor Collection Highland Park 1991 cask no. 8089 **(83.5) n21 t20.5 f21 b21.** A hotter, sharper version of cask 8089 where the murderous natural caramels have disposed of the smoky body. 54.6%

Duthies Highland Park 17 Years Old (92.5) n23 a curious touch of tobacco on the usual smoky-honey aroma: quite light and salty, too, with the heather/bracken in concentrate form; t23.5 something of the honeyed throat pastel as it sits in the mouth and massages all it touches; f23 long, lightly oiled and continues with the acacia honey buzz... b23 if you don't like this, you might as well turn to Cognac. Or meths. This is magnificent. 46%

⠐ **Hart Brothers Highland Park Aged 32 Years** dist Nov 77, bott Aug 10 (93.5) n23 bananas and custard and a few other notes displaying dotage; t24 that is a quite beautiful delivery: entirely unexpected from the nose. The very softest vanillas imaginable on a lightly oiled base plus sublime sugars nesting amid something approaching a lightly smoked gristiness; they say we return to childhood as we get older...; f22.5 hard to find more gentle vanillas if you searched every cask in Scotland... b24 even though grey haired and stooping somewhat, the elegance and good breeding is unmistakable. A beautiful whisky experience. 46%. sc.

James MacArthur's Old Masters Highland Park 1998 Aged 12 Years cask no. 5712, bott May 10 (86.5) n22.5 t22 f20.5 b21.5. Marginally less sympathetic cask than its twin, 5712, injecting a fair degree of natural caramel which tones down the smoky complexity. Pleasant, though, and well spiced. 573%

James MacArthur's Old Masters Highland Park 1998 Aged 12 Years cask no. 5713, bott Apr 10 (87.5) n23 watch out for the playful smoke; t22.5 a little bit of fizz and crackle can be heard over the usual honeyed melody; f20 a tad bitter; b22 at times, full of typical Highland Park mischief. 578%

⠐ **The MacPhail's Collection Highland Park 1987** (84.5) n22 t23 f18.5 b21. For all its obvious brilliance on the nose and delivery, helped along by a much higher degree of smoke than is the norm, it doesn't quite make it as an all round success story. The delivery is fabulous with its massive honey and peat. But the finish falls flat on its face by offering a bitterness entirely out of place with its early prospects. Of course the smoke on the nose helped paper over the cracks in the oak, but the degree of tightness did make you wonder... 43%

⠐ **Malts Of Scotland Highland Park 1986** bourbon hogshead, cask no. 2296, dist Jun 86, bott Feb 11 (95) n24.5 if there is a nose that encapsulates HP at its most delicate and understated, then this must be it: all the trademark flourishes, but seemingly in miniature. Perhaps the lightness of it all is emphasised by the lemon-citrus slant. Whatever, it is a thing of beauty; t24 one of the rare occasions where the nose and taste are an exact match: the citrus is plentiful and dilutes the honey and smoke into flavours which tantalise rather than dominate; there are soft vanillas, too, plus spice and barley juice. A little bitterness creeps into the late middle, docking half a point...; f22.5 even though the cask is showing the odd sign of fatigue at this point, there is still enough of the delicate sugars to ensure a charming glow... not unlike the effect of the sunset at midnight on June 30th at HP... b24 curses! Tasting this just a couple of days after the 25th anniversary of this being distilled: had I known, I would have shifted my tasting schedule to mark the occasion especially. And, believe me: with a malt like this, there is a lot to celebrate. 50.7%. ncf sc. 234 bottles.

⠐ **Master Of Malt Highland Park 13 Year Old** refill bourbon hogshead, dist 1997, bott 2010 (91) n23 waxy smoke; clever spices and Palma violets seriously up the intensity levels; a touch of physalis helps lighten them a little; t23.5 those spices are first out of the blocks and some heavy duty honey, backed by a ridge of natural caramel ensures all stays on the plump side; f21.5 plenty of vanilla and caramel; b23 everything you would expect from a sound HP cask. 57%. nc ncf sc. Master Of Malt. 281 bottles.

Murray McDavid Highland Park 1989 sherry/port (95) n23 t24 f24 b24. My tastebuds, having recovered from the unpleasant shock of having to analyse not one but two Dufftowns, have been amply rewarded by this truly magnificent malt. Stunningly haphazard, but everything – through either luck or design – falls into place gloriously. 46%

Old & Rare Highland Park Aged 30 Years dist Mar 78, bott Aug 08 (74.5) n19 t19 f18.5 b18. A real shame. There appears to be an astonishing degree of honey to this. But something has crept in to spoil the party. Any guesses what...? 55.1%. Douglas Laing. 302 bottles.

Old Malt Cask Highland Park Aged 12 Years refill hogshead no. DL 5611, dist Sep 97, bott Nov 09 (87.5) n22 unusual mixture of coal dust and crushed green leaves; t22 the honey missing on the nose romps over the taste buds, but always with that slightly unginaly vegetable note in tow; f21.5 attractive spices and more smoke; b22 some trademark HP characteristics, but absolutely refuses to conform to the norm. 50%. Douglas Laing. 222 bottles.

Old Malt Cask Highland Park 13 Years Old refill hogshead no. DL 5732, dist Sep 96, bott Jan 10 (92) n23 a little salt 'n' pepper on the honeydew melon; t24.5 as near enough perfect for a HP of this age: the honey is layered and blended with roasted sugars and then a fabulous spice development rumbles along like a minor earthquake; f22 an element of bitterness points to a less than perfect cask. But the spirit put into it must have been close on perfection; **b22.5** oh...yes...!!! 50%. Douglas Laing & Co Ltd. 325 bottles.

🍷 **Old Malt Cask Highland Park Aged 13 Years** refill hogshead, cask no. 6398, dist Sep 96, bott Jul 10 **(90) n22.5** intense with the barley prominent and the honey of the slightly forgotten in the jar variety; **t23** lovely delivery with decent body: like honey on porridge; **f22** long, with waxy vanilla fade; **b22.5** clean as a whistle: no scars from the cask at all (well, maybe the very faintest, almost negligible trace of later bitterness) and all the usual HP characteristics in perfect working order. 50%. nc ncf sc. Douglas Laing & Co. 388 bottles.

Old Malt Cask Highland Park Aged 15 Years dist Feb 94, bott Jul 09 **(88) n21.5 t22 f22.5 b22.** Lovely stuff with just the right degree of attitude. 50%

Old Malt Cask Highland Park Aged 26 Years sherry hogshead no. DL 5596, dist Mar 83, bott Nov 09 **(93) n24** wonderfully clean grape of the old school and still enough space for the obligatory honey and smoke; an unusual sprig of mint adds to the fun; **t23** now it enters the realms of fantasy whisky with a thick, viscous delivery. Some chewy cream toffee helps give a fudge and raisin middle; **f22.5** more fudge, more raisin...and a late injection of smoke; **b23** a long way from the normal clichéd HP. Delightfully different. 50%. 294 bottles.

🍷 **Old Malt Cask Highland Park Aged 27 Years** refill sherry hogshead, cask no. 6377, dist Mar 83, bott Jul 10 **(89) n23** clipped in some places; expansive in others: curious mix of smoky sherry trifle and a hoppy fruitiness. Very different; **t23** fills out with stunning depth. The grape is juicy for sure. But the main characteristic is the controlled sweetness. There are signs of a contrasting light bitterness but always brought under control in time. The middle produces a vague Jaffa cake effect; **f21** finally that bitterness creeps in. But, like the nose, it has something of the hop about it; **b22** old Beer cask, more like... 50%. nc ncf sc. Douglas Laing & Co. 247 bottles.

Premier Barrel Highland Park Aged 11 Years (90.5) n23.5 smoke...tick; honey...tick...; mosses and bracken...tick...HP on the sample label...tick...; **t23** those stunning strata of honey edge out the smoke for top billing; **f22** bitters slightly but some smoky spice kicks in; **b22** an Orcadian odyssey... 46%. nc ncf. Douglas Laing & Co Ltd. 180 bottles.

🍷 **Premier Barrel Highland Park Aged 12 Years (82.5) n20 t22 f20 b20.5.** Plenty of Golden Syrup and attractive, almost coppery metallic sharpness. But never settles or feels particularly happy with itself by HP standards. 46%. nc ncf sc. Douglas Laing & Co. 182 bottles.

🍷 **Premier Barrel Highland Park Aged 12 Years (85.5) n21.5 t22.5 f20 b21.5.** A slight bitter edge cannot entirely disturb the well entrenched honey and kumquat. 46%. nc ncf sc. Douglas Laing & Co. 370 bottles.

🍷 **Premier Barrel Highland Park Aged 13 Years (87.5) n22.5** ticks every HP box; **t23** some early smoke is blown away by the usual gathering honey forces **f20.5** falls away as the bitterness gains; **b21.5** wonderful nose and delivery combo. 46%. nc ncf sc. Douglas Laing & Co. 319 bottles.

Provenance Highland Park Aged 10 Years refill hogshead, dist Autumn 98, bott Autumn 08 **(87) n22** the lightness of the oak gives the peat a clear road; **t21.5** lively and bracing with a salty tang; **f22** long, sweetens and really comes into its own as the smoke re-emerges; late vanilla and soft chalk; **b21.5** good, delicate malt, for all the smokiness. 46%. Douglas Laing.

Provenance Highland Park Aged 10 Years dist Sep 98, bott Jul 09 **(89) n21.5 t23 f22 b22.5** A common and garden HP treat. 46%. Douglas Laing.

Provenance Highland Park Over 11 Years refill hogshead no. DMG 5744, dist Summer 98, bott Winter 2010 **(85) n21.5 t22 f20.5 b21.5.** Light, lilting and sweet, even the most delicate smoke has a strangely refreshing quality to it. 46%. Douglas Laing & Co Ltd.

🍷 **Provenance Highland Park Over 11 Years** refill hogshead, cask no. 7086, dist Autumn 99, bott Spring 2011 **(88) n22.5** all the usual honey, smoke and heather suspects. Just very low volume; **t22** juicy; a touch of green apple amid the honey; **f21.5** a hint of oak bitterness; **b22** HP at its most simple and easy going. 46%. nc ncf sc. Douglas Laing & Co.

🍷 **Provenance Highland Park Over 12 Years** refill hogshead, cask no. 6822, dist Autumn 98, bott Autumn 2010 **(77) n18.5 t21.5 f18 b19.** An OK-ish whisky. But by HP's mega-high standards, thin and less than convincing. 46%. nc ncf sc. Douglas Laing & Co.

🍷 **Provenance Highland Park Over 13 Years** refill hogshead, cask no. 7479, dist Autumn 97, bott Summer 2011 **(87) n20.5 t23 f21.5 b21.5.** A curious HP, this. Seams to splutter like a plane with a dodgy engine and just as it appears to be heading to earth, it starts up again and soars off to offer wonderful views. 46%. nc ncf sc. Douglas Laing & Co.

Rare Old Highland Park 1973 (78.5) n21.5 t20 f18.5 b19.5. Loses the battle against the oak. 43%. Gordon & MacPhail.

Scotch Malt Whisky Society Cask 4.141 Aged 10 Years 1st fill bourbon barrel, dist Apr 99 **(89.5) n22** whispering haystacks and crumbled German caramelised biscuit; **t23.5** crisp, clean, crunchy barley with more of that beautiful caramelisation...not so much the trademark honey but more brown sugars; **f22** thins and bitters a little; **b22** never tries to oversell itself or shout its worth. This is subtlety and quiet construction on the palate. But don't bother looking for the smoke. 58.9%. Scotch Malt Whisky Society. 253 bottles.

Scotch Malt Whisky Society Cask 4.143 Aged 20 Years refill hogshead, dist May 89 **(95) n25** if you want to know what HP should nose like, then go no further: grab one of these. The barley is shadowed by the lightest shade of lemon; the smoke is little more than suggestion and elsewhere other charming notes drift in and out, especially the glorious, honeyed, crushed gorse petal; **t24.5** so it naturally follows that what happens on the palate is the nose in liquid form: here the honey really does play a more significant part but the barley simply melts in the mouth while the smoke threatens something spicy, but never quite makes it. Single malt whisky at its most gentle...; **f22.5** perhaps because of the fragility of the body and flavours it is inevitable that a slight bitterness from the cask eventually makes itself heard...though those spices do finally form; **b23** one of those truly great whiskies that makes me want to take it home at the end of the day. HP as it should be... 51.4%. 241 bottles.

Scotch Malt Whisky Society Cask 4.148 Aged 10 Years 1st fill bourbon barrel, cask no. 800271, dist 2000 **(86) n21.5 t22.5 f21 b21.** Plenty of sweet, juicy character and spice. But you get the feeling the whole thing is half cooked. Indeed: if this is from a first fill bourbon barrel, then either it has been maturing in a snow drift for the last 10 years, or the cask had matured a bourbon for about 20 years... 59.9%. sc. 206 bottles.

Scotch Malt Whisky Society Cask 4.151 Aged 26 Years refill sherry butt, cask no. 1751, dist 1984 **(93) n23** plums and dates as well as grape here: pretty weighty for an HP; **t23** the impact is like being hit by a ton of grapey feathers; an appealing mix of natural caramels and fruit...shouldn't work, but just does, though it needs a generous dose of spices to inject a biting balance; **f23.5** long and highly impressive. Still there is no aggression, just continuing waves of fruit and nut chocolate; **b23.5** the distillery has a silky character at the best of times. Here it somehow marries substance with a near weightlessness: some trick! 53%. sc. 226 bottles.

Scott's Selection Highland Park 1981 bott 2011 **(97) n24** all the usual HP characteristics are here in almost clichéd amounts: the smoke, the heather, the honey... but this has an added extra: a delicate degree of jelly baby fruitiness, mainly lime but with the strains of a raspberry tartness to counter the sweeter honey, as well; I would use the word delicate, but that hardly begins to do it justice... **t25** a faultless delivery. The honey and maple syrup are diluted so not to overwhelm the Rich Tea barley; the spices dissolve on impact while the vanillas carry just enough oaky dryness to balance the sugars: this is a force of nature...; **f24** here you might reasonably expect a bittering from the oak to break the spell you are by now under. But it never arrives. Instead, we have yet more and more layering of honey and now natural caramels, but with the sugars and spices still dancing together in the background...; **b24** perhaps the most remarkable thing about this particular bottling, is that it is almost a distillation of the great Highland Park distillery itself. Absolutely nothing jumps out at you as being extra special. Conversely, I cannot find a single fault with it, either. It is as if this whisky in my glass is making a very simple statement: "This is why I have been one of the world's top five most consistent whiskies." It is quite impossible to even attempt to contradict it. Indeed, had it even gone further and told you that it is one of the top ten single cask whiskies you are likely to taste in your lifetime, I am not sure where the materials required for a counter argument could be found. This, ladies and gentlemen, is near as damn it as good as it gets... 48.5%. Speyside Distillers.

The Whisky Agency Highland Park 25 Years Old dist 1985, bott 2010 **(95) n23.5** so honey and heathery is this that it could almost be a send up of itself; **t24** now the honey is in league with maple syrup...sweet or what!!! **f24** settles down with an apologetic degree of peat creeping in through the back door. But the honey buzzes along delightfully; **b23.5** an HP do it yourself kit: honey – check. Heather – check. Soft smoke – almost. Go for it...!! 48%

The Whisky Agency Highland Park 1977 bott 2010 **(88.5) n23.5** astonishing how such little amounts of smoke can stay the course after so many years! Elegant and refined, even with the oak moving in; **t22** superb sweetness to the delivery aided by soft, vanilla-enriched oils; **f21** perhaps a little too much natural caramel; **b22** the shape of the whisky has been weathered by time. But its innate beauty remains fully recognisable. 52.3%. The Whisky Agency.

Whisky Doris Highland Park 1995 bourbon hogshead, cask no. 1468, dist Jul 95, bott May 10 **(89.5) n23** a beautiful concoction of clear honey spread over German white bread baked that morning...; **t23.5** try not to close your eyes and groan with pleasure: the delivery is about as close to the perfect honey sweetness and depth you are likely to find. The vanillas form quickly...; **f21** the bitterness of a tiring cask outmuscles even this sweetie; **b22** HP – Honeyed Perfectly... 55.8%. Whisky Doris.

IMPERIAL

Speyside, 1897. Chivas Brothers. Silent.

Imperial Aged 15 Years "Special Distillery Bottling" db (69) n17 t18 f17 b17. At least one very poor cask, hot spirit and overly sweet. Apart from that it's wonderful. 46%

Berrys' Own Selection Imperial 1989 (86) n22.5 t21.5 f21 b21. Textbook blending Speysider: the oak has had limited impact on the barley-rich nose and delivery but makes a bitter contribution at the death. Always juicy and attractive, though. 46%. Berry Bros & Rudd.

Cask Strength Imperial 1997 (72) n18 t19.5 f17 b17.5. An empire in revolt... Not a great cask. 61.6%. Gordon & MacPhail.

Duncan Taylor Collection Imperial 11 Years Old (87.5) n23.5 absolutely pristine barley sets the heart a flutter; t22 same again on delivery with the malt in almost three dimensional mode: early on it doesn't come cleaner, then the oaky bitterness clogs the middle; f20.5 light and bitter; b21.5 worth finding for the nose and delivery alone. 46%. Duncan Taylor & Co Ltd.

Duncan Taylor Collection Imperial 1990 cask no. 443 (92) n22.5 t23.5 f23 b23. A superbly made malt. Imperial often gets a bad press for its quality and occasionally perceived blandness. Nonsense! I have always rated this distillery, and here you can see why. This is simply fabulous. 55%

Duncan Taylor Collection Imperial 1990 cask no. 445 (91) n23 t23 f22.5 b22.5. Quite adorable. 53.1%. Duncan Taylor.

Duncan Taylor Collection Imperial 1990 cask no. 446 (86) n21.5 t22 f21.5 b21. A sharper, thinner, but no less malty version of cask 443. 53.7%

Duncan Taylor Collection Imperial 1990 cask no. 448 (88.5) n22.5 t23 f21 b22. Fades too quickly but a malty charmer. 55.7%

Duncan Taylor Collection Imperial 1990 cask no. 449 (86.5) n21.5 t22 f21.5 b21.5. Excellent barley theme and tense, at times, too. Plus a fine bourbony skit at the finish. A tad hot here and there, maybe. 53.4%. Duncan Taylor.

Duncan Taylor Collection Imperial 1990 cask no. 450 (83.5) n22 t21.5 f19.5 b20.5. Clearly not a malt designed for a second decade in the cask, this has all the exotic fruit oakiness of a whisky twice its age. Stylish early on, it descends into something pretty sawdusty, though. 53.9%. Duncan Taylor & Co Ltd.

Duncan Taylor The NC2 Range Imperial Aged 13 Years (86) n22 t22 f21 b21. Charming, grassy, citrusy, ultra fresh Speysider. 46%

Gordon & MacPhail Distillery Label Imperial 1991 (83) n22 t21 f20 b20. Lots of suet pudding with some nagging bitterness at death. Seriously easy going beside. 43%

⬩ **Gordon & MacPhail Distillery Label Imperial 1993** (88.5) n23 fruit and nut, bordering on farmhouse cake; t22 clean and flimsily bodied, there is an equal play between the garish malt and darker-toned fruit; f21.5 slightly off key but the vanilla works hard to restore the equilibrium; b22 enjoyable whisky, not least because you are never quite sure the direction it is taking next. 43%

⬩ **Old Malt Cask Imperial Aged 16 Years** refill hogshead, cask no. 7018, dist Apr 95, bott Apr 11 (85) n21 t21 f21.5 b21.5. Untaxing mega-malty Imperial showing all its blending colours. 50%. nc ncf sc. Douglas Laing & Co. 271 bottles.

Provenance Imperial Aged 12 Years refill hogshead, dist Summer 96, bott Spring 09 (84.5) n22 t21.5 f20 b21. Light, airy, malty. Juicy barley early on delivery. 46%. Douglas Laing.

Provenance Imperial Aged 12 Years refill barrel, dist Spring 96, bott Winter 08 (88) n22 t23 f21.5 b21.5. Tasting this and another Prov. Imp. 12 together, the difference a good cask can make is clearly defined. 46%. Douglas Laing.

INCHGOWER

Speyside, 1872. Diageo. Working.

Inchgower 1993 The Manager's Choice db (84.5) n21 t21.5 f21 b21. Like your malts subtle, delicate, clean and sophisticated? Don't bother with this one if you do. This has all the feel of a malt that's been spray painted onto the taste buds: thick, chewy and resilient. Can't help but like that mix of hazelnut and Demerara, though. You can stand a spoon in it. 61.9%

⬩ **Berry's Own Selection Inchgower 1982** cask no. 6968, bott 2010 (84.5) n21.5 t22 f20 b21. A knife and fork job with masses of dark sugars and spice. Fun, but bitters out and lacks the usual complexity. 56.2%. nc ncf sc. Berry Bros & Rudd.

Connoisseurs Choice Inchgower 1993 (87.5) n21 t22 f22.5 b22. Finding decent Inchgowers has been far from an easy task in recent years. Good ol' G&M have come to the rescue here, though, with a bottling bursting with character. 43%. Gordon & MacPhail.

⬩ **Malts Of Scotland Inchgower 1982** bourbon hogshead, cask no. 6969, dist Jun 82, bott Feb 11 (91.5) n23 leafy and dry, the oaks make their mark without offering the expected bourbony sugars; **t24** gazooks! The taste buds are absolutely over-run by the magnificence of the brilliantly spiced barley which is bolstered by a natural burned fudge; loads of custard topped by molten muscovado sugars... stunning; **f21.5** slightly too vigorously drying; **b22.5** this whisky happened to be made on the very same day as my chief researcher, Ally Telfer, was born. It is obvious which has matured more magnificently over the years... *57.2%. nc ncf sc. 212 bottles.*

⁘ **Old Malt Cask Inchgower Aged 28 Years** refill hogshead, cask no. 6455, dist Jun 82, bott Aug 10 **(91) n23.5** a fabulous battle between big, bourbon sweetness, freshly squeezed orange and sliced cucumber...; **t23.5** the barley beats its chest on arrival but, not surprisingly, those bourbon incantations on the nose can be heard again; sharp kumquat and deft marzipan complete the job; **f21.5** drying custard vanilla; **b22.5** a typically lusty Inchgower which revels in its bawdy brute force. But there is real quality here, too. A fabulous example of this distillery's finer moments. *50%. nc ncf sc. Douglas Laing & Co. 165 bottles.*

Old Malt Cask Inchgower Aged 34 Years dist Sep 74, bott Jul 09 **(91) n23 t22 f23 b23.** Dating from the days when the distillery was in its pomp. And it shows. *50%. Douglas Laing.*

The Whisky Agency Inchgower 1974 (87.5) n22 mildly feral but with an elegant oakiness; **t22** fiery and full bodied, there is an usual thickness to the body for its age; **f21.5** liquorice and drying oak; **b22** a teamed beast. *57.3%*

⁘ **The Whisky Agency Inchgower 1974** bott 2010 **(89) n21.5** salty and thick. A touch of molasses...of the unsweetest kind; **t23.5** luxurious mouthful; a touch of bite and attitude before relaxing into a more spicy character. Levels out with thick portions of date and walnut cake; **f22** reverts to a more molassed – and broodingly closed – type; **b22** an unusual malt for its age, having a dark, mysterious nature rather than one that has opened up over time. Compellingly different. *50.4%. The Whisky Agency.*

⁘ **The Whisky Castle Cask Collection No. 15 Inchgower 20 Years** American oak, cask no. 6987, dist 1990, bott 2011 **(89) n22** a real slap dash , oiled up beast full of sugared almonds and toast; **t23** sensuously sweet, but not in that appallingly cloying Dufftown or Mortlach manner. Here it grabs some spice to cause a degree of mayhem and a touch of greengage jam on the burnt fudge...it actually tastes as weirdly wonderful as it sounds...; **f22** settles for an easier life of creamed mocha; **b22** I have to say that this distillery as often as not comes up with a malt with an almost eccentric character. Here's another one. *46%. nc ncf sc. Angus Dundee for The Whisky Castle. 264 bottles.*

INVERLEVEN
Lowland, 1938–1991. Demolished.

Gordon & MacPhail Distillery Label Inverleven 1990 (87) n20 t23 f22 b22. Absolutely unique version from this lost distillery: if I was a gambling man I'd say that this was filled into an old Laphroaig or Ardbeg cask, for there is a delicate smoky element that was never intended during mashing. Odd, also because the nose reveals a mild, butyric flaw...as well as unmistakable hints of gin/jenever. But as soon as it hits the tastebuds...my, oh my..!!! *40%*

Gordon & MacPhail Distillery Label Inverleven 1991 (93.5) n24 beautifully clean, flawless, barley emboldened by a dash of tangerine; distant lavender quietly underscores the age; **t23.5** some really beautiful, understated threads of honey give this star quality; **f22.5** no major faults that such an age might threaten; **b23.5** handled the aging process with an accomplished performance. Surprisingly suave: one of the surprise packages of the year. *40%*

Rarest of the Rare Inverleven 1979 cask no. 5666 **(96) n23.5 t24 f24.5 b24.** Easily one of the best lowlanders I've come across in the last five years oozing nothing but sheer class. Beautifully made, wonderfully casked and no less than stunning in the glass. *56.2%*

ISLE OF ARRAN
Highlands (Island–Arran), 1995. Isle of Arran Distillers. Working.

The Arran Malt 8 Years Old Pinot Noir Finish db **(79.5) n19 t21 f19.5 b20.** Pleasant enough. But just seems to lack the trademark Arran balance and has a few lopsided moments to boot, especially at the death. *50%. Isle of Arran Distillers.*

The Arran Malt 8 Years Old Pomerol Wine Finish db **(87) n19** another Arran which strains against a fruity muzzle; **t23.5** that's much more like it!! All the harmony missing on the nose arrives in buckets as the trademark thickness of body takes on the spiced grape without missing a beat. Beautiful...; **f22** much drier, as it should be, but the chalkiness of the oak hardly makes a dent on the barley-grape surface. Just a slight wobble on the finish; **b22.5** Full bodied and lush. *50%. Isle of Arran Distillers.*

The Arran Malt Under 10 Years Old db **(89) n22** limp, lush barley of the butterscotch variety; **t23** those stunning soft oils are working overtime to spread the sweet barley; **f22** long, biscuity and balanced; **b22** this one's kicked its shoes and socks off... *43%*

The Arran Malt 10 Year Old db **(87)** n22.5 sharp and lively with an unusual (and unwelcome) fruity nip; no shortage of polished oak floors and big vanilla; t22.5 juicy with a number of lighter sugars in attendance; the barley forms the main thrust, but still a vague fruit character presses itself; f20 surprisingly dull with the vanilla working hard for attention; b22 it has been a while since I last officially tasted this. If they are willing to accept some friendly advice, I think the blenders should tone down on raising any fruit profile and concentrate on the malt, which is amongst the best in the business. 46%. nc ncf. ☺ ☺

The Arran Malt 12 Years Old db **(85)** n21.5 t22 f20.5 b21 Hmmmm. Surprise one, this. There must be more than one bottling already of this. The first I tasted was perhaps slightly on the oaky side but otherwise intact and salt-honeyed where need be. This one has a bit of a tang: very drinkable, but definitely a less than brilliant cask around. 46%

⋰⋰ The Arran Malt Aged 14 Years db **(89.5)** n22 light dusting of cumquat and physalis does not form quite a big enough umbrella to cope with the oaky storm clouds; t23.5 usual sublime weight to the body, but the oak makes its pitch several beats earlier than the norm. Fortunately there is still enough Demerara sugar and barley sugar to make for a massively juicy experience; f21.5 dries profoundly with the oak offering a chalky farewell; b22.5 a superb whisky, but the evidence that there has been a subtle shift in emphasis, with the oak now taking too keen an interest, is easily attained. 46%. ncf.

The Arran Malt 1996 'The Peacock' Icons of Arran bott 2009 **(96)** n24.5 oh my word: what a shame I have only three or four months to write this book: the degree of complexity will take that time to unravel. Both floral and fruity in almost perfect doses, the white pepper perfectly balances the light saltiness. The big weight is deceptive as the delicate sultana and perry sub plot appears to give more air and space to the overall picture. Outstanding...; t24.5 what a delicate creature this is: the juicy grape appears to be apparent on a couple of levels, sandwiching the honey and hickory bourbon notes between them; f23 long, now with that hint of pear on the nose re-surfacing as the finish nestles somewhere between butterscotch tart and buttered toast; b24 yet again this outstanding distillery delivers the goods: one of the most outstanding malts of the year and certainly one of the most complex. I would not be surprised if this was overlooked by some of you new to whisky: if you have not already discovered the faultless beauty on offer (not a single off note or hint of discord to be had from first to last!!) go back and try again with your palate as clean and unsullied as this magnificent malt demands and deserves. I've not yet spoken to the Arran guys about this, but would happily bet my house that this is a sublime mix of top bourbon cask and faultless sherry. As fabulous as this distillery unquestionably is, they will be hard pressed to keep this standard going... 46%

The Arran Malt 1996 Single Cask sherry butt, cask no. 1596, bott 2009 db **(88.5)** n22 a slight bubblegum effect to this, though the fruit appears closely tied up with weightier oak elements; t23 wow...!!! Now that's some delivery with the grape forming the most delicious degree of juiciness to perfectly match the natural glossy oiliness. The oaks are no pushover, either. The spicy crescendo is expected and doesn't disappoint...; f21 very dry with distinct signs of assertive over-oakiness; b22.5 excellent whisky. But no doubt the oak is a tad too domineering and the points here would have been higher if bottled a couple of years earlier. 54.4%

⋰⋰ The Arran Malt Single Sherry Cask 1996 cask no. 1073, dist 11 Dec 96, bott 31 Mar 11 db **(91.5)** n23 crystalline fruit, including a hint of banana to soften matters. Clean and, for those capable of sherried whisky hard-ons, about as arousing as it gets. I suspect... t24.5 rock solid barley wrapped in juicy grape. Spices arrive on demand and stay the course. The sugars are the stuff of future sugar hero worship... I doubt if those with the sherried hard-ons have made it to this point...; f21.5 crumbles slightly as it dries. Bitterness creeps in, but those sugars and spices do a pretty impressive job; b22.5 a rare case of a great whisky being let down slightly by the quality of the European oak itself, rather than any sulphur treatment. For the most part, glorious. 54.1%. nc ncf sc. UK exclusive. 264 bottles.

The Arran Malt Sherry Single Cask 1997 ex-sherry hogshead no. 410 db **(88.5)** n23 coastally complex: decidedly seaweedy, but not so much that the light layering of fresh grape and barley cannot be clearly detected. High class stuff... t22 dry delivery with the barley forcing its way through a surfeit of grape skin and tannin; f21.5 surprising degree of vanilla; b22 elegant. 52.2%

The Arran Malt Sherry Single Cask 1997 ex-sherry hogshead no. 435 db **(89)** n22.5 clumsy with the salt and grape tripping over each other; t23 sharp and massively salty delivery with the fruit being almost three dimensional; moves off into a malty middle ground; f21.5 lots of natural caramels; b22 lively and showing a pleasing edginess. 52.5%

The Arran Malt Sherry Single Cask 1997 ex-sherry hogshead no. 517 db **(86.5)** n22 t22 f21 b21.5. The occasional clap of thundering, salty malt, but the fruitiness tones the intensity down towards the middle and finish. 53.5%

The Arran Malt Sherry Single Cask cask no. 819, dist Jun 98, bott Jun 09 db (**91**) n23 wild strawberry; crushed, under-ripe green grape and a hint of something vaguely kiwi-fruitish. And, despite all this, the clarity is such that the malt is as plain as day...; t24 fabulously crisp and assertive: golden sugar sprinkled spiced sultana...with the spices hotting up as the salivating qualities multiply; f22 dulls down as the natural oak caramels dig in; b22 a thumpingly good sherry cask with not a single off note detectable. 57.7%

The Arran Malt 1997 Single Cask sherry hogshead no. 965, bott 2010 db (**93.5**) n24 fat with the oils evident. The grape quickly latches on to them, as do the drier vanillas: beautifully complex; t24 the type of malt which massages: initially sweet and rotund, but a few sleepy waves give way to something a little more charismatic as salt and spice begin to make some profound speeches; mouth filling and chewy all the way; f22.5 thins out somewhat abruptly, but perhaps that is inevitable considering the type of body on offer on delivery and through to the middle stages; b23 for those who like their grape a little seasoned. A celebration of what a good, untarnished sherry butt should be all about. What a star...!! 55%. Isle of Arran Distillers. Belgium.

The Arran Malt 1997 Single Cask sherry hogshead no. 1318, bott 2009 db (**95**) n24 a clever marriage of salty oak and dryish grape with an almost orange blossom sweetness providing the balance: elegant in the extreme; t24.5 so delicate that you are frightened to move it around the mouth in fear it might snap! Just a light sprinkling of icing sugar seems to see off any oaky excess; at times angular at others sleek, the complex components are forever moving around, the degree of sweetness fading and brightening like the star it is; f23 for a malt so dry, the finish is longer than first appears. It is the tight vanilla which hangs on longest, though; b23.5 the kind of sophisticated malt you could drop an olive into...but don't..!! 52.5% Japan.

The Arran Malt 1997 'The Rown Tree' Icons of Arran bott 2010 db (**77.5**) n18.5 t22 f18 b19. The key here is balance and harmony. And this, unusually for an Arran, possesses little of either. The bitter finish confirms the unhappiness hinted at on the nose. Someone was barking up the wrong tree when putting this one together and the malt, in this form, even for all the sweet, bright moments on delivery, is ready for the chop. 46% Isle of Arran Distillers

The Arran Malt 1998 Single Cask sherry butt no. 452, bott 2009 db (**93.5**) n23.5 textbook stuff. Not a sulphur atom in sight as the clean, thick-ish grape mixes delightfully with a prickling spice and barley; t24 a salty delivery with a fabulous texture to the creamy grape and sweeter barley. Spices throb fore and aft but it's that complex texture which really wins the day: one of the best sherried whisky mouthfuls I have encountered this year; f23 hollows out as the vanilla gets a grip. Ever tasted spiced chocolate? Here it's in liquid form; b23 wonderfully assertive yet always pays respect to the salty sub-plot. Complex, elegant and never short of character. A charmer bordering on the old school. 56.3% USA.

The Arran Malt 1998 Single Cask bourbon cask no. 650, bott 2009 db (**89**) n21.5 a bit of attitude to this: some vanilla-oak nip and a hint of fast distillation; t23 zippy and thinner than the norm for this distillery, it papers over the cracks with a beautiful lift of layered malt and citrus-fused vanilla. The spices, though, have the greatest say; f22 bitter-sweet with a real cocoa depth to the finish; b22.5 lacking the usual weight and showing signs of an impatient stillman, still this malt turns cartwheels on the taste buds. An entertainer. 57.6% USA.

The Arran Malt 1998 Single Cask bourbon cask no. 673, bott 2009 db (**87.5**) n21 elements of bourbon and blood orange; t22 the citrus-barley theme helps tame the more energetic vanillas; f22.2 lots of vanilla and chocolate; b22 many of the same attributes as cask 650; and my suspicion about some rapid distillation has been confirmed. 55.7% Norway.

The Arran Malt Bourbon Single Cask 1998 cask no. 671 db (**94.5**) n24 t24 f23 b23.5. My gut instinct is that Arran is just about at its best at 10-11 years in bourbon cask, and here is a bottling which does little to change my mind. Brilliantly made malt in a very fine bourbon cask. What a superstar. 58%

The Arran Malt Bourbon Single Cask 1998 cask no. 675 db (**85.5**) n22 t20.5 f22 b21. Similar, beautifully made malt to 671 (above) but the cask is more fragile and offers flattening caramels where the livelier citrus ought to be... 57.5%

The Arran Malt Bourbon Single Cask 1998 cask no. 682 db (**88.5**) n22 t21.5 f23 b22. At times conservative, there is enough life in the cask to lift the barley. 46%

The Arran Malt Single Sherry Cask 1998 ex-sherry butt cask no. 84 db (**72**) n18.5 t19 f16.5 b18. Nope...! 56%

The Arran Malt Single Sherry Cask 1998 cask no. 724 db (**73**) n17 t20 f18 b18. Massive – and what otherwise would certainly have been outstanding - sweet grape juice tries to fight off the worst of the sulphur excesses. But it is asking too much. 57.3%

The Arran Malt Single Sherry Cask 1998 cask no. 353 db (**94.5**) n25 t23.5 f22.5 b23.5. Oh, it is just so rare to come across sherry butts unspoiled by sulphur these days I could weep for joy when I find one like this. I immediately nosed its partner (724) afterwards and could thrash myself with a thorned twig because it is a complete negative of it. 53%

⁘ **The Arran Malt 1998 "The Westie" Icons Of Arran** oloroso cask, bott 2011 (85) n20.5 t22.5 f21 b21. Pleasant but, frankly, dull fayre, despite the spicy teasing on delivery. Such an oloroso cask may be fine for a commoner, but hardly fit for an emperor... 46%. nc ncf. 6000 bottles.

The Arran Malt 1999 Vintage 15th Anniversary Edition finished in amontillado, bott 2010 db (92.5) n24 sherry as you demand it shows on the nose. Clean, confident, a hint of sultana only as this is dry, yet always with enough finesse for the barley to come through loud and clear: an absolute treat...; t23.5 salivating from the off with a glittering delivery of fresh grape and spice. Waves of vanilla punch through and there is a fabulous malty flourish towards the middle. But those spices continue to pulse...; f22.5 drier, with vanilla pods and a buttery residue; b22.5 there is no mistaking excellence. And here it appears to flow freely. 54.6%

⁘ **The Arran Malt Open Day Single Bourbon Cask Bottling 2011** db (94) n23.5 unbelievable degree of fruit sitting alongside the rich barley and muscovado-enriched bourbon notes; t24 a match of spice and sugared barley made in heaven; f23.5 the earlier juiciness evaporates as the vanillas lay claim. But enough spices – and fruit again – remain for the finale to be anything but standard; b23.5 to me, Arran in a high class bourbon cask shows the distillery to its very finest advantage: my case rests... 52%. nc ncf sc. Sold at distillery during 2011 Open Day.

The Arran Malt 2005 Single Cask "The Peated Arran" bourbon cask no. 116 bott 2009 db (89) n22.5 some burnt toast on the peat; t22 sweet, gristy smokiness. Rampaging vanilla kicks in with a twist of bitter lemon; f21.5 oily, disjointed, dry but naggingly smoky; b22 for its tender years, it works uncommonly well. 57.7%

The Arran Malt Ambassador's Choice db (87.5) n22 t22 f21.5 b22. So heavy with oak I was amazed I could pick the nosing glass up... 46%

⁘ **The Arran Malt Amarone Cask Finish** db (94.5) n23 the buzzing black peppers leave you in no doubt what is to follow. As does the stunning clarity of the grape and crisp, business-like manner of the barley: stirring! t24 and so it is played out on the palate: the grape is juicy and sweet, the barley is firm and forms the perfect skeleton, the spices pop busily around the palate. No great age evident, but the oak also chimes in with a few choice cocoa notes; f23 a shard of bitterness, but nothing which subtracts from the gloss; b23.5 as cask finishes go, this one is just about perfect. 50%. nc ncf.

The Arran Malt Bourgogne Finish db (74) n18 t19 f18 b19. Arran Malt Vinegar more like... 56.4%

The Arran Malt Chianti Classico Riserva Cask Finish db (85) n19 t23 f21 b22. Mamma mia: there eeza poco zolfo ina mia malto!! Butta chicco d'uva, ee eez eccellente! 55%

The Arran Malt Fino Sherry Cask Finish db (82.5) n21 t20 f21 b20.5. Pretty tight with the bitterness not being properly compensated for. 50%

The Arran Malt Fontalloro Wine Cask Finish db (84.5) n20 t22 f21.5 b21. For a wine cask, the malt really does sing. 55%

The Arran Malt Lepanto PX Brandy Finish db (85) n22 t22 f20 b21. Tight, unusually thin for an Arran, but some lovely sweet fruit amid the confusion. Pretty oaky, too. 59%

The Arran Malt Madeira Wine Cask Finish db (77.5) n19 t21 f18.5 b19. The odd exultant moment but generally flat, flaky and bitter. 50%

The Arran Malt Moscatel Cask Finish db (87) n22 t21.5 f22 b21.5. Arran is pretty full bodied stuff when just left to its own devices. In this kind of finish it heads towards an almost syrupy texture. Luckily, the grape effect works fine. 55%

The Arran Malt 'Original' db (80.5) n19 t22 f19.5 b20. Not the greatest bourbon casks used here. 43%

The Arran Malt Pineau des Charentes Cask Finish db (94) n22.5 wispy barley clouds in a bright, sweet-grapey sky; t24 succulent and spicy. Delivery is first class, allowing full weight to the grassy barley before those fuller, fruitier notes close in. The spices are fabulously subtle and mildly puckering; f23.5 a real chocolate dessert helped by the slow build up of soft oils; b24 I may not be the greatest fan of cask finishes, but when one comes along like this, exhibiting such excellence, I'll be the first to doff my hat. 55%

The Arran Malt Pinot Noir Cask Finish db (73.5) n18 t19 f18 b18.5. A less than efficient cask from the Germans who produced it. Plenty of off key moments on nose and taste, but it does enjoy a too brief, barely redeeming Bird's Angel Delight chocolatey moment. 55%

The Arran Malt Pomerol Cask Finish Bordeux wine casks db (86.5) n20 t23 f22 b21.5. Although the cask is very marginally flawed, the relentlessness of the sweet, juicy grape and barley is a sheer delight. The odd cocoa note does no harm either. 50%

⟡ **The Arran Malt Port Cask Finish** db **(85.5) n21 t22.5 f22 b20.** One of the real problems with cask finishes is that there is no real or straightforward reference point to knowing exactly when the host flavours and the guest ones are in maximum alignment. For all this one's obvious charms, I get the feeling it was bottled when the balance was pretty low on the graph... *58.3%. nc ncf.*

The Arran Malt Premier Cru Bourgogne Cask Finish db **(86) n21 t22 f21 b22.** An entertaining dram which some would do somersaults for, but marks docked because we have lost the unique Arran character. *56.4%*

The Arran Malt Robert Burns 250 Years Anniversary Edition db **(91.5) n22.5** mainly floral with just a light touch from the barley; **t23.5** unusually light and flighty in body: most unArran...!! A dusting of castor sugar softens the vanilla even further: juicy, a touch spicy and quite wonderful; **f22.5** a few oils had formed towards the middle and follow through to the end. Again it is barley dominant with a squeeze of something citrussy; **b23** curiously, not that far away from the light Lowland style of malt produced in the 60s and 70s in Burns' native Lowlands. Not the usual Arran, but shows that it can change personality now and again and still be a total charmer. *43%*

The Arran Malt St. Emilion Cask Finish Grand Cru Classé wine casks db **(89) n24** huge aroma: thick grape and big fruitcake. The vanillas have a toasted feel to them; crisped hazelnut, too; **t22** almost too big and busy as the intensity of the grape and the roastiness of the oak clash. But a fabulous river of sweet barley flows freely enough once it gets past the early dam; **f21.5** muscovado and grapey sugars see off some threatening bitterness but it is still a bit on the heavy side; **b21.5** not the best balanced whisky you'll ever pour. But such is the sheer force of flavours, you have to doff your beret... *50%*

The Arran Malt Sassicaia Wine Cask Finish db **(92.5) n22.5 t23.5 f23 b23.5.** Unquestionably one of Arran's better wine finishes. *55%*

⟡ **The Arran Malt Sauternes Cask Finish** db **(86) n21 t23 f21 b21.** Plenty of sugars and allure. But natural caramels bring an abrupt halt to the complexity. *50%. nc ncf.*

The Arran Malt Sauternes Finish db **(84) n21 t22 f20 b21.** Strap yourself in for this one: eye-watering sultana and 240 volts of spice. Choked with oak, though. *56%*

⟡ **The Arran Malt "The Sleeping Warrior"** bott 2011 db **(84.5) n19 t22.5 f21.5 b21.5.** Zzzzzzzz. *54.9%. nc ncf. 6000 bottles.*

The Arran Malt Tokaji Aszu Wine Cask Finish db **(83) n20 t21.5 f21 b20.5.** Pleasant enough, but the wine dulls the more interesting edges. *55%*

Isle of Arran 'Jons Utvalgte' Aged 7 Years db **(87) n22** intense malt with trace vanilla; **t21.5** tangy malt thickens; **f22** a touch of spiced butterscotch and vanilla adds relief to the full on barley; **b21.5** The clean intensity of the malt is soup-like. *46%. Norway.*

⟡ **The Peated Arran "Machrie Moor"** 1st release db **(86.5) n22 t22 f21 b21.5.** A bit of a surprise package: I have tasted many peated Arrans over recent years, the majority voluptuous and generous in their giving. Yet this one is strangely aloof. The flavours and nuances have to be sought rather than presented for inspection and there is a hardness throughout which makes for a very solid dram. That said, it has many fine qualities, too. And the mouth-watering unravelling of its slightly cough-sweetish intensity is great entertainment. A fascinating, mixed bag. *46%. nc ncf. 9000 bottles.*

A. D. Rattray Cask Collection Arran Aged 12 Years puncheon no. 96.723, dist Jul 96, bott Nov 08 **(64) n15 t17 f16 b16.** Does its best to put a sweet face on things, but fatally held below the alcohol line by sulphur. *55.7%*

A.D. Rattray Arran 1996 cask no. 723 **(71.5) n17.5 t18 f18 b18.** Oops. A dodgy, sulphury, cask has slipped through the very early Arran net. *55.7%*

⟡ **Connoisseurs Choice Arran 1999 (90) n23** clean barley offers a squirt of citrus in just the right spots; **t22.5** fresh barley and newly cut grass; the oak takes a meandering course, offering the odd touch of natural caramels; **f22** butterscotch and delicate spice; **b22.5** outwardly simple malt. But spend a little time with it and drink in the understated complexity. *43%. Gordon & MacPhail.*

⟡ **McCulloch Arran 8 Years Old** oloroso hogshead, cask no. 772, bott Sep 10 **(86) n21.5 t23 f20 b21.5.** Those happy souls unable to detect sulphur should make a bee-line for this: before being treated in Jerez this probably would have qualified as one of the sherry butts of the year. *49%. nc ncf sc. Chester Whisky & Liquors. 305 bottles.*

Old Malt Cask Arran Aged 12 Years refill puncheon, dist Sep 96, bott Dec 08 **(73) n18 t19 f18 b18.** Furry, flat and out of sorts. *50%. Douglas Laing. 687 bottles.*

⟡ **Old Malt Cask Arran Aged 15 Years** refill hogshead, cask no. 7504, dist Jul 96, bott Jul 11 **(93) n24** spellbinding: so delicate, subtle and sophisticated it almost seems a shame to go on and taste: the barley is fresh but seemingly sharpened by a single shake of salt; the citrus notes are alive and alluring, hedging towards orange pith; the sugars refuse to be buttonholed: neither honey or dark brown, or a syrup. Or maybe a touch of all three...; **t23.5** mouth-watering from the off. A cascade of intense barley is followed by a thrilling delivery of massive spice. Again there is a shaft of sweetness that falls into no immediate category...perhaps nearer a gristy style; **f22.5** dips slightly as a little bitterness from the oak makes an entrance. But the spices stay buzzing and the barley continues its refreshing course; **b23** in some respects the best old Arran above ten years I have encountered. Friendly memo to my friends at Arran: please note... this is not a cask finish... 50%. nc ncf sc. Douglas Laing & Co. 321 bottles.

Premier Barrel Arran Aged 12 Years (81) n22 t21 f19 b19. Fine, malty nose and a juicy delivery but the cask cracks rather. 46%. Douglas Laing. 369 bottles.

Provenance Arran Aged 10 Years refill hogshead, dist Summer 98, bott Autumn 08 **(90) n22 t23 f22.5 b22.5.** This distillery appears to manage excellence effortlessly. 46%

Provenance Arran Aged 11 Years refill hogshead, dist Spring 97, bott Winter 09 **(87) n21 t22 f22.5 b21.5.** Not the distillery's finest hour, but enough in there to enjoy and savour. 46%

Provenance Arran Over 12 Years refill hogshead no. DMG 5998, dist Summer 97, bott Spring 2010 **(91) n22.5** toasty with attractive bourbon elements, especially the zesty orange bit; **t23** beautifully silky arrival with a big oak agenda but barley oozing every other available pore; **f23** long, full of liquorice and hazelnut oil. Improbably soft for its age with more bourbon notes evident on the attractive sheen; **b22.5** a superb offering which nutshells the distillery at this age pretty well. 46%. Douglas Laing.

⋅⋅⋅ **Provenance Arran Over 12 Years** refill hogshead, cask no. 6418, dist Autumn 97, bott Summer 2010 **(89) n21.5** mildly yeasty and, overall not quite right. But there are pockets of sweet spice which compensate; **t23** granny's cough sweets: a curious, massively juicy collection of herbs and spices flecked with light fruit; **f22** back to a more recognisable barley and vanilla mix; **b22.5** can't say I have ever encountered an Arran displaying this kind of personality before. But have to say: I like it! 46%. nc ncf sc. Douglas Laing & Co.

⋅⋅⋅ **Provenance Arran Over 12 Years** refill hogshead, cask no. 6824, dist Summer 98, bott Autumn 2010 **(80) n20 t21 f19 b20.** Along similar lines to cask 6418, but the missing sweetness and less meaningful spice exposes the oak's weaknesses. 46%. nc ncf sc.

⋅⋅⋅ **Provenance Arran Over 12 Years** refill hogshead, cask no. 7163, dist Summer 98, bott Spring 2011 **(89) n22** hint of a less than brilliant cask, but the excellence of the malt conquers all; **t23.5** one of the juiciest drams of the year: the barley is of the grassy but salty variety; the sugars take little encouragement to make an impression; **f21.5** more salt but a tightness of the cask restricts progress; **b22** fruity, fresh and frisky. 46%. nc ncf sc. Douglas Laing & Co.

Scotch Malt Whisky Society Cask 121.32 Aged 9 Years refill hogshead, dist Jan 00 **(88) n22** jagged, ragged and maltily gruff; **t23** how can you not adore this delivery...? There is a massive, salty mouth watering explosion with barley hitting every crevice; there is a salty tang, too **f21** evidence of light oil but also surprisingly bitter; **b22** Malty, salty and tasty. But perhaps a bit too course by Arran's high standards to make this a classic. 56.3%. Scotch Malt Whisky Society. 313 bottles.

Scotch Malt Whisky Society Cask 121.36 Aged 12 Years refill hogshead, dist Apr 97 **(85) n22 t22 f21 b20.** For those looking for a fruity-coffee combo. 57%. 224 bottles.

⋅⋅⋅ **Scotch Malt Whisky Society Cask 121.38 Aged 7 Years** refill sherry butt, cask no. 800397, dist 2002 **(69.5) n18.5 t19 f15.5 b16.5.** I could weep. All those magnificent casks of Arran out there and the judging panel, in their combined "wisdom", choose this sulphured dross. Astonishing. A great distillery, the Society's outstanding reputation and its members have all been done no favours whatsoever. 61.6%. sc. 668 bottles.

Victoria Single Malt Club Arran 10 Years Old sherry refill, cask no. 374, dist 1998, bott 2008 **(94) n23.5 t24 f23 b23.5.** Always one of the better experiences of whisky tasting when you come across an in-form Arran like this. 55.8%. Canada.

ISLE OF JURA
Highlands (Island–Jura), 1810. Whyte and Mackay. Working.

Isle of Jura 5 Years Old 1999 db **(83) n19 t23 f21 b20.** Absolutely enormously peated, but has reached that awkward time in its life when it is massively sweet and as well balanced as a two-hour-old foal. 46% The Whisky Exchange

Isle Of Jura Aged 10 Years db **(79.5) n19 t22 f19 b19.5.** Perhaps a little livelier than before, but still miles short of where you might hope it to be. 40% ☉ ☉

Isle of Jura Mountain of Gold 15 Years Old Pinot Noir cask finish db **(67.5) n15 t18 f17 b17.5.** Not for the first time a Jura seriously hamstrung by sulphur - for all its honeyed sweetness and promise: there are some amazingly brilliant casks in there tragically wasted. And my tastebuds partially crocked because of it. Depressing. 46%. 1366 bottles.

Isle of Jura Mountain of Sound 15 Years Old Cabernet Sauvignon finish db **(81)** n20 t21.5 f19.5 b20. Pretty quiet. 43%

Isle of Jura The Sacred Mountain 15 Years Old Barolo finish db **(89.5)** n21.5 t24 f21.5 b22.5 Hoo-bloody-rah! One of the three from this series has actually managed to raise my pulse. Not, it must be said, without the odd fault here and there. But there really is a stunning interaction between the grape and barley that sets the nerves twitching: at its height this is about as entertaining a malt as I've come across for some time and should be on everyone's list for a jolly jaunt for the taste buds. Just when I was beginning to lose faith in this distillery... 43%

Isle Of Jura Aged 16 Years db **(90.5)** n21.5 salty, coastal, seaweedy, but with an injection of honey; t23.5 carries on from the nose perfectly and then ups the stakes. The delivery is malt dependent and rich, the salty tang a true delight; f23 all kinds of vanillas and honeys carried on a salty wind; b23 a massive improvement, this time celebrating its salty, earthy heritage to good effect. The odd strange, less than harmonious note. But by far and away the most improved Jura for a long, long while. 43% ⊙ ⊙

⬧ **Isle of Jura Aged 21 Years 200th Anniversary** db **(74)** n19 t19 f18 b18. Don't know what to say. Actually, I do. But what's the point...? 44%

Isle of Jura 21 Years Old Cask Strength db **(92)** n22 t24 f23 b23. Every mouthful exudes class and quality. A must-have for Scottish Island collector... or those who know how to appreciate a damn fine malt 58.1%

Isle of Jura 30 Years Old db **(89)** n22.5 a touch of orange peel and mildly overcooked yam: soft, intriguing and pepped up further by the beginnings of a few sweet bourbony notes; t22.5 the delivery flutters onto the palate. It's a pretty delicate encounter, perhaps softened by a touch of cream toffee but there is enough life in the juicy citrus and layered barley to get the tongue exploring; spices soon begin to pop around the palate as some vanilla encroaches; f22 chewy, toffeed, fat and still a touch of spicy feistiness; b22 a relaxed dram with the caramel dousing the higher notes just as they started to get very interesting. If there is a way of bringing down these presumably natural caramels – it is a 30 years old, so who in their right mind would add colouring? – this would score very highly, indeed. 40%

Isle of Jura 40 Years Old finished in oloroso wood db **(90)** n23 a different species of Jura from anything you are likely to have seen before: swamped in sherry, there is a vague, rather odd smokiness to this. Not to mention salty, sea-side rockpools. As a pairing (sherry and smoke), the odd couple... which works and doesn't work at the same time. Strange... t22 syrupy sweet delivery with thick waves of fruit and then an apologetic 'ahem' from the smoke, which drifts in nervously. Again, everything is awkward... f22 remains soft and velvety, though now strands of bitter, salty oak and molasses drift in and out; b23 throw the Jura textbooks away. This is something very different. Completely out of sync in so many ways, but... 40%

Isle of Jura 1974 db **(87.5)** n23 t22.5 f20.5 b21.5. Stick your nose in this and enjoy those very first outstanding moments on delivery. 42%

⬧ **Isle Of Jura 1974** db **(85.5)** n22 t23 f18.5 b22. A case where the unhappy, bitter ending is broadcast on the nose. Talk about warts 'n all...!! 44.5%

⬧ **Isle of Jura 1976** db **(94.5)** n24.5 a fascinating wisp of smoke acts almost like a thread which stitches together myriad complex, barely discernable facets which make for a nose to be treasured. We are talking pastel shades here, nothing brash or vivid. Vanilla shapes the background but the light herbal notes, marrying with the deft, crushed between the fingers berries makes for the most teasing of experiences. Look out for gooseberries and a butterscotch/honey mix in particular; t24 works with rare magnificence from the go simply because the barley leads the way with such ease and there is neither OTT oils or oaks to blur the picture; varying types of sugars follow behind and spices are also in close attendance, again with a marvellous hint of smoke lingering; f22.5 shows an acceptable and understandable degree of oaky bitterness but the spices and barley still ride high; b23.5 absolutely beautiful whisky which carries its age with unfeigned elegance. 46.1%

Jura Boutique Barrels Vintage 1995 bourbon Jo finish db **(89.5)** n24.5 just how beautiful is that orange blossom? Could easily be mistaken for a high class bourbon...; t23.5 busy and lively enough to delight a million mouth nerve endings: the layering of the bourbon-rich oak is a wonder to behold; some lovely chocolate fudge, honeycomb and praline bond beautifully; f20 ...but the finish is a disappointment as the heavier distillation oils kick all else out of sync; b21.5 there are moments when you wonder if you have a possible malt of the year on your hands. Then the slip shows... Even so, one of the more memorable whiskies of the 2011 Bible. 56.5%

⬧ **Jura Boutique Barrels 1996** db **(78)** n21 t21.5 f17.5 b18. A clumsy whisky in which the fruit fits the malt in the same way a size 46 jacket fits a guy with a 40 inch chest. Either too cloyingly sweet or just too viciously bitter. 54%. 493 bottles.

Jura Boutique Barrels Vintage 1999 heavily peated, bourbon Xu finish db **(84) n21.5 t21 f20.5 b21.** Pretty peat. But not in the same league as the Prophecy, simply because the base spirit is nowhere near as good. 55%

Jura Elements "Air" db **(76) n19.5 t19 f18.5 b19.** Initially, I thought this was earth: there is something strangely dirty and flat about both nose and delivery. Plenty of fruits here and there but just doesn't get the pulse racing at all. 45%

Jura Elements "Earth" db **(89) n23.5 t22 f21.5 b22.** I haven't spoken to blender Richard Paterson about these whiskies yet. No doubt I'll be greeted with a knee on the nuts for declaring two of these as duds. My guess is that this is the youngest of the quartet by a distance and that is probably why it is the best. The peat profile is very different and challenging. I'd still love to see this in its natural plumage as the caramel really does put the brakes on the complexity and development. Otherwise we could have had an elementary classic. 45%

Jura Elements "Fire" db **(86.5) n22.5 t21.5 f21 b21.5.** Pleasant fare, the highlight coming with the vaguely Canadian-style nose thanks to a classic toffee-oak mix well known east of the Rockies. Some botanicals are there to be sniffed at while a few busy oaky notes pep up the barley-juiced delivery, too. Sadly, just a shade too toffee dependent. 45%

Jura Elements "Water" db **(73.5) n18.5 t19 f18 b18.** What a shame. Oranges by the box-full trying to get out but the mouth is sent into puckering spasm by the same sulphur which spoils the nose. 50%

Jura Prophecy profoundly peated db **(90.5) n23.5** something almost akin to birchwood in there with the peat and salt; there is a wonderful natural floral note as well as coastal elements to this one; **t23** impressively two-toned: on one side is the sharper, active barley and peat offering an almost puckering youthfulness and zest; on the other, a sweeter, lightly oiled buzz...a treat; **f22** thins as the vanillas enter; **b22** youthful, well made and I prophesize this will be one of Jura's top scorers this year... 46%

Jura Superstition db **(73.5) n17 t19 f18 b18.5.** I thought this could only improve. I was wrong. One to superstitiously avoid. 43% ⊙ ⊙

Connoisseurs Choice Jura 1995 (76.5) n19.5 t19.5 f18.5 b19. Pretty faithful to the default Jura style. 43% Gordon & MacPhail

Dun Bheagan Isle of Jura 12 Years Old Manzanilla Finish dist Jun 97 **(87.5) n23** various spices of a different hue Spring at you from every direction but all find themselves embedded in fruit wine gums; **t22** wonderful clarity to the duel layered barley and fruit juice; **f20.5** bitters out; **b22** one hell of a box of tricks before the finish. Certainly one of the better examples of spirit from the distillery for the last year or so and a much better cask would have seen this score handsomely in the 90s. 43% Ian Macleod

Duncan Taylor Collection Jura 1990 cask no. 6401 **(81.5) n20.5 t22.5 f18.5 b20.** Adorable malt delivery, if a little short-lived. 52.4% Duncan Taylor & Co Ltd

Old Malt Cask Jura Aged 16 Years refill barrel, dist Oct 92, bott Apr 09 **(91.5) n24 t23.5 f22 b22.** Ah...if only more Juras were like this... 50%. Douglas Laing. 323 bottles.

Old Malt Cask Jura Aged 18 Years refill hogshead, cask no. 5977, dist Mar 92, bott Mar 10 **(73) n17 t19 f18 b19.** This distillery does have the propensity to make one shudder. 48.8% Douglas Laing & Co Ltd. 328 bottles.

⋯ **Planeta Jura 12 Year Old Finished in Planeta Syrah Cask (86) n21.5 t23 f20 b21.5.** Some excellent finishing has allowed the malt to magnify all the juicy elements. Very rich and attractive whisky: impressed. 46%. sc. Enotria.

⋯ **Provenance Jura Over 11 Years** refill hogshead, cask no. 6827, dist Summer 99, bott Autumn 2010 **(77) n19 t20 f18.5 b19.5.** An extraordinary projection of great age is somehow made: so pine-like is it in its resonance. Some decent juicy malt but is all about sows ears and silk purses. 46%. nc ncf sc. Douglas Laing & Co.

⋯ **Provenance Jura Over 11 Years** refill hogshead, cask no. 6994, dist Summer 99, bott Winter 2011 **(73) n18.5 t19 f17 b18.5.** Takes time to get off the ground...and soon crashes. 46%. nc ncf sc. Douglas Laing & Co Ltd.

Scotch Malt Whisky Society Cask 31.18 Aged 20 Years refill hogshead, dist Apr 88 **(89) n21.5 t23 f22.5 b22.** A Jekyll and Hyde distillery at the best of times and here you get a feel of that in just one bottle. A fine, salty tang, though; like taking a mouthful of the Atlantic. 56.2%

KILCHOMAN

Islay, 2005. Kilchoman Distillery Co. Working.

Kilchoman Autumn 09 Release db **(85) n21 t22.5 f20 b21.5.** Still to completely find it's legs: a youthful malt is trying desperately hard to hit the high notes, but falling short. Or perhaps I should say flat as the fruit here is acting like caramel in dumbing down the more complex notes you know are in there somewhere...especially in the final third. Like the Inaugeral Release there is a feinty element to this, not all of it bad, but certainly marks the nose and finish. Also a charming gristiness: you feel as though you are standing there watching the barley being dried. But as yet doesn't quite have the early excellence that Arran, for instance, boasted. But these are early days in the distillery's life. And, for me, anything drinkable at all is a bonus... 46%

⸙ **Kilchoman Winter 2010 Release** fresh and refill bourbon db **(88) n23** peat with the kind of thickness one associates with the walls of Scottish castles...; a bit of dry pepper, too; **t22** sweet delivery: well oiled with a surprising degree of early oak caramels; the smoke is big though not to sure of the role it is supposed to play; **f21** a tad bitter; **b22** size doesn't really matter, apparently. Well that is certainly the case here. This may be a big boy, displaying a stonking 50ppm phenols, but its fails to match the overall elegance of the Kilchoman Inaugural 100% Islay...which is a p-challenged 15ppm. The Inaugural showed great purpose throughout. This is a big crash, bang wallop merchant. That said, fully enjoyable stuff! 46%. nc ncf.

⸙ **Kilchoman Spring 2011 Release** oloroso finish db **(93.5) n23.5** there is no doubting the enormity of the smoke, but that is matched by the deftness of the lightly molassed grape. What a surprisingly well suited marriage; **t24** and there we go again: juicy yet dry at the same time. The delivery offers outstanding early balance and control. Also, very hard to believe this is just three years old: behaves something nearer ten or twelve. Excellent soft oils which act as a reservoir for the melting muscovado sugar; **f22.5** garibaldi biscuit and coffee; the smoke does not act much like a 50ppm giant; **b23.5** have to admit: when I this was a 50ppm phenol malt finished in oloroso, my head was in my hands and my heart was filled with trepidation. This is a story that normally ends in tears... But what a surprise! A faultlessly clean butt helped, but the grape is by no means overplayed and its main function, apart from balance, appears to be to generate a feeling of extra age and tranquillity in the glass. A lovely and genuinely unexpected Islay experience. On this evidence, Kilchoman has well and truly arrived and can hold its head as high as the other Islay distilleries... 46%. nc ncf.

Kilchoman Inaugural Release db **(87.5) n21** the smoke lurks around like a detective under a streetlamp: trying to look casual but can be easily seen. A distant but distinct feintiness gives a mildly off kilter oiliness, but things are lightened by an effusive citrus note; **t23** the coppery evidence of a new still soon makes its mark but the fanning out of the phenols towards a vaguely hickory style, all underscored by sultry fruit notes, makes for a gentler experience than might have been earlier predicted on arrival; **f21.5** bitters out slightly as both the effect of the feints and stills combine; some very late spice has the last word; **b22** not by any means perfect but what could have been something of a bumpy ride has been helped along by some very good casks: like an excellent football referee, you don't notice it, but not only is it there, it makes the best of what is on offer. Not even remotely a great whisky. But a very promising start. 46%. nc ncf.

⸙ **Kilchoman Inaugural 100% Islay** 1st fill bourbon db **91.5 n23.5** a superb nose which takes full advantage of some excellent oak to give weight to the soft gristiness. Young, but no hint of a Bambi here: this has found its feet already...; **t24** fabulous delivery. Soft, genteel peats melt into a light citrus sweetness and then several waves of red-liquorice oak add just the right anchor; **f21.5** pleasant and vanilla-driven though slightly untidy, as one might reasonably expect; **b22.5** in a quite different world to the first two bottlings. Those, falteringly, gave reason for hope. But a slight degree of concern, too. This is unerringly fine: clean and purposeful and making a very clear and eloquent statement. 50%. nc ncf.

KNOCKANDO
Speyside, 1898. Diageo. Working.

Knockando Aged 12 Years dist 1994 db **(86) n22 t22 f21 b21.** An usually light bottling for Diageo. Here you get full exploration of the attractive, malty skeleton. But Knockando has a tendency towards dryness and the casks here oblige rather too well. A delicate dram all the same. 43%

Knockando Aged 12 Years dist 1995 db **(71.5) n16 t19 f18 b18.5.** If there was an award for Worst Nose of the Year, this must be somewhere in the running. 43%

⸙ **Knockando Aged 12 Years** dist 1996 db **(76) n18 t20.5 f18.5 b19.** Disappointing. As someone who knows this distillery perhaps as well as anyone working for its current owners, I had hoped for a dry, sophisticated dram to send me into various degrees of ecstasy. Instead, I am left lamenting a few poor casks which have distorted what this distillery stands for. 43%

Knockando Aged 18 Years sherry casks, dist 1987 db **(77) n19 t21 f18 b19.** Bland and docile. Someone wake me up. 43%

Knockando 1990 db **(83) n21 t22 f20 b20.** The most fruity Knockando I've come across with some attractive salty notes. Dry, but a little extra malty sweetness these days. 40%

Knockando The Manager's Choice Spanish sherry European oak, cask no. 800790, dist 1996, bott 2009 db **(94)** n23.5 I think my staff have poured me the wrong stuff: they've opened up some pot still Demerara, right...? Wrong. No, definitely from the Knockando sample. Well, well, well...let's just say it's a fruity, sugary, rich start on the nose...; **t25** actually, I don't care if this is rum or whisky. When you get flavours this beautifully defined, a body this sublimely structured...it really doesn't much matter. Oozes fruity, beautifully natural sweetened quality and complexity; **f22** a slight bitterness on the finish where, for the first time, there is a very minor blemish, but the array of sugars still make for something memorable...and absolutely 100% nothing like I have ever tasted from any previous Knockando...; **b23** I have been in the Demerara region Guyana, crawled around a rum warehouse at a rum distillery and opened a cask of rum which has less rum characteristics than this rumbustuous chappie. Quite a rum do. *58.6% 599 bottles.*

Old Malt Cask Knockando Aged 14 Years bourbon barrel, dist Sep 94, bott Jan 09 **(83.5)** n19 t22.5 f21 b21. Very sweet for a Knockando with a big barley sugar theme, despite the misfiring nose. *50%. Douglas Laing. 357 bottles.*

Provenance Knockando Over 9 Years sherry butt no. DMG 5738, dist Summer 00, bott Winter 2010 **(77)** n18 t21 f19 b19. Sweet. But no cigars to the stillman. *46%. Douglas Laing & Co Ltd.*

Provenance Knockando Over 9 Years sherry butt no. DMG 5442, dist Summer 00, bott Summer 09 **(82)** n19 t22 f21 b20. A vuvuzela of a whisky: one long, continuous malty note. *46%. Douglas Laing & Co Ltd.*

KNOCKDHU
Speyside, 1894. Inver House Distillers. Working.

AnCnoc 12 Year Old db **(94.5)** n24 so complex it is frightening: delicate barley; delicate spices; delicate butterscotch-vanilla, delicate citrus... and all the while the lightest discernible sugars melt into the malt; **t23** it had to be salivating... and is! Yet there is enough oaky-vanilla roughage to ensure the citrus and barley don't get their own way; **f23.5** a slow but telling arrival of spices fit hand in glove with the complex cocoa-barley tones; **b24.5** a more complete or confident Speyside-style malt you are unlikely to find. Shimmers with everything that is great about Scotch whisky... always a reliable dram, but this is stupendous. *40%* ⊙⊙

AnCnoc 13 Year Old Highland Selection db **(85)** n21 t23 f20 b21. A big Knockdhu, but something is dulling the complexity. *46%*

AnCnoc 16 Years Old db **(91.5)** n22 sharp, pithy, salty, busy...; **t23.5** those salts crash headlong into the taste buds and then give way to massive spice and barley; soft sugars and vanilla follow at a distance; **f23** salted mocha and spice; **b23** unquestionably the spiciest AnCnoc of all time. Has this distillery been moved to the coast..? *46%* ⊙⊙

AnCnoc 26 Years Old Highland Selection db **(89)** n23 t22 f23 b21. There is a little flat moment between the middle and finish for which I have chipped off a point or two. That apart, superb. *48.2%*

AnCnoc 30 Years Old db **(85)** n21 pipe smoke, old leather armchairs and a sprig of mint: this seems older than its years; **t23** wonderfully thick malt, beefed up in intensity by drawing in as much oak as it comfortably can; the honeycomb and molassed sweetness adds a lovely touch; **f19** big natural caramel and some pretty rough-stuff oak; **b22** seat-of-the-pants whisky that is just on the turn. Still has a twinkle in the eye, though. *49%*

⬩∷ **AnCnoc 35 Years Old** db **(86)** n21 t21 f22.5 b21.5. Tries to take the exotic fruit route to antiquity but headed off at the pass by a massive dollop of natural caramels. The slow burn on the spice is an unexpected extra treat, though. *43%*

An Cnoc 1993 db **(89)** n22 t21 f24 b22. Quite an odd one this. I have tasted it a couple of times with different samples and there is a variance. This one takes an oakier path and then invites the barley to do its stuff. Delicious, but underscores the deft touch of the standard 12-year-old. *46%*

AnCnoc 1994 db **(88.5)** n22.5 t22.5 f21.5 b22. Coasts through effortlessly, showing the odd flash of brilliance here and there. Just get the feeling that it never quite gets out of third gear... *46%. ncf.*

AnCnoc 1995 db **(84.5)** n21 t22 f20.5 b21. Very plump for a Knockdhu with caramel notes on a par with the citrus and burgeoning bourbon. Some barley juice escapes on delivery but the finish is peculiarly dry for the distillery. *46%*

Knockdhu 23 Years Old db **(94)** n23 t24 f23 b24. Pass the smelling salts. This is whisky to knock you out. A malt that confirms Knockdhu as not simply one of the great Speysiders, but unquestionably among the world's elite. *574%.*

Harrods Knockdhu Aged 12 Years (84) n19 t23 f21 b21. One can assume only that caramel (or an exceptional dull sherry cask) has been added here because it is otherwise impossible to find such a flat nose from a Knockdhu. However, the arrival on the palate is bliss, with dates combining with glossy honey and marzipan, but again the finish is only a dull echo of what it should be. Shackled greatness. 40%.

LAGAVULIN
Islay, 1816. Diageo. Working.

Lagavulin 12 Years Old 7th release, bott 2007 db (92.5) n23 t23 f23 b23.5. Brooding, enigmatic and just pulsing with quiet sophistication. A dram to drink quietly so all can be heard in the glass... 56.4%

Lagavulin 12 Years Old 8th release, bott 2008 db (94.5) n24 heady mixture of coal dust and peat reek, quite dry but not without some fried banana sweetness in the most delicate terms possible; t24.5 a lightly oiled landing allows the peats to glide around the palate with minimal friction; a light dusting of hickory powder works well with the big, but by no means brooding phenols; the sweetness levels are just about perfect; f22.5 surprisingly short with a dull toffee flourish to the smoke; b23.5 sensational malt: simply by doing all the simple things rather brilliantly. 56.4%

⁙ **Lagavulin 12 Years Old** 10th release, bott 2010 db (94.5) n23.5 a dusty, gristy combination. As though someone has swept up the remnants of an anthracite pile and mixed it in with powdered peat and grist. And then sprinkled liberally with hickory. Dry with sugars at a premium; t24 the arrival offers a surprising amount of juice: still enough rich barley still not under the influence of oak. The sugars, so shy on the nose, show all the bashfulness of a teenage wannabe on a TV talent show. Except these sugars do have talent...; all the while the smoke hangs around like reek on a windless winter morn; f23.5 long with a touch of melted molasses spread over a butterscotch tart; the peat could hardly be more gentile; b23.5 keeps on track with previous Releases. Though this is the first where the lowering of the ppms from 50 to 35 really do seem noticeable. Quite beautiful, nonetheless. 56.5%

Lagavulin 16 Years Old db (95) n24 morning cinders of peat from the fire of the night before: dry, ashy, improbably delicate. Just a hint of Demerara sweetness caught on the edge; t24 that dryness is perfectly encapsulated on the delivery with the light sugars eclipsed by those countless waves of ash. A tame spiciness generates a degree of hostility on the palate, but the mid-ground sticks to a smoky, coffee-vanilla theme; f23 light spicy waves in a gentle sea of smoke; b24 although i have enjoyed this whisky countless times socially, it is the first time for a while I have dragged it into the Tasting Room for professional analysis for the Bible. If anyone has noticed a slight change in Lagavulin, they would be right. The peat remains profound but much more delicate than before, while the oils appear to have receded. A different shape and weight dispersal for sure. But the sky-high quality remains just the same. 43% ☉ ☉

Lagavulin Aged 16 Years The Distillers Edition PX cask, dist 1991, bott 2007 db (83) n22 t21 f20 b20. I have oft stated that peat and sherry are uncomfortable bed-fellows. Here, the two, both obviously from fine stock and not without some individual attraction, manage to successfully cancel each other out. One is hard pressed to imagine any Lagavulin this dull. 43%

Lagavulin 21 Years Old bott 2007 db (96) n24.5 t24 f23 b24.5. Big peat and grape rarely work comfortably together and here we a have malt which struggles from the nose to finish to make some kind of sense of itself. There will be some Islayphiles who will doubtless drool at this and while certain aspects of the finish are quite excellent the balance never appears to come into focus. 56.5%

⁙ **Lagavulin Special Release 2010 12 Years Old** refill American oak db (94) n24.5 unambiguously Lagavulin: the mixture of chalkiness to the gristy peat, all ringed by light oil, is unmistakable. Clean, wonderfully shaped and disciplined in its use of spice; t24 the same can be said here as the nose: it absolutely screams Lagavulin and is bolstered by a clever injection of muscovado sugars which actually boosts rather than relieves the intensity. The oils are so soft, they could come from Leeds...; f22 just a shade of disappointing bitterness as tired cask cocks a snook at the continuing spices and forming cocoa; b23.5 Bloody hell! This is some whisky...! 56.5%. nc ncf. Diageo.

Lagavulin The Manager's Choice bodega sherry European oak cask no. 4446, dist 1993, bott 2009 (4th and final release) db (91) n24 not sure I've ever seen the pounding smoke from a Lagavulin quite this soft. Gently peated butterscotch tart with just a light teasing of pine; t22.5 fingers of smoke caress the palate; light oils and a slow integration of cream toffee notes; f22.5 the toffee becomes quite chewy while the delicate smoke clings to the roof of the mouth b22 a lot more toffee and oil than I expected. But the quality is beyond question: tastes like it's from the days when Lagavulin was a 50ppm merchant. 54.7% 597 bottles

LAPHROAIG

Islay, 1815. Beam Inc. Working.

Laphroaig 10 Years Old db **(90) n24** impossible not to nose this and think of Islay: no other aroma so perfectly encapsulates the island – clean despite the rampaging peat-reek and soft oak, raggy coast-scapes and screeching gulls – all in a glass; **t23** one of the crispiest peaty malts of them all, the barley standing out alone, brittle and unbowed, before the peat comes rushing in like the tide: iodine and soft salty tones; **f20.5** the nagging bitterness of many ex-Allied bourbon casks filled during this period is annoyingly apparent here... **b22.5** has reverted back slightly towards a heavier style in more recent bottling, though I would like to see that old oomph at the very death. Even so, this is, indisputably, a classic whisky. The favourite of Prince Charles apparently: he will make a wise king... 40% ⊙ ⊙

Laphroaig 10 Years Old Cask Strength batch no. 001 bott Feb 09 db **(91.5) n22.5** like a throbbing 6 litre engine below a still bonnet, you are aware of the peaty power waiting to be unleashed; **t23.5** a stunningly sublime, slightly watered muscovado sugar coating ensures the dry, phenolic explosion conjures myriad variances on a theme; **f23** a quite beautiful milk chocolate quality dovetails to excellent effect with the smoke; **b22.5** a Groundhog Day of a malt with the waves of smoke starting identically but always panning out a little differently each time. Fascinating and fun. 57.8%

Laphroaig 10 Years Old Original Cask Strength (with UK Government's Sensible Drinking Limits boxed on back label) db **(92) n22** a duller nose than usual: caramel reducing the normal iodine kick; **t24** recovers supremely for the early delivery with some stunning black peppers exploding all over the palate leaving behind a trail of peat smoke; the controlled sweetness to the barley is sublime; **f23** again there is a caramel edge to the finish, but this does not entirely prevent a fizzing finale; **b23** caramel apart, this is much truer to form than one or two or more recent bottlings, aided by the fresh, gristy sweetness and explosive spices. Wonderful! 55.7%

Laphroaig Aged 15 Years db **(79) n20 t20 f19 b20.** A hugely disappointing, lacklustre dram that is oily and woefully short on complexity. Not what one comes to expect either from this distillery or age. 43%

Laphroaig 18 Years Old db **(94) n24** multi-layered smokiness: there are soft, flightier, sweeter notes and a duller, earthier peat ingrained with salt and leather; **t23.5** perhaps it's the big leg-up from the rampant hickory, but the peat here offers a vague Fisherman's Friend cough sweet quality far more usually associated with Bowmore, except here it comes in a milder, Demerara-sweetened form with a few strands of liquorice helping that hickory to a gentler level; **f23** soft oils help keep some late, slightly juicy barley notes on track while the peat dances off with some spices to niggle the roof of the mouth and a few odd areas of the tongue; **b23.5** this is Laphroaig's replacement to the woefully inadequate and gutless 15-year-old. And talk about taking a giant step in the right direction. Absolutely brimming with character and panache, from the first molecules escaping the bottle as you pour to the very final ember dying on the middle of your tongue. This is as noisily Islay as a sky-blackening invasion of White-fronted Geese or rain pelting against your cottage windows. Relentlessly first class. 48% ⊙

Laphroaig Aged 25 Years db **(94) n23** the clean - almost prim and proper - fruit appears to have somehow given a lift to the iodine character and accentuated it to maximum effect. The result is something much younger than the label demands and not immediately recognisable as Islay, either. But no less dangerously enticing... **t24** the grapes ensure the peat is met by a salivating palate; particularly impressive is the way the sweet peat slowly finds its footing and spreads beautifully; **f23.5** no shortage of cocoa: a kind of peaty fruit and nut chocolate bar... **b23.5** like the 27-y-o, an Islay which doesn't suffer for sherry involvement. Very different from a standard, bourbon barrel-aged Laphroaig with much of the usually complexity reined in, though its development is first class. This one's all about effect - and it works a treat! 40%

⁘ **Laphroaig Aged 25 Years Cask Strength 2011 Edition** oloroso and American oak casks db **(96.5) n24** an immense nose with fruit and smoke dished out in equal measure: rarely have I located so much marmalade on a Laphroaig nose. An extraordinary degree of black pepper, too. The smoke, though intense, enjoys a wonderful degree of layering; **t24.5** the peat is, as is so often the case with this distillery, the first to show. But it does so with such a suave sophistication that one is tempted to bow at its majesty. The backdrop to this is a molassed cocoa depth. But it is the light oils bringing in the distinctive vanilla followed by the Jaffa cake orange...; **f24** lengthened by those most delicate oils, the vanilla still has a presence while the smoke forms circular patterns of almost feather-like substance; **b24** quite possibly the finest bottling of Laphroaig I have ever encountered. And over the last 35 years there have been a great many bottles... 48.6%

Laphroaig 27 Years Old sherry cask, dist 1980, bott 2007 db **(94.5) n24 t23.5 f23 b24.** One of the better examples of big sherry and big peat working in close harmony without the usual bristling stand off. A real class act. 57.4%. nc. 972 bottles.

Laphroaig Aged 30 Years db **(94) n24 t23 f23 b24.** The best Laphroaig of all time? Nope, because the 40-y-o is perhaps better still... just. However, Laphroaig of this subtlety and charm gives even the very finest Ardbeg a run for its money. A sheer treat that should be bottled at greater strength. 43%

Laphroaig Aged 40 Years db **(94) n23 t24 f23 b24.** Mind-blowing. A malt that defies all logic and theory to be in this kind of shape at such enormous age. The Jane Fonda of Islay whisky. 43%

➤ **Laphroaig Càirdeas Ileach Edition** ex bourbon Maker's Mark casks, bott 2011 db **(90) n23** a beautiful grist theme with spice and floral tones; **t22.5** lounges around the palate as though it owns the place. Just stretches out, brings a few brown sugar notes absent-mindedly into play and dozes off into a toffee-enriched land of nod; **f22** a few bitter oak notes, but the natural caramels and peaty spices tip toe around determined not to cause a scene; **b22.5** the name of the whisky means "friendship". And it is unlikely you will ever find a Laphraoig 101 any friendlier than this... 50.5%

Laphroaig Quarter Cask db **(96) n23** burning embers of peat in a crofters fireplace; sweet intense malt and lovely, refreshing citrus as well; **t24** mouthwatering, mouth-filling and mouth-astounding: the perfect weight of the smoke has no problems filling every crevice of the palate; builds towards a sensationally sweet maltiness at the middle; **f24** really long, and dries appropriately with smoke and spice. Classic Laphroaig; **b25** a great distillery back to its awesome, if a little sweet, self. Layer upon layer of sexed-up peatiness. The previous bottling just needed a little extra complexity on the nose for this to hit mega malt status. Now it has been achieved... 48% ☺ ☺

➤ **Laphroaig Triple Wood** ex-bourbon, quarter and European oak casks db **(86) n21 t21.5 f21.5 b21.** A pleasing and formidable dram. But one where the peat takes perhaps just too much of a back seat. Or, rather, is somewhat neutralised to the point of directional loss. The sugars, driven home by the heavy weight of oak, help give the whisky a gloss almost unrecognisable for this distillery. Even so, an attractive whisky in many ways. 48%. ncf.

➤ **A.D. Rattray Laphroaig '86** dist Feb 86, cask no. 2123 **(88) n21.5** surprisingly muddled with the peat uncertain just how to tackle the oak; **t23** enormous malt delivery. I sense here a rare case of the smoke and the malt itself becoming parted. The oils are much more fulsome than the norm for a laphroaig; **f22** a hint of oaky bitterness is headed off by a slow upping of the sugars; **b22.5** it's amazing how 60% abv can focus what matters in a malt when at first the paths have vanished... 60.6%. sc.

A.D. Rattray Laphroaig 1996 cask no. 7290 **(81) n19.5 t21 f20.5 b20.** Long finish, but should have quit whilst it was ahead... 60.3%

A.D. Rattray Laphroaig 1998 cask no. 80044, dist Mar 98, bott Mar 09 **(88.5) n23** pure peat ash... **t22.5** I know this is a 60+% abv cask, and that might give the impression of upping the peat levels. But believe me...this is very smoky: I've even had to turn off the alarms in my lab...; no shortage of sugars here, as well; **f21** when the vanillas finally break through, everything appears comparatively tame...; **b22** the usual phenol level for Laphroaig is 35ppm. This appears to be a little higher. Well, actually, a lot higher... Had the previous UK government known you could have this amount of fun legally, they would have banned it. 61.6%

Berry's Own Selection Laphroaig 1990 bott 2008 **(73) n17 t20 f18 b18.** Both nose and finish are disasters. Though there is a brief sweet peated revival on delivery, it is not enough to save this from being a rare Berry's dud. 55.6%. Berry Bros & Rudd.

Berry's Own Selection Laphroaig 1998 bott 2009 **(87) n21.5 t22 f21.5 b22.** Simple but effective. 58.7%. Berry Bros & Rudd.

➤ **Berry's Own Selection Laphroaig 1998** cask no. 700223, bott 2010 **(94) n24** Laphroaig showing that, given a good cask and the right number of years, it is the most iodiney of all the Islays...; **t23.5** a grippingly dry delivery where the peat smoke appears to soak up all the moisture on the palate; this is wonderfully countered by mere outlines of sugar adding balance; **f23** steadfastly remains dry but with attractive vanilla joining the powdery throng; **b23.5** another Berry's bottling with the unnerving ability to buttonhole the distillery's innate house style. 58.7%. nc ncf sc. Berry Bros & Rudd.

➤ **Berry's Own Selection Laphroaig 1998** cask no. 700254, bott 2010 **(82.5) n20 t22 f20 b20.5.** A pleasant, peaty experience for the most part. But that it will come to a vaguely bitter, muddled finish is foretold on the nose. 58.9%. nc ncf sc. Berry Bros & Rudd.

The Cooper's Choice Laphroaig 1999 Aged 10 Years refill butt no. 4211, bott 2009 **(85.5) n22; t22 f20 b21.5.** Playful, gristy smoke, light and shy to the point of being a little timid. Let down a little by the bitter finale. Pleasant enough, but goes through the paces a little. *46% nc ncf The Vintage Malt Whisky Co. Ltd.*

Duncan Taylor Collection Laphroaig 1997 cask no. 56363 **(88)** n22 green tea, grist and peat ash; t22 nervy start with little rhythm, but fun when the smoke and spices really get a grip; f22 moves towards a hickory-Demerara-cocoa finale; b22 a pea from the same pod as cask 56441, but more sweet cocoa and better balance. *54.7%*

Duncan Taylor Collection Laphroaig 1997 cask no. 56441 **(86.5)** n21.5 t21.5 f22 b21.5. After the powder-dry nose, seriously sweet. Decent complexity. *54.8%*

Duthies Laphroaig 11 Years Old (85) n22 t21 f21 b21. A smidgen oilier than the norm with some citrus scattered among the peaty ashes. *46% Wm. Cadenhead Ltd.*

Exclusive Casks Laphroaig 1996 Aged 12 Years (79.5) n22 t20 f18.5 b19. The charming nose gives a subtle hint of the impending fire waters to be overcome. This is bloody hot stuff...! *52.4%. Chester Whisky & Liqueur Co.*

Hart Brothers Laphroaig Aged 18 Years dist Apr 90, bott Jun 08 **(90.5)** n23.5 t23 f22 b22.5. High quality whisky with effortless complexity. *46%. Hart Brothers Limited.*

The John Milroy Selection Laphroaig 10 Years Old hogshead, dist 1998, bott 2009 **(85.5)** n22.5 t21.5 f20.5 b21. After the dry, demure, if vaguely citrusy, nose, this becomes engulfed in attritional in-fighting between the smoke and vanilla. *60.4% Berry Bros & Rudd.*

Kingsbury's Laphroaig 11 Years Old 1998 (93.5) n23 wow! Creamy peat...!!! So clean... t24 soft, docile delivery followed by a fabulous thickening of treacle-sweetened Laphroaig cream-rice; the middle fills with all kinds of chocolate fudge; f23.5 the smoke and chocolate continue their uniquely creamy way b23 a Laphroaig chocolate bar. Beautiful. And very different. *61.8% Japan Import System Celtic Series*

Kingsbury's Laphroaig 1990 18 Years Old Cask Strength (86) n22 t21.5 f21.5 b21. The tight, ashy nose – with circling light citrus - is followed by the most cramped of deliveries where the hot barley grunts firm peat. Only towards the finish, where some natural caramels soften and sweeten, is there any room for complexity; but in finding it, a slight bitter oak note is revealed, too. *53.9%. Japan Import System.*

Liquid Library Laphroaig 1998 bourbon hogshead, bott 2011 **(84.5)** n21 t21 f21 b21.5. Straightforward smoke fest. The tired cask means a relative silence in this library. *53.3%. The Whisky Agency.*

Liquid Sun Laphroaig 1991 sherry hogshead, bott 2011 **(91.5)** n22.5 the strands of peat and sherry refuse to meet; t24 sweet, viscous, ultra smoked fruitcake; even for those of us who are not great fans of this style, this is some experience... f22.5 dries and bitters slightly but neither the grape or phenols let up; b22.5 a battle of egos between smoke and sherry with each wielding mighty blows upon the other. Huge. *53.3%. The Whisky Agency.*

Liquid Sun Laphroaig 1998 bourbon hogshead, bott 2011 **(83)** n20 t21 f21 b21. Very similar in style to the Liquid Library '98 bottling due to a relatively inert cask. More spice evident here, though. *52.9%. The Whisky Agency.*

Malts Of Scotland Laphroaig 1990 bourbon hogshead, cask no. 2229, dist Mar 90, bott Feb 11 **(91.5)** n23 the unmistakable call of buttered kippers...unless you mistake it for a Laphraoig...; t23 you might as well use the knife and fork you had prepared for the kippers for this: thick with a fabulous deft molassed depth; an attractive wholemeal biscuit background; f22.5 a touch toasty and the last oils spreading the smoke as far as it can; b23 putting Laphroaig into a decent cask makes a huge difference. Here's one that was. *52.6%. nc ncf sc. 178 bottles.*

Malts of Scotland Laphroaig 1996 bourbon hogshead, cask no. 5382, dist Jan 96, bott Mar 09 **(95)** n23.5 when you aren't expecting a sherry cask – as I wasn't – the fresh and intact grape fair knocks you off your seat; t24 outstanding mouth-feel, with the grape managing to absorb the wilder punches of the thick smoke; the middle ground is a comfortable but complex mix of juicy date, busy sugars...and peat...; f23.5 very long with a thunder rumble of smoky spices and building vanillas and butterscotch; b24 this is a very classy bottling. I can see the Islayphiles fighting to the death over each and every bottle of this classic Laphroaig. *58.5%*

Malts Of Scotland Clubs Laphroaig 1996 bourbon hogshead, cask no. 7313, dist Oct 96, bott Apr 10 **(86)** n21.5 t23 f20. b21.5. Not perhaps the greatest oak at work, but the massive sugar compensates. *57.3%. nc ncf sc. Malts Of Scotland. 255 bottles.*

Malts of Scotland Laphroaig 1998 sherry butt, cask no. MoS 15, dist Dec 98, bott Jul 09 **(85)** n22 t21 f21 b21. Oily, sulkily peated and more tart than tartan. Sulphur-free, though, and a pat on the back for that alone. *55.5% 192 bottles.*

Malts Of Scotland Laphroaig 1998 bourbon hogshead, cask no. 700272, dist Jun 98, bott Jan 11 **(95.5)** n23.5 a stunningly beautiful portrait of smoke embers and liquorice; t24 at first compact, but then the molasses and smoke start to do their stuff. A playful butterscotch note begins to sing, but is almost immediately overcome by the gathering smoke; f23.5

remains guardedly intense but still those sugars keep searching for the whites of your eyes, carried on a wave of almost erotic oils; **b24.5** "hang on", I thought. "Have I tasted this whisky twice this year? Is age catching up on me as much as these malts?" Panic over. This is a very close approximation of the Old Master's 12, and on closer inspection I discover they are just a few casks apart... And the Old Master's ain't a bad whisky by any stretch of the imagination! However, this is even better ...much better: it is what the other might have been had not that slight oak interference. For scholars of whisky, you could do worse than buy both bottles and taste one beside the other. One excellent, the other bordering on one of the Islays of the Year. It is on two whiskies like this that you can cut your clinical teeth. *59.6%. nc ncf sc. 152 bottles.*

Old & Rare Laphroaig Aged 20 Years dist Mar 89, bott Aug 09 **(94) n23.5** both firm and rounded in its starchy vanilla opening; the smoke has faded over time and now appears happily integrated with the friendly oak; **t24** jam tart sweetness followed by a few waves of gristy peat and cocoa; **f23** just a succession of soft smoky vanilla plopping against the taste buds; even the mocha cannot be bothered to be anything other than perfectly sweetened; **b23.5** so comfortable, it's smoking a peaty pipe and wearing slippers. Brilliant. *58.1%. 174 bottles.*

⠿ **Old & Rare Laphroaig 21 Years Old** refill sherry hogshead, dist Mar 89, bott Jun 10 **(96) n24** Man sherry!! The most masculine sherry aroma imaginable with sultana fit to explode integrating with smoke fit to suffocate; fruitcake at its raunchiest; sherry trifle at its juiciest... and not even the hint of a hint of the feared "s" word... **t24** a to die for delivery: one of those massive moments that is so well controlled that it somehow momentarily seems smaller than it actually is. But close your eyes and feed into that wine and spine interplay – the smoky backbone will not be dominated by the juicy grape and vice versa; the spices sparkle while the sweeter barley shine; **f24** a long burn for the spice guarantees an even longer fade; the grape remains clean, confirming that this is one of those most rare phenomena - a quite faultless sherry butt - and juicy and between them butterscotch, hickory and tannin ply their considerable trade...; **b24** don't let this whisky deceive you: for all its finesse and faultlessness, for all its rounded edges, for all its good manners...this is a beast. This, one of the great whiskies of 2011, is a vixen dressed as a kitten; a vamp as the high school prefect. Not so much old and rare. But Old and Raring. *56.9%. nc ncf sc. 212 bottles.*

Old Malt Cask Laphroaig Aged 12 Years refill hogshead, dist Oct 96, bott Feb 09 **(76.5) n18 t20.5 f19 b19**. What little influence the cask has is not particularly positive. *50%*

⠿ **Old Malt Cask Laphroaig Aged 12 Years** refill butt, cask no. 7458, dist Mar 99, bott Jun 11 **(90.5) n22** thick, dense...not for the Islay amateur...; **t22.5** excellent delivery: a distinct molasses and liquorice heart with veins of honey. The ubiquitous smoke is both soft and firm; **f23** more of the same but now a little more butterscotch and a tinge of honeycomb; **b23** a superb cask, bipolar in personality, seemingly of smoked molasses... *50%. nc ncf sc. Douglas Laing & Co. 303 bottles.*

⠿ **Old Malt Cask Laphroaig Aged 12 Years** refill hogshead, cask no. 6539, dist May 98, bott Sep 10 **(79.5) n20 t21 f19 b19.5**. Dense smoke but weighed down further by bitter oak. *50%. nc ncf sc. Douglas Laing & Co. 262 bottles.*

⠿ **Old Malt Cask Laphroaig Aged 12 Years** refill hogshead, cask no. 6704, dist Apr 98, bott Oct 10 **(83.5) n22 t21.5 f19 b21**. Tries hard to find a rhythm despite the cask. Some milky cocoa helps. *50%. nc ncf sc. Douglas Laing & Co. 318 bottles.*

⠿ **Old Malt Cask Laphroaig Aged 13 Years** refill hogshead, cask no. DL 5612, dist Oct 96, bott Nov 09 **(85) n21 t22 f21 b21**. a very competent cask. Laphroaig offers arguably the driest of all Islay's peaty noses. And this one is dry even by this distilleries own standards. Excellent for a cold, rainy night, though...but there is a touch of the Bowmores in style on the finish. *50% Douglas Laing & Co Ltd. 313 bottles.*

Old Malt Cask Laphroaig Aged 15 Years refill hogshead, dist Mar 93, bott Aug 08 **(90) n22.5 t23 f22 b22.5**. A malt which benefits from a good quality cask to match the even higher distilling: a delightful and complex experience. What a shame the distillery's own 15-y-o could not match this. *50%. Douglas Laing. 352 bottles.*

⠿ **Old Malt Cask Laphroaig Aged 15 Years** refill hogshead, cask no. 7492, dist Jul 96, bott Jul 11 **(86.5) n22 t22 f21 b21.5**. Enjoyable and no slouch on the smoke front. A slight cough sweet character raises the eyebrows a little. *50%. nc ncf sc. Douglas Laing & Co. 308 bottles.*

Old Malt Cask Laphroaig Aged 16 Years refill butt, dist Apr 92, bott Jan 09 **(75) n17 t19.5 f19.5 b19**. Sweet, fat, rather shapeless and never quite gets its act together. *50%. 691 bottles.*

⠿ **Old Malt Cask Laphroaig Aged 17 Years** refill hogshead, cask no. 6630, dist Mar 93, bott Oct 10 **(82) n19 t22.5 f20 b21.5**. The trouble is, this is an old malt cask. Much older than the 17-y-o malt it contained. So the slight off key finale is foretold by the nose, as usual. The good news is that the delivery is a busy and delicious peat-spiced splendour with an admirable degree of sweetness. *48.2%. nc ncf sc. Douglas Laing & Co. 150 bottles.*

Old Malt Cask Laphroaig Aged 18 Years refill hogshead, dist Nov 89, bott Aug 08 **(92.5)** n23.5 t23.5 f22.5 b23. Classic for age and distillery. *50%. Douglas Laing. 229 bottles.*

⁙ **Old Malt Cask Laphroaig Aged 18 Years** refill hogshead, cask no. 7120, dist Mar 93, bott Mar 11 **(94.5)** n23.5 sensuous, sexy, salty...not sure if it is one's panting partner or a Laphroaig at its most alluring vivacious...; **t24.5** the low levels of smoke detected on the nose begin with the same laziness on delivery. However, with a minute or two the peat has not just built up a head of steam, but now there are spices buzzing in every direction; the light sugars also play an important part in bringing the oak into play; wonderful bourbony liquorice and raisin ensures the malt enters new levels of intensity and complexity; **f22.5** delicate traces of spice remain; burnt fudge and friendly oils do the rest; **b24** at times the balance and complexity between the outstanding bourbony oak and smoke cannot be bettered. Occasionally even strays into the world of pot still Demerara rum. What a quite magnificent experience. *50%. nc ncf sc. Douglas Laing & Co. 121 bottles.*

Old Malt Cask Laphroaig Aged 20 Years sherry hogshead, cask no. DL 5699, dist Mar 89, bott Dec 09 **(70)** n16 t19 f17 b18. A dose of the sulphurs, I'm afraid. *50%. Douglas Laing & Co Ltd. 286 bottles.*

Old Malt Cask Laphroaig Aged 20 Years sherry hogshead, dist Mar 89, bott Apr 09 **(91)** n23 t22 f23.5 b22.5. Weighty yet works with an improbable degree of harmony given the major players looking for top billing. *50%. Douglas Laing.259 bottles.*

Old Malt Cask Laphroaig Aged 21 Years refill hogshead, dist Nov 87, bott Jan 09 **(77.5)** n20.5 t20 f18 b19. Aggressive in part despite the sugary mask. *50%. 439 bottles.*

Old Malt Cask Laphroaig Aged 21 Years rum barrel, dist Mar 88, bott Apr 09 **(84)** n21 t20.5 f21.5 b21. Very sharp, very sweet and very brittle; the smoke gets lost somewhere along the way, re-emerging late on...very. *50%. Douglas Laing. 311 bottles.*

⁙ **Old Malt Cask Laphroaig Aged 21 Years** refill hogshead, cask no. 7459, dist Mar 90, bott Jun 11 **(90)** n22.5 pleasantly farmyardy, but they must be growing mint...; **t22.5** ...there we go: a flavour I've not enjoyed for a while – a Merlin's Brew mint and chocolate ice lolly. Which kind of fits in neatly with the mint on the nose... **f22.5** and the chocolate caramel on the finish...; **b22.5** deceptively smoky: a lot less peat on the palate than the nose suggests. *50%. nc ncf sc. Douglas Laing & Co. 122 bottles.*

⁙ **Old Masters Laphroaig 12 Years Old** cask no. 700233, dist 1998, bott Feb 11 **(93)** n23 Laphroaig, quite literally, in essence...; only a milky note which lives below ground, docks it a point; **t23.5** the overall clarity of the nose is now evident in the confidence of the clean-cut peat. Big, bold, yet refreshing and curiously delicate; **f22.5** the vanillas and the return of the milk fog up the previous clarity, but the smoke drifts to the end; **b23** a near exemplary cask. *57.2%. sc. James MacArthur & Co.*

⁙ **The Perfect Dram Laphroaig 1990** bott 2011 **(86.5)** n21.5 t22.5 f20.5 b22. Counters its slight nip and bite with an impressive interplay between the smoke, liquorice and mild molasses. A bit of bitterness creeps in at the death. An enjoyable dram. But "perfect"...? *56.3%*

Premier Barrel Laphroaig Aged 7 Years dist May 01, bott Feb 09 **(83.5)** n23.5 t21 f19 b20. Despite the tired, bitter cask finish, this is one to simply stick your snout in. *46%. 366 bottles.*

Premier Barrel Laphroaig Aged 7 Years **(85.5)** n20.5 t22 f22 b21. From an unprepossessing nose comes a malt with a lot to say for itself. The peat is orderly and the fudge on the finish is a smoky delight. *46%. Douglas Laing. 370 bottles.*

⁙ **Premier Barrel Laphroaig Aged 11 Years** **(78)** n19.5 t21 f18.5 b19. Lightly smoked with not quite enough about it to entirely overcome the bitter oak *46%. nc ncf sc. 264 bottles.*

Provenance Laphroaig Aged 8 Years refill hogshead no. 4203, dist Summer 99, bott Spring 08 **(88)** n22 t22.5 f22 b21.5. Very similar to the previous Prov Laphroaig. Quality identical, characteristics similar but reaches same point from slightly different direction. *46%. nc ncf.*

Provenance Laphroaig Aged 8 Years refill hogshead, dist Spring 01, bott Spring 09 **(88)** n21 t23 f22 b22. Lots of whisky to get your tastebuds round despite the limited oak influence. But clean and compelling throughout with just the right amount of oomph. *46%*

⁙ **Provenance Laphroaig Over 9 Years** refill hogshead, cask no. 6421, dist Winter 01, bott Summer 2010 **(85.5)** n22 t22 f20 b21.5. A very gentle, almost non-committal, farmyardy version which treads wearily with the oak and boosts the vanilla to high levels. *46%. nc ncf nsc.*

Provenance Laphroaig Aged 10 Years refill hogshead, dist Autumn 98, bott Winter 09 **(87.5)** n21 t22.5 f22 b22. A real pussycat. *46%. Douglas Laing.*

⁙ **Provenance Laphroaig Over 10 Years** refill hogshead, cask no. 7161, dist Spring 01, bott Spring 2011 **(89)** n23 salty, seaweedy and dry smoke; **t22** soft delivery with a bigger than norm smoke blast but an extra spoonful of Demerara; **f22** a lovely smoke-vanilla fade; **b22** excellent Laphroaig which differs from the distillery bottling by its relaxed simplicity, distinct lightness and an extra injection of sugars. *46%. nc ncf sc. Douglas Laing & Co.*

⇒ **Provenance Laphroaig Over 10 Years** refill hogshead, cask no. 6921, dist Winter 01, bott Winter 2011 **(80)** n21 t20 f19 b20. The usual problem of over-used old Allied casks is responsible for a degree of bitterness. But the high quality of the smoky distillate can still be marvelled at. *46%. nc ncf sc. Douglas Laing & Co.*

⇒ **Provenance Laphroaig Over 11 Years** refill butt, cask no. 6629, dist Winter 99, bott Autumn 2010 **(91)** n22.5 hard to imagine a more peaty Laphroaig than this; t23 silky delivery offering first a wave of juicy, peatless barley, then several squeezes of lemon and, finally, several oily layers of smoke f22.5 long, with a lovely manuka honey edge to the citrus and smoke; the oils seize every last complex opportunity; b23 obviously distilled from smoked lemons...and with no little success. Brilliantly different. *46%. nc ncf sc. Douglas Laing & Co.*

Scotch Malt Whisky Society Cask 29.82 Aged 10 Years refill hogshead, dist Jun 99 **(91.5)** n23.5 wonderful. No off notes. No threat of bitterness further down the line from a sub standard cask. Just an excellent salty vanilla/sweet smoke interplay, helped along by the softest of oils...; t23 my prayers were answered: on the nose I suspected and then fervently hoped the delivery would include some peaty spice prickle to ensure the oils don't dominate. f22.5 now the oils get a grip, but the lightly salted coastal theme is played to the very long end; b22.5 the detailed blueprint for how a 10-year-old Laphroaig might be expected to taste for age and bourbon cask type. *56.4% 297 bottles.*

Scotch Malt Whisky Society Cask 29.83 Aged 20 Years refill butt, dist Nov 89 **(78.5)** n20 t22.5 f17 b19. OK, I like it...sort of. And for some of you out there, that won't be enough. You'll be demanding to know why I'm not swooning just being in the same company as this stuff. Sure, it's sassy and dazzling and tripping over itself with all kinds of meaningful fruity-peaty stuff on delivery; and the mouth feel, the oils the sweetness ratio are spot on and such like. But there was a warning on the nose about the cask. Not sulphur. Just a poor cask. And the finish confirms it. Sorry: it's a bit of a dud. *52.2% 561 bottles.*

⇒ **Scotch Malt Whisky Society Cask 29.88 Aged 9 Years** refill butt, cask no. 334, dist 2001 **(75.5)** n18.5 t20.5 f18 b18.5. The nose tells you there is trouble down the line with a poor cask. And what follows doesn't disappoint. Or does, depending on your viewpoint. *60.9%. sc. 653 bottles.*

⇒ **Scotch Malt Whisky Society Cask 29.89 Aged 20 Years** refill butt, cask no. 12629, dist 1989 **(84.5)** n20.5 t21.5 f21.5 b21. A massive contribution from some granite-like muscovado sugar, aided by deft spice, saves the day against an uncompromising cask. *54.3%. sc. 605 bottles.*

⇒ **Scotch Malt Whisky Society Cask 29.92 Aged 10 Years** refill sherry butt, cask no. 700062, dist 2000 **(91.5)** n23 when the richness of the grape can be heard above the tinnitus of the peat, you really take note...; t23 lush grape and even a juicy barley blast. The peat is less than dominant; f22.5 long, with some fruit candy amid the hickory and smoke; b23.5 a rare marriage between grape and peat which appears blessed. *63.2%. sc. 584 bottles.*

⇒ **Scotch Malt Whisky Society Cask 29.94 Aged 11 Years** refill sherry butt, cask no. 2748, dist 1999 **(94)** n23 the nose is almost a replay of 29.92 but somehow manages to get the grape across with even greater clarity. What makes this even more remarkable is that the peat seems a whole lot heftier; t24 the delivery is one huge battle for supremacy between squelching grape and thumping peat. But this is pistols at 20 paces, rather than a wrestling match: pure elegance. f23 some real spice to the fade which now includes some major vanilla; b24 simply beautiful whisky. *58.8%. sc. 610 bottles.*

⇒ **Scotch Malt Whisky Society Cask 29.97 Aged 20 Years** refill butt, cask no. 10835, dist 1990 **(79)** n20 t21 f19 b19. Sweet. But another less than stupendous piece of oak making a poor contribution. *59.1%. sc. 608 bottles.*

⇒ **Scotch Malt Whisky Society Cask 29.103 Aged 13 Years** refill hogshead, cask no. 700064, dist 1998 **(87.5)** n21.5 light, grassy barley, modest smoke; citrusy; t22 clean, juicy and with the sugars in the ascendency; a little extra oil than normal; f22 big vanilla outweighs the smoke; b22 Grade A blending fodder. *57.5%. sc. 247 bottles.*

⇒ **Vom Fass Laphroaig 12 Years Old (90.5)** n22 a healthy, clean cask does little to interrupt the gentle, mildly salty smoky pulse; t22 how gentle is that? The smoke, the sugars, the butterscotch, even the oils...every element in a seemingly deliberate rhythm; f23.5 now I'm really hooked: the peat remains on best behaviour, but the rich liquorice melting into it is almost cruel...; b23 creeps up and seduces you like a young temptress in a smoky bar... *43%. sc.*

The Whisky Agency Laphroaig 8 Year Old dist 2001, bott 2009 **(89)** n22 t23 f22 b22. Exactly the kind of young, near flawless dram you should have in your hand at a ceilidh...and in the other, a woman of a similar description. *59.1%. The Whisky Agency, Germany.*

The Whisky Agency Laphroaig 11 Years Old dist 1998, bott 2010 **(86.5)** n21.5 t22.5 f21.5 b21. A lovely, if rather half-cocked whisky. All the fruit is there, the oils are in place and the smoke is ashy and delicate. But needs the missing ingredient of oak to bring it all together. *59.6%*

·::· **The Whisky Agency Laphroaig 11 Years Old** (75.5) n20 t19 f16 b17.5. Sadly, a malt of promise has been torpedoed by oak that has given way and now offers a milky note, which leads to a vivid bitterness. At a tasting recently, someone in the audience informed me they had been told that if you leave it in the glass, it goes away. If only! Yet more drivel spouted by so called experts, I'm afraid... *54.5%. The Whisky Agency.*

The Whisky Agency Laphroaig 12 Year Old dist 1996, bott 2009 (81) n23 t21 f18 b19. Superb nose with all kinds of complex ashy possibilities. But the cask errs on the unfriendly side with a disappointing degree of bitterness. *56.9%. The Whisky Agency, Germany.*

The Whisky Agency Laphroaig 18 Year Old dist 1990, bott 2008 (88) n22 t22 f22 b22. Not entirely complex of the flavour front, but certainly in composition and structure. *56%*

·::· **The Whisky Agency Laphroaig 1990** bott 2010 (81) n19 t21 f20 b21. Some anthracite in with the peat. Niggardly and thin for the most part; expansive and sweet on the rare occasions it has the mind. *52.8%. The Whisky Agency.*

·::· **The Whisky Agency Laphroaig 1990** bourbon hogshead, bott 2010 (94) n23 thumping iodine attached to butter spread on to a slightly burned piece of toast; t24 much sweeter delivery than expected: a light, sugary sheen coating the fomenting peat. Dries impressively in the middle phase while the peppers get to work; f23 dries exactly how it should, with the peat almost taking a powdery form but brown sugars ensuring balance and length; b24 an attractively shaped, slightly buttery version. Absolutely gorgeous, in fact. *56.1%*

·::· **The Whisky Castle Collection No. 12 Laphroaig 12 Years** sherry butt, cask no. 80017, dist 1998, bott 2011 (74) n18.5 t19 f18.5 b18. Imagine both the Berlin and London Symphony Orchestras being assembled to play Tod und Verklarung. One starts in C Major and the other in D flat... I could weep. Without the sulphur, this might well have been the best single cask of the year. Lovely people bottling a potentially stupendous whisky to be sold in probably the best whisky shop in Scotland... Like Strauss, what a story I might have told... *63.9%. nc ncf sc. A.D. Rattray for The Whisky Castle. 324 bottles.*

·::· **Whisky Doris Laphroaig 2000** bourbon hogshead, bott 2010 (80) n22 t21 f18 b19. Tries to spin an attractive, honeyed tale despite the remorselessly bittering oak. *59.1%*

The Whisky Fair Laphroaig 1998 bott 2009 (82) n21 t20 f21 b20. Peaty and pleasant. But far too fat, oily, sweet and graceless for greatness. *571%. The Whisky Fair, Germany.*

·::· **Wilson & Morgan Barrel Selection Laphroaig Twenty Years Old** cask no. 2348/49, dist 1990, bott 2010 (87.5) n22 thicker than a bed of nettles, with just as much sting...; t22 chewy, though barely oiled. The weight comes from a mix of vanilla and smoky grist, revealing a vibrantly young personality; f21.5 the sugars break out with the smoked butterscotch and cocoa; b22 almost impossible to believe this is 20 years old: at times you feel you can still spot the odd feinty note. *46%. Wilson & Morgan.*

LINKWOOD
Speyside, 1820. Diageo. Working.

Linkwood 12 Years Old db (94.5) n23.5 gorgeous malt absolutely bursting at the seems with barley-rich vitality; citrus and anthracite abound; t24 a quite stunning delivery with some of the clearest, cleanest, most crystalline malt on the market. The sugars are angular and decidedly Demerara; f23 a long play out of sharp barley which refuses to be embattled by the oaky vanillas; light spices compliment the persistent sugars; b24 possibly the most improved distillery bottling in recent times. Having gone through a period of dreadful casks, it appears to have come through to the other side very much on top and close to how some of us remember it a quarter of a century ago. Sublime malt: one of the most glittering gems in the Diageo crown. *43%* ⊙ ⊙

Linkwood 26 Year Old port finish dist 1981, bott 2008 db (85) n20 t24 f20.5 b20.5. Can't say that either nose or finish do it for me. But the delivery is brilliant: the enormity and luxurious sweetness of the grape leaves you simply purring and rolling your eyes in delight. *56.9%*

Linkwood 26 Year Old rum finish, dist 1981, bott 2008 db (89.5) n23.5 sharp, flinty; enticing nose prickle; t23.5 lots of juice, then a touch of spruce as the oak kicks in; the sweetness is delicate and softer on development than many rum finishes; f21 becomes dependent on cream toffee; b21.5 a real touch of the rum toffee raisin candy to this one. *56.5%*

Linkwood 26 Year Old sweet red wine, dist 1981, bott 2008 db (89) n22.5 punchy, salty and lively; distinct sherry-custard trifle; wine and oak together spin out the spice; t23 perky delivery, again with spice to the fore; juicy grape and a lively layering of oak; f21 dulls out slightly as it sweetens, again with a cream toffee softness; b22 juicy, spicy: doesn't stint on complexity. *56.5%*

Linkwood 1974 Rare Malt db (79) n20 t21 f19 b19. Wobbles about the palate in search of a story and balance. Finds neither but some of the early moments, though warming, offer very decent malt. The best bit follows a couple of seconds after – and lasts as long. 55%

A.D. Rattray Linkwood 1983 cask no. 5711 (86) n21 t22.5 f21.5 b21. Very sweet: white sugar cubes dropped into a whisky toddy. Pleasant and well spiced. 53%

⊰ **Adelphi Linkwood 26 Years Old** cask no. 5266, dist 1984, bott 2011 (94) n23.5 full on blood orange and rhubarb is fortified with wild spices; t23.5 textbook mouth-feel followed by x-rated spices which rip relentlessly into you. Some accommodating brown sugars dab a welcome degree of relief..; f23 a fabulous mixture of dark and brown chocolate (to be a little more precise a typical central American style with central German), while those peppers continue their assault; b24 Linkwood is one of those malts that is akin to going out on a blind date. You have no idea whether you are about to come face to face with something you wish not only to get to know intimately, but enjoy a night of joy without end. Or it might just be a characterless, vacuous ratbag you want to shove into a taxi and send home within the first ten minutes. Here's one I wouldn't mind spending a night alone with... and expect a bleeding back in the morning...576%. sc. Adelphi Distillery. 113 bottles.

Cadenhead's Authentic Collection Linkwood-Glenlivet 1989 port wood, bott Feb 10 (90.5) n22.5 a back-seat fruitiness allows the malt and spice to do the driving. Pretty weighty for a Linkwood; t23 a fabulous chewathon on delivery with the oak adding extra degrees of weight yet never compromising the understated sweetness; there is a vague pulpy fruitiness, too...more skin than meat; f22.5 long with a rich and very deep degree of medium roast Java coffee; b22.5 a genuine degree of complexity to this one. Beautiful. 554%. 256 bottles.

⊰ **Chieftain's Linkwood Aged 11 Years** German oak finish, dist Jun 99, bott 2011 (70) n20 t22 f19 b19. Before I read the details, I was on to them: "ha-ha!", I thought. "It's one of those sneaky German cask things, with all its tannin and sugars." But before those thoughts were set in stone, some slightly off-key better notes on the finish began to appear and I began to wonder. But I was right the first time, apparently. Always trust your instincts, I say... 57.1%. nc ncf.

Chieftain's Linkwood Aged 13 Years French oak (72) n19 t18 f17 b18. Overly sweet and latterly furry. 43%. Ian Macleod.

The Coopers Choice Linkwood 1995 Aged 13 Years (89) n22.5 just can't get enough of that grassy barley; t22.5 mouth-watering, crisp with just enough give for the gristy sugars to meet the light vanilla; f22 lots of natural but attractive caramel; b22 delightful and delicate. 46% The Vintage Malt Whisky Co. Ltd

Dun Bheagan Linkwood Aged 12 Years hogshead, dist Dec 97 (82) n20.5 t21.5 f19.5 b20.5. Above average spirit let down by a below average cask. 43%. Ian Macleod.

Fine Old Malt Whisky Linkwood 1973 bourbon cask (80) n21 t20 f19 b20. Here and there a graceful cameo is performed, especially by the odd highfaluting, debonair barley note. But this one is simply several Summers past its best. 49.7% Speciality Drinks Ltd. Bottled for TWE's 10th Anniversary.

Gordon & MacPhail Distillery Label Linkwood 15 Years Old (62.5) n16 t16.5 f15 b15. The trouble with bottling a 15-year-old from this distillery is that it falls right into the middle of the timeline when they were having a nightmare with their casks...and my word: doesn't this one just prove it..!! 43%. Gordon & MacPhail.

⊰ **Gordon & MacPhail Distillery Label Linkwood 25 Years Old** (91) n23 tangy, lively and refusing to admit its old age: a fabulous marriage of Palma violets and something much fruitier; t23.5 fabulously refreshing with a continuous retracing of its malty steps. A little curious salt sits comfortably with the oak; f22 much drier and vanillin pronounced; b22.5 if anyone is capable of making a Linkwood tick, it is G&M: wonderful! 43%

Gordon & MacPhail Linkwood 1972 (87) n22 t22 f21 b22. No yield to this hard-as-nails but fun bottling. 43%. Rare Vintage range.

Hart Brothers Linkwood Aged 10 Years dist Feb 98, bott Mar 08 (91.5) n23 t22.5 f23 b23. I had almost given up hope of seeing a Linkwood as good as this again. A ray of malty sunshine. 46%. Hart Brothers Limited.

⊰ **Hart Brothers Linkwood Aged 13 Years** dist Apr 97, bott Jan 11 (94.5) n23.5 thick barley riddled with sublime citrus and vanilla. Light oils add weight to the new mown grass; t24 silky and salivating as it had to be. Brilliant display of brown sugars and the most delicate hint of glazed ginger possible as the butterscotch mounts; f23 a long fade of all those previous characters and hardly a hint of oak bitterness but some spices for sure; b24 how much more of a Speyside can this be...? Of its style, just about perfect. 46%. sc.

⊰ **Hart Brothers Linkwood Aged 19 Years** dist May 91, bott Jan 11 (94) n22.5 despite a mild flaw, a beautiful mix of Dundee cake, apple pie with cinnamon and vanilla sponge... t23.5 full bodied delivery with the juicy grape and liquorice making an unlikely alliance; some spices and little honey are found in the chunky middle ground; f22.5 medium length with a pleasing pithy dryness; b23 maybe Hart's should buy Linkwood: they certainly know how to make it sing, even from a less than perfect cask... 46%. sc.

James MacArthur's Fine Malt Selection Linkwood Aged 12 Years bott Apr 10 (87.5) n23.5 if you are looking to discover what is meant by a "clean, grassy Speysider"...then you can do no better than this...especially if you are looking for a "nibble of citrus", too...; t22 clean... grassy and very...errr...Speysidey; f20.5 annoyingly bitter oak, but offset by late spice; b21.5 a reminder that when Linkwood is good, it can be quite charming... 40% For Harry's Pub Sweden.

Kingsbury's "The Selection" Linkwood 7 Years Old 1999 (84.5) n21.5 t21.5 f20.5 b21. Clean, light, refreshing and entirely non-taxing. 43% Japan Import System

⚗ **Kingsbury Single Cask Series Linkwood 20 Years Old** Valdespino's PX (86.5) n23 t21.5 f21 b21. While I would usually drink a PX aged 20 years in a whisky cask over a 20-y-o malt matured in a PX barrel at least 99 times out of 100, I must admit that this guy has some outstanding attributes. Especially the nose which offers just the right degree of spice to the rambling grapey sugar. The delivery is of the right stuff, too. But then, as is so often the case, enormity of the wine tends to befuddle all else. 46%. nc ncf sc. Japan Import Systems.

Malts of Scotland Linkwood 1989 bourbon hogshead no. 1826, dist Apr 89, bott Jan 10 (79.5) n20 t21.5 f18.5 b19.5. Malt, initially sweet, but a tad tangy. 53.5%. 192 bottles.

Old Malt Cask Linkwood Aged 13 Years bourbon cask no. DL 6309, dist May 97, bott May 10 (88) n23 excellent and quite elegantly clean malt; crisp and citrusy in the occasional house style; t22 much more richly textured than many examples from this distillery, with the story being exclusively about the malt; f21.5 love those late spices; b21.5 a beautiful, unassuming Speysider. 50% Douglas Laing. 276 bottles.

⚗ **Old Malt Cask Linkwood Aged 21 Years** refill butt, cask no. 6302, dist May 89, bott Jun 10 (62) n15 t17 f15 b15. Sulphur tainted. 50%. nc ncf sc. Douglas Laing & Co. 484 bottles.

Old Malt Cask Linkwood Aged 25 Years refill hogshead, dist Apr 83, bott Oct 08 (84.5) n22 t21.5 f21 b20. Proof that whiskies can be too sweet. This one is like molten sugar bedeviled by spice. Have to say it enjoyable, but you can get too much of a good thing...!! 50%.

⚗ **Old Malt Cask Linkwood Aged 26 Years** refill hogshead, cask no. 6627, dist Jan 84, bott Oct 10 (92.5) n23 pronounced grassy barley top dresses the milky oak; t23.5 every bit as juicy as the nose suggests but even displaying an extra degree of icing sugar; just a playful hint of spice and twist of citrus; f22.5 soft oils allow the same song to be repeated; b23.5 simplistic but everything it does is completed with a flourish and a touch of class. 50%. nc ncf sc. Douglas Laing & Co. 126 bottles.

⚗ **Old Malt Cask Linkwood Aged 28 Years** refill hogshead, cask no. 6499, dist Aug 82, bott Aug 10 (95) n24 excellent oak lead which fully celebrates the barley-rich freshness; more than a hint of freshly squeezed carrot juice underlines an earthy depth; t24 beautifully oiled, the forceful sugars cling to the barley as the spices make an impact; juicy and chewy for an age with massive liquorice and hickory notes which would not be out of place in the very finest bourbons; f23.5 dies as the oak and vanilla dominate but still so much to explore; b23.5 a memorable Linkwood which revels in its vivid beauty. A distillery classic. 50%. nc ncf sc. Douglas Laing & Co. 152 bottles.

⚗ **Old Masters Linkwood Aged 12 Years** cask no. 11650, dist 1998, bott Feb 11 (94.5) n23 wonderful sprinkling of allspice and bluebells on the big barley lead; t24.5 just so intact and composed as the malt forms a thick train of sharp and juicy barley which takes you into mega salivation mode; the weight nears perfection; f23.5 a fabulous display of spicy zestiness; b23.5 a quite masterful cask from the Old Master... 54.6%. sc. James MacArthur & Co.

Provenance Linkwood Aged 11 Years bourbon barrel, dist Spring 97, bott Autumn 08 (81.5) n20 t21 f20.5 b20. Sugared almonds. Untaxing. 46%. Douglas Laing.

⚗ **Provenance Linkwood Over 12 Years** refill hogshead, cask no. 6823, dist Spring 98, bott Autumn 2010 (84.5) n21 t21.5 f21 b21. Clean, lightly juiced, mega-simplistic malt designed to bulk up any decent blend. 46%. nc ncf sc. Douglas Laing & Co.

Private Collection Linkwood 1959 (90) n23.5 that peculiar hint of tinned tomatoes you sometimes get with pre-historic casks, especially sherry butts, is on full view here; also a hint of advocaat and cream strawberry sponge; t22 lush, but as it melts in the mouth, a few splinters are left high and dry; some major bourbon-style fingerprints all over this one; f22.5 bitters, but saved by a very lightly sugared, creamy mocha; b22 one of those which from the nose you know exactly how it is going to taste. And that means a lot of oak. Even so, a most agreeable very late night dram. 45% Gordon & MacPhail

Scotch Malt Whisky Society Cask 39.72 Aged 26 Years refill hogshead, dist Oct 82 (85) n21.5 t23 f20 b20.5. Perfectly enjoyable sweet malt delivery – even with a degree of early richness and fizz - but dulls out at the end considerably. 54.6%. 230 bottles.

The Secret Treasures Linkwood 1996 oak cask no. 8761, bott no. 372, dist Oct 96, bott Sep 07 **(89.5) n22.5 t22.5 f22 b22.5.** An aging second fill or young third fill cask allowing the barley to do its stuff. Charming. *43% Haromex Development GmbH, Germany. 492 bottles.*

The Whisky Agency Linkwood 1973 Aged 36 Years **(91.5) n22.5 t24 f22 b22.5.** Droolingly beautiful. *49.9%*

LITTLEMILL

Lowland, 1772. Loch Lomond Distillers. Demolished.

Littlemill Aged 8 Years db **(84) n20 t22 f21 b21.** Aged 8 Years, claims the neck of the dumpy bottle, which shows a drawing of a distillery that no longer exists, as it has done for the last quarter of a century. Well, double that and you'll be a lot closer to the real age of this deliciously sweet, chewy and increasingly spicy chap. And it is about as far removed from the original 8-y-o fire-water it once was as is imaginable. *40%.*

Littlemill 1964 db **(82) n21 t20 f21 b20.** A soft-natured, bourbony chap that shows little of the manic tendencies that made this one of Scotland's most-feared malts. Talk about mellowing with age... *40%*

Berry's' Best Lowland Littlemill 12 Years Old **(71) n17 t19 f17 b18.** Astonishingly tame by Littlemill standards. But, though bad form to speak ill of the dead, pretty naff. *43%*

Dun Bheagan Littlemill Aged 21 Years Sherry Finish **(74) n20 t19 f17 b18.** Mutton dressed as lamb. *46%. Ian Macleod.*

Hart Brothers Littlemill Aged 16 Years dist Feb 92, bott Dec 08 **(77.5) n18 t20.5 f18 b20.** Among some of the last Littlemill ever made, this isn't too bad with lots of light barley notes and not a single tooth in site, though you can see it is intrinsically flawed. Curiously, there is almost a touch of German malt to this, which is hardly surprising when you consider the type of still they were using. *46% Hart Brothers Ltd*

Hart Brothers Littlemill Aged 20 Years dist Oct 88, bott Dec 08 **(71.5) n18 t19 f16.5 b18.** Sweet. Firm. But...well...weird. Collectably so, I'd say...!! *46% Hart Brothers Ltd*

Malts of Scotland Littlemill 1990 bourbon barrel no. 915, dist Mar 90, bott Jan 10 **(91) n23** really not what I expected at all: a clean gristiness giving excellent weight to the quasi Canadian corn-oak notes. Adorably curious... **t23** now this is too good to be true: the taste buds simply salivate to the reverberating malt; a few dud oak notes but easily overcome by the marzipan; **f22.5** more of Lubek's best with a little spice, too...; **b22.5** Thomas Ewers has somehow bagged himself an eminently drinkable Littlemill. As if to prove, against the odds, that such a thing exists. He sometimes amazes me, that bloke. How does he do it...? *54.3% Malts of Scotland. 192 bottles.*

Old & Rare Littlemill Aged 19 Years dist Mar 90, bott Mar 09 **(76) n19 t20 f18 b19.** Some of the old distilled-from-razors faults are there, but the extra zeal on the barley has helped iron out the worst of the kinks over the years. *55.4%. Douglas Laing. 333 bottles.*

Old Malt Cask Littlemill Aged 17 Years refill hogshead, dist Mar 92, bott Mar 09 **(72) n18 t19 f16 b17.** Sweet barley but the finish is bitter: the kind of badly produced malt this distillery was once a byword for. *50%. Douglas Laing. 320 bottles.*

Old Malt Cask Littlemill Aged 18 Years refill hogshead no. DL 6201, dist Nov 91, bott May 10 **(68.5) n18 t18 f15.5 b17.** Can you imagine...? I am tasting this directly after the 18 year old Lochside. Probably what the term "from the sublime to the ridiculous" was invented for... *50% Douglas Laing. 174 bottles.*

⟐⟐ Old Malt Cask Littlemill Aged 19 Years refill hogshead, cask no. 6552, dist Nov 91, bott Nov 10 **(74) n20 t19 f17 b18.** Malty and juicy in part. But otherwise like chewing glass. *50%. nc ncf Douglas Laing & Co. 340 bottles.*

Scotch Malt Whisky Society Cask 97.19 Aged 19 Years 1st fill barrel, dist Mar 90 **(84) n21.5 t21.5 f20 b21.** Classic glue and paint stripper combo dissolves your teeth in seconds. For masochistic malt lovers with a sense of danger... *55.6% Scotch Malt Whisky Society. 80 bottles.*

Scotch Malt Whisky Society Cask 97.20 Aged 19 Years 1st fill barrel, dist Mar 90 **(87.5) n21** a light corn whisky style normally found in Georgia, USA...; **t22.5** delicate (now there's a term I never expected to use under this distillery) barley delivery which plays quietly with the gathering sawdusty oak; **f22** soft vanillas and natural caramels calm down a threatening spice attack but still enough barley around for a pleasant finish; **b22** much better behaved. Even a touch of elegance from this one. Hang on: it's Littlemill...I must have swallowed a few by mistake... *54.4% Scotch Malt Whisky Society. 48 bottles.*

⟐⟐ The Whisky Agency Littlemill 1989 sherry wood, bott 2011 **(89) n22.5** attractive bon bon aroma – real sweet jar stuff. Soft, fruity and alluring; **t22.5** a muzzled tiger: there is a little scratching to the throat, but it soon dies out as that boiled sweet fruitiness takes effect. Juicy...not sure whether to suck or chew...; **f21.5** a minor bitter blemish, but a hint of vanilla to the fruit; **b22.5** Wow! A Littlemill not showing its usual vampire tendencies. The right kind of sherry butt really can sooth the savage beast. If you see it, add to your collection! *47.1%*

LOCH LOMOND

Highlands (Southwestern), 1966. Loch Lomond Distillers. Working.

Craiglodge sherry wood cask 139, dist 26 Mar 98 db **(72) n17 t19 f18 b18.** Cloying, off-key, rough...and they're the good points. The nose of sherry and smoke don't gel and it never recovers. *45%*

Craiglodge Peated Cask No.137 Distillery Select sherry hogshead, dist 26 Mar 98, bott 09 May 07 db **(85) n18 t24 f21 b22.** A nose that defies description but demands witnesses so the tale can be passed on to future generations and an arrival to the palate which at once amazes, charms and, ultimately, mugs. *45%. 150 bottles.*

Croftengea cask no. 24, dist 22 Jan 97 db **(87) n22** pungent young peat, bracing, clean and even mildly salty; **t22** refreshing barley with coffee/smoke double act; **f21** vanilla and dry toast; **b22** what a difference a cask makes: entirely together and charming. *45%*

Croftengea American Oak Cask No. 32 dist Jan 97, bott Jun 07 db **(91) n21.5 t23.5 f23 b23.** A tad off key, but the enormity of the sweet oils and peat just wins your heart. This is big, mildly flawed, but stunningly enjoyable whisky. *45%. 410 bottles.*

Croftengea Heavily Peated Cask No.1 Distillery Select sherry butt, dist 03 Mar 03, bott 10 May 07 db **(94) n23 t24 f23 b24** Fabulous knife and fork malt that doesn't even try to look pretty on the plate...let alone the palate. *45%. 885 bottles.*

Glen Douglas Cask No. 1 Distillery Select madeira puncheon, dist 23 Sep 02, bott 08 May 07 db **(89) n22 t21 f23 b23.** Not exactly firing on all cylinders, with the odd note way out of tune. But very different... and delicious. *45%. 910 bottles.*

Inchfad 2001 Heavily Peated cask no. 665 dist 14 Feb 01 db **(80) n20 t21 f19 b20.** Pretty atypical of this particular malt. Missing the fruity ester kick that comes with the big peat. In fact, what big peat? An underwhelming example. *45%*

Inchfad 2001 Heavily Peated cask no. 666, dist 14 Feb 01 db **(87) n22 t23 f21 b21.** One cask on and so much more in tune. From the same distillate, but an excellent example of how a better quality cask can allow the malt to thrive. Perhaps the cask numbers are the wrong way round...!! *45%*

Inchfad Cask No. 4359 Distillery Select freshly charred American oak, dist 18 Dec 02, bott 2 May 07 db **(83) n20 t22 f20 b21.** A tad new- makey though the barley is slapped on thick and to eye watering effect. *45%. 445 bottles.*

Inchmurrin 12 Years Old db **(86.5) n21.5 t22 f21.5 b21.5.** A significantly improved dram which is a bit of a malt soup. Love the Demerara injection. *40%*

Inchmurrin Single Cask Distillery Select Madeira puncheon no. 1, dist May 02, bott Apr 07 db **(74.5) n18 t21 f17.5 b18.** Malty and fulsome. But feinty, too. *45% Loch Lomond Distillers. 685 bottles.*

Loch Lomond 18 Years Old db **(78.5) n19 t21 f19 b19.5.** A demanding, oily malt which is a long way from technical excellence but is no slouch on the chocolate nougat front. *43%*

Loch Lomond 21 Years Old db **(89.5) n22.5** a real chunky fella with all kinds of melted fruit and chocolate bar properties; a few oily nuts, too...; **t23** the usual fruitcake feel to this, plus the Demerara sugar topping; **f22** light oils carry vanilla and cocoa; **b22** a little while since I last tasted this, and pretty close to exactly how I remember it. Seems to revel in its own enormity! *43%*

Loch Lomond Copper Pot Still 1966 db **(92) n23** the naturalness of the interplay between clean, fresh grape and a bournony, kumquat-studded oak is enough to make you purr...; **t23.5** soft and sensual delivery, the grape entwines itself around the palate but without ever offering pressure; light spices and more tannin-enriched vanilla supply the weight; **f23** lightly sweetened barley, but still those spices fizz and the delicate mocha is a further treat...; **b22.5** shows remarkably little wear and tear for its great age. A gentleman of a whisky. *45%*

Loch Lomond Gavin's Single Highland Malt dist 1996, bott 2007 db **(90.5) n23 t23 f22.5 b22.** Ester-fuelled and fabulous. *45%. nc ncf.*

Loch Lomond No Age Statement db **(74.5) n18 t20 f18 b18.5.** Still feinty and out of sync, though the lively sugars try to compensate. *40%*

Loch Lomond Single Highland Peated Malt db **(74) n16.5 t20 f19 b18.5.** Feints and peat simultaneously: not something you happen upon very often. Thankfully. *46%*

Duncan Taylor The NC2 Range Rhosdhu 1995 Aged 11 Years (79.5) n18 t21 f20 b20.5 The feinty nose is compensated for somewhat, and logically, by the enormity of the body and corresponding oils. *46%*

LOCHSIDE
Highlands (Eastern), 1957–1992. Chivas Brothers. Demolished.

⠿ **Berry's Own Selection Lochside 1981** cask no. 777, bott 2011 (90) n23 vaguely molassed (dry rather than moist) a hint of burnt raisin...Garibaldi biscuits, really, with an extra dose of salt; t22.5 silky delivery with an immediate juicy flourish. Again dark sugars formulate, but now we have little fruit but charismatic barley and wave upon wave of vanilla; f22 melt-in-the-mouth vanilla and toffee; b22.5 the almost unerring palate of Mr Douglas McIvor has struck bull's-eye again...not a single off note to be had. 46%. nc ncf sc. Berry Bros & Rudd.

⠿ **Berry's Own Selection Lochside 1981** cask no. 808, bott 2011 (85) n21.5 t22 f20.5 b21. In some ways as aggressive as cask 777, is gentle. Much more roasty and bitter. The extra drama on the palate entertains but the odd note that doesn't quite harmonise. 46%. nc ncf sc.

Connoisseurs Choice Lochside 1991 refill bourbon barrel, dist 1991, bott 2008 (68) n18 t19 f15 b16. Sweet delivery and nutty at first. Then nasty. 43%. Gordon & MacPhail.

Old Malt Cask Lochside Aged 18 Years refill hogshead no. DL 6303, dist Oct 91, bott Jun 10 (96) n24 attractively floral with fabulous citrus byways; t24 the arrival is one of the most delicate caresses: although there is an immediate oily film, it is never thick enough to keep at bay an astonishing mosaic of delicate sugar tones and barley in imperious richness; the middle ground hints at wonderful bourbon-style liquorice and hickory f24 continues on its journey into the outer suburbs of Kentucky; now a few extra caramel and Demerara notes kick in and a few spices, too...; b24 another reason to weep at the loss of this distillery. Frankly, you will be hard pushed to find a malt and cask so easily in tune at this age... 50%. 289 bottles.

⠿ **Old Malt Cask Lochside Aged 19 Years** refill hogshead, cask no. 6653, dist Oct 91, bott Oct 10 (90) n21.5 something of the dank malting about this; a little mossy but sweet, also; t23.5 barley concentrate: about as intense malt (almost Malteser-like) as you are ever likely to find. Some salivating citrus and muscovado sugars ensure complexity; f22.5 simple malt and vanillas; b22.5 beautifully structured and deeply satisfying malt. Adorable. 50%. nc ncf sc. 315 bottles.

⠿ **Old Malt Cask Lochside Aged 21 Years** refill barrel, cask no. 6953, dist, Apr 89, bott Feb 11 (74) n17 t22 f17 b18. What a strange beast... I know there will be many who will swoon at this one. But there is something about it to me that is just a little uncouth. It has the front of a dandy, yet beneath the veneer we find the chancer flattering to deceive. It is the Mr Hyde to the 19-year-old's Jekyll. 48.2%. nc ncf sc. Douglas Laing & Co. 126 bottles.

The Whisky Agency Lochside 1981 sherry (86) n21 t22.5 f21 b21.5. Not exactly 100% free from treated cask interference, but at least here the grape adds a richness that its sister cask can only dream of and, despite the eye-watering sharpness, burnt fruitcake acridness has enough in reserve to leave you demanding a refill to your glass. 55.5%

The Whisky Agency Lochside 1981 sherry (82) n18 t21 f22 b22. Even though the sulphur does its level worst, such is the enormity of the chocolate, honey and toffee on show here that it is actually (once past the nose and early delivery) a very pleasant experience. 54%

LONGMORN
Speyside, 1895. Chivas Brothers. Working.

Longmorn 15 Years Old db (93) n23 curiously salty and coastal for a Speysider, really beautifully structured oak but the malt offers both African violets and barley sugar; t24 your mouth aches from the enormity of the complexity, while your tongue wipes grooves into the roof of your mouth. Just about flawless bitter-sweet balance, the intensity of the malt is enormous, yet – even after 15 years – it maintains a cut-grass Speyside character; f22 long, acceptably sappy and salty with chewy malt and oak. Just refuses to end; b24 these latest bottlings are the best yet: previous ones had shown just a little too much oak but this has hit a perfect compromise. An all-time Speyside great. 45%

Longmorn 16 Years Old db (84.5) n20.5 t22 f21 b21. This was one of the disappointments of the 2008 edition, thanks to the lacklustre nose and finish. This time we see a cautious nudge in the right direction: the colour has been dropped fractionally and the nose celebrates with a sharper barley kick with a peppery accompaniment. The non-existent (caramel apart) finale of yore now offers a distinct wave of butterscotch and thinned honey...and still some spice. Only the delivery has dropped a tad fast...but a price worth paying for the overall improvement. Still a way to go before the real Longmorn 16 shines in our glasses for all to see and fall deeply in love with. Come on lads in the Chivas lab: we know you can do it... 48%

Adelphi Longmorn 1992 Aged 17 Years bourbon hogshead, cask no. 48430, bott 2010 (86.5) n22 t22 f21 b21.5. Exceptionally stodgy for a Longmorn and at times seems like a convention for dark sugars. Even so, a little bitter at the death, though some half-hearted mocha tries to make amends. 53.9% 186 bottles.

Berry's Own Selection Longmorn 1996 bott 2008 (**91.5**) n22 t22.5 f23.5 b23.5. Now that Benriach is no longer a part of Chivas, will we be seeing more delightfully smoked Longmorns like this, only officially? *56.7%. Berry Bros & Rudd.*

Cärn Mör Vintage Collection Longmorn 1996 hogshead, cask no. 156794, bott 2009 (**82.5**) n20 t21 f21.5. Malty, gristy almost, and exceptionally young in style for its age. Not entirely representative of this distillery's usually excellent output. **b20** *46%.*

The Coopers Choice Longmorn 1997 Aged 12 Years (**88**) n23 rotund, with some oils clinging to the barley essential to broadening its scope and bringing on board the meatier elements; t22 again those oils play a vital role: this time marrying the juicier barley to the maple-esque sugars; f21.5 clean vanilla; b21.5 a dram which will never over tax you. But what it does do, it accomplishes with a degree of style. *46% The Vintage Malt Whisky Co. Ltd*

Dun Bheagan Longmorn Aged 11 Years Madeira Finish (**82**) n21 t22 f19 b20. A pretty whisky but, for all its mildly fruity make-up, lacks personality. *43%.*

Duthies Longmorn 19 Years Old (**93.5**) n24 one of those glorious noses which appears to have so much intensity, yet always understated and in control. Naturally, the vanillas hold the largest hand but the delicate custardy sweetness balances perfectly with a greengage barley and marshmallows... scrummy; t23.5 ditto the delivery... hugely intense, just somehow relaxed and refined. Again the vanillas lead the way, helped along by biscoito de polvilho which simply melts in the mouth; f23 more of the same, now with a little extra dryness **b23** the Longmorn of your dreams. For its age, just about faultless. *46% Wm. Cadenhead Ltd*

Gordon & MacPhail Distillery Label Longmorn 30 Years Old (**86**) n21 t23.5 f21.5 b20. Mind the very serious splinters amid the orange peel. Almost a parody of an over-the-top, over-aged malt. But strangely, and against all odds, it retains fragments of pure, indisputable deliciousness. *43% Gordon & MacPhail*

⁙ **Gordon & MacPhail Private Collection Longmorn 1964** (**86**) n22 t23.5 f21.5 b19 [That's on opening and tasting within first 15 minutes. Now leave for 45 mins minimum in warm room and this is what you get: (90.5) n24 t23 f22.5 b21...] I have been shot back 25 years to my days in Fleet Street. Now and then, as I did the rounds of the famous hostelries there, I would end up in El Vinos. And they would have their own single malt bottling, usually dripping in a sherry not so much sumptuous as pompous. And I would hate it. Today, after nearly 20 years of battling, often it appears single-handedly, against appalling sulphur-fucked casks, I tend to view these types of malt with a little more latitude than I once might. There is absolutely no sulphur at all; sadly, little sign of the whisky, either, which has been entirely lost under the mountainous weight of the lavish grape. But, nonetheless, I now wholeheartedly commend this whisky to you, where once I would have counselled a wide berth. Not for its greatness, but, rather, for its touching adherence to an ancient whisky style close to extinction and that is unlikely ever to be repeated. *51.9%*

⁙ **Gordon & MacPhail Longmorn 1968** (**95.5**) n23.5 marzipan with a fleck of ginger and thick cut marmalade: additional sugars of the honeycomb variety; t24 exceptional delivery: the oak-blooded spices arrive at the same moment as the honeyed barley for one memorable rush; stupendous grassy malt cleans the palate to make way for a slow cocoa-enriched burn...; f24 confirmation of a brilliant cask comes with this finale which is entirely free of any element of bitterness. Instead, the spices play a subdued role in keeping with the buttered coconut cake exit; a wondrous degree of cocoa and soft oil make it almost too good to be true; **b24** a fabulous malt which goes to prove just how good a preservative alcohol is. The higher strength does this malt no harm at all; indeed, it helps form a Longmorn of as high a quality for its age as you are ever likely to encounter. *60.5%. Exclusive bottling for The Whisky Fair.*

Gordon & MacPhail Longmorn 1969 Cask Strength refill butt no. 5305, bott 2009 (**94.5**) n24.5 spellbinding infusion of fruit, coffee and some thick bourbony notes. Sheer class; t23.5 punchy oak delivery, some seriously stavey moments, also burnt raisin and Demerara-sprinkled fruitcake makes for a eye-watering but, frankly, fabulous experience; f23 long with more mocha and overcooked, raisin-burned fruitcake; b23.5 every year I pray a malt like this turns up. And because of the quality of recent sherry butts, this kind of experience is not going to just get rarer but within a decade will be only a part of the memory. Enjoy while you still can. *57.7%. Gordon & MacPhail for TWE's 10th Anniversary.*

⁙ **Gordon & MacPhail Longmorn 1971** (**90**) n21 an over-tired bourbon...? t23 the sugars work overtime to keep the forest of oak grounded. The very mildest puff of smoke still detectable and some cocoa, too. The result, aided by soft barley oil, is a surprisingly well adjusted Longmorn; f22.5 the oaks creep back into play, but the spices team up with those gorgeous sugars to do the trick; b23.5 a much more integrated whisky than the G&M Rare

Vintage version. In fact, knowing the distillery and the frighteningly advanced age of the malt, this is very much an old dog showing new tricks... 43%

⟨ **Gordon & MacPhail Rare Vintage Longmorn 1971** (86.5) n21 t22.5 f21 b21.5. A pleasing old chap which is puffing a bit with all that oak it has to carry. But a moderate injection of maple syrup gives him the energy to carry on. 47.4%. Gordon & MacPhail. Exclusive bottling for The Whisky Agency.

James MacArthur's Old Masters Longmorn 1997 Aged 13 Years cask no. 156791, bott Oct 09 (86.5) n20.5 t22.5 f21.5 b22. Despite the limitations of the cask, this is sweet and malty and at times the chocolate fudge hits the spots. You fancy a bit of smoke has crept in there, too. 56.9%

Kingsbury's Finest and Rarest Longmorn 26 Years Old 1980 (88) n22.5 slightly tart but the elderflower and butterscotch is superb; t23 mouth watering, lightly sugared barley helps keep control of the usual big oak spice kick; f20.5 dries towards a milky mocha; b22 never settles for the easy ride at any given time. Busy and beautiful. 52.6%. Japan Import System.

Kingsbury's Finest & Rarest Longmorn 1980 (89) n21.5 t23.5 f22 b22. The big oak is well orchestrated in this chunky, stylish bottling. 52.6%. Japan Import System.

⟨ **Malts Of Scotland Longmorn 1976** bourbon hogshead, cask no. 5892, dist May 76, bott Jan 11 (80) n19 t20 f21 b20. Pleasant, but rather one dimensional after extracting all the natural caramels the cask possessed. 51.5%. nc ncf sc. Malts Of Scotland. 132 bottles.

⟨ **Masterpieces Longmorn 1978** bourbon cask (86) n22.5 t22.5 f20 b21. This has many things going for it – except maybe its age. I have never understood why Longmorn is not launched more often in something around the 8 to 14 years range, when it is at its most effervescent. Here we have another example of the malt hanging on to the cliff face by its finger nails. All the fun and complexity is found on the nose and delivery where the sugar and barley are still in play. Just. 58%. nc ncf sc. Speciality Drinks Ltd. 135 bottles.

Montgomeries Longmorn 1975 cask no. 3967, dist Mar 75, bott Jul 08 (94) n23 t23 f24 b24. This is exactly how you want to find your old whisky: showing age but the grey hairs are confined to the temples and the sophistication is effortless. 46%. Montgomerie's & Co. Ltd.

Old Malt Cask Longmorn Aged 14 Years refill hogshead, dist Oct 94, bott Dec 08 (83) n20 t23 f19 b21. The thin, unpromising nose is reflected in the stingy finish. However, it is impossible not to be amazed by the beauty of the rich malt delivery which is far more in keeping with the distillery's hallmark. 50%. Douglas Laing. 352 bottles.

Old Masters Longmorn Aged 12 Years cask no. 156777, dist 1996, bott 2008 (85) n22 t21.5 f20.5 b21. Natural caramels have a big say on this otherwise misty affair. 60.1%

Old Malt Cask Longmorn Aged 19 Years refill hogshead, dist Apr 89, bott Sep 08 (88) n22 t23 f21 b22. There is sometimes no keeping an excellent distillery down. 50%. 313 bottles.

⟨ **Provenance Longmorn Over 8 Years** refill hogshead, cask no. 6830, dist Autumn 02, bott Autumn 2010 (93) n23 the lightest possible strata of smoke shoehorns in a biscuit-like maltiness; t24 deft barley showing a surreal number of different sugar notes is happy to embrace the growing vanilla and butterscotch; light spice enters the fray; f23 a surprise hint of gooseberry does nothing to shake this off its intensely malty course...; b23 who gives a toss that this is an eight year old? Great whisky is just that...however old it may be. Adorable and, frankly, must have. 46%. nc ncf sc. Douglas Laing & Co.

Provenance Longmorn Aged 10 Years bott 2009 (79) n20 t20 f19 b20 Pleasant. Sweet but surprisingly dull. 46%. Douglas Laing.

Provenance Longmorn Over 10 Years refill hogshead no. DMG 5575, dist Summer 99, bott Autumn 09 (86) n21 t22.5 f21 b21.5. Thank heavens someone was willing to bottle this distillery at something other than a pensionable age. This one enjoys some serious sugary gloss to the intense barley. 46% Douglas Laing & Co Ltd

Scotch Malt Whisky Society Cask 7.58 Aged 19 Years refill barrel, dist Feb 90 (87) n22 vanilla ice cream, complete with caramelised cornet; t22 bright barley start is tempered with a quick surge of oak and massive spice; f21.5 an oaky rumble lightened by shards of sweet barley; b21.5 a recently excellent cask still with plenty to enjoy but on its way down. 51.5% Scotch Malt Whisky Society. 188 bottles.

Scotch Malt Whisky Society Cask 7.59 Aged 20 Years refill barrel, dist Feb 90 (79.5) n21 t20 f19 b19.5. Snatched from oaky jaws just a little too late... 48.7% Scotch Malt Whisky Society. 185 bottles.

Scotch Malt Whisky Society Cask 7.60 Aged 24 Years refill hogshead, dist Nov 85 (89) n22 the vanilla-barley relationship is simply so complex...; t22 juicy, salivating barley with no shortage of oaky pep and natural caramels; f22 long with this oak-barley battle going to the end, entirely unresolved; b23 one of those where a little bit of over-aging is not a bad thing. 52.3% 220 bottles

Scotch Malt Whisky Society Cask 7.56 Aged 25 Years refill hogshead, dist Oct 84 **(88.5)** n22 no shortage of cedar wood; t23.5 enormous! Fabulous strands of manuka honey seeing off an attempted oaky coup. The spices are pounding and ceaseless; f21 the fragile malt has difficulty keeping the oak in check, but manages...just; b22 a big whisky that is taken as far as it can by the oak. Saved, beautifully so, by the honey... *56.8% Scotch Malt Whisky Society. 193 bottles.*

Scotch Malt Whisky Society Cask 7.57 Aged 25 Years refill hogshead, dist Oct 84 **(86)** n21.5 t22 f21.5 b21. Another strikingly attractive malt and very much along the same lines as 7.56. However, here the oak is just a fraction too striking for greatness, though again the spices, softened by natural caramels, are a treat. *58.7% Scotch Malt Whisky Society. 243 bottles.*

Scotch Malt Whisky Society Cask 7.55 Aged 40 Years 1st fill sherry butt, dist Dec 68 **(94)** n24 oaky woodiness – the inside of old mahogany drawers comes to mind – but my goodness: just how clean is that intense grape? One of those great Chivas casks of the 1960s being taken to its utmost; t24.5 silk. No, silk just isn't as sleek and embracing. The taste buds are sent into mouth watering spasms as the oak and grape fight out the most seemly of battles. Neither wins...neither try as this is as harmonious as you could pray for; some stunning medium roast Mysore coffee threads its way through the ripe plum; f22.5 as usual the end shows a degree of over oaked bitterness. But still the oloroso sooths and caresses; b23 even though it is obvious that the oak has a little too much to say, such is the high standing of the sherry butt that not only is it capable of withstanding the onslaught but offers enough to ensure complexity. *54.9% Scotch Malt Whisky Society. 451 bottles.*

➤ **Scotch Malt Whisky Society Cask 7.65 Aged 21 Years** 2nd fill sherry butt, cask no. 18573, dist 1989 **(76)** n18 t21 f18 b19. I adore the defiant glow of honey and marmalade as another sherry butt bites the dust. *55.2%. sc. 164 bottles.*

➤ **Scotch Malt Whisky Society Cask 7.66 Aged 18 Years** refill hogshead, cask no. 48422, dist 1992 **(83)** n22 t21.5 f19.5 b20. A good example of a well made, firmly structured malt suffering somewhat at the hands of a cask not quite up to the task. *49.4%. sc. 215 bottles.*

➤ **The Whisky Agency Longmorn 33 Years Old** dist 1976, bott 2010 **(84.5)** n20 t22 f21 b21.5. Even though it is far too oaked for its own good, you cannot spend less than a good 20 mins on this one. Sweetened custard does its best to see off the oaky excess. *52.5%*

➤ **The Whisky Agency Longmorn 1975** bott 2010 **(94)** n24 once the haze of natural caramels clear, we are treated to about as clean a butterscotch tart with fruit topping as you are ever likely to find; the most delicate sugars are pure textbook; t23.5 a melt-in-the-mouth merchant. Some saltiness keeps you ever mindful of its age. But those near perfect sugars on the nose play a huge part in bringing every atom of barley to the fore; f22.5 superb vanilla and the most subtle of spices underlines the quality of the oak: not a single bitter note to be had...; b24 at first seems docile and immaculately mannered, like some Edwardian upper-class sloth. But time in the glass allows the magnificence of this dram to be played out. *52.5%*

➤ **The Whisky Agency Longmorn 1976** bott 2010 **(89.5)** n23 pungent, lively and is hardly subtle about its old age. Plenty of exotic fruit, though; t23 purringly excellent delivery with a wonderfully delicate introduction to the milky sugars; a touch of coconut water making the fruit even more exotic; f21.5 dries with a salty coffee effect; b22 deliciously piles on the exotic fruit. But the oak has a final, salty, say *50.2%. The Whisky Agency.*

The Whisky Society Longmorn 1990 bott Oct 08 **(92)** n23.5 big bourbony infusion of decaying kumquat and old leather...wonderful! t23 hold on to your hats as the first layer of enamel is scorched off by a searing spice attached to the molassed sugars; f23 quietens and the barley is back on track, against a lightly molassed emulsion and lightly charred vanillas; b22.5 a dram to bring a tear to the eye...for many reasons! *58% Speciality Drinks Ltd*

THE MACALLAN
Speyside, 1824. Edrington. Working.

The Macallan 7 Years Old db **(89)** n23 beautifully clean sherry, lively, salty, gentle peppers; t23 mouth-filling and slightly oily. Some coffee tones intertwine with deep barley and fruit; f21 unravels to reveal very soft oak and lingering fruity spice; b22 an outstanding dram that underlines just how good young malts can be. Fun, fabulous and in recent bottlings has upped the clarity of the sherry intensity to profound new heights. *40%*

The Macallan Fine Oak 8 Years Old db **(82.5)** n20.5 t22 f20 b20. A slight flaw has entered the mix here. Even so, the barley fights to create a distinctive sharpness. However, a rogue sherry butt has put paid to any hopes the honey and spice normally found in this brand. *40%*

The Macallan 10 Years Old db **(91)** n23 oloroso appears to be the big noise here, but clever, almost meaty, incursions of spice offer an extra dimension; fruity, yet bitter-sweet:

dense yet teasingly light in places; **t23** chewy fruit and the old Macallan silk is back: creamy cherries and mildly under-ripe plum ensures a sweet-sour style; **f21.5** traces of vanilla and barley remind us of the oak and barley, but the fruit reverberates for some while, as does some annoying caramel; **b23.5** for a great many of us, it is with the Mac 10 our great Speyside odyssey began. It has to be said that in recent years it has been something of a shadow of its former great self. However, this is the best version I have come across for a while. Not perhaps in the same league as those bottlings in the 1970s which made us re-evaluate the possibilities of single malt. But fine enough to show just how great this whisky can be when the butts have not been tainted and, towards the end, the balance between barley and grape is a relatively equal one. 40%

The Macallan 10 Years Old Cask Strength db **(85) n20 t22 f22 b21.** Enjoyable and a would give chewing gum a run for its money. But over-egged the sherry here and not a patch on the previous bottling. 58.8%. Duty Free.

The Macallan Fine Oak 10 Years Old db **(90) n23** finely tuned and balanced: everything on a nudge-nudge basis with neither fruit nor barley willing to come out and lead: really take your time over this to maximise the entertainment; **t22.5** brimming with tiny, delicate oak notes which just brush gently, almost erotically, against the clean barley; **f21.5** drier, chewier and no less laid-back; **b22** much more on the ball than the last bottling of this I came across. Malts really come as understated or clever than this. 40%

The Macallan Sherry Oak 12 Years Old db **(93) n24** thick, almost concentrated grape with a stunning degree of light spices. Topped with boiled greengage; **t23.5** clean sherry is heralded not just by vanilla-thickened grape but a deft muscovado sweetening and a light seasoning of spice; **f22.5** cocoa, vanilla and fudge. Remains clean and beautifully layered; **b23** I have to say that some Macallan 12 I have tasted on the road has let me down in the last year or so. This sample before me is virtually faultless. Virtually a time machine back to another era... 40% ⊙ ⊙

The Macallan 12 Years Old Sherry Oak Elegancia db **(86) n23 t22 f20 b21.** Promises, but delivers only to an extent. 40%

The Macallan Fine Oak 12 Years Old db **(95.5) n24** faultless, intense sherry light enough to allow the fabulous apple and cinnamon to blend in with the greengage and grape; **t24** near perfect entry: firm, rummy sugars are thinned by a barley-grape double act; juicy yet enough vanilla to ensure structure and layering; **f23.5** delicate spice keeps the finish going and refuses to let the muscovado-grape take control; **b24** a whisky whose quality has hit the stratosphere since I last tasted it. I encountered a disappointing one early in the year. This has restored my faith to the point of being a disciple... 40% ⊙ ⊙

Macallan Gran Reserva Aged 12 Years db **(92) n23** massive cream sherry background with well matured fruit cake to the fore: big, clean, luxurious in a wonderfully old-fashioned way. Oh, and a sprinkling of crushed sultana just in case the grapey message didn't get across... **t24** a startlingly unusual combination on delivery: dry yet juicy! The ultra fruity lushness is dappled with soft spices; oak arriving early-ish does little to alter the path of the sweetening fruit; just a hint of hickory reveals the oak's handiwork towards the middle; **f22** dry, as oloroso does, with a vaguely sweeter edge sparked by notes of dried date; the delicate but busy spices battle through to the toffeed end; **b23** well, you don't get many of these to the pound. A real throwback. The oloroso threatens to overwhelm but there is enough intrigue to make for a quite lovely dram which, as all good whiskies should, never quite tells the story the same way twice. Not entirely without blemish, but I'm being picky. A Macallan soaked in oloroso which traditionalists will swoon over. 45.6%

The Macallan Fine Oak 15 Years Old db **(79.5) n19 t21.5 f19 b20.** As the stock of the Fine oak 12 rises, so its 15-y-o brother, once one of my Favourite drams, falls. Plenty to enjoy, but a few sulphur stains remove the gloss. 43% ⊙ ⊙

The Macallan Fine Oak 17 Years Old db **(82) n19.5 t22 f19.5 b21.** Where once it couldn't quite make up its mind on just where to sit, it has now gone across to the sherry benches. Sadly, there are a few dissenters. 43% ⊙ ⊙

The Macallan Sherry Oak 18 Years Old db **(87) n24** near perfection as to regard the sherry: soft, oloroso led, the most playful spice prickle with the balance of sweet and dry almost faultless: stick your nose in this and abide a while... **t22** soft, silky...but without backbone. Limited development and caramel appears to outwit the malt; **f20** pretty dull and lifeless, caramel apart: I really can't get my head around this... **b21** an entirely underpowered dram. The body doesn't even come close to matching the nose which builds up the expectancy to enormous levels and, by comparison to the Independents, this at 43% appears weak and unrepresentative. Why this isn't at 46% at the very least and unambiguously uncoloured, I have no idea. 43% ⊙

The Macallan 18 Years Old dist 1991 db (87) n22 some seriously old-fashioned Macallan oloroso in finest, most expansive form...but a nagging light off-note just detectable; t22.5 the delivery through to the middle is just a succession of juicy, mega rich grape; but in the background... f21 a touch of Mysore enriches the fruit further...then a slight furry, bitter note...; b21.5 honestly: I could weep. Some of the sherry notes aren't just textbook...they go back to the Macallan manuals of the early 1970s. But the achievable greatness is thwarted by the odd butt of you know what... 43%. *Imported by Remy Cointreau, USA.*

The Macallan Fine Oak 18 Years Old db (94.5) n23.5 classic cream sherry aroma: thick, sweet but enlivened by a distinct barley sharpness; t24 juicy, chewy, clean and intense delivery. Strands of honey and syrup help pave the way for vanillas and spices to get a grip; the complexity levels are startling and the weight just about spot on; f23 a degree of blood orange bitterness amid the cocoa and raisin; the spices remain lazy, the texture creamy; b24 is this the new Fine Oak 15 in terms of complexity? That original bottling thrived on the balance between casks types. This is much more accentuated on a cream sherry persona. But this sample is sulphur-free and quite fabulous. 43% ☉☉

⠿ **The Macallan Masters Of Photography Albert Watson 20 Years Old** db (94.5) n24 if there is such a thing as a seismograph for measuring sherry, this would be bouncing from wall to wall. Concentrated noble rot, with a few roasted almonds and spices tossed in; t24.5 as soft as a 20-year-old sherry... without the whisky. It works beautifully as the required balance between sugars and spice is there in bundles; and as well as sherry trifle, there is blackcurrant on butterscotch, too; f22.5 just a hint of bitterness but plenty of over-ripe greengage and toasty vanilla to see you off; b23.5 it's one of those! (Bizarrely, as I wrote that, Milton Jones said exactly the same words on the radio...spooky!) Once I would have marked this down as being simply too sherry drowned. But since clean sherry butts are now at a premium, I am seeing whiskies like this in a very different light: certainly not in the negative... It can still be argued that this is far too sherry driven, with too much else overpowered. And maybe just a little too bitter on the finish. But of its once thought extinct type, staggering. 46.5%. *Edrington.*

The Macallan Fine Oak 21 Years Old db (84) n21 t22 f20 b21. An improvement on the characterless dullard I last encountered. But the peaks aren't quite high enough to counter the sulphur notes and make this a great malt. 43% ☉☉

The Macallan 25 Years Old db (84.5) n22 t21 f20.5 b21. Dry with an even drier oloroso residue; blood orange adds to the fruity mix. Something, though, is not entirely right about this and one fears from the bitter tang at the death that a rogue butt has gained entry to what should be the most hallowed of dumping troughs. 43%

The Macallan Fine Oak 25 Years Old db (90) n22 coal dusty: the plate of old steam engines; a speckle of raisin and fruitcake; t23.5 despite the early signs of juicy grape, it takes only a nanosecond or two for a much drier oak-spiced spine to take shape; the weight is never less than ounce perfect, however; f22 puckering, aged oak leaves little doubt that this is a malt of advanced years, but a few liquorice notes ensure a degree of balance; b22.5 the first time I tasted this brand a few years back I was knocked off my perch by the peat reek which wafted about with cheerful abandon. Here the smoke is tighter, more shy and of a distinctly more anthracitic quality. Even so, the sweet juiciness of the grape juxtaposes gamely with the obvious age to create a malt of obvious class. 43%

The Macallan Fine Oak 25 Years Old db (89) n23 cream soda meats cream sherry... but where is the smoke that was always apparent...? Are the remnants tucked away in those spices...? Lubeck marzipan makes a surprise appearance; t23 almost a drier version of the Fine Oak 18, with a little extra tannin; a distinctive honey and marmalade thread; f21 bitters to furry blood oranges; b22 very similar in make up to the Fine Oak 18. However, the signature smoke has vanished, as I suppose over time it must. Not entirely clean sherry, but much remains to enjoy. 43% ☉☉

The Macallan Fine Oak 30 Years Old db (81.5) n22 t22 f18 b19.5. For all its many riches on delivery, especially those moments of great bourbon-honey glory, it has been comprehensively bowled middle stump by the sherry. Gutted. 43% ☉☉

The Macallan 40 Years Old dist 10 May 61, bott 09 Sep 05 db (90) n23 no shortage of oak, as you might expect. But nutty, too (chestnut pure, to be precise). The scope is broadened with a distracted smokiness while oak maximizes the longer it stays in the glass; t23 soft and yielding, with a lovely dovetailing of vanillins and delicate sherry. The grape appears to gain control with a sweet barley sidekick before the oak recovers; f22 soft oils formulate with some laite and slightly salted, Digestive-style biscuit. Gentle spices delight; b22 very well-rounded dram that sees off advancing years with a touch of grace and humour. So often you think the oak will take control, but each time an element intervenes to win back the balance. It is as if the dram is teasing you. Wonderful entertainment. 43%

The Macallan 50 Years Old dist 29 Mar 52, bott 21 Sep 05 db **(90) n25** we all have pictures in our minds of the perfect grandmother: perhaps grey-haired and knitting in her rocking-chair. Or grandfather: kindly, gentle, quietly wise, pottering about in the shed with some gadget he has just made for you. This, then, is the cliched nose of the perfect 50-year-old malt: time-defying intensity and clarity; attractive demerara (rum and sugar!) sweetened coffee, a tantalizing glimpse at something smoky and sensationally rich grape and old fruit cake. So that the sweetness and dryness don't cancel each other out, but complement each other and between them tell a thousand tales. Basically, there's not much missing here... and absolutely all you could wish to find in such an ancient Speysider...; **t23** dry delivery with the oak making the early running. But slowly the grape and grain fights back to gain more than just a foot-hold; again telling wisps of smoke appear to lay down a sound base and some oily barley; **f19** now the oak has taken over. There is a burnt-toast and burnt raisin bitterness, lessened in effect marginally by a sweeter vanilla add-on; **b23** loses it at the end, which is entirely excusable. But until then it has been one fabulous experience full of passion and complexity. I nosed and tasted this for over an hour. It was one very rewarding, almost touching, experience. 46%

The Macallan Millennium 50 Years Old (1949) db **(90) n23 t22 f22 b23**. Magnificent finesse and charm despite some big oak makes this another Macallan to die for. 40%

⠿ **The Macallan Lalique III 57 Years Old** db **(95) n24.5** coffee and walnut cake. That's the simple way of looking at this one: but give yourself maybe half an hour and a slightly more detailed picture forms. The fruit conjures dates and walnuts — so walnuts and walnut oil is a pretty common thread here. And truffle oil, amazingly. The oak is toasty liquorice and overcooked fudge. But the delicate smoke I was expecting is conspicuous by its absence... until very late on. Only after a major degree of oxidisation does it add that extra delicate dimension; **t23** a soft landing in the canopy of the oaky trees with those coffee notes noticeable on the nose now really making a stir. Most beautiful, perhaps, is the lightness of the Demerara and muscovado sugar blend, damped in intensity by a sprinkling of vanilla. Some surprising oils form and make for a silky middle ground; **f23.5** some late spices, no more than a smattering, underline the oak without overstating the case while the sugars do their almost invisible job of keeping the dryer notes under control; like on the nose, a little smoke drifts in from seemingly nowhere; **b24** I chose this as my 1,000th new whisky tasted for the Jim Murray Whisky Bible 2012 not just because of my long-standing (36 years this summer) deep love affair with this distillery, but also because I honestly felt it had perhaps the best chance to offer not just a glimpse at the past but also the possibility of a whisky experience that sets the hairs on the back of my neck on end. I really wasn't disappointed. It is almost scary to think that this was from a vintage that would have supplied the whiskies I tasted when getting to first discover their 21-year-old. Then, I remember, I thought the malt almost too comfortable for its age. I expected a bit more of a struggle in the glass. No less than 36 years on, the same things concentrate the mind: how does this whisky find it so easy to fit into such enormous shoes? No experience with this whisky under an hour pays sufficient tribute to what it is all about. Checking my watch, I am writing this just two minutes under two hours after first nosing this malt. The score started at 88.5. With time, warmth, oxidation and understanding that score has risen to 95. It has spent 57 years in the cask; it deserves two hours to be heard. It takes that time, at least, to not just hear what it has to say to interpret it, but to put it into context. And for certain notes, once locked away and forgotten, to be slowly released. The last Lalique was good. But simply not this good. What a way to celebrate my 1,000th new whisky for the 2012 Bible...! What a whisky! 48.5%

The Macallan 1824 db **(88) n24 t23.5 f19 b21.5**. Absolutely magnificent whisky, in part. But there are times my job is depressing...and this is one of them.. 48%

⠿ **The Macallan 1824 Estate Reserve** db **(90.5) n22** excellent clean grape with an intriguing dusting of mint; **t23** almost a Jamaican pot still rum sheen and sweetness; beautiful weight and even some barley present; **f22.5** long, satisfying, gorgeously clean with very good vanilla-grape balance; **b23** don't know about Reserve: definitely good enough for the First Team. Superb! 45.7%

⠿ **The Macallan 1824 Select Oak** db **(82) n19 t22 f20 b21**. Soft, silky, sometimes sugary... and tangy. Not convinced every oak selected was quite the right one. 40%

The Macallan 1851 Inspiration db **(77) n19.5 t19.5 f19 b19**. Flat and uninspirational in 2008. 41%

The Macallan 1937 bott 1969 db **(92) n23** an outline of barley can eventually be made in the oaky mist; becomes better defined as a honeyed sweetness cuts in. Fingers of smoke tease. When nosing in the glass hours later the fresh, smoky gristiness is to die for ... and takes you back to the mill room 67 years ago; **t22** pleasantly sweet start as the barley piles in – even a touch of melon in there; this time the oak takes second place and acts as a perfect counter; **f24** excellent weight with soft peat softening the oak; **b23** a subtle if not overly complex whisky where there are few characters but each play its part exceptionally well. One to get out with a DVD of Will Hay's sublime Oh Mr Porter which was being made in Britain at the same time as this whisky and as Laurel and Hardy were singing about a Lonesome Pine on the other side of the pond; or any Pathe film of Millwall's FA Cup semi-final with Sunderland. *43%*

The Macallan 1937 bott 1974 db **(83) t19 t24 f20 b20.** It's all about the superb, silky initial mouth impact. *43%.*

The Macallan 1938 bott 1973 db **(90) n21 t23 f23 b23.** No hint of tiredness here at all: a malt that has all the freshness and charisma yet old-world charm and mystery of Hitchcock's The Lady Vanishes, which was made at the same time as this whisky. *43%*

The Macallan 1938 (31 Years Old) dist 1938, first bott 1969, re-bottled 2002 db **(83) n20 t22 f20 b21.** Some wonderful trills of barley early on but the oak dominates. *43%.*

The Macallan 1939 bott 1979 db **(90) n23** pleasing peaty edges to the thick malt; a touch of hickory for extra weight and Highland Park-esque heather-honey; **t22** spot on barley gives an unmolested mouthwatering performance; the oak tags on reluctantly drying towards cocoa at the middle; **f22** the integrity is kept as the oak backs off and little wisps of smoke re-surface; some brown sugar keeps the bitter-sweet pot boiling; **b23** enormous complexity confidence to a whisky distilled at a time of uncertainty; one to accompany the original Goodbye Mr Chips, though the whisky seems nothing like so faded. *43%*

The Macallan 1940 bott 1975 db **(83) n20 t22 f21 b20.** Easily the most modern style discernible from this distillery; a Macallan recogisable as an ancestor of today's famous dram, even with one or two warts apparent. *43%*

The Macallan 1940 (37 Years Old) dist 1940, first bott 1977, re-bottled 2002 db **(91) n22 t23 f23 b23.** Blind-tasting I would have declared this Irish, though slightly mystified by the distant hints of peat. Hard to believe that something so sublime could have been made by a nation under siege. Obviously nothing can distract a Scotsman from making great whisky... *43%*

The Macallan 1945 (56 Years Old) cask 262, bott 2002 db **(89) n22 t23 f22 b22** How can a whisky retain so much freshness and character after so long in the cask? This game never ceases to amaze me. *51.5%*

The Macallan 1946 Select Reserve db **(93) n25 t23 f22 b23.** I have never found a finer nose to any whisky. Once-in-a-lifetime whisky. *40%*

The Macallan 1946 (56 Years Old) cask 46/3M, bott 2002 db **(84) n21 t21 f20 b22.** The most peat-free '46 I've come across yet *44.3%*

The Macallan 1948 (53 Years Old) cask 609, bott 2002 db **(77) n18 t21 f19 b19.** Drinkable, but showing some major oaky cracks. *45.3%*

The Macallan 1948 Select Reserve db **(75) n22 t19 f17 b17.** What a fabulous nose! Sadly the package trails behind the '46. *40%*

The Macallan 1949 (53 Years Old) cask 136, bott 2002 db **(95) n23 t24 f24 b24.** Hold on to your trilbies: this punchy malt knows exactly where it is going. What a year: Carol Reed makes the incomparable The Third Man and Macallan can come up with something like this. Oh, to swap Orson Welles for H. G. Wells and his time machine. Sheer, unrepeatable class. *49.8%*

The Macallan 1949 (52 Years Old) cask 935, bott 2002 db **(82) n23 t21 f19 b19.** Faded and slightly tired, it has problems living up to the heaven-made nose. *41.1%*

The Macallan 1950 (52 Years Old) cask 598, bott 2002 db **(83) n22 t22 f18 b21.** Charmingly delicate peat but probably about two or three Summers past being a truly excellent whisky. *46.7%*

The Macallan 1950 (52 Years Old) cask no. 600, bott 2002 db **(91) n20 t24 f23 b24.** Only two casks apart, but this is almost a mirror image of the first, in the sense that everything is the other way round... *51.7%*

The Macallan 1951 (51 Years Old) cask 644, bott 2002 db **(93) n23 t24 f23 b23.** A malt instantly recognisable to Macallan lovers of the last two decades. Simply outstanding. *52.3%*

The Macallan 1952 (50 Years Old) cask no. 627, bott 2002 db **(80) n20 t20 f21 b19.** Good, clean sherry but it all seems a little detached *50.8%*

The Macallan 1952 (49 Years Old) cask 1250, bott 2002 db **(74) n19 t19 f18 b18.** Ye olde weirde Macallane. *48%*

The Macallan 1953 (49 Years Old) cask no. 516, bott 2002 db **(92) n22 t24 f23 b23.** Deliciously big and unflinching in its Christmas pudding intensity. *51%*

The Macallan 1954 (47 Years Old) cask 1902, bott 2002 db **(77) n19 t18 f21 b19.** The line between success and failure is thin: outwardly the '53 and 54 are similar but the 53 controls the oak much tighter. I love the coffee finale on this, though. *50.2%*

The Macallan 1955 (46 Years Old) cask 1851 49, bott 2002 db **(88) n21 t22 f23 b22.** Close call: one more Speyside August and this dram would have been matchwood. 45.9%

The Macallan 1958 (43 Years Old) cask 2682, bott 2002 db **(86) n17 t22 f24 b23.** One fears the worst from the sappy nose but the taste is sheer Highland Park in its honey depth. 52.9%

The Macallan 1959 (43 Years Old) cask 360, bott 2002 db **(79) n19 t21 f19 b20.** The oak is giving the malt a good hiding but it just hangs on to a delicious sub-plot. 46.7%

The Macallan 1964 (37 Years Old) cask 3312, bott 2002 db **(86) n24 t22 f20 b20.** Butterscotch and honey: a real chewing whisky if ever there was one. 58.2%

The Macallan 1965 (36 Years Old) cask 4402, bott 2002 db **(91) n22 t23 f22 b24.** If this was a woman it would be Marilyn Monroe. 56.3%

The Macallan 1966 (35 Years Old) cask 7878, bott 2002 db **(83) n21 t22 f20 b20.** a malt which never quite works out where it is going but gives a comfortable ride all the same. 55.5%

The Macallan 1967 (35 Years Old) cask 1195, bott 2002 db **(93) n23 t24 f23 b23.** This is what happens when you get a great sherry cask free of sulphur and marauding oak: whisky the way God intended. Unquestionably classic Macallan. 55.9%

The Macallan 1968 (34 Years Old) cask 2875, bott 2002 db **(92) n23 t23 f22 b24.** Possibly the most sophisticated and delicate malt in the pack despite the strength. 51%

The Macallan 1968 (33 Years Old) cask 5913, bott 2002 db **(84) n17 t23 f22 b22.** Flawed genius: how can a whisky with such a poor nose produce the goods like this? 46.6%

The Macallan 1969 cask 9369 db **(75) n19 t18 f20 b18.** One of those ungainly sherry butts that swamps everything in sight. 52.7%

The Macallan 1969 (32 Years Old) cask no. 10412, bott 2002 db **(76) n18 t20 f18 b20.** One small sip for man, one ordinary vintage for Macallan. Splinters. anybody? 59%

The Macallan 1970 (32 Years Old) cask no. 241, bott 2002 db **(95) n23 t24 f23 b25.** Brazil win the World Cup with the finest team and performance of all time, my girlfriend born there soon after and Macallan receive a butt from Heaven via Jerez. 1970 was some year ... 54.9%

The Macallan 1970 (31 Years Old) cask no. 9033, bott 2002 db **(81) n20 t20 f22 b19.** A butt bottled on its way down. 52.4%

The Macallan 1971 (30 Years Old) cask no. 4280, bott 2002 db **(86) n21 t22 f22 b21.** Imagine the trusty 10 years old from about 1980 with a grey beard ... 56.4%

The Macallan 1971 (30 Years Old) cask 7556, bott 2002 db **(91) n22 t22 f24 b23.** A complex dram that is comfortable with its age. 55.9%

The Macallan 1972 (29 Years Old) cask no. 4041, bott 2002 db **(92) n23 t24 f22 b23.** Once, I would have hated this type of malt. But I have come across so many sulphur-tainted casks over recent years that I have learned to have fun with monsters like this. Snatched from an awesome clutch of butts. 49.2%

The Macallan 1972 (29 Years Old) cask 4043, bott 2002 db **(93) n25 t24 f21 b23.** The sherry butt used for this was a classic. If, as Macallan claim, the sherry accounts for only 5% of the flavour, I'd like to know what happened to the other 95... 58.4%

The Macallan 1973 (30 Years Old) cask 6098, bott 2003 db **(93) n23 t24 f23 b23.** A superbly chosen cask for those with a sweet tooth in particular. If you know any women who claim not to like whisky, seduce them with this. 60.9%

The Macallan Gran Reserva 1981 db **(90) n23 t22 f22 b23.** Macallan in a nutshell. Brilliant. But could do with being at 46% for full effect. 40%

The Macallan Gran Reserva 1982 db **(82) n21 t22 f20 b19.** Big, clean, sweet sherry influence from first to last but doesn't open up and sing like the '81 vintage. 40%

The Macallan 1989 cask no 552 db **(94) n23 t23 f24 b24.** There are countless people out there who cut their whisky teeth 20 years ago on Macallan. Battle to get a bottle of this and the grey hairs will return to black, the eyesight will improve and your clothes will fit more easily. This is timewarp Macallan at its most dangerously seductive. 59.2%

Macallan Cask Strength db **(94) n22 t24 f24 b24.** One of those big sherry babies; it's like surfacing a massive wave of barley-sweetened sherry. Go for the ride. 58.6%. USA.

The Macallan Easter Elchies Seasonal Cask Selection Winter Choice 14 Years Old db **(94) n24 t24 f23 b23.** From a faultless cask and one big enough to have its own Postcode... 54%. Exclusive to visitor centre.

The Macallan Estate Reserve db **(84) n22 t22 f20 b20.** Doh! So much juice lurking about, but so much bitterness, too. ...grrrrr!!!! 45.7%

The Macallan Fine Oak Master's Edition db **(91) n23** one of the most delicate of all Macallan's house noses, depending on a floral scented theme with a sweetish malty tinge to the dank bracken and bluebells; **t23** so salivating and sensual! The tastebuds are caressed with sugar-coated oaky notes that have a devilish buzz about them; **f22** more malt and now vanilla with a bitter cocoa death... **b23** adorable. 42.8%

The Macallan Fine Oak Whisky Maker's Selection db (92) n22 t23 f23 b24. Those who cannot see Macallan in anything other than chestnut oloroso will be having sleepless nights: this is a dram of exquisite sophistication. The ultimate pre-prandial dram with it's coy, mildly cocoaed dryness, set against just enough barley and fruit sweetness here and there to see off any hints of austerity. Some great work has gone on in the lab to make this happen: fabulous stuff, chaps! 42.8%. Duty Free.

The Macallan Oscuro db (95.5) n24.5 the cleanest, most juicy grape dripping into a puddle of molten muscovado sugar: amazed I have not been attacked by wasps while nosing this; it would be too much on its own, but there is a sprinkling of spice to balance things beautifully; t24 and there you go: golden sultanas, ripe fig, exploding greengages and that muscovado sugar and spice again...unreal...; f23 just a little bitter, but probably from the oak which until now had hardly got a look in; some toasty vanilla makes a late entry but that juicy, lightly spiced fruit just keeps on going; b24 oh, if all sherried whiskies could be that mind - and taste bud-blowingly fabulous...! 46.5%

⟝ **The Macallan Royal Marriage** db (89) n23.5 unusually salty, with another happy marriage – this time between oak and grape. Tries to head off into the world of blissful, silky even-ness, but that salty-liquorice character is like a dog with a bone - thankfully; t22.5 black cherries make a fabulous statement on delivery, and right behind is that salty tang you just knew would be there; also a big caramel surge; f21 bitters and dries annoyingly: just like I am sure the marriage won't...; b22 some amazing moments to remember. 46.8%

The Macallan Select Oak db (83) n23 t21 f19 b20. Exceptionally dry and tight; and a little furry despite the early fruitiness. 40%

The Macallan Whisky Makers Edition db (76) n19 t20 f18 b19. Distorted and embittered by the horrific "S" element... 42.8%

The Macallan Woodlands Limited Edition Estate Bottling db (86) n21 t23 f21 b21. Toffee towards the finish brings a premature halt to a wonderfully mollased early delivery. 40%

⟝ **Alchemist Macallan 18 Years Old** (73) n18 t19 f18 b18. Ah, the alchemy of turning liquid gold into sulphur. A trick many a German palate will cherish... 46%. nc ncf. Alchemist.

Cadenhead's Macallan-Glenlivet 1989 bott Feb 10 (87.5) n22.5 sharp. Fruit Pastilles; t22 massive wave of grist. The softest fruit attachment; f21 delicate spice and a hint of milk chocolate before drying; b22 malty and even. 52.1% Wm. Cadenhead Ltd. 168 bottles.

The Càrn Mòr Vintage Collection Macallan 1988 hogshead no. 9171, bott 2009 (85) n22 t22.5 f20 b20.5. Crisp, clean citrus on the nose and delivery, backed up by juicy barley. But the oak bitters a little. 46% nc ncf 1048 bottles

Duncan Taylor Collection Macallan 1990 cask no. 18222 (87.5) n22 t23 f21 b21.5. Quite a confused and confusing malt, not quite sure what it wants to be, or where it wants to go. Luckily, it works out attractively. 54.1%

Duncan Taylor Collection Macallan 1991 cask no. 21437 (92.5) n23 t23.5 f23 b23. No doubting the quality on offer. 52.8%

Duncan Taylor Collection Macallan 1991 cask no. 21439 (86) n22 t21 f22 b21. Acacia honey escorts the barley and the interaction with the oak on the finish is pleasing, as is the intensity. But at times a little on the hot side. 55.1%

Duncan Taylor Collection Macallan 1991 cask no. 9714 (89) n22.5 perfectly structured malt. A little citrus adds to the clean, rounded forms; t22.5 beautiful arrival: fresher than you could think a near 20-y-o whisky could be; the malt layers out and thickens; f21.5 the oak remains in the background but does add a late bitter marmalade quality; b22.5 a well used bourbon cask but in excellent form. 55.3% Duncan Taylor & Co Ltd

Gordon & MacPhail Speymalt Macallan 1938 (94) n25 t22 f23 b24. This is nature-defying whisky, very much like the 62-year-old Dalmore. Few people will be lucky enough ever to taste this. But those that do will be one of the truly privileged. And that includes me. 41.4%

Gordon & MacPhail Speymalt Macallan 1950 (91) n24 t22 f22 b23. I always taste these ultra-ancient whiskies with trepidation. Nature suggests that malt should not be that good as barley – even with the aid of sherry – can see off only so much oak. But fortified with a delightful touch of peat, this holds itself together like an old Shakespeare first in original buckskin. It creaks. It's delicate. But take the time and handled carefully, this will amaze you. 43%

Gordon & MacPhail Speymalt Macallan 1967 (93) n23 t24 f22 b24. A mighty classy malt which has withstood the years with aplomb. 40%

Gordon & MacPhail Speymalt from Macallan 1971 (95) n23.5 weak honeycomb, weak barley, weak smoke, weak red liquorice, stewed fruit...yet all comes together for a powerful dose of yesteryear; t24.5 silky, melt-in-the-mouth malt is backed by light sultana juiciness; a few reminders of the timber but so very politely done and has much to do with the spices; f23.5 there is almost an inevitability to the fruit and nut chocolate finale... and the accentuating of the spice; **b23.5** one of most genteel and elegant whiskies of the year: a true classic. Remember to lift the glass with your little finger sticking out... 43%. Gordon & MacPhail.

❧ **Gordon & MacPhail Speymalt from Macallan 1990 (71) n18 t19 f16 b18.** S is for Speyside. And, alas, sulphur... 43%. Gordon & MacPhail.

Hart Brothers Macallan Aged 15 Years dist Dec 92, bott Jun 08 **(77.5) n18 t22 f19 b19.5.** What a shame! Loads of sweet juice and for a moment it really takes off with spices in tow. But dries and tightens. 46%. Hart Brothers Limited.

Hart Brothers Macallan Aged 17 Years 1st fill sherry butt, dist Jun 91, bott Jul 08 **(88.5) n22.5** succulent grape; a little clove and spice; **t23** sultana and apple juice; malt and vanilla begin to build a more solid foundation; **f21** spices; a bitter vanilla and grape note; **b22** light bodied for a Macallan but wonderfully juicy! 46%. Private bottling for Whisky World.

❧ **Hart Brothers Macallan Aged 19 Years** dist May 91, bott Jan 11 **(69) n17 t19 f16 b17.** sweet grapes by the bunch full. Sadly, sulphured. 46%. sc.

❧ **Hart Brothers Macallan Aged 19 Years** dist May 91, bott Jan 11 **(69) n18 t18 f16 b17.** Identical to the 46% but the profile coming from slightly different angles. 55%. sc.

Kingsbury's Single Cask Macallan Aged 17 Years 1991 (86) n22 t22 f21 b21. Attractive ginger gives the malt an extra lift. 46%. Japan Import System

Norse Cask Selection Macallan 1991 Aged 17 Years hogshead cask no. CM703, dist May 91, bott Jul 08 **(85) n21.5 t22 f20.5 b21.** Dusty in a few places, but the delivery sparkles bright barley. 57%. Qualityworld for WhiskyOwner.com, Denmark.

Old & Rare Macallan Aged 30 Years bott 2009 **(88.5) n22 t22 f22.5 b22.** A creaky old 'un, this. More ancient on the palate than its 30 years but a fair degree of juicy charm, too. 45.1%

Old Malt Cask Macallan Aged 15 Years dist Jun 93, bott Jul 09 **(83) n20.5 t22.5 f19 b21.** Far from perfect, but for a while the vivid sweetness of the noble rot grape hinted on the nose shines on the palate, too. 50%. Douglas Laing.

❧ **Old Malt Cask Macallan Aged 15 Years** refill butt, cask no. 6540, dist Oct 95, bott Oct 10 **(83.5) n21 t22.5 f18.5 b21.5.** Unusual for a Macallan in that the sherry offers a tangy sweetness for the main course as well as a bitter marmalade finish. 50%. nc ncf sc. 410 bottles.

Old Malt Cask Macallan Aged 18 Years refill hogshead, dist Aug 90, bott Feb 09 **(84) n20.5 t21 f21.5 b21.** Even with the dab of peat this one carries, it is pleasant and enjoyable rather than inspiring as a Macallan of this vintage hopefully should be. 50%. 292 bottles.

❧ **Old Malt Cask Macallan Aged 18 Years** refill hogshead, cask no. 7246, dist Jun 93, bott May 11 **(86.5) n22.5 t22.5 f20 b21.5.** One of those big natural caramel-laden jobbies that roars along the runway but is never quite able to take off. A delicious journey nonetheless. 50%. nc ncf sc. Douglas Laing & Co. 288 bottles.

Old Malt Cask Macallan Aged 19 Years rum finish refill hogshead, finished in rum cask, dist Nov 89, bott Nov 08 **(89.5) n22.5 t22.5 f22 b22.5** Classic crisp rum finishing. Excellent. 50%. Douglas Laing. 277 bottles.

Old Malt Cask Macallan Aged 19 Years refill hogshead no. DL 5603, dist Sep 90, bott Nov 09 **(92) n23** a wonderful concoction of grass and grape; **t23** fresh, spiced juiciness but the malt is almost crystal clear; excellent array of light sugars and grist; **f23.5** long, pulsing spices with the grape juicy to the end; **b22.5** a total joy. 50%. Douglas Laing. 347 bottles.

Old Malt Cask Macallan Aged 20 Years Wine Finish refill hogshead, finished in wine barrel, dist Jun 88, bott Oct 08 **(85) n21 t21 f21.5 b21.5.** Sweet, grapey, enjoyable. But could have been devised and matured in East Anglia of England rather than the Highlands of Scotland. 50%. Douglas Laing. 274 bottles.

❧ **Old Malt Cask Macallan Aged 20 Years** wine finished barrel, cask no. 5069, dist Aug 90, bott Jan 11 **(85.5) n22 t21 f21.5 b21.** Reminds me of a lady of loose morals who tests soap: amazingly clean, but still a little tart. 50%. nc ncf sc. Douglas Laing & Co. 318 bottles.

❧ **Old Malt Cask Macallan Aged 21 Years** refill hogshead, cask no. 7090, dist May 90, bott May 11 **(94.5) n23.5** a stunning amalgam of sultana and sweeter bourbon notes; the fruit also heads towards spiced yam and caramel; **t24** perfect delivery: the barley leaps from the first note and the juiciness just keeps on developing; the middle ground begins hinting of muscovado-sweetened mocha: outrageously refreshing for its age; **f23** long and more and more bourbon tones flex their muscles...with wonderfully good grace; **b24** looking for a magnificent, fault-free Macallan 21? Look no further... 50%. nc ncf sc. 160 bottles.

Old Malt Cask Macallan Aged 23 Years Rum Finish refill hogshead, finished in rum cask, dist Apr 85, bott Oct 08 **(86) n22.5 t21.5 f21 b21.5.** Scented but not quite soapy on the nose and a stirring, almost thirst-quenching juiciness on delivery. 50%. Douglas Laing.

Old Malt Cask Macallan Aged 24 Years refill hogshead, dist Apr 85, bott Apr 09 **(93.5) n23 t24 f23 b23.5.** How can a whisky be this sweet but not for a second either cloying or over the top? I defy anyone to say a bad word against this classic dram. 50%. 281 bottles.

⁘ **Premier Barrel Macallan Aged 8 Years** (89) n22.5 beautifully clean, intense barley with a mildly chalky and fruity coating: exemplary; t22 big, booming malt showing every lightly metallic sign of being born in a relatively small still; f22 dry, clean cocoa; b22.5 if someone asked me to draw you a picture of a clean Macallan at eight showing all its usual intense attributes, this would be it...; 46%. nc ncf sc. Douglas Laing & Co. 150 bottles.

Premier Barrel Macallan Aged 11 Years (86.5) n21.5 t22 f21.5 b21.5. A beautiful example of a well used barrel giving the distillery a chance to show its credentials: the barley is gristy-sweet and carried on a coppery-sharp oiliness. 46%. Douglas Laing. 376 bottles.

Premier Barrel Macallan Aged 12 Years (86) n21.5 t22 f21.5 b21. Pleasant, malty, but not much tread left in the barrel. 46%. nc ncf. Douglas Laing. 180 bottles.

Provenance Macallan Aged 11 Years refill hogshead, dist Winter 97, bott Autumn 08 (78.5) n20 t21 f18.5 b19. Low key with the barley working flat out against the bitter oak. 46%

Provenance Macallan Over 12 Years refill hogshead no. DMG 6191, dist Autumn 97, bott Spring 2010 (89) n23 refreshing, clean, and malty to infinity; t22 juicy, salivating barley: a mixture of grist sweetness and weak golden syrup; f22 remains of the simplistic but delightful fresh barley trail; b22 quite literally a breath of fresh air... 46%. Douglas Laing.

⁘ **Provenance Macallan Over 12 Years** refill hogshead, cask no. 6983, dist Autumn 98, bott Winter 2011 (90) n22.5 beautiful barley, clean, sharp and vaguely fruity; t22 wave upon wave of gorgeous barley; f22 carries on its simple course, but with an extra injection of chalky vanilla and citrus; b22.5 not overly taxing. But what it does, it does quite beautifully. 46%. nc ncf sc. Douglas Laing & Co.

⁘ **Provenance Macallan Over 12 Years** refill hogshead, cask no. 7087, dist Autumn 98, bott Spring 2011 (91) n22.5 crushed sultanas; t23 big spiced barley take off: the oak is prodigious for its age and chips in with a chewy mixture of fruit and bourbon honeycomb; f22.5 sugared almonds; b23 a quality cask offering a surprising degree of fruit. 46%. nc ncf sc.

⁘ **Provenance Macallan Over 13 Years** refill hogshead, cask no. 7201, dist Autumn 97, bott Summer 2011 (85.5) n21.5 t22 f21 b21. Sweet, mildly spicy and scarily easy going. 46%. nc ncf sc. Douglas Laing & Co.

Scotch Malt Whisky Society Cask 24.110 1st fill sherry butt, dist May 90 (77) n19 t21 f18 b19. Can the panel try to avoid sulphur tainted casks if you don't mind? I mean: I know this isn't as heavily treated as some but, surely, the trick for the members is to select for them one that's free of sulphur, right? Thank you. 57.1%. Scotch Malt Whisky Society.

⁘ **Scotch Malt Whisky Society Cask 24.114 Aged 21 Years** refill butt, cask no. 16520, dist 1989 (86) n21.5 t22 f21 b21.5. Thoroughly enjoyable whisky which perhaps just overdoes the sugary caramel to take it into the next level of excellence. 52.3%. sc. 165 bottles.

⁘ **Scotch Malt Whisky Society Cask 24.116 Aged 20 Years** 1st fill sherry hogshead, cask no. 278057, dist 1990 (91.5) n22.5 huge spiced sultana; the odd "s" atom or two, but those peppers and the promise of thick juice is pretty damn sexy; t23 an early puckering "s" note is blasted into the sidings by a staggering degree of explodingly fat sultana; the grape arrives in layers, as does a rich coffee note; f23 coffee cake complete with walnuts. And a few date thrown in for good measure; b23 not quite 100% free of impurity, but still a stonking cask! 55.8%. sc. 202 bottles.

Speymalt Macallan 1988 (88) n22 t22.5 f21.5 b22. A real Speyside feel to this one. 43%. Gordon & MacPhail.

Speymalt Macallan 1999 (72.5) n19 t19.5 f16 b18. Juicy early on but dulls as the flaws become apparent. 43%. Gordon & MacPhail.

⁘ **The Whisky Castle Old Malt Cask Macallan Aged 13 Years** refill hogshead, cask no. 7195, dist Oct 97, bott May 11 (86) n21 t22.5 f21 b21.5. Huge barley theme. And sweet enough to rot your teeth. Liqueur lovers will drag this off the shelf... 55.3%. nc ncf sc. Douglas Laing & Co for The Whisky Castle.

Wilson & Morgan Barrel Selection Macallan Aged 20 Years dist 1988, bott 2008 (79) n21 t20 f19 b19. Very tight. 46%. Wilson & Morgan.

Wilson & Morgan Barrel Selection Macallan 1998 Marsala Finish bott 2008 (82) n20.5 t21 f20.5 b20. Juicy yet dry and restrained. 46%. Wilson & Morgan.

MACDUFF

Speyside, 1963. John Dewar & Sons. Working.

Glen Deveron Aged 10 Years dist 1995 db (86) n19 t23 f23 b21. The enormity of the third and fourth waves on delivery give some idea of the greatness this distillery could achieve perhaps with a little more care with cask selection, upping the strength to 46% and banning caramel. We'd have a malt scoring in the low to mid 90s every time. At the moment we must remain frustrated. 40%

Glen Deveron Aged 15 Years db (88.5) n22 the vaguest hint of smoke curls around the foot of the honey; t22.5 one of the most delightful signatures of a Macduff is the softness of textures and a hint of honey lurking somewhere in close proximity. No disappointments here; f22 more lush, light sweetness but more than a hint of toffee; b22 for those who like whisky to caress rather than attack their taste buds. 40%

Berry's Own Selection Macduff 1984 (91.5) n22.5 anyone with a passion for Crunchie chocolate bars will appreciate this one...; t24 ...and on delivery, too, as the honeycomb makes a spectacularly grand entrance, flanked by rich barley and butterscotch; f22.5 some creaking oak, for sure, but the soft oils and continuing watering golden syrup makes amends. b22.5 MacDuff at its very best and the kind of wonderful dram which can compensate for watching your team lose in the Play Off semi-finals. 52.2%

Berry's Own Selection Macduff 1991 bott 2008 (88) n23 t22 f21 b22. Quite an unusual type of malt which needs three or four mouthfuls to get the measure of. 46%

Cärn Mòr Vintage Collection Macduff 2005 hogshead, cask no. 23, dist 2005, bott 2009 (78) n19 t21 f19 b19. Sweet malt on delivery, otherwise not picked at the best moment of its early life cycle. 46%. The Scottish Liqueur Centre.

Connoisseurs Choice Macduff 1989 (82) n19 t21.5 f20.5 b21. Not even its best attempts to rack up the honey can entirely overcome the slight technical flaw in the distillate. Plenty to chew over, though...literally! 43%. Gordon & MacPhail.

Duncan Taylor Collection Macduff 1969 cask no. 3668 (86.5) n22.5 t21 f21.5 b21.5. Lovely malt showing some knots of age but having the grace and wherewithal to allow the more elegant barley notes to take a bow. 40.8%

The Golden Cask Macduff 1984 cask no. CM143, bott 2009 (86.5) n22 t22 f21 b21.5. Some glorious strands of golden syrup and coconut with some late mocha, too. 55%. The House of MacDuff. 326 bottles.

∴ **L'Esprit Single Cask Collection Macduff 2000** first fill sherry butt, cask no. 5778, dist 15 Nov 00, bott 19 Oct 10 (75) n18 t22 f17 b18. Natural colour. Un-natural sulphur. 46%. nc ncf sc. Whisky & Rhum. 298 bottles.

∴ **L'Esprit Single Cask Collection Macduff 2000 Cask Strength** first fill sherry butt, cask no. 5778, dist 15 Nov 00, bott 19 Oct 10 (76) n18 t23 f17.5 b18.5. In whisky terms, a tragedy. I can only imagine the faultless, wondrous beauty of what would have been one of the finest oloroso casks in the entire bodega before its fateful encounter with that lighted candle. The fact that so many mountainous points of magnificent grape can still be seen above the sulphur clouds is astonishing: a lesser butt would have lost its identity entirely. 61.1%. nc ncf sc. Whisky & Rhum. 60 bottles.

Lonach Macduff 1969 (92) n23 t23 f23 b23. Uncompromised star quality throughout. One of those malts that makes writing this book so rewarding...!! 40.6%. Duncan Taylor.

∴ **Malts Of Scotland Macduff 1980** bourbon hogshead, cask no. 6107, dist Oct 80, bott Mar 11 (85) n21.5 t22.5 f20 b21. Tighter than a pair of 1980 disco trousers. Some eye-watering sweetness and an attractive nuttiness, too. But bitters out. 54.1%. sc.

∴ **Old Malt Cask For A Fine Cigar's Pleasure Macduff Aged 10 Years** sherry butt (85.5) n21 t22 f21 b21.5 MacPuff, surely... Sweet, syrupy and a real meal of a dram. But at least a sherried Macduff not showing signs of debilitating sulphur... give that whisky a cigar... 50%. nc ncf sc. Douglas Laing & Co. 319 bottles.

Old Malt Cask Macduff Aged 19 Years dist Mar 90, bott Jul 09 (69) n17 t18 f17 b17. MacDuff without the Mac. 50%. Douglas Laing.

∴ **Old Malt Cask Macduff Aged 21 Years** refill hogshead, cask no. 7149, dist Mar 90, bott Apr 11 (68) n16.5 t18.5 f16 b17. A MacDuff not to carry on with. Some of the whisky from this distillery from '89 and 90 were shockers. 50%. nc ncf sc. Douglas Laing & Co. 252 bottles.

Old Masters Macduff Aged 17 Years cask no. 1418 dist 90, bott 08 (68.5) n16 t18 f17 b17.5. Duff by name and nature. Noses do come worse than this...but not that often. 57.8%. James MacArthur & Co. Ltd.

∴ **Provenance Macduff Over 10 Years** refill hogshead, cask no. 6541, dist Winter 99, bott Autumn 2010 (81.5) n22 t21 f19 b19.5. An interesting guy full of a coppery sharpness blunted by oils. 46%. nc ncf sc. Douglas Laing & Co.

∴ **Provenance Macduff Over 10 Years** sherry butt, cask no. 6966, dist Autumn 00, bott Winter 2011 (84) n19 t22.5 f21 b21.5. Recovers with great panache from the slight flaw evident on the sherry butt. The levels of juicy fruit are delightful. 46%. nc ncf sc. Douglas Laing & Co.

∴ **Vom Fass Macduff 28 Years Old** (88.5) n23 quite superb: a sexy mix of orange-led fruit and various light herbs; t22 thirst-quenching freshness and bite for all its years. Sweet marmalade leads to a surprising spice avalanche; f21.5 lengthened by the spice; b22 a cask on the edge of tiredness has rolled out a wonderfully impressive malt full of delicate fruit. 40%

MANNOCHMORE
Speyside, 1971. Diageo. Working.

Mannochmore Aged 12 Years db (84) n22 t21 f20 b21. As usual the mouth arrival fails to live up to the great nose. Quite a greasy dram with sweet malt and bitter oak. 43%.

Mannochmore 1998 The Manager's Choice db (71.5) n18 t18 f17.5 b18. A very bad cask day... 59.1%

Chairman's Stock Mannochmore 1982 claret wood, bott Feb 10 (91.5) n22.5 very firm, crisp barley with the most lethargic smokiness; t23 juicy, firm and, as the sugars build, hardens by the second; f23 a distinct touch of green tea attaches itself to the vanilla and spice; about as crunchy as malt gets; b23 quite excellent whisky with a mind of its own. 58.4%. 221 bottles.

⋄ **Chieftain's Mannochmore Aged 28 Years** hogshead, dist Aug 82, bott 2011 (93) n23 gorgeous interplay between liquorice-honey bourbon notes and prime barley; t23 the honey remains but picks up some butterscotch along the way. A degree of toffee makes for a chewy middle ground; f23.5 you might have thought after 28 years the finish might just be getting a little tired. But no hint of it: even a degree of copper to ensure length and backbone to the fade; b23.5 ridiculously rich and lively. Would have scored even high had not the caramel gummed up the higher notes. 47.4%. nc ncf. Ian Macleod Distillers.

Connoisseurs Choice Mannochmore 1990 (85) n20 t22 f21 b22. Perhaps overly sweet and slightly featureless. 46%. Gordon & MacPhail.

⋄ **Gordon & MacPhail Connoisseurs Choice Mannochmore 1991** (88.5) n22 cucumber and black pepper; earthy; t22 simplistic, velvety malt with an appealing degree of juicy liveliness; f22 dries and spices up; late cocoa salvo; b22.5 understatedly ticks the right boxes. 46%

⋄ **Old Malt Cask Mannochmore Aged 13 Years** refill hogshead, cask no. 6567, dist Jun 97, bott Sep 10 (89) n21.5 playfully clean and malty; t22 salivating barley with a crystal clear, fresh grassiness. Lime and butterscotch fills the middle ground; f23 a beautiful spice and barley union. Really impressive; b22.5 if you are looking for a light, malty number which has juiciness and spice in equal proportion...here it is! 50%. nc ncf sc. 228 bottles.

Old Malt Cask Mannochmore Aged 18 Years refill barrel, dist Feb 91, bott Apr 09 (91) n22.5 t23 f22.5 b23. Modest in its intentions and delicate, it is never less than charming. 50%. Douglas Laing. 288 bottles.

⋄ **Old Malt Cask Mannochmore Aged 20 Years** refill hogshead, cask no. 6306, dist Feb 90, bott Jun 10 (91) n23.5 beautifully complex: freshly sliced runner beans, dank north-facing gardens, tannin and a hint of salt...; t23 at last some sweetness: the delivery shows an unexpected gristy quality and then a developing vanilla theme of varying depth; f22 long, with the salt returning but the confident oils spread the remaining sugars thickly; b22.5 on its day, Mannochmore can be an impressive malt. This is its day... 50%. nc ncf sc. 345 bottles.

⋄ **Provenance Mannochmore Aged 12 Years** (80) n20 t20 f20 b20. The perfect blending malt: virtually no character... just heaps of barley and some soft oil to big it up. 50%. nc ncf sc.

⋄ **Scotch Malt Whisky Society Cask 64.28 Aged 9 Years** 1st fill barrel, cask no. 1906, dist 2001 (81) n21.5 t21 f18.5 b20. Has much to say for itself and, though mainly inarticulate, proves pretty sharp-tongued and bitter. 58.3%. sc. 240 bottles.

⋄ **Scotch Malt Whisky Society Cask 64.30 Aged 22 Years** refill hogshead, cask no. 219079, dist 1988 (85.5) n20 t21.5 f22.5 b21.5. Plenty of crunchy sugars work well with the salty oak. Tries to be unimpressive, but just can't help showing some old world charm. 49.5%. sc. 260 bottles.

⋄ **The Whisky Agency Mannochmore 1982** bott 2010 (86.5) n21.5 t22 f21.5 b21.5. Requires time to settle and relax in the glass. When it does, the barley shows to a far greater extent than you might expect from a malt of almost 30 years. 49.9%. The Whisky Agency.

MILLBURN
Highlands (Northern), 1807–1985. Diageo. Demolished.

Millburn 1969 Rare Malt db (77) n19 t21 f18 b19. Some lovely bourbon-honey touches but sadly over the hill and declining fast. Nothing like as interesting or entertaining as the massage parlour that was firebombed a few yards from my office twenty minutes ago. Or as smoky... 51.3%

MILTONDUFF
Speyside, 1824. Chivas Brothers. Working.

Miltonduff Aged 15 Years bott code L00/123 db (86) n23 t22 f20 b21. Some casks beyond their years have crept in and unsettled this one. But some real big salty moments to savour, too. 46%

⊰∷⊱ **Berry's Own Selection Miltonduff 1998** cask no. 3604, bott 2010 **(87.5) n22** mildly Glen Grantish in its firm, no-nonsense maltiness. Clean with a delicate vanilla build; **t22** momentarily juicy on delivery, big spice thrust with training vanilla; **f21.5** remains firm with lots of cocoa; **b22** a very close approximation of the official 12 year old distillery version brought out by Allied in the days when they had no idea whatsoever what they were doing with their malts: a very decent, confident and well made Speysider. 46%. nc ncf sc.

⊰∷⊱ **Berry's Own Selection Miltonduff 1998** cask no. 3605, bott 2011 **(86) n21 t22 f21.5 b21.5**. As solid as cask 3605 but with its barley juiciness limited by what seems a fruitcake let loose with a flame thrower... Entertaining, to put it mildly... 57%. nc ncf sc. Berry Bros & Rudd.

The Càrn Mòr Vintage Collection Miltonduff 1998 hogshead no. 3620, bott 2009 **(87) n21.5** clean, under-developed gristy malt; **t23** stunningly beautiful malt with sheen due not lesst to the soft oils and delicate citrus sub plot; **f21** long malt before a vague tired oak bitterness creeps in; **b21.5** An outstanding example of just how well Miltonduff is made and how astoningly clean and juicy it's malt can be...and why so highly prized by blenders. Even in that exhausted old cask, the 24-carat quality of this under-rated distillery sparkles. 46%. nc ncf. 1224 bottles.

The Golden Cask Miltonduff 1998 cask no. CM140, bott 2009 **(74) n18 t19 f18 b19**. Dry, tight, bitter. 57%. The House of MacDuff. 258 bottles.

⊰∷⊱ **Malts Of Scotland Miltonduff 1980** bourbon hogshead, cask no. 12429, dist Sep 80, bott Jan 11 **(82) n19 t22.5 f19.5 b21**. A fine example of the distillery in all its blending finery: a few milky notes denoting a cask at the end of its tether but the enormity of the barley is there to be admired. 44.7%. nc ncf sc. Malts Of Scotland. 259 bottles.

Old Malt Cask Miltonduff Aged 12 Years refill hogshead, dist Mar 96, bott Sep 08 **(79.5) n19.5 t19 f21 b20**. Recovers with a malty-vanilla flourish after an uncertain, off-key start. 50%. Douglas Laing. 357 bottles.

Old Malt Cask Miltonduff Aged 28 Years refill hogshead, dist Sep 80, bott Feb 09 **(92) n24 t23 f22 b23**. Doesn't quite live up to the nose: it is hard to see how it might. Nosing must constitute at least 60% of the experience with this whisky, though it's no disappointment in the glass, either, showing elegance throughout. 44.5%

Old Masters Miltonduff Aged 13 Years cask no. 5563, dist 1996, bott 2009 **(81) n19 t21 f20.5 b20.5**. Not all the heat is generated by the alcohol. By no means unpleasant but its scope is limited. 57.2%. James MacArthur & Co. Ltd.

Provenance Miltonduff Aged 11 Years refill hogshead, dist Winter 98, bott Spring 09 **(74) n19 t19 f18 b18**. Sweetish, but never begins to gel. 46%. Douglas Laing.

Scotch Malt Whisky Society Cask 72.21 Aged 11 Years refill hogshead, dist Oct 97 **(90) n23 t22.5 f22 b22.5**. Refined and delicate but makes a big early statement. 56%

Scott's Selection Miltonduff 1988 bott 2008 **(83) n21 t22 f20 b20**. A pleasing malt with its entire emphasis on the early barley kick. 54.3%. Speyside Distillers.

The Whisky Agency Miltonduff 1980 hogshead, bott 2009 **(94) n23** chocolate orange and figs; **t23** stunning delivery and mouth feel; spot on oils lift the barley and fruit soup; light salt sharpens and intensifies; **f24** superbly long fade with the oak displaying a sweetened liquorice, fitting charmingly with the barley **b24** a cracking malt comfortable with its age and underscoring this distillery's latent talent. 49%

MORTLACH

Speyside, 1824. Diageo. Working.

Mortlach Aged 16 Years db **(87) n20** big, big sherry, but not exactly without a blemish or two; **t23** sumptuous fruit and then a really outstanding malt and melon mouthwatering rush; **f22** returns to heavier duty with a touch of spice, too; **b22** once it gets past the bold if very mildly sulphured nose, the rest of the journey is superb. Earlier Mortlachs in this range had a slightly unclean feel to them and the nose here doesn't inspire confidence. But from arrival on the palate onwards, it's sure-footed, fruity and even refreshing ... and always delicious. 43%

Mortlach 32 Years Old dist 1971 db **(88) n22 t22 f22 b22**. Big and with attitude... 50.1%

A.D. Rattray Mortlach 1990 cask no. 5950 **(79) n20 t20 f19 b20**. Monotoned malt syrup. 58.6%. A.D. Rattray Ltd.

Berrys' Own Selection Mortlach 1989 cask no. 5141, bott 2010 **(89.5) n23** not what I was expecting by a long shot: excellent weight to the malt with the sugars in support rather than swamping; even the vanillas have a smartness about them, especially with the light orange blossom attachment...unusually impressive...; **t22.5** a beautiful turn of malt on the palate with there being a splendid countering between malt and vanilla and malt and light salt; **f22** very equal vanilla again with the barely sweetened barley just hanging in there; **b22** there you go. Proof they exist: you can get seriously decent Mortlach after all. Well done Doug

McIvor for unearthing this rarity. I mean, it is Mortlach isn't it Doug...? Or were you so shell-shocked by Charlton's 4-0 mauling at the Lions' Den of Millwall, you went and put the wrong labels on...???? 46%. Berry Bros & Rudd.

Chieftain's Mortlach Aged 15 Years sherry wood **(69) n17 t18 f17 b17.** This sweet and sulphurous effort is one 69 I don't like... 46%. Ian Macleod.

The Coopers Choice Mortlach 1990 Sherry Wood Aged 18 Years sherry butt no. 4421, bott 2009 **(57) n14 t15 f14 b14.** Grimly sulphured for all the big grape breast-beating. 46% nc ncf The Vintage Malt Whisky Co. Ltd.

⠿ **Dun Bheagan Mortlach 12 Years Old** hogshead, dist Aug 98 **(90) n22** a surprising, slightly plumy fruitiness to this. The weight of the malt impresses; **t23** now that is a very complex delivery: the sweetness of the barley breaks down in almost orchestrated moves: the peeling of a malty onion. Clean, soft yet compact and exuding excellence; **f22.5** long with the softest of malty oils. The oaky balance shows no dodgy cask bitterness whatsoever; **b22.5** something of a workhorse malt, but in this form is showing there is more to it than the one dimensional thug we've had to endure for the last decade. This, from time to time, actually radiates some real charm. To see Mortlach as it hasn't been viewed for some while, go fetch! 43%. nc ncf.

Duthies Mortlach 16 Years Old (88.5) n22.5 t22.5 f21.5 b22. Easily one of the more enjoyable Mortlachs on the market. 46%. Cadenhead's for Germany.

Duthies Mortlach 21 Years Old (74) n19 t19 f18 b18. Tight, bitter and confined, with little scope for manoeuvre. 46% Wm. Cadenhead Ltd

The Golden Cask Mortlach 1994 cask no. CM115 **(76) n19 t20 f18 b19.** Syrupy and though sumptuous and hearty, enough of the mud from the cask sticks...especially on the finish. 55.1%. House of Macduff. 305 bottles.

The Golden Cask Mortlach 1994 cask no. CM148, bott 2009 **(86) n21 t22 f21 b22.** Above average for the distillery with a balanced oaky dryness to the usual thick, sweet barley. 57.5% The House of MacDuff. 329 bottles.

Gordon & MacPhail Distillery Label Mortlach 21 Years Old (84) n21 t22 f20 b21. Attractive, well weighted, malty and competent. 43%. Gordon & MacPhail.

Gordon & MacPhail Generations Mortlach 70 dist 1938 **(96.5) n24** the oak tried to play hardball but fails: instead a light bourbony touch arrives, which in turn is softened by a surprising turn of frutiness. Mainly figs and gooseberry but with a spoonful of chocolate mousse to keep it company. Meanwhile the most delightful and delicate smoke drifts aimlessly around...; **t24** the palate is treated to something unique and extraordinary: 70-y-o oak. But rather than trying to take over the show it is instead quite content to let the softest possible body allow the sultanas and playful smoke have the lion's share of the limelight; various thin brown sugars ensure the desired sweetness is maintained; **f23.5** long and at last some spices; small, fizzing and pernickety. The smoke continues its perambulations around the palate; the fruits remain subtle with the vaguest hint of something exotic and the vanillas are light and fragile; **b25** this is most probably the least likely whisky you are able to encounter. To stay 70 years in the barrel and remain intact after all that time defies logic. To actually go several stages further and become one of the world's most stupendous whiskies of the year defies belief. It is a freakish situation, where the body of the malt and the state of the cask must have been at a million to one state of readiness to have received and complimented each other over so long a period. Remember, when this was distilled, there had only ever been one world war. The whisky itself confirms how peat was used to a far greater scale in the average Speyside distillery than is the case today. And how the sherry casks, so clean and unspoiled, could add fruitiness and oak in just so amounts. It is impossible to have selected anything more spectacular to mark my 999th "new" whisky for the 2011 Bible: the 2012 edition will be hard pressed to trump this. But for those of you lucky enough ever to try it, once you have emptied the glass, DON'T wash it. Allow the aroma to grow for the next hour or two. If I scored the nose then, it would be a 25. Talk about "Rage,rage against the dying of the light"... 46.1%

Hart Brothers Mortlach Aged 18 Years 1st fill sherry butt, dist Jun 90, bott Dec 08 **(58) n15 t16 f13 b14.** Uncompromisingly sulphured. 46%. Hart Brothers Ltd.

Kingsbury's Mortlach 15 Years Old 1989 (61) n15 t16 f15 b15. Grim, even by Mortlach's undemanding standards. 56.7%. Japan Import System Celtic Series.

Old & Rare Mortlach Aged 17 Years dist Sep 92, bott Nov 09 **(87.5) n22** a rare subtlety (by Mortlach standards) to the sugars works a treat here, breaking up the usual porridge rather well; **t23** very decent weight, with a light liquorice, semi-boubony thread to the developing oils; big, thick layering, but well measured and attractive; **f20.5** bitters out as expected, but not with too much pain; **b22** my Pavlovian response to first seeing this was that it should be, preferably, bottled under "Old and Extinct". But, I have to say, I'm delightfully surprised with this one which is helped along the way by taking a buccaneering rummy route on the old flavour portfolio rather than its usual hopeless Speyside malt gubbins. Don't mind a second glass of this at all. 56.1%. Douglas Laing & Co Ltd. 28 bottles.

Old Malt Cask Mortlach Aged 12 Years refill butt no. DL 5559, dist Sep 97, bott Nov 09 **(72.5) n19 t19 f17 b17.5.** A brown sugar fest on delivery. 50%. 365 bottles.

Old Malt Cask Mortlach Aged 12 Years sherry butt no. DL 6074, dist Sep 97, bott Apr 10 **(71) n18 t18 f17 b18.** Pretty unforgiving. I think I need some SMWS 76.67... 50%. 330 bottles.

∴ **Old Malt Cask Mortlach Aged 13 Years** refill butt, cask no. 6574, dist Sep 97, bott Sep 10 **(80) n20 t19.5 f20.5 b20.** The technical flaws are outweighed by the vivid sharpness and intensity of the barley. Fun. 50%. nc ncf sc. Douglas Laing & Co. 424 bottles.

Old Malt Cask Mortlach Aged 16 Years sherry cask, dist Sep 92, bott Jan 09 **(81.5) n20.5 t22 f19 b20.** The old-fashioned trifle, grapey nose survives a sulphur scare, as does the initial, thick delivery. And even for a while we have a bit of a sultana festival. But that dreaded off note can't escape the finale, as is so often the case... 50%. Douglas Laing.

Old Malt Cask Mortlach Aged 16 Years sherry butt, dist Sep 92, bott Dec 08 **(73.5) n18.5 t19 f18 b18.** Grapey, sweet, lush...and flawed. 50%. Douglas Laing. 582 bottles.

Old Malt Cask Mortlach Aged 19 Years Gabriel Meffre red wine cask, dist Mar 89, bott Sep 08 **(85) n22 t21 f21 b21.** Pretty acceptable version of a malt which struggles from bottling to bottling. Here there are an extra few spoonfuls of Demerara on the Dundee cake and the big, fig biscuit chew ends up with a bit of Jammy Dodger. Silky but laid on with a trowel. 50%. Douglas Laing. 359 bottles.

Old Malt Cask Mortlach Aged 21 Years refill hogshead no. DL 6126 **(73) n17 t19 f19 b18.** Do you know, I wondered if I was being a little harsh on the Mortlachs...was I guilty of a personal dislike affecting my scores? Then I found this one, mis-filed amongst the Longmorns and nosed it thinking it was from that excellent Speyside distillery. I shrank back in horror and surprise until I took a closer look at the bottle, to realise what had happened. And it just underlined, in the most garish neon, what second rate whisky this distillery is continuously guilty of producing. Sorry. But it had to be said. 50% Douglas Laing & Co Ltd

Old Masters Mortlach 1989 Aged 16 Years cask no. 969 **(77) n19 t20 f19 b19.** Furry, bitter, harsh and hot: one of the better Mortlachs from this period... 56.5%. James MacArthur.

∴ **Planeta Mortlach 18 Year Old** planeta nero d'avola cask **(86) n21 t21.5 f22 b21.5.** A thick, soupy Mortlach showing all the refinement of a tattooed arm-wrestler. But though the grapey, sherryed fruit is all over this like a rash, there is not a single off note. The perfect malt for those who think style is a four-letter word. 46%. sc. Enotria.

∴ **Premier Barrel Mortlach Aged 12 Years (89) n22.5** the vaguest hint of anthracite amid the juiciest of barley aromas; **t23** almost a grotesque amount of Speyside malt: massive barley on levels that could make you drown in your own juices; light oils spreads the delicate sweetness to maximum effect; **f21.5** some of the less impressive distillate gets a word in at last; **b22** shows what an above average barrel can do to a below average distillery... 46%. nc ncf sc. Douglas Laing & Co. 175 bottles.

∴ **Premier Barrel Mortlach Aged 14 Years (84) n21 t22 f20 b21.** Teaming with natural caramels. Clean and vanilla-rich, too. 46%. nc ncf sc. Douglas Laing & Co. 180 bottles.

∴ **Provenance Mortlach Over 8 Years** montilla finish butt, cask no. 6929, dist Spring 01, bott Spring 2011 **(85) n20 t22 f21.5 b21.5.** A thoroughly enjoyable Speysider which shows the density of a black hole and the dexterity of a Saudi Arabian thief. I, for one, would still come back for a second glass, though. 46%. nc ncf sc. Douglas Laing & Co.

∴ **Provenance Mortlach Over 8 Years** sherry finished butt, cask no. 7265, dist Spring 03, bott Summer 2011 **(88) n21** mildly discordant but enough marmalade and raisin to offer promise; **t22.5** chewy, thick but a very pleasing balance between the oily, malty body, more playful fruits and light spice; **f22** some vanilla tacks onto the light spice; more malt at the death; **b22.5** an enjoyable heavyweight. 46%. nc ncf sc. Douglas Laing & Co.

Provenance Mortlach Aged 12 Years refill hogshead, dist Summer 96, bott Spring 09 **(81) n18 t20.5 f22 b20.5.** Treacle-sweet; recovers well with a bit of barley bite and spice, even, after the poor nose. 46%. Douglas Laing.

∴ **Provenance Mortlach Over 12 Years** refill butt, cask no. 6372, dist Autumn 97, bott Summer 2010 **(76) n18 t20 f18 b19.** Some lovely barley on impact, but does not possess the wherewithal to see off the off-colour oak. 46%. nc ncf sc. Douglas Laing & Co.

Sassenach's Dram Whisky Club Mortlach 14 Year Old (83.5) n22 t21 f20 b20.5. Excellent fresh, grassy barley on nose. 46%. Exclusively for Sassenach's Dram Whisky Club Ltd.

Scotch Malt Whisky Society Cask 76.67 Aged 10 Years 1st fill barrel, dist Jun 99 **(80) n20 t20.5 f19.5 b20.** Saccharine sweet. Kind of pleasant, in the same way that certain medicines are when you are a kid...even complete with mandatory bitter finish. 59.7% 243 bottles.

Scotch Malt Whisky Society Cask 76.70 Aged 15 Years 1st fill sherry butt, dist May 94 **(72)** n19 t18 f17 b18. Thick, glutinous, hot... One for me to take home...now creosote has been outlawed. 59% 627 bottles.

Scotch Malt Whisky Society Cask 76.71 Aged 20 Years 1st fill sherry butt, dist Aug 89 **(59)** n15 t15 f14 b15. One assumes this was bottled by the Society only to give its members an idea of what sulphured, truly awful whisky tastes like. 60.1% 606 bottles.

Scotch Malt Whisky Society Cask 76.66 Aged 23 Years refill hogshead, dist Apr 86 **(74.5)** n19.5 t20 f17 b18. The odd spice mixed in with the sugars. 59.1%

⁙ **Scotch Malt Whisky Society Cask 76.72 Aged 20 Years** 1st fill sherry butt, cask no. 3677, dist 1989 **(63)** n17 t16 f14 b16. That's my taste buds comprehensively screwed for another day... 59.2%. sc. 565 bottles.

⁙ **Scotch Malt Whisky Society Cask 76.77 Aged 16 Years** 1st fill sherry butt, cask no. 4848, dist 1994 **(61)** n17 t15 f14 b15. Bloody awful doesn't cover it. Another example of that well known whisky equation: Sherry + Mortlach = Disaster. 58%. sc. 604 bottles.

⁙ **Scotch Malt Whisky Society Cask 76.79 Aged 14 Years** 1st fill sherry butt, cask no. 7273, dist 1995 **(89)** n22 unusually firm and clean. This is Mortlach...??? t22 crisp barley with a developing raisiny softness and deft spice; f23 one of the better finishes from Mortlach for a while with some real high quality sultana juicing up the vanilla, cocoa and barley to the end; b22 enough all round grapey oomph and complexity to set the taste buds salivating. 56.3%. sc. 551 bottles.

⁙ **Vom Fass Mortlach 21 Years Old (74)** n18.5 t19 f18 b18.5. Syrupy, heavy-handed and not for a moment finds a happy rhythm. A dud on many levels, yet I know many who will prostrate themselves before it... 43%

⁙ **The Whisky Castle Old Malt Cask Mortlach Aged 13 Years** refill hogshead, cask no. 7196, dist Sep 97, bott May 11 **(83)** n21 t21.5 f20 b20.5. Any more syrupy and it would have serious pretensions of being a liqueur...Some lovely bold and mouth-watering moments, though. 56.9%. nc ncf sc. Douglas Laing & Co for The Whisky Castle. 120 bottles.

Wilson & Morgan Barrel Selection Mortlach Aged 18 Years Old butt no. 4422, dist 1990 **(74.5)** n18 t19 f19 b18.5. A typically mucky, lightly sulphured affair from this distillery. Oddly enough there is a strawberry jam attractiveness late on. 56.8%. Wilson & Morgan.

⁙ **Wilson & Morgan Barrel Selection Mortlach 20 Years Old** cask no. 4412, dist 1990, bott 2010 **(71)** n18 t17 f19 b17. Such an over-the-top, grizzly Mortlach, it is almost classic for the style. Some delightful mocha makes a game of it against the sulphur very late on. 56.5%. sc.

MOSSTOWIE
Speyside, 1964–1981. Chivas Brothers. Closed.
Rarest of the Rare Mosstowie 1975 cask no. 5816 **(90.5)** n23 t23 f22 b22.5. Talk about getting old gracefully... 48.4%. Duncan Taylor.

Rarest of the Rare Mosstowie 1975 cask no. 5817 **(81)** n21.5 t21.5 f19 b19. Pleasant, malty but hot and skeletal. 47.7%. Duncan Taylor.

Rare Old Mosstowie 1979 (84.5) n21.5 t21 f21 b21. Edging inextricably well beyond its sell by date. But there is a lovely walnut cream cake (topped off with brown sugar and spices) to this which warms the cockles. Bless... 43%. Gordon & MacPhail.

NORTH PORT
Highlands (Eastern), 1820–1983. Diageo. Demolished.
Brechin 1977 db **(78)** n19 t21 f18 b20. Fire and brimstone was never an unknown quantity with the whisky from this doomed distillery. Some soothing oils are poured on this troubled – and sometimes attractively honeyed – water of life. 54.2%

Connoisseurs Choice North Port Brechin 1982 bott 2008 **(79.5)** n21 t21 f18.5 b19. Although the oak has left a bitter mark, there is a jaunty fruitiness to this on both nose and delivery which speaks well of the barley. 43%. Gordon & MacPhail.

Rarest of the Rare North Port 1981 cask no. 779 **(95)** n24.5 t24.5 f22.5 b23.5. The old Brechin distillery is in danger of getting a good posthumous name for itself...this is what great whisky is all about. 56.5%

OBAN
Highlands (Western), 1794. Diageo. Working.
Oban 14 Years Old db **(79)** n19 t22 f18 b20. Absolutely all over the place. The cask selection sits very uncomfortably with the malt. I look forward to the resumption of normality to this great but ill-served distillery. 43% ⊙⊙

Oban Aged 15 Years The Distiller's Edition db finished in Montilla Fino casks, dist 1992, bott 2007 **(90)** n22.5 t23 f22.5 b22. This isn't all about complexity and layering. It's about style and effect. And it pulls it off brilliantly. *43%*

Oban Aged 15 Years The Distiller's Edition db finished in Montilla Fino casks, dist 1993, bott 2008 **(91.5)** n22 nutty, tight, a little musty; t24 much more assured: the dryness of the grape sports beautifully against the obviously more outgoing and sweeter barley: excellent balance between the two; f22.5 perhaps the Fino wins, as it dries and embraces the oak quite happily; b23 delicate and sophisticated whisky. *43%*

PITTYVAICH
Speyside, 1975–1993. Diageo. Demolished.

Pittyvaich Aged 12 Years db **(64)** n16 t18 f15 b15. It was hard to imagine this whisky getting worse. But somehow it has achieved it. From fire-water to cloying undrinkability. What amazes me is not that this is such bad whisky: we have long known that Pittyvaich can be as grim as it gets. It's the fact they bother bottling it and inflicting it on the public. Vat this with malt from Fettercairn and neighbouring Dufftown and you'll have the perfect dram for masochists. Or those who have entirely lost the will to live. Jesus... *43%. Flora and Fauna.*

Old Malt Cask Pittyvaich Aged 18 Years sherry butt, dist Jun 90, bott Jan 09 **(76)** n18.5 t21 f17.5 b19. If you find a more uncompromisingly sweet malt this year, let me know. *50%*

Rarest of the Rare Pittyvaich 1979 cask no. 5635 **(87)** n22.5 t23 f20 b21.5. I had to check the bottle for this one. Was this really Pittyvaich? Could it be that this mouth-filling, ultra-delicious beast is the prodigy of one of the world's most hopeless distilleries? It appears it is...!!!! The finish is up to scratch, though.. *48.3%. Duncan Taylor.*

Rarest of the Rare Pittyvaich 1979 cask no. 5640 **(81.5)** n21 t21 f19 b20.5. Big, rollocking barley flattened by natural caramels; hot and graceless with a splintering finish. But still much better than the norm. *50.2%. Duncan Taylor.*

Scotch Malt Whisky Society Cask 90.11 Aged 19 Years refill barrel, dist Mar 90 **(75.5)** n20 t20 f17 b18.5. Thin and impoverished, though the oak does its level best to beef up the barley: one can only imagine with a horror bordering on morbid fascination what this must have been like 19 years ago... *54.9%*

PORT ELLEN
Islay, 1825–1983. Diageo. Closed.

Port Ellen 1979 db **(93)** n22 mousy and retiring; a degree of oak fade and fruit on the delicate smoke t23 non-committal delivery but bursts into stride with a series of sublime, peat-liquorice waves and a few rounds of spices; f24 a surprising gathering of oils rounds up the last traces of sweet barley and ensures an improbably long – and refined – finish; b24 takes so long to get out of the traps, you wonder if anything is going to happen. But when it does, my word...it's glorious! *57.5%*

Port Ellen 29 Year Old 8th Release, dist 1978, bott 2008 db **(90.5)** n23 t22.5 f22.5 b22.5. The glory and charisma is still there to cast you under its spell, but some high notes are missed, the timing not quite what it was; yet still we stand and applaud because we recognise it exactly for what it is: beauty and genius still, but fading beauty; receding genius. Something which only those of us, ourselves now of a certain vintage, can remember as being that unique, almost naked, celebration of Islay malt whisky it once so beautifully and so gloriously was. *55.3%*

⁙ **Port Ellen 31 Years Old Special Release** refill American & European oak, dist 1978, bott 2010 db **(88.5)** n22 borderline OTT oak. That was perhaps to be expected: the vague hint of juniper wasn't. The twist of lemon seems to accentuate the gin nature, though the most delicate smoke possible coaxes you back to Scotland again...; t23 oak is pile-driven into the taste buds; molasses and hickory work well while the cocoa and peat are carried on the oils; f22 long with plenty of spices zipping around and cocoa on the warm fade; b21.5 shows some serious cracks now – though that can't be helped; this whisky was never made for this type of age. Still some moments to close the eyes to and simply cherish, however; *54.6%. nc ncf. Diageo. Fewer than 3000 bottles.*

Chieftain's Port Ellen 27 Years Old hogshead, dist May 82, bott 2009 **(92)** n24 stunning cocoa and spice intro to this. The peat is obviously about but tries not to dominate and even takes a back seat to the lemon curd tart; t23 busy delivery with spice and smoke on equal terms with the unusually early mocha; f22.5 lingering smoke and a real cranking up of the drier vanilla; b22.5 one of the best new Port Ellens I have tasted this year. *56.8%. nc ncf.*

Connoisseurs Choice Port Ellen 1982 **(89.5)** n23.5 floaty peat with still a hint of grist, lightened further by a twist of lemon; t23 stays on its ultra-light course. That lemony grist shows first, then a slow after-you, after-me build up of smoke and oak; **f21.5** slightly spicy and bittering oak; **b21.5** every aspect is gentle and understated. Wonderful. *43%*

⁂ **Dun Bheagan Port Ellen 28 Years Old** hogshead, dist May 82 **(86) n22 t22 f20 b22.** Some beautiful moments, especially with the lightness of touch with the smoke – and the unusual citrus notes for a malt so old – is fabulous. But the oak lets the side down somewhat. *50%. nc ncf. Ian Macleod Distillers.*

The Golden Cask Port Ellen 1983 cask no. CM155 **(74) n17 t20 f18 b19.** Sadly, more the yellow cask... *51.8%. The House of MacDuff.*

⁂ **Malts Of Scotland Port Ellen 1983** refill sherry butt, cask no. MoS66, dist Mar 83, bott Sep 10 **(95.5) n23** low res citrus helps break up the bigger smoke notes. Some serious anthracite amid the peat reek; **t23.5** light delivery – though not dull. The contrary as juicy barley lets rip with juicier grape. Mocha and praline combine for the middle, with a hint of Jaffa Cake; **f24.5** long with the mocha becoming more milky and spices now hitting home... but with supreme sophistication; **b24.5** quietly magnificent with much to shout about. *56%. nc ncf sc. 322 bottles.*

Norse Cask Selection Port Ellen 1983 Aged 24 Years hogshead cask no. CM016, dist 1983, bott Jul 08 **(92) n22 t23.5 f23 b23.5.** A very different PE, here in a form I'd say is unique. The story chops and changes from one minute to the next and though perhaps technically challenged from time to time, the result is as intriguingly different as it is enjoyable. *52.5%*

Old & Rare Port Ellen Aged 30 Years dist Sept 78, bott Jan 09 **(91.5) n21.5 t23 f24 b23.** Has stemmed the march of time impressively. *52.5%. Douglas Laing.*

Old & Rare Port Ellen Aged 30 Years dist May 79, bott Oct 09 **(92.5) n24** creaks and reeks with antiquity: pine, heather and honey have by now replaced the more pungent elements of the peat smoke; **t23** a Demerara-sweetened oak kick then the missing smoke from the nose rushes in like a silver screen hero untying the maiden bound to the tracks as the train thunders towards her. But here the smoke appears to release the cocoa and sugars before the oaky express claims everything before it. Complex, chewy and wonderfully balanced; **f22.5** vaguely smoked vanilla; **b23** seen off the years with rare aplomb. *52.1%. ncf. 190 bottles.*

Old Bothwell Single Cask Port Ellen 1979 cask no. 7087, bott Jul 10 **(82) n19 t22.5 f20 20.5.** Plenty of citrus, but a case of too much oak limiting the charm. *54.9%. Old Bothwell Wine & Spirits Co Ltd.*

Old Bothwell Single Cask Port Ellen 1982 cask no. 2852, bott Aug 10 **(84) n20 t22.5 f20 b21.5.** Silky, buttery and the smoke just a little shy with the peat offering an ashy dryness. Some most un-PE nip and bite here. *63.2%. Old Bothwell Wine & Spirits Co Ltd.*

Old Malt Cask Lochnagar Aged 19 Years sherry butt, dist May 90, bott Jul 09 **(85) n22.5 t21 f21 b20.5.** certainly no shortage of honey, or chocolate fudge. But it is all rather swimming in natural caramels. *50%. Douglas Laing.*

Old Malt Cask Port Ellen Aged 26 Years dist May 82, bott Oct 08 **(87) n23 t22 f20.5 b21.5.** Sees off the oaky challenge. *50%. Douglas Laing.*

Old Malt Cask Port Ellen Aged 26 Years refill hogshead, dist May 82, bott Oct 08 **(86) n20 t23 f21 b22.** A bit hot and oily. But this is much better than the slightly murky nose shapes up. The delivery is dense and beautifully peated. *50%. Douglas Laing. 263 bottles.*

Old Malt Cask Port Ellen Aged 26 Years refill butt no. DL 5398, dist Sep 82, bott Jul 09 **(92) n23** lively, tingling peat. An eggy cake batter offers sweetness; **t23** civilised delivery with gently intensifying malt and a few useful spices pinging around; **f22.5** the smoke drifts into the butterscotch finale; those light spices persist; **b23.5** a beautiful buzz to this one. *50%. Douglas Laing. 712 bottles.*

Old Malt Cask Port Ellen Aged 27 Years refill hogshead, dist Apr 82, bott Nov 09 **(83.5) n21 t21 f20.5 b21.** Not the first, and by no means the last PE to have slipped over the oaky edge. *55.2%. Douglas Laing for the Whisky Fair, Germany.*

⁂ **Old Malt Cask Port Ellen 27 Years Old** refill hogshead, cask no. 6397, dist Mar 83, bott Jul 10 **(92.5) n23.5** a leaf or two of mint adds further joy to the salty light smoke; **t23.5** excellent interplay between busy spice and smoky vanilla. Excellent deftness to the oil; **f22.5** the lingering smoke compensates for late tiredness; **b23** in wonderful nick. *50%. nc ncf sc. Douglas Laing & Co. 199 bottles.*

⁂ **Old Malt Cask Port Ellen 27 Years Old** refill hogshead, cask no. 6588, dist Feb 83, bott Sep 10 **(85.5) n22 t21.5 f21 b21.** A little hot and aggressive. Some unusual cough sweet tendencies to this one. *50%. nc ncf sc. Douglas Laing & Co. 225 bottles.*

⁂ **Old Malt Cask Port Ellen 27 Years Old** refill hogshead, cask no. 6702, dist Mar 83, bott Nov 10 **(89) n23** soft vanillas, softer smoke and barely audible citrus; **t22** silky, delicate oils, a hint of panting oak; **f21** liquorice fills the oaky fissures...; **b23** a genteel Islay. *50%. nc ncf sc. Douglas Laing & Co. 230 bottles.*

⌐ **Old Malt Cask Port Ellen 27 Years Old** refill hogshead, cask no. 6708, dist Mar 83, bott Oct 10 **(95)** n24.5 probably the most delicate, complex and sublimely weighted peat aroma this year. The interplay between the smoke, citrus and vanilla is truly the stuff of whisky legend. Frankly, impossible to ask for more; t23 nearly 30 years old and yet the delivery is that of melting grist! How the hell does that happen? Again, the peat is so deft you can barely measure it. The citrus notes have dissolved sugars... The oaks equally dissolve, showing just enough weight to count but doing nothing to dominate; f23.5 medium length due to lack of oils, but the fade is a beautiful dimming of the early glory; b24 I could do with a full bottle of this stuff. Not a single off note: what a way to visit a lost gem. 50%. nc ncf sc. Douglas Laing & Co. 217 bottles.

Provenance Port Ellen Aged 25 Years sherry butt, dist Winter 83, bott Autumn 08 **(90)** n23.5 t22.5 f21.5 b22.5. A lovely cask on the edge of its age range. 46%. Douglas Laing.

Provenance Port Ellen Over 26 Years sherry butt no. DMG 5746, dist Spring 83, bott Winter 2010 **(95.5)** n24 a wall of aroma: fruit and smoke in just about equal proportions, as is the sweetness against the drier vanillas. An all evening experience; t23 surprising degree of early oak, but this soon dissipates for the fruit and smoke to resume their dominance; f24.5 long, silky, burnt raisin and sultanas, Demerara sugars and smoky caresses to the very end; b24 strikingly beautiful whisky. 46%. nc ncf. Douglas Laing.

Provenance Port Ellen Over 27 Years refill butt no. DMG 6101, dist Spring 83, bott Spring 2010 **(89)** n22 dry oak tightening around the more delicate peat; a real bonfire feel to this nose; t22 a very soft oil base helps the barley and smoke merge in intensity and, aided by a blast of full on orange, see off the drier oak; f22.5 sweeter vanilla and late gristiness; b22.5 the Port Ellens I have tasted this year look as though age is beginning to tell. This one narrowly maintains its integrity. 46%. nc ncf. Douglas Laing.

Wilson & Morgan Barrel Selection Port Ellen 27 Years Old cask no. 2347, dist 1982, bott 2010 **(87.5)** n23 powdery peat; excellent sweet-dry balance with the vanillas just seeming to convey a little lime; t22.5 sweet, icing sugar sweetness then an immediate spice impact; oily and vanilla-tame through the middle; f20 traces of bitter oak; b22 the odd phrase in this is glorious. But the oak is just negating the more complex moves. 61.3%. Wilson & Morgan.

PULTENEY
Highlands (Northern), 1826. Inver House Distillers. Working.
⌐ **Old Pulteney Aged 12 Years** db **(90.5)** n22 pungent, busy and full of zesty zap. Enough salt to get your blood pressure up; t23 beautifully clean barley, again showing little shortage of saltiness; f22.5 the vanillas and cocoa carry out an excellent drying operation. The sea-breeze saltiness continues to hang on the taste buds...; b23 a cleaner, zestier more joyous composition than the old 43%, though that has less to do with strength than overall construction. A dramatic whisky which, with further care, could get even closer to the truth of this distillery. 40%

Old Pulteney Aged 12 Years db **(85)** n22 t23 f19 b21. There are few malts whose finish dies as spectacularly as this. The nose and delivery are spot on with a real buzz and panache. The delivery in particular just bowls you over with its sharp barley integrity: real pulse-racing stuff! Then... toffee...!!! Grrrr!!! If it is caramel causing this, then it can be easily remedied. And in the process we'd have a malt absolutely basking in the low 90s...! 43%

Old Pulteney Aged 15 Years db **(91)** n21 pretty harsh and thin at first but some defter barley notes can be detected; t24 an attention-grabbing, eye-wateringly sharp delivery with the barley in roasty mood and biting immediately with a salty incision; the barley-sugar effect is mesmerising and the clarity astonishing for its age; f23 long, with those barley sugars working overtime; a slight salty edge there but the oak behaves impeccably; b23 only on about the fourth or fifth mouthful do you start getting the picture here: enormously complex with a genuine coastal edge to this. The complexity is awesome. 54.9%

Old Pulteney Aged 17 Years db **(95)** n22 tight but does all that is possible to reveal its salty, fruity complexity with pears and lemons to the fore; t25 one of the softest, most beautifully crafted deliveries in the whisky world. Absolutely faultless as it picks the most fabulous course among the honeyed vanilla and barley which is so delicate words simply cannot do justice; f24 long with near perfect balance between the vanillas and delicate honeys; b24 the nose confirms that some of the casks at work here are not A1. Yet, even so, the whisky performs to the kind of levels some distillers could only dream of. What a fabulous whisky: there really is a heaven! 46% ☉ ☉

Old Pulteney Aged 21 Years db **(97.5)** n25 if you had the formula to perfectly transform salt, citrus, the most delicate smoke imaginable, sharp barley, more gristy barley, light vanilla, toasty vanilla, roasted hazelnut, thinned manuka honey, lavender honey, arbutus blossom and cherry blossom, light hickory, liquorice, and the softest demerera sugar into the aroma of a whisky, you still wouldn't quite be able to recreate this perfection...; **t24** the sugars arrive: first gristy and malt-laden, then Demerara. This is followed by a salty, nerve-tingling journey of barley at varying intensity and then a slow but magnificently complete delivery of spice...; **f24** those spices continue to buzz, the vanillas dovetail with the malt and the fruit displaying a puckering, lively intensity. Ridiculously long fade for a malt so seemingly light, the salts and spices kiss the taste buds goodnight...; **b24.5** by far and away one of the great whiskies of 2012, absolutely exploding from the glass with vitality, charisma and class. One of Scotland's great undiscovered distilleries about to become discovered, I think... and rightly so! 46% ☉☉

Old Pulteney 30 Years Old db **(92) n23.5** fabulous mix of Jaffa cake and bourbon, seasoned by a pinch of salt; **t23.5** an early, unexpected, wave of light smoke and silkier oak gives immediate depth. But stunning, ultra-juicy citrus and barley ensures this doesn't get all big and brooding; **f22** thinner and oakier with a playful oak-spice tingle; plenty of vanilla controls the drier aspects; **b23** I had to laugh when I tasted this: indeed, it had me scrambling for a copy of the 2009 Bible to check for sure what I had written. And there it was: after bemoaning the over oaking I conjectured, "As Pulteney has the fascinating tendency to radically shift style over not too long a period, I can't wait for the next instalment." And barely a year on, here it is. Pretty far removed from last year's offering and an absolute peach of a dram that laughs in the face of its 30 years... 45%

Old Pulteney Isabella Fortuna cask no. WK499, bott 2010 db **(91.5) n23** reminiscent of a breakfast I had in Grenada some years back: lots of slightly green banana, the lightly sweetened oiliness of mixed diced nuts and a light coastal saltiness in the air: just so wonderfully fresh...; **t23.5** wow! Pulteney rarely comes more unambiguously malty than this. For all the bite of the salt and oak – which is more a little nip and nibble, to be fair – it is the barley which shines proudest of all; both sweet and sharp in equal measures; **f22.5** a touch tangy; **b22.5** over the 30-odd years I have been tasting whisky from this distillery I have noticed that its quality simply continues rising, unlike a number of other whiskies I could name. Here's further proof. 52%. 18,000 bottles.

⁙ **Old Pulteney WK209** db **(71) n68.5 t18 f16.5 b17.** Could well be liked by the Germans. 46%

A.D. Rattray Old Pulteney 1982 cask no. 502 **(90) n23 t24 f21.5 b22.** You really can't keep an excellent distillery down... 47.7%

A.D. Rattray Pulteney 1982 cask no. 504, dist Apr 82, bott Mar 10 **(96) n24** good god! An albatross on a light house singing a sea shanty...; **t23.5** more early oak than the last Rattray '82 I sighted, but extra fruitcake, too, and this one has a fair degree of salt and Demerara in the recipe. Gorgeously handsome honeycomb fills the middle ground with the build up of something coffee-related there, too...; but still that coastal feel is never far from the surface; **f24.5** on this evidence I might just try salt in my coffee...not to mention more chocolate honeycomb, burnt raisin... and an albatross...; near perfection!! **b24** magnificent malt from a quite magnificent distillery. Easily one of the highlights of the Scotch whisky year. 53.5%

Cask Strength Old Pulteney 1995 (85) n22 t22.5 f19 b21.5. Big, toe-curling fruit. But not without the odd maturation flaw. And curious lack of the normal coastal breeze. 60.5%

Duncan Taylor Collection Pulteney 1977 cask no. 3976 **(88) n21 t23 f22 b22.** No doubting the class on show here. 55.9%

Duncan Taylor Collection Pulteney 1989 cask no. 10260 **(91) n22 t24 f22 b23.** Displays all the lucidity and verve missing from the distillery bottling at this age. 58%

Gordon & MacPhail Old Pulteney Aged 15 Years (87.5) **n22 t22 f21.5 b22.** Juicy and zesty. 40%. Gordon & MacPhail.

⁙ **Gordon & MacPhail Rare Vintage Old Pulteney 1980 (88.5) n23** boiled rhubarb with salt rather than sugar added; dainty vanilla; **t22.5** mouth-watering with an early announcement of big barley; **f21** light butterscotch softens the oak; **b22** rock steady, clean and fulsome. 43%

Kingsbury's 'The Selection' Pulteney 7 Years Old cask no. 800120 & 800121, dist Jun 01, bott Jun 08 **(83.5) n21 t21.5 f20 b21.** Gristy, sweet and very light. 43%. 658 bottles.

⁙ **Malts Of Scotland Old Pulteney 1998** bourbon hogshead, cask no. 1217, dist Feb 98, bott Jan 11 **(72) n16 t19 f18.5 b18.5.** Sweet malt with a touch of apple and pear. But limited by a flawed cask – unusual for these bottlers. 52.5%. nc ncf sc. Malts Of Scotland. 301 bottles.

Rare Vintage Old Pulteney 1974 (83) n21 t20 f21 b21. Sadly, even the great distilleries can radiate their untarnished brilliance for only a finite time. Some lovely old brown sugars seeing off the oaky excess here, but still a malt that needs a Zimmer to move about the taste buds. 43% Gordon & MacPhail.

Scotch Malt Whisky Society Cask 52.18 Aged 7 Years refill barrel, dist Jun 01 **(89) n22 t23.5 f21.5 b22.** I have long been a champion of bottling at this age: this is a good example as to why. 66.3%

∴ **The Whisky Castle Exclusive Old Pulteney Aged 14 Years** cask no. 1180, dist 1997, bott 2011 (82.5) n21 t22 f19 b20.5. A confident, impressive individual at times with plenty of kumquat and honey comb. But it's all a bit of a front: there is also a darker, more bitter, side... 58.9%. nc ncf sc. Gordon & MacPhail for The Whisky Castle.

ROSEBANK
Lowlands, 1840–1993. Diageo. Closed. (But if there is a God will surely one day re-open)

Rosebank Aged 12 Years db (95) n24 t24 f23 b24. Infinately better than the last F&bottling, this is quite legendary stuff, even better than the old 8-y-o version, though probably a point or two down regarding complexity. The kind of whisky that brings a tear to the eye... for many a reason... 43%. Flora and Fauna.

Rosebank 22 Years Old Rare Malts 2004 db (85) n22 t23 f19 b21. One or two Rosebank moments of joyous complexity but, hand on heart, this is simply too old. 61.1%

Rosebank 25 Years Old db (96) n24.5 t23.5 f24 b24. I had to sit back, take a deep breath and get my head around this. It was like Highland Park but with a huge injection of sweetened chocolate on the finale and weight – and even smoke – from a Rosebank I had never quite seen before. And believe me, as this distillery's greatest champion, I've tasted a few hundred, possibly thousands, of casks of this stuff over the last 25 years. Is this the greatest of all time? I am beginning to wonder. Is it the most extraordinary since the single malt revolution took off? Certainly. I have just looked at my watch: these tasting notes have taken one hour and 21 minutes to compile...where has the time flown, where have I been? Do I endorse it? My god, yes! 61.4%

Cadenhead's Rosebank Aged 20 Years dist 1989, bott 2009 (96) n24.5 t24 f23.5 b24. Even at this ridiculous age for a distillery which peaked so young, this is legendary whisky for the annals... and to tell your grandchildren you once tasted. 52.1%

Cask Strength Rosebank 1991 (67) n18 t18 f15 b16. A rare disaster from G&M...and Rosebank: not something you would have seen coming. Has this spent time in a sherry butt? Because some sulphur is seeping in from somewhere. And that on top of a ghastly butyric note. Oh dear...taste buds ruined, that's my tasting over for the day... A shocker. 55.3%

Chieftain's Rosebank 18 Years Old sherry butt, dist Feb 90 (91) n22 t23.5 f23 b23.5. Perhaps not quite in the element of when the malt was a decade younger, but this is unquestionably made of the very finest stuff. Wonderful, and once opened the type of bottle that empties quickly. 46%. Ian Macleod Distillers Ltd.

∴ **Dun Bheagan Rosebank 20 Years Old** French oak finish, dist Feb 90 (90.5) n23.5 can't think of a better way to start the day: honey and orange juice...oh, and some Rosebank...; a few tables away is a kipper...; t23 tip-top mouth feel with the firm barley offering the skeleton for the much fleshier fruits. The oils also carry a fabulous cracked pepper bite and the slight semblance of smoke that is fleetingly alluded to in the nose; f21.5 if you expect a degree of bitterness on the home straight of a French oak finish, then you will not be disappointed. Though this is much better than the norm. b22.5 so good, you could weep. 46%. nc ncf. Ian Macleod Distillers.

Hart Brothers Rosebank Aged 17 Years dist Jun 90, bott Mar 08 (92) n23.5 t23 f22.5 b23. Just one of those lovely malts which ticks all the right boxes. And look at the tasting notes for the Montgomerie's 1990 below: tasted a month or two apart and without note comparison... consistent whisky, or what! 46%. Hart Brothers Limited.

Hart Brothers Rosebank Aged 18 Years dist Jun 90, bott May 09 (91) n23 light honey sweetens the oak and barley theme; t23.5 a delightful dollop of lemon curd sharpens the lush barley; f22.5 a plethora of vanilla notes, always with a lightly sugared coating; b22 about as soft and sweet as a Lowlander gets. Glorious. 46% Hart Brothers

Old Malt Cask Rosebank Aged 18 Years refill butt, dist Feb 90, bott Sep 08 (87) n21 t22 f22 b22. Outwardly appears a little on the thin and shy side, the victim of a sluggish old cask. Slow investigation reveals something a whole lot more charming, however. 50%.

Old Malt Cask Rosebank Aged 19 Years refill butt, dist Feb 90, bott Feb 09 (88) n22 t22.5 f21 b22.5. Definitely on the simplistic side. But it does clean, sweet maltiness...and does it well!! 50%. 374 bottles.

Old Malt Cask Rosebank Aged 19 Years refill butt, dist Feb 90, bott Mar 09 (89) n22 t23 f21.5 b22.5. Rosebank doesn't always convert to old age with grace. Here, though, it has embraced a sweet character with relish. 50%. Douglas Laing. 444 bottles.

Old Malt Cask Rosebank Aged 19 Years refill butt no. DL 5700, dist Feb 90, bott Dec 09 (89.5) n22.5 the odd atom of phenol perks up an already lively citrus-engaged barley theme; t23 salivating and lightly spiced, the roll call of honey is well attended; f22 custard and rhubarb...while those light spices fizzle... b22 almost impossible not to be charmed by this one. Playful and expansive. 50% Douglas Laing & Co Ltd. 670 bottles.

Old Malt Cask Rosebank Aged 19 Years refill hogshead no. DL 5360, dist Jun 90, bott Jul 09 **(79)** n20 t21 f19 b19. Curiously sullen for a Rosebank with huge natural caramels at work. *50%. Douglas Laing & Co Ltd. 327 bottles.*

⋯ **Old Malt Cask Rosebank Aged 20 Years** refill hogshead, cask no. 6396, dist Feb 90, bott Jul 10 **(93)** n22.5 a few flakes of sandalwood help blunt the sharpness of the bourbon lead; over-ripe kumquat, nougat and crushed pistachio; even a very curious touch of gristiness; t23.5 a surprising depth to the juicy barley balances against the on schedule spice. The odd citrus note nibbles away; the midpoint is clean and nimble; f23.5 all kinds of oaky statements: not one of them drab or determined to get the upper hand of the rest; lightly sweetened vanillas keep the balance on track; b23.5 exquisite. *50%. nc ncf sc. 232 bottles.*

⋯ **Old Malt Cask Rosebank Aged 20 Years** refill butt, cask no. 6815, dist Feb 90, bott Nov 10 **(94.5)** n23.5 big citrus chorus; t24.5 initially sweet, friendly and barley-rich. Then the taste buds are at the receiving end of a massive spice kick; it is hard to imagine a Lowlander of this age offering so much; f23 cools considerably as the vanillas trot to the rescue. But some pulsing spices thankfully remain; b23.5 obviously from the very same stable as cask 6396, above. But this one revels in a spicy belligerence, perhaps railing against the injustice of being silenced when other distilleries, some of which are not fit to be mentioned in the same breath, continue to have the marketing men lavishing their money upon them. *50%. nc ncf sc. 449 bottles.*

Scotch Malt Whisky Society Cask 25.54 Aged 18 Years refill barrel, dist Jul 91 **(85.5)** n21.5 t22 f21 b21. Fails to roll out the usual Rosebank honeyed carpet. Chirpy, but a less than sympathetic cask reduces the charm. *54.6%. Scotch Malt Whisky Society.*

ROYAL BRACKLA
Speyside, 1812. John Dewar & Sons. Working.

Royal Brackla Aged 10 Years db **(73)** n18 t20 f17 b18. A distinct lowering of the colours since I last tasted this. What on earth is going on? *40%*

Cadenhead's Royal Brackla Aged 16 Years dist 1992, bott 2009 **(96.5)** n24 t24.5 f24 b24. Another quite awesome cask from Cadenhead's. After tasting the Rosebank, I cannot remember the last time I ever tasted two successive 96-ers: I have been spoiled... *54.7%*

Premier Barrel Royal Brackla Aged 9 Years **(86)** n20 t22.5 f22 b21.5. Deliciously one-dimensional. Excellently made, not a single off-note but the oak has barely made a mark. About as easy-drinking a whisky as you'll ever find. *46%. Douglas Laing. 374 bottles.*

Provenance Brackla Aged 9 Years dist Winter 99, bott Winter 08 **(84.5)** n20 t22 f21 b21.5. Oily, malty, juicy, refreshing, deftly spiced, Reisling-looking... and amoebically simple. *46%*

⋯ **Provenance Royal Brackla Over 11 Years** refill hogshead, cask no. 6819, dist Autumn 99, bott Autumn 2010 **(84.5)** n21 t21.5 f21 b21. Reminds me of a wartime whisky: all the richer flavours seem strictly rationed. *46%. nc ncf sc. Douglas Laing & Co.*

⋯ **Scotch Malt Whisky Society Cask 55.20 Aged 12 Years** 2nd fill hogshead, cask no. 10656, dist 1998 **(89)** n22 fleeting glimpses of citrus and green banana amid the barley; t23.5 some pretensions towards lushness but it is the lightly sweetened intense barley which enjoys star billing; f21.5 lightens and thins by comparison to the mega middle but a pleasant marmalade and cocoa fade; b22 had the finish carried on where the main body left off this would have been Royalty, indeed... *58.8%. sc. 202 bottles.*

ROYAL LOCHNAGAR
Highlands (Eastern), 1826. Diageo. Working.

Royal Lochnagar Aged 12 Years db **(84)** n21 t22 f20 b21. More care has been taken with this than some other bottlings from this wonderful distillery. But I still can't understand why it never quite manages to get out of third gear...or is the caramel on the finish the giveaway...? *40%*

Royal Lochnagar 1994 The Manager's Choice db **(89.5)** n23 a lovely fruit cocktail containing guava and lychee amid the grapey orange; t23.5 sensual delivery with the barley at first forming an oily base then a subtle layering of oak and light fruits; f21.5 mallow and mocha...but the toffee drowns out the higher notes; b21.5 much more intense and heavyweight than the norm. Also a bit of toffee on the finish brings down the marks slightly. Great stuff, even so. *59.3%*

Royal Lochnagar Selected Reserve db **(89)** n23 superb oloroso, clean and spicy with apples and pears; t23 stupendous spice lift-off which really starts showing the malts to great effect; f21 the malts fade as the toffee progresses; b22 quite brilliant sherry influence. The spices are a treat. *43%*

The Càrn Mòr Vintage Collection Royal Lochnagar 1986 hogshead, cask no. 1109, dist 1986, bott 2009 **(77)** n20.5 t19 f18.5 b19. Though this appears to be from the same batch as the Duncan Taylor bottlings, this one isn't in the same league. The slightly lactic nose does offer plenty of small still richness. But the delivery, though malty, errs on the bitter side. 46%.

Duncan Taylor Collection Royal Lochnagar 1986 cask no. 942 **(87.5) n22.5 t22 f21.5 b21.5.** One of the better Lochnagars on the market, showing elegance. 56.4%. Duncan Taylor.

Duncan Taylor Collection Royal Lochnagar 1986 cask no. 948 **(89) n23 t22 f22 b22.** A more lush, richer version than cask 942 and almost as good as has been seen from this distillery for a while. For the best try cask 951. 56.9%. Duncan Taylor.

Duncan Taylor Collection Royal Lochnagar 1986 cask no. 951 **(92) n21.5 t24 f23 b23.5.** The bitter-sweet balance is exemplary. Quite the little star. 53.8%. Duncan Taylor.

Duncan Taylor Collection Royal Lochnagar 1990 cask no. 356 **(75.5) n17.5 t19 f20 b19.** There are constant reminders here that the quality of this malt from this period can be variable. While the nose and delivery are technical train wrecks, just occasionally that small still charm attempts some damage limitation. 54.3%.

Duthies Royal Lochnagar 10 Years Old (89.5) n23 gosh!! Does malt get any fresher than this? Amazingly lively and effervescent; **t22.5** a tad on the hot side but the ultra refreshing lemony malt is stunning: not a dull moment...; **f22** perhaps the odd touch of second-rate cask, but still that citrussy malt abounds; **b22** now that was fun... 46%

Harris Whisky Co. Royal Lochnagar Aged 12 Years cask no. 519, dist Jul 96, bott Sep 08 **(89) n23 t23 f21 b22.** Big delivery of citrus on the nose and palate paves the way for a really charming malt. A very different Lochnagar. 46%. Harris Whisky Co.

Norse Cask Selection Royal Lochnagar Aged 12 Years Fino sherry butt no. 520, dist Jul 96, bott Nov 08 **(83.5) n20.5 t22.5 f20 b20.5.** An attractive smudge of malty honey through the middle, but the bitter finish unsettles the balance. 57.6%.

Norse Cask Selection Royal Lochnagar 1977 Aged 29 Years cask no. DL863 **(75) n20 t19 f18 b18.** A touch of soap on the nose and pencil shavings on the palate. But there is still some glossy barley to be had. 50.4%. WhiskyOwner.com, Denmark.

Old Malt Cask Lochnagar Aged 13 Years refill butt no. DL 6290, dist Jun 97, bott Jun 10 **(89) n22.5** perky barley of the most mouth-watering grassy variety...; **t23** ...and exactly the same again on delivery: there is even a big spice injection which is hardly the norm for a Lochnagar; **f21.5** the usual sma' still coppery tang; **b22** an excellent malt with which to check that your taste buds are alive and well... 50% Douglas Laing. 380 bottles.

Old Malt Cask Lochnagar Aged 32 Years refill hogshead, dist Jan 77, bott Jan 09 **(92.5) n23.5 t23.5 f22.5 b23.** Far, far better than I expected: the malt has stayed the course and, perhaps above all other similar distilleries, really does radiate the fact that the stills are circumferentially challenged... Great stuff!! 47.7%. 74 bottles.

Premier Barrel Royal Lochnagar Aged 11 Years dist Jun 98 **(86.5) n21.5 t22 f21.5 b21.5.** Fresher than a new-grown daisy. And sweeter, too. 46%. Douglas Laing. 270 bottles.

Provenance Royal Lochnagar 12 Years Old refill hogshead no. DL 5245, dist Summer 97, bott Spring 2010 **(89) n23** let me grab that sample bottle again: it is Lochnagar! With smoke...?? Virtually not a jot of oak present, so it's sweet, lightly phenolic barley all the way... lovely!! **t23** again, just the most mouth watering, oak-free experience you might ever have. The peat simply swirls about the taste buds, adding a bit of spice here and there and even some fizzing kiddies' purple Love Heart candy kicks in; **f21.5** barley and not much else; **b21.5** the serious limitations of the cask means this won't run off with many prizes. But a very unusual touch of smoke on this helps paper over the cracks and contributes to a delightful experience where the malts pull in many delicious directions. If you see it, grab it. A real collector's item. And one to be drunk... 46%. Douglas Laing & Co Ltd.

🔹 **Provenance Royal Lochnagar Over 12 Years** refill butt, cask no. 6374, dist Summer 98, bott Summer 2010 **(91.5) n23** an intriguing aroma of honey, carrot juice and very distant cordite; **t23.5** what a cracking marriage between barley sugar and busy, ever-growing spice. That cordite nose translates perfectly but it is the overall clarity and yield in delivery which really makes the heart sing; **f22** a little oak bitterness, but the spices do their job; **b23** so often a hit or miss distillery, there is no doubting the sheer quality here. A must have bottling for this tiny and temperamental distillery. 46%. nc ncf sc. Douglas Laing & Co.

The Whisky Fair Lochnagar 1972 (94.5) n23.5 apricots and almonds make for a sexy overture; **t23.5** beautiful oils heighten the bitter-sweet delivery; sharp kumquat and then a grassy bourbon sweet quickly followed by vanilla; **f23.5** a little cocoa on the vanilla an though it dries, does so with panache; **b24** a phenomenal cask which shows both the small still character and a distillery and cask absolutely on top of its game. 50.7%

Wild Scotsman Royal Lochnagar Aged 12 Years hogshead, cask no. CM118, dist 1996, bott 2008 **(85) n21 t21 f21.5 b21.5.** An attractively lightweight, refreshing dram with the older cask allowing some of the richer barley notes full scope. 46%. House of Macduff.

ST. MAGDALENE
Lowlands, 1798–1983. Diageo. Demolished.

Linlithgow 30 Years Old dist 1973 db **(70) n18 t18 f16 b18.** A brave but ultimately futile effort from a malt that is way past its sell-by date. *59.6%*

Berry's Own Selection St. Magdalene 1982 bott 2008 **(95.5) n24 t22.5 f25 b24.** When you get an old whisky from a dead distillery, you pray for something a little special; those prayers have been answered. Glorious: you have died and St Magdalene is waiting at the gates of heaven... *46%*

⬧ **Hart Brothers St. Magdalene Aged 28 Years** dist Sep 82, bott Jan 11 **(91) n22** busy barley with some excellent polished furniture; malt in an antique shop; **t23** gristy barley, at first fresh and then bowing under the weight of big honey and maple syrup; so much oilier than I have seen from this distillery...; **f23** a swatch of vanillas, some enjoying a degree of spiciness; **b23** one of my sons lives next to the site where this distillery used to be: I shall ensure he gets a bottle of this. I never, for one moment, believed all those years back that this distillery was able to stand up to such age so easily. Life never ceases to amaze... *46%. sc.*

Old Malt Cask St Magdalene Aged 26 Years refill butt, dist Sep 82, bott Oct 08 **(90) n23 t22.5 f22 b22.5.** Simply beautiful. *50%. Douglas Laing. 511 bottles.*

⬧ **Old Malt Cask St Magdalene Aged 27 Years** refill hogshead, cask no. 6478, dist Dec 82, bott Aug 10 **(92) n23** some black pepper seriously ups the ante. Lemon curd tart, whipped cream and barley sugar completes the attractive nose; **t23.5** beautifully weighted citrus works impressively with the juiciest barley imaginable; **f22.5** the black peppers on the nose were no illusion; **b23** when I used to talk to the guys at this long lost distillery, they told me they saw it as three- and five-year-old fodder for the blends. They would be quite astonished not just that this, like the 28-years-old below, made it this far, but was so damned good at the end of its unlikely journey. *50%. nc ncf sc. Douglas Laing & Co. 264 bottles.*

⬧ **Old Malt Cask St Magdalene Aged 28 Years** refill butt, cask no. 6810, dist Sep 82, bott Nov 10 **(94) n22.5** green olives dull the complexion of the buttery lemon barley; **t23.5** the vivid, mouth-watering barley is at odds with the nose; **f24** lightly oiled, delicately but positively spiced and ridiculously fresh for its age: memorable; **b24** another Lowland hero worthy of some kind of honour of achievement against the odds. This must have been stored in an exceptionally good cask. *50%. nc ncf sc. Douglas Laing & Co. 439 bottles.*

SCAPA
Highlands (Island–Orkney), 1885. Chivas Brothers. Working.

Scapa 12 Years Old db **(88) n23** honeydew melon, soft salt and myriad styles of barley: really complex with a sprinkling of coal dust on the fruit; **t22** truly brilliant mouth arrival: the most complex display of malt and cocoa, the fruit is ripe figs with a thread of honey; **f21** a slight bitterness with some developing toffee, but the malt stays the distance; **b22** always a joy. *40%*

Scapa 14 Years Old db **(88) n22** toasted oak, butterscotch and lime; **t22.5** fresh barley for its age, a few bands of light oak but some fruity notes towards the drying middle **f21.5** chalky but some toffee interferes with the usual sweeter finale; **b22** enormous variation from bottling to bottling. In Canada I have tasted one that I gave 94 to: but don't have notes or sample here. This one is a bit of dis-service due to the over-the-top caramel added which appears to douse the usual honeyed balance. Usually, this is one of the truly great malts of the Chivas empire and a classic islander. *40%*

Scapa 16 Years Old db **(81) n21 t20.5 f19.5 b20.** For it to be so tamed and toothless is a crime against a truly great whisky which, handled correctly, would be easily among the finest the world has to offer. *40%*

Scapa 'the' Orcadian 16 Years Old db **(87.5) n22** honey offering both density to the body yet a lightness of touch; distant smoke alongside a squeeze of satsuma and shake of salt; **t22** silky and gently spiced on delivery; a citrus and toffee follow through; a hint of honey lurks; **f21.5** the softness of touch persists though one is left waiting for the oak which seems unable to battle through the toffee-honey soup; **b22** a thin wisp of honey is key to the weight and balance of this malt. *40%. For the Swiss market.*

Gordon & MacPhail Scapa Aged 15 Years dist 1993, bott 2008 **(88.5) n22 t22 f22.5 b22.** Oh, had this been a bit nearer natural strength... *40%. Gordon & MacPhail.*

⬧ **Gordon & MacPhail Distillery Label Scapa 2000** **(81.5) n21.5 t21 f19 b20.** Very strange: Gordon and MacPhail have been bringing out magnificent bottlings of this malt for as long I can remember. Yet this vintage is, though apparently natural coloured and quite pleasant in its own way, not in the same league as previous incarnations. Perhaps a price is being paid for limited wood availability at the distillery during its stop-start days. Or perhaps an inconsistency in the distillate the open-closed policy of Allied was inevitably going to produce. This is a flat Scapa divest of the genius which set this distillery apart. But if anyone can get these bottlings back on track, I'm sure it will be G&M. *43%*

Old Malt Cask Scapa Aged 15 Years refill hogshead, dist Sep 93, bott Oct 08 (**87**) n22.5 t22 f21 b21.5. A curious creature: lighter than its years, yet oaky fingerprints everywhere. *50%*

Old Malt Cask Scapa Aged 15 Years Old refill hogshead no. DL 5245, dist Oct 93, bott Jun 09 (**85**) n22 t22 f20 b21 Though this falls away towards the end, there is a resounding salty edge to the barley to ensure a full-flavoured, slightly piquant experience. *50%*

Old Malt Cask Scapa Aged 16 Years refill hogshead, cask no. DL 5728, dist Oct 93, bott Jan 10 (**81**) n20 t20 t22.5 f18.5 b20. Exceptionally tart and quite oily. *50%*

⁂ **Old Malt Cask Scapa Aged 17 Years** refill hogshead, cask no. 6560, dist 93, dist Oct 10 (**86.5**) n21 t22 f21.5 b22. A very even marriage between the sharp barley and the slightly briny, toffee oak. *50%. nc ncf sc. Douglas Laing & Co. 314 bottles.*

⁂ **Old Malt Cask Scapa Aged 17 Years** refill hogsdhead, cask no. 6925, dist Oct 93, bott Feb 11 (**89**) n22 bright, lively and distinctly coastal – wherever it may have been warehoused! t23 fabulous, eye-watering barley. Intense, single minded and offering just enough sugar and salt to maximise impact; f22 natural caramels and delicate spices harmonise; b22 really enjoyable whisky which would have scored even more highly in a better cask. *50%. nc ncf sc. 333 bottles.*

⁂ **Scotch Malt Whisky Society Cask 17.28 Aged 8 Years** 2nd fill hogshead, cask no. 310, dist 2002 (**94.5**) n23.5 a wonderful salt and honey tapestry; marvellously refreshing; t24 quite magnificent. The delivery is another patchwork of honeys of varying intensity and sweetness but with the barley bobbling in and out at regular intervals; the salt and pepper background is sublime; f23 long with the spices prevailing and the honeys melting into a butterscotch and caramel morass; b24 worth becoming a member for a bottling like this one alone. Absolutely encapsulates the distillery at an age when it is at its most dynamic and in a cask type which is most sympathetic. An easily overlooked gem. *56.7%. sc. 253 bottles.*

SPEYBURN
Speyside, 1897. Inver House Distillers. Working.

Speyburn 10 Year Old db (**82**) n20 t21 f20.5 b20.5. A tight, sharp dram with slightly more emphasis on the citric. A bit of toffee on the finale. *40%* ☉

Speyside 12 Years Old db (**85**) n22 t22 f20.5 b21.5 Copious honey and malt on delivery. Simplistic, effective but a tad bitter on finish. *40%*

Speyburn Aged 25 Years db (**92**) n22 t24 f23 b23. Either they have re-bottled very quickly or I got the diagnosis dreadfully wrong first time round. Previously I wasn't overly impressed; now I'm taken aback by its beauty. Some change. *46%*

Speyburn Bradan Orach db (**76.5**) n19 t20 f19.5 b18. Fresh, young, but struggles to find a balance. *40%* ☉

Old Malt Cask Speyburn Aged 18 Years refill hogshead, finished in rum cask, dist Jan 90, bott Oct 08 (**84**) n22.5 t21 f20.5 b20. Speyburns at this kind of age are pretty rare in bottled form, so it's always a treat to come across a very different character. The green tea characteristic isn't exactly one I have come across in the lab with this distillery at 15 years and onwards, either. Pleasing, but perhaps too many lumps of sugar in it to lift it to greatness. *50%*

SPEYSIDE
Speyside, 1990. Speyside Distillers. Working.

Speyside 10 Years Old db (**81**) n19 t21 f20 b21. Plenty of sharp oranges around; the malt is towering and the bite is deep. A weighty Speysider with no shortage of mouth prickle. *40%*

Speyside 12 Years Old db (**85**) n22 t22 f20.5 b21.5 Copious honey and malt on delivery. Simplistic, effective but a tad bitter on finish. *40%*

The Speyside Aged 15 Years db (**75**) n19 t20 f18 b18. A case of quantity of flavours over quality. *40%* ☉ ☉

⁂ **Cu Dhub** db (**76**) n18 t20 f18.5 b19.5. Even in all the caramel mud you will find Speyside distillery's paw print. A colourful malt – if your colour is black. *40%. nc ncf.*

Drumguish db (**71**) n17 t19 f17 b18. This whisky could only improve. And, thankfully, it has. Even so, a long, long way to go on this. The nose is still flawed and, despite an injection of barley early on, it flatlines its way from the fourth taste wave to the end. *40%*

Cadenhead's Speyside Aged 15 Years dist 1994, bott 2009 (**92.5**) n23 t24 f22.5 b23. Speyside as in as fine nick as you've ever seen it. What are Cadenhead's doing...? Tipping honey into the casks...? Seriously, chaps: well done you for finding a classic from this notoriously temperamental distillery. *64.6%*

The **Cärn Mör Vintage Collection Speyside 1995** sherry butt, cask no. 18, dist 1995, bott 2009 **(85.5)** n21.5 t22.5 f20 b21.5. Some serious biscuity maltiness to this one, even sporting a gentle citrus freshness. Much better than some of what was around at the distillery at the time. 46%. *The Scottish Liqueur Centre.*

Dancing Stag 17 Years Old Speyside dist 1992 **(92.5)** n23 a beautiful mix of garibaldi biscuit dunked in coffee and dank caramelized biscuit; a miniscule touch of smoke can be found in the background; t23.5 astonishing texture, helped along the way by liberal doses of golden syrup, molasses and hickory; elsewhere some burnt Dundee cake chips in, complete with nuttiness; f23 long, robust with the molasses really taking hold, followed by a spiced up vanilla fade; b23 the oldest and probably finest whisky I have ever encountered from this distillery. 46%. *Robert Graham Ltd.*

Hart Brothers Speyside Aged 13 Years dist Jun 95, bott Oct 08 **(85)** n19 t22.5 f22 b21.5. Very simple malt. Built entirely around its mega-malty theme there is some serious juiciness. The feints on the nose come to help by adding extra oil and depth to the finish. 46%

Malts of Scotland Speyside 1993 sherry butt, cask no. 636, dist Oct 93, bott Jul 09 **(93.5)** n23 sharp, unsugared gooseberries and slightly under-ripe redcurrants; the thinnest stratum of smoke weaves through the remaining grapey fruit; t24.5 eye-watering, and not just because of the strength. The barley comes out and carelessly bounds around like fox cubs with their mum; a thicker fruit fudge offers a more sombre note; f23 the fudge continues to dominate at the death, though there is a Demerera and cherry jam edge to the late butterscotch; there is a very late dry, furry note but... b23 I am now looking at this distillery in a whole new light. Well, not quite. But this is a rare specimen, to be sure. 61.7%. 192 bottles.

SPRINGBANK
Campbeltown, 1828. J&A Mitchell & Co. Working.

Hazelburn Aged 8 Years 3rd Edition (triple distilled) bott 2007 db **(89)** n22 t22.5 f22 b22.5. Somewhat effete by comparison to last year's big malty number. Here there is a shade more accent on fruit. Very light, indeed. 46%

Longrow Aged 10 Years db **(78)** n19 t20 f19 b20. Seeing as I was one of the first people alive ever to taste Longrow from its very first bottling and used to track down – in my comparative youth – every expression thereafter (and still have some in my personal collection), you could say I am a fan. But this has completely bemused me: bereft not only of the usual to-die-for smoke, its warts are exposed badly, as this is way too young. Sweet and malty, perhaps, and technically better than the marks I'm giving it – but this is Longrow, dammit! I am astonished. 46%

Longrow Aged 10 Years 100 Proof db **(86)** n20 t23 f22 b21. Still bizarrely smokeless – well, maybe a flicker of smoke as you may find the involuntary twitching of a leg of a dying fly – but the mouthfeel is much better here and although a bit too oily and dense for complexity to get going, a genuinely decent ride heading towards Hazelburn-esque barley intensity. Love it, because this oozes class. But where's the ruddy peat...? Oi, mister. I want my peat back...!! 57%

Longrow Aged 14 Years db **(89)** n25 t21 f21 b22. Hard to get a bearing on this one. The nose, though... 46%. nc ncf.

Longrow Aged 18 Years db **(94)** n23.5 t23 f24 b23.5. Determined to hide its light under a bushel...but fails. The most subtle and sophisticated Longrow I've come across in 20 years... 46%

Longrow C.V db **(95.5)** n25 t24 f22.5 b23.5. A master-class in the art of subtle peat use. 46%

Longrow Gaja Barola Wood Expression Aged 7 Years db **(91.5)** n23.5 t22.5 f23 b22.5. Taking this on is like running around an asylum claiming you're Napoleon. But I have to admit; it's fun! An accidental classic that is unlikely to be repeated...even if they tried..!! 55.8%

Springbank Society Aged 9 Years Rum Wood bott Mar 07 db **(93.5)** n23 t23.5 f23 b24. A mere pup by Springbank standards. For once its comes through as a real winner in these tender years, doubtless aided by the mercurial charms of the rum and even an unexpected touch of smoke to make for one of the most complex and entertaining drams of the year. Don't expect anything too green, though... 60.2%

Springbank 10 Years Old db **(89)** n22 t22.5 f22 b22.5. Now that's more like it!! The last bottling I had really was all over the show. This is still slightly Bambi-ish. But there is some real meat here, too. On this showing, I am beginning to change my mind about younger Springbanks... 46%

Springbank Aged 10 Years (100 Proof) db **(86)** n21.5 t22 f21 b21.5. Trying to map a Springbank demands all the skills required of a young 18th century British naval officer attempting to record the exact form and shape of a newly discovered land just after his sextant had fallen into the sea. There is no exact point on which you can fix...and so it is here. A shifting dram that never quite tastes the same twice, but one constant, sadly, is the bitterness towards the finale. Elsewhere, it's one hell of a journey...! 57%

Springbank 11 Years Old Madeira Wood Expression db (88) n23 t22.5 f21.5 b21. Madeira perhaps as you've never seen it before: don't go thinking Glenmorangie or Penderyn with this one. As big as the fruit is, the smoke outguns it. 55.8%

Springbank 15 Years Old db (87.5) n22 t21.5 f22 b22. Pity again about the light sulphur kick which is louder on the palate than nose. Even so, there are so seriously graceful sherry moments. 46%

Springbank 18 Years Old db (89.5) n23 another dense offering, but here the fruit is playing a bigger role with blood orange and under-ripe fig adding to the barley. Not perfect but there is so much going on... t22 cautiously salivating. There is a buzz from the cask, but the barley ignores this and sings its own song, alternating between sharp and juicy; f22.5 that chocolate mousse finale that appears to not be uncommon from this distillery these days; b22 it's amazing that even at 18 years of age, you get the overwhelming feeling that this malt has barely cleared its throat...? 46%

Springbank Vintage 1998 cask no. 08/263, bott Jun 09 db (92) n24 strewth! You know how generations of Australian batsmen have chipped away single-mindedly at English bowlers for hours on end over the years...well you need that kind of dedication to get through the seemingly impregnable sherry here. When you do, you'll pick up some pretty amazing notes, perhaps the pick of the bunch being a glorious meeting of dried dates, Mysore coffee and molasses. And then you get to the grape itself, which helps form a Melton Hunt cake structure but with some pretty well cooked raisins...but there's plenty more to discover, so I don't see you declaring before the end of the second day on this one...; t23 how roasty is that...? Grape in both fresh juicy form and more bitter, pleasantly burned. More bite than the 46% abv would have you think its capable of and soothing hickory fills the middle ground; f22.5 long. Some molassed dregs keep the finish away from anything too bitter; b22.5when I started trying to unravel this one my beard was still black... 53.3% 612 bottles

Springbank 2000 cask no. 240, dist Oct 00, bott Apr 09 db (90) n23 a beautiful alloy of concentrated barley and thickish, condensed, oak and a much younger personality: barley still wet behind the ears and, though a little fruity, still waiting for its nuttiness to drop...; t23.5 again we have a concentrated display with the barley topped by all kinds of molten sugars so the pulses are sweet, vibrant and often; yet another strata offers a degree of bourbon honeycomb and hickory and this is interwoven with a thinner, pre-pubescent barley. Elsewhere are chewy, burnt raisin notes...some mixture...; f21.5 a little salty tang to this and a tad furry, too; b22 not your average eight- or nine-year-old Springbank and certainly not your average malt. Tuck in: there's a little bit for everyone in this one...except smoke lovers! 48% Specially bottled for Lia and Koos den Boef Vlaardingen. 110 bottles.

⁖ **Berry's Own Selection Springbank 1992** cask no. 61, bott 2011 (88) n22 coastal with salt sharpening the stewed celery; even a mildly earthy note to this; t23 a lovely delivery of honey and Ovaltine. The malt thickens out and becomes a tad one dimensional, though there is no denying how lovely that dimension is...; f21.5 just a little tired bitterness to the oak, but otherwise it is malt all the way. Oh, and a pinch of salt...; b21.5 not often a Springbank fades away. But this one does. 46%. nc ncf sc. Berry Bros & Rudd.

Berry's Own Selection Springbank 1993 bott 2009 (83.5) n22 t21 f20 b20.5. Doesn't quite live up to the lively, lovely pear drop nose. Emotionless fare. 46%. Berry Bros & Rudd.

Cadenhead's Authentic Collection Springbank 2001 cognac cask, bott Feb 10 (73.5) n18 t21 f17 b17.5. Uptight, wet-behind-ears, uncouth, bitter and displaying a marked inferiority complex. Though a tad smoky and offering a superficial charm, sadly a poor representative of Springbank in the way we know and love it. 58.5% Wm. Cadenhead Ltd

Duthies Hazelburn 9 Years Old (93.5) n23 get some concentrated barley...then concentrate it: you'll probably end up with this...; oak is huge, too. But just get that barley...; t23.5 firm, mouth-puckering barley radiating a delicately sugared juiciness; f23.5 the oak, which is always hanging thickly around the nose and delivery but without detracting from the barley's, at last gets its ten minutes of fame, with the toasty sugars a perfect joy; b23.5 pure star quality. 46%

Duthies Springbank 12 Years Old (84.5) n21.5 t21 f21 b21. Malty, sweet and enjoyable but with a limited degree of the usual background saltiness. 46%

Founder's Reserve Springbank Aged 17 Years (86) n22 t22 f21 b21. Another Springbank which sets off at an excellent pace with barley riches galore and then tires towards the end. Delicious in part, but the natural vanillas and caramels are simply too much to take it on to greatness. 46%. Japan Import System.

⁖ **Hart Brothers Springbank Aged 14 Years** dist Nov 96, bott Jan 11 (90.5) n23 any amount of honey...very limited fruit; t22.5 again the delivery and middle is all about acacia honey and a little liquorice; some mild sultana; **f22** intense vanilla and custard tart; **b23** thick, almost glutinous barley wins the battle over the grape hands down. Great fun; superb quality. 46%. sc.

🞜 **Hart Brothers Springbank Aged 14 Years** dist Nov 96, bott Jan 11 (73) **n19 t19 f17 b18.** I checked and was told that this was from the same cask as the Springbank. 46%. I don't know what to say, other than I didn't find any sulphur on that one... 55.2%. sc.

Old Malt Cask Springbank Aged 15 Years refill hogshead, dist Jun 93, bott Oct 08 (85.5) **n21.5 t21.5 f21 b21.5.** Big, enjoyable malt, sharp and happy to keep sweetness to a minimum. A thorough oaky buzz, too. 50%. Douglas Laing. 365 bottles.

Premium Scotch Importers Springbank 1998 small oak cask (95) **n24.5 t24 f23 b23.5.** The problem with Springbank is that it is such an enormous malt it needs big age or at least a major reaction with oak to bring the best out of it. So many malts up to the age of about 18 struggle to really be heard: the oak and barley cancel each other out. That has long been my theory and this wonderful, full-throttled bottling from Springbank filled into small casks to maximise the oak influence – a form of premature aging – goes a way to prove it. The best independent Springbank I have tasted in yonks. 53.3%. Premium Scotch Importers Pty Ltd, Australia.

Scotch Malt Whisky Society Cask 27.75 Aged 12 Years refill hogshead, dist May 96 (90.5) **n23.5** beyond intriguing: polished floors much older than the given 12 years; citrus ranging from diluted lemon to mildly furry old orange! The sugars seem to appear in caramelised biscuit crumb form and there, mega-intriguingly, is even a light strata of vague smoke; and then on another hand there is something of the under-ripe new make about this...a bit like a lad who still has that bumfluff he is refusing to shave ...astonishing...; **t23** the hint of smoke on the nose is there – to say in force would be overstating it – but wearing less of a malty niqab; most Springbanks under 15 tend to flail around a bit and this one doesn't exactly get into a groove, either, but there is a disarming beauty to the juicy barley and there is even a Bowmore-style Fisherman's Friend cough sweet tang to the late middle ground...; **f22** never had a Springbank finish like this in 30 years...; **b22** strictly for those who have a good hour or so. Springbanks at this age are not meant to be quite so absorbing or smoky...and had I not been told otherwise, I would have had this down as coming from another distillery entirely. 59%

🞜 **Scotch Malt Whisky Society Cask 27.84 Aged 12 Years** refill barrel, cask no. 733, dist 1997 (93) **n23** good god! Distilled sea water? The cask has been kept in a sea shore cave? I have very rarely come across a whisky so vividly displaying such a maritime personality; **t23** mouth-watering then a succession of intense barley soup. But beautifully seasoned; **f23.5** after the barley soup comes the dessert of honey; **b23.5** one of the better 12-year-old Springbanks I have tasted in a while, the salty injection helping to break down those thick caramels. I have no idea whether this was matured by the sea or not. But I would not be surprised if it was tenderly cared for by mermaids...! 58%. sc. 213 bottles.

🞜 **Scotch Malt Whisky Society Cask 27.89 Aged 10 Years** refill barrel, cask no. 122, dist 2000 (86) **n21 t22 f21.5 b21.5.** Enjoyable. But in so many ways indicative of why this distillery struggles at these relatively low ages to come close to its greatness of later years. Just a massive onslaught of natural caramels which are pleasant enough, but keeps any complexity in a straightjacket. The salty, sweaty armpit nose is worth discovering, though!! 55.9%. sc. 263 bottles.

Scotch Malt Whisky Society Cask 126.1 Aged 11 Years (Hazelburn) sherry butt, dist Jul 97 (85) **n22 t20 f23 b20.** This is a bit like tasting a 1986 Chateaux Latour just a few years after bottling: it needed time to reach its optimum complexity but wasn't granted it. So we have a grape-soaked malt not without charm and with no little Columbian coffee. And molasses. But no shape or direction. A fantastic cask: but one emptied way, way too soon... 56.7%

🞜 **Scotch Malt Whisky Society Cask 126.2 Aged 10 Years** (Hazelburn) refill barrel, cask no. 15, dist 2000 (95) **n23** salty bacon with grits; the sugars are light, the oaks perfectly mannered. A little prickle...this promises something special...; **t24** oh my word!!! And it really doesn't let you down. One of the best deliveries of a10-year-old malt I have tasted this year, helped by a controlled weight to die for. There are oils, but just enough to help spread the honeyed word; not enough to over-run all other character traits. Some salt sharpens the barley; a nibble of butterscotch hints of age it has not yet achieved; **f23.5** the faintest degree of cask bitterness, but it doesn't stand a chance against the continuing honey theme; **b24** the difference between a Springbank and Hazelburn at exactly the same age can be astonishing. Like this one. 54%. sc. 263 bottles.

The Secret Treasures Springbank 1970 sherry cask no. 1344, dist May 70, bott Sep 07 (94) **n23** exotic fruit is only half the story; soft peat mingles with over-ripe banana; **t24** brilliant delivery: all at once full and yielding yet firm, too. Equally the balance is sublime with the darker, oakier notes which threat over-age immediately met by a lighter, more lively fruitiness again, with smoke just drifting around binding the two; **f23.5** long, decadent, a procession of vanillas of varying sweetness, chocolate mousse and that most delicate of peats bringing with it, inevitably, some spices; **b23.5** should you need further confirmation that Springbank ages with almost uncanny beauty, here it is. *43% Haromex Development GmbH, Germany. 489 bottles.*

STRATHISLA
Speyside, 1786. Chivas Brothers. Working.

Strathisla 12 Years Old db (87.5) **n22.5** the smoke evident on the last few tastings of this has been largely usurped by a heavy fat-sultana grapiness. Back to its old heavyweight self of a few years back, except the malt-fruit balance is kinder to the nose and the merest whiff of smoke is still detectable; **t23.5** thick, sweet barley swamps the tastebuds early on but slowly nudged aside by the trademark sweet sultana; engaging chocolate honeycomb towards the middle; **f20** duller than before with some big caramels kicking in and the unmistakable furry signature of the odd dud sherry butt; **b21.5** still a big, chewy dram which is about as heavy in body as you are likely to find anywhere in Speyside. Very enjoyable, though you know deep down that some fine tuning could take this guy easily into the 90s. *43%*

Strathisla Distillery Edition 15 Years Old db (94) **n23** flawlessly clean and enriched by that silky intensity of fruity malt unique to this distillery; **t23** the malt is lush, sweet and every bit as intense as the nose; a touch of toffeespice does it no harm; **f24** just so long and lingering, again with the malt being of extraordinary enormity: these are simply wave upon wave of pure delight; **b24** what a belter! The distillery is beautiful enough to visit: to take away a bottle of this as well would just be too good to be true! *53.7%*

Duncan Taylor Collection Strathisla 1967 cask no. 2721 (88) **n24.5 t22 f20 b21.5.** Doesn't live up to the pin-up nose but the bourbony aspects are attractive. *48.3%. Duncan Taylor.*

Gordon & MacPhail Distillery Label Strathisla 25 Years Old (89) **n22.5 t22.5 f22 b22.** Beautifully crafted, the aging process, apparently threatening, has ultimately been kind. *40%*

Gordon & MacPhail Distillery Label Strathisla 30 Years Old (91) **n23 t23.5 f22 b22.5.** Old age doesn't equal great whisky – fact. But here, when there is a degree of drama involved, my word: it can be so enjoyable...!! *43%*

Gordon & MacPhail Distillery Label Strathisla 40 Years Old (84.5) **n23 t21 f20 b20.5.** Excellent exotic fruit nose, but the oak has taken too firm a grip here. *43%*

⁖ **Gordon & MacPhail Strathisla 1963** 1st fill sherry, bott 2011 (84) **n22 t22 f19.5 b20.5.** Like a marathon runner at the end of his endurance, staggers blindly across the finishing line. An exhausted malt, displaying enough salt for a heart attack. But the roasted raisins and burnt molasses still shows some impressive physique. *51.8%. For Limburg Whisky Fair.*

⁖ **Gordon & MacPhail Rare Vintage Strathisla 1970** (77.5) **n20 t22 f17 b18.5.** Were I a gambling man (which, most profoundly, I am not) I would wager that this whisky has been rounded off in a fresh sherry butt somewhere along the line to take out any oaky creases. I may be wrong, of course... *43%*

Gordon & MacPhail Distillery Label Strathisla 1997 (85.5) **n21.5 t22 f21 b21.** Strathisla offering all its full blown viscosity. *43%*

⁖ **Hart Brothers Strathisla Aged 13 Years** dist Jun 97, bott Jan 11 (85) **n21.5 t21.5 f21 b21.** A pretty love to form Strathisla heavyweight with the butterscotch-barley ruling the roost over the lighter citrus. Just a little oak laziness dulls the fun. *46%. sc.*

⁖ **Malts Of Scotland Strathisla 1970** sherry hogshead, bott Mar 11 (95) **n24.5** the raisins are burned, but not to a crisp, the figs are ripe, but not to exploding point while bourbon oak is present with thick liquorice but not without the balancing honeycomb. For a 40-year-old malt, it really doesn't get much better than this...; **t23.5** one is rendered speechless by the alcoholic bite of a malt of such age: this isn't meant to happen! It does no harm whatsoever in accentuating the grip of the fruit, its wonderfully integrated depth and yet the ease in which the oak and even strands of barley are brought on board. Light oils help coat the mouth with this complex soup of a dram and even a touch of salt helps bring the flavours to the boil; **f23** dries in the manner oloroso should. Keeps closer to the wine style than the delivery and absorbs the mocha oakiness with ease; **b24** an absolutely faultless oloroso butt weaves a wonderfully rich tapestry. In many ways a malt by which others of its ilk should be judged. *59.6%. sc. Malts Of Scotland. Joint bottling with The Whisky Agency.*

Murray McDavid Mission Strathisla 1967 bourbon/grenache banyuls (85) **n22 t21 f21 b21.** From the school of exotic fruit via bourbon college. Has just about controlled on the oak, but needed a few fruit salad/black Jack nails to help keep the lid on. *43.6%. 300 bottles.*

Norse Cask Selection Strathisla 1997 Aged 12 Years hogshead cask no. 47819, dist 1997, bott May 09 (86) **n22 t22 f21 b21.** Malty, juicy and chocolaty. But a bit on the fizzy side, showing a cask not quite on its full game. *57.7%. Qualityworld for WhiskyOwner.com, Denmark.*

Old Malt Cask Strathisla Aged 18 Years refill hogshead, dist Mar 91, bott Mar 09 **(85) n22 t22 f20 b21.** Juicy, regulation Strathisla in full blending colours. *50%.*

⸭ **Provenance Strathisla Over 10 Years** refill hogshead, cask no. 6301, dist Winter 99, bott Summer 10 **(72) n18 t18 f18 b18.** Starts off kilter and never corrects itself. *46%. nc ncf sc.*

Provenance Strathisla Aged 11 Years refill hogshead, dist Winter 96, bott Autumn 08 **(86) n20.5 t22 f21.5 b22.** The nose suggests a flagging cask but the delivery is pure Strathisla with the malt intense and gently sweetened to the point of excellence in part. *46%. Douglas Laing.*

Rare Vintage Strathisla 1953 (82.5) n22 t20 f20.5 b20. Resounding oaks from start to finish but just enough brown sugars to limit the damage. But the hints of pine and creosote tell their own story. *43% Gordon & MacPhail*

Rare Vintage Strathisla 1963 (89) n22 oak tries to take an instant stranglehold, orange blossom lightens the load; **t22.5** sharp, over the top oak offers a worrying intro, but the recovery is sublime with a cool minty sweetness ushering in praline and spicy fruitcake; **f22.5** the oak has been repelled, leaving behind layers of soft vanillas; **b22** a Lazarus of a dram, which on more than one occasion looked dead in the glass. Give it a good fifteen minutes between pouring and tasting...and no bloody water!!! *43% Gordon & MacPhail*

The Whisky Agency Strathisla 42 Year Old dist 1967, bott 2009 **(91) n23 t22 f23.5 b22.5.** This is great whisky on the very edge. Just as much a battle as a dram but the overall effect is startlingly attractive. *44.5%. The Whisky Agency, Germany.*

The Whisky Fair Strathisla 1967 (88.5) n23 a huge orange affair: marmalade and kumquat on heat; **t22** sharp and tangy: the oak is not shy coming forward; some pleasant mocha fills the middle; **f21.5** oily and vanilla-rich; **b22** a valiant, if somewhat orangey, attempt to stay the course over 40 plus years. Doesn't quite entirely succeed. *43%*

STRATHMILL
Speyside, 1891. Diageo. Working.

The Càrn Mòr Vintage Collection Strathmill 1990 hogshead, cask no. 2400, dist 1990, bott 2009 **(86) n21.5 t22 f21 b21.5.** So malty and clean it just screams "Speyside" at you... *46%.*

Old Malt Cask Strathmill Aged 16 Years dist Jan 93, bott Jul 09 **(80) n19 t20 f21 b20.** One of the great undiscovered Speysiders. But here it feels pretty restricted and bound in its own natural caramel. *50%. Douglas Laing.*

Old Malt Cask Strathmill Aged 35 Years dist May 74, bott Jul 09 **(89) n23 t21.5 f22.5 b22.** I am astonished how delicate, lightweight malts like these survive 35 years. Well, usually they don't truth be told. And this one's managed it by the skin of its cask. A real gray-haired charmer, though. *474%. Douglas Laing.*

⸭ **Old Malt Cask Strathmill Aged 36 Years** refill hogshead, cask no. 7186, dist May 75, bott May 11 **(91) n22.5** a stroll among the evening flowers is likely to bring together this combination of lavender and orchid. Powerful, but not overpowering; **t23** sweet, with a build up first of gristy barley and then richer, darker sugars; some spices play ball but vanilla hits the middle earlier than expected; **f23** anyone who spends time in Brazil will appreciate this: the most perfect biscoito de polvilho; **b22.5** defies the years and the odds to come out quite so sublime. I know this distillery's greatest ever advocate saw it as a provider of mainly youngish to mid-range malts. It is one of the great mysteries, as well as one of my profound regrets, that it is not found at ten to a dozen years old. In the meantime, this fabulous bottling shall have to suffice. *44.1%. nc ncf sc. 367 bottles.*

TALISKER
Highlands (Island-Skye), 1832. Diageo. Working.

Talisker Aged 10 Years db **(93) n22** Cumberland sausage and kipper side by side; **t23** early wisps of smoke that develop into something a little spicier; lively barley that feels a little oak-dried but sweetens out wonderfully; **f24** still not at full throttle with the signature ka-boom spice, but never less than enlivening. Some wonderful chocolate adds to the smoke; **b23** it is wonderful to report that the deadening caramel that had crept into recent bottlings of the 10-y-o has retreated, and although that extraordinary, that wholly unique finale has still to be re-found in its unblemished, explosive entirety, this is much, much closer to the mark and a quite stupendous malt to be enjoyed at any time. But at night especially. *45.8%* ⊙

Talisker 12 Years Old Friends of the Classic Malts db **(86) n22 t21.5 f21 b21.5.** Decent, sweet, lightly smoked...but the explosion which made this distillery unique - the old kerpow! - appears kaput. *45.8%*

Talisker Aged 14 Years The Distillers Edition Jerez Amoroso cask, dist 1993, bott 2007 db **(90.5) n23 t23 f22 b22.5.** Certainly on the nose, one of the more old-fashioned peppery

Taliskers I've come across for a while. Still I mourn the loss of the nuclear effect it once had, but the sheer quality of this compensates. 45.8%

Talisker Aged 20 Years db (95) n24 t24 f23 b24. I have been tasting Talisker for 28 years. This is the best bottling ever. Miss this and your life will be incomplete. 62%

Talisker 25 Year Old bott 2008 db (92) n23 lazy smoke drifts over a scene of light citrus and slowly forming ancient oaks; t23.5 soft vanillas arrive first, then a wave of muted peppers stinging only playfully as the sweet barley unfolds just so charmingly; f22.5 the oaks really are revving up, but the sweet barley provides the balance; peat and citrus provide an unlikely fade; b23 busy and creaking but a glass or two of this offers some classy entertainment for the evening. 54.2%

➤ **Talisker 25 Years Old** db (88.5) n23 fragile and frugal: the peat leads, but does so tamely. All other elements are likewise shy but with the exotic fruit and treacle just about audible; t22 sweet delivery with a muscovado-charged cream toffee dominating. Slowly, apologetically the spices begin to emerge; f21.5 tame toffee and vanilla; b22 another Talisker almost choked with natural caramels. Chewy and undoubtedly charming. 54.8%

Talisker 25 Years Old db (92) n23.5 t24 f22.5 b22.5. Fabulous stuff, even though the finish in particular is strangely well behaved. 58.1%

Talisker 30 Year Old bott 2008 db (89) n21 very tired oak; t23.5 who would have believed it...? The delivery shows no woody failings whatsoever, but silky-soft barley, with a touch of toffee, and a slow-motion deployment of half-hearted smoke: just the right degree of sweetness and chewiness; f22 remains soft with the toffee-vanilla dominant; b22.5 this malt seriously defies the nose, which gives every indication of a whisky about to peg it. The softness of the experience is memorable. 49%

➤ **Talisker 30 Years Old** db (84.5) n21 t21.5 f21 b21. Toffee-rich and pretty one dimensional. Did I ever expect to say that about a Talisker at 30...? 53.1%

➤ **Talisker Special Release 2010 30 Years Old** refill American & European oak db (93) n23 shards of honeycomb pierce the thin cloud of smoke; some bristling spice suggests daddy may be home...; t24 superb delivery: an explosion of rabid spices tear at the taste buds, though some astonishingly refined honey does its best to hold it back; there is a melt-in-the-mouth barley sub plot and the natural caramels one comes to expect from this guy; a late burst of garibaldi biscuit rounds things off efficiently; f23 relatively docile by comparison and perhaps over dependent on the caramel. But at least the spice keeps buzzing...; b23 at last! A Talisker with some snap, grunt and attitude. Attaboy!!! 57.3%. nc ncf. Diageo. Fewer than 3000 bottles.

Talisker 57 Degrees North db (95) n24 salty, smoky, coastal, breezy. The distillery's location in a nose... t24.5 peat encased in a muscovado sugar, in the same way a fly might be enveloped in amber, melts to allow the slow blossoming of a quite beautiful and peaty thing...; f23 some welcome whip and bite; the smoke and vanillas hang in there and even the odd hint of mocha puffs around a bit; b23.5 a glowing tribute, I hope, for a glowing whisky... 57%

Hart Brothers Talisker Aged 15 Years dist Dec 93, bott Jul 09 (49) n15 t15 f07 b12. An elementary mistake: I thought the geology around Talisker was known for its iron, not sulphur. 51.7% Hart Brothers Ltd

➤ **Old Malt Cask Talisker 10 Years Old** refill hogshead, cask no. 7409, dist Jun 01, bott. Jun 11 (88) n(22) the peat is sulking away somewhere; citrus notes are more playful; t(22) a little bit of cough sweet and then a very slow building of phenols. The sugars are of the cooked molasses variety; f(22) no shortage of natural caramels on the fade. Again the smoke goes into hiding...; b(22) one of the biggest whisky double takes, I have ever made...almost of James Finlayson proportions... Really had to look twice to see if this was Skye's finest at 10: very little discernable peat and arrives only at the finish. Well made, though, and from a pretty decent cask. 50%. nc ncf sc. Douglas Laing & Co. 245 bottles.

Old Malt Cask Tactical Aged 10 Years refill hogshead, cask no. 5704, dist Dec 99, bott Dec 09 (84.5) n21 t22 f20.5 b21. Talisker, at its maltiest, sweetest and least fiery. 50%

Old Malt Cask Tactical Aged 18 Years refill hogshead, dist Dec 90, bott Apr 09 (96) n24.5 t23.5 f24 b24. Talk about taking you back in time. A style lost to the present day distillery bottling, though this one is a tad sweeter than normal. No other distillery can offer this particular, spectacular, package on nose and tastebuds. 50%. Douglas Laing. 152 bottles.

Scotch Malt Whisky Society Cask 14.17 Aged 20 Years refill hogshead, dist Mar 89 (90.5) n23.5 white peppers tickle and bite; the kippery smoke appears to carry sugars into the air; salty and unambiguously coastal; t23 surprisingly sweet arrival, soft, well groomed and a little oily; some unexpected Lubec marzipan and jaffa cake orange before some light spices arrive; f22 the usual lift off is missing and instead we have slightly bitter vanillas b22 beautifully distilled but for all its class the usual explosion is muted. 57.2%

TAMDHU
Speyside, 1897. Ian Macleod Distillers. Mothballed.

Tamdhu (84.5) n20 t22.5 f21 b21. So-so nose, but there is no disputing the fabulous, stylistic honey on delivery. The silkiest Speyside delivery of them all. 40%

Tamdhu Aged 18 Years bott code L0602G L12 20/08 db (74.5) n19 t19 f18 b18.5. Bitterly disappointing. Literally. 43%.

Tamdhu 25 Years Old db (88) n22 citrus showing now a more orangey based style to the lemon of its youth; t22 typically fat and intense; the barley eventually escapes the gravitational pull of the oils to offer a wonderful barley sweetness; f21 dried dates vanilla; b23 radiates quality. 43%

A.D. Rattray Tamdhu 1967 cask no. 9, dist Jan 67, bott Sep 09 (95.5) n23.5 talk about pick 'n' mix...!!! Not so much fruity bonbons. But fruity bourbons... t24 ye-ha! If I ain't in ol' rib-eye steak sizzling Kentuck...no, hang on a mo: I'm in the heart of Mars Bar-frying Speyside...! What are all these hickory and chocolate honeycomb flavours doing here...? And these strung out juicy, over heated grapes. I'm confused...; t23 some burnt raisin...but is that from the sherry or just thick barley and sugar on the oak...???? b24 A.D. Rattray have been coming out with some stunners of late. But this one almost takes the corn biscuit...or is it sherry-raisin type Garibaldi ...???? 46.5%

Cadenhead's Tamdhu Aged 18 Years dist 1991, bott 2009 (85) n20 t22.5 f21 b21.5. A bit of attitude on the nose, but mainly dealt with by the tsunami of sweet barley on delivery. 58.3%

The Càrn Mòr Vintage Collection Tamdhu 1991 hogshead, cask no. 35093, bott 2009 (85) n21 t22 f21.5 b21.5. Well, if that doesn't clean the palate with an uncomplicated malty blast, nothing will... 46% 1159 bottles.

⟐ **Chieftain's Tamdhu Aged 16 Years** fino sherry butt, dist Mar 94, bott 2011 (89) n22 dry, clean and impressively true to cask type; t23 much better delivery with the oils spreading the grape to every corner; f22 very simplistic vanilla amid the light fruit: the barley has been bypassed; b22 an excellent butt, but the barley fails to make too many waves. Even so, you won't go wrong with this clever wee dram. 46%. nc ncf. Ian Macleod Distillers.

The Golden Cask Tamdhu 1991 cask no. CM123, bott 2008 (91) n22 banana sandwich; t24 explosive barley. Within about two seconds you are hit not just by faultlessly clean barley, but also spices which, for a brief moment, take a layer off the skin of your mouth. Sharp, eye-watering fresh grass and green apples. It's beautifully insane; f22.5 calms for a pleasant and gentle butterscotch and spice warm-down; b22.5 another golden malt from the Golden Cask. While the nose and finish may be pretty standard, the delivery makes the hairs on the back of your neck stand up. 55% The House of MacDuff. 535 bottles.

⟐ **Liquid Sun Tamdhu 1990** sherry butt, bott 2011 (73) n18 t20 f17 b18. A bit of a tragedy, this. Despite the obvious faults with the butt, the degree of honey and raisin on delivery point to a paradise lost. 48.1%. The Whisky Agency.

⟐ **The MacPhail's Collection Tamdhu 1971** (88) n23 blood orange plus mango and freshly diced crunchy green apple; how old is this...???? t22 the vanillas and natural caramels hit early and hard. A light peppery fizz, aided and abetted by a hint of oaky-pine which cannot find enough support to topple the fruit; f21.5 a distinct feel of weariness, but the natural caramels prop it up to the end; b21.5 a curious malt, with the palate never quite living up to the promise of the nose. But the fact it has survived intact at all is a miracle. 43%

⟐ **Malts of Scotland Tamdhu 1990** sherry butt, cask no. 8119, dist May 90, bott Mar 11 (93) n23.5 dates, walnut, toffee and all the other things you demand from a top-notch sherry butt. Only spice is missing...; t24 but it doesn't take long to arrive on delivery and does much to pep up the blood orange and pithy attack; plenty of mocha filling the middle; f22.5 the spices and molasses survive to the delicious death; b23 fabulous sherry butts at Tamdhu are hardly two-a-penny. Savour this rarity. 49.8%. sc. Malts Of Scotland.

Old & Rare Tamdhu Aged 19 Years dist Dec 89, bott Sep 09 (92.5) n24 some black pepper gives the nearly faultless grape some hostility; t24.5 if you could see me...or hear me...I am actually sighing, such is the absolute beauty of the marriage between the flawless grape and cherry and the dense but well controlled vanillas; f21.5 a late bitter and furry note; b22.5 the distillery had some critics in later years. But I well remember when its make really was of a very decent standard...and this confirms it. 57.1% Douglas Laing & Co Ltd. 235 bottles.

Old & Rare Tamdhu Aged 19 Years sherry cask, dist Dec 89, bott Mar 09 (94) n24 t24 f22.5 b23.5. Douglas Laing appear to have hit a rich seem of massive, memorable Tamdhus. Just one of those must-have drams. 55.8%.

Old & Rare Tamdhu Aged 20 Years dist Dec 89, bott Dec 09 (81) n21 t21.5 f18.5 b20. With its initial big grapey blast, does everything in its power to hit the high spots, but the faulty sherry butt won't allow it. 55.6% Douglas Laing & Co Ltd. 232 bottles.

⫶ **Old Malt Cask Tamdhu Aged 13 Years** wine finished barrel, cask no. 6906, dist Sep 97, bott Jan 11 **(64) n16 t17 f15 b16.** When they say "wine Finished", they really aren't joking... *50%. nc ncf sc. Douglas Laing & Co. 354 bottles.*

Old Malt Cask Tamdhu Aged 17 Years refill hogshead,dist Dec 91, bott Apr 09 **(84.5) n22 t21.5 f20 b21.** Good, honest, malty, lightly oily Speyside malt, though showing more like a 10-year-old. *50%. Douglas Laing. 320 bottles.*

Old Malt Cask Tamdhu Aged 18 Years sherry hogshead, dist Dec 89, bott Sep 08 **(95) n24 t24 f23.5 b23.5.** A steamroller of a dram, the sherry crushing everything in its path. Initially not a purists' dream, as complexity takes a backseat, but there is a slow dawning of myriad bitter-sweet complexities – though mainly sweet. It's like an old, clean, unsulphured Macallan cask of yesteryear has rolled down the hill and landed in the warehouse of Tamdhu. One for sherry lovers of the original Macallan school...*50%. Douglas Laing. 268 bottles.*

⫶ **Old Malt Cask Tamdhu Aged 21 Years** sherry hogshead, cask no. 6956, dist Dec 89, bott Mar 11 **(95) n24.5** you know when you visit an ancient castle and you spot the two-feet thick walls...well, this has that kind of substance: something from before our time where you know the people responsible knew what they were doing... almost a lost craft. The grape isn't quite impenetrable... it is pierced by a beam mildly acidic sugar. And molasses...; **t24** how many layers of grape? I lost count at six. Each with a varying degree of either fruit, such as juicy, over-ripe greengage or a pulpier, more bitter note... and molasses; **f23** long, layered with the drier, chalky oak tones acting as the cement to the grapey brick. The lasting sweetness is supplied by... the molasses **b23.5** what a rare and memorable year this is for classic Tamdhu sherry bottlings... But this might be a once in a lifetimer so far as this distillery is concerned. I don't do prices: I have no idea what a bottle of this goes for. But, whatever it may be, rip their arms off... *50%. nc ncf sc. Douglas Laing & Co. 154 bottles.*

⫶ **Whisky Doris Tamdhu 25 Years Old** refill hogshead, cask no. 2834, dist Oct 84, bott Jul 10 **(83.5) n20 t21 f21.5 b21.** If you are into uncompromising barley, and very tight oak, then this bottle has your name on it. Especially if your name is Doris. *50.1%. Whisky Doris.*

TAMNAVULIN
Speyside. 1966. Whyte and Mackay. Working.

Tamnavulin 1966 Aged 35 Years cream sherry butt db **(91) n24 t22 f23 b22.** For those who love great old sherry, this is an absolute. Perhaps too much sherry to ever make it a true great, but there is no denying such quality. *52.6%*

Connoisseurs Choice Tamnavulin 1990 (82.5) n20 t22 f20.5 b20. Chugs along pleasantly and maltily enough, but with an annoying lack of enterprise or complexity for a dram normally so good. *43%. Gordon & MacPhail.*

⫶ **Gordon & MacPhail Connoisseurs Choice Tamnavulin 1991 (76) n19 t20 f18 b19.** Massively malty but just a little tart in the areas which matter most. *43%*

Master of Malt Tamnavulin 16 Years Old Cask Strength (90.5) n22 t23 f23 b22.5. At first, not too sure about this one. Then just wears you down with its non-stop enormity. And bloody niceness! *55.1%*

Old Malt Cask Tamnavulin Aged 18 Years refill hogshead no. DL 6044, dist Dec 91, bott Apr 10 **(87) n21.5** despite a distant touch of butyric, there is enough Parma Violet and dank bluebell to keep anyone happy; **t22** a little bitter due to the cask, the intense barley fights back; **f21.5** custard powder sticking to the oils; **b22** you get the feeling that in a top cask, this would have been a stunner. Wish we could see more of this distillery in the market place. *50%*

Old Malt Cask Tamnavulin Aged 20 Years dist May 89, bott Jul 09 **(95.5) n24 t24 f23.5 b24.** As healthy a specimen of Speyside 20-years-old as you are likely to find. A corker. *50%*

⫶ **Old Malt Cask Tamnavulin Aged 21 Years** refill hogshead, cask no. 7502, dist Oct 89, bott Jul 11 **(88) n22.5** custard over the kind of exotic fruit notes usually reserved for a malt ten years older at least...some charming spices develop; **t22.5** a rich barley and custard mix makes for a lovely and unusual dram; **f21** dries out despite some thickening oils; **b22** by no means standard fare: at first appears considerably older than its age, then more youthful due to the big oil slick... *50%. nc ncf sc. Douglas Laing & Co. 206 bottles.*

Old Malt Cask Tamnavulin Aged 40 Years refill hogshead, dist Nov 68, bott Mar 09 **(86) n21.5 t21 f22 b21.5.** Not quite in the same league as the formidable OMC 30-y-o of last year. Yet though the oak leaves little doubt about the age there is a melodic sweetness, of the old fashioned boiled sweet school, that ensures the barley gets a good hearing. Pleasantly spiced and in better nick than some 40-year-olds I know...I don't mean whisky. *43.1%. 261 bottles.*

⫶ **The Whisky Agency Tamnavulin 1967** bott 2010 **(86.5) n22 t22 f21 b21.5.** Plenty of surprisingly youthful, almost zesty charm which, initially, defies the years. But the passing summers – and oak – catch up with it in the end. *41%. The Whisky Agency.*

TEANINICH

Highlands (Northern), 1817. Diageo. Working.

Berry's Own Selection Teaninich 1973 (83.5) n22 t21 f20 b20.5. Even accounting for the strength, thinner than you might expect with the timid malt entirely subservient to the oak. Some lovely leathery-honey notes here and there, though. *41.8%. Berry Bros & Rudd.*

⫶⫶ **Chieftain's Teaninich Aged 28 Years** hogshead, dist Dec 82, bott 2011 (85) n21 t22 f21.5 b21.5. A serious oaky infusion boasts enough sugar and salt to make for a complex, if rather over-aged, meal of a dram. Plenty to enjoy for a final nightcap, though. *46.8%. nc ncf.*

⫶⫶ **Old Malt Cask Teaninich Aged 27 Years** refill hogshead, cask no. 6454, dist Dec 82, bott Aug 10 (80) n21 t20 f19 b20. Still standing, maltilly, after all these years. Just. *50%. nc ncf sc. Douglas Laing & Co. 239 bottles.*

⫶⫶ **Scotch Malt Whisky Society Cask 59.40 Aged 27 Years** 2nd fill hogshead, cask no. 6758, dist 1983 (86.5) n22 t22 f21 b21.5. Sweet, malty and lusty, this doesn't want for personality. A shade on the hot side, though. *55%. sc. 186 bottles.*

The Secret Treasures Teaninich 1984 sherry cask no. 5950, bott no. 250, dist Nov 84, bott Sep 07 (88.5) n23 a plate of freshly diced kumquats mingles with a playful spice buzz; t22.5 mouth-watering, juicy and refreshing. If the barley could show more it would be superstar stuff; f21 a slight marmalade bitterness; b22 oh, the irony of finding an untainted sherry butt...and it's in Germany! Actually, not entirely without taint, but it arrives only at the very end. Otherwise a really lovely – and unusual – bottling. *43% Haromex Development GmbH, Germany. 774 bottles.*

TOBERMORY

Highlands (Island–Mull), 1795. Burn Stewart Distillers. Working.

Ledaig 10 Years Old db (85) n21.5 t22 f20 b21.5. Some gorgeous and beautifully weighted peat at play here, showcased in full glory on the nose and delivery. Has to paper over some cracks towards the finish, though. *46.3%.*

⫶⫶ **Ledaig Aged 10 Years** db (85.5) n20 t22.5 f21.5 b21.5. Almost a Bowmore in disguise, such are its distinctive cough sweet qualities. Massive peat: easily one of the highest phenol Ledaigs of all time. But, as usual, a slight hiccup on the technical front. Hard work not to enjoy it, though. *46.3%. nc ncf.*

Ledaig Aged 10 Years db (63) n14 t17 f15 b17. What the hell is going on? Even Gulliver on all his weird and wonderful travels would not have come across such a strange world as the one I am on while trying to come to terms with the whisky of Tobermory. Butyric and peat in a ghoulish harmony on nose and palate that is not for the squeamish. *43%*

Ledaig Aged 12 Years db (90) n23 serious farmyard aromas – and as someone who spent three years living on one, believe me...borderline butyric, but somehow gets away with it, or at least turns it to an advantage; t23.5 the staggering peat on the nose is no less remarkable here: chunky, clunking, entirely lacking poise and posture. And it obviously doesn't give a damn...; f21.5 strange gin-type juniper amid the smoke; b22 it has ever been known that there is the finest of lines between genius and madness. A side-by-side comparison of the Ledaig 10 and 12 will probably be one of whisky's best examples of this of all time... *43%*

Tobermory Aged 10 Years db (67.5) n16 t17 f17.5 b17. A less than brilliantly made malt totally bereft of character or charm. I have no idea what has happened here. I must investigate. Frankly, I'm gutted. *40%*

Tobermory 10 Years Old db (73.5) n17.5 t19 f18 b19. The last time I tasted an official Tobermory 10 for the Bible, I was aghast with what I found. And didn't taste again for the remainder of the day, I remember. So I prodded this sample I had before me of the new 46.3% version with all the confidence Wile E Coyote might have with a failed stick of Acme dynamite. No explosions in the glass or on my palate to report. And though this is still a long way short, and I'm talking light years here, of the technical excellence of the old days, the uncomplicated sweet maltiness has a very basic charm. The nose and finish, though, are still very hard going. *46.3%.*

⫶⫶ **Tobermory Aged 10 Years** db (85) n20 t22.5 f21 b21.5 Bracing, nutty and malty the oils perhaps overdo it a little but there are enough sugars on hand to steer this one home for an enjoyable experience overall. *46.3%. nc ncf.*

⫶⫶ **Tobermory Aged 15 Years** db (93) n23.5 dripping with fresh, clean, ultra high quality oloroso there remains enough tangy malt to underscore the island location; t23.5 a fabulous marriage of juicy grape and thick, uncompromising malt. It is an arm wrestle for supremacy between the two...but it is the delicate spices which win; f23 salty chocolate raisin; b23 a tang to the oils on both nose and finish suggests an over widened middle. But such is the quality of the sherry butts and the intensity of the salt-stained malt, all is forgiven. *46.3%. nc ncf.*

Tobermory Aged 15 Years Limited Edition db (72.5) n17 t18 f19 b18.5. Another poorly made whisky: the nose and delivery tells you all you need to know. 46.3%

Berrys' Own Selection Ledaig 2005 cask no. 900008 (86) n21 t22.5 f21.5 b20.5. A massively fruity/peaty number that, though engrossingly enjoyable and at times stops you in your tracks with the odd big surprise, struggles to find the rhythm and harmony to take it up a notch. 62.7%. Berry Bros & Rudd.

The Càrn Mòr Vintage Collection Tobermory 1994 sherry butt, cask no. 5125, bott 2009 (88.5) n21.5 t23 f22 b22. A sweetie. Literally! 46%

Chieftain's Ledaig 12 Years Old Acolon Wine Finish dist Mar 97, bott 2010 (75) n18 t20 f18 b19. Mutton dressed as spam. 55%. Ian Macleod.

Duthies Ledaig 13 Years Old (80) n19 t21 f20 b20. Ultra sweet and busy with the peat pleasantly reducing the effects of a less than brilliant distillate. 46%. Wm. Cadenhead Ltd.

⋙ **Malts Of Scotland Ledaig 1997** bourbon hogshead, cask no. 800029, dist Mar 97, bott Oct 10 (79) n18.5 t23 f18 b19.5. Usually I am an advocate of bourbon cask over sherry butt any day. But here is a prime example of where it allows the faults created in the distilling process full cry, where it would have been swamped and overcome by a massive sherry, such as the '98 bottling. Even so, the delivery is a beguiling treat. 60.3%. nc ncf sc. 303 bottles.

⋙ **Malts Of Scotland Ledaig 1998** sherry butt, cask no. 800025, dist Apr 98, bott Sep 10 (95.5) n23 no sulphur, no (negative) feints...nothing to do other than bathe in the glow of outstanding oloroso, a praline peatiness and brawny brininess... t24.5 mesmerising complexity on delivery and the first 20 or 30 flavours which crash into the taste buds. Lively, surprisingly youngish, smoky, salty...yet loads of Demerara and oils to counter anything the drier oloroso and saline notes might throw down... f23.5 long, with the Demerara and spices dancing together long into the night... b24.5 it has been many a year since encountering a Ledaig of such magnificence. I am blown away... 61.8%. nc ncf sc. 256 bottles.

Old Malt Cask Tobermory Aged 14 Years sherry butt, cask no. 5993, dist Feb 96, bott Mar 10 (81.5) n20 t21 f20 b20.5. Even with a sherry overcoat, still presents itself in too sugary and ill-disciplined a fashion. 50%. Douglas Laing & Co Ltd. 677 bottles.

Private Cellar Tobermory 1995 bott 2008 (86) n21 t22 f21.5 b21.5. Enjoyable, essentially honeyed and enjoys a coppery richness. 43%. Scott's Selection.

Provenance Ledaig Aged 8 Years (86) n21 t23 f21 b21. Thundering peat but new-makey and a tad feinty. An early juice-fest, though. 46%

⋙ **Robert Graham's Dancing Stag Tobermory 1996** hogshead, dist 16 Apr 96, bott Sep 10 (76) n18 t20 f19 b19. After tasting five stupendous whiskies in a row the sequence comes to a shuddering halt. The barley here is big and intense and the sugars are impressive. But something in its overall makeup just sits all wrong. 46%. nc ncf sc. 258 bottles.

⋙ **Robert Graham's Treasured Selection Tobermory 1996** hogshead (78) n18 t21 f20 b19. The treasure chest is not quite empty, but don't expect to find gold, either. Very similar to the dancing Stag, except here the sugars and oils add bearable intensity and lustre. 59.5%. nc ncf sc. Robert Graham. 100 bottles.

The Whisky Fair Tobermory 8 Years Old dist 2001, bott 2010 (86.5) n22 t21 f21.5 b22. A model lightly peated island whisky: Twiggy. 60.9%

Wilson & Morgan Barrel Selection Tobermory 1995 Port Finish bott 2008 (84.5) n21 t21.5 f21 b21. Eye-wateringly sharp fruit pierces the taste buds. A modicum of smoke confuses the issue further. 46%

⋙ **Wilson & Morgan Barrel Selection Tobermory 1995** refill sherry, bott 2011 (85) n19 t22.5 f22 b21.5. Strikingly firm for a Tobermory with a light coating of grape softening some of the harder edges. Love the delicate sweetness. 46%. Wilson & Morgan.

TOMATIN

Speyside, 1897. Takara, Shuzo and Okura & Co. Working.

Tomatin 12 Years Old db (85.5) n21 t21.5 f22 b21. Reverted back to a delicately sherried style, or at least shows signs of a touch of fruit, as opposed to the single-minded maltfest it had recently been. So, nudge or two closer to the 18-y-o as a style and shows nothing other than good grace and no shortage of barley, either. 40%

Tomatin Aged 15 Years ex bourbon cask, bott 2010 db (86) n21 t22 f21.5 b21.5. One of the most malty drams on the market today. Perhaps suffers a little from the 43% strength as some of the lesser oak notes get a slightly disruptive foothold. But the intense, juicy barley trademark remains clear and delicious. 43% Tomatin Distillery

Tomatin Aged 18 Years db (85) n22 t21 f21 b21. I have always held a torch for this distillery and it is good to see some of the official older stuff being released. This one has some serious zing to it, leaving your tastebuds to pucker up - especially as the oak hits. 40%

Tomatin 18 Years Old db (88) n22.5 a real clean sherry statement; t22 a bit of a finoesque kick to this, then the oily malts grab the fruit and slowly assimilate it into a fruity maltshake f21.5 unbelievably gentle and demure; b22 what a well-mannered malt. As though it grew up in a loving, caring family and behaves itself impeccably from first nose to last whimpering finale; 43%

Tomatin Aged 18 Years sherry finish, bott 2010 db (92.5) n22.5 busy, thick milkshake maltiness with a touch of fruitcake; t23.5 cream sherry: creamy + sweet barley + fruity = cream sherry...; f23 very long with a touch of controlled spicy fizz to the proceedings. But that indomitable barley signature sings to the end; b23.5 finished in quite superior sherry butts. A malt brimming with character and quality. What a treat! 46%. ncf. Tomatin Distillery.

Tomatin Aged 21 Years created using 6 refill American oak casks and the 7th an ex sherry butt, bott 2009 db (81) n22 t22.5 f18.5 b19. A clattering, chattering, cluttering malt never once getting into rhythm to tell a coherent story. The sherry-pitched nose is jumbled but attractive; the delivery is at first rampant and entertaining but the middle and finale fall away, with the odd negative note at the death. A good one to pour your friends while they are blindfolded: this will confuse them. 52% Tomatin Distillery. 2400 bottles.

Tomatin 25 Years Old db (89) n22 the trademark Tomatin 25 citrus nose – plus perhaps a dash of exotic fruit - proudly attacks and teases... t21 but we have a different lad on the palate: starts gently with the citric, mouth-watering maltiness but where once it famously vanished for a while, now a regiment of spices go on the attack; soft oils ensure a rich presentation; f21.5 a becalmed finale with the malt having found its voice again; b22.5 not a nasty bone in its body: understated but significant. 43%

Tomatin 30 Years Old db (91) n22 if there was a hint of the exotics in the 25-y-o, it's here, five years on, by the barrel load. Evidence of grape, but the malt won't be outdone, either; t23 silky and sultry, there is every suggestion that the oak is thinking of going too far. Yet such is the purity and intensity of the malt, damage has been repaired and/or prevented and even at this age one can only salivate as the soft oils kick in; f23.5 probably my favourite part of the experience because the sheer deliciousness of the chocolaty finale is awesome; b22.5 malts of this age rarely maintain such a level of viscosity. Soft oils can often be damaging to a whisky, because they often refuse to allow character to flourish. Yet here we have a whisky that has come to terms with its age with great grace. And no little class. 49.3%

⁙ **Tomatin 30 Year Old** European & American oak casks db (85.5) n21 t21 f22.5 b21. Unusually for an ancient malt, the whisky becomes more comfortable as it wears its aged shoes. The delivery is just a bit too enthusiastic on the oaky front, but the natural caramels soften the journey rather delightfully. 46%. ncf.

Tomatin 40 Years Old db (89.5) n21.5 a few oaky yawns because this old guy's feeling a bit tired; t22 for all the oak intrusion, for all the burntish honeycomb, for all the old aged spices coming through, for all the first-rate impression of a high-class old bourbon, somehow, eventually, it's the malt which really catches the eye; f23 still oily after all these years and though the oak tries to get a bit tough, it doesn't stand a chance: the sweet malt, and those oils see to that; b23 not quite sure how it's done it, but somehow it has made it through all those oaky scares to make for one very impressive 40-y-o!! Often it shows the character of a bourbon on a Zimmer. 42.9%

⁙ **Tomatin 1973** refill American oak cask, cask no. 25602 db (85) n21.5 t21 f21.5 b21 Like an heroic old soldier, mortally wounded, struggling yet determined to complete its mission, this ancient malt defies the odds to make a thoroughly enjoyable experience. Yes, it pegs out in the end, the victim of a thousand too many oaky arrows to the heart. But the juicy, lightly honeycombed big-barleyed battle it rages is worthy of a medal. 44%. ncf sc. 184 bottles.

⁙ **Tomatin 1982** refill sherry puncheon, cask no. 92 db (95) n24 deft spices, grape, oak and assorted sugars in proportions one usually only dreams about; t24 top marks for the mouth feel and delivery alone. The clarity of grape and spice confirm in the first nanosecond exactly what the nose tells you: no sulphur. And so uncluttered or ruined it carries on imperiously with the spices piling into the molasses and fruit caked bowels; f23 plum pudding with a superb sugary crust and, finally, some barley join the spices and burgeoning vanilla; b24 by far the most impressive puncheon I have seen since I watched Jason Puncheon score a hat-trick for Millwall against Crystal Palace earlier this year. Like that wonderful afternoon, this whisky is something to be savoured. In fact, of its type from this distillery it is peerless. 57%. ncf sc. 560 bottles.

Tomatin 1997 1st fill bourbon, bott 2009 db (93.5) n23.5 cranked up orangey notes. Some real bourbon DNA but without the heavier oakiness. Intense barley and oak mix with limited room for further complexity development; t24 seat gripping time as those citrus notes add a piquancy to the spices which let rip. Not a single dull moment with the sugars radiating the odd concentrated Demerara moment; **f23** even with the arrival of some calming vanilla, this still pulses on the palate; **b23** another outlandishly beautiful malt from this underrated distillery. Had they mixed in a few second fill casks into this, the complexity would have been fearsome and the stuff of legend. *57.1% Tomatin Distillery. 244 bottles.*

Tomatin 1999 refill American oak, Tempranillo finish, bott 2009 **(92) n22** nutty, tight. Enclosing oak and fruit stone – something of the slivovitz about this; **t23.5** good morning taste buds...!!!! Wow! Now this one has got their attention. Improbably lively following on from the dullish nose with the fruit notes still ricocheting around the palate. The spices are marked but by no means brutal; **f23** absolutely exemplary cocoa...with a touch of cherry perhaps; **b23.5** looking for something different? Want some fun? Give this a whirl around the palate. Fabulous. *57.1%. 302 bottles.*

⁘ **Tomatin Decades** European & American oak casks db **(91) n23** floral and earthy yet equally fruity and vivid: as if nosing in a greenhouse.. **t23** big malt but the strands of toffee become chewier as the oaky theme develops; light, vaguely peaty, spices open out on an increasingly vanilla landscape; **f22.5** big age as the oak, in curiously diverse forms, take control. Just love the sugars of the cream toffee; **b22.5** an intriguing onion of a malt, of which the layers can, with concentration, be stripped away. The light smoke is there, I am sure, to paper over the oaky cracks. And it does its job immaculately. A malt for those with an hour to spare... *46%. ncf. Marriage of 1967, 1976, 1984, 1990 and peated 2005 Tomatins.*

The Càrn Mòr Vintage Collection Tomatin 1987 hogshead no. 509, bott 2009 **(87.5) n22.5** beautiful, lightly peated grist; **t22** beautiful, lightly peated grist...that's been distilled...; **f21** soft puffs of smoke help see off the more bitter oak notes **b22** for those of you who don't like their peat to have any intensity. Simple...but had this been in better wood the score would have been a lot higher. *46% nc ncf 1065 bottles*

Celtic Heartlands Tomatin 1967 bott 2008 **(78) n19 t21 f18 b20** Decent malt kick but less than kind cask input. *47.7%. Bruichladdich Ltd. 523 bottles.*

⁘ **Chieftain's Tomatin Aged 13 Years** German oak finish, dist Apr 97, bott 2011 **(88) n22** usual distillery style of intense barley...but with a sugar-coated edge; **t22** begins like hundreds of previous Tomatins I have tasted before over the years...but then the middle ground changes course and moves to a very different form of oak intensity; **f22.5** a lovely layering of tannin, molassed and muscovado sugars...and burned fudge; **b21.5** much less about balance, but more about dramatic effect. A whole bunch of sugary moves you very rarely see. *50.2%. nc ncf. Ian Macleod Distillers.*

Connoisseurs Choice Tomatin 1988 refill American hogshead dist Dec 88, bott Nov 08 **(84.5) n21 t22 f20.5 b21.** Malty and sweetens brightly towards the middle. *43%.*

Duncan Taylor Collection Tomatin 1976 cask no. 6818 **(94.5) n23.5** a well weighted honeycomb-nutmeg mix; just the odd molecule of peat evident while the oak gives the first overture to what might have become a bourbon melody; **t24** just eye-closingly beautiful arrival of a honey and spice enriched butterscotch tart; then one wave after another of a delicately oiled bourbon-style sweetness, alternating between Demerara sugars and liquorice; **f23.5** long with the oak upping in vanilla yet still there remains a charming barley fade, untainted by age; **b23.5** flawless. *50.8%*

Hart Brothers Tomatin Aged 15 Years dist Jan 93, bott Jun 08 **(81) n20.5 t21 f19 b20.5.** Malty though it is, every evidence that this one's gone through the top: lactic nose, bitter finish. *46%.*

⁘ **Liquid Sun Tomatin 1976** sherry butt, bott 11 **(82.5) n21 t21 f19.5 b21.** Some of the sherry butt notes you might expect. And a few bitter ones you might not. *48.7%. The Whisky Agency.*

Mackillop's Choice Tomatin 1978 dist Jan 78, bott May 08 **(84.5) n23.5 t20 f20.5 b20.5** To taste, leaks oak badly. But the nose is something else: dried, pithy tangerine; the grassiest of barleys; the oak is equally gentle, radiating soft cassava; any more delicate and it'd crack. *46%*

⁘ **Old Malt Cask Tomatin Aged 40 Years** refill hogshead, cask no. 7273, dist Dec 70, bott May 11 **(93) n23** no doubting age given on label: this type of aroma, wallowing in its exotic fruitiness, comes only with a light malt reaching antiquity; **t23.5** luxurious and very comfortable in its fruity skin. The barley is still sound and welcomes the high quality vanillas with equanimity; **f23** the faintest degree of smoke attaches itself to the elegant vanilla fade: very old school; **b23.5** beautiful. Almost a blueprint for a fine old Speyside-style malt. *44.3%. nc ncf sc. Douglas Laing & Co. 168 bottles.*

⁘ **Rare Auld Tomatin 33 Years Old** dist 1976, cask no. 6822 **(91) n23** the oak attempts to bludgeon you. But a wonderful sugar-fruit density swings both towards a liquorice-bourbon theme and a grapey-apple freshness; the spice is spot on; **t22.5** mouth-watering barley and sugared fruit and then a massive surge of oaky mocha and blood orange; **f23** calms down so the sugars work a magic spells on the milk chocolate oak; **b22.5** this excellent whisky may be aged 33 years...but it seems considerably older. *51%. sc. Duncan Taylor & Co.*

The Scotch Single Malt Circle Tomatin 1976 cask no. 19085, dist Nov 76, bott Jan 08 **(89.5)** **n23 t23 f21.5 b22.** Needs a bit of time in the glass to oxidise and see off some of the worst of the oak. But the low voltage sweetness is simply charming. *49.6%*

Scott's Selection Tomatin 1976 bott 2008 **(87.5)** n23 t21.5 f22 b21. The malty notes scream Tomatin and handle the oak sometimes more comfortably than others. *50.9%. Speyside Distillers.*

⭳ **Scott's Selection Tomatin 1988** bott 2011 **(88)** n22 just the right amount of spice balancing the rhubarb and boiled candy; **t22.5** dainty and crisp start with an impressive gathering of barley and fruit. The spices are always around when needed; **f21.5** pretty sugary and toasty; **b22** one of those really lovely, if non-spectacular, whiskies offering so many key elements to a good dram, you really can't say no to another glass... *50.6%. Speyside Distillers.*

⭳ **The Whisky Agency Tomatin 1966** sherry butt, bott 2011 **(94)** n23 at first the aroma seems a touch claustrophobic, but let the air get to this one and the juiciness of the grape is unveiled before your very nose...; **t24** outstanding delivery with a touch of noble rot to the first wave or two, followed by a more traditional degree of fruitcake grapiness and then even a degree of oak-puckered barley; the subtle spices do a fabulous job; **f23.5** the big oak at first looks threatening but then a rainbow appears in the shape of high quality vanilla sprinkled with enough sugars to ensure a balanced finale; **b23.5** a textbook oldie but with all the twists and turns of a novel... *46.1%. The Whisky Agency.*

⭳ **The Whisky Agency Tomatin 1976** bott 2010 **(85.5)** n22 t22 f20.5 b21. Plenty of grey whiskers but a charming display of herb on the nose and spice on the palate does the trick. *51.1%*

Whisky Doris Tomatin 43 Year Old cask no. 20950, dist Nov 65, bott Mar 09 **(87)** n22 t22 f21.5 b21.5. Not a great 43-year-old: far too much oak for that. But the spice and honey intervention makes for a battle royale. *48.2%*

The Whisky Fair Tomatin 43 Year Old dist 1965, bott 2009 **(93)** n22.5 t24 f22.5 b24. Slightly overstretched age-wise for certain, but still has enough charm and sophistication, helped along by soft orange and cocoa, to make for an improbably beautiful dram which defies the ages. *48.1%. The Whisky Fair, Germany.*

TOMINTOUL

Speyside, 1965. Angus Dundee. Working.

Tomintoul Aged 10 Years db **(79)** n19 t21 f20 b19. The caramel is less bossy than before but, for all its sharpness and decent oak finale, still doesn't quite click. *40%* ⊙⊙

⭳ **Tomintoul Aged 12 Years Portwood Finish** db **(85)** n21.5 t22.5 f20 b21. Plenty of tangerines on the nose and a marmalade on burnt toast finish. But the star quality is in the delivery which shows superb early lushness to the malt. *46%. nc ncf.*

Tomintoul Aged 14 Years db **(95)** n24 curiously, there is a sea-weed saltiness attached to this one: not exactly what you expect to find from a malt made and (I think) matured in the centre of the Scottish Highlands. But it adds a compellingly attractive - if eyebrow raising – element to this delicately framed and gently structured, lightly honeyed malt fest. The oak splendidly keeps within the spirit of the style; **t24** just how many variations on a honeyed theme can you get? Here I count at least five, each wave coming in after the other with just the odd nip and tuck or expansion of its intensity; the very faintest smoke is detectable and just when the natural caramels appear to be getting too excited, the malt re-establishes itself; **f23** medium length, but sheer quality all the way: Bird's custard mixing dreamily with drier, playfully spiced, oaky vanillas. The lightest of oils spreads the grassy, sharper malts to ensure a wonderful lightness of touch; **b24** not a single weakness: no bitterness, no off notes, no caramels other than those naturally from the oak, no sulphur. Just magnificent whisky bottled exactly the way it is meant to be. An absolute corker from this little-known but outstanding distillery and one of the most delicately complex distillery bottlings of the year. *46%*

Tomintoul Aged 16 Years db **(94.5)** n24.5 a fruity concoction of apples and pears topped with vanilla ice cream; even the vaguest hint of something smoky...one of the noses of the year...; **t23.5** soft, indeed every bit as gentle as the label promises, as the light oils coat the palate with a fabulously intense and delicately sweetened barley skin. The skeleton is playful oak; **f23** a wonderful, multi-layered interplay between malt and oak-vanillas. Long, curiously spice-free, increasingly dry but hugely sophisticated...; **b23.5** confirms Tomintoul's ability to dice with greatness. *40%* ⊙⊙

⭳ **Tomintoul Aged 21 Years** db **(93.5)** n24 has all the hallmarks of a malt which contains casks a lot older than the stated age: the fruit is of the exotic variety and the manner in which those fruit and defter floral notes effortlessly intertwine confirms not just the magnificence of quality but also familiarity between oak and malt; **t24** silky and soft with the balance of the light sugars to barley almost perfect; the vanillas grow, as they should, but the freshness to the barley never diminishes; **f22** slightly on the furry side but now the vanillas dance and light spices begin to arrive; **b23.5** just how good this whisky would have been at cask strength or even at 46 absolutely terrifies me... 40%

Tomintoul Aged 27 Years db (87) n22 t22.5 21.5 b21. The last time I saw a colour like this was on antique expert David Dickinson's face. Still, lots of charm and character to go round... and on the whisky, too. 40%

Tomintoul Aged 33 Years bott 2009 (90.5) n21 not promising. A little touch of resin, even drying creosote...; some incongruous orange blossom lightens the load; t23.5 improbably juicy delivery. Whisky marmalade and figs melt in with the sweetened vanilla and intense barley; f23 long with barley-thickened molasses. A hint of kumquat at the death; b23 didn't see that coming; thought it was almost dead in the bottle on nosing. A Lazarus of a malt. 43%

Tomintoul With A Peaty Tang db (94) n23 t24 f23 b24. A bit more than a tang, believe me! Faultlessly clean distillate that revels in its unaccustomed peaty role. The age is confusing and appears mixed, with both young and older traits being evident. 40%

⠿ **Liquid Sun Tomintoul 1967** bourbon hogshead, bott 2011 (83.5) n21 t22 f20 b20.5 It should sometimes be remembered that whiskies do often become too old for greatness. This one would have been magnificent had it been bottled maybe eight or nine years ago. But it still shows the well-worn contours of its greatness and tries its best to see off the encroaching oak with a few defiant rays of honey. 49.8%. The Whisky Agency.

Mackillop's Choice Tomintoul 1966 Sherrywood dist Oct 66, bott May 07 (87) n22.5 t21.5 f21.5 b21.5. Filled into an above average whisky butt even for its day, this malt was never going to have a problem in making 40 years. Just. 41.5%. Iain Mackillop & Co Ltd.

Mackillop's Choice Tominoul 1989 cask no. 5990, dist Aug 89, bott Mar 08 (94.5) n23 t24.5 f23 b24. It will take a good five or six mouthfuls to get the measure of this. Once you do, this essay in complexity will be a dangerously hard bottle to put down... 43%

Norse Cask Selection Tomintoul 1992 Aged 15 Years hogshead cask no. CS059, dist Aug 95, bott Jul 08 (90) n22.5 t24 f21.5 b22. Though it finishes slightly off course, so much else about this is just so wonderful. 55.5%. Qualityworld for WhiskyOwner.com.

Old Malt Cask Tomintoul Aged 33 Years refill hoghead, dist Sep 75, bott Apr 09 (86) n22 t21 f22 b21. The oak is heavy, at times cumbersome, but the greater weight is lifted by a curious molten sugared thread and juniper. The lightest oils all help lessen the burden. Really enjoyable, especially when that late puff of smoke materialises. 43.6%. Douglas Laing. 151 bottles.

Old Malt Cask Tomintoul 36 Years Old refill hogshead no. DL 5733, dist Jun 73, bott Jan 10 (86.5) n24 t20 f21.5 b21. Sadly, the oak has taken hold and has way too big an agenda on the palate despite the malty sweetness. But the nose is an entirely different matter with its lavender and lime freshness and mercurial spices. 45.9% Douglas Laing. 215 bottles.

Old Malt Cask Tomintoul Aged 40 Years refill hogshead no. DL 6215, dist Jan 70, bott May 10 (90.5) n22.5 from the exotic fruit school. But with some spices tacked on; t23 classic oldie refusing to die! Some honeyed coconut has entered the fray to see off the weightier oaks; the oils are wonderful; f22.5 long, with the oak creaking back in, but enough honey and syrup to do the job; b22.5 you just can't keep a great whisky down! 50%. 168 bottles.

⠿ **The Whisky Castle Tomintoul Aged 21 Years** refill bourbon hogshead, cask no. 6544, dist 1989, bott 2010 (91.5) n22.5 ridiculously lively barley for its years: crisp, juicily fresh and owning a very unusual Sauternes-sweet quality – especially unusual as this is from bourbon...; t23.5 oh...I just love it! Again crisp, but well mannered enough to bend in the right places to allow the barley to find all those hidden nooks and crannies on the palate.. f22.5 vanilla, a slight fudge effect...but those beautiful, remorseless barley notes just carry on delighting...; b23 on this magnificent evidence, I am celebrating Tomintoul...and The Whisky Castle!! 50%. nc ncf sc. For The Whisky Castle. In celebration of Cairngorm's National Park. 144 bottles.

TORMORE

Speyside, 1960. Chivas Brothers. Working.

Tormore 12 Years Old db (75) n19 t19 f19 b18. For those who like whisky in their caramel. 40%

Tormore Aged 15 Years "Special Distillery Bottling" db (71) n17 t18 f19 b17. even a supposed pick of choice casks can't save this from its fiery fate. 46%

Provenance Tormore Aged 12 Years dist Winter 96, bott Winter 09 (82) n20 t21 f21 b20. Malty, pleasant, clean and entirely untaxing; excellent by Tormore standards. 46%.

Scotch Malt Whisky Society Cask 105.12 Aged 25 Years 1st fill sherry hogshead, dist Sep 83 (93.5) n23 rasping bourbon; t23.5 excellent brown sugars playing around with soft spices; f24 a fabulous coating of mocha still allows the bourbon and barley full depth; superbly weighted and helped by a delicate oil; **b23** the best bottled Tormore I have tasted in a very long while...and by a distance. *55.8%. Scotch Malt Whisky Society.*

Scotch Malt Whisky Society Cask 105.13 Aged 26 Years 1st fill sherry hogshead, dist Sep 83 **(82) n24 t21 f18 b19**. OK, so the taste is on the thin side; and the finish hardly sets the pulse racing, either. But I didn't expect a stupendous nose like this from a Tormore. With those wonderful variants of pear and kumquat, this is one worth nosing...but don't bother with the drinking bit. *56%*

TULLIBARDINE
Highlands (Perthshire), 1949. Tullibardine Ltd. Working.

⸭ **Tullibardine 1962** sherry hogshead, cask no. 3185, bott 2011 db **(95.5) n24** an astonishing marriage between faultless oak, firm malt and clean, rich but non-dominating fruit. Hugely unusual because after all these years a negative note is bound to creep in somewhere. However, this is faultless. The fruit pastel candy lead is just so fresh and fabulous...; **t24** the clarity of the grape tells only half the story. What works here is the layered development of the chocolatey oak, the barley sugar malt and the fruitcake mixed spices; **f23.5** vanilla and butterscotch as you might expect, but just the very faintest wisp of smoke hovering above the toasted sultana more than does the trick; **b24** I can scarcely believe a malt of such antiquity has passed through the years unscathed. I was enjoying my first ever full year at school, Millwall were winning the old Fourth Division, and the Tornados were wowing us on both sides of the Atlantic with Telstar. There are no sepia tones or scratches to this, however. Simply timeless. *41.8%. sc.*

⸭ **Tullibardine 1964** sherry hogshead, cask no. 3354, bott 2011 db **(89.5) n21** oak inflamed and a touch of pine. The malts try to redress the balance, but it is a battle...; **t22.5** where did that come from...? Much more delicate and salivating than the nose would even come close to admitting. Some heavy duty oak arrives towards the middle ground but there is enough fruit to cushion the blow; **f23** long with any number of sultana and fruitcake notes absorbing the burnt raisin of the oak; **b23** the faltering start on the nose sends false messages for the joy which is to follow. *42.1%. sc.*

Tullibardine 1968 hogshead no. 130, bott 2008 db **(85) n23.5 t21.5 f19 b21**. The ravages of time are here for all to see, especially towards the middle and finish. But the nose (like the first few clean waves of the delivery) is a treat. The oak is thick, but there is something of the Summer night garden to the sweet floral chorus. *40.3%. sc. 252 bottles.*

⸭ **Tullibardine 1976** sherry hogshead, cask no. 3161, bott 2011 db **(94.5) n23** dense spotted dog pudding style aroma with a vague farmhouse fruitcake edge; **t24** mouth-watering, the barley and fruit are in happy unison. Surprising degrees of malt detectable given the richness of the grape and the slow but assured development of the spices; **f23.5** those tingly spices now excel and the natural caramels from the oak act as an extra harmonious anchor; **b24** voluptuous and tactile, a fruity feast to take a good half hour over. Complex; simply magnificent. *50.2%. sc.*

Tullibardine 1988 John Black Edition 4 bott 2008 db **(91.5) n23.5** gosh!! How about this for ultra ripe figs and greengages? Wonderfully spiced, honeyed - in an intriguingly understated style - and clean for good measure. One of those you leave the empty glass to give any room's aroma a touch of class to for a few days... **t23** the grape cascades onto the taste buds in a thick, dizzying regiment of fruitiness, by no means all grape, either. The spices hinted at on the nose are here ramrod hard and unyielding; **f22.5** the intensity on delivery fades quite dramatically to leave an almost new-makey cocoa residue. Surprising...and delicious...; **b22.5** An altogether superior and much more complex animal to J B's disappointing No 3 Selection. *46%*

Tullibardine 1992 Rum Finish bott 2009 db **(89.5) n22** caramelized...but without the toffee, if you see what I mean...; **t23** crunchy, sugar-coated barley helped along the way with a lovely sheen; **f22.5** a mildly sweetened vanilla flourish; **b22** cracking stuff! *46%*

Tullibardine 1993 bott 2009 db **(91.5) n22** a touch of yeast underlines the ultra-light, delicate side of an otherwise weighty nose; **t23.5** a quietly weighty body but, like the nose, it is the lightness of touch with the barley which makes for a juicy and attractive malt; **f23** long with those softly spoken oils coming through with the oaked-up vanilla; **b23** intrinsically sweet barley. But spellbindingly charming all the way. *40%*

Tullibardine 1993 Moscatel Finish bott 2007 db **(92.5) n23.5** has the rare knack of belting out its rich, raunchy Moscatel roots, yet allows both oak and barley a pretty free hand: excellent...; **t23.5** wonderful sweet and sharp delivery with some really major grape insurgence. Almost something of the liquid honey-filled cough sweet about the delivery; **f23** simmers down for an elegant, oaky, slightly mocha-stained retreat; **b22.5** this really is how wine casks should integrate. A minor stunner. *46%*

Tullibardine 1993 Oloroso Sherry Finish bott 2008 db **(89)** n23 now that is oloroso!! Deep, unblemished grape with just a pinch of ginger spicing up the malt; t23 outstanding mouthfeel with the grape offering both soft juiciness and lively kick; f21 purely an age thing as toasty dryness bites; b22 almost a trip down Memory Lane: once a pretty standard sherry butt, but now a treat. 46%

Tullibardine 1993 Pedro Ximénez Sherry Finish bott 2009 db **(87)** n21 clean with waxy floorboards; t23 much better with excellent spice offering vibrancy to the thick dollop of grape; f20.5 big, weighty toffee-apple...but without the apple... b22.5 sticky and enjoyable. 46%

Tullibardine 1993 Port Finish bott 2008 db **(83.5)** n21.5 t21 f20 b21. A bumbling, weighty kind of dram with indistinct shape and purpose, even to the extent of displaying a more bourbony gait than a fruity one. Enjoyable, decently spiced but limited in scope. 46%

Tullibardine 1993 Sauternes Finish bott 2008 db **(84.5)** n22 t22 f20 b20.5. Sleepy and soft with the expected major grape input. Yet rather flattens out too early and to too great a degree. Pleasant, but a little disappointing, too. 46%

Tullibardine Aged Oak bott 2009 db **(86)** n21.5 t21 f22 b21.5. Aged oak maybe. But early on this is all about the malt which is faultless. Major oaky buzz later, but all about attractive simplicity. 40%

꤫ **Tullibardine Aged Oak Edition** bott 2010 db **(88)** n21 youthful, vaguely gristy and despite a slight vanilla interference the malt is unopposed in its dominance; t22 a beautiful array of deft sugars and playful spice enriches the charming malt; f22.5 remains youthful and lively to the end with seemingly fresh battalions of barley arriving from somewhere; b22.5 beautifully made malt which is full of life. 46%. nc.

꤫ **Tullibardine Banyuls Finish** bott 2011 db **(68)** n16 t18 f17 b17. I saw the sulphur coming on this. A steaming mug of intense black coffee and a cool glass of taste bud restorative coconut water wait in the wings. 46%. nc ncf.

꤫ **Tullibardine John Black** db **(84.5)** n20 t21.5 f22 b21. Young, clean and bursting with all kinds of delicious maltiness. An almost perfect first dram of the day. 40%. nc.

꤫ **Tullibardine John Black Edition No. 5** sherry hogshead, cask no. 15022, dist 1992, bott Nov 10 db **(93.5)** n23 toffee apple with some medium roast Java percolating in the background; crushed sultana and the very green apple has been bitten into; t24 a luxurious texture is still crisp enough to allow both the barley and fruit all the space it needs to develop; really does juice out beautifully and as natural caramels form on the middle, some rollicking spices arrive; f23 long with a delightful sherry trifle finale, topped lightly with cream; b23.5 the John Black Edition appears to get better year on year. Here there is no doubting the faultless sherry. 53.8%. nc ncf sc. 328 bottles.

꤫ **Tullibardine Premier Cru Classé Finish Chateau Lafite** casks, dist 1992, bott Nov 10 **(89.5)** n21.5 curiously spiky and fractured with the fruit and malt seemingly having their backs to each other. Both factions can be easily spotted; t22.5 salivating with layers of fresh barley squaring up to the invading fruit; elsewhere spices begin to gather; f23 long and curiously dry. The spices still prod and nip but the fruit has the greatest impact; b22.5 a quite fascinating whisky which will keep you entertained for hours. It's like having War Games in a glass. Curiously, I tasted this from the cask when it was a few months younger and at full strength. At the greater strength and with the malt having more telling depth and confidence there was more harmonisation. Proof that each of these type of bottlings are truly unique and impossible to replicate. 46%. nc ncf.

Tullibardine Pure Pot new make db **(90.5)** n24 t23 f21.5 b22. Pure delight! Not whisky, of course, but a great example of how new make malt should be. 69%

Tullibardine PX Finish dist 1993, bott 2008 db **(85)** n23 t22 f20 b20. A big, at times bone-hard, whisky which, like many which have spent time in Pedro Ximénez casks, have found it difficult to acquire the kind of balance hoped. The nose offers great promise with a real old-fashioned fruitcake flourish but after the melt-in-the-mouth delivery gets past the barley lead, the degree of bitterness outweighs the growing soft fig notes. For equilibrium, needed less – or more – time in cask: we'll never know. 46%

Tullibardine Vintage Edition Aged 20 Years dist 1988, bott 2008 db **(86)** n22 t22 f21 b21. The malt sparkles on the nose and delivery. Fades as caramels kick in. 46%

A.D. Rattray Tullibardine 1990 cask no. 6105, dist Sep 90, bott Sep 09 **(91.5)** n23 a beautiful gooseberry and soft bourbon buzz: a very recognizable, elegant distillery character; t23 biscuity, complete with soft oils, and a light citrus thread; f23 ridiculously clean with the naked barley sauntering to the finish line; b22.5 you know, for some reason Tullibardine has its fare share of detractors. Or at least I often hear it criticised. I have absolutely no idea why. Here is another malt of exceptionally high quality. 59.1%

Duthies Tullibardine 16 Years Old (87) n22 light, Canadian-style (but without the colouring!) with a touch of gooseberry; t22 the barley is almost elasticated and stringy, getting everywhere; f21 standard dry vanillas; b22 delicate, malty and beautifully assembled. 46%

The Golden Cask Tullibardine 1989 cask no. CM127, dist 1989 (86) n21.5 t22 f21 b21.5. A thick, lolling malt with some outrageously intense barley and shards of honey. The oak does bite now and again but the soft liquorice sub-plot ensures something to chew over. 56.7%

The Queen of the Moorlands Rare Cask Tullibardine 1994 Edition XV hogshead no. 676 (89) n23 t21 f23 b22. Pretty wild, and it has nothing to do with the strength. The delivery is scrambled but finds a rhythm late on and genuinely impresses. 57.7%

Scotch Malt Whisky Society Cask 28.21 Aged 18 Years refill hogshead, dist Jun 90 (88.5) n21.5 t23 f22 b22. Thick enough to make a malty milkshake from: a honeyed insertion enriches the still mildly juicy but typically intense barley. 54.8%

The Whisky Fair Tullibardine 1976 dark sherry, dist 1976, bott Sep 08 (96) n24 t24.5 f23.5 b24. You see, when you nose and taste this you get some idea of the unutterable paucity of the indefensible, sulphur-screwed bollocks which passes for an embarrassing percentage of sherry cask whisky today... 54.1%. The Whisky Fair.

The Whisky Fair Tullibardine 1976 light sherry, dist 1976, bott Sep 08 (94) n24 t24 f23 b23. Absolutely not a single sign of age damage. Superb malt. 54.3%.

UNSPECIFIED SINGLE MALTS (Campbeltown)

Cadenhead's Campbeltown Malt (92) n22 t24 f23 b23. On their home turf you'd expect them to get it right... and, my word, so they do!! 59.5%

Cadenhead's Classic Campbeltown (92) n23 t24 f22 b23. What a dram! Must be what they gave Lazarus... 50%

UNSPECIFIED SINGLE MALTS (Highland)

Asda Extra Special Highland Single Malt 12 Years Old (79.5) n21.5 t21 f18 b19. Performs well with a chunky body until it bitters dramatically at the finale. 40%

Cadenhead's Classic Highland (82) n19 t22 f21 b20. The trace of fusel oil on the nose guarantees a big delivery. Highly malty! 50%

Cadenhead's Highland Malt (90) n22 t23 f22 b23. Does barley come any more pure or intense than this...? 60.2%

∴ **Co-operative Highland Single Malt Aged 12 Years** (79) n22 t21 f17.5 b18.5. Guys! You have to tone down the caramel drastically – preferably remove it altogether. It is there in such enormity that after the first ripe cherry delivery on the palate, all else is entirely lost: the whisky vanishes completely. Such a shame, as the nose suggests we might have been in for something rather lovely. 40%. Co-operative UK.

∴ **Deerstalker Aged 10 Years** bott 06/05/11 (87.5) n22 so delicate it feels like it is breaking into a thousand pieces just on the nose. Very intense, though fragile, barley; even a hint of sherbet; t23 mouth-watering beyond belief. Immeasurable degree of barley that is as juicy as spring grass; some spices and caramels ensure a degree of pastures new and balance; f21 the danger of an ultra-light dram like this is that you are left prey to any lurking oak bitterness; b21.5 a 10 year old masquerading as a malt half that age. The deerstalker must belong to Holmes, who has done a pretty fine job tracking down some decent third fill casks. Possibly the most refreshing drams of the year and one of the few that might actually slake a thirst...! 40%. nc

Duncan Taylor Majesty Single Highland Malt 30 Years Old (93.5) n22.5 some grand old age brings out the exotic fruit and a squirt of liquorice...and a dash of smoky creosote; t24 a real shock as fresh barley goes on a salivating orgy; gristy sugars everywhere plus some watered golden syrup...beautiful...almost youthfully so; f23.5 long, with the syrup holding out until the vanilla takes control; b23.5 the nose suggests a malt past its sell by date. The reality on the palate is anything but. A thrilling way to mark the 800th new whisky for Bible 2011. 40%

Glenandrew Aged 10 Years (83.5) n22 t21 f20 b20.5. Soft chewy toffee. 40%

Glen Burn Single Highland Malt (81) n20 t20 f21 b20. Pleasant, gentle if simplistic pub fodder. 40%. Glen Burn Distillers.

Glenfinnan Highland Scotch Single Malt Over 12 Years Old (84) n22 t23 f19 b20. Starts beautifully with citrus and rose petals among other delights. But then stops dead just as you pass the middle. Damn!! 40%. Celtic Whisky Compagnie, France.

∴ **Glen Marnoch 12 Years Old** dist Mar 98, bott Oct 10 (83) n21 t21 f20 b21. Shards of honey try to penetrate the fog of caramel and coffee. 40%. Aldi.

∴ **Glen Marnoch 18 Years Old** bott Oct 10 (84.5) n21 t22.5 f20 b21. Some delicious dates, walnuts and spices are to be found in there somewhere. But just too thick and shapeless for a malt this age. 40%. Aldi.

Glen Torran Highland Single Malt 8 Years Old (75) n17 t21 f18 b19. Sparkles briefly on arrival, helped along the way by lovely spice. But the caramel on the nose and finish does it in. 40%. Roderick & Henderson for London & Scottish International.

Glen Turner Single Highland Malt Aged 12 Years (85) n21.5 t22.5 f20 b21. Pleasant enough. 40%. Glen Turner Distillery for La Martiniquaise, France.

Glen Turner Single Highland Malt Aged 18 Years (83) n19 t23 f20 b21. Some serious honey doing the rounds here and the fruitiness is at times impressive. But the nose and finish testifies that odd dodgy cask has been tipped into this, too. 40%. Glen Turner Distillery for La Martiniquaise, France.

❖ **The Grangestone Whisky Collection Highland Single Malt 12 Years Old** (87) n22 the distant aroma of raspberry jam spread on warm, slightly overcooked toast; but mainly it is big barley; t22 sweet, sugary delivery: gristy at times; a late juicy surge; f21 dries as we return to the burnt toast; b22 a safe bet. 40%. Quality Spirits International.

Matisse Aged 15 Years Highland Single Malt (83.5) n22 t21 f20 b20.5. Lots of toffee with fruit. Has rather upped the toffee delivery of late. 40%. Matisse Spirits Co. Ltd.

Matisse 19 Year Old Highland Single Malt bott Oct 09 (85) n22 t21.5 f21 b21.5. Even flavoured and tempered: a safe, malty, lightly fruity dram. 46% Matisse Spirits Co Ltd

Matisse 1996 Single Cask Highland Malt Special Scottish Parliament Edition bott Apr 10 (90) n23 marzipan with sugared eggs and flour: like an uncooked cake; t23 beautifully clean and refreshing: lemon juice freshens further thick, malty middle; f22 a quite astonishing degree of natural caramel and malt concentrate; b22 the nose wants to make you run your fingers around the inside of the glass and devour whatever you get...a whisky far too good to be wasted on mere politicians. 58.6%. Matisse Spirits Co Ltd. 222 bottles.

McClelland's Highland Single Malt (80) n21 t20 f19 b20. Easy going – until the bitter finish kicks in. 40%

Sainsbury's Single Highland Malt Aged 12 Years (88) n22 playful spices and banana skins; t22 juicy delivery showing a degree of youth and freshness; f22 long with plenty of caramel and vanilla. A few spices promised on the nose make a late entry; b22 hard to imagine a more easy drinking malt than this. What it loses in simplicity of character, it makes up for with a clean, steady degree of rich textures. 40%. UK. ☉☉

Tantallan 10 Years Old Highland Single Malt (86) n21.5 t22.5 f21 b21. Has kept impressively to its massively malted principles with a squirt here and there of fruit, too. But let down slightly by the bitterness of the odd tired bourbon barrel. 40%

Tesco Highland Single Malt 12 Years Old (88.5) n23 chunky and alluring with dates and chocolate marzipan starring; t23.5 superbly textured with magnificent muscovado sugar and light spice balance; still more marzipan dipped in plum brandy; f20 relatively disappointing despite the vanilla...just a little furry; b22 the odd flaw cannot undo a really lovely whisky brimming with weight and character. 40%. Tesco. ☉☉

Wemyss 1989 Single Highland "The Fruit Bowl" refill hogshead, bott Sep 09 (89.5) n22.5 light, flighty malt; stewed cooking apple; t23 full mouth feel with chunky malt and many stratum of juicy figs sweetened with molasses; f22 malty and mildly metallic b22 mild mannered and meandering. 46%. Wemyss Malts Ltd. 331 bottles.

❖ **Wemyss 1989 Single Highland "The Herb Garden"** bott Apr 09 (89) n24.5 dry, delicate, naughtily understated. Dried orange and chopped walnuts in groundnut oil. The vanillas are clean and unthreatening..this is one of the best aromas of the year; t24 a malty blast but with featherbed weight. Still nutty but the malts are salivating; the chocolate orange middle is sublime; f19 hits the buffers by comparison. Just the wrong type of fruit with a sharpness out of sync with the magnificence of before; b22.5 the nose and early delivery was the stuff of world whisky of the year. Doesn't manage to stay on course, but so worth discovering. 46%. sc. Wemyss Malts. 345 bottles.

❖ **Wemyss 1989 Single Highland "The Orange Tree"** hogshead, bott 2011 (92) n22 tapioca pudding with a blob of jam; t23.5 sensual and salivating a watered down freshly squeezed orange is sweetened by slightly burned molasses; f23 soft oils and cocoa; b23.5 well done to Wemyss: they have unearthed some stunners... and here is another! 46%. sc. Wemyss Malts. 272 bottles.

❖ **Wemyss 1990 Single Highland "Chocolate Plums"** bott Apr 09 (71) n17.5 t19 f17 b17.5. Plum duff... 46%. sc. Wemyss Malts. 345 bottles.

❖ **Wemyss 1990 Single Highland "Mocha Spice"** butt, bott 2011 (84.5) n20 t23.5 f20 b21. Not entirely without blemishes. And way too fruity for mocha (which tends to come from bourbon cask) but some juicy delights on offer. 46%. sc. Wemyss Malts. 732 bottles.

❖ **Wemyss 1990 Single Highland "Red Berry Cream"** butt, bott 2011 (71) n17.5 t18.5 f17 b18. Must have come from a feintyberry bush... 46%. Wemyss Malts. 865 bottles.

⊰⊱ **Wemyss 1990 Single Highland "Spiced Figs"** bott Apr 09 (93) n23 a distinctly grapey, almost plum brandy-esque aroma which straddles a degree of thinness with a sharper fruit quite beautifully; t24 still more of the slivovitz style: sharp, sweet, lightly bodied but fabulously layered with the vanilla arriving with a delicate degree of mocha; f22.5 the lightness of the structure allows the oak to have a big say but the spices ensure plenty of continuing activity on the palate; b23.5 forget the "figs". You won't find them as they aren't there. But one thing is certain: this is brilliant whisky! 46%. sc. Wemyss Malts. 345 bottles.

Wemyss 1990 Single Highland "Tropical Spice" refill butt, bott Sep 09 (95) n24.5 wow!! Now this makes you sit up and take notice. No sitting on fences here: a full broadside of intense oaky spice softened, yet thickened by an ultra rich fruit-barley combo of white knuckle intensity. The type of nose which takes a good hour to circumnavigate...; t24 the delivery is no less intimidating with a highly unusual charge of rich, sweet fruit and a much drier, austere almost, oakiness; the treacle candy is a treat; through all this the malt is never less than salivating; f23 long, playful background spice and sweetened hickory; b23.5 a peach of a barrel. Highly unusual in character and never seemingly the same any two times you taste it. 59.4%. Wemyss Malts Ltd. 767 bottles.

⊰⊱ **Wemyss 1997 Single Highland "Vanilla Summer"** hogshead, bott 2011 (93) n23 big bourbon signature; t23.5 an imposing flypast of various bourbony mainstays, with red liquorice and a delicate Demerara-vanilla to the fore; f23 dries elegantly towards a touch of butterscotch and honeycomb; b23.5 more like a Kentucky Spring... 46%. Wemyss Malts. 363 bottles.

Wilson & Morgan Sherry Cask Malt "Highland Heart" cask no. 4446, 4448 & 4450, dist 2001, bott 2009 (75.5) n18 t22 f17 b18.5. For a while the golden honey flies high and handsomely. Then a familiar sherry off note breaks my lowland heart. 43%

UNSPECIFIED SINGLE MALTS (Island)

Adelphi's Fascadale Aged 10 Years Batch 2 bourbon hogshead, bott 2010 (86.5) n22.5 t21.5 f21 b21.5. Punchy, peaty, and attractively aggressive. 46%. 3746 bottles.

Dun Bheagan Island Single Malt Aged 8 Years (93) n23 t24 f23 b23. As beautiful as a Scottish isle. 43%. Ian Macleod Distillers.

⊰⊱ **Isle Of Mull Aged 10 Years** (77) n16.5 t22 f19.5 b19. A balanced Ledaig defined...peat and feints in equal measure. 40%. Marks & Spencer UK.

Macleod's Island (85) n21 t22 f21 b21. A soft, toffee-fudged affair. Easy drinking. 40%

UNSPECIFIED SINGLE MALTS (Islay)

⊰⊱ **Adelphi Breath Of The Isles 15 Years Old** cask no. 1792, dist 1995, bott 2010 (94.5) n24 excellent honey-smoke combo; floral pollen-like notes; spices take a little time to arrive but when they do, they no more than complete the picture; t24 sublime honeycomb: actually breaks down honey constituents thanks to a manuka-acacia mix; a liquorice layer; f22.5 threatens to bitter up, but instead light spices and more honeycomb edge it closer to a bourbon-style finale; b24 take a breath of this every day and you'd live for ever... 58%. sc. 245 bottles.

Adelphi's Liddesdale Aged 18 Years Batch 1 sherry butt, bott 2010 (94) n23.5 crisp, brittle, crumbly peat partnering a more succulent fig and date fruitiness; t24 glorious delivery, with the fruit thick and jammy, then wave upon wave of manuka honey. Elsewhere, spices dance and the peat rumbles; f23 a tad bitter, both in a marmalade and burnt way, but now hickory and vanilla rise above the smoke; b23.5 an exceptional Islay where complexity and balance are the key. 46%. Distillery Ltd. 2962 bottles.

Asda Extra Special Islay Single Malt 12 Years Old (91) n23 classic peat ash and citrus-tinged smoke; t23 fabulous liquorice and Demerara-sweetened peat; toffee vanilla is in no short supply, either; f22.5 cough sweet, spices and toffee; b22.5 a high quality Islay from the old traditional school. 40%

⊰⊱ **Auld Reekie 10 Years Old** (90.5) n22 thumping peat, younger in style than its given age; t23.5 sweet, gristy, sugary peat which fair cleans the palate. How salivating is that...? f22.5 so many smoke signals. And every one single: youthful peat... b22.5 about as subtle as a Glasgow kiss followed by a knee in the nuts. Just a whole lot more enjoyable... 46%

Auld Reekie Islay Malt (95) n24 t24 f23 b24. My last whisky of the day and a dram I shall be tasting all the way to when I clean my teeth. On second thoughts... I'll do them in the morning. Only kidding. But this is a must have dram for Islayphiles: true genius. 46%

Berrys' Reserve Islay (86.5) n21.5 t22.5 f21 b21.5. Fat, sweet, chewy and particularly pleasing on delivery. Decent nip, too. 46%. Berry Bros & Rudd.

Blackadder Peat Reek (88) n23 t22 f21 b22. A clean, very gentle giant. 46%. Blackadder Int.

Cadenhead's Classic Islay (91) n23 t23 f22 b23. I admit: totally baffled by this one. Just can't read the distillery at all: a completely different take on any of them: kind of

Ardbegian, but a Lahphraogish blast and a hint of Caol Ila's oils. Yet it is all, yet none of them. Oddly enough, it reminds of Port Ellen when about eight years old. But, obviously, can't be. Classic, indeed! *50%*

Cadenhead's Islay Malt (84) n22 t21 f20 b21. Fat, well enough peated but lacks ambition and complexity. *58%*

Classic of Islay Single Malt Cask Strength (81) n20 t22 f19 b20. Fat, smoky, oily, very sweet, tight. Enjoyable, but lacking character development due mainly to the casks. *58%*

Dun Bheagan Islay Vintage 2000 (88) n22 dry, powdery peat ashes; t22.5 opens up on delivery with a charge of molasses and hickory. The smoke is lazy and drifts without shape; f21.5 more hickory, vanilla and burnt toast tang; b22 a plodding malt which reveals its considerable charms in slow motion. *43%. Ian Macleod for Canadian Market.*

Elements of Islay Ar2 (90.5) n22 dry, dusty smoke, some real singed toast to this one; t23.5 a peppery explosion on delivery, then a beautiful, molassed sweetness coats the mouth; f22.5 long, a touch of brine on the hickory and smoke; b22.5 sunshine one minute, storms the next... yep: this whisky about sums up the elements of Islay quite succinctly. *60.5%*

⌐:⌐ **Elements Of Islay Br1** (89) n22.5 refreshing, peat-free, vivid citrus and a sprinkle of salt; t22.5 barley gushes in the salivating delivery and then an immediate blanket of caramel; f22 caramel, vanilla and a lot of chewing; b22 absolutely delicious and clean but quietened by what appears to be a massive dose of natural caramels from the oak. Hang on: for an Elements of Islay, shouldn't rain be in there somewhere...? *53.6%. ncf. Speciality Drinks Ltd.*

Elements of Islay Cl1 (85.5) n21 t22.5 f21 b21. Molassed Fisherman's Friend cough sweet. Where have I tasted this style before? Simplistic, but a real meal. *62.9%*

⌐:⌐ **Elements Of Islay Lg2** (77) n19 t20 f19 b19. The storm? *58%. Speciality Drinks Ltd.*

Elements of Islay Lp1 (91) n23 the entire shape is hewn from smoked grape; t23.5 thick, juicy multi-layered with more than a single strata dedicated to mocha; the peat is windblown; f22 dries with dates and molasses keeping the balance; b22.5 a big, fruity Islay with few pretensions of subtlety. *58.8%. Speciality Drinks Ltd.*

Elements of Islay Pe1 (95.5) n24 absolutely classic dry, peat ash but enlivened by the most subtle heather and lavender; t24.5 if you heard a distant sigh on the 29th July 2010, it was me tasting this. Again, most of everything I am looking for: a touch of honey to enrich the peat, barley offering attractive juiciness, a countering dryness from the smoke...; f23.5 long with the inevitable vanillas entering with an almost perfect degree of weight and sweetness; confirmation that the cask it matured in is quite perfect; b23.5 this is a fabulous, nigh faultless, example of the purest element of Islay: its whisky... *58.7%. Speciality Drinks Ltd.*

Finlaggan Islay Single Malt 10 Years Old (82) n21 t21 f20 b20. Beautiful citrus notes mildly tempered with smoke: an enormous improvement from the caramel-ruined previous "Lightly Peated" bottlings. *40%. The Vintage Malt Whisky Co.*

Finlaggan "Old Reserve" Islay Single Malt (79.5) n19 t21 f19 b20.5. A smoky shadow of its once great self. *40%. The Vintage Malt Whisky Co Ltd.*

The Ileach Islay Single Malt (85) n20.5 t22 f21 b21.5. Not the dram it was. Once near faultless, now a highly smoked hotchpotch. Not without its lovely moments, but pray the next bottling is nearer its magnificent old self. *40%*

Islay Storm (76) n19 t20 f19 b18. More of a drizzle. *40%. C.S. James & Sons.*

Islay Storm 12 Years Old (81) n20 t21 f20 b20. Some lovely spice emphasis the seaweed kick. Decent oak weight, too. *40%. C.S. James & Sons.*

McClelland's Islay Single Malt (88) n22 delicate yet confident smoke; t22 light at first then livens as the smoke kicks in; f22 beautifully long and clean with tapering Fisherman's Friend; b22 no mistaking which distillery this little beaut is from: Bowmore anyone? *40%*

Macleod's Islay (84.5) n21 t22 f20.5 b21. Considering the raging bull of a malt this used to be, this appears to have been snipped in its prime. Toffee and coffee have as much impact as the peat, which offers more smoke than depth. *40%. Ian Macleod.*

⌐:⌐ **Marks and Spencer Islay Single Malt Aged 12 Years** (83) n21.5 t21 f20 b20.5. Entertaining rough-house malt which belies its strength. Cordite on the nose and beyond... *40%*

Pibroch Aged 12 Years (92) n23.5 t23 f22 b22.5. Chugs along beautifully... *43%*

Port Askaig Aged 17 Years (89) n22 t22.5 f22.5 b22. What it does, it does rather attractively and with minimum fuss. *45.8%. Speciality Drinks.*

Port Askaig Aged 25 Years (86) n22 t21.5 f21 b21.5. Distinctly Caol Ila in style, with big fat oils entirely running the show. The peat is curiously big and modest in the same show, but that has much to do with the sweet citrus and vanilla-enriched oils. Easy dramming. And perfect for keeping the most vicious of midges off you whenever sitting outside the Port Askaig hotel watching the ferry, as indeed I did when this was made 25 years ago... *45.8%*

Port Askaig Aged 30 Years (81.5) n19 t22.5 f20 b20. Some malts make it through to this age unscathed. Some don't. This falls into the latter category. Some exotic notes, but this always appears to work less well for Islays than mainlanders. The odd wonderful malt and caramel moment, even so. 45.8%. Speciality Drinks Ltd.

Port Askaig Cask Strength (89) n22 ash dry; t23.5 thumping peats which dominate until the sweet yam and muscovado muscles their way in on the soft oils; f21 bitters out; b22.5 surprisingly juicy after the nose. Profound. 57.1%. Speciality Drinks Ltd.

The Queen of the Hebrides Islay Single Malt Whisky (85) n22 t22 f20 b21. Big, rolling fat peats: any fatter and it'd be declared obese. 40%. Wine Shop, Leek; Islay Whisky Shop.

Robert Graham's The Hoebeg Single Islay Malt (88) n23 charming nose full of morning after the night before ashes of a peat fire; t22.5 fresh and chattering with all kinds of sugary smoke notes; f21 speedy fade leaving just sugars and smoky caramel behind; b21.5 what first appears to be a big, roaring Islay turns out to be a smoky kitten. 40%

Sainsbury's Single Islay Malt Aged 12 Years (92.5) n23 stupendously coastal with any number of salty shades working in harmony with the refreshing citrus. The smoke massages rather than confronts; t23.5 light vanillas manage to out manoeuvre the smoke while the juicy barley and fruits build and build; f22.5 the smoke virtually vanishes as the lightly oiled vanilla and citrus takes us to the close; b23.5 Islay malt has been Sainsbury's trump card for a little while. And here they have managed to trump themselves. Almost ridiculously delicate. 40%. UK. ☺☺

Smokehead Extra Black Aged 18 Years (94) n23 what a softie...delicate layers of dry peat ash and oils intermingle; extra oaky-floral life added by gentle hickory and a sprig of prickly lavender; t24 juicy, rock-hard delivery which is entirely divorced from the nose; almost a bourbon rye-led fruitiness until the peat slowly, methodically and irrevocably takes over in that beautiful dry, ashy style; f23.5 dry smoked, coffee-stained and with enough molassed sugars to comfortably see off any threat of OTT oak; b23.5 doubtless some will prefer the in-your-face standard version. This is for those seeking a bit of grey-templed sophistication. 46%

Smokehead Islay db **(92)** n24 even iodine doesn't come more iodiney than this. Also salty, youngish and bracing; t23 sweet grist at first, moves into sharp citrus and back into malt; f22 the complex peats begin to fade as vanilla and caramel kick on; b23 this company does this kind of whisky so well. A little gem. 43%. Ian Macleod.

Tesco Old Islay Single Malt 12 Years Old (80.5) n20 t21 f19.5 b20. Smoky for sure. But somehow thin and a little basic. 40%. Tesco. ☺☺

⫶⫶ **Wemyss 1981 Single Islay "Whispering Smoke"** hogshead, bott 2011 **(94)** n23 a beautiful meeting of butterscotch, salt, lemon peel and surprisingly crisp barley; t24 fabulous texture: a real golden syrup and burned fudge sweetness to the barley with busy spices popping around the palate; f23 earthy, chewy and wards off any oaky excess without breaking sweat; b24 just one of those really magnificent malts which cannot be ignored. 46%. Wemyss Malts. 228 bottles.

⫶⫶ **Wemyss 1984 Single Islay "Crumpets & Cordite"** bott Apr 09 **(90)** n23.5 playful smoke, sweetened with a touch of banana. Not quite cordite...more anthracite...; t23.5 genuinely complex: the barley is fresh and juicy; the smoke is both thick and lightly spiced but enjoys a lighter sub-plot, too; f20.5 just a slight wobble from the cask but enough spice to see it through; b22.5 I always fancy sophisticated, beautifully-shaped crumpet like this... 46%. sc. Wemyss Malts. 342 bottles.

Wemyss 1996 Single Islay "Burnt Heather" bott Apr 09 **(85.5)** n21 t23 f20 b21.5. An array of sugars do a wonderful job in balancing out the spices. Pure, juicy entertainment. 46%. sc. Wemyss Malts. 342 bottles.

Wemyss 1996 Single Islay "Honey Smoke" hogshead, bott Sep 09 **(85)** n21.5 t22 f20.5 b21. I was expected to find a smoked out hive. Instead, a rather salty dram where the sweetness is of a more muscovado sugar rather than honey variety. 59.6%. 425 bottles.

⫶⫶ **Wemyss 1996 Single Islay "Smoke On The Sea Shore"** hogshead, bott 2011 **(86)** n21.5 t22 f21 b21.5. Smoky, massively salty and with a refreshing twist of lemon. I doubt I have ever come across a malt with such a twee, chintzy name. But it just about does what it says on the tin... 46%. Wemyss Malts. 328 bottles.

⫶⫶ **Wemyss 1996 Single Islay "Smoke Stack"** hogshead, bott 2011 **(88)** n22.5 smoky bacon but chunky barley, too; t22 clean, sweet and some molassed smoke; delightful layering of juicy barley; f21.5 light vanilla; b22 sweet and well mannered. 46%. sc. 294 bottles.

Wemyss 1997 Single Islay "Autumn Leaves" refill bourbon, bott Sep 09 **(75)** n18 t19 f19 b19. Technically, not quite the greatest whisky: one I will leaf well alone... 46%

⫶⫶ **Wemyss 1997 Single Islay "Autumn Warmer"** hogshead, bott 2011 **(63)** n14 t18 f15 b16. Poorly constructed distillate to begin with. 46%. 360 bottles.

⸙ **Wemyss 1997 Single Islay "Bonfire Embers"** bott Apr 09 **(84) n22 t22 f19 b21.** As bonfires go, this is a very sugary one. Oh, and peaty... 46%. sc. Wemyss Malts. 342 bottles.

Wemyss 1997 Single Islay "Sandy Seaweed" bott Apr 09 **(84) n22 t22.5 f19 b20.5.** In the artificial light of my tasting bunker, on picking this up I thought it was new make. To my astonishment, it's been around longer than the Euro. As is often the case when exhausted old casks are deployed, the nose and delivery are excellent (and new makey/gristy) but the finish is bitter and off key. 46%. Wemyss Malts Ltd. 342 bottles.

⸙ **Wemyss 1997 Single Islay "Vanilla Smoke"** bott Apr 09 **(73.5) n17.5 t21 f17 b18.** Smoke. But dodgy wood means it just doesn't fire properly. 46%. sc. 342 bottles.

Wilson & Morgan House Malt "Born on Islay" cask no. 309928 & 309934, dist 2001, bott 2010 **(86) n21.5 t22 f21 b21.5.** A curious thick set Islay with a mildly industrial nose, revealing the oiliness of old workshops. The delivery is sweet but a little muted. 43%

⸙ **Wemyss 1999 Single Islay "Well Mannered Mint"** hogshead, bott 2011 **(92.5) n23** I say: how awfully delicate the smoke is...; **t23** frightfully gentle delivery with a sweet, juicy smokiness which slowly heads towards milky cocoa; **f23** frightfully chocolate-minty; **b23.5** anyone who remember's Merlin's Brew chocolate mint lolly will have more than a pang of nostalgia here. 46%. Wemyss Malts. 307 bottles.

⸙ **Wilson & Morgan House Malt "Born On Islay"** dist Aug 02, bott Jan 11 **(87.5) n22** big smoke: an interesting marriage of dryish grist and thick oils; **t22** a full bodied house with an outbreak of gristy sugars; **f21.5** bitters out; coffee and smoke; **b22** absolutely presentable, oily-smoked everyday dramming. A still-house malt with a good view... 43%. Wilson & Morgan.

Wm Morrison Islay Single Malt Aged 10 Years (84) n21 t22 f21 b20. A uniform Islay which, though pleasant and initially sweet, fails to trouble the imagination or pulse. 40%

UNSPECIFIED SINGLE MALTS (Lowland)

Cadenhead's Classic Lowland Bourbon wood **(82) n19 t21 f21 b21.** Much juicier and fortified with rich barley than the nose suggests. 50%

Cadenhead's Lowland Malt (90) n22 t23 f22 b23. One of the best lowlanders around. Fabulously fresh! 56.4%

Master of Malt 12 Years Old Lowland 2nd Edition (86.5) n22.5 t22 f20.5 b21.5. Lots of joined up aromas, with apple and liquorice character linking with drier elements quite effortlessly while the delivery offers attractive weaving between youthful maltiness and an older, slightly bourbony edge. 40%

UNSPECIFIED SINGLE MALTS (Speyside)

Asda Extra Special Speyside Single Malt 12 Years Old (76) n18.5 t19 f19 b19.5. The last time I tasted this, some thug attacked my office and smashed up neighbouring property. If only there could be some similar violence to my taste buds, as this is as docile and nondescript as it comes. 40%

Berrys' Reserve Speyside (88) n21.5 some under-ripe fruit tangles with the barley; **t22.5** silky, satisfying mouth feel, again with the barley dominating, though a little liquorice seeps in; **f22** a curious coppery small still feel as the gentle vanillas grow; **b22** entirely unspectacular, utterly lacking in star quality...and yet...a very pleasant, fault-free dram which hits the spot. 46%. Berry Bros & Rudd.

Celtique Connexion Monbazillac Finish Aged 14 Years dist 1994, bott 2009 **(88) n23 t22.5 f21 b21.5.** Clean, fabulously sulphur-free and quite substantial whisky, but the Monbazillac has gone Monballistic... 46%. Celtic Whisky Compagnie.

⸙ **Celtique Connexion Saussignac Double Matured 1997** bott 2010 **(95) n24** the vaguest degree of smoke drops anchor on the fruit. Freshly cleaned mature plums and tangy fruit cubes from the boiled sweet jar; Clean, lively, intense; **t24** thrilling delivery full of fresh, spicy grape, salivating barley and meaningful caramel; **f23** long with the caramels continuing the cream toffee theme, but with extra spices arriving late... and that irrepressible grape...; **b24** dreamy. Faultless. Just bloody fantastic! Displays more life, vitality and reasons to live than the entire main stand at Selhurst Park... 46%. nc ncf sc. Celtic Whisky Compagnie. 381 bottles.

Celtique Connexion Sauternes Finish Aged 13 Years dist 1995, bott 2008 **(95) n23.5 t24 f23.5 b24.** Top notch balance between spice and grape. Elegant. 46%

Celtique Connexion Vin de Paille du Jura Finish Aged 14 Years dist 1994, bott 2008 **(71) n17 t19 f17 b18.** It seems that many a whisky label with the word Jura on it is accursed: sulphur yet again! 46%. Celtic Whisky Compagnie.

⸙ **Cuidich'n Righ 10 Years Old (83.5) n21.5 t22 f20 b20.** About as simple as they come: the barley is sharp but the oak offers only so much support. 40%. Gordon & MacPhail.

GlenParker Speyside Single Malt (86.5) n21 t22.5 f21.5 b21.5. An enjoyable, bracing malt with plenty of backbone and bite. If you are looking for flavour and personality, you can do a lot worse. *40%. Angus Dundee.*

Macleod's Speyside (86) n21.5 t22 f21 b21.5. Friendly, malty and juicy. *40%*

Master of Malt 30 Year Old Speyside 3rd Edition (88.5) n23 t23 f20.5 b22. A character malt, performing all kinds of stunning Speyside tricks, but with the odd one falling flat on its face. Great fun. *40%. Master of Malt, UK.*

Master of Malt 40 Year Old Speyside 2nd Edition (92.5) n23 t24 f23 b22.5. Brinkmanship doesn't quite cover it...but the intense and multi-faceted sugars cope with the major splinters in there. *40%*

McClelland's Speyside (77.5) n20 t19 f18.5 b19. Remains stunningly inert. *40%*

Old Malt Cask Speyside's Finest Aged 41 Years sherry butt, cask no. 5515, dist Nov 67, bott Sep 09 (82) n22 t21 f19 b20. Salty biscuit and mocha. But buckles under the weight of oaky expectancy. *50% Douglas Laing & Co Ltd. 456 bottles.*

Old Malt Cask Speyside's Finest Aged 41 Years sherry cask (93) n23 t24 f23 b23. For all its wrinkles, a malt with great charm and personality *50%. Douglas Laing.*

Old Malt Cask Speyside's Finest Aged 42 Years sherry butt no. DL 6245, dist Nov 67, bott Jun 10 (88) n23 cherry fruitcake meets cherryade; a real touch of the cake shop about this one with a light spicy nip in the air; t21.5 friendly sumptuous fruit scores early but the hefty oaks fight back immediately to take the lead; f22 only late on do the fruit and oaks harmonise, though a touch of dry bitterness creeps in; b21.5 you know the elegant building in your town which is crumbling a bit and someone's tarted it up slightly in not quite the right colours...? *50%. Douglas Laing. 385 bottles.*

Old Malt Cask Speyside's Finest Aged 43 Years (83.5) n20 t22.5 f20 b21. A surprisingly juicy job for its age but not entirely flawless. *50%. Douglas Laing.*

Old Malt Cask Speyside's Finest Aged 43 Years sherry butt, dist Jun 66, bott Oct 09 (96.5) n24 one of those improbably clean sherry butts (for its age) that offers as much medium roast Mysore/Java mix roast as it does fruit. Only rarely can a cask take such an oaky punch and not even flinch; t24.5 how does it do it after 43 years...? The first note is freshly pressed grape juice. Not far behind comes a whole army of subsidiary characters, led by mocha and hickory, then some pithy tannins, a little salt and muscovado...the column is endless; f24 ...still this ensemble marches on into the finish; and still the coffee has a big say, though now the big oaky vanillas have given it a slightly creamy texture...; b24 as near as damn it faultless... *48.2%. Douglas Laing for The Whisky Show 2009.*

Sainsbury's Single Speyside Malt Aged 12 Years (89) n22.5 lively, vaguely fruity, orange pithy, with attractive, clean vanillas; t22.5 pure malt and custard delivery with a superb, lightly oiled, ultra soft texture; a light, juicy barley thread works wonders; f22 anyone for a malt milkshake? b22 you will do well to find a softer, more friendly malt. A creamy delight. *40%. UK.* ⊙⊙

Spey Single Malt Aged 12 Years (80) n20.5 t21 f18.5 b20. The over-ripe kumquat on the nose warns of some little imperfections to come, especially on the finish. *40%*

Spey Single Malt Aged 15 Years (84) n22 t21 f20 b21. Soft and safe, there is not a bump in the tangy-caramel ride. *46%. Harvie's of Edinburgh. Japanese market.*

Spey Single Malt Aged 21 Years (92) n24 t23 f22 b23. Oh, had only this wonderful dram been bottled at least 46%: it is like driving a Mercedes E class with an engine designed for a lawnmower... *40%. Harvie's of Edinburgh. Japanese market.*

Spey Single Malt 1956 (87.5) n24 t21.5 f21 b21. A case of a dram which has seen too much wood for its own good. Yet, as the magnificence of the nose shows, this cask still has something very special to offer. *45.8%. Harvie's of Edinburgh. Japanese market.*

Spey Single Malt 1991 (92) n23 t24 f22 b23. What a treat of an experience! Layered, complex and very high class. Those who enjoy the Glenfarclas style might enjoy this, too. *63.5%*

Spey Single Malt 'Chairman's Choice' (90) n22 t23.5 f22 b22.5. My experience over the years is that most Chairmen haven't got a clue which end of a barrel is which. This does appear to be an exception, though... *40%*

Tesco Speyside Single Malt 12 Years Old (88) n22.5 billowing barley: clean, extensive and gorgeously fresh; t22 absolutely spot on delivery of malt operating on both crisp and oily levels tinged with the lightest of sugar coatings; the middle is attractively vanilla dominant; f21.5 dryish but with the malt still pounding through; b22 a lovely whisky entirely devoid of the smoke promised on the label. Not remotely complex but very true to the regional style and thoroughly enjoyable. *40%. Tesco.* ⊙⊙

Wemyss 1990 Single Speyside "Toffee Apples" dist 1990, bott Apr 09 (70) n17 t18.5 f17 b17.5. "Sulphured Casks 1990" *46% Wemyss Malts Ltd. 335 bottles.*

Wemyss 1991 Single Speyside "Ginger Treacle" dist 1991, bott Apr 09 **(63.5) n16 t17.5 f15 b15.** "Sulphured Casks 1991" 46% Wemyss Malts Ltd. 335 bottles.

Wemyss 1995 Single Speyside "Spiced Apples" refill hogshead, bott Sep 09 **(91) n22.5** thick treacle toffee and honey; **t24** wonderful delivery and follow through: again, it's thick honey with a powering barley sub plot; beautifully lush mouth feel; **f22.5** toffees out as the vanilla enters the fray; **b22** a rich, satisfying, high quality dram. 46%. 386 bottles.

⌖ **Wemyss 1996 Single Speyside "Ginger Compote"** butt, bott 2011 **(69) n16 t18.5 f17 b17.5.** Ginger compost...? 46%. sc. Wemyss Malts. 767 bottles.

⌖ **Wemyss 1996 Single Speyside "The Honey Pot"** hogshead, bott 2011 **(88.5) n22** butterscotch tart; **t23** big barley signature with more than a hint of honey on toast; **f21.5** dries with vanilla and cocoa dominating; **b22** no so much a honey pot as a thimble full. But a real charmer. 46%. sc. Wemyss Malts. 299 bottles.

⌖ **Wemyss 1996 Single Speyside "Vanilla Oak"** butt, bott 2011 **(84.5) n21.5 t22 f20 b21.** Totally puzzled by the Vanilla oak tab: the oak plays only a supporting role to the outstanding barley. Not the greatest barrel and offers little positively on oaky front. But the quality of the distillate is exceptional. 46%. Wemyss Malts. 733 bottles.

The Whisky Agency Speyside Single Malt 39 Year Old dist 1970, bott 2009 **(96) n24.5 t25 f22.5 b24.** No one has told me what this is. But anyone who knows a Glenfarclas at this age in full flow will understand the type of outstanding whisky this is. In a nutshell: old sherry at its blemish-free olde worlde pre-sulphur ruining finest. 54.4%. The Whisky Agency, Germany.

⌖ **The Whisky Agency Speyside Single Malt 1969** bott 2010 **(92.5) n22** at first, appears weighed down with wood. But boiled molassed sweetness is evident, as well as overcooked gooseberry tart; **t24** fabulous delivery: grip tightly to your chair as the spices rip around your palate. But the balancing sugars do a near perfect job and we are back with hint of a fruit pie again...; **f23.5** calms down with a creamy mocha...with an extra sugar; **b23.5** one of the spiciest drams of the year. Delicious! 54.3%. The Whisky Agency.

UNSPECIFIED SINGLE MALTS (General)

⌖ **Chieftain's The Cigar Malt Aged 15 Years** hogshead, dist Apr 95, bott 2011 **(94) n24** a spicy affair: delicate with fascinating tangy tangerine oak complexity; **t22.5** a muddled delivery, but within a beat or two it has set its course. And that is to the heart of a cocoa bean. Massive waves of milky chocolate; **f23.5** fantastically long finish with deft oak spices piling on those sugars and cocoa; **b24** must be one of those chocolate cigars I used to eat when I was a kid. Seemingly distilled from 100% malted cocoa and matured in a cask coopered by the gods. A gun to the head would never induce me to smoke a cigar or even cigarette (I did once have one put to my head by a weirdo to force me to smoke dope, and I turned that down, too – but that's another story). But just try and stop me drinking this stuff... 46%. nc ncf. Ian Macleod Distillers. USA release.

Scottish Vatted Malts
(also Pure Malts/Blended Malt Scotch)

100 Pipers Aged 8 Years Blended Malt (74) n19 t20 f17 b18. A better nose, perhaps, and some spice on arrival. But when you consider the Speysiders at their disposal, all those mouth-wateringly grassy possibilities, it is such a shame to find something as bland as this. 40%

Ballantine's Pure Malt Aged 12 Years bott code. LKAC1538 **(88.5) n22.5** spicy mixture of honey, light smoke and added orange; **t23** stupendous mouth-feel with the fruit re-inserted alongside the honey; **f21** pretty thin with almost a grainy feel alongside the bittering oak; **b22** no sign of the peat being reintroduced to major effect, although the orange is a welcome addition. Remains a charmer. 40%. Chivas.

Barrogill (90) n22.5 t23 f22.5 b22. Prince Charles, who allows the name to be used for this whisky, is said to enjoy this dram. Hardly surprising, as its pretty hard not to: this is wonderful fun. Curiously, I have just read the back label and noticed they use the word "robust". I have employed "lusty". Either way, I think you might get the message. 40%

Barrogill North Highland Blended Malt Mey Selections bott code P012630 **(79) n18 t21 f20 b20.** Recovers attractively – helped by a mighty dose of concentrated maltiness - from the disappointing nose. 40%. Inver House Distillers for North Highland.

Bell's Signature Blend Limited Edition bott 2009, bott no. 42515 **(83.5) n19 t22 f21 b21.5.** The front label makes large that this vatted malt has Blair Athol and Inchgower at the heart of it as they are "two fine malts selected for their exceptionally rich character". Kind of like saying you have invited the Kray twins to your knees up as they might liven it up a bit. Well those two distilleries were both part of the original Bell's empire, so fair dos.

But to call them both fine malts is perhaps stretching the imagination somewhat. A robust vatting to say the least. And, to be honest, once you get past the nose, good back-slapping fun. *40%. 90,000 bottles.*

Berrys' Best Islay Vatted Malt Aged 8 Years (82) n20 t21 f20 b21. Smoky, raw, sweet, clean and massive fun! *43%. Berry Bros & Rudd.*

Berry's Best 14 Years Old Islay Vatted Malt bott 2009 (88) n22.5 takes a while for the peat to show – then it takes over; **t22** soft: excellently controlled sweetness and rolling, lightly oiled phenols; **f21.5** duller, a touch of spice but otherwise vanilla-led; **b22** a sleepy, clean vatting which talks in whispers. *43%. Berry Bros & Rudd.*

Berry's Own Selection Blue Hanger 4th Release bott 2008 (87) n22 t23 f21 b21. Its finest notes are very fine, indeed. *45.6%. Berry Bros & Rudd.*

⚜ **Berry's Own Selection Blue Hanger 5th Release** bott 2010 (81) n20 t21 f20 b20. Not a lot – but enough – sulphur has crept in to take the edge of this one. *45.6%. nc ncf. Berry Bros & Rudd.*

⚜ **Berry's Own Selection Islay Reserve 2nd Edition** (86.5) n22 t22 f21 b21.5. Maybe an Islay reserve but has enough smoky weight and hickory/chocolate charisma to be pushing for the first team squad. *46%. nc ncf. Berry Bros & Rudd.*

⚜ **Berry's Own Selection Speyside Reserve 2nd Edition** (79.5) n21 t21.5 f18 b19. Some excellent early sharpness and honey depth but falters. *46%. nc ncf. Berry Bros & Rudd.*

Big Peat (96) n25 magnificent array of salt and bitty peat; heavy yet light enough for the most delicate of citrus. Hard to find a nose which screams "Islay" at you with such a lack of ambiguity: it is, frankly, perfect. **t24** the delivery is constructed around a fabulous bourbon Demerara sugar and liquorice framework; the peat enters as soon as this is in place and in varying layers of oiliness and depth. The mid ground sees the re-emergence of the more complex Ardbeg and Port Ellen factions, a bourbon style, small grains busyness; **f23.5** long, softly oiled still and then a slow dissolving liquorice and spice; vanillas pop up very late, still accompanied by soft Demerara; **b23.5** I suppose if you put Ardbeg and Port Ellen together there is a chance you might get something rather special. Not guaranteed, but achieved here with the kind of panache that leaves you spellbound. The complexity and balance are virtually off the charts, though had the Caol Ila been reduced slightly, and with it the oils, this might well have been World Whisky of the Year. *46%. ncf Douglas Laing.*

The Big Smoke 40 (83) n22 t21 f20 b20. Pure grist. *40%* ⊙ ⊙

The Big Smoke 60 (92) n23 clean gristy lead with a freshly toasted bread depth; **t23.5** lovely sprightliness to the barley and zest to the peat; youthful but some impressive age lines, too; **f22.5** some coppery notes to the spicy, smoky finale; **b23** much more delicate and in touch with its more feminine self than was once the case. A real beauty. *60%. Duncan Taylor & Co.* ⊙ ⊙

Black Face 8 Years Old (78.5) n18.5 t22 f19 b19. A huge malt explosion in the kisser on delivery, but otherwise not that pretty to behold. *46%. The Vintage Malt Whisky Co Ltd.*

Burns Nectar (89.5) n22 honeycomb dipped in lime juice; **t22** glorious mouth feel to delivery: a soft, oily platform from which more honey can easily be detected; chewy toffee and vanilla, too; **f23** the lightest sprinkling of spice and some ginger cake to round off beautifully; **b22.5** a delight of a dram and with all that honey around, "Nectar" is about right. *40%*

Carme 10 Years Old (79) n21.5 t20 f18.5 b19. On paper Ardmore and Clynelish should work well together. But vatting is not done on paper and here you have two malts cancelling each other out and some less than great wood sticking its oar in. *43%*

Castle Rock Aged 12 Years Blended Malt (87) n22.5 grassy, under-ripe gooseberry; **t23** every bit as fresh and juicy as the nose suggests **f19.5** a creeping bitterness; **b22** stupendously refreshing: the finish apart, I just love this style of malt. *40%*

Cearban (79.5) n18 t21.5 f20 b19. The label shows a shark. It should be a whale: this is massive. Sweet with the malts not quite on the same wavelength. *40%. Robert Graham Ltd.*

Clan Campbell 8 Years Old Pure Malt (82) n20 t22 f20 b20. Enjoyable, extremely safe whisky that tries to offend nobody. The star quality is all on the complex delivery, then it's toffee. *40%. Chivas Brothers.*

Clan Denny (Bowmore, Bunnahabhain, Caol Ila and Laphroaig) (94) n24 t23 f23 b24. A very different take on Islay with heavy peats somehow having a floating quality. Unique. *40%*

Clan Denny Speyside (87) n22 big, big malt: exceptionally clean and soft. Oily, too; **t22** a charming sweetness to the barley helps counter the more bitter aspects of the approaching oak; delicate oils help make for an exceptionally soft delivery **f21** no shortage of vanilla as it bitters out; **b22** a Tamdhu-esque oiliness pervades here and slightly detracts from the complexity. That said, the early freshness is rather lovely. *46%. Douglas Laing.*

⚜ **Compass Box Canto Cask 10** bott Jul 07 (86.5) n20.5 t21 f23.5 b21.5. One the Canto collection which slipped through my net a few years back, but is still around, I understand.

Typical of the race, this one has perhaps an extra dollop of honey which helps keep the over vigorous oaks under some degree of control. Sublime finish. *54.2%. nc ncf. 200-250 bottles.*

Compass Box Eleuthera Marriage married for nine months in an American oak Hogshead (86) n22 t22 f20 b22. I'm not sure if it's the name that gets me on edge here, but as big and robust as it is I still can't help feeling that the oak has bitten too deep. Any chance of a Compass Box Divorce...? *49.2%. Compass Box for La Maison du Whisky.*

Compass Box Flaming Hart second batch, bottling no. FH16MMVII (95.5) n23.5 t24.5 f23 b24.5. The Canto range was, I admit, a huge over-oaked disappointment. This, though, fully underlines Compass Box's ability to come up with something approaching genius. This is a whisky that will be remembered by anyone who drinks it for the rest of their lives as just about the perfect study of full-bodied balance and sophistication. And that is not cheap hyperbole. *48.9%. nc ncf. 4,302 bottles.*

⁖ **Compass Box Flaming Heart 10th Anniversary** bott Sep 10 (92) n24 earthy, almost rustic in its smouldering stubble smokiness; a number of almost zingy fruity notes ensure the balance; t23 naturally, the smoke has an important early role and gets its lines away without a hitch; a light sliver of dark chocolate melts into the impressive oils; f22 lashings of vanilla though the oak may scare some, as might a light tanginess; b23 this one, as Flaming Heart so often is, is about counterweight and mouth feel. Everything appears just where it should be... *48.9%. nc ncf. 4186 bottles.*

Compass Box Lady Luck American white oak hogshead, bott Sep 09 (91) n22 earthy; tree bark; dank woods; an irrigated Taiwanese tomato field; t24 much lighter than the nose...and sweeter...and spicier...wow!!... f23 pure chocolate mousse before some bitterness descends; b22 just a shade too sweet for mega greatness like The Spice Tree, but quite an endearing box of tricks. *46%. Compass Box Whisky Co.*

⁖ **Compass Box Oak Cross** bott May 10 (92.5) n23 all kinds of bourbony red liquorice notes and drilled, oaky spices. But the butterscotch tart takes me back to my earliest school memories...; t24 a delivery which makes you gasp out loud: decent weight, but absolutely no pressure on the taste buds as it coats the mouth and the injection of maple syrup is to die for. The bitter-sweet interplay is exceptional, again keeping a big oaky butterscotch shape, but lightened by lemon curd tart; f22.5 now those oaky vanillas get a clearer sight of goal but the barley still fends off any excess; b23 the oak often threatens to be just too big a cross to bear. But such is the degree of complexity, and cleverness of weight, the overall brilliance is never dimmed. Overall, a bit of a tart of a whisky... *43%. nc ncf.*

⁖ **Compass Box The Peat Monster** bott May 10 (82) n21.5 t21.5 f19 b20. It is as though Victor Frankenstein's creation has met Bambi. Monsters don't come much stranger or more sanitised than this... *46%. nc ncf.*

Compass Box The Peat Monster Reserve (92) n23 comfortable, thickish smoke and a dusting of peppers: complex and well balanced; t23.5 silky soft malty oils cleverly disguise the big punchy peat which is to follow; lovely touch of golden syrup here and there, but mainly towards the delivery; f22.5 smoky sweetened mocha; b23 at times a bit of a Sweet Monster...beautiful stuff! *48.9%*

Compass Box The Spice Tree first-fill and refill American oak. Secondary maturation: heavily toasted new French oak (95.5) n24.5 quite paradoxical. First sniff and you think: "whoa! That's a big-un." Then you nose again, slowly and carefully you realise that whilst the nose does seem superficially big, it is actually made up of dozens of tiny aromas ganging together. The main theme is delicate tangerine and vanilla – almost like tangerine yogurt – but there are weightier spices to note, all of them fragments, especially the watery allspice and ginger...sublime...; t24.5 and now the palate continues with exactly the same theme: a million little flavour explosions, all timed to go off one after the other, but all on a sweet muscovado sugar bed created by the superb base malt of Clynelish; f23 thins rapidly into a more basic vanilla, though there is still a spice pulse and glow; just a little bitter at the death; b23.5 having initially been chopped down by the SWA, who were indignant that extra staves had been inserted into the casks, The Spice Tree is not only back but in full bloom. Indeed, the blossom on this, created by the use of fresh oak barrel heads, is more intoxicating than its predecessor – mainly because there is a more even and less dramatic personality to this. Not just a great malt, but a serious contender for Jim Murray Whisky Bible 2011 World Whisky of the Year. *46%*

Compass Box The Spice Tree Inaugural Batch (93) n23 t23 f23 b24. The map for flavour distribution had to be drawn for the first time here: an entirely different whisky in shape and flavour emphasis. And it is a map that takes a long time to draw... *46%. 4150 bottles.*

Co-operative Group (CWS) Blended Malt Aged 8 Years (86.5) n22 t22 f21 b21.5. Much, much better! Still a little on the sticky and sweet side, but there is some real body and pace to the changes on the palate. Quite rich, complex and charming. *40%*

⋅⋅⋅ **Cutty Sark Blended Malt** (92.5) n22 a salty, sweaty armpit doesn't fill you with confidence at first, but then light smoke descends as well as some prime grassy barley; t24 magnificent! The mouth feel is close to perfection, as there is a dazzling sheen to this one thanks to a just-so squirt of something a little oily; the vaguest of smoke wrestles with the more clear-cut barley; f23 thinner, but maintains the malty sheen, though dried now by vanilla; the building of the spices is quite wonderful; b23.5 sheer quality: as if two styles have been placed in the bottle and told to fight it out between them. What a treat! 40%. Berry Bros & Rudd.

Douglas Laing's Double Barrel Ardbeg & Glenrothes Aged 10 Years product no. MSW2685 (92) n22 a salty breeze apart, the curiously inconspicuous Ardbeg allows the Speysider to dominate; t24 but a different story on delivery where the malts are sharp, jagged and juicy while the smoke and oak, and even some rich dates from somewhere, hover in the background; with a metallic sheen and the nod spurt of honey here and there, this is different...and works a treat; f23 a deft smoke edge to the vanilla; b23 not what I was expecting. But a lovely experience nonetheless. 46%. Douglas Laing & Co Ltd.

Douglas Laing's Double Barrel Ardbeg & Glenrothes Aged 10 Years product no. DBS0003 (88.5) n23 great nose: delicate, playful smoke lightened by lime Rowntree's Fruit Gums; t22 firm barley with virtually no give but a slow unveiling of juicy barley; the smoke is also firm but flighty; f21.5 an oaky bitterness; b22 an uncompromising but fun way to bring up New Whisky no. 750 for Bible 2011... 46%. Douglas Laing.

Douglas Laing's Double Barrel Braeval & Caol Ila Aged 10 Years (78) n18 t21 f20 b19. The Mike and Bernie Winters of double barrelled whisky. 46%. Douglas Laing & Co Ltd.

Douglas Laing's Double Barrel Caol Ila & Braeval Aged 10 Years (84.5) n21 t22 f20.5 b21. It is probably impossible to find a malt which is more friendly and inoffensive. Or two malts which have done such a first class job of cancelling each other's personalities out. 46%

Douglas Laing's Double Barrel Glenrothes & Ardbeg Aged 10 Years 4th Release (89.5) n21.5 surprisingly angular and sharp; t23 and on delivery, too, though a soft caress of lightly oiled smoke helps. A few waves of honey hit the middle with some citrus thinning things down; f22.5 lightly smoked custard; b22.5 despite the average nose the charmingly effete palate is another matter entirely. 46%. Douglas Laing.

Douglas Laing's Double Barrel Highland Park & Bowmore (95) n23 pounding spices and dry smoke; t24.5 a passionate embrace of honeyed peat followed by waves of juicy barley almost gives you the vapours; f24 long, lip-smacking with the improbable degree of honey lasting the distance; the peat gives way to a stunning array of spices; b23.5 the vital spark of fury to this one keeps the palate ignited. A standing ovation for such a magnificent performance on the palate. 46%. Douglas Laing & Co Ltd.

Douglas Laing's Double Barrel Macallan & Laphroaig 5th Release (93) n23.5 rousing barley balances the light, flakey smoke; t24 the ultra delicate theme continues, with a lovely jam Swiss Roll sweetness mixing it with the gristy peat; juicy with a slow building of oil; f22.5 long with a sprinkling of grated chocolate in the vanilla and smoke; b23 as if born to be together. 46%

Douglas Laing's Double Barrel Macallan & Laphroaig Aged 9 Years (83.5) n21 t22 f20 b20.5. Curiously muted. Sweet with the natural caramels outweighing the smoke. 46%

Duncan Taylor Regional Malt Collection Islay 10 Years Old (81) n21 t22 f19 b19. Soft citrus cleanses the palate, while gentle peats muddies it up again. 40%

The Famous Grouse 10 Years Old Malt (77) n19 t20 f19 b19. The nose and finish headed south in the last Winter and landed in the sulphur marshes of Jerez. 40%. Edrington Group.

The Famous Grouse 15 Years Old Malt (86) n21 t22 f21.5 b21.5. Salty and smoky with a real sharp twang. 43%. Edrington Group.

The Famous Grouse 15 Years Old Malt (86) n19 t24 f22 b21. There had been a hint of the "s" word on the nose, but it got away with it. Now it has crossed that fine – and fatal – line where the petulance of the sulphur has thrown all else slightly out of kilter. All, that is, apart from the delivery which is a pure symphony of fruit and spice deserving a far better introduction and final movement. Some moving, beautiful moments. Flawed genius or what...? 40%

The Famous Grouse 18 Years Old Malt (82) n19 t21.5 f21 b20.5. Some highly attractive honey outweighs the odd uncomfortable moment. 43%. Edrington Group.

The Famous Grouse Malt 21 Years Old (91) n22 candy jar spices, green apple and crisp barley. t24 spot on oak offers a platform for the myriad rich malty notes and now, in the latest bottlings, enlivened further with an injection of exploding spice... wow! f22 flattens slightly but muscovado sugar keeps it light and sprightly; b23 a very dangerous dram: the sort where the third or fourth would slip down without noticing. Wonderful scotch! 43%. Edrington Group.

The Famous Grouse 30 Years Old Malt (94) n23.5 brain-implodingly busy and complex: labyrinthine depth within a kind of Highland Park frame with extra emphasis on grape and salt; t24 yesssss!!!! Just so magnificent with the theme being all about honeycomb...but on so many different levels of intensity and toastiness; so juicy, too...; **f23** now the spices dive in as the barley resurfaces again; long, layered with spot on bitter-sweet balance; **b23.5** whisky of this sky-high quality is exactly what vatted malt should be all about. Outrageously good. 43%

Glenalmond 2001 Vintage (82.5) **n22 t21.5 f19 b20.** Glenkumquat, more like: the most citrusy malt I have tasted in a very long time. 40%. *The Vintage Malt Whisky Co Ltd.*

Glenalmond "Everyday" (89.5) **n21.5** mainly malt; **t23.5** soft delivery which increases in barley intensity at a remarkably even rate; excellent gristy sugar-vanilla balance; **f22** remains on its malty crusade to the death; **b22.5** they are not joking; this really is an everyday whisky. Glorious malt which is so dangerously easy to drink. 40%

Glen Brynth Aged 12 Years Blended Malt (87) **n22.5 t23 f19.5 b22.** Deja vu...! Thought I was going mad: identical to the Castle Rock I tasted this morning, right down to the (very) bitter end ..!!! 40%. *Quality Spirits International.*

Glendower 8 Years Old (84) **n21.5 t21 f20.5 b21** Nutty and spicy. 43%

Glen Turner Pure Malt Aged 8 Years L525956A (84) **n20 t22 f22 b20.** A lush and lively vatting annoyingly over dependent on thick toffee but simply brimming with fabulously mouth-watering barley and over-ripe blood oranges. To those who bottle this, I say: let me into your lab. I can help you bring out something sublime!! 40%

-:·:- **Glen Orrin** (68) **n16.5 t17.5 f17 b17.** In its favour, it doesn't appear to be troubled by caramel. Which means the nose and palate are exposed to the full force of this quite dreadful whisky. 40%. *Aldi.*

Glen Orrin Six Year Old (88) **n22** a bit sweaty but the oranges delight. Some delicate background smoke is a surprising complement; **t23** big, chewy and rugged with outstanding soft-oiled lushness which helps to dissipate the youthfulness; **f21** delicate spice and arousing coffee-cocoa: a bigger age signature than you might expect **b22** a vatting that has improved in the short time it has been around, now displaying some lovely orangey notes on the nose and a genuinely lushness to the body and spice on the finish. You can almost forgive the caramel, this being such a well balanced, full-bodied ride. A quality show for the price. 40%

Hedges and Butler Special Pure Malt (83) **n20 t21 f22 b21.** Just so laid back: nosed and tasted blind I'd swear this was a blend (you know, a real blend with grains and stuff) because of the biting lightness and youth. Just love the citrus theme and, err...graininess...!! 40%

Imperial Tribute (83) **n19.5 t21.5 f21 b21.** I am sure – and sincerely hope – the next bottling will be cleaned up and the true Imperial Tribute can be nosed and tasted. Because this is what should be a very fine malt... but just isn't. 46%. *Spencer Collings.*

Islay Trilogy 1969 (Bruichladdich 1966, Bunnahabhain 1968, Bowmore 1969) Bourbon/Sherry (91) **n23 t23 f22 b23.** Decided to mark the 700th tasting for the 2007 edition with this highly unusual vatting. And no bad choice. The smoke is as elusive as the Paps of Jura on a dark November morning, but the silky fruits and salty tang tells a story as good as anything you'll hear by a peat fire. Take your time...the whiskies have. 40.3%. *Murray McDavid.*

J & B Exception Aged 12 Years (80) **n20 t23 f18 b19.** Very pleasant in so many ways. A charming sweetness develops quickly, with excellent soft honeycomb. But the nose and finish are just so...so...dull...!! For the last 30 years J&B has meant, to me, (and probably within that old company) exceptionally clean, fresh Speysiders offering a crisp, mouth-watering treat. I feel this is off target. 40%. *Diageo/Justerini & Brooks.*

J & B Nox (89) **n23** classy Speyside thrust, youthful and crisp with a wonderful strand of honey. Gentle oak balances pleasingly; **t23** the nose in liquid form: exactly the same characteristics with some extra, gently peppered toast towards the middle; **f21** dries just a little too much as the barley tires; **b22** a teasing, pleasing little number that is unmistakably from the J&B stable. 40%. *Diageo.*

John Black 8 Years Old Honey (88) **n21** vanilla to the fore; **t22.5** the promised honey arrives on delivery couched by fresh barley; **f22.5** light, delicate back to vanilla; **b22** a charming vatting. 40%. *Tullibardine Distillery.*

John Black 10 Years Old Peaty (91) **n21** salty and peaty; **t23** soft and peaty; **f22** delicate and peaty; **b23** classy and er...peaty. 40%. *Tullibardine Distillery.*

John McDougall's Selection Islay Malt 1993 cask no. 103 (94.5) **n23.5** peek-a-boo peat can barely make itself heard above the honeyed barley and lightly salted oak. 'Delicate' barely covers it... **t24.5** seductive beyond belief: the soft rounding off of the honey with a mint-chocolate peatiness, especially as it fills the middle ground, really is one for the collector's corner: unique and simply breathtaking, and with a Bowmore-ish Fisherman's Friend bite hitting for a couple of nano seconds, pretty intriguing, too; **f22.5** drier with soft peat embers giving way to the milk coffee and vanilla; **b24** complex, superbly weighted and balanced malt which just keeps you wondering what will happen next. 54.7%. *House of Macduff.*

Johnnie Walker Green Label 15 Years Old (95) **n24** kind of reminds me of a true, traditional Cornish Pasty: it is as though the segments have been compartmentalised, with the oak acting as the edible pastry keeping them apart. Sniff and there is a degree of fruit; nose again and there is the Speyside/Clynelish style of intense, slightly sweet maltiness. Sniff a third time and, at last you can detect just a hint of smoke. Wonderful... **t23.5** no compartmentalisation here as the delivery brings all those varying characters together for one magnificently complex malt event. Weightier than previous Green Label events with the smoke having a bigger say. But the oak really bobs and weaves as the palate is first under a tidal wave of juicy malt and then the fruit and smoke – and no little spice – take hold...; **f23.5** soft smoke and grumbling spice latch on to the fruit-stained oak; plenty of cocoa just to top things off; **b24** god, I love this stuff...this is exactly how a vatted malt should be and one of the best samples I've come across since its launch. 43%. Diageo.

Jon, Mark and Robbo's The Rich Spicy One (89) **n22 t23 f22 b22**. So much better without the dodgy casks: a real late night dram of distinction though the spices perhaps a little on the subtle side... 40%. Edrington.

Jon, Mark and Robbo's The Smoky Peaty One (92) **n23 t22 f23 b24**. Genuinely high-class whisky where the peat is full-on yet allows impressive complexity and malt development. A malt for those who appreciate the better, more elegant things in life. 40%. Edrington.

⊹ **Mackinlay's Rare Old Highland Malt** (89) **n22** mainly a vanilla structure on the nose with a mildly industrial oily heaviness lurking deep in its bowels. There is a hint of a hint of citrus and a more profound barley quality sweetened in the way a small puddle of molten sugar does the trick on porridge; **t22** much more weighty on delivery than the nose ever achieves. Back more now to the trademark W&M denseness (though without the usual accompanying toffee) with a thick soup of barley and oak thinned only by a slow development of vanilla. That distant industrial oil on the nose becomes a lot more profound from the early middle ground onwards; **f22** chewy with a mocha, vaguely smoked and oily finale; **b23** possibly the most delicate malt whisky I can remember coming from the labs of Whyte and Mackay. Thought it still, on the palate, must rank as heavy medium. This is designed as an approximation of the whisky found at Shackleton's camp in the Antarctic. And as a life-long Mackinlay drinker myself, it is great to find a whisky baring its name that, on the nose only, briefly reminds me of the defter touches which won my heart over 30 years ago. That was with a blend: this is a vatted malt. And a delicious one. In case you wondered: I did resist the temptation to use ice. 47.3%. Whyte & Mackay.

Matisse 12 Year Old Blended Malt (93) **n23.5** a wonderful variation of fruit but with the accent on citrus-orangey notes. As astonishing as it is beautiful... **t23** soft, delicate, melt-in-the-mouth delivery with those gentle fruits at the fore and the barley tagging on right behind; **f22.5** a quieter finale placing the accent on milky custard; **b23** succulent, clean-as-a-whistle mixture of malts with zero bitterness and not even a whisper of an off note: easily the best form I have ever seen this brand in. Superb. 40%. Matisse Spirits Co Ltd.

Matisse Aged 12 Years (79) **n17 t21 f20 b21**. Not sure if some finishing or re-casking has been going on here to liven it up. Has some genuine buzz on the palate, but intriguing weirdness, too. Don't bother nosing this one. 40%. The Matisse Spirits Co Ltd.

Milroy's of Soho Finest Blended Malt (76) **n18 t19 f20 b19**. Full flavoured, nutty, malty but hardly textbook. 40%. Milroy's of Soho.

⊹ **Mo'land** (82) **n21 t22 f19 b20**. Extra malty but lumbering and on the bitter side. 40%. Master Of Malt.

⊹ **Monkey Shoulder** batch 27 (79.5) **n21 t21.5 f18 b19**. Been a while since I lasted tasted this one. Though its claims to be Batch 27, I assume all bottlings are Batch 27 seeing as they are from 27 casks. This one, whichever it is, has a distinctive fault found especially at the finale, which is disappointing. Even before hitting that point a big toffeed personality makes for a pleasant if limited experience. 40%. William Grant & Sons.

"No Age Declared" The Unique Pure Malt Very Limited Edition 16-49 Years (85) **n22.5 t19.5 f22 b21**. Very drinkable. But this is odd stuff: as the ages are as they are, and as it tastes as it does, I can surmise only that the casks were added together as a matter of necessity rather than any great blending thought or planning. Certainly the malt never finds a rhythm but maybe it's the eclectic style on the finish that finally wins through. 45%. Samaroli.

Norse Cask Selection Vatted Islay 1992 Aged 16 Years hogshead cask no. QWVIM3, dist 92, bott 09 (95) **n24** a unique smorgasbord of dry, peat-reeky smoke and much oilier phenols. The interplay between sweet and dry is as startling and bamboozling is it is beautiful; **t24** melts-in-the-mouth – and then explodes into something like phenolic fire: talk about being lulled into a false sense of security...the sugars – mainly muscovado style – go into overdrive while those oils ensure that the palate is fully coated and the tongue keeps smacking around the mouth in enquiry; **f23** long, layered, not a single outbreak of anything even remotely bitter from the oak and still the phenols dance to varying tunes; **b24** the recipe of 60/35/5 Ardbeg/Laphroaig/Bowmore new make matured in one cask is a surprise: the oiliness here suggests a squirt of Caol Ila somewhere. This hybrid is certainly different, showing that the DNA of Ardbeg is unrecognisable when mixed, like The Fly, with others. Drinkable...? Oh, yes...!! Because this, without a single negative note to its name, is easily one of the whiskies of the year and a collector's and/or Islayphile's absolute must have. *56.7%*

Norse Cask Selection Vatted Islay 1991 Aged 12 Years (89) n24 t23 f21 b21. Fabulous, but not much going in the way of complexity. But if you're a peat freak, I don't think you either notice...or much care...!! *59.5%. Quality World, Denmark.*

Old St Andrews Fireside (88.5) n22 delicate, bright, the faintest hint of distant smoke; t22.5 sharp, clean and full of malty freshness; f21.5 custard creams dunked in spiced milk; b(22.5) beautifully driven... *40%. Old St Andrews Ltd.*

Old St Andrews Nightcap (89) n21.5 oak and spice plus the odd atom of smoke amid the Tunnock's caramel wafer...; t24 beautiful weight on delivery and the muscovado sugar edge is a pure delight; salivating and eye-wateringly sharp: a classic vatted malt early flavour profile...; f21 dries quickly amid the vanilla and caramel; b22.5 some delightful weight and mass but perhaps a bit too much toffee takes its toll. *40%. Old St Andrews Ltd.*

Old St Andrews Twilight (94.5) n24 fabulous: a classic clean, Speyside-juicy style which is quite irresistible. Not a single harsh or discordant note here...it is almost pure grist; t23.5 mirrors the nose to a tee...; f23 light, flaky vanilla and spice begins to take over; b24 less Twilight as Sunrise as this is full of invigorating freshness which fills the heart with hope and joy: Lip-smacking Scotch malt whisky as it should be. Anyone who thinks the vatted malt served up for golf lovers in these novelty bottles are a load of old balls are a fair way off target... *40%. Old St Andrews Ltd.*

Poit Dhubh 8 Bliadhna (90) n22.5 toffee-banana; t23.5 sublime delivery: perfect weight and chewability with light spice mixing with the cocoa-rich barley; f21.5 toffee fudge; b22.5 though the smoke which marked this vatting has vanished, it has more than compensated with a complex beefing up of the core barley tones. Cracking whisky. *43%. ncf. Pràban na Linne.* ☉ ☉

Poit Dhubh 12 Bliadhna (77) n20 t20 f18 b19. Toffee-apples. Without the apples. *43%. ncf. Pràban na Linne.* ☉ ☉

Poit Dhubh 21 Bliadhna (86) n22 t22.5 f21 b20.5. Over generous toffee has robbed us of what would have been a very classy malt. *43%. ncf. Pràban na Linne.* ☉ ☉

The Pot Still Scotch Vatted Malt Over 8 Years Old (90) n22 excellent oak sub plot to the ballsy barley; t24 goes down with all the seductive powers of long fingernails down a chest: the wonderful honey and barley richness is stunning and so beautifully weighted; f22 a lazier finale, allowing the chalky oaky notes to make folly of those tender years; b22 such sophistication: the Charlotte Rampling of Scotch. *43.5%. ncf. Celtic Whisky Compagnie, France.*

Prime Blue Pure Malt (83) n21 t21 f21 b20. Steady, with a real chewy toffee middle. Friendly stuff. *40%*

Prime Blue 12 Years Old Pure Malt (78) n20 t20 f19 b19. A touch of fruit but tart. *40%*

Prime Blue 17 Years Old Pure Malt (88) n23 clever weight and a touch of something fruity and exotic, too; t21 thick malt concentrate; f22 takes a deliciously latte-style route and would be even better but for the toffee; excellent spicing; b22 lovely, lively vatting: something to get your teeth into! *40%*

Prime Blue 21 Years Old Pure Malt (77) n21 t20 f18 b18. After the teasing, bourbony nose the remainder disappoints with a caramel-rich flatness. The reprise of a style of whisky I thought had vanished about four of five years ago *40%*

Sainsbury's Malt Whisky Finished in Sherry Casks (70) n18 t19 f16 b17. Never the greatest of the Sainsbury range, it's somehow managed to get worse. Actually, not too difficult when it comes to finishing in sherry, and the odd sulphur butt or three has done its worst here. *40%. UK.*

Scottish Collie (86.5) n22 t23 f20.5 b21. A really young pup of a vatting. Full of life and fun but muzzled by toffee at the death. *40%. Quality Spirits International.*

Scottish Collie 5 Years Old (90.5) n22.5 teasing interplay between grassy young malts and something just a little more profound and vaguely phenolic; t23 more of the same on delivery; an engaging sharpness keeps the tastebuds puckered; f22 long, with the accent on that wonderfully clean ,sweet and sharp barley; even the soft toffee can't get much of a toe-hold; b23 fabulous mixing here showing just what malt whisky can do at this brilliant and under-rated age. Lively and complex with the malts wonderfully herded and penned. Without colouring and at 50% abv I bet this would have been given a right wolf-whistle. Perfect for one man and his grog. *40%. Quality Spirits International.*

Scottish Collie 8 Years Old (85.5) n22 t21.5 f21 b21. A good boy. But just wants to sleep rather than play. *40%. Quality Spirits International.*

Scottish Collie 12 Years Old (82) n20 t22 f20 b20. For a malt that's aged 84 in Collie years, it understandably smells a bit funny and refuses to do many tricks. If you want some fun you'll need a younger version. *40%. Quality Spirits International.*

Scottish Leader Imperial Blended Malt (77) n20 t20 f18 b19. Now don't be confused here: this isn't Imperial malt from Speyside. And although it says Blended, it is 100% malt. What is clear, though, is that this is pretty average stuff. *40%. Burn Stewart.*

Scottish Leader Aged 14 Years (80) n21 t21 f19 b19. A cleaner, less peaty version than the no-age statement vatting, but still fails to entirely ignite the tastebuds *40%. Burn Stewart.*

Sheep Dip (84) n19 t22 f22 b21. Young and sprightly like a new-born lamb, this enjoys a fresh, mouthwatering grassy style wth a touch of spice. Maligned by some, but to me a clever, accomplished vatting of alluring complexity. *40%*

Sheep Dip 'Old Hebridean' 1990 dist in or before 1990 **(94)** n23 every aspect has the buoyancy of an anchor, the subtlety of Hebridean Winter winds. Thick peat offering both smoke and a kippery saltiness is embraced by honey; t24 big, weighty delivery with an immediate spice and honey delivery; a butterscotch barley theme appears and vanishes like a small fishing craft in mountainous waves; f23.5 that honey keeps the pace and length, while a beautiful bourbon red liquorice beefs up the vanilla; b23.5 you honey!! Now, that's what I call a whisky...!! *40%. The Spencerfield Spirit Co.*

The Six Isles Pomerol Finish Limited Edition French oak Pomerol wine cask no. 90631-90638, dist 2003, bott 2010 **(85.5)** n19 t23 f21.5 b22. What makes the standard Six Isles work as a vatted malt is its freshness and complexity. With these attributes, plus the distinctive distilleries used, we consistently have one the world's great and truly entertaining whiskies. With this version we have just a decent malt. The wine finish has levelled the mountains and valleys and restricted the finish dramatically, while the nose doesn't work at all. Perfectly drinkable and the delivery is extremely enjoyable. But as a Six Isles, delighted it's a Limited Edition. *46%. Ian Macleod. 3266 bottles.*

⋰ **S'Mokey (88)** n22.5 playful peat covering three, maybe four, levels of weight and intensity. Lively and opens well with a few citrus notes apparent; t22 sweet with a light oiliness spreading the weight and smoke efficiently; f21.5 remains on the light side with the vanilla levels rising as the smoke drops; b22 delicate, sweet and more lightly smoked than the nose advertises. *40%. Master Of Malt.*

Tambowie (84.5) n21.5 t21.5 f20.5 b21. A decent improvement on the nondescript bottling of yore. I have re-included this to both celebrate its newly acquired lightly fruited attractiveness...and to celebrate the 125th anniversary of the long departed Tambowie Distillery whose whisky, I am sure, tasted nothing like this. *40%. The Vintage Malt Whisky Co Ltd.*

Treasurer 1874 Reserve Cask (90.5) n23 huge oak: pungent and salty with a soupcon of peat; lightly molassed with a more telling imprint of maple syrup; t3 dense delivery: the wood is among the leaders, as is a pithy orange. But giant waves of malt break over the taste buds to claim control; the extra complexity is completed with busy spice; f22.5 toffee fudge and raisin; b22 some judicious adding has been carried out here in the Robert Graham shop. Amazing for a living cask that I detect no major sulphur faultlines. Excellent! *51%. Robert Graham Ltd. Live casks available in all Robert Graham shops.*

Vintner's Choice Speyside 10 Years Old (84) n21.5 t22 f20 b20.5. Pleasant. But considering the quality of the Speysiders Grants have to play with, the dullness is a bit hard to fathom. *40%. Quality Spirits International.*

Waitrose Pure Highland Malt (86.5) n22 t22 f20.5 b22. Blood orange by the cartload: amazingly tangy and fresh; bitters out at the finish. This is one highly improved malt and great to see a supermarket bottling showing some serious attitude...as well as taste!! Fun, refreshing and enjoyable. *40%*

⋰ **Wemyss Malts "The Hive" Aged 12 Years (93)** n23 a sumptuous combination of various honeys – including Manuka and lavender – which team with citrus and vanilla comfortably. The lightest breeze of smoke adds ballast; t24 no disappointments on delivery where the honey becomes almost liquid form. Indeed, the texture is divine and carries a ridiculous number of oaky layers, seemingly glued together with beeswax; a heavier liquorice thread works beautifully; f22.5 a degree of vague bitterness gives the effect of over toasted honeycomb; b23.5 mixing different malt whiskies is an art form – one that is prone to going horribly wrong. Here, though, whoever is responsible really is the bees-knees... *40%*

Wemyss Malts "Peat Chimney" 5 Years Old (82.5) n20.5 t21 f20 b21. Rougher than the tongue of a smoking cat. *40%. Wemyss Malts Ltd.*

Wemyss Malts "Peat Chimney" 8 Years Old (85) n21.5 t21.5 f21 b21. Delightful chocolate amid the attractively course peat. *40%. Wemyss Malts Ltd.*

⠿ **Wemyss Malts "Peat Chimney" Aged 12 Years** bott Oct 10 **(90.5) n22**.5 good vanilla depth to the clunking phenols: the peat is positively lashed to the aroma; **t23** beautifully made malt with an outstanding understanding between the light but silky oils, phenols and sympathetic sugars; **f22.5** the vanillas return but retain their smoky chaperone; **b22.5** gorgeous: does what it says on the tin... 40%. Wemyss Malts.

Wemyss "Smooth Gentleman" 5 Years Old (80) n20 t21 f19 b20. A bit of a schoolkid with an affectation. 40%. Wemyss Malts Ltd.

Wemyss Malts "Smooth Gentleman" 8 Years Old (89) n21 sweet but a little bland; **t23.5** much better arrival with a gorgeous barley-toffee impact assisted, naturally, by a spoonful of acacia honey; **f22** returns to a more middle-of-the-road character, but still deliciously soft and rich...and a little juicy; **b22.5** more of a Kentuckian George Clooney than a Bristolian Cary Grant. 40%. Wemyss Malts Ltd.

⠿ **Wemyss Malts "Smooth Gentleman" Aged 12 Years** 1st fill bourbon cask, bott Oct 10 **(88.5) n23** honeycomb and chocolate with a dash of ginger; **t22** big oak early on but the barley keeps it honest; **f21.5** vanilla and butterscotch...but dries big time; **b22** a very attractive and competent, vaguely spicy gentleman who has a bit of a penchant for butterscotch and chocolate. 40%. Wemyss Malts.

Wemyss Malts "Spice King" 5 Years Old (76) n18.5 t20 f18.5 b19. A little on the mucky, tangy side. 40%. Wemyss Malts Ltd.

Wemyss Malts "Spice King" 8 Years Old (87) n22 plenty of butterscotch and fudge; **t22** chewy toffee with a malty, honeyed strata; **f21.5** more toffee. Just when you start wondering where the spice is, it appears very late on through the tradesmen's entrance, though does the best it can not to disturb those at home; **b21.5** hard to believe this lush malt is in any way related to the 5-y-o...!! 40%. Wemyss Malts Ltd.

⠿ **Wemyss Malts "Spice King" Aged 12 Years** bott Oct 10 **(85) n22.5 t21 f21 b21.** Thoroughly enjoyable sugar edge to the decent smoke. A bit thin on the complexity front, though. 40%. Wemyss Malts.

Wemyss Vintage Malt The Peat Chimney Hand Crafted Blended Malt Whisky (80) n19 t22 f20 b19. The balance is askew here, especially on the bone-dry wallpapery finish. Does have some excellent spicy/coffee moments, though. 43%. Wemyss Vintage Malts Ltd.

Wemyss Vintage Malt The Smooth Gentleman Hand Crafted Blended Malt Whisky (83) n19 t22 f21 b21. Not sure about the nose: curiously fishy (very gently smoked). But the malts tuck into the tastebuds with aplomb showing some sticky barley sugar along the way. 43%

Wemyss Vintage Malt The Spice King Hand Crafted Blended Malt Whisky (84) n22 t22 f20 b20. Funnily enough, I've not a great fan of the word "smooth" when it comes to whisky. But the introduction of oily Caol Ila-style peat here makes it a more of a smooth gentleman than the "Smooth Gentleman." Excellent spices very late on. 43%. Wemyss Vintage Malts.

Wholly Smoke Aged 10 Years (86.5) n22.5 t22.5 f20 b21.5. A big, peaty, sweat, rumbustuous number with absolutely no nod towards sophistication or balance and the finish virtually disintegrates. The smoke is slapped on and the whole appears seemingly younger than its 10 years. Massive fun, all the same. 40%. Macdonald & Muir Ltd for Oddbins.

⠿ **Whyte & Mackay Blended Malt Scotch Whisky (78) n19 t22 f18 b19.** You know when the engine to your car is sort of misfiring and feels a bit sluggish and rough...? 40%. Waitrose.

Wild Scotsman Scotch Malt Whisky (Black Label) batch no. CBV001 **(91) n23.5** smoke hangs moodily in the glass; the atmosphere is heavy and humid with the oak in no mood to give way to the peat and the sugars in sticky, molassed form; even a separate layer of barley is thick and clearly means business...; **t23.5** sublime delivery with those molassed, sugary barley tones seeing to the form. But then the smoke comes crashing through followed shortly by some major oak. Elegant, soft, yet this is not a place for pussycats...; **f21** bitters out slightly as the oaks get a bit too cocky; **b23** the type of dram you drink from a dirty glass. Formidable and entertaining. 47%. House of Macduff.

Wild Scotsman Aged 15 Years Vatted Malt (95) n23 t24 f24 b24. If anyone wants an object lesson as to why you don't screw your whisky with caramel, here it is. Jeff Topping can feel a justifiable sense of pride in his new whisky: for its age, it is an unreconstituted masterpiece... 46% (92 proof). nc ncf. USA.

Mystery Malts

Chieftain's Limited Edition Aged 40 Years hogshead **(78) n22 t22 f16 b18.** Oak-ravaged and predictably bitter on the death (those of you who enjoy Continental bitters might go for this..!). But the lead up does offer a short, though sublime and intense honey kick. The finish, though... 48.5%. Ian Macleod.

Cu Dhub (see Speyside Distillery)

Scottish Grain

It's a bit weird, really. Many whisky lovers stay clear of blended Scotch, preferring instead single malts. The reason, I am often told, is that the grain included in a blend makes it rough and ready. Yet I wish I had a twenty pound note for each time I have been told in recent years how much someone enjoys a single grain. The ones that the connoisseurs die for are the older versions, usually special independent bottlings displaying great age and more often than not brandishing a lavish Canadian or bourbon style.

Like single malts, grain distilleries produce whisky bearing their own style and signature. And, also, some display characteristics and a richness that can surprise and delight. Most of the grains available in (usually specialist) whisky outlets are pretty elderly. Being made from maize and wheat helps give them either that Canadian or, depending on the freshness of the cask, an unmistakable bourbony style. So older grains display far greater body than is commonly anticipated.

Light whiskies, including some Speysiders, tend to adopt this north American stance when the spirit has absorbed so much oak that the balance has been tipped. So overtly Kentuckian can they be, I once playfully introduced an old single grain Scotch whisky into a bourbon tasting I was conducting and nobody spotted that it was the cuckoo in the nest ... until I revealed all at the end of the evening. And even had to display the bottle to satisfy the disbelievers.

Younger grains may give a hint of oncoming bourbon-ness. But, rather, they tend to celebrate either a softness in taste or, in the case of North British, a certain rigidity. Where many malts have a tendency to pulverise the taste-buds and announce their intent and character at the top of their voice, younger grains are content to stroke and whisper.

Scotch whisky companies have so far had a relaxed attitude to marketing their grains. William Grant had made some inroads with Black Barrel, though with nothing like the enthusiasm they unleash upon us with their blends and malts. And Diageo are apparently content to see their Cameron Brig sell no further than its traditional hunting grounds, just north of Edinburgh, where the locals tend to prefer single grain to any other whisky. And the latest news from that most enormous of distilleries...it is getting bigger. Not only are Diageo planning to up their malt content by building a new Speyside distillery, but Cameronbridge, never a retiring place since the days of the Haigs in the 1820s is set for even grander expansion. Having, with the now death-sentenced Port Dundas, absorbed the closure of a number of grain distilleries over the last 30 years something had to be done to give it a fighting chance of taking on the expansion into China, Russia and now, most probably, India. It is strange that not more is being done. Cooley in Ireland have in the last year or so forged a healthy following with their introduction of grain whiskies at various ages. They have shown that the interest is there and some fresh thinking and boldness in a marketing department can create niche and often profitable markets. Edrington have entered the market with a vatted grain called Snow Grouse, designed to be consumed chilled and obviously a tilt at the vodka market. The first bottling I received, though, was disappointingly poor and I hope future vattings will be more carefully attended to. All round, then, the news for Scottish grain lovers has not been good of late with the demolition of mighty Dumbarton and now, controversially, the pending closure of Port Dundas itself. With the expansion of Cameronbridge and a 50% stake in North British, Diageo obviously believe they have all the grain capacity they require.

The tastings notes here for grains cover only a few pages, disappointingly, due to their scarcity. However, it is a whisky style growing in stature, helped along the way not just by Cooley but also by Compass Box's recent launching of a vatted grain. And we can even see an organic grain on the market, distilled at the unfashionable Loch Lomond Distillery. Why, though, it has to be asked does it take the relatively little guys to lead the way? Perhaps the answer is in the growing markets in the east: the big distillers are very likely holding on to their stocks to facilitate their expansion there.

At last the message is getting through that the reaction to oak of this relatively lightweight spirit - and please don't for one moment regard it as neutral, for it is most certainly anything but - can throw up some fascinating and sometimes delicious possibilities. Blenders have known that for a long time. Now public interest is growing. And people are willing to admit that they can enjoy an ancient Cambus, Caledonian or Dumbarton in very much the way they might celebrate a single malt. Even if it does go against the grain...

Single Grain Scotch
CALEDONIAN

Clan Denny Caledonian Aged 44 Years dist Jan 65, bott Jul 09 **(94) n23** soft natural caramels caress the nose: toffee wafer with milk chocolate; **t23.5** velvety delivery of corn oil and custard pie; there is almost a bizarre hint of rye from the slightly harder fruity sub plot. Intriguing, if not impossible...; **f24** back to custard cream biscuits dunked in black coffee – and proceeds to melt in the mouth accordingly; **b23.5** I feared that after a gap of our years since last seeing a Clan Denny Caledonian, time might have taken a fatal toll. Not a bit of it! Every bit as gentle as those great drams of yesteryear, even though the oak has, as to be expected, gone up an extra notch. Track a bottle down and cherish it!! 45.8%

··∴·· **Clan Denny Caledonian 45 Years Old** bourbon barrel, cask no. HH6294, dist 1965 **(89) n22** some impressive nip for its strength; a touch of Canadian; **t23.5** quite superb degree of sweetness: some watered down syrup combines with a crescendo of intense corn and mocha; **f21.5** pretty thin corn; the barrel bitters out a small degree; **b22** for all its obvious tiredness, there is plenty of rich character. 46.1%. nc ncf sc. Douglas Laing & Co.

··∴·· **Clan Denny Caledonian 45 Years Old** refill hogshead, cask no. HH6228, dist 1965 **(96) n23.5** fascinating – and quite stunning – mix of light Canadian and deeper bourbon characteristics; almost a buttery quality to the corn; **t25** that is about as good as you might ever expect the delivery of an ancient grain to be: perfect weight, perfect balance between light sugars, oily corn and drier oak; perfect timing to its slow unveiling of its many complexities...in fact, simply perfect...; **f23.5** simplifies, as a grain really has to but those delicate sugars ensure the oak remains honest; **b24** Super Caley...my prayers have been answered... 47.6%. nc ncf sc. Douglas Laing & Co.

··∴·· **Scott's Selection Caledonian 1965** bott 2011 **(89.5) n24** glazed ginger; an unlicked bowl of cake mix remnants; highly polished leather; beeswax; dried orange peel; **t22.5** almost corn whisky at first, then heads off into the vanilla an toffee world of Canada. Softer than silk; **f20.5** some late citrus but bitters out just a little too powerfully; **b22.5** how about that? The nose belongs to Kentucky, the flavours carry a Maple Leaf flag. Aaah, pure Scotch! 45%. Speyside Distillers.

CAMBUS

··∴·· **Clan Denny Cambus Aged 36 Years** bourbon barrel, cask no. HH7252, dist 1975 **(89.5) n22** honey stirred into vanilla yogurt; **t23.5** spices arrive from nowhere – and then vanish almost as quickly; deliciously juicy and light for all the oils. Then the whole vanilla... **f22** ...and nothing but the vanilla. Except maybe a hint of mocha. **b22** flawless grain limited only by its simplicity. 52.1%. nc ncf sc. Douglas Laing & Co.

··∴·· **Clan Denny Cambus 45 Years Old** refill bourbon barrel, cask no. HH5638, dist 1965 **(88.5) n22** someone has left the boiled sweet jars open in the old candy shop... **t23** ... and tipped the sugary dregs into this whisky. Beautifully sweet start, then a vanilla-induced thump in the solar plexus; **f21.5** simplifies and reduces to thin vanilla in the most un-Cambus of ways...; **b22** a grain which has learned to deal with the impact of age in its very own, sweet way... 45.9%. nc ncf sc. Douglas Laing & Co.

··∴·· **Clan Denny Cambus 47 Years Old** bourbon barrel, cask no. HH7029, dist 1963 **(97) n24.5** a mesmeric blending of classic liquorice-bourbony tones, the vivid vanilla of a great Canadian and the sharp, lively precision of a massive scotch... **t25** if you spent a dozen years of your life trying to create a whisky with absolutely perfect weight on delivery, you'd still fail to match the natural genius of this. The oils have just enough body to coat the palate with a delicate fretwork of the finest light liquorice and honeycomb lustre, but whose fragility is exposed by the orange-citrus sharpness which etches its own, impressive course; the sugars mingle with the spices with 47 years of understanding...; **f23** after almost 50 years in the barrel, there is no surprise that a degree of bitter tightness comes into play. But the compactness of the vanilla keeps damage to a minimum; **b24.5** if this wasn't a Scotch single grain, it might just qualify as Bourbon of the Year. Proof that where a whisky is made, matured, or from makes absolutely no difference: it is the quality which counts. And there will be very few whiskies I taste this year that will outgun this one in the quality stakes... 49.7%. nc ncf sc. Douglas Laing & Co.

··∴·· **Scotch Malt Whisky Society Cask G8.1 Aged 21 Years** refill hogshead, cask no. 41759, dist 1989 **(85.5) n22.5 t22 f20 b21.** Decent enough, but a relatively underwhelming way to kick off the Society's account with this legendary grain distillery. A less than endearing piece of oak keeps any chance of the distillery's usual ability to tantalise with clever use of weight and complexity. A few kumquat and delicate clove notes do shake up the caramels on the nose, though. 61.2%. sc. 272 bottles.

CAMERONBRIDGE

⁘ **Clan Denny Cameronbridge 45 Years Old** bourbon barrel, cask no. HH6805, dist 1965 **(78) n21 t20 f18 b19.** Even grains can feel the cold hand of Father Time on their shoulder... 40.5%. nc ncf sc. Douglas Laing & Co.

Duncan Taylor Collection Cameronbridge 1978 cask no. 391150 **(92) n23** corn bread with a touch of stem ginger cake and vanilla cream; **t23.5** succulent Demerara-infused oils effortlessly carry the corn and spices; **f22.5** long with very acceptable drying oak input; **b23** clearly from a first class cask. Pretty good grain, too. 54.6% Duncan Taylor & Co Ltd

Duncan Taylor Collection Cameronbridge 1979 cask no. 46 **(85) n23 t21 f20 b21.** The nose is a celebration of seriously delicate bourbon (not Canadian); a sliver of lime off the soft corn and leathery honeycomb; the delivery shows its age. 50.3%

Duncan Taylor Collection Cameronbridge 1979 cask no. 3585 **(86) n22.5 t22 f20.5 b21.** Oak pounds into the grain, at first making very little difference on the early sugars but then taking control. 51.9%

Duncan Taylor Collection Cameronbridge 1979 cask no. 3586 **(84) n22.5 t21 f20 b20.5.** For those who prefer their grain old and dry. 51.2%

Duncan Taylor Collection Cameronbridge 1979 cask no. 3587 **(82) n22 t22 f18 b20.** The fun and flavour is all front loaded. 51.3%

⁘ **Rare Auld Grain Cameronbridge 32 Years Old** cask no. 3597, dist 1979 **(92) n23** quite lovely but there is a curious non-whisky edge to this one, though can't place how or why exactly. The oak is deep but controlled; **t23.5** got it! You'd swear this is a Geneva: a distinct juniper edge to the complex grain; the little barley present is sharp, puckering and juicy; a light layer of honey offers the required sweetness; **f22.5** busy grain again but now with a coppery metallic glow; again some late juniper is present at the death; **b23** anything but the norm. 48.8%. sc. Duncan Taylor & Co.

⁘ **Scott's Selection Cameron Bridge 1973** bott 2010 **(77) n19 t21 f18 b19.** Good grain + poor cask = 77. 41.4%. Speyside Distillers.

CARSEBRIDGE

⁘ **Clan Denny Carsebridge 29 Years Old** 1st fill hogshead, cask no. HH6609, dist 1981 **(82) n22 t22 f18 b20.** The intensity of the corn is profound. So too, alas, is the bitter retribution of the tired cask. 53.1%. nc ncf sc. Douglas Laing & Co.

Duncan Taylor Collection Carsebridge 1979 cask no. 33033 **(91) n23 t23 f22.5 b22.5.** A fabulous dram from this lost distillery and about as relaxing as they come. Indeed, I found this Carsebridge the perfect antidote to when my beloved Millwall lost at Wembley against Scunthorpe... 54.9%

Duncan Taylor Collection Carsebridge 1979 cask no. 33038 **(93.5) n23.5** a teasing aroma: powdered sugar on boiled fruit candy; a freshly opened bottle of lemon drops; **t24.5** crisp, brittle sugars and crunchy corn biscuit; a light topping of Demerara: just about perfect in grain whisky terms; **f22.5** fades with the usual chorus of vanillas; **b23** a Duncan Taylor Carsebridge bottling is usually one of the highlights of the whisky year. This one certainly doesn't disappoint. In fact, it's a belter...!!! 52.3%. Duncan Taylor & Co Ltd.

DUMBARTON

⁘ **Clan Denny Dumbarton 45 Years Old** refill hogshead, cask no. HH7001, dist 1965 **(89.5) n23** a serious injection of treacle, liquorice and light spice to the rich corn; **t23** quite beautiful delivery: firm yet silky texture make you purr and the sugars and brief juicy spice to the vanilla offer a degree of youthfulness; **f21.5** just a hint of puffing, bittering oak, but the vanillas stay in command; **b22** a lovely grain bottled in the nick of time and happy to display the remnants of its zesty vigour. 49.5%. nc ncf sc. Douglas Laing & Co.

⁘ **Scott's Selection Dumbarton 1986** bott 2011 **(94) n24.5** complex? Doesn't even touch upon what is going on here. Most ungrain like in the manner by which a complex prickle teases the nose. A bit like the small grains working wonders in a bourbon. Not overly sweet, but the cooked molassed sugars do add depth as well as balance; butterscotch in a mildly overcooked tart; **t24** initially a silkier delivery than the nose suggests will happen. But those corn oils are relatively brief and a combination of sugars, of varying degree of intensity, begin to box with the fizzing spices; **f22** some bitterness as one comes to expect from old Allied casks, but the clarity of the grain and now honeyed sugars negates the worst and has a little to spare; **b23.5** when this distillery was closed I was almost beside myself with disappointment...and rage. Following the closure of Cambus, this left Dumbarton as the brightest star in the collapsing grain whisky galaxy. This bottle will give you some insight into just why I treasured it so greatly; certainly more so than the bead counters at Allied who saw its potential as prime real estate over its ability to keep making arguably the best blended Scotch whiskies in the world. My main point of surprise now is why so few bottlings from this giant of a distillery ever see the shelves... 51.5%. Speyside Distillers.

GARNHEATH

❖ **Clan Denny Garnheath 43 Years Old** refill hogshead, cask no. HH6642, dist 1967 **(94) n24.5** a charming mix of very old Georgian corn whiskey and no less young Demerara column still rum; it would be hard to fine tune the spices to better effect; **t23.5** rare for a grain, the barley is detectable briefly but distinctly early on. It is then lost under a silo of corn but the juiciness never dissipates; **f22.5** fabulously controlled, bristling spice keeps a hint of oaky burnout to a minimum; **b23.5** what a treat: not just a whisky as rare as budgie teeth, but one in tip-top nick for its age. A rare delight. 44.4%. nc ncf sc. Douglas Laing & Co.

The Clan Denny Garnheath Vintage 1969 Aged 40 Years refill hogshead HH 5538 **(95) n25** a decidedly bourbony twist to this one with a blood orange, hickory and watered honey theme. On another level comes the berry fruits and apricot. Sensational...in every sense...!!! **t24** more bourbon on delivery and on the offshoot development: soft liquorice, the mildest honeycomb. It works so well because of the understatement and attention to elegance; **f22.5** bitters a little, with the odd flaw in the cask exposed as it enters its fifth decade. A soft red liquorice and vanilla depth, coupled with a charmingly tingling spice attack, does its best to compensate; **b23.5** one of the rarest experiences in Scotch whisky: even I have tasted different Garnheath only 30 to 40 times in my life. Few, though, have been as well rounded as this. The nose, especially, almost defies belief. Unquestionably grain of this and probably many a year... 47.9%. Douglas Laing & Co Ltd.

GIRVAN

Berrys' Own Selection Girvan 1989 cask no. 37531 **(84) n21.5 t22 f20 b20.5.** Stodgy on both nose and delivery with the grainy sharpness coming through briefly but to excellent effect. 45.1%. Berry Bros & Rudd.

❖ **Berry's Own Selection Girvan 1989** cask no. 37530/1, bott 2010 **(82.5) n21 t22 f19.5 b20.** Thick, sweet but a little on the tardy side... 45.1%. nc ncf sc. Berry Bros & Rudd.

Celtic Heartlands Girvan 1965 Aged 42 Years (83) n21 t22 f20.5 b20.5. I know that around about the time this was made some blenders in Scotland weren't over enamoured with Girvan – which is hardly the case today. Here you get a slight insight as to why some feathers were flying back then, with the sharpness of the firm grain at times biting pretty deep. However, after all these years, it is the oak making the loudest noise and the messages are mixed. Certainly the bitterness is entirely wood related. There is the odd window, though, especially just after initial delivery, through which the grain does show a rich shaft of golden promise. This is not a whisky without moments of great beauty. 45%

❖ **Clan Denny Girvan 45 Years Old** refill hogshead, cask no. HH6276, dist 1965 **(90) n23** thick with a big fruity overcoat spanning the richly bourboned main body; **t23.5** almost eye-wateringly sharp on delivery with a major grapey accent. Plenty of marmalade in there, too and then we are back to the bourbon basics; **f21.5** long and, though bittering out, a touch of butterscotch adds comfort and dignity; **b22.5** laid on with a golden trowel. 47.3%. nc ncf sc.

❖ **Clan Denny Girvan 45 Years Old** refill hogshead, cask no. HH6923, dist 1965 **(88.5) n23** teasingly light yet distinctly bourbony, with an extra spoonful of molassed sugar; **t23** straight down the line vanilla and corn, with a light sweetened liquorice side dish; **f20.5** tires and bitters; **b22** simplistic, certainly. But as you get older, you learn to appreciate the more simple things in life... 45%. nc ncf sc. Douglas Laing & Co.

The Clan Denny Girvan Vintage 1990 Aged 20 Years Bourbon Barrel hogshead no. 5794 **(88.5) n20.5** a touch of spice, otherwise non-committal; **t23** spice, indeed!! Sugared almonds add the balance as the oily spices take a delightful hold; **f22.5** lots of cocoa; **b22.5** the nose is quiet, but what happens on the taste buds is a joy. 59.3%. 246 bottles.

Scotch Malt Whisky Society Cask G7.1 Aged 18 Years refill barrel, dist Jul 90 **(86.5) n21 t23 f21 b21.5.** Subtly Canadian and slightly rich. Perhaps over indulges the caramels but weight, mouthfeel, degree of sweetness and spice impact are all very good. 54.2%

❖ **Scott's Selection Girvan 1964** bott 2011 **(92.5) n23.5** distant echoes of bourbon but also sports a non specific fruitiness. Beautifully clean with a little toffee and coffee for good measure; **t24** excellent and unexpected early arrival of spice which adds serious oomph to the buttery toffee that tries to lead. Golden syrup and maple syrup fight for the sugary context (and what a delight that is!); **f22** makes the usual attempt to bitter up you'd expect from a grain but the prevailing spices and vanillas, plus a little late mocha, counter impressively; **b23** Girvan, like Invergordon, is grain which takes full advantage of its sumptuous persona. Here, though, it adds some controlled sharpness. But it's the lordly sugars which really win the day. Superb. 48.8%. *Speyside Distillers.*

INVERGORDON

Berrys' Own Selection Invergordon 1971 (79.5) n20 t20.5 f19 b20. Buttery, but soapy and bitter, too. 48%. *Berry Bros & Rudd.*

Berry's Own Selection Invergordon 1971 bott 2009 (88) n22 t22 f22 b22. Steady as a rock; hard as a blancmange...; 48.2%. *Berry Bros & Rudd.*

⁖ **Berry's Own Selection Invergordon 1971** cask no. 2, bott 2011 (91.5) n24 more of a high quality column still rum than a whisky...; Demerara in both rum type and sugars evident with the vanillas showing a delicious citrus tinge; some real butterscotch in there, too; t23 back to being grain whisky now: toffee, toasted fudge and spices; some soft oils glue the busy flavours to the roof of the mouth; f22 the peppers keep peppering, but the toffee-vanillas dominate; b22.5 a beautiful experience. 46.7%. *nc ncf sc. Berry Bros & Rudd.*

⁖ **Clan Denny Invergordon 44 Years Old** refill barrel, cask no. HH4995, dist 1966 (95.5) n23.5 corn dough and carrot juice; a light smattering of spice ensures some real complexity here; t24 as soft and sweet as you might imagine an Invergordan to be. But also offers a surprising degree of countering sharpness with a salivating quality of a grain more than half its age f23.5 a wonderful build up of tingling, busy spice offers an excellent exit; b24.5 almost quicksand-ish in its softness. But an amazing degree of complexity, too. A true gem of a whisky. 46.8%. *nc ncf sc. Douglas Laing & Co.*

⁖ **Clan Denny Invergordon 45 Years Old** bourbon barrel, cask no. HH7254, dist 1966 (88) n22 a little salty; otherwise usual soft toffee-vanilla; t22 silky delivery with the toffee melting to allow in some tannins; f22 Cornish cream toffee; remains a real softy; b22 played with an absolutely straight bat: over 45 years every kink appears to have been ironed out. 47.1%. *nc ncf sc. Douglas Laing & Co.*

The Clan Denny Invergordon Vintage 1965 Aged 44 Years refill barrel HH 5576, dist 1965 (90.5) n23 fat, absolutely dense corn with some jumbled, half-hearted fruit notes; t23.5 how soft is that? The corn dissolves on arrival as it moves towards a lazy Canadian style. Almost one dimensional, but that is not a criticism as it does what it does superbly; f22 more of the same, but now in a much more simpering, vanilla-led way; b22 improbably simplistic and almost youthful for its age. You can't go wrong with this. 45.4%. *Douglas Laing.*

Duncan Taylor Collection Invergordon 1965 cask no. 15519 (94) n24.5 t23 f23 b23.5. Duncan Taylor have obviously struck upon a rich seam of outstanding Invergordon. 100% must buy whisky. 51.6%

Duncan Taylor Collection Invergordon 1965 cask no. 15528 (94) n24 passion fruit and gooseberry neatly wrapped in custard...stunning!!... t24 just the degree of melt-in-the-mouth yield you would expect from this distillery. Except here it not only shows its supine qualities, but a much more aggressive alter ego with first some punchy vanillas then a middle ground peppery spice; f22.5 a lovely interplay between the elegant spices and delicate vanillas; b23.5 it is very difficult to ask much more of a grain whisky of such advanced years, especially one that is determined not to go down the bourbony route. 50.8%. *Duncan Taylor & Co Ltd.*

Duncan Taylor Collection Invergordon 1965 cask no. 15532 (85.5) n21 t22.5 f20.5 b21.5. Good, simple entirely honest old grain. But here all the accent is on the vanilla and the complexity which wins heart and palate on 15519 is conspicuous by its absence. 52.7%

⁖ **Rare Auld Grain Invergordon 38 Years Old** cask no. 96251, dist 1972 (88.5) n22.5 attractively floral with a red liquorice nod to Kentucky; t22.5 salivating corn and light oaky spice; f21.5 sweet vanilla; b22 ramrod straight and beyond the nose eschews any grand design of complexity. 44%. *sc. Duncan Taylor & Co.*

⁖ **Scotch Malt Whisky Society Cask G5.2 Aged 17 Years** virgin toasted oak hogshead, cask no. 53285, dist 1993 (90.5) n23 one assumes they were still using corn, because along with the aid of the virgin oak, this could easily pass for a half decent bourbon. The intensity of the honey, as well as the honeycomb, is the star of the show; t23 sweet, oily and intense, we are treated to Lubec's finest, seemingly moistened with almond oil, but also a thick burst of caramels and red liquorice; f21.5 bitters somewhat and only the caramel, plus a burst of vanilla, is all that remains in the oily trail; b23 oils apart, barely representative of the distillery at this age but bourbon lovers will be thrilled. 65.3%. *sc. 248 bottles.*

⁖ **Scott's Selection Invergordon 1964** bott 2011 (92) n24 exceptional: some lovely rhubarb tart with vanilla topping; strands of Demerara with a slight salty flourish. Some Invergordon show Canadian tendencies, this is purely Kentuckian. Beguiling...; t24 pure silk. Typical of the distillery in its softness, but again bourbony characteristics loom large with fabulous honeycomb, creamed hickory and Demerara-sweetened oils; f21 grinds to a slightly uncomfortable halt as some bitterness arrives. But a few spices and a few lingering vanilla notes compensate; **b23** another which keeps faithfully to the distillery's yielding, melt-in-the-mouth style. But here we have a deep Kentucky drawl and a nose from heaven... *43.8%. Speyside Distillers.*

⁖ **The Whisky Agency Invergordon 1965** bott 2010 **(90) n23.5** fabulous sugar-salt interplay. Distinct Canadian whisky theme here with the vanillas as soft as you please; **t23** sweet and intense vanilla; a hint of butterscotch and manuka honey passes quickly as a light spicing settles; **f21** bitters out acceptably and expectedly; **b22.5** a glorious old timer, showing some quality Canadian-style manoeuvres. *44.7%. The Whisky Agency.*

LOCH LOMOND

⁖ **Rhosdhu 2008 Cask No. 2483** re-char bourbon, dist 17/03/08, bott 27/07/11 **(86.5) n22 t22 f21 b21.5.** Delicately clean barley with a touch of lemon and, though engagingly soft, is not beyond showing some sugary teeth. *45%. nc ncf sc.*

⁖ **Rhosdhu 2008 Cask No. 2484** bourbon barrel, dist 17/03/08, bott 27/07/11 **(84) n21.5 t21.5 f20.5 b21.** The barley battles with some aggressive oak, even at this tender age. The spice count is pretty high. *45%. nc ncf sc.*

NORTH BRITISH

Berry's Own Selection North British 2000 bott 2009 **(78) n19.5 t21 f18.5 b19.** Pock marked by the occasional sulphurous North British house style – this is to do with distillation, not maturation – and for all its brightness on delivery has a bit of problem shaking off the dogged late bitterness. *46%. Berry Bros & Rudd.*

The Clan Denny North British Vintage 1979 Aged 30 Years refill butt HH 5557, dist 1979 **(90) n22** pedestrian vanilla; corn oil with a sprinkling of icing sugar; **t24** absolutely everything you didn't expect from the nose: a flavour eruption of sharp, salivating corn and grass notes; vanilla towards the middle; **f22** bitters out as the cask begins to talk; **b22** I know a blender or two who will regret that such an effervescent cask for its age slipped through the net. *54.2%. Douglas Laing.*

Duncan Taylor Collection North British 1978 cask no. 38469 **(89) n21.5 t23 f22 b22.5.** Just charms you to death. *54.9%*

Duncan Taylor Collection North British 1978 cask no. 38472 **(84.5) n21 t22 f20.5 b21.** Many of the usual NB corn characteristics, but evidence of a mildly fatigued cask. *55.2%*

Duncan Taylor Collection North British 1978 cask no. Q247 **(95) n24 t24 f23 b24.** Golden proof that great grain is a match for anything. *54.7%*

Norse Cask Selection North British 1997 Aged 11 Years hogshead cask no. 18278, dist 1997, bott 2008 **(91) n22.5 t23.5 f22.5 b22.5.** An exemplary cask: exactly what you should expect from this distillery at this age. *64.9%. Qualityworld for WhiskyOwner.com, Denmark.*

Scotch Malt Whisky Society Cask G1.5 Aged 24 Years refill barrel, dist Apr 84 **(90.5) n23 t23.5 f21 b23.** Even after nearly a quarter of a century, this a powering beauty. *60.7%*

⁖ **The Whisky Agency North British 1962 (93) n24** sharp, punchy, a tad coastal by displaying a briny freshness..but, best of all, neither sweet nor dry. The thin molasses and honey balances the drier vanillas to an atom; **t23.5** crisp delivery. The sugars are firm, crunchy almost, but softened by the corn oil. The vanilla intensifies wonderfully and some lovely hints of Lubec marzipan adds a further flourish of class; **f22.5** no hints of bitterness. Just a light spice dusting stodging up the oiliness slightly **b23** full of traits and characteristics as rare as this type of whisky. But, above all, absolutely refuses to admit its age. This grain is an inspiration to us all... *47.9%. The Whisky Agency.*

NORTH OF SCOTLAND

The Clan Denny North of Scotland Vintage 1974 Aged 35 Years refill hogshead HH5562 **(80.5) n21.5 t21 f18 b20.** The more bitter elements of the cask have bitten deep but the Canadian style vanillas are shapely. *44.1%. Douglas Laing.*

⁖ **Late Lamented North of Scotland 37 Years Old (94.5) n23.5** sweet and nutty, there is a crisp sheen to the more sugary Canadian vanilla notes. Just a slight drizzle of something spicy makes for a beautifully balanced aroma; **t23.5** a sumptuous mouth feel cannot disguise the busy interplay between the weighty vanillas and slicker sugars, which run the range from refined to muscovado; ridiculously clean, allowing a rare clarity on the palate for a whisky of such great age; **f23.5** textbook complexity of an old-fashioned Canadian style. Beautiful corn dots the I and crosses the T, finding the spots still not filled by the sugary vanillas. An almost lazy, apologetic spiciness ramps up the complexity and the expected semi-gluey finale has a surprising mouthwatering quality; **b24** an astonishing whisky completely devoid of the bitterness often found in a whisky of such antiquity, or over the top oakiness. One of the great Scottish Single Grains of recent years and a bottling that Canadian whisky devotees of a near lost style of half a century ago will relish. Monumentally magnificent and, of its type, almost flawless. 44.2%

PORT DUNDAS

Scotch Malt Whisky Society Cask G6.1 Aged 28 Years refill hogshead, dist Dec 80 **(89.5)** n23 t22.5 f22 b22. About as friendly a dram as you will ever meet. 51%

◌ **Scott's Selection Port Dundas 1965** bott 2011 **(91)** n24 peaches and creamed toffee. Honeysuckle adds a sweet, floral note; the moistest of Dundee cakes; we are talking no more than hints of hints...; t23 less melts-in-the-mouth, as simply vanishes. Possibly the softest delivery of the year and then an entire gamut of vaguely honeyed, vaguely coffeed notes drying with peanut buttered toast. Vaguely... f21.5 dries and sticks to a butterscotch theme; b22.5 if you ever see a witch's chest in Holland...this is even flatter than that... No peaks or troughs. Just one flavour rolling, seemingly without a second glance, hesitation or join into the next... Not sure whether to adore this incredibly delicate whisky or try to thrash some life into it. Certainly, as I come up to tasting my 1,000th whisky of the year (this is no. 972) I can safely say there has been no other one quite like it. Which must be a good thing. So, upon reflection, one to get to know and love. For it is a thing of rare beauty. Flat chest or not... 43.3%. Speyside Distillers.

STRATHCLYDE

◌ **Clan Denny Strathclyde 33 Years Old** refill butt, cask no. HH6144, dist 1977, bott 2010 **(94.5)** n23.5 pithy grape and pepper; t23.5 fresh fruit and then an avalanche of pepper and bread pudding spices, complete with a topping of crunchy brown sugars; succulent mouth feel with a superb touch to the delicate oil; f24 so un-33-year-old! No tired oak and the spices still lightly buzz. But more fruity notes now draining away b23.5 I am not told it has been, but imagine an old grain finished in a lively, fresh and very clean wine cask... A stunner! 57.2%. nc ncf sc. Douglas Laing & Co.

The Clan Denny Strathclyde Vintage 1969 Aged 40 Years refill hogshead HH 5741 **(86.5)** n22 promising, thanks to some light citrus; t23 big, marauding grains; less oils than its peers giving a fresher delivery and middle; f21 thins and bitters out; b21.5 delightfully textured and possessing a wonderfully rich and mouth-watering delivery. One of those grains which still turns up hidden at the back of hotel bars: definitely worth blowing the dust off. 51.7%. Douglas Laing & Co.

Duncan Taylor Collection Strathclyde 1973 cask no. 74067 **(86)** n22.5 t22 f20.5 b21. An infinitely better cask than those previously in this series: the nose is almost identical to the Kentucky Tavern bourbon from the old Barton distillery a decade ago. 55.2%

Vatted Grain

◌ **Compass Box Hedonism** batch H29MMIX **(91)** n22 an unusual oak thrust to this; the lightness of the grain is exposed but not taken advantage of; t23.5 eye-watering freshness and a buzzing spice which one may associate with wheated whisky; f22.5 remains clean with the massive parade of sugars keeping the oak at bay; b23 with virtually all the grains launched being older than Zeus' granddad, it is such a relief to find one where you can still just hear the patter of tiny wheat... 43%. nc ncf. 4410 bottles.

Compass Box Hedonism Maximus (93.5) n25 the kind of aroma your nose was invented for: lots orich bourbony swirls, with butterscotch, liquorice and chocolate-covered honeycomb arriving – big time! – on cue...; oh, and a few gooseberries and greengages tossed in for an extra dimension: it just doesn't get any better... t22.5 the oak is a bit top heavy on arrival, but lush malt cushions its impact to a degree; still juicy and tongue-teasing; f23 retains its overtly bourbony character to the end with massive chewy oak extract, but always enough sweetness in reserve to cope; b23 Bourbon Maximus... 46%

Norse Cask Selection Inver Bridge Aged 29 Years hogshead cask no. QW-gr1108, dist 66 & 79, bott 08 **(88.5)** n23 t23 f21 b21.5. Hmmm, can't think which two distilleries this will have been made from... 46%. Qualityworld for WhiskyOwner.com, Denmark.

The Snow Grouse (70.5) n17.5 t18 f17 b18. Served normally, a tedious nonentity of a whisky. What little flavour there is, is toffee-based. On both nose and finish there are distant off notes, but in something so light louder than they might be. Surely...it can't be...? Served chilled as instructed on bottle: (79) n20 t21 f18 b20. Much, much better. Very sweet and the 's' word is confined, especially on the vodka-ish nose. The finish is still a give away though. 40%

Scottish Blends

Doubtless, the odd eyebrow or two was raised when it was last year announced that a blended scotch had again won Jim Murray's Whisky Bible World Whisky of the Year. For it meant the award has gone to blends as many times over the last five years as single malts.

That implies blended scotch is as good as single malt. And, for my money, that is entirely the case; and if the blender is really doing his job, it should often be better. However, that job is getting a little harder each year. Once it was the standard joke that a sulphured sherry butt that had once been marked for a single malt brand would be dumped into a large blend where it would work on BP Chief executive Tony Hayward's "drop in the ocean" principle. However, there is now a lot more than just the odd sherry butt finding their way in and blenders have to take guard that their blends are not being negatively affected. Certainly, during the course of writing the 2010, 2011 and 2012 Bibles I discovered this was becoming a much more common occurrence. Indeed, one or two brands which a few years back I would have expected to pick up awards on a regular basis have been hit badly: disappointing and a great loss to whisky lovers.

However, the fact that Ballantine's 17 – a blend that has been on a higher plane than most other world whiskies for a very long time – last year finally managed to pick up the big one, after regularly knocking at the door, confirms that there are still a great number of stupendous blends out there to go and discover. It still amazes me, though, how many scotch whisky enthusiasts I meet worldwide who rarely taste blends more than a handful of times a year, if ever at all.

Perhaps it is a form of malt snobbery: if you don't drink malts, then you are not a serious Scotch whisky connoisseur ... or so some people think. Perhaps it is the fact that over 90 out of every 100 bottles of Scotch consumed is a blend, and therefore rather common, that has brought about this cold-shouldering. Well, not in my books. In fact, perhaps the opposite is true. Until you get to grips with blends you may well be entitled to regard yourself knowledgeable in single malts, but not in Scotch as a whole. Blends should be the best that Scotland can offer, because with a blend you have the ability to create any degree of complexity. And surely balance and complexity are the cornerstones of any great whisky, irrespective of type.

Of course there are some pretty awful blends created simply as a commodity with little thought going into their structure – just young whiskies, sometimes consisting of stock that is of dubious quality and then coloured up to give some impression of age. Yes, you are more likely to find that among blends than malts and for this reason the poorest blends can be pretty nasty. And, yes, they contain grain. Too often, though, grain is regarded as a kind of whisky leper – not to be touched under any circumstances. Some writers dismiss grain as "neutral" and "cheap", thus putting into the minds of the uninitiated the perception of inferiority.

But there really is nothing inferior about blends. In fact, whilst researching The Bible, I have to say that my heart misses more than one beat usually when I received a sample of a blend I have never found before. Why? Well, with single malts each distillery produces a style that can be found within known parameters. With a blend, anything is possible. There are many dozens of styles of malts to choose from and they will react slightly differently with certain grains.

For that reason, perhaps, I have marked blends a little more strictly and tighter than I have single malts. Because blends, by definition, should offer more.

The most exciting blends, like White Horse 12 (why, oh, why is that, like Old Parr 18, restricted mainly to Japan?) Grant's and the perennially glorious Ballantine's show bite, character and attitude. Silk and charm are to be appreciated. But after a long, hard day is anything better than a blend that is young and confident enough to nip and nibble at your throat on its way down and then throw up an array of flavours and shapes to get your taste-buds round? Certainly, I have always found blends ultimately more satisfying than malts. Especially when the balance, like this year's Bible Blend Champion, Ballantine's 17, simply caresses your soul. And they do more: they paint pictures on the palate, flavour-scapes of extraordinary subtlety and texture. No two bottles are ever exactly the same, but they are usually close enough and further illustrate the fascination of a beautifully orchestrated variation on a theme.

With Blended Scotch the range and possibilities are limitless. All it takes is for the drinker not just to use his or her nose and taste-buds. But also an open mind.

Scottish Blends

"10 Years and a Bit" Blended Scotch (84) n21.5 t22 f20 b20.5. Matured in oloroso and finished in a Cognac quartercask. Explains why this blend lurches drunkenly all over the palate. Enough honeycomb, though, for a pleasant few minutes 42%. *Qualityworld, Denmark.*

100 Pipers (74) n18.5 t18 f19 b18.5. An improved blend, even with a touch of spice to the finish. I get the feeling the grains are a bit less aggressive than they for so long were. I'd let you know for sure, if only I could get through the caramel. 40%. *Chivas.*

Aberdour Piper (88.5) n22 t23 f21.5 b22. Always great to find a blend that appears to have upped the stakes in the quality department. Clean, refreshing with juicy young Speysiders at times simply showing off. 40%. *Hayman Distillers.*

Adelphi Private Stock Loyal Old Mature (88) n21 t23 f22 b22. A very attractive number, especially for those with a slightly sweet tooth. 40%

Antiquary 12 Years Old (92) n23.5 by some distance the smokiest delivery I have seen from this blend since my late dear friend Jim Milne got his hands on it. The last time I had hold of this it was Speyside all the way. Now peat rules; t23.5 immediate oils and smoke form a thick layer in almost Caol Ila style, but penetrating grains and juicier Speysiders ensure parity of style; f22 light with vanilla and echoes of peat; b23 a staggering about turn for a blend which, for a very long time, has flown the Speyside flag. I am not convinced that this degree of peatiness was intended. But it works! 40%. *Tomatin Distillery.*

Antiquary 21 Years Old (93) n23.5 as dense and brooding as an imminent thunderstorm: just a hint of a less than perfect sherry butt costs a point but manuca honey and crushed leaves, all helped along with a delicate peat-reek, ensure something sultry and wonderful; t23.5 improbably dense with a honeycomb maltiness you have to hack through; the grains offer lighter, bourbony touches; f23 softer vanillas and toffee, topped with the thinnest layer of molassed sugar and further bourbony notes; b23 a huge blend, scoring a magnificent 93 points. But I have tasted better, and another sample, direct from the blending lab, came with even greater complexity and less apparent caramel. A top-notch blend of rare distinction. 43%

Antiquary 30 Years Old (86) n22 t23 f20 b21. Decidedly odd fare but the endearingly eccentric nose and early delivery are sublime, with silky complexity tumbling all over the palate. 46%. *Tomatin Distillery.*

Antiquary Finest (79.5) n20 t21 f19 b19.5. Pleasantly sweet and plump with the accent on the quick early malt delivery. 40%. *Tomatin Distillery.*

Arden House Scotch Whisky (86) n19.5 t22 f22.5 b22. Another great bit of fun from the Co-op. Very closely related to their Finest Blend, though this has, for some reason or other, a trace of a slightly fatter, mildly more earthy style. If only they would ditch the caramel and let those sweet malts and grains breathe! 40%. *Co-Operative Group.*

Asda Blended Scotch Whisky (76.5) n19 t21 f17.5 b19. A scattergun approach with sweet, syrupy notes hitting the palate early and hard. Beware the rather bitter finish, though. 40%

Asda Extra Special 12 Years Old (78) n19 t21 f19 b19. Pleasantish but dragged down by the dreaded S word. 40%. *Glenmorangie for Asda.*

The Bailie Nicol Jarvie (B.N.J) (95) n24 the sharpest barley has been taken to a barley-sharpening shop and painstakingly sharpened; this is pretty sharp stuff...the citrus gangs together with the fresh grass to form a dew which is pretty well...er... sharp...; t24 mouth-watering, eye-closingly, mouth-puckeringly sharp delivery with the barley pinging off the tautest grain you can imagine; f23 softens with a touch of vanilla and toffee; the late run from the citrus is a masterpiece of whisky closing; b24 I know my criticism of BNJ, historically one of my favourite blends, over the last year or two has been taken to heart by Glenmorangie. Delighted to report that they have responded: the blend has been fixed and is back to its blisteringly brilliant, ultra-mouth-watering self. Someone's sharpened their ideas up. 40%

Ballantine's Aged 12 Years (84.5) n22.5 t22 f19 b21. Attractive but odd fellow, this, with a touch of juniper to the nose and furry bitter marmalade on the finish. But some excellent barley-cocoa moments, too. 43%. *Chivas.*

Ballantine's 12 Years Old (87) n21 t22 f21 b23. The kind of old-fashioned, mildly moody blend Colonel Farquharson-Smythe (retired) might have recognised when relaxing at the 19th hole back in the early '50s. Too good for a squirt of soda, mind. 40%. *Chivas Bros.*

Ballantine's 17 Years Old (97.5) n24.5 deft grain and honey plus teasing salty peat; ultra high quality with bourbon and pear drops offering the thrust; a near unbelievable integration with gooseberry juice offering a touch of sharpness muted by watered golden syrup; t24 immediately mouthwatering with maltier tones clambering over the graceful cocoa-enriched grain; the degrees of sweetness are varied but near perfection; just hints of smoke here and there; f24 lashings of vanilla and cocoa on the fade; drier with a faint spicey, vaguely smoky buzz; has become longer with more recent bottlings with the most subtle oiliness imaginable; **b25** now only slightly less weighty than of old. After a change of style direction it has comfortably reverted back to its sophisticated, mildly erotic old self. One of the most beautiful, complex and stunningly structured whiskies ever created. Truly the epitome of great Scotch. To the extent that for the last year, I have simply been unable to find a better whisky anywhere in the world. *43%. Chivas Bros.*

Ballantine's Aged 21 Years (93) n24 superbly intrinsic, relying on deft fruit and vanilla notes as the key; **t24** superbly textured with subtle layers of honey, juicy grasses and refined, slightly subdued, bourbony notes from the grain; **f22** flattens somewhat as the toffee evolves; **b23** one of the reasons I think I have loved the Ballantine's range over the years is because it is a blenders' blend. In other words, you get the feeling that they have made as much, and probably more, as possible from the stocks available and made complexity and balance the keystones to the whisky. That is still the case, except you find now that somehow, although part of a larger concern, it appears that the spectrum of flavours is less wide, though what has been achieved with those available remains absolutely top drawer. This is truly great whisky, but it has changed in style as blends, especially of this age, cannot help but doing. *43%*

Ballantine's Aged 30 Years (94) n23.5 satisfying interplay between spiced grape and vanilla-clad smoke; **t24** quite sublime: the delivery simply melts in the mouth. Mainly grain on show early, again with all the attendant vanilla, then a juicier network of sharper barley and fruit. The weight is outstanding; **f23.5** long, with a real grain-malt tug of war. Spices persist and the vanilla ups a gear; **b23.5** quite a different animal to that which I tasted last year...and the year before. Having come across it in three different markets, I each time noted a richer, more balanced product: less a bunch of old casks being brought together but more a sculpted piece from preferred materials. That said, I still get the feeling that this is a work in progress: a Kenny Jackett-style building of a team bit by bit, so that each compartment is improved when it is possible, but not to the detriment of another and, vitally, balance is maintained. *43%* ⊙ ⊙

⸫ **Ballantine's Christmas Reserve (72) n18 t19 f17 b18.** Not quite what I asked from Santa. A rare sulphury slip up in the Christmas day snow from the Ballantine's stable. *40%*

Ballantine's Finest (96) n24 a playful balance and counter-balance between grains, lighter malts and a gentle smokiness. The upped peat of recent years has given an extra weight and charm that had been missing; **t24** sublime delivery: the mouthfeel couldn't be better had your prayers been answered; velvety and brittle grains combine to get the most out of the juicy malts: a lot of chewing to get through here; **f23.5** soft, gentle, yet retains its weight and shape with a re-emergence of smoke and a gristy sweetness to counter the gentle vanillas and cocoa from the oak **b24.5** as a standard blend this is coming through as a major work of art. Each time I taste this the weight has gone up a notch or two more and the sweetness has increased to balance out with the drier grain elements. Take a mouthful of this and experience the work of a blender very much at the top of his game. *40%. Chivas Bros.*

⸫ **Ballantine's Limited** brown bottle, bott code D03518 **(94.5) n23.5** a gentle patchwork quilt of fruit and surprisingly nippy spices. The odd stewed greengage chimes in, as well as toffee apple. And there is something of the early opened bakers too, with that sweet smell of warm cakes and pies...; **t24** obscenely beautiful delivery, perhaps bordering on the delivery of the year. When you taste as many whiskies as I, you sometimes forget that it is, under exceptional circumstances, possible to create a mouth-feel so soft; icing sugars and diluted golden syrup offer moisture to the burnt raisin; **f23** a very slight bitter fade but there are now oaky vanillas to contend with, though they no more than breeze around the palate; **b24** when it comes to Ballantine's I am beginning to run out of superlatives. The last time I tasted Limited, I remember being disappointed by the un-Ballantine's-like bitter finish. Well, from nose to finale, there is a barely perceptible trace of a rogue cask costing half a point from each stage: indeed, it may have cost it World Whisky of the Year. But so magnificent are all those keeping it company there has been no such falling at the last hurdle here. This bottle, rather than finding its way back into my warehouse library, will be living at my home for offering an ethereal quality unmatched by any other whisky in the world. *43%. Chivas.*

Ballantine's Limited 75cl royal blue bottle **(89) n22** beautifully clean barley and soft fruits; a touch of vanilla and smoke in the distant background; **t24** a sumptuous delivery of melt-in-the-mouth grain followed by a slow unfurling of complex malt notes, from sweet barley to spicier cocoa-oak. Lovely fruit and a dab of smoke in the middle; **f21** bitters out impatiently; **b22** hadn't tasted this for a little while but maintains its early style and quite glorious delivery. *43%*

Ballantine's Master's (82) n21 t22 f19 b20. Excellent lively grain and chewy malt, but the always suspect, grain-drizzled finish has become even more nondescript in recent bottlings. *40%*

Ballantine's Rare Limited (89.5) n23.5 busy and weighty: light smoke compliments the bananas and raisins; **t22.5** thick and soupy; the delivery and follow through are both lush and viscous and moderately juicy. Again we have bananas in custard plus a more aggressive muscovado-sweetened fruitiness; **f21.5** spices gather as do drier oaks; **b22** a heavier, more mouth watering blend than the "Bluebottle" version. *43%. ncf Chivas.*

Bell's Original (91) n23 superb, old fashioned stuff: a few biting grains (as there should be), but kept in good order by a confident, smoky tapestry. Plenty of caramel but still quietly assertive; **t22.5** delivery offers a two-pronged attack of grinding grain and more sumptuous oils and smoke; quick to sweeten though never too far; caramel and vanilla offers a fanfare to a middle spice surge; **f22.5** long with the smoke lengthening the tail further. Usual butterscotch and caramel, but everything charmingly well tailored; **b23** your whisky sleuth came across the new version for the first time in the bar of a London theatre back in December 2009 during the interval of "The 39 Steps". To say I was impressed and pleasantly surprised is putting it mildly. And with the whisky, too, which is a massive improvement on the relatively stagnant 8-year-old especially with the subtle extra smoky weight. If the blender asks me: "Did I get it right, Sir?" then the answer has to be a resounding "yes". *40%*

Bells 8 Years Old (85) n21.5 t22.5 f20 b21. Some mixed messages here: on one hand it is telling me that it has been faithful to some of the Bells distilleries – hence a slight dirty note, especially on the finish. On the other, there are some sublime specks of complexity and weight. Quite literally the rough and the smooth. *40%. Diageo.*

Benmore (74) n19 t19 f18 b18. Underwhelming to the point of being nondescript. *40%*

Berrys' Blue Hanger 30 Years Old 3rd Release bott 2007 **(90.5) n23** ye olde oake, as one might expect from this olde companye, manifesting itself in sweet exotic fruit; **t22.5** bitter-sweet and tingly, from the very start the blend radiates fruit and big oak; **f22.5** long, spiced, a dash of something vaguely smoky but never tries to disguise its great age; saved at the death by a lush sweetness which sees off any OTT oak; **b22.5** much improved version on the last, closer to the original in every respect. Excellent. *45.6%. Berry Bros & Rudd.*

Big "T" 5 Years Old (75) n19 t20 f18 b18. Still doesn't have the finesse of old and clatters about the tastebuds charmlessly. *40%. Tomatin Distillery.*

Black & White (91) n22 t23 f22.5 b23.5 This one hasn't gone to the dogs: quite the opposite. I always go a bit misty-eyed when I taste something this traditional: the crisp grains work to maximum effect in reflecting the malts. A classic of its type. *40%. Diageo.*

Black Bottle (74.5) n18 t20.5 f17 b18. Barely a shadow of its once masterful, great self. *40% Burn Stewart.* ☺☺

Black Bottle 10 Years Old (89) n22 so age-weightedly peaty it could almost be a single malt: the grains make little discernible impact; **t23** soft, deft malt and firmer grain. The peat arrives after a short interval; **f22** more vanilla and other oaky tones; **b23** a stupendous blend of weight and poise, but possessing little of the all-round steaming, rampaging sexuality of the younger version...but like the younger version showing a degree less peat: here perhaps even two. Not, I hope, a start of a new trend under the new owners. *40%*

Black Dog 12 Years Old (92) n21 t23 f24 b24. Offering genuine sophistication and élan. This minor classic will probably require two or three glass-fulls before you take the bait... *42.8%*

Black Dog Century (89) n21 t23 f23 b22. I adore this style of no-nonsense, full bodied bruising blend which amid the muscle offers exemplary dexterity and finesse. What entertainment in every glass!! *42.8%. McDowell & Co Ltd. Blended in Scotland/Bottled in India.*

The Black Douglas bott code 340/06/183 **(84) n19 t20 f23 b22.** Don't expect raptures of mind-bending complexity. But on the other hand, enough chewability and spice buzz here to make for a genuinely decent whisky, especially on the excellent finish. Not dissimilar to a bunch of blends you might have found in the 1950s. *40%. Foster's Group, Australia.*

The Black Douglas Aged 8 Years bott code 348/06/187 **(79) n20 t21 f19 b19.** Slightly lacking for an 8-y-o: probably duller than its non-age-statement brother because of an extra dollop of caramel. *40%. Foster's Group, Australia.*

The Black Douglas Aged 12 Years "The Black Reserve" bott code 347/06/188 **(87) n21 t21 f23 b22.** The toffee does its best to wreck the show – but there sre simply too many good things going on to succeed. The slight smoke to the nose delights and the honeycomb middle really does star. *40%. Foster's Group, Australia.*

Black Grouse (94) n23 outwardly a hefty nose, but patience is rewarded with a glorious Demerara edge to the malt and oak: superb, understated stature; **t24** again the smoke appears to be at the fore, but it's not. Rather, a silky sweet delivery also covers excellent cocoa and spice **f23** so gentle, with waves of smoke and oak lapping on an oaky shore. Brilliant... **b24** a superb return to a peaty blend for Edrington for the first time since they sold Black Bottle. Not entirely different from that brand, either, from the Highland Distillers days with the smokiness being superbly couched by sweet malts. A real treasure. *40%*

Black Knight (85.5) n21 t22 f21 b21.5. More of a White Knight as it peacefully goes about its business. Not many taste buds slain, but just love the juicy charge. *43%. Quality Spirits Int.*

Black Ram Aged 12 Years (85) n21 t23 f21 b20. An upfront blend that gives its all in the chewy delivery. Some major oak in there but it's all ultra soft toffee and molasses towards the finish. 40%. *Vinprom Peshtera, Bulgaria.*

Blend No. 888 (86.5) n20 t21.5 f23 b22. Not to be confused with the Nantucket single malt by the same name (or number) – and by nose and taste cannot possibly be. Still, a good old-fashioned, rip-roaring, nippy blend with a fudge-honey style many of a certain age will fondly remember from the 60s and 70s. Love it! 40%. *The House of MacDuff.*

Broadford (78.5) n19 t19.5 f20 b20. So boringly inoffensive, you could punch it. Toffee anyone? 40%. *Burn Stewart.*

Buchanan's De Luxe 12 Years Old (82) n18 t21 f22 b21. Just don't recognize this as the usual ultra-classy blend you could put money on you'd normally get from this brand. The nose shows more than just a single fault and then the character simply refuses to get out of second gear. Certainly pleasant, and some of the chocolate notes towards the end are gorgeous. But just not the normal brilliant show-stopper. 40%. *Diageo.*

Buchanan's Red Seal (90) n22 clean with almost equal portions of grain, malt and oak; t23 wonderful malt clarity guarantees a rare charm; the grains are crisp and amplify the barley sweetness; f22 lovely sweet vanilla complements the persistent barley; b23 exceptional, no-frills blend whose apparent simplicity paradoxically celebrates its complexity. 40%. *Diageo.*

Budgen's Scotch Whisky Finely Blended (85) n21 t22 f21 b21. A sweet, chunky blend offering no shortage of dates, walnuts, spice and toffee. A decent one to mull over. 40%

Callander 12 Years Old (86) n21 t22 f21.5 b21.5. Cheery stuff. No shortage of malt sparkle and even a touch of tangy salt. Very attractive and enjoyable without ripping up trees. 46.3%. *Burn Stewart.*

Campbeltown Loch Aged 15 Years (88) n22.5 deft marzipan and smoke; t22.5 firm, with ever-increasing oak but never at the cost of the honeyed malt; at times sharp and puckering; f21 much grainier and firm; dries very slowly; b22 well weighted with the age in no hurry to arrive. 40%. *Springbank Distillers.*

Castle Rock (81) n20 t20.5 f20 b20.5. Clean and juicy entertainment. 40%

Catto's Aged 25 Years (87.5) n23 age pours from every molecule, but never in a negative way: teasing exotic fruit states that a significant part is played by the malts; there is toffee (I sincerely hope not from colouring for a 25-year-old whisky!!!) that dulls things a little – and turns it distinctly Canadian in style - but a kind of distant smoked bacon on the wind brings life back into things; t22.5 a soft, juicy arrival is punctuated by deliciously teasing spice; again there is a caramel kick which flattens things as they get interesting; f20.5 dull, toffee caramel... we have returned to the tundra of Canada; b21.5 at once a hugely enjoyable yet immensely frustrating dram. The higher fruit and spice notes are a delight, but it all appears to be played out in a padded cell of cream caramel. One assumes the natural oak caramels have gone into overdrive. Had they not, we would have had a supreme blend scoring well into the 90s. 40%

Catto's Deluxe 12 Years Old (79.5) n20 t21.5 f18 b20. Strange how a standard blend can completely out-manoeuvre its 12-year-old brother. Refreshing and spicy in part, but still a note in there which doesn't quite work. 40%. *Inverhouse Distillers.*

Catto's Rare Old Scottish (92) n23.5 the young Speysiders leap from the glass with joyous abandon while the grain looks on benevolently; t23.5 various shades of citrus and juicy grass make for a mouthwatering experience; a soft honey strand adds the slightest touch of weight and the most delicate of spices chime in; f22 medium length, with gentle vanillas balancing the sweeter notes; remains refreshing to the death; b23 currently one of my regular blends to drink at home. Astonishingly old-fashioned with a perfect accent on clean Speyside and crisp grain. In the last year or so it has taken on a sublime sparkle on the nose and palate. Of its style, an absolutely masterful whisky which both refreshes and relaxes. 40%. *James Catto & Co.*

Chequers Deluxe (78.5) n19.5 t20 f19 b20. Charm, elegance, sophistication...not a single sign of any of them. Still if you want a bit of rough and tumble, just the job. And make sure they serve it in a dirty glass... 40%. *Diageo.*

Chivas Regal Aged 12 Years (83.5) n20.5 t22.5 f20 b20.5. Chewy fruit toffee. Silky grain mouth-feel with a toasty, oaky presence. 40%. *Chivas.*

Chivas Regal Aged 18 Years (73.5) n11.5 t17.5 t20 f17.5 b18.5. The nose is dulled by a whiff of sulphur and confirmation that all is not well comes with the disagreeably dry, bitter finish. Early on in the delivery some apples and spices show promise but it is an unequal battle against the caramel and off notes. I keep being told that this is Chivas' flagship brand. Well, it's been a very long time since I last tasted a good one – and I've tried a few over the years, believe me. Maybe I'm constantly unlucky. Or just maybe it's probable that it ranks among the most over-rated whiskies in the world. 40%

Chivas Regal 25 Years Old (95) n23 exotic fruit of the first order: some pretty serious age here, seemingly older than the 25 years; t23.5 mesmerisingly two-toned, with a beautiful delivery of velvety grains contrasting stunningly with the much firmer, cleaner malts. Softly chewable, with a gentle spice fizz as the vanilla begins to mount; unbelievably juicy and mouth-watering despite its advanced age; f24 long, wonderfully textured and deft; some cocoa underlines the oak involvement, but there is not once a single hint of over-aging; b24.5 unadulterated class where the grain-malt balance is exemplary and the deft intertwining of well-mannered oak and elegant barley leaves you demanding another glass. Brilliant! 40%

Clan Campbell (86.5) n21.5 t22.5 f21 b21.5. I'll wager that if I could taste this whisky before the colouring is added it would be scoring into the 90s. Not a single off note; a sublime early array of Speysidey freshness but dulls at the end. 40%. *Chivas.* ⊙ ⊙

⋯ **Clan Gold 3 Year Old** (95) n23.5 shimmering elegance; delicate enough to allow both grain and malt a clear voice with a light mintiness and seasoned celery well at home with those gently honeyed vanilla-oaked notes; t24 an eye closing, mouth-puckering delivery as those fabulous, sharp Speyside-style barley notes get to work. Beyond the obvious malt come several layers of spices of varying intensity and a much drier oak signature; f23.5 seemingly dry at first but some late crystalised demerara and wave of pristine barley ensure a sublime balance; deserves a standing ovation; b24 a blend-drinkers blend which will also slay the hearts of Speyside single malt lovers; a charming preprandial, back from the office dram unashamedly celebrating an almost lost, old-school style which places the emphasis on youthful, unspoiled elegance and stunning flavour development over weightier, more cumbersome styles. For me, this is love at first sip... 40%

⋯ **Clan Gold Blended 15 Years Old** (91) n21.5 an intricately delicate fruit style. Soft green banana sweetness borders on sharpness; a wisp of citrus offers a juicy element; effortless complexity with a surprising degree of crispness; t23 mouth-watering, clean arrival with an early blast of juicy Speyside-style grassy, almost crystalline malt upping the salivation levels on either side of the tongue: a deeply satisfying experience for blend lovers; f23.5 exceptional. Long with fine strands of controlled spice expertly woven into the malty tapestry. The grains are lush and chewy and add a lustre to the light oaks. A fabulous, almost classical, fade with not a single discordant note to be heard; b23 an unusual blend for the 21st century, which steadfastly refuses to blast you away with over the top flavour and/or aroma profiles and instead depends on subtlety and poise despite the obvious richness of flavour. The grains make an impact but only by creating the frame in which the more complex notes can be admired. 40%

⋯ **Clan Gold Blended 18 Years Old** (94.5) n23 a light background coating of dusty oak but the freshness of the barley startles and pleases. Its trademark is the crushed green apple of a whisky almost half its age though the softening custardy sweetness is an unmistakable sign of antiquity; t24 bristles on the palate: all kinds of peppery spices lead the malty surge. Gloriously mouthwatering: the lushness of the grains make the hairs stand on end as the mouth feel is the stuff of dreams. Apples lead the fruity fray but that intense barley is never far away; a delightful formation of muscovado sugars, then more apples...; f23.5 chewy, clean and truly rejoicing in the complex dovetailing of the malt and chalk. The oak remains refined throughout, the grains polishing the last of the fading malts. The smattering of light muscovado sugar continues until near the end. Then the slightly drier oaks reintroduce the now intense spices apparent on delivery; b24 almost the ultimate preprandial whisky with its at once robust yet delicate working over of the taste buds by the carefully muzzled juiciness of the malt. This is the real deal: a truly classy act which at first appears to wallow in a sea of simplicity but then bursts out into something very much more complex and alluring. About as clean and charming an 18-year-old blend as you are likely to find. 40%

Clan MacGregor (92) n22 superb grains allow the lemon-fruity malt to ping around: clean, crisp and refreshing; t24 as mouthwatering as the nose suggests with first clean grain then a succession of fruit and increasingly sweet malty notes. A brilliant mouthful, a tad oilier and spicier than of old; f23 yielding grain; and now, joy of joys, an extra dollop of spice to jolly it along; b23 just gets better and better. Now a true classic and getting up there with Grant's. 43%

Clan Murray Rare Old (84) n18 t23 f21 b22. The wonderful malt delivery on the palate is totally incongruous with the weak, nondescript nose. Glorious, mouth-watering complexity on the arrival, though. Maybe it needs a Murray to bring to perfection... 40%. *Benriach Distillery.*

Clansman (80.5) n20.5 t21 f19 b20. Sweet, grainy and soft. 40%. *Loch Lomond.*

⋯ **Clansman** (78.5) n20 t21.5 f18 b19. Plenty of weight, oil and honey-ginger. Some bitterness, too. 43%. *Loch Lomond Distillers.*

The Claymore (85) n19 t22 f22 b22. These days you are run through by spices. The blend is pure Paterson in style with guts etc, which is not something you always like to associate with a Claymore. Even so, a livelier dram than it was with some delightful muscovado sugar at the death. Get the nose sorted (and do away with some toffee) and a very decent and complex whisky is there to be had. 40%. *Whyte & Mackay Distillers Ltd.*

⟐ **Compass Box Asyla** 1st fill American oak ex-bourbon, bott May 10 **(93)** **n24** crisp, complex and crystalline: a fascinating trade off between the grassier malts and the vanilla-clad grains; **t24** the house style of frighteningly fresh and salivating complexity. Here offers good early weight and texture. Vanillas abound towards the middle; **f22.5** surprisingly rabid grain, but of such excellent quality one can only admire; **b23.5** if you can hear a purring noise, it is me tasting this... 40%. *nc ncf.*

Compass Box Asyla Marriage married for nine months in an American oak barrel **(88)** **n22** a soup of a nose, though slightly over oaked for perfect harmony; **t23** a big, sweet cherry tart kick off with custard and spices galooped on top; **f21** warming, spiced vanilla; **b22** a lovely blend, but can't help feeling that this was one marriage that lasted too long. 43.6%. *Compass Box Whisky for La Maison du Whisky in commemoration of their 50th Anniversary.*

⟐ **Compass Box Double Single 10th Anniversary** refill and 1st fill American oak hogshead, bott Sep 10 **(95.5)** **n24** clean, juicy and peppery, there is a vividness here which near brings a tear to the eye: almost a mixed salad in its green-ness...with no shortage of watercress; **t24** magnificent clarity and weight to delivery. Just as mouth-watering as the nose broadcasts and those peppers don't take long to arrive, either. A lightly sugared sheen is the perfect foil to the delicate spice; **f23.5** long, with a very slow upping of the vanilla-dryness. Elegant and in keeping with the style; **b24** shows starkly what a little imagination and care can bring you in the way of blended scotch: sheer bliss... 53.3%. *nc ncf. 876 bottles.*

Consulate (89) **n22** **t22** **f22.5** **b22.5**. One assumes this beautifully balanced dram was designed to accompany Passport in the drinks cabinet. I suggest if buying them, use Visa. 40%

Co-operative Finest Blend (92.5) **n23.5** the stuff of time machines: I have been whizzed back to the late 1970s and here's a throwback for even then. Gorse, honey and light, melting oak; the style of grain has changed since then, but that is all; **t23** the trademark velvety grain one immediately associates with this brand is there as a crutch. But rather than being engulfed in delicate peat as before, we are now seduced by the most gorgeous honey-butterscotch theme. Weight and texture to die for; **f22.5** relatively long and still making the most of the very high quality grain. The vanillas are charming; **b23.5** a fabulous and fascinating blend which has divested itself of its peaty backbone and instead packed the core with honey. Not the same heavyweight blend of old, but still one which is to be taken seriously – and straight – by anyone looking for a classic whisky of the old school. 40% ⊙ ⊙

Co-operative Premium Scotch 5 Years Old (91.5) **n22** perhaps a little on the mucky side, there is enough date and walnut to be getting on with; **t24** wins hands down for its presentation on the palate: silky, fruity, earthy. The smoke has thinned dramatically from its old incarnation. And the caramel has a very big say, too. But those Demerara sugars, the main fingerprint of this blend, are not only still detectable but have upped the oily outline considerably. Real knife and fork stuff; **f22.5** the caramel plays a big part but some vanilla and honey battle gamely through; the grains, though, have the longest and final say...; **b23** from the nose I thought this blend had nosedived emphatically from when I last tasted it. However the delivery remains the stuff of legend. And though it has shifted emphasis and style to marked degree, there is no disputing its overall clout and entertainment value remains very high. Also, great to see that a blend I have been extolling the virtues of for years is receiving recognition elsewhere. 40% ⊙ ⊙

Craigellachie Hotel Quaich Bar Range (81) **n20** **t21** **f20** **b20**. A delightful malt delivery early on, but doesn't push on with complexity as perhaps it might. 40%

Crawford's (83.5) **n19** **t21** **f22** **b21.5**. A lovely spice display helps overcome the caramel. 40%.

Cutty Black (83) **n20** **t23** **f19** **b21**. Both nose and finish are dwarfed and flung into the realms of ordinariness by the magnificently substantial delivery. Whilst there is a taint to the nose, its richness augers well for what is to follow; and you won't be disappointed. At times it behaves like a Highland Park with a toffeed spine, such is the richness and depth of the honey and dates and complexity of the grain-vanilla background. But those warning notes on the nose are there for good reason and the finish tells you why. Would not be surprised to see this score into the 90s on a different bottling day. 40%. *Edrington.*

Cutty Sark (78) **n19** **t21** **f19** **b19**. Crisp and juicy. But a nipping furriness, too. 40% ⊙ ⊙

Cutty Sark Aged 12 Years (92) **n22** grain heavy, but crisp and clean; **t24** mountainous honey which had been hiding on the nose cascades onto the taste buds. The firm grain gives the honey and accompanying maple syrup a backbone with spices slowly gather; **f23** long and lush, toffee begins to absorb the honey; **b23** at last! Cutty 12 at full sail...and blended whisky rarely looks any more beautiful! 40%. *Edrington.*

Cutty Sark Aged 15 Years (82) **n19** **t22** **f20** **b21**. Attempts to take the honey route. But seriously dulled by toffee and the odd sulphured cask. 40%. *Edrington.*

Cutty Sark Aged 18 Years (88) n22 much oakier output than before with only fragments of sherry; herbal; **t22** a safe delivery of yielding grain with out-reaching fingers of juicier malt; decent spice buzz as a bitter-sweet harmony is reached; **f22** cream toffee and custard creams; **b22** lost the subtle fruitiness which worked so well. Easy-going and attractive. *43%*

Cutty Sark Aged 25 Years (91) n21 a sensational, luxurious, almost erotic but certainly exotic mix of the most delicate peat and juicy sub-Saharan dates. Molten muscovado sugar and light mocha is pelted by spice and you can't escape the sherry trifle-Christmas pudding duet, either...; **t23.5** the usual silkiness is there in layers. But the fruit content has been upped considerably. More sultana and though the normal honey is subdued, the smoky spice more than makes amends; for all its weight, remains impressively juicy; **f22.5** the grains come out in force and do a good job of giving a custardy edge to the very light furriness; **b23** magnificent, though not quite flawless, this whisky is as elegant and effortlessly powerful as the ship after which the brand was named... *45.7%. Berry Bros & Rudd.* ⊙ ⊙

Demijohn's Finest Blended Scotch Whisky (88) n21 strange, out of shape, but soft; **t22** salivating delivery with a wonderful firmness to the grain; the malts eventually mould into the style; **f23** remains tangy to the end, even with a touch of marmalade thrown in; **b22** a fun, characterful blend that appears to have above the norm malt. Enjoy. *40%. Adelphi.*

Dew of Ben Nevis Blue Label (82) n19 t22 f20 b21. A busier, lighter blend than the old Millennium one it replaced. The odd off-key note is handsomely outnumbered by deliciously complex, mocha tones with a touch of demerara. Ditch the caramel and you'd have a sizzler! *40%. Ben Nevis Distillery. Replacement for Dew of Ben Nevis Millennium Blend.*

Dew of Ben Nevis Special Reserve (85) n19 t21 f23 b22. A much juicier blend than of old, still sporting some bruising and rough patches. But that kind of makes this all the more attractive, with the caramel mixing with some fuller malts to provide a date and nuts effect which makes for a grand finale. *40%. Ben Nevis Distillery.*

Dew of Ben Nevis Supreme Selection (77) n18 t20 f20 b19. Some lovely raspberry jam swiss roll moments here. But the grain could be friendlier, especially on the nose. *40%*

Dewar's Special Reserve 12 Years Old (84) n20 t23 f19 b22. Some s... you know what... has crept onboard here and duffed up the nose and finish. A shame because elements of the delivery and background balance shows some serious blending went on here. *40%*

Dewar's 18 Years Old (93) n23 confident and complex, the nose makes no secret that its foundations are solid grain. From it hang a succession of nubile malty notes, weighty and not without a minor degree of smoke. The fruit has a strawberry jam presence, and there are spices, of course... **t24** entirely classical in its delivery: firm grain and rich, sweet malt linked arm in arm. Again the grain is bold and firm but tattooed into it is a buzzing busy maltiness, offering varying degrees of weight, sweetness and depth...; **f22.5** a build up of caramel begins to lessen the degree of complexity, though not the body and weight; **b23.5** here is a classic case of where great blends are not all about the malt. The grain plays in many ways the most significant role here, as it is the perfect backdrop to see the complexity of the malt at its clearest. Simply magnificent blending with the use of flawless whisky. *43%. John Dewar & Sons.*

Dewar's 18 Year Old Founders Reserve (86.5) n22.5 t22 f20.5 b21.5. A big, blustering dram which doesn't stint on the fruit. A lovely, thin seam of golden syrup runs through the piece, but the dull, aching finale is somewhat out of character. *40%. John Dewar & Sons.*

Dewar's Signature (93) n24 a stunning celebration of controlled grape: this is sweet-edged and of a distinctly sauternes style. Elsewhere the oak offers a light vanilla haze and the barley is clean and relaxed. Just doesn't come much more sultry and elegant than this; **t23.5** as luxuriant a mouthfeel as you could pray for, but with some spicy sparks flying. The fruit continues to dominate while the grain must be distilled satin; **f22** some custard tart is about as aggressive as the oak gets, though there is an unwelcome buzz from a sherry cask or two; **b23.5** a slight departure in style, with the fruit becoming just a little sharper and juicier. Top range blending and if the odd butt could be weeded out, this'd be an award winner for sure. *43%*

Dewar's White Label (78.5) n19 t21.5 f19 b19. When on song, one of my preferred daily blends. But not when like this, with its accentuated bitter-sweet polarisation. *40%*

Dimple 12 Years Old (86.5) n22 t22 f21.5 b21. Lots of sultana while the spice adds aggression. *40%. Diageo.*

Dimple 15 Years Old (87.5) n20 t21 f24 b22.5. Only on the late middle and finish does this particular flower unfurl and to magnificently complex effect. The texture of the grains in particular delight while the strands of barley entwine. A type of treat for the more technically minded of the serious blend drinkers among you. *40%. Diageo.*

⫸ **Drummer** (81) n20 t21 f20 b20. Big toffee. Rolos...? *40%. Inver House Distillers.*

Drummer Aged 5 Years (83) n19 t22.5 f20.5 b21. The nose may beat a retreat but it certainly gets on a roll when those fabulous sharp notes hit the palate. However, it deserves some stick as the boring fudge finishes in a cymbal of too much toffee. 40%. Inver House.

Duncan Taylor Auld Blended Aged 35 Years dist pre 70 (93) n23 a knife and fork nose appears too oaked but time in the glass allows some excellent marmalade and marzipan to appear; t24 glorious delivery: amazing silk, lots of gentle, natural caramel but topped with honeycomb; f22 chocolate malt and burnt toast; b24 only a handful of companies could come up with something like this. An infinitely better dram than previous bottlings, due mainly to the fact that the dangers of old oak appear to have been compensated for. 46%. 131 bottles.

Duncan Taylor Collection Black Bull 12 Year Old (88.5) n22.5 like many a Black Bull, this is muscular and with no shortage of attitude; it is also a touch oily but the malt is well represented; t22.5 beautifully chewy with all kinds of natural toffees mixing well with the creaminess and hazelnut; even a light spice to add to the balance; f21.5 toffee and vanilla; b22 Black Bulls enjoy a reputation for being dangerous. So does this: once you pour yourself a glass, it is difficult not to have another...and another... 50%. Duncan Taylor & Co Ltd.

Duncan Taylor Collection Black Bull Deluxe Blend Aged 30 Years (93) n24 fantastically rich: a real mish-mash of fruit, barley, smoke and, of course, oak...really has hit the bullseye; t24 one of the creamiest-textured deliveries I've come across this year. Again the smoke leads, but there is so much else slushing around in these soft oils; the bourbony liquorice in the middle ground is sublime; f22 long with a real tapering spiciness amid the molasses and vanilla b23 this pedigree Black Bull doesn't pull its horns in... 50%. Duncan Taylor.

Duncan Taylor Collection Rarest of the Rare Deluxe Blend 33 Years Old (94) n24 a heady fusion of rich bourbon and old Canadian characteristics beefed up further with diced exotic fruit and a dash of ancient Demerara rum Uitvlught to be precise; t24 the bourbon hits the track running, closely followed by some silky barley couched in velvet grain; invariably some spices pitch in to ramp up the complexity even further; f22 no great length, but no off notes, either. Instead the oak adds an unsweetened custardy grace; b23 outstanding and astounding blended whisky. An absolute must for blend lovers...especially those with a bourbony bent. 43.4%

Duncan Taylor Collection Black Bull 40 Year Old batch 1 (86.5) n23 t21 f21.5 b21. Almost certainly whisky which had dipped below 40%abv in the cask has been included in this blend. That would account for the occasional spasm of ultra intense natural caramels, a kind of tell-tale fingerprint indicating this is likely to have been done. The nose is exotic fruit; the delivery is a battle to keep the oak at bay. One which is happily won. 40.2%

⁙ **Duncan Taylor Collection Black Bull 40 Years Old** batch 2 (94) n23 a barrel-load of exotic fruitiness that is not unexpected from a whisky of this antiquity; light but with banana and custard the main theme; t24 ridiculously fresh delivery for its massive age with a brilliant eye-watering quality to the barley. Slightly coppery, too; f23 virtually no ill effect from the cask, as one might expect from something this delicate. Instead, we are treated to a touch of freshly squeezed orange alongside the lightly creamed mocha; b24 just sit back and marvel at something so old...yet so young at heart. 41.9%. Duncan Taylor & Co. 957 bottles.

⁙ **Duncan Taylor Collection Black Bull Special Reserve** batch 1 (86) n21 t22.5 f21 b21.5. Juicy in just the right areas. Some charming spice and vanilla, too. 46.6%

The Famous Grouse (89) n22 a weightier aroma than Grouse once was. Not quite so clean and crisp; now a slight smoke can be detected, while honey threads, once audible, have to fight to be heard; once you get used to it, it is quite lovely...; t23 a real surprise package for a Grouse, as this is no lightweight on delivery: the flavours come thick and fast – literally – though the intensity makes it hard to pick out individual notes; once acclimatised, there are distinct marmalade and custard qualities, but only after a brooding shadow of smoke moves out of the picture taking some honey with it; f21.5 lots of mocha and cream toffee with the vanilla adding a dusty quality; b22.5 it almost seems that Grouse is, by degrees, moving from its traditional position of a light blend to something much closer to Grant's as a middle-weighted dram. Again the colouring has been raised a fraction and now the body and depth have been adjusted to follow suit. Have to say that this is one very complex whisky these days: I had spotted slight changes when drinking it socially, but this was the first time I had a chance to sit down and professionally analyse what was happening in the glass. A fascinating and tasty bird, indeed. 40%. Edrington Group.

The Famous Grouse Gold Reserve (90) n23.5 ye gods! What an improvement on the last bottle of this I came across!! Really sexy complexity which, though showing decent weight, including delicate smoke, also celebrates the more citrussy things in life. At body temp the complexity of the structure and degree of layering goes through the roof...; t23 honeyed to start, then an injection of lime and ground cherry; some caramel tries to interfere and to some extent succeeds; **f21.5** the toffee effect immediately curtails further complexity, but there is a slight spice rumble very late on and even a light sprinkling of barley grist; **b22** great to know the value of the Gold Reserve is going up...as should the strength of this blend. The old-fashioned 40% just ain't enough carats. *40%. Edrington Group.*

The Formidable Jock of Bennachie (82) **n19 t22 f21 b20.** "Scotland's best kept secret" claims the label. Hardly. But the silky delivery on the palate is worth investigating. Impressive roastiness to the malt and oak, but the caramel needs thinning. *40%. Bennachie Scotch Whisky.*

⊰⊱ **Fort Glen The Blender's Reserve Aged 12 Years** (88.5) **n21.5** any British school kid dating back to WW2 will recognise the "Fruit Salad" sweet signature on this. Soft, delicate and evocative; **t23** and no less fruit on delivery as the salivating citrus makes way for a spicier, oilier middle **f21.5** thins out as the grain and vanilla set up camp; **b22.5** an entirely enjoyable blend which is clean and boasting decent complexity and weight. *40%*

⊰⊱ **Fort Glen The Distiller's Reserve** (78) **n18 t22 f19 b19.** Juicy, salivating delivery as it storms the ramparts. Draws down the portcullis elsewhere. *40%. The Fort Glen Whisky Company.*

Fraser MacDonald (85) **n21 t21.5 f21 b21.5.** Some fudge towards the middle and end but the journey there is an enjoyable one. *40%. Loch Lomond Distillers.*

Gairloch (79) **n19 t20 f20 b20.** For those who like their butterscotch at 40% abv. *40%*

Glen Brynth (70.5) **n18 t19 f16 b17.5.** Bitter and awkward. *43%*

⊰⊱ **Glen Gray** (84.5) **n20 t22.5 f21 b21.** A knife and fork blend you can stand your spoon in. Plain going for most of the way, but the area between delivery and middle enjoys several waves of rich chocolate honeycomb...and some of the cocoa resurfaces at the finale. *43%*

Glen Lyon (85) **n19 t22.5 f22 b21.5.** Works a lot better than the nose suggests: seriously chewy with a rabid spice attack and lots of juices. For those who have just retired as dynamite testers. Unpretentious fun. *43%. Diageo.*

⊰⊱ **Grand Sail** (87) **n21** nutty and teasingly nibbles; **t22** multi-layered and full of attitude. Spices abound, providing sharp teeth to the cuddly grain; **f22** long, with vanilla and toffee in the starring roles; **b22** a sweet, attractive blend with enough bite to really matter. *40%*

⊰⊱ **Grand Sail Aged 10 Years** (79) **n20 t(22.) f18 b19.** Pleasant and at times fascinating but with a tang that perhaps the next vatting will benefit from losing. *40%. China market.*

⊰⊱ **Grand Sail Rare Reserve Aged 18 Years** (94) **n23** slightly waxy and bourbony; **t24** fabulous grain delivery which offers 100% silk and no little early cocoa; as it moulds into the palate, the mix of corn and spice forms a beautifully textured layering to the roof of the mouth; brown sugars slowly form; **f23** long, as the earlier oils suggest, and the chocolate lightly sweetened by brown sugars go into overdrive; a desired degree of late bite, too...; **b24** indulgent and uses the grains to maximum effect though an upping of the strength would have brought even further all round rewards. Even so, a truly beautiful whisky which cuts effortlessly and elegantly through the taste buds... *40% Angus Dundee. China market.*

Glenross Blended (83) **n20 t22 f20 b21.** Decent, easy-drinking whisky with a much sharper delivery than the nose suggests. *40%. Speyside Distillers.*

Glen Simon (77) **n20 t19 f19 b19.** Simple. Lots of caramel. *40%. Quality Spirits International.*

The Gordon Highlanders (86) **n21 t22 f21 b22.** Lush and juicy, there is a distinctive Speysidey feel to this one with the grains doing their best to accentuate the developing spice. Plenty of feel good factor here. *40%. William Grant & Sons.*

Grand Macnish (79) **n19 t21 f19 b20.** Welcome back to an old friend...but the years have caught up with it. Still on the feral side, but has exchanged its robust good looks for an unwashed and unkempt appearance on the palate. Will do a great job to bring some life back to you, though. *43%. MacDuff International Ltd.*

Grand Macnish 12 Years Old (86) **n21 t22 f21.5 b21.5.** A grander Grand Macnich than of old with the wonderful feather pillow delivery maintained and a greater harmonisation of the malt, especially those which contain a honey-copper sheen. *40%. MacDuff.*

⊰⊱ **Grant's Aged 12 Years** bott 30/09/10 (89.5) **n23** vanilla laden and soft. Threads of acacia honey and jam sponge cake, and various other baker's aromas, offer a subdued, delicate and come hither sweetness...; **t23** the delivery, like the nose, is of feather pillow softness with a mildly bracing, slightly salty barley blast and even the most delicate hint of peat; **f21.5** caramels out rather too grandly though the spices stay the course; **b22** can't argue too much with the tasting notes on the label (although I contend that "full, rich and rounded" has more to do with its body than taste, but that is by the by). Beautiful whisky, as can be reasonably expected from a Grant's blend. If only the sharpness could be kept going through to the finish...wow! *40%. William Grant & Sons.*

⊰⊱ **Grant's Cask Edition No.1 Ale Cask Finish** Edinburgh ale casks (88.5) **n22 t23 f21.5 b22.** always loved this concept: a whisky and chaser in one bottle. This was has plenty of cheer in the complex opening, but gets maudlin towards the end. *40%. William Grant & Sons.*

Great MacCauley (81) n20 t20.5 f20 b20.5. Reminds me of another whisky I tasted earlier: Castle Rock, I think. Identical profile with toffee and spice adding to the juicy and youthful fun. 40%. *Quality Spirits International.*

Green Plaid 12 Years Old (89) n22 the smoke of old has been doused slightly, though mint comes through with the soft barley; t23 light oils coat the mouth with a gentle sweetness; f22 vanilla and a distant rumble of smoke; b22 a beautifully constructed, mouth-watering blend. 40%. *Inverhouse Distillers.*

Haddington House (85.5) n21 t21.5 f22 b21. Mouth-watering and delicate. 40%

Haig Gold Label (88) n21 somewhat sparse beyond a vague grapey-graininess; t23 begins light and unimpressive, but about three flavour waves in begins to offer multi-layered spices and juice aplenty; the sweet-dry ratio as the oak arrives is brilliant; f22 classy fade with a touch of Cadbury's Fruit and Nut in the mix as the spices persist; b22 what had before been pretty standard stuff has upped the complexity by an impressive distance. 40%. *Diageo.*

Hankey Bannister (84.5) n20.5 t22 f21 b21. Lots of early life and even a malt kick early on. Toffee later. 40%. *Inverhouse Distillers.*

Hankey Bannister 12 Years Old (86.5) n22 t21.5 f21 b22. A much improved blend with a nose and early delivery which makes full play of the blending company's Speyside malts. Plenty of toffee on the finish. 40%. *Inverhouse Distillers.*

Hankey Bannister 21 Years Old (93.5) n22.5 a fruity ensemble, clean, vibrant and loath to show its age; t23.5 every bit as juicy as the nose suggests, except here there is the odd rumble of distant smoke; mainly a firm, barley-sugar hardness as the grains keep control; f23.5 the arrival of the oak adds further weight and for the first time begins to behave like a 21-y-o; long, now with decent spice and with some crusty dryness at the very death; b24 a beautifully balanced blend that takes you on a series of journeys into varying styles and stories. Does the blend movement a great service. 43%. *Inverhouse Distillers.*

Hankey Bannister 25 Years Old (91) n22.5 a slight bourbony honey-hickory edge, to where the 21-y-o has fruit; t24 a swooning delivery: just about everything in exactly the right place and showing sympathetic weight to the other. The grains are soft, the malts are sturdier and more energetic, the oak docile...for the time being; f21.5 some bitter cocoa notes reveal the oak to be a little more militant but the light oils help the grains recover the position and balance; b23 follows on in style and quality to 21-year-old. Gorgeous. 40%

Hankey Bannister 40 Years Old (89) n22 t23 f22 b22. "This is some of the last whisky produced before England won the World Cup in 1966," Gareth Stanley of Inverhouse gleefully tells me. Yes, Gareth. Thanks for reminding me. But at least I can look Alex Salmond and his brothers straight in the eye and tell him: "Well, at least we once won the bloody thing..." This blend, though, has been put together to mark the 250th anniversary of the forging of the business relations between Messrs. Hankey and Bannister. And although the oak creaks like a ship of its day, there is enough verve and viscosity to ensure a rather delicious toast to the gentlemen. Love it! 44%. *Inverhouse.*

Hedges & Butler Royal (92) n22.5 curiously salty and coastal, yet peat-free; the grains couldn't get much crisper; t23.5 sharp, crisp grain working in complete harmony with the sprightly Speyside-style malts; all kinds of citrus, grassy notes; f23 a lemon zesty liveliness refreshes and cleanses; some chattering, drier cocoa very late on; b23 massively improved to become a juicy and charming blend of the very highest order. 40%

High Commissioner (88.5) n22.5 beautiful weight with a touch of the old-fashioned English sweetshop about the subtle sugar input; something lightly rummy about this; t22.5 star quality delivery and mouth-feel. Chewy with just the right degree of give. Again those sugars have a delightful say in proceedings; f20.5 shame about the bitter fade; b22.5 had to laugh. Picked up the wrong glass and nosed and tasted thinking it was Dewar's White Label. My notes read: "Bloody hell!!!! White Label has suddenly become High Commissioner on steroids"...! Then I noticed the White Label bottle was still full and unopened. And yes, I had picked up what turned out to be the High Commissioner sample without realising it was one of the set of blends to be tasted. Now I admit I had a hand in cleaning this brand up a couple of years back, giving it a good polish and much needed balance complexity. But I don't remember leaving it in quite this good a shape. Just a bitter semi-off note on the finish, otherwise this guy would have been in the 90s. What a great fun, three-course dram this is... 40%. *Loch Lomond Distillers.*

Highland Baron (85.5) n21 t22 f21 b21.5. A very clean, sweet and competent young blend showing admirable weight and depth. 40%. *Loch Lomond Distillers.*

Highland Bird (77) n19 t19 f19 b20. I've has a few of these over the years, I admit. But I can't remember one quite as rough and ready as this... 40%. *Quality Spirits International.*

Highland Black 8 Years Old Special Reserve (85.5) n22 t22.5 f20 b21. A lovely blend which has significantly improved since my last encounter with it. A touch too much grain on the finish for greatness, perhaps. But the nose and delivery both prosper from a honey-roast almond sweetness. 40%. Aldi. ⊙ ⊙

Highland Dream 12 Years Old bott Jan 05 **(94.5)** n23.5 t24 f23 b24. Now that is what I call a blend! How comes it has taken me two years to find it? A wet dream, if ever there was one... 43%. J & G Grant. 9000 bottles.

Highland Dream 18 Years Old bott May 07 **(88.5)** n22.5 t22.5 f21.5 b22. Perhaps doesn't get the marks on balance that a whisky of this quality might expect. This is due to the slight over egging of the sherry which, while offering a beautiful delivery, masks the complexities one might expect. Lovely whisky, and make no mistake: the type of which you'll find the bottle emptying very quickly during the course of a night before anyone quite realises. But, technically, doesn't match the 12-year-old for balance and brilliance. 43%. J & G Grant. 3000 bottles.

Highland Earl (77) n19 t20 f19 b19. Might have marked it higher had it called itself a grain: the malt is silent. 40%. Aldi. ⊙ ⊙

Highland Gathering Blended Scotch Whisky (78) n19 t20 f19 b20. Attractive, juicy stuff, though caramel wins in the end. 40%. Lombards Brands.

⋯ **Highland Glendon (87.5)** n21.5 fruity and well rounded; t22.5 adorable delivery: soft, chewy and making the most of some lush grains; f21.5 toasty but a surprising degree of honey comb at the death; b22 an honest, simple but effectively attractive blend. 43%. Quality Spirits International.

Highland Harvest Organic Scotch Whisky (76) n18 t21 f19 b18. A very interesting blend. Great try, but a little bit of a lost opportunity here as I don't think the balance is quite right. But at least I now know what organic caramel tastes like... 40%

⋯ **Highland Mist (88.5)** n20.5 a tad nutty and bruising; t23 total transformation on the palate to the nose: bristling with noticeable malt, including a deft smoke, but biting and nipping with glee...; salivating despite the toffee – some achievement! f22.5 nutty and chewy...but, unlike the nose, very clean and in control; b22.5 fabulously fun whisky bursting from the bottle with character and mischief. Had to admit, broke all my own rules and just had to have a glass of this after doing the notes... 40%. Loch Lomond Distillers.

Highland Piper (79) n20 t20 f19 b20. Good quaffing blend – if sweet - of sticky toffee and dates. Some gin on the nose – and finish. 40%

Highland Pride (86) n21 t22 f21.5 b21.5. A beefy, weighty thick dram with plenty to chew on. The developing sweetness is a joy. 40%. Whyte & Mackay Distillers Ltd.

Highland Reserve (82) n20 t21 f20 b21. You'll probably find this just off the Highland Way and incorporating Highland Bird and Monarch of the Glen. Floral and muddy. 40%

⋯ **Highland Reserve Aged 12 Years (87)** n21 sweet shop soft fruits and confident toffee plus an attractively sharp nip; t22 much to chew over. The sugars are well interspersed with lively spice; f22 beautifully chewy milk toffee pepped up by those light spices; b22 Anyone who has tasted Monarch of the Glen 12 will appreciate this. Maybe a bit more fizz here, though, despite the big caramel. 43%. Quality Spirits International.

Highland Warrior (77.8) n19 t19 f19.5 b20. Just like his Scottish Chief, he's on the attack armed with some Dufftown, methinks... 40%. Quality Spirits International.

Highland Way (84) n19 t20.5 f22.5 b22. This lovely little number takes the High Road with some beautiful light scenery along the way. The finish takes a charming Speyside path. 40%

Inverarity Limited Edition cask no. 698, dist 1997, bott 2009 **(84.5)** n20.5 t22 f21 b21. A heady, heavy-duty blend where honeycomb rules on the palate and thick dates offer a more intense sweetness. But don't go looking for subtlety or guile: those whose palates have been educated at the Whyte and Mackay school of delicate sophistication will have a ball. 40%

Islay Mist 8 Years Old (84) n20 t22 f21 b21. Turned into one heavy duty dram since last tasting a couple of years back. This appears to absorb everything it touches leaving one chewy, smoky hombre. Just a little tangy at the end. 40%. MacDuff International Ltd.

Islay Mist 12 Years Old (90) n22 Bowmore-style cough sweet dominates over the most gentle of grains; t23 decent smoke drive, intense at first then feathering out; remains sweet to the house style f22 long, back to cough sweet and a long fade of gristy, muscovado sugar; b23 adore it: classic bad cop - good cop stuff with an apparent high malt content. 40%

Islay Mist 17 Years Old (92.5) n22.5 reclusive peat can just be spotted amid the rich vanillas; t23.5 silky, mouth-watering delivery: a dream of a start for any blend with the light muscovado, semi-bourbony sugars keeping their shape; depth supplied by the shy peat and no less retiring oak; f23 long finish with a late spice prickle and sugared almonds. The smoke continues to play a teasing role; b23.5 always a cracking blend, this has improved of late into a genuine must have. 40%. MacDuff International Ltd.

Islay Mist Delux (85) n21.5 t22 f21.5 b20. Remains a highly unusual blend with the youthful peat now more brilliant than before, though the sugar levels appear to have risen markedly. 40%

Isle of Skye 8 Years Old (94) n23 Isle of Skye? Or Orkney? Honey and smoke play tag; the grain is firm and clean; t24 just so beautiful. Honeycomb and light fudge form a rich partnership, the smoke is little more than ballast and a shy spice; the grains play a fabulous role in allowing the maltier notes to ping around and increase the salivating qualities; f23.5 the spice is now pretty warming but the honeycomb and vanilla dominate the finale; b23.5 where once peat ruled and with its grain ally formed a smoky iron fist, now honey and subtlety reigns. A change of character and pace which may disappoint gung-ho peat freaks but will intrigue and delight those looking for a more sophisticated dram. 40%. Ian Macleod.

Isle of Skye 21 years Old (91) n21 sluggish: trying to work out its own stance; t23.5 sweet chocolate raisin, sumptuously brushed with a layer of soft smoke and demerara; f23 wonderfully deft spices nibble at the tastebuds like tiny fish at your feet in a rock pool; grains at last – soft and silky all the way; b23.5 what an absolute charmer! The malt content appears pretty high, but the overall balance is wonderful. A belter of a blend. 40%. Ian Macleod.

Isle of Skye 50 Years Old (82.5) n21.5 t21 f20 b20. Drier incarnation than the 50% version. But still the age has yet to be balanced out, towards the end in particular. Early on some distinguished moments involving something vaguely smoked and a sweetened spice. 41.6%

James Alexander (85.5) n21 t21.5 f21.5 b21.5. Some lovely spices link the grassier Speysiders to the earthier elements. 40%. Quality Spirits International.

James King (76.5) n20 t18 f20 b18.5. Young whiskies of a certain rank take their time to find their feet. The finish, though, does generate some pleasant complexity. 43%

James King Aged 5 Years (85) n21 t21.5 f21 b21.5. Very attractive, old fashioned and well weighted with a pleasing degree of fat and chewy sweetness and chocolate fudge. Refreshingly good quality distillate and oak have been used in this: I'd drink it any day. 40%

James King 8 Years Old (78.5) n18.5 t21.5 f19 b19.5. Charming spices grip at the delivery and fine malt-grain interplay through the middle, even showing a touch of vanilla. But such a delicate blend can't fully survive the caramel. 40%. Quality Spirits International.

James King 12 Years Old (81) n19 t23 f19 b20. Caramel dulls the nose and finish. But for some time a quite beautiful blend soars about the taste buds offering exemplary complexity and weight. 40%. Quality Spirits International.

James King 15 Years Old (89) n22 t23 f21.5 b22.5. Now offers extra spice and zip. 43%

James King 21 Years Old (87.5) n20.5 t23.5 f22 b22. Attractive blend, but one that could do with the strength upped to 46% and the caramel reduced if not entirely got rid of. One of those potentially excellent yet underperforming guys I'd love to be let loose on! 43%

James Martin 20 Years Old (93) n21 t23.5 f24.5 b24. I had always regarded this as something of an untamed beast. No longer: still something of a beast, but a beautiful one that is among the most complex found on today's market. 43%. Glenmorangie.

James Martin 30 Years Old (86) n21.5 t22 f21 b21.5. Enjoyable for all its exotic fruitiness. But with just too many creaking joints to take it to the same level as the sublime 20-y-o. Even so, a blend worth treating with a touch of respect and allowing time for it to tell some pretty ancient tales... 43%. Glenmorangie.

J&B Jet (79.5) n19 t20 f20.5 b20. Never quite gets off the ground due to carrying too heavy a load. Unrecognisable to its pomp in the old J&B days: this one is far too weighty and never properly finds either balance or thrust. 40%. Diageo.

J&B Reserve Aged 15 Years (78) n23 t19 f18 b18. What a crying shame. The sophisticated and demure nose is just so wonderfully seductive but what follows is an open-eyed, passionless embrace. Coarsely grain-dominant and unbalanced, this is frustrating beyond words and not worthy to be mentioned in the same breath as the old, original J&B 15 which, by vivid contrast, was a malty, salivating fruit-fest and minor classic. 40%. Diageo.

J&B Rare (88.5) n21.5 the most youthful J&B nose ever: young malts and grain integrate well, but those grains really do appear still to have milk teeth; t22.5 one thing about young whisky: it's packed with flavour. And here you go on salivatory overdrive as the sheer unopposed freshness sets the tastebuds goosebumps; f22 clean, grain layered with soft vanilla; b22.5 I have been drinking a lot of J&B from a previous time of late, due to the death of their former blender Jim Milne. I think he would have been pretty taken aback by the youthful zip offered here: whether it is down to a decrease in age or the use of slightly more tired casks – or both – is hard to say. 40%. Diageo.

Jim McEwan's Blended Whisky (86.5) n20 t22 f22.5 b22. Juicy and eye-watering with clever late spices. 46%. Bruichladdich.

John Barr (85.5) n20 t22 f21.5 b22. I assume from the big juicy dates to be found that Fettercairn is at work. Outwardly a big bruiser; given time to state its case and it's a bit of a gentle giant. 40%. Whyte & Mackay Distillers Ltd.

Johnnie Walker Black Label 12 Years Old (95.5) n23.5 pretty sharp grain: hard and buffeting the nose; a buffer of yielding smoke, apple pie and delicate spice cushions the encounter; t24.5 if there is a silkier delivery on the market today, I have not seen it: this is sublime stuff with the grains singing the sweetest hymns as they go down, taking with them a near perfection of weighty smoke lightened by brilliantly balanced barley which leans towards both soft apple and crème broulee; f23.5 those reassuringly rigid grains re-emerge and with them the most juicy Speysidey malts imaginable; the lovely sheen to the finish underlines the good age of the whiskies used; b24 here it is: one of the world's most masterful whiskies back in all its complex glory. A bottle like this is like being visited by an old lover. It just warms the heart and excites. 40%. Diageo.

Johnnie Walker Blue Label (88) n21 the old, cleverly peated nose has been lost to us and now the accent falls on fruit though this is hardly as cleanly endearing as it might be; t24 but the magnificence of the mouth arrival is back with a bang with the most sumptuous marriage of over-ripened figs, volumous malt and lightly sprinkled peat all bound together and then expanded by a brilliant use of firm and soft old grains. Spices also sparkle and tease. Magnificent...; f21 oh, so disappointing again, with the plot played on the arrival and there being insufficient reserve to see off the broodier elements of the slightly bitter oak; b22 what a frustrating blend! Just so close to brilliance but the nose and finish are slightly out of kilter. Worth the experience of the mouth arrival alone. 43%. Diageo.

Johnnie Walker King George V db (88) n23 delicate smoke and honey with green tea. Unusual, but it works; t22 good weight and spice buzz on delivery; melting grains help lighten the oak; f21 gets lost in toffee. Pity... b22 One assumes that King George V is no relation to King George IV. This has genuine style and breeding, if a tad too much caramel. 43%

Johnnie Walker Red Label (87.5) n22 such a crisp delivery of grain; toffee apple, too...with young apples...; t22 juicy and hard delivery, much in keeping with the nose; toffee arrives early, then a welter of malty blows; f21.5 crisp grain again and the vaguest hint of smoke joins the vanilla; b22 the ongoing move through the scales quality-wise appears to suggest we have a work still in progress here. This sample has skimped on the smoke, though not quality. Yet a few months back when I was in the BA Business Lounge at Heathrow's new Terminal Five, I nearly keeled from almost being overcome by peat in the earthiest JW Red I had tasted in over three decades. I found another bottle and I'm still not too sure which represents the real Striding Man. 40%. Diageo.

Kenmore Special Reserve Aged 5 Years bott code L07285 (75) n18 t20 f19 b18. Recovers to a degree from the poor nose. A must-have for those who prefer their Scotch big-flavoured and gawky. 40%

King Robert II (77) n19 t19 f20 b19. A bustier, more bruising batch than the last 40 per cent version. Handles the OTT caramel much better. Agreeably weighty slugging whisky. 43%.

Kings Blended 3 Years Old (83) n21 t21.5 f20 b20.5. A young, chunky blend that you can chew forever. 40%. Speyside Distillers.

King's Crest Scotch Whisky 25 Years Old (83) n22 t22 f19 b20. A silky middle weight. The toffee-flat finish needs some attention because the softly estered nose and delivery is a honey-rich treat and deserves better. 40%. Speyside Distillers.

Label 5 Aged 18 Years (84.5) n20.5 t22 f21 b21. A big mouthful and mouth-feel. Has changed course since I last had this one. Almost a feel of rum to this with its estery sheen. Sweet, simple, easy dramming. 40%. La Martiniquaise, France.

Label 5 Classic Black (75) n18 t20 f18 b19. The off-key nose needs some serious re-working. Drop the caramel, though, and you would have a lot more character. Needs some buffing. 40%. The First Blending for La Martiniquaise, France.

Label 5 Reserve No. 55 Single Cask sherry cask finish, bott code no. E-1067 (75) n19 t20 f18 b18. The cordite on the nose suggests fireworks. But somehow we end up with a damp squib. 43%. La Martiniquaise, France.

Lang's Supreme Aged 5 Years (93.5) n23.5 outstanding barley-grain interplay, with the vanillas in fine form; all this underpinned by the most delicate of smoky, mildly seaweedy notes; t23.5 a gushing early barley delivery confirms the relatively high malt content: Glengoyne's grassy fingers can be felt caressing the tastebuds before the gentle grain vanillas begin to soften things further; f23 the smoke which made no effort to interfere with the barley-grain love in, reinvents itself as a soft, purring spice; the finale is as deft as it is beautifully weighted though the odd fractious sherry note can be heard and brings the score down a point; b23.5 every time I taste this the shape and structure has altered slightly. Here there is a fraction more smoke, installing a deeper confidence all round. This is blended whisky as it should be: Supreme in its ability to create shape and harmony. It is the kind of whisky I like to have easily to hand around the home, a blend for every mood. 40%. Ian Macleod Distillers Ltd.

The Last Drop (96.5) n24 t25 f23.5 b24. How do you mark a whisky like this? It is scotch. Yet every molecule of flavour and aroma is pure bourbon. I think I'll have to mark for quality, principally, which simply flies off the graph. I'll dock it a point for not being Scotch-like but I feel a pang of guilt for doing so. This, by the way, is a blend that was discovered by accident. It had been put away many years ago for marrying – and then forgotten about in a warehouse. The chances of finding another whisky quite of this ilk are remote, though I'm sure the hunters are now out. It is a one off and anyone who misses this one will kick themselves forever. Astonishing. Unforgetable. A freak whisky at its very peak. *52%. The Last Drop Distillers Ltd.*

⸫ **The Last Drop 50 Years Old** (96.5) n25 where once there was bourbon only, now we have a cross fertilisation of aromas. Certainly, once you allow it to breathe, the grape engulfs most else. It is as if the whisky has undergone a fruity polish and shine. On first pouring, the oak has the ability to cause splinters; allow to settle for a while and we are talking a much softer, less senile Drop; and slowly the spices unravel...; **t24.5** if you could capture the first second and a half of the delivery somehow mass produce it and sell that to the world: everyone would have the chance, just once in their lives, to taste perfection. But it is a fleeting moment as soon the oak is delivered some stern truths about the wearisomeness of time, though does so with cut glass panache and inimitable, effortless style. Perhaps what is so astounding about this, is the way that the balance does not, even for a second, waiver under the occasional oaky onslaught: as it bites, from somewhere a grapey honeycomb flies in to the rescue offering just-so compensatory sugars which perfectly match the most delicate spices imaginable...; **f22.5** now we edge towards a drier finale than before. The original was remarkable for not having a degree of bitterness, though it had every right to be there. Now, alas, there is and with it slips the crown of World whisky of the Year, which was within its grasp until then. The bitterness is slightly furry and dusty, but to make amends we are treated to one very old Melton Hunt cake, indeed; **b24.5** call me old-fashioned. Call me conservative. Perhaps I speak with the mind of one with little love for gambling. Yet, there again, has lived an unconventional life which some might say was one entire gamble and where the norm would be entirely unrecognisable to any other on this planet. But I tend to stick to the old adage: if it isn't broke, don't fix it. However, I do admire what has been done here. Because it was a gamble for the right reasons, which has paid handsomely in many ways, yet has just fallen short in others. Here, they took a magnificent whisky which for no other reason than pure serendipity, like Adam Adament, had awoken in another age but instead of, like our Victorian hero, being lost in a strange new world, found itself in one ready to appreciate and embrace its manifold beauty. This whisky was thrown back for a few extra summers in oak to take it to 50 years. A bold move. And it remains a quite astonishing, for life-remembering dram of labyrinthine complexity. But it has clearly changed: it is a different animal. As I write this, one of the men behind it, the industry legend Tom Jago, is unwell. I raise the glass of this unique whisky to honour you, my old friend: may you soon be as well and vibrant as your glorious creation. *52%. 198 bottles.*

Lauder's (74) n18 t21 f17 b18. Well, it's consistent: you can say that for it! As usual, fabulous delivery, but as for the rest...oh dear. *40%. MacDuff International Ltd.*

Lauder's Aged 12 Years (93.5) n23 seemingly matured in an orange grove; blossom is everywhere; the grains are clean and crisp, the barley is unmolested and precise; **t24** that is stunning: the most delicate orange delivery melting in with the grassy barley; the grains are bright and act as a sublime mirror to the proceedings; **f23** soft oaky vanillas with some marzipan and Jaffa cake ensuring the controlled sweetness persists to the end; **b23.5** this is every bit as magnificent as the standard Lauder's isn't. A new whisky, as now at 43%, and with the extra alcohol has come a fresh, superbly balanced and quite elegant whisky. *43%*

Loch Lomond Blended Scotch (89) n22 beautiful balance: delicate with a simmering weightiness. Mainly grain apparent, but the malt chips in sweetly; **t22.5** excellent double thrust of crispness and velvety yield. Again the grains lead the way with toffee not far behind but the malt offers soft, barley-sharp contours; **f22** vanilla and caramel but so clean; **b22.5** a fabulously improved blend: now clean and precise and though malt is seemingly at a premium, a fine interplay. *40%. Loch Lomond Distillers.*

Lochranza (83.5) n21 t21.5 f21 b20. Pleasant, clean, but, thanks to the caramel, goes easy on the complexity. *40%. Isle of Arran.*

⸫ **Lochside 1964 Rare Old Single Blend** (94.5) n24 a real gamut of sensual citrus: thick cut marmalade thinned by delicate lime. Hints of bourbony liquorice fits the style perfectly; **t23.5** mainly a corn lead: sweet, yielding yet salivating. Momentarily shows signs of wilting under the oak, but responds almost immediately by slamming the door shut and upping the light fruit and vanillas; **f23** remains improbably delicate with the corn and vanilla dovetailing with aplomb; **b24** a unique and entirely fitting tribute to a distillery which should never have been lost. 42.1%. nc ncf. Speciality Drinks Ltd.

Logan (78.5) **n19 t19 f20 b19.5**. Entirely drinkable but a bit heavy-handed with the grains and caramel. It appears Logan's run continues, despite the fact this was meant to have reached the end of the line. 40%. Diageo.

Lombard's Gold Label (88) **n22 t22 f22 b22**. Excellently weighted with some wonderful honeycomb and spice making their mark. 40%. Lombards Brands.

Lord Hynett (88.5) **n21.5** a bit messy, but there is hope... **t23** which is fully justified by the enormity of the delivery. A bare knuckle fighter of a blend with a sublimely haphazard, random deliciousness; honey and spices don't give shape but purpose; **f22** long, spiced toffee; **b22** just perfect after a shitty day. 40%. Loch Lomond Distillers.

Lord Scot (77.5) **n18.5 t20 f19.5 b19.5**. A touch cloying but the mocha fudge ensures a friendly enough ride. 40%. Loch Lomond Distillers.

⋯⋯ **Lord Scot** (86.5) **n20 t22 f22.5 b22**. Apparently, the Lord Scot I was sent last year was not Lord Scot at all but some imposter, don't you know. Well this particular squire is a bit more of a toff than the previous blighter. But his jacket is still a little threadbare. Even so, the gorgeous lushness to the honey and liquorice middle and the easy charm but deep complexity would make him a welcome guest in the finer homes and polite society of Lexington, Ky. I, for one, would have no qualms in introducing him. 43%. Loch Lomond Distillers.

Mackessack Premium Aged 8 Years (87.5) **n21.5 t23 f21.5 b21.5**. Claims a high Speyside content and the early character confirms it. Shoots itself in the foot, rather, by overdoing the caramel and flattening the finish. 40%. Mackessack Gioventu. Italian Market.

Mac Na Mara (83) **n20 t22.5 f20 b20.5**. Absolutely brimming with salty, fruity character. But just a little more toffee and furriness than it needs. Enjoyable, though. 40%⊙⊙

Mac Na Mara Rum Finish (93) **n22** as is often the case, the rum has hardened the aroma; **t24** beautifully crisp with fragile malts clashing with equally crisp barley; the touch of golden syrup works wonders; **f23** serious depth to the malt; the grains soften out with vanilla; **b24** this is high quality blending, and the usage of the rum appears to have retained the old Mac Na Mara style. Sublime. 40%. Praban na Linne.

MacQueens (89) **n21.5 t22.5 f22.5 b22.5**. I am long enough in the tooth now to remember blends like this found in quiet country hotels in the furthest-flung reaches of the Highlands beyond a generation ago. A wonderfully old-fashioned, traditional one might say, blend of a type that is getting harder and harder to find. I could drink this all day every day. Well, not really, but you know what I mean... 40%. Quality Spirits International.

Master of Malt 8 Years Old (88) **n22.5 t22.5 f21 b22**. Understated and refined. 40%

Matisse 12 Years Old (90.5) **n23** vanilla and citrus make comfortable bedfellows; dry Lubeck marzipan perfects the balance; **t23** mouth-watering with little grain evidence: the malt is clear, almost shrill; **f22** gentle vanillas and caramels; the spices arrive late; **b22.5** moved up yet another notch as this brand continues its development. Much more clean-malt oriented with a Speyside-style to the fore. Majestic and charming. 40%. Matisse Spirits Co Ltd.

Matisse 21 Years Old (86) **n23 t22 f20 b21**. Begins breathtakingly on the nose, with a full array of exotic fruit showing the older bourbon casks up to max effect. Nothing wrong with the early delivery, which offers a touch of honeycomb on the grain. But the caramel effect on the finish stops everything in its tracks. Soft and alluring, all the same. 40%

Matisse Old (85.5) **n20 t23 f21 b21.5**. Appears to improve each time I come across it. The nose is a bit on the grimy side and the finish disappears under a sea of caramel. But the delivery works deliciously, with a chewy weight which highlights the sweeter malts. 40%

Matisse Royal (81) **n19 t22 f20 b20**. Pleasant, if a little clumsy. Extra caramel appears to have suppressed the spice. 40%. Matisse Spirits Co Ltd.

McArthurs (89.5) **n22** soft smoke rumbles about like distant thunder on a Summer's day: the grains and light barley are bright; **t22.5** silky delivery with a slow injection of peat as the storm moves overhead; the degree of sweetness to the soft vanillas is sublime; **f22** gentle fade with the smoke rumbling though; **b23** one of the most improved blends on the market. The clever use of the peat is exceptional. 40%. Inverhouse Distillers.

Michael Jackson Special Memorial Blend bott 2009 (89) **n24 t22.5 f20.5 b22**. Whenever Michael and I had a dram together, his would either be massively sherried or equally well endowed with smoke. This is neither, so an odd tribute. Even so, there is more than enough here for him to savour, though I'm not sure what he would have made of the finish. 43%. Berry Bros & Rudd. 1000 bottles.

Mitchell's Glengyle Blend (86.5) **n21.5 t22 f21.5 b21.5**. A taste of history here, as this is the first blend ever to contain malt from the new Campbeltown distillery, Glengyle. Something of a departure in style from the usual Mitchell blends, which tended to put the accent on a crisper grain. Interestingly, here they have chosen one at least that is soft and voluptuous enough to absorb the sharper malt notes. 40%. *Springbank Distillers.*

Monarch Of The Glen Connoisseurs Choice (80) n20 t21 f19 b20. Has changed shape a little. Positively wallows in its fat and sweet personality. 40%. *Quality Spirits International.* ⊙ ⊙

⠿ **Monarch Of The Glen Connoisseurs Choice Aged 8 Years** (76.5) n19 t20.5 f18 b19. Leaves no doubt that there are some malts in there... 40%. *Quality Spirits International.*

⠿ **Monarch Of The Glen Connoisseurs Choice Aged 12 Years** (88) n21.5 candy store mix of toffee and fruit bonbons; t22.5 gorgeously silky delivery with barley showing early and then a welter of light fruity punches; f22 tinned tangerine segments and a slow bitter build; b22 charming, fruity and a blend to put your feet up with. 40%. *Quality Spirits International.*

⠿ **Monarch Of The Glen Connoisseurs Choice Aged 15 Years** (83) n21 t22 f19 b21. Starts off on the very same footing as the 12-y-o, especially with the sumptuous delivery. But fails to build on that due to toffee and bitters at the death. 40%. *Quality Spirits International.*

Montrose (74.5) n18 t20 f18 b18.5. A battling performance but bitter defeat in the end. A bad year for Montrose: first they finish ten points adrift of the rest of the Scottish Football League...and now this... 40%. *Burn Stewart.*

Morrisons The Best 8 Years Old (87) n21 t23 f22 b21. I could almost weep: last year this was a blend to delight and win over converts. It was the whisky I was telling everyone to go out and get. This year, some of the traces of its excellence are still there, it remains highly drinkable, but that greatness has been lost in a tide of caramel. Yes, there was caramel used last year, but it had not crossed that fine line: here it has and paid the price and all the high notes have been ruthlessly flattened. When, oh when, are people going to understand that you can't just tip this stuff into whisky to up the colour – even minimally as in the case here – without causing a detrimental effect on the product? Is anybody listening? Does anyone care??? Someone has gone to great lengths to create a sublime blend – to see it wasted. Natural colour and this'd be an experience to die for. 40%

Morrisons Fine Blended Whisky (77) n18.5 t21 f18.5 b19. Sweet, chewy but a few rough edges. 40%. *Wm Morrison Supermarket.*

Muirheads (83) n19 t22 f23 b21. A beautifully compartmentalised dram that integrates superbly, if that makes sense. 40%. *MacDonald & Muir.*

⠿ **The Naked Grouse** (76.5) n19 t21 f17.5 b19. Sweet. But reveals too many sulphur tattoos. 40%. *Edrington.*

Northern Scot (68) n16 t18 f17 b17. Heading South bigtime. 40%. *Bruce and Co. for Tesco.*

Old Crofter Special Old Scotch Whisky (83) n18 t22 f21 b22. A very decent blend, much better than the nose suggests thanks to some outstanding, velvety grain and wonderfully controlled sweetness. 40%. *Smith & Henderson for London & Scottish International.*

Old Masters "Freemason Whisky" (92) n24 t23 f22 b23. A high quality blend that doesn't stint on the malt. The nose, in particular, is sublime. 40%. *Supplied online. Lombard Brands*

Old McDonald (83.5) n20 t22 f20.5 b21. Attractively tart and bracing where it needs to be with lovely grain bite. Lots of toffee, though. 43%. *The Last Drop Distillers. For India.* ⊙ ⊙

Old Mull (84.5) n22 t21 f20.5 b21. With dates and walnuts clambering all over the nose, very much in the house style. But this one is a shade oilier than most – and certainly on how it used to be – and has dropped a degree or two of complexity. That said, enjoyable stuff with the spices performing well, as does the lingering sweetness. 40%

Old Parr 12 Years Old (91.5) n21.5 firm and flinty with the grains comfortably in control; t23.5 no surprise with the mouthwatering juice: the grains help the barley and soft fruit element hit top gear; delicate, light, teasing yet always substantial; f23 mocha dominates with the vaguest hint of gentle smoke; the weight, length and complexity are stupendous b23.5 perhaps on about the fourth of fifth mouthful, the penny drops that this is not just exceptionally good whisky: it is blending Parr excellence... 40%. *Diageo.*

Old Parr Aged 15 Years (84) n19 t22 f21 b22. Absolutely massive sherry input here. Some of it is of the highest order. The nose, reveals, however, that some isn't... 43%

Old Parr Classic 18 Years Old (84.5) n21 t21.5 f21 b21. Decent, yet in the Old Parr scheme of things, just doesn't do it for me. A real jumbled, mixed bag with fruit and barley falling over each other and the grains offering little sympathy. Enough to enjoy, but with Old Parr, one expects a little more... 46%. *Diageo.*

Old Parr Superior 18 Years Old batch no. L5171 (97) n25 here's a nose with just about a touch of everything: especially clever smoke which gives weight but allows apples and bourbon to filter through at will. Perfect weight and harmony while the complexity goes off the scales; t25 voluptuous body, at times silky but the grains offer enough jagged edges for a degree of bite and bourbon; mouthwatering and spicey with the peats remaining on a slow burner. Toasty and so, so chewey; f23 the vanilla is gentle and a counter to the firmness of the combined oak and grain. A flinty, almost reedy finish with spices and cocoa very much in evidence; **b24** year in, year out, this blend just gets better and better. This bottling struck me as a possible Whisky of the Year, but perhaps only an outsider. Familiarity, though, bred anything but contempt and over the passing months I have tried to get to the bottom of this truly great whisky. Blended whisky has long needed a champion. This grand old man looks just the chap. This is a worthy, if unexpected (even to me), Jim Murray' Whisky Bible 2007 World Whisky of the Year. *43%. Diageo/MacDonald Greenlees.*

Old Smuggler (85.5) n21 t22 f21 b21.5. A much sharper act than its Allied days with a new honeyed-maple syrup thread which is rather delightful. Could still do with toning down the caramel, though, to brighten the picture further. *40%. Campari, France.*

⸙ **Old St Andrews Clubhouse (82) n18 t22 f21 b21.** Not quite the clean, bright young thing it was many years back. But great to see back in my nosing glass after such a long while and though the nose hits the rough, the delivery is as sweetly struck as you might hope for. *40%. Old St Andrews Ltd.*

Old Stag (75.5) n18.5 t20 f18.5 b18.5. Wants shooting. *40%. Loch Lomond Distillers.*

The Original Mackinlay (83) n19 t21 f22 b21. Upped a gear since I last tasted this. Still a hard nose to overcome and the toffee remains in force for those addicted to fudge. But now a degree of bite and ballast appears to have been added, giving more of a story to the experience. Having said that, some 30 years ago this was my daily dram. In style it has moved away significantly. *40%. Whyte & Mackay Distillers Ltd.*

Passport (83) n22 t19 f21 b21. It looks as though Chivas have decided to take the blend away from its original sophisticated, Business Class J&B/Cutty Sark, style for good now, as they have continued this decently quaffable but steerage quality blend with its big caramel kick and chewy, rather than body. *40%. Chivas.*

v **Passport (91) n23 23.5 f22 b22.5.** Easily one of the better versions I have come across for a long time and impressively true to its original style. *40%. Bottled in Brazil.*

v **Passport (91) n22.5 t22 f23.5 b23.5.** A lovely version closer to original style with markedly less caramel impact and grittier grain. An old-fashioned treat. *40%. Ecuador.*

Parkers (78) n17 t22 f20 b19. The nose has regressed, disappearing into ever more caramel, yet the mouth-watering lushness on the palate remains and the finish now holds greater complexity and interest. *40%. Angus Dundee.*

Prince Charlie Special Reserve (73) n17 t20 f18 b18. Thankfully not as cloyingly sweet as of old, but remains pretty basic. *40%. Somerfield, UK.*

Prince Charlie Special Reserve 8 Years Old (81) n18 t20 f22 b21. A lumbering bruiser of a dram; keeps its trademark shapelessness but the spices and lush malt ensure an enjoyable experience. *40%. Somerfield, UK.*

Real Mackenzie (80) n17 t21 f21 b21. As ever, try and ignore the dreadful nose and get cracking with the unsubtle, big bruising delivery. A thug in a glass. *40%. Diageo.*

Real Mackenzie Extra Smooth (81) n18 t22 f20 b21. Once, the only time the terms "Real Mackenzie" and "Extra Smooth" were ever uttered in the same sentence was if someone was talking about the barman. Now it is a genuine descriptor. Which is odd, because when Diageo sent me a sample of their blend last year it was a snarling beast ripping at the leash. This, by contrast, is a whimpering sop. "Killer? Where are you...???" *40%. Diageo.*

Red Seal 12 Years Old (82) n19 t22 f20 b21. Charming, mouthwatering. But toffee numbs it down towards the finish. *40%. Charles Wells UK.*

Reliance PL (76) n18 t20 f19 b19. Some of the old spiciness evident. But has flattened out noticeably. *43%. Diageo.*

Robert Burns (85) n20 t22.5 f21 b21.5. Skeletal and juicy: very little fat and gets to the mouthwatering point pretty quickly. Genuine fun. *40%. Isle of Arran.*

Robertson's of Pitlochry Rare Old Blended (83) n21 t20 f21 b21. Handsome grain bite with a late malty flourish. Classic light blend available only from Pitlochry's landmark whisky shop. *40%*

The Royal & Ancient (80.5) n20 t21.5 f19 b20. Has thinned out dramatically in the last year or so. Now clean, untaxing, briefly mouth-watering and radiating young grain throughout. *40%. Cockburn & Campbell.* ☉ ☉

⸙ **Royal Castle (84.5) n20 t22 f21 b21.5.** From Quality Street, or Quality Spirits? Sweet and very well toffeed! *43%. Quality Spirits International.*

Royal Castle 12 Years Old (84.5) n22 t22 f20 b20.5. Busy nose and delivery with much to chew over. Entirely enjoyable, and seems better each time you taste it. Even so, the finish crumbles a bit. *40%. Quality Spirits International.*

⸙ **Royal Clan Aged 18 Years (85) n21.5 t21 f21.5 b21.** For those giving up gum, here's something to really chew on. Huge degree of cream toffee and toasted fudge which makes for a satin-soft blend, but also one which ensures any big moves towards complexity are nipped in the bud. Very enjoyable, all the same. *40%. Quality Spirits International.*

Royal Household (90.5) n21.5 t23 f23 b23 We are amused. *43%. Diageo.*

Royal Salute 21 Years Old (92.5) n23 has persisted with the gentle, exotic fruit but less lush here with much more punch and poke; it even seems that the smoke which had been missing in recent years has returned, but in shadowy form only; **t23.5** yep! Definitely more bite these days with the grains having a much greater input, for all the juiciness, and the vanilla striking home earlier. Makes for a decent sweet/dry middle, the sweetness supplied by boiled sweet candy; **f23** plenty of cocoa and the very lightest dab of something smoky; **b23.5** if you are looking for the velvety character of yore, forget it. This one comes with some real character and is much the better for it. The grain, in particular, excels. *40%. Chivas.*

⋰ **Royal Salute 62 Gun Salute (95.5)** n24.5 the trouble with writing the Bible is that I have only a year in which to do it. And that doesn't seem quite enough time to get my head around this one. I was expecting exotic fruit, dates and all the other flags hoisted by old whiskies. They are not here. Instead we have prunes and apples plus a little cinnamon. And grapes, of course. All this in a bed of seemingly natural caramels. It is a smoke-free environment where every oak note is rounded and friendly, where you fancy you can still find the odd mark of barley and yet although being a blend, the grain is refusing to take it down a bourbon path, despite the peek-a-boo honeycomb. Is this where old whiskies go when they die...? **t24** but obviously not dead yet, for the delivery is alive and kicking. The oak is relatively full on, but early on adds a toasty quality to the marmalade and plum jam. The mid ground casts off any sherry-like clothes and heads for a more honey-rich, vaguely bourbon style without ever reaching Kentucky. Most masterful, though, is the body which somehow is soft yet firm at the same moment, like a proffered breast. Not a unique characteristic but one performed by only a handful of whiskies; **f23** the fade is purely on the gentle side with sugars dissolving against a slightly bittering background as some of the oak rebels, as you might expect at least one or two of these old timers to do. At the very death comes the one and only sign of smoke...that is some parting shot; **b24** now here's a trick. How do you get a bunch of varying whiskies in style, but each obviously growing a grey beard and probably cantankerous to boot, to settle in and harmonise with the others? A kind of Old People's Home for whisky, if you like. Well, here's how... I hear this guy doesn't come cheap. To be honest, I'm not surprised: a masterpiece barely does it justice. *43%. Chivas.*

Royal Salute The Hundred Cask Selection Limited Release No. 7 (92) n22 a mixture of Caperdonich-esque exotic fruit and slightly over cooked, lactic oak masquerading as rice pudding; **t23.5** the silky glide onto the palate you'd expect from the nose and previous experience; some groaning oak arrives pretty early on; **f23** sweet, muscovado-sprinkled cocoa; **b23.5** it would be rude to ask how old some of the whiskies that go into making this one up are...As blends go, its entire countenance talks about great age and elegance. And does so with a clipped accent. *40%. Chivas.*

Royal Silk Reserve (93) n22 classically light yet richly bodied under the clear, crisp ethereal grains. The freshly-cut-grass maltiness balances perfectly; **t24** crystal clear grains dovetail with intense, mouthwatering and refreshingly sweet malt to create a perfect pitch while the middle is heavier and livelier than you might expect with the very faintest echo of peat; **f24** delicate oils and wonderful grainy-vanilla ensures improbable length for something so light. Beautiful spices and traces of cocoa offer the last hurrah. Sheer bliss; **b23** I named this the best newcomer of 2001 and it hasn't let me down. A session blend for any time of the day, this just proves that you don't need piles of peat to create a blend of genuine stature. A must have. *40%*

Sainsbury's Basics Blended Scotch Whisky (78.5) n19 t20.5 f19.5 b19.5. "A little less refined, great for mixing," says the label. Frankly, there are a lot of malts out there far less enjoyable than this. Don't be scared to have straight: it's more than decent enough. *40%*

Sainsbury's Scotch Whisky (84.5) n20 t22 f21 b21.5. A surprisingly full bodied, chewy blend allowing a pleasing degree of sweetness to develop. No shortage of toffee at the finish – a marked improvement on recent years. *40%. UK.* ⊙⊙

Sainsbury's Finest Old Matured Aged 8 Years (86) n21.5 t21 f22 b21.5. A sweet blend enjoying a melt-in-the-mouth delivery, a silky body and toffee-vanilla character. The spices arriving towards the end are exceptionally pleasing and welcome. *40%. UK.* ⊙⊙

Sandy Mac (76) n18 t20 f19 b19. Basic, decent blend that's chunky and raw. *40%. Diageo.*

Scots Earl (76.5) n18 t20 f19 b19.5. It's name is Earl. And it must have upset someone in a previous life. Always thrived on its engaging disharmony. But just a tad too syrupy now. *40%. Loch Lomond Distillers.*

Scottish Chief (77) n19 t19 f19 b20. This is one big-bodied chief, and not given to taking prisoners. *40%. Quality Spirits International.*

Scottish Collie (77) n19 t19 f19 b20. Caramel still, but a Collie with a bit more bite. *40%*

Scottish Collie 12 Years Old (85) n22 t22 f20 b21. On the cusp of a really classy blend here but the bitterness on the finish loses serious Brownie points. *40%. Quality Spirits Int, UK.*

Scottish Collie 18 Years Old (92) n24 t23 f22 b23. This, honey-led beaut would be a winner even at Crufts: an absolute master class of how an old, yet light and unpeated blend should be. No discord whatsoever between the major elements and not a single hint of over-aging. Superb. *40%. Quality Spirits International, UK.*

Scottish Glory dist 2002, bott 2005 (85) n21 t21 f22 b21. An improved blend now bursting with vitality. The ability of the grain to lift the barley is very pleasing. *40%. Duncan Taylor.*

Scottish Leader Original (83.5) n17.5 t22.5 f21 b22.5. About as subtle as a poke in the eye with a spirit thief. The nose, it must be said, is not great. But I have to admit I thoroughly enjoy the almost indulgent coarseness from the moment it invades the palate. A real chewathon of a spicy blend with a wicked, in-yer-face attitude. Yet among all the rough-'n-tumble and slap-'n-tickle, the overall depth, weight, balance and molassed charm ain't half bad. Impressed. *40% Burn Stewart* ⊙⊙

Scottish Leader Aged 12 Years (91) n22.5 excellent bourbon notes: honeycomb and liquorice accompanied by light spices and toffee; t23 big and cream-textured: positively melts on the palate. Huge degree of toffee, but the honeycomb and dates are vibrant enough to be more than heard. Elsewhere the sugars take a positively datey shape and, with a soft nuttiness apparent, there is something about a Dundee cake about this one; f22 light, milky cocoa and vanilla; b22.5 absolutely unrecognisable from the Leader 12 I last tasted. This has taken a plumy, fruity route with the weight of a cannonball but the texture of mallow. Big and quite beautiful. *40% Burn Stewart* ⊙⊙

Scottish Leader 30 Years Old (87) n23.5 stylish: fruit and honey in pretty even measures. Not only is it soft but there is neither spice nor an alcohol prickle to disrupt the silky passage; t21.5 melt-in-the-mouth delivery with toffee and raisin theme; f20.5 way too much caramel; a touch of bitterness creeps in; b21.5 perhaps a little too docile ever to be a great whisky, but the nose is something rather special. A bit of attention on the finish and this could be a real corker. *40%. Burn Stewart.*

Scottish Leader Select (91.5) n23 gorgeous honey with a buzzing spice accompaniment; t23.5 beautiful delivery. Those honeys and spices gang together to make a delightful statement with the grains offering a beautiful custard-rich support; f22.5 firmer, but the sweetness persists; b22.5 had to do a James Finlayson double take on this one. Don't make the mistake of thinking this is just the 40% with three extra percentage points of alcohol. This appears to be an entirely different bottling with an entirely different personality the characters including a few handsome leads. A delight. *43%. Burn Stewart. For the South African Market.*

Scottish Leader Select (74) n18.5 t19 f18 b18.5. I assume the leader is Major Disharmony. *40%. Burn Stewart.*

Scottish Leader Supreme (72.5) n17 t19 f18 b18.5. Jings! It's like an old-fashioned Gorbals punch-up in the glass – and palate. *40% Burn Stewart* ⊙⊙

Scottish Piper (80) n20 t20 f20 b20. A light, mildly- raw, sweet blend with lovely late vanilla intonation. *40%*

Scottish Prince (83.5) n21 t22 f20 b20.5. Muscular, but agreeably juicy. *40%*

Scottish Reel (78.5) n19 t19 f20 b19.5. Non fussy with an attractive bite, as all such blends should boast. *40%. London & Scottish International.*

Scottish Rill (85) n20 t20.5 f22.5 b22. Refreshing yet earthy. *40%. Quality Spirits Int.*

Something Special (85) n21.5 t22 f20.5 b21. Mollycoddled by toffee, any murderous tendencies seem to have been fudged away, leaving just the odd moment of attractive complexity. Enough to make you think that there is a hit man in there somewhere just trying to get out... *40%. Chivas.*

Something Special Premium Aged 15 Years (89) n22 a vague, distant smokiness sits prettily with some fruity caramel; t23 boisterous delivery with unshackled malt adding a wonderful, zesty spiciness amid much more mouth-watering Speyside-style fresh grass; the grain offers the desired cut-glass firmness; f21 lots of vanilla and too much caramel, but remains busy and entertaining; b23 a hugely enjoyable, fun whisky which pops around the palate like a crackerjack. Fabulous malt thread and some curious raisiny/sultana fruitiness, too. A blend-lover's blend. *40%. Chivas/Hill Thompson, Venezuela.*

Spar Finest Reserve (90.5) n21.5 fabulously clean, young grain offering butterscotch and toffee; elsewhere something earthy rumbles; t22.5 brilliantly subtle delivery with silky grains ensnared in a sweet shell; towards the middle chocolate fudge and a distinctive smoky rumble forms; f23.5 one of the best "supermarket" finishes to be found with a stunning array of clean, dapper smoke notes which cling, like softly oiled limpets, to the tastebuds for an improbably long time: lush and beautifully layered, this is masterful blending...; **b23** one of Britain best value for money blends with an honest (or as honest as any whisky with caramel can be) charm which revels in the clean high quality grain and earthier malts which work so well together. 40%

Stewart's Old Blended (93) n22.5 apples and date and walnut cake; clean and more delicate than the early weight suggests; **t24** sublime silky delivery with the slow erection of a fruity platform; the yielding grain cushions the juicy malt aspects; **f23** bitters out as some oak makes its play but firmer malt and molasses compensate superbly; **b23.5** really lovely whisky for those who like to close their eyes, contemplate and have a damned good chew. Voluptuous and as that chunky style goes, absolutely top of its league. 40%

Swords (78) n20 t21 f18 b19. Beefed up somewhat with some early smoke thrusting through and rapier grains to follow. 40%. *Morrison Bowmore.*

Talisman 5 Years Old (85.5) n22 t22 f20.5 b21. Unquestionably an earthier, weightier version of what was once a Speyside romp. Soft peats also add extra sweetness. 40%

Teacher's Highland Cream (90) n23 firm, flinty grain; a tad fruity with gently smoked malt-ensuring weight; **t23** mouth-filling with a tender sweetness; the grains seem softer than the nose suggests; **f22** toffee and lazy smoke; **b22** not yet back to its best but a massive improvement on the 2005 bottlings. So harder grains to accentuate the malt will bring it closer to the classic of old. 40%

v **Teacher's Highland Cream** (90) n23 grain dominates, but not the old-fashioned sharp Dumbarton style. This is softer, sweeter with a topping of thick vanilla and butterscotch and delicate barley...where's the famous smoke...??? It's there, but the most distant echo; almost a dull background throb – for some Teacher's diehards, it is too well integrated...; **t22.5** as silky a delivery as the nose promises. Again the grain comes through loud and clear with the playful malts hanging on to its coat-tails. Only towards the middle do the two combine, and rather attractively and with style; **f22** much more spiced with a decided vanilla twirl; still virtually no smoke worthy of the name other than a vague oiliness; **b22.5** a very curious, seriously high grade, variant. Although the Ardmore distillery is on the label (though for the life of me I don't recognize it!), it is the only place it can really be seen. Certainly - the least smoky Teacher's I've come across in 35 years of drinking the stuff: the smoke is there, but adds only ballast rather than taking any form of lead. But the grain is soft and knits with the malts with ease to make for a sweeter, much more lush version than the rest of the world may recognize. 40%

·:· **Teacher's Origin** (88.5) n22 thick, treacle tart, nose. A pinch of salt ensures a certain piquancy and gentle peat reek on the breeze does no harm, either; **t23.5** thick, soupy and sweet, the delivery is muscular and manful. Toffee takes an early lead, but fabulous spice and several delicate layers of smoke add to the initial beauty; a slightly negative sherry-cask style influence begins to bite in towards the middle and dry things somewhat; **f21** that dryness continues and all other avenues are cut off with toffee; **b22** a fascinating blend which probably ranks as the softest on the market today. That is aided and abetted by the exceptionally high malt content, 65%, which makes this something of an inverted blend, as that, for most established brands, is the average grain content. What appears to be a high level of caramel also makes for a rounding of the edges, as well as evidence of sherry butts. The bad news is that that has resulted in a duller finish than perhaps might have been intended, which is even more pronounced given the impressive speech made on delivery. Lovely whisky, yes. But something, I feel, of a work in progress. Bringing the caramel down by the percentage points of the malt would be a very positive start... 42.8%. ncf. *Beam Global.*

Té Bheag (86) n22 t21 f21.5 b21.5. Classic style of rich caramels and bite. 40%. ncf. Pràban na Linne. ⊙⊙

Tesco Finest Reserve Aged 12 Years (74) n18.5 t19 f18 b18.5. The most astonishing thing about this, apart from the fact it is a 12 year-old, is that it won a Gold "Best in Class" in a 2010 international whisky competition: it surely could not have been from the same batch as the one before me. Frankly, you have to go a long way to find a whisky as bland as this and for a 12-y-o it is monumentally disappointing: a blend with not a single word to say. I expect so much more from a company as great as Tesco. Any more caramel and it should be sold on their toffee counter... 40%. ⊙⊙

Tesco Special Reserve Minimum 3 Years Old (78) n18.5 t21.5 f19 b19. Decent early spice on delivery but otherwise anonymous. 40%. *Tesco.* ⊙⊙

Tesco Value Scotch Whisky (83) n19 t21 f22 b21. Young and genuinely refreshing whisky. Without the caramel this really would be a little darling. 40%

Traquair (78) n19 t21 f19 b19. Young, but offering a substantial mouthful including attractive smoke. 46%. *Burn Stewart.*

⣿⣿ **The Tweeddale Blend Aged 10 Years** (89.5) n22 attractive and well-balanced mix of mint humbug and toffee; t23.5 beautifully weighted and structured. The non-filtration and 50% malt content combo has paid dividends as the weight and oiliness is highly unusual for a blended scotch. Chewy with an impressive degree of spice development which is in complete harmony with the increased sugar intensity; f21.5 dries as the oak begins to play its part and the grains begin to bite. Lots of toffee, too; b23 the first bottling of this blend since World War 2, it has been well worth waiting for. Cut down on the toffee and you'd really have a supreme whisky on your hands... 46%. ncf. 50% malt. Stonedean.

Ushers Green Stripe (85) n19 t22.5 f21.5 b22. Upped a notch or two in all-round quality. The juicy theme and clever weight is highly impressive and enjoyable. 43%. Diageo.

VAT 69 (84.5) n20 t22 f21 b21.5. Has thickened up in style: weightier, more macho, much more to say and a long way off that old lightweight. A little cleaning up wouldn't go amiss. 40%

White Horse (90.5) n22 busy, with a shade more active grain than normal. But the smoky depth is there, as is a gentle hickory, butterscotch and fruity thread; a few bruising malts can be picked up, too; t23 the usual sensual delivery, at first almost like a young JW Black, thanks to that soft billowing out towards the gentle honeys and juices; as it reaches the middle the clunking, muddied fist of some volumous malts can be easily detected; f22.5 gets no less complex or more subtle as it develops; playful spices dovetail with vanilla while the smoke reinforces the backbone; b23 a malt which has subtlety changed shape. Not just the smoke which gives it weight, but you get the feeling that some of Diageo's less delicate malts have been sent in to pack a punch. As long as they are kept in line, as is the case here – just – we can all enjoy a very big blend. 40%. Diageo.

White Horse Aged 12 Years (86) n21 t23 f21 b21. enjoyable, complex if not always entirely harmonious. For instance, the apples and grapes on the nose appear on a limb from the grain and caramel and nothing like the thoroughbred of old. Lighter, more flaccid and caramel dominated. Just don't recognize it from the glorious beast that so often sat within arm's length of me in my house. 40%. Diageo.

Whyte & Mackay 'The Thirteen' 13 Year Old (92) n22.5 a fruity barley edge to this one; soft and enticing; t23.5 a silky, mouth-watering delivery with some instant spices ensuring an immediate extra dimension. The sugars are muscovado toned, but with a pinch of molasses as a delicate bourbony sub plot develops below the tingling peppers; f23 drier with some beautifully integrated vanillas and mocha: clever stuff; b23 try this and your luck'll be in... easily the pick of the W&M blended range. 40%. Whyte & Mackay Distillers Ltd.

Whyte & Mackay Luxury 19 Year Old (84.5) n21 t22 f20 b21.5. A pleasant house style chewathon. Nutty, biting but with a tang. 40%. Whyte & Mackay Distillers Ltd.

Whyte & Mackay Supreme 22 Year Old (87) n21 t23 f20.5 b22.5. Ignore the nose and finish and just enjoy the early ride. 43%

Whyte & Mackay Oldest 30 Year Old (87.5) n23 blackjack candy, punchy vanilla and apples: heavy booted but all rather sexy... t23 the usual W&M full throttle delivery with fruity flavours galore; f20 the usual W&M finale which is all a bit flat, tangy and furry; b21.5 what exasperating whisky this is. So many good things about it, but... 45%

Whyte & Mackay Original Aged Blended 40 Years Old (93) n23 t24 f22 b24. I admit, when I nosed and tasted this at room temp, not a lot happened. Pretty, but closed. But once warmed in the hand up to full body temperature, it was obvious that Richard Paterson had created a quite wonderful monster of a blend offering so many avenues to explore that the mind almost explodes. Well done RP for creating something that further proves, and in such magnitude, just how warmth can make an apparently ordinary whisky something bordering genius. 45%

Whyte & Mackay Special (84.5) n20 t23 f20 b21.5. This has to be the ultimate mood blend. If you are looking for a big-flavoured dram and with something approaching a vicious left uppercut, this might be a useful bottle to have on hand. The nose, I'm afraid, has not improved over the years but there appears to be compensation with the enormity and complexity of the delivery, a veritable orgy of big, oily, juicy, murky flavours and tones if ever there was one. You cannot but like it, in the same way as you may occasionally like rough sex. But if you are looking for a delicate dram to gently kiss you and caress your fever'd brow, then leave well alone. 40%

William Grant's 12 Years Old Bourbon Cask (90.5) n23 lively and floral. The drier notes suggest chalky oak but the sweet spiciness balances beautifully; t22.5 flinty textured with both malts and grains pinging around the teeth with abandon; f22 remains light yet with a clever, crisp sweetness keeping the weightier oaks in check; b23 very clever blending where balance is the key. 40%

William Grant's 15 Years Old (85) n21 t23 f20 b21. Grain and, later, caramel dominates but the initial delivery reveals the odd moment of sheer genius and complexity on max revs. 43%

William Grant's 25 Years Old (95.5) n23.5 some serious oak, but chaperoned by top quality oloroso, itself thinned by firm and graceful grain; t24 sheer quality: complexity by the shovel-load as juicy fruits interact with darting, crisp barley; again the grain shows elegance both sharpening increasingly mouth-watering malt and softening the oak; **t24** medium length, but not a single sign of fatigue: the sweet barley runs and runs and some jammy fruits charm. Just to cap it all, some wonderful spices dazzle and a touch of low roast Java enriches; **b24** absolutely top-rank blending that appears to maximize every last degree of complexity. Most astonishing, though, is its sprightly countenance: even Scottish footballing genius Ally MacLeod struggled to send our Ayr Utd. sides with this kind of brio. And that's saying something! A gem. *40%*

William Grant's 100 US Proof Superior Strength (92) **n23** sublime chocolate lime nose, decent oak; **t24** big mouth arrival, lush and fruity with the excellent extra grain bite you might expect at this strength, just an extra degree of spice takes it into even higher orbit than before; **f22** back to chocolate again with a soft fruit fade; **b23** a fruitier drop now than it was in previous years but no less supremely constructed. *50% (100 US proof)*

William Grant's Ale Cask Reserve (89) **n21 t23 f22 b23**. A real fun blend that is just jam-packed with jagged malty notes. The hops were around more on earlier bottlings, but watch out for them. Nothing pint-sized about this: this is a big blend and very true in flavour/shape to the original with just a delicious shading of grain to really up the complexity. *40%*

William Grant's Family Reserve (94) **n25** this, to me, is the perfect nose to any blend: harmonious and faultless. There is absolutely everything here in just-so proportions: a bit of snap and bite from the grain, teasing sweet malts, the faintest hint of peat for medium weight, strands of oak for dryness, fruit for lustre. Even Ardbeg doesn't pluck my strings like this glass of genius can; **t23** exceptionally firm grain helps balance the rich, multi-layered malty tones. The sub-plot of burnt raisins and peek-a-boo peat add further to the intrigue and complexity (if it doesn't bubble and nip around the mouth you have a rare sub-standard bottling); **f22** a hint of caramel can be detected amid returning grains and soft cocoa tones: just so clean and complex; **b24** there are those puzzled by my obvious love affair with blended whisky - both Scotch and Japanese - at a time when malts are all the rage. But take a glass of this and carefully nurture and savour it for the best part of half an hour and you may begin to see why I believe this to be the finest art form of whisky. For my money, this brand - brilliantly kept in tip-top shape by probably the world's most naturally gifted blender - is the closest thing to the blends of old and, considering it is pretty ubiquitous, it defies the odds for quality. It is a dram with which you can start the day and end it: one to keep you going at low points in between, or to celebrate the victories. It is the daily dram that has everything. *40%*

William Grant's Sherry Cask Reserve (82) **n20 t22 f20 b20**. Raspberry jam and cream from time to time. Attractive, but somewhat plodding dram that's content in second gear. *40%*

William Lawson's Finest (85) **n18.5 t22.5 f22 b22**. Not only has the label become more colourful, but so, too, has the whisky. However that has not interfered with the joyous old-fashioned grainy bite. A complex and busy blend from the old charm school. *40%*

William Lawson's Scottish Gold Aged 12 Years (89) **n22 t23 f22 b22**. For years Lawson's 12 was the best example of the combined wizardry of clean grain, unpeated barley and good bourbon cask that you could find anywhere in the world: a last-request dram before the firing squad. Today it is still excellent, but just another sherried blend. What's that saying about if it's not being broke...? *40%*

Windsor 12 Years Old (81) **n20 t21 f20 b20**. Thick, walloped-on blend that you can stand a spoon in. Hard at times to get past the caramel. *40%. Diageo.*

Windsor Aged 17 Years Super Premium (89) **n23** a fabulous aroma which bombards the nose with both luxurious grain and a hint of something smoky above the butter-honey theme; **t22** sweet, as is the house style, with a Demerara coating to the crisp malt and gathering vanilla; silky and voluptuous throughout; **f22** a gentle, soft-textured landing with an echo of spice; **b22** still a little on the safe side for all its charm and quality. An extra dose of complexity would lift this onto another level altogether. *40%. Diageo.*

Windsor 21 Years Old (90) **n20** fruity and weighty but something a bit lactic and lethargic from some old bourbon casks has crept in; **t23** excellent oils surround the silk to help amplify the intensity of the fruit and drifting smoke; **f24** some spiciness that shows towards the middle really takes off now as drying vanilla counters the sweet grains; **b23** recovers fabulously from the broken nose and envelopes the palate with a silky-sweet style unique to the Windsor scotch brand. Excellent. *40%. Diageo.*

Ye Monks (86) **n20 t23 f21.5 b21.5**. Just hope they are praying for less caramel to maximize the complexity. Still, a decent spicy chew and outstanding bite which is great fun and worth finding when in South America. *40%. Diageo.*

Yokozuna Blended 3 Years Old (79.5) **n18.5 t20.5 f20 b20.5**. It appears the Mongols are gaining a passion for thick, sweet, toffeed, oily, slightly feinty whisky. For a nation breastfed on airag, this'll be a doddle... *40%. Speyside Distillers. Mongolian market.*

Irish Whiskey

Of all the whiskies in the world, it is Irish which probably causes most confusion amongst both established whisk(e)y lovers and the novices.

Ask anyone to define what is unique to Irish Whiskey – apart from it being made in Ireland – and the answers, if my audiences around the world at my tastings are anything to go by, are in this order: i) It is triple distilled; ii) It is never, ever made from peat; iii) They exclusively use sherry casks; iv) It comes from the oldest distillery in the world; v) It is made from a mixture of malted and unmalted barley.

Only one of those answers is true: the fifth. And it is usually the final answer extracted from the audience when the last hand raised sticks to his guns after the previous four responses have been shot down.

There was no shortage of Blarney when the Irish were trying to market their whiskey back in the 1950s and early 60s. Hence the triple distilled/non-peated myth was born. The Irish had had a thin time of it since the 1920s and seen their industry decimated. So the marketing guys got to work.

As much of Ireland is covered in peat, it is hardly surprising that in the 19th century smoky whiskey from inland distilleries was not uncommon. Like Scotland. Some distilleries used two stills, others three. Like Scotland. Sherry butts were ubiquitous in Ireland before World War 2. Just as they were in Scotland. And there are distilleries in Scotland older than Bushmills, which dates from 1784.

However, the practice of using malted and unmalted barley, begun so less tax had to be paid on malted grain, had died out in the Lowlands of Scotland, leaving it for Ireland to carry on alone.

It is hard to believe, then, that when I was researching my Irish Whiskey Almanac way back in 1993, Redbreast had just been discontinued as a brand leaving Green Spot, an ancient gem of a bottling from Mitchell and Son, Dublin's legendary high class wine and spirit merchants, as the sole surviving Pure Irish Pot Still Whiskey. At first Redbreast's owners refused to send me a bottle as they regarded it a pointless exercise, seeing as the brand had gone. After I wrote about it, first in my Almanac and then in newspapers and magazines elsewhere, they had no option other than to reverse their decision: interest had been whetted and people were asking for it once more.

When it was relaunched, the Pot Still came from Midleton. The Redbreast they were discontinuing was Pure Pot Still from the long defunct original Jameson Distillery in Dublin. Jameson may once have been locked in commercial battle with their neighbouring Power's distillery, but they united in the late 19th century when they brought out a book called: "The Truth About Irish Whiskey" in which they together, along with other Dublin distillers, fought against blended and other types of what they considered adulterated whiskey to tell the world that the only true Irish whiskey was Pure Pot Still.

How fitting, then, that this year's Jim Murray's Whisky Bible Irish Whiskey of the Year should fall to a new Pot Still from Midleton: Powers John's Lane, named after the old distillery. With Midleton's Barry Crockett's Legacy it represents a most welcome and long awaited extension to their Pot Still portfolio. For years I used to irritate former blender Barry Walsh by sitting on the end of his desk and asking him continuously when he was going to get another Irish Pot still launched. He would chide me that the cause had been put back years by my managing to persuade the directors to seriously up the Pot Still content in their standard Jameson brand so it again tasted like Irish whiskey.

Therefore Irish Pot still is a type of whiskey I know intimately and with more than a little affection. The fact that I gave the taste profile of John's Lane the top score of 25 reveals that in 25 years I have never tasted better.

But Irish is not all about Pot Still and Cooley continue to do a wonderful job of producing high quality grain and malt. Particulary worth finding is their peated and diverse bottling of Connemara and their unpeated 8-year-old for Sainsbury, Dun Leire, which is winning converts to Irish whisky at a remarkable rate of knots.

Next year I will be completely re-tasting the entire Irish section from fresh: it will be one of the highlights of the year. For however miserable the past twelve months may have been for the Irish people and their economy, there is certainly nothing that can be said against the overall quality of their whiskey. From what I have tasted this year, officially for the Bible and unofficially for my own enjoyment, it just seems to be getting better.

Bushmills

Londonderry●

NORTHERN
IRELAND   Belfast●

▲Cooley

Kilbeggan▲   Dublin●

REPUBLIC OF
IRELAND

Cork● ▲ Midleton

Key
● **Major Town or City**
▲ **Distillery**

Pure Pot Still
MIDLETON (old distillery)

Midleton 25 Years Old Pot Still db **(92)** n24 t24 f21 b23. A really enormous whiskey that is in the truest classic Irish style. The un-malted barley really does make the tastebuds hum and the oak has added fabulous depth. Interesting when tasted against an American rye – the closeness of the character is there to be experienced, but also the differences. A subtle mature whiskey of unquestionable quality. Superb. 43%

Midleton 30 Years Old Pot Still db **(85)** n19 t22 f22 b22. A typically brittle, crunchy Irish pot still where the un-malted grains have a telling say. The oak has travelled as far as it can without having an adverse effect. A chewy whiskey which revels in its bitter-sweet balance. An impressively tasty and fascinating insight into yesteryear. 45%

Midleton 1973 Pure Pot Still db **(95)** n24 t24 f23 b24. The enormous character of true Irish pot still whiskey (a mixture of malted and unmalted barley) appears to absorb age better than most other grain spirits. This one is in its element. But drink at full strength and at body temp (it is pretty closed when cool) for the most startling – and memorable effects. I have no idea how much this costs. But if you can find one and afford it... then buy it!! 56%

MIDLETON (new distillery)

∴ **Midleton Barry Crockett Legacy** db **(94)** n23.5 spices nip and thrust; delicate fruits form a series of gentle layers; a light bourbon liquorice adds depth...; t24.5 the delivery provides the sweetness missing from the nose but only after an early surge of oak and soft oils. The middle ground is a battlefield between spices and peachy fruit, with just a touch of honey moving in when it thinks no one is watching...; f22.5 relatively short and duller than you might expect. The caramels cap the higher points and though spices rumble there is little for it to echo against; b23.5 another fabulous Pot Still, very unusual for its clever use of the varied ages of the oak to form strata of intensity. One very sophisticated whiskey. 46%. ncf.

∴ **Powers John's Lane Release Aged 12 Years** db **(96.5)** n24 unmistakable. Unique. Utopian. Irish pure pot still at its most embracing and magnificent. That bizarre bipolar character of rock hard grain so at home in the company of silky, molten honey. Some light, non-specific fruit – a bit like boiled sweets in a candy shop. But a vague menthol note, too...; t25 as Irish whiskey goes: perfection! The delivery can come only from Irish Pot still – I have encountered it nowhere else. And it is a replay of the nose: soft, dissolve-on-the-palate honey and elsewhere strands of something much firmer – hardening more and more as it moves to the middle ground; **f23.5** wonderful fade: a distant medium roast Java, the Lubec marzipan which you just knew would be coming; a little caramel; some orangey notes... **b24** this is a style of Irish Pot Still I have rarely seen outside the blending lab. I had many times thought of trying to find some of this and bottling it myself. No need now. I think I have just tasted Irish Whiskey of the Year, and certainly one of the top five world whiskies of the year. *46%. Irish Distillers.*

Redbreast 12 Years Old db **(96) n23.5** lively and firm, this one offering a gentle fruity swetness not too dissimilar to a rye, ironic as there is light bourbony kick off the oak, too; **t24.5** wonderfully clipped and correct in delivery: firm at first - very firm!!! - but slowly the barley melts and light muscovado sugars dovetail with a flinty fruitiness and pillow-soft vanilla; incorrigibly mouthwatering and the build up of spices is just showing off; **f24** remains spicy but clean, allowing a clear view of those varying barley tones drifting away; **b24** Yess...!!! Back to its classically classy, brilliant best. No sulphur casks this time (unlike last year). Just juicy pot still all the way. An old loved one has returned... more gorgeous than ever. *40%. Irish Distillers.*

Redbreast 15 Years Old db **(94) n23 t24 f23 b24.** For years I have been pleading for Irish Distillers to launch a pot still at 46%, natural colour and unchillfiltered. Well, I've got two out of three wishes. And what we have here is a truly great Irish whiskey and my pulse races in the certain knowledge it can get better still... *46%. ncf. France.*

Green Spot (94.5) n23.5 mouthwatering and fresh on one level, honey and menthol on another; **t24** crisp, mouthwatering with a fabulous honey burst, alarmingly sensuous; **f23.5** the caramel has receded, leaving the finer, sharper pot still character to battle it out with the honey. The spices are now much clearer too; **b23.5** this honeyed state has remained a few years, and its shar ness has now been regained. Complex throughout. Unquestionably one of the world's greatest branded whiskies. *40%. Irish Distillers for Mitchell & Son, Dublin.* ☉ ☉

Green Spot 10 Year Old Single Pot Still dist 1993 **(92) n23 t22 f24 b23.** Launched to celebrate the 200th anniversary of this wonderful Dublin landmark, this is bottled from three mixed bourbon casks of Irish Pot Still. The extra age has detracted slightly from the usual vitality of the standard Green Spot (an 8-y-o) but its quality still must be experienced. *40%. Mitchell & Son. 1000 bottles.*

Green Spot 12 Year Old Single Pot Still dist 1991 **(93) n24 t24 f22 b23.** A single cask restricted to exactly 200 bottles to mark the 200th anniversary of the grand old man of Kildare Street, this is the first Middleton pot still I have seen at this strength outside of a lab. A one-off in every sense. *58%*

OLD COMBER

Old Comber 30 Years Old Pure Pot Still (88) n23 t24 f20 b21. A classic example of a whiskey spending a few Summers too many in wood: increasing age doesn't equal excellence. That said, always very drinkable and early on positively sparkles with a stunning mouthfeel. Out of respect for the old I have made the markings for taste cover the first seven or eight seconds... *40%*

Single Malt
COOLEY

Connemara bott code L9042 db **(88) n23** a bigger than usual salty, kippery tang; **t22.5** one of the more delicate and mouth-watering deliveries Connemara has given for a while: the peat is at once strident and meek but the subtle gristy sweetness is a constant and first class foil to the vanillas; **f20.5** rather short, toffeed and hurried; **b22** one of the softest smoked whiskies in the world which though quite lovely gives the impression it can't make its mind up about what it wants to be. *40%*

Connemara Aged 8 Years db **(85) n22.5 t21.5 f20 b21.** Another Connemara lacking teeth. The peat charms, especially on the nose, but the complexity needs working on. *46%*

Connemara Aged 12 Years bott code L9024 db **(85.5) n23 t21.5 f20 b21.** The nose, with its beautiful orange, fruity lilt, puts the shy smoke in the shade. *40%*

Connemara 1995 Sherry Cask cask no. V07/08 87, dist Oct 95, bott Oct 08 db **(76) n18 t20 f19 b19.** Sulphured butts respect no international boundaries...and particularly love to hide behind peat. *46%*

Connemara Cask Strength bott code L9041 db **(90) n21.5** a shrill peatiness fends off a determined, off-key vanilla attack; **t23** fabulous delivery: it's juicy, sharp, eye-watering malt all the way, with the smoke prodding the tastebuds here and there; spices as the smoke becomes a little more hostile; **f22** finally the vanilla gets to have its say; **b22.5** a juicy negative of the standard bottling: does its talking on the palate rather than nose. Maybe an absence of caramel notes might have something to do with that. 57.9%

Connemara Distillers Edition db (86) n22 t22.5 f20 b21.5. When I give whisk(e)y tastings around the world, I love to include Connemara. Firstly, people don't expect peated Irish. Secondly, their smoked whisky stock is eclectic and you never quite know what is going to come out of the bottle. This is a particularly tight, sharp style. No prisoners survived... 43%

Connemara Single Cask sherry finish, cask no. 112, dist Aug 92, bott Nov 09 db (92.5) n23 allotment bonfires and freshly opened pack of dates; t23.5 uncharacteristically silky for a Connemara! The fruit oozes around every crevice; the peat adds serious weight; decent flakey oak and grist through the middle; f23 smoked chocolate dates; some wonderful oils spin it out; b23 ladies and gentlemen: I have the pleasure of presenting to you Connemara wearing fruity clothes you may never have quite seen before. 46%. Approx 300 bottles.

⁙ **Connemara Turf Mór Limited Edition Small Batch Collection** bott code L10215 db (94) n23.5 t23.5 f23.5 b23.5. At Burnley FC, the wine served in their boardroom is The Claret's Claret, naturally. I will not be surprised to find this the whiskey on offer... The tasting notes to this just about perfectly match the ones above. 58.2%

Locke's Aged 8 Years bott code L9005 db (88) n22.5 excellent, rousing citrus; t22 begins bright fresh and sharp, clouds over slightly with caramel; f22 barley loses its toffeed marker from time to time to complete a juicy experience; b21.5 a beautiful malt at probably this distillery's optimum age. 40%

Locke's Aged 8 Years Crock (92) n23 pounding, intense, grassy-sweet barley; t24 excellent mouth arrival and almost immediately a honey-rich delivery of lush, slightly oily malt: wonderful, wonderful stuff! f22 soft oak tempers the barley and a degree of toffee digs in and flattens the...; b23 much, much better cask selection than of old: some real honey casks here. A crock of gold...! 40%

Locke's Aged 9 Years Grand Crew cask no. 700, dist Feb 00, bott Sep 09 db (91.5) n23 how delicate is that squeeze of lime juice on the crystal clear barley? t23.5 that typically Cooley sharp barley thrust lightened by traces of honey; a wonderful silky sheen to the barley, yet a countering bite, too; f22.5 a lovely, though brief, injection of ginger before the vanilla; b22.5 this took me back a few years. Having the three new Locke's lined up was like the days when I went through the Cooley warehouses looking for casks to put into Knappogue. This wasn't far off the style I was searching for. The right age, too. 58.9%. Cooley for The Irish Whisky Society. 233 bottles.

Locke's Aged 10 Years Premier Crew cask no. 713, dist Feb 00, bott Jul 10 db (88) n22 sharp barley, a bit of oak attitude; t23 fabulous malt explosion: barley in several guises and varying weights; f21 some cocoa but the hassle of the oak on the nose translates to a degree of bitterness; b22 the cask does its best to try and spoil the barley fun. Here's a tip: stick to younger malts. Cooley is brilliant and relatively undiscovered at between seven and nine years. And there is less time for cask to bite back... 46%. Cooley for The Irish Whisky Society. 292 bottles.

⁙ **Tullamore Dew Single Malt 10 Years Old** db (91.5) n23 when I was a child in the early '60s, an aunt used to bring me the odd bag of toffee. These toffees were studded with crystalised fruit and opening the bag was always a delight: it was something akin to this...; t23 soft-textured and delicate. Again the toffee is ubiquitous. But the juicy nature of this malt, coupled with a tingly spice, lifts it above the norm; f22.5 the caramels and spices play out the medium finish, perhaps with a hint of butterscotch too; b23 the best whiskey I have ever encountered with a Tullamore label. Furtively complex and daringly delicate. If only they could find a way to minimise the toffee... 40%. William Grant & Sons.

The Tyrconnell bott code L9074 db (86) n21 t22 f22 b21. Sweet, soft, chunky and with a finely spice finale. 40%

The Tyrconnell Aged 10 Years Madeira Finish bott code L8136 db (91) n23 a dull, rumbling marmalade bitter-sweetness; milk toffee and more delicate, twittering marzipan; t23 lush and fat, the sharpness is confined to the odd exploratory fizz of indeterminate fruit: purrs along very pleasantly; f22 toffee raisin; very late spiced apricot; b23 not quite the award-winning effort of a few years back, as those lilting high notes which so complimented the baser fruit tones haven't turned up here. But remains in the top echelon and still much here to delight the palate. 46%

The Tyrconnell Aged 10 Years Port Finish bott code L8167 db (81.5) n21.5 t21 f19 b20. Toffee all the way. 46%

The Tyrconnell Aged 10 Years Sherry Finish bott code L8168 db (84) n22 t21 f21 b20. Like the Port Cask in this present series we have a thick malt that is friendly, toffeed and generally flat. This one, though, does have the odd peak of grapey richness, but you have to travel through a few plateaux to reach them. 46%

Tyrconnell Aged 11 Years sherry cask finish, cask no. V09-10 #336 db **(95)** n23.5 my word! This bodes very well! Black pepper notes ginger up the intense marmalade and honey. Clean and brimming with undisguised intent; t24 magnificent. The palate is left salivating and, if you are not careful, you are left dribbling as a glorious delivery of rich grape and sweetened orange paste offers the juicy introduction while a slow rumbling of ever-increasing spice shakes you to the core; f23.5 long with a slow build up of oils and further fruit. Very late on a succession of bourbon-style honeycomb and molassed notes begin to make their mark; b24 a thrilling virtuoso performance. Those who bought a bottle of this when they had the chance are unlikely to have regretted it. 58.5%. Bottled for Whisky Live 2011.

The Tyrconnell Aged 14 Years cask no. 3179, rotation K92/25 db **(93)** n23 apple blossom (no, honestly!), cedar wood and still remnants of ultra clean barley; t23 refreshingly rich barley offering a shard of golden syrup to its perfectly lush delivery; f23 long, soft vanilla, a touch of tannin and those continuing gentle oils...sigh, what bliss!! b24 By rotation, K92 means it was distilled in 1992. Which just proves this distillery really has come of age, because, make no mistake, this is a belter... 46%

The Tyrconnell Aged 15 Years Single Cask cask no. 1854/92 db **(92.5)** n24 outstanding malt and vanilla interaction: the two poles have met and intertwined to offer maximum complexity; stunning, deft floral notes keep the odd squeak of citrus under control. One of the most beautifully structured Irish noses of the year; t23 like the nose, the weight is outstanding and the march of the juicy barley a treat; soft vanillas and engagingly shy spices fill in the middle ground; f22.5 biscuity sweetness before some exhibition cocoa; b23 infinitely more comfortable in its aging skin a similar malt I tasted in Canada last year. 46%

The Tyrconnell Aged 17 Years Single Cask cask no. 5306/92 db **(87)** n22 Lincoln biscuits; malty; t22 a frisson of sharpness to the simplistic barley; f21.5 soft caramel; b21.5 attractive barley all the way but barely deviates. 46%

The Tyrconnell Single Cask cask no. 9571/1992 db **(85.5)** n23 t21 f20.5 b21. The wonderful citrus notes on the nose are swamped by the oak further down the line. There is no doubting the age of this Cooley! 46%

Clonmel Peated Aged 8 Years db **(86)** n22 t23 f20 b21. Take the toffee away and you would have one hell of an Irish. Claims to be "Pure Pot Still". It isn't (in Irish terms): it's malt. 40%

Craoi na Mona Irish Malt Whiskey **(68)** n16 t18 f17 b17. I'm afraid my Gaelic is slipping these days: I assume Craoi na Mona means "Feinty, badly made smoky malt"... (that's the end of my tasting for the day...) 40%

Glen Dimplex **(88)** n23 solid malt with a hint of honey; charming, blemish-free; t22 gentle development of the malts over simple dusty vanilla; f21 quite dry, spiced and a little toffeed; b22 overall, clean and classically Cooley. 40%

Knappogue Castle 1990 **(91)** n22 t23 f22 b24. For a light whiskey this shows enormous complexity and depth. Genuine balance from nose to finish; refreshing and dangerously more-ish. Entirely from bourbon cask and personally selected and vatted by a certain Jim Murray. 40%. nc. Great Spirits.

Knappogue Castle 1991 **(90)** n22 t23 f22 b23. Offers rare complexity for such a youthful malt especially in the subtle battles that rage on the palate between sweet and dry, malt and oak and so on. The spiciness is a great foil for the malt. Each cask picked and vatted by the author. 40%. nc. Great Spirits.

Knappogue Castle 1992 **(94)** n23 t23 f24 b24. A different Knappogue altogether from the delicate, ultra-refined type. This expression positively revels in its handsome ruggedness and muscular body: a surprisingly bruising yet complex malt that always remains balanced and fresh – the alter-ego of the '90 and '91 vintages. I mean, as the guy who put this whiskey together, what do you expect? But it's not bad if I say so myself and was voted the USA's No. 1 Spirit. Virtually all vanished, but worth getting a bottle if you can find it (I don't receive a penny – I was paid as a consultant!). 40%. nc. Great Spirits.

Knappogue Castle 1993 (see Bushmills)

Knappogue Castle 1994 (see Bushmills)

Magilligan Cooley Pure Pot Still Single Malt **(91)** n22 slightly waxy and honeyed: Cooley at its softest; t22 beautiful arrival of highly intense, spotlessly clean malt. The sweetness level is near perfect; f24 spiceless – unlike the previous bottling. Now just the longest fade-out of malt concentrate in Irish whiskey...and with a touch of honey for good measure; b23 ... or maybe not..!! 43%. Ian MacLeod Distillers.

Magilligan Irish Whiskey Peated Malt 8 Years Old **(89)** n21 old, blackening banana and peat; t23 lush, sweet barley, wonderfully oiled with the softest injection of smoke; f22 long,

long fade with those oils working wonders. The smoke gathers in intensity considerably before dispersing; **b23** such a different animal from the docile creature that formally passed as Magilligan peated. Quite lovely...and very classy. *43%. Ian Macleod Distillers.*

Merry's Single Malt (83) n20 t22 f20 b21. Ultra-clean barley rich nose is found on the early palate. The finish is flat, though. *40%*

Michael Collins Irish Whiskey Single Malt db **(68)** n17 t18 f17 b16. Bloody hell, I thought. Didn't anyone get my message from last year? Apparently not – and it's our fault as the tasting notes above were accidentally edited out before they went in. Sorry. But the caramel in the latest bottling has been upped to take the whisky from deep gold to bronze. Making this among the most over-coloured single malt I have tasted in years. Please guys. For the love of whiskey. Please let us taste exactly what a great malt this could be. *40% (80 proof)*

⋰ **Sainsbury's Single Malt Irish Whiskey** bott code L10083/16 **(87.5)** n22 a lively nose which makes no disguise of its youth: fresh, with the barley out-punching the oak; more than a squeeze of citrus; **t22** sherbet lemon: sharp, piercing and mouth-watering. The barley again makes the most of the limited oak interference for a charming display of light, clean sugars; **f21.5** a touch of caramel and late spice; **b22** classic Cooley showing its big, malty depth. *40%. UK.*

Sainsbury's Dún Léire Aged 8 Years Single Malt (95.5) n24 the score for this crept upwards as I investigated the aroma like the thermometer in a back garden on a bright Summer's day. The first thing to throw itself at you is Seville blood orange, backed up by a clever layering of barley at varying intensity and sweetness; the delicate oak acts as no more than a buffer in between; **t24** just about the perfect mouth feel: silky and melting on the palate. Again, it was an orangey citrus first to show, then again followed by some stunning malt. Everything dissolves: you don't have to do anything but close your eyes and enjoy, indeed: marvel...but it is hard work to stop yourself chewing; **f23.5** dries slightly, but the bitterness threatened on the label fails to materialise...thankfully. The fruit and barley ride off into the sunset in tandem; **b24** when I read "notes of bitter orange" on the label I feared the worst and expected a sulphurous whiskey. Well maybe there is a molecule or two hanging around, but so minor is it, it is impossible to tell exactly where it comes from. This is one of the great whiskeys from Cooley, ever. And as a supermarket Irish...unsurpassed. One of the surprise packages of world whisky for 2010. Magnificent. *40%. Cooley for Sainsbury's Supermarket.*

Shannahan's (92) n23 beautifully young, fresh and zesty: this distillery's best style; **t22** refreshing, clean barley that tries to be little else; **f24** excellent late complexity as some first-class soft vanilla appears; more citrus cleans the palate; **b23** Cooley natural and unplugged: quite adorable. *40%*

Slieve Foy Single Malt Aged 8 Years bott code L9108 **(88)** n23 so delicate, you feel it could snap if you sniffed at it too hard: beautiful lemony malt with fudge and advocaat mix; **t22.5** pure silk. Juicy young barley that just keeps you salivating. Fudge and vanilla begin to edge their way into the frame; **f21** tame spices and toffee; **b21.5** never deviates from its delicate touch. *40%. Cooley for Marks & Spencer.*

⋰ **Vom Fass Cooley Irish Single Malt 8 Years Old (88)** n22 light, clean barley; **t22.5** refreshing, zesty, delicate sugars and malt; **f21.5** a little bit of a tang but good late spices; **b22** a very decent, if undemonstrative, example of the distillery at an age which well suits. *40%*

The Wild Geese Single Malt (85.5) n21.5 t21 f22 b21. "A Rare Blend of Pure Aged Irish Malt Whiskies" says the front label. Yet it is a single malt. Confusing. And very unhelpful to a whiskey public already being totally bamboozled by the bizarre and misguided antics of the Scotch Whisky Association. It is not a blend. It is a mixing of Cooley malt whiskey, as I understand it. The back label's "Smoother Because We Distil it Longer" is also a bit of a blarney. It's made in a pot still and whilst it is true that if you distil faster (by higher temperatures) you could well end up with "hot" whiskey, I am not aware of this being distilled at a significantly slower rate than at either Bushmills or Midleton. Or do they mean the cut of the run from the spirit still is longer, which would impart more oils – not all of them great? Just ignore the Wild Goose chase the labels send you on and enjoy the malt, with all its failings, for what it is (and this is pretty enjoyable in an agreeably rough and ready manner, though not exactly the stiff of Irish whiskey purists): which in this case for all its malt, toffee and delicate smoke, also appears to have more than a slight touch of feints - so maybe they were right all along...!!! *43%. Cooley for Avalon.*

OLD KILBEGGAN

Kilbeggan Distillery Reserve Malt matured in quarter casks, batch no. 1, bott Jun 10 db **(89)** n22.5 wonderfully delicate with a distinctive light nutty sweetness to the malt; the youth is well camouflaged behind a curious (considering you can't get any more inland than this distillery) coastal saltiness and a weak, nondescript fruit; **t22.5** a sugary delivery to boost the thin malty line; quick vanillas and toffee; **f22** mainly fudgy and flat but a light lemon postscript; a late spice buzz; **b22** an endearingly soft malt to see Kilbeggan distillery back into the whiskey world. Shame it has been reduced to 40%, as this one demanded to be at least 46% - indeed, preferably naked - and allowing those delicate, elegant but marginalised characters a chance to bloom. But welcome back...and I look forward to many an evening with me tasting you as you blossom, as I am sure you will. It has been nearly 20 years since I first discovered the beauty of Kilbeggan Distillery and I have countless times since dreamed of that moment. *40%. 1500 bottles. Available only in the distillery gift shop.*

The Spirit of Kilbeggan 1 Month (90.5) n22 t23 f23 b22.5. Wow!! They are really getting to grips with the apparatus. Full bodied and lush small still feel to this but radiating complexity, depth, barley and cocoa in equal measures. The development of the oils really does give this excellent length. Impressed! *65.5%*

The Spirit of Kilbeggan 1 Year (85) n20.5 t21 f22 b21.5. A veritable Bambi of a spirit: a typical one year old malt which, as hard as it tries, just can't locate its centre of gravity. Even so, the richness is impressive and some highly sugared chocolate mousse near the end is a treat. *62.7%*

The Spirit of Kilbeggan 2 Years (84) n20 t21 f22 b21. A tad raw and a little thin. There is some decent balance between oak and malt, but the overall feeling is that the still has not yet been quite mastered. *60.3%*

OLD BUSHMILLS

Bushmills 10 Years Old matured in two woods db **(90) n22.5** for the first time in living memory there is real grape detectable on the nose; it appears to be of the crushed sultana school of fruitiness with a few minor honeyed notes also around; **t23** a fulsome delivery again with the grape at the vanguard; soft vanilla trundles along at Antrim speed; spices arrive with just a touch of cocoa for company; **f22** soft with the work being done by the grape and toffee; **b22.5** this malt has now changed character enormously...and certainly not for the worse. Until recently it was traditionally a chalky effort, dry-ish with the accent on the barley and oak. Now the sherry is the major shareholder in terms of all round shape and depth. And very good sherry butts they are, too. A great leap forward: this is lush and lovely whiskey. *40%*

Bushmills 12 Years Old Distillery Reserve db **(86) n22.5 t22.5 f20 b21.** This version has gone straight for the ultra lush feel. For those who want to take home some 40% abv fruit fudge from the distillery. *40%*

Bushmills Select Casks Aged 12 Years married with Caribbean rum cask db **(95) n23** unusual moist rum and raisin cake effect: effective and just enough spice to deliver extra complexity. Just the very slightest hint of bourbon, too; **t24** adorable malt richness; biscuity and stupendously seasoned yet always remains fresh and mouthwatering. The sweetness is very cleverly controlled; **f24** there are just so many layers to this: the oak is a growing force, but restricts itself to a vanilla topping; **b24** one of the most complex Bushmills in living memory, and probably since it was established in 1784. *40%*

Bushmills Aged 16 Years db **(90) n24.5** one of the most complex fruit aromas in the world: explodingly ripe greengage and gooseberry; those who love sauternes finishes will appreciate the spiced apricot and layered sweetness. Back to top form with a masterful brilliance; **t22.5** the arrival is pretty two-toned: on one hand is a juicy, sensual, fruit-tinged maltiness. By its side is a more bitter toffee kick; throughout is a fabulous spice rhythm; **f21.5** almost treacle tart toffeeness; **b21.5** a confusing malt: we have a nose that half the blenders of the world would give their right nostril for. And then we have a performance on the palate that promises but does not deliver to its expected potential. Lovely whisky, for sure, and it gets a 90, which means this really is the dbs – and I don't mean distillery bottlings. But I wonder if anything can be done about those duller toffee notes. *40%*

Bushmills Rare Aged 21 Years db **(95) n25** one of the cleanest fruit noses of any whiskey in the world and it needs to be: only then can you get a clear enough view and therefore a chance to see what the hell is going on. Grape notes come at you with different intensity in spice and sweetness; barley somehow makes the odd, firm guest appearance and there is a drifting medium roast Java to the oak. But it is the grape which intrigues and entirely seduces... **t23.5** silky, yet charismatic enough to confidently show you the spicier side to its personality early on; the grape ranges from burnt raisin to chocolate sultana; **f23** remains juiced and spiced to the end with a rummy-style bitterness to the sugars; **b23.5** I manage to get round to tasting this, socially, twice a year top whack. But whenever I do, I find myself spending more time nosing this than drinking it. And this sample is absolutely no exception. It almost redefines complexity. But, please, don't forget to taste it. I mean, you can have only so much foreplay... there again, maybe not. *40%*

The Old Bushmills Single Cask 1989 Bourbon Barrel cask 7986 **(88) n**22 **t**23 **f**21 **b**22. Perhaps a better malt than the early nose suggests, but very unusual in style for this distillery and would mark higher but for the debilitating toffee. *56.5%. ncf. Specially selected for Canada.*

The Old Bushmills Distillery Single Cask Bourbon Barrel 1989 cask 8139 db **(88) n**21 **t**23 **f**22 **b**22. Old Bushmills really Springing a surprise with its depth for the age. *56.5%. USA.*

The Old Bushmills Distillery Single Cask Bourbon Barrel 1989 cask no 8140 db **(84) n**20 **t**22 **f**21 **b**21. Quite a fiery number, closed early on but with excellent cocoa finale. *56.5%. USA.*

The Old Bushmills Distillery Single Cask Bourbon Barrel 1989 cask no 8141 db **(88) n**20 **t**23 **f**23 **b**22. The only one of the three bourbon casks to scream "Old Bushmills" at you for its unique style. *56.5%. USA.*

The Old Bushmills Distillery Single Cask Rum Barrel 1989 cask no 7110 db **(81) n**21 **t**20 **f**20 **b**20. Big, biting and hot but some serious malt. *53.7%. USA.*

The Old Bushmills Distillery Single Cask Rum Barrel 1989 cask no 7112 db **(84) n**20 **t**21 **f**22 **b**21. Sweet and attractively simple with excellent late malt. *53.7%. USA.*

The Old Bushmills Single 1989 Rum Barrel cask no. 7115 **(93) n**22 **t**24 **f**23 **b**24. Some in Canada may have seen me taste this for the first time with the country's most effortlessly beautiful and charming tv presenter Nancy Sinclair. I said then I thought we had a great malt on our hands, and a later tasting of it under more controlled – and private – conditions confirmed those initial suspicions. A real honey: elegant, deeply desirable, lip-smacking, memorable and something to get your tongue round and experience slowly at least once in your lifetime. And the whiskey's not bad, either... *53.7%. ncf. Canada.*

The Old Bushmills Distillery Single Cask Sherry Butt 1989 db cask no 7429 **(90) n**22 passion fruit among the citrus. Sensual and gentle; **t**22 gets into a malty stride from go then a slow burning sherry fuse; **f**23 delightful finish that is long, vanilla-rich but with the most subtle interwoven fruit and barley and natural caramel; **b**23 charismatic, charming, self-confident and supremely elegant. *53.7%. USA.*

The Old Bushmills Distillery Single Cask Sherry Butt 1989 cask no 7430 db **(91) n**21 slightly sweaty armpit but a good malt recovery **t**23 sweet, enormously malty for a sherry-influenced dram **f**24 mildly salty, with many layers of sweet malt and spice that go on almost endlessly **b**23 this is a massively complex and striking Bushmills well worth finding: casks 7429 and 7430 could be almost twins...!! *53.7%. USA.*

Clontarf Single Malt (90.5) n23 barley concentrate with a squeeze of orange and distant juniper; **t**23 beautifully fresh barley, almost barley sugar, with light sinews of oak; **f**22 long, intense barley but with the vanilla standing tallest at the death as welcome spices finally gather; **b**22.5 beautiful in its simplicity, this has eschewed complexity for delicious minimalism; *40%. Clontarf Irish Whiskey Co.*

The Irishman Single Malt bottle no. E2496 **(83) n**20 **t**21 **f**21 **b**21. Highly pleasant malt but the coffee and toffee on the finish underline a caramel-style whiskey which may, potentially, offer so much more. *40%. Hot Irishman Ltd.*

Knappogue Castle 1990 *(see Cooley)*
Knappogue Castle 1991 *(see Cooley)*
Knappogue Castle 1992 *(see Cooley)*

Knappogue Castle 1993 (91) n22 **b**22 **f**23 **b**24. A malt of exceptional character and charisma. Almost squeaky clean but proudly contains enormous depth and intensity. The chocolate finish is an absolute delight. Quite different and darker than any previous Knappogue but not dwarfed in stature to any of the previous three vintages. Created by yours truly. *40%. nc. Great Spirits.*

Knappogue Castle 1994 lot no. L6 **(89) n**23 **t**24 **f**20 **b**22. A wonderful whiskey in the Knappogue tradition, although this one was not done by its creator. That said, it does have an Achilles heel: the finish. This is the most important bit to get right, especially as this is the oldest Knappogue yet. But not enough attention has been paid to getting rid of the oak-induced bitterness. *40%. Castle Brands.*

Knappogue Castle 1995 bott 2007 **(88) n**23 banana skins and custard; soft barley but drier and dustier than any other Knappogue nose; **t**22 early mouthwatering barley fades; a sugary sheen is quickly usurped by an impatient oaky bitterness; **f**21 dry-ish and bitter but with a soft barley residue; some ultra late spices; **b**22 a charming malt showing Old Bushmills in very unusual colours. Lacking the charisma, clarity and complexity of the first Knappogues simply because they were designed to extol the virtues of young (8-year-old) malt. Naturally, extra oak has crept in here, forcing out – as it must – the sharpness and vitality of the barley. A decent effort, but perhaps more should have been done to keep out the aggressive bitterness. *40%*

Single Grain
COOLEY

Cooley 1991 16 Years Old 1st fill bourbon cask no. 12441, dist Nov 91, bott Feb 08 **(89.5)** n22.5 some solid oak, but a fruity, soft oiliness smooths the ruffled feathers; t23 a sweet silkiness with bite: love it!! f22 gentle fade with the corn offering a sweeter edge to the oak; b22 it hardly makes sense that Cooley grain appears to absorb the years better than their malt! Great stuff. 46%. Milroy's of Soho. 264 bottles.

Greenore 6 Year Old bott code L9015 db **(89)** n23.5 even at such tender age this has more to do with bourbon than Irish: gentle, sweet red liquorice, toffee apple, and hot even the slightest hint of bitterness...; t22.5...but tastes of pure Canadian, especially with the over-enthusiastic caramels; sweet with an amazingly yielding texture; f21 lightly burnt toast and more toffee; b22 very enjoyable whiskey. But two points: cut the caramel and really see the baby sing. And secondly, as a "Small Batch" bottling, how about putting a batch number on the label...? 40%. Cooley.

Greenore 8 Year Old bott code L8190 db **(86.5)** n20 t22 f23 b21.5. The vague hint of butyric on the nose is more than amply compensated by the gradual build up to something rather larger on the palate than you might have expected (and don't be surprised if the two events are linked). The corn oil is almost a meal in itself and the degree of accompanying sugar and corn flour is a treat. 40%. Cooley.

Greenore 10 Years Old dist 1997, bott 2007 db **(87.5)** n22 pretty standard Canadian style: plenty of corn digging in, a touch of toffee sweetness and a degree of bite; t22 lightly oiled corn and vanilla; the oak dips in and out; f21.5 pleasantly sweet at times yet amazingly docile, knowing what this grain is capable of... b22 well made grain and always enjoyable but perhaps not brought to its fullest potential due to some less than inspired oak. 40%. 3000 bottles.

Greenore 15 Years Old bott code L8044 **(90)** n23 the depth of ingrained oak mixed with corn meals you in the direction of Canada; a few spicy folds and golden syrup edges ensure a lovely simple elegance; t22.5 just the right dosage of spice to counter the sugars; f22 oaky bitterness outgunned by those marauding dark sugars; b22.5 the advent of the Kilbeggan 15 reminded us that there must be some grain of that age around, and here to prove it is a superb bottling of the stuff which, weirdly, is a lot better than the blend. Beautiful. 43%

⁘ **Greenore 18 Years Old** db **(91)** n22.5 like a fine Canadian there is superb harmony between the vanilla and soft oils. A custard tart sweetness; t22.5 lush, silky, improbably mouth-watering; f23 a really lovely spice zips around, balancing charmingly with the sugars and oils; b23 this continuous still at Cooley should be marked by the State as an Irish national treasure. One of the most complex grains you'll ever find, even when heading into uncharted territory like this one. 46%. ncf. 4000 bottles.

Blends

Bushmills 1608 anniversary edition **(94)** n23.5 the grain barely gets a look in as the malt and oak dominates from the first whiff. Toasted oak and bread form a dense background, sweetened by muscovado sugar melting on porridge; t23.5 now that's different: how many blends do you know kick off with an immediate impact of sweetness that offers about four or five different levels of intensity, and each accompanied by a toasted oakiness? Very, very different, charming, fascinating...and delicious; f23 long, mocha with the emphasis on the coffee and then, at the very end some firm grains at last get a toe-hold; b24 this whiskey is talking an entirely different language to any Irish blend I have come across before, or any blend come to that. Indeed, nosed blind you'd not even regard it a blend: the malt calls to you like a Siren. But perhaps it is the crystal malt they have used here which is sending out such unique signals, helping the whiskey to form a thick cloak of roasty, toasty, burnt toffeed, bitter-sweetness which takes your breath away. What a fabulous whiskey! And whether it be a malt or blend, who cares? Genius whiskey is genius whiskey. 40%

Bushmills 1608 400th Anniversary (83) n21 t21.5 f20 b20.5. Thin-bodied, hard as nails and sports a peculiarly Canadian feel. 46%. Diageo.

Bushmills Black Bush (91) n23 a firmer aroma with less evident malt and the spices have also taken a back seat. But the gentle, toffee apple and night garden scent reveal that the malt-grain interaction is still wonderfully alluring; t23 busy delivery, much softer than the nose indicates with the malt first to show. The oak is no slouch either, offering excellent spices; some burnt, raisiny notes help confirm this is Black Bush on song; f21.5 still over the top caramel interfering but not before some honeycomb makes a small stand; b23.5 this famous old blend may be under new management and even blender. But still the high quality, top-notch complexity rolls around the glass and your palate. As beautiful as ever. 40%

Bushmills Original (80) n19 t21 f20 b20. Remains one of the hardest whiskeys on the circuit with the Midleton grain at its most unflinching. There is a sweeter, faintly maltier edge to this now while the toffee and biscuits qualities remain. 40%

Cassidy's Distiller's Reserve bott code L8067 **(84.5)** n21.5 t22 f20 b21. Some salivating malt on flavour-exploding delivery, but all else tame and gentle. 40%. Cooley.

Clancey's bott code L8025 **(87)** n22 sweet malt bounces off the firmer grain; young, lively and a touch floral; t21 early toffeed delivery then a parade of vanilla and varied grains, barley most certainly included; f22 burnt fudge and some teasing spice; b22 remains an excellent blend for all the toffee. The spice balance excels. 40%. Cooley for Wm Morrison.

Clontarf Classic Blend (86) n18 t23 f23 b22. This has to be treated as a new whiskey. Many moons back I created this as a 100% grain from Cooley, a velvet-soft job of real subtlety. These days, with me having no involvement, the whiskies are from Irish Distillers. This is no longer all grain, though the malt content is no more than fractional. And it really underscores the difference in style between Midleton and Cooley grain. For every degree Colley is soft and yielding, Midleton is unremittingly rigid. The nose (though not the taste) is recognizable to devotees of White Bush and Paddy. Which means aroma-wise, with the caramel, it's pretty austere stuff. But you cannot fault the delivery which is crisp, salivating and offering surprising sweetness and big citrus. Not bad once you adapt: in fact, seriously entertaining.

⠿⠿ **Delaney's (85.5)** n20 t21.5 f22 b22. Young, clean, citrusy, refreshing and proud. Thoroughly enjoyable and dangerously moreish. 40%. Cooley for Co-operative UK.

Delaney's Special Reserve (84) n21.5 t20.5 f22 b21. An attractive blend with a big late spicy blast. The toffee dominates for long periods. 40%. Cooley for Co-operative Group.

Feckin Irish Whiskey (81) n20 t21 f20 b20. Tastes just about exactly the feckin same as the Feckin Strangford Gold... 40%. The Feckin Drinks Co. ⊙

Golden Irish bott code L7064 **(93)** n23 do I nose before me spice? And syrup-dripping coconut candy tobacco from childhood days? Yep, that and citrussy vanilla; t23 near perfect mouthfeel helps stoke up the malt intensity. The grain simply moulds into the palate bringing with it an odd twist of cocoa even by the middle; f23.5 milky chocolate and Demerara make for a long, pleasing, almost breakfast cereal-type finale; b23.5 by far one of the most enjoyable Irish blends around. Simple, but what it does, it does well – and deliciously well at that...!! 40%. Cooley.

The Irishman Rare Cask Strength bott 2010 **(81.5)** n20 t22.5 f19 b20. Fabulous crescendo of weighty malt on delivery. But just too much bitterness and toffee hits this one. 53%. Hot Irishman Ltd. 2850 bottles.

The Irishman Rare Cask Strength bott 2009 **(85.5)** n22 t21.5 f21 b21. A lovely, brawny malt which for all its strength feels that it has never quite slipped out of third gear. A chewy sweetness dominates but the caramel certainly has clipped this whiskey's wings. 56%. Hot Irishman Ltd. 1,800 bottles.

The Irishman Rare Cask Strength (93.5) n23 a wonderful combination of soft bourbony notes and a light malty sub-plot. No shortage of honey and a lighter sprinkling of the ginger which, if memory serves me correctly, is a feature of the mere mortal 40% bottling; t24 absolutely brilliant! It's not just the strength, although there are few whiskies that are so enormously affected. No, it's the immediate balance with the grains going in strong, but of such high quality and rich character that the gentle bourbon persuasion continues; softly oiled, very lightly malted, the arrival of the drier oak offers the perfect bitter-sweet foil; f23 long, chocolate rich and sophisticatedly spiced; b23.5 just so wonderful to come across a full strength blend. Better still when that blend happens to be as quite beautiful and characterful as this. A hot whisky alright: this should be burning a way into most blend lovers' homes. Quite exceptional, to be sure. 56%. Hot Irishman Ltd. 1400 bottles.

⠿⠿ **The Irishman Rare Cask Strength** bott 2011 **(94.5)** n23 flecks of honey intermingle perfectly with the lightest blush of greengage. A touch of bourbon liquorice is sweetened by a hint of molasses; a piquancy is added by a sprinkle of salt; seemingly light, yet weighty...; t24 excellent body with the soft barley circling around the more rigid middle. This profound gentle-firm balance is the main feature, but those salty sugars also dazzle. Egg custard tart middle makes for a friendlier environment; light honey is threaded throughout; f23.5 more vanilla and custard, but now some excellent light spices, too; b24 the back labels of Hot Irishman whiskeys are always entertaining, not least for their unique use of the English language. A free Jim Murray's Whisky Bible 2012 for the first person to e-mail in and tell us what the cock-up is on this label. Back to the whiskey: this blend of malt whisky and Pure Irish Pot still, is a mildly more lilting, more lightly coloured, version of Writer's Tears. And, just like the first bottling, a must-have stunner. 53%. Hot Irishman. 2400 bottles.

The Irishman Superior Irish Whiskey bott code L6299L059 **(93)** n23 chunky caramel perhaps, but the apple is green and inviting; even an inclusion of soft manuka honey and ginger – most un-Irish; t23 lush, with a distinct malt carabee before the caramel and oaky spice arrive; f23 those spices really tick, accentuated by the contrasting molasses and more honey but doused in vanilla; b24 what a quite wonderful blend: not of the norm for those that have recently come onto the market and there is much more of the Irish Distillers about this than most. Forget about the smoke promised in the tasting notes on the label...it gives you everything else but. And that is one hell of a lot!! 40%. Hot Irishman Ltd.

Jameson (95) n24.5 Swoon...bizarrely shows even more Pot Still character than the Redbreast I tasted yesterday. Flinty to the point of cracking. The sherry is there but on reduced terms, allowing the firm grain to amplify the unmalted barley: truly brilliant; t24 mouth-watering delivery and then wave upon wave of diamond-hard barley and grain; the odd eclectic layer of something sweetish and honeyed, but this is eye-watering stuff; f22.5 an annoying touch of caramel creeps in, costing points, but even beyond that you still cannot other than be charmed by the layering of cocoa, barley and light grape; b24 I thought I had detected in bottlings I had found around the world a very slight reduction in the Pot Still character that defines this truly classic whiskey. So I sat down with a fresh bottle in more controlled conditions...and was blown away as usual. The sharpness of the PS is vivid and unique; the supporting grain of the required crispness. Fear not: this very special whiskey remains in stunning, truly wondrous form. 40%

Jameson 12 Years Old Special Reserve (88) n22 caramel, lazy sherry, musty; enlivened by a splash of sharper pot still; t23 the grape shows little sign of shyness, aided by a bitter-sweet element; good body and layering; f21 dulls out as the caramel arrives; dusty, drying; b22 much more sherry than of late and the pot still makes inroads, too. Just needs to lose some of the caramel effect; 40%

Jameson 18 Years Old Limited Reserve eighth batch bott code JJ18-8 **(91)** n23 pure bourbon as oak dispenses myriad honey-leather-hickory notes with the Pot Still doing the job of the fruitier "rye"; t22.5 firm and juicy, gentle spice but a caramel-trimmed middle; f22.5 the redoubling of the juicier barley notes cuts through the vanilla and caramel to set up a long, delicately weighted finale; b22.5 the astonishing degree of bourbon on the nose thankfully doesn't make it to the palate where Ireland rather than Kentucky rules. 40%

Jameson Gold Reserve (88) n22 a touch of menthol has crept into this much weightier nose: creaks with age as bourbony elements drift in and out of the grape; t23 sweet, sexily spiced delivery; hardens towards the middle but the grains are surprisingly lush and softly oiled; f20 glutinous and plodding; b22 enjoyable, but so very different: an absolute re-working with all the lighter, more definitively sweeter elements shaved mercilessly while the thicker oak is on a roll. Some distance from the masterpiece it once was. 40%

Jameson Rarest 2007 Vintage Reserve (96) n24.5 the crispest, cleanest, most beautifully defined of all the Jameson family: orange peel, hickory, spotted dog pudding, lavender – they're all there mushed around and in near-perfect proportions; t24 ditto the arrival with the mouth puckering under the onslaught of very old Pot Still: the bitter-sweet sharpness one would expect from this is there in spades; oak present and correct and edged in thin muscovado layer; f23.5 vanilla by the barrel-load, pithy fruit and softly spiced barley b24 is this the whiskey where we see a blender truly come of age. Tall green hats off to Billy Leighton who has, as all the better blenders did in the past, worked his way from quality-testing barrels on the dumping room floor to the lab. With this stupendous offering we have a blender in clover for he has earned his Golden Shamrocks. If the blending alone wasn't stellar enough, then making this a 46%, non chill-filtered offering really does put the tin hat on it (so Billy: you really have been listening to me over the years...!!!) This is truly great whiskey, among the pantheon of the world's finest. 46%

Jameson Signature Reserve (93) n23.5 adore the sharp citrus notes which bore, shrapnel-like, into the firm, though lighter than normal pure Pot Still: supremely balanced; the degree of honey is exemplary...and enticing; t23.5 gossamer light delivery despite the obvious Pot Still presence. Some caramel momentarily dulls the middle but the flavours return for a beautifully constructed middle with alternating waves of citrus and pot still, occasionally honeyed, much as the nose predicts; the grains are softer than an Irish bog and simply dissolve without fuss: most un-Midleton f22.5 beautiful: the vanilla does pulse with acacia honey; the Pot still stands firm and lightly fruity; b23.5 be assured that Signature, with its clever structuring of delicate and inter-weaving flavours, says far more about the blender, Billy Leighton, than it does John Jameson. 40%. Irish Distillers.

⋄ **Kellan** American oak cask **(84)** n21 t22 f20 b21. Safe whisky which is clean, sweet and showing many toffeed attributes. Decent spices, too. 40% (80 Proof). Cooley.

Kilbeggan bott code L7091 **(86)** n21 t22 f21.5 b21.5. A much more confident blend by comparison with that faltering one of the last few years. Here, the malts make a significant drive towards increasing the overall complexity and gentle citrus style. *40%. Cooley.*

Kilbeggan 15 Years Old bott code L7048 **(85.5)** n21.5 t22 f21 b21. My word! 15 years, eh? How time flies! And on the subject of flying, surely I have winged my way back to Canada and am tasting a native blend. No, this is Irish albeit in sweet, deliciously rounded form. However, one cannot help feeling that the dark arts have been performed, as in an injection of caramel, which, as well as giving that Canadian feel has also probably shaved off some of the more complex notes to middle and finish. Even so, a sweet, silky experience. *40%. Cooley.*

⬩⬩⬩ **Kilbeggan 18 Year Old** db **(89)** n23 enough caramel to launch a thousand Mars bars. But beneath it can be found a wonderful Jaffa cake orange/chocolate theme and the most delicate of spices; t21.5 that caramel does no harm in ensuring a lush texture. A string of light sugary notes deal with any encroaching oak; f22.5 dries, allowing the spices to return for the excellent vanilla finale; b22 although the impressive bottle lavishly claims "From the World's Oldest Distillery" I think one can take this as so much Blarney. It certainly had my researcher going, who lined this up for me under the Old Kilbeggan distillery, a forgivable mistake and one I think he will not be alone in making. This, so it appears on the palate, is a blend. From the quite excellent Cooley distillery, and it could be that whiskey used in this matured at Kilbeggan... which is another thing entirely. As for the whiskey: apart from some heavy handedness on the toffee, it really is quite a beautiful and delicate thing. *40%*

Kilgeary bott code L8063 **(79)** n20 t20 f19 b20. There has always, and still proudly is, something strange about this blend. Cold tea on the nose and a bitter bite to the finish, sandwiches a brief flirtation with something sweet. *40%. Cooley.*

Locke's bott code L8056 **(85.5)** n21 t22 f21.5 b21. Now, there you go!! Since I last really got round to analysing this one it has grown from a half-hearted kind of a waif to something altogether more gutsy and muscular. Sweeter, too, as the malts and grains combine harmoniously. A clean and pleasant experience with some decent malt fingerprints. *40%*

Michael Collins A Blend (77) n19 t20 f19 b19. Michael Collins was known as the "big fellow". This pleasant, impressively spiced dram, might have enjoyed the same epithet had it not surrendered to and then been strangled by caramel on the finish. *40% (80 proof). Cooley.*

Midleton Distillery Reserve (85) n22 t22 f20 b21. A whiskey which, for all its muscovado sweetness offers some memorable barley moments. *40%. Irish Distillers Midleton Distillery only. Was once bottled as Jameson Distillery Reserve exclusive to Midleton. Changes character slightly with each new vatting. This one is some departure.*

Midleton Very Rare 1984 (70) n19 t18 f17 b16. Disappointing with little backbone or balance. *40%. Irish Distillers.*

Midleton Very Rare 1985 (77) n20 t20 f18 b19. Medium-bodied and oily, this is a big improvement on the initial vintage. *40%. Irish Distillers.*

Midleton Very Rare 1986 (79) n21 t20 f18 b20. A very malty Midleton richer in character than previous vintages. *40%. Irish Distillers.*

Midleton Very Rare 1987 (77) n20 t19 f19 b19. Quite oaky at first until a late surge of excellent pot still. *40%. Irish Distillers.*

Midleton Very Rare 1988 (86) n23 t21 f21 b21. A landmark MVR as it is the first vintage to celebrate the Irish pot-still style. *40%. Irish Distillers.*

Midleton Very Rare 1989 (87) n22 t22 f22 b21. A real mouthful but has lost balance to achieve the effect. *40%. Irish Distillers.*

Midleton Very Rare 1990 (93) n23 carrying on from where the '89 left off. The pot still doesn't drill itself so far into your sinuses, perhaps: more of a firm massage; t23 solid pot still again. There is a pattern now: pot still first, sweeter, maltier notes second, pleasant grains third and somewhere, imperceptibly, warming spices fill in the gaps; f24 long and Redbreast-like in character. Spices seep from the bourbon casks; b23 astounding whiskey: one of the vintages every true Irish whiskey lover should hunt for. *40%. Irish Distillers.*

Midleton Very Rare 1991 (76) n19 t20 f19 b18. After the Lord Mayor's Show, relatively dull and uninspiring. *40%. Irish Distillers.*

Midleton Very Rare 1992 (84) n20 t20 f23 b21. Superb finish with outstanding use of feisty grain. *40%. Irish Distillers.*

Midleton Very Rare 1993 (88) n21 t22 f23 b22. big, brash and beautiful – the perfect way to celebrate the 10th-ever bottling of MVR. *40%. Irish Distillers.*

Midleton Very Rare 1994 (87) n22 pot-still characteristics not unlike the '93 but with extra honey and ginger; t22 the honeyed theme continues with malt arriving in a lush sweetness; f21 oily and a spurt of sharper, harder pot still; b22 another different style of MVR, one of amazing lushness. *40%. Irish Distillers.*

Midleton Very Rare 1995 (90) n23 big pot still with fleeting honey; t24 enormous! Bitter, sweet and tart all together for a chewable battle of apple and barley. Brilliant; b21 some caramel calms proceedings, but Java coffee goes a little way to restoring complexity. b22 they don't come much bigger than this. Prepare a knife and fork to battle through this one. Fabulous. 40%. Irish Distillers.

Midleton Very Rare 1996 (82) n21 t22 f19 b20. The grains lead a soft course, hardened by subtle pot still. Just missing a beat on the finish, though. 40%. Irish Distillers.

Midleton Very Rare 1997 (83) n22 t21 f19 b21. The piercing pot still fruitiness of the nose is met by a countering grain of rare softness on the palate. Just dies on the finish when you want it to make a little speech. Very drinkable. 40%. Irish Distillers.

Midleton Very Rare 1999 (89) n21 malt and toffee: as sleepy as a nighttime drink; t23 stupendous grain, soft enough to absorb some pounding malt; f22 spices arrive as the blend hardens and some pot still finally battles its way through the swampy grain; b23 one of the maltiest Midletons of all time: a superb blend. 40%. Irish Distillers.

Midleton Very Rare 2000 (85) n22 t21 f21 b21. An extraordinary departure even by Midleton's eclectic standards. The pot still is like a distant church spire in an hypnotic Fen landscape. 40%. Irish Distillers.

Midleton Very Rare 2001 (79) n21 t20 f18 b20. Extremely light but the finish is slightly on the bitter side. 40%. Irish Distillers.

Midleton Very Rare 2002 (79) n20 t22 f18 b19. The nose is rather subdued and the finish is likewise toffee-quiet and shy. There are some fabulous middle moments, some of flashing genius, when the pot still and grain combine for a spicy kick, but the finish really is lacklustre and disappointing. 40%. Irish Distillers.

Midleton Very Rare 2003 (84) n22 t22 f19 b21. Beautifully fruity on both nose and palate (even some orange blossom on aroma). But the delicious spicy richness that is in mid launch on the tastebuds is cut short by caramel on the middle and finish. A crying shame, but the best Midleton for a year or two. 40%. Irish Distillers.

Midleton Very Rare 2004 (82) n21 t21 f19 b21. Yet again caramel is the dominant feature, though some quite wonderful citrus and spice escape the toffeed blitz. 40%.

Midleton Very Rare 2005 (92) n23 t24 f22 b23. OK, you can take this one only as a rough translation. The sample I have worked from here is from the Irish Distillers blending lab, reduced to 40% in mine but without caramel added. And, as Midleton Very Rares always are at this stage, it's an absolute treat. Never has such a great blend suffered so in the hands of colouring and here the chirpiness of the pot still and élan of the honey (very Jameson Gold Label in part) show just what could be on offer given half the chance. Has wonderful natural colour and surely it is a matter of time before we see this great whiskey in its natural state. 40%

Midleton Very Rare 2006 (92) n22 real punch to the grain, which is there in force and offering a bourbony match for the pot still; t24 stupendously crisp, then a welter of spices nip and sting ferociously around the palate; the oaky coffee arrives early and with clarity while the barley helps solidify the rock-hard barley; f23 usually by now caramel intervenes and spoils, but not this time and again it's the grain which really stars; b23 as raw as a Dublin rough-house and for once not overly swamped with caramel. An uncut diamond. 40%

Midleton Very Rare 2007 (83) n20 t22 f20 b21. Annoyingly buffeted from nose to finish by powering caramel. Some sweeter wisps do escape but the aroma suggests Canadian and insufficient Pot Still gets through to make this a Midleton of distinction. 40%. Irish Distillers

Midleton Very Rare 2008 (88.5) n22 t23 f21.5 b22. A dense bottling which offers considerably more than the 2007 Vintage. Attractive, very drinkable and without the caramel it might really have hit the heights. 40%. Irish Distillers.

Millars Special Reserve bott code L8069 (86) n21 t22 f21.5 b21.5. Now that's some improvement on the last bottling of this I found, with spices back with abandon and grains ensuring a fine mouthfeel. Even the chocolate fudge at the death is a treat. 40%. Cooley.

Morrisons Irish Whiskey bott code L10028 (78) n19 t20 f19 b20. Sweet, pleasant and inoffensive. 40%. Wm Morrison Supermarket.

Paddy (74) n18.5 t20 f17.5 b18. Cleaned its act up a little. Even a touch of attractive citrus on the nose and delivery. But where does that cloying sweetness come from? As bland as an Irish peat bog but, sadly, nothing like so potentially tasty. 40%. Irish Distillers.

Powers (91) n23 rugged pot still and beefed up by some pretty nippy grain; t24 brilliant mouth arrival, one of the best in all Ireland: the pot still shrieks and attacks every available tastebud; f22 pulsing spices and mouthwatering, rock-hard pot still. The sweetness is a bit unusual but you can just chew that barley; b22 is it any coincidence that in this bottling the influence of the caramel has been significantly reduced and the whiskey is getting back to its old, brilliant self? I think not. Classic stuff. 40%. Irish Distillers.

Powers Gold Label (87) n22 Powers? Really? I had to look twice and re-pour the sample to ensure this was the right stuff. Where is the clunking pot still? Soft, grainy caramel; t22 attractively sweet with a distinct candy tobacco golden syrup but a serious departure from the ancient style. It's grain all the way, soft and silky as she goes; f21 more lightness and caramel; maybe some semblance of pot still but you have to hunt to find it; b22 the solid pot still, the very DNA of what made Powers, well, Powers is vanishing in front of our very noses. Yes, still some pot still around, but nothing like so pronounced in the way that made this, for decades, a truly one-off Irish and one of the world greats. Still delightful and with many charms but the rock hard pot still effect is sadly missed. What is going on here? 40%. Irish Distillers.

Redbreast Blend (88) n23 some genuinely telling pot-still hardness sparks like a flint off the no less unyielding grain. Just love this; t23 very sweet and soft, the grain carrying a massive amount of vanilla. Barley offers some riches, as does spice; f20 a climbdown from the confrontational beginnings, but pretty delicious all the same; b22 really impressed with this one-off bottling for Dillons the Irish wine merchants. Must try and get another bottle before they all vanish. 40%. Irish Distillers for Dillone IR (not to be confused with Redbreast 12 Years Old Pure Pot Still)

Sainsbury's Blended Irish Whiskey (86.5) n22 t22 f21 b21.5. A beautifully relaxed blend showing pretty clearly – literally, thanks to an admirable lack of colouring - just how good the Cooley grain whiskey is even at no great age. Clean with a deceptively busy and intense flavour profile. Far too good for the cola the back label says this should go with... 40%. UK. ⊙ ⊙

St Patrick bott code L030907 (77) n19 t20 f19 b19. Good grief! No prisoners here as we have either a bitter oakiness or mildly cloying sweetness, rarely working in tandem. A few gremlins for the Kremlin. 40%. Cooley for Russia.

Strangford Gold (81) n20 t21 f20 b20. A simplistic, exceptionally easy drinking blend with high quality grain offering silk to the countering spice but caramel flattens any malt involvement. 40%. The Feckin Drinks Co.

Tesco Special Reserve Irish Whiskey bott code L8061 (89.5) n21.5 gentle caramels try – and fail – to intervene as the vivid malts and seductive grains fuse; t23.5 Irish blends don't come any softer: Cooley grain is as good as it gets anywhere in the word and here embrace and amplify the malts wonderfully; f22 gentle, soft, sweet and clean; b22.5 a cracker of a blend which allows the malts full scope to do their juicy bit. Possibly more malt than usual for a Cooley blend, but as they say: every little bit helps. 40%. Cooley.

Tullamore Dew (85) n22 t21.5 f20.5 b21. The days of the throat being savaged by this one appear to be over. Much more pot still character from nose to finish and the rough edges remain, attractively, just that. 40%. Campbell & Cochrane Group.

Tullamore Dew 10 Years Old (81.5) n21 t21.5 f19 b20. A bright start from this new kid on the Tullamore block. Soft fruit and harder pot still make some kind of complexity, but peters out at the death. 40%. Campbell & Cochrane Group.

Tullamore Dew 12 Years Old (84.5) n21.5 t21.5 f20 b21.5. Silky thanks to some excellent Midleton grain: there are mouthwatering qualities here that make the most of the soft spices and gentle fruit. An improved whiskey, if still somewhat meek and shy. 40%. Campbell & Cochrane Group.

⁖ **Tullamore Dew Black 43** (85) n19 t22 f22.5 b21.5. "Black". Now there's an original name for a new whiskey. Don't think it'll catch on, personally: after all, who has ever heard of a whisky being called "This or That" Black...?? But the whiskey might. Once you get past the usual Tullamore granite-like nose, here even more unyielding than usual, some rather engaging and complex (and especially spicy) things happen, though the caramel does its best to neuter them. 43%. William Grant & Sons.

Tullamore Dew Heritage (78) n20 t21 f18 b19. Tedious going with the caramel finish a real turn off. 40.0%. Campbell & Cochrane Group.

⁖ **Waitrose Irish Whiskey** (86.5) n21.5 t22 f21.5 b21.5. Cooley's grain whiskey, about as good a grain made anywhere in the world, is in fine voice here. Pity some toffee stifles it slightly. 40%

Walker & Scott Irish Whiskey "Copper Pot Distilled" (83) n20 t22 f20 b21. A collectors' item. This charming, if slightly fudgy-finished blend was made by Cooley as the house Irish for one of Britain's finest breweries. Sadly, someone put "Copper Pot Distilled" on the label, which, as it's a blend, can hardly be the case. And even if it wasn't a blend, would still be confusing in terms of Irish whiskey, there not being any traditional Irish Pot Still, that mixture of malted and unmalted barley. So Sam's, being one of the most traditional brewers in Britain, with the next bottling changed the label by dropping all mention of pot still. Top marks, chaps! The next bottling can be seen below. 40%. Sam Smith's.

Walker & Scott Irish Whiskey (85) n21 t22 f21 b21. Oddly, sharper grain has helped give his some extra edge through the toffee. A very decent blend. 40%

The Whisky Fair Connemara 2001 bott 2009 **(90.5) n22** a golden toast dryness to the honeyed smoke; **t23.5** goes into overdrive with some unexpected and unusual oils bulking up the sweetness; the drier points are hammered home with spicy intent; **f22.5** vanilla and butterscotch with a hazelnut oil topping still can't quite master the powering phenols; **b23** not your Irish bog-standard Connemara: extra doses of complexity and oil – not two things which normally go hand-in-hand. 59.2%. The Whisky Fair, Germany.

The Wild Geese Classic Blend (80.5) n20 t21 f19.5 b19. Easy going, pretty neutral and conservative. If you are looking for zip, zest and charisma you've picked the wrong goose (see below). 40%. Cooley for Avalon.

The Wild Geese Limited Edition Fourth Centennial (93) n23 sensationally clean and with the citrus really taking a starring role; vanillas abound, but in the soft, playful form; light and just so enticing; **t23.5** barley notes peck around the tastebuds entirely unfettered by more tactile and heavier elements; lithe and lean, there is no fat on this goose and the vanilla lives up to its best expectation given on the nose while the mouth is drenched in salivating promises – simply stunning; **f23** just so light, the clarity of the barley sugar and vanilla leaves you purring; **b23.5** a limited edition of unlimited beauty. One of the lightest, subtle, intriguing and quite simply disarming Irish whiskeys on the market. As a bird and whiskey lover, this is one goose that I shall be looking out for. 43%. Cooley for Avalon.

The Wild Geese Rare Irish (89.5) n22 some toffee, yes, but the excellence of the vanilla is there to behold; just a light layering of barley but the gentle citrus caresses with the more exquisite touch... **t23** superb arrival on the palate; the grain displays nothing other than excellence in both weight and control, and while the oaks and caramels are a tad bitter, the sweeter barley compensates wonderfully; **f22** a silky, almost metallic sheen to the finale which complements the drying vanillins; **b22.5** just love this. The Cooley grain is working sublimely and dovetails with the malt in the same effortless way wild geese fly in perfect formation. A treat. 43%. Cooley for Avalon.

Writers Tears (93) n23.5 a glossy Pot Still character: rather than the usual fruity firmness, the recognisable Pot Still traits are shrouded in soft honey tones which dovetail with lightening kumquat-citrus tones. Quite a curious, but always deliciously appealing animal...; **t24** works beautifully well: the arrival is an alternating delivery of hard and soft waves, the former showing a more bitter, almost myopic determination to hammer home its traditional pot still standpoint; the sweeter, more yielding notes dissolve with little or no resistance, leaving an acacia honeyed trail; towards the middle a juicier malt element mingles with soft vanilla but the Pot Still character never goes away; **f22** relatively short with perhaps the Pot Still, with an old-fashioned cough sweet fruitiness, lingering longest, though it does retain its honeyed accompaniment for the most part; **b23.5** now that really was different. The first mix of pure Pot Still and single malt I have knowingly come across in a commercial bottling, but only because I wasn't aware of the make up of last year's Irishman Blend. The malt, like the Pot Still, is, I understand from proprietor Bernard Walsh, from Midleton, but the two styles mixed shows a remarkably similar character to when I carried out an identical experiment with pure pot still and Bushmills the best part of a decade ago. A success and hopefully not a one off. Which is more than I can say for the label, a whiskey collectors – sorry, collector's – item in its own right. There is a wonderfully Irish irony that a whiskey dedicated to Ireland's extraordinary literary heritage should be represented by a label, even a brand name, so punctually inept; it's almost brilliant. The reason for the Writers (sic) Tears, if from the spirits of James Joyce, Samuel Beckett, George Bernard Shaw, Oscar Wilde and perhaps even Maurice Walsh, whose grandson became a legendary blender at Irish Distillers, will be open to debate: we will never know whether they laughed or cried. As far as the actual whiskey is concerned, though, I am sure they, to a man, would have no hesitation but to pen the most luminous and positive critiques possible. 40%. Writers Tears Whiskey Co.

Writer's Tears Cask Strength bott 2011 **(90.5) n23** a thick nose with honey and butterscotch, but dulled by caramels; **t22** a mouth-watering delivery is mildly out of context with the degree of acceleration of toffee and vanilla **f22.5** livens up towards the finish as some world-class spices begin to fizz. More accent on the hard-guy/soft-guy approach the two Pure Irish Pot still and malt whiskey styles evoke; **b23** sometimes seems a rabble of whiskey, with the flavours and shapes never quite deciding where it wants to go. But the randomness of the style is also a strength as you are entertained from first to last, though the caramels do keep the lid on some of the more honeyed moments. And memo to brand proprietor Bernard Walsh: only one mistake on your back label this time... 53%. Hot Irishman. 1200 bottles.

American Whiskey

Not that long ago American whiskey meant Bourbon. Or perhaps a very close relation called Tennessee. And sometimes it meant rye. Though nothing like often as it did prior to prohibition. Very, very rarely, though, did it ever get called single malt, because virtually none was made on the entire North American continent. That was a specialist - and very expensive - type left to the Scots and, to a lesser extent, the Irish. Or even the Japanese if a soldier or businessman was flying back from Tokyo.

I say "virtually" none was made because, actually, there was the odd batch of malt produced in America and, in my library, I still have some distilled at a rye distillery in Maryland in the early 1970s - indeed, I remember drinking the stuff there back in 1974. But it was hardly a serious commercial concern and the American public were never made greatly aware of it.

Now, though, at last count it appears that there are at least 25 distilleries doing their best to make whiskey mainly from malted barley but sometimes from rye and corn, too. Some still have much to learn, others have shown that they are well on their way to possible greatness. One distillery, Stranahan's in Colorado, has in a very short space of time managed to bring out a series of bottlings which left no doubt that they have joined McCarthy's of Oregon and Anchor of California in achieving it with another Portland distiller, Edgefield, not that far behind.

But as a collective movement it is by far the most exciting in the entire whisky world, despite what is happening in certain parts of Europe, especially Germany, Austria and Switzerland, where there is an even bigger movement. It appears to me that the better "micro distillers" are just a little more advanced in the US and have a stronger urge to grow. Some new wave American distillers, doubtless, will fall by the wayside while others will take their place. But those at the vanguard are likely to act as the spur to keep the others moving onwards and it is a situation I shall monitor very closely. There are squabbles about whether enzymes should be used for fermentation, a question I have been asked about many times. My view is that they should be avoided, although I can understand the reasons for their employment. However, when you are witnessing the birth of an entirely new whiskey life form it is always fascinating to see how it naturally develops. Usually the strongest live and the weakest die. In this survival of the fittest it will soon become apparent which methods are the ones that will succeed - and they tend to be the ones which have served distillers well over the last couple of centuries.

There is no little irony, however, that as we take a closer look at the alternative distilling world within the United States, it is the old order which is now really catching the eye. As I suspected, my award to Sazerac Rye 18 Years Old as Jim Murray's Whisky Bible 2010 World Whisky of the Year bemused quite a number of whisky lovers because it represents a style of whiskey they have never as much seen, let alone tasted. Doubtless Thomas Handy rye being named the world's second best for the 2011 Whisky Bible also caused consternation in some quarters.

Once upon a time, though, rye whiskey was seen as the embodiment of indigenous American spirit and the preferred choice in the country. After falling out of favour following Prohibiton and then World War II the traditional rye distillers in Pennysylvania and Maryland closed, production of the spirit shrank to a week's fermentation a year, if that, in a few Kentucky distilleries and until recently it was seen only as a rare alternative to bourbon in American liquor stores, often hidden on the end of shelves, or at the bottom. And often, ignominiously, both - with giveaway prices to add insult to injury.

Rye whiskey, where a minimum 51 per cent of the mashbill is made from rye - as opposed to bourbon where 51 per cent must be from corn - has long been my favourite whisk(e)y style. What matters isn't is the stuff which constitutes the flavoured "bourbons" which have been filling up valuable shelf space all over the USA. I was going to include them in the Bible – even though scores of less than 20 were not uncommon – but decided against it. For they are simply not bourbon whiskey, though the industry in watching sales go through the liquor stores' roof are not too upset to see the flavoured version standing shoulder to shoulder with traditional names. This, for me, is a major problem as it far from makes clear in the minds of drinkers exactly what bourbon is. But for the average liquor store manager, if cases of the stuff are selling each week: does he care? I can understand if he doesn't...

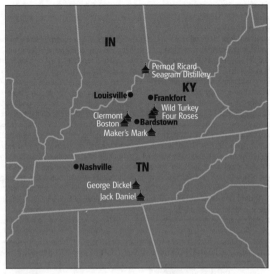

Bardstown
- Heaven Hill†
- Tom Moore

Frankfort
- Buffalo Trace

- Woodford Reserve

Louisville
- Early Times
- Bernheim
- Stitzel Weller

Bourbon Distilleries

Bourbon confuses people. Often they don't even realise it is a whiskey, a situation not helped by leading British pub chains, such as Wetherspoon, whose bar menus list "whiskey" and "bourbon" in separate sections. And if I see the liqueur Southern Comfort listed as a bourbon one more time I may not be responsible for my actions.

Bourbon is a whiskey. It is made from grain and matured in oak, so really it can't be much else. To be legally called bourbon it must have been made with a minimum of 51% corn and matured in virgin oak casks for at least two years. Oh, and no colouring can be added other than that which comes naturally from the barrel.

Where it does differ, from, say Scotch, is that the straight whiskey from the distillery may be called by something other than that distillery name. Indeed, the distillery may change its name which has happened to two this year already and two others in the last three or four. So, to make things easy and reference as quick as possible, I shall list the Kentucky-based distilleries first and then their products in alphabetical order along with their owners and operational status.

TOM MOORE Bardstown. Sazerac. Operating.

BUFFALO TRACE Leestown, Frankfort. Sazerac. Operating.

BROWN-FORMAN Shively, Louisville. Brown-Forman. Operating.

FOUR ROSES Lawrenceburg. Kirin. Operating

HEAVEN HILL BERNHEIM DISTILLERY Louisville. Heaven Hill. Operating.

JIM BEAM Boston and Clermont. Fortune Brands. Operating.

WOODFORD RESERVE Near Millville. Brown-Forman. Operating.

MAKER'S MARK Loretto. Fortune Brands. Operating.

WILD TURKEY Lawrenceburg. Campari Group. Operating.

Bourbon

Ancient Age (74.5) n18 t18.5 f19 b19. Basic: no frills and certainly no thrills until some late oils and spices kick in. 40% ⊙⊙

⋅⋅⋅ **Ancient Age 90 Proof (86.5) n21 t23 f21.5 b22.** If this is supposed to be the same whiskey as standard AA, but with just extra strength, you wouldn't know it. Here the oils have reduced considerably and in their place a quite beautiful tapestry of lively spice and rich, sweetened tannins arrive from the first moment...and last most of the course. More than just a passing nod to this distillery's glory. 45%

Ancient Ancient Age 10 Star (94.5) n23 no pussyfooting here: an immediate lurch into oranges and a firmer, fruitier rye foundation. Of its type (the quiet and understatedly sophisticated) about as good as it gets, nose-wise; **t24** those fruit tones on the nose hit the taste buds running: fresh but allowing the lightly oiled texture to let the soft corn and strapping rye melt together; plenty of chocolate and fudge to entertain, too; also, the spices - which again attack early - do so with rare chivalry; **f23.5** long, with the emphasis always on the custardy oak but the rye notes refuse to go down without a last hurrah; **b24** a bourbon which has slipped effortlessly through the gears over the last decade. It is now cruising and offers so many nuggets of pure joy this is now a must have for the serious bourbon devotee. Now a truly great bourbon which positively revels in its newfound complexity: a new 10 Star is born... 45% ⊙⊙

⋅⋅⋅ **Ancient Age Bonded (92) n23** showing off big time with a fabulous marriage of iron glove and velvet: pounding rye is the glove, a medley of delicate citrus and even, astoundingly, rose petals represents the velvet...; **t24** sumptuous and mouth-filling, the corn adds first flavours and then the oils. Not far behind comes a beautiful mixture of rye-fruitiness and cocoa and then relaxed but serious pounding of light spices; **f23** just loses its depth to a degree as the chalkier elements of the oak take hold; even so, just enough time for some blood orange to arrive and mingle with the spiced chocolate; **b23** unmistakably Buffalo Trace bourbon...with balls. 50% (100 Proof)

Ancient Ancient Age 10 Years Old (96) n23.5 busy, tangy, sharp, rounded, sweet in part - dry in others...an aroma full of contrasts but sings faultlessly for the duration; **t24** almost impossible to spit...the flavours just are so complex, the weight so astonishingly even. This is a marriage between the AAA 10 of about 20 years ago when the story was all about the subtlety of the delicate oak and the more recent version which is an oilier, more robust rye and weightier tannin...viva la difference...!! viva la sameness...!!; **f24** lightens with several degrees of custardy vanilla serving to accentuate the power of the juicy rye; the oils act as ballast for the almost mesmeric, butterfly-like flightiness of the smaller grains and accompanying, lightly scorched, Demerara sugars **b24.5** this whiskey is like shifting sands: same score as last time out, but the shape is quite different again. Somehow underlines the genius of the distillery that a world class whiskey can reach the same point of greatness, but by taking two different routes...However, in this case the bourbon actually finds something a little extra to move it on to a point very few whiskeys very rarely reach... 43% ⊙⊙

Baker's Aged 7 Years bott no. L1074CLA **(89.5) n23** chocolate orange and honey dew melon... pretty attractive even though the oak is taking no prisoners; **t22.5** much more oak than you might expect from a 7-year-old: high roast coffee lightened by a sprinkling of sugar and vanilla; **f22** the toasty hickory and soft corn oil makes for a slightly bitter but soft landing; **b22** infinitely more intense and complex than a few years back: further proof that Beam whiskey is very much improving. Superb whiskey but, if anything, too old for its age... 53.5% ⊙⊙

Basil Hayden's 8 Years Old (78) n20 t20 f19 b19. A thin bourbon which never quite finds anchor. Certainly one of the most citrusy bourbons around, but, overall, more Basil Fawlty as this is a bit of a strange, mildly neurotic character. 40% ⊙

Benchmark (86) n21 t22 f21.5 b21.5. Unquestionably a better whiskey than once it was with now an entirely well constructed vanilla-sugar depth adding ballast where once there was none. Lovely unexpected spices, too. A real surprise after not having tasted for a couple of years...as, frankly, it hadn't been worth it. Now it is... 40%

Benchmark No. 8 (79) n20 t21 f19 b19. Conspicuously thinner in body and character than the standard Benchmark. Papery aspects to the sweetness, but little of the balancing spice of its stablemate. 40% ⊙

Benjamin Prichard's Double Barrelled Bourbon 9 Years Old (94.5) n24.5 double chocolate, it appears... as usual a stunning nose from Prichards: do they know how to do anything else? Crisp rye and crisper apple teams with equally firm Demerara and liquorice but that chocolate plus corn and vanilla offers the countering softness required; a mega bourbon nose...; **t24.5** like the nose, absolutely breathtaking intensity which spells bourbon with every atom; spellbinding balance between the maple syrup sweetness and the drier vanillas; the corn really does have a major input in flavour **f22** oils and dries out a fraction and some cocoa returns, but remains chewy; **b23.5** if only they could bottle that nose...oh, they have...!!! Just wonderful whisky. 40% ☉ ☉

⋙ **Blanton's** (92) **n21.5** strangely quiet and a little dusty...; **t24** ...but not anymore...!! Ye-haaa!! What a fabulous kick. On the spice front certainly – and more importantly with the onslaught of flavours which begins with a big red liquorice and honey display, moving onto a paprika and nougat number and finally a liquorice-cocoa middle. The cocoa by now is a constant, but we also have varying dark sugars playing the field, too... **b23.5** if it were not for the sluggish nose this would be a Whisky Bible Liquid Gold award winner for sure. On the palate it shows just why little can touch Buffalo Trace for quality at the moment... 40%

⋙ **Blanton's Gold Original Single Barrel** (96.5) **n24** a thumping barrage of old honey forgotten in a jar with lavender and leather; **t24.5** rarely does a flavour profile follow the nose so faithfully. Here it also confirms the weight and texture; this is pure chewability. One of the most honeyed middles on the circuit with liquorice, usually ballast, here actually thinning things down a little; the spices hit an early crescendo and then buzz contentedly; **f24** long and remains absolutely unblemished and on a steady course. The honey remains intact; soft vanillas joins the liquorice while the spices just carry on...and on... **b24** it is improbable that a whiskey this enormous and with so many star turns can glide so effortlessly over the palate. One of the best Blanton's in years, this is true Gold standard... 46.5% (93 Proof)

⋙ **Blanton's 80 Proof** (89) **n22** thin honey; **t23** loads of honey..which has been thinned out a bit more; decent spices and toffee-vanilla; **f22** more honey, but not in concentrate form; flaky, oaky, dry vanilla at the death; **b22** Simplistic, soft and full of water-down honey. I doubt you'd say no to a second one... 40%

⋙ **Blanton's Takara** (91.5) **n24.5** fabulous orange blossom mingles delightfully with candyfloss wisps of vanilla and icing sugar. A threat of vanilla, celery and spice add the only weight required. One of the most delicate, sexy noses of the whiskey year... **t23** here we go...as expected, almost so light, the flavours land on the taste buds with all the force of feathers settling on the ground from ripped pillow; it is those soft sugars which lead the way, but dissolving before reaching the middle leaving the vanilla in charge; **f22** a little bitterness creeps in with the marmalade; **b22** not quite how many people might envisage a bourbon: certainly not butch enough to keep the wild west gunslingers happy. No this is a bourbon which searches for your feminine side. And being so light, leaves itself open for any off-key bitter notes which might just happen along the way. 49% (98 proof)

Blanton's Uncut/Unfiltered (96.5) **n25 t24 f23.5 b24.** Uncut. Unfiltered. Unbelievable. 65.9%

⋙ **Booker's 7 Years 4 Months** batch no. C03-1-17 (95.5) **n24** a mountain of dates and walnuts topped with kumquats and even the lightest hint of newly laid tarmacadam: sweet, earthy and near mesmerising; **t25** faultless: the weight and distribution of the oils is textbook, the balance between the sweet Demeraras and drier liquorice and hickory is almost to atomic precision...just take one bloody big mouthful, keep on the palate for a minute and simply discover how good life can get; **f22.5** somewhat thinner than might be expected from the delivery and middle. But still enough dried dates and almost smoky earthiness to make the experience complete; **b24** the best Booker's I have tasted for a very long while, probably ever. Absolutely world class whiskey. 64%

⋙ **Bowman Brother's Virginia Straight Bourbon** (90) **n21** strangely dry and dusty; **t23** deceptively rich, with a pulsing honey and spice theme; **f23** long. The dark sugars melt impressively into the drier vanillas; **b23** quietly confident and complex: a bit of a gem waiting to be discovered. 45% (90 proof)

Buffalo Trace (89.5) **n22** a corn-utopia of lightly sugared oils; plenty of custard, too...; **t23** juicy and salivating delivery then many long, slow waves of corn crashing over the oak; traces of light liquorice and muscovado sugars; **f22** huge vanilla and a real silkiness to the profound corn; **b22.5** easily one of the lightest BTs I have tasted in a very long while. The rye has not just taken a back seat, but has fallen off the bus. 45% ☉ ☉

⋙ **Buffalo Trace Experimental Collection 1989 Barrels Rediscovered** white oak with seasoned staves, dist Nov 89, bott Dec 10 (91.5) **n24** egg custard tart seasoned with cloves and hickory: very fine; **t23** astonishingly soft with the corn leading the way, surfing its very own oils. Chewy and remarkable for its refusal to find any meaningful spice; **f22.5** a long fade of (old, blackened) banana-related sugars and sawdusty vanilla; **b22.5** a whispering bourbon of exceptional subtlety which makes minimum fuss of its antiquity. 45% (90 Proof)

⋙ **Buffalo Trace Experimental Collection 1991 Barrels Rediscovered** white oak with seasoned staves, dist Oct 91, bott Dec 10 (93.5) **n24** thick liquorice and demerara with all the trimmings; **t23.5** creamy, rich-textures with a charming date and walnut cake middle and burnt raisin later in; **f23** spices develop and punctuate the vanilla; **b23** pretty classic stuff. 45%

⫶ **Buffalo Trace Experimental Collection 1993 Barrels Rediscovered** white oak with seasoned staves, dist May 93, bott Dec 10 (89) n24 big citrus hullo from Kentucky: most un-BT!! The sugars are about as delicate as they come, lightening the vanilla almost into cream soda; t22 mouth-filling, as you would expect with the vanillas thick and spiked by spice; f21 here's the cream from the cream soda... b22 a long way from the BT norm. *45% (90 Proof)*

⫶ **Buffalo Trace Master Distiller Emeritus Elmer T Lee Collector's Edition** bott. 06/09/11 (96) n24.5 no shy rye here with a firm, slightly peppery attack and a honeyed counter balance. Sublime... t24 the spices grab the taste buds by their throats...and then promptly gives the soft, lightly corn-oiled, delicately honeyed kisses. A few shafts of liquorice confirms there is some very serious bourbon-ness going on here; f23.5 long, with the accent on dry oaks, a burnt caramel sweetness and a re-entering of the firm rye which seals the deal b24 simply spellbinding. One of the best BT bottlings I have even enjoyed for bourbon rarely comes more understatedly complete and complex than this. This is the bottle with a nickel coin glued to it. And each complex character within this whiskey gets more than its five cents worth... *45%*

⫶ **Buffalo Trace Single Oak Project Barrel #132** (a1yA1 *see key below*) db (95) n24 busy rye: at once sharp and fruity while simultaneously displaying impressive layers of caramel and liquorice. Complex, exceptionally well profiled and leaves no ambiguity as to regard its high class status; t23.5 the delivery, like the nose, appears to enjoy two simultaneous entry levels. At the same moment those sharp rye notes appear to be messages carved in granite; this surrounded by a light caramel fog, seemingly ungraspable yet obviously there and having an effect. The next round of flavour centre on varied cocoa notes as well as a variance of textures, especially as the corn oil seeps in; as usual for this distillery, the sugars are of a crisp Demerara/muscovado type, vivid at first but happily becoming background noise as the complexity levels increase; f23.5 long, with the vanilla, cocoa and corn now dominating to the fade, the rye little more than a distant echo; b24 this sample struck me for possessing, among the first batch of bottlings, the classic Buffalo Trace personality. Afterwards they revealed that it was of a profile which perhaps most closely matches their standard 8-year-old BT. Therefore it is this one I shall use as the tasting template. *45% (90 Proof)*

⫶ **Buffalo Trace Single Oak Project Barrel #3** (a2xA1) db (90.5) n22.5 t23 f22.5 b22.5. Nutty, dry aroma; apple fruitiness and brown sugars. *45% (90 Proof)*

⫶ **Buffalo Trace Single Oak Project Barrel #4** (a2yA1) db (92) n23 t23 f23 b23. Exceptionally crisp; sharp rye, honeycomb, big liquorice. *45% (90 Proof)*

⫶ **Buffalo Trace Single Oak Project Barrel #29** (a3xB2*) db (91) n23 t22.5 f23 b22.5. Crisp rye nose; more precise grain. Excellent spices. *45% (90 Proof)*

⫶ **Buffalo Trace Single Oak Project Barrel #31** (a3xB2) db (87.5) n22 t22 f21.5 b22. Dull, rumbling and herbal; oily caramel and sugars. Soft. *45% (90 Proof)*

⫶ **Buffalo Trace Single Oak Project Barrel #35** (b3xA1) db (89.5) n22 t22 f23 b22.5. Soft mint, yeasty; soft toffee delivery, builds in spice. *45% (90 Proof)*

⫶ **Buffalo Trace Single Oak Project Barrel #36** (b3yA1) db (91.5) n23 t23 f22.5 b23. Vague rum and toffee; bold, salivating, slow spice. *45% (90 Proof)*

⫶ **Buffalo Trace Single Oak Project Barrel #61** (b3xB2*) db (94.5) n24 t23 f23.5 b24. Classic spiced wheat; Demerara sugars and spices abound. Big. *45% (90 Proof)*

⫶ **Buffalo Trace Single Oak Project Barrel #63** (b3xB2) db (95.5) n24 t23 f24 b24.5. Subtle dates, spice, cocoa; gentle, oily, perfect spice build. Ultra complex. *45% (90 Proof)*

⫶ **Buffalo Trace Single Oak Project Barrel #67** (a2xA1) db (89.5) n22 t23 f22 b22.5. Blandish nose; tart, tight, sharp, some toffee raisin. *45% (90 Proof)*

⫶ **Buffalo Trace Single Oak Project Barrel #68** (a2yA1) db (92) n22.5 t23 f23.5 b23. Rye depth; deeper, warmer spices, liquorice and light molasses. *45% (90 Proof)*

⫶ **Buffalo Trace Single Oak Project Barrel #93** (a2xB2*) db (89) n22.5 t22 f22 b22.5. Soft rye and sugars; juicy grain, tangy citrus, muscovado. *45% (90 Proof)*

⫶ **Buffalo Trace Single Oak Project Barrel #95** (a2xB2) db (94) n23 t23.5 f23.5 b24. Citrus, banana; soft vanilla, profound rye sharpness, spices. Big. *45% (90 Proof)*

⫶ **Buffalo Trace Single Oak Project Barrel #99** (b2xA1) db (86.5) n22 t22 f21 b21.5. Malty, vanilla; thin maple syrup, caramel. Dull. *45% (90 Proof)*

⫶ **Buffalo Trace Single Oak Project Barrel #100** (b2yA1) db (94) n23 t23.5 f23.5 b24. Busy, green, fresh; big juicy, vanilla, muscovado, spices. *45% (90 Proof)*

⫶ **Buffalo Trace Single Oak Project Barrel #125** (b2xB2*) db (93) n24 t22 f22.5 b22.5. Heavy oak, spices; firm, juicy. Softer caramel fade. *45% (90 Proof)*

⫶ **Buffalo Trace Single Oak Project Barrel #127** (b2xB2) db (85.5) n21.5 t22 f21 b21. Off balance, citrus; juicy at first, bitters later. *45% (90 Proof)*

⫶ **Buffalo Trace Single Oak Project Barrel #131** (a1xA1) db (92.5) n23 t23 f23.5 b23. Relaxed vanilla, light tannin; corn oily, icing sugars, marzipan. *45% (90 Proof)*

··· **Buffalo Trace Single Oak Project Barrel #132** *See above.*
··· **Buffalo Trace Single Oak Project Barrel #157** (a1xB2*) db (84.5) n21 t21.5 f20.5 b21.
Vague butyric; sharp, juicy corn with slow rye build. Bitter. *45% (90 Proof)*
··· **Buffalo Trace Single Oak Project Barrel #159** (a1xB2) db (88) n20.5 t22.5 f22 b22.5.
Vague butyric; firm sugars then watery, confident spices, soft honey. Complex. *45% (90 Proof)*
··· **Buffalo Trace Single Oak Project Barrel #163** (b1xA1) db (90) n23 t22.5 f22 b22.5.
Citrus, bubble gum; spiced muscovado sugars at first, bitters. *45% (90 Proof)*
··· **Buffalo Trace Single Oak Project Barrel #164** (b1yA1) db (94.5) n23.5 t23 f24 b24.
Citrus and vanilla; massive spice, building. Demerara. Warm and complex. *45% (90 Proof)*
··· **Buffalo Trace Single Oak Project Barrel #189** (b1xB2*) db (88.5) n24 t22 f21 b21.5.
Complex citrus, delicate yet big; tart, sweet, fresh, strangely off balance. *45% (90 Proof)*
··· **Buffalo Trace Single Oak Project Barrel #191** (b1xB2) db (94.5) n23 t23.5 f24 b24.
Big, spicy, classic; firm wheaty spiciness, juicy, thick caramels. Complex. *45% (90 Proof)*

Key to Buffalo Trace Single Oak Project Codes
Mash bill type: a= rye; b= wheat **Entry strength:** A=125; B=105
Tree grain: 1= Course; 2= Average; 3=Tight **Seasoning:** 1=Six Months; 2= 12 Months
Tree cut: x=top half; y=bottom half **Char:** All #4 except *=#3

··· **Bulleit Bourbon** (89) n23 how subtle is that? A pretty noticeable input from the small grains as the rye chips in with a distinguished degree of firm fruitiness and spice; t23 and the rye is first to show on delivery, offering a crystallised sugar base which the corn oil is happy to lap around; f21 custard pie and light cocoa; b22 a very easy going bourbon which makes the most of any rye in the recipe. Dangerously drinkable. *45%*

Charter 101 (95.5) n23.5 standard Charter 101 evening flowers? Check. Usual spices? Check. Obvious lack of honey on the nose? We have a negative, Frankfort. This is just brimming with all the pollen collected from those evening flowers... t24.5 the lush mouth feel betrays the strength of this bourbon. Again, this has much to do with the honey which absolutely oozes into every crevice of the mouth it can find. Honey was always around on Charter 101, but never like this. Emboldened, it seems, by beautiful blending of lively liquorice and voluptuous vanilla...all with a softly spoken spiciness. But once that settles – even allowing in a chewy fudge sweetness – those honey notes begin to blow you away... simply adorable stuff; f23.5 long? How long have you got? A sublime layering of Demerara and muscovado sugars embraced by custardy oak...with a cocoa edge throughout. But once that melts you are back to the soft honeyed centre...; b24 now here is a whiskey which has changed tack dramatically. In many ways it's like the Charter 101 of a year or two back. But this bottling suggests they have turned a warehouse into a giant beehive. Because few whiskeys offer this degree of honey. You can imagine that after all these years, rarely does a whiskey genuinely surprise me: this one has. No wonder there is such a buzz in the bourbon industry right now... *50.5%* ☉ ☉

··· **Colonel E. H. Taylor Old Fashioned Sour Mash** (94) n24 how can something be so light yet possess such gravitas all at the same moment? The corn offers a wonderful butterscotch-honey blend while the rye and oak, though hardly enormous on their own, combine to strengthen, firm and enrich. One of the most subtle aromas of the year; t23.5 another dual attack: salivating and puckering at once. And also sweet and bitter. Plus rounded and spicy. The rye ensures a lustre to the sugary corn while the oak offers hickory; the mouth feel and weight are exceptional; f23 long, a very light layer of corn and several more stratum of cocoa and honey; the spice tingle lasts to the very death; b23.5 when they say "old fashioned" they really aren't joking. This is a style which takes me back to my first bourbon tasting days of the mid 1970s. And, at the moment, it is hard to name another bourbon offering this unique, technically brilliant style. Outstanding! *50% (100 Proof)*

··· **Colonel Lee** (70) n17.5 t18.5 f17 b17. The Colonel and I have known each other for a great many years, though it has been a while since I last spent time in his company. A few minutes of his very limited conversation is all I need to remember why... *40%*

Corner Creek Reserve (86) n22 t22 f21 b21. Honeyed with some striking small grain action. *44%. Corner Creek Distilling Company.*

Cougar Bourbon Aged 5 Years (95) n25 t24 f23 b23. If Karl Kennedy of Neighbours really is the whisky buff he reckons he is, I want to see a bottle of this in his home next to Dahl. By the way: where is Dahl these days...? (And by the way, Karl, the guy who married you and Susan in London is a fan of mine. So you had better listen up...!) *37% (74 proof). Foster's Group, Australia.*

Daniel Stewart 8 Years Old (92.5) n22 t23 f23.5 b24. Stellar sophistication. Real complexity here, and, as 8-year-olds go, probably among the most complex of them all. A deep notch up on the previous bottling I encountered. *45%*

⋙ **Eagle Rare Aged 10 Years Single Barrel (89)** n21.5 attractively floral but with a big signature of corn syrup; t23 early oils as expected, then a surprising change of gear towards a rye-Demerara mix which firms and then moves towards a much spicier, kumquat inclined middle than the nose suggests; f22 long, with more corn and a little oak bitterness; b22.5 a surprising trip, this, with some dramatic changes en route. *45%*

⋙ **Eagle Rare Kentucky Straight Bourbon 17 Years Old** bott Fall 2010 **(92.5)** n24 the rye makes a powering speech from the off; just bristling with solid, flinty intent, there is a fabulous Palma violet and clove contrast: nosed blind and you could mistake this for a rye; t23.5 one of the firmest of all the Buffalo Trace bourbons I have come across in 35 years of tasting the stuff: there is a fabulous backbone of steel which, again, is the rye in overdrive but now aided and abetted by a gathering of dense oak which finds an escape route through some prickly spice; f22 a tad too dry for perfection with a gloomy bitterness; the cocoa is charming though; b23 the corn hardly makes itself heard and oil's at a premium. But for those who love bourbon in their rye...wow!! Oddly enough, while tasting this I am watching, from my sample room, a pair of black vultures circling a bluff at Frankfort, Ky, a short glide from the distillery where this whiskey was made. They are not exactly eagles, I grant you. But, with its eagle-esque deportment and chunkiness, close enough for the moment not to be lost...The Turkey Vultures, meanwhile, are probably waiting until I start on the samples from Lawrenceburg... *45%*

Elijah Craig 12 Years Old (79) n20 t21.5 f18.5 b19. Once upon a time this whiskey was as resolute, dependable, unshakable and constant as the cliffs which guide the mighty Kentucky River. And every bit as impressive and memorable. Those were in the days when the bourbon was made at Bardstown, with its massive copper input from unerringly fine stills. Then came the fire. And the distillery was lost. So 13 years after the event the whiskey had to change: there was no way it could not. This bottling is a considerable distance in style from the original. Superficially, plenty of rye and Demerara sugars. But it is hot and untidy. So unlike Elijah Craig 12... *47%* ⊙ ⊙

⋙ **Elijah Craig 18 Years Old Single Barrel** barrel no. 3328, dist 8/9/91 **(94.5)** n25 one of the most complex noses of the year with its busy, light warbling of rye, high quality marzipan and honey notes as well as freshly crushed brazil nut and very lightest Jamaican Blue Mountain coffee: as it oxidizes, delicate citrus and leather notes appear. Incredible...; t23.5 the oak is upfront, as you might expect at this age, but the ryes immediately counter and very juicily so; outstanding weight and the vanillas go very gently; f22.5 you would expect some negatives at the death from a whiskey of this age. But, instead, it just rolls out the sugared, lightly creamed mocha; b23.5 masterful. Don't even bother opening the bottle unless you have an hour to spend... *45%*

Elmer T Lee Single Barrel (91) n22 almost seems like a little smoke on the toffee apple and honey...but that just proves to be the tannins riding high; t23.5 fabulously rich and fulsome, the early lead is a pleasing hotch-potch of liquorice and cream toffee, a dab of acacia honey here and there while the middle heads very much towards burned fudge; f(22.5) long, with a steady stream of honey and fudge; lightly spiced butterscotch steers us home at the death; b23 a sturdy, dense bourbon with above average sweetness. So effortless, it is hard to immediately realise that greatness has entered your glass. *45%* ⊙ ⊙

Elmer T. Lee 90th Birthday Limited Edition (93.5) n23.5 t23.5 f23 b23.5. Age has mellowed the whiskey's top class, complex, slightly fiery character...a bit like an old friend and bourbon legend I could name. This sample has come directly from the bottle Elmer gave me after I had the honour of sitting beside him at his 90th birthday bash. Sadly, a member of my staff opened it by mistake for my sampling. Though it was the first new whisky I tasted after completing the 2010 Bible, I have made this the 1,056th whisky to officially taste for the 2011 Whisky Bible. Because tell me: how can you follow an Elmer T Lee...? *45%*

Evan Williams (76.5) n18 t20 f19 b19.5. Unrelentingly sweet and simplistic. *43.3%*

Evan Williams 12 Years (90) n21.5 a touch of the new HH Character, but compensated by a real old fruitcake kick; t23.5 brilliant mouth arrival with the spices boldly leading the way. Juicy, fruity rye isn't too far behind and the liquorice notes begin to up the ante at just the right time; f22.5 varying dark sugar tones are sprinkled over the drier vanillins and chalky oakiness; b22.5 perhaps not the force it recently was, but enough grunt here to emphasise the important bits. Namely the enormity of the rye and the sharp spices. Much more at home than, say, the 12-year-old Elijah Craig, for so long its match for quality. *50.5%* ⊙

Evan Williams 23 Years Old (94) n22 coffee anyone...? A hardly subtle mix of Ethiopian high roast and Java medium roast would probably do the trick here as there is a lightly acidic kick to the following spices and liquorice; **t23.5** way too much oak on delivery, for sure. But after that goes again we have a milky coffee softness aided by a wonderful mix of Demerara and molasses; the middle ground is full of mocha and intense vanilla...almost like some kind of dessert; **f24.5** comes into its own and with massive style as all the above characteristics begin to show a degree of understanding for each other and merrily interface: the years seems to disappear... **b24** it has been three years since I last tasted this fellow and it has to be said that first impressions suggested time had caught up with him a bit. Then he strutted his stuff, refusing to allow age to slow him or dim the shine from his glowing grains. Now oak has taken its toll. This seems older than its 23 years... Or so I first thought. Then a light shone in my soul and it occurred to me: hang on...I have wines going back to the last century. For the older ones, do I not allow them to breathe? So I let the whiskey breathe. And, behold, it rose from the dead. This Methuselah of a whiskey had come alive once more...and how!! 53.5% ⊙⊙

Evan Williams 1783 (81) n19 t20.5 f21 b20.5. Much improved and now an exceptionally spicy offering. 43% ⊙⊙

Evan Williams Single Barrel Vintage 2000 dist Mar 00, bott Oct 09 **(90) n24 t23 f21.5 b21.5.** Beautiful bourbon for sure. But when you get that type of aroma and this kind of strength... Well, let's say that it's like owning a Corvette and finding a lawnmower engine under the hood. 43.3% (86.6 proof)

◦⋰· **Evan Williams Single Barrel Vintage 2001** dist Jul 01, bott Oct 10, barrel no. 001 **(85) n21.5 t21 f21 b21.5.** One thing is for absolute certain: this was not distilled at the long lost Heaven Hill distillery in Bardstown. Those were whiskeys which leapt at you from the glass and pulled your face into its enormity. This, by contrast, is most un-Single Barrel-esque. It is a huge outpouring of cream toffee. Enlivened by some layering of delicate citrus. But all rather sweet and monosyllabic...and soft. 43.3% (86.6 Proof)

Fighting Cock Aged 6 Years (82.5) n21 t21.5 f20 b20. I have just gone straight from Virgin Bourbon to Fighting Cock...such are the vagaries of my life. But while the virgin seduced or, rather, raped me, this old Cock leaves me underwhelmed. With its rich colour I had expected untold layering and depth. Instead, it is all rather corn-led and slightly OTT bitter oak. 51.5% ⊙⊙

Four Roses (Yellow Label) (89) n23 subtlety is the key here: small grains bristling and jostling for position against the softer honeyed vanilla; **t23** steady on, there! The delivery is much weightier and altogether thicker than a couple of years back and that honey note (yes, I do mean honey!) is contrasting vitally against the crisper rye; **f21** the fog of vanilla descends; **b22** seriously impressed: this whiskey was always pleasant but afraid to say boo to a goose. Now a honey injection has actually helped ramp up the rye content and the complexity has benefitted. The nose and delivery are exceptional. 40% ⊙⊙

Four Roses (Black Label) (88) n20 t23 f23 b22. A whiskey which starts falteringly on the nose recovers with a sublime delivery of all things bourbon. 40%

◦⋰· **Four Roses Single Barrel** warehouse US cask no. 10-2A **(96.5) n25** the perfect bourbon nose: floral (pansies/daffs) meets spice (ginger/pepper/clove) meets honey (acacia) meets fruit (redcurrant/dates) and at the confluence red liquorice and walnut oil is thrown in for good measure. Simply majestic; **t24.5** there are some rye whiskies which don't show this much of that most startling of grains. Clean delivery, almost like crystallised brown sugar melted by the increasing warmth of the spice. The oak adds a degree of liquorice but absolutely no bitter back chat; **f23** long, continues along the same lines but runs out of steam; **b24** if you have ever wondered if Four Roses has the wherewithal to play amongst the super-elite of the whiskey world, then track down this particular bottling and all will be revealed...For me, the finest Four Roses I have ever come across. 50%

Four Roses Small Batch (86) n20.5 t22.5 f21 b21.5. It is odd that while the standard Yellow Label has massively increased its personality, this one has, if anything, moved towards a more neutral stance thanks to the vanillas dominating the nose and finish. The delivery is by no means so restricted, though. Good spice, too. 45% (90 proof) ⊙⊙

Four Roses Marriage Collection 2009 (88.5) n23.5 t22 f21.5 b21.5. Not sure of the barrel number for this one, but could do with a little less toastiness if in search of true greatness. Even so, lovely stuff. 58% (116 proof)

◦⋰· **Four Roses 2010 Limited Edition Barrel Strength (88) n22.5** thumping rye and hickory; **t23.5** hides its strength well as the rye goes bananas...literally. Some over-ripe banana defuses the ticking small grain; some decent cocoa hits the middle ground; **f20** annoyingly over assertive vanilla; **b22** talk about a gentle giant...! The rye within the mashbill asserts itself monumentally but the vanillas fight back rather too well. 55.1% (110.2 proof)

George T. Stagg (96) n24 t24.5 f23.5 b24. On first tasting this at the distillery last year, my knee-jerk reaction was that this was a fair distance behind the Weller. However, with whiskey this massive, it takes four or five hours to unravel its mysteries. Taste this only if you can give it the time. *70.7% (141.4 proof). ncf.*

⟨∞⟩ **George T Stagg (97.5) n24** huge: profound, rich and seemingly distilled in the Blue Mountains of Jamaica; hickory and clove in close harmony, lightened with the merest (and I mean tiniest!) dash of redcurrant jelly; **t25** thick oak, yet so well honed are the molasses and Demerara notes that every aspect just seems to slide into place. Juicy, too, as the sub-plot rye makes some bold, sharp statements. And we haven't even reached in about a third of the way. However, the perfect weight, the magnificence of the corn and the marriage between the corn, its oils and the proud tannins is the stuff of legend...; meanwhile, the Jamaican Blue Mountain (mid and heavy roast mix) percolates sublimely...; **f24** a few dim spices are etched delicately into the vanilla but the coffee stays the course assisted by the big vanillas and fabulous Demerara-hickory combo....; **b24.5** astonishing how so much oak can form and yet have such limited negative impact and so few unpleasant side effects. These tasting notes took nearly four hours to compile. Yet they are still in a simplified form to fit into this book... George T Stagg is once again... staggering. *71.5% (143 Proof). ncf.*

Hancock's Reserve Single Barrel (92) n25 huge corn with rye apparent only if you really look hard; creamed rice pudding with a dollop of acacia honey slapped in the middle; a hint of evening gardens...all sewn together by the thinnest thread of liquorice: to die for... **t23** melts-in-the-mouth with an array of light oak and strands of coconut dipped in treacle; a sudden paroxysm of spice before heading towards a surprisingly dry middle; **f21.5** a disappointing finish with the oak taking a rough-handed control... **b22.5** a slightly quieter example of this consistently fine brand. The nose, though, is the stuff of wet whiskey dreams... *44.45% ⊙⊙*

Heaven Hill Old Style Bourbon (81) n20 t20 f21 b20. a sweeter, more citrusy number than before. Still a lightweight, but offers much more entertainment and style. *40% ⊙⊙*

Heaven Hill 6 Years Old (83) n20 t20 f22 b21. An infinitely more satisfying bourbon than its Old Style stable mate at this age. The battle between crisp rye and compact caramel is intriguing and pretty tasty to boot. *40%*

Heaven Hill Old Style Bourbon 6 Years Old Bottled in Bond (81.5) n18 t21.5 f21 b21. What a strange beast. Sluggish on the nose and vanilla-bound on the finish it tends to hurtle around the palate without thought. The delivery, though, is sharp and enjoyably mouth-watering. *50% ⊙⊙*

Heaven Hill Mild and Mellow (90) n22 solid depth with liquorice and honeysuckle; **t23** mouth-filling and oily, the small grains break out with gusto. It's enough to make you dribble, such is the salivating effect of the juicy rye. Pretty big stuff; **f22.5** the oak infuses all the spice this needs and the corn keeps it there; **b22.5** you never know what you are going to get with this one: for that it is consistent. This version is full of colour and vitality and is a real (very pleasant) surprise package. A corker. *43% ⊙⊙*

Heaven Hill Ultra Deluxe Aged 36 Months (80) n20 t21 f19 b20. I remember a surprising liquorice backbone to this last time out. Not now. Lighter all round with corn dominating but the delicate spices are a treat. *40% ⊙⊙*

⟨∞⟩ **Henry McKenna Aged 10 Years Single Barrel** barrel no. 642, dist 11/08/11 **(86) n21 t22.5 f21.5 b21.** Much more interesting than the last bottle of this I sampled. Here, as before, the sugars are king. But there is a charming kumquat note on both nose and delivery which burrow into the ever thickening liquorice. Superficially, appears to have much in common with the Virgin 7. But tasted side by side... Even so, good stuff. *50%*

⟨∞⟩ **Hogs 3 (86.5) n21.5 t22 f21 b22.** Have to say this is above average 3-year-old fare, with generous lashings of honey and red liquorice at regular intervals. A note about the label: the commendable sweetness of the whisky comes from the sugars that have melted into the alcohol from the oak and nothing, as claimed, from the water. But that nonsense apart, top-range for age, high-class daily bourbon. *40% (80 Proof). Quality Spirits International.*

Jefferson's Reserve batch no. 84 **(91) n23 t23.5 f22 b23.** Once a 15-year-old, no age statement now. But this has seen off a few Summers, and sweetened with each passing one. *45.1%. 2400 bottles.*

Jim Beam (86) n21 t21 f22 b21. After a few years kicking its heels, JB White Label has returned to something closer to how I remember it a couple of decades back. Not just a welcome degree of extra weight, but much more honey intensifying and lengthening: someone has been climbing higher up in the warehouse to find this four-year-old... Impressed. *40% ⊙⊙*

Jim Beam Black Aged to Perfection (89.5) n22 softer, less pungent than the 8-y-o version; **t23** the accent on the sugars with the usual rye boldness taking a back seat behind the sweeter corn, though by no means invisible; **f22.5** gentle vanilla and more molasses with some puckering liquorice towards the finale; **b22.5** Jim Beam Black. But, teasingly, with no age statement! Does it live in the shadow of the sublime 8-years-old? Well, perhaps not quite.

Lacks the lushness and the peaks and troughs of complexity. But, though a lot more even in temperament, it never fails to delight, even if the standard rye kick is conspicuous by its absence. As a bourbon, excellent. As a Jim Beam Black, a little disappointing. *43% (86 proof)*

Jim Beam Black Double Age Aged 8 Years (93) n23 a fraction lighter than usual with a most un-JB milky mocha note braking up the trademark fruitcake and liquorice fingerprint; a few glazed cherries thrown in for sweetness; **t24** again, the intensity has shifted somewhat. This really is polite fayre compared to the usual Black Label character. But no less beguiling with the rye notes playing peek-a-boo with the building Demerara sugars and juicy dates, and the liquorice arriving in slow motion; the middle is fabulously sumptuous and complex, especially now the spices can be heard; **f22.5** thinner than usual with the liquorice and sugars winding down until the vanilla dominates; **b23.5** rather than the big, noisy, thrill-seeking JB Black, here it is in quiet, reflective, sophisticated mode. Quite a shift. But no less enjoyable. *43%* ⊙⊙

Jim Beam Choice Aged 5 Years (89) n22 t22 f23 b22. A hugely improved whiskey which is no longer betwixt and between but now strikingly makes its own bold statements. Makes noises on both nose and palate way above its five years. A bourbon to grab whilst in this expansive and impressive mood. *40%*

Jim Beam Devil's Cut 90 Proof (89) n22.5 subtle spearmint notes in decent harmony with the hickory and Demerara: deceptively weighty and complex; **t24** dream-like delivery! The weight is close on perfection as the corn oils steam in ahead with the rye, sharp and bright, close behind. The Demerara sugars also make telling contribution early on, helping to accentuate the middle spices; **f20.5** a bit scruffy and untidy as the vanillas dry a little too rapidly **b22** beautifully thrusting with the palate both ran ragged and soothed by a devilish degree of silky complexity and intensity. The finish, though, needs a little attention. *45%*

John J Bowman Virginia Straight Bourbon Single Barrel (94) n23 Dense and intense; John J means business...plenty of liquorice to accentuate the oak. Dry and toasty; **t24** the delivery is an essay in deportment: big weight, but so evenly balanced that the burnt honey and spice have no problems in showing to the full...chewy and multi-layered; **f23** long with the drying processes giving the honey all the time it needs to make its exit; **b24** one of the biggest yet most easily relaxed and beautifully balanced bourbons on the market. *50% (100 proof)*

Johnny Drum (Black Label) 12 Years Old (78) n20 t22 f18 b18 Attractive early, crusty sugars. But bitters out and loses balance later on. *43%*

Johnny Drum (Green Label) (87.5) n21.5 thick with over-ripe banana and vanilla with no little liquorice input; **t22** soft and succulent with the middle filling with toasty oak and honeyed hickory; no shortage of corn evident; **f22** long, significantly oiled and a decent bitter-sweet fade; **b22** has changed direction since I last tasted this one. Now true as a die. And even outperforms the Johnny Drum Black! *43% (86 proof)*

Johnny Drum Private Stock (90.5) n22.5 another aroma you could stand a spoon in: lots of toffee and vanilla but enough corn oil to bathe in...; **t22.5** excellent early sugars immediately squares up to the threatening liquorice. Where they meet proves a touch tart; the oils arrive just as the nose foretells; **f23** gracefully complex and truly offering weight and that tell-tale touch of quality; **b22.5** one of those bourbons where a single glass is never quite enough. Great stuff! *50.5% (101 proof)*

Kentucky Gentleman (86) n19 t22.5 f22 b22.5. Once you get past the disjointed nose, you are in for a very pleasant surprise. The highlight is the delivery on palate and follow-through: a silky-textured (hazelnut) nutty experience with a delightful honeycomb wake. There is a lovely small grain busyness, too. A minor gem of a gentleman. *40%*

Kentucky Supreme Number 8 Brand (76) n18 t19 f20 b19. Simplistic and undemanding with massive emphasis on a barley sugar-style tartness and sweetness. *40%* ⊙

Kentucky Tavern (84) n20 t22 f21 b21. Another juicy little number which appears almost to have a young malt feel to it. Clean, with just the right amount of rye sparkle to offer buzz and complexity. *40%* ⊙

Kentucky Vintage batch 08-72 **(94.5) n23.5** delicate to the point of brittle. Playful spice prickles as the small grains dance and tease; beautiful citrus notes are just showing off; **t24.5** the whole thing just melts in the mouth. No grating oak nor rabid spices. No bitter char. Just an intricate and delicate mix of grain and vanilla interweaving...and then melting along with some accompanying butterscotch and muscovado sugar. Quite stunning; **f23** both the bitterness and spices grow. But all is balanced and genteel; **b23.5** staggered! I really didn't quite expect that. Previous bottlings I have enjoyed of this have had hair attached to the muscle. This is a very different Vintage, one that reaches for the feminine side of a macho whiskey. If you want to spend an hour just getting to know how sensitive your taste buds can be, hunt down this batch... *45%* ⊙⊙

Knob Creek Aged 9 Years (94.5) n23.5 almost arrogantly consistent: you know pretty well what you are going to get...and there it is. In this classic whiskey's case a whole bunch of honeycomb and vanilla, always more delicate than it first appears...; t24 salivating delivery with rye and barley absolutely hammering on the palate. The corn oil is there not for flavour but effect – it is a fabulous mixture of dates and Demerara rum having the biggest say; f23.5 wonderfully long with the oak toastiness now really beginning to bite...; b23.5 no whiskey in the world has a more macho name, and this is not for the faint-hearted. Big, hard in character and expansive, it drives home its point with gusto, celebrating its explosive finish. 50% ⊙⊙

⊹⊱ **Knob Creek Aged 9 Years Single Barrel Reserve** bottling batch no. L1017CLH (89) n22.5 thick, almost single layered coffee and fruit cake; t22.5 huge corn oil and spice; sweet and sticky; f22 plenty of treacle and oak...chewy to the very last coffee dregs; b22 the point often overlooked by people, even in the industry, is that a single cask is often a part of the sum. So this bottling just shows a single fragment into what will make up the usual Knob Creek small batch bourbon. This particular barrel – and sadly they don't name which one it is for further comparison (a bit of a marketing mistake that, as there are thousands out there dying to compare different styles) is all about depth and weight. Complexity, therefore, does not play a significant role, especially with the rye taking a back seat. Even so, an impressive ride. 60%

Maker's Mark (Red Seal) (91) n22.5 the liquorice oak arrives early and with more force than you would expect from a Maker's. A bunch of vanilla notes of mixed sweetness try to dampen down the effect; t23.5 honey...!!! Even more than usual, but this time winning the battle over the wheated spice. A silky mouthfeel and an attractive walnut subplot fits in pleasantly; f22 the vanilla returns with a little caramel for a sleepy finale; b23 the big honey injection has done no harm whatsoever. This sample came from a litre bottle and the whiskey was darker than normal. What you seem to have is the usual steady Maker's with a helping hand of extra weight. In fact this reminds me of the old Maker's Gold wax. 45% ⊙⊙

⊹⊱ **Maker's 46** (95) n23.5 crushed toasted hazelnuts dappled with honeycomb and delicate hickory; beautifully even and well mannered; t24.5 quite superb: an initially thick, intense delivery which fans out in directions; excellent weight as those honeycomb notes go into overdrive; a dotting of wheaty and oaky spices but it's the way the softest of silky and highly complex flavours crash feather-like into the taste buds which cranks up the points; f23 surprisingly light and simplistic with the accent firmly on vanilla; b24 some people have a problem with oak staves. I don't: whisky, after all, is about the interaction of a grain spirit and oak. This guy is all about the nose and, especially, the delivery. With so much controlled honey on show, it cannot be anything other than a show-stopper. Frankly, magnificent. I think I've met my Maker's... 47% (94 proof)

Most Wanted Kansas Bourbon Mash Whiskey (83) n18 t20 f23.5 b21.5. A sweaty armpit nose is the unlikely overture for an attractively flavoursome and delicately sweet bourbon. Highly unusual and rather gristy in style, the superb finish offers hugely attractive chocolate. One that really grows on you. 40%

⊹⊱ **Noah's Mill** batch 10-170 (93) n23.5 classic big aged bourbon: toasted glazed cherry and liquorice to the fore, significant corn oil offering a vanilla and Demerara sugar balance; outstanding weight and poise; t23.5 again, everything about this signals significant age. But also style and class. Sweetened hickory, a shed load of tannins but all countered by just so dark sugar reinforcements. Enormous whiskey, but totally in tune; f23 just a little toasty bitterness on the finale deprives this of supreme greatness. Yet there is just enough sugar in the tank to keep the balance on track; b23 this monster of a bourbon just rumbles along the palate like one of the four thunderstorms I have encountered in Kentucky today... 57.15% (114.3 proof)

Old 1889 Royal Aged 12 Years (78) n19 t20 f19 b20. A curiously ineffectual and ultimately frustrating bourbon which still needs to feel loved for its small grain complexity but succeeds only in demanding a slap for being so lily-livered. In the end it falls between the delicate and full-blown fruity stools. 43%

⊹⊱ **Old Bardstown Black Label** (85.5) n20 t22.5 f21.5 b21.5. Lush and overtly simplistic there is enough oiled honey and busy small grains to keep you very pleasantly entertained. 43%

⊹⊱ **Old Bardstown Black Label** (88) n21.5 a corn oil convention; t23 an oil slick on the palate involving corn and chattering rye; some liquorice underlines the oak; f21.5 remains long with light sugars countering the building spice; b22 forget about the 2% difference in strength. On this showing, a whiskey with a different mindset and a more muscular body and liberal use of spice. I'm a sucker for this style of bourbon: love it! 45%

⊹⊱ **Old Bardstown Estate Bottled** (86.5) n22.5 t22.5 f21 b20.5. Just a tad too sweet for greatness, though there is plenty to enjoy along the way. Can't help feeling the complexity levels are lost en route. 50.5%

⋄ **Old Bardstown Gold Label** (83) n20.5 t21.5 f20 b21. Sweet, citrusy, juicy, uncomplicated, session whiskey. 40%

Old Charter 8 Years Old (78) n19 t22 f18 b19. Sweetened up of late and even has a bit of pulse early on. But the finish is dull. 40% ⊙ ⊙

Old Charter 10 Years Old (84) n20.5 t23 f19.5 b21. From a dazed Brontosaurus, as I described it previously, to one that's been prodded awake. Still cumbersome, but now attacks those citrus and liquorice leaves with a spicy relish. Dozes off again at the end, though, for all the chocolate. 43% ⊙ ⊙

⋄ **Old Crow Reserve Aged 4 Years** (86) n21.5 t22.5 f21 b21. Huge colour for a 4-year-old. Loads of mocha and fruit on the nose and plenty of toffee on the finish. But the star attraction is the big, oily, fat delivery full of liquorice and brown-sugared coffee. 43% (86 proof)

Old Fitzgerald (83.5) n19 t21 f22 b21.5. A greatly improved bourbon that is beginning to feel more at home in its sweet, vaguely spicy surroundings. 43% ⊙

Old Fitzgerald's (85.5) n21 t22 f21 b21.5. That's much more like it! After a time in the doldrums, this bourbon has fought back in style. Still one of the sweetest on the market. But the intensity of the spice and the manner in which it dovetails with the Demerara sugars is most enjoyable. Fitz beautifully... 45% ⊙ ⊙

Old Fitzgerald Very Special 12 Years Old (93) n24 lively and energetic, there is a wonderful interweave between liquorice-led ancient notes and something much younger in style. A real freshness, accentuated by the peppery wheat: wow! t23.5 the sugars are off running – mostly muscovado. But there is a fruit fudge element, too, with the inevitable peppers popping up almost from the first beat and then continuing unabated; f22.5 the corn floods back adding a custardy element. The spices cannot be tamed, though; b23 there is always something that makes the heart sing when you come across a whiskey which appears so relaxed in its excellence. At the moment my heart is in the shower merrily lathering itself... 45% ⊙ ⊙

Old Forester Birthday Bourbon dist Spring 93, bott 2005 (94) n24 t23 f23 b24 One of the most rye-studded stars in the bourbon firmament and wholly in keeping with the fabulous quality for which this brand has now become a byword. 40%

Old Grand-Dad (90.5) n22 t23 f23 b23.5. This one's all about the small grains. A busy, lively bourbon, this offers little to remind me of the original Old Grand-Dad whiskey made out at Frankfort. That said, this is a whisk(e)y-lover's whiskey: in other words the excellence of the structure and complexity outweighs any historical misgivings. Enormously improved and now very much at home with its own busy style. 43%

Old Grand-Dad Bonded 100 Proof (94.5) n22.5 light rye spices and citrus fruit pop around the glass. One of those weighty yet delicate bourbons, but here the small grain appear at full throttle; t24 impossible not to be blown away. Exactly like the nose, you are expecting from first impact thundering, almost bullying oak. Instead your taste buds are mesmerised by a fabulous infusion of busy rye: a thousand tiny, crisp explosions in every quarter of the mouth followed by a layering of coconut strands dipped in lightly charred, molten sugars...; f23.5 very toasty with the oak now unflinchingly taking the rye on; b24.5 obviously Old Grand-dad knows a thing or two about classy whiskey: this is a magnificent version, even by its own high standards. It was always a winner and one you could bet your shirt on for showing how the small grains can impact upon complexity. But this appears to go a stage further. The base line is a touch deeper, so there is more ground to cover on the palate. It has been a whiskey-lover's whiskey for a little while and after a few barren years, has been inching itself back to its great Frankfort days. The fact that Beam's quality has risen over the last decade has played no insignificant part in that. 50% ⊙ ⊙

Old Heaven Hill Bottled in Bond (79) n18.5 t20.5 f20 b20. Doesn't have much to choose from flavour-wise. But what it has, it has in spades...especially the maple syrup and vanilla. 50% ⊙ ⊙

Old Heaven Hill Very Rare Old Aged 8 Years (88) n23 such a busy little nose! Rye showing various degrees of weight and very attractive marmalade notes I wouldn't normally associate with this brand; t22 a strange interplay between thin rye and a fuller, oiler thrust; f21 tires towards the end and falls back to a safer vanilla mode; b22 now that is very different! In fact, I can't say I have ever come across a flavour profile quite like it. Maybe it's all from one distillery. I may be wrong, but I get the feeling that the complexity indicates the influence of more than DSP type. 43% ⊙ ⊙

Old Heaven Hill Very Rare Old Aged 10 Years Bottled In Bond (77.5) n19 t20 f19 b19.5. Good Heavens...!! What happened here? I remember this as the mad dog of the whiskey world, thrashing around my palate like something demented. Now it appears the men in the white coats have injected a sedative. Plenty of goody-two-shoes corn and vanilla...but where's the chemistry? 50% ⊙ ⊙

◦◦◦ **Old Kentucky Aged 4 Years** (84) n22 t22.5 f19 b20.5. Hugely enjoyable, busy bourbon where the small grains run amuck for a while. Perhaps over-sweetens towards the middle and runs out of steam towards the end. But as 4-year-olds go, quite a little treat. 40% (80 proof)

Old Rip Van Winkle 10 Years Old (93) n24 absolutely benchmark 10-y-o bourbon to nose: a kaleidoscope of warmed walnut, a vague hint of juniper, more than a twist of citrus and a friendly corn oil carrying vanillas and liquorice. Glorious...; t23 soft corn oils here, too. Guarantees a baby's bum softness before the spices kick in to ensure a lively welcome for the more graceful molassed notes; f23 still those oils persist and hold in place the richer elements of the delivery for a good while with cocoa nudging its way in alongside some late sugars; b23 a much sharper cookie than it once was. And possibly a Maryland Cookie, too, what with the nuts and chocolate evident. As graceful as it is entertaining. 45% (90 Proof). Buffalo Trace ⊙ ⊙

Old Taylor Aged 6 Years (89) n23 marzipan and Seville orange offer a delightful lightness of touch and teasing complexity; t23 almost a hint of single malt about the lightness of touch to the honey here; the arrival is sweet and busy with just enough oaky depth to add ballast; f21 almost vanishes off the palate though the rye and spice stick around to impress; b22 the curiously thin finish is in telling contrast to the superbly honeyed middle that simple dances with small-grain charm. So much lighter than the original Old Taylor (see below) of McCracken Pike. But certainly has enough weight and fruit punch to make this better than the cheap brand it is perceived to be. 40% ⊙

Old Virginia Aged 6 Years (79) n20 t21 f18.5 b19.5. Old Virginia because of the drying tobacco leaf on the aroma? Sweet, but a lot flatter than the state... 40%. La Martiniquaise.

Old Virginia Aged 8 Years L434401A (85) n22 t21 f21 b21. Vanilla-rich and never quite lives up to the bold nose. 40%. La Martiniquaise, France.

Old Weller Antique 107 (96) n24.5 only pour this one if you have a good half hour to spare: the nose absolutely mesmerises as it changes shape and depth continuously. The honeys are soft and graceful, never dominating but rounding edges. The spices are well mannered yet condiment. The fruit takes the direction of apple and mango. Together they create a near faultless harmony; t24 the wheat is vibrant, pressing bold spices into a honeyed core. The layering accentuated by the liquorice and hickory which balance the sweeter elements with rare panache; f23.5 long with varying textures of oak. Never dries too much while refusing to allow the bountiful sugars the upper hand. All the time the spices throb... b24 this almost blew me off my chair. Always thought this was pleasant, if a little underwhelming, in the past. However, this bottling has had a few thousands volts past through it as it now comes alive on the palate with a glorious blending of freshness and debonair aging. One of the surprise packages of 2012. 53.5% ⊙ ⊙

Pappy Van Winkle's Family Reserve 15 Years Old (96) n24.5 the usual blood oranges by the cartload...the lilting mix of plum juice and white bread kneaded until it has become a sweet, sugary ball. All that plus a shy spiciness and some broad oak. But what makes it all work is the lightness of the mix...so big...yet so delicate...; t23.5 lush but with those threatening oaks on the nose exploding on impact. For a moment just a little OTT, but then several huge waves of cocoa-lined vanilla and marmalade puts the world to rights again...; f24 long and back to unbridled elegance. Cocoas flit around, as do these wheated softly, softly spices and layers of thinned manuka honey... stunning...; b24 at a book signing in Canada earlier this year a Bible enthusiast asked me which well-aged, wheated bourbon he should look for. I told him Pappy 15. He looked at me quizzically and said: "Well, that's what I thought, but in the Bible you have it down as rye-recipe." I told him he was wrong... until I checked there and then. And discovered he was right. Of course, Pappy has always been wheated and the lushness on the palate and spices radiating from it has always confirmed this. I'll put it down to not spitting enough. Or perhaps the speed at which I type whilst tasting. Sometimes you mean one thing – then another word comes out. Like when a member of my staff asks for a pay rise. I mean no. But somehow say yes. So apologies to any other I fooled out there. For not only is this a wheated bourbon. With its improbable degree of deftness for something so big, it has edged up a notch or two into a truly world great whiskey...whatever the recipe. 53.5% (107 proof) ⊙ ⊙

Pappy Van Winkle's Family Reserve 20 Years Old (85) n19.5 t22 f22 b21.5. Definitely a marked improvement upon recent years with the sugars and spices finding far better synchronisation and harmony than in many previous bottling. And the lushness to the mouth feel has distinctly improved. But the oak remains too powering, thereby upsetting the balance. I know I am a loan voice among commentators here, but... 45.2% (90.4 proof) ⊙ ⊙

Pappy Van Winkle's Family Reserve 23 Years Old (78) n18 t24 f17 b19. If I remember correctly, the last time I tasted this guy, the nose was a turn on while the body left me pretty cold. Bit of an about face here. Now the aroma shows signs of some of the soapier elements of the oak being exposed (much like a Scotch malt which has lived too long in a third-filled cask), and that in turn has, as is usually the case, a negative knock-on effect with the finish. But the delivery, vibrant with spice and trade mark blood orange, is nothing short of stunning. *47.8% (95.6 proof)* ⊙ ⊙

Parker's Heritage Collection (94.5) n22.5 t24 f24 b24. A bourbon for men – and probably women – with hairs on their chests. The bottle suggests you add water to this. Yeah, if you're a gutless wimp. I have known Parker Beam since before the barrels selected for this was a wicked glint in the old distiller's eye. And I can't believe he didn't pass many a barrel by before he chose those which have given us one of the best new whiskeys of the year. An instant classic. And a new must have bourbon is born. *64.8% (1296 proof)*

Parker's Heritage Collection Second Edition Aged 27 Years bott 2008 **(93)** n23 t23 f23.5 b23.5. An improbably excellent bourbon from the oldest commercial bottling I can remember ever seeing. To be honest, I expected the worst and if someone was to ask me prior to tasting this what hope I would have for bourbon of this age hitting the heights, my answer would not have been particularly positive. However, I have now known Parker Beam for more years than I care to admit and am 100% confident in his sound values: he is without a shadow of doubt in the highest echelon of whiskey and whisky men there have been in our generation. It was he who selected the casks so I was intrigued (also in why they didn't bring out 100 single barrel bottlings rather than dump them together for a one-off, but that's another story), to put it mildly. And the result of 27 years in the barrel are an entirely unique experience not even close to being similar to any other whisky in the world. Indeed, it as if it has not so much entered another whisky world but a parallel universe. Normally I'd shudder at the thought of so much oak. However, this works - and some! I hear it's going for 200 bucks a bottle. I don't normally comment on price but, believe me, for its uniqueness of style alone it's a snip. *48% (96 proof)*

Parker's Heritage Collection Third Edition 2009 "Golden Anniversary" (96.5) n24.5 t24.5 f23 b24.5. A whiskey entirely befitting Parker, a quiet colossus not just in the bourbon industry but the world whisky stage. This whiskey, like the man, is the real deal. *50% (100 proof)*

Parker's Herritage Collection Fourth Edition Aged 10 Years wheated bourbon **(95.5)** n25 t24 f23 b23.5. Here we go again: you know if a whiskey has Parker's name on it, you have to strap yourself in and go for the long haul. One of those bourbons which starts off as though it is going to overwhelm you, but calms down to show it's just a good, well-mannered boy at heart and the epitome of great bourbon. A bit like Parker, I guess... *63.9% (1278 proof).* Heaven Hill. 4800 bottles.

⋄⋄⋄ **Parker's Heritage Collection Wheated Mash Bill Bourbon Aged 10 Years (97)** n24 a faultless aroma: dried fruits (mainly dates and plums) with crushed pine nuts and a sensual spiciness. The sugars are relaxed and, naturally, of the darkened variety, softening the mocha; t24 magnificent bite on delivery, showing this is not a showcase whiskey, but a living and breathing bourbon. The muscovado sugars are in molten form; the honey is manuka and no other while the spices set about their task with relish. The oils are light but weighty enough to spread the word with ease; f24.5 long and now more refined...as a finish should always be. Some evidence of vanilla but the liquorice and honeycomb gang together with purpose and poise; b24.5 hard to find the words that can do justice. I know Parker will be immensely proud of this. And with every good reason: I am working exceptionally hard to find a fault with this either from a technical distillation viewpoint or a maturation one. Or just for its sheer whiskeyness...A potential World Whisky of the Year. *62.1% (124.2 Proof).* ncf. 4800 bottles (est)

Peach Street Bourbon (86) n19 t22 f23 b22. The nose, though the weak link, is not without its charms; the delivery offers excellent spice and a real fruit cake quality, complete with juicy dates. The finish, as the oak finds a home, really is a joy. Impressive stuff from a small batch distiller and a two-year-old bourbon. *43% Peach Street Distillers, Colorado.*

⋄⋄⋄ **Pure Kentucky Batch 10-96 (77)** n20 t20 f19 b18. Surprisingly fruity but lacks cohesion and direction from first to last. *53.5% (107 proof)*

Ridgemont Reserve 1792 Aged 8 Years (94.5) n23.5 throbbing, pulsing oak is kept comfortably in check with a soft honey and mint restraint. Fabulous depth and even a hint of salt to season the effect; t24 Barton's unique rye and Demerara combo is in full swing here and contrasts fascinatingly with the deeper, vaguely bitterish oak notes; f23.5 back to a vanilla and rye thread here, oscillating where the pulsing of the spice is sublime; b23.5 now here is a whiskey which appears to have come to terms with its own strengths and, as with all bourbons and malts, limitations. Rarely did whiskey from Barton reach this level of maturity, so harnessing its charms always involves a bit of a learning curve. Each time I taste this it appears a little better than the last...and this sample is no exception to the rule. Excellent. *46.85% (93.7 Proof)* ⊙ ⊙

Rock Hill Farms Single Barrel (85.5) n22 t22 f20 b21.5. An interesting, but perhaps little known point, is that I never read tasting notes of a brand from previous years until after I have tasted the present whiskey. I can usually remember anyway. But this struck me as being a bit odd, even before I referred back, as it seemed to have an extra summer or two to ramp up the intensity, especially of the sugared-marmalade delivery. But the finish still struck me as typically corn led and stubbornly docile. Pleasant, though, if pretty true to type. 50% ☉ ☉

·⋙· **Rowan's Creek** batch 10-109 (67) n17.5 t19 f15 b16 Pity: the odd barrel in here should not have got through. Definite soapy quality on the nose is countered by a big maple syrup kick on delivery. But the finish confirms all is not well. Talk about up the creek... 50.05% (100.1 proof)

Russell's Reserve Small Batch 10 Year Old (92.5) n24.5 in many ways, one of the most beguiling and intriguing of all bourbon noses. As a small batch I had expected my tasting notes to be different from the last. Yet each time I picked out gooseberries present, though here I also spot some high quality Danish marzipan, complete with a light, vaguely milky cocoa note. Raspberries are around, too, while the Demerara sugars so normally prevalent are happy to take a back seat. There is plenty of toffee and vanilla but it never gets in the way of this improbable bourbon story...; t23 that toffee and vanilla on the nose has a far bigger say on the palate and though bolstered by several shock waves of spice, only occasionally allows some rye to pucker through; f22 creamy textured, busy spice and so much vanilla...; b23 had the quality and complexity on the palate followed on from the nose I may well have had the world's No 1 whisky for 2012 in my glass. Just slum it with something quite wonderful, instead. Still waiting for an official explanation as to why this is a miserly 90 proof, when Jimmy Russell's preferred strength is 101, by the way... 45%. Wild Turkey. ☉ ☉

·⋙· **Sainsbury's Kentucky Bourbon 3 Year Old** (76.5) n19 t19.5 f19 b19. About the most caramel-flattened bourbon I have tasted in a very long time. 40%. Sainsbury's UK.

Speakeasy Select dist 28 Jan 93 (87) n22 t22.5 f21.5 b21. pleasant, but one or four Summers too long for this barrel. 58.1%. Steelbach Hotel, Louisville, Kentucky.

Ten High (68) n17.5 t16.5 f17 b17. Always one of the lighter bourbons, now sporting a curious sweetness which does little to engage. Still a good mixer, though. 40% ☉

Tom Moore (85.5) n20 t22 f21.5 b22. An improved and engaging whiskey happy to display its increased fruit and complexity. The babbling on the palate of the small grain is a treat. 40% ☉ ☉

·⋙· **Tom Moore 100 Proof** (88.5) n21 a beautiful mixing of custard and rye; look out for the citrus, too; t23 superb! Thick on the palate, but it immediately melts down to its constituent small grain and rough oak parts; some cocoa invades the middle ground; f22 mocha, sweetened by Demerara sugar but the late spice attack stars; b22.5 another bourbon showing the inimitable Barton 1792 Distillery house style. The majority entertain but fall short in one department or another. Here, thanks to a little less water added in the bottling hall, we can really see how this whiskey can really tick. 50% (100 Proof)

Van Winkle Special Reserve 12 Years Old lot B (77.5) n18.5 t22 f18 b19. A very curious bottling: the nose and finish are both lacking in substance. But the delivery offers brief, spicy, slightly jammy riches. 45.2% (90.4 proof) ☉ ☉

Van Winkle 23 Years Old (89.5) n23 big oak impact but still breathing with some soft coffee notes; a freshly opened bag of Liquorice Allsorts candy; t23 sweet muscovado sugars help the liquorice see off some probing pine notes; pulsing spices and diced, slightly burnt apple pie; f21.5 burnt French toast; b22 more of a Van Wrinkle: this is showing a lot of age. But enough of a pulse for one last enthralling show. 57% (114 proof). Buffalo Trace.

Very Old Barton (85.5) n21 t22 f21 b21.5. A fair slab of vanilla to go with the busy-ish spice. Attractive, but nothing like as complex as the 6-y-o label. 40% (80 proof) ☉

·⋙· **Very Old Barton 90 Proof** (94) n23 a bit of mint in the tea this time. And perhaps an extra spoonful of sugar; t24 the rye and small grain have gone into overdrive. One of the busiest Kentucky whiskeys with no shortage of layering...and spice; f23.5 tons of vanilla to bring the curtain down on the budding history and liquorice; b23.5 one of the most dangerously drinkable whiskeys in the world... 45% (90 proof)

·⋙· **Very Old Barton 100 Proof** (86) n22 t22 f21 b21. Enjoyable and well made for sure. But by VOB standards pretty dense and one dimensional with the light liquorice-vanilla note having too big a say. Lacking the usual small grain and rye intensity, this cannot be explained by the extra strength alone. 50% (100 proof)

Very Old Barton 6 Years Old (92) n23 I think this is an aroma in the past I have compared to Sahara's camp fires and green tea. Not surprising, really...because that experience is conjured yet again by the very distinct nose. Here, though, a little extra (brown) sugar is added, which I don't remember last time out...; t23 a slightly oilier delivery than normal, but the usual small grain/rye firmness is soon evident and entertaining; f23 elegant vanilla and spices; **b23** one of those seemingly gifted bourbons that, swan-like, appears to glide at the surface but on closer inspection has loads going on underneath. *43%* ☉ ☉

Virgin Bourbon 7 Years Old (96.5) n24 so Wild Turkey-esque in style it is almost untrue: just loads of honey spilling out of the glass, backed up by big rye and leathery oak; **t24.5** hold on to the arm of your seats...the mouth feel is massive with chocolate honeycomb surrounded by juicy dates and figs; liquorice has been piled high with really thick molasses...quite incredible; **f24** the corn oils carry the sugars to the very end. But like distant thunder beyond the limestone hills, comes the spices and that liquorice, now with a touch of hickory, rumbling to the last...; **b24** this takes me back nearly 40 years to when I first began my love affair with bourbon and was still a bit of a whisky virgin. This was the very style that blew me away: big, uncompromising, rugged...yet with a heart of honeyed gold. It is the type of huge, box-ticking, honest bourbon that makes you get on your hands and knees and kiss Kentucky soil. *50.5% (101 proof)* ☉ ☉

Virgin Bourbon 15 Years Old (92.5) n23.5 t23 f23.5 b23. The kind of bourbon you want to be left in a room with. *50.5% (101 proof)*

⋰ **Virginia Gentleman (90.5) n22** curiously yeasty yet quite full bodied. Plenty of corn but it is the fruit-oak marriage which wins hands down; **t23** the full gamut of delicate citrus notes are eventually overpowered by the increasing cocoa; **f23** charming oaks add depth to what might have been an overly-sweet, sugary finish; impressive oils last the course; **b23.5** a Gentleman in every sense: and a pretty sophisticated one at that. *40% (80 Proof)*

Walker's DeLuxe 3 Years Old (86) n22 t22 f21 b21. Excellent by 3-y-o standards. *40%*

Weller Special Reserve 7 Years Old (83) n20 t21 f21 b21. Pleasant stuff which sings a fruity tune and is ably backed by subtle spice. Perhaps a little too sweet, though. *45%* ☉

Weller 12 Years Old (93) n24 there always appears to be fruit on the nose of this guy and here it is again: green, crunchy toffee apple, apricot and young melon. A little Swiss milk chocolate yodels its presence while the spices tease and prickle. All rather yummy...; **t23.5** silk with attitude: corn oil, honey and a few tongue-withering peppers; **f22.5** dries, allowing a full look at the 12 years of oak...and that milk chocolate is back; **b23** sheer quality. And an enormous leap in complexity and grace from the 7-y-o. *45%* ☉ ☉

Wild Turkey (77) n19 t19 f20 b19. As sweet and simple as bourbon gets. Shows few of the qualities that make it such astonishing whiskey when older. *40% (80 proof)*

Wild Turkey 101 (91) n22 the nose still appears to have a big vanilla cap on it. But now a few traces of sugar and spice can be detected while the orange blossom blooms...a vast improvement; **t23.5** luxurious mouth feel. But those spices really get cracking early on and immediately pepper the shafts of sugary light which try to reach the oaky depth; **f22.5** remains chewy with a big vanilla swirl at the death; **b23** by far the best 101 I have tasted in a decade: you simply can't do anything but go weak at the knees with that spice attack. *55.5% (101 proof)* ☉ ☉

Wild Turkey American Spirit Aged 15 Years (92) n24 t22.5 f22.5 b23. A delightful Wild Turkey that appears under par for a 100 proofer but offers much when you search those nooks and crannies of your palate. *50.0% (100 proof)*

⋰ **Wild Turkey Kentucky Spirit Single Barrel** barrel no. 96, bott. 5/13/09, warehouse F rick 16 **(86.5) n21.5 t22.5 f21 b21.5.** More dense from nose to finish than the type of forest the real Wild Turkey prefers to inhabit. Lots of delicious butterscotch and mocha on show, but surprisingly little development. *50% (100 proof)*

Wild Turkey Rare Breed bott code L0049FH **(94) n22.5** the oak and fruit is of that firm, almost smoky, variety that will be readily recognised and appreciated by devotees of Oregon Pino Noit. However, this is a very different bird to the one I last spotted: the butterscotch and honey are absent leaving berry fruits to dominate. Attractive but very odd; **t24.5** much more like it! The puckering oaks are immediately set upon by pots of acacia honey and slightly overcooked butterscotch tart. Reminiscent of the Rare Breed of the early 2000s with the oak pulling up trees, so to speak. The rye notes kick in at about midpoint and dig in satisfyingly deeply; **f23** very long with the burned elements offering the required gravitas. Also overcooked prunes are lightened by under-ripe dates...; **b24** it is hard to credit that this is the same brand I have been tasting at regular intervals for quite a long while. Certainly nothing like this style has been around for a decade and it is massively far removed from two years ago. The nose threatens a whiskey limited in direction. But the delivery is as profound as it is entertaining. Even on this bottling's singular though fabulous style, not perhaps quite overall the gargantuan whiskey of recent years. But, seeing as it's only the nose which pegs it back a point or two, still one that would leave a big hole in your whiskey experience if you don't get around to trying. *54.1%* ☉ ☉

Wild Turkey Tradition Aged 14 Years db **(89) n23 t21.5 f22.5 b22.** Something of a departure in style for a Wild Turkey (which is why it is a little odd it is called "Tradition"): this one makes a point of being an old bird. *50.5% (101 proof)*

⌐ **Willett Pot Still Reserve** barrel no. 2421 **(95.5) n24.5** gorgeous honey daubed over a Maryland cookie, with nuts and cocoa showing just ahead of the lightest of spice; just a touch of pine denotes the aging; as near as damn it faultless... **t23** and, just as the nose suggests, it is as soft as it gets with its soothing honeycomb countering the liquorice but layers of spice injecting zest and life; all kinds of rich, sherried fruitcake notes towards the middle...in fact something of a sherry trifle; **t24** finishes like a throat lozenge: more melting honey and a hint of a little menthol...beautifully delicate for all the weight; **b24** another quite fabulous whiskey from Willett. You can so often trust them to deliver and here they have given us a bourbon showing serious oak injection, yet a sweetness which counters perfectly. *47%. 273 bottles.*

Willett Straight Kentucky Bourbon Aged 17 Years white oak barrel no. 1599, bott no. 9 of 36, dist Apr 91 **(86) n22 t22 f21 b21.** An overdose of natural caramels puts a cap on the complexity. Thoroughly enjoyable, but follows few trails. *53.6%. Heinz Taubenheim.*

Willett Straight Kentucky Bourbon Aged 17 Years Barrel Proof white oak barrel no. 1598, bott no. 6 of 72, dist Apr 91 **(95) n23.5 t24.5 f23.5 b24.** Truly great, memorable bourbon. No argument. *60.5% (121 Proof). Heinz Taubenheim.*

Willett Straight Kentucky Bourbon Aged 19 Years Barrel Proof white oak barrel no. 8552, bott no. 5 of 5, dist Mar 90 **(77) n21 t18 f20 b17.** This is so outrageously over oaked it nearly pulls it off! *63.9% (127.8 Proof). Heinz Taubenheim.*

William Larue Weller (97) n24 t24 f25 b24. Among the best wheated mash bill bourbon I have ever encountered. Why some whiskeys work better than others is the stuff of long debate. The reason for this particular bottling is relatively simple: you have an almost breathless intensity, yet somehow the constituent parts of the complexity can be individually identified and savoured. That is quite rare in any whiskey with this degree of weight. *67.4% (134.8 proof). ncf.*

⌐ **William Larue Weller** bott. 2010 **(93) n24** the forest of oak is penetrable and once you reach the clearing it is easier to see the dank, earthy bluebells and cinnamon apple. Big, spicy and almost claustrophobically dense; **t23.5** at first the Demerara sugars give the taste buds a gentle welcome, but puckering oak is not far behind. No surprise, with the wheat recipe, that spices come galloping in scything down all before it; finally a jammy, fruity middle is reached...but you are still left chewing splinters; **f22** mocha and liquorice dominate at first but those drier oaks inevitably take control; **b23.5** there is a fine line between over oaking and greatness. This one has just a little too much barrel for it to reach the magnitude of the previous year's bottling which I rate the second best whisk(e)y in the world. Still a five course meal of a bourbon and one to savour. *63.3% (126.6 proof)*

⌐ **Winn Dixie Bourbon (84.5) n19 t22 f21.5 b22.** An entirely agreeable and more-ish bourbon which makes the most of its delicious kumquat and spice backbone. *40%*

Woodford Reserve Master's Collection Four Grain (95) n24 t24 f23 b24. Sod's law would have it that the moment we removed this from the 2006 Bible, having appeared in the previous two editions without it ever making the shelves, it should at last be belatedly released. But a whiskey worth waiting for, or what? The tasting notes are not a million miles from the original. But this is better bourbon, one that appears to have received a significant polish in the intervening years. Nothing short of magnificent. *46.2%*

⌐ **Zachariah Harris (89) n22** light, layered oak with a clean, sweet depth; **t23** busy, lots of small grains with a pounding rye and oak contrast; a background hum of honey and a rich oil base; **f22** long, the honey now intensifying with the vanilla; **b22** very good quality, not overly taxing fayre where the spices harmonise comfortably with the generous honey on show. Lovely, every day drinking. *40%*

Tennessee Whiskey
BENJAMIN PRICHARD

⌐ **Benjamin Prichard's Tennessee Whiskey (83) n21.5 t21 f20 b20.5.** Majestic fruity rye notes trill from the glass. Curiously yeasty as well; bounding with all kinds of freshly crushed brown sugar crystals. Pleasant enough, but doesn't gel like Prichard's bourbon. *40%*

GEORGE DICKEL

George Dickel Superior No 12 Brand (90.5) n22.5 the tannins have been ramped up here and there is no shortage of molasses to compensate; quite floral in part and a touch of green tomato, too! **t23** much bigger delivery than a year or so back: again it's all oak and molasses up front forming an impressive, chewy clump. Spices swirl around with the corn oil; the middle is mocha; **f22.5** long, with the mocha finale taking on a slightly creamy texture; **b22.5** a slightly different story told by George from the last one I heard. But certainly no less fascinating. *45%* ⊙ ⊙

JACK DANIEL
Gentleman Jack Rare Tennessee Whiskey (77) n19 t20 f18 b19. A Tennessee that appears to have achieved the impossible: it has got even lighter in character in recent years. A whiskey which wilfully refuses to say anything particularly interesting or go anywhere, this is one for those prefer their hard liquor soft. 40%. Brown-Forman.

Jack Daniel's (Green Label) (84) n20 t21 f22 b21. A light but lively little gem of a whiskey. Starts as a shrinking violet, finishes as a roaring lion with nimble spices ripping into the developing liquorice. A superb session whiskey. 40% (80 proof)

Jack Daniel's Old No. 7 Brand (Black Label) (87) n21 thick, oily, smoky, dense, corn syrupy ... it's Jack Daniel; **t23** sweet, fat, chewy, various types of burnt notes: tofffee, toast etc. etc; **f21** quite a sweet, fat and toffeed finale; **b22** a quite unique whiskey at which many American whiskey connoisseurs turn up their noses. I always think it's worth the occasional visit; you can't beat roughing it a little. 40% (80 proof). Brown-Forman.

Jack Daniel's Single Barrel barrel no.7-3915, bott 28 Sep 07 **(87)** n21.5 t22 f22 b21.5. Pleasant, yet perhaps not the most inspiring single cask I have come across from JD. This one refuses to offer up the usual oily weight. 45%. Brown-Forman.

Corn Whiskey
Dixie Dew (95) n22.5 corn whiskey...???? Really...??? The corn oils form a bit of a sweet blob, but elsewhere it is all about graduated degrees of cocoa and hickory...and all rather lovely. **t24** good grief!! Have not tasted a profile such as this: healthy corn oils but then a welter of Columbian Santander Cacao and rye-rich spices interject. Absolutely unique and astonishing...; **f24** the corn plays out its long farewell but the spices don't listen and take up the main ground; a few juicy sultanas fly in...from goodness knows where; **b24.5** I have kept in my previous tasting notes for this whiskey as they serve a valuable purpose. The three matured corn whiskeys I have before me are made by the same distillers. But, this time round, they could not be more different. From Mellow Corn to Dixie we have three whiskeys with very differing hues. This, quite frankly, is the darkest corn whiskey I have ever seen and one of world class stature with characteristics I have never found before in any whiskey. Any true connoisseur of whisk(e)y will make deals with Lucifer to experience this freak whiskey. There is no age statement...but this one has gray hairs attached to the cob... 50%

Georgia Moon Corn Whiskey "Less Than 30 Days Old" (83.5) n21.5 t22 f20 b20. If anyone has seen corn whiskey made – either in Georgia or Kentucky – then the unique aroma will be instantly recognisable from the fermenters and still house. Enjoyable stuff which does exactly what it says on the jar. 50% ⊙⊙

J. W. Corn (92.5) n23 I have long associated this brand with sophistication...and still do. The spice and cocoa layering is sublime, the injection of citrus startling; **t23.5** sweet, very graciously oiled; corn leads the charge but the oak backed by vanilla and butterscotch is not far behind; **f23** back to a nutty chocolate number with a clever sub plot of dates and red liquorice; **b23** in another life this could be bourbon. The corn holds the power, for sure. But the complexity and levels are so far advanced that this – again! – qualifies as very high grade whiskey. Wonderful that the normal high standard is being maintained for what is considered by many, quite wrongly, as an inferior spirit. 50% ⊙⊙

Mellow Corn (83) n19 t21 f22 b21. Dull and oily on the nose, though the palate compensates with a scintillating array of sweet and spicy notes. 50% ⊙

Single Malt Rye
ANCHOR DISTILLERY
Old Potrero Single Malt Hotaling's Whiskey Aged 12 Years Essay MCMVI-MMVII (96) n24 t25 f23 b24. I have tasted this Essay against the previous one, and whilst there are the odd subtle differences, this is the closest in style I have ever found two Potreroes to be: their likeness, in general terms, is uncanny. This one has perhaps the slightly drier finish but on the complexity front there is nothing to compare in the whisky world. I am not, remotely, an advocate of whisky and food. But I could murder a beautifully marbled T bone at my third favourite steak joint in the world, Harris's of San Francisco (still has a little way to go to match the incomparable The Ring in Portland and, at a shorter distance, Barbarian's in Toronto), and follow after a delicate pause with a glass of this local super whisky. Life rarely, if ever, gets better than that. 50% (100 proof)

Old Potrero Single Malt Straight Rye Whiskey Essay 10-SRW-ARM-E (94) n24 t23 f24 b23 The whiskey from this distillery never fails to amaze. With the distillery now under new management it will be fascinating to see what lands in my tasting lab. Even at 75% quality we will still be blessed with astonishing whiskeys. 45% (90 proof)

Straight Rye

Abraham Bowman Limited Edition dist 4/3/98, bott. 12/15/09 **(85) n21 t22 f21 b21.** For those who like rye with their vanilla. *63.2%*

Bulleit 95 Rye (96) n25 only the rye from the Lawrenceburg Indiana distillery can conjure a perfect rye aroma such as this...and that is exactly where it is from. Cinnamon and crunchy muscovado sugar crystal on green apple...so soft...so rigid...so unique...; **t24.5** exactly as the nose is fashioned, so is the delivery. At once litingly soft yet absolutely granite hard... the rye offers both fruity and spicy branches...both lead to a salivating trunk; **f22.5** echoes of firm grain and fruit but pretty quick by comparison to what has gone on before...**23.5** this is a style of rye, indeed whiskey, which is unique. Buffalo Trace makes an ultra high-quality rye which lasts the course longer. But nothing compares in nose and delivery to this...in fact few whiskies in the world get even close... *45%. Straight 95% rye mash whiskey.*

Cougar Rye (95) n25 t24 f23 b23. The Lawrenceburg, Indiana Distillery makes the finest rye I have ever tasted - and that is saying something. Here is a magnificent example of their astonishing capabilities. Good luck hunting the Cougar. *37%. Foster's Group, Australia.*

Devil's Bit Seven-Year-Old Single Barrel (93.5) n22.5 t24 f23 b24. A must-find rye from one of the most impressive small distilleries in the world. *47.7%. Edgefield Distillery.*

Fleischmann's Straight Rye (87.5) n22 a pipette drop of honey goes a long way; **t22.5** straight down the line rye: firm with a vaguely juicy bent while the honey really does begin to shine; **f21.5** pleasant enough, but surprisingly inert and dusty; **b21.5** one of the most spiceless ryes I have come across. But a lovely mouth-watering touch. *40%*

High West Rendezvous Blend of Straight Rye Whiskies Batch No. 78 (79) n18 t22 f19 b20. Virtually identical in style to their Double Rye (see below) *46%*

High West Double Rye (78.5) n18 t21.5 f19 b20. The strange tobacco-encrusted nose is compensated by the sharp rye and cocoa delivery. *46%*

High West 12 Years Old Rye (92.5) n22 oak and citrus appear to douse the higher rye notes; **t24** fabulous! Stunning and frighteningly brittle delivery where the rye is determined at impact every inch of the palate: the spices are contained but perfectly harmonised; **f23** a cocoa sub plot very much plays second fiddle to the insistent rye; some serious tannins make themselves heard; **b23.5** a very clever rye which will hit a chord of appreciation for those who savour this whiskey style. *46%*

High West Rocky Mountain 16 Years Old Rye (86.5) n20 t22.5 f22 b22. Here and there, the nose being a good example, the rye and vanilla cancel each other out. But there is enough viperfish spice and juicy fruit to keep you salivating for a good while. *46%*

High West Rocky Mountain 21 Year Old Rye (95) n23 how sexy is that dance between the milky cocoa and the piercing rye...? **t25** just about everything you could wish for: the rye (as is the case in the very best ones) offers a dual role: it both firms up and fruit enriches, and here refuses to overly play either hand. The sugars are pure melt in the mouth; honeydew melon and liquorice dry out towards a toasty butterscotch-hickory middle; **f23** relaxes to let the vanillas (aided by a little cocoa) take charge; **b24** bizarrely, tastes a whole lot younger than the 16-years-old. Lighter in both colour and character, here you get to see the full personality of an absolutely outstanding rye whiskey. *46%*

Jim Beam Rye (89) n22.5 the odd ray of rye pokes through the cloud of vanilla; occasionally the fruity rye builds into fruity clusters, then vanish again...intriguing doesn't quite cover it... **t23** mouth-watering delivery with those firm rye notes of yesteryear making a bold attempt at dominance. But sweetens out quickly and vanishes beneath the vanilla; **f21.5** a pleasant, spicy afterglow; **b22** it seemed that when Beam changed the colour of the label from bright, road-marking, yellow to a wash-out, over milked custard hue, the vividness had also mysteriously – and tragically - vanished from the rye. Still more caramel than the glory days of old, but unquestionably a very welcome, if limited, move back to its sharper old self. Great stuff once more...now let's see what they can do about the label... *40%* ⊙⊙

Old Overholt Four Years Old (85) n22 t21 f21 b21. Still little sign of this returning to its old rip-roaring best. Duller and less challenging with a frustrating dustiness to the procedings. *40%*

Pappy Van Winkle's Family Reserve Rye 13 Years Old (94) n24 outwardly, the aroma basks in a crisp rye flourish; scratch below the surface and there are darker, more sinister oaky forces at work; **t23.5** crisp, almost crackling rye offers both the fruity-clean and burned fruitcake options; **f23** dulls out a bit as the liquorice/toffee oak takes hold but remains alluringly spicy and sensual; **b23.5** uncompromising rye that successfully tells two stories simultaneously. A great improvement on the Winkle rye of old. *478%*

Pikesville (77.5) n17.5 t21.5 f19 b19. The freshness is absent here and instead we have a grumpy dustiness which limits development. Know when you have left your car lights on all night and you can't start engine next day? Yep...it's that flat... *40%* ⊙⊙

Rathskeller Rye dist 1983 **(95)** n24 t24 f23.5 b23.5. A beguiling rye of genuine beauty and charm which electrifies and excites; that complex, yielding hardness so typical of a great rye is something the tongue was invented for. Further exploration needed on my return to the hotel: just hope the bar still has it! 65%. *Steelbach Hotel, Louisville, Kentucky.*

⋯⊱ **(rī)**[1] **(94)** n23 now that's more like it from Beam: the rye is a solid mass, radiating all kinds of fruity notes. But there are intriguing spices, too, ranging from light cloves to varying peppers; t24 spot on delivery: as stark as a Kentucky cliff face and just as porous, too: the rye is crisp for sure and the citrus-induced salivating levels sublime. There is a slow build up of mildly milky chocolate, occasionally bordering on praline; f23.5 the cocoa continues all the way, now with vanilla edging its way in but those light citrus notes balancing against the increasing spice presence...just so complex... b23.5 (ri)ght up my alley. A fabulous meeting of crispy rye and much softer cocoa: an irresistible and ultra high quality addition to Kentucky's rye whiskey cannon. 46%

Rittenhouse (78.5) n18.5 t21.5 f19 b20. Juice and spice but lacking sharpness. 40% ⊙ ⊙

Rittenhouse 100 Proof Bottled in Bond (86.5) n20 t23 f21.5 b22. The nose labours for a Rittenhouse 100. But the salivating delivery and sweetly fashioned and richly-spiced rye makes a delightful impact on the palate. 50% ⊙ ⊙

Rittenhouse Very Rare Single Barrel 21 Years Old (91) n25 t23 f21 b22. I may be wrong, but I would wager quite a large amount that no-one living has tasted more rye from around the world than I. So trust me when I tell you this is different, a genuine one-off in style. By rights such telling oak involvement should have killed the whisky stone dead: this is like someone being struck by lightning and then walking off slightly singed and with a limp, but otherwise OK. The closest style of whisky to rye is Irish pot still, a unique type where unmalted barley is used. And the closest whiskey I have tasted to this has been 35 to 50-year-old pot still Irish. What they have in common is a massive fruit base, so big that it can absorb and adapt to the oak input over many years. This has not escaped unscathed. But it has to be said that the nose alone makes this worthy of discovery, as does the glory of the rye as it first melts into the tastebuds. The term flawed genius could have been coined for this whisky alone. Yet, for all its excellence, I can so easily imagine someone, somewhere, claiming to be an expert on whiskey, bleating about the price tag of $150 a bottle. If they do, ignore them. Because, frankly, rye has been sold far too cheaply for far too long and that very cheapness has sculpted a false perception in people's minds about the quality and standing of the spirit. Well, 21 years in Kentucky equates to about 40 years in Scotland. And you try and find a 40-year-old Scotch for £75. If anything, they are giving this stuff away. The quality of the whiskey does vary from barrel to barrel and therefore bottle to bottle. So below I have given a summary of each individual bottling (averaging (91.1). The two with the highest scores show the least oak interference...yet are quite different in style. That's great whiskey for you. 50% (100 proof). ncf. Heaven Hill.

Barrel no. 1 (91) n25 t23 f21 b22. As above. 50%

Barrel no. 2 (89) n24 t23 f20 b22. Dryer, oakier. 50%

Barrel no. 3 (91) n24 t23 f22 b22. Fruity, soft. 50%

Barrel no. 4 (90) n25 t22 f21 b22. Enormous. 50%

Barrel no. 5 (93) n25 t23 f22 b23. Early rye surge. 50%

Barrel no. 6 (87) n23 t22 f20 b22. Juicy, vanilla. 50%

Barrel no. 7 (90) n23 t23 f22 b22. Even, soft, honeyed. 50%

Barrel no. 8 (95) n25 t24 f23 b23. The works: massive rye. 50%

Barrel no. 9 (91) n24 t23 f22 b22. Sharp rye, salivating. 50%

Barrel no. 10 (93) n25 t24 f22 b22. Complex, sweet. 50%

Barrel no. 11 (93) n24 t24 f22 b23. Rich, juicy, spicy. 50%

Barrel no. 12 (91) n25 t23 f21 b22. Near identical to no.1. 50%

Barrel no. 13 (91) n24 t24 f22 b22. Citrus and toasty. 50%

Barrel no. 14 (94) n25 t24 f22 b23. Big rye and marzipan. 50%

Barrel no. 15 (88) n23 t22 f21 b22. Major oak influence. 50%

Barrel no. 16 (90) n24 t23 f21 b22. Spicy and toffeed. 50%

Barrel no. 17 (90) n23 t23 f22 b22. Flinty, firm, late rye kick. 50%

Barrel no. 18 (91) n24 t24 f21 b22. Big rye delivery. 50%

Barrel no. 19 (87) n23 t22 f21 b21. Major coffee input. 50%

Barrel no. 20 (91) n23 t24 f22 b22. Spicy sugar candy. 50%

Barrel no. 21 (94) n24 t23 f24 b23. Subtle, fruity. 50%

Barrel no. 22 (89) n23 t22 f22 b22. Mollased rye. 50%

Barrel no. 23 (94) n24 t23 f24 b23. Soft fruit, massive rye. 50%

Barrel no. 24 (88) n23 t22 f21 b22. Intense oak and caramel. 50%

Barrel no. 25 (93) n25 t22 f23 b23. Heavy rye and spice. *50%*
Barrel no. 26 (92) n23 t23 f23 b23. Subtle, delicate rye. *50%*
Barrel no. 27 (94) n25 t23 f23 b23. Delicate rye throughout. *50%*
Barrel no. 28 (96) n25 t24 f23 b24. Salivating, roasty, major. *50%*
Barrel no. 29 (88) n23 t22 f21 b22. Hot, fruity. *50%*
Barrel no. 30 (91) n24 t23 f22 b22. Warming cough sweets. *50%*
Barrel no. 31 (90) n25 t22 f21 b22. Aggressive rye. *50%*

Rittenhouse Rye Single Barrel Aged 25 Years bott Nov 09 (93.5) n24.5 cinnamon on apple crumble. That's perhaps the easy way of describing something which is almost too astonishingly complex for words. Remember how, with very good justification, I was blown away by the 21-year-old a few years back...? Well this has actually upped the game and taken the rye, nose-wise into a new dimension. When you are playing with old whiskies like this it is too easy for the cask to run away with itself; for an off note or a sign of tiredness to begin an unstoppable journey of destruction. It simply hasn't happened here: what we have is one of the ultimate experiences of truly great spirit being filled into entirely compatible top-drawer barrels and time being allowed to coax every last degree of complexity and beauty possible. Beyond that cinnamon, away from that apple crumble, we have so much more. Like ultra high quality Jamaican medium high ester pot still of advanced years from Long Pond; or lighter efforts from Hampden. There is a golden honey and coconut thread to this, a touch of leathery hickory, too. But we keep getting back to that rye-ramped fruitiness, the key to aroma puzzle... it really is a thing of ridiculous complexity and beauty. And, frankly, mystery... t24 an immediate arm locking of firm, rock-hard rye in the form of a candy-like fruited, crystalline Demerara sugar, and much more aggressive oak with a real thick hickory/camp coffee assertiveness: one heck of a confrontation; f22 long with a definite oak drawl but still a fruity juiciness fighting off the worst of the aging; b23 this is principally about the nose: a thing of rare beauty even in the highest peaks of the whiskey world. The story on the palate is much more about damage limitation with the oak going a bit nuts. But remember this: in Scottish years due to the heat in Kentucky, this would be a malt well in excess of 50 years. But even with the signs of fatigue, so crisp is that rye, so beautifully defined are its intrinsic qualities that the quality is still there to be clearly seen. Just don't judge on the first, second or even third mouthful. Your taste buds need time to relax and adjust. Only then will they accommodate and allow you to fully appreciate and enjoy the creaky old ride. At this age, though, always worth remembering that the best nose doesn't always equal the best tasting experience... 50% (100 proof). Heaven Hill.

Barrel no. 1 (93.5) n24.5 t24 f22 b23. As above. *50%*
Barrel no. 2 (88) n22 t24 f20 b22. Intense. Crisp, juicy; a tad soapy, bitter. *50%*
Barrel no. 3 (89.5) n23 t23.5 f21.5 b21.5. Fabulously crisp. Fruity. Mollassed. *50%*
Barrel no. 4 (85) n21.5 t21.5 f21 b21. Subdued fruit. Massive oak. *50%*
Barrel no. 5 (90.5) n25 t22.5 f21.5 b21.5. Complex. Mega oaked but spiced, fruity. *50%*
Barrel no. 6 (91.5) n24.5 t22 f23 b22. Tangy. Honeyed and hot. Spiced marmalade. *50%*
Barrel no. 7 (83.5) n20 t22 f20.5 b21. Treacle toffee amid the burnt apple. *50%*
Barrel no. 8 (90) n23.5 t23.5 f21 b22. Flinty, teeth-cracking rye. Crème brulee. *50%*
Barrel no. 9 (91) n23.5 t23.5 f22 b22. Massive ryefest. Mocha coated. *50%*
Barrel no. 10 (86.5) n22 t23 f20 b21.5. Early zip and juice. Tires towards caramel. *50%*
Barrel no. 11 (89) n24 t22 f21 b22. Honeycomb. Hickory. Caramel. Oil. *50%*
Barrel no. 12 (84.5) n22.5 t21 f20 b21. Delicate. Vanilla and caramel. Light. *50%*
Barrel no. 13 (89.5) t22.5 t23 f22 b22. Succulent. Yet rye remains firm. *50%*
Barrel no. 14 (88) n22 t23 f21 b22. Very similar to 13 but with extra caramel. *50%*
Barrel no. 15 (86) n21 t23 f20.5 b21.5. Lazy grain. Warming but flat. Caramel. *50%*
Barrel no. 16 (92) n23 t23 f23 b23. Sculpted rye: sugared fruit; a twist of juniper. *50%*
Barrel no. 17 (86.5) n22.5 t21.5 f21 b21.5. Fizzy, fruity spice calmed by caramel. *50%*
Barrel no. 18 (91) n23.5 t23.5 f21.5 b22.5. Pristine rye. Spice. Juicy molasses. Crisp. *50%*
Barrel no. 19 (96) n24 t23.5 f24.5 b23.5. Concentrated honeycomb and chocolate. *50%*
Barrel no. 20 (89.5) n23 t22 f22.5 b22. Cream toffee. Fruit and spice. *50%*
Barrel no. 21 (85) n21 t20 f23 b21. Severe oak delivery. Recovers with mocha toffee. *50%*
Barrel no. 22 (81) n20 t20 f21 b20. Mild sap. Fruity. Oily. *50%*
Barrel no. 23 (94) n23.5 t24 f23.5 b23. Rich. Fruity. Juicy. Clean. Corn oil. Cocoa. *50%*
Barrel no. 24 (88.5) n22.5 t22 f21 b22. Huge vanilla. Slow spice. *50%*
Barrel no. 25 (88) n22.5 t21.5 f22 b22. Custard and sugared fruit. Sharpens. *50%*
Barrel no. 26 (90.5) n22 t23 f23 b22.5. Classic crisp rye. Big, manageable oak. *50%*
Barrel no. 27 (88) n23 t22 f21.5 b21.5. Huge, honeyed oak. Oily. Dries at end. *50%*
Barrel no. 28 (91) n22.5 t23.5 f22.5 b22.5. Exemplary honeycomb-rye delivery. Spices. *50%*
Barrel no. 29 (94) n23.5 t24 f23 b23.5. Juicy rye; crisp sugar-vanilla-hickory fade. *50%*

Barrel no. 30 (94.5) n23 t24 f24 b23.5. Thick rye. Cocoa. Spices. *50%*
Barrel no. 31 (79) n21 t20 f19 b19. Lethargic. Bitter. *50%*
Barrel no. 32 (88) n21.5 t22.5 f22 b22. Relaxed honeycomb. Hint of mint. *50%*
Barrel no. 33 (88.5) n22.5 t22 f22 b22. Powering oak-rye battle. *50%*
Barrel no. 34 (84) n23 t21 f20 b20. Thick oak throughout. Corn oil. *50%*
Barrel no. 35 (93.5) n22.5 t23.5 f24 b23.5. Big rye. Demerara-hickory. Complex. *50%*
Barrel no. 36 (77) n21 t19 f18 b19. Bitter oak. *50%*

⠄⠢⠄ **Russell's Reserve Rye 6 Year Old Small Batch** bott. code L0194FH) (93.5) n24 superb balance better the hammer-homed firm fruity rye and the mintier, more vanilla defused elements; t23.5 juice and spice equal partners on the impact; more cocoa where there was once honey. But plenty of dark sugars...; f22.5 soft vanilla and spice make for a well behaved exit; b23.5 has lost none of its wit and sharpness: in fact has improved a notch or two in recent times. Wonderful! *45% (90 proof)*

Sazerac Kentucky Straight Rye Whiskey 18 Years Old bott Fall 2009 (95.5) n24 t24 f23.5 b24. Another year, another dip into the metal vats... and another different result. Fabulous whiskey worthy of the finer moments in your life, though somehow not quite matching the genius and improbable freshness of the Fall 08 version. *45% (90 proof)*

⠄⠢⠄ **Sazerac Kentucky Straight Rye Whiskey 18 Years Old** bott Fall 2010 (95) n23.5 a much thicker, oakier than norm version full of the more profound oaky elements; here there are dank bluebell woods to vie with the fruitier firmness of the rye itself; t24 dry with oak piling in from the first moment with the juicier rye playing catch up. It does, arrive, of course, and brings with it a coffee and Demerara nuance which is quite beautiful; f23.5 complex, lightly oiled and carries the now mocha and rye to the last, tingling moments; b24 some ego-driven, know-nothing commentators who for some mysterious reason claim an expertise with whiskey wonder how people can give different scores each year for a rye which has been living in a stainless steel vat. Of course, it would not occur to them that each time the vat is stirred before bottling the mix reveals subtle differences, depending on where the molecules fall. Line up Sazerac 18, one after the other from the last few years, and tell me which one is identical to the other. They are all quite different, and this one appears to have more than its fair share of sawdust and tannin. *45% (90 Proof)*

Templeton Prohibition Era Recipe Rye batch 2, barrel 122, bott 2008 (93) n24 t23.5 f22.5 b23. There is no doubt that whoever made this knew exactly what they were doing, and were doing it in stills that needed no proving. Wonderful and truly singular. *40%*

⠄⠢⠄ **Thomas H. Handy Sazerac Rye** (95.5) n24 angular, crystal, cut-glass molasses, sharpened further by a glint of muscovado; but really this is the cloves' show. As the nose opens, the cloves intensify dramatically and alluringly, sweetened along the way by kumquat; t23.5 grips the palate like a lion clings to a wildebeest by the throat: big vanilla trail and natural toffees. Takes little time for the fruitier, sharper rye aspects to surface which are as salivating as they are delicious; f24 a long, luxurious fade with a seemingly endless supply of oils and cocoa; b24 now you live and learn. I happened to stumble across this particular bottling from Fall 2009 when giving a tasting at the unparalleled Victoria Whisky Festival in BC last January. I was about to put the three top whiskies from the 2010 Bible through their paces when I spotted the change in strength. Luckily, Harlen Wheatley, the Buffalo Trace distiller, was at hand to check it out and discover there had been more than the one bottling... intriguing. Had I been sent this bottling, rather than the 129 proof version, Handy wouldn't have grabbed second spot last year. But this is still unambiguously magnificent whiskey, just a little short of the complexity of its twin for sure, but offering more than enough to dazzle and seduce. *63.45% (126.9 proof). ncf.*

Thomas H. Handy Sazerac Straight Rye Whiskey (97) n24 seriously heavy duty: thick enough to use for armour plating. Takes time, but slowly the notes become identifiable, the dense, obvious rye apart. On hand warming, concentrated cocoa notes emerge, as well as spiced kumquat. But that is only the beginning: light cloves and molasses confirm the oak's impact; t25 massively thick with the oils of rye and corn forming a surprisingly lush field. The cocoa on the nose is re-introduced, this time as molten chocolate while the juicy fruity rye fizzes and forms mini lakes as the salivation factor goes through the roof (of the mouth); massive infusion of Demerara sugar, but these do no more than balance the gathering spice intensity: perfection...; f24 calms down quite dramatically as the natural caramels and vanillas begin to impact. But still those heady chocolate-rye notes continue their delicious seduction of the taste buds; b24 it has taken me over three hours to taste this. Were all whiskies and whiskeys like this, the Bible, quite simply, would never see the light of day. Beyond enormous. A whiskey which located taste buds I had no idea I actually possess... Just like his near namesake, Thomas Hardy, Thomas Handy has come up with a rambling, immortal classic. *64.5% (129 proof). ncf.*

⌐ **Van Winkle Reserve Rye Aged 13 Years Old** (94.5) n23.5 beautiful amalgamation of floral and fruit; t24.5 juicy, crisp brown sugar laced with hickory and then a storming middle of spice, tannin and toffee-liquorice; so like an ultra first class Jamaican pot still rum...; f23 with so little corn evident the twilight is shortish, but the sunset is nothing but pure dazzling rye; b23.5 magnificent. 45% (90 proof)

Wild Turkey (80.5) n18 t22.5 f20 b20. Shackled by a dusty, cocoa-vanilla lethargy, breaks out into its sparkling old self only on delivery. Just not in the same league as the current Russell's Reserve... 50.5% ⊙ ⊙

⌐ **Willet Family Estate Bottled Rye Barrel Proof Single Barrel 3 Years Old** (91.5) n23.5 a curious salt and pepper mix...but there is no doubting the clean freshness of the rye; t24 firm, brittle and explosive: salivating and firm with spices taking a little while to mount a challenge, but when they do they take few prisoners; f21.5 surprisingly light and vanilla thick; b22.5 what it loses in complexity, it makes up for in bay-faced freshness and charm. Ryes rarely come more juicy or puckering than this...a must locate rye! 57.7% (115.4 proof)

Straight Wheat Whiskey

Bernheim Original (91.5) n22 smouldering toast from that-day-baked bread. Mealy, too with a little salt added for effect; t23 that peculiar salty tang on the nose transfers with little difficulty to the palate. It joins a citrusy throng and a delightful sharpness which counters the sweeter, oilier nature of the beast; f23 a classy finale where we are back to toast, if a little burned, and dissolving sugars but, mainly, a crackling firmness which appears to be a stand off between the wheat and the oak; b23.5 by far the driest of the Bernheims I have encountered – and this is about the 11th – showing greater age and perhaps substance. Unique and spellbinding. 45% ⊙

American Small Batch
ALLTECH Lexington, Kentucky.
⌐ **Pearse Lyon's Reserve Malt Whiskey** (87) n22 the malt appears to be in three or four different layers of intensity and sweetness; a decent twist of lemon for diversity; t22 had this whiskey come from Speyside I would not have batted an eyelid: the mashing appears to have been extremely successful, as does the yeast use...it's just pure malt...; f21 a light smattering of something oaky and spicy and a little bitter, but otherwise short; b22 one of the maltiest whiskeys produced in the US today. Very much reminds me of an old Maryland single malt from the early 1970s. 40% (80 Proof)

AMERICAN CRAFT WHISKY DISTILLERY Redwood Valley, California.
⌐ **Low Gap Clear Malted Bavarian Wheat Whiskey** batch 2010/3B, dist 30/07/10, aged 357 minutes in oak (90.5) n23 oh, the oak...the oak!! Way too much...not really: just kidding. Rich, slightly cut on the heavy side but thoroughly acceptable. The wheat chips in monumentally with an attractively sweet spiciness; t23 frankly, beautiful. Gloriously rich in texture with those oils doing the trick in coating the mouth and ensuring the toffeed cake is fully heard. Chewy and lightly spiced; f22 just a little bit of bitterness, confirming the wide-ish cut. But now a decent bitter-sweet balance; b22.5 in 20 years of doing this professionally, I'm pretty sure I have never come across something that has spent so little time in the oak. Very impressed and pray they have set some of this distillate aside for proper maturation. 42.7%

BALCONES DISTILLERY Waco, Texas.
⌐ **Balcones Baby Blue Corn Whisky** batch no. BB10-15, bott 28/06/10 (78) n18 t20 f19 b19. Proudly sporting a Double Gold Medal sticker from a Spirits Competition, one can only assume (and sincerely hope!) it wasn't this batch which somehow wowed the judges. Feinty and frugal, I have already tasted enough from this distillery to know that it can do a lot, lot better than this. Proof of just how carefully you have to keep your eye on the ball... 46%

⌐ **Balcones Brimstone Texas Scrub Oak Smoked Corn Whisky** batch no. BRM11-2, bott. 1/11/11 (94) n23 a distinctly European style, one savoured by the Germans in particular. Few, though, get the smoke quite so complete and offer such magnificent structure in the process. Something below that smoke is sweet and sugary and dying to be heard. Adorable...; t23.5 bingo! There are those sugars on first bite. A wide cut gives every chance for the oils to bury into the palate but the golden syrup accompanying it is tempered by a much drier oak thrust and some polite spices. The smoke babbles happily in the background; f24 long, with smoke hanging contentedly around. The spice recedes and we are left with a rich honeycomb and cocoa finale. Oh, with some delicious smoke thrown in... b23.5 if, like me, you begin your tasting very early in the day...then you can't beat a bit of bacon. Smoked bacon lovers, or devotees of Rupp smoked Alpine cheese, will be in their element. 53%

:·: **Balcones True Blue Cask Strength Corn Whisky** batch no. TB10-5, bott. 11/05/10 **(93.5) n22** clever, enticing marriage between manuka honey and maple syrup is a clever and enticing one and though just the most distant of all feint notes has crept in, something more teasing in the dark recesses makes you wonder if they may be ok...; **t23.5** wonderful! An explosion of demented Demerara sugars litters the palate with fragments of honeycomb and chocolate almond. Every single note from the nose onwards tells me the cut was too wide, that technically things are a little amiss. But in this case it has paid dividends: those extra oils have bolstered the body and complexity beautifully. Next time they may not be so lucky...; **f24.5** one of the finest finishes I have discovered from any small distiller in the world. This is where their whiskies normally unravel, very often with the feints biting back. Here, though, it simply enters a new level and the layering and texture appear to shed off its infant clothing and offers something a lot more grown up. Near perfect in its balance and structure, the interplay between the chocolate fudge and walnut cake is enough to drive any man (or woman) on a diet to distraction...; **b23.5** made from 100% Blue Corn, you could call this cornagraphic. It is certainly naked and gives you a rough, full-bodied ride...but also seduces you and caresses more tenderly than you could ever believe. A fabulous experience that will have you gasping for more...Believe me: a Texas star is born.. 63%

:·: **Balcones Single Malt Whisky (87) n21** abstract echoes of their Brimstone smokiness here gives the malt a peculiar – indeed, unique - edge. Takes the third or fourth visit to begin to understand and appreciate...should appeal to dentists, or those with toothache as the clove statement is pretty bold; **t22** usual huge delivery which fills the mouth with an oily glow. Minimum malty sweetness to see off the oak, then it's cocoa all the way; **f22** attractive vanilla and chocolate; **b22** these guys so remind me of Mackmyra in Sweden in their formative days.. 46%

BENJAMIN PRICHARD'S DISTILLERY Kelso, Tennessee.
Benjamin Prichard's Double Barrelled Bourbon 9 Years Old (see bourbon section)
:·: **Benjamin Prichard's Lincoln County Lightning Tennessee Corn Whiskey (89) n24 t22.5 f21 b22.** Another white whiskey. This one is very well made and though surprisingly lacking oils and weight has more than enough charm and riches. 45%
Benjamin Prichard's Tennessee Whiskey (see Tennessee whiskey)

BERKSHIRE MOUNTAIN DISTILLERS Great Barrington, Massachusetts.
:·: **Berkshire Bourbon Whiskey (91.5) n23** beautiful marriage of mocha and mint. But it's the shameless exuberance of the rye which wins the heart...; **t23.5** ...and not content in dominating the nose, it's there at the delivery, firm but fair, and ushering in the caramel and butterscotch; **f23** some oaky spice digs in, and the rye has a hand in that, too: what do you expect? **b23** a bourbon bursting with character: I am hooked! Another micro-gem. 43%
:·: **New England Corn Whiskey (73) n18 t19 f18 b18.** Not remotely in the same league as their bourbon, either technically or through character. Plenty of corn oil early on in the delivery. 43%

BRECKENRIDGE DISTILLERY Breckenridge, Colorado.
:·: **Breckenridge Colorado Bourbon Whiskey Aged 2 Years (86) n22.5 t22 f20.5 b21.** Full of character, big-hearted, chewy, slightly rugged bourbon where honey and cocoa thrives and spices make a telling impact. How apposite that probably the one and only town in Colorado named after a Kentuckian should end up making bourbon. Being close on 10,000 feet above sea level you'd think ice would come naturally with this one. But it does pretty well without it, believe me... 43%

CATOCTIN CREEK DISTILLERY Loudoun County, Virginia.
:·: **Mosby Organic Spirit Whisky (87.5) n22 t22.5 f21 b22.** Clean, well made, juicy and beautifully structured white dog 50%
:·: **Roundstone Rye (81) n20 t21 f20 b20.** No shortage of bristling spice from the rye. But not as soundly made as their organic spirit. 50%

CHARBAY DISTILLERY Napa Valley, California.
Charbay Hop Flavoured Whiskey release II, barrels 3-7 **(91) n22 t22 f23 b24.** Being distilled from beer which includes hops, it can – and will - be argued that this is not beer at all. However, what cannot be disputed is that this is a rich, full-on spirit that has set out to make a statement and has delivered it. Loudspeaker and all. 55%

CLEAR CREEK DISTILLERY Portland, Oregon.
McCarthy's bott Oct 08 **(94.5)** n24 t24 f23 b23.5. The upping of the strength from 40% has done this whisky no harm whatsoever and at 46% it would be better still. Proof that consistent drams can come from small stills. An American masterpiece – and now an institution. Haven't seen there stuff for a while, though. *42.5%*

COPPER FOX DISTILLERY Sperryville, Virginia.
⠿ **Copper Fox Rye Whisky Aged 12 Months** bott. 02/22/11 **(83)** n23.5 t21.5 f19 b19. Bizarrely, doesn't work as well as the spirit, though seemingly made from the same 66% rye mash bill and smoked with the same applewood/cherrywood combination. The sophisticated nose is the star turn, but the flavours never appear to harmonise, save a brief fruity interlude half way through. Very dry finish. *45%*

⠿ **Wasmund's Distiller's Art Series Single Malt Spirit** dist 03/03/11, less than 30 days old **(92)** n23.5 t23 f22.5 b23. The light smoke of 60% applewood and 40% cherrywood really makes itself count, especially on the quite sexy nose. A beautifully characterful and superbly weighted spirit. *62%*

⠿ **Wasmund's Distiller's Art Series Rye Spirit** dist 15/01/11, less than 30 days old **(85.5)** n21 t23.5 f20 b21. An ugly duckling of a spirit which lurches and crashes around the palate without any indication of where it has just been or is about to go. Love it. *62%*

Wasmund's Rappahannock Single Malt Batch No. 32 (91.5) n22 t23 f23.5 b23. One of the highlights since completing the 2010 Bible was driving over to Rick Wasmund's rambling Copper Fox distillery in Virginia. His was the first I had been to where they had turned chap maturation into an art form. Some of his earlier bottlings were testing. With practice, especially in the malting department, he appears to be getting the balance right. Batch 32 here, for instance, is a cracker by any standards. *48% (96 proof). ncf.*

⠿ **Wasmund's Single Malt Whisky 14 Months Old Batch No. 52 (91.5)** n22 some of the old Wasmund character there for sure...but don't worry about that! The glazed cherry fruitcake compensates rather well; t23 mouth-filling in the house style. But now the sugars arrive in procession: some of them fruity and back to dark cherry, other lighter...closer to maple syrup. The vanilla has a big say, too; f23 slow burning spices fizz, making a late impact and sitting brilliantly with the butterscotch and late honey; b23 makes a huge lightly honeyed statement: superb! *48%. ncf.*

⠿ **Wasmund's Single Malt Whisky 42 Months Old Batch No. √-3 (90)** n23 quite honestly, I can say this is a unique aroma: the combination of the smoke and the finish has appeared in no other whisky I have ever found. The fruitiness, along with the chocolate fudge, is a winner..; t24 salivating and full of vigour, you think you are in for a big ride. But then it relaxes to allow a beautifully spiced grape juice to massage your palate...; f21 annoyingly bitter and dry... preventing it from true, award-winning greatness; b22 Rick Wasmund is the chuckling, mad professor of American whisky...always seeing what he can cook up next with his experimentations. This one is an oldie by his standards and as well as getting the usual applewood/cherrywood smoke treatment, has also subjected this to a toasted French oak wine stave finish. If he had a chat with either Doctors Frankenstein or Jekyll, he'll discover that not all experiments are guaranteed to be a success. This one, somehow, and against all probability, is. It seriously helps if you allow the whisky to oxidise in the glass for a good ten minutes to give it a chance to unravel. But then sit back and allow one of the silkiest malt whiskies yet created in the USA to dance nubile and erotically all over your taste buds. Well done, prof... This is the 205th – and last – whisky I have tasted for the Bible while in Kentucky. After tasting this, where can you go from here...? *48%*

CORSAIR ARTISAN DISTILLERY Nashville, Tennessee.
⠿ **Corsair Rye Moon (85)** n20 t22.5 f21 b21.5. A sweet, well-weighted white dog with surprisingly little bite. The odd intense, crystalline rye moment is a joy. *46% (92 proof)*

⠿ **Corsair Aged Rye (73.5)** n18 t18 f19 b18.5. Hot and anarchic, not as well made as the Rye Moon. But has enough playful character to keep you guessing what's coming next. *46% (92 proof)*

⠿ **Corsair Triple Smoke (92.5)** n24 just about a unique smoke fingerprint: certainly one of the most delicate in the world with a mixture of wood smoke and Arbroath Smokies...so tantalising... t23 the sugars melt almost immediately leaving a big malty pool on the palate; those delicate smoke tones keep on shifting; f22 virtually smoked vanilla with a thread of spice; b23.5 the odd technical flaw, to pick nits. But, overall, a lovely whiskey with a curiously polite smoke style which refuses to dominate. Teasingly delicate and subtle...and different. *40% (80 proof)*

DELAWARE PHOENIX DISTILLERY Walton, New York.

❀ **Rye Dog Batch 11-1 (78.5) n19 t21.5 f18 b19.** Sweet, distinctive rye tang but a little short on copper sheen. *50% (100 proof)*

DOWNSLOPE DISTILLING Centennial, Colorado.

❀ **Double Diamond Whiskey (73) n17 t19 f18 b19.** A rum-like sweetness is emphasised by the oils from the width of cut. And, as we know about diamonds, it is the way they are cut which makes all the difference... *40%*

EDGEFIELD DISTILLERY Troutdale, Oregon.

Edgefield Hogshead (94) n23.5 t23.5 f23 b24. This little distillery has very much come of age. This is fabulous malt that makes no attempt to confuse complexity with no-holds-barred enormity. Big, ballsy and just about flawless. No bottling or batch date, but believed to be bottled 2008. *46%*

FINGER LAKES DISTILLING Burdett, New York.

❀ **Glen Thunder Corn Whiskey (92.5) n23.5 t23 f23 b23.** Beautifully distilled, copper rich, Formula 1 quality, absolutely classic corn white dog. The Scotch Whisky Association in particular will love it... *45% (90 proof)*

❀ **McKenzie Wheat Whiskey (82) n20 t22 f19.5 b20.5.** A few heads and tails in there certainly up the body and help make the sugar-honey notes sing. *45.5% (91 proof)*

❀ **McKenzie Bourbon Whiskey (78) n19 t18 f21 b20.** Gets off to an oily, rocky start as it struggles to find its balance. But once it gets going, pretty late on, the compensation is worth the wait as the toffee honey becomes a real chewathon. Good late spice, too. *45.5% (91 proof)*

❀ **McKenzie Rye Whiskey (85.5) n18 t23 f22.5 b22.** No awards for grace and style. But for sheer content and charisma it is a great whiskey to find. The nose shows a little bit of distilling naivety, but the delivery proffers rye like an old 'un. Big oils, but then a thumping wall of firm, fruity muscovado sugars and light liquorice. Some superb spices and chocolate, too. *45.5% (91 proof)*

GARRISON BROTHERS Hye, Texas.

❀ **Garrison Brothers Texas Straight Bourbon Whiskey Aged Two Years** dist 2008, bott. Spring 2011 **(88) n21** as is the norm with a new distillery, the feints have a bit too much to say for themselves. But those notes are countered by a gripping oaky red liquorice topped with honeydew melon and a pretty sexy spiciness...it has promise...; **t22.5** big and oily as the nose tell you it will be. The palate is coated with a rich demerara and marzipan mix, balanced by toasty oak. You can chew your tongue off...; **f22** those feints return as is expected, but the sweetness still grips to the corn oils and the sugars become just a little more toffeed and toasty; **b23**...despite the odd technical fault, it is very hard not to love this as you might a Texas steak. Plenty of chewing and flavour and fat. For a first bottling, quite wonderful. Another Texas star is born... *47% (94 proof)*

GREAT LAKES DISTILLERY Milwaukee, Wisconsin.

❀ **KinnicKinnic A Blend of American Whiskies (87) n21.5** honey and nougat; **t22.5** gets away with the obviously wide cut by again conjuring up honey a thousand bees would be proud of; **f21** bitters out, as expected; **b22** pronounced Kin-i-nuh-nik, this is one of the most honey-copper resplendent whiskeys from the USA. Follows a distinctive German-style pattern. *43% (86 proof)*

HIGH WEST DISTILLERY Park City, Utah.

❀ **High West Silver Oat (86) n20 t22 f22 b22.** A white whiskey which at times struggles to find all the copper it needs. But so delicious is that sweet oat – a style that has enjoyed similar success in Austria – that some of the technical aberrations are forgiven. Soft and friendly. *40%*

KOVAL DISTILLERY Chicago, Illinois.

❀ **Lion's Pride Millett Whiskey (84) n20 t22 f20.5 b21.5.** Now I know what Borat, my budgie used to get all excited about. The nose takes a little getting used to: decidedly green, like sweetened spinach. But the delivery, apart from being a whole new whiskey experience, delivers an oily custard tart sweetness (or is that custard sweet tartness?) which is unconventional and enjoyable. So who's a pretty whiskey, then...? *40% (80 Proof). Made from 100% millett.*

❀ **Lion's Pride Dark Millett Whiskey (86) n19 t23 f22 b22.** Borat, my late and deeply missed budgie, was occasionally known to stick his beak in a glass of whisky when I was looking...and always tried to come back for more. Well, we'd be fighting over this one. Again the nose is hardly enticing. But this time on the palate we have shards of honeycomb getting in among some tangy spices. Much more oil, too, which helps the finish distribute the sugars to the very death. Get the nose cleaned up, and this would be a whiskey worth squawking about. 40% (80 Proof). Made from 100% millett.

⁛ **Lion's Pride Spelt Whiskey** (77) n19 t22 f17 b19. My experiences with Spelt whiskey, wherever in the world it is made, have rarely been happy ones. Actually, this is better than expected. Certainly no problems with the delivery which positively oozes an oily sugary sheen as a fanfare to a milk chocolate middle. Then it all rather falls away. 40% (80 Proof). Made from 100% spelt.

⁛ **Lion's Pride Dark Spelt Whiskey** (72.5) n18 t19 f17.5 b18. There is no shortage of juicy sweetness to locate and for a while enjoy. Sadly it is no match for the bitter theme. 40%. Made from 100% Spelt.

⁛ **Lion's Pride Wheat Whiskey** (79) n20 t20 f20 b19. OK, not technically pulling up trees. But proof there is better things to do than make bread with it: the oil-driven layering early on is quite a delight. Improves in the glass: a warm room helps melt some of the higher alcohols. 40% (80 Proof). Made from 100% wheat.

⁛ **Lion's Pride Dark Wheat Whiskey** (72) n18 t18 f18 b18. No shortage of sweetness and good mouth feel. But an underlying bitterness undoes some of the good work. 40% (80 Proof). Made from 100% wheat.

⁛ **Lion's Pride Oat Whiskey** (77) n22 t21 f16.5 b17.5. Sugar melting on porridge for the excellent nose. The delivery also stands up...then those bitter oils develop, alas... 40% (80 Proof). Made from 100% oat.

⁛ **Lion's Pride Dark Oat Whiskey** (87.5) n21.5 chocolate and ginger fudge melting on porridge this time t22 wow! Impressive weight and oils, evenly spreading the molten sugars. The oats interplay with vanilla and make for a relatively complex ride; f22 long, a very light burst of spice and returns to the elegant porridge and sugar theme; b22 a pretty sexy way to get your oats. The best I have found in this distillery's range: quite lovely whiskey. 40% (80 Proof). Made with 100% oat.

⁛ **Lion's Pride Rye** (88) n21 only a cursory nod towards the rye; t23 huge cascade of sugars and it appears malt. The rye notes are as hard to locate as a Kentucky warbler in the thickest of undergrowth... f22 a lovely wood-spice fade; b22 a really enjoyable, well distilled whiskey. But you'd never guess it was a rye.. 40% (80 Proof)

⁛ **Lion's Pride Dark Rye** (73) n19 t18 f17 b18. The bitter-sweet element is rather too well accentuated. 40% (80 Proof)

MOYLAN'S DISTILLING COMPANY Petaluma, California.

⁛ **Moylan's Rye Whiskey** (89.5) n22.5 with its sweetened clove and clean fruits, a highly attractive, classic rye aroma; t23.5 again it is the rye which stars...big time. So crisp you expect it to break the glass; yummilly mouth-watering and goes easy on the sugars but there is still plenty of molassed tannin to make it a joy; f21.5 short, clipped and little ceremony; b22 a beautifully businesslike rye which accentuates the grain's crisper aspects. 49.5% (99 proof)

⁛ **Moylan's Single Malt** (73) n17 t19 f18.5 b18.5. A sweet, spicy but unusually off key affair. 43%

⁛ **Moylan's Single Malt Cask Strength** (86.5) n21 t22.5 f21.5 b21.5. Tangy and entertaining, this appears to harness all the malt's sweeter qualities and offers enough oil to make them stick. A genuine mouthful of a malt. 60.8% (121.6 proof)

⁛ **Moylan's 2004 Cherry Wood Smoked Single Malt Cask Strength** (94) n24 easily one of the most subtle of all America's micro distillery whiskeys and is unusual in not trying to make an early statements of intent. The smoke does no more than furnish a thin, earthy gloss to the delicate array of lightly fruited vanillas: absolutely beguiling; t23.5 more of the same: a distinctive sharp kumquat note injects life into the vanilla; f23 long yet without a hint of oil with light spices and cocoa playing happily together; again there is a faint, fruity glass to the finale; b23.5 a top drawer, quite beautifully distilled and matured, malt which goes much easier on the smoke than you'd expect but is bubbling with personality...and quality. Bravo! 49.5% (99 proof)

⁛ **Moylan's Bourbon Cask Strength** (89.5) n21 clean but a little vanilla heavy; t23.5 much more like it: the corn oil provides all the weight required to make the flavours stick. Sugars and spices radiate in just about spot on proportions; f21.5 back to a big vanilla statement with a very late hint of bitters; b23 these guys certainly know how to distil: technically an excellent whiskey. Yet another very high quality distillate from this truly promising distillery. 57.25% (114.5 proof)

NEW HOLLAND BREWING COMPANY Holland, Michigan.

Brewers' Whiskey Double Down Barley batch 01, (83.5) n21 t22 f19.5 b21. A huge caramel swipe – unquestionably of that sweeter style found from oak. The barley and vanilla quietly fight for the upper hand, but the finish is somewhat suspect. There is no doubt that New Holland's Dennis Downing knows how to distil: this is a marvellous composition. But when I get over to his distillery, hopefully quite soon, I must find out where those hoppy, bitter notes are coming from. 45% (90 Proof)

Zeppelin Bend Straight Malt Whiskey barrel no. 4, 5 & 6, bott Feb 10, (86.5) n19 t23 f22 b22.5. Another hugely attractive malt from the Zep. Just like the previous bottling, the nose (at times offering a salty, sea-shore character) is a little off course. But the delivery is pure, malty joy with a fabulous caramel-muscovadoo richness to drive home its depth and makes the most of its increased alcohol. The finish offers additional spice. But, overall, there is a feeling of a hoppy-bitter ghost haunting the proceedings. 45% (90 Proof) 140 bottles.

ROCK TOWN DISTILLERY Little Rock, Arkansas.

Arkansas Lightning (89.5) n22 t23 f22.5 b22.5. Superbly made. Clean, oily and very impressive. Intrigued by the vaguest hint of sweet fresh shrimp on the nose. Will make a fine whiskey if placed in high quality oak. 62.5%. New, clear spirit pot distilled from Arkansas corn and wheat mash.

ROUGHSTOCK DISTILLERY Bozeman, Montana.

Roughstock Montana Whiskey (81) n19 t20 f22 b20. A very sweet, almost gristy malt which fairly shakes the taste buds to its foundations with its outrageous oily yet rock solid stance. The spices towards the back end are worth a second glass alone...; 45%

Roughstock Spring Wheat Whiskey (88.5) n21.5 a wisp of tobacco but otherwise a lovely sweetness to the dusting of cocoa; t22 mouth-filling with that so typical sweet softness which is so peculiar to wheat; surprising degrees of vanilla; f23 now hits the high spots as the spices begin to rise and vanilla dovetails with the figs; b22 mon dieu! What is a rollicking great whiskey like this from Montana doing being finished in French oak cask. Survives the experience...and has a wonderful tale to tell. 45%

Roughstock Black Label (92.5) n22.5 the sugars are thumping, but is it all oak induced? I don't think so... The barley floats merrily around, threatening. Big but quite manageable...; t23.5 one suspected this would happen on the palate...and it does...! Fabulous delivery with a silky softness for all the body and strength. Malt concentrate which sends you off to another barley-rich universe...; f23 long, with a fine balance between the sturdy vanillas and profound malt; b23.5 a very beautiful malt whiskey very well made which underlines the happy marriage between barley and virgin oak. A stunner! 64%

ST GEORGE SPIRITS Alameda, California.

St George Single Malt Lot 10 (90) n22 a touch oily from a widening cut. But the apples see off any potential negatives. If I didn't know better, I'd have said there was rye in that there glass... t23 crisp to the point of cracking, those oils really come into play offering a certain chocolate mousse quality. But again it is a fruity rye style that stars and juices up the taste buds mercilessly; f22.5 long, oily and all the developing spice you need; b22.5 welcome back, my old friend! One of the grand-daddies of the micro distilling world and sticking to its guns for one of the fruitiest of all the malts out there. Even if not technically perfect, this is a three course meal of a malt. And so fruity, this one will appeal to rye lovers, too. In fact, it'll slay you.. 40%

SAINT JAMES SPIRITS Irwindale, California.

Peregrine Rock (83.5) n21 t20.5 f21.5 b20.5. Fruity and friendly, the wine and smoke combo work well-ish enough but the thumping oak injection highlights that maybe there isn't quite enough body to take in the aging. Perhaps less time in the barrel will reduce the bitter orange finale. 40%

SANTA FE SPIRITS Santa Fe, New Mexico.

Silver Coyote Pure Malt Whiskey (72.5) n16 t21 f17.5 b18. This is made from malted barley, has never seen the inside of an oak barrel yet is called whiskey. Most probably there is some law I am unaware of regarding definitions of whiskey...especially in New Mexico. Even so, not a bad first attempt and on delivery gives a pretty good account of itself as the oils kick in. But somewhere along the line, to significantly up the quality, they have to, among other things (like sorting out the cut), get the spirit to enjoy a lot more contact with copper. A noble effort and I am sure they will improve as they get to know their distillery. Good luck, guys! 40% (80 Proof)

STRANAHAN DISTILLERY Denver, Colorado.

❖ **Stranahan's Colorado Whiskey Small Batch** dist Dec 05, cask no. 225 **(94.5)** n24 complex stuff: slight this and that, not big anything. But look carefully enough and you'll find cucumber...and salty moist skin. As well as the blackberries smeared on the hand, cherry cake, vanilla, honey and muscovado sugars. Keep seeking and ye shall find... **t23.5** for the first five minutes in the glass little more than caramel shows. Give it time to open and we have, youthful malt apart, a juicy barley fanfare to cream toffee and the usual butterscotch middle. Remarkable, though, is the sharpness of the oak and a thick liquorice statement, too; **f23** long, hanging onto the confident oils with a wonderful flowering of the spices; **b24** absolutely magnificent; a malt which never stays still in the glass. By the way, boys: the message on the label to me brought a lump to my throat. Thank you. 47% (94 Proof). sc.

❖ **Stranahan's Snowflake Cab Franc** dist Sep 05 **(95.5)** n24 not a great fan of marriage, personally. But when honey-hickory bourbon notes gel so sublimely with spiced fruit salad, could be converted. Well, maybe not...; **t24.5** silky delivery with a near perfect engagement, once again, between the fruits and the malty/bourbon effect. One loses count of the sugar notes: they are all there from natural caramels to more forceful molasses. The honey arrives in light honeycomb and acacia form. But there is also a juicy barley attack, though at times it has to be searched for among the general hubbub; **f23** long, with a distinct degree of spices, but just a little bitterness; **b24** what a quite fabulous way to mark my 1,100th new whisky for the 2012 Bible. Not only is it a celebration of great whiskey, but a profound statement of what the small distilleries of the USA are capable of. 47% (94 Proof). sc.

❖ **Stranahan's Snowflake Solitude** dist Mar 08 **(93)** n23 I must be getting punch drunk. But if I didn't know better I'd swear there was something smoky in there: Arbroath Smokies on the salty sea wind. Not much – I mean a fraction of a wisp. But enough to engage with soft, plummy fruits and light molasses; **t23** salivating with perfect oils to polish the barley and copper beautifully; **f23.5** spices and a return of some juicy fruits; **b23.5** I chose this as my 1,111th new whisky of the 2012 Bible, because there is a lot of ones in that. And when you spend the best part of three months on your own, virtually cut off from all others, one is number you get used to. So sampling a whisky called "Solitude" strikes home...whatever it tastes like... 47% (94 Proof). sc. Stranahan's.

❖ **Stranahan's Snowflake Paladise/Grand Mesa** dist Apr 05 **(94)** n23 a beautiful confection of boiled sugar candy with the emphasis on spice and mixed fruits; **t24** gently embracing like no other Stranahan I have tasted before. Magnificent and compelling cask influence with the fruits – with boiled greengage at the fore – ensuring a stunningly complex mix between spice and those caramelised fruits; **f23** for the first time the caramels from the oak make a big play; light oils ensure it has staying power; **b24** seriously impressive. I know this distillery makes something a little special, but this is such a sure footed move away from the norm I am stunned. This is my first-ever Stranahan Snowflake...so named because it simply dissolves on touch...? 47% (94 Proof). sc.

❖ **Stranahan's Snowflake Triple Wood** dist Dec 07 **(86)** n21.5 t21.5 f22 b21. Pulsing with varying degrees of sugar. Juicy and busy, but never quite settles down. 47% (94 Proof). sc.

❖ **Stranahan's Snowflake Hungarian White Oak Cask Finish** dist Dec 07 **(77)** n17.5 t21 f19 b19.5. Chunky, oily, sugary and about as faultless as a Monty Python Hungarian Phrase Book. 47% (94 Proof). sc.

Stranahan's Colorado Whiskey Batch No. 24 dist May 05 db **(87)** n21.5 t22 f21.5 b22. Hints of aggression, and then offers a bunch of honey-scented flowers to make amends. 47%

Stranahan's Colorado Whiskey Batch No. 25 dist May 05 db **(93.5)** n23.5 t24 f23 b23. Unmistakable, unmissable, unique and truly gorgeous. 47% (94 proof)

Stranahan's Colorado Whiskey Batch No. 26 dist May 05 db **(89.5)** n22.5 t23 f22 b22. They obviously don't take prisoners in Colorado: you take this one on at your own peril... 47%

Stranahan's Colorado Whiskey Batch No. 27 dist May 05 db **(94.5)** n23 t24.5 f23 b24. Talk about a gentle giant... 47% (94 proof)

Stranahan's Colorado Whiskey Batch No. 28 dist Jun 05 db **(83)** n20 t22 f20 b21. A Beam...? No, just a fraction off beam. Attractive trademark honey, but too wide a cut. 47%

Stranahan's Colorado Whiskey Batch No. 29 dist Jul 06 db **(86)** n21 t22 f22 b21. Another oily version. A thick layering of muscovado sugars and vanilla. 47% (94 proof)

Stranahan's Colorado Whiskey Batch No. 30 dist Nov 06 db **(89.5)** n22 t22 f23 b22.5. An errant malt but the fruit and intense honey compensate outrageously well. 47%

Stranahan's Colorado Whiskey Batch No. 31 dist Jul 05 db **(90.5)** n23.5 t23 f22 b22. A show off whisky: everything it does it does big and vividly. 47% (94 proof)

Stranahan's Colorado Whiskey Batch No. 32 dist Nov 06 db **(92.5)** n22.5 t23.5 f23 b23.5. Variation on a theme. But some of those variations can leave you drooling. 47% (94 proof)

Stranahan's Colorado Whiskey Batch No. 33 dist Nov 06 db (85.5) n20.5 t22 f22 b21.
Lots of chocolate nougat...and chewing...!! 47% (94 proof)

Stranahan's Colorado Whiskey Batch No. 34 dist Sep 06 db (91.5) n22 t24 f23 b22.5.
Haven't a clue what has gone on here. But whatever it is, it works. 47% (94 proof)

Stranahan's Colorado Whiskey Batch No. 35 dist Jul 06 db (88) n22 t22 f22 b22.
Uncomplicted. But the intensity means there is no chance of a dull moment. 47% (94 proof)

Stranahan's Colorado Whiskey Batch No. 36 dist Sep 06 db (89) n23 t23 f21.5 b21.5.
Delicious. Starts out at full throttle but reaches the finish line in third gear. 47% (94 proof)

Stranahan's Colorado Whiskey Batch No. 37 dist Sep 06 db (76.5) n20 t19 f18.5 b19.
Thin and gruff; every sign of a still worked faster than usual. 47% (94 proof)

Stranahan's Colorado Whiskey Batch No. 38 dist Sep 06 db (88.5) n23 t22 f21.5 b22.
Excellent muscovado signature. Quite a clever whiskey without probably meaning to be. 47%

Stranahan's Colorado Whiskey Batch No. 39 dist Oct 06 db (87) n21.5 t23 f21.5 b21.
I've heard that some men, such as whiskeys likes this, get so excited it's over in seconds. 47%

Stranahan's Colorado Whiskey Batch No. 40 dist Feb 07 db (81.5) n22.5 t22 f18 b19.
You don't find many from this distillery with an off-key finish. Here's one. 47% (94 proof)

Stranahan's Colorado Whiskey Batch No. 41 dist Jan 07 db (94) n23.5 t24 f23 b23.5.
After a period of unusually ordinary batches we are back to something world class. 47%

Stranahan's Colorado Whiskey Batch No. 42 dist Mar 07 db (88) n22 t23 f21 b22.
Attractively angular in shape and delivery thanks to the lack of usual oils. 47% (94 proof)

Stranahan's Colorado Whiskey Batch No. 43 dist Jun 07 db (86) n21.5 t21 f22 b21.5.
Firm with the grain and cocoa really chiselling their way about the mouth. 47% (94 proof)

Stranahan's Colorado Whiskey Batch No. 44 dist Jun 07 db (87.5) n22.5 t22 f21 b22.
Another bottling that feels as though it's holding back somewhat. On puberty, too. 47%

Stranahan's Colorado Whiskey Batch No. 45 dist Apr 07 db (90.5) n22.5 t23.5 f22 b22.5.
Stranahan's is back singing its honeyed, complex, magnificent song. 47% (94 proof)

Stranahan's Colorado Whiskey Batch No. 46 dist Jul 07 db (89.5) n22 t22 f23 b22.5.
An elegant whiskey. Doffs its cap to youth, but shows maturity in all the right places. 47%

Stranahan's Colorado Whiskey Batch No. 47 dist Jul 07 db (90.5) n23 t23 f22.5 b22.
A real complex, mildly schizophrenic bottling which just entertains all the way. Superb! 47%

Stranahan's Colorado Whiskey Batch No. 48 dist Jun 06 db (87.5) n23 t21.5 f22 b21.
Quite a different bottling. Great fun without ever really settling into a rhythm. 47% (94 proof)

Stranahan's Colorado Whiskey Batch No. 49 dist Oct 07 db (94.5) n23.5 t24 f23.5 b23.5.
Required tasting for anyone thinking that great age is the key to great whiskey... 47%

Stranahan's Colorado Whiskey Batch No. 50 Oct 07 db (89) n22.5 t23 f21.5 b22.
A fascinating whiskey: the most bitter-sweet yet. 47% (94 proof)

Stranahan's Colorado Whiskey Batch No. 51 dist Nov 07 db (82) n21 t22 f19 b20.
Full bodied and not too bothered about frills and complexity. Good spice, though. 47%

Stranahan's Colorado Whiskey Batch No. 52 dist Jan 07 db (81.5) n20.5 t21 f20 b20.
Evidence of a wider than normal cut. But enough sugars to give you a toothache. 47%

Stranahan's Colorado Whiskey Batch No. 53 dist Jan 08 db (85.5) n21 t21.5 f22 b21.
Absolutely chock-a-block with honey-nougat. Everything dense and in concentrate. 47%

Stranahan's Colorado Whiskey Batch No. 54 dist Jan 08 db (91.5) n23.5 t23 f22.5 b22.5.
Much more like it!!! 47% (94 proof)

Stranahan's Colorado Whiskey Batch No. 55 dist Mar 08 db (88.5) n22 t23 f21.5 b22.
First gives your taste buds a good slap, then offers them a gentle dusting down. 47%

⋯ **Stranahan's Colorado Whiskey Batch No. 56** dist Dec 07 (87.5) n22.5 buzzzzz; t22.5
buzzzz. Buzzzzz; f21 sting; b21.5 Plenty of bees at work here. Chewy, big and spicy but
shows a generous cut. 47% (94 proof)

⋯ **Stranahan's Colorado Whiskey Batch No. 57** dist Apr 08 (87) n21 a few early feints,
which blew away quickly, then a succession of honey and butterscotch notes; t22 big oils,
but even bigger manuka honey. You know the honey you sometimes get as the soft centre of
a throat lozenge...? Now you get the picture..; f22 long with a little maple syrup thinning the
honey. High quality vanilla balances; b22 has to be the distillery's closest two consecutive
batches in style: this is obviously a wanna bee... 47% (94 Proof)

⋯ **Stranahan's Colorado Whiskey Batch No. 58** dist Jun 08 (89) n22 plenty of liquorice
with custard on butterscotch tart; t22 fat, waves of thick malt and then a much more profound
offering of spiced vanilla; light touches of honey here and there; f22.5 very long indeed, again
thanks to the oils. But the balance between the mocha and fudge is superb; b22.5 back to
its more complete self. 47% (94 Proof)

⋯ **Stranahan's Colorado Whiskey Batch No. 59** dist Jul 08 (92) n21.5 big and oily. Slightly
out of sync, but you have the feeling something extraordinary is lurking...; t24 oh my god...

I'm getting good at this: maybe I should do it for a living... Those hidden signs on the nose come up trumps – and how! The very first second or two on delivery makes me think I've got it wrong. Then the mist clears and we are left with a staggeringly beautiful build up of slightly fudgy, lightly oiled honeycomb. But all this is done with more than a nod to the finest bourbons; **f23** long with the usual vanilla-butterscotch trait. The oils, though, ensure continuing depth; **b23.5** very complex. Very classy. The interplay of the sugars and spice is utterly world class and the bourbon notes which sing are regular intervals do so with a very clear voice. 47%

➤ **Stranahan's Colorado Whiskey Batch No. 60** dist Jul 08 (94.5) **n23** much better nose than Batch 59, boasting a sublime nutty, marzipan trait and, overall, much more oak interference; again it registers that certain indescribable something that signals lift off later down the line; **t24.5** a really beautiful delivery from the off: monumental mix of honey and molasses with a few strands of liquorice. The spice grows quickly; from time to time salivating barley...wow! **f23** long, big vanilla and fudge but the honeycomb lingers; a shard of ginger seals the magnificence; **b24** two whiskeys obviously distilled on the same day (see Batch 59)...and a fascinating variance... This is Stranahan at its most communicative. And brilliant! 47% (94 Proof)

➤ **Stranahan's Colorado Whiskey Batch No. 61** dist Aug 08 (90.5) **n22** oranges and lemons...; **t22.5** mouth-watering with the barley in fine fettle. A tad oily maybe from a wide cut, but the butterscotch and fudge are top class; **f23** late spices and more sophistication; even a degree of coffee cake; the orange returns in Jaffa Cake form; **b23** back to its mega fudge state. Lovely whisky. 47% (94 Proof)

➤ **Stranahan's Colorado Whiskey Batch No. 62** dist Sep 08 (92) **n23** moist ginger cake topped with honey; a warm few sliced toasted almonds don't hurt, either...; **t23.5** big, lush yet this time with an inner steel which guarantees a sublime firmness. A thread of lime waves between the barley and honey; a burgeoning fudge character fills the middle; **f22.5** back to spiced butterscotch with some sharp marmalade; **b23** they appear to have hit a rich seem of consistency. My word: I love this distillery...! 47% (94 Proof)

➤ **Stranahan's Colorado Whiskey Batch No. 63** dist Sep 08 (83.5) **n21 t21.5 f20 b21.** Spicy, more aggressive than normal; a distant vegetable hit suggests another wider cut. 47%

➤ **Stranahan's Colorado Whiskey Batch No. 64** dist Oct 08 (85) **n21 t22 f20.5 b21.5.** By Colorado standards, this is a straight up and downer. Enjoyable, though limited, malt with the emphasis on caramel. A few toasty sugars and spices stretch the flavour profile out a little. 47%

TRIPLE EIGHT DISTILLERY Nantucket, Massachusetts.
The Notch Aged 8 Years dist 2000, bott Aug 08 db (93) **n24 t23.5 f22.5 b23.** Very few distilleries make their international bow with a single malt this sublime and superbly constructed. $888 dollars a bottle it may be, but for a taste of America's very first island malt... well, is there really a price? A head turner of a whisky, and every time it's towards the glass. Do we have a world classic distillery in the making...? 44.4% (88.8 proof)

The Notch Aged 8 Years db (95.5) **n24.5** a veritable fruitfest: name one, look hard enough and you'll find it. Topping the bill, though, are apricots and peaches in full juicy ripeness. A sprinkle of salt reminds you this is an island whisky and traces of vanilla underscores the aging. Oh, and you can't help but trip over the malt; **t24.5** as juicy fruits tend to do, this just melts the mouth. The malt is phenomenal in its clarity and intensity, like the fruit, mouth-watering to an improbable degree; a very fine oil embraces the taste buds and ensures the structure and layering stay in place; **f23** a dignified exit, full of toasty oakiness, the drier balancing act to the juicy opera of before; **b23.5** only six bottles of this were produced for a special dinner at the distillery. It is possible one escaped. I admit I had a hand in putting this one together, selecting samples from about half a dozen casks on the warehouse and blending them to certain percentages. Perhaps the closest it might be compared to is a Cardhu, though with a touch extra fruit. For the doubters, proof that this distillery is quite capable of whisky of the very highest calibre. 40% (80 proof)

Triple Eight Distillery db (90) **n23 t23 f21.5 b22.5.** A beautifully-made malt but keeps very much to a lighter style. Almost classically elegant. 44.4% (88.8 proof)

WILLIE HOWELL SPIRITS
➤ **WH32137** (73.5) **n15 t21 f18.5 b19.** As big and intense as you'd expect from any spirit with a cut as wide as this. Very sweet corn oil ensures an uplifting body. 42.5%

WOODSTONE CREEK DISTILLERY Cincinnati, Ohio.
➤ **5 Grain Bourbon White Dog** (63) **n14 t17 f16 b16.** Barking up the wrong tree. 47%
➤ **Woodstone Creek Blended Whisky** (85) **n20 t22.5 f21 b21.5.** Pretty sharp and keeps you on your toes. A very different herbal aroma, by the way. 42.5%

:::: **Woodstone Creek Barrel Aged Biershnapps** (76) n20 t20 f18 b18. Pretty sure this has hops, which rules this out as a whiskey and is marked down accordingly. As distilled hopped beer, pretty decent. 42.5%

:::: **Woodstone Creek 5 Grain Bourbon** (76.5) n17 t20 f19 b19.5. Hard to get past the municipal swimming pool aroma. This one's taken a high dive... 42.5%

Woodstone Creek Single Barrel #1 (92) n24 earthy, salty peat much more rendolent of Islay than Cincinnati; t23 the silkiness on the palate stuns: all is understated yet the clarity of the riches never fades. Lots of fruit, but the even sweeter peat circles in clouds and dovetails with drier oak-led incursions; a tantalising saltiness gives this a curious coastal dimension...; f22 surprisingly brittle at the finish, but the smoke shows little sign of abating; b23 Islayphiles will be confused by this one because it displays so many coastal characters. A massive well done for a first bottling from this new distillery! 47%

:::: **Woodstone Creek 10 Year Old Peated Malt** (92) 24 23 22 23. Just read the previous tasting notes. There is nothing I can either add nor subtract. Quite, quite wonderful... 46.25%

YAHARA BAY DISTILLERY Madison, Wisconsin.

:::: **Sample No 1** (87) n22.5 clean with the accent on a maltshake intensity; a squirt of some citrus lightens the experience; t22 beautifully soft delivery which coats the mouth without the use of higher alcohols. Lovely array of rich barley sugars on a yielding field of corn; f20.5 comes to an abrupt halt as the odd bitterness creeps in; b22 a disarmingly elegant whiskey. 40% (80 Proof)

American/Kentucky Whisky Blends

Ancient Age Preferred (73) n16.5 t19 f19.5 b18. A marginal improvement thanks mainly to a re-worked ripe corn-sweet delivery and the cocoa-rich finish. But still preferred, one assumes, by those who probably don't care how good this distillery's whisky can be... 40% ⊙⊙

:::: **Beam's Eight Star** (69.5) n17 t18 f17 b17.5. If you don't expect too much it won't let you down. 40%

:::: **Bellows** (67) n17 t17.5 f16 b16.5 Just too thin. 40%

:::: **Calvert's Extra** (79) n19 t20 f20 b20. Sweet and mega-toffeed. Just creaking with caramel but extra marks for the late spice. 40%

:::: **Carstair's White Seal** (72) n16.5 t18.5 f19.5 b17.5 Possibly the cleanest blend about even offering a cocoa tang on the finale. Pleasant. 40%

:::: **Hobble Creek** (64) n16 t17 f15 b16. Sweet, soft, easy drinking. Total shortage of complexity. 40%

:::: **Kentucky Dale** (64) n16 t17 f15 b16. Thin and spineless, though soft and decently sweet on delivery. The grain spirit completely dominates. 40%

:::: **Kessler** (84.5) n20 t21 f22 b21.5. "Smooth As Silk" claims the label. And the boast is supported by what is in the bottle: a real toffee-mocha charmer with a chewy, spicy depth. 40%

:::: **PM Deluxe** (75) n18 t18 f19 b18. Pleasant moments as the toffee melts in the mouth. 40%

:::: **Sunny Brook** (79.5) n20 t21 f19 b19.5. An entirely agreeable blend with toffee and lightly oiled nuts. Plus a sunny disposition... 40%

Other American Whiskey

Buffalo Trace Experimental Collection 1995 American Oak Chips Seasoned dist Apr 95, bott Aug 10 (92) n24 t23 f22.5 b22.5. Fascinating. BT as you will never have quite seen it before. The muted sugars gives us a rare insight to the other, firmer aspects of the whiskey. 45%

Buffalo Trace Experimental Collection 1995 French Oak Barrel Aged dist Apr 95, bott Jul 10 (94.5) n23.5 t24.5 f23 b23.5. A memorable knife and fork job which is required drinking for anyone who prefers their whiskey to take your taste buds to the limit. Just outlandish fun! 45%

:::: **Buffalo Trace White Dog Mash #1** (93) n23 t23 f24 b23. Exceptionally high quality spirit, fabulously weighted, neither too sweet nor dry and with the distinctive cocoa character of the very best grain distillate. Beats the crap out of vodka. "White Dog" is the name for spirit which has run off the still but not yet been bottled: "New Make" in Scotland. It is not, therefore, whiskey as it has not been in any form of contact with oak. But what the hell... It must be at least 15 years ago that I told the old plant manager, Joe Darmond, that he should bottle this stuff as it would sell fast. BT brought it out initially for their distillery shop...and now it is in demand worldwide. ???? !!!! If you are reading this... what did I tell you... and about rye come to that...!!! 62.5% (125 proof)

:::: **High West Bourye** (84.5) n21.5 t22 f20 b21. With the caramels dominating, exceptionally soft and sweet with the rye much more shy than one might have imagined. A very late in the day spice helps it along. 46%. A mixing of bourbon and rye whiskey.

Canadian Whisky

It is becoming hard to believe that Canadian was once a giant among the world whisky nations. Dotted all over its enormous land large distilleries pumped out thousands upon thousands of gallons of spirit that after years in barrel became a clean, gentle whisky.

It was cool to be seen drinking Canadian in cocktail bars on both sides of the pond. Now, sadly, Canadian whisky barely raises a beat on the pulse of the average whisky lover. It would not be beyond argument to now call Canadian the forgotten whisky empire with column inches devoted to their column stills measured now in millimetres. It is an entirely sad, almost heartbreaking, state of affairs though hopefully not an irreversible one. The finest Canadian, for me, is still whisky to be cherished and admired. But outside North America it can be painfully hard to find.

Especially seeing how whiskies containing the permitted 9.09% of non-Canadian whisky (or whisky at all) had been barred from the European market. So just to ensure Jim Murray's Whisky Bible remained on the ball I spent two spells last year in Canada tasting every Canadian whisky I could find on the market. The result, as ever, was illuminating. This latest blitz reconfirmed there was now a clear divergence of styles between traditionalist whisky like Alberta Premium and a more creamy textured, fruit-enhanced product once confined to the USA but now found in Canada itself.

BRITISH COLUMBIA

ALBERTA

MANITOBA

● Vancouver

🔺 Alberta
Calgary
🔺 Okanagan †

🔺 Palliser

Gimli 🔺

Key

● Major Town or City
🔺 Distillery
† Dead Distillery

However, there is no doubt that we are seeing a change in the perception of Canadian by drinkers who had previously confined themselves to top quality Scotch malt. Following my award of Jim Murray's Whisky Bible Canadian Whisky of the Year 2006 to Alberta Premium, I had the chance to spend time in television and radio studios around the country talking about the exceptionally high quality of top Canadian whiskies. It led to a string of emails from readers telling me they had since tasted Alberta and been somewhat shocked to find a world classic whisky lurking so unobtrusively - and cheaply - on their shelves. For many, this had led to further exploring of Canadian, and uncovering of further gems. One of those to really light up the Canadian scene was Danfield's 21-year-old while a Whisky Bible Award went to another showing great complexity and balance: Wiser's Red Letter. For the Jim Murray's Whisky Bible 2012 Crown Royal Reserve retains its crown. The Wiser's had taken advantage of a rare form blip from Alberta Premium. This year, though, Alberta was back to its brilliant self, showing just how good the Crown Royal Reserve had to be to get top billing. Working out which thrilled me most was one of the highlights of my whisky year.

Perhaps one of the things that makes Canadian whisky compelling is its ever-changing face. Many brands do have a tendency to move around in style slightly more than you might expect. However, there is an interesting development from Kentucky which contradicts that in an unorthodox manner. Buffalo Trace have decided to bottle some casks of Canadian in their inventory as a single barrel product. They sent me and others some samples back in their developmental stage and asked us for our input. Now, contrary to what anyone tells you, or claim they know, a Canadian single cask whisky called Bush Pilot was around some 15 years ago, the product of Canadian Club's Okanagan distillery. And each bottling was natural and fascinatingly different. The same can't quite be said for the new Caribou Crossing, a pleasant enough whisky which sports a thumping degree of unionizing caramel while the Canadian whisky lover, or potential convert, is little helped by every bottle looking identical with no cask details. BT have done little wrong in the last decade; indeed, in that time have become the most consistently excellent and exciting distillers in the world taking both bourbon and rye to new heights in my lifetime, and in Drew Mayville (a Canadian, incidentally) they have a blender at the top of his game. But the usual BT sure-footedness appears to have found a hole in the ice - for you can't help thinking that this perfect chance to win over hearts and minds to Canadian has not been fully grasped. Both Drew and I learned our Canadian from the very same school of past Canadian blending masters – and I use the term carefully – so we tend to have very similar views on matters Canadian/Canadien. When last in Frankfort I was unable to discuss this with him as we had the small matter of the Single Oak Project to dissect. Next time though I will be locking friendly Caribou horns with him.

ONTARIO

QUEBEC

Glenora

NOVA SCOTIA

●Quebec

Valleyfield ●Montreal

Canada Mist ▲ ●Toronto

▲Kittling Ridge

▲Walkerville

Canadian Single Malts
GLENORA

Glen Breton db (81) n19 t21 f20 b21. Enormously sweet malt, in almost concentrated form with a tantalising whiff of smoke hanging around; mildly spiced and slightly oily, soapy finale. 43%

Glen Breton Rare db (80) n18 t21 f20 b21. Caramel nose a bit soapy but the buttery, sweet malt, with its vanilla fizz, makes for a pleasant experience. 43%

Glen Breton Rare Aged 10 Years (75) n15 t21 f20 b20. Lashings of butterscotch help put out of the mind the feinty nose (those who tasted the original Sullivan's Cove from Australia will be suffering serious déjà vu here...). Full bodied, as wide-cut whiskies tend to be, and for all the cuts, bruises and plasters, there is enough complexity here to make for an entertaining Canadian - once the nose has been negotiated. 40%

Glen Breton Ice Aged 10 Years (85.5) n21.5 t21 f22 b21. Tasting both a full strength bottled Canadian, and one that had been matured in Icewine barrels, I was nearly blown through the back of my seat and into the wall. One of the biggest shocks to hit you on the Canadian whisky scene today, there is no denying that this whisky offers sufficient panache and lucidity to genuinely impress. Hardly an exercise in perfect balance, it certainly celebrates the art of surprise and, late on, charm. The cocoa-dusted butterscotch really is a rare treat and, thanks to the fruity world it finds itself in, a truly unique and enjoyable experience. 57.2%

⁙ **Glen Breton Battle Of The Glen Aged 15 Years Special Edition** (94) n23.5 apologetic honey fuses with the more confident oaky vanillas: a few non-specific fruity notes dance mysteriously, as though naked before a full moon; t23.5 soft, mouth-watering and now a slow, quite astounding build up of light sugars and vanillas. Melt-in the mouth icing sugar at first (sharpened with a tangy lime) and heads to a more earthy maple syrup and butterscotch; f23 gentle spices boost the length and impact of the finale greatly, as do some late, light oils; b24 I really did know they were capable of bottling something this good: there isn't a single barrel of this vintage I have not tasted in their warehouse at one time or another during its maturation cycle. This watermark bottling from then is an essentially sweet whisky, tasting all the sweeter as it marks the little distillery's victory over the Goliath that is the Scotch Whisky Association in their rightful battle to retain the right to use the name of their brand. Just sometimes there is evidence there just may be a god... 43% 4200 bottles.

OKANAGAN

Long Wood 8 Years Old Malt db (74) n19 t20 f17 b18. There are no discernable off notes and a pleasant liquorice-spice prevails. But the true life has been strangled out if it by caramel. A tragedy, in whisky terms, as this is very rare malt from a lost distillery. 40%. Germany.

Canadian Blended Whisky

Alberta Premium (95.5) n24 throbbing, pulsing rye on a variety of levels: full and juicy, dull and dusty, firm and flinty. Unique and unmistakable; t25 my first whisky of the day – and it needs to be. The tastebuds are given such a working over that they need to be fully tuned and fit to take this on. Again it is all about the rye: the first, second and third flavours to pound the mouth are all rye-related. The very first are juicy with a minute sweetness. The second, hanging onto the coattails of the first are Rockies hard and brittle, clattering into the tastebuds with zero yield. Next comes a quick follow through of explosive peppers, but again leaving in their wake a semi-sweet juicy, fruitiness, almost certainly from the malted rye. No other whisky in the world unleashes this combination of grainy punches around the palate in this way. Beautiful and complex: just words, and ones that don't even begin to do this whisky justice; f22.5 dulls down, probably because of the needless caramel added, but there is slightly more depth than before thanks most probably to the malted rye. The spices continue to fizz as the Demerara-tipped vanillas make their mark; b24 it has just gone 8am and the Vancouver Island sky is one of clear blue. My windows are open to allow in some chilly, early Spring air and, though only the first week of March, an American robin sits in the arbutus tree, resplendent in its now two-toned leaves, calling for a mate, as it has done since 5.15 this morning, his song blending with the lively trill of the house finches and the doleful, maritime anthem of the gull. It seems the natural environment of Alberta Premium, back here to its rye-studded best after a couple I tasted socially in Canada last year appeared comparatively dull and restrained. (Indeed, I am tasting this from Bottle Lott No L93300197: it is classic, generating all I expect and now demand. Another bottle here, L00180007 offers something caked in caramel and is by, AP standards, inert and scores only 88.) Now L933 is calling from the glass, like the robin and finches from the

Arbutus, true to nature: it is a true rye whisky, not a misnomer like the rest. The 100% rye grain used, fortified in its mouth-watering delivery by the usage of a degree of malted rye, offers flavours unlimited. Alberta Premium is no longer just a great Canadian whisky. It has become a national treasure. *40%*

Alberta Premium 25 Years Old (95) n24 t23 f23 b25. Faultless. Absolutely nothing dominates. Yet every aspect has its moment of conquest and glory. It is neither bitter nor sweet, yet both. It is neither soft nor hard on the palate yet both elements are there. Because of the 100% rye used, this is an entirely new style of whisky to hit the market. No Canadian I know has ever had this uncompromising brilliance, this trueness to style and form. And, frightening to think, it could be improved further by bottling at least 46% and un-chillfiltered. For any whisky lover who ever thought Canadian was incapable of hitting the heights among the world's greats, I have previously recommended Alberta Premium. I still do. But if they want to taste something that will amaze then they can do worse than this. The question will now rage: which is the better of the two? For me, perhaps the Premium, because it also has bite as well as guile and slakes thirsts as well as outrageously entertains. Having made love to a young vixen this, though, is perhaps closer to spending a night in the arms of a sultry lady of greater experience. Passion or elegance? We are back to whisky being a mood thing. And if this doesn't get you in the mood, nothing will. *40%. Alberta Distillers.*

Alberta Premium 30 Years (88.5) n23 an awfully refined nose: a picture of etiquette. Neither the firmer, fruitier rye elements wish to dominate, nor to the vanilla-rich oak. So it's after you, no after you all the way... A charming weight, though; t23.5 here we go again: both the juicy, semi-crisp ryes and the drier, almost banana-laden oak step on each other's toes. Teaming with complexity and marked by gorgeously structured layering, all set firm by delightful, coconut- and vanilla-rich oils; f20 a rather bitter affair now, with some of the more ruthless tannins playing havoc with the gentile rye; b22 when you get a whisky this delicate on the nose and delivery, it doesn't take much to tip the balance. Five extra years in the cask has nudged the oak just a little too far. However, savour the nose and delivery which are to die for. *40%*

Alberta Springs Aged 10 Years (88) n23 t23 f20 b22.5. The intense, disappointing vanilla-toffee fade, plus a curious candy sweetness, robs this otherwise delicious whisky of greatness. *40%*

Barton's Canadian 36 Months Old (78) n19 t20 f19 b20. Sweet, toffeed, easy-going. *40%. Barton.*

Bowman's Canadian Whisky (90.5) n22 clean but no shortage of attractive vanilla; t22 lightly oiled and mouth-clinging. Loads of early chocolate and even a hint of praline; f23.5 long, distinguished and with the lightly spiced chocolate content heading through the roof; b23 a delicious, honest Canadian for chocoholics. *40%*

Black Velvet (78) n18 t20 f20 b20. A distinctly off-key nose is compensated for by a rich corn and vanilla kick on the palate. But that famous spice flourish is a distant memory. Another big caramel number. *40%*

Campbell & Cooper Aged a Minimum of 36 Months (84.5) n21.5 t22 f22 b21. Huge flavour profile. An orchard of oranges on the nose and profound vanilla on delivery. *40%*

Canadian Club 100 Proof (89) n21 t23 f22 b23. If you are expecting this to be a high-octane version of the standard CC Premium, you'll be in for a shock. This is a much fruitier dram with an oilier body to absorb the extra strength. An entertaining blend. *50%.*

Canadian Club Premium (78.5) n19 t21.5 f18 b20. The ashy nose is hardly a come on, but the delivery – remaining on the fruity course it has taken of late – compensates. The bitter, unhappy finish is dried further by heavy caramel. *40%*

Canadian Club Aged 6 Years (88.5) n21.5 t22 f22.5 b22.5. Not at all bad for a Canadian some purists turn their nose up at as it's designed for the American market. Just brimming with mouth-watering enormity and style. Dangerously moreish. *40%*

Canadian Club Reserve 10 Years of Age (93) n22.5 t24 f23 b23.5. The perfect antidote after the disappointing standard CC I have just tried. This is a real charmer of a Canadian; the sweetness, though profound, is always controlled and kept in line by that fabulous spice. A surprise package to the natives not least because of the clever interplay between fruit and oak. I suppose the law of averages dictates that one fruited Canadian is going to be pretty damn good: well, this is it! *40%*

Canadian Club Classic Aged 12 Years (91.5) n22 fruity, firm, a sprinkle of cinnamon yet a touch closed, even with maximum coaxing; t24 beautifully coated with honey and grain oils, allowing for a juicy chewiness to gain momentum before delicate spices strike: they don't come much more luxuriant than this; f21.5 long with a similar copper-honey character to the standard CC. Crushed sultana and sharper raisin, but it's not all fruit as some grains deliver some more fiddly, intrinsic notes. Lots of chalky vanilla confirms the age; a point dropped for the slight furry bitterness at the death; **b23.5** a confident whisky which makes the most of a honeycomb theme. 40%

Canadian Club Aged 20 Years (92.5) **n24** bread pudding and sherried fruit cake combine. Some real fizzle and entertainment – oh, and some class – make for one of the best Canadian noses around; **t21** a very tame delivery, with soft oils confused by the fruit; pleasant enough but almost a cancelling out of character; **f23.5** readjusts and reinvents itself brilliantly and we are back to the same bread pudding my mum used to make; as those spices settle, some marauding cocoa also goes for it...and then a return to soft corn oil... it's bitter sweet all the way and, as finishes go, this is a bloody long way...!! **b23** in previous years, CC20 has ranked among the worst whiskies I have tasted, not just in Canada, but the world. Their current bottling, though, is not even a distant relation. Sure, it has a big sherry investment. But the sheer elan and clever use of spice make this truly magnificent. Possibly the most pleasant surprise in my latest trawl through all Canada's whiskies. 40%

Canadian Club Sherry Cask batch no. SC-018 (76) **n18 t20 f20 b18.** Twice as strong as you can normally buy Sherry yet somehow has only half the body. As I say, I really don't know what to make of this. Nor do I get the point. 41.3%

Canadian Five Star Rye Whisky (83) **n21 t22 f20 b20.** An entirely tame, well behaved Canadian which celebrates the inherent sweetness of the species. That said, the immediate impact on the palate is pretty delicious with a quick, flash explosion of something spicy. But it is the deft, satin-soft mouthfeel which may impress most. 40%

Canadian Hunter (85.5) **n20.5 t21 f22 b22.** Remains truly Canadian in style, But the toffee has diminished slightly, allowing far more coffee and cocoa to ensure a delightful middle and finish. 40% ☉ ☉

Canadian Mist (78) **n19 t20.5 f18.5 b20.** Much livelier than previous incarnations despite the inherent, lightly fruited softness. 40%

Canadian Pure Gold (82) **n21.5 t20.5 f20 b20.** Full-bodied and still a notably lush whisky. The pure gold may have more to do with the caramel than the years in cask but the meat of this whisky still gives you plenty to chew over. I especially enjoy the gradual building of spices. 40%

Canadian Spirit (78) **n20 t20 f19 b19.** A real toffee-fest with a touch of hard grain around the edges. 40%. Carrington Distillers (Alberta Distillers).

Caribou Crossing Single Barrel (84) **n20 t22.5 f20 b21.5.** While the nose offers an unholy battle between some apple-fruity rye notes and dry, dusty caramel, there is a real pulsating delivery with the sharper spices helped along the way by the silkiness of the body. Though the caramel offers a toffee-fudge backdrop, a countering dry date sweetness does more than enough to keep it at bay. However, the finish dulls out as the caramel gains the upper hand, though the twitching spices do ensure a light, throbbing beat. An enjoyable Canadian, undoubtedly, I am somewhat perplexed by it. There is no reference to the barrel number so you won't know if you are buying from different casks. Also, if it is single barrel what is the point of the caramel? If it is to make all the casks taste the same, or similar, then why not just blend them together. A badly missed opportunity. 40%. Sazerac.

Centennial 10 Year Limited Edition (88.5) **n21.5** light, oaky sawdust with a gentle powdering of sweet vanilla; **t23** clean with a beautifully complex, delicate spice and honey chorus; **f22** the spices continue their trademark buzz; **b22** retains its usual honey-flavoured breakfast cereal style, but the complexity has unquestionably increased. A busy and charming whisky throughout. 40%

Century Reserve 8 Years Old Premium (82) **n20 t21 f20 b21.** Clean vanilla caramel. 40%

Century Reserve Custom Blend 15 Years Plus (88.5) **n21.5 t22 f23 b22.** After two days of being ambushed in every direction, or completely steamrollered by Canadian caramel, my tastebuds are in total shock. Caramel kept to an absolute minimum so that it hardly registers at all. Charming and refined drinking. 40%

Century Reserve 21 Years Old (91.5) **n23.5** a beautiful mix of banana and soft oak; a teasing spice prickle is offset by a light liquorice and sugar cane juice sweetness: impressively delicate and refined; **t23** the slight hint of rum on the nose is emphatically underscored on delivery: back to sugar cane and the inevitable Highwood distillery spices; **f23** continues on the vanilla-spice theme and, for all the obvious age present, that rum character continues throughout. Lovely strands of honey and even coconut balance the drier elements; **b22** quite beautiful, but a spirit that is as likely to appeal to rum lovers as whisky ones. 40%

Century Reserve Custom Blend lot no. 1525 (87) **n21.5** light buttery grains tangle with a delicate, yet still more forceful fruitiness; **t22** a gorgeous mouth-feel: the weight is excellent and the grains clean and confident; a wheaty spiciness gets the buzz going..; **f21.5** the spices dominate on an otherwise arid, grainy backdrop; a touch of caramel helps reduce further complexity; **b22** an enjoyable whisky which doesn't quite reach its full potential. 40%

Corby's Canadian 36 Months Old (85) n20 t21 f22 b22. Attractive with fine bitter-sweet balance and I love the late spice kick-back. 40%. *Barton. Interesting label: as a keen ornithologist, I had no idea there were parrots in Canada. Must be related to the Norwegian Blue.*

Crown Royal (87) n20 dry and grapey, like a puckering fino. The grains, once the fluttering flag of the old CR nose, are hardly anywhere to be seen; t22 the grain wizardry which once mapped out every nuance on the palate has now completely vanished. This is about fruity contours peaked by busy, chattering spices; f22.5 dries and bitters out; pithy and sharp; b22.5 it looks as though we have waved goodbye to the old multi-layered rich grained CR for ever: I'll have to pop over to Vancouver and raid the library of Mike Smith for those. But this brand has come a long way in the last year or so and there is now a confidence and shape to the blending that had been badly missing. Still a bit of a shock to us long-time (and I'm talking decades here) CR lovers, but a very decent whisky nonetheless. 40%

⋅∴⋅ **Crown Royal Black** (85) n22 denser than a Canadian rainforest: red liquorice and sugared breakfast cereal abounds; soft and teasing for all its intensity; t23 rich doesn't even begin to tell the story: the mouth is coated with an attractive and complex legion of sugar of the dark and toasted variety; a satisfying controlled counter bitterness ensures equilibrium; plenty of oak in the middle ground has a drying effect; f18.5 very much the Achilles heel: lots of resins and vanillas make for a gluey finale; b21.5 not for the squeamish: a Canadian which goes for it with bold strokes from the off which makes it a whisky worth discovering. The finish needs a rethink, though. 45%

Crown Royal Cask No 16 Finished in Cognac Casks (85.5) n21.5 t21 f22 b21. Clean cut and exceptionally grapey. The nose is unique in the whisky world: it is one of Cognac. But otherwise this struggles to really find its shape and rhythm. A perfect Canadian for those who prefer theirs with an air of grace and refinement but very limited depth. In fact, those who prefer a Cognac. 40%

Crown Royal Limited Edition (88) n22 dry, dusty caramels and fudge but perked up with a vanilla and apple topping; t22.5 a much firmer mouth-feel than of old, though the buttered toffee character remains. This is joined now by a vaguely toasty grain component and scattered spices; f21.5 remains on that attractively bitter-sweet road with a mild overdependence on the spice; b22 a much happier and productive blend than before with an attractive degree of complexity. 40%

Crown Royal Special Reserve (96) n24 a clean and attractively spiced affair with cinnamon and the faintest pinch of allspice leading the way: rye at work, one presumes; the fruit is clean and precise with weightier grape overshadowing a green apple freshness; t24 a spicier element to the usual rye and fruit delivery, much more in keeping with the nose, but that fabulous, contrary mouth-feel of harder grain and softer fruit continues to do the business. The spices build slowly but with an impressive evenness and determination: one of the most outstanding Canadians on the palate of them all; f24 the finish has been tidied up and with stunning effect: no more sawdust and eye-watering dryness. Both grain and soft fruit ensure a magnificently mouth-watering end to an amazing journey; b24 complex, well weighted and simply radiant: it is like looking at a perfectly shaped, gossamer clad Deb at a ball. The ryes work astonishingly well here (they appear to be of the malted, ultra-fruity variety) and perhaps to best effect after Alberta Premium, though now it is a hard call between the two. 40%

Crown Royal XR Extra Rare lot no. L7064 N4 (93.5) n24 t23 f23 b23.5. Just about identical to the previous bottle above. The only difference is on the finish where the rye, fortified with spice, decides to hang back and battle it out to the death; the toffee and vanilla make a controlled retreat. Either the same bottling with a slightly different stance after a few years in the bottle, or a different one of extraordinary high consistency. 40%

Danfield's Limited Edition Aged 21 Years (95) n24 t24 f23.5 b23.5. A quite brilliant first-time whisky. The back label claims this to be small batch, but there is no batch number on the bottle, alas. Or even a visible bottling code. But this is a five star performer and one of this year's whiskies of the world. 40%

Danfield's Private Reserve (84.5) n20 t21.5 f22 b21. A curious, non-committal whisky which improves on the palate as it goes along. An overdose of caramel (yawn!!) has done it no favours, but there is character enough for it to pulse out some pretty tasty spice. Seamless and silky, for all the toffee there underlying corn-rich clarity is a bit of a turn on. 40%

8 Seconds Small Batch (86) n20 t22 f22.5 b21.5. Fruity, juicy, luxurious. And perhaps one of the few whiskies on the market anywhere in the world today which could slake a thirst. 40%. *Frank-Lin Distillers.*

Forty Creek Barrel Select (75) n20 t21 f16 18. Sadly, still appears to be sulphur-tainted, especially at the death. The nose, though, is better than of old and the delivery really does give you a rich lift...then the dreaded S-word strikes. Blast!!! 40%

⋰⋰ **Forty Creek Confederation Oak Reserve Canadian** white oak, lot 1867 (91) n22.5 I'm sure I have encountered this bubblegum aroma at this distillery before. Thought here it is hardly a negative force and appears to underline an attractive depth of fruit; t23 soft and grainy and then a wonderful interplay between the fruits and vanilla. The mouth feel and weight is near enough perfect, especially as a little oaky cocoa broadens the anchor; f22.5 spicy butterscotch with a burnt raisin accompaniment; b23 refuses to stint on depth and richness. Excellent and endearing. 40%. 16,800 bottles.

Forty Creek Double Barrel Reserve lot no. 242 (83.5) n20 t21.5 f21 b21. One of those whiskies which has that James Finlayson double-take moment. At first you think: hmmmm, bubble gummy, fruity but flat. But then the spices begin to gather with intent and before you know it you are on your fifth mouthful trying to find exactly what is going on here. Certainly there is oak and there is fruit. And for all the softness and palate caressing there is a grainy trail-off harder than silicon. 40%

⋰⋰ **Forty Creek Double Barrel Reserve** lot 246 (86) n21.5 t21 f22 b21.5. Much better than the last one of these I tasted: this one has some yield and integration where previously it was pretty bipolar fare. At various moments spices, juicy grape and cocoa star. 40%

Forty Creek Port Wood Reserve lot no. 60 (88) n21.5 the usual Kittling Ridge fruit fest in full flow, the grape displaying a mildly shrivelled, sweet character while the vanilla and spice somehow find space to breathe; a distinctive Spanish-style brandy character kicks in; t22.5 for all the soft juiciness, this is not shy on the palate, as spices literally pepper the taste buds. A light viscosity allows these spices to gain a decent foothold as the chocolate raisin middle develops; f22 soft waves of spice continue but now the vanilla gets a late say; b22 a strange though thoroughly entertaining beast with as many elements of brandy as there are whisky. 45%

Forty Creek Three Grain (76) n19 t20 f18 b19. Not quite as well assembled as some Three grains I have come across over the last few years. There is a lopsidedness to this one: we know the fruit dominates (and I still haven't a clue why, when surely this of all whiskies, just has to be about the grains!) but the bitterness interferes throughout. If there have been sherry casks used here, I would really have a close look at them. 40%

Gibson's Finest Aged 12 Years (79) n19 t20 f20 b20. You can't help getting the feeling that here is a decent whisky sitting on the fence, just not knowing which way to go. Pleasant, but in the same way as that boring neighbour you are happy to offer a cheery hullo to but not invite round for dinner. Bitter-sweet, but strangely lacking complexity or depth. Has fallen behind sterling for entertainment value. 40%

Gibson's Finest Rare Aged 18 Years (95.5) n24 close your eyes and sniff and you would swear you have a bourbon-rye mix: simultaneously crisp and soft, the sharpness of the rye and apple-style fruitiness is sublime and as enticing as it gets; t24.5 and a perfect transfer onto the palate: spectacularly juicy with all kinds of clean rye and corn notes bobbling around in a gorgeous gentle Demerara sugar backdrop; f23.5 impressive vanilla and long strands of grain and bitter liquorice; b23.5 so far ahead of both Sterling and the 12, it is hard to believe they are from the same stable. But make no mistake; this is pure thoroughbred: truly world class. 40%

Gibson's Finest Canadian Whisky Bourbon Cask Rare Reserve (89) n23 t21 f23 b22. A much better version than the first bottling, the depth this time being massively greater. 40%

Gibson's Finest Sterling (81) n20 t20 f20.5 b20.5. Lightened and loosened up dramatically of late. There are even strands of corn detectable amid the surprising complexity. Even the old off-key bitterness has changed to something far more tangible and attractive: in this case sharp marmalade. 40%

Gibson's New Oak (88) n22 t21 f23 b22. Distinctly different from any other Canadian doing the rounds: the oak influence makes a wonderful and clever impact. 40%

Highwood Pure Canadian (84) n20 t21 f22 b21. A decent, ultra-clean Canadian with markedly more character than before. Certainly the caramel has been seriously reduced in effect and the wheat ensures a rather attractive spice buzz while the cane juice sweetness harmonises well. Perhaps most delightful is the wonderful and distinct lack of fruit. 40%

Hiram Walker Special Old (93) n22.5 granite-hard with softer, oilier, more citrusy notes being trampled underfoot by almost impermeable grain; t24 textbook delivery with the rye offering both yielding juice and granite. Absolutely no let up in the spice development which works outstanding well with the hard skeleton. The sweetness is more upfront now with the honey petering out towards the late middle; just gone up an impressive notch; f23 drier now with the grain offering rich vanilla though the muscovado sugar signature subtlety remains; the caramel is present but doing a little less damage b23.5 even with the extra degree of all-round harmony, this remains the most solid, uncompromising Canadian of them all. And I love it! Not least because this is the way Special old has been for a very long time with obviously no intentions of joining the fruity bandwagon. Honest, first class Canadian. 40%

⋄ **James Foxe** (77.5) n20 t19.5 f19 b19. James could do with putting some weight on... 40%

Lord Calvert (72.5) n19 t18.5 f17 b18. Truly eccentric aristocracy, this. Comes from the most noble of homes, Alberta Distillery, and the pedigree of the rye is evident in patches on both nose and delivery. Then marries something very fruity well beneath its class. 40%

McGuinness Silk Tassel (79.5) n20 t21 f19.5 b19. Silk or satin? The corn oils offer a delightful sheen but still the caramel is over enthusiastic. 40%

Wm Morrison Imported Canadian Rye (87.5) n22 lavender and still a hint of something in the area of rye. Certainly bold and big; t22 firm, big and chewy but the caramels deliver much earlier these days; f21.5 a touch of oak-spice buzz; the toffee dominates the death; b22 still a lovely Canadian, though the toffee needs toning down. Not sure what "Full Strength" is doing on the label when bottled at 40%, though... 40%.

Mountain Rock (87) n22 t20.5 t22.5 b22. Still a soft Canadian cocking a melt-in-the-mouth snook at its name. But this time the fruit is just over anxious to be heard and a degree of its old stability has been eroded. 40%. Kittling Ridge.

Pendleton Let'er Buck (91.5) n22.5 t23 f22.5 b23.5. A significantly improved whisky from the ultra-sweet, nigh on syrupy concoction of before. Here the surprisingly complex and sensual grains take star billing, despite the caramel: it almost makes a parody of being Canadian, so unmistakable is the style. For those who affectionately remember Canadian Club from 20-30 years ago, this might bring a moistening of the eye. 40% (80 proof). Hood River Distillers.

Potter's Crown (83) n19 t21.5 f21.5 b21. Silky and about the friendliest and most inoffensive whisky on this planet. The dusty aroma and thick, chewy toffee backbone says it all but still impossible not to enjoy! 40%

Potter's Special Old a blend of 5 to 11 year old rye whisky (91) n23.5 t23 f22 b22.5. More Canadian than a hockey punch-up – and, for all the spice, somewhat more gentle, too. 40%

Potter's Special Old Rye (85.5) n21 t23.5 f20 b21. Not quite the force majeure of a year or two back, the grains are now thinner and starker despite the beautifully striking delivery on the palate. The soft honey tones are an attractive compensation but the austerity on nose and finish takes a little getting used to when remembering previous incarnations. 40%

Rich and Rare (79) n20 t20 f20 b19. Simplistic and soft. One for toffee lovers. 40%

⋄ **Rich and Rare Reserve** (86.5) n19.5 t21 f23.5 b22.5. Actually does what it says on the tin, certainly as to regard the "Rich" bit. But takes off when the finish spices up and even offers some ginger cake on the finale. Lovely stuff. 40%

Royal Canadian (87.5) n22 fruit shortbread biscuit and vanilla; t22.5 chewy and soft, then an attack of tangerine and spice; f21 toffee vanilla; b22 Now there's a whisky which is on the up. 40% ⊙⊙

Royal Canadian Small Batch (88) n22 intense, thickly oaked, big caramels and spices; t22.5 rich and silky, the honeycomb leads from the front; the spices cut through the toffee and firmer grains; f21.5 bitters dramatically under those oaks and caramels; b22 a big Canadian with a pleasing silk and steel pulse. 40%. Sazerac.

Royal Reserve (84.5) n19 t22.5 f21.5 b21.5. No question that the delivery is much richer, fresher and entertaining than before with the spices, dovetailing with subtle fruit, ensuring a complexity previously lacking - especially at the death. Frustratingly, the caramel seems to be biting deeper on the nose, which has taken a backward step. A much more enjoyable and satisfying experience, though. 40%

Royal Reserve Gold (94.5) n24 this was already one of the better Canadian noses. And with this latest bottling the grain complexity has moved up a gear. Bereft of the tacky toffee which dulls so many Canadian whiskies, we have here a joyous mixture of rye and citrus notes beautifully embedded in decent, vanilla-clad oak and the most tantalising of light honey tones; t23.5 a glorious composition of juicy, salivating rye in tandem with a honey-biscuit note gets this off to a stupendous start. It gets better still as the spices lift off and that honey begins to stick to the roof of the mouth; f23 magically light: a dusting of oak gives a nod towards a respectable, aged dryness but then this acts only as a foil to the delicate lime and Fruit Pastille juiciness and late, radiating rye; b24 retains its position as a classy, classy Canadian that is an essay on balance. Don't confuse this with the much duller standard bottling: this has been moulded in recent years into one of the finest – and among its country's consumers - generally most underrated Canadians on the market. 40%

Sam Barton Aged 5 Years (83.5) n19 t21.5 f22 b21. Exceptionally sweet session whisky with a lovely maple syrup glow and some complexity on the finish. Friendly, hospitable and impossible not to like. 40%. La Martiniquaise, France.

Schenley Golden Wedding (92) n22 t24 f22 b23. Like a rare, solid marriage, this has improved over time. Always been a consistent and pleasant whisky, but now there appears to be a touch of extra age and maturity which has sent the complexity levels up dramatically. Quite sublime. 40%

Schenley OFC (90) n22 t22.5 f23 b22.5. Notice anything missing from this whisky? Well the 8-year-old age statement has fallen off the label. But this is still a truly superb whisky which would benefit perhaps from toning down the degree of sweetness, but gets away with it in spectacular fashion thanks to those seductive oils. Not as complex as the magnificent old days, but a whisky that would have you demanding a refill nine time out of ten. 40%

Seagram's Canadian 83 (86.5) n21 t22 f21.5 b22. A vastly improved blend which has drastically cut the caramel to reveal a melt-in-the-mouth, slightly crisp grain. There are some citrusy edges but the buttery vanilla and pleasing bite all go to make for a chic little number. 40%

Seagram's VO (91) n22 dried banana skin, a touch of waffle and a complex layering of drier, oaky notes; t23.5 mouth-filling, lush corn oil and a slow, sensual build up of brown sugar and spice; f22.5 back to its oaky promise on the nose as it dries with a mixture of niggly spice and vanilla; b23 with a heavy heart I have to announce the king of rye-enriched Canadian, VO, is dead. Long live the corn-dominant VO. Over the years I have seen the old traditional character ebb away: now I have let go and have no option other than to embrace this whisky for what it has become: infinitely better than a couple of years back; not in the same league as a decade ago. But just taking it on face value, credit where credit is due. This is an enjoyably playful affair, full of vanilla-led good intention, corn and complexity. There is even assertive spice when needed and the most delicately fruity edge...though not rye-style. Thoughtfully blended and with no little skill, I am impressed. And look forward to seeing how this develops in future years. A treat which needs time to discover. 40%

❖ **Snake River Stampede 8 Years Old** dist 12 Dec 99, bott. 18 Jul 08 (87.5) n22.5 fruit and spice rounding off the vanilla backbone; t22.5 wow! As silky as a cowboy's kerchief. Pure corny Canadian all the way and showing some decent oaky intent; f21 bitters out through oak rather than anything more sinister to do with the sherry; b21.5 I was a bit concerned when I read in the blurb that they finish this Canadian whisky in sherry butts. But no need; as clean as a perfectly lassoed colt. A Canadian with great character. 40%

Tangle Ridge Aged 10 Years (69) n18.5 t19.5 f15 b16. Decidedly less in your face than of old, unless you are thinking custard pies. For all the cleaned up aroma and early injection of spiced sultana, the uncompromisingly grim finish remains its usual messy self. An unpleasant reminder as to why I only taste this when it's Bible time... 40%

Tesco Canadian Whisky (75) n18 t18 f20 b19. Sweet, clean, uninspiring. 40%

White Owl (77.5) n19 t19.5 f20 b19. White whisky: in others words, a whisky the same colour as water. To both nose and taste somewhat reminds me of the long gone Manx whisky which was casks of fully matured scotch re-distilled and bottled. Sweet and pleasant. But I doubt if connoisseurs will give two hoots... 40%

Windsor (85.5) n21 t22 f21 b21.5. A whisky you could usually bet your week's wages on for consistency and depth. Here, though, the usual rye fruity, crispness has been dumbed down and though there are enough spices to make this a pleasant affair, the impact of the caramel is a tad too significant. The usual custard sweetness has also changed shape and dry vanilla at the death is the compromise. 40%

Windsor (86) n20 t21 f23 b22. Pleasant but with the majority of edges found on the Canadian edition blunted. Some outstanding, almost attritional, spice towards the middle and finale, though. Soft and desirable throughout: a kind of feminine version of the native bottling. 40%. For US market.

❖ **Winn Dixie Canadian Whisky** (80) n19 t20 f21 b20. Soft, sweet, toffeed and boasting a little spice...but with minimum fuss. 40%

Wiser's 18 Years Old Limited Release (93.5) n24 a variation on a wonderful, familiar theme: the green apples and sultana are there in abundance but a firmer, grainier note keeps it all anchored. The usual clarity remains and now there appears an extra degree of delicacy; t24 quite brilliant: the grains now cut loose to bombard the taste buds with myriad crisp, peppery notes. Less rye apparent than before but a significant upping in the Demerara coating; f22.5 cleaner and grainier, with the fruit jettisoned for a more minimalist finale, concentrating on the vanilla and corn; b23 like most of the Wiser's family, an improved, more carefully thought out blend than of a year or two back. Thoughtful, top quality blending resulting in a whisky which holds its head high on the world stage. 40%. 3500 bottles.

Wiser's Very Old 18 Years Old (90.5) n24 t23 f21.5 b22. Much better than the last bottling I encountered, which in itself was no slouch. Here, though, the blender has written bolder what he is trying to achieve. 40%

Wiser's De Luxe (86) n20 t22.5 f21.5 b22. A whisky which never sits still: I have noticed over the last few years that the shape of this whisky has changed and changed again. Once, it was my everyday drinking Canadian: pale coloured though 10 years old and absolutely brimming with grain-oak complexity. Then the age guarantee vanished. And the colour got darker and darker until today it is unrecognisable. Still nothing like the classic, ultra-charming and almost fragile-delicate Wiser's of old. But this present bottling has got its head partly out of the sand by injecting a decently oaked spiciness to the proceedings and one might even fancy detecting shards of fruity- rye brightness beaming through the toffeed clutter. Definitely an impressive turn for the better and the kind of Canadian with a dangerous propensity to grow on you. If they had the nerve to cut the caramel, this could be a cracker... 40%

Wiser's Legacy (95) n24 even by Canadian standards, a little different: coriander and juniper give a slight gin-style edge to this, though waiting in the wings is a subtle, spicy wine quality. The teasing sweetness, not entirely without a bourbon style new-oakiness and hint of rye-fruitiness, has all the intensity of Mona Lisa's smile...; **t24.5** there is a crystalline quality to the nose, and it transfers immediately to the palate. One is reminded of absolutely unblemished First Growth Bordeaux in the way the grape–fruitiness announces itself before progressing into greatness. After that, it takes, thankfully, a very different course except perhaps in the way the spices unfold: first no more than a shadow, then blossoming out into something profound, deep and always in sync with all else that is going on. Cocoa notes arrive early and stay while the grains offer a salivating edge...nothing short of glorious...; **f22.5** serious but high quality and contained oak: dry and toasty but always a light dusting of slightly sweetened vanilla; **b22.5** when my researcher got this bottle for me to taste, she was told by the Wiser's guy that I would love it, as it had been specially designed along the lines of what I considered essential attributes to Canadian whisky. Whether Mr Wiser was serious or not, such a statement both honoured and rankled slightly and made me entirely determined to find every fault with it I could and knock such impertinence down a peg or two. Instead, I was seduced like a 16-year-old virgin schoolboy in the hands of a 30-year-old vixen. An entirely disarming Canadian which is almost a whisky equivalent to the finest of the great French wines in its rich, unfolding style. Complex beyond belief, spiced almost to supernatural perfection, this is one of the great newcomers to world whisky in the last year. It will take a glass of true magnificence to outdo this for Canadian Whisky of the Year. 45%

Wiser's Red Letter (95) n24 the complexity is enough to make you weep: the accent is on elegance, achieved by offering near perfect servings of all you hope to see in a great Canadian. An orangey citrus element is in turn caressed by small grain embedded in a field of soft-oiled corn, which sports a light grape hillside. The toffee-caramel has a flattening effect, sadly: otherwise near perfection in complexity; **t24** a wave of soft corn oil spreads over the roof of the mouth; both juicy and chewy in equal measure, the vanilla starts making delightful speeches while the most delicate of rye injections cranks up the complexity further; **f23.5** the caramel which builds on the nose does likewise on the finale to form a toffee dam. At least some spices filter through; **b23.5** the recent trend with Canadian whisky has been to do away with finesse and cram each bottle with fruit. This returns us to a very old fashioned and traditional Canadian style. And had the rye been upped slightly and the caramel eschewed entirely it might have been a potential world whisky of the year...Even in this form, however, it is certainly good enough to be Jim Murray's Whisky Bible Canadian Whisky of the Year 2010. 45%

Wiser's Reserve (75) n19 t20 f18 b18. Something very strange has happened to this. The nose offers curious tobacco while the palate is uneven, with the bitterness out of tandem with the runaway early sweetness. In the confusion the fruit never quite knows which way to turn. A once mighty whisky has fallen. And I now understand it might be the end of the line with the excellent Wiser's Small Batch coming in to replace it. So if you are a reserve fan, buy them up now. 43%

Wiser's Small Batch (90.5) n21.5 much bigger in the fruit department than of yore with the grains struggling to be heard; soft to the point of borderline flat; **t24** that's more like it!! Back online with the huge, salivating, juicy, mouth-enveloping delivery. The spices spark and ark around the palate and for a while the fruits are lost. Layers of grain dominate and the balance between the brown sugar sweetness and the pounding peppers is sublime; **f22** much harder and crisp with the fruit having now fallen by the wayside. Even the spices burn out leaving firm vanilla; **b23** a real oddity with the nose and taste on different planets. The fruity onslaught promised by the drab nose never materialises – thankfully! – and instead we are treated to a rich, grainy explosion. It's the spices, though, that take the plaudits. 43.4%

Wiser's Special Blend (78) n19 t20 f19 b19. A plodding, pleasant whisky with no great desire to offer much beyond caramel. 40%

Japanese Whisky

At Edinburgh Castle in 2010 a fanfare of pipes heralded the launch of the first 70-year-old whisky certainly within living memory. A Speyside scotch single malt, it deservedly brought great acclaim and an enormous degree of publicity. Elsewhere, sneaking in through the back door, came a Japanese single malt bottled by the Whisky Exchange in London as part of their 10th anniversary celebrations. It was 42 years old and from the Karuizawa distillery.

Now Japan tends to get hot... very hot. Certainly a lot hotter than anywhere in Scotland. And though the Winters can sometimes be equally if not more cold than Speyside, I would be quite confident in saying that 42 Japanese Summers is worth at least 70 Scottish in terms of whisky maturation. Ironically, I sat next to WE's owner, Sukhinder Singh, at the Edinburgh event but didn't have time to chat about the Karuizawa. Perhaps the Mortlach edges it in terms of finesse and overall star quality, but for sheer fun the freaky Karuizawa 1967 wins hands down and, for me, and despite its obvious oaky input, was the Japanese Whisky of the Year. I am not the only one praying that this has opened the door for other grandiose Japanese malts to follow.

Yet still there is a great frustration that the myriad types of Japanese whisky is unlikely to be seen outside the mother country, so slow has been the expansion of their whisky empire.

I have met a number of whisky shop owners around the world who will stock only a handful of Japanese simply because they cannot get assurances that what they are being sent does not contain Scotch. Certainly, these mind-blowing single malts which had lorded it with the world's elite were 100% from the land of the rising sun. But until exchanging whiskies within Japanese companies becomes a natural part of their culture it is hard to see how the confidence generated by the excellence of the single malt and grains available as singletons can be extended to the blends.

Part of the problem has been the Japanese custom of refusing to trade with their rivals. Therefore a Japanese whisky, if not made completely from home-distilled spirit, will instead contain a percentage of Scotch rather than whisky from fellow Japanese distillers.

This, ultimately, is doing the industry no favours at all. The practice is partly down to the traditional work ethics of company loyalty and an inherent, and these days false, belief that Scotch whisky is automatically better than Japanese. Back in the late 1990s I planted the first seeds in trying to get rival distillers to discuss with each other the possibility of exchanging whiskies to ensure that their distilleries worked more economically.

In the meantime word is getting round that Japanese whisky is worth finding. It is now not uncommon for me to discuss with whisky lovers at a fair or book signing the merits and differences of Yoichi and Hakushu, two distilleries which are now being correctly recognised for their world-class brilliance. And, increasingly, Yamazaki which has moved away from a comfort zone it operated in for many years and is now offering malts of great magnitude: indeed, it was recently the producer of one of the two

Yamazaki ▲
●Osaka

●Fukuoka

Japanese whiskies which was considered as a
possible Whisky Bible World Whisky of the Year. And
I still get a small thrill when I hear Yoichi's name mentioned
around the world: I'm proud to have first brought it to the world's
attention way back in 1997 – though these days the distillery, like all others in Japan, has to
be a little more careful with their use of sherry.

Mind you, the same didn't have to be said about the Karuizawa 1967. That may have been
matured in a sherry butt, but it was filled in the good old days when they were sent from
Jerez to Japan still full of the fortified wine, so arrived fresh. Further evidence that there is just
no beating the old traditions...

Finally, though by no means an afterthought, the great earthquake and tsunami which
devastated the east coast of Japan on 11th March 2011, causing a barely imaginable loss of
life. Although the Miyagikyo Distillery at Sendai was close to the worst affected areas of the
disaster, miraculously none at the distillery sustained injury. Indeed, all of Japan's distilleries
and their workers appeared to escape what is believed to be have been one of the five
biggest earthquakes ever recorded. I and all of the Whisky Bible team would like to send our
many friends in Japan, be they within the industry or readers, our condolences for any loss of
loved ones they endured; our thoughts and very warmest wishes remain with you.

Single Malts
CHICHIBU

Golden Horse Chichibu db (80) n19 t21 f20 b20. Light, toasty and delicate yet the oak is prominent throughout. Good balancing sweet malt, though. 43%. Toa.

Golden Horse Chichibu 10 Years Old Single Malt db (82) n19 t22 f21 b20. Developing citrus notes lighten the weight as the oak and sweet malt go head to head. 43%. Toa.

⌐ **Golden Horse Chichibu Aged 12 Years** bott July 08 db (95.5) n24 a majestic nose: crushed nuts on a big malt plane; diced Slovakian milk chocolate and a bourbon injection of mild honeycomb, hickory and toasty Demerara. Sounds like bourbon, but there is a certain something that is purely Japanese. Meanwhile, a slab of drying dates guarantees immortality, despite a inter-planetary distant, nagging bitterness. Sublime... t24.5 a fruity delivery intensified by spice and a build up of oils that borders on the obscene. I am salivating and having my mouth coated with intense barley all at the same moment: a near unique experience; the letters at the command of my keyboard can't quite describe the depth of the honey or the subtle layering of sugars; f23 the malt and vanillas become inseparable while the spices ramp up an extra couple of gears. The delicate sugars and drier oaks absolutely match each other stride for stride. Some very late bitterness, but it hardly matters (actually, it probably does), especially when the honeycomb is making a late comeback. How long can a finish be...? b24 immaculate, faultless (OK, nearly faultless), whisky. And, rarely for Japanese, bottled at exactly the right age. Had this not been bottled in 2008, a contender for World Whisky of the Year. Guys! You have to get this to me sooner!!! For the record, it kind of took me back to the mid 1970s when I was first studying whisky, for here I felt I was learning about this distillery for the very first time...Oh, and for the best effects: don't bother warming in the glass – just pour...and score... 56%

Chichibu 14 Years Old Single Malt db (89) n20 tangerine peel and rice: two years older than the 12-y-o, that hint of bourbon has now become a statement; t23 brilliantly eclectic arrival on the palate with no organisation at all to the flurry of malt and bourbony oak and tangerine-fruity spices that are whizzing around; f23 pretty long with firm vanilla and a distinctive oiliness. Something approaching a whiff of smoke adds some extra ballast to the oak; b23 we are talking mega, in-your-face taste explosions here. A malt with a bourbony attitude that is unquestionably superb. 57%. Toa.

⌐ **Chichibu Single Malt 2008** bourbon barrel, bott 2011 db (89) n22.5 young, but a veritable bouquet of barley; t23.5 even more youthful, but how can you not fall to your knees and kiss the feet of the intense gristy sugars; f21.5 bitters out surprisingly for such a babe; b22.5 lovers of young malty Bunnahabhains will appreciate this doppelganger! Youthful, especially on delivery, but proof –as I have long argued in Japan – that their whisky doesn't have to be of Scottish value ages to excel...A three year old Japanese classic...and how many times have you heard of one of those? 61.8%. For 'Whisky Live Tokyo 2011'.

⌐ **Chichibu Peated Single Malt 2008** refill hogshead, bott 2011 db (84.5) n19 t21 f22 b21.5. Maybe the right age, just the wrong kind of cask. Love the liquorice on the smoke, though. 62%. For 'Whisky Live Tokyo 2011'.

Chichibu Single Malt Newborn Double Matured cask no. 447, dist 2008, bott 2009 db (81) n18.5 t22.5 f20 b20. A toffee fest. Seeing as it was distilled only a year or two ago, I'm amazed it is quarter matured, let alone double matured... 61.3%

Chichibu Single Malt Newborn Heavily Peated cask no. 451, dist 2009, bott 2009 db (84) n21.5 t22 f20.5 b20. Chewy, peaty toffee. 61.3%

Ichiro's Malt Chichibu Newborn cask no. 127, dist 2008, bott 2008 db (80) n18.5 t21 f20.5 b20. A fierce, juicy, fruity, barley-oil intense semi new make which appears to have spent a limited time in cask. Not entirely free of feints, it is not lacking in character for that and while technically challenged, is flavourful fun. 62.5%. Number One Drinks Co.

FUJI GOTEMBA 1973. Kirin Distillers.

The Fuji Gotemba 15 Years Old db (92) n21 diced nuts, especially pistachio with vanilla and a sprinkling of sugar; t23 mouth watering from the start with a sensational development of sweet malt; f24 plateaus out with textbook spices binding sweet malt and dry oak. The length is exemplary; b24 quality malt of great poise. 43%. Kirin.

The Fuji Gotemba 18 Years Old db (81) n20 t19 f21 b21. Jelly-baby fruitiness, complete with powdered sugar. Big, big age apparent. 43%. Kirin.

Fuji Gotemba 20th Anniversary Pure Malt db (84) n21 t20 f22 b21. The nose is a lovely mixture of fruit and mixed oak; the body has a delightful sheen and more fruit with the malt. Handsome stuff. 40%. Kirin.

HAKUSHU 1973. Suntory.

Hakushu Heavily Peated Aged 9 Years bott 2009 db (92.5) n22.5 lightly heavily peated with a now lost Port Ellen style gristy sweetness; t23.5 ultra sweet barley bang on cue and a slow radiation of spice, citrus and sympathetic oak; f23 drier, oakier but still some sugared lime for balance and freshness. The smoke is distant and barley involved; b23.5 nothing like as heavily peated as some Hakushus it has been my pleasure to sample over the years. But certainly superbly orchestrated and balanced. 48%

Hakushu Single Malt Whisky Aged 10 Years bott 2009 db (87.5) n22 a much more lumbering gait with both barley and oak; t23 sprightly barley at first, which immediately sweetens deliciously. The oak and toffees become a brooding presence; f20.5 pretty flat and oak-fuelled; b22 duller than of old. 40%

⌘ **Hakushu Single Malt Whisky Aged 10 Years** bott 2011 db (88) n22.5 lovely interlocking between citrus, worty grist (some offering delicate smoke) and natural caramels; some walnut oils ramp up the complexity further; t22 the vaguest smoke imaginable offers extra weight to the juicy barley and cream toffee; f21.5 simple toffee; b22 quite youthful and beautiful: a fruitier affair than the last Hakushu 10 I came across. 40%

Hakushu Single Malt Whisky Aged 12 Years db (91.5) n22.5 t23.5 f22.5 b23. Just about identical to the 43.3% bottling in every respect. Please see those tasting notes for this little beauty. 43.5%

Hakushu Single Malt Aged 12 Years db (91) n22 revitalising barley with smoke as distant as a cloud over Fuji; t23 multi-layered barley with so many levels of sweetness; the very faintest hint of smoke on the middle; f23 long with the accent now on vanilla and soft, developing oil and spice; b23 an even more lightly- peated version of the 40%, with the distillery's fabulous depth on full show. 43.3%

⌘ **Hakushu Single Malt Whisky Aged 12 Years** bott 2011 db (95.5) n24 light but offering enough to really get the nose twitching: complex oaky tones offering subdued vanilla as a platform for the brighter barley, some of which is offering little more than a soupcon t23.5 salivating, crisp malt turns towards a sugary, gristy very mildly smoky form; spices engage the vanilla in the middle ground; f23.5 subtle, teasing spices infiltrate the soft lemon jelly and vanilla sponge cake; b24.5 a prime example of what makes this such a magnificent distillery. One of the most complex and clever 12 year old malts to be found anywhere in the world this year: a great whisky that could be easily overlooked. 43%

The Hakushu Single Malt Whisky Aged 15 Years Cask Strength db (95) n24 pure, unmistakable Hakushu: intense, powering, yet clean and refined. Loads of citrus to lighten matters but the local oak ensures enormity; t23 big, initially oak-threatened but the barley comes flooding back with light oils helping to soften the early scratchiness; first mouthful is dry, the second shows a much truer picture; f24 now goes into complexity overdrive as all those fruity-barley-oaky- elements continue to jostle for supremacy, only for late spices and gorgeous milky mocha to come in and steal the thunder; b24 last time round I lamented the disappointing nose. This time perhaps only a degree of over eagerness from the oak has robbed this as a serious Whisky of the Year contender. No matter how you look at it, though, brilliant!! 56%

Hakushu Single Malt Whisky Aged 18 Years bott 2009 db (86) n20 t23.5 f21 b21.5. Wow! Where has all this oak come from? Appears to have gone gray overnight...The delivery, though, makes this a malt worth finding because for 20 seconds or so we have absolutely everything in complete harmony, and the degree of barley sweetness is just about perfect. Then all is lost to the duller oak tones again. 43%

⌘ **Hakushu Single Malt Whisky Aged 18 Years** bott 2011 db (86) n23 t21.5 f20.5 b21. Never quite finds either the main story or the punch line. Enjoyable but, knowing the capabilities of the distillery, I expected more. Enormous degree of toffee here. The nose, though, is a charmer. 43%

The Hakushu Single Malt Whisky Aged 25 Years db (93) n23 some blowhard oak is pegged back by an intense barley-fruit mix; thick yet complex; t24 a wonderful combination of silk and barley sheen juxtaposed with busy but light spice; soft fruits adorn the higher places within the palate while a subtle earthiness rumbles below; f23 improbably long. Even though some serious extraction has taken place from the oak, the integrity of the barley makes you sigh with pleasure. Now the spices change in nature to soft and playful to warm and rumbling; b23 a malt which is impossible not to be blown away by. 43%

⌘ **Hakushu Single Malt Whisky Aged 25 Years** bott 2011 db (91) n23.5 mesmeric dates and crushed walnuts, but little overall sweetness as the oloroso does the job it should. The most vague hint of a treated butt; the overall poise of the aroma is stunning, though; t23.5

again, the deportment of the delivery is textbook, helped by the lightest smoke drift. Delicate sugars form in slow motion; **f21** bitters out with burnt raisin and a renegade cask; **b23** just one slightly off butt away from total magnificence. 43%

Hakushu 1984 db **(95) n22** delicate banana and malt with a gentle fly-past of peat. The oak is unbowed but sympathetic; **t25** staggeringly beautiful: wave upon wave of astonishing complexity crashes against the tastebuds. The malt is intense but there is plenty of room for oak in varying guises to arrive, make eloquent speeches and retire. The intensity of spice is spot on – perfect; **f24** long, more spice and greater malt intensity as the oak fades. Only the softest hints of smoke; mouthwatering to the last as mild coffee appears; **b24** a masterpiece malt of quite sublime complexity and balance. The sort of experience that gives a meaning to life, the universe and everything... 61%

Hakushu 1988 db **(92) n21** overtly peaty and dense, pleasant but lacking usual Hakushu complexity; **t24** mouthwatering start with massively lively malt and fresh peating hanging on to its coat-tails. Some amazing heather–honey moments that have no right to be there; the peat intensifies then lightens; **f23** lots of rich peat and then intense vanilla; crisp and abrupt at the finale with late bitter chocolate; **b24** like all great whiskies this is one that gangs up on you in a way you are not expecting: the limited complexity on the nose is more than compensated for elsewhere. Superb. If this were an Islay malt the world would be drooling over it. 61%

Hakushu 1989 Sherry Cask bott 2009 **(88) n22** there must be some whisky in there somewhere... **t22** ...yep... no... yep... there it is: just seen it coming up for the second time... **f22** ...no gone for good now... **b22** a malt whisky drowned in a sea of thick sherry. Enjoyable, though! 62%. Speciality Drinks Ltd bottled for TWE's 10th Anniversary.

Hakushu Vintage Malt 1990 db **(89) n22** firm barley and firmer oak; **t23** serious intensity on delivery, this time with all the action being enjoyed by the concentrated, grassy barley; **f22** layers of vanilla add balance to the fade; **b22** warming in places with the tastebuds never getting a single moment's peace. 56%. Suntory.

Scotch Malt Whisky Society Cask 120.05 Aged 17 Years 1st fill barrel, dist Dec 91 **(94) n23** subtly peated in a way Hakushu possibly does best of all; **t24** it's all there: the most deft smoke; firm, eye-watering barley; explodingly over-ripe cherries; an Arbroath Smokie saltiness; oil laced with honey...; **f23.5** remains bullet hard and mercurially smoky to the last departing atom; **b23.5** amazingly, this is a less than perfect cask deployed. But so absurdly good was the spirit filled into it, you barely notice...or care. 59%. 104 bottles.

Suntory Pure Malt Hakushu Aged 20 Years db **(94) n23** fresh, mildly grapey fruit combined with subtle waves of peat; **t24** the peat is now less subtle: wave upon wave of it bringing with it flotsam of drifting oak and then a very sharp malt tang; **f23** long, sweet spice but the oak forms a chunky alliance with the firm peat. The bitter-sweet compexity almost defies belief; **b24** a hard-to-find malt, but find it you must. Yet another huge nail in the coffin of those who purport Japanese whisky to be automatically inferior to Scotch. 56%

HANYU

Hanyu 1990 cask no. 9511, dist 1990, bott 2007 db **(91) n23 t23 f22 b23.** Leaves you in no doubt how outstanding this stuff can be when found nowhere near a sherry butt... 55.5%

⁘ **Hanyu Single Malt 2000** hogshead refilled into Japanese oak, bott 2011 db **(91.5) n21.5** a bit messy and off key: not from bad distilling, but the oak doesn't appear to know which way to turn; some attractive crystalised sugars; **t24** muscovado sugars melt into a malty morass before sweetening the mocha; anyone who knows such a thing as a coffee Walnut Whip will recognise this...; **f23.5** the coffee vanishes to leave the milky cocoa and muscovado; **b23.5** about as sweet a whisky can go and still be in total control. An after dinner malt if ever there was one... 60.9%. For 'Whisky Live Tokyo 2011'.

Full Proof Europe Hanyu 1988 butt no. 9307, bott 2008, **(74.5) n19 t20.5 f18 b18.** Some bright honeyed moments can't entirely contain the sulphur. 55%. nc ncf. 534 bottles.

Ichiro's Card "Ace of Diamonds" 1986 cream sherry butt finish, cask no. 9023, dist 1986, bott 2008 **(94.5) n24 t23.5 f23 b24.** Another big sherry finish. But again sulphur free and here provides sufficient spice to make the whole thing rock. High grade Japanese. And even higher grade finishing... 56.4%. Venture Whisky Ltd.

⁘ **Ichiro's Card "Eight of Clubs" 1998** American oak puncheon finish, bott 2011 **(88.5) n22** a curious bourbon honeycomb effect mixed with drifting smoke. Odd, but rather lovely; **t23** salivating barley on delivery, a small puff of smoke spreads in all directions and then a massive display of sweet caramel; **f21.5** the caramel persists allowing only a few sugars and some smoke to emerge; **b22** vanishes in a cloud of caramel, but has much to say first. 57.5%

Ichiro's Card "Eight of Diamonds" Spanish oak oloroso finish, dist 1991, bott 2009 **(77.5) n20 t21 f18 b18.5.** Wild cherry with some fizz and bite. But bitter and off key, too. *57.1%*

Ichiro's Card "Eight of Spades" 2000 cask no. 9301, dist 2000, bott 2008 **(66.5) n16 t18 f16 b16.5.** The sulphur reduces this to a deuce. *58%. Venture Whisky Ltd.*

Ichiro's Card "Five of Clubs" Mizunara hogshead finish, dist 1991, bott 2009 **(84.5) n22 t21.5 f20 b21.** A fruitier number but with a blemish on the finish. *57.4%. Venture Whisky Ltd.*

‹❖ **Ichiro's Card "Four of Diamonds" 2000** PX finish, bott 2011 **(79) n19.5 t22 18 b19.5.** One of the few things harder than diamond is trying to persuade PX casks to work with whisky. Add sulphur into the equation and there is no hope at all. Even when the sulphur is as little as found here. Drinkable, though, against all the odds. *56.9%. Venture Whisky Ltd.*

Ichiro's Card "Four of Spades" Japanese oak "Mizunara" puncheon finish, dist 2000, bott 2010 **(95) n24** big bourbon character: not just honey and liquorice, but an almost rye-like fruity (cherry) hardness, too; **t24.5** glorious arrival with a manuka and clear honey mix plus a landslide of warming spices. Then it's back to pure bourbon again with the liquorice, molassed and succulent, kicking in; **f23.5** long, at last with an element of maltiness but the butterscotch and vanilla hints at honeycomb, too; **b23.5** I have often heard the Japanese accused of trying to mimic scotch whisky. On this evidence, it's the Kentuckians who should be looking over their shoulder... *58.6%. Venture Whisky Ltd.*

Ichiro's Card "Jack of Hearts" red oak hogshead finish, dist 1991, bott 2010 **(86) n22.5 t22 f20.5 b21.** A knave of a dram. Lulls you into thinking this is going to be a honeyed gem, then mugs you with its rock hard, biting malt. *56.1%. Venture Whisky Ltd.*

‹❖ **Ichiro's Card "King of Clubs" 1988** cognac cask finish, bott 2011 **(83) n21 t22 f20 b20.5.** Cognac casks have the unfortunate habit of tightening and strangling the best out of a whisky...and this petit assassin is no exception. Pleasant in part with the odd strand of peat and molasses escaping. But the bitterness is another disappointment. Anyway, being from cognac cask, the Emperor of Clubs rather than "King", surely... *58%. Venture Whisky Ltd.*

Ichiro's Card "King of Hearts" PX finish, dist 1986, bott 2009 **(95.5) n23.5** big and fruity: strawberry and figs; more than a trace of smoked oak; some ginger and clove sprinkled in, too; **t24** superb spice delivery, accompanied by soft peat, followed by a salivating salvo of ultra sharp greengages. Finally the barley begins to soak into the middle ground accompanied by that luxurious smoke; **f24** smoked chocolate mousse; **b24** this King of Hearts had some smoky tarts...delicious and complex almost beyond measure! *55.4%*

‹❖ **Ichiro's Card "Nine of Spades" 1990** cream sherry butt finish, bott 2010 **(77) n18 t20.5 f18.5 b19.** Creamy for sure. But time for some sulphur-removing raspberries. *52.4%*

Ichiro's Card "Queen of Spades" port pipe finish, dist 1990, bott 2009 **(83.5) n22.5 t22 f19 b20.** Lots of toffee; the finish is furry and bitter. *53.1%. Venture Whisky Ltd.*

‹❖ **Ichiro's Card "Seven of Diamonds" Hanyu 1991** PX finish, bott 2010 **(81.5) n21 t22 f19 b19.5.** Some kind of sulphur note lurks (with intent), but there is also date and walnut in previously undiscovered quantities. Quite literally a bitter sweet experience. *54.8%*

Ichiro's Card "Six of Clubs" cream sherry butt finish, dist 2000, bott 2009 **(66) n17 t18 f15 b16.** A sulphurous deuce. *57.9%. Venture Whisky Ltd.*

Ichiro's Card "Ten of Clubs" 1990 sherry butt finish, cask no. 9032, dist 1990, bott 2008 **(85) n22.5 t21.5 f21 b20.** Tempted to give this one extra marks just for finding a non-sulphured cask. But also have to say that the sherry here, though profound and clean, is having too big a say. Some of the grape is formidably beautiful. But there is too much of a good thing, and vital complexity is lost. That said, a whisky worth investigating. *52.4%. Venture Whisky Ltd.*

‹❖ **Ichiro's Card "Ten of Hearts" Hanyu 2000** Madeira hogshead finish, bott 2011 **(91) n22.5** no off notes from arguably the best wine cask type used in the whisky industry today. A beautiful softness allows barley to flourish amid the grape...; light spices tickle the nose; **t23** sumptuous delivery! Leave in the glass for a while and spices arrive much earlier – and to dramatic effect. Again barley gets a word – no an entire sentence – in before being enveloped by the juicy, warming grape. **f22.5** the spices continue and now enjoy a raisin fudge accompaniment: tops off a gorgeous experience. **b23** thank you, Madeira... *61%*

‹❖ **Ichiro's Card "Three of Hearts" Hanyu 2000** Port pipe finish, bott 2010 **(90) n23** spicy plums and warmed marzipan with a Jaffacake type orange filling; **t23.5** fabulous fruit bonbon delivery, with the sugars splitting, allowing the intense fruit to ooze out; soon a big fudge middle arrives, along with coffee-flavoured revels; cream toffees are not in short supply; **f21** a little biting bitterness (not entirely unexpected with a few recognisable noises on the nose and delivery) adds angst to the big caramel; **b22.5** delicious, but an astonishing degree of toffee is created in the process. *61.2%. Venture Whisky Ltd.*

Ichiro's Card "Two of Hearts" Madeira hogshead finish, dist 1986, bott 2009 **(86) n22 t23 f20 b21.** Big, sweeping, delicious statements: some malty, some bourbon. But, overall, just a shade on the hot and rough and ready side. 56.3%. *Venture Whisky Ltd.*

⟐ **Ichiro's Card "Two of Spades" Hanyu 1990** Port hogshead finish, bott 2011 **(84.5) n21 t22 f20.5 b21.** Enjoyable. But bizarrely one-dimensional. Another Hanyu lost in a storm of toffee. Just the odd off-key note, too. 55.8%. *Venture Whisky Ltd.*

Ichiro's Malt Aged 15 Years 4th bottling **(89.5) n23.5** lively, saline tang to the spicy marmalade; **t23** another, typically Hanyu, sugar-malt juicy salvo; **f21** a degree of tangy buzz; **b22** oozes character and quality. 46%. *Venture Whisky Ltd.*

⟐ **Ichiro's Malt Aged 20 Years (95.5) n24** a magnificent portrait of complexity. The malt stands proud and clean, offering a mildly crusty light sugariness; the oaks are a model of good manners: vanilla and honey, but in the most modest amounts; here and there the odd molecule of smoke; **t24** a delivery to pray and die for: such spices, such juiciness after so many years: remarkable. The middle ground is taken up by a quite glorious concentrated Malteser candy...but with better milky cocoa than found in the bag; **f23.5** long and brimming with so many layers of barley the head spins. The Malteser story continues; **b24** no this finish; no that finish. Just the distillery allowed to speak in its very own voice. And nothing more eloquent has been heard from it this year. Please, all those owning casks of Hanyu: for heaven's sake take note... 57.5%. *Venture Whisky Ltd.*

Ichiro's Malt Aged 23 Years (92.5) n23 salty; obvious age and some less obvious smoke; **t23.5** beautifully salivating delivery with rich, focussed barley; **f23** long, with a stream of ever-sweetening vanilla; **b23** a fabulous malt you take your time over. 58%

Ichiro's Malt The Final Vintage of Hanyu Aged 10 Years cask no. 6067 **(89.5) n22.5** slight vegetable edge to the thick malt; **t24** wow! That malt is thick! Beefed up with plenty of oak and maple syrup; **f21.5** on the bitter side; **b21.5** if it's a quiet glass of whisky you're after, give this one a miss... 60.8%. *Venture Whisky Ltd.*

One Single Cask Hanyu 1990 cask no. 9305, bott 2009 **(90.5) n23** an injection of orange peel where and when needed; **t23** powering barley/oak mix: the intensity of the sweetly sapped oak is every bit as mouth-watering as fresh barley; **f22.5** an enormous surge of sharp vanilla; **b22** huge whisky but borderline OTT oak. The infused sugars do the trick. 53.4%

One Single Cask Hanyu 1991 Japanese malt, cask no. 370, bott 2009 **(91.5) n22** spices nestle amid the dry oak; **t23.5** glorious delivery: honeycomb in its densest form with some marauding spices intensifying by the second; **f23** long, a catwalk for varying types of vanilla, but decent sugars offer balance; **b23** unmistakable style: I found myself muttering " ah, local oak!" to myself (tasting close on 800 malts in a couple of months does that to you...) before I spotted the label. Quite beautiful. 57.3%. *Number One Drinks Co.*

KARUIZAWA 1955. Mercian.

Karuizawa 1967 Vintage sherry cask, bott 2009 **(96) n24** spiced Mysore coffee sweetened with Demerara; a little hickory and peat thing going on, too; remarkably, for its age, not an off note in sight... **t24.5** back to that style I have encountered so many times over the years from this distillery: grape and malt followed by waves of burnt raisin, yet somehow drenching the palate in salivating barley and green grape, too : is this for real...???? **f23.5** seemingly infinitely long, with a playful liquorice finale, giving way to some improbably late Demerara; **b24** another engaging, engrossing and, frankly, brilliant malt from this distillery, equalling the oldest I have ever encountered from Karuizawa. If you find it, sell your body, sell your partner's body... anything...just experience it! 58.4%. *Bottled for TWE's 10th Anniversary.*

Karuizawa 1971 cask no. 6878, dist 1971, bott 2008 **(94) n24 t23.5 f23 b23.5.** It's not just Scotch which goes all exotic fruity on us when it gets towards being an antique malt. By the time you have grappled and overcome this one your tastebuds and brain are pretty knackered. But it's so worth the battle...! 64.1%. *Number One Drinks Company.*

Karuizawa 1972 sherry butt finish, cask no. 7290, dist 1972, bott 2008 **(87.5) n24 t20 f22 b21.5.** A bizarre whisky, not helped by its strength and spirit-driven punch. But clean and hammers home its finer points if you are able to listen. It's the nose, though, which stars. 65%. *Number One Drinks Co.*

Karuizawa 1982 sherry, bott 2009 **(90) n23** latticed cherry tart; a light spice and smoke dart around the periphery; **t24** profound grape, sharp at first, then a quite enthralling, shocking, almost unique, wave of ultra-rich malted vanilla..."beautiful" doesn't quite do it justice; **f22** bitters out slightly; **b22** forget the sherry. Forget the distant, nagging "S" word. Just home in on that astonishing middle: like a million Maltesers dissolving in your mouth all at once...there is nothing else like it in the whisky world. And no other distillery is capable. Alas. 56.1%. *Speciality Drinks Ltd bottled for TWE's 10th Anniversary.*

Karuizawa 1985 Vintage Single Cask cask no. 7017, bott 2009 db (78.5) n19 t22.5 f18 b19. Sherry preserve spread over slightly burnt toast. Pity about that sulphur. *60.8%*

Karuizawa 1986 cask no. 7387, dist 1986, bott 2008 (82.5) n20 t22 f20 b20.5. For a malt so obviously trying to overcome a sulphurous handicap it holds its head high with a vivid barley thrust. Lots of caramel on the finish, too. *60.7%. Number One Drinks Company.*

Karuizawa 1991 cask no. 3318, dist 1991, bott 2007 (85) n19 t21.5 f22.5 b22. Aggressive barley tries to help compensate for the over extraction from the oak. Never less than high quality, though, and blessed with delicious molasses all the way. *62.5%*

Karuizawa 1992 cask no. 3330, dist 1992, bott 2007 (92) n23 t22.5 f23.5 b23.5. Flawed, certainly. But in genius, it's just about forgivable.. *61.5%. Number One Drinks Company.*

Karuizawa Pure Malt Aged 12 Years (85) n18 t23 f22 b22. A recent Gold Medal Winner at the IWSC, but surely not by sporting a fractured nose like this. Thankfully the delivery is quite superb with the emphasis on silky honeycomb. *40%*

Karuizawa Pure Malt Aged 15 Years (76) n17 t21 f20 b18. Some vague sulphur notes on the sherry do no favours for what appears to be an otherwise top-quality malt. (Earlier bottlings have been around the 87–88 mark, with the fruit, though clean, not being quite in balance but made up for by an astonishing silkiness with roast chestnut puree and malt). *40%*

Karuizawa Single Malt Aged 17 Years (87.5) n23 juicy dates in the rich, molassed fruitcake; t23 almost ridiculously soft on delivery: it's all about fruit, for sure, but the roast coffee and dark molassed sweetness do give it a required dimension; f20 despite the clarity of grape, still a dry, bitter note develops; b21.5 a beautiful malt in so many ways, but one less-than-wonderful sherry butt has robbed this of greatness. How many times has this happened this year...? *40%*

Karuizawa Pure Malt Aged 17 Years (90) n20 bourbony, big oak and pounding fruit; t24 enormous stuff: the link between malt and fruit is almost without definition; f23 amazingly long and silky. Natural vanilla melts in with the almost concentrated malt; b23 brilliant whisky beautifully made and majestically matured. Neither sweetness nor dryness dominates, always the mark of a quality dram. *40%*

Noh Whisky Karuizawa 1976 cask no. 6719, bott 2009 (91) n22 tight, spiced grape; t24 enveloping grape dovetailing with thick stratum of malt; impressive early sugars and a mouth feel to die for; the laid back juiciness is a treat; f22.5 delicate hickory and plenty more rich barley; b22.5 sticks religiously to the malty house style despite the grape trying to enter from every angle. A beautiful whisky, reminding me what a special year 1976 was for Japan. Happy 35th in April...x. *63%. Number One Drinks Co.*

Noh Whisky Karuizawa 1977 cask no. 4592, dist 1977, bott 2010 (75) n19 t19 f18 b19. The bizarre dark colour and aggressive sharpness of nose and flavour suggests a small iron nail dropped into the cask at some time in its long life. Pity, for the grape is quite wholesome. *60.7%. Number One Drinks Co.*

Noh Whisky Karuizawa 1995 Japanese wine cask finish no. 5004, dist 1995, bott 2008 (93.5) n23.5 t23 f23.5 b23.5. Seatbelts needed for this enormous ride. An unusual malt which doesn't entirely add up...but comes to the right numbers!! *63%. Number One Drinks Co.*

KIRIN

Kirin 18 Years Old (86.5) n22 t22 f21.5 b21. Unquestionably over-aged. Even so, still puts up a decent show with juicy citrus trying to add a lighter touch to the uncompromising, ultra dense oak. As entertaining as it is challenging. *43%. Suntory.*

KOMAGATAKE

Komagatake 10 Years Old Single Malt db (78) n19 t20 f19 b20. A very simple, malty whisky that's chewy and clean with a slight hint of toffee. *40%. Mars.*

Komagatake 10 Years Old Sherry Cask db (67) n16.5 t17 f16.5 b17. Torpedoed by sulphur. Gruesome. *40%. Mars.*

Komagatake 1988 Single Cask sherry cask, cask no. 566, dist 1988, bott 2009 db (62.5) n15 t16.5 f15 b16. I can assume only that this has been "finished" in a relatively recent sherry butt. "Finished" is putting it mildly. A sulphur horror show. *46%. Mars.*

Komagatake 1989 Single Cask American white oak cask, cask no. 617, dist 1989, bott 2009 db (88) n23 t22.5 f21 b21.5. A fine but bitty malt which feels its age at times. *46%. Mars.*

Komagatake 1992 Single Cask American white oak cask, cask no. 1144, dist 1992, bott 2009 db **(93.5) n24.5 t23 f22.5 b23.5.** You know when you've had a glass of this: beautiful and no shrinking violet. *46%. Mars.*

MIYAGIKYO *(see Sendai)*

SENDAI 1969. Nikka.

Miyagikyo batch 24H20B db **(89) n22** sweet chestnut and marzipan share the nutty honours; **t23.5** beautiful delivery, superbly weighted: the malt really has some backbone and some toffee liquorice makes for a chewy middle ground; **f21.5** perhaps a touch too much toffee; **b22** another high quality malt from this improving distillery. *43%*

Miyagikyo 10 Years Old batch 06I08C db **(83) n19 t22 f21 b21.** Much better than the sharp nose warns, with some juicy, fruity moments. A little flat, though. *45%*

Miyagikyo 12 Years Old batch 08I28A db **(89) n22.5** that familiar gooseberry nose with barley and custard; **t23** juicy and sweetens superbly mainly with gristy barley, though that oaky vanilla lurks nearby; **f21** drier, a hint of bitterness, but that persistent sweet barley compensates; **b22.5** in many ways, absolutely 100% recognisable as the distillery house style; in another this has much more confidence and charisma than of old. *45%*

Miyagikyo 15 Years Old batch 02I10D db **(91.5) n23** fruity, as is the expression's style. But now lighter with much more emphasis on a Sauternes-style sultana; **t23.5** pulsing fruit, but the barley is sharp and wonderfully juicy; **f22** vanillas balance the barley and still a residual sweet grape can be found; a mild degree of very late bitterness; **b23** a much lighter, more refined and elegant creature than before. Despite a minor sherry butt blemish, fabulous. *45%*

Miyagiko Key Malt Aged 12 Years "Fruity & Rich" db **(90) n22** fruit biscuits with burnt raisin and sugar; **t23** wonderful lift-off of sultana and burnt raisin on a sea of chewy barley. Towards the middle, a brief expression of oak and then much sweeter – and oilier – barley. Fruity; **f22** rich! **b23** a very comfortable whisky, much at home with itself. *55%. Nikka.*

Miyagiko Key Malt Aged 12 Years "Soft & Dry" db **(85) n22 t21 f21 b21.** Perhaps needs a degree of sweetness... *55%. Nikka.*

Miyagikyo 15 Years Old batch 20C44C db **(84) n20 t21 f22 b21.** Very typically Sendai: light body and limited weight even with all the fruit. Clean and gathers in overall enjoyability, though. *45%*

Sendai 12 Years Old code 06C40C db **(83) n17 t22 f23 b21.** To put it politely, the nose is pretty ordinary; but what goes on afterwards is relative bliss with a wonderful, oily, fruity resonance. For those thinking in Scotch terms, this is very Speysidey with the malt intense and chewy. *45%. Nikka.*

Sendai Miyagikyo Nikka Single Cask Malt Whisky 1986 dist 16 May 86 bott, 05 Dec 03 db **(88) n22 t20 f24 b22.** Little to do with balance, everything about effect. *63.2%*

Sendai Miyagikyo Nikka Single Cask Malt Whisky 1992 dist 22 Apr 92, bott 05 Dec 03 db **(84) n19 t20 f24 b21.** Very strange whisky: I would never have recognised this as Sendai. I don't know if they have used local oak on this but the fruity, off-balance nose and early taste is compensated by an orgy of mouth-watering, softly smoked barley that sends the taste buds into ecstasy. A distinct, at times erratic, whisky that may horrify the purists but really has some perzaz and simply cannot be ignored. *55.3%*

SHIRAKAWA

Shirakawa 32 Years Old Single Malt (94) n23 ripe mango meets a riper, rye-encrusted bourbon. We are talking a major aroma here; **t24** the most intense malt you'll ever find explodes and drools all over your tastebuds. To make the flavour bigger still, the oak adds a punchy bourbon quality. Beautiful oils coat the roof of the mouth to amplify the performance; **f23** long, sweet and malty. Some fruitiness does arrive but it is the oak-malt combination that just knocks you out; **b24** just how big can an unpeated malt whisky get? The kind of malt that leaves you in awe, even when you thought you had seen and tasted them all. *55%. Takara.*

WHITE OAK DISTILLERY

White Oak Akashi Single Malt Whisky Aged 8 Years bott 2007 db **(74.5) n18.5 t19.5 f17.5 b19.** Always fascinating to find a malt from one of the smaller distilleries in a country. And I look forward to tracking this one down and visiting, something I have yet to do. There is certainly something distinctly small still about his one, with butyric and feintiness causing damage to nose and finish. For all the early malty presence on delivery, some of the off notes are a little on the uncomfortable side. *40%*

YAMAZAKI 1923. Suntory.

Yamazaki 1984 bott 2009 db (**94**) **n24** massive: more dates and walnut – the occasional distillery style - only here in concentrate form; **t24** big. But you'd never know it. Superbly weighted grape is full, buxom and ripe. But gathers in with almost honeybun-bourbony oak with something approaching tenderness. Juicy and weaving between bourbony and sherried channels with aplomb; **f22.5** a slight buzz to the finale shows we don't have perfection, but the vanillas remain intact; **b23.5** if you like your whisky boringly neutral, lifeless and with nothing to say other than that it has been ruined by sulphur, then this will horrify you. Though there is a little blemish at the very death, there is still no taking away from this being a sublime 25-year-old. When this distillery is on form it makes for compelling whisky and here we have a bottling showing Yamazaki at its brightest. *48%*

The Yamazaki Single Malt Whisky Aged 10 Years bott 2009 db (**87.5**) **n21.5** a mixed bag of big vanilla, barley and plummy bananas; **t22** whisky doesn't come softer on delivery but there is a price; the toffees seem to flatten any higher notes but there is still a tangible fruitiness drifting on from somewhere which is very attractive; **f22** remains lightly sweet, with raisins and vanilla the softness continues; **b22** returned to some of its fruitier root. But if it's silky whisky you want, look no further. *40%*

⌐ **The Yamazaki Single Malt Whisky Aged 10 Years** bott 2011 db (**84**) **n22 t22 f19 b20.** Plenty to enjoy, especially the intensity of the malt and its happy balance with the oak. But the finish needs a little attention. *40%*

⌐ **The Yamazaki Single Malt Whisky Aged 12 Years** bott 2011 db (**90**) **n23** has retained its sherry trifle character, though now with more custard; **t22** firm delivery: the barley thumps home confidently. It takes the grapes, sugars and a few trailing spices a little while to catch up; **f22.5** the surprising late arrival of oils give the fruit ample time make their mark, especially the sugary banana. The late spices are a treat. **b22.5** A complex and satisfying malt of a very high standard. *43%*

The Yamazaki Single Malt Whisky Aged 15 Years Cask Strength db (**94**) **n23** just a hint that its gone OTT oak-wise, but there is a wisp of smoke to this, too. All in all, wonderful brinkmanship that pays off; **t24** stunning: a massive injection of bourbon-style liquorice and honeycomb plays perfectly against the softer malts. The most controlled of malty explosions... **f23** long, lascivious, the tastebuds are debauched by ingots of honeycomb, molasses and dark sugary notes balanced by the drier oaks; **b24** an extraordinary bottling that far exceeds any previous version I have encountered. Stunning. *56%*

⌐ **The Yamazaki Single Malt Whisky Aged 18 Years** bott 2011 db (**89**) **n23.5** very different from of old: now chocolate encased exotic fruit with kumquat, blood orange and toasted raisin completing the dazzling array; the tannins are almost those found in a fine wine; **t23** lighter delivery than you could possibly expect, the oak backing off leaving delicate barley to go it alone. Soon an ever-increasing number of rich, fresh fruity notes of excellent sweetness; **f20.5** disappointingly furry; **b22** a very slight sulphur flaw takes the edge of what is a remarkably beautiful whisky for most of the time. *43%*

The Yamazaki Single Malt Whisky Aged 25 Years db (**87**) **n23 t22 f20 b22.** It has taken me over an hour to taste this. And still I don't know if I have marked it too high. You'll either love it or hate it – but you'll find nothing else like it..!! *43%*

The Yamazaki Sherry Cask Aged 10 Years bott 2009 db (**82.5**) **n21 t22 f19.5 b20.** Very tight. The grape, initially impressive, is domineering leaving the malt's wings clipped. There are those who will adore this. But, technically and balance-wise, not quite right. *48%*

The Cask of Yamazaki 1990 Sherry Butt cask no. 0N70646, dist Feb 90, bott Jun 08 db (**97**) **n24.5 t24 f24 b24.5**. Such is the state of sherry butts today – including in Japan – that the first thing to report is that it is entirely sulphur-free...and some!! Without blemish, this is a rare treat. Once, slightly over the top grape-wise. These days a joyous relief! Beyond that, it is gargantuan. Few whiskies this year have covered such a wide variety of flavours and aromas with such panache: the structure and complexity for its type are close to perfection. Even more telling, is the fact that it is hard to believe that one of this company's Scottish distilleries could have come up with something quite so brilliant. *61%. 506 bottles.*

The Cask of Yamazaki 1993 Heavily Peated Malt white oak puncheon cask, dist May 93, bott Oct 07 db (**95**) **n23.5 t25 f23 b23.5**. When they say "Heavily Peated" they mean heavily. Like some kind of new phenol isotope, this is heavy peat whisky. Like probably twice as thick as the average peaty whisky you come across. It is, shall we say...peaty. Strap yourself in for the ride: only the fittest will survive... *62%. 574 bottles.*

The Cask of Yamazaki 1993 Heavily Peated Malt white oak puncheon cask no. 3Q70048, dist May 93, bott Jun 08 db **(89) n22 t21.5 f23 b22.5.** Takes a long time to get going thanks to an initially unattractive oily coating. But on finding its feet becomes a cracker. *62%. 503 bottles.*

Suntory Pure Malt Yamazaki 25 Years Old db **(91) n23** quite intoxicating marriage between grapey fruitiness and rich oak: supremely spiced and balanced with a wave of pure bourbon following through; **t23** big, big oloroso character then an entrancing molassed, burnt raisin, malty richness; **f22** subtle spices, poppy seed with some late bitter oak; **b23** being matured in Japan, the 25 years doesn't have quite the same value as Scotland. So perhaps in some ways this can lay claim to be one of the most enormously aged, oak-laden whiskies that has somehow kept its grace and star quality. *43%*

Suntory Single Malt Yamazaki Aged 12 Years db **(87) n22** delicate, chalky vanilla with a squeeze of kiwifruit and butterscotch; **t23** a wonderfully light touch with fresh house-style mouth-watering barley and transparent fruit setting up the busy middle spice; **f20** pretty dry with oak and toffee; **b22** this was the 2006 bottling which somehow missed entry into the Bible, although tasted. A fruity little babe. *43%*

YOICHI 1934. Nikka.

Hokkaido 12 Years Old db **(87) n23 t22 f21 b21.** Full-flavoured malt with absolutely zero yield. Just ricochets around the palate. *43%. Nikka.*

Yoichi batch 04H10D **(87.5) n22.5 t22 f21.5 b21.5.** Very drinkable, though you get the feeling it is performing well within itself. *43%*

Yoichi batch 04I10D db **(81.5) n21.5 t21.5 f18.5 b20.** A very hard malt: crisp, sweet at first but with limited yield. The apparent sulphur on the finish doesn't help. *43%*

Yoichi 10 Years Old batch 08I16C db **(83.5) n21.5 t21 f20.5 b20.5.** Good grief! What has happened to this whisky? Actually, I think I can tell you: too much sherry and caramel makes for a dull malt. Pleasant. Drinkable. But dull. *45%*

Yoichi 12 Years Old batch 08I18B db **(75.5) n19 t19 f18.5 b19.** Fruity but flat and sulphury; some smoke perhaps, but all rather hush-hush...and very disappointing, though had you been at the distillery some dozen years ago not entirely surprising. One feared this day might come...and it has. *45%*

Yoichi Key Malt Aged 12 Years "Peaty & Salty" db **(95) n23** the peat rumbles like distant thunder, difficult to pinpoint but letting you know that it is there. The oaky tones suggest a mixing of Kentucky and something local; soft fruits make an almost apologetic appearance; **t25** there is perfect distribution of peat. It rumbles around the palate offering bitter-sweet depth, and a salty, coastal tang emphasises the richness of the malt; **f23** waves of vanilla begin to outflank the soft peat: the finish is long and there is no victor between the sweet malt and the more bitter, salty oak; **b24** of all the peated whiskies of the world, only Ardbeg can stand shoulder to shoulder with Yoichi when it comes to sheer complexity. Here is an astonishing example of why I rate Yoichi in the best five whiskies in the world. Forget the odd sulphur-tarnished bottling. Get Yoichi in its natural state with perfect balance between oak and malt and it delivers something approaching perfection. And this is just such a bottling. *55%. Nikka.*

Yoichi Key Malt Aged 12 Years "Sherry & Sweet" db **(80) n19 t22 f19 b20.** Sad to report that this should be called "Very Slight Sulphur and Sweet". A real pity because it is obvious that had the Spaniards not molested these butts, they would have been absolutely top-of-the-range. And probably would have scored in the low to mid 90s. I could weep. *55%. Nikka.*

Yoichi Key Malt Aged 12 Years "Woody & Vanillic" db **(83) n21 t22 f20 b20.** Pretty decent whisky. Not sure about creating one that sets out to be woody: that means balance has been sacrificed to concentrate on a particular essence to the whisky that should be used only as a component of complexity. Still, there is enough sweet malt on arrival to make this a dram to be enjoyed. *55%*

Yoichi Single Malt 12 Years Old batch 14F36A db **(91) n22** soft smoke and under-ripe fruit; **t23** profound, chewy barley; lots of small still coppery sharpness and then a gentle awakening of peat; **f23** sweet peats dusted with demerara; it takes some time for the chalky oak to finally have a say; **b23** best when left in the glass for 10-15 minutes: only then does the true story emerge. *45%*

Yoichi 15 Years Old batch 06I08B db **(91.5) n22** surprisingly quiet and well behaved considering the light smokiness drifting about; **t23.5** nutty, chewy and with lots of early toffee. Juices up to puckering effect as the barley and phenols strikes home; **f23** sweet and spicy in the right places as the malt begins to find its legs and goes up a notch or two **b23** for an early moment or two possibly one of the most salivating whiskies you'll get your kisser around this year. Wonderfully entertaining yet you still suspect that this is another Yoichi reduced in effect somewhat by either caramel and/or sherry. When it hits its stride, though, becomes a really busy whisky that gets tastebuds in a right lather. But I'm being picky as I know that this is one of the world's top five distilleries and am aware as anyone on this planet of its extraordinary capabilities. Great fun; great whisky – could be better still, but so much better than its siblings... 45%

Yoichi 20 Years Old db **(95) n23 t23 f25 b24.** I don't know how much they charge for this stuff but either alone or with mates get some for one hell of an experience. What makes it all the more remarkable is that there is a slight sulphury note on the nose: once you taste the stuff that becomes of little consequence. *52%. Nikka.*

Yoichi 20 Years Old batch 06l06A db **(87) n22** an enormous statement from the glass. Immediately the odd sulphur note is detected, but the grape and high roast Java (possibly with medium Mysore) comes to its aid. The result is thick and very warehousy; **t22.5** much lighter delivery than nose: the barley actually shows first and juices up. Soon after though, the dark coffee clouds form; spicy in part, but something niggles away... **f20.5** that off key note gains strength amid a mocha recovery; **b22** bitter-sweet experience, both in taste and perception. Not unusual to find sulphur on this guy, but a shame when it alters the course of the malt. *52%*

Yoichi 1987 batch 22G26B **(89.5) n22** juicy grape somehow outperforms the delicate peats; **t23.5** again the grape is first to show: sweet and juicy and then gives way slightly as some peated chocolate arrives – almost like a smoked fruit chocolate bar: delicious... **f21.5** a few signs of the cask tiring, but the fruit and smoke provide the required sticking plaster; **b23** having tasted from quite a number of casks from this year at the distillery itself, I was a bit worried when I saw that sherry butts had been used. However, no great signs of sulphurous ruination here and the marriage of the varying styles of peat and grape has created the desired degree of complexity. *55%*

Nikka Whisky Yoichi (78) n18 t20 f21 b19. Not often I'm lost for words...but this one left me stunned. Nothing like I expected. Not least because it seems either very young. Or not remotely short of feints. Or both. And the whole thing is propped up by caramel. The best bit is the late spice attack...but this is like nothing I would have expected from one of the top five distilleries in the world. As my one time Japanese girlfriend would have said: "I am shocked..." *43%*

Nikka Whisky Yoichi 1986 20 Years Old (94) n23 age, the salty sea air of Hokkaido and sweet oak have accounted for the more excessive possibilities of the peat: weighty but restrained; **t24** no holding back here, though, as the delivery is one first of juicy fruit and then silky waves of peat; chunky heavy-duty stuff which, for some reason, appears to float about the palate; the spices shoot on sight; **f23** a sweeter, more sober finale with liquorice and molasses joining forces with the salty oakiness to keep the lid on the smoke; **b24** now this is unambiguous Yoichi :exactly how I have come to know and adore this distillery. *55.0%*

Scotch Malt Whisky Society Cask 116.12 Aged 21 Years refill hogshead, dist Jul 86 **(87.5) n22 t22 f21 b22.5.** Attractive and works to the limitations of the cask itself. *54.2%*

Scotch Malt Whisky Society Cask 116.14 Aged 25 Years 1st fill hogshead, dist Sep 83 **(96.5) n23.5 t24.5 f24 b24.5.** What a bloody whisky...!!! There are times, when tasting one sulphur-stuffed whisky after another, I wonder why I do this. Then something as beautiful as this comes along and you remember the exact reason. Whisky can be, and should be, the dark matter of our appreciation of the senses. The reason why so many millions of people worldwide have switched on to whisky is because they have discovered that, if made, matured or mixed the right way, it can bring sensations of joy that we previously thought only possible on a bed, or swinging from a chandelier. So whiskies like this have an exotic and erotic element to them, but to make them sexier still there has to be a cerebral quality, too. In other words, all your senses are being stimulated. Few whiskies stimulate them quite as well as this one. *59.4%*

Scotch Malt Whisky Society Cask 116.15 Aged 25 Years Japanese oak, dist Sep 83 **(89) n23.5 t22 f21.5 b22.** One of the problems with Japanese oak is that whilst it can add an extra, and quite unique, zing to a malt at conventional Japanese ages, when it gets to 25 years it has perhaps added a little too much. Here is a case of a Japanese oak not exactly doing Japanese oaky sort of things. All that said...a really delightful whisky and one which takes you into fascinating, unexplored lands...!!! *58.9%*

Unspecified Malts

"Hokuto" Suntory Pure Malt Aged 12 Years (93) n22 trademark delicate lightness; fleeting barley chased by soft vanilla; **t24** melt-in-the-mouth malt arrival; hints of honey work well with the loftier barley and earthier oak; **f23** honey on toast with just a little toffee; **b24** another example of Suntory at its most feminine: just so seductive and beautiful. Although a malt, think Lawson's 12-y-o of a decade ago and you have the picture. 40%

Nikka Whisky From the Barrel (89) n20 carries some weight; good age and subtle malty sugars; **t23** exemplary mouthfeel: delightful oils and nipping spices but the malt remains clean and very sweet; **f22** some dryer oakiness but the malt keeps its balancing sweetness; **b24** a whisky that requires a bit of time and concentration to get the best out of. You will discover something big and exceptionally well balanced. 51.4%. Nikka.

Nikka Whisky From the Barrel batch 02F26A (82) n20 t22 f20 b20. Some attractive honey notes and caramel, but a bit laboured. 51.4%

Nikka Whisky From the Barrel batch 12F32C db (91) n22 date and brazil cake; **t24** monumental delivery with soft smoke melting into the most glorious honeycomb known to man; tingly spices and toffee-apple, too; **f22** caramel kicks in slightly but some butterscotch rounds it off wonderfully; **b23** truly great whisky that mostly overcomes the present Japanese curse of big caramel finishes. 51.4%

Nikka Whisky Single Coffey Malt 12 Years (97) n23.5 forget all about the malt: it's the big bourbony, hickory and honey sweet oak which wins hands down; **t25** hold on to your hats: it's flavour explosion time...on first tasting it's simply too much to comprehend. Only on third or fourth mouthful do you really get an idea. First, the delivery is pretty close to perfection: the soft oils seem to draw every last nuance from the barley; then when it has done that, it manages to mix it with myriad delicate sweet notes radiating from the oak. This includes some of those allied to bourbon, especially chocolate honeycomb and very deep molassed notes usually associated with Demerara Coffey still rum; a unique combination absolutely perfectly displayed; **f24** long...just so long. One mouthful, especially at 55%, last for about six or seven minutes. So impressive here is the delicacy of the fade: after a delivery so large, the finesse is extraordinary. The flavours in effect mirror the earlier delivery. Except now some vanilla does come in to dry things a little; **b24.5** the Scotch Whisky Association would say that this is not single malt whisky because it is made in a Coffey still. When they can get their members to make whisky this stunning on a regular basis via their own pots and casks, then perhaps they should pipe up as their argument might then have a single atom of weight. 55%

Vatted Malts

All Malt (86) n22 t21 f21 b22. The best example by a mile of an almost unique style of vatted whisky: both malt and "grain" are distilled from entirely malted barley, identical to Kasauli malt whisky in India. Stupendous grace and balance. 40%. Nikka.

All Malt "Pure & Rich" (89) n22 honeycomb and liquorice with some thumping oak; **t24** beautifully mouthfilling, and "rich" is an understatement. Barley sugar and molten brown sugar combine and then there is a soft gristiness. Big...; **f21** vanilla and caramel with some residual malt; **b22** my word, this has changed! Not unlike some bottlings of Highland Park with its emphasis on honey. If they could tone down the caramel it'd really be up there. 40%. Nikka.

All Malt Pure & Rich batch 14F24A (77) n19 t20 f19 b19. My former long term Japanese girlfriend, Makie (hope you enjoyed your 30th birthday in April, by the way), used to have a favourite saying, namely: "I am shocked!" Well, I am shocked by this whisky because it is much blander than the previous bottling (04E16D), with all that ultra-delicate and complex honeycomb lost and lovely gristiness removed. For me, one of the biggest surprises – and disappointments - of the 2007 Bible. But proof that, when using something so potentially dangerous as caramel, it is too easy to accidentally cross that fine line between brilliance and blandness. Because, had they gone the other way, we might have had a challenger for World Whisky of the Year. 40%. Nikka.

Hokuto Pure Malt Aged 12 Years (86) n20 t22 f22 b22. An oaky threat never materialises: excellent finish. 40%. Suntory.

Ichiro's Malt Double Distilleries bott 2010 (86.5) n22.5 t22 f21 b21. Some imperious barley-rich honey reigns supreme until a bitter wood note bites hard. 46%. Venture Whisky Ltd.

Ichiro's Malt Mizunara Wood Reserve (76) n19 t21 f18 b19. I have my Reservations about the Wood, too... 46%. Venture Whisky Ltd.

Malt Club "Pure & Clear" (83) **n**21 **t**22 **f**20 **b**20. Another improved vatting, much heavier and older than before with bigger spice. 40%. *Nikka.*

Mars Maltage Pure Malt 8 Years Old (84) **n**20 **t**21 **f**21 **b**22. A very level, intense, clean malt with no peaks or troughs, just a steady variance in the degree of sweetness and oak input. Impossible not to have a second glass of. 43%. *Mars.*

Nikka Malt 100 The Anniversary Aged 12 Years (73) **n**18 **t**19 **f**18 **b**18. The depressing and deadly fingerprint of sulphur is all over this. Shame, as the spices excel. 40%

Nikka Pure Malt Aged 21 Years batch 08I18D db (89) **n**23 profound, clean, over-ripe grape with some lovely nip and prickle; weighty with a liquoricy bourbony element, too; **t**22.5 soft at first then a steady build up of malt and spice. The fruit is never far away; **f**21.5 toasty vanilla and a light buzz from the sherry; **b**22 by far the best of the set. 43%

Nikka Pure Malt Aged 17 Years batch 08I30B db (83) **n**21 **t**21 **f**20 **b**21. A very similar shape to the 12-years-old, but older - obviously. Certainly the sherry butts had a big say and don't always do great favours to the high quality spirit. 43%

Nikka Pure Malt Aged 12 Years batch 10I24C db (84) **n**21.5 **t**21 **f**20 **b**21.5. The nose may be molassed, sticky treacle pudding, but it spices up on the palate. The dull buzz on the finish also tells a tale. 40%

Pure Malt Black batch 02C58A (95) **n**24 an exquisitely crafted nose: studied peat in luxuriant yet deft proportions nestling amid some honeyed malt and oak. The balance between sweet and dry is faultless. There is neither a single off-note nor a ripple of disharmony. The kind of nose you can sink your head into and simply disappear; **t**23 for all the evident peat, this is medium-weighted, the subtlety encased in a gentle cloak of oil; **f**23 long, silky, fabulously weighted peat running a sweet course through some surging malt and liquorice tones with a bit of salt in there for zip; **b**25 well, if anyone can show me a better-balanced whisky than this you know where to get hold of me. You open a bottle of this at your peril: best to do so in the company of friends. Either way, it will be empty before the night is over. 43%. *Nikka.*

Pure Malt Black batch 06F54B (92) **n**24 great balance to the nose with a careful sprinkling of barley, honey, peat and oak – but never too much of any; **t**24 massive, ultra-intense sweet malt with a delicate sub-stratum of smoke; a spiced fruitiness also cranks up the weight and depth; **f**21 vanilla kicks in as it thins surprisingly fast; **b**23 not the finish of old, but everything else is present and correct for a cracker! 43%. *Nikka.*

Pure Malt Red batch 02C30B (86) **n**21 **t**21 **f**22 **b**22. A light malt that appears heavier than it actually is with an almost imperceptible oiliness. 43%. *Nikka.*

Pure Malt Red batch 06F54C (84) **n**21 **t**22 **f**20 **b**21. Oak is the pathfinder here, but the oily vanilla-clad barley is light and mouth-watering. 43%. *Nikka.*

Pure Malt White batch 02C30C (92) **n**23 massive, Islay-style peat with a fresh sea kick thanks to brine amid the barley; **t**24 again, the peat-reek hangs firmly on the tastebuds from the word go, the sweetness of the barley tempered by some drying oaky notes suggesting reasonable age. Lots of subtle oils bind the complexity; **f**22 liquorice and salt combine to create a powerful malty-oak combo. An oily, kippery smokiness continues to the very end; **b**23 a big peaty number displaying the most subtle of hands. 43%. *Nikka.*

Pure Malt White batch 06J26 (91) **n**22 soft peat interrupted by gentle oak; **t**23 biting, nippy malt offering a degree of orangey-citrus fruit amid the building smoke; **f**22 sweet vanilla and light smoke that dries towards a salty, tangy, liquorice finish; **b**24 a sweet malt, but one with such deft use of peat and oak that one never really notices. Real class. 43%

Pure Malt White batch 10F46C (90) **n**23 the quality of the delicate peat is beyond reproach; some attractive kumquat juices it up nicely; **t**23 wonderful balance between silky-soft and nail-hard malts with some tasty local oak getting in on the act; **f**22 the smoke lessens to allow vanilla and toffee dominance; a sawdusty dryness brings down the curtain; **b**22 there is a peculiarly Japanese feel to this delicately peated delight. 43%

Southern Alps Pure Malt (93) **n**24 bananas and freshly peeled lemon skin: one of the world's most refreshing and exhilarating whisky noses; **t**23 crisp youngish malts, as one might suspect from the nose, mouthwatering and as a clean as an Alpine stream; **f**22 some vanilla development and a late slightly creamy flourish but finished with a substantial and startling malty rally boasting a very discreet sweetness; **b**24 this is a bottle I have only to look at to start salivating. Sadly, though, I drink sparingly from it as it is a hard whisky to find, even in Japan. Fresh, clean and totally stunning, the term "pure malt" could not be more apposite. Fabulous whisky: a very personal favourite. 40%. *Suntory.*

Super Nikka Vatted Pure Malt (76) **n**20 **t**19 **f**19 **b**18. Decent and chewy but something doesn't quite click with this one. 55.5%. *Nikka.*

Taketsuru Pure Malt 12 Years Old (80) n19 t22 f19 b20. For its age, heavier than a sumo wrestler. But perhaps a little more agile over the tastebuds. Lovely silkiness impresses, but lots of toffee. 40%. Nikka.

Taketsuru Pure Malt 17 Years Old (89) n21 firm oak, but compromises sufficiently to allow several layers of malt to battle through with a touch of peat-coffee; t22 massive: a toasted, honeyed front gives way to really intense and complex malt notes; f23 superb. Some late marmalade arrives from somewhere: the toast is slightly burnt but the waves of malty complexity are endless; b23 not a whisky for the squeamish. This is big stuff – about as big as it gets without peat or rye. No bar shelf or whisky club should be without one. 43%. Nikka.

Taketsuru Pure Malt 21 Years Old (88) n22 middle-aged bourbon with a heavy, vaguely honeyed malt presence; t21 the oak remains quite fresh and chewy. Again, the malt is massive; f22 sweet, oily and more honey arrives; b23 a much more civilised and gracious offering than the 17-y-o: there is certainly nothing linear about the character development from Taketsuru 12 to 21 inclusive. Serious whisky for the serious whisky drinker. 43%. Nikka.

Zen (84) n19 t22 f22 b21. Sweet, gristy malt; light and clean. 40%. Suntory.

Japanese Single Grain

∴ **Kawasaki Single Grain** sherry butt, dist 1982, bott 2011 db (95.5) n23.5 clean thick grape offering several layers of depth and intensity. Salty and sharp, too. My god, this is very much alive and kicking...; t24 classic! Faultless grape arm in arm with rich, fruity fudge. Some spices arrive on impact and slowly spread out with the marauding sugars; f24 chocolate fudge and garibaldi biscuit...carried far on usual oils for a grain...amazing! b24 my usual reaction to seeing the words "sherry" and "whisky" when in the context of Japanese whisky, is to feel the heart sinking like the sun. Sulphur is a problem that is no stranger to their whiskies. This, however, is a near perfect sherry butt, clean and invigorating. Grain or malt, it makes no difference: excellent spirit plus excellent cask equals (as often as not) magnificence. 65.5%. For 'Whisky Live Tokyo 2011'.

Nikka Single Cask Coffey Grain Whisky Aged 12 Years "Woody & Mellow" (93) n22 delicate vanalins and tannins; t24 sweet and yielding (probably corn) with layers of drying spices. Stupendous; f23 long, with subtle oils lengthening the grain effect and spice; more vanilla at the very death...eventually. Vague bourbony tones towards the finale; b24 exceptional grain whisky by any standards – and helps explain why Japanese blends are so damn good!! 55%. Nikka.

Nikka Single Cask Coffey Grain 12 Years Old 70th Anniversary (85) n20 biting, nose, tingling oak; t22 massive oak delivery sweetened and soothed by the rich grain; lush and brilliantly weighted throughout; f22 long liquorice and cocoa tones are met by some bitter, zesty, oaky notes; b21 more woody than the "woody and mellow". 58%. Nikka.

Nikka Single Cask Coffey Grain Aged Over 13 Years batch 20 116399, dist 1992, bott 2005 db (85) n22 t23 f20 b20. Distinctly subdued by this brand's normal high standards, though the early bourbon riches are mesmerizing. The finish, though attractive, is too simplistic. 62%. sc.

Nikka Single Cask Coffey Grain Whisky 1991 dist 1 Oct 91, bott 12 May 03 db (93) n22 t24 f23 b24. I have tasted much Japanese straight grain over the years but this is the first time in bottled form for public consumption. And Nikka have exceeded themselves. Forget the word "grain" and its inferior connotations. This is a monster whisky from the bourbon family you are unlikely ever to forget. Use the first couple of mouthfuls for a marker: once you get the idea, life will never quite be the same again. Track down...and be consumed. 61.9%

Nikka Single Cask Coffey Grain 1992 dist 31 Feb 92, bott 25 Jul 06 db (95) n24 a curious mixture with hints of Japanese oak (from the cask heads?) and a bourbony, hickory edge. Rich and rousing; t24 sweet, flushed with maize and a silky body, almost verging on demerara. Honeyed and revelling in its bourbon theme; f23 vanilla layers, again with a deep, delicious touch of molasses; b24 make no mistake: this grain is as entertaining as any malt. Those loving high-class bourbon will be thrilled. 57%. France.

Blends

Ajiwai Kakubin (see Kakubin Ajiwai)

Black Nikka Aged 8 Years (82) n20 t21 f21 b20. Beautifully bourbony, especially on the nose. Lush, silky and great fun. Love it! 40%. Nikka.

The Blend of Nikka (90) n21 a dry, oaky buzz infiltrates some firm grain and sweeter malt; t23 brilliant! Absolutely outstanding explosion of clean grassy malts thudding into the tastebuds with confidence and precision: mouthwatering and breath-catching; **f22** delightful grain bite to follow the malt; **b24** an adorable blend that makes you sit up and take notice of every enormous mouthful. Classy, complex, charismatic and brilliantly balanced. *45%*

Evermore (90) n22 big age, salt and outstanding malt riches to counter the oak; **t23** more massive oak wrapped in a bourbony sweetness with glorious malts and a salty, spicy tang; **f22** long, sweet malt and crisp grains: plenty to chew on and savour; **b23** top-grade, well-aged blended whisky with fabulous depth and complexity that never loses its sweet edge despite the oak. *40%. Kirin.*

Ginko (78.5) n20.5 t20 f19 b19. Soft – probably too soft as it could do with some shape and attitude to shrug off the caramel. *46%. Number One Drinks Company.*

Golden Horse Busyuu Deluxe (93) n22 some decent signs of age with some classy oak alongside smoke: sexy stuff; **t24** enormous flavour profile simply because it is so fresh: massive malt presence, some of is peaty, bananas and under-ripe grapes; **f23** clean malt and some sharpish grain with a touch of bite, continuing to tantalise the tastebuds for a long time; **b24** whoever blended this has a genuine feel for whisky: a classic in its own right and one of astonishing complexity and textbook balance. *43%. Toa. To celebrate the year 2000.*

Hibiki (82) n20 t19 f23 b20. The grains here are fresh, forceful and merciless, the malts bouncing off them meekly. Lovely cocoa finale. A blend that brings a tear to the eye. Hard stuff – perfect after a hard day! Love it! *43%. Suntory.*

⟐ **Hibiki Aged 12 Years** bott 2011 **(89) n22.5** fruity, full and fat; some Demerara sugars work well with the fruit; **t22** lush and complex with a huge vanilla-butterscotch theme; semi-salivating; **f22** long, fruity and with a touch of oily boiled sugar candy; **b22.5** a sensual whisky full of lightly sugared riches. *43%. Suntory.*

⟐ **Hibiki Aged 17 Years** bott 2011 (84.5) n22 t21 f20.5 b21. Big oaks and a clever degree of sweetness. But takes the lazy big toffee option. *43%. Suntory.*

Hibiki 50.5 Non Chillfiltered 17 Years Old (84) n22 t22 f20 b20. Pleasant enough in its own right. But against what this particular expression so recently was, hugely disappointing. Last year I lamented the extra use of caramel. This year it has gone through the roof, taking with it all the fineness of complexity that made this blend exceptional. Time for the blending lab to start talking to the bottling hall and sort this out. I want one of the great whiskies back...!! *50.5%. Suntory.*

⟐ **Hibiki Aged 21 Years** bott 2011 **(96) n24** cherry fruitcake...with more black cherries than cake. Spiced sherry notes embrace the oak with a voluptuous richness; **t24.5** virtually perfect texture: seemingly silk-like but then a massive outbreak of busy oaky vanilla and juicy barley; the creamy mouth feel supports a mix of maple syrup and muscovado sugars; the middle moves towards a walnut oiliness; **f23.5** long, spicy with a gentle date and walnut fade; **b24** a celebration of blended whisky, irrespective of which country it is from. Of its style, it's hard to raise the bar much higher than this. Stunning. *43%. Suntory.*

Hibiki Aged 30 Years (88) n21 less smoky than before, a touch of soap and no shortage of bourbon honeycomb; **t22** sweet delivery with that Kentuckian drawl to the middle; **f22** long, with some extra molasses to the finale; a few extra splinters of oak, too; **b23** still remains a very different animal from most other whiskies you might find: the smoke may have vanished somewhat but the sweet oakiness continues to draw its own unique map. *43%. Suntory.*

Hokuto (86) n22 t24 f19 b21. a bemusing blend. At its peak, this is quite superb, cleverly blended whisky. The finish, though, suggests a big caramel input. If the caramel is natural, it should be tempered. If it is added for colouring purposes, then I don't see the point of having the whisky non-chillfiltered in the first place. *50.5%. ncf. Suntory.*

Ichiro's Blend Aged 33 Years (84) n20 t22 f21 b21. Silky and sweet. But the creamy fudge effect appears to wipe out anything important the oak may have to say. Pleasing spices towards the end, though. *48%. Venture Whisky Ltd.*

Imperial (81) n20 t22 f19 b20. Flinty, hard grain softened by malt and vanilla but toffee dulled. *43%. Suntory.*

Kakubin (92) n23 lemon zest and refreshing grain: wonderful; **t23** light, mouthwatering, ultra-juicy with soft barley sub-strata; true melt-in-the-mouth stuff; **f22** long, with charming vanilla but touched by toffee; **b24** absolutely brilliant blend of stunningly refreshing and complex character. One of the most improved brands in the world. *40%. Suntory.*

Kakubin Ajiwai (82) n20 t21 f20 b21. Usual Kakubin hard grain and mouthwatering malt, with this time a hint of warming stem ginger. *40%. Suntory.*

Kakubin Kuro 43° (89) n22 a confusing but sexy mix of what appear to be old oak and burnt toffee; **t23** fabulous weight on arrival with again the oak in the vanguard but controlled by a malty, chewy-toffee arm; **f22** long with soft vanillins and toffee; **b22** big, chewy whisky with ample evidence of old age but such is the intrusion of caramel it's hard to be entirely sure. *43%. Suntory.*

Kakubin New (90) **n21** gritty grain with very hard malt to accompany it; **t24** stunning mouth arrival with heaps of mouthwatering young malt and then soft grain and oil. Brilliant stuff; **f21** some beautiful cocoa notes round off the blend perfectly; **b24** seriously divine blending: a refreshing dram of the top order. *40%. Suntory.*

Kirin Whisky Tarujuku 50° **(93)** **n22.5** some prickly oak and prickly pear; **t24** what a delight...! A delivery from the heavens: the combination of malt, grain and oak all appear to be equally divided here, but rather than arriving in layers they erupt upon the palate together. The shockwaves are sweet ones, with subtle molasses infiltrating the oak; **f23** long, cleverly oiled and still with those lightly sugared vanillas having much to say. The balance isn't for one second compromised; **b23.5** a blend not afraid to make a statement and does so boldly. A sheer joy. *50%. Kirin Distillery Co Ltd.*

Master's Blend Aged 10 Years (87) **n21 t23 f22 b21.** Chewy, big and satisfying. *40%. Mercian/Karuizawa.*

New Kakubin Suntory *(see Kakubin New)*

Nikka Master Blend Blended Whisky 12 Years Old 70th Anniversary (94) **n24** nothing shy or retiring here: big oak, big sherry. A little nervousness with the smoke, maybe; **t23** lush, silky grain arrives and then carries intensely sweet malt and weightier grape; **f24** dries as the oak takes centre stage. But the peripheral fruit malt, gentle smoke and grain combine to offer something not dissimilar to fruit and nut chocolate; **b23** an awesome blend swimming in top quality sherry. Perhaps a fraction too much sweetness on the arrival, but I am nit-picking. A blend for those who like their whiskies to have something to say. And this one just won't shut up. *58%. Nikka.*

The Nikka Whisky Aged 34 Years bott 1999 **(93)** **n23 t23 f24 b23**. A Japanese whisky of antiquity that has not only survived many passing years, but has actually achieved something of stature and sophistication. Over time I have come to appreciate this whisky immensely. It is among the world's greatest blends, no question. *43%. Nikka.*

Nikka Whisky Tsuru Aged 17 Years (94) **n23** the usual fruity suspects one associates with a Tsuru blend, especially the apple and oranges. But the grains are now making a bourbony impact, too; **t24** advanced level textbook here because the marriage between fruit, grain and oak is about as well integrated as you might wish for; simperingly soft yet enough rigidity for the malts to really count and the palate to fully appreciate all the complexities offered; **f23** brushed with cocoa, a touch of sultana and some gripping spices, too; only the caramel detracts; **b24** unmistakingly Tsuru in character, very much in line, profile-wise, with the original bottling and if the caramel was cut this could challenge as a world whisky of the year. *43%*

Robert Brown (91) **n22.5** the grain really has kicked this one on towards a leathery bourbon; **t23** clean, sweet, brown sugars with a juicy sub plot; **f22.5** lovely spices accompany the custardy vanilla; **b23** just love these clean but full-flavoured blends: a real touch of quality here. *43%. Kirin Brewery Company Ltd.*

Royal 12 Years Old (91) **n23** chalky and dry, but malt and oranges – and now some extra juicy grape - add character; just a soupcon of smoke adds the perfect weight; **t23** fabulously complex arrival on the palate with some grainy nip countered by sparkling malt and where once there was smoke there is now ultra clean sherry; **f22** the grains and oak carry on as the spice builds; **b23** a splendidly blended whisky with complexity being the main theme. Beautiful stuff that appears recently to have, nose apart, traded smoke for grape. *43%*

Royal Aged 15 Years (95) **n25** soft ribbons of smoke tie themselves to a kumquat and sherry flag; supremely well weighted and balanced with the grains and malts united by invisible strands; **t24** few whiskies achieve such a beautifully soft and rounded delivery: there is no dominance on arrival as the tastebuds are confronted by a silky marriage of all that is found on the nose, aided and abetted by luxurious grain; **f22** a degree of toffee slightly hinders the fade but the lightness of touch is spellbinding; **b24** unquestionably one of the great blends of the world that can be improved only by a reduction of toffee input. Sensual blending that every true whisky lover must experience: a kind of Japanese Old Parr 18. *43%*

Shirokaku (79) **n19 t21 f20 b19**. Some over-zealous toffee puts a cap on complexity. Good spices, though. *40%. Suntory.*

Special Reserve 10 Years Old (94) **n23** magnificent approach of rich fruit buttressed by firm, clear grain. Some further fruity spices reveal some age is evident; **t24** complex from the off with a tidal tsunami of malt crashing over the tastebuds. The grain holds firm and supports some budding fruit; **f23** a touch of something peaty and pliable begins to take shape with some wonderful malty spices coating the mouth; **b24** a beguiling whisky of near faultless complexity. Blending at its peak. *43%. Suntory.*

Special Reserve Aged 12 Years (89) n21 peaches and cream with a dollop of caramel; **t24** luxurious delivery of perfect weight and softness to body; the barley sweetness works beautifully with the buzz of oak and yielding grains; **f21** caramel-coffee crème from a box of chocs; **b23** a tactile, voluptuous malt that wraps itself like a sated lover around the tastebuds, though the complexity is compromised very slightly by bigger caramel than the 10-y-o. *40%. Suntory.*

Suntory Old (87) n21 dusty and fruity. Attractive nip and balance; **t24** mouthwatering from the off with a rich array of chewy, clean fresh malt: textbook standard, complete with bite; **f20** thins out far quicker than it once did leaving the vanilla to battle it out with toffee; **b22** a delicate and comfortable blend that just appears to have over-simplified itself on the finale. Delicious, but can be much better than this. *40%*

Suntory Old Mild and Smooth (84) n19 t22 f21 b22. Chirpy and lively around the palate, the grains soften the crisp malts wonderfully. *40%*

Suntory Old Rich and Mellow (91) n22 very lightly smoked with healthy maltiness; an extra touch of older oaks in the most recent bottling helps the balance and works wonders; **t23** complex, fat and chewy, no shortage of deep malty tones, including a touch of smoke; **f23** sweeter malts see off the grain, excellent spices; **b23** a pretty malt-rich blend with the grains offering a fat base. Impressive blending. *43%*

Super Nikka (93) n23 excellent crisp, grassy malt base bounces off firm grain. A distant hint of peat, maybe, offers a little weighty extra; **t23** an immediate starburst of rich, mouthwatering and entirely uncompromising malt that almost over-runs the tastebuds; **f23** soft, fabulously intrinsic peaty notes from the Yoichi School give brilliant length and depth. But the cocoa notes from the oak-wrapped grain also offer untold riches; **b24** a very, very fine blend which makes no apology whatsoever for the peaty complexity of Yoichi malt. Now, with less caramel, it's pretty classy stuff. However, Nikka being Nikka you might find the occasional bottling that is entirely devoid of peat, more honeyed and lighter in style (21-22-23-23 Total 89 – no less a quality turn, obviously). Either way, an absolutely brilliant day-to-day, anytime, any place dram. One of the true 24-carat, super nova commonplace blends not just in Japan, but in the world. *43%. Nikka.*

Super Nikka Rare Old batch 02I18D **(90.5) n22** toffeed but no shortage of lively barley bouncing against firm grain; some playful fruit, mainly greengages, ensures extra freshness; **t23** superb arrival with a shimmering barley sweetness fending off the drier vanillas: the balance is spot on here. Remains delicately mouth-watering though it is milky mocha which arrives, not the peat I normally find here; **f22.5** remains happily on its vanilla course but some soft cocoa and fruit also plays along; **b23** beautiful whisky which just sings a lilting malty refrain. Strange, though, to find it peatless. *43%. Nikka.*

Torys (76) n18 t19 f20 b19. Lots of toffee in the middle and at the end of this one. The grain used is top class and chewy. *37%. Suntory.*

Torys Whisky Square (80) n19 t20 f21 b20. At first glance very similar to Torys, but very close scrutiny reveals slightly more "new loaf" nose and a better, spicier and less toffeed finale. *37%. Suntory.*

Tsuru (93) n23 apples, cedar, crushed pine nuts, blood oranges and soft malt, all rather chalky and soft – and unusually peatless for Nikka; **t24** fantastic grain bite bringing with it a mouthwateringly clean and fresh attack of sweet and lip-smacking malt; **f22** a continuation of untaxing soft malts and gathering oak, a slight "Malteser" candy quality to it, and then some late sultana fruitiness; **b24** gentle and beautifully structured, genuinely mouthwatering, more-ish and effortlessly noble. If they had the confidence to cut the caramel, this would be even higher up the charts as one of the great blends of the world. And with Japanese whisky becoming far more globally accepted and sought after, now would be a very good time to start. As it is, in my house we pass the ceramic Tsuru bottle as one does the ship's decanter. And it empties very quickly. *43%. Nikka.*

The Whisky (88) n22 t22 f21 b23. A rich, confident and well-balanced dram. *43%. Suntory.*

White (80) n19 t21 f20 b20. Boring nose but explodes on the palate for a fresh, mouth-watering classic blend bite. *40%. Suntory.*

Za (79) n19 t21 f19 b20. Some lively boisterous grain offers a suet-pudding chewiness. A little bitter on the finish. *40%. Suntory.*

European Whisky

The debate about what it means to be European is one that seemingly never ends. By contrast, the discussion on how to define the character of a European whisky is only just beginning.

And as more and more distilleries open throughout mainland Europe, Scandinavia and the British Isles the styles are becoming wider and wider.

Small distillers in mainland Europe, especially those in the Alpine area, share common ground with their US counterparts in often coming into whisky late. Their first love, interest and spirit had been with fruit brandies. It seemed that if something grew in a tree or had a stone when you bit into it, you could be pretty confident that someone in Austria or California was making a clear, eye-watering spirit from it somewhere.

Indeed, when I was writing Jim Murray's Complete Book of Whisky during 1996 and 1997 I travelled to the few mainland Europe distilleries I could find. Even though this was before the days of the internet when research had to be carried out by phone and word of mouth, I visited most – which was few – and missed one or two... which was fewer still.

Today, due mainly to the four solid months it now takes to write the Bible, I can scarcely find the time to go and visit these outposts which stretch from southern Germany to Finland and as far abreast as France to the Czech Republic. It is now not that there is just one or two. But dozens. And I need my good friend Julia Nourney to whizz around capturing samples for me just to try and keep up to date.

It is a fact that there is no one style that we can call European, in the way we might be able to identify a Kentucky bourbon or a Scotch single malt. That is simply because of the diversity of stills – and skills – being deployed to make the spirit. And a no less wide range of grains, or blends of grains, and smoking agents, from peat to wood types, to create the mash.

The distillers who have made major financial investments in equipment and staff appear to be the ones who are enjoying the most consistent results. In the Premier League we have the now firmly established Mackmyra in Sweden and Penderyn in Wales, both of whom use female blenders or distillers, curiously. Newly promoted to the highest tier comes St George's in England and just joining them quality-wise, though not quantity, alas, is their British counterpart Hicks and Healey who this year launched their maiden bottling. This eight year old malt has to be the oldest first whisky of any new distillery outside Scotland I can remember in the last 20 years. It is also a distillery which turned European tradition on its head. Throughout mainland Europe you will find small distillers with a serious shortage of the knowledge, money, capacity or will to ferment their own mash. So they will hop along to their local brewery, often old historic ones, and get them to make their wash for them, sans hops.

Hicks and Healey came about quite the other way round. The excellent and historic St Austell Brewery in Cornwall decided to make whisky. So they persuaded a pot-still owning cider brandy maker from within the county to distill their wash for them. With the whisky maturing for eight years in a cellar containing casks of cider brandy, it is little wonder the whisky has a distinct and compelling apple-sharpness to it.

This year also witnessed the first bottling of a maturing spirit from a distillery which promises to be making some impression over the coming years. The Stauning Distillery in Denmark has made a distinctly spicy rye spirit which, in this initial batch, reveals great character even though there is a touch of getting-to-know-you evident between the still and stillman. But other samples of later batches I tasted at the distillery are more relaxed and precise. It will not be long before they are first leaguers.

Another distillery which maintains exceptionally high standards is the Belgian Owl. This is smaller concern than some, but the output of their single malt is consistent, beautifully made, and brimming with personality. It may be true that you can count internationally famous Belgians on one hand, but the whisky-loving world would immediately recognise two fingers of its owl... Some of the most remarkable whisky came from Liechtenstein, the country which was once unable to furnish me – anywhere within its borders – with a decent hotel but this year presented me with a three-year-old malt which, but for the wideness of its cut, nearly walked off with an award. The Telser distillery has a long history and its move into whisky has been an impressive one: its Telsington IV being the most impressive of all. Perhaps that big, malty, slightly oily and lush style is something of an Alpine trait: another distillery to watch is Interlaken with their Classic, Swiss Highland Single Malt. Which, with a brand name like that, is as likely to stir up the good folk at the Scotch Whisky Association as anything else.

AUSTRIA
ACHENSEE'R EDELBRENNEREI FRANZ KOSTENZER Maurach. Working.

Whisky Alpin Grain Whisky Hafer bott code L1/2005 db **(92) n24 t22 f23 b23.** If you are looking for a whisky with a personality, you've just found it... *44%*

Whisky Alpin Rye & Malt bott code L1/2005 db **(87.5) n21.5 t23 f21 b22.** Despite the feinty sub plot, this is one very impressive distillery. *40%*

⋙ **Whisky Alpin Single Malt Rye** db **(87.5) n20** more nougat than rye; **t23.5** silky, oily delivery. Slowly the feinty clouds part and fabulous, ultra intense and fruity rye pours down onto the taste buds; natural caramel arrive, but the rye holds its own; **f21.5** worn down somewhat by the returning oils from the wide cut; some late, busy spices; **b22.5** not until the delivery gets into full stride does the rye ram home. And then it celebrates – in style! *45%. 100% Rye Malt*

BRENNEREI EBNER Absam. Working.

Absamer Whisky bott code L2305 db **(79.5) n23 t17 f21.5 b18.** This job of mine prepares you for most things. But not this. What the bloody hell has just hit me...? Whatever it was, the balance between sweet and dry was pretty bang-on and the complexity levels were falling off the page. And then, on delivery, it seared my taste buds like a blowtorch. *50%*

BRENNEREI LAGLER Kukmirn. Working.

Best Korn Burgenland bott 2007 db **(84) n20 t22 f21 b21.** A strange paprika and hop nose, though the body is fruity and sweet. *43%*

Pannonia Korn Malt bott 2007 db **(85.5) n21.5 t21.5 f21 b21.5.** Easy drinking whisky with a charming, stimulating sweetness and light though lush finish. *40%*

Pannonia Blend bott 2008 db **(83.5) n19 t22 f21 b21.5.** The strength means this is not actually whisky by native European standards. And you fear the worst with the feinty nose. But pans out pleasantly and sweetly, as is the house style. *38.5%*

DESTILLERIE GEORG HIEBL Haag. Working.

George Hiebl Mais Whisky 2004 db **(93) n23 t23.5 f23 b23.5.** More bourbon in character than some American bourbons I know...!! Beautifully matured, brilliantly matured and European whisky of the very highest order, Ye..haahhhh!! *43%*

George No. 1 Aged 5 Years db **(86) n22 t22 f20 b22.** Much more perfumy and oily with honeycomb rather than honey. *40%*

George No. 2 Aged 5 Years bott code L1/09 db **(84.5) n21.5 t21 f22 b20.** Very pleasant in part. But much of its bourbony personality seems to be shaped from laying in a bed of caramel...making it rather Canadian *41.8%*

DESTILLERIE KAUSL Mühldorf, Wachau. Working.

Wachauer Whisky "G" Single Barrel Gerste (Barley) bott code L6WG db **(90.5) n22 t23 f22.5 b23.** Absolutely charming and well made malt. *40%*

Wachauer Whisky "H" Single Barrel Hafer (Oat) bott code L1WH db **(88) n21.5 t21.5 f23 b22.** I can safely say that no whisky in the world has quite this signature. A unique and ultimately very enjoyable whisky. *40%*

Wachauer Whisky "R" Single Barrel Roggen (Rye) bott code L2WR db **(86.5) n21 t22 f23.5 b21.** A real eyebrow-raiser. Bloody hell!! Where do I start...? OK: butyric nose... not good. Way, way too much oak...not good. Yet...also on the nose: superb fruitiness to the unmistakable rye; ditto the sharp juiciness on delivery. This really is rye whisky with knobs on. Like others from this distillery, there is a lovely mocha-coffee slant to the, frankly, astonishing finish. Technically, an absolute nightmare that should be taken out and shot. In effect – and as much as I hate to say it...bloody delicious...!!! *40%*

Wachauer Whisky "W" Single Barrel Weizen (Wheat) bott code L1WW db **(76.5) n19 t18.5 f20.5 b18.5.** A feinty heavyweight which has real problems finding its direction and balance. Only when some molasses and cocoa form towards the end does it take shape. *40%*

DESTILLERIE ROGNER Rappottenstein. Working.

Rogner Waldviertel Whisky No. 2 db **(86) n21.5 t21 f22 b21.5.** Toasted almonds and light molasses make for enjoyable and oily whisky. I wish more of their whiskies were as good as this. *42.7%*

⋙ **Rogner Waldviertel Whisky 3/3** db **(86.5) n20 t22 f22.5 b22.** Plane sailing once you get past the tight nose. A beautiful display of crisp sugars and come-back-for more grainy juiciness. Lovable stuff, for all its gliches. *41.7%. ncf.*

Rogner Waldviertel Whisky 3/3 db (77.5) n17.5 t20 f21 b19. Once you get past the startling nose, which is more akin to certain forms of Scandinavian aquavit than whisky, the rest of the journey is sweet and easy. Though still pretty unwhisky-ish. 42%

Rogner Waldviertel Whisky 3/3 Malz db (87.5) n19.5 t23.5 f22 b22.5. Hang on to your hats: this one plays for shocks. Look forward to visiting this distillery to work out what the hell they are up to there. Absolutely love it! 65%

Rogner Waldviertel Rye Whisky No. 13 db (83) n20 t21.5 f20.5 b21. Drying tobacco nose and not quite the cleanest delivery. But an attractive rye fruitiness does has something to say, aided and abetted by some toffee and oil. 41%

⋄ **Rogner Waldviertel Rye Whisky No. 13** db (80) n18.5 t20 f21 b20.5. If memory serves, the last time I had this guy I was met by an oily tobacco note. It is a unique feature and this reminds me of it. 42.5%. ncf.

DESTILLERIE WEUTZ St. Nikolai im Sausal. Working.

⋄ **Black Peat** bott code. L070205/01 db (73.5) n18.5 t16 f20 b19. Well...!!! That was different – literally! Apparently the well used for the making of this whisky supplies a water rich in various nutrients. Including iodine and sulphur. Anyone who has taken the waters at Bath will have some kind of idea what we are talking about. The result is something the likes of which I have never before encountered. The delivery is simply bloody awful...but, once you acclimatise, the late middle is quite tolerable, and the finish enjoyable! Possibly the healthiest whisky I have ever tasted! 41.4%. sc.

⋄ **Franziska** bott code. L070206/02 db The 5% elderflower means this is 100% not whisky. But a fascinating and eye-opening way to create a spirit very much in the young Kentucky rye style, especially in the nose. They certainly can do delicious... For the record, the scoring for enjoyment alone: (93) n23.5 t23 f23.5 b23. 48%. Malt refined with 5% elderflower.

Hot Stone Single Malt db (88) n21.5 t23 f21.5 b22. The Arnold Schwarzenegger of Austrian whisky: huge, muscle-bound...and a bit of a friendly giant. Technically, the finish needs some attention; and it could do with a tweak here and there from nose onwards, really. But just one of those drams that demands a second glassful – even when you are still like to be in a state of wonder and shock from the very first arrival. Delicious! 67.1%

Hot Stone Single Malt Single Cask bott code L 041411/01 db (88.5) n21 t23 f22 b22.5. Exhausting to taste, as the brain has to go into overdrive to work out what the hell is going on! 42.1%

⋄ **St. Nikolaus** bott code. L072004/01 db (86) n20 t22 f22 b22. Not quite up there with their previous Hot Stone whiskies, but not far off. Certainly enjoys a biscuit style maltiness, which puts me in mind of it slightly. Only really let down by the sweaty armpit nose. 40%. sc.

⋄ **White Smoke** sherry finished, bott code. L062411/01 db (90) n22.5 confident, biting spices cut their way through the cleanest grape imaginable; salty, as though stuck in a warehouses lashed by a wild Hebridean sea...in land-locked Austria...!! t22.5 a silk glove but with some sharp claws protruding; the grape is big but isn't allowed to have its own way as a vague dry oakiness ensures some chewing is to be done; f22 salty with a huge amount of grape pips and skins having a further drying effect; b23 at times, seems more like sherry finished in whisky. Not a single off note from the cask (though the same can't quite be said for the actual spirit itself) – a completely sulphur free experience. Wonderful and borderline sophisticated. 40%

REISETBAUER Axberg, Thening. Working.

Reisetbauer Single Malt 7 Years Old Chardonnay and sweet wine cask, bott code LWH 099 db (85.5) n19 t21 f23.5 b22. Well it takes some time. But it gets there in the end. A less than impressive nose is followed by a rocky delivery. But the panning out is truly spectacular as harmony is achieved with a rich honey and nougat mix, helped along the way with pecan nuts and figs. The finish is like a top rank trifle and fruitcake mix. A whisky of two halves. 43%

Reisetbauer Single Malt 12 Years Old Limited Edition db (85) n18.5 t21.5 f23 b22. A remarkably similar story to the 7-y-o, though a touch silkier, with less sweetness and not quite so much complexity at the death. Even so, a dram to find. 48%

WHISKY-DESTILLERIE J. HAIDER Roggenreith. Working.

Single Malt J.H. L3/03 db (86) n21 t21.5 f22.5 b21. Rich and robust, for the odd brief moment it displays the character of a malt heading somewhere towards its 40th birthday: the oak certainly makes an impact here. Plenty of honeycomb to delight. 41%

Special Single Malt "Karamell" J.H. L2/03 db **(80.5) n19 t21 f20.5 b20.** The sugars, most of them dark and rich, appear to be welded on to the malty body. I am sure I have grown a few extra hairs on my chest, taking on this oily slugger. *41%*

Single Malt Selection J.H. L7/02 db **(86) n22 t21 f21.5 b21.5.** A pretty, layered, nose, sporting excellent oak integration. Doesn't quite hit the same heights on the palate where sugars and certain oils, some bitter, dominate. Good biscuity tail off, alternating between caramelized dunking fare and sweet digestive. Molasses abounds. Deceptively enjoyable. *46%*

Original Rye J.H. L2/02 db **(82) n20.5 t21 f20.5 b20.** Some quiet spice and aggression amid the sleepy toffee. *41%*

Original Rye-Whisky J.H. L5/03 db **(93.5) n24** one of the cleanest rye noses ever from the distillery: I could be in Kentucky!! Beautifully fruity and entirely unambiguous; **t23.5** mouth-watering rye that's just a little softer on delivery than you'd expect. Reigns supreme for a comparatively short time before the oak enters with an egg-custard flourish; **f23** long finish with some spicy candy balls **b23** a masterpiece from a distillery located in an area named after rye... how fitting! *41%*

⸭ **Original Rye Whisky J.H.** L19/05 db **(91.5) n23.5** had I been handed this in Kentucky, my only thought was that it had been a slightly wider cut than normal. But the fresh fruitiness of the grain is textbook; **t23** those oils evident on the nose do an amazing job of harnessing together the richer aspects of this whisky. So the middle ground is back to Kentucky with its liquorice and honeycomb and the cascading caramels. But the feel is entirely different; **f22** long with a fruity toffee fudge fade; **b23** their Original Rye was last year close to bringing home to Austria the Bible's European Whisky of the Year. This is another outstanding bottling. Perhaps not as sharp and mouth-watering as last time, but the marriage between the rye and toffee-honeycomb is a blissful one. Superb yet again! *41%*

Pure Rye Malt J.H. L6/03 db **(83) n18.5 t22 f21 b21.5.** Here's a "Nougat" one, too, though they've advertised "caramel"! Butyric in part, there is still enough wholesome rye percolating through to give the taste buds a charming, sugar-crisp rye platform from which to watch the developing vanillas, mochas and caramels. After the shock of the nose, enjoyable. *41%*

⸭ **Pure Rye Malt J.H.** L10/05 db **(87.5) n20.5** off key, but enjoyable chocolate raisin; **t22.5** recovers superbly on delivery with the palate awash with thick rye-studded oil. There's those chocolate raisins again; **f22.5** feinty whisky usually has the benefit of a big finish. No let down here, with some oils conjuring extra spices, too; **b22** to get the best out this distillery's whisky, it is advisable to either warm the glass or leave for a good 15 minutes or so. This is to burn off the feints which can be apparent. They are here. But the whisky always has the ability to enthral and reveal an inner beauty. I am not sure of it is like a plain-faced woman having a beautiful body, or a gorgeous looker not quite shaping up for Miss World. Oh, and those comments are, above all, for the enjoyment of the young lady who described me as "sexist" to a mutual friend: might as well get hung for a sheep... *41%*

Pure Rye Malt J.H. L14/02 db **(92) n23 t23.5 f22.5 b23.** Some of the most beautifully made whisky I have come across for a little while. This is absolutely top grade European rye whisky. And all the better when left in the glass for 20 minutes before drinking. *41%*

Special Rye Malt "Nougat" J.H. L1/03 db **(77.5) n17 t21 f19.5 b20.** A huge, oily beast of a whisky. For "Special" and "Nougat" read feinty... *41%*

⸭ **Special Rye Malt "Nougat" J.H.** L7/05 db **(72.5) n17 t19 f18 b18.5.** Now this guy is a traditionally feinty beast. This time, though, some butyric pops up. Odd thing, though, the finish possesses a lovely rye "g" spot. *41%*

⸭ **Special Single Malt Peated J.H. Limited Edition** auslese Chardonnay wine cask, bott code. L3/08JU db **(79.5) n19 t20 f21.5 b19.** Ironically, this is technically the best distilled spirit they have ever put into bottle. Virtually no feints or butyric. Just excellent spirit. But, from a flavour perspective, something of a train wreck. The ashy peat and the grape are really not great friends, though they do end up on speaking terms by the finish. Compellingly different. *46%. ncf.*

⸭ **Special Single Malt Peated J.H. Limited Edition** auslese cuvee wine cask, bott code. L2/08LEI db **(84) n19 t20.5 f24 b21.5.** In case the distilling family are wondering: once they enter into this type of whisky, they are marked accordingly. And again we have another malt which begins with no steering wheel as it arrives on the palate, but navigates its way to what must be the equivalent of Austria's chocolate festival for a finish you'll never forget. If you are looking for a whisky with character and something different to say...this might be it. *46%. ncf.*

DESTILLERIE WEIDENAUER Kottes. Working.

Waldviertler Single Malt db **(75) n18 t19 f19 b19.** Heavy, lush oily with a big oak signature. The feel is that the cut taken has been very wide, indeed. *42%*

Waldviertler Dinkelmalz (2008 award label on neck) db **(77.5) n18.5 t21 f19 b19.** A bit rough round the edges from time to time, though the citrus on delivery charms. *42%*

Waldviertler Dinkelmalz (A La carte label on neck) db **(89) n22.5 t23 f21.5 b22.** Now that's far more like what I expect from this usually excellent distillery. *42%*

Waldviertler Dinkel (2008 Silber Medaille label on neck) db **(90) n19.5 t23 f23.5 b24.** The nose apart, the odd feint note here and there can't seriously detract from this majestically attractive whisky and towards the end even helps! Classy, classy whisky...!!! *42%*

Waldviertler Hafer (2007 Silber Medaille label on neck) db **(83.5) n19 t22 f21 b21.5.** A unique flavor profile from these oats. A touch more bitter than usual, perhaps, but there is a superb mouthwatering quality which counters the woody impact. *42%*

Waldviertler Hafer-Malz (2007 Gold Medaille label on neck) db **(91) n22 t22.5 f23 b23.5.** One of those whiskies that just gets better the longer it stays on the palate. Also, a master class in achieving near perfection in the degree of sweetness generated. *42%*

Waldviertler Hafer-Malz (2008 award label on neck) db **(76.5) n20 t19.5 f18 b19.** The big oaks do their best to compensate. But the damage has been done by making the cut here a little too wide and flooding the usual complexity with heavy oils. *42%*

BELGIUM
THE BELGIAN OWL

The Belgian Owl Single Malt 1st fill bourbon cask, bott Oct 09 db **(89.5) n22** some early feints, so minor the worst burns off quickly in a warm room or glass, cannot upstage the lemon peel and barley theme; **t22.5** the lightest delivery yet with sweet malt flooding into the taste buds; a really lovely sweet-dry undulation to the barley-vanilla middle; **f22.5** a hint of chocolate nougat; **b22.5** one very relaxed owl. An easy-drinking joy with no shortage of charisma. *46%*

⁘ **The Belgian Owl Single Malt Age 3 Years** 1st fill bourbon cask, bott code L060111 db **(88.5) n22.5** youthful and zesty, but old enough to enjoy good oak complexity; **t22** again, youthful but the mouth-watering quality of the barley is fabulous; **f22** a lovely spicy fade; **b22** a juicy joy. *46%. nc ncf.*

⁘ **The Belgian Owl Single Malt Age 4 Years** 1st fill bourbon cask, bott code L140211 db **(89.5) n21** extra caramel but, strangely, more citrus youth than normal; stays balanced, though; **t22.5** fabulous delivery: a really unusual blend of oils and juicy barley. The sugars, of the muscovado variety, melt delightfully; **f23** long, thanks to those extra oils, with the barley rather than oak dominating into the last seconds, though some superb liquorice plays a wonderful cameo part; **b23** brimming with Belgian vitality: high quality stuff. *46%. nc ncf.*

⁘ **The Belgian Owl Single Malt Age 4 Years** 1st fill bourbon cask, bott code. 270910 db **(94.5) n24** gorgeous marriage between delicate oak and even more delicate barley. Dissolved Lubeck marzipan melts into a lime jam. Youthful, yet almost impossible to see how a four-year-old malt could possibly be more attractive; **t23.5** silky, vaguely juicy maltiness and then any number of complex oaky tones. Again, a light fruitiness threads its way into the picture; **f23** much drier, though both the caramels and oaks remain light; a hint of Belgian chocolate...? **b24** a Belgian treat. *46%. nc ncf.*

⁘ **The Belgian Owl Single Malt Age 4 Years** 1st fill bourbon cask, bott code. L121110 db **(80.5) n19.5 t21 f20 b20.** Surprisingly thin. Also, seems as though the extra time in the cask has resulted in the overall balance struggling to keep the extra caramels under control. *46%. nc ncf.*

⁘ **The Belgian Owl Single Malt Age 4 Years** 1st fill bourbon cask, bott code. L250511 db **(83) n21 t21 f20 b21.** Soft with mild toffee. But will have benefitted with more time in the cask. *46%. nc ncf.*

⁘ **The Belgian Owl Single Malt Age 4 Years** 1st fill bourbon cask, bott code. L201210 db **(87.5) n22** bitty oaks and muscovado sugars ensure excellent complexity...though very youthful; **t22** and that oak is there in delivery, in the form of cream toffee; **f21.5** more caramels and a surprising touch of minor bitterness; **b22** beautifully distilled, some exceptionally clean caramel and more oils than might be expected. *46%. nc ncf.*

The Belgian Owl Single Malt Spirit Aged 24 Months 1st Fill Bourbon cask no. 4275997, bott Feb 10 db **(89) n22.5 t22 f22.5 b22.** Some of the best spirit to have come from this distillery. Signs that the distiller and apparatus have a better understanding of each other. Not just malty, but the cut, and therefore weight, appears more in tune with the spirit's capabilities even though it remains a little on the hefty side. *46%*

The Belgian Owl Single Malt Spirit Aged 44 Months 1st fill bourbon cask no. 4275966, bott Oct 09 db **(95.5) n23.5** massive bourbon theme on the nose; liquorice and spiced honey blows hot and sweet; **t23.5** near perfect weight on delivery. Those oils make the landing of a 74%abv whisky just about painless. But what works so well is the degree of sweetness:

the muscovado sugars are balanced with just-so degrees of vanillas to ensure an improbable degree of balance and complexity to a whisky quite so enormous; **f24.5** now goes into owly overdrive and benefits from the slightly wider than normal cut. Especially when the nougat-mocha notes kick in. Again the sugars remain in total sync and harmony and allow the barley the clearest of paths to make a late, juicy stand. Astonishingly beautiful... **b23.5** this owl is hunting every taste bud you have. What a wonderful experience...and whatever species this may be, a Little Owl, it isn't... *74.2%*

⁛ **The Belgian Owl Single Malt 48 Months** 1st fill bourbon cask no. 4275933 db **(90.5)** **n22.5** it is as though the big alcohol has burrowed into the oak – like a Burrowing Owl, in fact – and extracted vanilla notes very rarely seen. A delicious sweetness, almost like sugared coffee from a distance, **t23** how many layers can a whisky have? How many waves of flavour can a palate withstand? Plenty of caramel, as you might suspect, and those coffee notes start escalating; **f22** the coffee transforms into mocha. A minor degree of bitterness, but that is well met by any number of delicate sugars; **b23** this is quite probably the most powerful bottled whisky I have encountered anywhere in the world in my entire career. Perhaps what is most remarkable is the beautifully delicate nature of the nose and flavour profile, despite the scary alcohol levels. A unique and, if you have the nerve, wonderful experience. *76.5%. nc ncf sc.*

⁛ **The Belgian Owl Single Malt Age 55 Months** 1st fill bourbon cask no. 4275890 db **(92.2)** **n22** sweetish marmalade; fudge and vanillas abound; **t23.5** quite faultless delivery: the oils are firm and seem to help the alcohol to fully magnify the superb barley-oak balance. Not a single discordant note, no bitterness, no battling between flavour factions. Just a revelry of delicate flavours presented in a big way; **f23.5** long, with some major toasted fudge and Demerara notes. Also noticeable is a copper sharpness and both a metallic firmness plus a third dimensional sharpness. From somewhere dates and cocoa appear at the very death. The cocoa I understand..but the dates...? **b23.5** fantastic whisky with more twists and turns than a corkscrew. At times like the Hubble telescope looking back to the Belgian Big Bang – the beginning of the dedicated whisky universe in the country. The picking up of extra copper shows it is getting closer to those very first moments at Belgian Owl... *74.3%. nc ncf sc.*

⁛ **The Belgian Owl Single Malt Age 53 Months** 1st fill bourbon cask no. 4275986 db **(90.5)** **n23** more fudge and Bassetts chocolate liquorice sandwich than Belgian cocoa bonbons; some of the most profound oak yet found from this distillery...; **t23** intense (surprise, surprise) sugars and, also, metallic coppery notes – suggesting small (new?) stills. The barley is also wonderfully intense, clean and precise in its sharpness. Mouth-watering and just so delicious and well weighted; **f22** a late build up of massive natural caramels; **b22.5** enormous whisky, unsurprisingly, as deeply satisfying. *74.1%. nc ncf sc.*

DESTILLERIE RADERMACHER
Lambertus Single Grain Aged 10 Years db **(44)** **n12 t12 f10 b10.** This is whisky...? Really???!!!!????? Well, that's what it says on the label, and this is a distillery I haven't got round to seeing in action (nor am I now very likely to be invited...). Let's check the label again... Ten years old...blah, blah. Single grain... blah, blah. But, frankly, this tastes like a liqueur rather than a whisky: the fruit flavours do not seem even remotely naturally evolved: synthetic is being kind. But apparently, this is whisky: I have re-checked the label. No mention of additives, so it must be. I am stunned. *40%*

FILLIERS DISTILLERY
Goldly's Belgian Double Still Whisky Aged 10 Years db **(88)** **n21.5 t23 f21.5 b22.** Having actually discovered this whisky before the distillers – I'll explain one day...!! – I know this could be a lot better. The caramel does great damage to the finish in particular, which should dazzle with its complexity. Even so, a lovely, high-class whisky which should be comfortably in the 90s but falls short. *40%*

CZECH REPUBLIC
Single Malt
RUDOLF JELÍNEK DISTILLERY
⁛ **Gold Cock Single Malt Aged 12 Years "Green Feathers"** bott 27/05/09 db **(89.5)** **n22** lovely butterscotch and citrus embroidery to the clean barley; **t23.5** clean, refreshing with a charismatic outpouring of gristy sugars, topped with muscovado and some gorgeous, caramel laden oak; **f22** thins slightly, but the vanillas enjoy a light, nutty finale; **b22** from my first ever malt-related trip to the Czech Republic nearly 20 years ago, it was always a pleasure to get hold of my Gold Cock. I was always told it went down a treat. And this is no exception. Not a particularly big whisky. But since when has size counted? *43%*

STOCK PLZEN - BOZKOV S.R.O.

Hammer Head 1989 db (88.5) **n22** light with as much accent on the clean oak as there is the crystal clear barley; **t22.5** a re-run of the nose, except here the malt is richer, biscuity and much more intense; **f22** a lovely oily malt film clings to the palate...and lasts... **b22** don't bother looking for complexity: this is one of Europe's maltiest drams...if not the maltiest... 40.7%

Blends

:::· **Gold Cock Aged 3 Years "Red Feathers"** bott 22/06/09 (86) **n22 t21 f21.5 b21.5.** Sensual and soft, this is melt-in-the-mouth whisky with a big nod towards the sweet caramels. 40%. Rudolf Jelínek.

:::· **Granette Premium** (82) **n21 t22 f19 b20.** Lighter than the spark of any girl that you will meet in the Czech Republic. Big toffee thrust. 40%

Printer's Aged 6 Years (86.5) **n21.5 t22.5 f21 b21.5.** Blended whisky is something often done rather well in the Czech Republic and this brand has managed to maintain its clean, malty integrity and style. Dangerously quaffable. 40%

DENMARK
STAUNING DISTILLERY Skjern. Working.

:::· **Stauning Rye First Impression** dist 09 & 10, bott 2011 (88) **n21.5 t22.5 f22 b22.** Not a whisky, as it is too young. But another experience which almost brings a tear to my eye. Even before these guys got their stills underway, I suggested they go for a rye whisky, a grain entirely befitting Denmark. This they have done. Not quite technically perfect, as no first distillation has any right to be. But it still bombards the senses with a major degree of complexity and beauty... and any amount of spice. The fact it is rye is beyond dispute: the grain comes through loud, proud and clear. A few feints have to be disposed of by warming and then the fun, especially with the cinnamon and apple, really begins. Salivating and spicy, it is a quite superb first effort. And having tasted the maturing spirit of a number of later casks there, I can tell you this wonderful whisky distillery-to-be is just clearing its throat... 52.5%. nc ncf. 857 bottles.

ENGLAND
HEALEY'S CORNISH CYDER FARM Penhallow. Working.

:::· **Hicks & Healey Cornish Single Malt 2004 Cask #29** (94.5) **n24.5** quite possibly an aroma I could spend all day getting to know. The interweaving between the soft apples and the softer honeys alone is enough to keep you entertained for a good hour at least. What makes this so special is the shading and texture; this is not a simple canvas on which one side is painted an apple in still life, the other honey. Every hue imaginable appears to be in there; the apples, for instance, appear from crisp green form to sluggish, sweeter brown and bruised. And just to intrigue you further is the slow showing of the spices. Not quite cinnamon, which might have been just too much of a cliché (though in the mix there appears to be a kind of relation), but a dribble of clove oil and linseed. These seem tied in with a burgeoning bourbon characteristic as the red liquorice grows beside the waxed leather. Faultless and almost beautiful beyond words...; **t24** after that astonishing nose it just had to be mouth-watering...and my word, it is! The spices make an immediate impact, first feisty and then backing off. The delicate fruits refuse to take control and the lightly oiled barley has a bigger role here than on the nose. Again the honey (mainly of the clear, runny English type) waxes and wanes, like on the nose, from one moment being rich and bold, to watery and delicate the next; after a hint of cocoa a few cream caramel notes begin to fill the middle ground; **f22.5** just a hint of oaky bitterness arrives, but the natural caramels are now in the ascendency and offer the desired countering sweetness; late vanilla signs the whisky off; **b23.5** fascinatingly, picking up much more apple here than I did at the distillery, mainly because of the ambient aromas around me there: a great example why all tasting notes I carry out are in controlled environments. Back in January I headed down to the distillery and after going through their casks suggested this one was, like their very finest apples, exactly ripe for picking. The most noticeable thing was that there, in the still house, I picked up only a fraction of the apple I get here in the controlled environment of my tasting room. The distillery makes, above all else, cider brandy, so the aroma is all pervasive. However, my instincts were probably correct, for the apple (doubtless absorbed from the environment of maturing with apple brandy casks, something like the fruit apparent on the whisky of St George's distillery, California) to be found here only contributes positively rather than detracts, especially on the nose...which I have upgraded from excellent then to near faultless now. As new distilleries go, this rates among the best debut bottlings of the last decade. That is not least because most distillers try and launch on three years to get money back as soon as possible. Here they have more than doubled that time and are reaping the benefit...with interest. A dram, then, to keep your nocturnal cinema going on classic mode: "Last night I dreamt I went to Penhallow again." Hang on: twelve syllables... I feel a book coming on... and a film... *61.3%. sc.*

ST. GEORGE'S Rowdham. Working.

The English Whisky Co. Chapter 6 English Single Malt (unpeated) batch no. 001 (**90**) n22.5 youthful, delicate barley. The occasional catch of new make disappears behind a weightier vanilla and citrus blast; this screams at you that despite its youth, it is exceptionally well made; t23 melts in the mouth on contact. A plethora of barley notes mingle with a vanilla-caramel spine. Barley juices continue to flow; f22.5 surprisingly long and chewy. The faintest move towards spice and then a very late honey-toffee sweetness; b22 we had to wait over 100 years for it to happen. But, at last, another English whisky on the market. Was it worth the wait? On the evidence of this first-ever bottling, then unquestionably. The firm and expert hand of former Laphroaig distillery manager Iain Henderson was on the tiller when this spirit was made three years ago and his fingerprints are all over this precocious and ultra high quality bottling. Adorable clarity to this malt which is, considering its youth, without weakness or blemish and, for its tender years, an uncommonly fine whisky. The 1,000th new whisky for the 2011 Bible. As an Englishman, could there have been any other? *46%. nc ncf.*

The English Whisky Co. Chapter 6 English Single Malt (unpeated) cask no. 163, 165, 171 & 173, dist May 07, bott Jun 10 db (**91**) n22 much firmer and flintier barley than the previous bottling; less evident oils. The citrus is now closer to tangerine than lemon; t23 crisp, sharp and brimming with fresh barley...as you might expect. Even room for a hint of milky mocha to come through on the middle. But it is the juicy barley quality and a light spicy touch which steals the show; f23.5 superb interplay between the continuing crisp barley and polite vanilla, though what oils there are now assemble to stretch the finish: fabulous; b22.5 further confirmation that this distillery is on course for true excellence. Here, by comparison to earlier bottlings, the distillate shows some evidence that the stills have been run just a little faster and the cut thinned a little, meaning a laser-sharp crispness to the barley. So reminds me of Glen Grant at this age. *46%*

⸭ **The English Whisky Co. Chapter 7 Rum Finish** ASB & rum cask nos. 024/025, dist Mar 07, bott Oct 10 db (**94**) n23.5 a sweet roll call of delicate sugars, including grist; clean and offering just the right amount of balancing spice; t24 as the nose suggests it might, the whisky simply melts into the palate while the citrusy vitality of the barley generates all the required energy; f23 just a little cask bitterness for the sugars to contend with, but nothing they can't handle; b23.5 absolutely exceptional. A near faultless whisky where the youth of the malt and the sweet finesse of the rum casks were born for each other. The kind of light and juicy whisky I, frankly, adore. *46%. nc ncf.*

The English Whisky Co. Chapter 9 English Single Malt (peated) cask no. 102, 115, 124 & 144, dist May 07, bott May 10 db (**93.5**) n23 the softest vanillas imaginable vanish into a delicate, beautiful peat reek; exceptional in its clarity; t23.5 quite fabulous delivery and follow through: a surprising hickory note thickens the peat; gristy notes offer a near perfect degree of sweetness; f24 lengthens as the oils gather and spices begin to bubble and nip. Demerara sugars arrive from somewhere...and still that peat persists; b23 frankly, it would be churlish to ask any more of a malt whisky of this age. Three years old only, yet going through the gears of complexity like an old 'un. The secret, though, is in the quality of the distillation and the very decent casks used. So exceptional is this, you would almost think that this was created by the guy who made Laphroaig for many a year... *46%*

⸭ **The English Whisky Co. Chapter 10 Sherry Finish** Oloroso sherry hogshead, cask no. 488/489, dist Oct 07, bott Oct 10 db (**91**) n23.5 crusty oloroso in its purest dry form; almost a hint of salty crushed olive; of the malt and oak...there is no sign...; t23 a dry delivery followed – at last –by a trilling infant barley sweet juiciness; the tangy sharpness follows the salty path signposted on the nose; f22 dry with a soupcon of vanilla doing its level best to add a degree of age; a little spice buzz, but from the grape, I suspect; b22.5 a spotlessly clean oloroso cask ensures a beautiful malt, though not quite hitting the very highest forms of excellence as the host whisky has not yet formed sufficient muscle to carry the grape without the odd sideways stagger. That said, not a whisky you'd ever say "no" to the offer of a top-up. *46%. nc ncf.*

⸭ **The English Whisky Co. Chapter 11 "Heavily Peated"** ASB cask no. 645/647/648, dist Mar 08, bott May 11 db (**92**) n23 t23.5 f22.5 b23. As the full strength *59.7%* version below. Only for wimps. *46%. nc ncf.*

∴ **The English Whisky Co. Chapter 11 "Heavily Peated" Cask Strength** ASB cask no. 645/647/648, dist Mar 08, bott May 11 db **(94)** n23.5 although "heavily peated" it is light enough to allow the more citrusy elements of the young barley to ensure a sublime counter lightness. Curiously salty for a land-locked distillery...but just so sexy; **t24** melts in the mouth on impact. No doubting the youth as there is a real greenness to the barley. But it strangely works in its favour because, like on the nose, it generates a sublime counter to the smoke; **f23** just the odd disagreement between the oak and barley, as whiskies of this age have a tendency to do. But once the toy has been put back in the pram, we have a spicy fade which makes your toes curl...; **b23.5** what can you say? A whisky only three years old yet carrying itself with the wisdom of an elder statesman. The pace of the peat is absolutely textbook; the marriage between the smoke and sugars the stuff of dreams. Proof that great – or even intermediate - age is not always the deciding factor. Sometimes, when a distiller has got all his sums right, a whisky can be plucked from the cask at a positively infantile age and still it can have the capacity to knock you off your chair. As this, indeed, does. And if you require proof that adding water to whisky doesn't do a whisky many favours, just try the 46% version... 59.7%. nc ncf.

The English Whisky Co. Limited Edition "Ibisco Decanter" bourbon cask, dist Nov 06, bott Dec 09 db **(91.5)** n22 decidedly childish: the nose is still in short trousers as the oak makes limited headway into the slightly citrusy, juicy barley, but it's well-made stuff; **t24** forget the first mouthful, which gives you only beefed up new make: put all your energy into concentrating on the second onwards which is the most refreshing barley you will taste in a long while. Soft oil helps with the intensity, while a squeeze of lemon juice underscores the freshness and creates a subtle layering; **f23** remains clean and uncomplicated as some half-hearted vanilla inches into the picture; **b22.5** quite adorable. Beautifully made whisky from stills small enough to add almost invisible but vital weight. One of the true fun whiskies of the year which further raises the expectations of what this distillery is capable of. And mark my words: it will be a lot... 46%

∴ **The English Whisky Co. Royal Marriage** db **(86.5)** n21 t23 f21.5 b21. A charming, juicy and superbly made whisky showing the barley in varying weights and textures. But of all their bottlings yet, this is the one which most tellingly reveals its tender years. 46%

FINLAND
PANIMORAVINTOLA BEER HUNTER'S Pori. Working.

Old Buck cask no. 4, dist Mar 04, bott Apr 10 db **(95)** n24 t23 f24 b24. Just read the tasting notes to the second release because, a dose of what almost seems like corn oil and ancient Demerara rum combined apart, oh - and an extra dose of oak, there is barely any difference. I will never, ever forget how I got this sample: I was giving a tasting in Helsinki a few months back to a horseshoe-shaped audience and a chap who had been sitting to my right and joining in with all the fun introduced himself afterwards as I signed a book for him as non other than Mika Heikkinen, the owner and distiller of this glorious whisky. I had not been told he was going to be there. His actual, touchingly humble words were: "You might be disappointed: you may think it rubbish and give it a low score. It just means I have to do better next time." No, I am not disappointed: I am astonished. No, it isn't rubbish: it is, frankly, one of the great whiskies of the year. And if you can do better next time, then you are almost certainly in line for the Bible's World Whisky of the Year award. 70.6%

TEERENPELI

Teerenpeli Single Malt Whisky Aged 5 Years db **(86)** n21.5 t22 f21 b21.5. No shrinking violet, this impressive first bottling from Teerenpeli. It radiates the chunkier qualities often found with smaller stills, yet still manages to harness the richer barley notes to enjoyable effect. Weighty and a touch oily, the sweet barley which is briefly announced on arrival soon makes way for a more rumbustious combination of oak and higher oils. I look forward to getting there at last to see how it is done...though I think I can already imagine...!! 43%

FRANCE
Single Malt
DISTILLERIE BERTRAND

Uberach db **(77)** n21 t19 f18 b19. Big, bitter, booming. Gives impression something's happening between smoke and grape... whatever it is, there are no prisoners taken. 42.2%

DISTILLERIE DES MENHIRS

Eddu Gold db **(93)** n22 t23 f24 b24. Rarely do whiskies turn up in the glass so rich in character to the point of idiosyncrasy. Some purists will recoil from the more assertive elements. I simply rejoice. This is so proud to be different. And exceptionally good, to boot!! 43%

DISTILLERIE GLANN AR MOR

Glann Ar Mor Aged 3 Years 1st fill bourbon barrel db **(85)** n21.5 t22 f20.5 b21. The slight feints, so typical of European small still whisky, works well in upping the weight, structure and chewability. Juicy barley and cocoa dominate, but tasting after it has sat in an open glass for half an hour works wonders. 46%. Celtic Whisky Compagnie.

Glann Ar Mor Taol Esa 1 an Gwech 09 db **(88)** n21 dank hay; decidedly grassy; t22 a wider spectrum of oil on delivery and with it a thick surge of buttery malt; f23 long and the now familiar mocha arrives in good shape; just a squeeze of citrus barley very late on; b22 not quite as cleanly made and technically brilliant as their last bottling, but still a whisky to be reckoned with. Even with a slightly wider cut, remains delicate and engrossingly structured. 46%. Celtic Whisky Compagnie, France.

⁙ **Glann Ar Mor Taol Esa 1 an Gwech 11** db **(72)** n18 t19 f17 b18. F is for French. F is also for Feinty... 46%. nc ncf sc. Celtic Whisky Compagnie. 336 bottles.

⁙ **Kornog Single Malt Whisky Breton Sant Ivy 2011** db **(94)** n23 had I just opened a bottle of Caol Ila, this is pretty much what I would have expected. Telling but not overpowering peat, light oils and big vanillas... t24 now this is getting scary. The gristy sugars are right out of the Caol Ila repertoire and then, to cap it all, a truck load of lime and sugars. I last saw on a young Port Ellen back in the days when my beard barely sported a greying hair...; f23.5 long oils and spices while the smoky fug and the sugars just keep on seducing...; b23.5 the nose, at least, says it was distilled on Islay. To a Frenchman, is that an honour or an insult...? For I have to say, this is the closest to a Scotch whisky I have ever tasted outside those cold, windswept lands..To be honest, this is better than your average Caol Ila, as the oak is of finer quality. Frankly, this is a never to be forgotten whisky. 57.8%. nc ncf sc. Celtic Whisky Compagnie. 249 bottles.

Kornog Taouarc'h Kentan db **(94.5)** n24 now, when was the last time I came across peat this delicate yet profound? A glorious chocolate note mixes imperiously with the drifting smoke; the sweet-dry ratio cannot be bettered; t24 sizable oil on delivery but it brings with it malt on two fabulous levels. Just ahead of the other is a standard juicy, biscuit barley, then directly behind arrives the charmingly weighted peat; the middle ground is filled with a chocolate toffee biscuit...but enveloped in light smoke; f23 a few vanillas build up and there is a light treacle flourish to the lingering smoke; b23.5 not sure there has been this number of perfectly rhapsodic notes coming out of France since Saint Sans was in his pomp... 57.1%

DISTILLERIE GUILLON

Guillon No. 1 Single Malt de la montagne de Reims db **(87)** n22 t21 f22 b22. Right. I'm impressed. Not exactly faultless, but enough life here really to keep the tastebuds on full alert; By and large well made and truly enjoyable. Well done, Les Chaps! 46%

DISTILLERIE MEYER

Meyer's Whisky Alsacien Blend Superieur db **(88.5)** n22.5 t22.5 f21.5 b22. Impressively clean, barley-thick and confident: a delight. 40%

DISTILLERIE WARENGHEM

Armorik db **(91)** n23 t22 f23 b23. I admit it; I blanched, when I first nosed this, so vivid was the memory of the last bottling. This, though ,was the most pleasant of surprises. Fabulous stuff: one of the most improved malts in the world. 40%

Armorik Single Malt 5 Years Old bourbon casks & Breton oak casks, sherry finish, bott 2009 db **(83)** n18 t21.5 f22 b21.5. The standard Armorik is a rewarding whisky to find. This version, though attractively juicy and chewy in part, is a reminder that playing with sherry butts, even good ones, can result in a levelling of the higher points and an ultimately duller whisky. 42%

⁙ **Armorik Single Cask** sherry butt **(88)** n20 toffee nougat and little sign of grape...; t23 ...which can't be said on delivery as the juices crash spicily into the taste buds. Excellent Demerara sugar reinforcement; f22.5 the sugars, spices and vanillas pulse to the end with just a minor nod towards the fruit; b22.5 now that is seriously enjoyable! An unexpected nougat on the nose but the delivery and flowing richness is a real shock. 55%. sc.

Breizh Whisky Blended 50% malt/50% grain db **(85.5)** n22 t21 f21 b21.5. A safe, pleasant whisky which happily remains within its sweet, clean and slightly citrusy parameters. 42%

DOMAINE MAVELA DISTILLERIE ARTISANALE

P&M Pure Malt Whisky bott 2005 db **(91)** n23 t23 f22 b23. An outstanding whisky which, being French, seems to offer a style that is entirely different from anything else around. I have been told there is chestnut within the grist which, strictly speaking, means this is not whisky as we know it. My French is not good enough to discover the truth of this. Between now and the 2008 Bible I shall travel to the distillery in Corsica to get to the bottom of this. In the meantime, though, I shall occasionally enjoy this delicious dram! 42%

WAMBRECHIES DISTILLERY

Wambrechies Single Malt Aged 3 Years db **(78.5)** n19 t19 f21 b19.5. Sweet with a Malteser candy touch. A few feints just dampen the overall effect. There is also an aroma on the nose I kind of recognize, but... 40%

Wambrechies Single Malt Aged 8 Years db **(83)** n20 t21 f21 b21. There's that aroma again, just like the 3-y-o. Except how it kind of takes me back 30 years to when I hitchhiked across the Sahara. Some of the food I ate with the local families in Morocco and Algeria was among the best I have ever tasted. And here is an aroma I recognize from that time, though I can't say specifically what it is (tomatoes, maybe?). Attractive and unique to whisky, that's for sure. I rather like this malt. There is nothing quite comparable to it. One I need to investigate a whole lot more. 40%

Blends

P&M Blend Supérieur (82) n21 t21 f20 b20. Bitter and botanical, though no shortage of complexity. 40%. Mavela Distillerie.

P&M Whisky (89) n22 light, lemony, mildly Canadian wheated in style; t23 beautiful, sharpish citrus ensures a salivating experience; f22 soft oak lowers the sweetness levels; b22 no mistaking this is from a fruit distillery. Still quite North American, though. 40%

GERMANY
AV BRENNEREI ANDREAS VALLENDAR Wincheringen. Working.

Threeland Single Malt 2006 db **(93)** n23 t23.5 f23 b23.5. On this evidence, one of the technically best distillers of malt on mainland Europe. Sensational...!!! 46%

Threeland Whisky dist 2007, bott code L-Wtr200701 db **(83)** n19.5 t22.5 f20 b21. Whilst pleasant and malty enough in its own right, my eyes opened up at this one, as I remember last year's bottling as being one of the best from anywhere in Europe. That, I recall, was so wonderfully fresh and clean. This one, sadly, is bigger and oilier with evidence that the distiller has included some heads and tails which were excluded last time out. Still malty and mouth watering. But a useful lesson in learning the vital difference between good and great whisky. 46%

Threeland Whisky Sherry Fino Finish dist 2007 db **(88.5)** n22.5 beautifully malty and clean with the Fino having a very limited input; t22 virtually sleep walks over the taste buds, soft and quiet but with some heavier oils and dates meeting at the midpoint; f22 much more assertive now with a spiciness chattering in the fruity distance; all kinds of fudge, some with a vague hint of cocoa; b22 again not exactly a picture of technical perfection, but the relationship between the malt and fruit makes for very enjoyable tasting. 52.5%. 352 bottles.

BIRKENHOF-BRENNEREI Nistertal. Working.

Fading Hill 4 1/2 Years American and French oak, cask no. 09 & 11, dist Nov 05, bott Apr 10 db **(74)** n18 t20 f17.5 b18.5. One of those peculiar malts which sends out mixed messages. On one hand, there is a curiously attractive damp hay character and for the more fanciful, orange blossom. On the other, signs, confirmed by the finish, that not all is right or happy. 45.7%. 680 bottles.

❧ **Fading Hill 2005 Meets 2007** cask no. 14 & 19, dist Nov 05 & Oct 07 db **(85.5)** n20 t21 f23 b21.5. Nothing fading about its character: a feinty chap early on but the finish is the best part by a mile: those oils go on forever, bringing some magnificent molten Demerara and cocoa. 45.7%. nc. 690 bottles.

BOSCH EDELBRAND Unterlenningen. Working.

Bosch Edelbrand Schwäbischer Whisky lot 9105 db **(83.5)** n19 t22.5 f21 b21. Needs to make the cut a little more selective: has the promise to become a pretty high quality whisky. This shows some outstanding depth and honey for some time after the first, impressive delivery. 40%

BRANNTWEINBRENNEREI WEINBAU ADOLF KELLER Ramsthal.

A.K Whisky bott code L10209 db **(89.5)** n22 t23 f22 b22.5. Hardly faultless from a technical point of view. But if you can't enjoy something as raunchy and ribald as this, you might as well stop drinking whisky. 40%

A.K Whisky bott code L11110 db **(67) n15 t18 f17 b17.** I think the A.K. stands for the rifle which is required to shoot this ultra fruity, bizarrely scented whisky... 40%

BRENNEREI ANTON BISCHOF Wartmannsroth. Working.

Bischof's Rhöner Whisky bott code L-12 db **(75.5) n18 t19.5 f19 b19.** Rich and chewy, especially the toffee, but all a tad too feinty. 40%

Bischof's Rhöner Whisky bott code L-24 db **(75.5) n17.5 t20 f18 b19.** That unique blend of feints and intense, biscuity grains. Just checked: I see I gave it the same score as last year. Not only unmistakable, but consistently so! 40%

BRENNEREI DANNENMANN Owen. Working.

Danne's Schwäbischer Whisky dist 2002 db **(89) n22** crisp, clean and obviously well made. A light, grainy exoskeleton protects the delicate fruit; **t23** superb mouth feel with a textbook countering of a sweet, juicy lushness and a much firmer, well spiced character not so much a sub plot, but more an entirely different story; **f22** the usual bitterness, but aided by some playful spices; **b22** an exhausting whisky to try and understand. You crack the code only when you fathom that there are two entirely different songs being played at the same time. 54.6%

Danne's Schwäbischer Whisky dist 2002 db **(78) n19 t21.5 f18.5 b19.** A recognisable style of pungent, full-flavoured central and northern European spirit I have experienced over the many years, though not always associated with whisky. There is both a fruit and vegetable character here but the begrudging and short-lived juicy sweetness is, I assume, the brief bow towards the grain. The finish could almost be a full blown, old-fashioned Swedish or Norwegian aquavit. 43%

Schwäbischer Whisky vom Bellerhof db **(88) n21 t22 f23 b22.** Easy drinking clean and deliciously sweet malt with that indelible touch of class. 43%

Schwäbischer Whisky vom Bellerhof db **(88) n23 t22 f21 b22.** An entirely different route to the same high quality whisky...! 47.4%

BRENNEREI ERICH SIGEL Dettingen. Working.

Original Dettinger Schwäbischer Whisky db **(88) n21.5** sharp; egg-custard tart and a supine touch of pine; **t22.5** sugared almonds; body is silky and sweetens gently; **f22** heaps of vanilla and a slow build up of juicy barley notes and spice **b22** softly sophisticated. 40%

BRENNEREI FABER Ferschweiler. Working.

Whisky aus der Eifel Aged 6 Years American oak, dist 2003 db **(91) n23** mint and lavender crushed in the fingers; a little orange peel, too; **t23** exceptional weight with the barley forming a sweet layer at the top and more solid cocoa, caramel and tannin in the sediment; **f22.5** long, lightly oiled, subtly fused with a citrus sweetness and weightless spices; **b22.5** a riveting whisky of uncommonly high quality. 46%

BRENNEREI FRANK RODER Aalen - Wasseralfingen. Working.

Frank's Suebisch Whisky dist 2005 db **(86) n21 t22.5 f21 b21.5.** Impossible not to be charmed by the disarming citrus note. Every aspect of this whisky is low key and delicate. 40%

BRENNEREI HACK Pinzberg. Working.

Walburgis Franken db **(78) n17 t20 f21 b20.** While the nose puts the 'aahhhh!' in nougat, the sweet walnut-cake nuttiness on delivery and beyond makes some amends. 40%

BRENNEREI HÖHLER Aarbergen, Kettenbach. Working.

Whesskey Caramell-Malz bott code 2 db **(83) n18 t21.5 f22 b21.5.** This distillery makes whisky of remarkably consistent quality, even though the styles are slightly different. This one uses all the extra alcohol to give the grain extra spice and momentum to push through the rich cream caramel. 58%

⋅⋅⋅ **Whesskey Hessischer aus Caraaroma Malz** db **(87) n17.5** dreadful. Every distilling fault under the sun... yet...; **t24** possibly the biggest whisky of the year. Every whisky comes in waves. Here, I lose count just how many lap at a scary pace against my taste buds. And it's molassed chocolate fudge all the way...; **f22.5** more vanilla, with charming cocoa-dusted oils. About as far removed from the nose as you can get, though very late on some of the butyric notes can be felt...; **b23** what a pity my tasting of this whisky wasn't filmed. Then it would have been recorded me doing this: nosing...head in hands. Nosing again...shaking head and saying out loud to myself: "either you are going to be a bloody nightmare or something pretty amazing." Tasting it, tasting it for a second time and then, after slumping back in the chair, ejaculating: "you beautiful ugly bastard!" For all the feints and butyric on the dire nose, these somehow (as I suspected) come back to offer on the palate a massive malt. Certainly, no whisky on this planet has a bigger jump in quality from nose to delivery. *62%. nc ncf. Drei Jahre alt Faßtärke.*

⟐ **Whesskey Hessischer aus Caraaroma Malz und Rauchmalz** db **(86.5) n19 t21 f24.5 b22.** These guys specialise in outrageous whiskies which stick two fingers up to you. Again the nose is lacking. And again the whisky fights back with a dazzling exhibition of intense barley and Demerara flavours. The finish is relentless and, full of mocha and barley, a thing of beauty. *57.5%. nc ncf. Drei Jahre alt Faßtärke.*

⟐ **Whesskey Hessischer aus Rauchmalz** dist Jan/Feb 08, bott 25/02/11 db **(85) n19 t21.5 f22.5 b22.** Now there's a weird thing. When I blended some of their Caraaroma and Rauchmalx whiskies together, the nose and flavour profile I created was virtually identical to this. Weirder still, when you put the two poor noses together, they actually improve...two negatives, obviously. Big, chewy, chocolatey stuff. *44%*

⟐ **Whesskey Hessischer aus Rauchmalz Faßtärke** dist Jan/Feb 08, bott 25/02/11 db **(80.5) n18.5 t22 f20 b21.** Big and fruity...like attending a Sultana Fest. With a bar of chocolate as your guest. Some wonderful spices. But, overall, pays the price for a little sloppy distilling with the same faults as seen elsewhere, but this time unable to escape the consequences. *57%. ncf.*

⟐ **Whesskey Hessischer aus Stammwürze 4 Years Old** db **(90) n21** some feinty notes take about five minutes to burn off, leaving spiced peach and sultana; **t22.5** juicy and spicy as promised on the nose, but with an astonishing layer of concentrated barley grist; **f24** some oak at last gets into the fray and adds complexity, layering and decorum. And yet all the time it remains juicy and lip-smacking: fabulous! **b22.5** I have to get to this distillery. I want to meet the people behind this. None other in the world offer anything quite as idiosyncratic: it is the Surprise Symphony of whisky. There are so many things right with this whisky, but you also get the feeling – even when it as amazing as this - that something is wrong. Either way, bottling like this enliven any evening and give tired taste buds a new lease of life and a will to live... *57%*

Whesskey Hessischer Blended Whiskey bott code 114/150, dist Spring 07, bott May 10 db **(82) n18 t21 f22 b21.** A substantial jump in quality from Hohler's blend of last year. Curiously enough, reminded me of the Loch Lomond single malt I tasted earlier in the day, but gets over the feinty hump more easily and with a better display of controlled sugars. Cream toffeed and enjoyable. *42%. 150 bottles.*

Whesskey Hessischer Mais Whisky bott code 62/250, dist Feb 07, bott May 10 db **(82.5) n19 t22 f20.5 b21.** Intriguingly dense whisky with stewed nettles and celery on the nose and a curiously metallic delivery despite the pea soup consistency of the grain. Not for one second dull... *44%. 250 bottles.*

⟐ **Whesskey Hessischer Mais Whisky** dist Feb 07, bott Nov 10 db **(84.5) n22 t21.5 f21.5 b19.5.** Well, that was weird. For once they get the nose right. Then it begins to fall apart on the palate... I assume some kind of wine cask, as there is a profound grape and spice presence. But rarely are the cask and spirit on speaking terms. *44%*

Whesskey Special Blend db **(77) n17.5 t21 f19.5 b20.** One of those odd creatures which surface from time to time in this part of the world. The flavor profile – even taking into account the massive cream toffee caramel style – isn't quite like anything you've encountered before. You kind of like it, admire the deft spice delivery, but... *41%*

BRENNEREI HÜBNER Stadelhofen, Steinfeld, Working.

Fränkischer Whisky db **(67.5) n15 t17.5 f18 b17.** Well, that was different. Can't really give you tasting notes as such, as I don't really have a reference point as to where to start. Quite simply, a bunch of bizarre aromas and flavours, the vast majority of which I have never encountered before. Another distillery I must seek and visit to find out what all this is about... *40%*

Hubner Los Nr 3 db **(80.5) n20 t22.5 f18 b20.** Overwhelmed by fruit as far as complexity is concerned, but there is a distinctive smoky, salivating theme to this nonetheless. The balance has been trashed and if it were a novel, you'd have to read it three times...and still make no sense of it. A David Lynch film of a whisky...and I love it, though I have no idea why. *40%*

BRENNEREI LOBMÜLLER Talheim. Working.

Schwäbischer Whisky Single Grain cask no. 6 db **(83) n20 t22 f20.5 b20.5.** A big toffee presence softens the impact and helps steer this towards a gentle, pleasantly sweet whisky. *41%*

Schwäbischer Whisky Single Grain cask no. 7 db (86.5) n20 t22.5 f22 b22. A friendly, big-hearted, soul full of toffee-chocolate chewiness. Highly enjoyable. 41%

BRENNEREI MARTIN MEIER Neuravensburg. Working.
Mein 9. Fass db (84) n19 t21.5 f22 b21.5. The light spices and dissolving sugars melt beautifully into the malt. Nose apart, this is a ja, nicht ein ein... 42%

BRENNEREI MARTIN ZIEGLER Baltmannsweiler. Working.
Esslinger Single Malt Aged 8 Years db (85) n20.5 t22 f21 b21.5. Malty, nutty, a decent degree of sweetness and toffee marzipan. A well-made malt which you appreciate more as you acclimatise to its compact style. 42%

BRENNEREI RABEL Owen. Working.
Schwäbischer Whisky db (76.5) n17 t21.5 f18 b20. Here's something different. While the nose, or at least the getting it right, is a work in progress, the delivery and body are much more on the ball thanks mainly to a rich treacle and prune element which sees off the thicker distillate. The finish, though, confirms the fault lines.

BRENNEREI VOLKER THEURER Tübingen-Unterjesingen. Working.
Black Horse Ammertal db (83) n21 t21.5 f20 b20.5. A big puncher, this, with a coastal saline, phenolic uppercut amid the sugary jabs. 40%

Black Horse Ammertal bott code BL-2010 db (79) n18.5 t21 f19 b20.5. The wider cut used in the distilling means this Black Horse has put on a little bit of weight from the BL2008 I tasted last year. The light phenols have gone but the sugars have increased. 40%

Sankt Johann Single Barrel Aged 8 Years bott code BL-2010 db (85) n19.5 t22 f21.5 b22. Fabulous fun. Once it gets over the drying tobacco nose the inevitable nougat is delivered. But it comes with a milk-creamy mocha which develops in intensity and with just the right doses of treacle to keep the sweetness at desired levels. Good background spices too. A very likeable character, this Saint Johann. 46.5%

BRENNEREI ZAISER Köngen. Working.
Zaiser Schwäbischer Whisky db (83) n23 t21.5 f19 b19.5. Surprisingly dry and constricted in development considering the beautiful soft sugars on the nose which also boast excellent clarity. 40%

DESTILLERIE DREXLER Working.
Drexler Arrach No. 1 Bayerwald Single Cask cask no. 262, dist May 07, bott May 10 db (88.5) n21 a tad confused with a hint of kumquat and spices more recognisable at the local Indian takeaway; t23 much more at home on the palate where the grain and oak appear to harmonise pretty effortlessly; f22 fades pleasantly; b22.5 very good bitter-sweet marriage, but better still is the luxuriant mouth-feel. A well constructed malt. 46%. 210 bottles.

DESTILLERIE HERMANN MÜHLHÄUSER Working.
Mühlhäuser Schwäbischer Whisky aus Korn db (90.5) n23 as usual with Herman's whisky I am taken back to a farm. This time it is like when the freshly harvested corn is being unloaded into the silo and the dust of Summer is floating in the air...; t23 mouth wateringly fresh (and cleaner than last year) the grains and oak appear to harmonise instantly; the delicate nature of the sweetness wants to make you applaud; f22 at last a few stray feints gather, but they also help ramp up the spices; b22.5 another stunning bottling from this excellent distiller. You have to admire the subtlety of the complexity of this whisky. 41%

Mühlhäuser Schwäbischer Whisky aus Korn db (90) n22.5 t23 f22 b22.5. So different! If you are into this, it'll be pastoral perfection. 40%

EDELBRENNEREI PETER HOHMANN Nordheim, Rhön. Working.
Rhöner Grain Whisky Aged 6 Years db (89) n21 heady and bready. A distinct spice buzz; t22.5 delicate body with wispy strands of treacle and spice; f23 the peppery spices hit full flow as the vanillas enter; the late liquorice, honey and hickory is superb; b22.5 impressively made and matured with a quite lovely marriage between the sugars and spices. 40%

EDELOBST-BRENNEREI ZIEGLER Freudenberg. Working.
AVREVM db (83) n21.5 t21 f20 b20.5. A most peculiar, though not unattractive, marriage of marmalade and hops. 43%. 1000 bottles.

FEINBRENNEREI SEVERIN SIMON Alzenau-Michelbach. Working.
Simon's 10 Years Old Bavarian Pure Pot Still db (86.5) n21.5 t21.5 f22.5 b21. Not a whiskey to rush. Takes several hours to get to know this chap. When they say Pure Pott Still, I am sure they mean a mixture of malted and unmalted barley. Because that is the only style that offers a whiskey as rock hard as this with virtually no give on the palate. If there is any yield, it comes in a vaguely fruity form but this is a whiskey which sets up an impenetrable barrier and defies you to pass. Fascinating and very different. *40%*

GUTSBRENNEREI AGLISHARDT Nellingen. Working.
HFG Gutsbrennerei Aglishardt db (86.5) n22 t21 f22 b21.5. Clean, fruity and not entirely without some Fisherman's Friend phenol. A real juicy job. *40%*

HFG Dinkelwhisky Single Cask No 2 db (87.5) n21.5 well weighted oak with light layers of honey and nougat; t22 mouth watering and immediately chewy. Gristy sugars hold control; f22 long with a light spice addition to the vanilla; b22 good, honest whisky with plenty of charm from the grain. *41.5%*

HFG Schwäbischer Whisky db (72.5) n18 t19 f17.5 b18. Dry and spicy. But let down by the cask. *40%*

HAMMERSCHMIEDE Zorge. Working.
Glen Els Single Hercynian Malt dist May 06, bott May 10 db (86.5) n22 t22.5 f20.5 b21.5. Loads of baked yam and fresh barley on nose; clean and a touch of the Malteser candy on palate. Thoroughly enjoyable, and doubtless the SWA will love it even more... *51%. 570 bottles.*

HELMUT SPERBER Rentweinsdorf. Working.
Sperbers Destillerie Malt Whisky dist 2002 db (76.5) n17.5 t19 f21 b19. Great finish with the house cocoa/mocha style. But some of the other characteristics seem other worldly. *46%*

Sperbers Destillerie Malt Whisky dist 2002 db (77.5) n17.5 t20 f21 b19. Very similar to the 46% except the sugars are much more eccentric. *59%*

Sperbers Destillerie Single Grain Whisky dist 2002 db (76) n17 t21 f19 b19. Once you get past the butyric nose the mouth feel and slow cocoa development is rather lovely. *40%*

KINZIGBRENNEREI MARTIN BROSAMER Biberach. Working.
Kinzigbrennerei Martin Brosamer Single Malt oak cask, dist Apr 05, bott Sep 08   d   b (84) n20.5 t21 f21.5 b21. For all the obvious nougat, the barley is given a clear stage from which to make its sweet speech. *42%. 120 bottles.*

KLEINBRENNEREI FITZKE Herbolzheim-Broggingen. Working.
Schwäbischer Whisky 4-Korn-Malz db (75) n18 t19.5 f18.5 b19. Hard to have fun picking out the various ingredients when the distillate is this heavy. A thinner cut would have given us a better chance. *43%*

Schwäbischer Whisky Buchweizen db (83) n22 t21 f19 b21. With buckwheat being a plant and not a cereal crop, the spirit distilled from it cannot be called a whisky...whatever the label says. The spirit here is pleasant enough with an attractive vegetable nose and plenty of spices ducking in and out of the sugars. *43%*

⁘ **Schwarzwälder Whisky Emmermalz** bott code. L6807 db (91) n21 sharp and seemingly off the pace. But when left in the glass for a while, a grassy, straw-dust aroma develops; t23 after the initial very minor feints on delivery, the next five or six waves are giant ones. Some carry the oils, the others the gorgeously bitter-sweet grain which generates some major salivating; f23.5 a build up of delightful spice amid the mocha and walnut cake; b23.5 the ancient grain of emmerkorn is not a usual component of whisky, though as it was used for beer in prehistory it is about time something was done with it in the still. And on this evidence it has been worth waiting for. A magnificently characterful malt. Generally well distilled and beautifully matured, to boot. *43%*

Schwäbischer Whisky Dinkelmalz db (85.5) n22 t21 f21.5 b21. A fabulous whisky to find. The style is uncompromisingly different and it takes a little while for one's nose and taste buds to fall into line. But once you get into stride with it, the brittleness is a joy as is the attractively sour-grain note and the light cocoa finale. *43%*

⁘ **Schwarzwälder Whisky Hafermalz** bott code. L6707 db (70) n17 t18 f17 b18. Sweet. But way off key. *43%*

Schwäbischer Whisky Hirse db (88.5) n22 unique. A touch of the chewing gum about this. A mixture of molten sugar, prune juice and kind of stewed leaf concoction I had in Africa once; **t22** wow! So intense: a green tea bitterness to this but elsewhere a dense sugar and spice counters quite forcefully; **f22** exactly more of the same, but just fading with those tealeaves hanging in to the end; **b22.5** not every day you come across a whisky distilled from sorghum (if, indeed, it officially can be), though I am no stranger to Maotai, China's equivalent which does not taste remotely like this. A pity. *43%*

⚜ **Schwarzwälder Whisky Gerstenmalz** bott code. L5406 db **(84.5) n18.5 t21.5 f22.5 b22.** Juicy and possessing a plump and shapely body with plenty of spicy and chocolate curves. Especially towards the excellent sugared almond finish. *43%*

⚜ **Schwarzwälder Whisky Mais** bott code. L6305 db **(82.5) n18.5 t21 f22 b21.** Once past the, well...bizarre, nose it is relatively easy going, especially towards the impressive, attractively sticky, end. *43%*

⚜ **Schwarzwälder Whisky Roggenmalz** bott code. L5606 db **(87) n22** firm, no-nonsense rye with little fat or backchat; **t21.5** juicy and crisp and again focussing on the grain. Some vanillas try to gain a foothold but the rye remains aloof; **f22** a touch of honeycomb and liquorice softens and sweetens the encounter; **b21.5** hard as nails. *43%*

⚜ **Schwarzwälder Whisky Weizenmalz** bott code. L5706 db **(94) n23** clean distillation allows the spices full play; **t23** juicy, mouth-watering; a delightful custard sweetness patrols the middle ground; **f24** heads out in a more chocolaty direction. But those juicy spices continue to fizz; the softest oils ensure the encore keeps going; **b24** superbly made whisky with thumping character despite its fresh and delicate nature. One of Europe's finest, for sure. *43%*

KORNBRENNEREI WAGNER Dauborn. Working.

Golden Ground Grain Whisky Original Dauborner dist 2005 db **(84) n21 t21.5 f21 b20.5.** Lots of latent honey, yet the sum total offers a pretty dry experience. *40%*

Golden Ground Grain Whisky Original Dauborner dist 2005 db **(88) n21** wide cut but sweet and spicy; **t23** superbly weighted with genuine honey attaching to an almost pasty graininess which works through the complexity gears with ease; **f22** late spices work well with the drier distillate and oak; **b22** a little extra feints has worked well for the rich and complex body. *46%*

KOTTMANN´S EDELDESTILLAT-BRENNEREI Bad Ditzenbach. Working.

Schwäbischer Whisky lot no. 120705 **(78.5) n19 t20 f19 b19.5.** Heavy, oily and with much nougat to chew on. *40%*

MÄRKISCHEN SPEZIALITÄTEN BRENNEREI Hagen. Working.

⚜ **Bonum Bono New Make** db **(86) n21 t21.5 f22 b21.5.** Light, citrusy, attractively oiled, juicily malty and lip-smacking. I have also tasted their malt which in several months has upped colour and intensity to superb levels and will be bottled shortly. Can't wait! *55%*

NORBERT WINKELMANN Hallerndorf. Working.

⚜ **Fränkischer Rye Whisky** db **(93.5) n24** classic rye. The crisp fruitiness is refreshing, light and heavy, sweet and spicy. Magnificent...; **t24** the excellence of the nose, which suggested ultra high class, feint-free distilling, is confirmed here. The grain is classically crunchy, with the sugar candy sweetness and the contrasting fruit juiciness enough to set you on a jig of delight; **f22.5** spices pound and buzz though there are shades of feinty, oily bitterness that are apparent for the first time as the intensity of the rye fades; **b23** for the record, the nose is so good to this that I kept it with me one evening after a badly sulphured cask from another distillery had ruined my tasting for the day. The fruity beauty of this was not just balm, but a reminder of just how wonderful whisky should touch you. *42%*

Fränkischer Whiskey Strong Single Malt db **(78) n17.5 t20.5 f20 b20.** A huge whisky, but mainly because the cut has been nothing like so judicial as the rye. *48%*

OBSTBRENNEREI MÜCK Birkenau. Working.

⚜ **Old Liebersbach Smoking Malt Whisky** bott code. L1105 db **(83.5) n21 t21.5 f21 b20.** Good heavens! Don't find many whiskies like this one around the world. Almost a Sugar Fest in part, especially in the earlier stages, then bitters out with an almost shocking suddenness. Fascinating and dramatic, though perhaps not for the purist. *43%*

PRIVATBRENNEREI SONNENSCHEIN Witten-Heven. Demolished.

Sonnenschein 15 db **(79.5) n19.5 t21 f19 b20.** So, it's back!! In its youth, this was a tough whisky to entertain. Many years on and some of the old faults remain, but it has picked up a touch of elegance along the way. *41%*

BRENNEREI REINER MÖSSLEIN Zeilitzheim. Working.

Fränkischer Whisky db (91) n23 quite extraordinary: stick your head in a dank, warm bale of hay and you won't be far off this; on the other side, there is hint of emulsion paint, too...; t23 the lightest possible coating of maple syrup helps temper the intense oak statement of intent; the weight and body are exemplary; f22.5 long, clean; a more pronounced liquorice edge and just a hint of spice; b22.5 rich, earthy, pungent, full of unique character and quite adorable. Might be an acquired taste for single malt stick-in-the muds, though... 40%

SLYRS Schliersee-Neuhaus. Working.

Slyrs Bavarian Single Malt 2006 lot No. L26752, bott 2009 db (87.5) n22 malt thick enough to cut with a knife; a slightly sharp fruity, yeasty note, too; t22 friendly sugars join the melt-in-the-mouth gristy barley; f21.5 some oils and oaky dryness; b22 a very friendly, malty and well made greeting from Bavaria. 43%

⁙ **Slyrs Bavarian Single Malt 2008** lot no. 012341 (87.5) n18.5 feinty. and malty. In that order. t23.5 think of a shapely Bavarian beer server, and you get some idea of the curves and overall grrrr-ness of this malt. Chewy in the extreme, but what really blows you away is the intensity of the toffee and maple syrup. Not as sweet as it sounds, but one mouthful, and you'll know exactly what I mean...; f23 long with just more stuff as before; b22.5 I know it sounds strange, but one of my highlights of writing the Whisky Bible is to taste the latest offering from one of the pioneers of European whisky, Slyrs. I have high regard for their whisky, though it has the habit of being cut just a little too wide. Here that has certainly affected the nose. But, for the palate, it ensures rare and beautiful riches. A delight. 43%

SPREEWALD-BRENNEREI Schlepzig. Working.

Sloupisti 4 Years db (88.5) n22 t22 f22 b22.5. Very much grows on you: it is obvious the distillers have worked very hard to get both distillation and maturation right. 40%

Sloupisti 4 Years (Cask Strength) db (94) n23 t24 f23 b24. A mind-blowing fruitfest. Just love the clarity to the flavours. This is such great fun...!! 64.8%

Spreewälder "Sloupisti" Single Malt No. 1 db (89.5) n23 complex and busy. The vaguest hint of pine amid the citrus and diluted muscovado; t22.5 sweetened tangerines; a couple of sugars in the mocha; f22 thin but with an attractive malty-sweet, slightly buttery fade; b22 very clean malt which refuses to venture into the realms of bitterness despite the early threat of oak. 40%

Spreewälder "Sloupisti" Single Malt No. 1 db (88) n22.5 a slight touch of air freshener about this one but a little nip and spice and extra muscovado gives the nose the come hither treatment; appears rather wet-behind the ears...; t22 big, young, brash new-make-type maltiness; f21.5 remains strictly pre-pubescent, malty but lacking the usual oaky signature; b22 usually, whisky is easy to interpret yet I have to admit it: I'm entirely confused. Both labels are identical, except the strength. And they have both been marked as single Malt No 1. Yet the 62.2%, though beautifully made, strikes me as a youngster whilst the weaker version offers some evidence of maturity. Another point: how can the same malt, 50% weaker in strength than its twin, actually have more colour...? Really lovely whisky, but an enigma. 62.2%

STAATSBRAUEREI ROTHAUS AG Grafenhausen-Rothaus. Working.

Black Forest Single Malt Whisky dist Sep 06, bott Mar 10 db (74.5) n19 t20 f17.5 b18. Black Forest...Green Whisky. In fact I haven't seen anything with this green a tinge since I discovered these now legendary Green Whiskies in the warehouse of Springbank some 20 years ago, and the stuff at the Murree distillery in Pakistan about six years later. Just like the Springbank there is a sugary rum-like sheen to this, except here we are treated to a peculiar hoppy note, too, on both nose and finish. 43%

⁙ **Black Forest Single Malt Whisky** bourbon cask, dist Dec 07, bott Mar 11 db (79.5) n19 t20.5 f20 b20. This is one of the distilleries in Germany I haven't yet visited. So puzzled by what was in my glass, I called my dear friend Julia Nourney who sent me the sample. "Julia. Do they distill from beer, including the hops?" "You asked me exactly the same question last year", she replied. I had forgotten, until she reminded me. Apparently they don't. But it kind of tells a story in itself. 43%

STEINWÄLDER BRENNEREI SCHRAML Erbendorf. Working.

Stonewood 1818 dist 1999 db (91) n22.5 t23 f22.5 b23. Consistant throughout with a superb and endearing degree of sweetness. High quality stuff. 45%

Stonewood 1818 Bavarian Grain Whisky 10 Jahre dist 2000 db (84) n19 t22 f21.5 b21.5. Comes out all guns blazing spraying juicy citrus in every direction. 45%

UNIVERSITÄT HOHENHEIM Working.

Hohenheim Universität Single Malt (82) n21 t20 f20 b21. The aroma is atractively nutty, marzipan even, and clean; the taste offers gentle oak, adding some weight to an otherwise light, refreshing maltiness. Pleasant if unspectacular. 40%. *Made at the university as an experiment. Later sold!*

WEINGUT MÖßLEIN Kolitzheim. Working.

⁘ **Weingut Mößlein Fränkischer Whisky** db **(78) n20 t20.5 f18.5 b19.** Doesn't quite gel, sadly. The nose is a strange one: hints of butyric, tobacco and honeycomb... But for all the apparent fruit, never hits its stride. 40%

WHISKY DESTILLERIE LIEBL Bad Kötzting. Working.

⁘ **Coillmór American Oak Single Cask** cask no. 34, dist Sep 06, bott code. LC309 db **(78.5) n17 t19 f22.5 b20.** After the off centre nose and delivery it improves dramatically, especially in the spicy and quite delicious latter stages. 46%. sc. 420 bottles.

Coillmór American Oak Single Cask cask no. 45, dist Sep 06 db **(71) n17 t18 f18 b18.** If you are smoker – which I have never been – you might enjoy this one: stale cigarette smoke amid the sharp barley. 43%

Coillmór American Oak Single Cask cask no. 45, bott code LA0110, dist Dec 06 db **(72) n17 t18 f19 b18.** Well, 10/10 for consistency. Another cask which fails to work on many levels. That period in 2006 will not go down as the distillery's finest. 46%

Coillmór Bavarian Single Malt sherry cask, dist May 06 db **(90) n21.5 t23.5 f22 b23.** Excellent: that seriously works...!!! Oh, if only the Scots could come up with a sherry butt of such faultless beauty... 55%

⁘ **Coillmór French Oak & Sherry Single Cask** dist Nov 07, bott code. LD210 db **(86) n19 t22 f23 b22.** Twenty years in this game has given me something of a Pavlovian outlook on some whiskies. So, from vividly nasty experience indelibly lasered into my brain, I automatically shied away from a whisky which had the words "sherry" and "French oak" on the same label: this had the potential of being the double bill from hell. But, ironically, it is the quality of the oak involvement which manages to overcome the worst of some sloppy distilling and ensure, once the nose is out of the way, a joyous riot of fruity juiciness. Impressed! 46%. sc. 1002 bottles.

⁘ **Coillmór Kastanie Single Cask** chestnut cask, cask no. 19, dist 24 Feb 06, bott code. LB0311 db **(91.5) n22** slight feints, but acceptable thanks to the nutty, sweet chestnut quality; a hint of kumquat, too; **t23** the extra oils ensure a stunning delivery bursting with what appears to be natural caramels and Demerara sugars. Sweet, but entirely in context with the big barley middle; **f23.5** long and now offering sophistication with spices showing alongside the thickening nuttiness; **b23** this is a distillery capable of making whisky at both ends of the quality scale. This beautifully intense malt is the best yet produced by the distillery and most definitely Bundeslige...! Hang on! Just noticed it is from a chestnut cask (hence the chestnuts????) Bugger! It ain't whisky, folks! 50.2%. 60 bottles.

Coillmór Peat & Smoke Aged 3 Years cask no. 80 db **(79.5) n19 t20 f20.5 b20.** Major novelty value: peat and cigarette smoke...? 46%. 920 bottles.

⁘ **Coillmór Sherry Single Cask** cask no. 84, dist 30/31 Oct 07, bott code. LA0111 db **(76.5) n18.5 t19 f20 b19.** Takes a while for the sweet grape to overcome the heavier oils. 46%. sc. 960 bottles.

Coillmór Sherry Single Cask Aged 3 Years cask no. 81 db **(87.5) n21.5** seriously thick grape; **t22.5** huge grain again, but just a little marzipan, too, like the inside of a fruitcake; **f21.5** a little furry dryness; **b22** moments of delightful revelation. 46%

WHISKY-DESTILLERIE ROBERT FLEISCHMANN Eggolsheim. Working.

⁘ **Austrasier Single Cask Grain** cask no. 1, dist Jun 98, bott May 11 db **(91) n22** displays some of the spices not unknown in a Swedish Akvavit **t22.5** the 40% is immediately evident: very light entry for a Fleischmann whisky. Then, from nowhere, a thunderstorm of sugars, spices and prune juice...; **f23.5** copious amounts of Demerara and dates. Inevitably, we are reunited with those spices, and a sliver of dark chocolate; **b23** i really don't know whether the Germans are able to knight someone for their services to whisky. But if they can't they should change the law. Another wonderful piece of high quality whisky fun. 40%. sc.

Blaue Maus Single Cask Malt db **(84.5) n18 t22 f22.5 b22.** Beautifully molassed with a big burnt fudge finale. 40%

Blaue Maus Single Cask Malt cask no. 2, dist Jun 98, bott May 10 db **(86) n22 t22 f21 b21.** For those who love their fruitcake to have something of the sherry trifle about it. Brimming with clean grape, though curiously out of sync with the body of the spirit. The bitterness at the death is unexpected. *40%*

⸭ **Blaue Mause Single Cask Malt** cask no. 4, dist Jun 99, bott May 11 db (**88**) n21.5 heavy, with a hint of peanut butter on burnt toast and thick liquorice; **t22** rumbling oils spreading delicate sugars; **f22.5** more sugar, much darker in style – almost like an old-fashioned Scottish sweet stout but without the hops; **b22** an almost perfect exhibition of complex toasted brown sugars. *40%. sc.*

Blaue Maus Single Malt 20 Jahre cask no. 1, dist Jul 88, bott May 08 db (**91**) n22 t23 f22.5 b23.5. Complex and superbly balanced, the age is never in doubt while the management of the old oak is sublime. *40%*

Blaue Maus Single Malt 25 Jahre dist 1983, bott 2008 db (**95.5**) n24 t24 f23.5 b24. My 1,400th whisky for the 2009 Bible. And what better way to celebrate than by tasting Robert Fleischmann's special bottling to mark his 25th anniversary as a whisky distiller. I first tasted it with Robert earlier in the year at the Munich Whisky Festival. Back on neutral territory it tastes no worse than the stunning whisky he poured for me then. Quite dazzling and a magnificent way to mark this momentous anniversary. Because if a better German single malt has ever been bottled, then I have missed it. Which is rather unlikely... *40%*

Blaue Maus Single Cask Malt Fassstärke cask no. 1, dist Apr 92, bott May 08 db (**89**) n20 t23 f23 b23. A massive experience: The Blaue Max. *58.6%*

Blaue Maus 2. Fassfüllung Single Cask Malt cask no. 1, dist Jun 97, bott May 10 db (**84**) n20 t22 f21 b21. Thick and soupy on both nose and palate, the malt showing juicy personality despite the weight. Decent exploitation of delicate brown sugar trait. *40%*

⸭ **Blaue Mause Single Cask Malt 2 Fassfüllung** cask no. 1, dist May 98, bott May 11 db (**92.5**) n22.5 moist Jamaican ginger cake...; **t24** exceptionally moist Jamaican ginger cake...; **f23** somewhat dried out Jamaican ginger cake; **b23** methinks Blau Mause has sailed recently to Jamaica. *40%. sc.*

Blaue Maus Single Cask Malt Fassstärke db (**91.5**) n19.5 t24.5 f23.5 b24. Tasting whisky from this unique distillery is always fun. And it appears distiller Robert Fleischmann is really doing this with a smile on his face. This is really what world whisky is all about: what entertainment...what fantastic bloody fun...!!!! *56.3%*

Elbe 1 Single Cask Malt cask no. 1, dist Jul 96, bott May 10 db (**77**) n19 t19 f18 b19. A long way removed from the normal house style, the accent decidedly floral and dry: almost London gin-like. *40%*

⸭ **Elbe 1 Single Cask Malt** cask no. 1, dist Jun 96, bott May 11 db (**81.5**) n19 t21 f20.5 b21. The wall between success and comparative failure can be so thin. This ticks many of the correct boxes. There is vanilla aplenty and a chugging molasses. But something in the distillation is just slightly awry. A must, though, for those looking for an ultra dry dram. *40%. sc.*

Grüner Hund Single Cask Malt cask no. 3, dist Aug 97, bott May 10 db (**92.5**) n23.5 t24 b22.5. Somehow you get a feeling that here is a man enjoying the making of whisky. And I am certainly a man who enjoys tasting it...especially when it reaches these fun-filled heights. *40%*

⸭ **Grüner Hund Single Cask Malt** cask no. 3, dist Jul 98, bott May 11 db (**86.5**) n21 t22.5 f21.5 b21.5. Juicy barley assisted by chocolate nougat and molasses. Plenty of heavy oils, too. *40%. sc.*

Grüner Hund Fassstärke Single Cask Malt cask no. 1, dist May 96, bott May 10 db (**81.5**) n21.5 t21 f19 b20. Dry with plenty to chew over. But then when the cut has been made this wide, letting the nougat-rich feints surge in, that is hardly a surprise. *48.9%*

Krottentaler Single Cask Malt cask no. 1, dist Mar 97, bott Jan 09 db (**77.5**) n17 t21 f19.5 b20. Loads of sweet cocoa for all its obvious weaknesses. *40%*

New Make lott no. 1, dist Mar 09, bott May 10 db (**89**) n22.5 t23 f21.5 b22. High quality new make where, despite the strength, the malt goes on a salivating route. Better than one or two scotch single malt commercially sold. And excellent for dissolving your plaque...and probably enamel. *85.2%*

Old Fahr Single Cask Malt cask no. 1, dist Jul 00, bott Jan 09 db (**89**) n19.5 t23.5 f23 b23. Quite simply a beautiful whisky. *40%*

⸭ **Old Fahr Single Cask Malt** cask no. 2, dist Jun 00, bott May 11 db (**94.5**) n23.5 one of the finest noses ever from this distillery: oily and thick but with enough honey, chocolate-liquorice and sugar-toasted almonds to have you searching for more; **t23.5** near perfect weight on delivery with sublime sugars melting into the soft oils. Again, a bourbon honey-hickory edge sets up the finale; **f24** long with Demerara sugars in perfect harmony with the spiced butterscotch and vanillas; **b23.5** an object lesson in excellent whisky making. Robert, you have excelled...! *40%. sc.*

Old Fahr Single Cask Malt cask no. 3, dist Jul 00, bott May 10 db **(89.5)** n22.5 less nougat than of old and much more hickory and toffee fudge; t22 drier than expected with a real silky body. There is a subdued honeycomb, the sweeter edges rounded by vanillin; f23 the perfect finale for those who prefer the chocolate-flavoured Liquorice Allsorts; b22 beautifully complex and delightfully weighted with the odd technical imperfection which works in its favour. A late night treat. 40%

Otto's Uisge Beatha cask no. 1, dist Mar 07, bott May 10 db **(88.5)** n22 the Scottish malt is more than evident with some thick, crusty smoke flying about; t23 very different and damned tasty: gristy, smoky and roasty, but with a bizarre semi-nougat attachment; sweet, lusty and busty...; f21.5 the bawdiness of the delivery calms as the vanilla and nougat toffee get a grip; b22 Germany meets Scotland. Just as well it's in whisky and not football, otherwise this could have been embarrassing. Or something as grim as the days of Berti Vogts. 40%

⋰ **Otto's Uisge Beatha** cask no. 1, dist Oct 07, bott May 11 db **(73.5)** n17 t19 f18.5 b19. Incredibly sweet. Incredibly oily. And incredibly out of tune. Sorry, Otto! 40%. sc.

⋰ **Otto's Uisge Beatha Fassstärke** cask no. 1, dist Sep 07, bott May 11 db **(79)** n18 t20 f21 b20. Otto: a second chance for glory – and you've blown it again! Much better than the last bottling, with the sugars in better formation. But still too slack and indisciplined. 474%. sc.

Schwarzer Pirat Single Cask Malt cask no. 2, dist Jun 96, bott Jan 09 db **(86.5)** n20 t22.5 f22 b22. Honey and nougat all the way. 40%

⋰ **Schwarzer Pirat Single Malt** cask no. 2, dist May 00, bott May 11 db **(87.5)** n22 uber complex nose: bluebells, tree bark... dank, early spring woods. Offset by a shaft of manuka honey and marzipan breaking through the canopy; t22 big oils with Bassett's chocolate liquorice in abundance; f21.5 takes a little while to work out its direction: the oils could go anywhere but settle on a more vanilla-rich context, but still that chocolate-liquorice (with a marked emphasis on the chocolate!) hangs around like a ghost; b22 technically incorrect, but pure entertainment! 40%. sc.

⋰ **Seute Deern Single Cask Malt** cask no. 1, dist Jul 97, bott May 11 db **(85)** n20.5 t22 f21 b21.5. Massively enjoyable whisky. But just one too many hefty oils for greatness. Another showing some classy touches of stem ginger. The sugars are mesmeric. 40%. sc.

Spinnaker Single Cask Malt cask no. 1, dist Aug 93, bott Jan 09 db **(89)** n19.5 t23 f23.5 b23. Stunning chocolate fudge. 40%

⋰ **Spinnaker Single Cask Malt** cask no. 2, dist Jul 99, bott May 11 db **(93)** n22 oily but no off notes, carrying thick barley and cocoa in equal measures; some dark sugars evident, too; t23.5 excellent delivery and those sugars hinted on the nose arrive en masse, along with liquorice and some of the oils from the wider part of the cut; f24 long, with a dark liquorice frame and any number of drying, pleasingly bitter, coffee and cocoa notes; b23.5 aha! Spinnaker's back! Seams a couple of years since I last had a new bottling of this German whisky mainstay. A much cleaner version than I remember: none of the normal nougat and better distillation. Quite superb! 40%. sc.

Spinnaker Single Cask Malt 2 Fassfüllung cask no. 1, dist Jun 95, bott Jan 09 db **(86.5)** n18 t23.5 f22.5 b22.5. Ignore the nutty nougat/butyric nose and you have a sublime malt absolutely bursting out of the glass with cocoa-laden barley. Fabulously beautiful in every department, other than the aroma. (Note: all Blaue Maus whiskies can be improved by allowing the whisky stand in heat for a while to burn off the feints) 40%

LATVIA
LATVIJAS BALZAMS Riga. Working.
L B Lavijas Belzams db **(83)** n20 t22 f20 b21. Soft and yielding on the palate, this is said to be made from Latvian rye, though of all the world's rye whiskies this really does have to be the softest and least fruity. I'll be astonished if there isn't a fair degree of thinning grain in there, too. 40%

LIECHTENSTEIN
TELSER Triesen. Working.
Telsington db **(94)** n23 t23.5 f23.5 b24. Now here's a conundrum if not irony. The first ever whisky from probably the most land-locked country in the whole of Europe, and it has the aroma of a rock pool found on a Hebridean island of about the same, tiny size. As for the whisky? What can I say? The last time I stayed in this beautiful, idiosyncratic country I had no option other than to spend the night in the worst hotel I have encountered in the western world. Thankfully the new distillery does not perform to such pitiful standards. This is not just good whisky, it is outstanding: far, far better than it has any right to be at first attempt. Obviously a fourth visit to Vaduz is now called for: this whisky is worth another night of misery

and rudeness. I seriously need to shake the hand of the distiller...this is the most entertainingly delicious whisky I have tasted from mainland Europe this year. *40%*

⟶ **Telsington II 3 Years Old** dist 2007 db **(86) n21.5 t22 f21 b21.5.** A firm, big malted fellow with a delicious nuts and treacle sub plot. At its best when left in the glass for a short while, this one doesn't have some high quality grape to help it along like the first-ever bottling. However, a clearer look at the inner working of this whisky makes for a fascinating – and impressive – experience. A few phenols appear to have popped up from somewhere. *42%. sc.*

⟶ **Telsington III 4 Years Old** dist 2007 db **(89) n22** rich, intense and displaying a controlled enormity. Sugars are of the dried dates variety; the oak offers marzipan and vanilla. Improves with warmth and time in the glass. The vaguest smoke imaginable...atoms of the stuff amid the weighty oils; **t22.5** malt concentrate and nougat. A big, massively chewy beast of a whisky, a little tart here and there, but displaying a lovely Malteser candy personality, complete with milk chocolate; **f22** like spiced fruitcake... without the fruit; **b22.5** very similar to the Telsington II, only has moved on with extra oak. Some of the technical wrinkles have been ironed out with the extra year, though not quite enough to prevent it keeping its craggy character. *42%. sc.*

⟶ **Telsington IV 3 Years Old** dist 2008 db **(94) n23.5** complex: a salty, curiously semi-phenolic trait helps embroider shape, texture and relief into the otherwise silky fruits; **t23** one of the best deliveries from mainland Europe this year: possibly the best. Truly three dimensional with a juicy fruit character shoulder to shoulder with equally salivating barley and oaky spices. The grape is fabulously clean and offering a spiced dryness of devilish sophistication: whether it is or not, a highest grade Fino style to this; **f23.5** continues along those same beautiful salty, malty, fruity contours, the spices building if anything; **b24** it seemed only right that the 999th new whisky for the 2012 Whisky Bible, a very big number I think you agree, should come from the world's smallest whisky distilling nation. And also because they have the ability to make above average spirit and this, technically, is their best yet. For good measure they have matured it in a first rate cask. The result is a distinguished malt of rare sophistication worthy of the trust I placed in it. *42%. sc.*

THE NETHERLANDS
US HEIT DISTILLERY Bolsward. Working.

Frysk Hynder Frisian Single Malt Whisky dist 05 Nov 03, bott 01 Dec 06 db **(87) n22.5 t21.5 f22 b21.5.** Doesn't even begin to try to be complex. Almost opulently simplistic with its thick barley-oak theme. But well made and perhaps too easily quaffable. *40%.*

ZUIDAM Baarle Nassau. Working.

⟶ **Zuidam Dutch Rye Aged 5 Years** cask no. 446-683, bott no. 81, dist Jan 05, bott Aug 10 **(92.5) n23.5** there is something so sexy and alluring about the nose of a good rye whisky, and this is no exception. Fruity with cinnamon candy spiciness; the oak counters with a bludgeoning heavy-handed liquorice; **t23** no eider down pillow could afford this degree of softness on delivery: the oils from the wide-ish cut work their best and absorb all the fruity grains and natural toffees have to throw at it; juicy, though the grain disappears under the huge caramel. A fruity spiciness begins the fight back, but it takes a while; **f22.5** more settled with the grain showing greater confidence; **b23.5** this bottle stays in my dining room. There is a new classic European to be found. *40%*

⟶ **Zuidam Millstone French Oak** cask no. 358-359, bott Jan 00, dist Sep 10 **(74.5) n18 t20 f18.5 b19.** A huge fug of oily toffee. I think it would be a fair assessment to conclude that their distilling skills in 2000 don't quite match their abilities of 2005... *40%. Pure Pot Still.*

⟶ **Zuidam Millstone 5 Years Old** cask no. 1129+/m1133, dist Apr 05, bott Jun 10 **(89) n22** one of the most citrusy noses on the market today: mainly lemon with a hint of lime. Clean with a very slow build up of barley; **t22** oily textured with a creeping toffee and spice character; the sugars are delicate an help along the custard tart middle; **f22.5** now the oils are dominant and ensure a long finale. A late return of citrus, sharpening the toffee-lemon sponge cake; **b22.5** a thoughtfully made and matured whisky. The evidence is that the still is small and the cut on the wider but fully acceptable side. A joy. *40%. Pure Pot Still.*

⟶ **Zuidam Millstone 8 Years Old** cask no. 913t/m915, dist Jan 00, bott Sep 09 **(89) n22** busy, very slightly piney and old beyond its years. But the barley and well made spirit is balm on troubled oak; **t23** a pretty even match between thick, at times juicy, barley and toffee; one of the chewiest whiskies in Europe; **f22** the oak wins, but now tones down to more inviting vanillas and spice; **b22** for their French oak bottling, I had a bit of swipe at the quality of the distillate. I may, however, have been wrong about their ability to make good whisky in 2000. This technically ticks all the boxes with not a single off note – anywhere! *43%. Pure Pot Still.*

Zuidam Millstone Peated cask no. 570571, dist Feb 05, bott Sep 10 **(72)** n18.5 t17.5 f18 b18. Zuidam have joined the noble and endless list worldwide who have found making a peaty whisky a little harder than they thought. Perhaps closer to coal tar soap on the nose and wanders in all directions over the palate. Another heroic failure. Heads up: better luck next time, chaps. *40%. Pure Pot Still.*

SPAIN

DYC Aged 8 Years (90) n22 a charming meeting of delicate barley and equally light vanilla; t23 more of the same, with a silky soft grain element totally in tune with the clean juiciness of the malt; f22.5 more of the same, with a Victoria sponge creamy strawberry note; b22.5 I really am a sucker for clean, cleverly constructed blends like this. Just so enjoyable! *40%*

DYC Pure Malt (84.5) n20 t21 f21.5 b21. I admit it's been a few years since I visited the distillery, but from what I then tasted in their warehouses I am surprised that they have not brought out their own single malt to mark the 50th anniversary of the place. This, which contains a percentage of Scotch I believe, is OK. But no better than what I remember sampling. *40%*

DYC Selected Blend (86) n21.5 t22 f21 b21.5. Although still a bantamweight and remains its old refreshing self, has definitely muscled out slightly on nose, delivery and finish...with a distinct hint of smoke. Unquestionably a bigger DYC than before. *40%*

MAG'5 (80.5) n19 t21.5 f20 b20. Much more Alonso than Puyol... *40%. Destillerias MG.*

SWEDEN

MACKMYRA Gästrikland. Working.

Mackmyra Brukswhisky db **(95.5)** n24 deceptively heavy nose, or deceptively light? At first thin golden syrup, but a lovely rumbling counterweight of light oil, toasty grain and red liquorice; t24 just fabulous: so delicate and complex as varying levels of busy oak pop around the palate. Bourbony in some senses but the juiciness of the grain has an entirely different character. The molten honeycomb and drier hickory has a familiar feel; f23.5 long, spicy, chocolatey, honeyed, vanillary; b24 one of the most complex and most beautifully structured whiskies of the year. A Mackmyra masterpiece, cementing the distillery among the world's true greats. *41.4%*

Mackmyra Moment "Drivved" bott code MM-003 db **(89)** n22.5 distilled from lime? Big, sharp citrus kick in the caramels; a touch salty, bracing: as the naked wind from the sea... t22.5 a big outbreak of toffee sugars which appears to perfectly counter the agile young barley; f22 those youthful oils carry the toffee vanilla to the last, lingering moments; b22 young and, after the nose, simplistic, with a limited degree of true complexity. But these Mackmyras are on a different plane to anything they have done before and you cannot be anything other than awestruck. *55.5%*

Mackmyra Moment "Jord" bott code MM-004 db **(93)** n23 a detached fruitiness, like the sugars from big sultanas; but it's those red liquorice bourbon notes, And spices...mmmm! t24 huge. Not a prisoner to be seen. I think the weight and oils border perception. The sugars are also so sublimely well weighted and balanced with the drier vanillas, it is hard to know how you could improve upon this; f23 the spices up the pace a notch or two, but still those bourbon notes now with a degree of cocoa dryness, which are in complete control; thick cream toffee oozes from the oak...; b23 anyone with a fondness for bourbon might just have to get a case of this... hard to believe better casks have been used in maturation anywhere in the world this year. *55.1%*

Mackmyra Moment "Medvind" bott code MM-001 db **(87)** n22.5 mixed messages of young malt and more senior roast almonds set in toasted mallows; t22 clean, still youthful though the oak is injecting as much old-aged sugars as possible to catch up; f22 some extra oils arrive, as does a citrus-vanilla edge, so we are at last getting genuine complexity; b22 very few whiskies out there show pre-pubescent youth and a grey beard at the same time... *48.6%. 967 bottles.*

Mackmyra Moment "Urberg" bott code MM-002 db **(95)** n24 probably the most delicate and complex nose from Europe this year: light, yet somehow there is a real weight to the barley; the oak is one of those red-blooded, tannin rich affairs which somehow doesn't come even close to taking control; t23.5 what a fabulous delivery: all kinds of bourbon traits and characters, like the nose. The barley stands tall and intense; a slow gathering of muscovado sugars; f23.5 and so it continues; more of the same, with perhaps more vanillas and cocoa and a late, tingling spice; b24.5 beautifully distilled, superbly matured, clever flavour profile, first-rate packaging: the complete deal. Certainly one of the most intense, complex, compelling and simply enjoyable whiskies I have tasted this year. Truly a magic Moment... *55.6%*

Mackmyra Privus 04 Ratta Virket bott 28 Jan 08 db **(95)** n24 t24 f23 b24. Wonderfully raw, almost untamed, around the edges and quite impossible not to love. *55%*

Mackmyra Special: 01 eminent sherry, bott Winter 08 db **(87.5)** n21.5 t22.5 f22 b21.5. Enjoyable and chewy, but you feel the whisky tries to break free of the dull grape. *51.6%*

Mackmyra Special: 02 bott Summer 09 db **(78.5)** n20 t20.5 f18 b20. Feinty. Some barley and cocoa. But simply nowhere near up to this distillery's usual, brilliant standard. *50.6%*

Mackmyra Special: 03 bott Jul 09 db **(91)** n23 a compelling mixture of the lightest smoke, wine gums, a rather thicker than technically demanded cut from the stills (though it works!!), marmalade, and much more besides make for a slightly eclectic aroma, but one so beguiling you almost forget to taste the thing...; t23.5 a creamy, sweet bourbon edge to the delivery. Muscovado sugars do battle with the liquorice, then the grains battle their way in; f22 just a touch of marmalade bitterness; b23 after the last two less than special Specials, it's great to see Mackmyra right back on track with this glorious, typically characterful whisky which simply blows you away. *48.2%*

Mackmyra Special: 04 double dip bourbon, bott Summer 2010 db **(89.5)** n23 the kumquat school of bourbony oak: busy, spicy, bitty, malty. Just never sits still; t22.5 sharp, bubbling delivery soon gives way to a more relaxed, natural cream toffee; f22 pretty even though the oak begins to show a marked tannin-bitter persona; b22 for those who like big oak but without the feeling of over aging: a very different style of whisky. *53%*

⁘ **Mackmyra Special 05: "Jaktlycka" (Happy Hunting)** bott Autumn 2010, bott code MS-005 db **(89)** n23 it's the old vanilla and butterscotch one-two which usually denotes age, though here it simply heralds sublime oak. A rejuvenating citrus note courses through the aromas like blood through young veins; t21 on delivery, a rare moment of inexactitude for a Mackmyra: the citrus and barley are stumbling over each other. Only after a minute or so do the oaks move in to restore order...; f23 after the messy opening, what a finish! All traces of youth are expunged and now we are in a world of honeydew melon and Demerara-embraced hickory; we appear to have found ourselves in Kentucky...; b22 the youthfulness of the whisky at times causes problems in harmony, as is experienced on delivery. But all else is simply wonderful... *47.2%*

⁘ **Mackmyra Special 06: "Sommaräng" (Summer Meadow)** bott. Summer 2011 bott code MS-006 db **(83.5)** n20.5 t21.5 f21 b20.5. The name of the malt sounds like a Beethoven symphony. But as someone who spends his very rare moments of non-whisky related freedom walking through, up, down and over the countryside of various countries and continents, I can't say this whisky brings to mind the seemingly random but heart-thrilling trilling overhead of the invisible lark; or barley, with its copper shroud glowing against the green sheen of the sprouting grasses, dancing in the fleeting summer breeze. This is too earthy. Too heavy and base. Too one dimensional against the secret hidden textures and pastels of the uplifting summer meadow. An enjoyable malt, for sure. But one for the black moods of winter, with the rain beating its irregular, reassuringly depressing rhythm against the tear-stained window and, as the irrepressible caramels descend, so equally does the darkness of the looming winter equinox. "Winter Wastelands". By the marshes, with the forlorn call of the curlew more like... *46.8%*

SWITZERLAND
BRAUREREI LOCHER Appenzell. Working.

Säntis Malt Swiss Highlander Edition Dreifaltigkeit db **(96.5)** n24 fantastic mixture of apple-wood style smoke (this is very similar, almost identical in fact, to the smell from the bonfires burned by my late father at his Surrey allotment in the early 60s, and, yes, I think old branches from our apple tree often went up in smoke) and something a bit earthier – obviously the peat. Like a Rupp Cheese of malty heat; t24.5 this is truly astonishing: the weight of oil on the palate is gentle but sufficient to coat the mouth; next comes a layer of mixed smoke, both woody and earthy; this is followed by a layering of caramelized molasses; an indecipherable fruitiness makes itself heard, while spices pepper the palate like so many small asteroids hitting a small planet... f24 a near faultless finale (perhaps a degree of overenthusiastic bitterness), though the experience is so long and seamless, it is hard to know where the main body of the flavours are and when the finish begins... b24 this is one of the whiskies of the year, without question. Such is the controlled enormity, the sheer magnitude of what we have here, one cannot help taste the whisky with a blend of pleasure and total awe. *52%*

Säntis Malt Swiss Highlander Edition Säntis oak beer casks db **(88)** n22.5 t23 f20.5 b22. Light, fruity and impressive. *40%*

Säntis Malt Swiss Highlander Edition Sigel oak beer casks db **(91.5)** n23.5 t23 f22 b23. High quality whisky which balances with aplomb. *40%*

BRENNEREI HOLLEN Lauwil. Working.

Hollen Single Malt Aged Over 6 Years matured in red wine casks db **(89)** n23 t22.5 f21.5 b22. Perhaps the fruit is rather too emphatic and, a late show of spice apart, some of the other forms of character development you might wish to see are lacking. Apparently peatless. Possibly, but not entirely convinced. 42%

Hollen Single Malt Aged Over 6 Years smoke malt, matured in white wine casks db **(92)** n23.5 t23 f22.5 b23. You just can't really fault this stuff. 42%

Hollen Single Malt Aged Over 6 Years matured in white wine casks db **(90.5)** n23 t23.5 f21.5 b22.5. Many facets to its personality, the nose especially, shows more rum characteristics than malt. A won't-say-no glassful if ever there was one, though, and made and matured to the highest order. Indeed, as I taste and write this, my BlackBerry informs me that Roger Federer is on his way to another Wimbledon title: the similarities in the quiet dignity, elegance and class of both Swiss sportsman and whisky is not such a corny comparison. 42%

Hollen Single Grain Aged Over 6 Years db **(86.5)** n22.5 t21.5 f21 b21.5. Big, sharp and bruising. The odd feint kick here and there, but there is a pleasing chocolate fruit and nut touch to this one, too. 51.6%

Hollen Single Wheat Malt Aged Over 6 Years db **(74)** n18 t19.5 f18 b18.5. Oooops! Bitter, off-key...Even Federer has his off days...and I've just read that over at Wimbledon Roddick is storming to the fourth set...these things happen. 42% (see Hollen White Wine Cask)

BRENNEREI SCHWAB Oberwil. Working.

Bucheggberger Single Malt cask no. 23, bott no. 10 db **(74)** n17 t21 f17 b19. Decent malty lead, but the intensely bitter finish makes hard work of it. 42%

BRENNEREI URS LÜTHY Muhen. Working.

Dinkel Whisky pinot noir cask db **(92.5)** n23 lusty, clean fruit: the grapes appear to be sultana-sweet and beautifully spiced; clean and complex t24 lush, warmingly-spiced grape – as promised on the nose – medium-thick oils and a wonderful transformation into a coffee and fruit cake mix; the barley scuttles out from this enormous mix to make its mark near the middle ground; f22 a touch of bitterness creeps in, but some mocha-grape holds firm; b23.5 a big, striking malt which is not afraid to at times make compellingly beautiful statements. 61.5%

Wyna Whisky Original No. 2 dist Apr 06, bott Apr 09 db **(79)** n21 t21 f18 b19. Fruity, but seriously overcooks the bitterness. 43%. 489 bottles.

BURGDORFER GASTHAUSBRAUEREI Burgdorf. Working.

Reiner Burgdorfer 5 Years Old cask no. 4 db **(82.5)** n18 t22 f21 b21.5. Recovers from the mildly feinty nose to register some wonderfully lush cocoa notes throughout the coppery, small still development on the palate. 43%

DESTILLERIE EGNACH Egnach. Silent.

Thursky db **(93)** n24 all kinds of big fruit-edged bourbon notes; liquorice and honeydew melon; some lychee and marzipan add wonderfully to the mix; even a slightly rummy style to this; t23.5 silky, estery with a controlled sweetness; again there is a lovely bourbon-fruit interaction, perhaps more on the red liquorice honeycomb bourbon style; f22.5 some oak begins to bite but the honeyed sheen and light mint-cocoa dusting keeps the whisky honest; b23 beautifully even whisky! I am such a sucker for that clean fruity-spice style. Brilliant! 40%

BRENNEREI-ZENTRUM BAUERNHO Zug. Working.

Swissky db **(91)** n23 young, clean, fresh malt which sparkles with a hint of apple: one of the best noses on the European scene; t23 stunningly clean arrival and then the most delicate of malty displays that all hinges around a juicy youth to the barley. The sweetness is controlled, evenly and evenly distributed; a soft oiliness helps to lubricate the tastebuds; f22 no less soft and simple with the oak offering the kind of weight that can barely be detected; b23 while retaining a distinct character, this is the cleanest, most refreshing malt yet to come from mainland Europe. Hats off to Edi Bieri for this work of art. Moving stuff. 42%

Swissky Exklusiv Abfüllung L3365 db **(94)** n23 t23 f24 b24. A supremely distilled whisky with the most subtle oak involvement yet. Year after year this distillery bottles truly great single malt, a benchmark for Europe's growing band of small whisky distillers. 40%

ETTER SOEHNE AG Zug. Working.

⮮ **Johnett** db (89) n22 attractive vanilla and barley mix, with the character of the casks and the stills on public view; citrus drifts in and out; **t22.5** soft, lightly oiled and an ever-increasing build up of quite beautiful and clean barley. Also delicate, nutty sugars, occasionally hinting of praline, sometimes marzipan; one of those malts that prefers to hint rather than state; **f22** a little peach melba on the vanilla and custard tart goes a long way and faithfully sticks to the script;; **b22.5** a sane, beautifully crafted malt which, due to its delicate nature, makes no attempt to hide its few imperfections. An elegant, articulate every day whisky. *42%*

HAGEN DISTILLERY Hüttwilen. Working.

Hagen's Best Whisky No. 2 lot no. 00403/04-03-08.08 db (87) n19 t23.5 f22 b22.5. Much more Swiss, small still style than previous bottling and although the nose isn't quite the most enticing, the delivery and follow through are a delight. Lovely whisky. *42%*

Hagen's Best Whisky Oak Special lot no. 3031/03.03 -12.07 db (84) n21 t21.5 f20.5 b21. A very well made, sweet, uncomplicated malt matured in a thoroughly used bourbon barrel – or so it seems. Not sure if this is a compliment or not, but could easily be mistaken for some kind of Speyside single malt whisky destined for a young blend. *42%*

HR Distillery lot no. 10099, dist Dec 99, bott Jan 05 db (88) n21 t23 f22 b22. Again we have an enormously impressive whisky from Switzerland. Here we have a classic case of a whisky that has matured for a few years side by side with fruit spirit (probably apple) and has breathed in some of those delicate elements. *42%*

HUMBEL SPEZIALITÄTENBRENNEREI Stetten. Working.

Farmer's Club Finest Blended db (85.5) n22 t22 f20.5 b21. Clean, well made, astonishingly Scotch-like in its style. In fact, possibly the cleanest whisky made on mainland Europe. Lashings of butterscotch and soft honey; even a coppery sheen while the oak makes delightful conversation. But there appears to be lots of caramel which dulls things down somewhat. *40%*

Ourbeer Single Malt db (84) n21 t20.5 f21.5 b21. Once more very well made with some entertaining spice. But the caramels have way too much to say for themselves *43%*

RUGENBRAU AG Matten bei Interlaken. Working.

⮮ **Interlaken Swiss Highland Single Malt "Classic"** oloroso sherry butt db (95) n23.5 moist raisins on a toasted teacake; **t24** the palate is engulfed by about as soft and friendly a blanket of light grape you could imagine. But what really impresses is the structure of the lightly honeyed vanilla, enriched by the walnut oil and Bassett's chocolate liquorice on which the grape is embedded; **f23** plateaus out with those soft oils but the lightest dusting of spice allows the drying of the oak a natural progression; **b24** hugely impressive. I have long said that the finest whiskies made on mainland Europe are to be found in Switzerland. Game, set and match... *46%*

⮮ **Top Of Europe Swiss Highland Single Malt "Ice Label"** bott 2011 (93.5) n23 a hint of noble rot on this intense grape aroma. The clean wine allows maximum clarity for the clever spices; **t24** mouth-filling, momentarily over thick delivery. Soon, though, it thins sufficiently for the spiced, juicy sultana sugars to pour through. This mingles with a stunning barley; **f23** long with vanilla and caramel forming alongside a mocha richness which envelops the finale **b23.5** I get a lot of stick for heaping praise on European whisky. OK, there is the odd technical flaw in the distillation – though in some ways it works to its advantage. But how many casks do you find like this in Scotland? For sheer quality of its output, this distillery must rate as high as an Alpine peak... *58.9%. sc.*

SPEZIALITÄTENBRENNEREI ZÜRCHER Port. Working.

Zürcher Single Lakeland 3 Years Old dist Jul 06, bott Jul 09 db (88.5) n21.5 t23 f21.5 b22.5. This distillery never fails to entertain. Not as technically perfect as usual, but none of the blemishes are seriously damaging and even add a touch of extra character. *42%*

Zürcher Single Lakeland Malt Whisky 3 Years Old dist Sep 04, bott Sep 07 db (83) n21 t22 f20 b20. Enjoys some highly attractive moments when that famous grape-barley gets into full swing. But a sub-standard barrel has done a little damage here. *42%*

Zürcher Single Lakeland Malt Whisky 3 Years Old dist Jun 05, bott Jun 08 db (91.5) n23 t23 f22.5 b23. Stunning clarity to the fruit ensures a malt which simply sings on the palate. The fruit-barley balance is quite exceptional, though not surprising from this highly impressive distillery. *42%*

WHISKY CASTLE Elfingen. Working.

Castle One Single Malt Edition Käser cask no. 455, dist Jan 05 db **(86) n19 t22 f23 b22.** Technically, not the best from this distillery with the nose an OTT clash between feints and withering oak . But the extra weight from the extended cut has given the spirit enough muscle to take the weight of the enormous wood influence. The result is demanding, especially at full 68%abv throttle, but ultimately delicious when the Demerara sugars kick in. *68%*

Double Wood Castle Hill Single Malt cask no. 400 db **(83) n21 t20 f21 b21.** Oily, fruity, a tad feinty. *43%*

Edition Käser Castle One Single Malt cask no. 406 db **(94) n23 t23.5 f23.5 b24.** Another astonishing whisky from this top-rate distillery. *70.6%*

Smoke Rye Whisky Castle Single Malt cask no. 338 db **(90.5) n21.5 t23.5 f22.5 b23.** This will not be to everyone's liking: the distinctive nose alone is not entirely blemish free (though leave a glass of it in a very warm room for about half an hour and most of those blemishes will have vanished) but, like the tale which unfurls on the palate, it is very different, never less than fascinating and sometimes hits the point of high deliciousness. *43%*

Smoke Spelt Whisky Castle Single Malt cask no. 336 db **(71) n16 t19 f18 b18.** Never, ever, have I smelt the countryside so emphatically in a glass than with this whisky. Fusty hay. In concentrate. Amazing: liquid Constable. Also parts of the aroma is pure malting floors. Sadly, though, I am not convinced all this is entirely intentional: it also appears like some kind of infection has got in somewhere during the brewing process. If there is confirmation, it is from the slightly rancid nut oil on the taste. Yet for all the low scores and negatives, I also recognize certain elements on both nose and taste which are beautiful, or at least potentially so. Certainly unique. There again, I can't remember the last time I came across smoked spelt...I really want to see these guys try this one again and see what happens. Maybe this is the way it does turn out. Or maybe it will prove to be an invaluable and idiosyncratic addition to the whisky lexicon. The earth may or may not move for you with this one. But at least there is proof that it is still going round... *43%*

⋰ **Whisky Castle Sauternes Cask** db **(88) n21** heavy, oily grain locks horns with thick, sweet grape...**t22** had I been a castle under attack like this I might have waved the white flag by now: the intensity of barley and grape have to be tasted to be believed.; **f23** at last calms sufficiently for some poached greengages to a touch of gentility. But the barley remains in concentrate form and the massive natural caramels refuse to be outdone; **b22** a distillery that has the ability to storm your ramparts. This is no exception. *43%*

Whisky Castle Terroir cask no. 477, dist Sep 06 db **(71.5) n16 t18 f19 b18.5.** Butyric and wildly off target. *43%*

Whisky Castle Vintage cask no. 485, dist Sep 06 db **(90.5) n22 t23 f23 b22.5.** Imagine a whisky angel gently kissing your palate...this is all about very good spirit (with a slightly wide cut) spending time in what appears to be either a high quality virgin cask, or something very close to one. Brimming with character and charisma. *43%*

WALES
PENDERYN Penderyn. Working.

Penderyn bott code Jul 09 db **(94) n23.5 t24 f23 b23.5.** In many ways the essential Penderyn, showing its true colours and at times perplexing complexity. *46%*

Penderyn bott code Aug 09 **(77) n19 t21 f18 b19.** Not sure what happened here. The Edward Hyde to the July 09's Henry Jekyll. Hot and thin, the usual charm and complexity is in very short supply. *46%*

Penderyn bott code Sep 09 db **(89.5) n22 t23 f22.5 b22.5.** Much more like it. A seductive, silky glove glides around the palate. *46%*

Penderyn bott code Oct 09 db **(91) n22.5 t23.5 f22.5 b22.5.** Good grief! The most Madeira dominated standard bottling of them all. *46%*

Penderyn bott code 01 Nov 09 db **(92.5) n22 t24 f23 b23.5.** My, oh my: what a treat this is! The consistency of bottling after bottling, not so much in style but quality, almost defies belief: this is the Golden Age of Welsh whisky... *46%*

Penderyn bott code 02 Nov 09 **(85) n21.5 t22 f20 b21.5.** Fat with varying layers of grape; vanilla hits the middle ground running. *46%. ncf.*

Penderyn bott code Nov 09 db **(88) n22** Tunnock's mallow and jam... **t23.5** succulent, virile grape. Sharp, mouth-watering barley forms a delicious ally; **f21** late oaky bitterness; **b21.5** disappointing fade but the delivery is pure Welsh magic. *46%*

Penderyn bott code 01 Dec 09 db **(88) n22 t23 f21 b22.** The dullish finish cannot eclipse the bright, complex delivery. *46%*

Penderyn bott code Dec 09 db **(86.5) n22.5 t22 f21 b21.** Toffee and vanilla. *46%*

Penderyn bott code Jan 10 db **(78)** n19 t21 f19 b19. Pleasant. But a few cylinders failing to fire. *46%*

Penderyn bott code Feb 10 db **(85.5)** n21 t22.5 f21 b21. Chubby, attractive spices and fruitily simplistic. *46%*

Penderyn Madeira bott code Mar 10 db **(88.5)** n22.5 docile bourbony oak with a full gamut of citrus fruits and spice: a Welsh gentlemen's Cologne (or an Aberfeldy, I think they call it)... t23 hard as Welsh slate on delivery and then a fabulous eruption of varying coffee notes; f21 mocha with strictly no sugar...; b22 oh, if only they had managed to inject some sweetness into the finish of this one, it would have been one for the collection. *46%*

Penderyn Madeira bott code Apr 10 db **(94.5)** n24 now that is one of the most upfront Madeira finishes I have come across from this distillery for a little while: while the fruit is dripping from the glass, there is much more bourbon influence, too, with a serious touch of the Kentuckys about this...; t23.5 mouth-filling and lusciously malty, it is no time at all before the spices explode, lighting up the rich fruit middle. All around cocoa notes fly, as do some strategic muscovado sugars and delicate liquorice, underlining the big bourbon thread on this; the degree of accommodating oils nears perfection; f24 almost ridiculous in its length and complexity. Those oils which develop mid range can go on for many minutes more, carrying with them the light sugars and soft spearmint which so well matches that delicate mocha. Long, flakey and wonderfully complex; b23 now that IS a classic! Does what all the previous bottlings tried to do, but much more thoroughly and with confidence abounding. Big whisky, for something so seemingly delicate. *46%*

Penderyn Madeira bott code May 10 db **(90)** n21 lots of Kentucky again, on the nose through drying tobacco leaves; t23.5 much better assembled: in fact, pure entertainment! Seriously complex, at first just needing a slightly more telling degree of early sweetness to achieve excellence and then getting there with the super slow-motion assembling of juicy grape notes and then a hickory/Demerara ensemble...makes you purr like a contented dragon... f23 that softly fruited and big-spiced personality powers through for a superb – and very long - finale; b22.5 when at last the sweetness of the Madeira and malt can be heard we have an exceptionally complex whisky on our hands. *46%*

Penderyn Madeira bott code Jun 10 db **(84.5)** n21.5 t22 f20.5 b21. Perfectly enjoyable, if somewhat dry, whisky for stirring the bones on getting home in the evening from the pits and clearing the coal dust from the taste buds. Or having just seen your football team lose. But for a Penderyn, even for a wonderful mid-range surge of Madeira, it just doesn't hit the right notes at the end with the early promise never quite being fulfilled. Still, should provide the kind of jolt back to life Swansea City fans needed after the footballing lesson they received, especially from Tam Mkandawire, on the chilly evening of Friday 10th December 2010. *46%*

∴ **Penderyn Madeira** released 7 Jul 10 db **(92)** n21.5 zesty with crushed grape pips; chalky vanilla; t23.5 really engrossing delivery and one of the most structured developments on the palate I have seen from this distillery. The malt and fruit might as well be holding hands, the way they dovetail so effortlessly. Much more grape than the norm leading to a fruit and nut chocolate bar middle ground; f23.5 distinctly fuller bodied than is usual for this part of the experience allowing the sweetness to counter the oak to much more purposeful effect... b24 this bottling is a testament to how far this whisky has moved over the years. There appears to be much more Madeira influence than was once the case, indicating that the malt is being allowed a little longer to mature. This is lush, beguilingly complex whisky of the very top order. *46%. ncf.*

∴ **Penderyn Madeira** released 4 Aug 10 db **(89)** n21 dry lead with a fruity afterthought; t22.5 earlier spice and then a surge of natural caramels; f23 some bitter marmalade anchors the much juicier fruit which makes a late surge; b22.5 understated, clever and sophisticated. *46%. ncf.*

∴ **Penderyn Madeira** released 9 Sep 10 db **(91)** n21.5 pithy, crushed almond on a layer of drying grapeskin; t23.5 sensual and full bodied mouth feel with some early, sugared, milky cocoa easing the spices into place; f23 playful spices still, but this is all about relaxed fruit and continuing fine balancing between the sweeter malt and drier fruits and oaks; b23 practically a re-run of the July bottling, with the odd tweak here and there. My curiosity spiked, I contacted the Welsh Whisky Company who confirmed they were now, as I was very much suspecting, using a tank to store the vatted casks before bottling... and thus creating a minor solera system. This explains the continuity of style with the slight variation from month to month, rather than the sometimes violent lurches in style from one bottling to the next that had hitherto been the hallmark of Penderyn. Higher quality, for sure... if slightly less excitement and nosing into the unknown for me...! I shall miss its Russian roulette idiosyncrasy... *46%. ncf.*

⠿ **Penderyn Madeira** released 4 Oct 10 db (92.5) n22 t23.5 f23.5 b23.5. Very much in the same mould as the September release, above, but here the fruit has a warmer, softer, say while the milk chocolate is ramped up a notch or two. A very classy act. 46%. ncf.

⠿ **Penderyn Madeira** released 5 Nov 10 db (89.5) n21.5 t22 f23.5 b22.5. Busy on delivery and the creamy development. The finish is dreamy stuff with a wonderful, gradual injection of spice to add a delicate fizz to the usual fruit-chalk interplay. 46%. ncf.

⠿ **Penderyn Madeira** bott code 8 Dec 10 db (90) n22 t23 f22.5 b22.5. I believe this saw the light of day only in miniature form. But there is no challenging the size of the whisky: Penderyn in its silkiest mode and allowing the fruit massive scope for flexing its grapy muscle...which it does with style. Big but simply charming. 46%. ncf.

⠿ **Penderyn Madeira** released 1 Jan 11 db (85.5) n21 t22 f21 b21.5. Comparatively niggardly on the fruit front and has really gone to town on the drier, pithy notes. Bit like the old days... 46%. ncf.

⠿ **Penderyn Madeira** released 1 Feb 11 db (94.5) n23.5 light liquorice holds the bourbon flag aloft while the juicy fruit of figs, greengages and grapes whisper volumes; t23.5 it is hard to remember a standard Penderyn landing being this soft and juicy: a rich custardy sweetness perfectly engulfs the mouth-watering fruit; the molten muscovado sugar is simply being wicked; f23.5 a slow lingering unveiling of that has gone on before, but some spices adding another delicious dimension; b24 one of the great standard Peneryn bottlings. 46%. ncf.

⠿ **Penderyn Madeira** bott code. Mar 11 db (92) n22.5 t23 f23.5 b23. Almost like a chocolate mousse poured over a fruit pudding. And a spicy one at that. Not quite hitting the overall heights of the previous monster bottling. But sensational nonetheless. 46%

⠿ **Penderyn Madeira** bott code. Apr 11 db (88.5) n21.5 t22 f23 b22. A much closer relation in style to the Penderyn 41 of March 2011 than the previous standard bottling. Lighter and less lusty with the fruit playing only a bit part by comparison. More room for some of the oakier spices to flourish and help make for a more salivating, feistier and, one might even argue, sophisticated malt. Delicious. 46%

⠿ **Penderyn Madeira** bott code. May 11 db (87.5) n20.5 t23 f22 b22. Similar score and enjoyment level as the previous month's bottling, but gets there by taking a different route. Indeed; this really is like the Penderyn 41 with more fruit and oils here and, whether it is the case or not, the impression of greater youth. The spices are a treat. 46%

Penderyn bott code 092909 (93.5) n23 here we go: soft traces of apricot and distilled fruit stone, caressed by vanilla and with the most delicate of bourbon-sweet edges; t23.5 mouth watering, lush, an early sprig of mint and then onto a much more powdery middle where both fruit and oak are eyeing each other up warily; f24 decides on the course it wishes to take, then rumbles along forever. Just a continuous interplay between sweet fruit and drier vanilla, but a light molassed caress to ensure the fruit stones never quite bitter out; the raisin dusted in cocoa powder on the finish is almost being cocky; b23 just couldn't have been more Welsh than any potential offSpring of Catherine Zeta Jones by Tom Jones, conceived while "How Green Is My Valley" was on the DVD player and a Shirley Bassey CD playing in the background. And that after downing five pints of Brains bitter after seeing Swansea City play Cardiff City at the Liberty Stadium, before going home to a plate of cawl while watching Wales beating England at rugby live on BBC Cymru. Yes, it is that unmistakably Penderyn; it is that perfectly, wonderfully and uniquely Welsh. 46%. ncf. Imported by Sazerac Company.

Penderyn bott code 1131008 (750ml) db (93.5) n22.5 a dark, baritone undercurrent to this one: the mushy fruit occasionally flies off on a high one but elsewhere there is more persistent deep murmur of beautifully fused grape and cocoa; t23.5 exactly the same on delivery: not often outside fresh oloroso that the evident fruit offers such deep base; the odd sparkier high notes carrying both grape and vanilla with aplomb. The middle ground fills in beautifully, shaped by soft oils and embracing the lightest of praline chocolate wafers; f23.5 no high notes at all here: a long, persistent rumble of fruit and praline with a spot-on degree of sweetness. A creaseless experience: a gentle, almost erotic massaging of the tastebuds ...; b24 the light cocoa infusion just tops this off perfectly. A truly classic Penderyn; more charm than Tom Jones, hitting just as many pure notes...and just being a fraction of his age 46%. US Market.

Penderyn 41 db (91.5) n22 delicate peach and bitter almond; a touch of apricot, too; t23 the Madeira coats the palate with first a light layer of soft grape, then a heavier one of skin and stone. Against the drier vanillas, the gristy sweetness of the barley is supported by the constant grape; f24 a charming fade of spiced butterscotch and lightly sweetened cocoa; b22.5 don't think for one moment it's the reduction of strength that makes this work so well. Rather, it is the outstanding integration of the outlandishly good Madeira casks with the vanilla. At usual strength this would have scored perhaps another couple of points. Oh, the lucky French for whom this was designed... 41%

Penderyn 41 bott code Sep 09 db **(91.5) n22** dry vanilla ice cream with peach and apricot ripple; **t23.5** luxurious delivery with a splendid diversity of delicately sweetened vanilla and soft fruit notes. Complex and sublimely balanced with a playful peppering of spices; **f23** varying levels of fruit and nut chocolate; **b23** tells a slightly different story to the first version of the "41", but tells it no less brilliantly. *41%*

Penderyn 41 code Feb 10 db **(89.5) n21** crushed fruit stones; **t23.5** soft and fruity delivery with a slow growth of sweeter sugars to spar with the spices; **f22.5** excellent oil development hangs on the gristy and dilute treacle sweetness to the not so bitter end; **b22.5** this sweeter bottling opts for a much more understated and easy-going approach with a notably more emphatic fruit input. A hat-trick of ultra-complex stunners from Penderyn...astonishing! *41%*

⋯ **Penderyn 41** released 3 Nov 10 db **(88) n21.5 t22 f22.5 b22.5**. Very similar to the Novemeber 1910 Release except fewer oils to carry the fruit and a bigger part played by drier, cocoa notes. *41%. ncf.*

⋯ **Penderyn 41** bott code. Mar 11 db **(84.5) n20 t21 f22 b21.5**. Had me worried at first: the nose and, to a lesser extent, delivery were unusually thin and niggardly. But recovers from the mid ground onwards with its usual fruity charm. *41%*

⋯ **Penderyn Bourbon Matured Single Cask** dist 2000 **(96) n24** although this has spent its entire life in what I assume to be a first fill bourbon cask, one of the sweeter notes here is more likely to be associated with a sauternes cask: that's the one with sticky honey and fruit in equal abundance. Elsewhere we are treated to a plethora of liquorice notes, both of the red and black variety, sandalwood coconut in treacle and, if you have enough hours in the day to devote to such matters, much else besides...; **t24.5** the delivery is an explosion of sugar and barley but the biggest bang reserved for the immediate spices; a number of vanilla and tannin notes arrive earlier than you might expect, while the oiliness is quite different to what is usually associated with this distillery; **f23.5** thins, by comparison, once the sugars have exhausted themselves. Dries as the oak gains the upper hand, but never so much that the barley is entirely lost or balance is compromised; **b24** Penderyn as rarely seen, even by me. This is as old a Welsh whisky that has been bottled in living memory. And it is one that will live in the memory of this current generation. For I have encountered very few whiskies which revels in a controlled sweetness on so many levels. This is so good, it is frightening. *61.2%*

Penderyn Peated Edition bott code Apr 08 db **(78) n18.5 t20 f19.5 b19**. Oily, clanking, thick whisky. Pleasant in part but something here just doesn't add up – on the nose especially. The most unsubtle Penderyn of them all. *46%. ncf.*

Penderyn Peated Edition bott code May 09 db **(92) n23.5 t23 f22 b23.5**. For those not of a peaty disposition, don't let the nose worry you: it plays only a character rather than leading role on the palate. Beautiful, anytime whisky. *46%*

Penderyn Peated Edition bott code Sep 09 db **(93.5) n23** you can almost count the peat molecules... **t24** a tantalising dusting of smoke over the juicy Chinese pear and an oilier malt thread; reaches its zenith at the midpoint when all these flavour profiles are still in play but joined also by mocha and raspberry jam; youthful and lithe; **f23** very long finish for a whisky which, for all its delicate smoke, always remains light and dextrous; **b23.5** a definitive case of where less is more: just the lightest smoke infusion helps cloak any disjointed notes, but is never heavy enough to allow the main flavour players full run. Fabulous. *46%*

Penderyn Peated Edition bott code Dec 09 db **(86) n21 t21 f22.5 b21.5**. Shows attitude throughout and an early over sweetness. Some rough edges are never quite blunted by the smoke and though the finish in particular keeps you entertained, it never gets close the magnificence of the September peated version. *46%*

Penderyn Peated Edition bott code May 10 db **(84) n21 t20 f22 b21**. The smoke at times can barely bother registering. When it does it tends to rail against fruits and oak to create a heated whisky in every sense. Stirring, enjoyable, roughhouse stuff and never for a moment a glass you can relax with. *46%*

Penderyn Port Wood Edition cask no. PORT 13 db **(96.5) n24 t24 f24 b24.5**. If you have five minutes to try a great whisky, don't bother with this one. This is a full half hour job. At least. One of those malts which never sits still, changing shape and form and refuses to tell quite the same story twice. Classic doesn't quite cover it...I doubt if even Swansea's much vaunted beautiful football is quite as beautiful as this: that was Spanish inspired...this is Portuguese perfection. *60.4%*

Penderyn Port Wood Edition cask no. PT26 db **(81) n18 t22 f21 b20**. Enormous, eye-watering, fruit delivery which all but bludgeons the taste buds into submission. Tightens alarmingly on arrival and then again towards the middle ground and finish. For all its might and magnitude, and occasional lip-smacking deliciousness, at times bitter, grouchy, cramped and, overall, just not in the same league as the previous, legendary, Port Wood Penderyn.

Having said all that, so different you just have to try it...!! One for the world's Whisky Clubs: I'd love to be a fly on the fall of the debates around this one... 60.6%

Penderyn Rich Madeira Limited Edition cask no. M3 **(96) n24.5 t24.5 f23 b24.** This whisky has moved on since that extraordinary bottling was presented to Prince Charles. In some ways it has gained, in others lost. But, quality-wise, it is impossible to separate them by anything wider than the width of a grape skin. Unquestionably one of the world whiskies of the year, and if anything crops up better in Europe we will have found something truly exceptional. This is the kind of whisky where if you can only get a bottle by swearing allegiance to the Principality of Wales, I for one would re-name my house Yaki Dah, eat nothing but leak soup and go back to find that girl I knew in Maesteg and have lots of Welsh-born sprogs. Second thought... giving up my Millwall season ticket for a Swansea one...now you're asking a bit too much... 54.3%

Penderyn Sherrywood Edition bott code Dec 09 db **(94.5) n22** firm; maybe a subtle hint of bitter cherry; **t24.5** envelops the mouth with a bosomy embrace: fat, succulent and something to alternately nibble and chew...; fruits pop into every crevice and spices aren't far behind; **f24.5** a quite beautiful spice pulse beats to the lip-smacking, cocoa-encrusted end; no bitterness, no off notes, just wave upon wave of unbelievable complexity: one of the greatest finishes in Wales since Ivor Allchurch was strutting his stuff at The Vetch; **b23.5** one of those whiskies which on first taste you think: Hmmm, a bit quiet. Ordinary..." On second taste you think: "hang on...what's going on here...?" Third taste: "ooh, I say..." Funny how it's the quiet ones you have to watch... 46%

⫶⫶⫶ **Penderyn Sherrywood Edition** released 1 Jan 11 db **(94) n23** a hint of salty olives and an almost apologetic, half-hearted move towards something vaguely sweet in the barley and fruit department. Sophisticated hardly covers it...; **t23.5** the wine immediately fills the palate but the oak has a great deal to say. Everything is clean, clearly defined and oozing quality and quiet confidence; **f23.5** more moody swings between salty dry and vaguely sweet – the gap between the two is severe; **b24** drier than the lips of a Welsh Male Voice Choir singing in the Sahara. But a whole lot more harmonious. If James Bond was into whisky, it would be this. 46%. ncf.

⫶⫶⫶ **Penderyn Sherrywood Limited Edition** cask no. 546 db **(95) n24** sticky toffee pudding, dates, mildly overcooked Christmas pudding, molasses, unsugared stewed apples...clean, complex and celebrating its own controlled enormity; oh, and those spices... mmmmm!!!! **t24** massive oils coat the mouth to ensure maximum impact with the exploding grape and almost earthy depth. Chocolate fudge, yet no hint of toffee, a fusion of medium roast Java with crisp Nicaraguan cocoa...yet somehow the barley, seemingly roasted, appears to come through amid the middle ground to make a telling impact...of its style, it simply doesn't get any better...; **f23** just a mere excellent finish – a bit of a letdown. The sharper more bitter elements of the grape are exposed...luckily enough there is any number of sugar style to make amends...; **b24** this is one of the world great whiskies of this and many a year. Penderyn's consultant, Jim Swan, is responsible for the use and selection of this cask. As was the case with the other single cask selections. It has meant an entire four hour tasting afternoon has been spent simply analysing those three astonishing casks. If all the world's whiskies were this good I'd never be able to get even close to completing the Bible. Welsh whisky has gone up an extra notch in the last year. The three single casks included here confirm that Penderyn has entered the stratosphere of magnificent whisky. Ignore this distillery entirely at your peril. 50%. ncf sc.

⫶⫶⫶ **Scotch Malt Whisky Society Cask 128.1 Aged 6 Years** 1st fill port barrique, cask no. PT3, dist 2003 **(93.5) n21.5** all kinds of fruit notes, few of which are even close to being in alignment with the other...; **t24.5** ...which is certainly not the case on the fantastic delivery. Gosh! I am reeling in my chair trying to come to terms with the enormity and faultless richness of all that is happening on my palate. Exploding grape, over-ripe greengages and sugar-laden dates. All that with a deep coffee and molassed note at the heart. One of the whisky mouthfuls of the year; **f23.5** the fruit seem to have generated their own oils and energy. The finish is so long, there is plenty of time for things to go wrong – but they don't. Dries, becomes toasty...but the magnificence barely diminishes..; **b24** for those single malt fundamentalists who think the SMWS have welshed on their ideals, here is confirming proof: Welsh whisky. But tell me. The drunken nose apart, which has probably robbed it of an award, just which part of this whisky is not fabulous...? 55.6%. sc. 233 bottles.

⫶⫶⫶ **Scotch Malt Whisky Society Cask 128.2 Aged 7 Years** 1st fill Madeira hogshead, cask no. M13, dist 2002 **(86.5) n22.5 t21 f22 b21.** A strange reversal to 128.1. The nose disintegrates but displays a rare magnificence on the palate while this has a very good nose but doesn't quite find its stride on the palate. Some serious bite, though. 60.5%. 227 bottles

World Whiskies

I have long said that whisky can be made just about anywhere in the world; that it is not writ large in stone that it is the inalienable right for just Scotland, Ireland, Kentucky and Canada to have it all to themselves. And so, it seems, it is increasingly being proved. Perhaps only sandy deserts and fields of ironstone can prevent its make physically and Islam culturally, though even that has not been a barrier to malt whisky being distilled in both Pakistan and Turkey. While not even the world's highest mountains or jungle can prevent the spread of barley and copper pot.

Outside of North America and Europe, whisky's traditional nesting sites, you can head in any direction and find it being made. South America may be well known for its rum, but in the south of Brazil, an area populated by Italian and German settlers many generations back, malt whisky is thriving. In even more lush and tropical climes it can now also be found, with Taiwan and Thailand leading the way.

Japan has long represented Asia with distinction and whisky-making there is in such an advanced state and at a high standard Jim Murray's Whisky Bible has given it its own section. But while neighbouring South Korea has ended its malt distilling venture, further east, and at a very unlikely altitude, Nepal has forged a small industry to team up, geographically, with fellow malt distillers India and Pakistan. The one malt whisky from this region making inroads in world markets is India's Amrut single malt. Actually, inroads is hardly doing them justice. Full-bloodied trailblazing, more like. So good now is their whisky they were, with their fantastically complex brand, Fusion deservedly awarded Jim Murray's Whisky Bible 2010 Third Finest Whisky in the World. That represented a watershed not just for the distillery, but Indian whisky as a whole and in a broader sense the entire world whisky movement: it proved beyond doubt that excellent distilling and maturation wherever you are on this planet will be recognised and rewarded.

Africa is also represented on the whisky stage. There has long been a tradition of blending Scotch malt with South African grain but now there is single malt there, as well. Two malt distilleries, to be precise, with a second being opened at the Drayman's Brewery in Pretoria. I was supposed to have visited it a little while back, but the distiller, obviously not wanting to see me, went to the trouble of falling off his horse and breaking his thigh the actual day before. Wimp.

One relatively new whisky-making region is due immediate further study: Australia. From a distance of 12,000 miles, the waters around Australia's distilleries appear to be muddied. Quality appears to range from the very good to extremely poor. And during the back end of 2004 I managed to discover this first hand when I visited three Tasmanian distilleries and Bakery Hill in Melbourne which perhaps leads the way regarding quality malt whisky made south of the Equator. Certainly green shoots are beginning to sprout at the Tasmania Distillery which has now moved its operation away from its Hobart harbour site to an out of town one close to the airport. The first bottlings of that had been so bad that it will take some time and convincing for those who have already tasted it to go back to it again. However, having been to the warehouse – and having tasted samples from every single cask they have on site – I reported in previous Bibles that it was only a matter of time before those first offerings would be little more than distant – though horrific – memories. Well, as predicted, it is now safe to put your head above the parapet. The last cask strength bottling I tasted was a bloody beaut. For this year's Jim Murray's Whisky Bible 2012, I have again managed to taste the latest whiskies from the Timboon Railway Shed, The Nant and the Great Southern distilleries, each of which managed to offer something which, for the second year running, scored above 90. Together they represent one of the highlights of world whisky. That is a quite staggering achievement and one which means that I now have no option but to start thumbing through an Atlas and flight timetable to get back over there pronto. The remaining casks of Wilson's malt from New Zealand are disappearing fast and when in New Zealand I discovered the stills from there were not just making rum in Fiji but whisky as well. We are all aware of the delights of island whisky, but a Pacific Island malt? Which leaves Antarctica as the only continent not making whisky, though what some of those scientists get up to for months on end no one knows.

ARGENTINA
Blends
Breeders Choice (84) n21 t22 f21 b20. A sweet blend using Scottish malt and, at the helm, an unusually lush Argentinian grain. 40%

AUSTRALIA
BAKERY HILL DISTILLERY 1999. Operating.
Bakery Hill Classic Malt cask no. 2308 db (87) n22 t22 f21.5 b21.5. Enjoyable. But not a patch on its cask strength version. 46%

Bakery Hill Classic Malt cask no. 3009 db (81) n21 t21.5 f18.5 b20. Malty and sawdusty. Feints inject some weight and bitters. 46%

Bakery Hill Classic Malt cask no. 3108 db (82) n20 t21 f20.5 b20.5 More than a hint of feints amid the oily barley. 46%

Bakery Hill Classic Malt Cask Strength cask no. 2308 db (92) n23 t23.5 f22.5 b23. Here's incontrovertible proof that whisky does not necessarily improve with the addition of water. Where the 46% version of this is bitty and just keeps itself together for a decent innings, this one has all the oils in full flow ensuring something rich and magnificent. 60.2%

Bakery Hill Classic Malt Cask Strength cask no. 3108 db (82.5) n20.5 t21 f20.5 b20.5. Cask strength feintiness. 60.2%

Bakery Hill Classic Malt Cask Strength bourbon cask no. 4510 db (89) n23 big barley with a thick liquorice and caramelised ginger strata; t22.5 crystallised barley sugar on delivery; fattens as the oils arrive, as does the light honey and spice; f22 a thick coating of malt clings on forever; b22 talk about going back in time: it is 1994 and I am in a warehouse in Dunedin going through the earliest existing casks of Lammerlaw New Zealand malt. The closest thing to it. 60.5%

Bakery Hill Classic Malt Cask Strength bourbon cask no. 5710 db (83) n21.5 t21.5 f19.5 b20.5. One seriously sweet bottling. Plenty of nougat and honey. 60.5%

Bakery Hill Double Wood cask no. 3536 db (78.5) n21 t20 f18 b19.5. Citrus and feints. 46%

Bakery Hill Double Wood bourbon & French oak cask no. 5855 db (86.5) n22.5 t22.5 f20.5 b21. Substantial whisky with a delightful chocolate fruit and nut core. Chewy and enjoyably macho. 46%

Bakery Hill Peated Malt cask no. 2408 db (86.5) n22 t21.5 f21.5 b21.5. Very lightly peated, this actually has more of a Cadbury's Whole Nut character than an all out smoky one. Chewy and very enjoyable. 46%

Bakery Hill Peated Malt cask no. 2507 db (83) n21 t22 f19 b21. Another big mouth filler with the smoke little more than a distant cloud. Pretty bitter at the death. 46%

Bakery Hill Peated Malt bourbon cask no. 6209 db (88.5) n22 firm, flinty phenols; t23 crisp barley; crunchy brown sugars alongside the peat; f21 over-baked caramelised biscuit b22.5 spic and span, matter of fact malt. 46%

Bakery Hill Peated Malt Cask Strength cask no. 2507 db (84.5) n20.5 t22 f20.5 b21.5. Again a much more rotund and confident malt at this strength with a sweetness that falls between chocolate-liquorice and light molasses. But the nose, like the finish, has some unresolved issues. 60.7%

Bakery Hill Peated Malt Cask Strength French oak cask no. 6009 db (92.5) n23.5 heavyweight stuff: fruity and phenolic; a few spices march around; t24 and those spices come up trumps on delivery: a huge arrival with a big soft juicy backdrop acting as a stark contrast; the smoke resurfaces gingerly; f22.5 elegant fade with the fruit having been vanquished by the vanilla, spices and soft smoke; b22.5 I remember when Talisker had this kind of spice attack. Virtually every phase of this malt works fabulously: a truly wonderful piece of distilling and maturation. 60%

Bakery Hill Peated Malt Cask Strength bourbon cask no 6810 db (87) n22.5 the peat is so distant, it could be on the other side of the world...; t22 the mouth is washed in sweet barley. Some smoke nonchalantly hangs around; f21 bitter oak; b21.5 not the kindest cask, but the peat is intriguing. 60%

BOOIE RANGE DISTILLERY
Booie Range Single Malt db (72) n14 t20 f19 b19. Mounts the hurdle of the wildly off-key nose impressively with a distinct, mouth watering barley richness to the palate that really does blossom even on the finish. 40%

LARK DISTILLERY
The Lark Distillery Single Malt Whisky cask LD38, bott Apr 09 db (88.5) n22.5 a few feints, but some sexy mocha is the bait... t22 oily (no surprise there given the nose) but a

real cranking up of intense barley and cocoa; **f22** sweetens with a touch of dry molasses with an oily vanilla-barley fade; **b22** distiller Kristy Lark has taken a liberty or two here with her cut...and somehow got away with it. That's women distillers for you... *43%*

The Lark Distillery Single Malt Whisky Cask Strength cask no. LD100, bott Oct 08 db **(93.5) n23.5** I remember celery was part of the profile a little while back: here it is again, peppered rather than salted; **t24** fabulous fruit take off: juicy from a grape as well as a barley perspective, roasty and a late build up of intense spice; **f23** vanilla injection but the white peppers hangs around the tongue for quite some while... **b23** a stupendous bottling from Larks, brimming with impossible character and probably the best of theirs I have ever encountered. Did Kristy accidentally leave a pepper pot in the still or something...? *58%*

The Lark Distillery Single Malt Whisky Cask Strength cask no. LD140, bott Feb 10 db **(80) n19.5 t18.5 f22 b20.** From tip to tail there is a note on this I can't quite put my finger on, or say I much approve of. But there is also a real coppery small still feel to this, bolstered by a late-developing honeycomb and Demerara sheen. *58%*

The Lark Distillery Single Malt Whisky Distillers Selection cask LD99, bott Feb 09 db **(82) n21 t19 f21 b21.** Well there's one to get your kisser round! The nose has almost a toothpaste-y, minty edge and though the delivery doesn't seem quite on the button it recovers impressively enough for a real ol' oak and cocoa dust up further down the track. Not quite up to this distillery's usual high standards, though. *46%*

The Lark Distillery Single Malt Whisky Distillers Selection cask no. LD109, bott Apr 10 db **(86.5) n21.5 t21 f22.5 b21.5.** A chunky affair with some attractive nougat and orange; the star turn is the Rolo candy finale. *46%*

LIMEBURNERS

Limeburners Single Malt Whisky Barrel M23 bott no. 78 db **(90.5) n22.5** firm, grapey brandy with a wine gum sweetness; on another level, young barley pulses its malty theme; **t23.5** beautiful mouth feel: my word, this is well made spirit! Silky and no spirit burn despite the strength, with the taste buds bathed in uncluttered grape and powering malt; **f22** long with a dash of liquorice to thicken the grape further; **b22.5** first time I've tasted anything from this Western Australian mob. G'day fellas! I have to admit, thought it might have been from France at first, as the aroma on nosing blind reminded me of brandy. And not without good reason, it transpires. This no age statement malt spent an unspecified amount of time in American brandy cask before being finished in bourbon casks. Does it work? Yes it does. But now that's torn it lads. You are supposed to start off with a bloody horrible whisky and get better. Now you have gone and made a rod for your own back. Good on you! *61%*

Limeburners Single Malt Whisky Barrel M27 bott no. 47 db **(73) n18 t19 f17 b19.** Malty, but feinty, too. Probably not had the happiest fermentation, either. *43%*

Limeburners Single Malt Whisky Barrel M31 bott no. 293 db **(85.5) n21.5 t22 f21 b21.** Pouting, semi-spiced up sultana fruitcake, complete with a delicate nuttiness; full on in part, yet curiously weightless. *43%. ncf. Great Southern Distilling Co.*

⠿ **Limeburners Single Malt Whisky M64 Muscat Finish** db **(92) n23.5** another big grapey statement from Limeburners. The fruit is thick, clean, sugar-soaked and dripping from the barley; the playful spices on the oak are to die for; **t23** the big alcohol combines perfectly with the seemingly bigger grape and muscular malt. On one hand puckering, on the other, too juicy to be true; **f22.5** a salty finale sits well with the persistent clean grape; **b23** macho malt keeps in touch with its feminine side. Tasty and beautifully made. *61%. ncf.*

⠿ **Limeburners Single Malt Whisky M67 Sherry Butt Finish** db **(86) n21.5 t22 f21 b21.5.** a huge whisky. However, a few cracks which aren't quite papered over despite the magnificent body and chewiness. The main cocoa theme is a corker. *61%. ncf.*

THE NANT DISTILLERY

The Nant Single Malt First Release bott 2010 db **(91.5) n24** all the hallmarks of virgin oak giving it large; beautifully supported by medium roast Java and dreamy fruit: there's a statement of intent for you...; **t23** juicy, intense...and yet that big oak only serves to whip the complexity, with a kumquat and liquorice thread tying in to that persistent coffee perfectly; **f22** some fizzing spice and vanilla; **b22.5** beyond excellent for a first go. The flavours and style could not be more clearly nailed to the mast. I'll be watching this distillery closely. *43%*

⠿ **The Nant 3 Year Old** American oak/Port db **(91.5) n22.5** the aroma of a wine cask hit twice a day by the incoming tide; the odd kumquat sideshow; **t22** delicate evolving of fruit, though the barley remains in control; the oak drives some caramel into the fray, but with excellent understatement; **f23** confirmation of the big salt statement on the nose: some late oils (from the slightly wider cut they managed to get away with) drags some late barley into the picture **b24** beautifully well made whisky. Has the sophistication of a dry martini, but without the olive...yet maintaining the salt. Last year I set out to keep my eyes on these chaps. Not a bad move. *43%*

⟨⋰⟩ **The Nant 3 Years Old Cask Strength** American oak bourbon db **(95.5) n23** several layers of honey and a Sauterenes cask style fruitiness. Where is that coming from...? So big and voluptuous: you don't know whether to go on and drink it or make love to it...; **t24** I'm drinking it: good choice! The malt is obviously young because how else can you get this degree of barley enormity? Juicy, thick and, though carrying a little bit of feint, adorable for its profound richness. Again, some fruit notes wander in from somewhere, and once more they are the kind of orangey-grapey notes one usually associates with Sauterenes. Very odd. **f24** Ridiculously long. You can almost wear your tongue out against the roof of your mouth. Soft muscovado sugars with the lightest touch of honey, liquorice and maple syrup. The vanillas build and then give way to tasty butterscotch; **b24.5** I have really got to get back to Oz to visit these guys. Something majestic is happening here. Whatever it is they are doing, I have to discover first hand...World class. *61.6%*

SMALL CONCERN DISTILLERY

Cradle Mountain Pure Tasmanian Malt db **(87) n21** curiously vivid bourbon character; sweet vanilla with hints of tangerine and hazelnut. Really very, very attractive; **t22** an almost perfect translation onto the palate: gloriously sweet and gently nutty. The mouthfeel and body is firm and oily at the same time, the barley sparkles as the oak fades. Exceptionally subtle, clean and well made; **f21** pretty long with some cocoa offering a praline effect; **b23** a knock-out malt from a sadly now lost distillery in Tasmania. Faultlessly clean stuff with lots of new oak character but sufficient body to guarantee complexity. *43%*

SOUTHERN COAST DISTILLERS

⟨⋰⟩ **Southern Coast Single Malt Batch 001** db **(92.5) n23** crisp with varying layers of muscovado sugars; clean (well, a little bit of forgivable wide-ish cut apart, offering haystack barley amongst other delights) yet with a distinct Highland Park style honey and heather; **t24** magnificently crisp, sugar-crusted barley. Some fabulous oils (from that cut) counter the firm, spicy nature; **f22** more spice but with vanilla and cocoa; **b23.5** "a hint of bushfire in the barley" claims the back label. Well, that one's got me stumped: I pride myself in nosing anything and everything, but that particular aroma has passed me by. Perhaps they mean the heather aroma...? Mind you, I did get pretty close to some scary forest fires near Marseilles nearly 30 years ago, but probably not the same thing... Anyway, back to this fabulous first effort. Wow! Could ask for more in a study of crisp brown sugars and sweet cocoa...; *46%*

⟨⋰⟩ **Southern Coast Single Malt Batch 002** db **(96) n24** I am in Guyana. I am tucked into a warm warehouse. And I have my head stuck in a 20- possibly 25-year-old barrel of pre-caramelised pot still rum. Right...? Wow. Magnificent. **t23.5** OK. That coffee flavour. The toffees. The soft oils and broiling sugars. The immeasurable juices. I am still in Guyana. Right? **f24.5** the kind of coffee and confident but fragile elegance you find in a Guyanan pot still; sultanas and burnt raisins run amok; walnut cake and cream...bloody hell...???? What is this...????? **b24** is this the best Australian whisky ever to shamelessly masquerade as Demerara pot still rum? I should think so. Will it ever be beaten? I doubt it. In fact, just how many Demerara rums have I ever tasted of this refinement. One or two, at most. And I have probably tasted more than anyone in the whisky trade living. One of the most astonishing whiskies it has been my honour to taste. Frankly, I am on my knees... *46%*

⟨⋰⟩ **Southern Coast Single Malt Batch 003** db **(79.5) n18 t19 f23 b19.5.** Third time unlucky. Lots of oils and berserk honey. But too feinty, though this went to some finishing school, believe me...! *46%. ncf.*

TASMAN DISTILLERY

Great Outback Rare Old Australian Single Malt db **(92) n24** I could stick my nose in a glass of this all day. This is sensational: more a question of what we don't have here! The malt is clean, beautifully defined and dovetails with refined, orangey-citrus notes. The oak is near perfection adding only a degree of tempered weight. I don't detect peat, but there is some compensating Blue Mountain coffee; **t24** just so beautifully textured with countless waves of clean, rich malt neither too sweet nor too dry. This is faultless distillate; **f21** lightens considerably with the oak vanilla dominating. **b23** What can you say? An Australian whisky distillery makes a malt to grace the world's stage. But you can't find it outside of Australia. This will have to be rectified. *40%*

TASMANIA DISTILLERY

Old Hobart db **(69) n16 t19 f17 b17**. The nose still has some way to go before it can be accepted as a mainstream malt, though there is something more than a little coastal about it this time. However, the arrival on the palate is another matter and I must say I kind of enjoyed its big, oily and increasingly sweet maltiness and crushed sunflower seed nuttiness towards the end. Green (and yellow) shoots are growing. The whisky is unquestionably getting better. 60%

Sullivan's Cove db **(61) n13 t15 f17 b16**. Some malt but typically grim, oily and dirty; awesomely weird. 40%. Australia.

⁖· **Sullivan's Cove Bourbon Matured Cask Strength Single Cask** barrel no: HH0602, barrel date 21 Feb 01, bott 10 Sep 09 **(81) n18 t24 f20 b19**. An outrageous maltfest, for all its obvious faults. "Distilled with Conviction" the label proudly states, a reference to Tasmania's penal past. But it looks as though the stillman has made his escape as the nose suggests the eye wasn't being kept on the ball as feints abound. Ironically, the resulting extra oils mean the youthful but hugely intense malt simply blows you away. Technically, a nightmare. But you know what? I just love it...!!! (To ramp it up about five or six points, pour into a glass and place in hot water to burn off the higher alcohols. What remains after about five minutes, depending on the temperature of the water, is a much cleaner, more honeyed version). 60%

TIMBOON RAILWAY SHED DISTILLERY

Timboon Single Malt Whisky port cask, dist May 08, bott Jun 10 db **(85) n22.5 t20.5 f21 b21**. Fruity and edgy, almost closer to the botanicals in gin (minus juniper) than single malt. There is a background rumble which is quite unique. Ever seen those war films where the guy manning the radar on the sub detects something, yet despite all his experience cannot quite fathom what it is that ping is telling him? Well that's me with this whisky: I need to get out there to find out what this one is all about. In the meantime, not to be confused with Tim Boon, the England cricket coach who helped plot the downfall of the Aussies in the 2005 Ashes series... 40%

⁖· **Timboon Single Malt Whisky** dist Aug 08, bott May 11 db **(93) n24.5** quite possibly the most complex nose I have come across for a while. Certainly the most fragile. Sometimes I can barely hear what is being said. The orange blossom, bedecked in wisps of thin acacia honey, is stunning; **t23** pastel shades of honey and barley. A little amplification might see off the dogmatic oak; **f22** sawdusty vanilla...and more hints of orange and honey; **b23.5** imagine Tim Boon, the cricketer, going out to face the current England pace attack with one of those foot-long bats used exclusively for players to sign. That, basically, is what we have here with a malt underpowered for the type of job it is capable of doing. Yes, its technique is extraordinary. Certainly, it has moved to the pitch of the barley and is in line with what's coming with rare textbook elegance. But the strength is too feeble to translate into the highest score that it deserves. That said, quality is quality. And this is strictly First Class. 40%

YALUMBA WINERY

Smith's Angaston Whisky Vintage 1997 Aged 7 Years db **(88) n20** an attractive, if not entirely faultless, combination of barley and fruit sewn together by honey; **t22** an almost implausible silkiness to this: the barley and honey tip-toe over the tastebuds using a touch of oil to help them glide as well; **f23** now we have some serious complexity with the fruits showing a berry-like sharpness, but it's all very effete; **b23** easily one of the most delicate whiskies of the year and one that puts Samuel Smith on the map. Perfect for the hipflask for a night at the ballet. 40%

Smith's Angaston Whisky Vintage 1998 Aged 8 Years db **(86) n20 t22 f22 b22**. Perhaps conscious that their first offering, a genuine touch of culture that it was, wasn't quite Bruce enough to called Australian, this one's showing bit of aggression. And I mean a bit, as this is no tackle from Lucas Neil. Because after the delivery it's back to the girlie stuff with some admittedly delicious Swiss Roll filling fruitiness. Lovely malt from a distillery I'm going to have to keep my eyes on. 40%

Vatted Malts

Tasmanian Double Malt Whisky Unpeated (87.5) n22 muscovado sugar and vanilla; **t22** delightfully slick mouth with feel egg yolks and sugar: half way to a cake mix...; sugared vanillas form the mid ground; **f21.5** powdery oak with a spurt of lemon; **b22** not a chance of getting bored with this guy. A sweet tooth would be useful. 43%. The Nant Distillery.

BRAZIL
HEUBLEIN DISTILLERY
Durfee Hall Malt Whisky db (81) n18 t22 f20 b21. Superbly made whisky; the intensity of the malt is beautifully layered without ever becoming too sweet. Very light bodied and immaculately clean. Good whisky by any standards. *43%*

UNION DISTILLERY
Barrilete db (72) n18 t19 f18 b17. Nothing particularly wrong with it technically; it just lacks vitality. Thin but extremely malt intense. *39.1%*

Blends
Cockland Gold Blended Whisky (73) n18 t18 f19 b18. Silky caramel. Traces of malt there, but never quite gets it up. *38%. Fante.*

Drury's Special Reserve (86.5) n21.5 t22 f21 b22. Deceptively attractive, melt-in-the-mouth whisky; at times clean, regulation stuff, but further investigation reveals a honeycomb edge which hits its peak in the middle ground when the spices mix in beautifully. One to seek out and savour when in Brazil. *40%. Campari, Brasil.*

Gold Cup Special Reserve (84.5) n21 t22.5 f20 b21. Ultra soft, easily drinkable and, at times, highly impressive blend which is hampered by a dustiness bestowed upon it by the nagging caramels on both nose and finish. Some lovely early honey does help lift it, though, and there is also attractive Swiss roll jam towards the finish. Yet never quite gets out of third gear despite the most delicate hint of smoke. *39%. Campari, Brasil.*

Gran Par (77) n19.5 t22 f17.5 b18. The delivery is eleven seconds of vaguely malty glory. The remainder is thin and caramelled with no age to live up to the name. And with Par in the title and bagpipes and kilt in the motif, how long before the SWA buys a case of it...? *39%*

Green Valley Special Reserve batch 07/01 (70) n16 t19 f17 b18. A softly oiled, gently bitter-sweet blend with a half meaty, half boiled sweet nose. An unusual whisky experience. *38.1%. Muraro & Cia.*

Malte Barrilete Blended Whisky batch 001/03 (76) n18 t20 f19 b19. This brand has picked up a distinctive apple-fruitiness in recent years and some extra oak, too. *39.1%.*

Natu Nobilis (81.5) n22.5 t20 f19 b20. The nose boasts a genuinely clean, Speyside-style malt involvement. But to taste is much more non-committal with the soft grain dominating and the grassy notes restricted the occasional foray over the tastebuds. Pleasant, but don't expect a flavor fest. *39%. Pernod Ricard, Brasil.*

Natu Nobilis Celebrity (86) n22.5 t22 f20.5 b21. A classy blend with a decent weight and body, yet never running to fat. Some spice prickle ensures the flavor profile never settles in a neautral zone and the charming, citrus-domiated malt on the nose is immediately found on the juicy delivery. A cut above the standard Natu Nobilis and if the finish could be filled out with extra length and complexity, we'd have an exceptionally impressive blend on our hands. Another blend to seek out whenever in Brazil. *39%. Pernod Ricard, Brasil.*

O Monge batch 02/02 (69) n17 t18 f17 b17. Poor nose but it recovers with a malty mouth arrival but the thinness of the grain does few favours. *38.5%. Union Distillery.*

Old Eight Special Reserve (85.5) n20 t21 f22.5 b22. Traditionally reviled by many in Brazil, I can assure you that the big bite followed by calming soft grains is exactly what you need after a day's birding in the jungle. *39%. Campari, Brasil.*

Pitt's (84) n21 t20 f22 b21. The pits it certainly aint!! A beautifully malted blend where the barley tries to dominate the exceptionally flinty grain whenever possible. Due to be launched later in 2004, this will be the best Brazil has to offer – though some fine tuning can probably improve the nose and middle even further and up the complexity significantly. I hope, when I visit the distillery early in 2005, I will be able to persuade them to offer a single malt: on this evidence it should, like Pitt's, be an enjoyable experience and perfect company for any World Cup finals. *40%. Busnello Distillery.*

Wall Street (84) n23 t22 f19 b20. Fabulous nose with a sexy citrus-light smoke double bill. And the arrival on the palate excels, too, with a rich texture and confident delivery of malt, again with the smoke dominating. But falls away rather too rapidly as the grains throw the balance out of kilter and ensures too much bitter oak late on. *38%. Pernod Ricard, Brasil.*

INDIA
AMRUT DISTILLERY
Amrut Single Malt bott 2008 db (91.5) n22.5 t23.5 f22.5 b23. Taking it up that extra 6% abv has made a significant difference as this is stupendous stuff! I had a little moan with

the distillers about the slight use of caramel here which helps neither the nose nor finish. They called back the next day to tell me they had considered my comments and decided to drop the use of caramel in all future bottlings of Amrut altogether: Power to the Whisky Bible! 46%

Amrut Single Malt oak barrels, bott no. 15, bott Feb 10 db **(93.5) n23** Malted Milk biscuits dunked in coffee; the distinctive aroma of melting Demerara sugar adds a piquancy to the sweetness, as do the sharp kumquats; **t24** that is so beautiful: about as relaxed and confident a malt as you'll find anywhere in the world. The malt is refreshing, though in concentrated malt shake form, but this is punctuated by a busy but understated oak infusion, led again by that distinctive orangey-citrus note found on the nose; **f23** long, with a late bourbon liquorice flourish, but creamy and light with those sugars lasting the distance with ease; **b23.5** as good as their word: Amrut with no colouring as promised following a campaign by the Whisky Bible. And it pays off as the astonishingly intrinsic qualities of this fine whisky, fudgeless for the first time, is now there for all to see. Incredibly similar to their cask strength bottling of a year or two ago, proving there really is a formulated house style. 46%

⁙ **Amrut Single Malt** batch 27, bott Mar 11 db **(92.5) n23** wow! How weird was that? Put the glass under my nose and...Lammerlaw! I was flown to New Zealand and taken back the best part of 20 years as the aroma showed so many aspects of the malt from that now sadly defunct distillery. Never noticed it on any Amrut before, even when I went through their stocks in the distillery warehouses. Beautifully light with the vanillas dancing on a malty, lightly salty breeze; the bourbon casks are tipping in just-so amounts of hickory; where the Lammerlaw effect comes into its own is with the citrusy haze to the sawdusty oak: a long time since I last encountered that particular timbre **t24** stunning sugars melt effortlessly into the honey-lemon theme; a succession of bourbon-style tones – honeycomb, hickory and liquorice mainly – melt effortlessly into the mix; spices, too...well, it is Indian... **f22.5** light and a little lazy, some spices think about adding to the vanilla, but can't be too fussed; **b23.5** an assured, elegant malt which now strides greatness with nonchalance. 46%. nc ncf.

Amrut Cask Strength oak barrels, bott no. 01, bott Jul 09 db **(89.5) n23** some alpha oak whips up an orangey lead and some major caramels; **t22.5** surging, eye-watering barley: sharp, grassy and youthful at first. Then onrushing caramels make for a much softer second half; **f22** sweet, with a relatively simple barley-caramel fade; **b22** another big malty tale from India. But there is a big surge of natural, oily caramels to this one which keeps the complexity levels marginally down. 61.8%

⁙ **Amrut Cask Strength** batch 5, bott Jun 10 db **(84) n21 t22 f20 b21.** Just a little extra aging here has brought a telling degree of caramel into play, swamping much else. Pleasant, but a reminder of just how fragile the line between greatness and just plain, old-fashioned good. 61.8%. nc ncf.

Amrut Double Cask ex-bourbon cask no. 2874/2273, bott no. 44, bott Feb 10 db **(96) n23** a parade of delicate, natural caramels does not detract from the complexity: dried dates and figs offer a thickening sweetness; there is even room for a more floral note...perhaps befitting how this is from the India's garden city...; **t24.5** now defies belief: a combination of thumping, heady oaks but miraculously offset by the softest yet juiciest barley and intense vanilla and biscoito de polvilho so you barely notice the impact; the spices are pandering to the taste buds by offering a playful excursion from the growing sweetness; some quietly chattering orangey notes add further complexity and balance; **f24** long, not a shard of bitterness as might be expected from the demands upon the barrels, which means those vanillas, increasingly nutty and oily, have a perfect chewy journey to the finish; **b24.5** frankly, a malt I thought I'd never see: how can a whisky survive seven years under the unremitting Bangalore sun? I am proud of the very small part I played in seeing this wonderful whisky see the world: I tasted both casks, containing the oldest whisky Amrut had ever produced, in a cellar at the distillery earlier in the year and passed both not only fit but exceptional. But I made the observation that they would certainly be better still if mixed together as the personalities of both casks very much complimented the other. On the day the younger of the two casks turned seven years old, this they did and bottled it. And just to show how wonderful this whisky is, from now what must surely be from one of the top two or three malt whisky distilleries in the world, simply leave an empty glass of it by your bedside table and smell it first thing in the morning. 46%. 306 bottles.

Amrut Fusion batch no. 01, bott Mar 09 db **(97) n24** heavy, thickly oaked and complex: some curious barley-sugar notes here shrouded in soft smoke. Big, but seductively gentle, too... **t24** the delivery, though controlled at first, is massive! Then more like con-fusion as that smoke on the nose turns into warming, full blown peat, but it far gets its own way as a vague sherry trifle note (curious, seeing how there are no sherry butts involved) – the custard presumably is oaky vanilla - hammers home that barley-fruitiness to make for a bit of a free-for-all; but for extra food measure the flavours develop into a really intense chocolate fudge middle which absolutely resonates through the palate; **f24** a slight struggle here as the mouthfeel gets a bit puffy here with the dry peat and oak; enough molassed sweetness to see the malt through to a satisfying end, though. Above all the spices, rather than lying down and accepting their fate, rise up and usher this extraordinary whisky to its exit; **b25** one of the most complex and intriguing new whiskies of the year that needs about two days and half a bottle to get even close to fathoming. Not exactly a textbook whisky, with a few edges grinding together like tectonic plates. And there is even odd note, like the fruit and a kind of furry, oaky buzz, which I have never seen before. But that is the point of whiskies like this: to be different, to offer a unique slant. But, ultimately, to entertain and delight. And here it ticks all boxes accordingly. To the extent that this has to be one of the great whiskies found anywhere in the world this year. And the fact it is Indian? Irrelevant: from distillation to maturation this is genius whisky, from whichever continent... *50%*

⁘ **Amrut Fusion** batch 10, bott Mar 11 db **(94.5) n24** playful smoke mingles with Slovakian milk chocolate and crushed almond; for all the brooding oak much lighter than the original bottling but still an essay in complexity; **t24** the sugars are the first to show: the molten stuff on porridge variety. The barley has its big moment four or five flavour-waves in when it turns up the juicy volume; the vanillas grab the middle ground while the smoke hesitates; **f22.5** compared to the first bottling relatively short, though those spices, the remnants of the smoke, continue to buzz - if a little shy about it. Soft, sweetened cocoa marks the fade; **b23.5** superb whisky, though to be plotted on a different map to the now legendary Whisky Bible award-winning Batch 1. This is a much more delicate affair: more hints and shadows rather than statements and substance. Still, though, a fabulous malt whisky in Amrut's best style. *50%. nc.*

⁘ **Amrut Herald** cask no. 2857 db **(92) n23** nutty, north German marzipan smeared with bourbony liquorice; toasty and weighty; **t24** that unique, near perfect Amrut texture on delivery: softly oiled with more than a hint of crème brulee; however, it is the second round of flavours – a spice and molasses mix which really gets the taste buds tingling; **f22** big cream toffee with a dab of lingering spice; **b23** here is the news: Amrut have come up with another fabulous whisky. Actually, the news these days is when they don't... *60.8%. sc. 231 bottles.*

Amrut Intermediate Sherry Matured bott no. 01, bott Jun 10 db **(96.5) n24.5** instead of the usual biscuit aroma, we now get moist cake. And my word: is it fruity and spicy!! Love the freshly waxed oak floor, too. Brain-explodingly complex and multi-layered with one of the most intriguing sherry-style-bourbon-style marriages on the market; **t24** cracking delivery and entirely unique in form. The structure is decidedly oak-based, but acts as no more than a skeleton from which the juicy sultana and spices drape. Salivating, too, as the barley kicks in powerfully. But the liquorice-orangey-honeycomb bourbon theme quietly shapes the flavour profile; the spices pulse and glow; **f23.5** quite a chunk of natural caramel quietens the more exuberant characteristics; long and elegant; **b24.5** how do you get three freshly emptied oloroso butts from Jerez to Bangalore without the casks spoiling, and not use sulphur? Answer: empty two cases of Amrut cask strength whisky into each of the butts before shipping them. Not a single off note. No bitterness whatsoever. And the fruit is left to impart its extraordinary riches on a malt matured also in American oak. Amrut is spoiling us again... *57.1%*

Amrut Peated batch no. 1, bott Sep 08 db **(94) n23** unusually dry peat; not dissimilar to peat reek absorbed by an old leather armchair; a hint of citrus, too; **t24** despite the nose, the immediate sensation is one of being caressed by molassed sugar and then a ratching up of the peat notes. As they get more forceful, so the experience becomes that little bit drier and spicier, though not without the molasses refusing to give way; **f23.5** you can tell the quality of the distillate and the barrels it has been matured in by the crystalline depth to the finish. Everything is clear on the palate and the butterscotch vanillas wrap the phenols for a comfortable and clean finale; **b23.5** absolutely everything you could ask for a peated malt at this strength. The length and complexity are matched only by a train journey through this astonishing country. *46%*

Amrut Peated Cask Strength bott Apr 08 db **(92) n22** gristy smoked barley, kippers with a salted butter, peppered bite; **t22.5** the delivery is youthful and barely reaching puberty then suddenly an intensely malty ascendancy followed by a healthy dose of drier oaks; **f24.5** a sublime finale for its sheer delicacy and elegance; the peat no more than oozes, there are cups galore of sugarless medium roast Mysore and finally, as a bourbony trail is discovered, soft liquorice and molassed sugar – easily the highlight of the experience: one of the best finishes of the year... **b23** a touch of youth to this guy but the finish, entirely uncluttered by unnatural caramel or deprived by filtration, confirms a degree of greatness. By the way: if you want to experience something really stunning, trying mixing the 2007 and 2008 peated. When you get the proportions right...well, watch out Islay...!! *62.78%*

⋄ **Amrut Portonova** db **(93)** n22 a thick pudding of a nose; fruit and caramel have merged into one slightly over-oaked soup; burnt apple pie; **t24** this is essentially a port pipe sandwich...and it shows. The spicy, jammy fruit is interwoven through any amount of caramel while the oaky saltiness gets the taste buds both salivating and puckering until you run dry; **f24** long, massive oak with quite evident traces of the virgin barrels now detectable. And more of a cocoa hue as it progresses. At last some muscovado sugars arrive to supplant the berry fruits; **b23** this is a whisky so big, so blinding that when I first tasted it I was so dazzled I could barely see a thing. It was like coming out of the pitch black into a fierce light. My first instincts, while recoiling, was that there was too much oak at work. Only on acclimatisation did I work out what was going on here...and fall helplessly in love. There is still way too much oak, however you look at it and the nose, which neither improves nor worsens over time confirms that. Indeed, the entire thing is outrageous: I have never come across such a flavour profile before anywhere in the world. But my word: what a statement this makes... Unique. *62.1%*

Amrut Two Continents Limited Edition bott Feb 09 db **(95)** n23.5 t24 f23.5 b24. Here we have a malt distilled in India and matured first on the sub-continent and then Scotland. Let's just say that it is a malt which has travelled exceptionally well...and arrived at greatness. This is exactly how I like my whisky to be. *46%. 786 bottles.*

⋄ **Amrut Two Continents 2nd Edition** bott Jun 11 db **(95)** n23.5 suet pudding – spotted dog. Some oils and banana milkshake, too; **t24** voluptuous delivery. A stunning meeting of juicy barley, soft fruits and delicate yet persistent spices; a light oiliness helps the more complex notes glide to all parts of the palate and some muscovado sugars make light of any oaky encroachment; the middle ground heads towards chocolate milkshake; **f23.5** long with the slowest build up of oaks on record. The spices continue to flit and fizz and finally vanilla takes hold; **b24** I didn't expect their 2nd edition of this to get anywhere near the first in quality: it has. Not because of any loss in faith in the distillery – quite the contrary, in fact – but because, if I have learned anything in 20 years reviewing whisky, distillers find it near enough impossible to recreate the sublime. This is a vaguely fruitier effort and all the more fascinating for that. *50%. nc ncf. 892 bottles.*

Amrut 100 Peated Single Malt ex-bourbon/virgin oak barrels db **(92)** n23 youthful barley integrates effortlessly with the hickory and smoke: outrageously delicate for a nose so big; **t23** the virgin oak used has injected some major Demerara sugars. The smoke is not quite big enough to keep it all under control, nor the rising tide of vanillins; **f23.5** all kinds of milky mocha notes work well with that soothing smoke; **b22.5** ironically, though one of the older whiskies to come from this distillery, the nose shows a little bit of youth. A quite different style from Amrut's other peated offerings and it was obviously intended. Further proof that this distillery has grown not only in stature but confidence. And with very good reason. *571%. nc ncf.*

⋄ **Blackadder Amrut Rum Cask Finish** cask BA5/2009, bott Jul 09 **(91.5)** n23 thick, almost syrupy; an oak and sugar paste; **t24.5** as massive as expected. Plenty of sugars added to the mocha which punches through to occupy the middle ground; **f21.5** thins out surprisingly; **b22.5** for every action there is an equal and opposite reaction; so sweet to start, so dry on the finish. *62.%. nc ncf. 245 bottles.*

Milroy's of Soho Amrut 2003 cask no. 08/08/30-1, dist Jul 03, bott Jan 09 **(84)** n21 t22 f20 **b21.** Juicy in part and very malty. But this whisky struggles at this kind of age with the oak, especially through the flattening natural caramels, dumbing the beauty down. *46%. 210 bottles.*

The Ultimate Amrut 2005 Cask Strength bourbon barrel no. 1641, botto no. 174, dist Dec 05, bott Apr 10 db **(94.5)** n23.5 high phenols and proud of it: dank and earthy, bluebells in full bloom; slightly musky with neither the sweet or dry notes enjoying the upper hand; **t24** eye-closingly beautiful: the waves of sweet peat roll uncontainably over the taste buds; the gristy sweetness merge with Demerara sugars and other sub bourbon notes; meanwhile the prickly peat continues its quiet rampage; **f23.5** long, a smoky spice buzz and countless strands of vanilla; **b23.5** it makes no difference whether made and matured in Islay or India, great malt whisky is just that. And this is near faultless. And, what's more, it appears to have a character and personality all its own. *62.8%*

PONDA DISTILLERY

Stillman's Dram Single Malt Whisky Limited Edition bourbon cask no. 11186-90 **(94)** n23 beautifully soft peats fuse with lime-led citrus notes. At once delicate and enormous; **t23** softly smoked malts dissolve into honeyed pools on the palate. Sexier and more relaxing than a Goan foot massage; **f24** the way the delicate oak washes gently against the palate, the manner in which the soft peats build to a crescendo - and yet still refuse to overpower – the entrancing waves of muscovado-sweetened coffee, all make for a sublime finale; **b24** well, I thought I had tasted it all with the Amrut cask strength. And then this arrived at my lab...!! I predicted many years back that India would dish out some top grade malt before too long. But I'd be stretching the truth if I said I thought it would ever be this good... *42.8%. McDowell & Co Ltd, India.*

Blends

Antiquity blend of rare Scotch and matured Indian malts, bott Feb 06 **(79) n20 t21 f19 b19.** Uncluttered but clever in places with a silky and distinctly malty delivery on the palate; the oak – not noticeable on the nose - dominates the finish intertwined with toffee-caramel. Attractive, but never quite works out which direction it is going. *42.8%. Shaw Wallace Distilleries, India. No added flavours.*

Peter Scot Malt Whisky (84) n20 t21 f22 b21. Enjoyable balance between sweetness and oak and entertainingly enlivened by what appears to be some young, juicy malt. *42.8%.*

NEW ZEALAND
THE SOUTHERN DISTILLING CO LTD

The Coaster Single Malt Whiskey batch no. 2356 **(85) n20 t22 f21 b22.** Distinctly small batch and sma' still with the accent very much on honey. Nosed blind I might have mistaken as Blue Mouse whisky from Germany: certainly European in style. Recovers well from the wobble on the nose and rewards further investigation. *40%*

The MacKenzie Blended Malt Whiskey (85) n20 t22 f21 b22. A vaguely spicier, chalkier, mildly less honeyed version of Coaster. Quite banana-laden nose. I have flown over Timeru many times, half way as it is between Christchurch and Dunedin. By the time you read this, there is more than even chance I shall have driven there and visited this distillery. I'll let you know on the website. *40%*

WILSON DISTILLERY

Milford Aged 10 Years batch 321M42, dist 1993, bott 2004 db **(89) n20 t23 f23 b23.** What a shame that the Wilson distillery is not still extant and rich new make was being filled into some high quality bourbon casks. *43%. 4780 bottles.*

Milford Aged 15 Years batch 89M414, dist 1988, bott 2004 db **(91) n21 t24 f23 b23.** Quality whisky though slightly flattened by age but shows enough early on to confirm its class. *43%. 1878 bottles.*

Cadenhead's World Whiskies Lammerlaw Aged 10 Years bourbon, bott Sep 07 **(91.5) n22 t23.5 f23 b23.** Stunning bottlings like this can only leave one mourning the loss of this distillery. *48.9%. 198 bottles.*

Blends

Kiwi Whisky (37) n2 t12 f11 b12. Strewth! I mean, what can you say? Perhaps the first whisky containing single malt offering virtually no nose at all and the flavour appears to be grain neutral spirit plus lashings of caramel and (so I am told) some Lammerlaw single malt. The word bland has been redefined. As has whisky. *40%. Ever-Rising Enterprises, NZ, for the Asian market.*

Wilson's Superior Blend (89) n22 t23 f21 b23. Apparently has a mixed reception in its native New Zealand but I fail to see why: this is unambiguously outstanding blended whisky. On the nose you expect a mouthwatering mouthful and it delivers with aplomb. Despite this being a lower priced blend it is, intriguingly, a marriage of 60% original bottled 10-y-o Lammerlaw and 40% old Wilson's blend, explaining the high malt apparent. Dangerous and delicious and would be better still at a fuller strength...and with less caramel. *37.5%. Continental Wines and Spirits, NZ.*

SOUTH AFRICA
JAMES SEDGWICK DISTILLERY

Three Ships 10 Years Old db **(83) n21 t21 f20 b21.** Seems to have changed character, with more emphasis on sherry and natural toffee. The oak offers a thrusting undercurrent. *43%*

❖ **Three Ships Aged 10 Years Single Malt Limited Edition** db **(91) n22.5** hints of smoke and cocoa, but some course oak has something to say, too; **t22.5** very much like a blend in style: there is bite and a touch of spite. But a soft fruitiness to stem the bleeding; **f23** for a while you think there will be some fruity civility, at times laid on with a red carpet. Then the cat is back, scratching and pawing at you with oaky talons – my word, I love it...! **b23.5** if you are looking for a soft, sophisticated malt whose delicate fingers can sooth your troubled brow, then don't bother with this one. On the other hand, if you are looking for a bit of rough, some entertaining slap and tickle: a slam-bam shag of a whisky - a useful port in a storm -

then your boat may just have sailed in... Beware: an evening with this and you'll be secretly coming back for more... 43%

Bain's Cape Mountain Single Grain Whisky db (85.5) n21 t22 f21 b21.5. A lively, attractively structured whisky with more attitude than you might expect. Some lovely nip and bite despite the toffee and surprising degree of soft oils. 43%

Blends

Drayman's Solera (86) n19 t22 f23 b22. For a change, the label gets it spot on with its description of chocolate orange: it is there in abundance. If they can get this nose sorted they would be on for an all round impressive dram. As it is, luxuriate in the excellent mouthfeel and gentle interplay between malt and oak. Oh and those chocolate oranges... 43%. Drayman's Distillery. South African/Scotch Whisky.

Harrier (78) n20 t20 f19 b19. Not sure what has happened to this one. Has bittered to a significant degree while the smoke has vanished. A strange, almost synthetic, feel to this now. 43%. South African/Scotch Whisky.

Knights (83) n20.5 t21 f20 b20.5. While the Harrier has crashed, the Knights is now full of promise. Also shows the odd bitter touch but a better all-round richer body not only absorbs the impacts but radiates some malty charm. 43%. South African/Scotch Whisky.

Knights Aged 3 Years (87) n22 bourbony vanillas and toffee; t22 a superb bite to this with a salivating, sweet and oily follow through; f22 wonderfully textured vanilla and caramel; b22 this now appears to be 100% South African whisky if I understand the label correctly: "Distilled Matured and Bottled in South Africa." A vast improvement on when it was Scotch malt and South African grain. Bursting with attitude and vitality. When next in South Africa, this will be my daily dram for sure. Love it. 43%. James Sedgwick Distillery.

Three Ships Bourbon Cask Finish (90) n22 t23 f22.5 b22.5. A soft, even whisky which enjoys its finest moments on delivery. Clean with a pressing, toasty oakiness to the sweeter malt elements. Always a delight. 43% ⊙

Three Ships Premium Select Aged 5 Years (93) n23 personality change alert: soft smoke offers an elegant sweetness; t23.5 the silkiest delivery south of the equator. The grains dominate the mouth feel, but rule with gentle wisdom. The smoke takes a little time to form in any great weight and certainly helps the spices beautifully; f23 soft enough to melt but with sufficient oils, smoky weight and milk chocolate Maltesers to take the finish into extra time; b23.5 what a fabulous whisky. The blender has shown a rare degree of craft to make so little smoke do so much. Bravo! 43%. James Sedgwick Distillery. ⊙ ⊙

Three Ships Select (81) n19 t21 f20 b21. Busy and sweet. But I get the feeling that whatever South African malt may be found in Knights does a better job than its Scotch counterpart here. 43%. James Sedgwick Distillery. ⊙ ⊙

TAIWAN
KAVALAN DISTILLERY

Kavalan db (91) n23 predominantly fruity: plums and raisins topped by mint; a lovely dried date background; t23 firm, flinty, juicy delivery with thudding malts soothed and comforted by lighter fruits; the mid ground moves towards a more lush, velvety texture and the first signs an oaky weight; f22 a light buzz on the tongue points to a less than perfect sherry butt somewhere, but the compactness of the barley against the expansiveness of the delicate fruit remains a source of enjoyment; b23 a high quality, confident malt which underline's this distillery's enormous potential. 40%

Kavalan Concertmaster Single Malt Port cask finish db (87) n22 proud, juicy grape spread over some toasty vanilla; a slight, dull hint of a lesser cask; t23 voluptuous entry: the silkiness of the malt is matched by the salivating, sharper tones of fruit; the middle ground is diminuendo and more introspective; f20.5 a familiar buzz of an off-key cask; b21.5 a malt which will split its audience. In Germany, for instance, the light sulphur note will win all kinds of standing ovations; however, to the purist there will be a preference that it was not there. Because this piece has many moments of beauty as the malt and grape mingle and interlink: together they are company, anything else is a crowd. Even so I envisage many an encore for this... 40%

Kavalan King Car Conductor db (89.5) n22.5 complex, nutty, salty and vibrant, this conducter has decided to belt this one out, yet leave room for a bit of pathos when necessary...; t23 a sublime mingling of salty oaks; there is something of the cocktail olive about this; elsewhere clean grapey oaks rule the roost; f22 sharpens slightly too vividly for comfort but again fruit comes to a crisp rescue; b22 not quite sure where the salt comes from; this distillery is far enough inland not to be affected. But it is there and does no harm whatsoever. Not quite technically perfect, as at least some of the characteristics are so contra they occasionally jar. But still fabulous whisky and a journey entirely worth embarking on. *46%*

⠏ **Kavalan Solist Barique** db cask no. W080218037 **(90.5) n23** wild hedge fruits over ripening; big salt and vanilla yogurt; dry and creamy...; a little dry note which we might see later...; **t24** the delivery is one of puckering spice and fruit. Juicy, busy, profound. Makes the hairs on your neck stand on end. As they do, a big cocoa middle forms and the raisins appear to roast on your palate; **f21** just wilts slightly with a vaguely over sharp note predicted on the nose; **b22.5** this distillery is, in all the world, my favourite to visit. The drama of the geology in which it is set appears matched only by what one discovers from time to time in their warehouses. It has the potential for true world greatness, though this bottling, for all its magnificence, only nudges rather than grasps at the prospect. *59.2%. nc ncf sc. 237 bottles.*

Kavalan Solist Fino Sherry Cask db cask no. S060814045, bott no. 079/500 **(95) n24.5** textbook aroma: one of those almost now extinct species of sherried malt where the grape neither dominates nor offers sulphur in any degree. Being a fino there is an underlying dryness to the entire nose, yet as the malt and a bourbon-esque oak both have a say, there is a countering sweetness, too. The result is a rich texture, but one never straying towards heavy. The fruits aren't just white grape, either, but tomato and papaya, too. To add to the fray, delicate spices, most notably white pepper, pulse; **t24.5** one of the great deliveries of the year: how can something so seemingly clean be teaming with such extraordinary life? The taste buds go through about half a dozen flavour gear changes in the space of about a minute, yet there is no lurching or power surging: it's just one graceful glide all along the way. It is instantly juicy, the salivation factor going through the roof as a fabulous combination of fresh malt and grape offer a monumental double whammy. Next comes several layers of oak of varying degrees of intensity and sweetness; indeed at times we are on a roller-coaster ride of sweet-dry-sweet-dry with the sweeter notes offering a strata of bourbon brown sugars, the drier, a chalkier counter balance. But always in the background is that soft, regal grape; **f22.5** perhaps distilled before they widened the cut a little, the finish isn't quite as long as the glorious nature of the delivery might have you expect. The oils present seem to prefer the oak to the fruit, but the tailing off is as gradual as it graceful; **b23.5** when Dr Jim Swan, the distillery's consultant, told me he thought he'd found a cask which could well be a world-beater, I had mixed feelings. On one hand he'd been right when he'd said the same thing when he found a port pipe for Penderyn which has now entered Welsh whisky folklore. But, on the other, there are many times during the year when those I have long known in the game, including some good friends, have called me after reading my review and asked why I had marked their Great Hope down. Jim, though, has got this one spot on. The natural colour is astonishingly un-fino-esque and the overall experience is one that you come across only too rarely in life – especially with sherry butts. The marriage between the sweeter malt and drier grape notes is a thing of not just beauty, but awe. This is a bottling which will place the King Car Yuan-Shan distillery on the world map of truly great distilleries. Because having an exceptional cask is one thing. You also have to have a spirit excellent enough to maximize the potential of that cask and not be overwhelmed by it. That is exactly what you have here. A great new whisky dynasty has been born... *58.5%. ncf nc.*

⠏ **Kavalan Solist Fino Sherry Cask** db cask no. S060814021 **(97) n24.5** faultless fino: the dry, slightly salty grape offers both a sweet juiciness and a weightier dry pulpiness; delicate, strictly piano but entirely open for key spices to emerge allegro; **t24** the intermezzo is brief and soon we are once more into full blooded spices in which white peppers take the leading role. The malt, astonishingly, can still be heard rumbling among the bases but it is the dry, biting grape and oak which takes the breath away; **f24** the finale, as to be expected, is no half hearted affair; no withering away. This remains sophisticated to the very last, allowing some delicate sugars from the oak to counter and lengthen and add tone; **b24.5** it might be argued that the one and only thing that makes this exceptional is the quality of the cask, rather than the actual malt it contains. Well, let me set the record straight in this one. Earlier this week I made a very rare escape from my tasting room and visited the Royal Albert Hall for the 34th Prom of the 2011 season. The highlight of the evening was Camille Saint-Saens Symphony No 3 – "Organ". Now some critics, when they can find time to extract themselves from their own rear ends, dismiss this as a commoners' piece; something to amuse the plebeian. What they appear to not have is neither the wit nor humanity to understand that Saint-Saens sewed into this work a degree of such subtle shade and emotion, especially in the less dramatic second movement, that it can, when treated correctly, affect those capable of normal warmth and feeling. With so many nerve endings tingling and nowhere to go Saint-Saens recognised that he required something profound – in this case the organ – to create a backbone. And someone able to use it to maximum effect. And there we had it the other day: the Royal Albert Hall's awe-inspiring organ, and Thomas Trotter to make it come alive: The Solist. And this is what we have here: a perfect fino sherry selected by the maestro Dr Jim Swan. But able to display its full magnificence only because the host spirit is so beautifully composed. Good whisky is, without question, a work of art; great whisky is a tone poem. And here, I beg to insist, is proof. 58.4%. nc ncf sc. 513 bottles.

Kavalan Solist Single Cask Strength ex-Bourbon Cask cask no. B070319060 db **(90.5)** n23 an unusual array of dry toast, walnut oil, grated chocolate and even dried banana skin: an attractive compilation; t23 beautiful delivery with a multi-faceted richness. The oils are soft and wonderfully useful for getting the vanilla-driven complexity across. Fabulous, prickly spices abound while the sweet, juicy malts play the perfect foil; f22 returns to its drier self; the vanillas now really going into an almost chalky overdrive; a vague bitter marmalade on slightly burned toast bites home as a late surprise; b22.5 wow...!!! The first single cask from this excellent new distillery has much to say for itself. And most is seriously worth listening to. Much more of a soloist than a solist, I'd say. What's more how can you not adore the natural Eastern Cattle Egret breeding colour of the whisky...? 57.3%. ncf nc.

Kavalan Solist Single Cask Strength Sherry Cask cask no. S080821033 db **(92)** n22.5 t24 f22.5 b23. One of those fabulous sherry butts marked by a mild sulphury shadow but has so much else going on, that much, if not all, can be forgiven. 57.3%

Other Brands Available In Taiwan

Eagle Leader Storage Whisky (81.5) n20 t21 f21 b20.5. Attractively smoky with a surprisingly long finish for a whisky which initially appears to lack body. By no means straightforward, but never less than pleasant. 40%

Golden Hill Single Malt (75) n18 t20 f19 b18. An unwieldy heavyweight. 40%

Golden Knight All Malt (61) n17 t16 f12 b16. Amazingly thin for a malt with all the weight provided by caramel. 40%

Golden Shield Storage Whisky (62.5) n17.5 t16 f14 b15. Tarnished gold. Grim. 40%

Good Deer (in Chinese Characters) see McAdams Rye Whisky

Louis Dynasty (66.5) n16 t16 f17.5 b17. A very strange concoction. Certain elements leave much to be desired, offering a most peculiar mouth feel. Yet there is also the odd smoke note which beds down the sweeter, firmer notes. 40%

McAdams Rye Whisky bott Nov 09 (85.5) n21 t22 f21.5 b21.5. Thoroughly delicious stuff absolutely brimming with juicy, crisp grain notes. The body is lightly oiled and shapely while the finish is sweet and attractive. The odd green apple note, too. 40%. Note: Says it's made in Taiwan, but possesses a maple leaf on the label.

Sea Pirates (77) n18 t21 f19 b19. More Johnny Depp than Errol Flynn. Attractive smoke, though. 40%

URUGUAY

⋰ **Dunbar Anejo 5 Anos** (85.5) n20 t22.5 f21.5 b21.5. A clean, mouth-wateringly attractive mix where the grain nips playfully and the Speyside malts are on best salivating behaviour. Decently blended and boasting a fine spice prickle, too. 40%

⋰ **Seagram's Blenders Pride** (83) n20.5 t22 f20b20.5. The busy, relatively rich delivery contrasts with the theme of the silky grains and caramel. Easy drinking. 40%

MISCELLANEOUS

Jaburn & Co Pure Grain & Malt Spirit (53) n14 t13 f13 b13. Tastes like neutral grain and caramel to me. Some shop keepers, I hear, are selling it as whisky though this is not claimed on the label. Trust me: it isn't. 37.5%. Jaburn & Co, Denmark.

House of Westend Blended Whisky (67) n17 t18 f16 b16. No more than OK if you are being generous; some tobacco-dirty notes around. Doesn't mention country of origin anywhere on the label. 40%. Bernkasteler Burghof, Germany.

Prince of Wales Welsh Whisky (69) n17 t18 f17 b17. Syrupy aroma is compounded by an almost liqueurish body. Thin in true Scotch substance, probably because it claims to be Welsh but is really Scotch with herbs diffused in a process that took place in Wales. Interestingly, my "liqueur" tasting notes were written before I knew exactly what it was I was tasting, thus proving the point and confirming that, with these additives, this really isn't whisky at all. 40%

Shepherd's Export Finest Blend (46) n5 t16 f12 b13. A dreadful, illdefined grain-spirit nose is softened on the palate by an early mega-sweet kick. The finish is thin and eventually bitter. Feeble stuff. 37.2%. "A superb blend of Imported Scotch Malt whiskies and Distilled N.Z. grain spirit", claims the label which originally gives the strength as 40%, but has been over-written. Also, the grain, I was told, was from the USA. Southern Grain Spirit, NZ.

Slàinte

It seems as though you can't have a Bible without a whole lot of begetting. And without all those listed below – vast warehouses full of all the world's whisky people – this Jim Murray's Whisky Bible 2012 would never have been begot at all. A huge amount of blood, sweat and tears go into the production of each edition, more than anyone not directly involved could even begin to comprehend. So, as usual, I must thank my amazing team: James Murray, Ally Telfer, Billy Jeffrey, David Rankin, Dani Dal Molin and Mark Hunt. Also special thanks to Julia Nourney for again descending on the distilleries of Europe on my behalf. My appreciation goes to the staff and management of The Capital Plaza Hotel in Frankfort, Kentucky, for somehow finding a suite big enough for me carry out my US tastings and, as usual, their counterparts at The Empress Hotel, Victoria, BC, for my Canadian work. And, of course, I must thank all those not mentioned below by due to oversight (or, more likely, a crashed computer...) who have helped by getting samples across to us from far and wide. Finally, once more I hug my wonderful friends and supporters: Heiko Theime, Birgit Bournemeier and Barbara Smith. But it is with profound sadness I must say goodbye to Mike Smith, the most loyal and kind of friends, who passed away whilst this edition was being written. Thank you, Mike. For everything. You will never be forgotten by us at The Whisky Bible.

Tomo Akaike; Esben Andersen; Ichiro Akuto; Iain Allan; Jens-Uwe Altmann; Justin Apthorp; Raymond Armstrong; Paul Aston; Sarah Bailey; David Baker; Duncan Baldwin; Nicola Ball; Melanie Balmer; Kevin Balmforth; Hazel Barnes; Rachel Barrie; Edward Bates; Keith Batt; Lars Benjaminsen; Barry Bernstein; Jim Beveridge; Marilena Bidaine; John Black; Frank Michael Böer; my beautiful Borat, RIP; Etienne Bouillon; Neil Boyd; Shane Bramell; Jens Breede; Stephen Bremner; David Brisset; Ken Bromfield; Marie Broomer; Morag Brotherton; Karen Brown; Kim Brown; Mike Brown; Sara Browne; Alex Bruce; Corinne Bucchioni; Mikki Burgers; Andy Burns; Jim Busuttil; Emily Butcher; John Campbell; Jenny Cantrell; Tina Carey; Chris Carlsson; Alex Carnie; Ian Chang; Ian Chapman; Candy Charters; Hunter Chavanne; Suzanne Chester; Duncan Chisholm; Ashok Chokalingam; Julie Christian; Karen Christie; Ricky Christie; Nick Clark; Margaret Mary Clarke; Melissa Colman; Susan Colville; Kris Comstock; Rick Connolly; Andy Cook; Robin Cooke; Paula Cormack; Andy Cornwall; Silvia Corrieri; Isabel Coughlan; Graham Coull; James Cowan; David Cox; Ronnie Cox; Jason Craig; Kathleen Crammond; Georgie Crawford; Katherine Crisp; David Croll; Andy Crook; Andrew Currie; Peter Curry; Ewa Czernecka; Bob Dalgarno; Andre Dang; Craig Daniels; John Dannerbeck; Kimberley Davenport; Jancine Davies; Stephen Davies; Mark Dawkins; Martin Dawson; Zara D'Cotta; Herbert Debbeler; Jürgen Deibel; Alex Delaloye; Nathalie Desmedt; Eve Dewar; Marco Di Ciacca; Steve Dobell; Gordon Doctor; Ed Dodson; Aleta Donaldson; Chris Donaldson; Jean Donnay; Simon Downs; Lucy Drake; Jonathan Driver; Mike Drury; Hayley Dunn; Peter Dunne; Charles Du Pré; Colin Dunn; Peter Dunne; Frances Dupuy; Gavin Durnin; Lucy Egerton; Carsten Ehrlich; Ben Ellefsen; Brent Elliot; Pat Ellis; Duncan Elphick; Per Eriksson; James Espey; Richard Evans; Roy Evans; Jennifer Eveleigh; Lucy Evrington; Tracy Ewart; Thomas Ewers; Lucy Farber; Bruce Farquhar; Joanna Fearnside; Bernie Fennerty; Angus Ferguson; David Findlay; Giles Fisher; Alex Fitch; Erik Fitchett; David Fitt; Keira Fitzpatrick; Robert Fleischmann; Aude Florentin; Sally Forbes; Angela Forsgren D'Orazio; Seth Fox; Georgina Fowler; Tim French; Barry Frieslander; Alan Galloway; Luis Garcia Burgos; Stephen Gardiner; Nick Garland; Dan Garrison; Keith Geddes; Carole Gibson; Emma Gill; Fiona Gittus; John Glaser; Gregg Glass; John Glass; Alyson Goodenough; Jim Gordon; Richard Gordon; Bob Gorton; Jess Graber; Ed Graham; Isabel Graham-Yooll; George Grant; Lynn Grant; Miaochen Gray; Virginia Gray; Jonathan Greene; Hardus Greyling; Ken Grier; Christian Gruel; Jasmin Haider; Johann Haider; Monika Haider; Olga Haley; Anna Hall; John Hall; Archie Hamilton; Claudia Hamm; Wendy Harker; Jay Harman; David Harper; Wendy Harries Jones; Mark Harris; Susan Harris; Alistair Hart; Andy Hart; Donald Hart; Lily Hassan; Julian Haswell; Christopher Hayman; Michael Heals; Samantha Heaney; Mika Heikkenin; CJ Hellie; Jim Helsby; Lincon Henderson; Grace Henwood; Irene Hemmings; Anne Hempstock; John Hempstock; William Henderson; Robert Hicks; Jennifer Higgins; Vincent Hill; Aaron Hillman; Roland Hinterreiter; Sarah-Jane Hodson; Karl-Holger Hoehler; Alexa Hopkins; Gillian Howell; Steve Hoyles; David Hudson; Mark Hunt; Emma Hurley; Ford Hussain; David Hynes; Sandy Hyslop; Kai Ivalo; Sean Ivers; Ily Jaffa; Dee Jacques; Vivienne Jawett; Kate Johansen-Berg; Richard Joynson; Ben Kagi; Joanne Kain; Sonia Kalia-Sagoo; Shane Kalloglian; Naofumi Kamaguchi; Lara Karakasevic; Larry Kass; Caitriona Kavanagh; Colin Keegan; Halley Kehoe; Jaclyn Kelly; Bob Kennedy; Sheila Kennedy; Keiko Kinoshita; Brian Kinsman; Phillip J. Kirk; Sare Kotze; Lex Kraaijeveld; Peter Krause; Libby

Lafferty; Cara Laing; Fiona Laing; Fred Laing; Stuart Laing; Bill Lark; Kristy Lark; Lynne Lark; Liske Larsen; David Larsson; Rohna Lawson; Megan LeBoeuf; Walter Lecocq; Patricia Lee; Harvey Lees; Anne Marie Le Lay; Guy Le Lay; Billy Leighton; Darren Leitch; Gilles Leizour; Lars Lindberger; Graeme Lindsay; Cheryl Lins; Lochy; Andrew Long; Jim Long; Martin Long; Alistair Longwell; Linda Love; Jason Low; Andreas Lübberstedt; Bill Lumsden; John Lunn; Gillian Macdonald; Jane MacDuff; Stuart MacDuff; Frank MacHardy; Roderick Mackenzie; Lorne Mackillop; Stephanie Macleod; Grant MacPherson; Rosalyn MacRae; Iseabail Mactaggart; Lesley-Ann Maguire; Patrick Maguire; Chris Maile; Dennis Malcolm; Ellen Malinski; Pekka Marjamaa; Tracy Markey; Linda Marks; Gillian Marshall; Tim Marwood; Elaine Masson; Norman Mathison; Larry Mattingly; David Maxwell-Scott; Chris Maybin; Iain McCallum; Antony McCallum-Caron; Steve McCarthy; Clark McCool; Tom McCulloch; Mhairi McDonald; John McDougall; John McDonough; Barbara McEwan; Jim McEwan; Lynne McEwan; Julie McFadden; Sarah McGhee; Paul McGinlay; Helen McGinn; Alister McIntosh; Doug McIvor; Dominic McKay; Anne McKerrow; Brian McKenzie; Thomas McKenzie; Jaclyn McKie; Margaret McKie; Lorne McKillop; Morna McLelland; Kirsty McLeod; Fred McMillan; Janice McMillan; Steven McNeil; Alan McConnachie; Laura McVicar; Lee Medoff; Clare Meikle; Jon Metcalf; Rick Mew; Stephanie Middleton; Paul Miles; Robbie Millar; Ann Miller; Bill Miller; Ester Miller; Patrick Millet; Tom Mills; Jack Milroy; John Milroy; Tatsuya Minagawa; Andre Miron; Elaine Mitchell; Euan Mitchell; Matthew Mitchell; Michael Moane; Jürgen Moeller; Takeshi Mogi; Zubair Mohamed; Rainer Mönks; Glen Moore; Les Morgan; Chris Morris; Jemma Morris; Ian Morrison; Joanna Morrow; Mary Morton; Edelle Moss; Gordon Motion; Arthur Motley; Helen Mulholland; Malcolm Mullan; Anna Murby; Jayne Murphy; Alison Murray; Andrew Murray; Bert Murray; Charles Murray; David Murray; Karen Murray; Stacey Murray; Elaine Mutch; Arthur Nagale; Kamiguchi Naofumi; Shin Natsuyama; Marc Neilly; Jill Nelson; Andrew Nelstrop; Alie Newton; Mark Newton; Alex Nicol; Margaret Nicol; Graham Nicolson; Thrivikram G Nikam; Micke Nilsson; Kate Nimmo; Bryan Nolt; Edel Nørgaard; Johannes Nørgaard; Lis Nørgaard; Søren Nørgaard; Jake Norris; Tom O'Connor; Gerry O'Donnell; Catherine O'Grady; Deirbhile O'Grady; Aoife O'Sullivan; Barbara Ortner; Wolfram Ortner; Linda Outterson; Casey Overeem; Bill Owens; Ian Palmer; C R Parker; Richard Parker; Micheal Patterson; Robert Patterson; Richard Paterson; Rupert Patrick; Siobhan Payne; Rosa Pedley; Nadège Perrot; John Peterson; Plamen Petroff; Justin Petszaft; Stefan E. Petszaft; Catharine Pickering; Elisa Pierato; Edi Pierri; Simon Pointon; Nick Pollachi; Steve Poore; Henry Pratt; Amy Preske; Ashley Presser; Warren Preston; Sabina Pringle; Lucy Pritchard; Annie Pugh; Scott Pugh; Roland Puhl; Bernadette Quinn; David Radcliffe; John Ramsay; Caroline Randu; David Rankin; Robert Ransom; Aaron Rasmussen; Kaye Rawlings; Kelly Rayney; Alan Reid; Clémence Réveilhac; Carrie Revell; Mark Reynier; Kay Riddoch; Jeannie Ritchie; Christine Roberts; Patrick Roberts; Allan Robertson; James Robertson; Jennifer Robertson; Pamela Robertson; Maureen Robinson; Geraldine Roche; Jim Rogerson; Johanne Rolland; Claire Ross; Colin Ross; Duncan Ross; Fabio Rossi; David Roussier; Ronnie Routledge; Jim Roy; Leonard S Russell; Suzy Russell; Jim Rutledge; Caroline Rylance; Richard Salmond; Silvano S. Samaroli; Courtney Sandora; Christine Sandys; Jacqui Sargeant; Virginie Saudemont; Trish Savage; Leander Schadler; Ian Schmidt; Felix Schnappauf; Bryan Schultz; Yossi Schwartz; Bob Scott; Kendra Scott; Tara Serafini; Euan Shand; Rubyna Sheikh; Yuko Shimoda; Naomi Shooman; Sam Simmons; Joy Simpson; Alistair Sinclair; Fred Sinclair; Sukhinder Singh; Michael Slevin; David Sloan; Ian Smart; Allan Smith; Barbara Smith; Michelle Smith; Mike Smith; Phil Smith; Robert Hill Smith; Isa Sneddon; Emanuel Solinsky; Squeak Sparrow; Jeremy Speirs; Sue Stamps; Rory Steel; Barry Stein; Florian Stetter; Tamsin Stevens; David Stewart; Karen Stewart; David Stirk; Kathleen Stirling; Katy Stollery; Kaj Stovring; Derek Strange; Johanna Strasser; Ivar Svensson; Henning Svoldgaard; Noel Sweeney; Kier Sword; Shogo Takagi; Katsuhiko Tanaka; James Tanner; Michelle Tansley; Chip Tate; Marko Tayburn; Graham Taylor; Elizabeth Teape; Jack Teeling; Jo Terry; Celine Tetu; Sarah Thacker; Volker Theurer; Heiko Thieme; Jens Tholstrup; Corinna Thompson; Stuart Thompson; Terry Threlfall; Drew Tiffin; Nick Tilt; Margrat Mary Timson; Una Tomnay; Jeff Topping; Hamish Torrie; Kimitaka Toyoma; Angela Traver; Sarah True; Joanie Tseng; Rob Tuer; Matthew Turner; Ben Upjohn; Ian Urquhart; Mr Vannan; Patrick van Zuidam; Johan Venter; Stefanu Venturini; Kenneth Vernon; Alistair Viner; Christine von Allwörden; Hans von Essen; Alistair Walker; Billy Walker; Jamie Walker; Karen Walker; Leesa Walker; Barry Walsh; Bernard Walsh; Christopher Watkin; Claire Watson; Joanna Watson; Mark Watt; Andy Watts; Susan Webster; Peter Wheeler; Oswald Weidenauer; Ian Weir; Chris Weld; Bill Welter; Isabella A Wemyss; Jan H Westcott; Kerry White; Nick White; Sian Whitelock; Jack Wiebers; Lars-Göran Wiebers; Alex Williams; Anthony Wills; Pamela Wils; Anna Wilson; David Wilson; Lisa Wilson; Arthur Winning; Lance Winters; Tony Wise; Jeff Wiseman; David Wood; Léonie Wood; Steve Worrall; Gordon Wright; Graham Wright; Kate Wright; Pete Wright; Vanessa Wright; Chi-Min Wu; Junko Yaguchi; Takashi Yamagami; Venita Young; Daniel & Ursula Zurcher.